Encyclopedia of

Library and Information Sciences, Fourth Edition

Volume 6

Encyclopedias from the Taylor & Francis Group

Print	Online

Agriculture

Encyclopedia of Agricultural, Food, and Biological Engineering, 2nd Ed., 2 Vols. — Pub'd. 10/21/10
K10554 (978-1-4398-1111-5) | K11382 (978-1-4398-2806-9)

Encyclopedia of Animal Science, 2nd Ed., 2 Vols. — Pub'd. 2/1/11
K10463 (978-1-4398-0932-7) | K10528 (978-0-415-80286-4)

Encyclopedia of Biotechnology in Agriculture and Food — Pub'd. 7/16/10
DK271X (978-0-8493-5027-6) | DKE5044 (978-0-8493-5044-3)

Business and Computer Science

Encyclopedia of Computer Science & Technology, 2nd Ed., 2 Vols. — Pub'd 12/21/2016
K21573 (978-1-4822-0819-1) | K21578 (978-1-4822-0822-1)

Encyclopedia of Information Assurance, 4 Vols. — Pub'd. 12/21/10
AU6620 (978-1-4200-6620-3) | AUE6620 (978-1-4200-6622-7)

Encyclopedia of Information Systems and Technology, 2 Vols. — Pub'd. 12/29/15
K15911 (978-1-4665-6077-2) | K21745 (978-1-4822-1432-1)

Encyclopedia of Library and Information Sciences, 4th Ed. — Publishing 2017
K15223 (978-1-4665-5259-3) | K15224 (978-1-4665-5260-9)

Encyclopedia of Software Engineering, 2 Vols. — Pub'd. 11/24/10
AU5977 (978-1-4200-5977-9) | AUE5977 (978-1-4200-5978-6)

Encyclopedia of Supply Chain Management, 2 Vols. — Pub'd. 12/21/11
K12842 (978-1-4398-6148-6) | K12843 (978-1-4398-6152-3)

Encyclopedia of U.S. Intelligence, 2 Vols. — Pub'd. 12/19/14
AU8957 (978-1-4200-8957-8) | AUE8957 (978-1-4200-8958-5)

Encyclopedia of Wireless and Mobile Communications, 2nd Ed., 3 Vols. — Pub'd. 12/18/12
K14731 (978-1-4665-0956-6) | KE16352 (978-1-4665-0969-6)

Chemistry, Materials and Chemical Engineering

Encyclopedia of Chemical Processing, 5 Vols. — Pub'd. 11/1/05
DK2243 (978-0-8247-5563-8) | DKE499X (978-0-8247-5499-0)

Encyclopedia of Chromatography, 3rd Ed. — Pub'd. 10/12/09
84593 (978-1-4200-8459-7) | 84836 (978-1-4200-8483-2)

Encyclopedia of Iron, Steel, and Their Alloys, 5 Vols. — Pub'd. 1/6/16
K14814 (978-1-4665-1104-0) | K14815 (978-1-4665-1105-7)

Encyclopedia of Plasma Technology, 2 Vols. — Pub'd 12/12/2016
K14378 (978-1-4665-0059-4) | K21744 (978-1-4822-1431-4)

Encyclopedia of Supramolecular Chemistry, 2 Vols. — Pub'd. 5/5/04
DK056X (978-0-8247-5056-5) | DKE7259 (978-0-8247-4725-1)

Encyclopedia of Surface & Colloid Science, 3rd Ed., 10 Vols. — Pub'd. 8/27/15
K20465 (978-1-4665-9045-8) | K20478 (978-1-4665-9061-8)

Engineering

Dekker Encyclopedia of Nanoscience and Nanotechnology, 3rd Ed., 7 Vols. — Pub'd. 3/20/14
K14119 (978-1-4398-9134-6) | K14120 (978-1-4398-9135-3)

Encyclopedia of Energy Engineering and Technology, 2nd Ed., 4 Vols. — Pub'd. 12/1/14
K14633 (978-1-4665-0673-2) | KE16142 (978-1-4665-0674-9)

Encyclopedia of Optical and Photonic Engineering, 2nd Ed., 5 Vols. — Pub'd. 9/22/15
K12323 (978-1-4398-5097-8) | K12325 (978-1-4398-5099-2)

Environment

Encyclopedia of Environmental Management, 4 Vols. — Pub'd. 12/13/12
K11434 (978-1-4398-2927-1) | K11440 (978-1-4398-2933-2)

Encyclopedia of Environmental Science and Engineering, 6th Ed., 2 Vols. — Pub'd. 6/25/12
K10243 (978-1-4398-0442-1) | KE0278 (978-1-4398-0517-6)

Encyclopedia of Natural Resources, 2 Vols. — Pub'd. 7/23/14
K12418 (978-1-4398-5258-3) | K12420 (978-1-4398-5260-6)

Medicine

Encyclopedia of Biomaterials and Biomedical Engineering, 2nd Ed. — Pub'd. 5/28/08
H7802 (978-1-4200-7802-2) | HE7803 (978-1-4200-7803-9)

Encyclopedia of Biomedical Polymers and Polymeric Biomaterials, 11 Vols. — Pub'd. 4/2/15
K14324 (978-1-4398-9879-6) | K14404 (978-1-4665-0179-9)

Concise Encyclopedia of Biomedical Polymers and Polymeric Biomaterials, 2 Vols. — Pub'd. 8/14/17
K14313 (978-1-4398-9855-0) | KE42253 (978-1-315-11644-0)

Encyclopedia of Biopharmaceutical Statistics, 3rd Ed. — Pub'd. 5/20/10
H100102 (978-1-4398-2245-6) | HE10326 (978-1-4398-2246-3)

Encyclopedia of Clinical Pharmacy — Pub'd. 11/14/02
DK7524 (978-0-8247-0752-1) | DKE6080 (978-0-8247-0608-1)

Encyclopedia of Dietary Supplements, 2nd Ed. — Pub'd. 6/25/10
H100094 (978-1-4398-1928-9) | HE10315 (978-1-4398-1929-6)

Encyclopedia of Medical Genomics and Proteomics, 2 Vols. — Pub'd. 12/29/04
DK2208 (978-0-8247-5564-5) | DK501X (978-0-8247-5501-0)

Encyclopedia of Pharmaceutical Science and Technology, 4th Ed., 6 Vols. — Pub'd. 7/1/13
H100233 (978-1-84184-819-8) | HE10420 (978-1-84184-820-4)

Routledge Encyclopedias

Encyclopedia of Public Administration and Public Policy, 3rd Ed., 5 Vols. — Pub'd. 11/6/15
K16418 (978-1-4665-6909-6) | K16434 (978-1-4665-6936-2)

Routledge Encyclopedia of Modernism — Pub'd 5/11/16
Y137844 (978-1-135-00035-6)

Routledge Encyclopedia of Philosophy Online — Pub'd. 11/1/00
RU22334 (978-0-415-24909-6)

Routledge Performance Archive — Pub'd. 11/12/12
Y148405 (978-0-203-77466-3)

Encyclopedia of

Library and Information Sciences, Fourth Edition

Volume 6

From: *Physical Sciences and Mathematics Literature and Their Users* To: *Special Librarianship*

Encyclopedia Edited By

John D. McDonald

and

Michael Levine-Clark

CRC Press
Taylor & Francis Group
Boca Raton London New York

CRC Press is an imprint of the
Taylor & Francis Group, an **informa** business

First published 2018 by CRC Press

Published 2019 by CRC Press
Taylor & Francis Group
6000 Broken Sound Parkway NW, Suite 300
Boca Raton, FL 33487-2742

First issued in paperback 2020

© 2018 by Taylor & Francis Group, LLC
CRC Press is an imprint of the Taylor & Francis Group, an informa business

No claim to original U.S. Government works

ISBN-13: 978-1-4665-5259-3 (HB Set)
ISBN-13: 978-0-8153-8633-9 (Vol. 6) (hbk)

ISBN-13: 978-0-3675-7010-1 (PB Set)
ISBN-13: 978-0-3675-7021-7 (Vol. 6) (pbk)

Visit the Taylor & Francis Web site at
http://www.taylorandfrancis.com

and the CRC Press Web site at
http://www.crcpress.com

Encyclopedia of Library and Information Sciences, Fourth Edition

Brief Contents

Encyclopedia of Library and Information Sciences, Fourth Edition

Editors-in-Chief

John D. McDonald
Analytics and Assessment, EBSCO Information Services

Michael Levine-Clark
University of Denver Libraries, Denver, Colorado

Editorial Advisory Board

Contributors

June Abbas / *School of Library and Information Studies, University of Oklahoma, Norman, Oklahoma, U.S.A.*

Richard Abel / *Portland, Oregon, U.S.A.*

Eileen G. Abels / *College of Information Science and Technology, Drexel University, Philadelphia, Pennsylvania, U.S.A.*

Tia Abner / *American Medical Informatics Association (AMIA), Bethesda, Maryland, U.S.A.*

Donald C. Adcock / *Dominican University, River Forest, Illinois, U.S.A.*

Kendra S. Albright / *School of Library and Information Science, University of South Carolina, Columbia, South Carolina, U.S.A.*

Mikael Alexandersson / *University of Gothenburg, Gothenburg, Sweden*

Joan M. Aliprand / *Cupertino, California, U.S.A.*

Jacqueline Allen / *Dallas Museum of Art, Dallas, Texas, U.S.A.*

Romano Stephen Almagno / *International College of St. Bonaventure, Rome, Italy*

Connie J. Anderson-Cahoon / *Southern Oregon University Library, Ashland, Oregon, U.S.A.*

Karen Anderson / *Archives and Information Science, Mid Sweden University, ITM, Härnösand, Sweden*

Rick Anderson / *University of Utah, Salt Lake City, Utah, U.S.A.*

Silviu Andrieş-Tabac / *Institute of Cultural Heritage, Moldova Academy of Sciences, Chişinău, Republic of Moldova*

Peng Hwa Ang / *Wee Kim Wee School of Communication and Information, Nanyang Technological University, Singapore*

Hermina G.B. Anghelescu / *School of Library and Information Science, Wayne State University, Detroit, Michigan, U.S.A.*

Leah Arroyo / *American Association of Museums, Washington, District of Columbia, U.S.A.*

Terry Asla / *Senior Lifestyles Researcher, Seattle, U.S.A.*

Shiferaw Assefa / *University of Kansas, Lawrence, Kansas, U.S.A.*

Ilse Assmann / *Radio Broadcast Facilities, SABC, Johannesburg, South Africa*

Maija-Leena Aulikki Huotari / *University of Oulu, Oulu, Finland*

Henriette D. Avram / *Library of Congress, Washington, District of Columbia, U.S.A.*

Sven Axsäter / *Department of Industrial Management and Logistics, Lund University, Lund, Sweden*

Murtha Baca / *Getty Research Institute, Los Angeles, California, U.S.A.*

Roger S. Bagnall / *Institute for the Study of the Ancient World, New York University, New York, New York, U.S.A.*

Nestor Bamidis / *GSA-Archives of Macedonia, Thessaloniki, Greece*

Franz Barachini / *Business Innovation Consulting—Austria, Langenzersdorf, Austria*

Rebecca O. Barclay / *Rensselaer Polytechnic Institute, Troy, New York, U.S.A.*

Judit Bar-Ilan / *Department of Information Science, Bar-Ilan University, Ramat Gan, Israel*

Alex W. Barker / *Museum of Art and Archaeology, University of Missouri, Columbia, Missouri, U.S.A.*

John A. Bateman / *University of Bremen, Bremen, Germany*

Marcia J. Bates / *Department of Information Studies, Graduate School of Education and Information Studies, University of California, Los Angeles (UCLA), Los Angeles, California, U.S.A.*

Philippe Baumard / *School of Engineering, Stanford University, Stanford, California, U.S.A., and University Paul Cézanne, Aix-en-Provence, France*

David Bawden / *City, University of London, London, U.K.*

Jennifer Bawden / *Museum Studies Program, Faculty of Information Studies, University of Toronto, Toronto, Ontario, Canada*

David Bearman / *Archives & Museum Informatics, Toronto, Ontario, Canada*

William K. Beatty / *Northwestern University Medical School, Chicago, Illinois, U.S.A.*

A.R. Bednarek / *University of Florida, Gainesville, Florida, U.S.A.*

Clare Beghtol / *Faculty of Information Studies, University of Toronto, Toronto, Ontario, Canada*

Lori Bell / *Alliance Library System, East Peoria, Illinois, U.S.A.*

Danna Bell-Russel / *Library of Congress, Washington, District of Columbia, U.S.A.*

William Benedon / *Benedon & Associates, Encino, California, U.S.A.*

Anna Bergaliyeva / *Kazakhstan Institute of Management, Economics and Strategic Research (KIMEP), Almaty, Kazakhstan*

Sidney E. Berger / *Phillips Library, Peabody Essex Museum, Salem, Massachusetts, U.S.A.*

Andrew J. Berner / *University Club of New York, New York, New York, U.S.A.*

Sean F. Berrigan / *Policy, Library and Archives Canada, Ottawa, Ontario, Canada*

John W. Berry / *NILRC: Network of Illinois Learning Resources in Community Colleges, Dominican University, River Forest, Illinois, U.S.A.*

Michael W. Berry / *Department of Electrical Engineering and Computer Science, University of Tennessee, Knoxville, Tennessee, U.S.A.*

Suresh K. Bhavnani / *Center for Computational Medicine and Bioinformatics, University of Michigan, Ann Arbor, Michigan, U.S.A.*

Tamara Biggs / *Chicago History Museum, Chicago, Illinois, U.S.A.*

Frank Birkebæk / *Roskilde Museum, Roskilde, Denmark*

Ann P. Bishop / *Graduate School of Library and Information Science, University of Illinois at Urbana-Champaign, Urbana, Illinois, U.S.A.*

Julia Blixrud / *Association of Research Libraries, Washington, District of Columbia, U.S.A.*

Gloria Bordogna / *Italian National Research Council, Institute for the Dynamics of Environmental Processes, Dalmine, Italy*

Steve Bosch / *Administration Department, University of Arizona, Tucson, Arizona, U.S.A.*

Kimberly S. Bostwick / *Ecology and Evolutionary Biology, Cornell University Museum of Vertebrates, Ithaca, New York, U.S.A.*

Natalia T. Bowdoin / *University of South Carolina Aiken, Aiken, South Carolina, U.S.A.*

Patrick J. Boylan / *Department of Cultural Policy and Management, City University, London, U.K.*

Amy E. Brand / *CrossRef, Lynnfield, Massachusetts, U.S.A.*

Judy Brooker / *Australian Library and Information Association, Deakin, Australian Capital Territory, Australia*

Terrence Brooks / *iSchool, University of Washington, Seattle, Washington, U.S.A.*

Vanda Broughton / *School of Library, Archive and Information Studies, University College London, London, U.K.*

Cecelia Brown / *School of Library and Information Studies, University of Oklahoma, Norman, Oklahoma, U.S.A.*

Jos de Bruijn / *Digital Enterprise Research Institute, University of Innsbruck, Innsbruck, Austria*

Steve Bryant / *BFI National Archive, Herts, U.K.*

Alan Bryden / *International Organization for Standardization, Geneva, Switzerland*

Jeff E. Bullard / *Free Library of Philadelphia, Philadelphia, Pennsylvania, U.S.A.*

Kathleen Burns / *Beinecke Rare Book and Manuscript Library, Yale University, New Haven, Connecticut, U.S.A.*

Brenda A. Burton / *Library, Kirkland & Ellis LLP, Chicago, IL, U.S.A.*

E. Burton Swanson / *Anderson School of Management, University of California, Los Angeles, Los Angeles, California, U.S.A.*

Donald I. Butcher / *Canadian Library Association, Ottawa, Ontario, Canada*

Kevin Butterfield / *Wolf Law Library, College of William and Mary, Williamsburg, Virginia, U.S.A.*

Alex Byrne / *University of Technology, Sydney—Sydney, New South Wales, Australia*

Brian Byrne / *Discipline of Psychology, School of Behavioural, Cognitive and Social Sciences, University of New England, Armidale, New South Wales, Australia, Australian Research Council Centre of Excellence in Cognition and its Disorder, Australia, and National Health and Medical Research Council Centre of Research Excellence in Twin Research, Australia*

Bernadette G. Callery / *School of Information Sciences, University of Pittsburgh, Pittsburgh, Pennsylvania, U.S.A.*

Paul D. Callister / *Leon E. Bloch Law Library, University of Missouri-Kansas City School of Law, Kansas City, Missouri, U.S.A.*

Perrine Canavaggio / *International Council on Archives, Paris, France*

Sarah R. Canino / *Dickinson Music Library, Vassar College, Poughkeepsie, New York, U.S.A.*

Robert Capra / *School of Information and Library Science, University of North Carolina, Chapel Hill, North Carolina, U.S.A.*

Nicholas Carroll / *Hastings Research, Inc., Las Vegas, Nevada, U.S.A.*

Ben Carterette / *Department of Computer and Information Sciences, University of Delaware, Newark, Delaware, U.S.A.*

Vittorio Castelli / *T.J. Watson Research Center, IBM, Yorktown Heights, New York, U.S.A.*

Jane Rosetta Virginia Caulton / *Library of Congress, Washington, District of Columbia, U.S.A.*

Richard Cave / *Formerly at the Public Library of Science, San Francisco, California, U.S.A.*

Roderick Cave / *Loughborough University, Loughborough, U.K.*

Marcel Caya / *Department of History, University of Quebec at Montreal (UQAM), Montreal, Quebec, Canada*

Frank Cervone / *Purdue University Calumet, Hammond, Indiana, U.S.A.*

Leslie Champeny / *Alaska Resources Library and Information Services (ARLIS), Anchorage, Alaska, U.S.A.*

Lois Mai Chan / *School of Library and Information Science, University of Kentucky, Lexington, Kentucky, U.S.A.*

Sergio Chaparro-Univazo / *Graduate School of Library and Information Science, Simmons College, Boston, Massachusetts, U.S.A.*

Mary K. Chelton / *Graduate School of Library and Information Studies, Queens College Flushing, New York, U.S.A.*

Hsinchun Chen / *Department of Management Information Systems, University of Arizona, Tucson, Arizona, U.S.A.*

Jianhua Chen / *Computer Science Department, Louisiana State University, Baton Rouge, Louisiana, U.S.A.*

Eric R. Childress / *OCLC, Dublin, Ohio, U.S.A.*

Michael A. Chilton / *Department of Management, Kansas State University, Manhattan, Kansas, U.S.A.*

TzeHuey Chiou-Peng / *Spurlock Museum, University of Illinois at Urbana-Champaign, Urbana, Illinois, U.S.A.*

Hyun-Yang Cho / *Department of Library and Information Science, Kyonggi University, Suwon, South Korea*

Jae-Hwang Choi / *Department of Library and Information Science, Kyungpook National University, Daegu, South Korea*

Carol E.B. Choksy / *School of Library and Information Science, Indiana University, Bloomington, Indiana, U.S.A.*

Su Kim Chung / *University Libraries, University of Nevada–Las Vegas, Las Vegas, Nevada, U.S.A.*

James Church / *University Libraries, University of California, Berkeley, Berkeley, California, U.S.A.*

Barbara H. Clubb / *Ottawa Public Library, Ottawa, Ontario, Canada*

Arlene Cohen / *Pacific Islands Library Consultant, Seattle, Washington, U.S.A.*

Barbara Cohen-Stratyner / *New York Public Library for the Performing Arts, New York, U.S.A.*

Edward T. Cokely / *Center for Adaptive Behavior and Cognition, Max Planck Institute for Human Development, Berlin, Germany*

Arthur H. Cole / *Harvard University, Cambridge, Massachusetts, U.S.A.*

John Y. Cole / *Center for the Book, Library of Congress, Washington, District of Columbia, U.S.A.*

Patrick Tod Colegrove / *DeLaMare Science & Engineering Library, University Libraries, University of Nevada, Reno, Reno, Nevada, U.S.A.*

Edwin T. Coman, Jr. / *University of California, Riverside, California, U.S.A.*

Nora T. Corley / *Arctic Institute of North America, Montreal, Quebec, Canada*

Sheila Corrall / *Department of Information Studies, University of Sheffield, Sheffield, U.K.*

Erica Cosijn / *Department of Information Science, University of Pretoria, Pretoria, South Africa*

Richard J. Cox / *School of Computing and Information, University of Pittsburgh, Pittsburgh, Pennsylvania, U.S.A.*

Barbara M. Cross / *Records and Information Management, Sony Pictures Entertainment, Culver City, California, U.S.A.*

Kevin Crowston / *School of Information Studies, Syracuse University, Syracuse, New York, U.S.A.*

Adrian Cunningham / *National Archives of Australia (NAA), Canberra, Australian Capital Territory, Australia*

Judith N. Currano / *University of Pennsylvania, Philadelphia, Pennsylvania, U.S.A.*

Susan Curzon / *University Library, California State University–Northridge, Northridge, California, U.S.A.*

Ingetraut Dahlberg / *Bad Koenig, Germany*

Nan Christian Ploug Dahlkild / *Royal School of Library and Information Science, Copenhagen, Denmark*

Jay E. Daily / *University of Pittsburgh, Pittsburgh, Pennsylvania, U.S.A.*

Kimiz Dalkir / *Graduate School of Library and Information Studies, McGill University, Montreal, Quebec, Canada*

Prudence W. Dalrymple / *Drexel University College of Computing & Informatics, Philadelphia, Pennsylvania, U.S.A.*

Marcel Danesi / *Department of Anthropology, University of Toronto, Toronto, Ontario, Canada*

Xuan Hong Dang / *Computer Vision and Image Understanding, Institute for Infocomm, A* STAR, Singapore*

Yan Dang / *Department of Management Information Systems, University of Arizona, Tucson, Arizona, U.S.A.*

Evelyn Daniel / *School of Information and Library Science, University of North Carolina at Chapel Hill, Chapel Hill, North Carolina, U.S.A.*

Richard A. Danner / *School of Law, Duke University, Durham, North Carolina, U.S.A.*

Regina Dantas / *Museu Nacional, HCTE, Universidade Federal do Rio de Janeiro, Rio de Janeiro, Brazil*

Daniel C. Danzig / *Consultant, Pasadena, California, U.S.A.*

Robert Allen Daugherty / *University Library, University of Illinois at Chicago, Chicago, Illinois, U.S.A.*

Charles H. Davis / *Indiana University, Bloomington, IN, U.S.A., and School of Library and Information Science, Indiana University, Bloomington, Indiana, U.S.A.*

Gordon B. Davis / *Carlson School of Management, University of Minnesota, Minneapolis, Minnesota, U.S.A.*

Mary Ellen Davis / *American Library Association, Chicago, Illinois, U.S.A.*

Peter Davis / *International Centre for Cultural and Heritage Studies, Newcastle University, Newcastle upon Tyne, U.K.*

Sheryl Davis / *University Library, University of California, Riverside, Riverside, California, U.S.A.*

Ronald E. Day / *School of Library and Information Science, Indiana University, Bloomington, Indiana, U.S.A.*

Cheryl Dee / *School of Library and Information Science, University of South Florida, Tampa, Florida, U.S.A.*

Robert DeHart / *Department of History, Middle Tennessee State University, Murfreesboro, Tennessee, U.S.A.*

Brenda Dervin / *School of Communication, Ohio State University, Columbus, Ohio, U.S.A.*

Brian Detlor / *Information Systems, McMaster University, Hamilton, Ontario, Canada*

Don E. Detmer / *American Medical Informatics Association (AMIA), Bethesda, Maryland, U.S.A.*

Stella G. Dextre Clarke / *Information Consultant, Oxfordshire, U.K.*

Catherine Dhérent / *National Library of France, Paris, France*

Anne R. Diekema / *Gerald R. Sherratt Library, Southern Utah University, Cedar City, Utah, U.S.A.*

Susan S. DiMattia / *DiMattia Associates, Stamford, Connecticut, U.S.A.*

Gloria Dinerman / *The Library Co-Op, Inc., Edison, New Jersey, U.S.A.*

Jesse David Dinneen / *School of Information Studies, McGill University, Montreal, Quebec, Canada*

Bernard Dione / *School of Librarianship, Archivists Information Science (EBAD), Cheikh Anta Diop University, Dakar, Senegal*

Dieyi Diouf / *Central Library, Cheikh Anta Diop University of Dakar, Dakar, Senegal*

Keith Donohue / *National Historical Publications and Records Commission, Washington, District of Columbia, U.S.A.*

Ann Doyle / *X̱wi7xwa Library, First Nations House of Learning, University of British Columbia, Vancouver, British Columbia, Canada*

Carol D. Doyle / *Government Documents Department and Map Library, California State University, Fresno, California, U.S.A.*

Marek J. Druzdzel / *School of Information Sciences and Intelligent Systems Program, University of Pittsburgh, Pittsburgh, Pennsylvania, U.S.A., and Faculty of Computer Science, Bialystok Technical University, Bialystok, Poland*

Kathel Dunn / *National Library of Medicine, Bethesda, Maryland, U.S.A.*

Luciana Duranti / *School of Library, Archival and Information Studies, University of British Columbia, Vancouver, British Columbia, Canada*

Joan C. Durrance / *School of Information, University of Michigan, Ann Arbor, Michigan, U.S.A.*

Maria Economou / *Department of Communication and Cultural Technology, University of the Aegean, Mytilini, Greece*

Gary Edson / *Center for Advanced Study in Museum Science and Heritage Management, Museum of Texas Tech University, Lubbock, Texas, U.S.A.*

Mary B. Eggert / *Library, Kirkland & Ellis LLP, Chicago, IL, U.S.A.*

Daniel Eisenberg / *Florida State University, Tallahassee, Florida, U.S.A.*

Innocent I. Ekoja / *University Library, University of Abuja, Abuja, Nigeria*

Sarah Elliott / *International Centre for Cultural and Heritage Studies, Newcastle University, Newcastle upon Tyne, U.K.*

David Ellis / *Department of Information Studies, Aberystwyth University, Wales, U.K.*

Jill Emery / *Portland State University Library, Portland, Oregon, U.S.A.*

Zorana Ercegovac / *InfoEN Associates, Los Angeles, California, U.S.A.*

Timothy L. Ericson / *School of Information Science, University of Wisconsin-Milwaukee, Milwaukee, Wisconsin, U.S.A.*

Elena Escolano Rodríguez / *National Library of Spain, Madrid, Spain*

Leigh S. Estabrook / *Graduate School of Library and Information Science, University of Illinois at Urbana- / Champaign, Champaign, Illinois, U.S.A.*

Mark E. Estes / *Alameda County Law Library, Oakland, California, U.S.A.*

Beth Evans / *Library, Brooklyn College, City University of New York, Brooklyn, New York, U.S.A.*

Joanne Evans / *Centre for Organisational and Social Informatics, Monash University, Melbourne, Victoria, Australia*

Dominic J. Farace / *Grey Literature Network Service, TextRelease/GreyNet, Amsterdam, The Netherlands*

David Farneth / *Special Collections and Institutional Records, Getty Research Institute, Los Angeles, California, U.S.A.*

Sharon Fawcett / *Office of Presidential Libraries, National Archives and Records Administration, College Park, Maryland, U.S.A.*

Dieter Fensel / *Institute of Computer Science, University of Innsbruck, Innsbruck, Austria, and National University of Ireland, Galway, Galway, Ireland*

Thomas L. Findley / *Leo A. Daly/Architects & Engineers, Omaha, Nebraska, U.S.A.*

Karen E. Fisher / *Information School, University of Washington, Seattle, Washington, U.S.A.*

Nancy Fjällbrant / *Chalmers University of Technology Library, International Association of Technological University Libraries, Gothenburg, Sweden*

Julia Flanders / *Brown University, Providence, Rhode Island, U.S.A.*

Nancy Flury Carlson / *Westinghouse Electric Corporation, Pittsburgh, Pennsylvania, U.S.A.*

Roger R. Flynn / *School of Information Sciences and Intelligent Systems Program, University of Pittsburgh, Pittsburgh, Pennsylvania, U.S.A.*

Helen Forde / *Department of Information Studies, University College London, London, U.K.*

Douglas J. Foskett / *University of London, London, U.K.*

Susan Foutz / *Institute for Learning Innovation, Edgewater, Maryland, U.S.A.*

Christopher Fox / *Department of Computer Science, James Madison University, Harrisonburg, Virginia, U.S.A.*

Carl Franklin / *Consultant, Columbus, Ohio, U.S.A.*

Jonathan A. Franklin / *Gallagher Law Library, University of Washington, Seattle, Washington, U.S.A.*

Thomas J. Froehlich / *School of Library and Information Science, Kent State University, Kent, Ohio, U.S.A.*

Steve Fuller / *Department of Sociology, University of Warwick, Coventry, U.K.*

Crystal Fulton / *School of Information and Communication Studies, University College Dublin, Dublin, Ireland*

Carla J. Funk / *Medical Library Association, Chicago, Illinois, U.S.A.*

Jonathan Furner / *Department of Information Studies University of California, Los Angeles, Los Angeles, California, U.S.A.*

Dennis Galletta / *Katz Graduate School of Business, University of Pittsburgh, Pittsburgh, Pennsylvania, U.S.A.*

D. Linda Garcia / *Communication Culture and Technology, Georgetown University, Washington, District of Columbia, U.S.A.*

Holly Gardinier / *Honnold/Mudd Library, Libraries of The Claremont Colleges, Claremont, California, U.S.A.*

Sally Gardner Reed / *Association of Library Trustees, Advocates, Friends and Foundations (ALTAFF), Philadelphia, Pennsylvania, U.S.A.*

Janifer Gatenby / *Online Computer Library Center (OCLC), Leiden, The Netherlands*

Ramesh C. Gaur / *Kalanidhi Division, Indira Gandhi National Centre for the Arts (IGNCA), New Delhi, India*

Lee Anne George / *Association of Research Libraries, Washington, District of Columbia, U.S.A.*

David E. Gerard / *College of Librarianship Wales, Cardiganshire, Wales, U.K.*

Malcolm Getz / *Department of Economics, Vanderbilt University, Nashville, Tennessee, U.S.A.*

Mary W. Ghikas / *American Library Association, Chicago, Illinois, U.S.A.*

Nicholas Gibbins / *School of Electronics and Computer Science, University of Southampton, Southampton, U.K.*

Gerd Gigerenzer / *Center for Adaptive Behavior and Cognition, Max Planck Institute for Human Development, Berlin, Germany*

Tommaso Giordano / *Library, European University Institute, Florence, Italy*

Lilian Gisesa / *Kenya National Archives, Nairobi, Kenya*

Edward A. Goedeken / *Iowa State University, Ames, Iowa, U.S.A.*

Warren R. Goldmann / *National Technical Institute for the Deaf, Rochester Institute of Technology, Rochester, New York, U.S.A.*

David Gordon / *Milwaukee Art Museum, Milwaukee, Wisconsin, U.S.A.*

David B. Gracy II / *School of Information, University of Texas at Austin, Austin, Texas, U.S.A.*

Karen F. Gracy / *School of Library and Information Science, Kent State University, Kent, Ohio, U.S.A.*

Renny Granda / *Universidad Central de Venezuela, Caracas, Venezuela*

Paul Gray / *School of Information Systems and Technology, Claremont Graduate University, Claremont, California, U.S.A.*

Jane Greenberg / *Metadata Research Center, School of Information and Library Science, University of North Carolina at Chapel Hill, Chapel Hill, North Carolina, U.S.A.*

Karen Greenwood / *American Medical Informatics Association (AMIA), Bethesda, Maryland, U.S.A.*

Jill E. Grogg / *Libraries, University of Alabama, Tuscaloosa, Alabama, U.S.A.*

Melissa Gross / *School of Information, Florida State University, Tallahassee, Florida, U.S.A.*

Andrew Grove / *Guest Faculty, Information School, University of Washington, Seattle, Washington, U.S.A.*

Dinesh K. Gupta / *Department of Library and Information Science, Vardhaman Mahaveer Open University, 3 Kota, India*

Laurel L. Haak / *Open Researcher and Contributor ID, Inc. (ORCID), U.S.A.*

Kate Hagan / *American Association of Law Libraries, Chicago, Illinois, U.S.A.*

Kathleen Hall / *Leon E. Bloch Law Library, University of Missouri-Kansas City School of Law, Kansas City, Missouri, U.S.A.*

Virginia M.G. Hall / *Center for Educational Resources, The Sheridan Libraries, Johns Hopkins University, Baltimore, Maryland, U.S.A.*

Wendy Hall / *Intelligence, Agents, Multimedia Group, University of Southampton, Southampton, U.K.*

Stuart Hamilton / *International Federation of Library Associations and Institutions, The Hague, The Netherlands*

Maureen L. Hammer / *Knowledge Management, Batelle Memorial Institute, Charlottesville, Virginia, U.S.A.*

Jong-Yup Han / *Research Information Team, KORDI, Seoul, South Korea*

Debra Gold Hansen / *School of Library and Information Science, San Jose State University, Yorba Linda, California, U.S.A.*

Derek L. Hansen / *University of Maryland, College Park, Maryland, U.S.A.*

Eugene R. Hanson / *Shippensburg State College, Shippensburg, Pennsylvania, U.S.A.*

Jane Hardy / *Australian Library and Information Association, Deakin, Australian Capital Territory, Australia*

Julie Hart / *American Association of Museums, Washington, District of Columbia, U.S.A.*

Hiroyuki Hatano / *Surugadai University, Saitama, Japan*

Robert M. Hayes / *Department of Information Studies, University of California, Los Angeles, Los Angeles, California, U.S.A.*

Caroline Haythornthwaite / *Graduate School of Library and Information Science, University of Illinois at Urbana- / Champaign, Champaign, Illinois, U.S.A.*

Penny Hazelton / *Gallagher Law Library, University of Washington, Seattle, Washington, U.S.A.*

P. Bryan Heidorn / *Graduate School of Library and Information Science, University of Illinois at Urbana-Champaign, Champaign, Illinois, U.S.A.*

Helen Heinrich / *Collection Access and Management Services, California State University–Northridge, Northridge, California, U.S.A.*

Doris S. Helfer / *Collection Access and Management Services, California State University–Northridge, Northridge, California, U.S.A.*

Markus Helfert / *School of Computing, Dublin City University, Dublin, Ireland*

Jean Henefer / *School of Information and Communication Studies, University College Dublin, Dublin, Ireland*

Steven L. Hensen / *Rare Book, Manuscript and Special Collections Library, Duke University, Durham, North Carolina, U.S.A.*

Pamela M. Henson / *Archives, Smithsonian Institution, Washington, District of Columbia, U.S.A.*

Peter Hernon / *Graduate School of Library and Information Science, Simmons College, Boston, Massachusetts, U.S.A.*

Dorothy H. Hertzel / *Case Western Reserve University, Cleveland, Ohio, U.S.A.*

Francis Heylighen / *Free University of Brussels, Brussels, Belgium*

Randolph Hock / *Online Strategies, Annapolis, Maryland, U.S.A.*

Theodora L. Hodges / *Berkeley, California, U.S.A.*

Sara S. Hodson / *Huntington Library, San Marino, California, U.S.A.*

Judy C. Holoviak / *American Geophysical Union, Washington, District of Columbia, U.S.A.*

Aleksandra Horvat / *Faculty of Philosophy, University of Zagreb, Zagreb, Croatia*

Ali Houissa / *Olin Library, Cornell University, Ithaca, New York, U.S.A.*

Pamela Howard-Reguindin / *Library of Congress Office, Nairobi, Kenya*

Han-Yin Huang / *International Centre for Cultural and Heritage Studies, Newcastle University, Newcastle upon Tyne, U.K.*

Kathleen Hughes / *American Library Association, Chicago, Illinois, U.S.A.*

Betsy L. Humphreys / *National Library of Medicine, Bethesda, Maryland, U.S.A.*

Charlene S. Hurt / *University Library, Georgia State University, Atlanta, Georgia, U.S.A.*

Sue Hutley / *Australian Library and Information Association, Deakin, Australian Capital Territory, Australia*

John P. Immroth / *University of Pittsburgh, Pittsburgh, Pennsylvania, U.S.A.*

Peter Ingwersen / *Royal School of Library and Information Science, University of Copenhagen, Copenhagen, Denmark*

Vanessa Irvin / *Library and Information Science Program, Information and Computer Sciences Department, University of Hawaii at Mānoa, Honolulu, Hawaii, U.S.A.*

Karla Irwin / *University Libraries, University of Nevada–Las Vegas, Las Vegas, Nevada, U.S.A.*

October R. Ivins / *Ivins eContent Solutions, Sharon, Massachusetts, U.S.A.*

Kalervo Järvelin / *School of Information Science, University of Tampere, Tampere, Finland*

Jean Frédéric Jauslin / *Federal Department of Home Affairs (FDHA), Swiss Federal Office of Culture, Bern, Switzerland*

V. Jeyaraj / *Hepzibah Institute of Conversion, Chennai, India*

Scott Johnston / *McPherson Library, University of Victoria, Victoria, British Columbia, Canada*

Trevor Jones / *Mountain Heritage Center, Western Carolina University, Cullowhee, North Carolina, U.S.A.*

William Jones / *Information School, University of Washington, Seattle, Washington, U.S.A.*

Jay Jordan / *OCLC Online Computer Library Center, Inc., Dublin, Ohio, U.S.A.*

Corinne Jörgensen / *School of Information Studies, Florida State University, Tallahassee, Florida, U.S.A.*

Gene Joseph / *Aboriginal Library Consultant, Langley, British Columbia, Canada*

Daniel N. Joudrey / *School of Library and Information Science, Simmons College, Boston, Massachusetts, U.S.A.*

Heidi Julien / *Library and Information Studies, State University of New York–Buffalo, Buffalo, New York, U.S.A.*

Janet Kaaya / *Department of Information Studies, University of California, Los Angeles, California, U.S.A.*

Philomena Kagwiria Mwirigi / *Kenya National Library Service (KNLS), Nairobi, Kenya*

Athanase B. Kanamugire / *Library Consultant, Dhahran, Saudi Arabia*

Paul B. Kantor / *School of Communication and Information, Rutgers University, New Brunswick, New Jersey, U.S.A.*

Sofia Kapnisi / *International Federation of Library Associations and Institutions, The Hague, the Netherlands*

Nelson Otieno Karilus / *Kenya National Library Service (KNLS), Nairobi, Kenya*

Amy M. Kautzman / *University of California, Berkeley, Berkeley, California, U.S.A.*

Karalyn Kavanaugh / *Account Services Manager, EBSCO Information Services, Birmingham, Alabama, U.S.A.*

Caroline Kayoro / *Kenya National Library Service (KNLS), Nairobi, Kenya*

Andreas Kellerhals / *Federal Department of Home Affairs (FDHA), Swiss Federal Archives, Bern, Switzerland*

John M. Kennedy / *Indiana University, Bloomington, Indiana, U.S.A.*

Kristen Kern / *Portland State University, Portland, Oregon, U.S.A.*

Christopher S.G. Khoo / *School of Communication and Information, Nanyang Technological University, Singapore*

Tapan Khopkar / *University of Michigan, Ann Arbor, Michigan, U.S.A.*

Irene Muthoni Kibandi / *Kenya National Library Service (KNLS), Nairobi, Kenya*

Ruth E. Kifer / *Dr. Martin Luther King, Jr. Library, San Jose State University, San Jose, California, U.S.A.*

Seong Hee Kim / *Department of Library and Information Science, Chung-Ang University, Seoul, South Korea*

Pancras Kimaru / *Kenya National Library Service (KNLS), Nairobi, Kenya*

Karen E. King / *Washington, District of Columbia, U.S.A.*

William R. King / *University of Pittsburgh, Pittsburgh, Pennsylvania, U.S.A.*

Susan K. Kinnell / *Consultant, Santa Barbara, California, U.S.A.*

Laurence J. Kipp / *Harvard University, Cambridge, Massachusetts, U.S.A.*

Thomas G. Kirk, Jr. / *Earlham College Libraries, Earlham College, Richmond, Indiana, U.S.A.*

Breanne A. Kirsch / *Library, Emerging Technologies, University of South Carolina Upstate, Spartanburg, South Carolina, U.S.A.*

Vernon N. Kisling, Jr. / *Marston Science Library, University of Florida, Gainesville, Florida, U.S.A.*

Adam D. Knowles / *San Diego, California, U.S.A.*

Rebecca Knuth / *Library and Information Science Program, University of Hawaii, Honolulu, Hawaii, U.S.A.*

Michael Koenig / *College of Information and Computer Science, Long Island University, Brookville, New York, U.S.A.*

Jesse Koennecke / *Cornell University Library, Cornell University College of Arts and Sciences, Ithaca, New York, U.S.A.*

Jes Koepfler / *Museum Studies Program, Faculty of Information Studies, University of Toronto, Toronto, Ontario, Canada*

Amelia Koford / *Blumberg Memorial Library, Texas Lutheran University, Seguin, Texas, U.S.A.*

Toru Koizumi / *Library, Rikkyo University, Tokyo, Japan*

Josip Kolanović / *Croatian State Archives, Zagreb, Croatia*

Sjoerd Koopman / *International Federation of Library Associations and Institutions, The Hague, the Netherlands*

Donald Kraft / *Department of Computer Science, U.S. Air Force Academy, Colorado Springs, Colorado, U.S.A.*

Allison Krebs / *University of Arizona, Tucson, Arizona, U.S.A.*

Judith F. Krug / *Office for Intellectual Freedom, American Library Association, Chicago, Illinois, U.S.A.*

D.W. Krummel / *Emeritus, Graduate School of Library and Information Science, University of Illinois at Urbana-Champaign, Champaign, Illinois, U.S.A.*

Carol Collier Kuhlthau / *Department of Library and Information Science, Rutgers University, New Brunswick, New Jersey, U.S.A.*

Krishan Kumar / *Former Head, Department of Library and Information Science, University of Delhi, New Delhi, India*

Sanna Kumpulainen / *Library, Tampere University of Technology, Tampere, Finland*

Michael J. Kurtz / *National Archives at College Park, U.S. National Archives and Records Administration, College Park, Maryland, U.S.A.*

Zhenhua Lai / *Department of Management Information Systems, University of Arizona, Tucson, Arizona, U.S.A.*

Mounia Lalmas / *Department of Computing Science, University of Glasgow, Glasgow, U.K.*

Heather M. Lamond / *Massey University Library, Palmerston North, New Zealand*

F.W. Lancaster / *Graduate School of Library and Information Science, University of Illinois at Urbana-Champaign, Urbana, Illinois, U.S.A.*

Ronald L. Larsen / *School of Information Sciences, University of Pittsburgh, Pittsburgh, Pennsylvania, U.S.A.*

Ray R. Larson / *School of Information, University of California—Berkeley, Berkeley, California, U.S.A.*

Jesús Lau / *Library Services Unit USBI Veracruz (USBI VER), University of Veracruz, Veracruz, Mexico*

Judith V. Lechner / *Department of Educational Foundations, Leadership, and Technology, Auburn University, Auburn, Alabama, U.S.A.*

Christopher A. Lee / *School of Information and Library Science, University of North Carolina at Chapel Hill, Chapel Hill, North Carolina, U.S.A.*

Janet Lee / *University of Denver, Denver, Colorado, U.S.A, and Regis University, Denver, Colorado, U.S.A.*

Catherine Leekam / *Museum Studies Program, Faculty of Information Studies, University of Toronto, Toronto, Ontario, Canada*

Kjell Lemström / *Department of Computer Science, University of Helsinki, Helsinki, Finland*

Timothy F. Leslie / *Department of Geography and Geoinformation Science, George Mason University, Fairfax, Virginia, U.S.A.*

Noémie Lesquins / *Scientific Mission (DSR), National Library of France, Paris, France*

Rosalind K. Lett / *Information-2-Knowledge, Atlanta, Georgia, U.S.A.*

Allison V. Level / *Colorado State University, Fort Collins, Colorado, U.S.A.*

Michael Levine-Clark / *Penrose Library, University of Denver, Denver, Colorado, U.S.A.*

Anany Levitin / *Department of Computing Sciences, Villanova University, Villanova, Pennsylvania, U.S.A.*

Marjorie Lewis / *Canaan, New York, U.S.A.*

Elizabeth D. Liddy / *School of Information Studies, Syracuse University, Syracuse, New York, U.S.A.*

Silje C. Lier / *Software & Information Industry Association, Washington, District of Columbia, U.S.A.*

Jane E. Light / *Dr. Martin Luther King, Jr. Library, San Jose Public Library, San Jose, California, U.S.A.*

Paul M. Lima / *Canadian Heritage Information Network (CHIN), Gatineau, Quebec, Canada*

Louise Limberg / *Swedish School of Library and Information Science, University of Borås and University of Gothenburg, Borås, Sweden*

Shin-jeng Lin / *Department of Business Administration, Le Moyne College, Syracuse, New York, U.S.A.*

Sarah Lippincott / *Educopia Institute, Atlanta, Georgia, U.S.A.*

Peter Johan Lor / *School of Information Studies, University of Wisconsin-Milwaukee, Milwaukee, Wisconsin, U.S.A., and Department of Information Science, University of Pretoria, Pretoria, South Africa*

Beth Luey / *Fairhaven, Massachusetts, U.S.A.*

Joseph Luke / *Kazakhstan Institute of Management, Economics and Strategic Research (KIMEP), Almaty, Kazakhstan*

Claudia Lux / *Central and Regional Library of Berlin (ZLB), Berlin, Germany*

Marianne Lykke / *Information Interaction and Architecture, Royal School of Library and Information Science, Aalborg, Denmark*

Elena Macevičiūtė / *Faculty of Communication, Vilnius University, Vilnius, Lithuania, and Swedish School of Library and Information Science, University of Borås, Borås, Sweden*

Juan D. Machin-Mastromatteo / *Universidad Central de Venezuela, Caracas, Venezuela*

Barbara A. Macikas / *American Library Association, Chicago, Illinois, U.S.A.*

Leslie Madsen-Brooks / *Boise State University, Boise, Idaho, U.S.A.*

William J. Maher / *Archives, University of Illinois at Urbana-Champaign, Urbana, Illinois, U.S.A.*

Thomas Mann / *Library of Congress, Washington, District of Columbia, U.S.A.*

Sylva Natalie Manoogian / *Department of Information Studies, University of California, Los Angeles, Los Angeles, California, U.S.A.*

Daniel Marcu / *Information Sciences Institute, University of Southern California, Marina del Rey, California, U.S.A.*

James W. Marcum / *Fairleigh Dickinson University, Madison, New Jersey, U.S.A.*

Francesca Marini / *School of Library, Archival and Information Studies, University of British Columbia, Vancouver, British Columbia, Canada*

Johan Marklund / *Department of Industrial Management and Logistics, Lund University, Lund, Sweden*

Dian I. Martin / *Small Bear Technical Consulting, LLC, Thorn Hill, Tennessee, U.S.A.*

Susan K. Martin / *Lauinger Library, Georgetown University, Washington, District of Columbia, U.S.A.*

Paul F. Marty / *College of Communication and Information, Florida State University, Tallahassee, Florida, U.S.A.*

Dan Marwit / *Lee H. Skolnick Architecture + Design Partnership, New York, New York, U.S.A.*

Laura Matzer / *Arizona Museum for Youth, Mesa, Arizona, U.S.A.*

Robert L. Maxwell / *Special Collections and Metadata Catalog Department, Brigham Young University, Provo, Utah, U.S.A.*

Hope Mayo / *Houghton Library, Harvard University, Cambridge, Massachusetts, U.S.A.*

Sally H. McCallum / *Network Development and MARC Standards Office, Library of Congress, Washington, District of Columbia, U.S.A.*

Gavan McCarthy / *eScholarship Research Centre, University of Melbourne, Melbourne, Victoria, Australia*

Ian McGowan / *Former Librarian, National Library of Scotland, Edinburgh, U.K.*

Roger McHaney / *Department of Management, Kansas State University, Manhattan, Kansas, U.S.A.*

I.C. McIlwaine / *University College London, School of Library, Archive and Information Studies, London, U.K.*

Sue McKemmish / *Centre for Organisational and Social Informatics, Monash University, Melbourne, Victoria, Australia*

Marie E. McVeigh / *JCR and Bibliographic Policy, Thomson Reuters - Scientific, Philadelphia, Pennsylvania, U.S.A.*

Linda Mboya / *National Museums of Kenya, Nairobi, Kenya*

Judith Adams Meadows / *State Law Library of Montana, Helena, Montana, U.S.A.*

K. van der Meer / *Faculty of Electrical Engineering, Mathematics and Computer Science, Delft University, the Netherlands; Information and Library Science, IOIW, Antwerp University, Belgium; and D-CIS, Delft, The Netherlands*

Bharat Mehra / *School of Information Sciences, University of Tennessee, Knoxville, Tennessee, U.S.A.*

Margaret Ann Mellinger / *OSU Libraries & Press, Oregon State University, Corvallis, Oregon, U.S.A.*

Elizabeth E. Merritt / *American Association of Museums, Washington, District of Columbia, U.S.A.*

David Millman / *Academic Information Systems, Columbia University, New York, U.S.A.*

Jack Mills / *North-Western Polytechnic, London, U.K.*

Kevin L. Mills / *National Institute of Standards and Technology, Gaithersburg, Maryland, U.S.A.*

Staša Milojević / *Department of Information Studies, University of California, Los Angeles, Los Angeles, California, U.S.A.*

Marla Misunas / *Collections Information and Access, San Francisco Museum of Modern Art, San Francisco, California, U.S.A.*

Joan S. Mitchell / *OCLC Online Computer Library Center, Inc., Dublin, Ohio, U.S.A.*

Yoriko Miyabe / *Rikkyo University, Tokyo, Japan*

Diane Mizrachi / *University Libraries, University of California–Los Angeles, Los Angeles, California, U.S.A.*

William Moen / *Texas Center for Digital Knowledge, University of North Texas, Denton, Texas, U.S.A.*

Abdul Moid / *University of Karachi, Karachi, Pakistan*

Hermann Moisl / *Center for Research in Linguistics, University of Newcastle upon Tyne, Newcastle upon Tyne, U.K.*

Ole Magnus Mølbak Andersen / *Danish State Archives, Copenhagen, Denmark*

Mavis B. Molto / *Utah State University, Logan, Utah, U.S.A.*

Philip Mooney / *Heritage Communications, Coca-Cola Company, Atlanta, Georgia, U.S.A.*

Reagan W. Moore / *San Diego Supercomputer Center, University of North Carolina at Chapel Hill, Chapel Hill, North Carolina, U.S.A.*

Mersini Moreleli-Cacouris / *Department of Library Science and Information Systems, Technological Educational Institute (TEI) of Thessaloniki, Sindos, Greece*

Paul K. Moser / *Department of Philosophy, Loyola University Chicago, Chicago, Illinois, U.S.A.*

Clara C. Mosquera / *Library, Kirkland & Ellis LLP, Chicago, IL, U.S.A.*

David J. Muddiman / *Leeds Metropolitan University, Leeds, U.K.*

Nancy C. Mulvany / *Bayside Indexing Service, Fort Collins, Colorado, U.S.A.*

Sue Myburgh / *School of Communication, University of South Australia, Adelaide, South Australia, Australia*

Elli Mylonas / *Brown University, Providence, Rhode Island, U.S.A.*

Jeremy Myntti / *J. Willard Marriott Library, Salt Lake City, Utah, U.S.A.*

Jacob Nadal / *ReCAP: The Research Collections and Preservation Consortium, Princeton, New Jersey, U.S.A.*

Diane Nahl / *Information and Computer Sciences Department, University of Hawaii, Honolulu, Hawaii, U.S.A.*

Robert Nardini / *Vice President, Library Services, ProQuest Books, La Vergne, Tennessee, U.S.A.*

Arnold vander Nat / *Department of Philosophy, Loyola University Chicago, Chicago, Illinois, U.S.A.*

Charles M. Naumer / *Information School, University of Washington, Seattle, Washington, U.S.A.*

Sophie Ndegwa / *Kenya National Library Service (KNLS), Nairobi, Kenya*

Dixie Neilson / *University of Florida, Gainesville, Florida, U.S.A.*

Sarah Beth Nelson / *School of Information and Library Sciences, University of North Carolina at Chapel Hill, Chapel Hill, North Carolina, U.S.A.*

Stuart J. Nelson / *National Library of Medicine, Bethesda, Maryland, U.S.A.*

Stephanie Nemcsok / *Museum Studies Program, Faculty of Information Studies, University of Toronto, Toronto, Ontario, Canada*

Ken Neveroski / *College of Information and Computer Science, Long Island University, Brookville, New York, U.S.A.*

Jennifer Ng / *Museum Studies Program, Faculty of Information Studies, University of Toronto, Toronto, Ontario, Canada*

Melissa Niiya / *Portland Public Schools, Portland, Oregon, U.S.A.*

Angela Noseworthy / *Museum Studies Program, Faculty of Information Studies, University of Toronto, Toronto, Ontario, Canada*

Barbara E. Nye / *Ictus Consulting, LLC, Pasadena, California, U.S.A.*

Charles Nzivo / *Kenya National Library Service (KNLS), Nairobi, Kenya*

Dennis O'Brien / *Maps and Wayfinding, LLC, Mystic, Connecticut, U.S.A.*

Karen Lynn O'Brien / *American Library Association, Chicago, Illinois, U.S.A.*

Kieron O'Hara / *Intelligence, Agents, Multimedia Group, University of Southampton, Southampton, U.K.*

Elizabeth O'Keefe / *Morgan Library and Museum, New York, U.S.A.*

Denise I. O'Shea / *Fairleigh Dickinson University, Teaneck, New Jersey, U.S.A.*

Douglas W. Oard / *College of Information Studies, University of Maryland, College Park, Maryland, U.S.A.*

Maria Oldal / *Morgan Library and Museum, New York, U.S.A.*

Lorne Olfman / *School of Information Systems and Technology, Claremont Graduate University, Claremont, California, U.S.A.*

Bette W. Oliver / *Austin, Texas, U.S.A.*

Annette Olson / *Biological Resources Division, U.S. Geological Survey, Reston, Virginia, U.S.A.*

Hope A. Olson / *School of Information Studies, University of Wisconsin-Milwaukee, Milwaukee, Wisconsin, U.S.A.*

Lawrence J. Olszewski / *OCLC Library, Dublin, Ohio, U.S.A.*

Kok-Leong Ong / *School of Information Technology, Deakin University, Burwood, Victoria, Australia*

Tim Owen / *Chartered Institute of Library and Information Professionals (CILIP), London, U.K.*

John C. Paolillo / *School of Informatics and School of Library and Information Science, Indiana University, Bloomington, Indiana, U.S.A.*

Eun Bong Park / *Library Service Department, National Library of Korea, Seoul, South Korea*

Soyeon Park / *Department of Library and Information Science, Duksung Womens University, Seoul, South Korea*

Gabriella Pasi / *Department of Informatics, Systems and Communication, University of Studies of Milano Bicocca, Milan, Italy*

Norman Paskin / *Tertius Ltd., Oxford, U.K.*

Christiane Paul / *Whitney Museum of American Art, New York, U.S.A.*

Ellen Pearlstein / *Information Studies and UCLA / Getty Program in the Conservation of Ethnographic and Archaeological Materials, University of California, Los Angeles, Los Angeles, California, U.S.A.*

Kathleen de la Peña McCook / *School of Library and Information Science, University of South Florida, Tampa, Florida, U.S.A.*

Steve Pepper / *Department of Linguistics, University of Oslo, Oslo, Norway*

Manuel A. Pérez-Quiñones / *Department of Software and Information Systems, University of North Carolina, Charlotte, North Carolina, U.S.A.*

Paul Evan Peters / *University of Pittsburgh, Pittsburgh, Pennsylvania, U.S.A.*

Jakob Heide Petersen / *Danish Agency for Libraries and Media, Copenhagen, Denmark*

Mary Jane Petrowski / *American Library Association, Chicago, Illinois, U.S.A.*

Katharine J. Phenix / *Northglenn Branch, Rangeview Library District, Northglenn, Colorado, U.S.A.*

Robert B. Pickering / *Gilcrease Museum, and Museum Science and Management Program, University of Tulsa, Tulsa, Oklahoma, U.S.A.*

Janice T. Pilch / *Rutgers University Libraries, Rutgers University, New Brunswick, New Jersey, U.S.A.*

Thomas E. Pinelli / *Langley Research Center, National Aeronautics and Space Administration (NASA) Hampton, Virginia, U.S.A.*

Daniel Pitti / *Alderman Library, Institute for Advanced Technology in the Humanities, University of Virginia, Charlottesville, Virginia, U.S.A.*

Elena Ploşniţă / *Science Department, National Museum of Archaeology and History of Moldova, Chisinau, Republic of Moldova*

Gabriela Podušelová / *Slovak National Museum, Bratislava, Slovak Republic*

Danny C.C. Poo / *School of Computing, Department of Information Systems, National University of Singapore, Singapore*

Martine Poulain / *Department of Libraries and Documentation, National Institute for the History of Art (INHA), Paris, France*

Tammy Powell / *National Library of Medicine, Bethesda, Maryland, U.S.A.*

Stephen Prine / *Library of Congress, Washington, District of Columbia, U.S.A.*

Mary Jo Pugh / *Editor, American Archivist, Walnut Creek, California, U.S.A.*

Ajit K. Pyati / *University of Western Ontario, London, Ontario, Canada*

Aimée C. Quinn / *Government Publications Services, Brooks Library, Central Washington University, Ellensburg, Washington, U.S.A.*

Jennie Quiñónez-Skinner / *University Library, California State University–Northridge, Northridge, California, U.S.A.*

Debbie Rabina / *School of Library and Information Science, Pratt Institute, New York, New York, U.S.A.*

Katalin Radics / *Research Library, University of California—Los Angeles, Los Angeles, California, U.S.A.*

Carl Rahkonen / *Harold S. Orendorff Music Library, Indiana University of Pennsylvania, Indiana, Pennsylvania, U.S.A.*

Jocelyn Rankin / *Centers for Disease Control and Prevention Library, Atlanta, Georgia, U.S.A.*

Samuel J. Redman / *Department of History, University of California, Berkeley, Berkeley, California, U.S.A.*

Thomas C. Redman / *Navesink Consulting Group, Little Silver, New Jersey, U.S.A.*

Barbara Reed / *Recordkeeping Innovation, Sydney, New South Wales, Australia*

Marcia Reed / *Getty Research Institute, Los Angeles, CA, U.S.A.*

CarrieLynn D. Reinhard / *Department of Communication, Business, and Information Technologies, Roskilde University, Roskilde, Denmark*

Harold C. Relyea / *Congressional Research Service, Library of Congress, Washington, District of Columbia, U.S.A.*

Steve Ricci / *Department of Information Studies/Film and Television, University of California–Los Angeles, Los Angeles, California, U.S.A.*

Ronald E. Rice / *Department of Communication, University of California–Santa Barbara, Santa Barbara, California, U.S.A.*

John V. Richardson, Jr. / *Department of Information Studies, University of California, Los Angeles, Los Angeles, California, U.S.A.*

Soo Young Rieh / *School of Information, University of Michigan, Ann Arbor, Michigan, U.S.A.*

Kevin S. Rioux / *Division of Library and Information Science, St. John's University, Queens, New York, U.S.A.*

Julian Roberts / *Wolfson College, University of Oxford, Oxford, U.K.*

Lyn Robinson / *City, University of London, London, U.K.*

Diane Robson / *University Libraries, Media Library, University of North Texas, Denton, Texas, U.S.A.*

Michael Rodriguez / *Michigan State University Libraries, East Lansin, Michigan, U.S.A.*

Juraj Roháč / *Department of Archival Science and Auxiliary Historical Sciences, Comenius University in, Bratislava, Slovak Republic*

Mark Roosa / *Pepperdine University, Malibu, California, U.S.A.*

Jonathan Rose / *Department of History, Drew University, Madison, New Jersey, U.S.A.*

Howard Rosenbaum / *School of Library and Information Science, Indiana University, Bloomington, Indiana, U.S.A.*

Catherine Sheldrick Ross / *Faculty of Information and Media Studies, University of Western Ontario, London, Ontario, Canada*

Shannon Ross / *Canadian Heritage Information Network (CHIN), Gatineau, Quebec, Canada*

Richard Rubin / *School of Library and Information Science, Kent State University, Kent, Ohio, U.S.A.*

Lynne M. Rudasill / *University of Illinois at Urbana-Champaign, Champaign, Illinois, U.S.A.*

Michael Rush / *Beinecke Rare Book and Manuscript Library, Yale University, New Haven, Connecticut, U.S.A.*

Mariza Russo / *Faculty of Administration and Accounting Sciences (FACC), Federal University of Rio de Janeiro, Rio de Janeiro, Brazil*

Athena Salaba / *Kent State University, Kent, Ohio, U.S.A.*

Romelia Salinas / *California State University, Los Angeles, Los Angeles, California, U.S.A.*

Airi Salminen / *Department of Computer Science and Information Systems, University of Jyväskylä, Jyväskylä, Finland*

Michael J. Salvo / *Department of English, Purdue University, West Lafayette, Indiana, U.S.A.*

Robert J. Sandusky / *University Library, University of Illinois at Chicago, Chicago, Illinois, U.S.A.*

Tefko Saracevic / *School of Communication and Information, Rutgers University, New Brunswick, New Jersey, U.S.A.*

Chris Sauer / *Said Business School, University of Oxford, Oxford, U.K.*

Rejéan Savard / *School of Library and Information Science, University of Montreal, Montreal, Quebec, Canada*

Reijo Savolainen / *School of Information Sciences, University of Tampere, Tampere, Finland*

Barbara Schaefer / *Geneseo, New York, U.S.A.*

Silvia Schenkolewski-Kroll / *Department of Information Science, Bar-Ilan University, Ramat Gan, Israel*

Lael J. Schooler / *Center for Adaptive Behavior and Cognition, Max Planck Institute for Human Development, Berlin, Germany*

Joachim Schöpfel / *Department of Library and Information Sciences (IDIST), GERiico Laboratory Charles de Gaulle University Lille 3, Villeneuve d'Ascq, France*

Catherine F. Schryer / *Department of English Language and Literature, University of Waterloo, Waterloo, Ontario, Canada*

Marjorie Schwarzer / *Museum Studies Department, John F. Kennedy University, Berkeley, California, U.S.A.*

Jo Ann Secor / *Lee H. Skolnick Architecture + Design Partnership, New York, New York, U.S.A.*

Sara Selwood / *Department of Cultural Policy and Management, City University, London, U.K.*

Frank B. Sessa / *University of Pittsburgh, Pittsburgh, Pennsylvania, U.S.A.*

Mark Sgambettera / *Bronx County Historical Society, Bronx, New York, U.S.A.*

Ayman Shabana / International Institute, University of California, Los Angeles, Los Angeles, California, U.S.A.

Nigel Shadbolt / *School of Electronics and Computer Science, University of Southampton, Southampton, U.K.*

Kalpana Shankar / *School of Informatics, Indiana University, Bloomington, Indiana, U.S.A.*

Debora Shaw / *School of Library and Information Science, Indiana University, Bloomington, Indiana, U.S.A.*

Conrad Shayo / *Department of Information and Decision Sciences, California State University—San Bernardino, San Bernardino, California, U.S.A.*

Elizabeth Shepherd / *Department of Information Studies, University College London, London, U.K.*

Beverly K. Sheppard / *Institute for Learning Innovation, Edgewater, Maryland, U.S.A.*

Ross Shimmon / *Faversham, U.K.*

Snunith Shoham / *Department of Information Science, Bar-Ilan University, Ramat Gan, Israel*

Lyudmila Shpilevaya / *New York Public Library, New York, New York, U.S.A.*

David Shumaker / *School of Library and Information Science, Catholic University of America, Washington, District of Columbia, U.S.A.*

Judith A. Siess / *Information Bridges International, Inc., Champaign, Illinois, U.S.A.*

John Edward Simmons / *Museologica, Bellefonte, Pennsylvania, U.S.A.*

Anestis Sitas / *Aristotle University of Thessaloniki, Thessaloniki, Greece*

Roswitha Skare / *Institute of Culture and Literature, UiT The Arctic University of Norway, Tromsø, Norway*

Katherine Skinner / *Educopia Institute, Atlanta, Georgia, U.S.A.*

Lee H. Skolnick / *Lee H. Skolnick Architecture + Design Partnership, New York, New York, U.S.A.*

Mette Skov / *Department of Communication and Psychology, Aalborg University, Aalborg, Denmark*

Bobby Smiley / *Vanderbilt University, Heard Libraries, Nashville, Tennessee, U.S.A.*

Linda C. Smith / *School of Information Sciences, University of Illinois at Urbana-Champaign, Champaign, Illinois, U.S.A.*

Lois Smith / *Human Factors and Ergonomics Society, Santa Monica, California, U.S.A.*

Lori Smith / *Linus A. Sims Memorial Library, Southeastern Louisiana University, Hammond, Louisiana, U.S.A.*

Patricia A. Smith / *Colorado State University, Fort Collins, Colorado, U.S.A.*

Scott A. Smith / *Langlois Public Library, Langlois, Oregon, U.S.A.*

A. Patricia Smith-Hunt / *Science Library, Preservation Services, University of California, Riverside, Riverside, California, U.S.A.*

Karen Smith-Yoshimura / *Online Computer Library Center (OCLC), San Mateo, California, U.S.A.*

Diane H. Sonnenwald / *University College Dublin, Dublin, Ireland*

Nour Soufi / *Library Cataloging and Metadata Center, University of California, Los Angeles, Los Angeles, California, U.S.A.*

Barbara M. Spiegelman / *Churchill Associates, Pittsburgh, Pennsylvania, U.S.A.*

Robert P. Spindler / *Department of Archives and Manuscripts, Arizona State University, Tempe, Arizona, U.S.A.*

Joie Springer / *Information Society Division, UNESCO, Paris, France*

Suresh Srinivasan / *National Library of Medicine, Bethesda, Maryland, U.S.A.*

Guy St. Clair / *Knowledge Management and Learning, SMR International, New York, New York, U.S.A.*

Cheryl L. Stadel-Bevans / *National Archives and Records Administration, College Park, Maryland, U.S.A.*

Jill Stein / *Institute for Learning Innovation, Edgewater, Maryland, U.S.A.*

Marcia K. Stein / *Museum of Fine Arts, Houston, Houston, Texas, U.S.A.*

Jela Steinerová / *Department of Library and Information Science, Comenius University in, Bratislava, Slovak Republic*

Dick Stenmark / *Department of Applied IT, IT University of Gothenburg, Gothenburg, Sweden*

Andy Stephens / *OBE, Board Secretary, Head of International Engagement, The British Library, London, U.K.*

Margaret Stieg Dalton / *School of Library and Information Studies, University of Alabama, Tuscaloosa, Alabama, U.S.A.*

Katina Strauch / *Addlestone Library, College of Charleston, Charleston, South Carolina, U.S.A.*

Robert D. Stueart / *Graduate School of Library and Information Science, Simmons College, Boston, Massachusetts, U.S.A.*

Paul F. Stuehrenberg / *Yale Divinity Library, New Haven, Connecticut, U.S.A.*

Brian William Sturm / *School of Information and Library Sciences, University of North Carolina at Chapel Hill, Chapel Hill, North Carolina, U.S.A.*

Anna Suorsa / *University of Oulu, Oulu, Finland*

Brett Sutton / *Aurora University, Aurora, Illinois, U.S.A.*

Sarah Sutton / *Mary and Jeff Bell Library, Texas A&M University-Corpus Christi, Corpus Christi, Texas, U.S.A.*

Destinee Kae Swanson / *Adams Museum & House, Inc., Deadwood, South Dakota, U.S.A.*

H.L. Swanson / *GSOE, University of California, Riverside, California, U.S.A.*

Miriam E. Sweeney / *School of Library and Information Studies, University of Alabama, Tuscaloosa, Alabama, U.S.A.*

Shelley Sweeney / *University of Manitoba, Winnipeg, Manitoba, Canada*

Jean Tague-Sutcliffe / *Graduate School of Library and Information Science, University of Western Ontario, London, Ontario, Canada*

Masaya Takayama / *National Archives of Japan, Tokyo, Japan*

Sanna Talja / *Department of Information Studies and Interactive Media, University of Tampere, Tampere, Finland*

G. Thomas Tanselle / *Vice President, John Simon Guggenheim Memorial Foundation, New York, New York, U.S.A.*

Ivan Tanzer / *Museum Studies Program, Faculty of Information Studies, University of Toronto, Toronto, Ontario, Canada*

Melissa Terras / *UCL Department of Information Studies, UCL Centre for Digital Humanities, University College London, London, U.K.*

Mike Thelwall / *School of Computing and Information Technology, University of Wolverhampton, Wolverhampton, U.K.*

Lynne M. Thomas / *Rare Books and Special Collections, Northern Illinois University, DeKalb, Illinois, U.S.A.*

Lawrence S. Thompson / *University of Kentucky, Lexington, Kentucky, U.S.A.*

Jens Thorhauge / *Danish Agency for Libraries and Media, Copenhagen, Denmark*

Anne Thurston / *International Records Management Trust, London, U.K.*

Michael Tiemann / *Open Source Initiative, Chapel Hill, North Carolina, U.S.A.*

Christinger Tomer / *School of Information Sciences, University of Pittsburgh, Pittsburgh, Pennsylvania, U.S.A.*

Elaine G. Toms / *Faculty of Management, Dalhousie University, Halifax, Nova Scotia, Canada*

Jack Toolin / *Whitney Museum of American Art, New York, U.S.A.*

Jennifer Trant / *Archives & Museum Informatics, Toronto, Ontario, Canada*

Barry Trott / *Williamsburg Regional Library, Williamsburg, Virginia, U.S.A.*

Alice Trussell / *Hale Library, Kansas State University, Manhattan, Kansas, U.S.A.*

John Mark Tucker / *Abilene Christian University, Abilene, Texas, U.S.A.*

James M. Turner / *School of Library and Information Sciences, University of Montreal, Montreal, Quebec, Canada*

Louise Tythacott / *Centre for Museology, University of Manchester, Manchester, U.K.*

George Tzanetakis / *Department of Computer Science, University of Victoria, Victoria, British Columbia, Canada*

Franklyn Herbert Upward / *Centre for Organisational and Social Informatics, Monash University, Melbourne, Victoria, Australia*

Richard Urban / *Graduate School of Library and Information Science, University of Illinois, Champaign, Illinois, U.S.A.*

Rachel E. Vacek / *University of Michigan, Ann Arbor, Michigan, U.S.A.*

Ron Van den Branden / *Centre for Scholarly Editing and Document Studies, Royal Academy of Dutch Language and Literature, Gent, Belgium*

Sydney C. Van Nort / *The City College of New York, The City University of New York, New York, U.S.A.*

Edward Vanhoutte / *Centre for Scholarly Editing and Document Studies, Royal Academy of Dutch Language and Literature, Gent, Belgium*

Rebecca Vargha / *Information and Library Science Library, University of North Carolina at Chapel Hill, Chapel Hill, North Carolina, U.S.A.*

Jana Varlejs / *School of Communication, Information and Library Studies, Rutgers University, New Brunswick, New Jersey, U.S.A.*

Jason Vaughan / *Library Technologies, University of Nevada, Las Vegas University Libraries, Las Vegas, Nevada, U.S.A.*

Dale J. Vidmar / *Southern Oregon University Library, Ashland, Oregon, U.S.A.*

Diane Vizine-Goetz / *OCLC Online Computer Library Center, Inc., Dublin, Ohio, U.S.A.*

Ellen M. Voorhees / *Information Technology Laboratory, National Institute of Standards and Technology, Gaithersburg, Maryland, U.S.A.*

Sharon L. Walbridge / *Libraries Washington State University, Pullman, Washington, U.S.A.*

Stephanie Walker / *Brooklyn College, City University of New York, Brooklyn, New York, U.S.A.*

Virginia A. Walter / *Department of Information Studies, University of California, Los Angeles, Los Angeles, California, U.S.A.*

Mark Warschauer / *School of Education, University of California, Irvine, CA, U.S.A.*

Nigel M. Waters / *Department of Geography and Geoinformation Science, George Mason University, Fairfax, Virginia, U.S.A.*

Kathryn M. Wayne / *Art History/Classics Library, University of California, Berkeley, California, U.S.A.*

Frank Webster / *City University, London, U.K.*

Jeff Weddle / *School of Library and Information Studies, University of Alabama, Tuscaloosa, Alabama, U.S.A.*

Judith Weedman / *School of Library and Information Science, San Jose State University, Fullerton, California, U.S.A.*

Stuart L. Weibel / *Office of Research and Special Projects, OCLC Research, Dublin, Ohio, U.S.A.*

Jennifer Weil Arns / *School of Library and Information Science, University of South Carolina, Columbia, South Carolina, U.S.A.*

Bella Hass Weinberg / *Division of Library and Information Science, St. John's University, Queens, New York, New York, U.S.A.*

Volker M. Welter / *Department of the History of Art and Architecture, University of California, Santa Barbara, Santa Barbara, California, U.S.A.*

Caryn Wesner-Early / *ASRC Aerospace & Defense, US Patent & Trademark Office, Alexandria, Virginia, U.S.A.*

Lynn Westbrook / *School of Information, University of Texas at Austin, Austin, Texas, U.S.A.*

Howard D. White / *College of Computing and Informatics, Drexel University, Philadelphia, PA, U.S.A., and College of Information Science and Technology, Drexel University, Philadelphia, Pennsylvania, U.S.A.*

Layna White / *San Francisco Museum of Modern Art, San Francisco, California, U.S.A.*

Michael J. White / *Engineering and Science Library, Queen's University, Kingston, Ontario, Canada*

Sarah K. Wiant / *School of Law, Washington and Lee University, Lexington, Virginia, U.S.A.*

Stephen E. Wiberley, Jr. / *University of Illinois at Chicago, Chicago, Illinois, U.S.A.*

Gunilla Widén-Wulff / *Information Studies, Åbo Akademi University, Åbo, Finland*

Bradley J. Wiles / *Hill Memorial Library, Louisiana State University, Baton Rouge, Louisiana, U.S.A.*

Mary I. Wilke / *Center for Research Libraries, Chicago, Illinois, U.S.A.*

Barratt Wilkins / *Retired State Librarian of Florida, Tallahassee, Florida, U.S.A.*

Peter Willett / *Department of Information Studies, University of Sheffield, Sheffield, U.K.*

Kate Williams / *University of Illinois at Urbana-Champaign, Champaign, Illinois, U.S.A.*

Kirsty Williamson / *Caulfield School of IT, Monash University, Caulfield, Victoria, Australia and School of Information Studies, Charles Sturt University, Wagga Wagga, New South Wales, Australia*

Concepción S. Wilson / *School of Information Systems, Technology and Management, University of New South Wales, Sydney, New South Wales, Australia*

Ian E. Wilson / *Librarian and Archivist of Canada 2004–2009, Ottawa, Ontario, Canada*

Kristen Wilson / *North Carolina State University Libraries, Raleigh, North Carolina, U.S.A.*

Thomas D. Wilson / *Publisher/Editor in Chief, Information Research, U.K.*

Catherine C. Wilt / *PALINET, Philadelphia, Pennsylvania, U.S.A.*

Charles Wilt / *Association for Library Collections and Technical Services (ALCTS), Chicago, Illinois, U.S.A.*

Niels Windfeld Lund / *Institute of Culture and Literature, UiT The Arctic University of Norway, Troms , Norway*

Michael F. Winter / *Shields Library, University of California, Davis, California, U.S.A.*

Erica Wiseman / *Graduate School of Library and Information Studies, McGill University, Montreal, Quebec, Canada*

Steve W. Witt / *University of Illinois at Urbana-Champaign, Champaign, Illinois, U.S.A.*

Blanche Woolls / *iSchool, San Jose State University, San Jose, California, U.S.A.*

Louisa Worthington / *Public Library Association, Chicago, Illinois, U.S.A.*

Jadwiga Woźniak-Kasperek / *Institute of Information and Book Studies, University of Warsaw, Warsaw, Poland*

Judith Wusteman / *School of Information and Communication Studies, University College Dublin, Dublin, Ireland*

Iris Xie / *School of Information Studies, University of Wisconsin–Milwaukee, Milwaukee, Wisconsin, U.S.A.*

Yiyu Yao / *Department of Computer Science, University of Regina, Regina, Saskatchewan, Canada, and International WIC Institute, Beijing University of Technology, Beijing, China*

Janis L. Young / *Library of Congress, Washington, District of Columbia, U.S.A.*

Priscilla C. Yu / *University Library, University of Illinois at Urbana-Champaign, Urbana, Illinois, U.S.A.*

Jana Zabinski / *American National Standards Institute, New York, New York, U.S.A.*

Lisl Zach / *iSchool, Drexel University, Philadelphia, Pennsylvania, U.S.A.*

Olga Zaitseva / *Kazakhstan Institute of Management, Economics and Strategic Research (KIMEP), Almaty, Kazakhstan*

Marcia Lei Zeng / *School of Library and Information Science, Kent State University, Kent, Ohio, U.S.A.*

Yi Zeng / *International WIC Institute, Beijing University of Technology, Beijing, China*

Višnja Zgaga / *Museum Documentation Center, Zagreb, Croatia*

Jun Zhang / *Pitney Bowes, Shelton, Connecticut, U.S.A.*

Yulei Zhang / *Department of Management Information Systems, University of Arizona, Tucson, Arizona, U.S.A.*

Kai Zheng / *Department of Health Management and Policy, University of Michigan, Ann Arbor, Michigan, U.S.A.*

Ning Zhong / *Department of Life Science and Informatics, Maebashi Institute of Technology, Maebashi-City, Japan, and International WIC Institute, Beijing University of Technology, Beijing, China*

Maja Žumer / *University of Ljubljana, Slovenia*

Vladimir Zwass / *Computer Science and Management Information Systems, Fairleigh Dickinson University, Teaneck, New Jersey, U.S.A.*

Encyclopedia of Library and Information Sciences, Fourth Edition

Contents

Volume I

Volume I (*cont'd.*)

Volume I (*cont'd.*)

Volume II

Volume II (*cont'd.*)

Volume III

Volume III (*cont'd.*)

Volume III *(cont'd.)*

Volume IV

Volume IV (*cont'd.*)

Volume V

Volume V (*cont'd.*)

Volume VI

Volume VI (*cont'd.*)

Volume VI (*cont'd.*)

Volume VII

Volume VII (*cont'd.*)

Introduction to the Encyclopedia of Library and Information Sciences, Fourth Edition

How to Use This Encyclopedia

Entries are arranged alphabetically in this encyclopedia (see end papers for alphabetical list). The editors of this edition (ELIS-4) have decided to forego the Topical Table of Contents that was provided in ELIS-3 by editors Marcia Bates and Mary Niles Maack. At the time of publication of ELIS-3, the Topical TOC was crucial for readers to get a sense of how subjects were grouped and an understanding of the field or subfield through the clustering of categorical entries in the print edition. ELIS-4 is envisioned as a primarily online reference work where a Topical TOC does not serve the same purpose. The print edition is served well by the main TOC as well as the detailed index, while entries in the online version are easily discoverable through title, author, keyword, and full text searches.

In sum, relevant entries can be found by
1. Entry title (alphabetical arrangement of entries in the encyclopedia or listing in the end papers)
2. Specific name or keyword, including the index at the end of each volume

If the first name or keyword searched is not found, try several more variations—either different words or a different order of words. Most topics are described in several ways in the literature of a discipline, and the first term or phrase that comes to mind may not be the one used here.

Scope of the Encyclopedia

The title of the third edition, *Encyclopedia of Library and Information Sciences*, ended with the letter "s" because the encyclopedia was broadened to cover a spectrum of related and newly emerging information disciplines, including archival science, document theory, informatics, and records management, among others. The fourth edition continues this trend but with an extensive focus on the aspects of library and information sciences that have been heavily impacted by the adoption and reliance on online information distribution. This focus is reflected in the inclusion of numerous new entries such as digital preservation, altmetrics, web-scale discovery services, demand-driven acquisitions, and global open knowledgebases. Alongside these entries based on entirely new topics, the expanded use of the Internet for information has led to new treatment of traditional LIS topics such as resource description and access (RDA) that reflects the adoption of new standards for cataloging.

ELIS-4 also seeks to build upon the description of professional practice to round out the theoretical perspective that previous editions covered very well. Both current editors are academic research librarians and thus, focused heavily on addressing gaps in the encyclopedia related to academic research information while still relying heavily on the structure established by editors of ELIS-3. For example, ELIS-3 introduced country profiles and ELIS-4 builds upon that with new entries for New Zealand and a third on Brazil, in addition to revisions for Slovakia, Netherlands, Canada, Belarus, Kazakhstan, and Brazil among others. This edition also expands the number of entries for named cultural and information entities that did not appear in previous editions, such as the National Library of Medicine, North American Serials Interest Group (NASIG), the International Association of Scientific, Technical and Medical Publishers (STM), and ASLIB, as well as entities like the HathiTrust that have been established since the last edition was published. A number of new entries describing important information conferences such as the Acquisitions Institute at Timberline, the Charleston Conference, and Electronic Resources in Libraries (ER&L) also help round out the encyclopedia and further the description of the current state of academic research librarianship.

ELIS-4 also continues the tradition of designating important entries of historical or theoretical importance as "ELIS Classics." These are entries by major figures in the library and information sciences or those that describe core concepts in LIS theory, practice, or education that appeared in earlier editions of the encyclopedia. The current editors preserved the approximately 40 previous "ELIS Classics" and designated 13 previous entries as new "ELIS Classics."

There are more than 550 entries, of which more than 20 are new, another 93 are revisions to prior entries that have been brought up to date by their authors or by new authors, about 30 are ELIS Classics, and about 400 are reprinted from an earlier edition since they have remained relevant to the present. It is important to note that the editors also had to make some choices related to retiring entries that were no longer relevant—due to the passage of time and the development of the field, the technologies and theories described in those entries were deemed to be out of scope for the new edition and thus not revised or reprinted.

Encyclopedia Authors

As in past editions, the authors writing for the encyclopedia are major researchers, librarians and practitioners, and leaders in the fields and subfields in the disciplines in which they are writing. Noted scholars are well represented, and a number of authors are former leaders in LIS associations, including the American Library Association (ALA), the Association for College and Research Libraries (ACRL), the International Federation of Library Associations and Institutions (IFLA), the American Society for Information Science and Technology (ASIS&T), and the American Association of Library and Information Science Education (ALISE). In addition, there are many contributors who are current or former directors of major institutions. As in past editions, the editors are very proud of the range and diversity of authors who have written these entries for the encyclopedia and we thank them for sharing their expertise with the current and future readers and researchers in the field.

Finally, the editors for ELIS-4 have grappled with the challenges of entry generation that was noted by previous editors in nearly every edition: that not all ideas, topics, and potential entries were able to be completed for publication in this edition. While we made a valiant attempt to include entries identified by ELIS-3 editors but not secured for publication in that edition, we sometimes could not find authors willing to take those topics on. Similarly, we were sometimes unable to secure revisions to entries from new authors when previous authors were unable to perform that task. To the greatest extent possible, we endeavored to replace authors when entries were deemed important enough to appear in ELIS-4 but initial or previous authors had to decline or defaulted. No doubt, the editors of ELIS-5 will also pick up the mantle and attempt to round out the encyclopedia with entries for anything that ELIS-4 missed. As noted by editors Bates and Niles Maack in ELIS-3, this problem of missing topics was also acknowledged by Allen Kent, editor of the first edition of ELIS. Kent stated in 1973, "I have prepared this presentation to make sure the lessons of Diderot-d'Alembert are recalled in terms of encyclopedia-making as an exercise in the art of the possible."

Background and Development of the Encyclopedia

The first edition of ELIS, under the editorship principally of Allen Kent and Harold Lancour, was published between 1968 and 1982. The 33 volumes of the first edition were published in alphabetical sequence during those years. After the "Z" volume appeared in 1982, a number of supplements were published at roughly the rate of two per year, up to and including volume 73, which appeared in 2003. Miriam Drake was appointed editor for the second edition, which appeared in 2003, both online and in paper. The second edition came out at one time in four large-format volumes, with a supplement in 2005 [3]. Kent and Lancour covered a wide range of librarianship, information science, and some computer science topics. Drake, an academic library director, emphasized academic libraries, and the ELIS-2 volumes contained many profiles of major academic libraries and professional library associations.

The third edition, under the editorship of Marcia Bates and Mary Niles Maack, reflected a growing convergence among the several disciplines that concern themselves with information and the cultural record. As information science educators and noted researchers in the field, their focus was on growing the encyclopedia in the theoretical fields of information sciences as well as drawing together the associated information and cultural disciplines such as archival sciences and museum studies within the overall field of LIS.

For this edition, we have focused on developing the encyclopedia to reflect the changing nature of information production and consumption through online and digital forms. We have also endeavored to fill in gaps in the description of important people, places, and theories in the information sciences, and further enhanced the description of important concepts related to the provision of research information and the field's major institutions.

We continue to see the audience for the encyclopedia just as previous editors have: as principally consisting of 1) the educated lay person interested in one or more of its topics, 2) students learning about a topic, and 3) professionals and researchers in the several fields who want to learn about something new, or to be refreshed on a familiar topic.

We honored the previous editors by reengaging their superb Editorial Advisory Board with significant new additions of experts known to the current editors. (See listing in the front matter.) These leaders and experts from as many disciplines as are in the encyclopedia provided excellent guidance and feedback for the editors as they began the process of new topic generation, evaluation of previous entries, and offering to author or review numerous entries throughout the process of publication.

All new and revised entries were reviewed by one or more outside expert reviewer as well as one or more of the editors. Referees provided invaluable feedback to authors, including noting errors or omissions as well as making suggestions on additional aspects of the topic to cover. While we made every reasonable attempt through this process to check the accuracy of every entry and every fact, undoubtedly readers will find some topics explained more thoroughly or accurately than others. Indeed, due to the time frame from the beginning of the generation of the fourth edition and the time of publication, readers will reasonably note that some topics have been quickly superseded due to this passage of time, so the date of acceptance of the entry will be noted on each entry since several years may have passed since the writing of the entry and the publication of this edition.

Acknowledgments

This edition of the encyclopedia was possible only through the countless hours that the editors, John McDonald and Michael Levine-Clark, spent reviewing the previous encyclopedia entries, outlining the topics that were missing or that were newly emerging in the field, and identifying appropriate expert authors to write those new entries. In addition, the editors devoted extensive time to corresponding with previous authors encouraging them to revise their entries, and finding replacement authors for important entries that needed revisions but whose original authors were unavailable.

Both editors wish to acknowledge the expertise of each other and their knowledge of our field, their extensive network of contacts, and their ability to work closely together to ensure the success of this encyclopedia. Neither of them could have completed this project alone.

They acknowledge and thank the Taylor & Francis Group editors, Claire Miller and Rich O'Hanley, as well as Susan Lee, who passed away at the early stages of the preparation of this edition, and more recently, Alexandra Torres, who supported and kept the editors and authors on track over the course of the years of work on this edition of the encyclopedia.

The editors thank the authors who wrote and revised entries, and the huge number of reviewers who refereed the entries. Without their dedication, expertise, and willingness to share their knowledge with others, there would be no encyclopedia. They also wish to thank the Editorial Advisory Board for their advice, suggestions of topics and authors, their hours spent writing or reviewing for the final edition. They also wish to thank the previous editors, Marcia Bates and Mary Niles Maack, whose organization and structure for ELIS-3 provided an excellent blueprint for ELIS-4.

Encyclopedia of Library and Information Sciences, Fourth Edition

Volume 6

Pages 3637–4360

Physical–Primary

Print–Qualitative

Rare–Reference

Regional–School

Science–Semantic

Semiotics–Slovakia

Smithsonian–Society

Sociology–Special

Physical Sciences and Mathematics Literatures and Their Users

Cecelia Brown
School of Library and Information Studies, University of Oklahoma, Norman, Oklahoma, U.S.A.

Abstract

The literatures of the physical sciences and mathematics are as diverse as the information wants and needs of their users while serving the common purpose of disseminating their research findings. The peer-reviewed journal is the hallmark of scholarly communication for physicists, astronomers, chemists, and mathematicians yet each discipline has its own unique information sharing practices. This entry discusses the information behavior of physical and mathematical scientists and the ways in which their literatures mesh with their distinctive research activities. Although physicists and astronomers were among the earliest adopters of electronic modes of scholarly communication, chemists and mathematicians have been slower to embrace digital information sharing. This entry therefore also considers the influence of electronic distribution of physical science and mathematical information on the ways in which their intended audiences access and manage the plethora of digital resources. Recent initiatives designed to facilitate access to the literatures of physics, astronomy, chemistry, and mathematics are also surveyed.

INTRODUCTION

Physical scientists study nonliving matter and energy through the lenses of the disciplines of physics, astronomy, and chemistry. Employing the scientific method, physical scientists develop concepts and theories to explain the physical world. Mathematicians are interested in numbers, quantities, and magnitudes and their relationships as well as the properties of space. Using methods involving logical reasoning and symbolic notation mathematicians investigate applied and theoretical problems in algebra, analysis, arithmetic, calculus, geometry, and trigonometry. The peer-reviewed journal is the hallmark of scholarly communication among both physical scientists and mathematicians; however, there are variations in the ways in which physicists, astronomers, chemists, and mathematicians access the information they want and need to support their research and creative activities. These differences in information behavior are reflected in the ways in which the different literatures of astronomy, physics, chemistry, and mathematics are organized, disseminated, accessed, and archived.

Beginning with a discussion of the traditional model of scientific communication, this entry describes the information behaviors of three groups of physical scientists: astronomers, physicists, and chemists, as well as the information behavior of mathematicians. Also considered are the ways in which the physical sciences and mathematics literatures mesh with their intended audience's information access and delivery preferences. Attention is given to the ways in which physical scientists and mathematicians handle the burgeoning body of information generated via high-output, cutting-edge scientific techniques plus their usage and acceptance of scholarly information that has not

only recently become accessible electronically but also that which is born digitally. This entry provides librarians and information scientists with an overview of the current understanding of the ways in which physical scientists and mathematicians access and use information to support their scholarly work. This understanding will enable the design and creation of products and services that facilitate, enhance, and improve the management, organization, and provision of information resources that not only meet, but also match, the specific information requirements and behaviors of physical scientists and mathematicians.

MODELS OF SCIENTIFIC COMMUNICATION

William Garvey and Belver Griffith discovered in the early 1970s through the observation of psychologists that scientists' information behavior is intimately tied to the ways in which they conduct their scientific work.[1] Garvey and Griffith's model of scientific communication delineates the path scientific results travel from the laboratory to citations in the peer-reviewed journal literature. Along the way scientific results are disseminated locally at seminars and colloquia, followed by presentations at regional, national, and perhaps even international, scientific meetings. After vetting the results in these venues, the results may be deemed worthy for submission to a peer-reviewed scientific journal for publication consideration. Once a report of scientific findings has successfully traversed the gauntlet of peer review and become published, indexing and abstracting services catalog the article's bibliographic information to provide the scientific community with an entree to the results. Subsequent researchers whose projects are informed by the published reports then

Encyclopedia of Library and Information Sciences, Fourth Edition DOI: 10.1081/E-ELIS4-120044373

cite the article in their scholarly publications thereby furthering the accessibility to the scientific results through reference linking. Running in tandem with Garvey and Griffith's model of scientific communication is an informal form of discourse described over 40 years ago by Price and Beaver as the "invisible college."[2] Similar to the prototypical office water cooler, informal, yet highly valuable, communication among scientists takes place in the hallways of academia, at social gatherings during professional conferences, as well as over the telephone and through written correspondence. In contrast to formal scientific communication, which can be traced through the journal literature and via indexing and abstracting tools, informal scientific communication is difficult to track as it is not codified and archived even though its impact on scientific information behavior can be significant.

Moving forward in time to the beginning of the twenty-first century, Garvey and Griffith's model still holds true with the peer-reviewed journal remaining the coin of the realm for dissemination of scientific research findings. However, the advent of the Internet and the World Wide Web has impacted the ways in which physical scientists and mathematicians not only access, but also create and share, the results of their research endeavors. The creation of public and private online repositories of scientific data allows scientists and mathematicians to exchange information with a wide array of collaborators, as it is being generated, without having to first pass through the peer-review gauntlet. Electronic preprint servers and online journals deliver up to date scientific information to scientists' desktops around the clock. Online forums and electronic mail allow physical scientists to discuss issues of scientific importance with their colleagues without constraints of

borders, time zones, and languages. The model of electronic scientific communication proposed by Lancaster[3] and revised by Hurd[4] as presented in Fig. 1 incorporates these modes of electronic communication suggesting that the flow of scientific information will soon circumvent printed journals, indexes, and abstracting tools and will eventually be entirely digitized. Even though electronic communication facilitates information sharing and dissemination among physical scientists and mathematicians, the forecasted completely digital model of information flow has received varying degrees of acceptance by physicists, astronomers, chemists, and mathematicians.

THE LITERATURES AND THEIR USERS

A major task for all physical scientists and mathematicians is discovering, collecting, and reading articles about their area of research. Tenopir and colleagues found that time spent in reading by physicists, astronomers, and chemists, ranges from 144 to 198 hours per year.[5] To access their literatures, physical scientists and mathematicians have at their disposal a myriad of indexing and abstracting services which employ an array of organizational schemes and offer a variety of access points. Providers include the American Association for Mathematics, a nonprofit professional society, as well as the scientific publishing powerhouse, Elsevier. Physical scientists and mathematicians have the option to access their literatures using not only sophisticated citation searching techniques through the Institute for Scientific Information's (ISI) *Science Citation Index* but also via simple, yet powerful, keyword searches

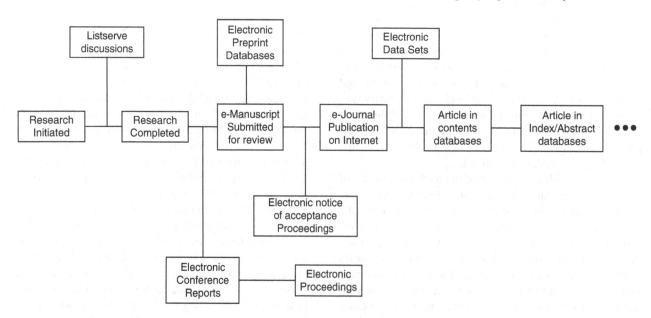

Fig. 1 Hurd's revised Garvey/Griffith model.
Source: From Hurd,[4] on p. 22.

using Chemical Abstracts Service's *SciFinder*. The information yielded ranges from bibliographic data for monographs and journal articles to full-text page views and research related data. The wide variety of bibliographic services available gives physical scientists and mathematicians great latitude in finding tools that meet their information seeking preferences and needs. Of note in the scholarly communication cycle of physical scientists and mathematicians are the prestigious journals, *Science* and *Nature*, published by the American Association for the Advancement of Science and the Nature Publishing Group, respectively. Also worthy of mention is the *Proceedings of the National Academy of Sciences*, published by the National Academy of Sciences of the United States, a scientific and engineering honor society dedicated to furthering science and technology for the benefit of the general public. These interdisciplinary publications are highly sought after venues for publication of research findings for all physical scientists, as well as mathematicians, and are the cornerstone of any science information collection. Even though the ultimate goal is the publication of research results in a peer-reviewed journal; physicists, astronomers, chemists, and mathematicians exhibit different information behaviors that are tightly aligned with their field of study and also the characteristics of their literatures.

Physics

Physics is considered to be the most basic of the physical sciences as physicists ask fundamental questions about energy and the structure of matter and their interactions in the universe. Physicists study physical phenomena within systems as large as the Milky Way galaxy or as small as the subatomic quark. Approximately 20% of physics research involves collaboration between several scientists around the world using large equipment with substantial support from private and federal agencies. Often referred to as "Big Science," this is particularly the case for research in high-energy physics where it is not unusual for over 50 scientists from several universities and research institutions to author a single journal article. Notable for a high volume of research and publications are the Stanford Linear Accelerator Center and the Fermi National Accelerator Laboratory, which employ thousands of scientists and engage in worldwide collaboration with many more. The majority of physicists, however, work individually or within smaller groups in one of several physics subfields including chemical, condensed matter, and molecular physics where funding remains critical but the research is less equipment intensive. Regardless of the size of the project or group, or the topic of investigation, physicists strive to disseminate their results via peer-reviewed journals.

Two scientific societies, the American Institute of Physics (AIP) and the Britain-based Institute of Physics (IOP), are responsible for publishing, indexing, abstracting, and archiving a significant fraction of the physics literature. The freely available *Scitation* from the AIP provides references to 1 million documents in scholarly journals, magazines, and conference proceedings from a range of scientific societies and technical publishers. Coverage is not limited to physics or the AIP and full-text is available to subscribers. Also accessible by subscribers from AIP is *Searchable Physics Information Notices (SPIN)*, which hosts more than 1.5 million article abstracts including publications indexed in *Scitation*. The AIP makes it possible for subscribers to search both *Scitation* and *SPIN* simultaneously for a comprehensive search of the physics literature. Additionally, the American Physical Society, a member of the AIP, has a free searchable Web interface for mining the contents of its suite of journals. The IOP similarly allows users to search their journals without charge plus users may freely download all papers published by the IOP for 30 days from the date of online publication. Physicists interested in issues related to engineering and technology make use of the Institution of Engineering and Technology's (IET) *Inspec* database. A new institution formed in 2006 by the joining together of the Institution of Electrical Engineers and the Institution of Incorporated Engineers, IET indexes and abstracts more than 3500 scientific and technical journals and 2000 conference proceedings, plus books, reports, and dissertations. The suite of IET journals is freely searchable via the *IET Digital Library*. Large, profit-generating publishing houses such as Springer, Elsevier, Taylor & Francis, and John Wiley & Sons also publish the research findings of physics and make the bibliographic information freely searchable via sophisticated Web interfaces; however, users must engage in licensing agreements to access full-text publications.

The commitment of physics scientific societies and publishers to make experimental results accessible online is reflected by the discipline's early adoption of electronic information dissemination. Physicists were among the first physical scientists to embrace electronic publication of their research findings with the IOP and AIP creating digital journal archives with searchable interfaces in the early 1990s. Perhaps the most significant indicator of acceptance of digital distribution of research findings by physicists is the extensive use of the online preprint server, *arXiv.org*. A preprint is the precursor to an article that is in the process of being submitted or has been submitted for publication consideration in a peer-reviewed journal. Physicists, particularly high-energy physicists, have been disseminating their research results via preprints for over four decades to facilitate large international collaborations, to avoid duplication of effort, and to bypass lengthy journal publication schedules.[6] Before the widespread adoption of the Internet, the paper preprint was used to share physics research information; however, the electronic preprint, or eprint, has replaced this classic mode of information exchange. The transition to eprints was a natural one for computer literate physicists who value the immediacy, efficiency, and simplicity of electronic communication. Developed by physicist Paul Ginsparg in 1991 for use by a group of 200 physicists at Los Alamos National Laboratory, *arXiv.org* has grown to be a repository of approximately 430,000 eprints and is connected to by approximately 450,000 visitors around the globe per day. Encompassing eight subfields of physics in addition to four areas of high-energy physics, *arXiv.org* also archives eprints in the areas of mathematics, computer science, quantitative biology, and statistics. Other eprint servers available for the high-energy physics community include *Stanford Public Information Retrieval System (SPIRES)* and the Central European Research Network's (CERN) document server. Physicists' acceptance of eprints in their scholarly communication cycle is indicated by the similar citation rate of eprints from *arXiv.org* and *SPIRES* to that of peer-reviewed journal articles.[7]

Originally a purely physical science, physics has become interdisciplinary in nature with overlap in many areas including astronomy, computer science, mathematics, medicine, chemistry, biology, and engineering. As a result, physics research has both theoretical and practical arms with the research results being dispersed across the literature of several scientific disciplines. For example, physicists who partner with medical colleagues to develop new techniques for cancer detection using noninvasive scanners employing magnetic resonance imaging (MRI) techniques may find a medical journal to be the best outlet for their results. Although there are journals that concentrate on interdisciplinary issues in physics such as the IoP's *Physics in Medicine and Biology* and the AIP's *Journal of Chemical Physics*, physicists engaged in interdisciplinary research are nonetheless required to be cognizant of the need to search beyond the physics literature to inform their research activities. Helpful in this endeavor is the National Library of Medicine's (NLM) index to the biomedical journal literature, *Medline*, which is also known as *PubMed*. The terminology used to assign topic headings to the articles within *Medline* is available in NLM's *Medical Subject Headings (MeSH)* database. A MeSH search for the three main physics terms: physics, health physics, and nuclear physics also locates several subheadings such as radiation protection, biophysics, and rheology and retrieves over 150,000 articles. Databases available from ISI also facilitate interdisciplinary work in physics. Of specific utility is *Science Citation Index* which was conceived by Eugene Garfield in 1955 as a tool for searching forward in time from a known article to articles citing that article. A cited reference search in the online version, *Web of Knowledge*, for Albert Einstein's 1906 *Annalen Der Physik* publication about the theory of Brownian motion yields a list of more than 500 publications that cite the seminal work thereby highlighting not only the paper's importance to the field of physics but also

denoting other works that further inform the reader about the random movement of particles.

Astronomy

Perhaps the oldest of the physical sciences, the study of astronomy has classically involved the structure, relative positions, and motions of the bodies in the universe including the earth. More recently, astronomers have turned their attention to the physical properties of astronomical objects to gain an understanding of the development, composition, and evolution of galaxies and planetary systems. Similar to high-energy physicists, astronomers collect data using very large-scale equipment such as the earth bound Mauna Kea Telescope in Hawaii or the orbiting Hubble Space Telescope. Before 1957, astronomy was a small field, where both amateur and professional astronomers studied and recorded observations of the sky. The launch of Sputnick by the Soviet Union stimulated the United States to establish the National Aeronautics and Space Administration (NASA) in 1958 thus beginning the era of "Big Science" in astronomy.[8]

Research in astronomy is highly data driven and technology dependent. Several scientists collaborate together on expensive, equipment-intensive projects like NASA's Mars Exploration Rover Mission while smaller groups and individuals purchase research time from observatories to collect information about the formation of black holes, the death of stars, and the rate of the universe's expansion. Whether the project involves several scientists or a single professor and their students, astronomers collect large volumes of data, often over prolonged time periods, which require extensive computing capability to house, organize, and maintain. The information amassed ranges from images and spectrographs to astrometric and photometric data all of which retain their value indefinitely thereby causing data preservation to be critical for the life of the project and beyond. Astronomers require access to not only research findings published in peer-reviewed journals but also to the original raw data. This access has classically been provided through astronomical catalogs that present data compiled from completed projects in a static print or CD-ROM format. Examples include Francis Wollaston's *A Specimen of a General Astronomical Catalogue* published in 1789 and the more recent *Second US Naval Observatory CCD [Charged Coupled Device] Astrograph Catalog* published for the American Astronomical Society (AAS) by the AIP in 2003, the final volume of which is expected in 2009. The Internet now affords access to dynamic sets of data via several online repositories that rapidly provide highly specific information to support astronomers' research activities using sophisticated search interfaces. The spectrum of repositories is constantly changing and growing with foremost projects including *NASA/IPAC Infrared Processing and Analysis Extragalactic Database* (*NED*), operated by the

California Institute of Technology's Jet Propulsion Laboratory, and *Set of Identifications, Measurements, and Bibliography for Astronomical Data* (SIMBAD), overseen by the Strasbourg Astronomical Data Center. Recently updated in March of 2007, *NED* provides spectral and photometry data for over 80,000 objects plus links to over 1 million journal and thesis abstracts. Equally impressive are *SIMBAD*'s current collection of over 3.5 million objects, 200,000 bibliographic references, and 5.5 million citations to objects in journal articles.

Recognizing the challenges of staying abreast with the highly dynamic nature, as well as the increasing magnitude, of online astronomy data repositories, nine astronomers at seven institutions across the globe merged their personal lists of online resources in 1994 to create *AstroWeb*. In addition to listing data resources, *AstroWeb* also links astronomers to astro-phy, the astrophysics archive of *arXiv.org*, and *ADS*, the Smithsonian/NASA Astrophysics Data System, which acts as a freely searchable portal to the astronomy and physics literature. Although subscriptions are needed to access most of the peer-reviewed content, when possible *ADS* provides a direct link to the *arXiv.org* eprint. Similar to physicists, astronomers appreciate the immediacy, ease of use, and free availability of eprints and are loyal users of and contributors to *arXiv.org* with 18.5% of submissions to the eprint server being to the astrophysical subject section. In addition to accessing the astronomy literature via *ADS* and *arXiv.org*, astronomers can also search the *Astronomisches Rechen-Institut Bibliographical Database (ARIBIB)*. A freely available online database, *ARIBIB* is based on the printed bibliography, *Astronomy and Astrophysics Abstracts*, however much of content in *ARIBIB* is also indexed in IET's *Inspec* database. The AIP's *Scitation* and ISI's *Web of Knowledge* are additional valuable resources for tapping the astronomy literature.

The limited number of astronomy-specific bibliographic databases is reflected in the narrow range of astronomy journals with the Royal Astronomical Society of Britain's *Monthly Notices of the Royal Astronomical Society* and the AAS's three publications: *Astronomical Journal*, *Astrophysical Journal*, and *Astrophysical Journal Letters*, being among the most highly read in the field. This small corpus of astronomy journals helped contribute to the ease with which the astronomy community adopted electronic publication of their scholarly works. The AAS, like their physics counterparts IOP and AIP, was a leader in electronic scholarly publication by offering their *Astrophysical Journal* online in the mid-1990s, with the online dissemination of their other publications following shortly thereafter. The small body of astronomy literature is enriched by its interweaving with that of physics. The tight relationship between the astronomy and physics communities is exemplified by AIP's publication of the journals *Astronomy Letters* and *Astronomy Reports* as well as EDP Science's, *Astronomy and Astrophysics*. Also

extending the astronomy literature is that of cosmology, the study of the universe as a whole, as illustrated by the research reports published in IOP's highly rated, *Journal of Cosmology and Astroparticle Physics*. In addition to physics and cosmology, astronomers are embracing additional disciplines such as paleontology, biology, and chemistry as they strive to understand the origins of life in the universe. The journal *Astrobiology*, launched in 2001 by Mary Ann Liebert Inc., exemplifies this trend by publishing articles about astropaleontology, bioastronomy, and cosmochemistry.

Chemistry

Chemistry is the physical science concerned with the properties, composition, and structure of matter and how it can be transformed from one substance to another. The subfields of chemistry include organic, inorganic, physical, analytical, and biological. Biochemistry, the chemistry of living things, has its own distinct, vast literature and biochemists possess unique information needs and information behaviors that differ from the other branches of chemistry. This entry emphasizes the information behavior and literatures of chemists who are considered to be physical scientists rather than that of biochemists. In all fields of chemistry, the literature is expanding at a swift pace with the American Chemical Society (ACS) currently publishing approximately 30,000 articles per year. As a result chemists download, view, and read far more journals than any other physical scientists.[9,10] Chemists, who primarily work individually or in small groups with equipment needs ranging from basic balances and pipettes to more expensive ultracentrifuges and mass spectrophotometers, universally require immediate and thorough access to up-to-date research findings that are primarily presented in short articles containing explicit methodologies and graphical data displays.

Similar to the fields of physics and astronomy, the ACS began making their journal content available on their website to subscribers in the mid-1990s beginning with the *Journal of Physical Chemistry*. In the fall of 1997 all of the ACS journals became available from 1996 forward. Ultimately in 2002, the ACS Journal Archives made the entire suite of 35 journals containing over 750,000 articles available online from the first published issue and volume beginning in 1879. The ACS journals are among those most highly cited in the field of chemistry, particularly the multidisciplinary *Chemical Reviews*, *Accounts of Chemical Research*, and the *Journal of the American Chemical Society*. The ACS also publishes several journals in each subfield of chemistry including the important titles *Analytic Chemistry*, *Organic Letters*, *Chemistry of Materials*, and *Inorganic Chemistry*. The Royal Society of Chemistry (RSC), ACS's older European counterpart, publishes over 20 prestigious titles in a variety of areas of chemistry. The RSC online gateway allows subscribers to reach the full-text of more than 240,000 articles published from 1841 to present. Titles range from the multidisciplinary *Chemical Society Reviews* and *Chemical Communications* to the discipline-specific *Journal of Materials Chemistry* and *Natural Product Reports*. Both societies offer a free Web-based search interface to gain bibliographic access to their journals; however, the primary database for comprehensive searching of the chemistry literature is *Chemical Abstracts*. Produced by Chemical Abstract Service (CAS), a division of the ACS, *Chemical Abstracts*, in addition to several other ACS databases, is searchable online via CAS's online portal, *SciFinder*. Even though *SciFinder* is expensive and access is complicated by firewalls and convoluted downloading procedures, *SciFinder* is nonetheless the premier search interface for accessing the chemical literature. Bibliographic information is not restricted to the publications of the ACS but rather strives to include all publishers of chemistry information from John Wiley & Sons and the Nature Publishing Group to the Indian Institute of Chemical Engineers and the Polish Academy of Science. Full-text is available to titles to which the user's institution subscribes. For individuals and institutions whose budget cannot afford the yearly subscription fee and/or who only need occasional access, the CAS databases are available for a per-search fee via ACS's online search service *STN* and ProQuest's Dialog.

A discussion of the products available from the 100-year-old CAS is critical in understanding the information behavior of chemists. Housed in Columbus, Ohio, CAS's 2000 employees index and abstract the extensive literature of chemistry. Access is provided to 9500 journals and patents from 1840 to the present in a manner that aligns with the way chemists work. The *SciFinder* interface offers access to more than 13 million chemical reactions through *CASREACT* as well as information about suppliers of commercially available chemicals via *CHEMCATS*. The information in *SciFinder* is accessible not only by simple keyword and author queries but also by chemical structure and molecular formula, the fundamental language of chemistry. Information can also be located using a CAS Registry number from the *CAS REGISTRY* database, which provides a unique numeric identifier for more than 31 million organic and inorganic substances. Originally a unique feature from CAS, the powerful ability to look for information using the standard CAS Registry number has recently met with competition from the National Institute of Health's (NIH) *PubChem*, a free online repository for storing records of small organic molecules. Although created for accessing biomedical resources, *PubChem* is remarkably similar to *CAS REGISTRY* in that it is based on a system of unique Chemical Identification Numbers (CIDs), which are housed in NIH's *ChemID* database. Information is available for over 380,000 chemical records, including 260,000 chemical structures, and is searchable using a wide range of options including CAS Registry number, molecular formula, and chemical structure. The NIH considers the free *PubChem* to be directed toward a different audience than, and therefore is complementary to the subscription only *CAS REGISTRY*. Nonetheless, the ACS is concerned about the impact NIH's free service will have on their organization's endeavors. While NIH and CAS debate the issue, *CAS REGISTRY* and *PubChem* continue to thrive and provide chemists with a controlled vocabulary with which to identify chemical compounds and their properties thereby facilitating access to their literature.

To standardize and support worldwide chemical communication the scientific, nongovernmental International Union of Pure and Applied Chemistry (IUPAC) was formed in 1919 to create a common chemical language. The IUPAC is considered the world's authority on chemical nomenclature and terminology plus the standardized methodologies for collecting measurements, atomic weights, and several other forms of data. The IUPAC core series of four publications, commonly referred to as the Red, Blue, Green, and Gold Books, provide rules for the nomenclature of organic and inorganic compounds, lists of quantities, units and symbols in physical chemistry, and definitions of technical terms used in chemistry. Updated information is provided in the quarterly *Journal of Physical and Chemical Reference Data* which is published by the AIP for the National Institute of Standards and Technology (NIST). Although the journal is not a typical peer-reviewed publication of original experimental results, it is a critical reference source for chemists as well as physicists. Two additional indispensable tools for chemists are the *Beilstein Handbook of Organic Chemistry* and its inorganic counterpart, *Gmelin*. First published as monographic series, the two resources are now available together in the online product, *Crossfire*, through which chemists can search structures, properties, and literature references for organic, inorganic, and organometallic compounds using Elsevier's MDL Crossfire Commander client software. Similarly, Springer's *Landolt–Börnstein* series of data handbooks provides chemists with mechanical, electrical, and thermodynamic property data for inorganic and organic substances. A freely searchable online interface allows chemists to use molecular and elemental formulae, CAS Registry numbers, or chemical names to find the volume within the *Landolt–Börnstein* series in which the desired information can be found.

In addition to requiring access to data about chemical compounds and to the journal literature, chemists also need the ability to search national and international patent repositories. This is especially critical for chemists working in the pharmaceutical, petrochemical, and agricultural industries, as well those in academia, who must be knowledgeable of current developments to retain a competitive edge. The United States Patent and Trademark Office's free online database indexes patents issued in the United States since 1790. A comprehensive and global patent search is available through CAS's *SciFinder* which allows chemists to simultaneously look for patents from 50 international patent-issuing authorities while also exploring the journal literature. Additional access to the patent literature is available through Thomson Scientific's *Derwent World Patents Index* (DWPI) which provides value-added expert analysis including a "Novelty" paragraph outlining the less than obvious technology improvements over previous patents as well as a "Technology Focus" abstract highlighting technological perspectives of the invention. Access to DWPI is available on a per-use or subscription basis via several platforms including ProQuest's Dialog and *Westlaw*, and CAS's *STN*. It is also possible to search and discover patents issued around the world using ISI's *Web of Knowledge* in tandem with a search for journal articles.

In contrast to physicists and astronomers, chemists do not wholeheartedly embrace eprints as part of their scholarly communication. The *Chemistry Preprint Server (CPS)* produced by Elsevier was active from only 2000 to 2004 even though chemists believed the eprints posted to be of high quality and appreciated the forum provided by the *CPS* for open discussion of current chemical research.[11] Despite the positive reception of the *CPS*, chemists' concern about the lack of peer review and the uncertain permanence of eprint storage, coupled with the refusal of editors of the top chemistry journals to subsequently publish papers previously posted on the server, the *CPS* was destined to fail. The chemistry related holdings in *arXiv.org* are limited to a small microcosm of eprints in the field of chemical physics. Even though chemists are reluctant to capitalize on free eprint distribution of their work, the ACS has a long tradition of making research-related data available to its readers, first as microfilm and now as free electronic files in the ACS *Electronic Supporting Information* archive. Similarly, the RSC's *Electronic Supporting Information (ESI)* service allows authors to deposit repetitive experimental details and large data sets including color diagrams, three-dimensional molecular models, and movies in this free repository. This practice of making research-related data openly accessible enhances chemists' scholarly communication by giving readers free access to potentially useful information while saving valuable journal page space.

Mathematics

Mathematicians study magnitude, quantity, and numbers and their relationships, as well as the properties of space, using logical reasoning methods and symbolic notation. Branches of mathematics include geometry, algebra, analysis, and applied mathematics. It is contended that mathematics is a philosophy rather than a science as mathematics involves the rational investigation of questions about existence and knowledge rather than being a process for evaluating empirical knowledge. In practice, though, mathematics is a combination of philosophy and science

depending on the nature of the problem being studied. Problems in mathematics can be purely theoretical in nature where patterns or relationships are studied for the knowledge yielded or they can be highly practical wherein the patterns and relationships are used to develop solutions for traffic flow issues or to create a data categorization scheme. Similar to astronomy information, information in the mathematical sciences retains its relevance for many decades as classical techniques and theories are frequently utilized for finding solutions to modern day problems. As a result the information needs of mathematicians range from historical theorems to cutting-edge computer modeling techniques, which they acquire by browsing information published in both journals and monographs. A very unique aspect of mathematics is that it is a support discipline for virtually all other sciences including the social sciences wherein phenomena can be described, or problems solved, using mathematical formulae or theories.

Mathematics research is similar to that in chemistry as mathematicians tend to work individually or in small groups. However, despite their solitary work style, mathematicians highly value attendance at conferences and personal discussions with colleagues to develop and augment their research ideas and processes.[12] This is supported by the range of mathematical societies that hold conferences, fund research in mathematics, and publish mathematics journals. The American Mathematical Society (AMS), the premier mathematics society in the United States, lists 110 national and international mathematics societies, associations, and groups on their Web site. The list includes the Estonian and Hellenic Mathematical Societies as well as the Clay Mathematics Institute in Cambridge, Massachusetts and the International Society of Dynamic Games in Finland. This breadth and diversity of mathematics-related organizations are evidences of the great importance of social networking in the daily work of mathematicians.

As is the case of the physical scientists discussed above, the peer-reviewed journal is the hallmark of dissemination of research information among mathematicians. The AMS publishes their suite of journals in a combination of print and electronic formats and includes the highly rated *Journal of the American Mathematical Society*, an outlet for articles about both pure and applied mathematics. Princeton University's top ranked *Annals of Mathematics* publishes reports of pure mathematical research while a wide array of field-specific titles such as *Geometry & Topology*, the *Journal of Differential Equations*, and the *Journal of Functional Analysis* provide researchers studying highly specific problems a venue to share their findings. Applied mathematics researchers find a prime outlet in the titles published by the Society for Industrial and Applied Mathematics (SIAM) including the very specific *SIAM Journal on Matrix Analysis and Application* and the more general *SIAM Review*. Most mathematics journals are available in both print and electronic formats with some exceptions such as the AMS's *Conformal Geometry and Dynamics* and *Representation Theory*, which are both published purely electronically. In an effort to make global research more accessible to its members, the AMS has a long-standing practice of translating mathematics journals into English from other languages especially Russian and Japanese. Currently four translation journals are fully searchable on the AMS online search interface: *St. Petersburg Mathematics Journal*, *Sugaku Expositions*, *Theory of Probability and Mathematical Statistics*, and the *Transactions of the Moscow Mathematical Society*.

A unique aspect of mathematics scholarly communication is the key role played by monographs and monographic series. For example, Springer's *Graduate Texts in Mathematics* series is comprised of over 240 titles providing advanced-level introductions to research in a wide variety of topics including group theory, complex analysis, and lie groups. The Oxford University Press publishes a similar series titled *Oxford Graduate Texts in Mathematics*, albeit on a smaller scale. Also of note is Springer's *Lecture Notes in Mathematics* series, published since 1964, which presents lectures about new fields of mathematics as well as fresh perspectives on classical mathematics. The expository presentation style of the *Graduate Texts* and *Lecture Notes* is echoed in the AMS's *Bulletin* and *Notices* journals. The *Bulletin* publishes peer-reviewed articles about current research topics written for the nonexpert while the *Notices* serves as a current awareness vehicle for mathematicians while including explanatory articles about current developments in mathematics research. Additionally, the AMS publishes 17 monographic series ranging from a sequence of research volumes generated from the Fields Institute for Research in Mathematical Sciences to *What's Happening in the Mathematical Sciences*, a series devoted to describing cutting-edge research in modern pure and applied mathematics at a level accessible to those with a high school mathematics education. Furthering the worldwide scholarly exchange in mathematics are the AMS's series of research and expository monographs that have been translated from Japanese, French, and Russian into English. One example is the series of *SMF/AMS Texts and Monographs* which is copublished with the Société Mathématique de France (SMF) and includes translations of the well-regarded series, *Astérisque*.

Mathematicians use two very distinctive tools to gain access to their literature: *Zentralblatt MATH* (*Zbl*) and *Mathematical Reviews* (*MR*), which not only index and abstract, but also review, the literature of mathematics. The reviewing feature is further illustrative of the high value mathematicians place on discourse with their colleagues around the world. Although the reviews are not fully equivalent to face-to-face, real-time interaction, they do provide a forum for assessing and discussing a work, a feature that sets these apart from traditional bibliographic

tools. Originally titled *Zentralblatt fur Mathematik* (*Zbl*), became available in 1931 and is edited by the European Mathematical Society, the Heidelberger Academy of Sciences, and Fachinformationszentrum or Specialized Information Center (FIZ) Karlsruhe. Published by Springer-Verlag, *Zbl*'s coverage extends from 1868 to the present with some full-text availability. The reviews in *Zbl* are primarily in English, with some French and Russian content, by approximately 5000 scientists who analyze over 2000 journals, conference proceedings, and monographs per year. Similarly, AMS's *MR* provides mathematicians with bibliographic and selected full-text access to the mathematical sciences literature that is augmented by more than 60,000 new expert reviews each year. Reaching back to 1864, the online equivalent of *MR*, *MathSciNet*, holds 2 million items with direct links to over 700,000 articles. Since 1991, the citations in both *Zbl* and *MR* have been organized according to the *Mathematics Subject Classification* (*MSC*) which was updated in 2000 in a collaborative effort between the editors of *Zbl* and *MR*. The classification scheme was devised to facilitate access to the mathematics literature and employs two-, three-, and five-digit classification codes that correspond to a discipline of mathematics. For example, the *MSC* code for partial differential equations is 35 while the code 35B can be used to find information about qualitative properties of solutions. Even greater specificity can be gained by using the code 35B40 to locate information about the asymptotic behavior of solutions. The search interfaces of both *Zbl* and *MathSciNet* allow users to search for information using the code that corresponds to their area of interest. Also organized according to the *MSC* is AMS's *Current Mathematical Publications* (*CPS*), which serves as an index of forthcoming mathematics publications. Published in print every 3 weeks and updated daily in *MR*, *CPS* is compiled by the editors of *MR*, and is searchable online via *MathSciNet*.

Although mathematicians are beginning to embrace electronic access to their literature, they continue to appreciate the browsing capability they believe to be distinctively afforded by printed information.[13] The browsing behavior of mathematicians is similar to humanities scholars in that both groups look for connections between wide ranging information sources that they can apply to the problems they are currently studying. Another complaint voiced by mathematicians about purely electronic access is the maintenance of the archive in perpetuity.[12] To help resolve this issue, as well as that of the ever-increasing issue of inadequate library shelf space, the nonprofit organization, *JSTOR*, is committed to creating and maintaining a stable archive of full-text scholarly journals, including 54 mathematics titles. The page images in *JSTOR* have been scanned to retain their original format and have been found to be a reasonable alternative to print journals for some mathematicians.[13] Titles available via *JSTOR* include publications from both AMS and SIAM as well as Springer and the National Council of Teachers of Mathematics. Although mathematicians find an electronic-only environment hampers their ability to browse the literature, they are the fastest growing group of authors submitting their research reports to *arXiv.org*'s mathematics archive. More than 1000 new submissions were posted to *arXiv.org*'s mathematics archive per month in 2008, surpassing the rate of 750 per month submitted to the high-energy physics archive, traditionally the most active archive of *arXiv.org*. The mathematics archive of *arXiv.org* contains eprints from 1991 to the present that are organized into 32 categories including logics, spectral theory, and combinatorics. The growing submission rate to the mathematics eprint archive, plus the availability of several other mathematics eprint repositories from institutes and universities worldwide, including the Mathematics Sciences Research Institute in Berkeley, California, Florida State University, and Hokkaido University, indicates an increasing acceptance of eprints by mathematicians. To date, however, the role of eprints in the scholarly communication of mathematics remains to be fully investigated.

OPENLY ACCESSIBLE PHYSICAL SCIENCES AND MATHEMATICS LITERATURES

The information behavior of physicists, astronomers, chemists, and mathematicians is deeply rooted in the way in which they conduct their scholarly work. Although the peer-reviewed journal model is the highly sought after end product, new formats and modes of information flow in the physical sciences and mathematics are quickly emerging in response to the desire for electronically delivered information. The ability to freely access scholarly information online allows scientists to expand and enrich their traditional modes of scholarly communication while helping to combat the ever rising cost of acquiring scholarly scientific journals. For example, to temper the high cost of scientific journals, the Association of Research Libraries formed the Scholarly Publishing and Academic Resources Coalition (SPARC), in 1998. Fuelled by the belief that inordinately high-scientific journal costs restrict the scientific community's ability to access, share, and use scholarly information, SPARC has forged partnerships with over 220 academic and research libraries to support promotion of and access to quality journals free of charge or for a nominal cost. In their commitment to reducing subscription prices SPARC publishes titles such as the affordably priced, yet peer-reviewed *Geometry & Topology* and the all-electronic, freely available *New Journal of Physics*, as alternatives to similar, yet much higher priced, titles distributed by the for-profit sector. Further reducing price barriers to physical science and mathematics scholarly information is the *Directory of Open Access Journals* (*DOAJ*). Supported in part by SPARC and the Open

Society Institute, the *DOAJ* is additionally funded and maintained by Lund University Libraries and provides access to peer-reviewed or editorially controlled journals. Currently 15 astronomy, 52 physics, 87 chemistry, and 132 mathematics titles are available at no cost through the *DOAJ* portal. HighWire Press, a division of Stanford University Libraries, is another leader in providing unfettered access to the scientific literature. Beginning with the *Journal of Biological Chemistry* in 1995, HighWire Press works with scholarly societies, university presses, and publishers to create a fully searchable, online collection of the research literature. Although the focus is on the life sciences, physical scientists and mathematicians will find access to the full-text of several prestigious titles including *Science* and the *Proceedings of the National Academy of Sciences*, and the *Proceedings of the London Mathematical Society* via HighWire Press's easy to use search interface.

Although the efforts of SPARC, *DOAJ*, and HighWire Press are making great strides in ensuring continued access to critical research information in the face of rising subscription costs and shrinking library budgets, physical scientists and mathematicians still require access to information beyond the reach of these progressive services. Consequently, several institutions, including the University of Wisconsin at Madison and Trinity University, are experimenting with a pay-per-view model where scientists request the articles they wish to read on a per-article basis rather than acquiring a subscription to the complete journal. The direct desktop delivery of articles as PDFs (Portable Document Formats) complete with legible diagrams, clear scientific notations, and color images provided by the pay-per-view model aligns well with physical scientists' and mathematicians' information needs and desires. Of concern with this mode of delivery is the maintenance and storage of the downloaded article, as these functions now become the burden of the user rather than the library or information center. Additional complications include the user's rights to share the article with their colleagues and to archive the article for an extended time. The pay-per-view option is available through several providers including HighWire Press, Elsevier, and Ingenta.

To simplify sharing of science information, Science Commons, a branch of the nonprofit Creative Commons, began establishing standardized licenses in early 2004 through which scientists can enter into agreements to share their research results. Two large open access publishers, the Public Library of Science (PLoS) and BioMed Central have adopted the "some rights reserved" licensing advocated by Science Commons. In the spirit of Science Commons, college and universities throughout the world are establishing their own online repositories of research related materials produced by their faculty and researchers. An excellent example is *Purdue e-Scholar*, a digital repository of e-books, papers, reports, dissertations, journal articles, research data sets, and data files by Purdue authors and researchers. Also of note is OhioLINK'S *Digital Resource Commons* which is committed to managing and preserving educational and research materials such as preprints, working papers, and dissertations from OhioLINK members and other Ohio institutions. On a national scale is the National Science Foundation's (NSF) National Science Digital Library (NSDL) which was created in 2000 to act as a dynamic repository of high-quality resources to support teaching and learning at all levels of science, technology, engineering, and mathematics education. Access to the free, well-organized resources are intended primarily to support science education; however, the research articles and data sets available from the NSDL are also of relevance to physical scientists and mathematicians. Furthering capitalizing on the Internet to facilitate and enhance the dissemination of scientific information is *SciVee*, an online multimedia repository where scientists can augment the content of their published works with narration, slides, and videos. Although still in its infancy, *SciVee*, the result of a partnership between the PLoS, the NSF, and the San Diego Supercomputer Center (SDSC), is contributing to the shift in scientific information dissemination from a one-dimensional article model to a multifaceted, interactive platform.

The rich and powerful online tools and services developed over the past decade are a boon to the scholarly communication of physical scientists and mathematicians, however, as their magnitudes and numbers intensify, the task of information seeking becomes highly complex. In 2000, several leading publishers of scholarly information including AIP, the Nature Publishing Group, Wiley, and Elsevier jointly formed the nonprofit, independent organization, Publishers International Linking Association, Inc. to promote the development and cooperative use of new and innovative technologies that speed and facilitate scholarly research. The result of the union is *CrossRef*, a collaborative reference linking service that helps users find additional articles of interest. Facilitated by Digital Object Identifiers (DOI), which are assigned to an article by participating publishers, *CrossRef* acts as a digital citation-linking network where, by clicking on a reference in an article, researchers are instantly directed to the cited article. Although *CrossRef* does not provide full-text access, it provides bibliographic information for millions of articles in journals of interest to physical scientists and mathematicians ranging from RSC's *PhysChemComm* to Elsevier's *Topology and its Applications* and IOP's *Chinese Journal of Astronomy and Astrophysics*. Elsevier is further working to facilitate the task of online searching across disparate scholarly resources with their science specific search engine, *Scirus*. The freely available service allows users to search over 415 million science-specific Web sites for scientific data, technical reports, peer-reviewed articles, patents, and eprints from providers like IoP, SIAM, and NASA. Perhaps the most promising and exciting new technology for managing digitalized

scientific resources is the *Google Scholar* library links program. The program, currently a beta service from the extremely popular search engine *Google*, allows libraries to link their holdings to *Google Scholar* thereby making it possible for scientists to mine the resources their institution has licensed using a single entryway. Scientists at universities including Northwestern, MIT, and Emory are able to use the familiar and straightforward *Google* interface to search their libraries' holdings and directly connect to full-text articles to which their institution subscribes, regardless of provider.

Although the reception and use of these forward thinking services by physicists, astronomers, chemists, and mathematicians remains to be fully elucidated, innovative programs like *SciVee*, *CrossRef*, and *Google Scholar* library links have great potential to facilitate the task of information seeking as digital access becomes the norm for scientific discourse. Regardless of format, delivery of scientific information in a mode physical scientists and mathematicians will utilize is critical to promoting and supporting innovation and progress in the physical sciences and mathematics. Physicists, astronomers, chemists, and mathematicians depend upon library and information centers to provide fast, comprehensive, and persistent access to information to support their research and creative activities. This has traditionally been the role of librarians and information scientists since the first libraries emerged 5000 years ago and remains the cornerstone of service in the emerging digital era. Continued awareness of the information behaviors and preferences of physical scientists and mathematicians is key to enabling the efficient and effective access to information products and services that scientists can rely on for the foreseeable future.

REFERENCES

1. Garvey, W.D.; Griffith, B.C. Communication and information processing within scientific disciplines: Empirical findings for psychology. Inform. Storage Ret. **1972**, *8*(3), 123–136.
2. Price, D.J.D.; Beaver, D.D. Collaboration in an invisible college. Am. Psychol. **1966**, *21*(11), 1011–1018.
3. Lancaster, F.W. *Toward Paperless Information Systems*, Academic Press, Inc.: New York, 1978.
4. Hurd, J.M. Models of scientific communication systems. In *From Print to Electronic: The Transformation of Scientific Communication*; Crawford, S.Y., Hurd, J.M., Weller, A.C., Eds.; Information Today: Medford, NJ, 1996; 9–33.
5. Tenopir, C.; King, D.W.; Boyce, P.; Matt Grayson, M.; Paulson, K.-L. Relying on electronic journals: Reading patterns of astronomers. J. Am. Soc. Inform. Sci. Technol. **2005**, *56*(8), 786–802.
6. Kreitz, P.A.; Addis, L.; Galic, H.; Johnson, T. The virtual library in action: Collaborative international control of high-energy physics pre-prints. Publish. Res. Q. **1997**, *13*(2), 24–32.

7. Brown, C.M. The evolution of preprints in the scholarly communication of physicists and astronomers. J. Am. Soc. Inform. Sci. Technol. **2001**, *52*(3), 187–200.

8. Crawford, S.Y. Astronomy, astrophysics, and space physics. In *From Print to Electronic: The Transformation of Scientific Communication*; Crawford, S.Y., Hurd, J.M., Weller, A. C., Eds.; Information Today: Medford, NJ, 1996; 77–96.

9. Tenopir, C.; King, D.W.; Boyce, P.; Grayson, M.; Zhang, Y.; Ebuen, M. Patterns of journal use by scientists through three evolutionary phases. D-Lib Mag. **2003**, *9*(5), Available at http://www.dlib.org/dlib/may03/king/05king.html (accessed August 2007).

10. Davis, M.P.; Solla, R.L. An IP-level analysis of usage statistics for electronic journals in chemistry: making inferences about user behavior. J. Am. Soc. Inform. Sci. Technol. **2003**, *54*(11), 1062–1068.

11. Brown, C.M. The role of electronic preprints in chemical communication: analysis of citation, usage and acceptance in the journal literature. J. Am. Soc. Inform. Sci. Technol. **2003**, *54*(5), 262–371.

12. Brown, C.M. Information seeking behavior of scientists in the electronic information age: astronomers, chemists, mathematicians, and physicists. J. Am. Soc. Inform. Sci. **1999**, *50*(10), 929–943.

13. Newby, J. An emerging picture of mathematicians' use of electronic resources: the effect of withdrawal of older print volumes. Sci. Technol. Libr. **2005**, *25*(4), 65–85.

BIBLIOGRAPHY

1. Casey, M.E.; Savastinuk, L.G. Service for the next generation library. Libr. J. **2006**, *131*(14), 40–42.

2. Flaxbart, D. Conversations with chemists; Information-seeking behavior of chemistry faculty in the electronic age. Sci. Technol. Libr. **2001**, *21*(3–4), 5–26.

3. Harter, S.P.; Park, T.K. Impact of prior electronic publication on manuscript consideration policies of scholarly journals. J. Am. Soc. Inform. Sci. Technol. **2000**, *51*(10), 940–948.

4. Lynch, C. The shape of the scientific article in the developing cyberinfrastructure. CTWatch Quart. **2007**, *3*(3), 5–10, Available at http://www.ctwatch.org/quarterly/articles/2007/ 08/the-shape-of-the-scientific-article-in-the-developing-cyber infrastructure/ (accessed August 2007).

5. Tenopir, C.; King, D.K. *Towards Electronic Journals: Realities for Scientists, Librarians, and Publishers*; SLA Publishing: Washington, DC, 2000.

6. Youngen, G.K. Citation patterns to traditional and electronic preprints in the published literature. Coll. Res. Libr. **1998**, *59*(5), 448–456.

INTERNET RESOURCES

The following is a list of the URLs for the resources referred to in this entry organized according to the field of study plus those mentioned in the "Openly Accessible Literatures" section.

Physics

1. American Institute of Physics' Scitation & SPIN (Searchable Physics Information Notices): http://www.scitation.aip.org.
2. American Institute of Physics: http://www.aip.org.
3. CERN (Central European Research Network): http://www. public.web.cern.ch/Public/Welcome.html.
4. Elsevier-Science Direct: http://www.sciendirect.com.
5. IET Digital Library: http://www.ietdl.org.
6. Inspec: http://www2.theiet.org/inspec/index.cfm.
7. Institute of Engineering & Technology: http://www.theiet. org.
8. Institute of Physics: http://www.iop.org.
9. John Wiley & Sons Interscience: http://www.interscience. wiley.com.
10. MeSH (Medical Subject Headings): http://www.nih.nlm. gov/mesh/.
11. NLM (National Library of Medicine): http://www.nih.nlm. gov.
12. SPIRES (Stanford Public Information Retrieval System): http://www.slac.Stanford.edu/spires/index.shtml/spires.
13. Springer Verlag: http://www.springer.com.
14. Taylor & Francis: http://www.taylorandfrancisgroup.com.
15. ISI web of Knowledge: http://www.iswebofknowledge.com.

Astronomy

1. AAS (American Astronomical Society): http://www.aas.org.
2. ADS (Smithsonian/NASA Astrophysics Data System): http://www.adsabs.harvard.edu.
3. ARIBIB (Astronomisches Rechen-Institut Bibliographical Database): http://www.ari.uni-heielberg.de/aribib.
4. AstroWeb: http://www.cv.nrao.edu/fits/www/astronomy.html.
5. NASA (National Aeronautics and Space Administration): http://www.nasa.gov.
6. NED (NASA/IPAC Extragalactic Database): http://nedwww. ipac.caltech.edu.
7. Royal Astronomical Society of Britain: http://www.ras.org.uk/.
8. SIMBAD (Set of Identifications, Measurements, and Bibliography for Astronomical Data).

Chemistry

1. ACS (American Chemical Society): http://www.chemistry. org.
2. ACS Electronic Supporting Information: http://pubs.acs. org/supmat/suppdoc.html.
3. CAS (Chemical Abstracts Service): http://www.cas.org4.
4. CPS (Chemistry Preprint Server): http://www.sciencedirect. com/preprintarchive.
5. IUPAC (International Union of Pure and Applied Chemistry): http://www.iupac.org.
6. Landolt–Boernstein: http://lb.chemie.uni-hamburg.de/.
7. NIST (National Institute of Standards and Technology): http://www.nist.org.
8. PubChem: http://pubchem.ncbi.nlm.nih.gov/.
9. RSC (Royal Society of Chemistry): http://www.rcs.org.

10. SciFinder: http://www.cas.org/products/scifoindr/index.html.
11. STN: http://www.cas.org/products/stnfamily/index.html.
12. ProQuest Dialog: http://www.dialog.com.
13. USPTO (United States Patent and Trademark Office): http://www.uspto.gov.

Mathematics

1. AMS (American Mathematical Society); http://www.ams.org.
2. JSTOR: http://www.jstor.org.
3. MR (Mathematical Reviews): http://www.ams.org/mathscinet.
4. MSC (Mathematics Subject Classification): http://www.ams.org/msc.
5. SIAM (Society for Industrial and Applied Mathematics): http://www.siam.org.
6. Zbl (ZentralblattMATH): http://www.zblmath.fiz-karlsruhe.de/MATH/home.

Openly Accessible Literatures

1. BioMed Central: http://www.biomedcentral.com.
2. Creative Commons: http://creativecommons.org.
3. CrossRef: http://www.crossref.org.
4. DOAJ (Directory of Open Access Journals): http://www.doaj.org.
5. Google Scholar Library Links: http://scholar.google.com/intl/en/scholar/librarylinks.html.
6. HighWirePress: http://highwire.stanford.edu.
7. MIT Open Courseware: http://web.mit.edu/ocw.
8. National Science Digital Library: http://nsdl.org.
9. OhioLINK's Digital Resource Commons: http://info.drc.ohiolink.edu/projects/.
10. PLoS (Public Library of Science): http://www.plos.org.
11. Purdue eScholar: http://e-scholar.lib.purdue.edu.
12. Science Commons: http://sciencecommons.org.
13. Scirus: http://www.scirus.com.
14. SciVee: http://www.scivee.tv/.
15. SPARC (Scholarly Publishing and Academic Resources Coalition): http://www.arl.org/sparc/.

Piracy in Digital Media

Stephanie Walker
Brooklyn College, City University of New York, Brooklyn, New York, U.S.A.

Abstract

Piracy of digital media refers to the unauthorized copying, usage, and sale or distribution of copyrighted materials in digital form, excluding materials which have been created or are distributed either specifically as fully "open access" materials, or those which have been licensed under some form of "open access" license (such as, for example, that offered by Creative Commons—see http://creativecommons.org/). These materials may include software, audio files, music, video files, movies or TV shows (in their entirety or in part), or electronic versions of books, journal articles, or databases. The term "piracy" itself remains somewhat controversial, as it carries a pejorative connotation, and not all copying for which authorization is not specifically obtained constitutes any form of theft; many forms of copying are legal, including copying of fully open access materials or materials licensed under Creative Commons or similar organizations. Also, there are ongoing and long-standing debates on what constitutes "fair use"; however, these issues are complex and are, in many cases, still before the courts and the legislators. However, for simplicity's sake, we will use the term "piracy," as described above, with the noted exceptions, throughout this entry.

Piracy can be accomplished through a variety of means, including copying materials from one medium to another, e-mailing zipped copies of files, downloading materials from servers, and many more elaborate schemes. Piracy is a global phenomenon, which costs software producers, recording artists, movie and TV production companies, publishers, and others considerable revenue; the exact amounts are near impossible to determine and frequently under dispute. Legislation governing copyright and technology has tended to lag behind the pace of technological developments, and much newer legislation is controversial. There have been numerous lawsuits against companies and individuals purportedly engaged in piracy; individual companies and artists have launched such lawsuits, as have the Recording Industry Association of America (RIAA), the Motion Picture Association of America (MPAA), and various other organizations. However, many of these cases are in process or pending, and the legal issues remain unclear. The situation is similar in many other countries as well, and there are great variances in copyright law, laws governing Internet Service Providers (ISPs), filtering, and other issues that affect piracy matters. Technological solutions designed to halt or limit piracy have proven generally unworkable, and legislative issues are thorny and remain unclear in many ways.

INTRODUCTION

Piracy, when used in discussions of digital media, refers to the unauthorized copying, usage, and often sale or distribution of copyrighted materials (or materials for which some party has other intellectual property rights) in digital form, excluding materials which have been created or are distributed either specifically as fully "open access" materials, or those which have been licensed under some form of "open access" license (such as, for example, that offered by Creative Commons—see http://creativecommons.org/). Also excluded are materials or portions of materials deemed to have been utilized under "fair use" provisions of copyright law (though "fair use" is, in the digital world, sometimes a disputed concept). A full discussion of "fair use" is beyond the scope of this entry; the interested reader is referred to Section 107 of the U.S. Copyright Act (title 17, U.S. code, online at http://www.copyright.gov/title17/92chap1.html#107), or to a discussion of fair use on the Web site of the U.S. Copyright Office, at http://www.copyright.gov/fls/fl102.html, and the topic has been discussed at length in legal, technical, and library literature.

Any discussion of piracy in digital media must necessarily encompass several major categories of digital media. There are common issues in discussing piracy across various types of digital media, but there are also specific considerations for various categories of media. Media and issues are outlined briefly here, but will be discussed in greater detail in the following section. Major types of digital media for which piracy is an issue include software (including various business applications), audio files/music, and video-based materials, including movies and television shows. Publishers who have ventured into e-books also have concerns about piracy. Indeed, digital intellectual property of any kind, from e-books to online lectures and classes to full-length creative works such as music albums or movies, is vulnerable to piracy. Piracy can be accomplished through a variety of means, from

Encyclopedia of Library and Information Sciences, Fourth Edition DOI: 10.1081/E-ELIS4-120044298

simple copying of material to a portable media device such as a "flash" drive or CD to much more elaborate schemes. Piracy is a global phenomenon; where there are computers, Internet access, and digital materials, there is piracy at some level, though its prevalence varies greatly from one country to another. There are a number of factors that have been identified or posited as contributing to the likelihood of piracy being widespread, including economic factors, cultural factors, and more, along with factors which inhibit widespread piracy. Piracy of digital media can cause economic harm to producers and inhibit development of new software or artistic creations. However, digital hosting, sharing, or transmission of files can also provide a means by which lesser known or previously unknown content creators can gain exposure for their work, and potentially attract future sales. Some well-known musicians (including highly popular bands such as Radiohead, Oasis, and Nine Inch Nails, to mention just a few) have also utilized digital sharing of files or offered portions of their work at low or reduced prices or even at no cost, or have offered to allow users to pay what they wish. There are strong arguments that such sharing increases music fan bases and in some cases frees musicians from restrictive contract agreements.[1] However, as has also been extensively reported in the media, major associations for the software, music, movie, and publishing industries have been taking aggressive (and frequently controversial) legal action to fight back against piracy.

PIRACY OVERVIEW: MEANS, PREVALENCE, AND COSTS

Software

Software can be quite vulnerable to piracy. Common business productivity software, especially, is often purchased by a single person, who then shares his one legal copy with friends, family, or colleagues.[2] There are also numerous sites where unlicensed or illegally copied software is available for free or greatly reduced costs, either by downloading or by placing an order for a copy which is then delivered or sent to the user upon receipt of payment. In some countries, the rates of software piracy exceed 90%—meaning that for every 100 copies of software, only 10 (or fewer) have been legally purchased and installed (see below). The rest are illegal copies, sometimes known as warez.[3] This affects software publishers' revenues, and many publishers claim this leaves a lower level of funds available for investment and research in new or updated software applications. As long ago as the year 2000, Ram D. Gopal and G. Lawrence Sanders (who have written extensively on piracy-related issues) provided some specific and surprising details on the widespread and dramatic problems associated with software piracy.

They reported that as early as 1997, the Software Publishers Association estimated that losses due to piracy for business application software in the United States alone reached $2.8 billion, and that worldwide, the revenue losses were estimated at $11.4 billion, and in some countries, including Kuwait, Pakistan, Indonesia, Bulgaria, China, Turkey, Egypt, Bolivia, and El Salvador, the rate of piracy was estimated to approach or exceed 90%.[2] Furthermore, because of a number of unique characteristics, software and other digital goods are particularly vulnerable to piracy: it is expensive to produce the first copy, but inexpensive to reproduce and distribute additional copies, and it is easy to share without impacting the value of the original product. "These idiosyncratic traits of software and related digital products," they write,

> have facilitated their illegal distribution worldwide. Several countries in the world are referred to as "one-legitimate-copy" countries, where one legal copy of a software package is sufficient to meet the demands of an entire nation. The advent of the Internet has amplified the problem. There are numerous warez (colloquial reference to pirated and cracked software) Web sites that permit customers to select from a menu of pirated software up to the 650 MB capacity of a CD. For around $30–$60, payable via credit card, the warez vendor will burn the CD and deliver it to the customer's doorstep.[3]

In the intervening years, there have been some changes in copyright law and there have been efforts by the U.S. government and by professional and business organizations to persuade other countries to take measures to lessen piracy rates, but they have met with mixed success, and in some cases with none. (It should also be noted that the Software Publishers Association merged with the Information Industry Association to become the SIIA—the Software and Information Industry Association.) "Many countries, particularly those without a viable local software industry, find it counterproductive to thwart piracy," Gopal and Sanders argue.

> While the threats of trade sanctions have arm-twisted many countries to enact copyright laws, they are rarely enforced. … China, for example, has recently cranked up raids against CD factories that manufacture bootlegged copies of software and confiscated the CD presses (each worth as much as $1 million). The suspicion, however, is these presses are put back into service in government-owned factories to manufacture CDs containing pirated software.[4]

Meanwhile, the costs of piracy continue to rise. In 2006, the Business Software Alliance (BSA) estimated total costs of software piracy worldwide at $40 billion, and reported that piracy rates have discouraged investment by software producers in some countries, such as the Philippines, where the BSA reports a piracy rate of 71% since

2004.[5] However, in the same article, representatives of such major software publishers as Symantec, Alcatel-Lucent, and Adobe Systems are quoted as providing statements to the effect that piracy is a concern, but does not determine strategic direction and is not the primary concern, and that they have made various adaptations to fight piracy and continue to do so.[5] Doubtless, piracy has an effect on revenue and on product distribution and development strategies; how much of an effect seems difficult to determine, and dependent on sources and methods.

Audio Files/Music

Piracy of audio files (especially music) is probably the best known area of digital piracy, due to heavy publicity surrounding court cases and activities by the RIAA and various music companies directed at stopping piracy, and due to statements by many artists on both sides of the file-sharing issues. The issues of pirated music, the services and tools which facilitate music file sharing and downloading, and the industry and legislative responses to such activities, have been widely reported in newspapers, magazines, and professional journals. Certainly not all shared music is pirated music; as aforementioned, many musicians support file-sharing or make portions of their music available for free or at reduced costs via various methods. As well, many users remember the days in the 1970s when the music industry claimed vociferously that home taping was killing music, and tried to discourage people from taping songs from the radio or sharing a homemade mixed cassette tape with a friend. It didn't work, and in reality, music sales grew. "Before the advent of home taping," writes Peter Martin, Economics Editor of the Canberra Times,

> Americans bought around 2.5 long-playing records a year. After two decades of home taping, they were buying 4.5 recorded cassettes and LPs a year. Stan Liebowitz, a Professor of Economics at the University of Texas, argues forcefully that the explosion in recorded music sales wasn't accidental. It was caused by the introduction of the cassette. Before then, music listening was limited to one room in each house—the one with the record player. The advent of the cassette made it possible to listen in the car, while jogging, in the garden, practically anywhere.[6]

Today, one commonly hears stories about the decline of the recorded music industry.
In a 2007 Washington Post article, Frank Ahrens reported that

> The music industry experienced the greatest one-year loss in sales of compact discs last year, and rising revenue from songs and albums bought on the Internet failed to offset the consumer flight from CDs. Revenue from CD sales was down 13 percent last year compared with 2005, the

Recording Industry Association of America reported yesterday. The drop-off exceeds that of any year during the Napster era of 2001 to 2004, when the file-sharing service and its descendants—such as Kazaa and Grokster—allowed users to download music for free. Meanwhile, online sales of singles from services such as Apple's iTunes were up 60 percent last year. However, because online sales remain a small percentage of all music sales, the industry's total revenue—for tangible and online products—was down 6.2 percent compared with 2005, the RIAA reported. … The music industry has blamed piracy for the dive in CD sales and began suing downloaders and the file-sharing services in retaliation in 2003.[7]

A lengthier discussion of legislative responses is included later in this entry; however, it is worth noting at this point that on December 22, 2008, an Associated Press report confirmed that the RIAA

> … has abandoned its policy of suing people for sharing songs protected by copyright and will work with Internet Service Providers (ISPs) to cut abusers' access if they ignore repeated warnings. The move ends a controversial program that saw the RIAA sue about 35,000 people since 2003 for swapping songs online. Because of high legal costs for defenders, virtually all of those hit with lawsuits settled, on average for around $3,500. The RIAA's legal costs, in the meantime, exceeded the settlement money it brought in.

This applies to individuals only; there is no current indication that organizations will no longer be sued.[8]
Yet even in claims that music sales are being "destroyed" by illegal downloading, there appears to be conflicting information. Again in the Canberra Times, in response to a request by the Australian Recording Industry Association to have the Minister of Communications enact a "three strikes and you're out" law which would ultimately allow users to be cut off from Internet access if they were caught three times illegally downloading material, Peter Martin reported that according to the Australian Recording Industry Association's own sales figures, in 1982, sales of recorded music were at the level of 29 million units, and have risen steadily; now, "… after the most recent five years of sustained CD-burning, intensive file swapping, the introduction of the iPod, wringing by the industry, we bought 99 million— easily an all-time record and an impressive jump of 23 per cent on the year before."[6] This includes not only 44 million units of physical CDs sold in that year, but also sales of new formats for music, including ring tones, digital albums, single tracks, music videos, and more. "The industry," Martin argues,

> will argue that it would be selling even more if it wasn't for illegal downloading. It's hard to prove. Certainly it would be selling less if it turned back the clock to before

illegal downloads began. And it is highly likely that illegal downloads stimulate sales. That used to be the function of CD-singles—loss-making samplers that would introduce consumers to new music and new bands. CD singles are all-but extinct. At the start of the decade the industry sold 12 million. It now sells just 2.5 million, having ceded the promotional business to the file sharing sites it claims to hate. Without those sites we would be exposed to a lot less new music and we might buy less. . . . In the face of zero evidence that illegal downloads are hurting music sales or drying up the supply of music, the industry wants the Minister for Communications to empower our ISPs cut us off from the web if it finds we have been downloading something it does not want us to.[6]

Again, we find conflicting reports from various sources on the effects which downloading (whether illegal or not) is having on the music industry, and thus on the effects of piracy on digital music.

However—to return to basics, including procedures and methods, and a brief history of music downloading—how precisely are music files shared? Music files are widely shared in many ways, including peer-to-peer networks which allow users to permit access a portion of their computer; networks and services which host files and allow for storage on their site; file-sharing services which allow users to post a file and notify a friend that the file is there for them to retrieve; or simple e-mailing of compressed files.

In some peer-to-peer networks, one must apply for "membership" to the network. One example of a way to apply for membership might be to offer to share rare or desirable files; this was the model followed by a service known as Hotline. If your application is approved by the site organizers, then you can access other files available through the network. But you must upload the promised files, or permit network members to access a secured portion of a server where these files are located. Many files shared via such services were not illegally obtained or even copyright protected, and often materials were not uploaded to servers owned by the company, but naturally, copyrighted and pirated materials were sometimes available. However, the idea was that responsibility for copyright clearance would fall upon the users, as would liability for infringements. There were many such networks and services that facilitated file sharing, and many persist. Such services, however, never obtained the notoriety or popularity of later incarnations such as Napster.

Napster was started by Shawn Fanning, a young programmer and student at Northeastern University in Boston, MA, and ultimately released by Fanning and two friends, Jordan Ritter and Sean Parker. It was the first well-known (and wildly popular) peer-to-peer file-sharing service. The service was unveiled broadly in 1998. The difference between Napster and many earlier peer-to-peer sites was that users could upload music files to, and download music files from, Napster itself, and the files were hosted on Napster servers. Users liked the cost (free), the ease of use, and the ability to download only songs they liked and create their own compilation CDs. Musicians could also post their own songs on Napster, and many did so in hopes of stimulating growth in their audience; it was a means of marketing their material and hopefully stimulating radio play and future sales. However, music industry players soon launched multiple lawsuits against Napster, claiming that Napster's actions and services were illegal and facilitated theft; certainly, some of the material that users posted on Napster was copyrighted, non-open access material, for which permission to post had not been sought. The RIAA launched a lawsuit against Napster in December 1999. The band Metallica was infuriated that some of their work was circulating on Napster, and shortly thereafter being played on radio stations, even before it was even released for commercial sale. Dr. Dre, Madonna, and other artists soon followed suit. In 2000, A & M Records sued Napster under the Digital Millennium Copyright Act (DMCA). The plaintiff's lawyers contended that Napster's users were directly infringing copyright, that Napster was liable for contributory copyright infringement, and that Napster was liable for vicarious copyright infringement.[9]

Napster argued that it was not liable for users' breaches of copyright, and that it could be used for many noninfringing purposes as well. Many users also contended that file sharing would help sales by allowing users to hear music and decide if they liked it before purchasing. However, the court found Napster guilty on all counts. Napster appealed to the Court of Appeals for the 9th Circuit but lost, though the appeals court recognized that Napster could be used for many purposes which did not constitute or facilitate copyright infringement. Napster was ordered to block access to infringing materials, but found this technologically and practically unfeasible; they shut down in July 2001 and eventually filed for bankruptcy. The service was restarted some time later under new ownership as Napster 2.0, a service offering legal copies of music files for sale, but it has never regained the popularity it had enjoyed as a free service.

Today, there are numerous services which offer legal copies of music. One popular example is the iTunes music store, which sells songs to be played on its popular iPod music players. Microsoft offers a similar service, as do many other companies. There are also still many copyright-infringing sites and services, both better and lesser known; some will be briefly discussed later in this entry. Lawsuits continue as each one is discovered by the music industry, and the music industry and other industries continue to lobby government for changes to legislation and harsher penalties for copyright infringement and theft of intellectual property. But it is difficult to keep up with the sheer volume of such sites, and some are better than others at hiding their activities from unwanted eyes.

Currently, BitTorrent is one popular technology used for downloading files. There are near-innumerable sites which make use of BitTorrent technology, for legal purposes or otherwise. While some such sites (such as the now-defunct Oink) have been shut down, others proliferate. It is impossible, in any practical way, to keep up with the sheer volume of sites which offer material (both legal and in violation of copyright) for downloading. In BitTorrent sites, the site acts as an organizer and indexer, and does not provide files for downloading. Rather, BitTorrent sites offer metadata giving the location of files being offered for downloading, and checksums which can be used to verify the integrity of the file once a download is completed. Pirate Bay, one popular BitTorrent tracker (as systems offering BitTorrent technology, file metadata and locations, and checksums are called), offers indexes to sites where one can download music, movies, games, and software. Pirate Bay has been the subject of repeated legal actions, but the founders assert that they are not participating in copyright violation. Peter Sunde Kolmisoppi, speaking on behalf of Pirate Bay to *Wired* magazine, compared Pirate Bay to Google, saying "We're just a general purpose search engine and torrent-tracking system. You can put whatever you want on the Pirate Bay. We don't participate in how the people communicate with each other. We only participate in bringing the possibility to communicate and share files."[10] Lawyers for various plaintiffs disagree.

As well, some sites are located in other countries, and therefore not bound by U.S. law; many countries (notably Russia) refuse to recognize many international copyright agreements or restrictions. Other sites have relocated to, or are located in, countries where they feel they are less likely to be prosecuted for copyright infringement. Pirate Bay moved to a double-blind distributed server model; the founders provided servers to other people without telling them the content included Pirate Bay, and those people rented space for the material without telling the founders where the servers were.[10]

Another way in which music files (and many other types of files) can be shared is through file-sharing services which allow users to post a file and notify a friend that the file is there for them to retrieve. These function in a manner somewhat analogous to a post office. One person uploads a file to the site, specifying a single person or a group of addressees to whom notification should be sent. One such service is known as YouSendIt. The recipient receives a notice via e-mail, much like the slip that the post office puts in your mailbox to tell you that a large parcel has been delivered to your local post office and is awaiting pickup. The addressee then clicks on the link in the e-mail or goes to the appropriate URL and enters specific information, and then retrieves the file. YouSendIt and similar services are popular as a means of avoiding the file size restrictions on attachments which are common to many e-mail systems. This avoids any issue of posting a file to a server and making it widely available, and there is nothing illegal about offering services such as YouSendIt provides, but there are still no guarantees that the file being sent is legally obtained or copied or perhaps is open access.

A similar type of service allows you to upload a file to a server and leave it there, and then tell other people, by e-mail or by posting a notice on a blog or wiki, or in any number of other ways, to go to a certain link and download the file. Many music blogs provide links to uploaded files, and a wide array of search tools is available for use in locating such blogs. Finally, users can simply compress or zip files and send them directly to friends and colleagues as well. Such services are a highly convenient means of sharing information, and certainly not inherently illegal in any way; the question of illegality would arise only when considering the contents of a file attachment and whether permission to copy or share any materials for which such permission was even required had been granted.

One more way in which material is made widely available is through the creation and sale of pirated, illegal copies of CDs. This is an issue for software and for music alike, and for movies, there are pirated copies of videos, DVDs, or Blu-ray discs. This is an international concern, deeply disturbing to the associated industries—music companies, software producers, film companies, and others. In many countries, one can easily find the latest CDs from popular recording artists selling for a fraction of the price that would be charged in the United States, often before the official release dates. Pirated music or movies are not necessarily of the same quality as those that are legitimately produced: quality can vary widely, depending on a number of factors. Some copies are created from original tapes or files or other original materials that have been leaked to counterfeiters; some movies are copied simply by a person who sits through a viewing of a legitimate copy of a movie in a theater, with an illegal handheld video device, and then sells copies of the resulting movie. Similarly, copies of downloaded audio files may vary. RealAudio files purportedly were of poorer quality than purchased, legitimate CDs; however, with the advent of the MP3 standard, there have been considerable improvements in quality. Many people claim the quality of MP3 audio files remains inferior to legitimate CDs, but the popularity of downloading (whether legal or illegal) attests to the fact that many users consider it adequate. Pirated copies of music and movies are also not limited to foreign countries: one need only walk down the streets of New York (to use just one example) to find street vendors selling CDs and DVDs for far less than one would expect. Some may be legal, but police have frequently cracked down on pirated and counterfeit copies being sold.

Video: Movies, TV Shows, and More

Video sharing sites are among the most popular destinations on the Web. YouTube, Yahoo! Video, and many others offer users the opportunity to upload videos to their servers, and make them publicly available. Many people upload perfectly legal materials—home videos or other materials for which they own the copyright or for which they have obtained permission, or open access materials. Libraries have posted training and orientation videos, promotional videos, and much more on YouTube, sometimes as a way to avoid the bandwidth restrictions in place at their institutions, or simply as a way to ensure widespread distribution of their materials. One simple example of a YouTube video explaining how to use the library catalog of Brooklyn College is located at http://www.youtube.com/watch?v=zLq1BzASsGU; many libraries have posted extensive orientation and training videos. Companies post materials: to provide just one example, ARTStor, an art image database, has posted a video showing people how to register with and use their service at http://www.youtube.com/watch?v=oAIQsiINlAA. Political campaigns and political action groups post videos highlighting the achievements and purported virtues of some candidates, or pointing out the alleged deficiencies of others; the 2008 U.S. Presidential Election saw an explosion of material from individual voters and advocates, action groups, and even the campaigns of the candidates themselves; there were even "YouTube" debates, where during a number of the official debates, candidates took questions from voters who had posted their questions via their own YouTube videos. But there are also many instances of copyrighted materials being posted without permission having been obtained, in violation of the policies of the host site. These can be subject to takedown, but by the time the offending material is removed it may have been further copied or distributed.

YouTube has received a number of takedown notices under the DMCA. Several entertainment companies claimed that the site contained full-length versions or long clips from a number of popular TV programs, and that these had been posted by users who had not obtained permission from rights holders.[11] YouTube was also sued by private individuals such as Robert Tur, who captured on tape the beating of trucker Reginald Denny during the 1992 riots in Los Angeles, and noted that this footage appeared on YouTube without his permission. Interestingly, "Tur did not claim that the site violated the DMCA. Instead, he invoked the 2005 Supreme Court decision in MGM v. Grokster and accused YouTube of building a network through the promotion of copyright infringement—i.e., piracy."[11]

However, YouTube had one advantage which had previously been unavailable to Napster. Congress has since added a provision to the DMCA, known as the Online Service Provider Safe Harbors provision (Section 512(c)).

Under this provision, YouTube is not liable for the actions of its users if it has posted a clear notice and takedown provision, which indicates that if copyright-infringing material is found and YouTube is notified that material on its site infringes copyright, it will remove the material. YouTube has such a posting, and removes infringing material when it is notified. This has not entirely stopped lawsuits: in July 2008, a lawsuit in the amount of $779 million (USD) was filed against YouTube (owned by Google since 2006) by the Italian broadcaster Mediaset.[12] In 2007, a $1 billion copyright infringement lawsuit was filed against Google itself; the plaintiff was Viacom, which owns MTV networks and Paramount Pictures.[12]

There are also a number of smaller sites that offer content which potentially infringes on copyright (presuming permission to post/distribute has not been sought). In 2007, Michael Arrington, coeditor of the popular Techcrunch weblog, wrote that:

> Full length copies of well known TV shows and/or movies are readily available on a number of YouTube competitors. Watch, for example, *The Office* on DailyMotion, *Scrubs* on GoFish, or *South Park* on Veoh (update: GoFish and Veoh have apparently removed the shows . . .). And if searching for the shows on these sites is just too much work, there are other sites that aggregate and organize this content, and embed it on their own sites. Watch any episode from any of the 11 seasons of *South Park* on Allsp.com. And new site VideoHybrid is in a class of its own, with dozens of full length movies and virtually every popular TV show. VideoHybrid even gives statistics showing exactly how many times copyrights have been violated.[13]

The MPAA and various entertainment companies and television producers have been watching YouTube, Yahoo! Video, and many other sites, but not all well-known sites have yet been targeted. "It's not clear if the MPAA and networks just aren't focusing on these smaller video sharing sites yet," Arrington also states, "or if DMCA notices are simply being ignored. These sites aren't hiding out and trying to evade the law—they're funded by well known venture capitalists and, in Veoh's case, copyright holders. And GoFish is actually a public company."[13]

As noted, the sale of pirated counterfeit DVDs and Blu-ray discs of movies, whether internationally or locally, is of great concern to the motion picture industry. Companies get no revenue from pirated movies, and many claim that the sometimes poor quality of the counterfeit materials could damage the movie producers' reputations and standards. But again, it appears to be nearly impossible to determine or even estimate with any degree of certitude how much piracy is taking place. The entertainment industry claims that "piracy costs the United States between $200 and $250 billion annually in lost sales, and 750,000 jobs."[14] However, there does not appear to be independent verification of these figures.

Published Works

Creators and distributors of other published works, such as book publishers and authors, are also concerned about issues of piracy. If the published works are normally in electronic form, the potential piracy issues and opportunities are similar to those for other digital materials. If the published works are in print, digitized copies of the original print works are at issue. (Of course, book "piracy" can also be accomplished by making additional print copies of print volumes, via such means as obtaining books and creating copies or additional print runs for sale. However, since this entry focuses on piracy in digital media, this will be excluded from discussion.)

One example of controversy surrounding digitized copies of print works is the Google Print Library Project. When Google announced in late 2004 that it would be working with the University of Michigan, Harvard University, Stanford University, the New York Public Library, and Oxford University to scan all of or portions of their collections (Harvard, for example, provided only a portion of their vast collections, and included no books which were in copyright), the reaction was swift. The Authors Guild, which is the largest society of published writers in the United States, termed this project a "brazen violation of copyright law"[15] and promptly sued Google. The Association of American Publishers (AAP) and their president, former Democratic congresswoman Patricia Schroeder, agreed, arguing that Google's business model for this project was to "take everything you create, for free, and sell advertising around it."[16] Five major publishers (McGraw-Hill Cos., Pearson Education Inc., Penguin Group (United States) Inc., Simon & Shuster Inc., and John Wiley & Sons Inc.) filed suit as well, and the French Publishers Association (representing over 400 French publishers) and La Martiniere Group also filed suit. Google argues that only material which is out of copyright will be freely available to all users; that books which are indexed in this project and which are still under copyright will be held to a limited display of "snippets" of text; and that creation of an index such as they avow the Google Print Library Project to be constitutes fair use under copyright law. As well, they state that any publishers who do not wish their books included can request removal of individual titles by contacting Google. Some authors support the lawsuits, but others have opposed it, arguing that it can only help them if potential readers find it easier to discover their books, even in "snippet" form. Several additional university libraries later joined the Google Print Library Project. The entire project, including other stakeholders in addition to libraries, became known as the Google Book Search project.

On October 28, 2008, Google announced that it had reached a settlement with U.S. publishers and authors, for $125 million.[17] The settlement agreement runs to approximately 300 pages, not all questions have been resolved, and reactions have been decidedly mixed. Harvard University Librarian Robert Darnton asserted that potential limitations on access to and use of materials could make it impossible for Harvard to continue to participate; Paul Courant of the University of Michigan wrote that the agreement changed Google from a "universal digital library" to a "universal digital bookstore" because of fees which would be charged to access more than small portions of books in copyright.[18] Other reactions, positive and negative abound. A discussion of the settlement could be fodder for an entire book in itself, and is beyond the scope of this entry, but it is worth noting that issues of fair use were not resolved for one and all. Writing a legal analysis for the Electronic Frontier Foundation (EFF), Fred von Lohmann asserts that

... this outcome is plainly second-best from the point of view of those who believe that Google would have won the fair use question at the heart of the case. A legal ruling that scanning books to provide indexing and search is a fair use would have benefited the public by setting a precedent on which everyone could rely, thus limiting publishers' control over the activities of future book scanners. Instead, only Google gets to rely on this settlement, and the agreement that makes many concessions that a fair user shouldn't have to make.[19]

By contrast, the Open Content Alliance, a book scanning project sponsored by Microsoft and Yahoo and working with a number of other academic libraries, including libraries from Columbia University and the University of Toronto among others, deals only with books currently in the public domain. Google News Search was also entangled in a lawsuit in Belgium, where Copiepresse, an organization managing a number of Belgian newspapers, was objecting to its use of content, including headlines, in Google News Belgium. The decision in that case went against Google, and Google was ordered to remove Copiepresse articles. Other legal action is still pending.

Another example of a controversy surrounding books and journals is the lawsuit against Georgia State University (GSU), launched in 2008 by the American Association of University Publishers (AAUP). GSU made available, through electronic reserves and its password-protected course management system, digital copies of articles in journals to which they subscribed. The AAUP claims as well that professors linked directly to some of the resources through open Web pages; however, at the time of this writing, it is unclear whether or not specific examples of this latter practice were available. The lawsuit alleges widespread copyright infringement; GSU counters that these practices are permissible under fair use. The case remains before the courts. Many universities and colleges have made deals with publishers to permit e-reserves, either in response to threatened lawsuits or in efforts to avoid them;

Cornell University, in particular, was an early player, and developed a set of comprehensive electronic course content guidelines, available online at http://www.copyright.cornell.edu/policy/Copyright_Guidelines.pdf.[20]

LEGISLATIVE FRAMEWORK

Before 1964, laws relating to piracy of intellectual property covered only printed works; in 1964, the U.S. Copyright Office began including software for registration. In 1974, the National Commission on New Technological Uses (CONTU) began to try to determine whether new technology growth was out-pacing existing copyright law, and what protection should be extended; in 1980, the Copyright Act was amended to explicitly include computer programs. In 1990, Congress approved the Software Rental Amendments Act, which "prohibits the commercial rental, leasing or lending of software without the express written permission of the copyright holder. An amendment to Title 18, of the United States Code, was passed by congress in 1992. This amendment, known as Public Law 102-561, made software piracy a federal offence and instituted criminal penalties for copyright infringement of software."[21]

In 1998, the DMCA became law. The reasoning behind this law was that copyright holders needed better laws to protect their rights and combat piracy.

DMCA provided those tools – and also created a whole new class of crime that causes unfortunate side effects. The Electronic Frontier Foundation (http://www.eff.org) posted *Unintended Consequences: Three Years Under the DMCA* in May. The executive summary argues that DMCA's anti-circumvention provisions (Section 1201) have not been used as Congress envisioned. Congress was after pirates and wanted to ban black boxes, but the provision has been used to stifle legitimate activities. According to EFF's report, Section 1201 chills free expression and scientific research, jeopardizes fair use, and impedes competition and innovation. The summary provides examples of otherwise-legitimate activities made impossible by Section 1201 (e.g. fast-forwarding through commercials before a DVD movie), real-world examples of the harm done by DMCA, including self-censorship for fear of violating the act, scientists unwilling to come to the U.S., the assault on fair use represented by copy-protected pseudo-CDs, and more.[22]

As one media education professor complains, "The DMCA trades the broad fair use doctrine for a series of narrowly defined exemptions"[23] and there is no exemption for media education; theoretically, for every usage of media work for educational purposes, a media education professor would need to research the rights holders and obtain written, explicit permission—a tiresome and lengthy process. Also in 1998, shortly after the passage of

the DMCA, the *Sonny Bono Copyright Term Extension Act* was passed into law. This law extended copyright terms by 20 years, causing many materials to take much longer to become available in the public domain.

In May, 2008, the U.S. District Court in Seattle ruled in favor of a man named Timothy S. Vernor who had posted a copy of Autodesk software on the Internet auction site eBay for resale. Autodesk had requested summary judgment against Vernor for contributory copyright infringement, but the Court ruled in his favor, and stated that the first sale doctrine of copyright law applied. The Court found that first sale applied.[24] This is the same principle as that by which used book stores operate: the publisher of a book gets nothing when a reader resells his copy of a novel to a used book store, as the publisher has already benefited from revenues received from the first sale. The case may be appealed, though, and there is much remaining confusion as to what constitutes legal or illegal practice regarding resale of technology. It is confusing, because contributory copyright infringement is essentially that with which Pirate Bay was charged. Pirate Bay charges nothing (and various materials loaded on its servers may not be under copyright, or may be open access), and Mr. Vernor was reselling a piece of software. Yet each was charged similarly, in very different environments. The legislative framework for copyrighted, non-open access software is often still unclear—as is indeed the case for other copyrighted materials. Additionally, the legislative structure in which intellectual property exists and operates varies widely depending on the country in which the property is created or utilized. Laws can be quite different from one country to the next, and international law is not accepted everywhere.

Pirate Bay is currently facing charges that it is "promoting other people's infringement of copyright laws"[10] and there is a movement by Swedish Culture & Justice ministers to give Swedish courts the power to force ISPs to reveal the Internet Providers (IPs) of their subscribers, in order to charge the subscribers themselves for copyright infringement.[25] Pirate Bay continues to face charges in Swedish courts, and people and organizations continue to appeal to the Swedish government to address the issues raised by Pirate Bay, even though they have ostensibly moved all of their servers out of Sweden.

According to some reports, in China, "bootleggers selling 75 cent DVDs dominate 95 per cent of the market"[26] and in an effort to combat this trend (which the studios claim cost them up to $3.8 billion a year), some companies have begun slashing the prices of legitimate DVDS. For example, "Time Warner is reducing the price further, to $1.50 or less, and releasing movies in as little as 15 days after theater runs."[26]

The Software Industry Association of America (SIAA) monitors auction sites, and insists that pirated materials be removed, "either the DMCA's notice-and-takedown process or eBay's VeRO (Verified Rights Owner) program."[27] Microsoft has launched several lawsuits against vendors using auctions sites to sell pirated software; "suits were brought in the U.S., Germany, the Netherlands, France, and Britain, as well as Argentina, Australia, Belgium, Korea, Mexico, and Poland."[28] FileMaker, Symantec, and other companies have also launched similar suits.

In the European Union (EU), however, the top court (the European Court of Justice) recently ruled, in a dispute between the Spanish music rights holders association Promuiscae and Spain's top telecom operator Telefonica, that EU countries were permitted to refuse to disclose names of file sharers on the Internet in civil cases. Telefonica argued that it was only required to disclose subscriber information in criminal cases, and the court said that "Community law does not require the member states, in order to ensure the effective protection of copyright, to lay down an obligation to disclose personal data in the context of civil proceedings."[29] In Belgium, Copiepresse won its lawsuit against Google news; in Italy, the lawsuit against YouTube proceeds. Requirements of service providers to reveal information about customers vary widely, and legal decisions regarding fair use and copyright continue to vary as well from country to country.

In the United States, various commercial ISPs have been accused of BitTorrent throttling—refusing to allow access to known BitTorrent sites, regardless of whether material being accessed is legal or copyright-free, or of choking access to such an extent as to reduce download speed to a crawl, in hopes of limiting or discouraging user access. ISPs generally deny this practice is occurring, but some are currently under investigation for the practice. Notably, Comcast has been cited for BitTorrent throttling, and the Federal Communications Commission (FCC) asserts that this practice violates Net Neutrality rules. However, it is unclear whether the FCC has authority to actually do anything about BitTorrent throttling, or take any action against Comcast.[30] ISPs have also sometimes been asked to turn over subscriber information, especially when there are allegations of piracy or other illegal practices, and some have complied, while others have refused and taken the issue to court, with varying results. In some countries, notably China, the Internet is filtered, and many sites cannot be accessed; Pirate Bay is apparently among those blocked by the Chinese government.

Universities and colleges have in many cases become perplexed not just about what they can legally provide in terms of electronic course reserves, but also about what professors may do in terms of excerpting materials for their classes. How large a clip from a film can they show to their class, for example, without having to obtain public performance rights? Will they risk being accused of piracy, or potentially charged, if the clip is too large? With so much still before the courts and the government, and many laws and regulations still unclear, many potential users of materials are afraid of risking a lawsuit, and claims of a "chilling effect" are common. In an attempt to alleviate this, the Center for Social Media of the School of Communication of American University has created a set of guidelines for copyright and fair use in documentary film, available online at http://www.centerforsocialmedia.org/resources/fair_use.[31] However, especially in the digital world, the exact parameters of fair use remain difficult to ascertain. A number of organizations which dispute the strong actions of many copyright holders or organizations representing copyright holders claim that not only does strict enforcement infringe upon fair use and cause a chilling effect, it also infringes upon free speech, as writers and artists and filmmakers may be unwilling to risk being sued.[32]

The legislative structure in which music, TV, and motion picture companies attempt to protect their material from unauthorized distribution or piracy is also somewhat unclear. The DMCA seems to lean heavily toward support for rights holders (some claim to the detriment of other stakeholders) but the Online Provider Safe Harbor clause does protect sites and their owners from unauthorized behavior by their users, if they have a clear "notice and takedown" policy. And yet, video and music sharing sites proliferate, and many offer free and easy access to copyrighted material. Is the MPAA not focusing on smaller sites? Or are the sites getting takedown notices, and ignoring them? Why, as aforementioned, are some of the sites public companies, or "funded by well known venture capitalists and, in Veoh's case, copyright holders"[13] if there is fear of legal reprisals? As well, the RIAA in particular has focused strong efforts on targeting universities and colleges, asserting that students are heavy users of pirated music. On May 3, *Wired* magazine noted "universities in the US are experiencing a '20-fold increase' in the number of takedown notices from the RIAA in the last ten days. Indiana University reports 80 notices a day, but they say their traffic hasn't increased significantly over the same time period."[32] There have been mixed responses from the universities and colleges that have been thus targeted; various responses and recent changes to RIAA actions will be discussed in the next section.

Finally, there is also a lack of clarity surrounding access to and distribution of electronic copies of journals, journal articles, and books. Back in the days when all books and journals were published in print form, libraries had long-established and clear policies and procedures. They might vary from library to library—but you knew what to do, whether you were a publisher, a librarian, or a researcher. Books and journals were published and sold in print form. Libraries purchased the materials (whether outright or via a standing order or subscription), and processed them according to whatever procedures they had established. Materials were made accessible to library patrons—again, according to whatever policies the library had established. Some institutions had "open stacks" and patrons could browse; others had closed stacks and library staff would retrieve requested materials. When photocopiers came into existence and became commonly used in libraries, researchers might copy articles or chapters they needed. Hopefully they would follow fair use principles as to the amount of material that could be copied, but whether they did or not, the principles and legal issues were generally fairly clear, and libraries frequently posted signs informing patrons of any restrictions. Interlibrary loan departments receiving article requests knew how much they could copy and send.

In a digital world, the legislative issues are again somewhat murky, and many questions have arisen. Articles in electronic form are much more easily transferred, copied, and shared. This is perfectly legal in many circumstances, but often there are disputes. For example, some licenses for electronic journals and databases refuse to permit libraries to use articles within these databases for interlibrary loan purposes, or they may place a variety of restrictions on the usage of the articles. Some will permit a library to print a copy of an article from an e-journal and use the printed copy to fill the request, but will not permit an electronic copy to be e-mailed. There are many possible permutations of restrictions that can be imposed. Some publishers wish to restrict access to their e-journals and databases by imposing such restrictions as limiting access to a single terminal or a set number of terminals within a library; some publishers refuse to permit remote access. As well, some publishers require institutions, including libraries, to sign agreements which require them to keep the terms of particular licenses confidential—so theoretically, you cannot even compare the deal your library has signed with that signed by another library.

As for e-books, procedures and restrictions vary by publisher here as well. Many publishers place restrictions on how much of a book can be saved, downloaded, and/or printed by a particular user or from a particular computer IP address. Some put restrictions on the number of simultaneous users for each item. Some object to e-books being used by entire classes unless multiple copies or user licenses are purchased. Some attempt to restrict access to e-books or e-journals in course management systems or online course systems such as Blackboard.

Again, one need only look to the aforementioned lawsuit against GSU for one example of a dispute between publishers and an academic institution as to how electronic materials may be used for online courses; many institutions (such as Cornell University and its libraries, for example) have worked out detailed agreements. Publishers are concerned about potential lost sales if their product is copied or shared—and this is much easier to accomplish when the material in question is in electronic format.

The recent settlement in the Google Book Search seems to impose a number of restrictions on access to and usage of works in their database, and reactions have been mixed. Many people have praised the increased overall access to digital copies of books. However, in an editorial

written for the online *Library Journal*, Editor in Chief Francine Fialkoff criticizes restrictions that will affect libraries and their patrons:

> One public access terminal per public library building. Institutional database subscriptions for academic and public libraries that secure once freely available material in a contractual lockbox, which librarians already know too well from costly e-journal and e-reference database deals. No remote access for public libraries without approval from the publisher/author Book Rights Registry, set up to administer the program. And no copying or pasting from that institutional database, though you can print pages for a fee. Of course, you can always purchase the book, too.

> Those are just a few of the choice tidbits from the 200-page settlement in the Association of American Publishers (AAP) and Authors Guild three-year-old suit against Google, drawn from Jonathan Band's "Guide for the Perplexed: Libraries and the Google Library Project Settlement."[33]

Fialkoff emphasizes that the settlement document does include provisions and specifications that outline what libraries are and are not permitted to do, and that in many instances, access to materials should become more widespread. However, she continues by stating that

> ultimately, it is the restrictions that scream out at us from the miasma of details. Even the libraries that were initial partners (or those that become partners) in the Google scan plan don't fare well. They get a single digital copy of each book from their collection—mind you, they've paid for these books already—and can print a replacement copy only if a new copy isn't available at a "fair price." They can allow faculty and students to "read, print, download, or otherwise use five pages of any book in its LDC" (library digital copy set) for books "not commercially available," but they can't use the LDC for interlibrary loan or e-reserves. There are all kinds of potentially costly, nightmarish administrative minutiae, including a security plan and annual audits of usage and security.[33]

Intellectual property and the rights of creators, publishers, vendors, and users are all tied in closely with issues of piracy and other (sometimes arguably) unauthorized or illegal access to and usage of digital materials of all types.

A related controversy is the issue of whether research which is accomplished and published partially or wholly with the assistance of public funding, such as grants, should be free of charge, either immediately or after a period of time. One interesting, and ongoing, case in point is the controversy surrounding the National Institutes of Health (NIH) Public Access Policy. In December 2007, the United States Congress and President George W. Bush authorized the NIH to require that any articles which were a result of research that had received public funding (such as an NIH grant, for example) be deposited, after a period of one year, in the PubMed Central archive. Articles need not be deposited immediately; a lag period of one year from time of publication was granted. This allowed publishers of the scientific journals which had accepted and printed the articles to continue to have sales of their journals, but researchers who were willing to wait a year would ultimately be able to obtain free access to the specific articles containing research results which had been supported by public funding. The American Association of Publishers fiercely opposed the NIH Public Access Policy. Subsequently, on September 9, 2009, Representative John Conyers (then Chairman of the House Judiciary Committee) introduced a bill (H.R. 6845, the Fair Copyright in Research Works Act) "designed to strike down the NIH Public Access Policy and prevent other federal agencies from implementing similar policies. According to the text of the bill, 'No Federal agency may, in connection with a funding agreement, impose or cause the imposition of any term or condition that requires the transfer or license to or for a Federal agency of any right provided under' copyright law."[34] Of course, if the Public Access Policy is struck down, then articles resulting from publicly funded research would be treated as any other articles, and "piracy" of such materials (or any other unauthorized action) would be subject to the same laws and penalties.

In December 2007, the Prioritizing Resources and Organization for Intellectual Property Act (variously shortened and referred to as PROIPA or PRO IP Act or PRO-IP Act) was introduced. In May 2008, it passed the House Judiciary Committee; this is the first step, though, and if the bill fails to pass both the House and the Senate before the end of the year, it would need to be brought forward anew in 2009. The bill is cosponsored by many legislators, including the Chair of the House Judiciary Committee, Representative John Conyers, Jr. and the Chair of the Subcommittee on Courts, the Internet, and Intellectual Property, Representative Howard Berman. Some of the provisions of PROIPA include massive reforms to copyright and patent enforcement. Statutory damages would be raised, and there would be a lower threshold for prison terms for copyright offenses.

In its initial form, the bill included a controversial rule which allowed litigants to stop treating compilations of copyrighted works as a single work. Thus, a music label could seek many times the normal statutory damages if they sued someone for copyright violation involving copying an album: every song would be treated separately. Similarly, for magazines or newspapers, every article would be treated separately. This rule, Section 104, was removed by Representative Berman before the bill went to the full Committee, after hearings during which proponents of the section argued that allowing works to be treated as compilations devalued individual articles or songs or other portions of a compilation. Opponents of the provision argued that statutory provisions for damages were already high, and that there was no proof any rights holder had ever been injured by insufficient compensation due to the existence of the compilations rule. Accordingly, the provision was removed.[35] The bill also provides for the establishment of an Intellectual Property Enforcement Division in the U.S. Justice Department.

Issues of copyright, intellectual property, piracy, and related issues (such as the issue of whether open access to publicly funded research shall be mandated or optional) continue to be issues of hot debate and ongoing interest to a wide variety of stakeholders.

RESPONSES

Library associations, intellectual property scholars, technology associations, and many others are unified in opposition to the PROIPA legislation and to various provisions of the DMCA. The Library Copyright Alliance, the Computer & Communications Industry Association, and the EFF, among others, have all written to Congress to express this opposition and dispute various claims made (such as claims about how widespread piracy is, and how great its costs are). In an essay on the difficulties created by raising the bar on getting permissions for usages that were clearly previously considered fair use, Peter Decherney argues that "If you are a documentary filmmaker, insurance companies and distributors have raised the permission bar to an impossibly high level. Documentary filmmakers are frequently expected to clear every use of copyrighted and trademarked material even when those uses are plainly allowed by the law."[23] He also goes on to describe the difficulties now inherent when professors wish to show clips of movies for classes; in many cases, they risk being in violation of copyright, though usage of portions of work for nonprofit, educational purposes had generally been considered to fall within the range of fair use in predigital times. As previously mentioned, GSU is battling the AAUP, which claims that copyright was infringed by the way in which GSU made electronic course reserve materials available.

Some ISPs are also unhappy—and not just those who have been accused of BitTorrent throttling. In the United States, to date, ISPs have generally not been held responsible when copyrighted materials are illegally made available via their servers. They must comply with takedown notices, but are not held responsible for the behavior of their users in posting the infringing materials in the first place. But this is not the case everywhere. In February 2008, *Business Week* reported that proposed legislation in Britain could turn ISPs into a different kind of ISP—Internet Service Policemen. ISPs would be held responsible for the behavior of their customers, ISPs who failed to halt illegal downloads would be sanctioned, and ISPs could be compelled to turn over information about customers who infringed intellectual property rights.[36] These proposals are still in their early stages. However,

> the tough ISP stance has already set off alarms. Industry analysts and legal experts warn the proposals could hurt legitimate downloading of Internet content and saddle ISPs already suffering from thinning margins with much higher costs. Equally important, the proposal raises privacy and free-speech issues. Under long-standing common carrier principles, communication companies aren't legally responsible for the content of the traffic they carry over their wires and wavelengths even if it's a conversation between robbers planning a crime or somebody downloading child porn. Britain's ISP plan could upend this bedrock principle by turning carriers into cops.[36]

At present, it is not technologically possible to distinguish between legal and illegal content being carried across the ISPs; imposing such restrictions could lead to extensive content monitoring by ISPs, jeopardizing user privacy. And even if the content of every file was monitored, who is to say that a user transmitting a file containing a research article, a scanned chapter of a book, a song, a video, or any other digital material, has not obtained permission to do so?

Universities and colleges are themselves ISPs, to their large communities of faculty, staff, and students. The RIAA has targeted postsecondary educational institutions, claiming that music piracy is rampant among students. Tactics espoused by the RIAA have included sending letters to university administrators demanding that the university reveal the identities of students using computers with various IP addresses; demanding that universities filter their Internet access to exclude peer-to-peer sites; and sending notices to universities asking them to pass along to individual students prelitigation letters demanding that they pay up to $3000 or face prosecution in court. Since February 2007, the RIAA "has provided some 4,000 such letters to more than 150 colleges and universities. The letters offer the students what they call bargain settlements if they act fast, by punching in a credit card number at http://www.p2plawsuits.com."[32] The RIAA is also "backing legislation in states such as Illinois and Tennessee that would require schools that get a certain number of notices to begin installing deep packet monitoring equipment on their internet and intranets."[32] As well, the RIAA had hired a company called MediaSentry to gather information about students and other potential music copyright infringers. MediaSentry would "troll the Internet in search of people who upload large amounts of music. The information that MediaSentry collected became an integral part of the RIAA's aggressive litigation strategy."[37]

However, MediaSentry was the cause of considerable controversy, including allegations by lawyers acting (for students and for some academic institutions opposing the RIAA in court) of invasion of privacy. In a report in the *Wall Street Journal*, Ray Beckerman, a lawyer who "maintains the Recording Industry vs. the People blog and who has represented more than a dozen clients fighting the RIAA"[37] was quoted as citing "MediaSentry's practice of looking for available songs in people's file-sharing folders, downloading them, and using those downloads in court as evidence of copyright violations. He says MediaSentry couldn't prove defendants had shared their files with anyone other than MediaSentry investigators."[37] Other tactics MediaSentry allegedly employed included "scan[ning] for anyone downloading files through LimeWire and Ares."[38] In 2008, the RIAA ended its agreement with MediaSentry, without disclosing its reasons, switching instead to Danish firm DtecNet Software ApS. Officially, the RIAA stood by the methods MediaSentry used, "citing University of Washington research released last year that concluded the company's methodology incorporates 'best practices.'"[37]

Responses (to RIAA actions) from colleges and universities have varied widely. In some cases, the university in question has simply immediately turned over all student information. Of course, this is easier if the student is always using the same computer, i.e., in a dorm room. Even in these cases, though, if there are two students sharing a dorm room, the RIAA has been known to sue both students, though only one may be guilty of infringement. This was the case when, in 2004, the RIAA sued two students attending Portland State University. The University responded to the subpoena from the RIAA by providing personal identifying information about two roommates. It could not determine which student was using the computer in the room, so it provided information on both students. One student, Delaney Conway, was not the person using the computer at all, yet the record company lawyers insisted that she pay $4500. She refused, and determined to fight the case. The case against Ms. Conway was finally dropped, and her roommate paid a settlement fee. Other universities have refused to provide any identifying information, citing either student privacy issues or, in some cases, the impossibility of telling which student was using which computer. The latter is particularly difficult to determine when the computers are public, or available to many people, as is the case in a computer lab or library.

Some universities have fought back on behalf of their own students, or, in one case, on behalf of non-students accused of piracy. The University of Maine's Cumberland Legal Aid Clinic has fought back against the RIAA on behalf of its students. In Oregon, the University of Oregon, with support from the State Attorney General, filed a motion to quash the RIAA's subpoena demanding student identities, explaining that

> it is impossible to identify the alleged infringers from the information the RIAA has presented: 'Five of the seventeen John Does accessed the content in question from double occupancy dorm rooms at the University. With

regard to these Does, the University is able to identify only the room where the content was accessed and whether or not the computer used was a Macintosh or a PC ... The University cannot determine whether the content in question was accessed by one occupant as opposed to another, or whether it was accessed instead by a visitor.'

The AG's motion further argues that "Plaintiffs' subpoena is unduly burdensome and overbroad. It seeks information that the University does not readily possess."[39] The University of San Francisco School of Law has taken action against the RIAA even further, and attorneys-in-training from its Intellectual Property Law Clinic, under the supervision of law professors, are helping clients outside of their own community, pro bono. "They reached out 3000 miles to get involved in Elektra v. Torres and Maverick v. Chowdhury, two cases going on in Brooklyn, NY, against non-college defendants."[40] Some additional complications include the fact that the Family Education Rights Protection Act (FERPA) makes it illegal to reveal most private information about students; that IP addresses of individual computers may be dynamically allocated, rather than static, and thus it can be impossible to identify with any certainty who used what computer at what time, and for what purpose; and that IP addresses can be falsified by clever people wishing to hide their identities and actions.

Results to such cases have been mixed. In some cases, various privacy arguments have not held; in others, judges have strenuously objected to some RIAA tactics and actions, even to the extent where some judges have threatened to fine RIAA lawyers. There have been allegations in court that MediaSentry violated privacy and engaged in unlicensed data mining to gather information about defendants or those suspected of engaging in illegal downloading. A defendant named Tanya Anderson filed an amended complaint against the RIAA, seeking to stop them from "continuing to engage in criminal investigation of private American citizens."[41] Again, this case is ongoing; it had begun as a the countersuit to the lawsuit where "RIAA lawyers tried to grill a 10-year-old girl, only later to drop their case for lack of evidence and have the mother sue them for malicious prosecution."[41] In a case involving four Boston University students, the EFF filed a brief in support of the students, who were represented by other lawyers. In that case, the *Boston Globe* reported on April 4, 2008 that

> US District Judge Nancy Gertner ruled this week that the university cannot turn over the names of students to several major record companies that sued for the information until she can do a more in-depth review. The ruling, for the moment, quashes the companies' efforts to hold the students liable for copyright infringement, which could have resulted in thousands of dollars in fines. Laywers who supported the students said the decision would make

it harder for record companies to win some 20,000 similar cases they have brought nationwide.[38]

Judge Gertner's ruling forbade Boston University from "turning over names until it shows her its Internet service agreement with students so that she can review what privacy protections, if any, it affords."[38] One recent development in the RIAA strategies is especially interesting. In December 2008, the RIAA decided to cease filing lawsuits against individuals engaging in downloading, though it plans to continue with cases currently filed; instead, it will continue its discussions with ISPs to attempt to reach agreements on file monitoring.

FUTURE DIRECTIONS AND CONCLUSIONS

Illegal downloading of music, software, visual images, videos, films, electronic books, electronic journal articles, or any digital material is theft. But what constitutes "illegal" downloading? This is, in many instances, unclear. "Fair use" has long been part of copyright law, and some allegations of piracy are met with a defense that the copying or usage or sharing falls within fair use. What, in a digital environment, constitutes fair use? There are many complications to various cases, and many debates about the appropriateness of various responses and actions. Arguments have become quite heated on all sides, in the courts and in the popular press. There are many details to be worked out by the courts, and it is likely that these battles will continue for some time.

Many technological solutions have been attempted, including copy protection added to DVDs and CDs; thus far, all solutions seem to have been vulnerable to hacking, and none appears to have succeeded. It may indeed be illegal to circumvent such protective technology; that does not mean it is not possible, and once a means to circumvent the protection is devised, one can be fairly well assured that it will be posted all over the Internet within hours.

Solutions have been proposed that would see ISPs held legally responsible for the content of what is posted on their services; arguments made against this include considerations such as privacy rights or freedom of speech. There have been suggestions that persons caught illegally downloading music or films should lose access to their Internet service; some schools have instituted such policies, and there are proposals being floated to have commercial ISPs follow suit. Alternatively, there have been proposals to have ISPs levy monthly fees on broadband customers and turn these fees over to the RIAA, the MPAA, the SIIA, the BSA, and/or other groups. Fees have been proposed on blank media, such as recordable CDs, as well. In some cases, reducing the prices of software, music, and movies is being attempted; the success of this strategy has not been fully documented to date. The only certainty appears to be that digital piracy (and even the definition of what constitutes digital piracy) will remain a controversial subject for many years to come.

REFERENCES

1. Bands rushing to ditch labels and embrace free: Are the floodgates opening? October 8, 2007 issue. http://www.techdirt.com/articles/20071008/154529.shtml (accessed January 6, 2009).
2. Gopal, R.D.; Sanders, G.L. Global software piracy: You can't get blood out of a turnip. Commun. ACM **2000**, *43* (9), 84.
3. Gopal, R.D.; Sanders, G.L. Global software piracy: You can't get blood out of a turnip. Commun. ACM **2000**, *43* (9), 85.
4. Gopal, R.D.; Sanders, G.L. Global software piracy: You can't get blood out of a turnip. Commun. ACM **2000**, *43* (9), 86.
5. Ramos, M.G.S. Investors discouraged by rampant software piracy, says group. Bus. World October 23 2007, S1–S3.
6. Martin, P. Music industry's false note. Canberra Times. (Final Edition) April 1 2008; 11.
7. Ahrens, F. Despite drop in CD sales, music industry is upbeat. Washington Post (Suburban Edition) April 18 2007, D01.
8. Associated Press. No more file-sharing suits for RIAA. Daily Variety December 22, **2008**; 5.
9. A&M Records, Inc. v. Napster, Inc., 239 F.3d 1004, 1013, 1020 (9th Cir. 2001).
10. Kravets, D. Pirate bay says it can't be sunk, servers scattered worldwide. Wired Blog Network, http://blog.wired.com/27bstroke6/2008/02/the-pirate-bay.html (February 1, 2008 issue, accessed March 28, 2008).
11. Decherney, P. From fair use to exemption. Cinema J. **2007**, *46* (2), 126.
12. Day, M. Mediaset logs lawsuit vs. YouTube. Daily Variety July 31, **2008**, 6.
13. Arrington, M. Forget YouTube: Go to these sites if you want hard core copyright infringing content. Techcrunch, April 4, 2007. http://www.techcrunch.com/2007/04/04/forget-youtube-go-to-these-sites-if-you-want-hard-core-copyright-infringing-content/ (accessed December 2007).
14. Library Journal Academic Newswire, May 6, 2008. http://www.libraryjournal.com/info/CA6562808.html (accessed May 20, 2008).
15. Mills, E. Authors Guild sues Google over library project. C-Net News.com, http://business2-cnet.com/2102-1030_3-5875384.html?tag=st.util.print (September 21, 2005 issue, accessed November 2007).
16. Bray, H. Publishers battle Google book index: Suit joins action filed by authors over copyright. Boston Globe (online), October 20, 2005. http://www.boston.com/business/technology/articles/2005/10/20/publishers_battle_google_book_index.html (accessed October 2007).
17. Bray, H. Google search starts new chapter with $125M deal. Boston Globe October 29, 2008, B5.
18. Albanese, A. Harvard slams Google settlement; others react with caution. Libr. J. Acad. Newswire October 30, 2008. http://www.libraryjournal.com/article/CA6610115.html?nid=2673&rid=reg_visitor_id&source=title (accessed January 8, 2009).
19. Von Lohmann, F. Google book search settlement: A reader's guide. Electronic Frontier Foundation, http://www.eff.org/deeplinks/2008/10/google-books-settlement-readers-guide (accessed January 8, 2009).
20. http://www.copyright.cornell.edu/policy/Copyright_Guidelines.pdf (accessed August 2008).
21. Hamade, S.N. Piracy and terrorism in the Arab world. Dig. Middle E. Stud. **2006**, *15* (2), 2.
22. Crawford, W. Copyright out of whack II: Control run amok. October 2002, 42–43.
23. Decherney, P. In focus: Fair use and film. Cinema J. **2007**, *46* (2), 119.
24. Vernor v. Autodesk, No. 07-1189 (W.D. Wash. May 20, 2008), http://www.scribd.com/doc/3077102/Vernor-v-Autodesk-No-071189-WD-Wash-May-20-2008. (accessed January 8, 2009).
25. *Sweden to Give Courts New Power to Hunt IP Infringers*; Slashdot.org, http://yro.slashdot.org/article.pl?sid=08/03/16/0046228 (March 16, 2008 issue, accessed March 2008).
26. Berretta, D. Pirate tactics. Foreign Policy 2006, 115, 92.
27. Kupferschmid, K. SIIA gets tough on software piracy. Inform. Today **2007**, *24* (7), 52.
28. Kupferschmid, K. SIAA gets tough on software piracy. Inform. Today **2007**, *24* (7), 54.
29. *EU Court Says File Sharers Don't Have To Be Named*; Slashdot.org, http://yro.slashdot.org/article.pl?sid=08/01/29/2025257 (January 29, 2008 issue, accessed January 2008).
30. McCullagh, D. FCC probably can't police Comcast's BitTorrent throttling. C-Net News.com, http://news.cnet.com/8301-13578_3-10000821-38.html (accessed July 2008).
31. American University School of Communications Center for Social Media. *Fair Use and Free Speech Resources*; http://www.centerforsocialmedia.org/resources/fair_use (accessed August 2008).
32. *Massive Increase in RIAA Copyright Notices*; Slashdot.org, http://yro.slashdot.org/article.pl?sid=08/05/02/0350227 (May 2, 2008 issue, accessed May 2008).
33. Fialkoff, F. Google deal or rip-off? Librarians need to protect the public interest. Library Journal.com, December 15, 2008. http://www.libraryjournal.com/article/CA6618842.html (accessed January 9, 2009).
34. Peek, R. The battle over PubMed central continues. Inform. Today November **2008**, *25* (10), 17.
35. Anderson, N. Rep. Berman pulls controversial "compilations" rule from PRO-IP Act. Ars Technica, http://arstechnica.com/news.ars/post/20080306-rep-berman-pulls-controversial-compilations-rule-from-pro-ip-act.html (March 6, 2008 issue, accessed October 30, 2008).
36. Scott, M. Anti-piracy plan threaten free speech: Proposed legislation in Britain aimed at curtailing illegal web downloads would turn ISPs into "internet service policemen." Business Week Europe (online), February 22, 2008. http://www.businessweek.com/globalbiz/content/feb2008/gb20080222_084238.htm?chan+globalbiz_europe+index+page_top+stories (accessed February 2008).

37. McBride, S. Changing tack, RIAA ditches MediaSentry. Wall Street Journal, (online), January 5, 2009. http://online.wsj.com/article/SB123109364085551895.html (accessed January 9, 2009).

38. Levenson, M. Music downloaders win round in court. In Boston Globe April 4, **2008**, A1.

39. Dawson, K. *Arizona Judge Shoots Down RIAA Theories*; Slashdot.org, April 30, 2008. http://news.slashdot.org/article.pl?sid=08/04/29/1840250 (accessed April 2008).

40. *University of San Francisco Law Clinic Joins Fight Against RIAA*; Slashdot.orgFebruary 29, 2008. http://yro.slashdot.org/article.pl?sid=08/02/29/0120224&tid=123 (accessed February 2008).

41. *Lawsuit against RIAA Tries to Stop Them All*; Slashdot.org, April 1, 2008. http://news.slashdot.org/article.pl?sid=08/04/01/0731209 (accessed April 2008).

Plagiarism of Print and Electronic Resources

Zorana Ercegovac
InfoEN Associates, Los Angeles, California, U.S.A.

Abstract

This entry discusses plagiarism of printed and electronic resources, explores definitions of plagiarism, and provides a literature review. The entry then discusses the following issues: how prevalent plagiarism is, faculty's attitudes toward plagiarism in general, cyber-plagiarism in particular, predictors that correlate with plagiarism, and how to cope with plagiarism. The entry offers suggestions for future research on the topic of plagiarism.

INTRODUCTION

This entry concerns itself with plagiarism of printed and electronic media. It starts off by reviewing literature on definitions of plagiarism, and answering questions as to how prevalent plagiarism is, faculty's attitudes toward academic dishonesty in general, and plagiarism in particular. Predictors that associate with acts of plagiarism are discussed under the headings of social factors and individual differences. To answer the question, what is done to cope with increase of plagiarism incidents, this author summarizes theories of ethical reasoning as well as various approaches, such as instructional techniques and software detection programs. The entry concludes with an agenda to be considered for future research.

DEFINITIONS OF PLAGIARISM

Merriam-Webster's Collegiate Dictionary[1] defines plagiarism as the act of stealing and passing off (other creators' ideas as expressed in words, pictures, music) as one's own; use (another's production) without crediting the source; to commit literary theft: present as new and original an idea or product derived from an existing source. The *Oxford English Dictionary*[2] defines plagiarism as the "wrongful appropriation or purloining, and publication as one's own, of the ideas, or the expression of the ideas (literary, artistic, musical, mechanical, etc.)." The OED cites numerous sources that mention plagiarism in different historical contexts starting with a citation from 1621.

Many articles that write about the concept of plagiarism also talk about related, but very distinct topics such as fabrication, academic integrity in the context of ethics and moral development; vocabulary also pertains to fair use, copyright and intellectual property, various cheating behaviors, and honor code violations by different user populations in different countries. While the acts of stealing, corruption, lying, piracy, and forgery are normally punished by law, stealing intellectual or artistic content (e.g., textual, musical, visual, software code) from another person and passing them off as one's own, sometimes remains undetected and unpunished. Dames in his 2007 article "Understanding plagiarism and how it differs from copyright infringement," states that "plagiarism allegations can be much more damaging [than copyright infringement that can result in financial damages or even jail] to a person's professional reputation than allegations of copyright infringement" (p. 26)[3].

Numerous other writers have attempted to define the concept of plagiarism. In an excellent bibliography on plagiarism that reviews nearly 700 books and scholarly articles written in English between 1900 and 1995, Anderson discusses different definitions in the historical, cultural, and disciplinary contexts.[4] The annotated bibliography is organized chronologically, following an extensive Introductory section, and discussed under four sections: 1) trends in definition; 2) follow the money; 3) detection, proof, and punishment; and 4) protecting one's property.

Angélil-Carter, in her work *Stolen Language? Plagiarism in Writing* (2000), discusses the historical development of the notion of plagiarism, along with copyright.[5] From the British perspective, she tries to convey that plagiarism is an elusive concept and has been treated differently in different contexts. As Angélil-Carter writes in her Introduction, she wanted to "understand plagiarism differently," and to communicate that understanding to teachers and writers of academic discourse (p. 3).

Two college English professors, Rebecca Moore Howard and Margaret Price also address the concept of plagiarism from multiple perspectives. Howard discusses plagiarism from the perspectives of authorship, pedagogy, and scholarship; in closing, she proposes policy on plagiarism, as well as advice for students and teachers.[6] Howard characterizes plagiarism as "patchwriting" if students are "copying from a source text and then deleting some words, altering grammatical structures, or plugging in one synonym for another." (p. xvii)[7]. Price considers

Encyclopedia of Library and Information Sciences, Fourth Edition DOI: 10.1081/E-ELIS4-120044510

plagiarism in a given time, academic community, workplace, defined in a specific discipline, rather than as an absolute concept across different cultures and communities.[8]

Not All plagiarism Is Perceived Equally

Burke distinguishes among the four forms of cheating: *Cheating*, according to Burke, is "intentionally using or attempting to use unauthorized materials, information, or study aids in any academic exercise." *Fabrication*, Burke writes, is "intentional and unauthorized falsification or invention of any information or citation in an academic exercise." *Facilitating academic dishonesty* is defined as "intentionally or knowingly helping or attempting to help another to commit an act of academic dishonesty," and *plagiarism* is defined as "intentionally or knowingly representing the word of another as one's own in any academic exercise."[9]

The Council of Writing Program Administrators, CWPA, thinks of plagiarism as a deliberate use of "someone else's language, ideas, or other original (not common-knowledge) material without acknowledging its source." This definition is extended to printed and digital materials, manuscripts, and other works.[10] The Council's statement on Best Practices suggests a five prong strategy: to explain plagiarism and develop clear policies; to improve the design and sequence of assignments; to attend to sources and the use of reading; to work on plagiarism responsibility; and to take appropriate disciplinary action.

The following studies investigated various forms of plagiarism pertaining to college students. For example, Klausman makes three distinctions between direct plagiarism, paraphrase plagiarism, and patchwork plagiarism.[11] Lasarenko offers exercises to help students understand the differences between summarizing and paraphrasing practices, and how both can result in plagiarism if the original sources are not cited.[12] Birnbaum and Goscilo[13] (cited in Kaltenbaugh[14] distinguish direct copying, rearranged copying, selective omission, copying selective words or phrases, paraphrasing, not citing a secondary source within a primary work, and making attribution unclear. In two separate studies with college students at St. John's University, New York, Roig asked students to determine which of 10 rewritten versions were plagiarized.[15] He found that 40–50% of the students did not identify plagiarized versions. Roig suggested that students in his tests were unclear as to what plagiarism meant.

The idea of "inadvertent plagiarism" or unconscious plagiarism has been examined in young and older adults.[16] From the perspectives of memory as well as psychology and aging, experiments have established that older adults were more likely to plagiarize inadvertently than did younger adults. McCabe, Smith, and Parks conclude that the primary cause of the age differences in plagiarism is the nature of the retrieval processes involved in monitoring for plagiarism errors, including age-related declines in recall of studied exemplars and/or to age-related declines in working memory.

WHAT DOES THE LITERATURE ON PLAGIARISM TELL US?

Literature on the topic of plagiarism is scattered, mostly descriptive, anecdotal, and has not as yet received a unique and deserving place in the scholarly literature it warrants. The reviewed literature asks important questions but the methodology used to study many of the questions is wanting in validity and applicability.

Plagiarism is a moral issue which is at the heart of the educational enterprise. It cuts across multiple disciplines, all sectors of the society, and hinges upon learning, teaching, levels of moral development, and applying ethical behavior in our everyday lives. This problem is reflected in the nature of literature that reports on plagiarism; it is spread out across library and information science, education, technology, social sciences, sciences, and ethics. How many English teachers read history or library-related literature? How many college instructors read literature especially targeted to secondary school teachers, technology coordinators, administrators, or to engineers and scientists? We have not made wide strides across disciplinary lines or between higher and secondary school education on plagiarism prevention. While the problems are basically the same, we see fragmentation along professions and educational status; professional conferences are designed around these lines, and literature follows the same structure. We need to learn much from one another, to share research results, evaluate models, and apply them in practice.

When this author searched ProQuest Platinum (thereafter ProQuest) database on the topic of plagiarism in peer-reviewed full-text articles, she retrieved the following distribution of results summarized in Table 1. It suggests a trend toward a significant increase in published articles on plagiarism since Internet has become widely available in various educational institutions. The numbers show rise of published literature at more than sevenfold in ProQuest Platinum database since the Web has become an ubiquitous and widely affordable information resource at all levels.

Plausible explanations are that: 1) plagiarism has started to receive the attention it deserves in the literature; 2) there are more cases of plagiarism detected, and with the advent of cyber-media in schools, colleges, and work places, more allegation cases are reported in the literature; and 3) it is easier to detect plagiarism as more electronic submissions are requested by publishing houses, and therefore it has become easier to compare texts on similarity strings and detect plagiarized contents.

Besides ProQuest and JSTOR, this author searched *Library and Information Science Abstracts*, Online

Table 1 Search results from ProQuest Platinum on plagiarism

Results on "plagiarism"— before and after the Internet era. The cutoff date was set for January 1, 1993	Proquest Platinum (2300+ periodical titles in all disciplines with about 43% full-text coverage)
Pre-Internet era	49
Internet era	377

Computer Library Center (OCLC)'s *FirstSearch* databases, such as *ArticleFirst, PapersFirst, Library Literature,* and *Dissertation Abstracts Online*. The retrieved items are published in journals, newspapers, reports, dissertations, and conferences. In addition to the information obtained from database searches just described, this author reviewed published bibliographies. The Center for Teaching and Learning maintains compilation of articles from a variety of sources on plagiarism-related issues. Other bibliographies are in books, such as in Harris[17] and in Marsh.[18] For example, a brief content analysis of 154 entry bibliography on plagiarism demonstrates that the topic is largely fragmented and domain-centered with little or no attention given to the domains outside the scope of authors' own. Bill Marsh, an English language instructor, in his book titled *Plagiarism: Alchemy and Remedy in Higher Education*, covers literature from 1874 to 2004 with about 70% pieces published since 1992 from the perspectives of electronic media composition techniques, education, rhetoric, print history, and communication.

Previous editions of *Encyclopedia of Library and Information Science* (ELIS)[19,20] contain articles under headings of copyright-related issues such as fair use and piracy. In volume 2, Jay Daily defines the word "piracy" as an "unauthorized publication of works," and taken to mean differently from plagiarism in that the "original author may be given credit for the intellectual content" p. 263.[19] In the 1988 Supplement to ELIS (volume 43), W. Z. Nazri's article titled "Federal actions against plagiarism in research," reviews "policies and specific cases involving plagiarism in federally funded research" including such agencies as the Office of Research Integrity of the U.S. Public Health Service and the Office of Inspector General of the National Science Foundation.[20] The article gives definitions of plagiarism as adopted by the research agencies, frequency of plagiarism allegations, process, findings, and actions taken against plagiarists.

The literature reviewed for this entry is primarily focused on plagiarism issues among secondary school students and college students.[9,11,15,21,22] A subset of that literature is concerned with issues among professional school students.[23–28] Articles cover scenarios of single case plagiarism-related issues in individual educational institutions, ranging from secondary schools, higher education institutions, research labs, professional schools such as nursing, business, engineering, and science. Though interesting, these reports cannot be generalized to populations outside a single case study or a

single school described in any given report. Other articles in newspapers, magazines, and search engine alerts continue to report sensational cases that involve paper mills, software companies, stories about prominent figures in journalism, writing composition, research, and academe.

The author examined literatures for effective pedagogical approaches that instructors can use to design specific academic integrity programs that would be appropriate for secondary schools and colleges. Since students at different levels of their cognitive development reason differently when presented with specific moral dilemmas,[29] educators need to customize academic integrity programs to make them sensitive to and compatible with students' levels of moral reasoning.

HOW PREVALENT IS PLAGIARISM?

Under the "Extent of the Problem," Kibler reviews literature that demonstrates that various forms of academic dishonesty have been with us since ancient civilizations, and that academic dishonesty, for a variety of reasons, has increased.[21] More recently, literature has shifted its attention from the student behavior toward a more robust approach to academic integrity taking into consideration a broader environment of teaching and learning.[30]

In terms of K-12th grade educational level, the *Center for Academic Integrity* consortium of more than 300 institutions at Clemson University, South Carolina, publishes valuable reports such as "Smart & Good High Schools: Integrating Excellence and Ethics for Success in Schools, Work, and Beyond."[31] Josephson Institute's "2008 Report Card on the Ethics of American Youth," reveals that young people are almost anonymous in saying that ethics and character are important on both a personal level and in business but they express very cynical attitudes about whether a person can be ethical and succeed.[32] Based on a survey of 29,760 students in public and private high schools across the United States, the *Report* found that 64% cheated on a test within the past 12 months, up from 60% in 2006. There were no gender differences on the issue of cheating on exams. However, students attending independent schools reported the lowest rate (47%) compared to those attending religious schools (63%). The lowest cheating rate was reported in the Midwest (59%) compared to the Southeast (70%). Thirty-six percent of the surveyed students copied an Internet document to a classroom assignment within the past 12 months compared to 32.9% in 2006.

Working with a smaller set of secondary school children, an exploratory study examined students' understanding, their attitudes, and general practices toward cyberplagiarism.[33] The article, based on a sample of availability, surveyed 37 high school juniors and framed questions in the context of information literacy standards and respective performance indicators. The study used a self-reported paper-and-pencil questionnaire to obtain data on content knowledge (what students say they know), students' attitudes toward cyber-plagiarism-related issues (what students feel), and students' practices (what students are telling us they actually do). Among the interesting findings was the extent of difficulties students had with regard to giving credit to creators of nonbook resources. Examples included photographers, choreographers, and cartoon artists. Equally confused were the students with respect to attributing to computer code, information obtained through e-mail transcripts, and personal communication. To gauge the question, "Is the Google generation information literate?," a case study looked at information-seeking behaviors of 105 middle school students.[34] The surveyed students are fluent with digital cameras, iPhones, Blackberries, Facebook, MySpace, YouTube, and Amazon's Kindle interfaces; their first best sources, regardless of the nature of inquiry, included search engines, (wiki)cyclopedias, books, and primary (digital) sources. Their perception was that 80% or more of everything that has been published is available on the Web. Other findings include problems with attribution, especially of digital resources, understanding what primary sources are, how to critically separate good sources from inappropriate or unreliable ones, and how to find those golden nuggets from the deluge of data. The surveyed students have both conceptual and mechanical problems in deciding when to give credit and how to do it properly; many come from elementary schools confused as to the differences between quoting and paraphrasing. More than 8 out of 10 surveyed students would give credit in order to "avoid plagiarism-related issues" (82%). Clearly, there is a gap between the surveyed students' understanding of the concepts of the ethical use of information and the belief that provided the basis for the newly created information literacy *Standards for the 21st-Century Learner*—that ethical behavior in communicating information is crucial.[35]

There have been a number of studies of college students in the context of plagiarism-related questions. Roberts, Anderson, and Yanish found that in the self-reported 1997 surveys of 422 college students at a midsized 4 year public university, 91.7% reported that had engaged in at least one type of academic misconduct during the surveyed year.[36] Virginia Polytechnic Institute reported that various forms of academic cheating have more than tripled, from 80 in 1995/1996 to 280 in 1997/1998. Virginia Tech is one among numerous campuses that has seen a rise of plagiarized information stolen from the Internet, e-mail, and other digital communication services. Ten years later, however, Virginia Tech has developed their Undergraduate Honor Code System which functions are to communicate the meaning and importance of intellectual honesty to all students of the University; to articulate and support the interest of the community in maintaining the highest standards of conduct in academic affairs; and to

identify, sanction, and educate those who fail to live up to the stated expectations of the university community with regard to these standards.[37]

Authors from Harvard University and University of Illinois at Urbana-Champaign found that in their introductory political science course in the spring of 2000, about one out of eight papers seemed problematic.[38] In the spring of 1999, a University Honor Council survey found that 54% of Penn students "considered copying homework to be cheating," and 61% of the students indicated that they would not "report a case of cheating to the Office of Student Conduct."[39]

In the scientific world, several recent incidents reported that stellar scholars at two highly regarded research institutions (Bell Labs, and separately at the Lawrence Berkeley National Lab), faked data. In his article, "Peer trouble: How failsafe is our current system at ensuring the quality and integrity of research? Not very," says Crace.[40] The author reports on a recent study by the University of Minnesota of 4000 researchers "that one in three scientists plagiarized, 22% handled data "carelessly" and 15% occasionally withheld unfavorable data." Most recently, Ben Martin, in his editorial article, details a case of a serial plagiarist, Hans Werner Gottinger (management/economy) who had been caught numerous times; each time he confronted the problem by moving to different research labs and academic institutions in the United States and Europe, and by apologizing, retracting his papers, and repeating all over again at his next affiliations.[26] In an anonymous article, "Policing Integrity," scientific misconduct, especially plagiarism, has been discussed.[41] Oversight organizations of the Office of Research Integrity at the Health Department, and by the Nation Science Foundation (NSF) in the United States are contrasted with those in Britain, France, Italy, and Germany. Standler, an attorney at law, marshals examples of statutes from 14 states about sales of term papers; he gives detailed accounts of plagiarism by students, professors, and cases against commercial agencies that sell papers.[42]

ATTITUDES OF FACULTY TOWARD ACADEMIC DISHONESTY

As we have seen above, the literature suggests some disturbing facts on the state of academic dishonesty in the United States, especially the growing prevalence of plagiarism. Other related research offers insight into the attitudes of faculty toward plagiarism. In his 1997 dissertation, Burke studied factors that influence faculty response to academic dishonesty at a multicampus, 2 year college. His "research investigated faculty: 1) perceptions of the extent of academic honesty; 2) perceptions of, and attitudes toward Academic Dishonesty Policy and policy implementation; 3) responses to academic dishonesty; 4) attitudes concerning values education; and 5) attitudes about responsibility for reducing academic dishonesty"

(p. 3).[9] The study delineated perceptions, responses, and attitudes among faculty grouped by employment status, campus, seniority, and discipline. Seven hundred and forty two faculty members completed a 25-question survey. The results indicated that faculty do not perceive academic dishonesty to be a serious problem. Faculty believed themselves to be familiar with current policy and procedure, and are not concerned with policy implementation. The surveyed faculty members believe that they have a primary role in values education. Of the faculty surveyed, 86% have suspected, and 65% have been certain of, academic dishonesty in their classrooms. The majority of the surveyed members do not regularly follow institutional policy; most handle incidents of cheating and plagiarism on the individual basis. They believe that the responsibility for reducing academic dishonesty lies primarily with students and individual faculty. The fact that 86% of the studied faculty have suspected academic dishonesty in their classrooms, and did not perceive this to be a major problem, should be investigated further.

Marcoux's doctoral work studied college faculty's awareness level of the Kansas State University's honor code and cheating policies.[43] The faculty's responses varied and indicated that they had not received training in how to handle cases of academic cheating.

Freedman[44] reports his experience with preservice elementary school science teachers; some plagiarists were apologetic, others were offensive. He proposes prevention rather than detection as a new paradigm to combat plagiarism. For example, Freedman asks his student teachers to find an existing lesson plan, and creatively adapt for his or her students, language, and programs; another technique requires students to reflect on the relevancy of selected lessons with regard to diversity, assessments, and inquiry-based teaching. While we have no data on evaluation of the proposed program, it seems reasonable to assume that teachers will benefit in many ways to access information, critically evaluate source lesson plans, acknowledge the sources, and adapt to suit their needs.

Johnston's article reflects on a moral dilemma she dealt with relating to cheating that occurred during one of her unproctored exams in her Moral Development and Education course by some upper division students at Colgate University in New York.[45] She decided to use that incident as a teaching challenge and "role-taking" technique. When Johnston confronted her class, she was alarmed with the range of students' responses. Some were surprised if no one cheated, some did not know how to deal with cheating if it occurred, many students rated cheating on a continuum, some viewed cheating as "refreshing the memory," others were bothered that students majoring in education in that particular class cheated. Students were equally divided about moral decision making as a group. Johnston's analysis of cheating takes her to search for causes of cheating behaviors beyond pressure and individual integrity. She writes, "it occurs because students do it if they won't 'get caught' and being caught by their peers is not problematic" (p. 290). Ethical behavior is often assumed among professionals, such as teachers, managers, scientists, and other scholars. However, as Hall and Berardino point out, this set of skills unless taught cannot be taken for granted.[25] Teaching professional behaviors (e.g., punctuality, honesty, cell phone usage, and appropriate appearance) is an important, complex, and underestimated area in general educational systems. It seems that there is a lack of alignment between offences and punishment, and lack of communication between administrators, faculty, parents, and students. Other problems are related to students' state of readiness to understand issues involved in academic dishonesty and plagiarism, and in relationships with peers, teachers, and as part of their educational climate as a whole.

CAN WE PREDICT ACADEMIC DISHONESTY?

The reviewed literature identified specific variables of learners in ethical uses of information.

Social Factors as Predictors of Academic Dishonesty

In a broader context, we sought to find societal indicators that strongly and positively correlate to academic dishonesty. Again, we turned to *The State of Americans: This Generation and the Next* to find possible answers to this question.[46] There is evidence to support that nuclear family correlates positively and strongly with students' academic performance (GPA scores), cheating behavior, drug use, and teenagers' trust in others.

In competitive classrooms across the board, under parents' pressure to produce high grades, many students, including those from professional schools, have been found guilty of academic misconduct and plagiarism. Kibler divides his literature review into *Personal Characteristics of Cheaters* and *Situational Factors Involved in a Student's Decision Whether to Cheat*.[21] Among the situational factors, important ones include unproctored tests, penalty systems, teaching styles (authoritarian style incites cheating, overly difficult tests, hopelessness, soft teachers), climate of the school, and "likely to get caught" (pp. 257–259). Schab writes that high school graduates cheat due to "fear of failure," because "parents demand and expect good grades" in order for their children to be admitted to top universities; other reasons given were that everyone cheats, and that teachers were "too soft on these issues" (p. 840).[47]

Individual Differences as Predictors of Academic Dishonesty

In the study mentioned earlier, Roberts, Anderson, and Yanish examined the relationship between demographic variables and academic dishonesty among undergraduates.[36] A total of 422 students from 22 classes completed a 27-item self-reported survey that was designed to measure their involvement in 17 types of academic misconduct. The survey also obtained data on class standing, age, gender, GPA, and college major. Results revealed that being male and/or younger than 24 years of age were characteristics associated with greater involvement in academic misconduct. The authors did not find significant difference in self-reported academic misconduct between students and respective GPA scores.

In an earlier study, the authors used a questionnaire to obtain data on self-reported frequency of 21 cheating behaviors ($n = 943$) sophomores and juniors from 19 disciplines).[48] This "first large-scale study of cheating carried out in the United Kingdom" (p. 238) calculated the frequency with which each reason was given for both cheating and for not cheating. Reasons given for cheating include time pressure, to get a higher grade, because everybody does it, to help a friend, and laziness. Students gave reasons for not cheating "because it is immoral," "situation did not arise," "it was unnecessary," and "personal pride" (p. 233). The study found that men cheated more, that cheating declines with age, and that it occurs more frequently among science and technology majors than among other disciplines.

Pennycook writes about some of the complexities of text, ownership, memorization, and plagiarism.[49] The author suggests that plagiarism needs to be understood in terms of relationships between text, memory, learning, literacy, and cultural differences.

Six hundred and ninety-eight college students from nine universities completed a survey on Internet plagiarism. A substantial minority of the surveyed students reported they used the Internet to copy and paste text into their own papers without giving credit to sources they used in their writings. Buranen in her piece, "But I wasn't cheating: Plagiarism and cross-cultural mythology," presents experiences with ESL (English as a Second Language) students and their writing problems and practices.[50] In many cases, students lack a combination of vocabulary skills, factual knowledge, and bibliographic conventions. According to Buranen, cultural differences may also influence students' attitudes toward "borrowing" and "'ownership' of ideas or of text" (p. 66). Cultural perspective has been further explored by Dryden in the context of Japanese education (pp. 75–85).[51]

Angélil-Carter writes about developing writing skills in general and not limited to non-English language students.[52] She writes, "This is what is so difficult for the novice writer of academic discourse (or for any writer)—it is the control of the voices so that the authorial voice speaks through them..." (p. 35). Nearly 70 years earlier, Edwards wrote about "good and bad borrowing," differences between imaginative and unimaginative borrowing, and those between a derivative artist and a thief.[53]

COPING WITH PLAGIARISM

In his chapter on "The Moral Atmosphere of the School," Kohlberg summarizes important findings by educational sociologists, such as Emile Durkheim, Philip Jackson, Robert Dreeben, and Edgar Friedenberg.[53] Kohlberg introduces us to a concept of "hidden curriculum" in which characteristics of the crowds, the praise, and the authority are of major influences on the development of children. "After the family the school is the first social institution an individual must deal with, the place in which he learns to handle himself with strangers" (Friedenberg, *Coming of Age in America*, 1963, p. 149).[53] Kohlberg's research builds on that tradition and on the notions of Dewey and Piaget, and finds that the development of moral reasoning is sequential progression through distinct stages. Kohlberg believes that the role of the teacher is to translate moral ideology into a working social atmosphere in which students understand the meaning of the "hidden curriculum" based on the universal principle of justice underlining respect of all people. In this context, teachers have considerable flexibility to implement "hidden curriculum" within respective school cultures. Theories of ethical reasoning are in line of combating plagiarism through teaching, information literacy units on ethical use of information, and campus-wide honor code policies. Another line of coping with plagiarism has been through detection tools and adjudication of student plagiarism. These two perspectives are described next.

Ethical Reasoning

Granitz and Loewy studied theories of ethical reasoning that students invoke when they defend their plagiarism behavior.[54] The researchers used a content analysis of written records of students formally charged with plagiarism. The authors classified case studies based on six types of reasoning students gave as justification for their academic misconduct. These were deontology, utilitarianism, rational self-interest, Machiavellianism, cultural relativism, or situational ethics. The authors found that students predominantly invoke deontology (41.8%), followed by situational ethics (19.9%) and Machiavellianism (18.4%). Under *deontology*, students typically justify their dishonest behavior by saying that they didn't know what plagiarism was or that it was wrong. The *Machiavellianism* reasoning considers the act successful if they can get away with it without being caught. The *situational* plagiarism blames a given situation for dishonest activity (e.g., being late, being poor, inequity, stress). For each of the six reasoning theories underpinning plagiarism, Granitz and Loewy recommend prevention techniques: have honor code, teach proper citation techniques, act as a role model, and avoid standardized assignments. Based on responses obtained from 2200 students on 21 college campuses,

McCabe and Trevino concluded that schools with honor codes had fewer repeat offenders.[55] This finding has policy implications, and honor codes have been widely practiced in numerous campuses.

Online Instruction

Among plagiarism prevention Web-based tutorials within information literacy units, Jackson assessed data from 2829 student quiz scores on their understanding of plagiarism.[56] The study found that students have difficulties with paraphrasing, don't understand the concept of plagiarism, and mechanics of citing sources. The article concludes that online tutorials should be considered a part of a broader educational framework in the area of intellectual property and academic integrity.

Plagiarism Prevention Techniques

An approach taken in Harris's *Handbook*[17] against plagiarism is to teach students about plagiarism-related issues rather than to assume that they know what plagiarism is. He uses anecdotes, cartoons, and plain language to demonstrate differences between plagiarism and copyright issues, good citing practices and careless note-taking techniques, differences between paraphrasing, summarizing, and copying sentences and paragraphs. An important section is directed toward explaining reasons why plagiarism is unethical, and the benefits of citing sources. McKenzie suggests specific ways in order to "prevent highway robbery in an electronic age:" distinguish between levels and types of research, give instruction to educators to go beyond "just factual" scavenger hunts and challenge students to use facts to explain, solve problems, and make decisions; go beyond "conventional thinking;" encourage students to "emphasize essential questions;" learn how to paraphrase, summarize, and cite the sources of ideas or information; use of color-coded text to differentiate between the ideas of others (black ink) and students' fresh ideas, reactions, or insights (green ink).[57] Niels reports that the entire academic program at the Central Park East Secondary School (CPESS) in New York City is organized around the five main questions: Whose viewpoint is being described? What evidence is there? How is this connected to other things? What are the alternatives? How is this relevant? Niels develops an argument that in order to deal with various forms of cheating behavior, we need to look at contextual factors that influence cheating, which is moral education.[58]

Brown and Howell, both with the University of St. Andrews, Scotland, studied the effectiveness of policy statements of plagiarism on students' behaviors.[59] The study concluded that there was a positive influence between students who read carefully worded statements of plagiarism and respective academic behaviors.

Software Detection Programs

In their two 90-student sections in Introduction to Political Science course at the University of Illinois at Urbana-Champaign, Braumoeller and Gaines used assignment sheets with: 1) explicit written and verbal warnings not to plagiarize in one section; and 2) plagiarism detection software in another section.[37] The investigators found that while verbal and written warnings not to plagiarize had a negligible effect on rates of plagiarism, plagiarism detection software proved to be successful in discouraging students to plagiarize. Policing plagiarism in any of the environments seems to be of mixed success.[60] This author has long been in line with those who strongly feel that software tools such as turnitin and eve are at the end of plagiarism pipeline, and therefore limited. As Evans states, trust and student honesty remain central to a successful academic scholarship.[59]

CONCLUSIONS

Plagiarism has always been known, although not adequately understood and reported, to teachers, administrators, behavioral psychologists, and sociologists. Literature has reported cases of plagiarism, under various names, including research misconduct, lack of academic integrity, academic dishonesty, misappropriation of intellectual property, and fabrication. This is not only a serious issue among students in secondary schools and colleges. It is rampant and on the increase among researchers, professors, and other professionals regardless of their age, discipline, seniority status, culture, and geographical region. Many have attributed its rise of epidemic proportions to a growing number of paper mills on the Web, "cut and paste" techniques, and educational culture as a whole; this has manifested itself through various ways in schools, such as instructors' inconsistent treatment and overall attitudes toward cheating, lack of plagiarism prevention strategies, uncertainty to interpret and apply honor codes, detect instances of plagiarism in print and electronic media, and customize teaching units on ethical use of information to meet students' uneven moral developmental capacities. In the higher education, plagiarism audits have been dealt with inconsistently and reported through peer review process, doctoral committee members, by individual readers, publishers, editors, and funding agencies. Much progress has been made about understanding of plagiarism and how to deal with at various levels of educational ladder. We need more effective pedagogical tools to engage students in real-life dilemmas at their levels of moral reasoning. We have illustrated paradigm shifts that have taken place between pre-Web and the Web era in Table 2.

Research is needed to study predictors that might suggest students' behavioral patterns at different phases of their reasoning development. Attention is also needed in

Table 2 Paradigm shifts in dealing with plagiarism

Paradigm shifts in plagiarism	Pre-Web era	The Web era
Medium and format	Piracy of mainly *printed texts*	Piracy of *multimedia*
Method of copying	*By hand*, purchase papers	"*Cut and paste*," paper mills
Domain: discipline and level of educational institutions	*English* teachers mainly at *college* level	*Multiple disciplines* (e.g., library literature, science, and professional schools) at different levels including secondary schools
Combating plagiarism in educational domains	*Mechanical* techniques: template-based bibliographic citations; detect and punish; however, some authors write about plagiarism preventions in pre-Web era (e.g., Daniels[65], Saalbach[66], and Carroll[67])	*Conceptual* techniques: Focus on the *reasons* to give credit to sources; scenario-based discussion prior to mechanics (how to apply templates to specific cases)
Pedagogical approach as represented in Information Literacy Standards	Legalistic approach, need for educational approach (see, for example, Drum[68])	Intellectual property and digital rights management → Learning Standards.[35]

the areas of mapping research results to pedagogical experiences and specific subject (and interdisciplinary) authentic scenarios and lesson plans, diagnostic and assessment tools that instructors can customize for individual curricular needs.

FUTURE RESEARCH

Doctoral level work in the context of moral reasoning and development starting with seminal works by, for example, John Dewey,[61] Jean Piaget,[62] and Lawrence Kohlberg[29] can advance our understanding and give us a conceptual framework around which to design research with specific questions in mind. Reporting beyond anecdotal stories would be useful in order to study trends of various segments in our society, reasons "plagiarism is on the rise," factors affecting these behaviors, as well as prevention strategies that might be considered and put in practice. In summary, plagiarism is not an isolated problem to any particular discipline.[26,63,64] It is systemic issue of epidemic proportions requiring the entire educational community to mobilize, to study the problem from different angles, communicate findings, propose models, verify, and translate into best practices across the educational ladder.

REFERENCES

1. *Webster's College Dictionary*; Random House: New York, 1991.
2. *Oxford English Dictionary*, 2nd Ed.; Simpson, J., Weiner, E., Eds.; Clarendon Press: Oxford, U.K., 1989.
3. Dames, M.K. Understanding plagiarism and how it differs from copyright infringement. Comput. Libr. **2007**, *27* (6), 25–27.
4. Anderson, J. *Plagiarism, Copyright Violation, and Other Thefts of Intellectual Property: An Annotated Bibliography with a Lengthy Introduction*; McFarland: Jefferson, NC, 1998.
5. Angélil-Carter, S. *Stolen Language? Plagiarism in Writing*; Pearson Education Limited: Harlow, England, 2000.
6. Howard, R.M. Plagiarism, authorship, and the academic death penalty. Coll. Engl. **1995**, *57* (7), 788–806.
7. Howard, R.M. *Standing in the Shadow of Giants: Plagiarists, Authors, Collaborators. Vol. 2 in the Series Perspectives on Writing: Theory, Research, Practice*; Ablex Publishing: Stamford, CT, 1999.
8. Price, M. Beyond 'gotcha!': Situating plagiarism in policy and pedagogy. Coll. Compos. Commun. **2002**, *54* (1), 88–115.
9. Burke, J.L. Faculty perceptions of and attitudes toward academic dishonesty at a two-year college; Unpublished doctoral dissertation: Athens, GA, ED431486, 1997.
10. Council of Writing Program Administrators (WPA). Defining and avoiding plagiarism: the WPA statement on best practices. http://www.wpacouncil.org (accessed December 22, 2008).
11. Klausman, J. Teaching about plagiarism in the age of the Internet. Teach. Engl. Two-Year Coll. December **1999**, *27*, 209–212.
12. Lasarenko, J. Teaching, paraphrase, summary, and plagiarism: An integrated approach. Exer. Exc. **1996**, *41*, 10–12.
13. Birnbaum, D.J.; Goscilo, H. Avoiding plagiarism 2002. http://dover.slavic.pitt.edu/02–1/plagiarism.html (accessed December 11, 2007).
14. Kaltenbaugh, A. Plagiarism: The technological, intellectual, and personal facets of the principles of attribution, use, and acknowledgment. J. Inform. Ethics **2005**, *14* (2), 50–60.
15. Roig, M. Can undergraduate students determine whether text has been plagiarized? Psychol. Rec. Winter **1997**, *47*, 113–123.
16. McCabe, D.P.; Smith, A.D.; Parks, C.M. Inadvertent plagiarism in young and older adults: The role of working memory capacity in reducing memory errors. Mem. Cogn. **2007**, *35* (2), 231–241.
17. Harris, R.A. *The Plagiarism Handbook: Strategies for Preventing, Detecting, and Dealing with Plagiarism*; Cartoons by Vic Lockman, based on ideas by the author; Pyrczak: Los Angeles, CA, 2001.

18. Marsh, B. *Plagiarism: Alchemy and Remedy in Higher Education*; State University of New York Press: Albany, NY, 2007.

19. Daily, J.E. Piracy. In *Encyclopedia of Library and Information Science*; Kent, A., Lancour, H., Daily, J.E., Eds.; Marcel Dekker: New York, 1977; Vol. 22, 263–266.

20. Nasri, W.Z. Copyright and the information professionals. In *Encyclopedia of Library and Information Science*; Kent, A., Ed.; Marcel Dekker: New York, 1988; Vol. 43 (Supplement 8), 79–93, 2003. Federal actions against plagiarism in research, also in ELIS, 132–146.

21. Kibler, W.L. Academic dishonesty: A student development dilemma. NASPA J. Summer **1993**, *30*, 252–267.

22. Lathrop, A.; Foss, F. *Student Cheating and Plagiarism in the Internet Era. A Wake-up call*; Libraries Unlimited: Englewood, CO, 2000.

23. Goett, J.A.; Kenneth, E.F. Cultivating student research and study skills in Web-based learning environments. J. Geogr. High. Educ. **2000**, *24* (1), 92.

24. Goffe, W.L.; Kim, S. Teaching with technology: May you live in interesting times. J. Econo. Educ. **2005**, *36* (3), 278 (14 pages).

25. Hall, A.; Berardino, L. Teaching professional behaviors: Differences in the perceptions of faculty, students, and employers. J. Bus. Ethics **2006**, *63*, 407–415.

26. Martin, B.R. Keeping plagiarism at bay—A salutary tale. Res. Policy **2007**, *36* (7), 905–911.

27. Skeikh, A. Publication ethics and the research assessment exercise: Reflections on the troubled question of authorship. J. Med. Ethics **2000**, *26* (6), 422(5 pages).

28. Tanner, C.A. Moral decline or pragmatic decision making? Cheating and plagiarism in perspective. J. Nurs. Educ. **2005**, *43* (7), 291.

29. Kohlberg, L. Moral stages and moralization: The cognitive-developmental approach. In *Moral Development and Behavior: Theory, Research, and Social Issues*; Lickona, T., Ed.; Holt, Rinehart & Winston: New York, 1976.

30. *Academic Integrity in the Twenty-first Century: A Teaching and Learning Imperative*; Gallant, T.B., Ed. Association for the Study of Higher Education (ASHE) Higher Education Report, 2008; Vol. 33 (5), 1–143. Available from ERIC Clearinghouse on Higher Education, EJ 791635.

31. Center for Academic Integrity: Ruthland Institute of Ethics. Clemson University, SC. *Smart & Good High Schools: Integrating Excellence and Ethics for Success in Schools, Work, and Beyond*; http://cortland.edu/character/highschool/ (accessed January 3, 2009).

32. Josephson Institute: Center for Youth Ethics. *2008 Report Cart on the Ethics of American Youth*; http://charactercounts.org/programs/reportcard/index.html (accessed January 3, 2009).

33. Ercegovac, Z. What students say they know, feel, and do about cyber-plagiarism and academic dishonesty? A case study. In *Proceedings of the American Society for Information Science and Technology (ASIST)*, 2005; Charlotte, NC, October 28–November 2, 2005. http://www.asis.org/Conferences/AM05/abstracts/42.html (accessed January 3, 2009).

34. Ercegovac, Z. Is the Google generation information literate? In People *Transforming Information—Information Transforming People*; Presented at the Annual Meeting of the American Society for Information Science and Technology (ASIST) 2008, Columbus, OH, October, 24–29, 2008.

35. American Library Association. American Association of School Librarians. *Standards for the 21st-Century Learner*; ALA: Chicago, IL, 2008. http://www.ala.org/ala/mgrps/divs/aasl/aaslproftools/learningstandards/standards.cfm (accessed January 3, 2009).

36. Roberts, P.; Anderson, J.; Yanish, P. *Academic Misconduct: Where Do We Start?* In Paper presented at the *Annual Conference of the Northern Rocky Mountain Educational Research Association*, Jackson, WY, 27. Report No: ED 415 781, October, 1997. http://reading.indiana.edu (accessed January 3, 2009).

37. Virginia Tech. Office of the Provost. Undergraduate Honor System; http://www.honorsystem.vt.edu/ (accessed January, 2009).

38. Braumoeller, B.F.; Gaines, B.J. *Actions Do Speak Louder Than Words: Deterring Plagiarism With the Use of Plagiarism-Detection Software*; APSANET (The American Political Science Association Online), December 2001, http://www.apsanet.org/PS/dec01/braumoeller.cfm?option=print (accessed August 31, 2008).

39. Clarke-Pearson, M. *Download. Steal. Copy. Cheating at the University*; (Posted Nov 17, 2001). The Daily Pennsylvanian, 2009. http://www.dailypennsylvanian.com/ (accessed January 3, 2009).

40. Crace, J. *Peer Trouble: How Failsafe is Our Current System at Ensuring the Quality and Integrity of Research? Not Very*; The Guardian, February 11 2003. http://education.guardian.co.uk/print/0,4602456–48826,00.html (accessed January 3, 2009).

41. Anonymous Policy integrity. Nature **2005**, *435*, 248.

42. Standler, R.B. *Plagiarism in Colleges in USA*, 2000. http://www.rbs2.com/plag.htm (accessed January 2, 2009).

43. Marcoux, H.E. Kansas State University faculty perspectives, opinions, and practices concerning undergraduate student academic dishonesty and moral development; Unpublished doctoral dissertation, Kansas State University: Kansas, 2002.

44. Freedman, M.P. A tale of plagiarism and a new paradigm. Phi Delta Kappa **2004**, *85* (7), 545.

45. Johnston, K.D. Cheating: Reflections on a moral dilemma. J. Moral Educ. **1991**, *20* (3), 283–291.

46. Bronfenbrenner, U.; McClelland, P.; Wethington, E.; Moen, P.; Ceci, S.J. *The State of Americans: This Generation and the Next*; The Free Press: New York, 1996.

47. Schab, F. Schooling without learning: Thirty years in high school. Adolescence **1991**, *23*, 681–687.

48. Neustead, S.E.; Franklyn-Stoes, A.; Armsted, P. Individual differences in student cheating. J. Educ. Psychol. **1996**, *88*, (2), 229–241.

49. Pennycook, A. Borrowing others' words: Text, ownership, memory, and plagiarism. TESOL Q. **1996**, *30*, 201–230.

50. Buranen, L. 'But I wasn't cheating': Plagiarism and cross-cultural mythology. In *Perspectives on Plagiarism and Intellectual Property in Postmodern World*; Buranen, L., Roy, A.M., Eds.; Foreword by A. Lunsford, State University of New York Press: Albany, NY, 1999; 63–74.

51. Dryden, L.M. A distant mirror or through the looking glass? Plagiarism and intellectual property in Japanese education.

In *Perspectives on Plagiarism and Intellectual Property in a Postmodern World*; Buranen, L., Roy, A.M., Eds.; State University of New York Press: Albany, NY, 1999; 75–85.

52. Edwards, W.A. *Plagiarism: An Essay on Good and Bad Borrowing*; Gordon Fraser, The Minority Press: Cambridge, England, 1933.

53. Kohlberg, L. The moral atmosphere of the school. In *Readings in Moral Education*; Peter, S., Ed.; with introduction by Lawrence Kohlberg; Winston Press: Minneapolis, MN, 1978; 149–163.

54. Granitz, N.; Loewy, D. Applying ethical theories: Interpreting and responding to student plagiarism. J. Bus. Ethics **2006**, *72*, 293–306.

55. McCabe, D.L.; Trevino, L.K. Honesty and honor codes. Academe **2002**, *88*, 37+.

56. Jackson, P.A. Plagiarism instruction online: Assessing undergraduate students' ability to avoid plagiarism. Coll. Res. Libr. **2006**, *67* (5), 418–428.

57. McKenzie, J. The new plagiarism: Seven antidotes to prevent highway robbery in the electronic age. Educ. Technol. J. **May 1998**, *7*. http://www.fno.org/may98/cov98may.html (accessed January 9, 2009).

58. Niels, G.J. *Academic Practices, School Culture and Cheating Behavior*; updated August 1 2002; Unpublished report. http://winchester-thurston.org/files/cheating.pdf (accessed January 3, 2009).

59. Brown, V.J.; Howell, M.E. The efficacy of policy statements on plagiarism: Do they change views. Res. High. Educ. **2001**, *42*, 103–118.

60. Evans, R. Evaluating an electronic plagiarism detection service. Active Learn. High. Educ. **2006**, *7* (1), 87–99.

61. Dewey, J. *Moral Principles in Education*; reprinted from the 1909 edition by permission of the Philosophical Library: Greenwood Press: New York, 1969.

62. Piaget, J. *The Moral Judgment of the Child*; Simon & Schuster: New York, 1997.

63. Abbot, A. with additional reporting by Cyranoski, D.; Feresin, E.; Lenotti, C.; Academic accused of living on borrowed lines, Nature **2007**, *448*, 632–633.

64. Ercegovac, Z.; Richardson, J.V. Jr. Academic dishonesty, plagiarism included, in the digital age: A literature review. Coll. Res. Libr. **2004**, *65* (4), 301–318.

65. Daniels, E.F. The dishonest term paper. Coll. Engl. **1960**, *21* (7), 403–405.

66. Saalbach, R.P. Critical thinking and the problem of plagiarism. Coll. Compos. Commun. **1970**, *21* (1), 45–47.

67. Carroll, J.A. Plagiarism: The unfun game. Engl. J. **1982**, *71* (5), 92–94.

68. Drum, A. Responding to plagiarism. Coll. Compos. Commun. **1986**, *37* (2), 241–243.

Poland: Libraries and Archives

Jadwiga Woźniak-Kasperek
Institute of Information and Book Studies, University of Warsaw, Warsaw, Poland

Abstract
This entry discusses the role and status of Polish libraries and other information institutions during the two decades following the collapse of Communist rule in 1989. Although the focus is contemporary issues, a short historical overview is included. Special attention is paid to the National Library, its collections, activities (including the compiling of the national bibliography), and the Polona National Digital Library project. Other Polish digital libraries are also briefly described, as well as the first fully computerized union catalog called NUKAT. Major topics discussed include library legislation, public, school and research libraries, library networks, and professional education. There is also a brief section concerning archives and a briefer discussion of museums.

INTRODUCTION

Poland is a republic in Central Europe bordered by Germany to the west, Belarus and Ukraine to the east, the Czech Republic and Slovakia to the south, and Lithuania, Russia, and the Baltic Sea to the north. It has a population of 38,500,696 (July 2008 estimate) making it the sixth most populous country in the European Union, which it joined in 2004 (Fig. 1).

Historical Background

The history of Polish libraries began with the Christianization of the country in 966 and the adoption of Latin culture. Cracow's (Polish: Kraków) capitulary library inventories of 1101 and 1110 are the earliest book lists in Slavic Europe. In 1364 King Casimir the Great founded a university in Cracow, which was first called Cracow Academy. This institution was the second university to be established in Central Europe, after Prague (1348). From 1400 onward the library collections of individual colleges started to accumulate quickly. The most prestigious among the colleges was Collegium Maius, which had an important book collection by the sixteenth century, and therefore started to be acknowledged as the main university library. During its entire history, the university in Cracow played an important role in the history of book culture in Poland. The most important function of Polish libraries in the first period of their existence was book collecting, and sometimes book production (copying, illuminating, binding, etc.) Yet the social impact of the collections established at royal or ducal courts, or in religious institutions, was limited to a narrow elite.

The sixteenth century—a time of the Renaissance and the Reformation—has often been called the golden age of Polish culture. This cultural flowering was stimulated by the spread of printing, and this in turn initiated a new phase of library development. Outstanding humanists, lay and church dignitaries, created their own private libraries; even wealthier burghers started to collect books. The library of King Sigismundus Augustus (d. 1572), which included over 4000 volumes, holds a prominent place among the Polish book repositories of the time. Later on, this extremely valuable collection was dispersed.

During the sixteenth century, Western influence stimulated a new type of library development in Poland: municipal libraries established by city councils. The Renaissance also fostered a deeper understanding and love of books, and elitist bibliophily flourished. Nonetheless the dominant trend was a pragmatic one. Most books purchased were primarily of utilitarian character, in the broadest meaning of the term: professional, intellectual, and ideological. School libraries also appeared during the sixteenth century after the arrival of the Jesuits in Poland in 1565.

The beginning of the seventeenth century is a distinct turning point in the history of Polish printing and librarianship. The Polish–Swedish wars (1601–1639 and 1655–1660) drastically diminished the holdings of Polish libraries. The wars not only brought about an end to some of the private collection (for example, that of the royal Vasa family) they also brought losses and instability to institutional libraries belonging to churches, monasteries, and schools.

The university library in Cracow also was changing during the seventeenth and eighteenth centuries. Even though the Collegium Maius Library was acknowledged as the main university library, separate collections of individual colleges still existed. However, during the eighteenth century, Hugo Kołłątaj (writer, politician, philosopher, and school reformer) initiated the process of

Encyclopedia of Library and Information Sciences, Fourth Edition DOI: 10.1081/E-ELIS4-120043627

Fig. 1 Map of Poland.
Source: CIA World Factbook.https://www.cia.gov/library/publications/the-world-factbook/geos/pl.html.

bringing them together, which resulted in the present day Jagiellonian Library.

The eighteenth century brought chaos and the military defeats of the Saxon period (1697–1763) led to the partitioning of Poland among the neighboring powers of Russia, Prussia, and Austria (1772, 1793, 1795). These events ultimately led to the total annihilation of the Polish–Lithuanian Commonwealth. At the same time, the eighteenth century brought about the flourishing of Enlightenment and the reforms of the country during the reign of King Stanislas Augustus Poniatowski (notably the Constitution of May 3, 1791). The Enlightenment was the time when all types of libraries developed. Eighteenth-century ideology, science and teaching subjected all earlier concepts and ideas to criticism and revision by reason. Book repositories were an essential element in this process. The end of the eighteenth century saw a national uprising orchestrated by Tadeusz Kościuszko (1794), that led to the foundation of modern Polish society, interested in new forms and ideas in culture. School librarianship underwent substantial changes too. This intellectual ferment prevailed in spite of partitions during the subsequent period of national captivity.

Libraries and books played an important part of all those turbulent changes. The institution which impressed its mark on the history and character of Polish librarianship the most, was the Library of the Polish–Lithuanian Commonwealth, commonly referred to as the Załuski Library (in commemoration of the brothers Andrzej Stanisław and Józef Załuski, who founded it). That library

was also a school of professional librarianship. Its holdings brought together a large collection of unique value, abundant in rare prints and exceptional bibliophile specimens. On the basis of that collection, Józef Andrzej Załuski compiled, the nearly complete, multivolume national bibliography: *Bibliotheca Polona Magna Universalis*, the first national bibliography in Polish history. *Bibliotheca Polona Magna Universalis*, which remained in manuscript form, was annihilated alongside the other works of Załuski and the manuscript catalogs of the library in 1944, after the Warsaw Uprising. Only the partial, printed catalogs and bibliographies prepared by Jan Daniel Janocki, librarian, are still in existence.

The Załuski Library formed the foundations of the Polish National Bibliography and of the Polish National Library. The Załuski Library ceased to exist in 1795 when as a measure of repression, after the Kościuszko Uprising it was confiscated and transported to St. Petersburg, where it became part of the Imperial Public Library and several other Russian libraries. Some of its holdings were returned to Poland after the Riga Peace Treaty of 1921, only to be destroyed during World War II. Today, only individual books are in existence.

The most modern of Polish school libraries was the one of the Warsaw Collegium Nobilium (1765–1794). Throughout the country, truly novel solutions, even by international standards, as to managing school libraries were introduced by the National Commission of Education (1773–1794). It created a network of school libraries after the dissolution of the Jesuits' monasteries in 1773, reorganized two university libraries [in Cracow and in Wilno (currently, the capital city of Lithuania)], and set up district and province elementary school libraries. Hence, it can be summarized that the eighteenth century in Poland brought about important developments in librarianship, chief among which were the appearance of public libraries, organization of a network of school libraries, secularization, creation of the Library of the Collegium Nobilium, modernization of collections, cataloging and access, establishment of librarianship as a profession and recognition of its legal status, beginnings of library law, national bibliography, proliferation of bibliophiles, and collecting attitudes.

During the whole of the nineteenth century Poland was partitioned between its three neighbouring countries—Russia, Prussia, and Austria. This had a lasting negative impact on library development. But there were also a positive impact on book culture and libraries. For example, one can observe the development of collecting attitudes among the educated classes, chiefly in the form of bringing together all types of publications concerning Poland, with the intention of preserving Polish culture. The nineteenth century was also the time that works such as the *Bibliograficznych ksiąg dwoje* (1823–1826; Bibliographical Book Duo) by Joachim Lelewel were produced. This outstanding work includes the foundations of the theory and methodology of the bibliography and its importance cannot be overestimated. Unfortunately it has never been translated into foreign languages.

In the part of Poland occupied by Austria, an impressive public library was opened in Lwów (1827) under the name of the Zakład Narodowy im. Ossolińskich—bibliotheca patria (Ossoliński National Institution—bibliotheca patria). In Prussian Poland, Count Edward Raczyński donated his family collection, chiefly from his Rogalin residence, to the nation. From 1868 Karol Estreicher Sr., author of the monumental national retrospective bibliography (*The Polish Bibliography*) and the reformer of Polish librarianship to the German model, worked on shaping the Jagiellonian Library in Cracow into a modern, European library.

Immediately after World War I, when Poland regained its independence, new libraries were established. The most important was the opening in Warsaw of the National Library (1928), under the direction of Stefan Demby (d. 1939). Some of the specialized libraries, which still exist, were organized in that time: the Library of the Central Statistical Office (1918), the Central Military Library (1919); the Library of Parliament (1919), and The Library of the Silesian Parliament in Katowice (1924). The number of libraries affiliated with higher education institutions rose during the interwar period from 10 to 32. In 1917 the Association of Polish Librarians came into being. Two important journals devoted to library issues started publication: *Przegląd Biblioteczny* (*Library Review*; since 1927) and *Bibiotekarz* (*The Librarian*; since 1919 primarily under the title: *Biuletyn Biblioteki Publicznej m. st. Warszawy—Bulletin of the Warsaw Public Library*). Designated libraries started receiving legal deposit copies from publishers.

World War II and the German occupation inflicted grave losses upon Polish cultural heritage in general and Polish libraries and books in particular. The losses are estimated at approximately 75% of all Polish library collections. Many librarians and professionals linked with books and literature were killed. As had happened in the past, during difficult times the activities of the Polish émigrés supplemented the book culture in Poland and were of great assistance.

Polish librarianship made considerable progress again after World War II. New libraries of all types were opened and functioned for the benefit of society. The establishment of the Polish Academy of Sciences in 1950 began a new period in Polish library history. It created new types of libraries that required a different kind of information services. The Library Act of April 9, 1968 provided the legal foundations for modern librarianship in Poland, including the specialization of libraries, interlibrary cooperation, and regulations concerning the licensing of librarians. The current binding act is The Library Act of June 27, 1997. Work is in progress to replace it due to its many shortcomings.

The Communist regime, in accord with its principles, took control over all book collections. During the whole postwar period, until 1989, preventive censorship was enforced by the Main Bureau for the Control of the Press, Publications and Performances in Warsaw, and by its delegations in individual provinces. Repressive censorship also existed. Nevertheless, from 1976 until 1990 (the official end of censorship in Poland) books were often issued outside the official system.

An unquestionable achievement during this period was the creation and upkeep of a network of numerous stable public libraries. Despite the fact that the administrative system changes in Poland did not always have a beneficial effect on the network, the country has provided the means (however modest they were) for the development of public libraries.

Research libraries were also developing due to industrialization and progress in research. This development however was hampered by the political isolation of Poland, problems with access to publications from outside of the Socialist Block and lack of access to technology.

Computerization of library and information processes began in the 1970s but progress was slow. In 1971 the appearance of further legislation, paved the way for the implementation of the National System of Scientific, Technical and Organizational Information SINTO. In practice, however, the system generally remained a concept, not a reality. Work on computerization of libraries was substantially accelerated two decades later. At present, the vast majority of Polish libraries, of all types, are computerized and their catalogs can be searched via the internet. Digital libraries and digitalization have become common practice and all services are directed for benefit of the public they serve. In the 1990s several major library buildings were constructed, among them the new facilities of the University Library in Warsaw (Fig. 2), which have already become an integral part of the largest Polish university and its capital city. In general Polish libraries have made significant progress and simultaneously have developed to better serve a new, democratic society (Fig. 3).

LIBRARIES

Library Legislation

The goals and areas of responsibility of different types of libraries are stipulated in the Library Act of June 27, 1997. The act introduces the concept of a national library network. In 2007 the network encompassed all public libraries (their participation is obligatory) and approximately 20 others, mainly those belonging to higher education institutions. One of the obstacles to the process of extending the network is the obligation imposed by Polish library law, which requires that a library willing to enter the network must apply through their founding bodies, (e.g., ministries,

Fig. 2 The University Library in Warsaw—outdoor sight.
Source: Courtesy of the University Library in Warsaw.

universities, local governments, and The Polish Academy of Science). Only the future will tell whether the national library network will be revived and what shape it will take.

During the transition from the communist system in Poland, which began in 1989, there have been many changes in the spheres of science, education, and culture and in the field of law, with respect to libraries. The following acts were passed:

- An Act concerning organization and conduct of cultural activities (October 25, 1991; amended in 1994, 1996, and 1998).
- An Act concerning libraries (June 27, 1997).
- An Act concerning the changes of some acts defining the competences of the agencies of public administration with respect to changes in the administrative division of the country (July 24, 1998).
- Amendment of library law (July 27, 2001) which introduced the prohibition of combining libraries with other institutions.

With regards to these matters, the role of the Krajowa Rada Biblioteczna (National Library Council), an advisory body to the Ministry of Culture and National Heritage has been the key. It provides a meeting place for those in authority to learn more about public opinion.

Public Libraries

Public libraries in Poland are open to the general public and their resources are accessible free of charge. Should the need arise to charge the user for any kind of services, such as photocopying or scanning, the payment cannot exceed the costs of the service. Public libraries are simultaneously cultural institutions and information centers. They are organized in such a way as to facilitate easy access to library materials and information for the inhabitants of a given region. Public libraries in Poland are closely connected with and dependent on governmental and/or local administrations. Their activities are financed by the state or by local councils; in most cases they draw upon both sources simultaneously.

Fig. 3 The University Library in Warsaw—interior.
Source: Courtesy of the University Library in Warsaw.

As a result of such close ties with the administration, each change in the administrative structure of the country requires respective changes in the public library network. The last reform of the administrative division of Poland in 1999 introduced a three level system. The number of provinces (Polish: *województwo*) were reduced from 49 to 16, which were then broken down into districts (Polish: *powiat*; previously nonexistent as an administrative unit), and then each district was divided into councils (Polish: *gmina*—the smallest territorial unit). The current network of public libraries therefore consists of three levels reflecting the territorial division of the country. The lowest level is the level of council or local libraries. Each council is required to organize and support at least one public library with an appropriate number of branches and library outlets. The district is also required to organize and provide for at least one district public library, while the self-governing authorities of a province are obliged to organize and support at least one provincial public library. Professional guidance for all public libraries is the responsibility of the National Library.

In 1989 there were 10,313 public libraries, 3342 of which were located urban areas, and 6971 in rural areas. In 2007 there were 8489 libraries (2871 urban and 5618 rural). The decline in total numbers equals about 17%. On occasion small libraries are closed and their responsibilities are taken over by larger libraries. In some cases the reasons for dissolution of a library are cost savings. There are eighteen provincial libraries (two of the provinces have two provincial public libraries each). In 2008 due to the importance of their holdings, their activities and the qualifications of their staff, 12 provincial public libraries were awarded the status of public research libraries.

The number of registered readers is slowly but steadily rising. In 2007 about 6.7 million readers (commonly known as borrowers) were registered, most of them in urban areas. (For context, the total number of the Polish citizens is about 38.5 million). Looking at the statistics of the age of users of public libraries, we find that the largest group consists of those aged 19 or younger and these school age users make up almost half of the total. Persons 60 years of age or older represent the smallest group of library users. A review of readers' professions demonstrated that farmers are the least interested in public libraries (0.9% of the total).

A section for children and young adults (below 15 years old), can be found within public libraries; sometimes there are also separate collections for children. In urban areas there are some branch libraries especially for children and young adults. Some public libraries function as a part of another institution, such as a school (as joint public/school library) or a cultural center. These libraries do not have independent legal status because they are an integral part of the parent institution. In 2006, there were 2002 public libraries functioning within the structures of other institutions, including 250 joint public/school libraries.

From the point of view of the average person, public libraries are the most important type of libraries in Poland because they are legally mandated to be open to everybody without regard to his/her nationality, place of residence, educational status, or social background. Public libraries respond to the needs of the largest groups of users, thus forming an image of "the library" in most minds.

One can follow the most recent developments thanks to the bulletin *Public Libraries in Figures*, an invaluable publication to be found on the Internet (http://www.bn.org.pl/doc/bpwl_2006_pl.pdf), although the latest issue shows the data from 2006. National statistics that include libraries, museums, archives, etc. are available on the Internet on the Web page of the Central Statistical Office: http://www.stat.gov.pl/gus/45_737_PLK_HTML.htm The current list of libraries in Poland is available on the Internet http://www.ebib.info/biblioteki.

School Libraries

The activities of public libraries are complemented by school libraries. School libraries are the most numerous type of library; they are administered by the Ministry of Education. Every school in Poland is obligated to have a library, often called a media center. Their holdings consist of 156 million volumes; 151.8 million of these volumes are in schools for children and young adults, i.e., 20 million volumes more than in the public libraries network. This gives an average of 22 books for every student (in schools for children and young adults: 24) and for every school an average of 3907 volumes (in schools for children and young adults: 4577). Through their efforts in promoting reading and the use of other media, and through offering training in information literacy skills, school libraries play a key role in the preparation of future readers, media users and information seekers. School librarians in Poland enjoy the status of teachers and the title of "teacher-librarian." Other teachers are assisted by the librarians in their daily teaching work, in continual training, development and upgrading of their own skills and knowledge, and in introducing new forms and methods of teaching. School libraries also cooperate with parents, school staff, and other libraries.

RESEARCH LIBRARIES

Research libraries hold an important place in the Polish library system. Among these we distinguish the National Library, the libraries of the Polish Academy of Sciences, libraries of research and development units, and other libraries which support research and conduct research activities themselves, like those of higher education institutions. A library receives research library status on the basis of the character of its holdings, types of users served, its activities, and the qualifications of its staff. In 1999 there were 1209 research libraries; this figure includes: the National Library; 981 libraries in higher education institutions; 98 libraries in research units of the Polish Academy of Sciences; 92 branch research and development units, and 9 public libraries.

In 2005 there were 1219 research libraries, which included 1 National Library, 1005 higher education institutions, 82 research units of the Polish Academy of Sciences, 89 branch research and development units, and 42 others, including 12 public research libraries.

One of the largest and most famous research libraries in Poland is the *Jagiellonian Library* (Polish: *Biblioteka Jagiellońska*, commonly known as *Jagiellonka*). Already in 1364 the Jagiellonian Library was considered the main library for the entire university. During the partition of Poland, the library continued to grow thanks to the efforts of such people as Jerzy Samuel Bandtkie, and Karol Estreicher Sr. Its collections were made public in 1812. In 1932, the Library was granted legal deposit status and obtained the right to receive a copy of every book printed in Poland by a Polish publisher. It has a large collection of medieval manuscripts, among them is the famous *De Revolutionibus orbium coelestium* by Copernicus. In 2007 the Library holdings were about 6.3 million volumes and on average 650,000 people visit the Library each year.

The Jagiellonian Library together with the Medical College Library and the departmental and chair libraries make up the library-information system of the Jagiellonian University. Thanks to its importance, its extensive collection of Polish publications and staff qualifications, the Jagiellonian Library is known as another national library. Currently, the Library collects and archives all Polish publications printed in Poland and abroad. The Library also collects foreign scholarly literature in fields related to the University's areas of research and coursework. Priorities include cultural studies, linguistics, literary studies, art, and religious studies. In the 1990s several priceless books (including Galileo, Johannes Kepler, Basilius Bessarion) were stolen from the library, presumably in order to be sold outside Poland. Some of them were recovered from an auction in one of the German auction houses.

The largest group among research libraries consists of the libraries of higher education institutions. These are organized in the form of an academic library network, which includes: the main library, libraries of individual faculties, institutes, chairs, centres, etc. The holdings of the main library cover all the fields of knowledge studied at the institution as opposed to the other libraries of the school's network, which are specialized.

There are also research libraries in nongovernmental institutions of higher education. In 2007 there were slightly more than 300 such institutions, but only one-third of them had a library.

Many of the research libraries cooperate to create a union catalog called NUKAT (Polish: Narodowy Uniwersalny Katalog Centralny—National Universal Union Catalog; http://www/nukat.edu.pl). NUKAT is managed by the NUKAT Centrum which is an organizational unit of the University Library in Warsaw. The objectives of NUKAT are

1. Furnishing information concerning documents and their location.
2. Allowing for copying by local catalogs of bibliographic and authority records.
3. Acceleration of the cataloging efforts in individual libraries.

NUKAT is a catalog with a single, extensive central database of bibliographic and authority records. In mid-February 2009 the NUKAT database contained 1,231,492 bib records (almost 52,000 of which were for periodicals) and nearly 2,555,873 authority records (both name and subject headings). Over 900 librarians, employed in 60 libraries (chiefly in institutions of higher education), cooperate in the ongoing creation of NUKAT. Since 2005 this body had also included the National Library. However as of August 1, 2007 the National Library withdrew from the project. NUKAT primarily contains bibliographic records of recently acquired materials (since July 2002) of the cooperating libraries; in addition there are a certain, still growing, number of records which are the effect of retroconversion. Since 2006 NUKAT cooperates with OCLC. However, if one is looking for a document issued prior to 2002, it is better to use the search engine *KaRo* (http://www.karo.umk.pl).

Since 1992 some of the research libraries also cooperated on creating the subject headings system KABA, which is a universal system, with a relatively large vocabulary. Initially it was supposed to be compatible with the three subject headings systems used internationally: the American Library of Congress Subject Headings, the French RAMEAU, and the Canadian RVM. From 2006 the requirement of compatibility started to be treated less seriously. There are 22 libraries creating the KABA system, which was being implemented by a 30 additional libraries. In mid-February 2009, the KABA authority files (http://www.nukat.edu.pl/nukat/pl/kaba.phtml?sm=5&poz=3&id=73), which have never had a hard copy version, contained about 265,000 records for topical headings and about 1,126,000 records for heading-subdivision combinations.

The National Library

The National Library – Polish: Biblioteka Narodowa (http://www.bn.org.pl). At present, the National Library (Figs. 4 and 5) is under the authority of the Ministry of Culture and National Heritage. It is regulated by The Act concerning libraries, and by the Statute of the National Library, issued by ordinance No. 4 of the Minister of Culture and National

Fig. 4 The National Library in Warsaw—outdoor sight.
Source: Courtesy of the National Library in Warsaw.

Heritage (July 6, 2000). The above-mentioned legislation stipulates that the National Library is the central book repository of the country and one of the main cultural institutions of the nation. The National Library is responsible for conducting library, bibliographical, research, informational, conservational, advisory, editorial, and service activities. In particular, it is responsible for

1. Collecting, cataloging, informing, and preserving library materials, produced in Poland, and those published outside the country, if they are related to Poland.
2. Preparation and publishing of the national bibliography.
3. Conducting research in the field of librarianship, book, and related sciences.

Fig. 5 The National Library in Warsaw—interior.
Source: Courtesy of the National Library in Warsaw.

4. Improving the functioning of libraries in Poland and Polish libraries outside of Poland.

5. Administering the centers responsible for assigning ISBN, ISSN, and ISMN.

The National Library collects manuscripts, old prints released by Polish publishers, contemporary publications, graphical, audiovisual, and electronic documents, as well as Polish publications issued outside of Poland, and foreign publications concerning Poland.

The initial basis for the creation of a complete archive of national publications is the law promulgated in 1927, by which the National Library received a legal deposit copy of all documents issued in Poland. Under current law The National Library receives two copies of every book, periodical, newspaper, musical notation, atlas, Brail publication, musical recording, audiovisual document, and electronic materials, leaflets, and gray literature. Currently work is in progress to take over the collections of the National Film Repository in Warsaw. As a consequence of this, the National Library will also receive a copy of every cinema and television production. Each year the National Library receives between 140,000 and 170,000 documents of various types, 75% of which belong to the category of legal deposit copies. The remainder are purchased, received as a bequest, or obtained through exchange programs. Through purchasing old works pertaining to national heritage, which appear on the antiquarian market, the library is rebuilding its former collections that were destroyed during times of war. All the Polish publications and valuable foreign items constitute a National Library Archive, and are therefore under additional protection. All Polish printed work and those which are related to Poland are gathered in at least two copies, one of which, listed as "A"-type copy, is accessible to the reader only in exceptional cases and exclusively in the reading rooms. The "A"-type objects form the archival, specially protected, holdings of the National Library.

The National Library is in possession of the oldest specimens of writing in the Polish language: the *Świętokrzyskie Sermons* (mid-fourteenth century), *St.-Florian Psalter* (Fig. 6) (late-fourteenth century), and the *Przemyskie Meditations* (fifteenth century). Among the more valuable manuscripts that represent the European literary heritage are

- The *Braniewo New Testament* (late-eighth to the early ninth centuries).
- The *Evangeliary of Anastasia* with a silver, binding adorned with gold plate (twelfth century).
- The *Wilanów Psalter* (ca. mid-thirteenth century).
- The *Roman de la Rose*, fourteenth century.
- The *Calendarium Parisiense*, fourteenth century.
- The *Revelationes sanctae Brigittae* fourteenth century.
- The *Legenda aurea* (ca. 1480).
- The *Cosmographia* (1467)—an early copy of Ptolemy's Geography.

Fig. 6   Florian Psalter.
Source: Courtesy of the National Library in Warsaw.

(cf. *More Precious than Gold*—http://www.bn.org.pl/doc/nzd_eng.pdfore).

The materials in the National Library are of special interest to the historians of the Napoleonic era and of the history of the November Uprising (1830–1831), for art historians and for those working on the history of the Polish peasantry at the turn of the nineteenth and twentieth centuries, as well as for those interested in the history of the Polish socialists. The collection of over 10,000 volumes that belonged to the Schaffgotsch family of Cieplice, has substantially supplemented the Silesian materials. The library of the freemason lodge B'nei Brith, which was dissolved prior to World War II contributed numerous (2600) volumes of freemason publications. Philologists and historians of literature are particularly interested in those books, which came from collections belonging to Polish writers and bibliophiles. The collection of Polish scientific and technical literature, in particular with respect to older works, is less comprehensive than in other fields.

There are numerous periodicals from the early nineteenth century. The same applies to the January Uprising (1863–1865), with the caveat that this collection is supplemented by an extremely valuable set of periodicals, circulated illegally during the years 1861–1864 and a collection of émigré periodicals of the nineteenth century in general. There are also rare complete sets of nineteenth century socialist publications, as well as agricultural periodicals of the same period and a formidable collection of calendars, taken over from the former Krasiński Family Library.

In spite of the gaps—the results of war losses—there is a fairly complete set of Polish periodicals from the interwar period, in particular those issued during the years 1927–1939. The collection of World War II conspiratorial periodicals ranks among the most extensive in the country. In addition, the National Library is in possession of the largest collection of microforms in Poland, which at the end of 2005 numbered nearly 242,000 units. Within this collection are 2500 units of unified sets of Polish periodicals that are of special value, encompassing materials beginning with seventeenth century special issues through to twentieth century journals. Single existing copies of these periodical issues were found in various collections and microfilmed, thus providing a full run and enabling wider access and scholarly use. Among the collections of ephemera, one can find leaflets dating back from 1801 to 1930 (e.g., parliamentary speeches, military orders, tsarist proclamations); from the November Uprising of 1830–1831; the Cracow Revolution of 1846; the Spring of Nations (1848); the January Uprising of 1863–1865 (proclamations, circulars, and manifestos of the National Government), and from World War I. There is an abundance of materials from World War II: the September Campaign in Poland (1939) and the German occupation.Finally, there are numerous valuable and rare posters.

By the end of 2007, the National Library contained more than 7 million items;

5,795,710 belonging to the main collection
- 2,496,480 volumes of books issued after 1801.
- 869,200 volumes of periodicals issued after 1801.
- 2,202,259 items such leaflets, grey literature, etc.
- 215,157 items of bibliological (book studies) special collections.
- 12,614 electronic documents.

1,385,934 items from special collections
- 26,810 manuscripts.
- 161,879 volumes of old prints.
- 119,257 units of printed musical notations.
- 106,935 units of musical and audiovisual units.
- 482,769 units of iconographical documents.
- 119,058 cartographical units.
- 266,993 microforms.

In 2002, with preservation in mind, as well as to create wider access and in accord with global trends, the National Library started to digitize its collections. In January 2003 a special agreement was signed with the University Library in Warsaw, aimed at creating a Digital Collection of Polish Periodicals. This collection of nineteenth century Polish periodicals is being created on the

basis of the microfilms made in the University Library. On October 11, 2006, with both library and Internet users in mind, the National Library launched the Polonal National Digital Library project (Polish: cyfrowa Biblioteka Narodowa Polona, cBN Polona; http://www.polona.pl/dlibra). The admission of Poland to the European Union in 2004 opened new areas of research and information activity. The National Library, as one of the ten national libraries of the new member states, participates in the TEL-ME-MOR project, aimed at unifying the access to the electronic holdings of the European national libraries and library services. As a result it became a partner of The European Library (TEL), and the holdings of the Polish National Library can be researched through the TEL portal.

NATIONAL BIBLIOGRAPHY

The current Polish national bibliography registers all documents published in Poland, notwithstanding their language or the nationality of the authors. It also registers documents published outside Poland, but related to her by subject matter, language, or the origins of the author. The aim is to provide as much as possible, a complete picture of the publishing production of the nation and the country. The current Polish national bibliography consists of four parts, all of which are prepared by the staff of the Bibliographical Institute of the National Library:

1. *Przewodnik Bibliograficzny* (Bibliographical Guide).
2. *Bibliografia Wydawnictw Ciągłych* (Bibliography of Periodicals).
3. *Bibliografia Zawartości Czasopism* (Bibliography of the Contents of Periodicals).
4. *Polonica Zagraniczne. Bibliografia* (Polonica Published Outside Poland: A Bibliography).

Przewodnik Bibliograficzny is a continuation of the interwar *Urzędowy Wykaz Druków wydawanych w Rzeczypospolitej Polskiej* (Official List of Printed Matter Published in the Republic of Poland), which was revived in 1946. At first it appeared irregularly, but since 1948 it has been published weekly. It is based primarily on the legal, signal copies sent to the National Library by the publishers. According to internationally acknowledged guidelines a national bibliography is to register books and the first issues of periodicals. *Przewodnik Bibliograficzny* registers also cartographical documents (maps and atlases, but not contour maps), musical prints (scores, songbooks, musical notations), graphics (but without single page prints), conference materials notwithstanding the number of copies issued, nor the physical form (e.g., bound folder), scholarly theses, notwithstanding their editorial form and destination, as well as bibliographical lists and Braille editions. It is not a complete bibliography. Iconographical documents are not included, neither are sound recordings (since 1990 they are registered in the database called The bibliography of sound recordings), nor gray literature, while electronic documents have only been registered since 2001 (Bibliography of Electronic Documents; a supplement to the *Przewodnik Bibliograficzny*). Each year, approximately 25,000 bibliographic entries are registered. It is estimated that about 15% of the books and other materials issued in Poland are not registered in the bibliography due to the fact that the publishers fail to send in the legal deposit copies to the National Library. Starting in 1986, *Przewodnik Bibliograficzny*, has also been available in an electronic form, through the home page of the National Library. *Przewodnik Bibliograficzny* has a bimonthly supplement, which has appeared since 1976, registers new and suspended periodicals as well as title changes. During recent years it has registered about 1300 titles of periodicals.

Bibliografia Wydawnictw Ciągłych until 1981 appeared under the title: *Bibliografia Czasopism i Wydawnictw Zbiorowych* (Bibliography of Periodicals and Collective Editions); It is currently an annual publication that registers periodicals appearing in Poland. This bibliography registers approximately 5000 titles every year and has appeared regularly since 1996. Retrospective materials, which did not appear in print as current yearly volumes, are accumulated and prepared for publication as single volumes covering 5 years.

Bibliografia Zawartości Czasopism is a monthly publication that has appeared since 1947. It registers approximately 55,000 bibliographic units, mainly articles, each year deriving from over 1300 periodicals (chiefly scholarly). It covers all subject matter, although some of the topics (e.g., medicine, agriculture, military) are very sparsely represented, due to the existence of appropriate specialized bibliographies. Since 1996 this bibliography has also been available on CD ROM, and since 2005 it has been published exclusively in an online version.

Polonica Zagraniczne. Bibliografia is published annually and has appeared independently since 1956. Initially foreign polonica was registered together with the current bibliography of books. At present this bibliography registers about 2400 bibliographic descriptions every year, half of which are taken from 30 foreign national bibliographies and databases. It encompasses books, musical notations, maps, individual literary pieces published in collective publications and larger fragments of book publications in the Polish language, by Poles, or related to Poland by subject matter.

Apart from those mentioned above, a number of specialized bibliographies appear regularly:

- *Bibliografia Filozofii Polskiej* (Bibliography of the Polish Philosophy).
- *Polska Bibliografia Lekarska* (Polish Medical Bibliography).
- *Polska Bibliografia Literacka* (Polish Literary Bibliography).
- *Polska Bibliografia Wojskowa* (Polish Military Bibliography).
- *Polska Bibliografia Prawnicza* (Polish Legal Bibliography),
- *Polska Bibliografia Ekonomiczna* (Polish Economical Bibliography).
- *Polska Bibliografia Bibliologiczna* (Polish Bibliography of Library Science).

There are also numerous retrospective bibliographies, like the *Bibliografia polska* (The Polish Bibliography) initiated in 1870 by Karol Estreicher, Sr. and continued by his son Stanisław, and then by his grandson Karol Jr.; *Bibliografia historii polskiej* (Bibliography of Polish History) by Ludwik Finkel; *Literatura polska od początków do powstania styczniowego* (Polish Literature from the Beginnings to the January Uprising) by Gabriel Korbut (the second edition brought it chronologically until World War I); *Bibliografia literatury polskiej: "Nowy Korbut"* (Bibliography of Polish Literature: "The New Korbut").

All these bibliographies, despite the extensive expertise and precision of their compilers, usually still have one common weakness—they have no online version.

Digital Libraries

The first digital library in Poland, the Polska Biblioteka Internetowa (http://www.pbi.edu.pl), was unsophisticated from a technological standpoint, usually employing simple html Web sites with links to individual publications. As the digital libraries grew in size, they were supplied with search engines and metadata systems. They are orientated toward scanning and making available the generally recognized canon of culture (literary classics, historical heritage) no longer protected by copyright law. A major breakthrough came with the advent of the dLibra software (original Polish product). Its first implementation was the Wielkopolska Biblioteka Cyfrowa (2002). In mid-February 2009 the number of dLibra libraries exceeded 30.

There is no doubt that the most important implementation of dLibra is Polona by the National Library. The objective of the project is providing free of charge broad, general access to digital holdings. The unique character of the collections of the National Library was the chief factor considered in working through the guidelines for Polona. The highest priorities for digitization were the most valuable holdings, such as rare manuscripts, old prints, first editions of great works of Polish literature, and the conspiratorial World War II documents—all of which are seldom displayed in public. Such documents are no longer protected by copyright law. These publications are described using the Dublin Core Metadata Set. It was decided that the documents digitized and published in

Polona will not receive an independent bibliographic and library registration, therefore they will not be treated as separate entries in the catalog of the National Library. Exceptions to this rule will be made for documents enhanced in some way with respect to the original, e.g., created from selected fragments of the original, or compiled of several original documents. In such cases they will be considered as new publications. Full-time work on the creation of Polona commenced in July 2006. By the end of January 2009 the library numbered almost 16,000 units.

Over the last few years global tendencies in digital libraries have pointed to the centralization of smaller projects and the creation of great national or even international virtual libraries. Europe has the European Library (TEL) and the European Digital Library (EDL). Do we see the same tendencies in Poland? The network of digital libraries, which operates in Poland now, demonstrates that the collections available on the Internet are strongly regionalized. Should this process be assisted and preserved? It is hard to answer.

In the context of digitalization it is worthy of mention that in Poland there is only one periodical devoted to library issues published exclusively in electronic form: the *Biuletyn EBIB*, appearing in monthly intervals since April 1999. Each issue has a thematic character dealing with current matters and a different editor. This journal is an element of a wider Internet service for librarians—the electronic platform of the Association of Polish Librarians (http://ebib.oss.wroc.pl).

Professional Education and Training of Librarians

In contemporary Polish, the term "librarian" means a qualified employee of a library. The qualifications in question encompass either a diploma in library and information science from a higher education institution or higher education in another field and a postgraduate course in library and information science. In Poland, one still finds library personnel with professional training at the secondary level, but this group is constantly diminishing in numbers. There is also another category of library staff, librarians of higher professional status (commissioned librarians and commissioned specialists in documentation and information science), who are research workers. To achieve commissioned status one is required to have a degree, have an appropriate length of employment in libraries or information centers, publish scholarly works, attend conferences, have certified knowledge of at least one foreign language, and pass an exam before a state commission authorized by the Minister of Science and Higher Education.

The first chair in library science, to train librarians, was established at the Humanities Faculty of the University of Łódź in 1946; it was headed by Jan Muszkowski. Next came the Chair of Library Science opened by Aleksander Birkenmajer within the Philological Faculty of the

University of Warsaw (1951) and a similar institution supervised by Karol Głombiowski at the Philological Faculty of the University of Wrocław (1956). In 2008 there were 13 units in Poland, which offer programs in library and information science (University of Warsaw, University of Wrocław, Jagiellonian University in Cracow, Silesian University in Katowice, Marie Curie-Skłodowska University in Lublin, Białystok University, Szczecin University, Adam Mickiewicz University in Poznań, Nicholas Copernicus University in Toruń, University of Warmia and Mazury in Olsztyn, Gdańsk University, University of Łódź, King Casimir the Great University in Bydgoszcz, Pedagogical University in Cracow, and Świętokrzyska Academy in Kielce). Training is offered in the form of standard MLIS studies, consisting of two levels (a 3-year BLIS and a 2-year MLIS), both regular and part-time (extramural) studies. Post-master courses for university graduates in other fields wishing to pursue a library career are also available. Some of the aforementioned university centers, e.g., Institute of Information and Book Studies of the Univerisity of Warsaw, also offer post-master PhD studies. The quality of training is overseen by an independent interuniversity commission and a state commission (Państwowa Komisja Akredytacyjna—State Commission for Accreditation) authorized by the Ministry of Science and Higher Education.

The largest Polish library school is the Institute of Information and Book Studies of the University of Warsaw. In 1999 the 5-year masters program was divided into two independent cycles: 3-year BLIS and 2-year MLIS studies. Moreover, the Institute runs four post-master professional programs and doctoral studies. In 2007, approximately 1500 students, including approximately 350 full-time, 850 extramural, and 300 students in postgraduate studies attended the Institute. The Institute employs 38 full-time and 3 part-time research and didactic staff, including 16 full professors. (Fig. 7)

Organizations Supporting the Activities of Libraries and Librarians

There are several organizations that support librarians and libraries, including

- Stowarzyszenie Bibliotekarzy Polskich (Association of Polish Librarians).
- Polskie Towarzystwo Informacji Naukowej (Polish Society of Scientific Information).
- Polskie Towarzystwo Bibliologiczne (Polish Bibliological Society).
- Konferencja Dyrektorów Bibliotek Szkół Wyższych (Conference of the Directors of Higher Education Libraries).
- Towarzystwo Nauczycieli Bibliotekarzy Szkół Polskich (Polish Schoolteachers–Librarians Society).

Fig. 7 The Institute of Information and Book Studies of the University of Warsaw—logo.
Source: Courtesy of the Institute of Information and Book Studies of the University of Warsaw.

The Association of Polish Librarians is the largest and the most important among these organizations and was established in 1917. It brings together over 9000 members representing various types of libraries, although most members are from public libraries. Members of the Association can join task teams which are dedicated to particular issues of library theory and practice. Among the most important of these 16 task teams are the following: the Subject Cataloging and Classification Commission, the Automation Commission, the Private Higher School Libraries Section, the Regional Bibliography Team. The Association publishes five journals devoted to library and information science of national character. These are: *Bibliotekarz* (*The Librarian*, a monthly published since 1919 in cooperation with The Warsaw Public Library); *Przegląd Biblioteczny* (*Library Review*, a quarterly published since 1927); *Poradnik Bibliotekarza* (*Librarians' Guide*, a monthly published since 1949); *Zagadnienia Informacji Naukowej* (*Journal of Information Science*, published twice a year since 1963 in cooperation with the Institute of Information and Book Studies, University of Warsaw), *Biuletyn Zarządu Głównego Stowarzyszenia Bibliotekarzy Polskich* (a quarterly published since 1993). In all, about 40 library and information science periodicals of scholarly, popular, and professional character appear in Poland. The Association of Polish Librarians also has a publishing office, which is especially known for the series *Science–Didactics–Practice*.

In Poland libraries themselves are members of a group of cultural institutions. Of special interest are: the Book Institute (http://www.instytutksiazki.pl), National Film Library (http://www.fn.org.pl), and the Polish Audiovisual Publishers (http://www.pwa.gov.pl).

MUSEUMS

The first museum in Poland was established by Duchess Izabela Czartoryska in 1801. At the end of 2007 there were 720 museums and nearly 300 art galleries in Poland, and among one can find the Museum of Children's Literature, a branch of The Warsaw Public Library (The Central Library of Mazovian Province) which was opened in 1938. Its collections encompassed 42,000 volumes of books and periodicals: Polish fiction for children and young adults, works of popular science (excluding school textbooks), periodicals for children, works on the theory of children's literature, biographies, bibliographies, and dictionaries. Literary classics and books bestowed by acknowledged international institutions are among the foreign literature found there. The foreign language section forms approximately 30% of the holdings. In accord with its name the Museum collects books of antiquarian value. It possesses numerous rare volumes published prior to 1900. The Museum is also conducting publishing activities, by issuing a new volume of the *Bibliografia z zakresu historii i krytyki literatury dla dzieci, bibliotekarstwa i czytelnictwa dziecięcego* (Bibliography of history and critics of children literature, librarianship, and readership) every year.

ARCHIVES

State archives in Poland are supervised by the General Director of State Archives, who in turn is answerable to the Minister of Culture and National Heritage. The General Director controls the state archives through his Head Office of State Archives (Polish: Naczelna Dyrekcja Archiwów Państwowych; http://www.archiwa.gov.pl). The main responsibilities of this office are the supervision and protection of the state archival holdings. In 2007, the archival network in Poland included: 30 state archives, 48 regional branches and 4 affiliated units of state archives, 3 central archives (Central Archives of Historical Records, Central Archives of New Records, National Digital Archives) and the State Archives of Personal and Payment Documentation. These repositories gather materials produced by local and central state institutions, law courts, self-governing administrations (including acts of town authorities), commercial and manufacturing organizations, family archives, landed estates, private persons, and regional institutions. Most of the materials kept in archives come from the nineteenth and twentieth centuries; however, in some cases charters can date as far back as the Middle Ages. It is perhaps worth mentioning, that during the communist regime, there were no archives for local governmental institutions in Poland (or at least that is what was said). Archives for local government institutions, officially came into existence only after 1989.

In addition to those mentioned above, there are also other types of archives:

1. Specialized archives (11), which are responsible to respective ministries (e.g., the Archives of the Ministry of Foreign Affairs; Central Military Archives; Archives of the Parliament) and collect documents produced by those ministries and their organizational units.
2. Archives with deposited collections (for limited and unlimited periods of time).
3. Archives of individual state administrative units (offices, institutions, industrial organizations), which gather materials produced by their mother institutions (including records destined for perpetual keeping);
4. Archives of political parties, trade unions, public organizations and associations, churches, and religious organizations. Archival materials are also to be found in numerous libraries (mainly research libraries) and museums run by the state and by local governments.

Three of the central archives are located in Warsaw:

1. Archiwum Główne Akt Dawnych (Central Archives of Historical Records; http://www.agad.archiwa. gov.pl).

    The Central Archives of Historical Records were established during the Napoleonic period in 1808, as the General Archives of the Country. At present it stores the records of central and regional authorities produced prior to 1918, archives of the more important Polish families, and cartographic collections (seventeenth to twentieth centuries). As a result of the losses inflicted during World War II, this archive consists of only 7 km. of acts. It also includes a library consisting of over 22,000 volumes of books and periodicals, and about 600 titles of old prints.
2. Archiwum Akt Nowych (Central Archives of New Records; http://www.aan.gov.pl);

    The Central Archive of New Records, was established in 1919 as a Military Archive. This archive has been known under its current name since 1930. It currently holds records of central government institutions, produced after 1918, and all national institutions and associations, as well as important individuals in political and public life.

3. Narodowe Archiwum Cyfrowe (National Digital Archives; http://www.nac. gov.pl).

    On March 8, 2008, the Archives of Audio-Visual Records, founded 1955, have been transformed into the National Digital Archives (NDA). The aim of NDA is to provide digital files as a response to the development of recording, storing, and access technologies. NDA is obliged to
    - Archive digital materials, including digital documents.
    - Archive photographs, films, and sound recordings.
    - Create digital files of hard copy materials.
    - Share information about archives and make the collection accessible online.

In addition to the digital collection, the NDA also manages traditional archive materials. The NDA's collection contains almost 14 million photographs (including the oldest tintypes and daguerreotypes), 30,000 sound recordings, and 2500 films.

Until the late 1980s, Polish archives did not have any computers at their disposition. As time progressed this situation gradually started to change. The computerization of the state archives is supported by the Centralny Ośrodek Informacji Archiwalnej (Centre for Archival Information), a section of the Head Office of State Archives. In 2003 the Head Office of State Archives conceptualized the idea of an Integrated Digital System of the National Archival Holdings. The goals of the system were stated as follows: enhancement of the effective management of the national archival holdings; design of an effective and user-friendly system of archival information; facilitation of access to digital archives; attaining compatibility of the archives with the needs of online governmental administrations; and creation of an archival research network, which would integrate archival information holdings, with the holdings of library and research networks.

The archives have at their disposal a certain number of databases that enhance, to a certain extent, the exchange of archival information and provide better management of archival holdings. The databases in question are as follows: SEZAM (system of organising of archival holdings), PRADZIAD ("grandfather "birth, marriage, and death records register), SCRINIUM (register of documents dated prior to 1800), IZA (register of inventories of archival fond), KITA (technological computer information), ELA (people registering in archives), SUMA (system of archival material accessing), NADZÓR, RAP (register of archival research).

As of 2007, approximately half of the state archives had their own Web sites. The Central Archive of Historical Records is an exemplary case, with numerous inventories in the Encoded Archival Description (EAD) format accessible through the Internet or the Crown Metrica search engine, which enables researching prepartition act registers, of the Polish central government (http://www.agad.archiwa.gov.pl/metodyka/metodyka.html). This archive is currently developing an online order form for accessing archival records.

Computerization confronted the Polish archives with new challenges. Information systems require precision and therefore standardization becomes a necessity. Works on the Polish standard FOPAR were started in 1987. In practice, the archives did not choose the FOPAR standard, but adhered to the ISADAG (International Standard Description—General). Decision No. 4 of the General Director of the State Archives issued on February 1, 2005 concerning the structure and contents of the computer databases created and managed by the state archives, obliged the archives to use the ISADAG standard (http://archiwa.gov.pl/repository/decyzje/dec_4_2005.pdf).

The ISAD(G) standard has its Polish version. Six elements of the original have been considered as important for the international exchange of information and have been made compulsory: country code, archive, fond, shelf mark, title, date, level of description, size, and creator. The other elements of the description of the archival object are optional. The information on the object is inscribed into the EAD standard , which is managed by the American Library of Congress. ISAD (G) and EAD enable the description of archival objects at the level of the fond, series, subseries, inventory unit, and even individual document. Such a description can be supplemented by a digital object.

BIBLIOGRAPHY

Key Works in Polish:

1. Bieńkowska, B. *Książka na przestrzeni dziejów*, Warszawa, 2005.
2. Kołodziejska, J. *Szerokie okno biblioteki*, Warszawa, 2006.
3. *Praca zbio-rowa pod red. Jadwigi Woźniak-Kasperek i Jerzego Franke*, Warszawa, 2007; Biblioteki cyfrowe: projekty, realizacje, technologie.
4. *Praca zbiorowa pod red. Elżbiety Barbary Zybert i Doroty Grabowskiej*, Warszawa, 2008; Książka, biblioteka, informacja w kręgu kultury i edukacji.
5. Wojciechowski, J. *Bibliotekarstwo: kontynuacje i zmiany*, Kraków, 2001; Wyd. 2.

Key Works in English:

1. Drewniewska-Idziak, B.; Stachowska-Musiał, E. Preservation of collections in Polish libraries and archives. Pol. Libr. **2007**, 78–89 Today.
2. Hollender, H. Polish research libraries in their contemporary context. Pol. Libr. **2007**, 19–30 Today.
3. Nikisch, J.A.; Górny, M. Regional digital libraries in Poland. Elec. Libr. **2005**, *23* (4), 474–479.
4. *Polish Libraries Today*, Published irregularly since 1991. Available at: http://www.bn.org.pl/index.php?id=5&czasop=4&elektr.
5. Potęga, J.; Ślaska, K. Polona Digital National Library. Pol. Libr. **2007**, *7*, 73–77 Today.
6. Wołosz, J. Changes in public librarianship in Poland after the political transformation of 1989. Pol. Libr. **2007**, 139–144 Today.

Politics of Representation in Museums

Louise Tythacott
Centre for Museology, University of Manchester, Manchester, U.K.

Abstract
This entry begins by examining key words, "politics," "power," and "representation," as they relate to the museum. It then moves on to explore how the politics of representation have been manifested in displays. A range of exhibitions is examined, particularly in national, art, and ethnographic museums. The entry posits the case that museums are not simply neutral containers of objects, but are ideologically loaded spaces, and it demonstrates how museum displays have, over the past decades, become politically charged battlegrounds between differing communities.

INTRODUCTION

The political implications of representation in museums have come under mounting scrutiny over the past 20 or so years. The authority of the museum has been disputed, with the exhibitions becoming increasingly the subject of debate. This entry begins by reviewing theories of power and representation in the museum. It examines how these institutions have traditionally reflected the values of societal élites. It will be argued that museums are not neutral frames through which objects are viewed, but places where ideologies are manifested through the positioning and interpretation of objects on display.

The focus moves to the documentation of key exhibitions where the politics of display has come to the forefront of debate. Sections are organized around different museum types—national museums, art museums, science museums and finally, and perhaps most controversially, ethnographic museums.

MUSEUMS, POWER, POLITICS

Displays of power have always been what museums do.[1]

If we consider the premise that, at its most general level, politics is associated with the workings of power,[2] then museums have always been "political." Since their inception these institutions have been embedded within, and represented, power structures in society. Many cabinets of curiosities of the sixteenth to seventeenth centuries (which were the precursors of the modern museum) began as elitist institutions designed to limit access to privileged classes.[3] Such early collections often operated as status symbols for the aristocracy and royalty in Europe.[4]

The modern museum emerged in the late eighteenth to early nineteenth centuries in an era of global politics and colonial domination, and when the vast collections of Royal families in Europe were transferred to public ownership. The most renowned instance of the transformation of a formerly private collection to a politically charged symbol of a new regime is the Musée du Louvre, which opened in Paris in 1793. By the end of the nineteenth century, every Western nation had at least one major public museum. As collections shifted from private to public, so museums consolidated their social status, becoming bastions of European society. For authors such as Tony Bennett, "...their central message was to materialize the power of the ruling class...in the interest of promoting a general acceptance of ruling-class cultural authority."[5]

While museums historically formed part of systems of prestige, they continue to be associated with status and power today. Just as in the nineteenth century in Europe and North America when museums were established to consolidate wealth, so in places such as China, new building projects—in Beijing, Nanjing, and Shanghai—are being harnessed to assert China's growing influence in the twenty-first century. There will be 1000 new museums built in China in the next decade and Shangai alone is planning to open 150 by 2010.[6] Macdonald characterizes such contemporary museums as "global symbols" through which "status" and "community" are expressed.[7]

A number of influential authors have analyzed the operations of power in the museum. For example, Tony Bennett argues that in the nineteenth century museums became an important component of cultural governance, involved in processes of regulating the moral, mental, and behavioral characteristics of the population.[8] Bennett notes that the spatial configuration of the nineteenth century museum—the balconies and courtyards, and display cases arranged along evolutionary ideas of progress—enabled them to function as a means for knowledge-control and the observation and control of behavior. Bennett characterizes museums as "agents for establishing and policing norms of public conduct."[9] By indoctrinating visitors with the current political ideology, they were able

Encyclopedia of Library and Information Sciences, Fourth Edition DOI: 10.1081/E-ELIS4-120044117

to regulate the population: "Going to a museum, then as now is not merely a matter of looking and learning: it is also. . .an exercise in civics."[10] Bennett's work draws on that of Michel Foucault in examining cultural technologies for exercising "disciplinary" or "governmental" power. According to a Foucaultian perspective, museums would be considered part of a system reinforcing the state's hegemony.

Pierre Bourdieu too sees the art museum as closely tied to power structures.[11] Working in the 1960s, he conceptualized the art museum as the exclusive domain of the cultivated classes, arguing that it was only those equipped by education who have a mastery of the codes and who are able to decipher the works on display. For Bourdieu, the art museum is a place through which the middle-classes and élites in society reinforce their sense of cultural distinction, perpetuating the notion of high art as exclusionary.[12] Culture, power, and class are related here, legitimating social differences and reproducing relations of power. As an important cultural site for the definition of distinction and taste, museums in this view become instruments of class hegemony.[13] Carol Duncan also conceptualizes the art museum as a "social, political and ideological instrument."[14] For her, like Bennett, they are "performative" environments. In particular, her writing focuses on their role as ceremonial sites that use display arrangements to promote national pride.[15] The visitors to an art museum perform a "ritual," which constructs them as ideal bourgeois citizens.[16]

Museums, of course, may be read in ways other than as articulations of social and political power. Witcomb argues for a position in which museums are not always considered to be concerned with power relations and puts forward alternative readings of the museum.[17] The notion of museum as an organ of the state may be clearly manifested in national museums but not particularly

evident in small, local sites—in community run or private museums. While acknowledging that many different types of museum exist, and that there is a range of funding regimes and sizes, here the focus is on exhibitions in larger museums, which are more clearly tied to systems of power and have been more consistently the subject of political debate.

Large civic or national museums have "status-conferring" roles: they are expected to present "authorized or established pictures of a nation's history and culture."[18] Such museums are perceived to represent socially approved definitions of reality. As Riegel notes: "People look to museums as the arbiters of 'high class' taste, a source to be relied upon when it comes to matters of culture."[19] The social power of museums derives from this belief that their views are sanctioned by the state. Displays that represent a culture, a people, a religion, even a nation, as we see in a later section, assume considerable social authority.

One of the most obvious ways in which museums emanate power is through architecture and position. Often collections are housed in imposing buildings which have been likened to ceremonial monuments that emulate classical temples, medieval cathedrals, or Renaissance palaces.[20] In the nineteenth century many were built in the style of Greek temples with columns, porticos, and steps (Fig. 1). Such architecture was intended to standout in the cityscape, marking these as sites of cultural significance. Riegel notes how the Royal Ontario Museum (ROM) in Canada, "exudes authority: the architecture is monumental, the technical aspects of exhibits are superbly executed."[19] This observation applies equally to such edifices as the British Museum, the Louvre, the Metropolitan Museum, New York, and indeed many of the large national institutions, or what have been termed "universal museums."

Fig. 1 National Archaeological Museum, Athens.
Source: Photograph taken by the author, 2008.

The location of museums is also important. In the nine-teenth century, many were built in the centre of towns or cities, near other places of civic authority, such as the town hall and library. Giebelhausen refers to this as the "symbolic geography of power."[21] The siting of major museums in visually prominent positions continues today—one thinks immediately of Bilbao's Guggenheim, Te Papa Tongarewa in New Zealand, the National Museum of Australia, or London's Tate Modern.

It is not only external architecture but the inner codes and conventions that are indicative of the authority that museums wield. Bennett refers to these as the "regulation of conduct"[22]—the silence imposed, the hushed conver-sations, the prohibition of daily activity, the slow and careful movements, the sense of reverence. Behavior inside is marked by a particular type of receptivity and contemplation that Carol Duncan likens to a ritual[23]—and most of us conform to this. As well as the modification of behavior, the messages imparted through display exert powerful effects. Exhibitions are generally not authored or dated, and seem intended to be read as the anonymous "voice" of the institution. The workings of the museum—the decisions made about how to display objects, who decides on themes, and why—are usually left opaque. Lavine and Karp argue that it is precisely the "neutrality" of museums that enables them to become instruments of power.[24] People think that what they are looking at in a large public museum is the undisputed "truth."

REPRESENTATION IN THE MUSEUM

Let us now examine the relationship between museums and representation. Stuart Hall defines representation as the "production of meaning through language,"[25] and museum displays, he argues, can be seen as "systems" or "practices of representation," in which objects stand for verbal concepts.[26] Rather than "words or images," then, the elements of this system of signification are things—their arrangement and display within a physical space.[26]

It is through objects and exhibitions that museums construct their most powerful representations. Hooper-Greenhill argues that displays are "visual public state-ments" of an institution.[27] The selection of certain objects and the exclusion of others, their arrangement on display, the type of language chosen for text panels, the use of photographs, lighting, display devices (cases, plinths, etc.) and interactives all function to construct cer-tain images: "Every choice—to show this rather than that, to show this in relation to that, to say this about that—is a choice about how to represent."[26] For Hall, museum rep-resentations can never be objective, neutral, or value-free: they will always articulate particular perspectives. Bennett,[23] Duncan,[23] and others argue also that the museum is a place that manifests dominant ideologies: they do not passively display objects but actively construct

the spaces in which things can be viewed. Being able to order the representation of the world carries with it a certain authority—"the power to name, define, classify and re-present."[28]

Hall maintains that politics has to do with the *effects* and *consequences* of representation.[29] It is the way the objects, the texts, and the spaces are read by visitors that enables them to become political. For some, the entire structure of display is permeated with power relations. Riegel argues that the practices of representing culture through imagery is:

> ...an inherently political act which separates those who view the exhibit from those who are on display. The act of viewing is related to the acts of ordering, defining and representing according to categories of the 'viewing' culture.[30]

Lavine and Karp too believe that the very nature of exhibiting makes it a contested terrain: "Decisions are made to emphasize one element and downplay others, to assert some truths and to ignore others."[31] While museums promote particular perspectives, they also, inev-itably, conceal others. Museums have the power to include and exclude, to interpret objects, peoples, and cultures in specific ways. In the nineteenth century, many ethno-graphic museums, for example, placed the material culture of non-Western peoples in evolutionary sequences in order to promote the idea of a hierarchy of progress from "primitive" to "civilized." Such a system of representa-tion, now politically unacceptable, was a product of the ideology of the time.

Over the past 20 or so years, the museological literature has been increasingly concerned with the processes of representation and its political effects.[32–39] Since the 1980s, in particular, the authority of the museum has been challenged and groups have questioned the right of insti-tutions to control how their cultures are displayed.[31] Communities and individuals have raised questions relat-ing to power, authority, and representation. Who decides on what should be selected for exhibition and why? Who authors displays? Who should represent and speak about cultures? Whose voices are heard? Whose voices are excluded? What are the languages of representation? Who is empowered and who is disempowered by particu-lar methods of display?[40] (Fig. 2).

The above discussion has outlined a framework for considering the museum as a site of power and a place of representation. Next let us examine some examples.

NATIONAL MUSEUMS: POWER, IDENTITY, AND THE NATION

More than any other, a national museum may be consid-ered part of a state's political apparatus of representation.

Fig. 2 Mahayana Buddhism case, World Cultures gallery.
Source: Photograph taken by National Museums Liverpool, 2008.

Large "nationals" play important roles in expressing established values and sanctioning the images a nation wishes to convey of itself. Some national museums are utilized overtly for political purposes, as tools of the state or instruments of propaganda. For example, the Museum of the Chinese Revolution, which opened in Tiananmen Square in Beijing in 1960, is a political institution, serving the interests of the Chinese Communist Party.

But what exactly is meant by the idea of the nation and how can this be manifested in a museum? Benedict Anderson famously argued that the concept of "nation" is imagined because "members of even the smallest nation will never know most of their fellow-members, meet them, or even hear of them. ..."[41] The "nation," for him, is created by people to serve specific purposes. It is abstract and anonymous and needs symbols as a way to manifest itself—flags, coins, monuments, uniforms, and, of course, museums, give the idea of the nation a physical presence. In this sense, national museums function to create bonds between individuals and the abstract political concept of the state. Exhibitions—or representations—within these buildings assume a particular social significance.

We saw earlier how there was a trend in the eighteenth and nineteenth centuries for the private collections of the aristocracy and royalty in Europe to be transformed into national museums. This was also a key period in the formation of modern nation-states in Europe, and museums were often established, then harnessed, as manifestations of national pride.[42,43] In other parts of the world, national museums have been created in response to radical political change or independence. Throughout the nineteenth and twentieth centuries a host of countries, in throwing off the yoke of colonial rule, used museums as a way to articulate a new sense of national identity. Greece is a good example. The year the Greek state was legally established, in 1834, the first National Archaeological Museum was constructed in Athens.[44] The new Greek nation was characterized by its fascination with the classical past, and

museums in particular were mobilized as political symbols of a new independent identity. In Mexico too, museums and archaeological objects became entangled in the processes of nation-building after the Revolution. Four years after independence from Spain, in 1825, a decree was issued for the establishment of a National Museum (though it would not be until 40 years later that the museum was built, in the city centre, near the presidential palace).[45] By the early twentieth century, the state had begun to take more direct control of the representation of the country, as the president, Porfirio Díaz (r. 1876–1880 and 1884–1911) patrolled the national museum, approving or disapproving the content of exhibition halls.[46]

This pattern between political independence and the establishment of national museums continued into the twentieth century. The National Museum of India in Delhi, for example, was created the same year as independence in 1947. The National Museum of Pakistan in Karachi was set up shortly after, in 1950. The first National Museum of Nigeria was opened in 1952. (Nigeria became independent in 1960). Though these links must not be overstated—for countries gain independence and do not construct national museums—these institutions nevertheless are clearly considered a means to articulate new nationhood. Patrick Boylan has even suggested that building a national museum is one of the top four priorities for newly independent governments. The four are: 1) a national defence force; 2) a national broad casting service; 3) a national museum; 4) a national university.[47]

The National Museum of Scotland is worthy of consideration here—this too is an institution that emerged at a key moment in Scottish political history. It opened in Edinburgh in 1998, seven months before the British Queen opened the first session of the Scottish Parliament in July 1999. Donald Dewar, the First Minister of Scotland, in fact drew a parallel between the museum and the new Scottish Parliament, describing both as "symbols for a cultural renaissance in Scotland."[48] As the plans progressed all "non-Scottish" elements were deleted. The museum became more rigorously thematic, documenting the story of the nation. It starts with *Beginnings*, (geological foundations and early wildlife), moving on to *Early Peoples; The Kingdom of the Scots; Scotland Transformed* (eighteenth century); *Industry and Empire* (nineteenth century); *Victorian and Edwardian Life* and, finally, *The Twentieth Century*. The choices and the arrangement of the galleries and their associated interpretation are deliberately configured to promote narratives of Scottishness (Fig. 3).

Since the mid-1980s, a number of new national museums have emerged offering different political representations of a country's history, culture, and identity. What seems to distinguish the national museums of the late twentieth to early twenty-first centuries is that they consciously celebrate diversity and equality. The idea of the nation tends to be defined as a blend of voices and groups marginalized through dominant white narratives of history are prominently addressed. Former colonial powers, in particular, have come under pressure to reappraise their representations of the past, especially those related to imperialism. The National Museum of Australia, in Canberra, which opened in 2001, is a good example, a place that consciously celebrates the Aboriginal peoples and their contribution to, and place within, the nation. This is also evident at the National Museum of New Zealand—Te Papa Tongarewa—which opened in 1998. Te Papa is a "bicultural" institution, with a Maori name, and it celebrates the Maori presence in New Zealand as never before. The museum calls itself a "gateway, or an encounter with the essence of New Zealand's land and people," its key task being to preserve and present the *taonga* (treasures) of New Zealand's indigenous people.[49]

Such national museums operate on a political level, as symbols of newly configured nationhood. It is evident that objects and collections here may be manipulated for ideological purposes. We now turn to examine how politics has been reflected in other museum types—firstly those devoted to art.

INSTITUTIONAL CRITIQUE AND "SENSATION": THE POLITICS OF REPRESENTATION IN ART MUSEUMS

It is in the art museum, with its predominant focus on the singularity of the object, that the codes of behavior seem most pronounced, the rituals of visiting heightened and the reverence of things most evident.[23] When this hallowed world and contemporary issues clash, the politics of representation is intense.

From the 1960s, artists started to explicitly engage with the idea that the gallery environment is socially, politically, and institutionally conditioned. Marcel Broodthaers, Daniel Buren, and Hans Haacke were associated with what came to be known as "Institutional Critique," a fundamental questioning of the practices of the art museum. In their various ways, they drew attention to the power of the museum apparatus in promoting taste and value, and used visual means to expose the ideological underpinnings of this institution.[50] More recently, in the 1990s, Fred Wilson's work has exposed the racial and political implications of display in installations such as "Mining the Museum" at the Maryland Historical Society.[51]

Hans Haacke's documentation of high art's corporate affiliations is perhaps the most overtly political. In 1970 he created an installation at the Museum of Modern Art (MoMA) in New York which asked "Would the fact that

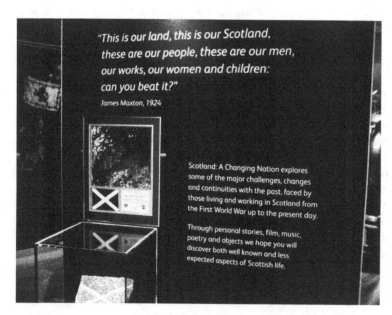

Fig. 3   Display at the National Museum of Scotland.
Source: Photograph taken by Kostas Arvanitis, 2008.

Governor Rockefeller has not denounced President Nixon's Indochina Policy be a reason for you not voting for him in November?" with two ballot boxes: there were twice as many "Yes" as "No" ballots. The installation also criticized a board trustee, and MoMA itself. The following year, Haacke planned a show at the Guggenheim Museum to expose the questionable transactions of a real-estate businessman, Harry Shapolsky, and his links with the museum's trustees, but this was cancelled by the Director. In another exhibition at the Museum of Modern Art in Oxford in 1978, Haacke's "A Breed Apart" criticized British Leyland for exporting vehicles for military use in apartheid South Africa.

Not only have artists deliberately drawn attention to political injustices—Mark Wallinger's installation "State Britain" at Tate Britain in early 2007 is a good example, a 40 m long replica of the minipeace camp run by Brian Haw opposite the Houses of Parliament—but art exhibitions themselves have become (sometimes unwittingly) entangled in wider political debates. "Sensation: Young British artists from the Saatchi Collection" is a notable case. In 1997 the display created a stir at the Royal Academy, London, because it included the painting, "Myra," an image of the child murderer, Myra Hindley, by Marcus Harvey, made up of hundreds of copies of a child's handprint. Winnie Johnson, the mother of one of Hindley's victims, asked for the portrait to be excluded. Along with supporters she picketed the show during its first day. Despite the protests, the painting remained on exhibition. Windows at the Royal Academy were smashed and demonstrators threw ink and eggs at the picture. It was taken off display for conservation and upon return, was placed behind glass and guarded by security officers.

"Sensation" traveled to the Brooklyn Museum of Art in New York City (October 2, 1999 to January 9, 2000) and here too it was met with political protest, this time focusing on a different image and issue. A public battle erupted around a painting, "The Holy Virgin Mary," by Chris Ofili. The press incited controversy by reporting that the work had been smeared with elephant dung. New York Mayor, Rudolph Giuliani, declared the show to be "insulting to Catholics." Protesters outside the museum handed out vomit bags and threw manure in protest. As a precautionary measure, the museum placed "The Holy Virgin Mary" behind protective glass. Even so, on December 16, 1999, a 72-year-old man was arrested for "criminal mischief" after smearing it with white paint. The Catholic League for Religious and Civil Rights issued press statements asking for a boycott of the museum and asking citizens to write to New York City Council demanding that the museum have its grant withdrawn. Two days before the opening, New York City Hall indeed severed its funding and threatened to evict the exhibition from the building. A court ruled against this on the grounds of freedom of expression.

"ENOLA GAY": HISTORY, WAR, AND POLITICS

Science museums too have become sites for the struggle over representation—the most renowned example being the display of "Enola Gay" at the Smithsonian's National Air and Space Museum (NASM) in Washington, D.C. in 1995, which aroused levels of controversy comparable to "Sensation."

The fuselage of "Enola Gay," the B-29 bomber that dropped the atomic bomb on Hiroshima, went on exhibition to commemorate the end of World War II, and the aeroplane's role in securing Japanese surrender. An earlier planned exhibition "The Crossroads: the End of World War II, the Atomic Bomb and the Origins of the Cold War" had been cancelled and after much discussion, the fuselage alone was allowed a public airing.[52] Yet this created huge controversy, particularly amongst veterans and the Air Force Association (AFA), who attacked the Smithsonian's interpretation for being "pro-Japanese" and "anti-American."

Dubin notes how the display was significant in coinciding with a period when Japan was a major U.S. trading partner, and sensitivities had to be handled carefully.[53] The exhibition texts were monitored and went through many amendments—some of which were requested by the AFA.[54] Both veterans and the AFA in fact accused the curators of only wanting to show the devastation the bomb had caused, and exaggerating Japanese suffering. They complained that the Japanese were being turned into tragic victims, or, worse still, heroes, and that the Allies by contrast were demonized as ruthlessly aggressive. The loan of material from Hiroshima and Nagasaki and planned videotape testimonies about the bomb's legacy came under particular attack.[55] It would not be possible, they argued, to display a balanced perspective if only the "last act" was shown.[56] The curators were accused of political bias. The House Speaker, Newt Gingrich argued: "Political correctness may be okay in some faculty lounge, but...the Smithsonian is a treasure house that belongs to the American people, and it should not become a plaything for left-wing ideologies."[57] Veterans wanted to counteract curatorial "bias" by including information on the Japanese war camps, the numbers of Allies lost in the Pacific, images of disabled veterans, and the numbers of lives saved because the bomb brought the war to an end.[58] Fundamentally, of course, their concern was to legitimize the bombing and pay tribute to the bravery of their comrades. Eight conservative members of the House of Representatives were outraged by the low figures suggested by curators for American casualities had the bomb not been dropped, and called for the Director, Martin Harwitt to resign. Harwitt indeed left in the wake of controversy.[59–61]

Peace campaigners were also enraged. On the opening day, 21 people were arrested during a demonstration, some bearing signs urging "Never Again" or "No More

Hiroshimas." Four days later, the museum closed for 90 min after three protestors poured human blood and two bags of ashes on the fuselage. The protestors were charged with, and found guilty of, felony destruction of government property.[62]

During the development of the exhibition, some had wanted the plane to be displayed without comment, so that it "could speak for itself"[63]: "Critics came to prefer a display of the aircraft in minimalist interpretative dress— precisely because they did not want to impose any particular reading on museum visitors."[64] One pilot, for example, said it should be displayed alone.[64] Yet, as we saw earlier, objects can never be interpreted neutrally. The apparatus of the museum will always influence the angle from which an exhibition is understood. The choice of words on texts and the other associated documentation— the information that is included *and* excluded—work to produce certain readings.

This particular exhibition demonstrates the difficulty of representing opposing points of view in the public space of the museum, particularly in such a culturally authoritative institution as the Smithsonian.[65] These controversies revolved around the perspective from which the war should be recounted. Critics were concerned about the authorship of the texts and whether they were biased. They wanted to know who was being celebrated—the Americans or the Japanese? Who was being blamed? Whose voices were being heard?

It is significant that the display was mounted at the Smithsonian, one of America's most powerful national museums. As an American Legion Spokesman noted, "this is. . .a public institution, where the impression is that anything it says is official history."[66] The authority of this museum functioned to underline the idea that the "truth" was being presented—and this is the reason why exact interpretations were so carefully monitored. In the next section we examine other groups whose historic injustices have created impassioned debate within a very different type of museum, and we see how controversial racial imagery was taken to be the officially sanctioned view due largely to its display in one of North America's most authoritative institutions.

REPRESENTING "OTHER" CULTURES: POLITICS IN THE ETHNOGRAPHIC MUSEUM

While museums in general have come under increasing attack in recent decades, it is in the sphere of ethnographic exhibitions that the political dimensions of display have come under the sharpest scrutiny. Ethnographic museums, above all others, have become targets of controversy. Hooper-Greenhill writes that, "the negotiation and contestation of museum authority has been at its most evident in relation to colonial collections"[67] (Fig. 4).

Why should this be? In many ways it is due to the historical formation of collections. Many ethnographic collections were created in the nineteenth to early twentieth centuries as a direct result of colonialism—and under such regimes, it is well documented that a great number of objects and collections were taken by force. The display strategies of ethnographic museums in the nineteenth century were also clearly linked to colonial ideology. Early ethnological galleries promoted dominant beliefs in the superiority of Western cultures. In particular, evolutionary displays visualized unequal power relations between peoples and implied the need for progress from "primitive" to "civilized." By the end of the nineteenth century, evolutionism had come to dominate the arrangement of non-Western objects in ethnographic museums.[68]

While evolutionary displays were largely abandoned in the twentieth century, ethnographic museums continued to be the keepers of other people's material and the interpreters of their histories. Museums continued to assume the undisputed power to speak for and represent other people. Here indigenous groups never had a voice: they were discussed, exhibited, and interpreted, but were never able to "talk back." As a result, for some, they became symbols of white power and domination, perceived ". . .to serve a cultural élite, staffed primarily by whites, reflecting white values, and excluding from the interpretative process the very peoples whose cultures were represented in the collections."[69]

In the 1980s, alongside wider social and political changes, indigenous peoples started to challenge the authority of museums to represent their cultures. Communities began to demand a greater voice in how they were being displayed. A series of exhibitions at this time resulted in the politics of representation being fore-grounded as never before—such exhibitions became implicated in politics because of tensions between who was doing the exhibiting and who was being exhibited.[70]

This section documents three exhibitions in the 1980s that illustrate well the climate of the times.

The earliest was "Te Maori" (literally "the Maori") which toured the United States between 1984 and 1986, before returning to New Zealand in 1986 and 1987.[71] This is considered a turning point in museum presentations of Maori culture and more widely in the relationship between Maori and museums.[72,73] For the first time, Maori people were consulted about their tribal *taonga* or treasures.[74] Not only did the exhibition combine Maori objects from museum collections all over the world, it also created links between collections and contemporary Maori people. It also brought to the surface issues over who should control the representation of their heritage. Elders and scholars, who were actively involved in setting up the exhibition, made recommendations to museum professionals in the light of the show—one of which was that the Maori should determine how their *taonga* is to be interpreted.[75] As a result of the exhibition, a conference was held in 1990 in

Fig. 4 Entrance to the World Cultures Gallery, World Museum Liverpool.
Source: Photograph taken by the author, 2005.

Wellington, where plans were launched for the creation of a museum of New Zealand, Te Papa Tongarewa, which, as we saw in an earlier section, opened in 1998.

Another exhibition in which politics came to the fore was the "Spirit Sings: Artistic Traditions of Canada's First Peoples" at the Glenbow Museum, Calgary, Canada in 1988. This was organized in association with the Calgary Winter Olympics and was designed to highlight the rich artistic and cultural traditions of Canada's native peoples. However, the exhibition became caught in the cross fire of a political campaign to support land claims by the Lubicon Lake Cree of northern Alberta. The Lubicon were demanding a boycott of the Winter Olympics in order to draw attention to their 50-year dispute with the Canadian government. At the same time they called for a boycott of the exhibition. The group was particularly incensed by the sponsorship of Shell Canada Ltd., who were actively involved in harmful drilling activities on land the Lubicon claimed as their own.[76] The exhibition created a great deal of publicity and, perhaps for the first time, made people realize that museums cannot simply ignore contemporary issues such as land claims when presenting an exhibition of the cultures of indigenous peoples. As a direct result of the show a First Peoples–Canadian Museums Association Task Force was established jointly sponsored by the Assembly of First Nations (the preferred term for indigenous peoples in Canada) and the Canadian Museums Association.[77] After several meetings, it produced recommendations on how to improve relations between First Nations and museums. Since this date there has been a dramatic change in power relationships—a shift from Canadian museums telling First Nations about their cultures, to dialogue, and inclusion.

A year later, in Canada, an exhibition at the ROM turned out to be the most politically controversial in its history (November 1989–August 1990). It was curated by a cultural anthropologist, Jeanne Cannizzo, who set out to show the origins of the ROM's African collection within the context of Canadian imperialist history. However local Afro-Caribbean communities were highly offended by it, labeling it racist. They formed an ad hoc group, the Coalition for Truth about Africa, and held protests every Saturday afternoon outside the museum. They also petitioned the ROM for the exhibition text to be changed or the exhibition to be closed, but the museum did neither. The main problem was that the displays represented the voices of "white" people—Canadian soldiers and missionaries—without incorporating African voices. There was ambiguity in messages in texts and the catalog, and an impression that the exhibition was celebrating rather than critiquing the role of missionaries and colonists in Africa.[78] The use of irony in text panels, in particular, was misunderstood. Although Cannizzo italicized terms such as "barbarous" and "savage customs" with the intent of questioning them, the placement of such problematic language in italics next to visual images was not taken as a critique, but rather as an affirmation of this problematic imagery.[79] This museum—one of Canada's most prestigious and powerful—was simply thought to be condoning contentious colonial and racist perspectives.[80]

The lack of consultation with African communities at a time when they were demanding a voice only inflamed anger.[81] Communities contested the ROM's right to ownership of its African collection, as well as the museum's ability to present an exhibition of Africa. They questioned the authority and ability of Cannizzo—a white cultural anthropologist—to "represent" Africa.

MUSEUMS AS "CONTACT ZONES"

As a result of these exhibitions and the wider critiques that emerged in the 1980s, museums became, in James

Clifford's words, "contact zones."[82] The historic aloofness and neutrality of the museum seemed to have been broken open by communities who had previously been ignored. Questions of power and authority came to the fore, as did questions about who has the right to speak for and represent whom. Ethnographic museums started to realize that they had to redefine their practices and strategies of display. In becoming sensitized to the political implications of their role, some began to acknowledge the unequal power relations that their collections and historic representations had been predicated upon.

The changes taking place within ethnographic museums have had a significant impact on the work of curators. Over the past decade or more, a new type of museum professional has emerged, who see themselves as "facilitators" or "stewards" of collections on behalf of communities. New forms of curatorship are increasingly sensitive to multiple voices and diverse audiences (Fig. 5). In ethnographic museums today, it is often the case that curators are not the sole voices of authority in interpreting and displaying objects, but acknowledge an obligation to involve source communities in the care and representation of collections.[83] Emphasis is placed on the active involvement of indigenous curators, consultants, or advisors, especially in North America, New Zealand, and Australia.

One of the most significant developments here is the National Museum of the American Indian in Washington, D.C. Opening in 2004, it represents an unprecedented collaboration between the Smithsonian and Native Americans. The museum was authorized by Congress in 1989, and from its inception was a political creation. It has three facilities: The George Heye Center, Manhattan opened in 1994; the Museum building itself in Washington, D.C. and a Cultural Resources Centre in Maryland.[85] Native peoples had the authoritative role in approving the architecture, design, and displays. The interpretation and

presentation of the collection was planned in consultation with tribal groups, and special regard was given to the exhibition of sacred or sensitive material. Material culture and sacred traditions are presented by native people in ways that reflect *their* values and viewpoints.[84]

What we are seeing in the twenty-first century is a transformation in the power relations in ethnographic museums. Clifford describes this as "... a shift from a 'colonial' to a 'cooperative' museology."[85] Museums and indigenous peoples have started to work together to redress the imbalances of cultural representation, using collections for promoting cross-cultural awareness. Yet such changes have been uneven, with museums in the United States, Canada, Australia, and New Zealand being much more active than those in Europe. In certain places, however, museums have indeed become institutions through which indigenous peoples now finally have a "voice."[86]

CONCLUSION

In this entry we have seen how museums have been intimately related to power and politics, traditionally reflecting the interests of those dominant in society. We have looked at how the authority of the museum emanates from a range of structures—architecture, location, the historical formation and ownership of collections, the themes and arrangements of exhibitions, the selection of objects, the authorship of displays, and the inclusions and exclusions in textual interpretation. We have also seen how the power of the museum is evident in its operation as a social space that modifies public behavior and how museums "represent" through the display of objects.

The museum as an institution has come increasingly under attack in the past 20 or more years, with previously marginalized groups questioning its traditional authority.

Fig. 5 Visitors to the Weston Discovery Centre, World Museum Liverpool.
Source: Photograph taken by the author, 2005.

Increasingly exhibitions have become the subjects of criticism and, at times, impassioned debate. Some shows, as we have seen, have unleashed dramatically opposing views. Controversy can erupt over the display of an aeroplane, a painting or the representation of "Africa"—particularly when touching upon topics such as war, religion, and race. In the ethnographic museum—and in other places too—the power issues often lie in the discrepancy between those who control access to, and those who want to have access to, collections. As exhibitions become more concerned to address contemporary concerns, it seems inevitable that they will become more controversial.[87] Increasingly, in the twenty-first century, museums are politically charged spaces, not neutral sites of display.

REFERENCES

1. Dubin, S.C. *Displays of Power: Controversy in the American Museum from the Enola Gay to Sensation*; New York University Press: New York, 1999; 227.
2. Macdonald, S. Exhibitions of power and powers of exhibition: An introduction to the politics of display. In *The Politics of Display: Museums, Science, Culture*; Macdonald, S., Ed.; Routledge: London and New York, 1998; 3.
3. Ames, M. *Cannibal Tours and Glass Boxes: The Anthropology of Museums*; University of British Columbia Press: Vancouver, BC, 1992; 89.
4. Bennett, T., Ed. *The Birth of the Museum: History, Theory, Politics*; Routledge: London and New York, 1995; 27.
5. Bennett, T. *The Birth of the Museum: History, Theory, Politics*; Routledge: London and New York, 1995; 109.
6. Emery, A. Give the people what they want?—Global museums in the 21st century. Orientations, Hong Kong **2008**, June *39*(5), 93–94.
7. Macdonald, S. Introduction. In *Theorizing Museums: Representing Identity and Diversity in a Changing World*; Macdonald, S., Fyfe, G., Eds.; Blackwell Publishers/The Sociological Review: Oxford, 1996; 2.
8. Bennett, T. *The Birth of the Museum: History, Theory, Politics*; Routledge: London and New York, 1995; 21.
9. Bennett, T. *The Birth of the Museum: History, Theory, Politics*; Routledge: London and New York, 1995; 101.
10. Bennett, T. *The Birth of the Museum: History, Theory, Politics*; Routledge: London and New York, 1995; 102.
11. Bourdieu, P. *The Love of Art*; Polity Press: Oxford, 1991.
12. Prior, N. *Museums & Modernity: Art Galleries and the Making of Modern Culture*; Berg: Oxford and New York, 2002; 51.
13. Bourdieu, P. *Distinction: A Social Critique of the Judgement of Taste*; Routledge: New York and London, 2003.
14. Duncan, C. *Civilising Rituals: Inside Public Art Museums*; Routledge: London and New York, 1995; 5.
15. Prior, N. *Museums & Modernity: Art Galleries and the Making of Modern Cultur;* Berg: Oxford and New York, 2002; 26.
16. Duncan, C. *Civilising Rituals: Inside Public Art Museums*; Routledge: London and New York, 1995; 49.
17. Witcomb, A., Ed. *Re-imagining the Museum: Beyond the Mausoleum*; Routledge: London and New York, 2003; 17.
18. Ames, M. *Cannibal Tours and Glass Boxes: The Anthropology of Museums*; University of British Columbia Press: Vancouver, 1992; 100–101.
19. Riegel, H. Into the heart of irony: Ethnographic exhibitions and the politics of difference. In *Theorizing Museums: Representing Identity and Diversity in a Changing World*; Macdonald, S., Fyfe, G., Eds.; Blackwell Publishers/The Sociological Review: Oxford, 1998; 87.
20. Duncan, C. Art museums and ritual of citizenship. In *Exhibiting Cultures: The Poetics and Politics of Museum Display*; Karp, I., Lavine, S.D., Eds.; Smithsonian Institution: Washington, DC, 1991; 903.
21. Giebelhausen, M., Ed. *The architecture of the museum: Symbolic structures, urban contexts*; Manchester University Press: Manchester and New York, 2003; 5.
22. Bennett, T. *The Birth of the Museum: History, Theory, Politics*; Routledge: London and New York, 1995.
23. Duncan, C. *Civilising Rituals: Inside Public Art Museums*; Routledge: London and New York, 1995.
24. Karp, I.; Lavine, S.D. *Exhibiting Cultures: The Poetics and Politics of Museum Display*; Smithsonian Institution: Washington, DC, 1991; 14.
25. Hall, S., Ed. *Representation: Cultural Representations and Signifying Practices*; Sage Publications: London, 1997; 28.
26. Hall, S., Ed. *Representation: Cultural Representations and Signifying Practices*; Sage Publications: London, 1997; 8.
27. Hooper-Greenhill, E. *Museums and the Interpretation of Visual Culture*; Routledge: London and New York, 2000; 101.
28. Riegel, H. Into the heart of irony: Ethnographic exhibitions and the politics of difference. In *Theorizing Museums: Representing Identity and Diversity in a Changing World*; Macdonald, S., Fyfe, G., Eds.; Blackwell Publishers/The Sociological Review: Oxford, 1998; 85.
29. Hall, S., Ed. *Representation: Cultural Representations and Signifying Practices*; Sage Publications: London, 1997; 6.
30. Riegel, H. Into the heart of irony: Ethnographic exhibitions and the politics of difference. In *Theorizing Museums: Representing Identity and Diversity in a Changing World*; Macdonald, S., Fyfe, G., Eds.; Blackwell Publishers/The Sociological Review: Oxford, 1998; 83.
31. Karp, I.; Lavine, S.D. *Exhibiting Cultures: The Poetics and Politics of Museum Display*; Smithsonian Institution: Washington, DC, 1991; 1.
32. Barringer, T., Flynn, T., Eds. *Colonialism and the Object: Empire, Material Culture and the Museum*; Routledge: London and New York, 1998.
33. Clifford, J. *The Predicament of Culture*; Harvard University Press: Cambridge, MA, 1988.
34. Hooper-Greenhill, E. *Museums and the Interpretation of Visual Culture*; Routledge: London and New York, 2000.
35. Karp, I.; Lavine, S.D. *Exhibiting Cultures: The Poetics and Politics of Museum Display*; Smithsonian Institution: Washington, DC, 1991.
36. Macdonald, S. Introduction. In *Theorizing Museums: Representing Identity and Diversity in a Changing World*; Macdonald, S., Fyfe, G., Eds.; Blackwell Publishers/The Sociological Review: Oxford, 1996; 1–18.

37. Macdonald, S., Ed. *The Politics of Display: Museums, Science, Culture*; Routledge: London and New York, 1998.
38. Introduction. In *Museums and Source Communities: A Routledge Reader*; Peers, L., Brown, A., Eds.; Routledge: London and New York, 2003.
39. Vergo, P. *The New Museology*; Reaktion Books Ltd.: London, 1997.
40. Macdonald, S., Ed. *The Politics of Display: Museums, Science, Culture*; Routledge: London and New York, 1998; 4.
41. Anderson, B., Ed. *Imagined Communities*; Verso: London and New York, 1991; 6.
42. Macdonald, S. Introduction. In *Theorizing Museums: Representing Identity and Diversity in a Changing World*; Macdonald, S., Fyfe, G., Eds.; Blackwell Publishers/The Sociological Review: Oxford, 1996; 7.
43. Prior, N. *Museums & Modernity: Art Galleries and the Making of Modern Culture*; Berg: Oxford and New York, 2002; 38.
44. Avgouli, M. The first Greek museums and national identity. In *Museums and the Making of Ourselves: The Role of Objects in National Identity*; Kaplan, F., Ed.; Leicester University Press: London and New York, 1994; 254.
45. Morales-Moreno, L.G. History and patriotism in the national museums of Mexico. In *Museums and the Making of Ourselves: The Role of Objects in National Identity*; Kaplan, F., Ed.; Leicester University Press: London and New York, 1994; 177.
46. Morales-Moreno, L.G. History and Patriotism in the national museums of Mexico. In *Museums and the Making of Ourselves: The Role of Objects in National Identity*; Kaplan, F., Ed.; Leicester University Press: London and New York, 1994; 182.
47. *Museums Journal*, Museums Association: London, 1990; October; 30.
48. Bryden, M. Shaping and selling the idea: How the product was presented. In *Heritage and Museums: Shaping National Identity*; Fladmark, J.M., Ed.; Donhead Publishers: Dorset, 2000; 31.
49. McCarthy, C. *Exhibiting Māori: A History of Colonial Cultures of Display*; Berg: Oxford and New York, 2007; 1.
50. Sherman, D., Rogoff, I., Eds. *Museum Culture: Histories, Discourses, Spectacles*; Routledge: London, 1994; xv.
51. Karp, I.; Wilson, F. Constructing the spectacle of culture in museums. In *Thinking about Exhibitions*; Greenberg, R., Ferguson, B., Nairne, S., Eds.; Routledge: London and New York, 1996.
52. Gieryn, T. Balancing acts. Science, Enola Gay and history war at the Smithsonian. In *The Politics of Display*; Macdonald, S., Ed.; Routledge: London and New York, 1998; 197.
53. Dubin, S.C. *Displays of Power: Controversy in the American Museum from the Enola Gay to Sensation*; New York University Press: New York, 1999; 220.
54. Gieryn, T. Balancing acts. Science, Enola Gay and history war at the Smithsonian. In *The Politics of Display*; Macdonald, S., Ed.; Routledge: London and New York, 1998; 201, 204.
55. Dubin, S.C. *Displays of Power: Controversy in the American Museum from the Enola Gay to Sensation*; New York University Press: New York, 1999; 221.
56. Gieryn, T. Balancing acts. Science, Enola Gay and history war at the Smithsonian. In *The Politics of Display*; Macdonald, S., Ed.; Routledge: London and New York, 1998; 204.
57. Dubin, S.C. *Displays of Power: Controversy in the American Museum from the Enola Gay to Sensation*; New York University Press: New York, 1999; 219.
58. Gieryn, T. Balancing acts. Science, Enola Gay and history war at the Smithsonian. In *The Politics of Display*; Macdonald, S., Ed.; Routledge: London and New York, 1998; 205.
59. Zolberg, V. Museums as contested sites of remembrance: The Enola Gay affair. In *Theorizing Museums: Representing Identity and Diversity in a Changing World*; Macdonald, S., Fyfe, G., Eds.; Blackwell Publishers/The Sociological Review: Oxford, 1998; 72.
60. Zolberg, V. Museums as contested sites of remembrance: The Enola Gay affair. In *Theorizing Museums: Representing Identity and Diversity in a Changing World*; Macdonald, S., Fyfe, G., Eds.; Blackwell Publishers/The Sociological Review: Oxford, 1998; 74.
61. Gieryn, T. Balancing acts. Science, Enola Gay and history war at the Smithsonian. In *The Politics of Display*; Macdonald, S., Ed.; Routledge: London and New York, 1998; 201.
62. Dubin, S.C. *Displays of Power: Controversy in the American Museum from the Enola Gay to Sensation*; New York University Press: New York, 1999; 222–223.
63. Dubin, S.C. *Displays of Power: Controversy in the American Museum from the Enola Gay to Sensation*; New York University Press: New York, 1999; 212–213.
64. Gieryn, T. Balancing acts. Science, Enola Gay and history war at the Smithsonian. In *The Politics of Display*; Macdonald, S., Ed.; Routledge: London and New York, 1998; 206.
65. Gieryn, T. Balancing acts. Science, Enola Gay and history war at the Smithsonian. In *The Politics of Display*; Macdonald, S., Ed.; Routledge: London and New York, 1998.
66. Dubin, S.C. *Displays of Power: Controversy in the American Museum from the Enola Gay to Sensation*; New York University Press: New York, 1999; 222.
67. Hooper-Greenhill, E. *Museums and the Interpretation of Visual Culture*; Routledge: London and New York, 2000; xi.
68. Clifford, J. On collecting art and culture. *The Predicament of Culture*; Harvard University Press: Cambridge, MA, 1988; 227.
69. Simpson, M. *Making Representations*; Routledge: London and New York, 1996; 9.
70. Hall, S., Ed. *Representation: Cultural Representations and Signifying Practices*; Sage Publications: London, 1997; 8.
71. McCarthy, C. *Exhibiting Māori: A History of Colonial Cultures of Display*; Berg: Oxford and New York, 2007; 137.
72. Tamarapa, A. Museum Kaitiaki: Maori perspectives on the presentation and management of Maori treasures and relationships with museums. *Curatorship: Indigenous Perspectives in Post-Colonial Societies*, Canadian Museum of Civilization with the Commonwealth Association of Museum and the University of Victoria, 1996; 162.

73. McCarthy, C. *Exhibiting Māori: A History of Colonial Cultures of Display*; Berg: Oxford and New York, 2007; 146.

74. Tamarapa, A. Museum Kaitiaki: Maori perspectives on the presentation and management of Maori treasures and relationships with museums. *Curatorship: Indigenous Perspectives in Post-Colonial Societies*, Canadian Museum of Civilization with the Commonwealth Association of Museum and the University of Victoria, 1996; 102.

75. Tamarapa, A. Museum Kaitiaki: Maori perspectives on the presentation and management of Maori treasures and relationships with museums. *Curatorship: Indigenous Perspectives in Post-Colonial Societies*, Canadian Museum of Civilization with the Commonwealth Association of Museum and the University of Victoria, 1996; 103.

76. Clifford, J. Museums as contact zones. In *Routes: Travel and Translation in the Late Twentieth Century*; Clifford, J., Ed.; Harvard University Press: London and Cambridge, 1997; 205.

77. Nicks, T. Partnerships in developing cultural resources: lessons from the task force on museums and first nations. Culture **1992**, *12*(1), 88.

78. Riegel, H. Into the heart of irony: Ethnographic exhibitions and the politics of difference. In *Theorizing Museums: Representing Identity and Diversity in a Changing World*; Macdonald, S., Fyfe, G., Eds.; Blackwell Publishers/The Sociological Review: Oxford, 1998; 92.

79. Riegel, H. Into the heart of irony: Ethnographic exhibitions and the politics of difference. In *Theorizing Museums: Representing Identity and Diversity in a Changing World*; Macdonald, S., Fyfe, G., Eds.; Blackwell Publishers/The Sociological Review: Oxford, 1998; 93.

80. Simpson, M. *Making Representations*; Routledge: London and New York, 1996; 26.

81. Clifford, J. Museums as contact zones. In *Routes: Travel and Translation in the Late Twentieth Century*; Clifford, J., Ed.; Harvard University Press: London and Cambridge, 1997; 207.

82. Clifford, J. Museums as contact zones. In *Routes: Travel and Translation in the Late Twentieth Century*; Clifford, J., Ed.; Harvard University Press: London and Cambridge, 1997; 211.

83. Introduction. In *Museums and Source Communities: A Routledge Reader*; Peers, L., Brown, A., Eds.; Routledge: London and New York, 2003; 1–16.

84. Rosoff, N. Integrating Native views into museum procedures: Hope and practice at the National Museum of the American Indian. In *Museums and Source Communities: A Routledge Reader*; Peers, L., Brown, A., Eds.; Routledge: London and New York, 2003; 76.

85. Clifford, J. Four northwest coast museums. In *Routes: Travel and Translation in the Late Twentieth Century*; Clifford, J., Ed.; Harvard University Press: London and Cambridge, 1997; 120.

86. McKenzie, M. Comments. *Curatorship: Indigenous Perspectives in Post-Colonial Societies*, Canadian Museum of Civilization with the Commonwealth Association of Museum and the University of Victoria, 1996; 216.

87. Simpson, M. *Making Representations*; Routledge: London and New York, 1996; 25.

Popular Literature Genres

Barry Trott
Williamsburg Regional Library, Williamsburg, Virginia, U.S.A.

Abstract
This entry defines the concept of "genre" in relation to popular reading. It then briefly reviews the eight traditional genre categories, discussing their forms, structures, history, major subgenres, and trends. The increasing interest in narrative nonfiction and its relation to genre is explored. Three emerging genres are then discussed as examples of new developments in the field. The topic of reading interests versus genre is examined, and cross-genre writing and genre separation are discussed.

INTRODUCTION

The idea of genre provides readers and librarians a convenient mechanism for categorizing and providing access to fiction writing. As Ursula K. Le Guin notes, "The concept of genre is a valid one. We need a method for sorting out and defining varieties of narrative fiction, and genre gives us a tool to begin the job."[1] Understanding genre fiction allows librarians to analyze

> the stylistic elements that authors use that will appeal to readers—of fantasy, Westerns, romances, mysteries, etc. The concept of genre is useful here because it defines a set of precepts that describe a certain style of writing. This knowledge allows librarians to connect readers to books that they will enjoy. In fact, it is an understanding of what the appeals of a particular genre are that will allow librarians to make connections between books and authors that may be separated by genre classification.[2]

A readers' advisor who grasps the broad concepts of genre appeal will be able to make reading suggestions both within genres and across genres, expanding the range of possible titles to offer readers. Here, genre becomes a useful tool for offering suggestions to readers. It is a concept that most readers understand. Librarians frequently hear from their users, "I like mysteries," "I love to read Regency romances." As an increasing number of authors (Michael Chabon, Audrey Niffeneger, Mary Doria Russell, and Cormac McCarthy to name only a few) write novels that blend genres, an understanding of the appeals of the various genres becomes even more essential to the provision of readers' advisory services to the reading public.

In the library world, genre has also been an important mechanism in collection arrangement. As in bookstores, many libraries separate some parts of the fiction collection by genre. Most commonly, libraries offer sections of mysteries, romances, science fiction, and so on. Breaking out large fiction collections into smaller, more browsable units may offer readers an easier time in locating desired materials. Sharon Baker's book *The Responsive Public Library: How to Develop and Market a Winning Collection* does a good job of summarizing the research done on genre separation and shelving.[3] Baker notes that in addition to increasing reader satisfaction, separating genre fiction collections generally results in higher circulation of library materials.

As in all areas of fiction, genre writing generally has a set of characteristics that can be defined and described. These patterns offer a sense of familiarity to the reader, and make a substantial contribution to the continuing popularity of genre fiction among readers. Like the structures of formal poetry, the structures of genre fiction create a frame within which authors can develop stories that will appeal to a wide range of readers. Crime fiction, most commonly centers around the concept of bringing order and justice to a chaotic world. Within that frame, mysteries stories can vary from the cozy to the graphic, and from the lyrical to the terse. Similarly, fantasy and science fiction writing allows the reader to ponder on the structure of the world. In these speculative genres, the author asks the reader to consider the question of whether society has to be as it is now.

In their landmark work on readers' advisory services, Joyce Saricks and Nancy Brown developed the concept of using appeal characteristics to more logically connect readers to the stories that they are seeking.[4] When looking at genre fiction, two of Saricks and Brown's appeal factors are of particular importance to readers of genre fiction. The appeal of character is clearly a major draw for readers of genre fiction. Readers come to identify with the character, whether that is the detective in a mystery, the sword-wielding hero of a quest fantasy, or the love-struck protagonist of a romance. Furthermore, the importance of character to genre readers is seen in the affection that many readers of genre fiction have for series characters. The pleasure of following a particular character from book to book is clearly one that genre readers enjoy. The second important appeal factor to consider in

Encyclopedia of Library and Information Sciences, Fourth Edition DOI: 10.1081/E-ELIS4-120043671

looking at genre fiction is the setting, both geographic and chronological. Many readers of genre fiction look to be transported to other places and times. This factor can be a manifestation of an interest in learning something new about a historical period or a particular place, or simply a desire to travel vicariously to a different locale that the reader enjoys. The other appeals discussed by Saricks and Brown also all apply to the enjoyment of genre fiction. Mood, tone, language, and story are as important to genre readers as they are to readers of other fiction.

Most discussions of popular genre fiction separate the field into eight areas: Adventure, Crime Fiction, Fantasy, Historical Fiction, Horror, Romance, Science Fiction, and Westerns. The next section will examine each of these traditional genres, looking at their basic structures, their foundations, their major subgenres, and their primary appeals to readers.

ADVENTURE

Novels that fall in the adventure genre are invariably fast-paced, plot-driven stories. These are stories that appeal to readers who enjoy breath-taking escapes, hair-raising exploits, and resourceful heroes. Though enjoyed by both male and female readers, the protagonists of adventures tales tend to be male, usually blending the intelligence of a Sherlock Holmes with the athleticism of an Olympic star. Readers come to these stories looking for action and suspense. At their most elemental, adventure stories present a main character, frequently on his own, with little assistance, who finds himself in danger and spends the rest of the story extricating himself from the problem. In the course of finding safety, the hero generally also saves some portion of society from the machinations of the evil-doers. Often these heroes exhibit powers of physical strength, intellectual acumen, and recuperation that are beyond the norm. Readers surrender disbelief here in order to enjoy the thrilling narrative. In many stories in the adventure genre, a secondary appeal is in the intricate details the author uses to construct the story. The minutiae of weaponry and equipment are frequently important to readers, and they look for authenticity as well as for action. In other adventure novels the particulars of legal or medical proceedings draw the reader into the tale. Adventure novels can be grouped into several subgenres, each of which has its readers. Military adventures can be either contemporary (Tom Clancy) or historic (Patrick O'Brian). The espionage subgenre has survived the end of the Cold War, and flourishes again with the rise of global terrorism. Legal and medical thrillers, such as those written by John Grisham or Robin Cook examine corrupt practices and frightening pandemics. Inspirational thrillers blend Christian themes with action-packed adventure (see Frank Peretti or Tim Lahaye). In all cases though readers are looking for an adrenaline jolt that will keep them glued to the pages.

CRIME FICTION

Crime fiction is one of the most pattern driven of the genres. Readers are drawn to these stories for the sense of resolution that they bring. The seeking out of justice is at the heart of the crime novel. The typical storyline features the commission of a crime (usually, but not exclusively, a murder), the arrival of the detective (amateur or professional), the investigation of the suspects, the solution of the crime, and the bringing of the criminal to justice. As in all genre fiction though, the way the author chooses to follow this pattern varies widely. The subgenres of crime writing are numerous, though they all reflect the basic structure outlined above. The early days of crime fiction (in the early twentieth century) were predominated by the puzzle mystery (Agatha Christie's Hercule Poirot and Miss Marple mysteries being typical examples), where the author sprinkled clues to the crime throughout the story, and the reader could solve the crime along with the detective. These cozy mysteries often featured an English setting and an amateur detective. Following the First World War, a new, harder-edged mystery story came to prominence, and readers began to enjoy the exploits of the hard-boiled detective, who solved crimes with his fists as much as his intellect. Here, the puzzle was less important and the reader began to follow the exploits of the detective rather than solving the crime in tandem with the detective. Writers such as Raymond Chandler and Dashiell Hammett led the way here. In the last quarter of the twentieth century, crime writing expanded its scope even further. Women and minorities started appearing as detectives, and a host of subgenres grew in popularity, including the heist caper (usually told through the eyes of the criminal, see Donald Westlake's Dortmunder series), historical mysteries (taking detection as far back as the days of the pharaohs, Ellis Peters's Brother Cadfael books did much to promote this subgenre), forensic thrillers (featuring the often grisly details of pathologists as central to the story, Patricia Cornwell and Kathy Reichs both are key authors here), police procedurals (for readers who enjoyed the details of policing, P.D. James, in England, and Ed McBain, in the United States provide benchmarks for police crime fiction), paranormal mysteries (blending elements of fantasy and science fiction with crime stories, see Kim Harrison, Jim Butcher, or Eric Garcia), and the new cozies (with a range of amateur detectives solving crimes while running B&Bs, herb shops, quilt stores, etc. among the leading authors here are Susan Wittig Albert, Earlene Fowler, and Carolyn Hart). As the twentieth century ended, there were several new developing trends in crime writing in addition to the expansion of the subgenres. Authors began to take a much more realistic approach to crime, resulting in darker, more violent, stories (George Pelecanos, Dennis Lehane, and Ken Bruen among others). Societal concerns began to be reflected in the crime fiction of such writers as Sara Paretsky and Marcia Muller. The rise of the serial killer novel paralleled the reporting of this sort of crime in the media. In the early twenty-first century, terrorism at home and abroad has become a central theme in much crime fiction. In addition to darker themes, crime fiction also has seen an increasing interest in the lives of the detectives. Crime writing now is often as much about the development of a series character as about the solution of the crime. The lives of the detectives are of great interest to readers, and family relationships and other personal details are sought out. Investigators are frequently dealing with problems in their own lives as well as with the misdeeds of others. Along with this trend toward darker detectives, contemporary crime novels frequently have a more ambiguous sense of justice. The criminal may never be brought to trial or serve time. Sometimes it is a corrupt state that allows criminals to get off, but it is not uncommon for extra-judicial justice to be meted out by the detective or by the victim's family or friends. It is this sense of order restored that is at the heart of the crime novel.

FANTASY

The story of a struggle between good and evil unites much of the writing in the fantasy genre. From the earliest times, people have told tales of the conflict between the dark and the light in order to reassure themselves that there is some chance to bring order out of the chaotic world. Fantasy novels continue to offer this hope to readers. In most fantasy fiction new worlds are created, or the existing world is reshaped, in order to provide the backdrop for the story. Fantasy invites its readers to suspend their understanding of the natural world and enter into a new place where the unexpected becomes real, and where magic replaces science as a source of power. The level of magic in the story may be quite variable. Earlier fantasy stories were often centered around the use and misuse of magic (Tolkein's Ring series for instance). In later fantasy fiction, magic often has a more ambiguous and less central role, with the exercise of power taking a toll on those who choose to use it. Although myths and tales of magic have been in circulation as long as people have been telling stories, beginning in the late nineteenth century a style of writing, typified in the works of George MacDonald and Lord Dunsany, emerges that would be recognizable to today's fantasy reader. The popularity of these early titles encouraged the growth of the genre, and by the end of the twentieth century, fantasy writing was flourishing among readers. In the early twenty-first century, much fantasy writing is looking at darker themes, and it is frequently more challenging to distinguish between good and evil than it was in the early days of fantasy writing. Much of the appeal of the fantasy genre comes from the intricate worlds created by the authors. Writers such as Robert Jordan and Lois McMaster Bujold create sprawling,

multi-title series featuring recurring characters who move from novel to novel. Readers come back again and again to these stories to discover what is going to happen to the characters. Character is complex in fantasy, with a multiplicity of fantastic creatures in addition to the human characters. Fantasy is also frequently concerned with things— rings, swords, helmets, jewels, etc. These sorts of potent icons give power to those who wield them, and feature prominently in much of fantasy writing. Fantasy fiction has a variety of subgenres of interest to readers. Much early fantasy was of the "swords and sorcery" variety, featuring swashbuckling heroes and powerful wizards. The quest, popularized by J.R.R. Tolkein's *Lord of the Rings*, continues to be a common theme in fantasy writing. An increasingly popular subgenre is the political fantasy, where the struggles for power within an invented world predominate, and magic has a secondary role (George R.R. Martin). Alternate histories continue to thrive as writers and readers explore the "what if" of various real times. The urban fantasies of writers such as China Miéville and Tannith Lee have grown increasingly popular, featuring dark and gritty city settings and equally ambiguous characters. At the opposite end of the fantasy spectrum, high fantasy invites the reader into a world of elevated speech, rhetorical flourishes, and courtly practices. Here, readers still enjoy classic authors such as E.R. Eddison as well as newer practitioners such as Guy Gavriel Kay or Patricia Wrede. Whatever the subgenre, fantasy allows the reader to visit a new world where things are rarely as they seem, and where characters are fighting the good fight.

HISTORICAL FICTION

In the historical fiction genre, readers are usually seeking stories with a strong sense of time and place. The key appeals here are those aspects of the novel that take the reader back in time to a specific period and/or to a specific geographic location. In order to do this successfully, the authors of historical fiction often provide intricately detailed stories that are the result of extensive research. The quality of this research is important, as many readers of historical fiction are also readers of historical nonfiction. These readers will be the first to note any details that are inappropriate to the period under discussion. Many readers will dismiss an historical novel out of hand if they discover anachronisms. This attention to detail also is important in considering the author's use of language. Historical fiction readers will be put off by language that sounds to them more modern than the setting of the book. An eighteenth century maid who talks like a Valley Girl will lead many readers to close the book. One reason that these sorts of period details are so essential to the success of historical fiction is that many readers come to these stories to learn something about a particular time or place.

This educational experience is diminished if the reader is not confident about the accuracy of the story. The accrual of details in historical fiction often means that these are long works that readers can sink themselves into. Though not as common as in fantasy and crime fiction, series titles also make their appearance in the historical genre, especially in the form of family sagas (e.g., John Jakes's North and South series or Jean Auel's Earth's Children titles). Historical fiction must, by definition, be set in the past. But there is no strong consensus about how far back the tale must take place. For some readers it may relate to their own age. For a reader born in the 1980s, a novel set in the 1960s might be considered historical. The same novel read by someone born in the 1930s may not have as strong an historical feel. In most cases, it is accepted that the story needs to be set in a time prior to the period of its writing. So Tolstoy's novels are not historical fiction, but are simply older examples of contemporary fiction. It is generally accepted that the earliest examples of historical fiction are the works of Sir Walter Scott. In novels such as *Waverly*, Scott used period details and an eighteenth century setting to frame his story of love and politics during the Jacobite rebellions. Since that time, historical fiction has seen a steady readership, with specific time periods or subgenres waxing and waning to the rhythm of cultural interests. There are several popular subgenres of historical fiction, including military stories (e.g., Bernard Cornwell or C.S. Forrester), with their focus on details of battles and campaigns. Historical mysteries became increasingly popular in the last quarter of the twentieth century, as readers enjoyed the period details of historical fiction blended with the elements of a crime novel (Ellis Peters, Bruce Alexander, and Anne Perry are all benchmark authors here). The early twenty-first century has seen a number of popular titles that blended history with fantastic elements, especially Diana Gabaldon's Outlander titles. Although not really subgenres, historical mysteries can also be subdivided by geographic location, time period, and the focus on real or fiction characters. Regardless of the specific period of interest, historical fiction readers continue to seek out the genre for its blend of detail and story.

HORROR

The horror genre is at heart about fear. Readers come to horror fiction looking for a visceral reaction to the story. While these reactions can range from a cold chill up the back of the neck to a sweat-drenched panic, to be successful, horror must induce a sense of dread in the reader. Horror fiction arises out of the Gothic novels of the late eighteenth century, in particular, the dark and fear-shrouded *Castle of Otranto* by Horace Walpole. The macabre tales of Poe and other nineteenth century novelists continued the trend. Bolstered by the popularity of horror titles in the pulp publications of the 1930s and

1940s, horror continued to build a dedicated, though perhaps limited, following. Unlike fantasy fiction, which can at times be frightening, horror fiction sustains a sense of dread throughout the entire story. The reader also has a feeling that these things could really be happening. As Joyce Saricks notes in *The Readers' Advisory Guide to Genre Fiction*, there are two paths that horror fiction generally uses to create an atmosphere of dread.[5] The first is the psychological thriller, what Saricks calls "Storyteller Horror." Here, the terror is a reflection of a dark and menacing atmosphere that becomes increasingly oppressing as the story progresses. The characters, and the readers, are drawn into an evermore frightening situation as they move through the novel. There may or may not be physical violence involved in the resolution, but it is the overwhelming and progressive sense of fear that draws readers to these tales. The ghost stories of Peter Straub or the classic tales of H.P. Lovecraft exemplify this subgenre. The other path chosen by horror writers is the graphic and gory tale which appeals to the reader's fears of physical violence (Saricks's "Visceral Horror"). Here, the fear comes more from the actual events than from the anticipation of those events. The works of writers such as Clive Barker and John Connolly are benchmarks here. In much of horror writing, the fear of "the other" dominates. Monsters are common in horror fiction, and whether they are imagined or real, they create the chaotic events that mark the story. Unlike most other genre fiction that closes with a clear resolution to the story, horror novels often have an open ended feel. As horror has developed, some subgenres can be identified. While less popular than in earlier days (M.R. James is a classic here), the ghost story continues to have its readers (see Joe Hill, Stephen King's son). The late twentieth and early twenty-first centuries saw an increasing number of horror stories focusing on the undead, particularly vampires, though zombies and werewolves also have their followers (Ann Rice and Laurell K. Hamilton stand out here). Splatterpunk, which arose as a horror subgenre in the 1980s, is known for its extremely graphic violence, its realistic urban settings, and its grim tone (see David Schow, Jack Ketchum). The late twentieth century also saw an increasing level of eroticism in horror fiction, exemplified by some of the stories of Poppy Z. Brite or Tannith Lee, that continues to exist alongside more traditional tales of terror. Though horror readers do not make up as large a percentage of the genre audience as crime or romance readers, the demand for fear-inducing fiction is still a driving force.

ROMANCE

In 2007, statistics from the Romance Writers of America indicate that romance fiction made up about 12.9% of book sales.[6] Like horror fiction, romance novels also arose out of the Gothic literature traditions. Here though, the path led not toward the macabre and horrific, but to the dark castles inhabited by brooding dukes who fell hopelessly in love with young women of dubious backgrounds. These Gothic tales eventually led to historical romances by writers such as Georgette Heyer that dominated the romance market in the first half of the twentieth century and that eventually led to the contemporary romance novel. At the core, romances are the most optimistic of genre fiction. They tell the story of two people falling in love. Like crime fiction, romances follow a pattern that is consistent throughout the genre. In a typical romance, the male and female protagonists are introduced at the start of the book. In most cases, there is some source of conflict between these characters. This conflict may be personal, the result of social constraints, or have its roots elsewhere in the characters' lives. The story then deals with the overcoming of these obstacles, allowing the couple to find a measure of happiness together. In the traditional romance story, this resolution is marriage, though more contemporary romances sometimes settle for some form of committed relationship. Many readers find the commitment to traditional values of family and marriage an appealing piece of the romance genre. The happy ending is essential to the success of the story for the reader. While the positive outcome of the relationship is a primary appeal to romance readers, other appeals also draw readers to these stories. Romances generally feature strong female characters who take responsibility for their own lives and fates. This is particularly true in the work of writers such as Linda Howard and Sandra Brown, who write in the increasingly popular romantic suspense subgenre. As romances developed in the last part of the twentieth century, authors such as Nora Roberts, Karen Kingsbury and Susan Wiggs began exploring difficult societal issues, including abortion, spousal abuse, alcoholism, single parenting, and other challenging topics. These elements add another layer to the traditional romance story. Romances can vary widely across time periods and geographic settings, and readers are often drawn to particular writers for these details. Romances also vary on the amount and the graphicness of sexual content, moving from the chaste to the erotic. As societal norms have loosened, romance fiction has become more open to graphic depictions of sexuality by writers such as Bertrice Small and Rochelle Alers. In addition to these looser categories of romance fiction, there are some well-defined subgenres that attract readers. Historical romances have been an important area for many years, and continue to have a strong following. In particular, stories set in England during the Regency period are much sought after. The previously mentioned romantic suspense novels continue to command a wide audience. Lori Wick and Karen Kingsbury among others have crafted inspirational romances that feature evangelical Christian themes and stories and have a large readership, especially among readers looking for more chaste stories. The fantasy or paranormal romance also is increasingly popular in the early twenty-first century as is seen in the interest in stories by writers such as Diana Gabaldon and Debbie Macomber. As the sales of romance novels reflect, these tales of requited love continue to inspire readers.

SCIENCE FICTION

Readers who are interested in questions of where society is going and what the future has to offer have always found much to enjoy in the science fiction genre. Throughout its history, science fiction has explored the possibilities and challenges of technology, and in particular what changes technological innovation brings to human society. Like other genre fiction writing, science fiction is shaped by cultural trends and changes. The earliest science fiction writers in the late nineteenth century, among them Jules Verne, H.G. Wells, looked at the technological advances of the industrial revolution and posited where those advances would lead. Throughout the first half of the twentieth century, science fiction writing explored the themes of space travel, exploration, and colonization, particularly in the pulp magazine of the period. As the world entered the Atomic Age, science fiction took a darker turn, and many writers produced dystopian novels of the end of human culture. The rise of computers in the last quarter of the twentieth century saw an equivalent rise in science fiction writing that looked at issues of technology and personal identity. In all cases though, science fiction uses the theme of technological advancement to explore the world. Much of science fiction writing is concerned with ideas, examining the nature of society, and the role of technology in society. There is also a strong component of science fiction writing that delves into the intricate details of science. As a result the character appeal, so common in much of genre fiction, is often less central to traditional science fiction writing. Over the years, the trend in science fiction writing has been a move from the adventure-based novels of exploration and conquest of space to philosophical stories that examine the consequences of actions in a more nuanced fashion. Some critics have speculated whether science fiction will be able to thrive as real science continues to uncover the secrets of the universe. As the elements of hard science become less important, and the more philosophic approach becomes common, character has become more central to science fiction writing, and the early twenty-first century has seen a rise in the publication of science fiction titles that concern themselves with the impact of the future not only on civilizations but also on individuals. Like the other genres, science fiction has a number of subgenres that attract readers. The space operas of Lois McMasters Bujold or Larry Niven bring together a large cast of characters and usually features themes of exploration and conquest. Space travel is also an essential part of the colonization subgenre, where alien worlds come into contact (see the novels and short fiction of Ursula K. Leguin). Post-apocalyptic tales of dark futures have already been mentioned as has computer-centered science fiction. The cyberpunk subgenre, exemplified in the work of Bruce Sterling and William Gibson, is an offshoot of these computer-based stories, and blends dystopian views and information technology. Military science fiction such as that of David Drake or Robert Heinlein appeals to readers looking for tactics and strategy on a galactic scale. Some readers place alternative histories, for example, Harry Turtledove's *American Empire* series in the science fiction genre, particularly those that include the introduction of modern technologies into earlier days. Although real scientific work has taken much of the mystery out of the world, science fiction readers are still captivated by the genre's exploration of the possibilities and the challenges of technology.

WESTERNS

In both the traditional and the contemporary Western novel the setting is the main appeal for most readers. The open spaces and the wide views across the prairies and deserts of the American West in the work of classic Western writers such as Louis L'Amour and Zane Grey continue to attract readers. The history of the western is rooted in the dime novel tales of outlaws, mountain men, cowboys, and other denizens of the early days of the westward expansion. These stories featured tough men who often found themselves in dangerous situations, and used their skills to extricate themselves from danger. In addition to the action/adventure themes though, many westerns have an elegiac feel as well. The stories tell of the incursion of the modern world into a seemingly idyllic life on the range. The coming of the railroads, fences, and towns all become challenges to the heroes of western novels. This concept of "hero" is essential to the western. The popular western novels of the twentieth century generally featured a lone hero who finds himself fighting against evil and corruption. Often battered, but rarely broken, this hero cleans up the problem and then moves on to the next task. A strong influence from western films can be seen in many of the novels of the West. The visual nature of the films, with sweeping views becomes part of the visual scene painting of the western writers. Contemporary westerns, such as those written by Elmer Kelton and Larry McMurtry, have seen a move toward expanding the role of the hero beyond cowboys. The perspectives of Native Americans and women characters are occasionally seen, and some writers have explored social and environmental issues in their stories. In addition to the traditional western, readers can find western romances, inspirational westerns, and mysteries with strong western settings and characters, as well as novels of the contemporary west. Many librarians note a decline in the popularity of the western since its apogee in the 1960s. In the future, Westerns may come to be considered a subgenre of historical fiction. Although the circulation of westerns has declined, there is still a dedicated body of readers looking for these tales of western adventure.

NARRATIVE NONFICTION

Although readers' advisory work has generally focused on fiction reading, the early twenty-first century saw a shift toward working with readers of narrative nonfiction as well. Narrative nonfiction blends the narrative style of fiction writing with facts, capturing characters, and telling stories with intricate plots and detailed settings. These are books that tell a story, and that are read for pleasure by a wide assortment of readers. Writers such as John McPhee, Sebastian Junger, Sue Hubbell, and Tracy Kidder are among the many prominent practitioners of this style. Like its fictional counterparts, narrative nonfiction is centered around the idea of story. All of the appeal factors that can be derived from fiction writing are applicable to narrative nonfiction. Readers in this area respond to variations in character, story, setting, language, and mood in the same way fiction readers do. The development of the structure of narrative nonfiction as a genre is still fluid at the end of the first decade of the twenty-first century. Several attempts have been made to organize the broader world of narrative nonfiction writing into more accessible, genre-like, areas. Some of these areas mirror or share characteristics with fiction genres—True Adventure, True Crime, History, Science. Other areas are not reflected in fiction writing—Food, Travel, Microhistories, Sports. Ongoing work with nonfiction readers will shape the future direction of narrative nonfiction as a genre, but given the wide readership and the interest of the publishing industry in works in this area, narrative nonfiction will continue to grow in importance in the popular reading world.

EMERGING GENRES

The late twentieth century witnessed not only an explosion in the popularity of traditional genre fiction, but also the emergence of some new directions in genre. Whether these emerging genres will stand the test of time or prove to be short-lived remains to be seen.

Chick Lit

The mid-1990s saw the development of a new type of fiction, dubbed "chick lit," that has gained acceptance as a popular genre over the past decade. Helen Fielding's *Bridget Jones's Diary* was among the first chick lit stories to attain popular success, and she has had many imitators in the years since. Although it is sometimes classed as a subgenre of romance, chick lit's themes set it apart from the romance genre. Chick lit tells the stories of the lives and loves of young, urban women who are trying to find a place for themselves in the professional world. The stories are filled with pop culture references to hip clothing, fashion accessories, and drinks. While romantic relationships may form a part of the story, the successful resolution of relationships that is crucial to romances is not necessarily a part of a chick lit tale. Success here may as likely be dumping a boyfriend as marrying him. The story here is not about romantic accomplishment, but about a young woman learning to stand on her own. Friends play an important role in these stories as supports for the main character. A variety of urban settings spreads the appeal of chick lit across ethnic and geographic boundaries.

Slipstream

The last decade of the twentieth century produced a number of writers whose works bridged the gap between literary fiction and speculative fiction. These novels are imbued with a sense of the surreal. The settings are mainly contemporary and based in reality, but these stories manage to twist reality in ways that "simply makes you feel very strange,"[7] as writer Bruce Sterling who coined the term "slipstream" notes. There may be occasional elements of science fiction or fantasy in these works, but these novels do not follow the usual patterns of those genres, and may not be as satisfying to a dedicated science fiction or fantasy fan. The idea of the surreal intruding on everyday life finds its roots in the magical realism of Latin American fiction and even in earlier works that created a feeling of unease in the reader. Sterling's essay goes on to question whether slipstream will succeed as a genre, but thus far it continues to gain readership. In addition to Sterling, other notable slipstream authors include, Jonathan Lethem, Paul Auster, Aimee Bender, and Cory Doctorow.

Street Lit/Urban Fiction

The burgeoning street lit genre tells hard-edged stories of African American life in bleak urban settings. Street lit arises out of the 1970s autobiographical fiction of drug dealing and prison life by authors such as Donald Goines and Iceberg Slim as well as the tradition of African American romance and erotica. Contemporary street lit features all the elements of "gangsta" culture—flashy jewelry, big cars, drugs, prostitution, and guns. Like the emerging chick lit genre, the stories feature a lot of name-checking of expensive or hip brands and pop culture trends. The stories tend to be graphic in language, violence, and sexuality. Street lit is notable for featuring strong protagonists, both male and female. There has been some controversy over the genre, with some condemning the romanticization of criminal culture and others noting the moral lessons that can be drawn from the stories. Street lit seems to be diverging into two main streams. The first are the gangsta novels that center around drugs, money, and guns. The second are the more relationship-centered stories, still set in the violent street world, but focusing more on romantic issues. Benchmark authors here include Chunichi, K'wan, and Nikki Turner.

GENRE OR READING INTEREST

In addition to looking at genre as a way to define popular reading tastes and areas, it can also be useful to consider divisions that are more logically termed "reading interests" (the phrase used for these areas in Libraries Unlimited's Genreflecting series). Reading interest is a broader term, and identifies a theme-related group of books or authors whose writings can be found in many genres. Three major reading interests to examine are Inspirational, African American, and Multicultural. In each of these areas, readers and librarians will find authors who write stories in most if not all of the traditional and emerging genres. What ties these disparate authors and their books together in the mind of readers, librarians, and publishers is an overarching theme. In the case of inspirational fiction it is the evangelical Christian outlook that is at the heart of the story, regardless if it is a mystery, romance, or legal thriller. With African American fiction, the unifying theme is the story of the lives of an ethnic minority in the broader American culture. Multicultural fiction details of the lives and concerns of a broad range of ethnic groups across the world, either in their own countries or as immigrants to a new society. In all these cases, the application of a genre label would be difficult since each of these reading interests encompasses the entire world of genre fiction.

CROSS-GENRE PHENOMENON

There has always been a certain amount of cross pollination between genres. Historical mysteries may appeal to both readers interested in crime fiction as well as readers with an interest in history. Similarly, many readers of Regency romances enjoy the period details as much as the satisfaction of a good love story. However, the trend toward cross-genre writing has exploded in the early twenty-first century. The popular success of titles such Mary Doria Russell's *The Sparrow* (which uses a very literary style to explore space travel and the issues of alien encounters and colonization) or Diana Gabaldon's Outlander series (which blends time travel, romance, and history) have exposed many readers to styles of writing they would not necessarily have tried otherwise. Blending of paranormal elements usually found in horror fiction with crime fiction, romances, and chick lit tales has become common. For librarians, the cross genre publishing phenomenon has raised certain challenges. One difficulty that arises is how to categorize a particular book for a specific reader. Is a mystery that features a vampire detective more appealing to a crime fiction reader or a horror or fantasy reader? Another concern is the tendency of some readers to use genre not as a system of classification but as a method to reject titles that they do not wish to read. Assigning *The Sparrow* to the science fiction genre may deter some readers who aver that they never read science fiction. Ursula Le Guin notes that it is when genre begins to be used to make value judgments about a particular work that the system leads to "arbitrary hierarchies" that promote "ignorance and arrogance."[1] The cross genre trend has led to renewed discussion in the library profession about the value of separating out genres in the fiction collection (see p. 33–38).[2] Decisions on what genres to separate out from the main fiction collection and how to assign cross genre titles to a particular area will continue to be debated as the trend toward blending genres grows.

CONCLUSION

An understanding of fiction genres and their characteristics enables librarians to organize and locate materials that will meet the needs of their users. Awareness of emerging genres and trends in popular reading tastes will continue to be important for collectors, readers' advisors, and other library staff working with popular fiction collections.

REFERENCES

1. Le Guin, U.K. Genre: A word only a Frenchman could love: A speech given at the PLA preconference on genre Seattle February, 2004 Public Libraries, 2005; January/February 44(1), 21 (accessed August 1, 2006).
2. Trott, B.; Novak, V. A house divided? Two views on genre separation. Ref. User Serv. Quart. 46(2), 34.
3. Baker, S. *The Responsive Public Library: How to Develop and Market a Winning Collection*; Libraries Unlimited: Englewood, CO, 2002; 66–68 and 282–286.
4. Saricks, J. *Readers' Advisory Service in the Public Library*, 3rd Ed.; ALA Editions: Chicago, IL, 2005.
5. Saricks, J. *The Readers' Advisory Guide to Genre Fiction*; ALA Editions: Chicago, IL, 2001; 113.
6. Romance Writers of America, *Romance Literature Statistics: Overview*. Available at http://www.rwanational.org/cs/the_romance_genre/romance_literature_statistics/industry_statistics (accessed September 17, 2008).
7. Sterling, B. *Slipstream*. Available at http://w2.eff.org/Misc/Publications/Bruce_Sterling/Catscan_columns/catscan.05 (accessed April 3, 2008).

BIBLIOGRAPHY

1. Bouricius, A. *The Romance Readers' Advisory: The Librarian's Guide to Love in the Stacks*, American Library Association: Chicago, IL, 2000.
2. Burgess, M. Bartle, L.R. *Reference Guide to Science Fiction, Fantasy and Horror*, Libraries Unlimited: Englewood, CO, 2002.
3. Cords, S.S. *The Real Story: A Guide to Nonfiction Reading Interests*, Libraries Unlimited: Westport, CT, 2006.
4. Dawson, A. van Fleet, C. *African American Literature: A Guide to Reading Interests*, Libraries Unlimited: Englewood, CO, 2004.
5. Fonseca, A.J. Pulliam, J.M. *Hooked on Horror: A Guide to Reading Interests in Horror Fiction*, Libraries Unlimited: Englewood, CO, 2000.
6. Herald, D.T. *Genreflecting: A Guide to Popular Reading Interests*, 6th Ed. Libraries Unlimited: Englewood, CO, 2005.
7. Herald, D.T. Kunzel, B. *Fluent in Fantasy: The Next Generation*, Libraries Unlimited: Westport, CT, 2008.
8. Hollands, N. *Read On...Fantasy Fiction*, Libraries Unlimited: Westport, CT, 2007.
9. Hooper, B. *Read On...Historical Fiction*, Libraries Unlimited: Westport, CT, 2006.
10. Johnson, S.L. *Historical Fiction: A Guide to the Genre*, Libraries Unlimited: Westport, CT, 2005.
11. Mort, J. *Christian Fiction: A Guide to the Genre*, Libraries Unlimited: Englewood, CO, 2002.
12. Mort, J. *Read the High Country: A Guide to Western Books and Films*, Libraries Unlimited: Westport, CT, 2006.
13. Niebuhr, G.W. *Make Mine a Mystery*, Libraries Unlimited: Westport, CT, 2003.
14. Pulliam, J.M. Fonseca, A.J. *Read On...Horror Fiction*, Libraries Unlimited: Westport, CT, 2006.
15. Ramsdell, K. *Romance Fiction: A Guide to the Genre*, Libraries Unlimited: Englewood, CO, 1999.
16. Saricks, J.G. *Readers' Advisory Guide to Genre Fiction*, American Library Association: Chicago, IL, 2001.
17. Trott, B. *Read On...Crime Fiction*, Libraries Unlimited: Westport, CT, 2008.
18. Wyatt, N. *The Readers' Advisory Guide to Nonfiction*, ALA Editions: Chicago, IL, 2007.

WEB RESOURCES

1. *Dark Echo Horror*, Available at http://www.darkecho.com/darkecho/index.html.
2. Dorothy-L. *Mystery fiction list*, Available at http://www.dorothyl.com/.
3. *Fantastic Fiction*, Available at http://www.fantasticfiction.co.uk/.
4. Fiction-L. *Readers' advisory list*, Available at http://www.webrary.org/rs/flmenu.html.
5. *Historical Fiction Network*, Available at http://www.histfiction.net/.
6. *Locus Magazine Online. Science Fiction and Fantasy*, Available at http://www.locusmag.com/.
7. *Overbooked: A Resource for Readers*, Available at http://www.over booked.org/.
8. *Read West*, Available at http://www.readwest.com/.
9. *The Romance Reader*, Available at http://www.theromancereader.com/.
10. *Romance Writers of America*, Available at http://www.rwanational.org/.
11. *Science Fiction and Fantasy Writers of America*, Available at http://www.sfwa.org/.
12. *Stop You're Killing Me*, Available at http://www.stopyourekillingme.com/index.html.

Precision and Recall *[ELIS Classic]*

F. W. Lancaster
Graduate School of Library and Information Science, University of Illinois at Urbana-Champaign, Urbana, Illinois, U.S.A.

Abstract

F.W. Lancaster's work has been immensely influential in library and information science. He has written on indexing and information system evaluation, and has been looked to as a pioneer in many areas. Here he describes precision and recall, the two most fundamental and widespread measures of information retrieval effectiveness.

—*ELIS Classic*, from 1978

INTRODUCTION

The terms "precision" and "recall" refer to measures that are commonly used to evaluate the performance of a literature search, especially a search conducted in some type of information retrieval system. These measures are probably best explained in the context of the well-known 2 × 2 table of search results, as illustrated in Table 1. When a search is conducted in most information retrieval systems, the system divides up the document collection into two parts. The documents that match the search strategy used to interrogate the system are *retrieved* $(a + b)$, and all the documents that fail to match this strategy are *not retrieved* $(c + d)$. this dichotomous partitioning of the document collection may be regarded as a form of system relevance prediction. The system, in a sense, predicts that certain documents are likely to be relevant and others are likely not to be relevant. It retrieves the former and holds back the latter.

OVERVIEW

In almost all situations, the number of documents retrieved by a search will be quite small in relation to the total collection size. Put differently, in almost all searches, $a + b$ will be quite small but $c + d$, the number of items not retrieved, will be very large. A search might, for example, retrieve 80 document references from a total file of 500,000 references. In this case, $a + b = 80$, while $c + d = 499,920$.

The other dimension of the 2 × 2 table relates to the relevance decisions of the system user (i.e., the person for whom the search is conducted). A perfect search would retrieve all the documents in the database that the user judges to be relevant $(a + c)$ and would not retrieve any that he judges not to be relevant $(b + d)$. In this case, there is perfect coincidence between the user relevance assessments and the system relevance predictions. That is, $b = 0$ and $c = 0$. We would say that this search has achieved 100% recall and 100% precision.

Recall relates to the ability of the system to retrieve relevant documents and *precision* relates to its ability not to retrieve irrelevant documents. The degree of recall achieved in a search, and the degree of precision achieved in a search, may both be expressed as ratios. The *recall ratio* is defined as

$$\frac{\text{Number of relevant documents retrieved}}{\text{Total number of relevant documents in the collection}} \times 100$$

In terms of Table 1, the recall ratio is

$$\frac{a}{a + c}$$

The *precision ratio* is defined as

$$\frac{\text{Number of relevant documents retrieved}}{\text{Total number of documents retrieved}} \times 100$$

In terms of Table 1, the precision ratio is

$$\frac{a}{a + b}$$

The precision ratio and the recall ratio, used jointly, express the filtering capacity of the system: its ability to let through what we want and hold back what we don't want. Neither one on its own gives a complete picture of the success of a search because, clearly, it would always be possible to get 100% recall if we retrieved enough of the total collection; if we retrieved the entire collection $(a + b + c + d)$, we would certainly achieve 100% recall. Unfortunately, however, precision would be extremely low in this situation because, for any typical request, the great majority of the items in the collection will not be relevant.

The precision ratio may be viewed as a type of cost factor. It is a cost factor in user time—the time required to

Encyclopedia of Library and Information Sciences, Fourth Edition DOI: 10.1081/E-ELIS4-120009003

Table 1 2 × 2 Table of results of a literature search

| System relevance prediction | User relevance decisions | | |
	Relevant	Not relevant	Total
Retrieved	a	b	$a+b$
Not retrieved	c	d	$c+d$
Total	$a+c$	$b+d$	$a+b+c+d$

separate the relevant citations from the irrelevant ones in the output of a search. Consider, as an illustration, a search request for which there are 20 relevant documents in a particular database. Suppose that one uses three different search strategies to interrogate the system and that each strategy retrieves 15 of the 20 relevant items (i.e., recall is 75%). In the first search, the total number of items retrieved is 30; in the second, it is 60; and in the third, it is 150. The precision ratio in these three searches is 50%, 25%, and 10%, respectively. In the first search, the user has to examine only 30 citations to find the 15 of relevance; in the second he must examine 60; and in the third, 150. All other things being equal, it will take him longer to separate the relevant from the irrelevant in the second search and considerably longer in the third. It is in this sense that we can regard the precision ratio as a measure of user effort or cost. A search that achieves 75% recall at 50% precision is more efficient than one that achieves 75% recall at 25% precision, and this is more efficient than one that achieves 75% recall at 10% precision.

As stated earlier, these ratios measure the degree of coincidence between the user relevance assessments and the system relevance predictions. In a perfect search, these will exactly coincide. Unfortunately, such perfect searches are relatively rare. We are more likely to get a situation in which there is partial coincidence between the set $a+c$ and the set $a+b$, as shown in Fig. 1. In this diagram, the total collection is represented by the solid rectangle and the set of items retrieved by the dotted rectangle. The hypothetical, but very typical, search has retrieved most, but not all, of the relevant documents and has avoided retrieval of most, but not all, of the irrelevant documents.

Recall and precision tend to be related inversely. By this we mean that when we broaden a search, to achieve better recall, precision will tend to go down. Conversely, when we narrow the scope of a search, in order to improve

its precision, recall will tend to deteriorate. For a particular group of, say, 50 requests, we could conduct each search at a number of different levels, from an extremely broad search designed to get very high recall, to an extremely narrow one, designed to get high precision. If we derived recall and precision ratios for each of these search approaches, we could reduce the results to a plot of recall versus precision. The resulting plot would look something like that of Fig. 2. It represents the average of the recall and precision ratios for all 50 searches, with each search being conducted at four different "levels." It can be seen that when the searches are conducted very generally (point A), a very high recall of around 90% is achieved; the precision, however, is very low. When, on the other hand, the searches are made very specific, a high-precision, low-recall result (point D) is achieved. The points B and C represent compromise strategies between these two extremes.

The curve of Fig. 2 represents the *average* of the results for 50 searches when each search is deliberately conducted at four different levels. But, in this situation, as in others, averages may be quite misleading. The performance figures for the individual searches are unlikely to fall on this curve. In fact, they are likely to be widely scattered, as shown in Fig. 3. Here we can see some very good results (top right-hand corner of the plot), some very poor results (bottom left-hand corner), some high recall–low precision results, some high precision–low recall results, and some completely middle-of-the-road results. When we average out all of these, we arrive at average performance figures and an average performance curve, A–D.

Recall and precision ratios are two important measures that can be used in the evaluation of an information retrieval system. Their major value lies in the fact that they can be used to determine under what conditions the system seems to operate best. Consider Fig. 3 again. What we really want to know is why some searches have produced very good results and some very poor results. In

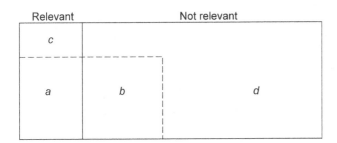

Fig. 1 Results of a typical search in a retrieval system.

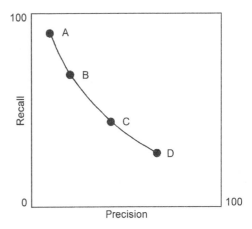

Fig. 2 Typical plot of recall versus precision.

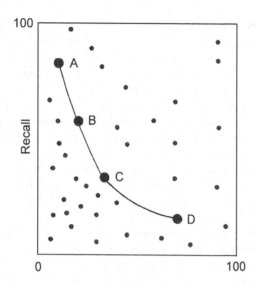

Fig. 3 Scatter diagram of search results.

other words, "what makes a good search good" and "what makes a bad search bad"? One way of approaching an answer to this question is to divide up all the searches according to various characteristics and to produce a family of curves for the various sets of searches thus created. In Fig. 4, we see the average performance curves for three groups of searches. Clearly, Group 1 has produced the best results and Group 3, the worst. The curves shown in Fig. 4 may represent searches conducted in different subject fields, searches conducted by different processing centers, searches conducted for different types of users, searches conducted for requests arriving in various ways (by mail, by telephone, by personal visit), and so on.

An analysis of this type might indicate weaknesses in the system and ways in which the performance might be improved. For example, if the Group 3 curve represents searches in a particular subject area, these poor results might indicate inadequacies in the vocabulary of the

system in this subject field. The evaluation has pinpointed this weakness and thus allows us to take appropriate corrective action. It should be pointed out, however, that we are likely to need a fairly large number of searches (many more than 50) to conduct, with any level of statistical confidence, the type of comparison exemplified by Fig. 4.

Recall and precision ratios have another important use. Each ratio is likely to indicate a certain number of failures and this permits us to conduct an analysis to determine why these failures occurred. To take a simple example, suppose that a particular search has performed as follows:

1. 7/10 = 70% recall
2. 7/28 = 25% precision

These results indicate 3 recall failures (instances in which a relevant item was not retrieved by the search) and 21 precision failures (instances in which irrelevant items were retrieved by the search), and these failures must be analyzed to determine why they occurred. Failure analysis of this type is the diagnostic element in an evaluation program. It is the most important part of the entire evaluation activity. Failure analysis requires an examination of the document involved, how it was indexed, the request statement, the search strategy, and the vocabulary of the system. The objective is to determine why the failure occurred and to attribute the failure to the appropriate component of the total retrieval system (the indexing, the search strategy, the vocabulary, or the user-system interface).

So far in this article, we have assumed that it is relatively simple to obtain recall and precision ratios for a search in a retrieval system. It is relatively easy to obtain a precision ratio for a search, but, it is not at all easy to measure recall. Consider another 2 × 2 table, Table 2, this time with some hypothetical results entered. Some of the results in this table are directly observable, others can be obtained through the cooperation of the requester, and some can only be estimated.

The database represented in this table contains 500,000 items, and this hypothetical search has retrieved 50 items and has not retrieved 499,950. This is a typical result. For any search in a retrieval system, the great majority of the items in the collection are not retrieved. To obtain a precision ratio for the search, we need to discover how many of the 50 items retrieved are "relevant." We can obtain this

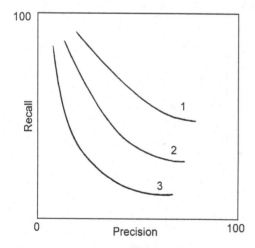

Fig. 4 Family of curves representing results for groups of searches of different "types."

Table 2 Results of a hypothetical search in an information retrieval system

System relevance prediction	User relevance decisions		
	Relevant	Not relevant	Total
Retrieved	10	40	50
Not retrieved	5	499,945	499,950
Total	15	499,985	500,000

figure by submitting these items to the person requesting the search and asking him to assess their relevance to the information need that prompted the request to the system. In this hypothetical case, he judges only 10 to be relevant. The precision ratio is thus 10/50, or 20%. We have assumed here that it is the requester who should make these relevance assessments. Not everyone accepts this assumption, however, and some would have relevance assessments made by an independent observer or possibly a jury of such observers.

We are still left with the problem of estimating recall, and this is not particularly easy. To establish recall, we need to determine how many of the documents not retrieved by the search are, in fact, relevant to the search request. There is only one way of determining absolute recall for a search and that would involve the examination of each and every item not retrieved. This is an impossible task in any but a very small, experimental situation. In the case of the search represented in Table 2, 499,950 documents would need to be examined. Random sampling does not improve the situation very much. In the case of this hypothetical search, we would need to examine a sample of 499,950/5 items, almost 100,000, in order to have any chance of finding even one relevant item purely at random.

Since it is virtually impossible to determine absolute recall, we must usually be satisfied with an estimate of recall. The most satisfactory of these is to base the recall estimate on some subset of documents known to exist in the database and known to be relevant. The situation is represented in Fig. 5. For any request *R*, the collection *I* contains a set of documents *A* that the initiator of the request would judge relevant if he saw them. That is, they are the set *a* + *c* of Table 1. Unfortunately, we do not know the identity of the documents in this set. For a very large collection, we will never know it. We can, however, estimate recall on the basis of a subset *A1* of the set *A*. The subset *A1* consists of a group of documents that we know to be relevant and we know to exist in the database. This subset could consist of relevant documents known by the requester before the search is conducted, it could consist of items found by a parallel search in one or more other indexes (e.g., printed indexes) and judged relevant by the requester, or it could be derived from a combination of these two sources. However we arrive at it, the recall ratio

of the search is estimated on the basis of the number of this subset *A1* that are retrieved. To take a very simple example, suppose that the subset *A1* consists of 3 documents known to be relevant and known to be in the collection. The search retrieves 2 of the 3 and our recall estimate is, therefore, 66%. In the case of the hypothetical search of Table 2, we know that 10 relevant documents have been retrieved. Our recall estimate indicates that 10 is approximately 66% of the total of relevant documents in the database. Our estimate of the number of relevant documents missed, then, is 5.

The subset *A1* is the *recall base* by which we estimate the recall ratio for a search. It is obvious that with very small recall bases we can have little statistical confidence in the recall estimate for a single search. But when we apply this technique to a large number of searches, we can create quite a large composite recall base and, as shown by Shumway,[1] we can achieve quite a high degree of confidence in the results for the entire set of searches or for large groups of these searches. This technique was used by Lancaster in the largest evaluation so far conducted.[2] This study was an evaluation of MEDLARS, the computer-based system of the National Library of Medicine. Some 300 searches were used in this study, and the combined recall base for these searches consisted of almost 2,000 known relevant documents.

DIFFERING REQUIREMENTS FOR RECALL AND PRECISION

Not everyone needs high recall all of the time. Different users will have different requirements for recall and precision, and a particular individual will have different requirements at different times. The precision tolerance of the user is likely to be directly related to his recall requirements. At one end of the spectrum, we have the individual who is writing a book, preparing a review article, or beginning a long-term research project. He is likely to want a comprehensive (high recall) search, and he may tolerate a fairly low precision in order to assure himself that he has not missed anything of importance. At the other end, we have the typical user of, say, an industrial information service who needs a few recent articles on a subject and needs them right away. This individual does not need high recall, but he will expect high precision in the search results. Other individuals may prefer a compromise; they would like a "reasonable" level of recall at an "acceptable" level of precision.

It seems rather pointless to use the recall ratio as a measure of the success of a search in which high recall is unimportant. This has led some writers to suggest the use of some measure of proportional recall (or relative recall) in which the success of the search is expressed in terms of the number of relevant documents retrieved over the number of relevant documents wanted by the requester. For example,

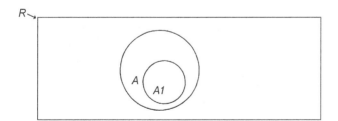

Fig. 5 Method of estimating recall by subset of relevant documents known to exist in the database.

the requester specifies that he needs five relevant documents but the search retrieves only three. The proportional recall ratio is, therefore, three-fifths or 60%. This measure, while attractive on the surface, is rather artificial in that very few requesters will be able to specify in advance just how many documents they want from the system.

Another limitation of the recall ratio is that it assumes, more or less, that all relevant documents have approximately equal value. This is not always true. A search may retrieve 5 relevant documents and miss 10 (recall ratio = 33%) but the 5 retrieved may be much better than the 10 missed. They could, for example, be more up to date and might in fact make the other 10 items completely redundant. The recall ratio, while important, must therefore be used with some caution in the evaluation of information services.

ALTERNATIVE PERFORMANCE MEASURES

The 2×2 table (Table 1) contains all the data that we really need to know about a search in a retrieval system for evaluation purposes. One way of expressing the results of this table is by the recall ratio and the precision ratio, used jointly. But there are several other measures of performance that can be derived from this table, and there are various ways in which these results can be presented. Before we mention some alternative measures, it may be desirable to give some names to the various cells of Table 1. The set *a* we can refer to as the *hits*, the set *c* as the *misses*, the set *b* as the *noise* (in the communications sense), and *d* as the set *correctly rejected*.

From Table 1, all of the following measures can be derived:

$a/(a+c)$ The *recall ratio*, also known as the *hit rate*. The measure was apparently first suggested by Perry, who referred to it as the *recall factor*.[3] Swets calls it the *conditional probability of a hit*.[4] Goffman and Newill have called it *sensitivity*.[5]

$c/(a+c)$ This is the complement of recall. Fairthorne has called it a *snobbery ratio*.[6] Swets terms it *conditional probability of a miss*.

$a/(a+b)$ This is the *precision ratio*, sometimes referred to as the *relevance ratio*. Again, Perry seems to have introduced the measure.[3] Perry called it the *pertinency factor*. Others have referred to it as an *acceptance rate*.

$b/(a+b)$ This is the complement of the precision ratio, called, by Perry, the *noise factor*.

$b/(b+d)$ This measure seems to have been first suggested by Swets, who referred to it as the *conditional probability of a false drop*.[4] Cleverdon et al. have since named it the *fallout ratio*.[7] It has also been referred to as *discard*.

$d/(b+d)$ The complement of *fallout*. Goffman and Newill have called it *specificity*.[5] Swets names it the *conditional probability of a correct rejection*.

Each one of these measures can be referred to as a *single measure* of merit for a search. When two measures are used together (as in a plot of recall versus precision or recall versus fallout), this has been referred to as a *twin variable measure*. When an attempt is made to combine two of these separate measures into a single measure (e.g., one reflecting both recall and precision), the result is known as a *composite measure* or, possibly, a *single figure of merit*.

These measures are appropriate for use with a retrieval system that merely divides a collection into two parts, those items retrieved and those not retrieved by a particular search. But certain systems will do more than this. They will generate a "ranked output" of documents in order of probable relevance to a request. Ranking systems should be evaluated in a somewhat different way because here we need an indication of the success of the ranking procedure. Various measures that have been applied to ranking systems include *rank recall*, *log precision*, *normalized recall*, and *normalized precision*. These measures, introduced by Salton, essentially compare the actual ranking achieved by the system with an ideal ranking.[8] That is, the measures reflect the degree to which the ranking matches the ideal situation.

CONCLUSION

Rather complete discussions of evaluation measures, methods of averaging results, and methods of presenting results of retrieval tests have been provided by Keen[9,10] and by Robertson.[11,12] Recall ratios and precision ratios have been the measures most used in evaluations of information retrieval systems. These measures were popularized by Cleverdon in the ASLIB Cranfield Project.[13] Many other writers, however, have presented reasons why other measures may be regarded as more accurate or more informative. Robertson's paper provides a useful analysis of the pros and cons of the various measures that have been proposed or used.

REFERENCES

1. Shumway, R.H. Some estimation problems associated with evaluating information retrieval systems. In *Evaluation of Document Retrieval Systems: Literature Perspective, Measurement, Technical Papers*; Westat Research Inc.: Bethesda, MD, 1968; 78–96.
2. Lancaster, F.W. *Evaluation of the MEDLARS Demand Search Service*; National Library of Medicine: Bethesda, MD, 1968.
3. Perry, J.W. Operational criteria for designing information retrieval systems. Am. Doc. **1955**, *6* (2), 93–101.
4. Swets, J.A. Information retrieval systems. Science **1963**, *141*, 245–250.

5. Goffman, W.; Newill, V.A. *Methodology for Test and Evaluation of Information Retrieval Systems*; Western Reserve Univ., Center for Documentation and Communication Research: Cleveland, OH, 1964.

6. Fairthorne, R.A.**1965**. Personal communication.

7. Cleverdon, C.W.; Mills, J.; Keen, E.M. *Factors Determining the Performance of Index Languages*; College of Aeronautics: Cranfield, England, 1966; 3 vols.

8. *The SMART Retrieval System: Experiments in Automatic Document Processing*; Salton, G., Ed.; Prentice-Hall: Englewood Cliffs, NJ, 1971.

9. Keen, E.M. Evaluation Parameters. In *The SMART Retrieval System: Experiments in Automatic Document Processing*; Prentice-Hall: Englewood Cliffs, NJ, 1971; 74–111.

10. Keen, E.M. *Measures and Averaging Methods Used in Performance Testing of Indexing Systems*; ASLIB Cranfield Research Project: Cranfield, England, 1966.

11. Robertson, S.E. The parametric description of retrieval tests. J. Doc. **1969**, *25* (1), 1–27.

12. Robertson, S.E. The parametric description of retrieval tests. J. Doc. **1969**, *25* (2), 93–107.

13. Cleverdon, C.W. *Report on the Testing and Analysis of an Investigation into the Comparative Efficiency of Indexing Systems*; ASLIB Cranfield Research Project: Cranfield, England, 1962.

Presidential Libraries

Sharon Fawcett
Office of Presidential Libraries, National Archives and Records Administration, College Park, Maryland, U.S.A.

Abstract

The National Archives and Records Administration (NARA) administers a nationwide network of Presidential libraries beginning with the 31st President of the United States, Herbert Hoover. These are not traditional libraries, but rather repositories for preserving and making accessible the papers, records, and other historical materials of U.S. Presidents. When a President leaves office, NARA establishes a Presidential project until a new Presidential library is built and transferred to the Government. Presidential libraries and museums are great treasures of our nation's history. They are important sources for historians and other researchers studying our presidents and our history. In addition to archiving and preserving presidential papers and objects, presidential libraries and museums bring history to millions of visitors from around the world.

BRIEF HISTORY OF THE PRESIDENTIAL LIBRARY SYSTEM

Sixty years ago, Franklin D. Roosevelt proposed creating a Presidential Library that would be part of an institution whose growth he had shepherded—the National Archives. Roosevelt suggested a creative approach—he would donate the land, build the library with private funding, and then give the library and his papers to the National Archives. On June 30, 1941, as the war in Europe threatened democracy, Roosevelt dedicated his library at Hyde Park. His words of dedication express as well today as then the importance of records in the nation's history and the nation's future.

> To bring together the records of the past and to house them in buildings where they will be preserved for the use of men and women in the future, a Nation must believe in three things.
>
> It must believe in the past.
>
> It must believe in the future.
>
> It must, above all, believe in the capacity of its own people so to learn from the past that they can gain judgement in creating their own future.[1]

The Roosevelt Library is the only Presidential Library built, dedicated, and used while the president was still in office. It became the model for the Presidential Library system. Privately constructed and donated to the government, Presidential Libraries provide extensive services for their researchers, an expansive collection of presidential materials, and incorporate a museum experience for hundreds of thousands of visitors each year. Geographically dispersed around the country, Presidential Libraries allow more students and the public to learn about the election process; how government works; leadership, decision making, and the role of the presidency; and historical events that have taken place in much of the twentieth century.

In 1952, President Truman, deploring the scattering of presidential papers in the past, stated "[the President's papers] ought to be accessible in one place…where the scholars and archivists can get to them without difficulty. I hope we will have that in the future." He went on to say that he wanted the "state papers of President Roosevelt and myself properly cared for."[2] Originally, Truman considered depositing his papers at the National Archives, in Washington, DC, but by 1950, he decided on a Presidential Library in his hometown of Independence, Missouri. Truman strongly believed that Presidential Libraries were not to be monuments to a president but centers for the study of the presidency. The Truman Institute, established to build and support the library, has a long history of sponsoring intellectual exchanges through conferences and the Truman Grants program for the study of the presidency.

Dwight D. Eisenhower's clear support of the development of a library at the site of the already established Eisenhower Museum in Abilene, Kansas, prompted Congress to pass The Presidential Libraries Act of 1955 (44 U. S.C. § 2108). The legislation had full bipartisan support, and was hailed by scholars and educators. This act provided continuing legal authority for the government to accept the gift of a Presidential Library without seeking legislative authority for each new library.

President Hoover had originally given his papers to Stanford University, but responded favorably to a request of a citizens committee from his hometown for the

Encyclopedia of Library and Information Sciences, Fourth Edition DOI: 10.1081/E-ELIS4-120014742

development of a library in West Branch, Iowa. His library became the third added to the system in 1962. The Eisenhower Library was also opened in 1962, and a pattern, which has remained unbroken, was established.

Over time, however, the venue for a Presidential Library shifted from the president's hometown, to larger metropolitan areas or a university campus. The Lyndon B. Johnson Presidential Library and Museum became the first Presidential Library located on a university campus. President Johnson sought to place his library in a university environment convenient for students and faculty where materials housed in the library could be used to promote the study of history, economics, political science, public affairs, and numerous other academic pursuits. Along with building the library, the Lyndon Baines Johnson Foundation established to provide additional support for the library also supports the LBJ School of Public Affairs located next door to the library.

This has meant that this remarkable public–private partnership that builds and supports the libraries has often expanded into three- and even four-way partnerships, as the library foundation, the university, and the local community come together to build a presidential center that can be turned over to the government. The Presidential Libraries Act of 1955 presciently enabled this by authorizing the government to enter into agreements with any state or political subdivision, universities and institutions of higher learning, and institute or foundation for the purposes of using land, buildings, and equipment for a Presidential Archival Depository. The John F. Kennedy Library is adjacent to the University of Massachusetts; the Lyndon B. Johnson Library and Museum is on the campus of the University of Texas at Austin; the Gerald Ford Library is at the University of Michigan; the Jimmy Carter Library is near the campus of Emory University; the George Bush Library is part of Texas A&M University; and the William Clinton Library will be affiliated with the University of Arkansas at Little Rock.

Overseeing these institutions for the National Archives and Records Administration (NARA) is the Office of Presidential Libraries established as a permanent part of NARA in 1964. Until then, the functions of supervision, coordination, and administration of Presidential Libraries had been handled directly out of the office of the Archivist of the United States. Herman Kahn, who had been the director of the Roosevelt Library, became the first Assistant Archivist for Presidential Libraries. His job was to establish and coordinate policies with regard to Presidential Libraries, including programs for acquisition, preservation, and use of historical materials appropriate for deposit in the Presidential Libraries, and to maintain liaison with the incumbent administration and with officials of former administrations with regard to organization, storage, and reference service on presidential papers and other historical materials. The current Assistant Archivist for Presidential Libraries, appointed in November 2001, is

Richard Claypoole who now oversees a system of 10 Presidential Libraries, the Clinton Presidential Project, the Nixon Presidential Materials Staff, and the Presidential Materials Staff.

In 1986, Congress passed various amendments to the 1955 Presidential Libraries Act to reduce the costs of operating Presidential Libraries. 44 U.S.C. § 2112 requires that an endowment equal to 20% of the cost of the building be transferred to the government at the time the library is turned over to the government. Libraries larger than 70,000 square feet are to be accompanied by an endowment that increases geometrically in accordance with the size of the building. The George H.W. Bush Library is the first library required to have an endowment. On the day the Bush Library was dedicated, the Bush Foundation presented a check for $4 million to the National Archives Trust Fund. Interest on the endowment is now used to offset part of the cost of operating the library. The act also required the Archivist to promulgate architectural and design standards for the preservation of materials and the inclusion of adequate research facilities. Architectural and design standards for Presidential Libraries address program and siting requirements and standards for structures, security, fire and life safety, lighting, electrical, and HVAC design.

The 1986 act did not change the requirement that the Archivist submit a written report to Congress prior to accepting a library, but it did set forth the specific information required in the report. The Archivist may not accept the library until the expiration of a period of 60 days of continuous session of Congress beginning on the day the Archivist transmits the report. The report must include:

- A description of the proposed gift
- A statement specifying the total cost and the amount to be deposited in an endowment
- A general description of any papers, documents, or historical materials proposed to be deposited in the library
- An estimate of the increase in the total annual cost to the United States of maintaining, operating, and protecting the depository
- A certification that the depository and the equipment therein will comply with the standards promulgated by the Archivist

PRESIDENTIAL MATERIALS

Throughout the eighteenth, nineteenth, and well into the twentieth century, no one questioned the private ownership of presidential papers by the president. Former presidents could donate them to a library or archives, or not, as they saw fit. Fortunately, many presidential papers were donated and are available for historical research today. However, many were accidentally or purposely destroyed. Biographers of George Washington snipped out pages of Washington's diaries. Chester Arthur burned his papers. Former presidents and their families exercised considerable discretion in what they donated resulting in selective donation and selective destruction. One very powerful reason the National Archives wanted libraries built and given to the National Archives was that the donation of a library meant the National Archives would also receive the president's papers. In its time, this system of donation worked very well. Although there was nothing mandatory in the legislation for Presidential Libraries requiring that presidents systematically preserve their presidential papers, the legislation assured a president who donated his materials to the National Archives that the integrity of his papers would be preserved. The papers would be cared for by a professional archival staff and made available to all as historical records.

The handling of presidential materials began to change again with President Nixon's resignation in 1974. Congress enacted the Presidential Recordings and Materials Preservation Act (PRMPA; 44 U.S.C. § 2111) to ensure that no evidence in President Nixon's papers, tapes, or other historical material relating to Watergate would be destroyed. The PRMPA seized the Nixon presidential materials and gave the National Archives and Records Service, now the NARA, legal custody and control over them.

Historians, journalists, and Congress now raised serious questions about the ownership of presidential materials, suggesting instead they be treated as government records. PRMPA had established the National Study Commission on Records and Documents of Federal Officials to explore topics of ownership, control, disposition, and preservation of historic materials. The report of the commission, completed in March 1977, made two basic recommendations:

1. All documentary materials received or made by federal officials in discharge of their official duties should be considered the property of the United States.
2. Federal officials should be given the prerogative to control access to their materials up to 15 years after the end of their federal service.

In 1978, Congress acted on the report and passed the Presidential Records Act (44 U.S.C. § 2201-2207). This act created and defined a new category of records—presidential records—and established the terms of access to these records. The act clearly established that these records are owned by the United States. After conclusion of a president's tenure, the custody of presidential records is transferred to the Archivist of the United States. The former president retains the right to impose specific restrictions outlined in the Presidential Records Act statute

on the records until 12 years after he has left office. Executive Order 13233 signed by President George W. Bush outlines a process for notification and review for executive privilege of presidential records proposed for opening.

Government archivists and curators preserve, process, and provide access to the presidential materials in their care. The process for providing access to donated historical materials and the process for providing access to presidential records vary somewhat in implementation because of the statutory and regulatory requirements. However, the mission of the government staff in each library is the same—to preserve and process the materials, and to provide access as fully and promptly as the law or deed and resources permit.

The 10 Presidential Libraries, the Nixon Presidential Materials Staff, and the Clinton Presidential Materials Project maintain more than 400 million pages of textual materials; more than 24 million photographs; 14.5 million feet of motion picture film; 103,000 hours of disc, audiotape, and videotape recordings; nearly 500,000 museum objects; and 40 million e-mail messages. In addition, the Clinton Presidential Materials Project has available on its website (http://www.clinton.archives.gov), four snapshots of the Clinton White House website.

The most important materials in each library are those the president and his staff create in the course of their official duties. In recently established Presidential Libraries, these documents can also be in electronic form. Researchers find that each library contains a rich audiovisual and photographic record of a president at work. Taken together, these historical materials form the substantive record of public policy in each administration. Libraries also house numerous museum objects including family heirlooms, items collected by the president or his family, campaign memorabilia, awards, and the many gifts given to the president by American citizens and foreign dignitaries. The latter include Head of State gifts under The Foreign Gifts and Decorations Act (22 U.S.C. § 264), and gifts received by the president from private citizens and accepted by him for eventual deposit in his presidential library (44 U.S.C. § 2111–2112). These gifts range in type from homemade items to valuable works of art. Curators in Presidential Libraries and in other museums throughout the country draw upon these collections for historical exhibits.

Other significant holdings include the personal papers and historical materials donated by individuals associated with the president. These individuals may include cabinet officials, envoys to foreign governments, political party associates, and the president's family and personal friends. Several libraries have undertaken oral history programs that have produced significant tape-recorded memoirs. A third body of materials comprises the papers accumulated by the president prior to, and following, his presidency. Such collections include documents relating to Franklin Roosevelt's tenure as Governor of New York and Dwight Eisenhower's long military career.

Each of the libraries has available on its website detailed information about their holdings. Many also provide copies of significant documents, photographs, and oral histories from their collections online. To access library websites, visit http://www.archives.gov and click on "Presidential Libraries" for links to each website.

Many historians, educators, and other users have offered their testimonials on the value of Presidential Libraries and the dedicated staff that preserve, process, and assist them in using the materials. Countless forwards to well-known historical works over the past 50 years refer to the importance of these materials for exploring and understanding historical themes and issues of our time. In a recent *Washington Times* article (2/28/00), the reporter noted that "As far as scholars, educators and the U.S. government are concerned, the libraries are among the most important research sites in the United States." In the same article, Page Miller, former director of the National Coordinating Committee for the Promotion of History, is quoted saying, "All you have to do is check the footnotes of major prize-winning books and monographs dealing with presidents and you'll see they all reference presidential libraries." Anna Nelson, a long-time user of archives, has found that "in all these presidential libraries the archivists are splendid," a view widely shared by other professionals who use the libraries.

The materials in Presidential Libraries are among this nation's most important documents. Presidential records are often open for research long before the records of other departments and agencies of government are even transferred to the National Archives. Political scientists study the different approaches and processes used by presidents to govern, and then make recommendations to new presidents on what works and does not work. Economists study the impact of presidential decisions on economic indicators and project what will happen in the future. The media searches for examples from our past to inform the public about current events. Hundreds of thousands of children visit libraries each year to learn about how presidents make decisions, how laws are passed, how wars were fought, how our civil rights have been ensured, and how their ancestors lived. More than 1 million visitors each year view the human drama of the presidency through the power of objects and documents displayed in the libraries.

PUBLIC AND EDUCATIONAL PROGRAMS

Each library offers various public and educational programs designed to give visitors a better understanding of the president, the institution of the presidency, and the American political system as a whole. Exhibits, conferences, and lectures funded by privately endowed library foundations are among the special events that help to define a library, and enhance its role as a

repository and cultural institution. Museum exhibits use library holdings to depict the stages of a president's life, the important policy decisions of his administration, and the various world and national events that occurred during his term.

Libraries work with educators to encourage the use of primary source materials by students, and sponsor public lectures, film series, and other events of historical or current interest. Conferences are another way in which the libraries serve the public and examine various topics ranging from public affairs and domestic policy to foreign affairs and world wars.

In 1973, James B. Rhoads, then Archivist of the United States, told an education symposium at the Lyndon Baines Johnson Library, "Presidential Libraries would be fulfilling their purpose if they did nothing more than preserve and provide access to the papers they contain...but their charters are broad and their possibilities for service are unlimited." However broad their charters may be, the libraries face limitations imposed by financial reality. Taxpayers are under no obligation to fund a temporary exhibit on the Civil War, a conference on civil rights, or educational efforts aimed at high school students, admirable and useful as these undeniably are to the public. These efforts are funded by the libraries' support organizations, which constitute much of the financial support received by the Presidential Libraries. Congressionally appropriated funds cover many of the personnel costs; program costs, such as collections maintenance, preservation, and access to records; building operations and maintenance; and repair and restoration. In 2001, actual obligations from appropriated funds totaled nearly $40 million for the Presidential Library system.

LIST OF PRESIDENTIAL LIBRARIES

Dwight D. Eisenhower Library
  200 SE 4th Street
  Abilene, KS 67410-2900
Franklin D. Roosevelt
  4079 Albany Post Road
  Hyde Park, NY 12538-1999
George Bush Library
  1000 George Bush Drive, West
  College Station, TX 77845
Gerald R. Ford Library
  1000 Beal Street
  Ann Arbor, MI 48109-2114
Gerald R. Ford Museum
  303 Pearl Street, NW
  Grand Rapids, MI 49504-5353
Herbert Hoover Library
  210 Parkside Drive
  P.O. Box 488
  West Branch, IA 52358-0488

Harry S. Truman Library
   500 West U.S. Highway 24
   Independence, MO 64050-1798
John Fitzgerald Kennedy Library
   Columbia Point
   Boston, MA 02125-3398
Jimmy Carter Library
   441 Freedom Parkway
   Atlanta, GA 30307-1498
Lyndon Baines Johnson Library
   2313 Red River Street
   Austin, TX 78705-5702
Nixon Presidential Materials Staff
   8601 Adelphi Road, Room 1320
   College Park, MD 20740-6001
Presidential Materials Staff
   700 Pennsylvania Avenue, NW
   Washington, DC 20408-0001

Ronald Reagan Library
   40 Presidential Drive
   Simi Valley, CA 93065-0699
William J. Clinton Presidential Materials Project
   1000 LaHarpe Boulevard
   Little Rock, AK 72201

REFERENCES

1. Freidel, F. Roosevelt to Reagan: The birth and growth of presidential libraries. Prologue **Summer 1989**, *21*, 113.
2. President Truman's remarks to the Eighth Annual Institute on the Preservation and Administration of Archives, June 18, 1952.

Primary Records: Future Prospects *[ELIS Classic]*

G. Thomas Tanselle
Vice President, John Simon Guggenheim Memorial Foundation, New York, New York, U.S.A.

Abstract

G.T. Tanselle probes deeply into the nature of primary records. He addresses many contextual questions about their future prospects in the light of current trends to microfilm and digitize documents and destroy pre-existing versions of them.

—ELIS Classic, from 2003

INTRODUCTION

When one speaks of "the future of primary records," there are at least four questions implicit in the phrase. One is, "Will people in the future have any interest in primary records?" An assumption that records of some kind will be needed leads to a second question, "What will be the form of the primary records that are created in the future?" A third question, looking backward to earlier records, is, "Will the primary records created in the past have a future usefulness as objects from the past?" This question asks, in other words, whether the perceived content of earlier records will be transferred to new forms employing the same technology as the newer records; and, if so, whether there is a reason to continue using the original physical objects as well. A fourth question, independent of the third but closely related to it, is, "Will the presently surviving physical objects that transmitted texts in the past continue to be available?" Do they—that is to say—have a future in the most basic sense: will they survive? And if they do survive, can they be found in accessible locations?

All of these questions are obviously interconnected. An object cannot be used unless it exists; and though it may exist without being used, its chances of survival are greater if it is perceived to serve a function. As technology changes, the function of earlier objects is brought into question, because there is a convenience in having all materials in compatible forms, and because the newer forms are likely to be regarded, by a great many people, as superior to the older ones. But if no one sees any function for records from the past, and if, therefore, no one has any interest in them, then their survival is not a matter of concern in any case. Although the questions continually impinge on each other, taking them up separately can be an aid to clear thinking. The late twentieth century has seen a great deal of discussion of the whole subject, but much of the commentary has been vitiated by a failure to think through, in a methodical way, the complexity of issues necessarily involved. The following responses to the four questions posed here constitute an attempt to provide a logical framework for further discussion.

INTEREST IN PRIMARY RECORDS

Any concern for the future of primary records presupposes a future interest in them; and such an interest does not seem self-evident to everyone. A necessary foundation, then, for discussing this topic is an understanding of the inevitability—almost by definition, one might say—of an interest in primary records. It is essential, therefore, to know what definition of the term "primary record" leads to that conclusion; and the process of defining it reveals many of the issues that make the subject complex.

The word "record" is ambiguous in the same way that "book" is: sometimes it refers to a physical object, sometimes it denotes what is regarded as the content of a physical object, and sometimes its meaning shifts from one to the other within a single discussion, producing a confused argument. If a literary critic first employs "book" to mean "literary work" (as we all do when we speak of a "good book") and then quotes from or discusses "the text of the book," referring to the particular text physically present in the copy being read, the result is fundamentally flawed by its unexamined assumption that a verbal work is identical to any given text of it.[1] The two are theoretically distinct, because a verbal work, made of language, is intangible and cannot reside in physical form. Each tangible object that carries a verbal text, such as a printed book, is one effort to transmit an intangible work, to make it transportable across time. But, each may be deficient, in one way or another, according to any of various possible standards for judging what ought to be there. The distinction between these senses of "work" and "book" is a necessary one, whatever terms one chooses to use. In coherent discussion, therefore, "book" must be used in only one way, and it seems sensible to employ the word to refer to a physical object, not to the intangible work that the object aims to transmit.

"Record" is simply a more encompassing term that includes "book" as one of its subcategories. Archivists are likely to think of "record" as denoting unprinted or unpublished material (especially when created as a by-product of the activities of an institution or individual).

Encyclopedia of Library and Information Sciences, Fourth Edition DOI: 10.1081/E-ELIS4-120008652

But the extension of this archival term, and "archive," to include printed artifacts has been common, as in phrases like "the print record" or "the national printed archive." Archivists are no less guilty than literary critics of blurring the distinction between physical text and intangible work: they may think of a "record" initially in physical terms, but when they include microfilming as a procedure for "record management," they have obviously switched to a concept of a "record" as a disembodied text. (The same switch applied to the word "materials" occurs in this sentence from a library newsletter: "Most brittle materials can be returned to usable condition by reformatting—transferring the information to another medium."[2]) If, to avoid this problem, we restrict "record," like "book," to the physical, it denotes a wider range of objects than books, from all kinds of handwritten and printed ephemera to business ledgers and card files. What links all of these objects is that they are the vehicles by which compositions in intangible media are transported. To make the compositions tangible, they are converted to notations that can be presented visually on physical surfaces—such notations as musical scores, choreographic diagrams, mathematical formulas, or alphabetical and numerical characters arranged to represent words and calculations.

A "record," then, for present purposes, can be defined as an artifact carrying a text that represents in physical form an intangible work. (The word "document" can be used synonymously with it.) Such objects are aptly called "records," because they do not contain the works themselves but only "records" of those works. There are other artifacts, of course, that convey works made up of physical media. They are not usually called "records," because the works actually exist in them or are identical to them. Paintings, sculptures, and buildings, which use physical media, exist as physical objects. One might, for certain purposes, wish to think of them as "records" of human activity rather than as works of art, but in either case, one would be examining the same objects. Reproductions of paintings, sculptures, or buildings could also be thought of as "records"; but, as long as the works survive, the reproductions do not provide the sole means for approaching them, because the works can be apprehended directly. Tangible records of intangible works, on the other hand, are essential for reconstructing and experiencing those works, because there is nowhere else to turn (except, in some cases, to oral tradition, which poses analogous problems).[3]

One might think, then, that the future of such records would be considered in the same terms as that of works in physical media, but by and large, it is not. Art historians and museum curators would scarcely condone the destruction of the artifacts they study, and their discussions of the future of those artifacts focus on preservation. But persons who deal with intangible works—from readers of literature to economic historians studying company archives—frequently believe that the content of what they are concerned with can be separated from the physical objects in which it has appeared. To these persons, preservation is less likely to mean saving physical records than maintaining their "content" in some form. Discussions of records, as defined above, therefore, involve explaining the value of physical details in a way that would usually seem superfluous when talking about other kinds of artifacts.

This is where the concept of "primary" evidence comes in, though adding the word "primary" to "record" presents further complications. "Primary" means simply "first-hand"—that is, not derived or reported. Whether it also refers to physical evidence depends on the context. The term "primary record," when used by those persons who equate records with intangible works, would not signify any physical details; it would mean a direct quotation from the figure being discussed or from an eyewitness account of an event, rather than a restatement made by someone farther removed from the subject of the discussion. From this point of view, an original manuscript and a microfilm of it would equally be primary records. If, however, one takes "record" to refer to an artifact, as we are doing here, then a "primary record" is a specific object containing a particular text of a work—the object being one directly connected with the historical moment that is the focus of one's attention. Under this definition, if an author's manuscript or a business ledger were considered a primary record, no copy of the texts in them—whether produced by handwriting, typewriting, photography, xerography, electronic scanning, or any other means—would be primary, because all such copies would constitute different physical objects.

One must remember, however, that an object regarded as primary for one purpose is not necessarily primary for another. Although an author's manuscript (the manuscript itself, that is, not a photocopy of it) is a primary record for the study of the author's method of working, it is not primary for an examination of the public influence of the work represented by the text in that manuscript. For that purpose, the primary record is made up of copies of the published edition. Similarly, to understand a particular critic's response, one must have access to the edition, and preferably the specific copy of it, used by the critic. F.O. Matthiessen's famous mistake in discussing Melville's *White-Jacket* illustrates the point. He wrote about the phrase "soiled fish of the sea" rather than "coiled fish of the sea,"[4] because he was using the Constable edition of 1922 rather than the original English and American editions of 1850.[5] The Constable edition in its original 1922 printing—not in the 1963 Russell & Russell reprint, which did not exist when Matthiessen wrote—is therefore a primary record for the purpose of studying Matthiessen's work, though it is not primary for understanding Melville's intention. Because the latter is what Matthiessen was interested in, it is fair to say that his failure to look behind the Constable edition was a mistake.

If his purpose had instead been to investigate the reception of Melville's work in the 1920s, not only the Constable edition but also the other Melville editions available in the 1920s would have been primary records for him. But later reprintings or photocopies of those editions would not have offered primary evidence of what readers in the 1920s had in front of them, because all reproductions are new documents with their own distinctive characteristics. Although the features of any document are subject to alteration over the years, a document surviving from the moment one is concerned with nevertheless provides evidenceunobtainable elsewhere for understanding that moment. Therefore, every textual artifact, however it may be classed in terms of "originals" or "reproductions," is potentially worthy of future study as a primary record. Even a private xerographic copy can be a primary record if a person who used it becomes a subject of historical inquiry—or, of course, if one's topic is the history of reproductions.

The definition of "primary record" adopted here is obviously not the only one possible. But, because the distinction between intangible works and physical texts is logically essential, limiting "record" to only one of them is conducive to rigorous discussion. If we agree to use "primary record" to mean *a physical object produced or used at the past moment that is the subject of one's inquiry*, we can further say that there must always be an interest in primary records, simply because no derived record can automatically be assumed to be trustworthy as a guide to what the original contains. Financial records, for example, will continue to be produced, in some form, as a by-product of a company's activity. Settling disputes over billing will require, in the future as in the past, recourse to those original documents, regardless of their form. In the same way, a questioned word or note in a verbal or musical text necessitates research into the most authoritative document available, because anything short of that (whether newly keyboarded or photographically reproduced) may be misleading, through human error or mechanical flaw. Obviously, primary documents may be untrustworthy as a record of what was intended, but they are the final authority for the texts that are actually present in them.

Of course, not everyone is, or needs to be, interested in historical accuracy. If one wishes to approach a text as a given arrangement of elements existing in the present, not as a link with a past time, one need not be concerned with distinguishing originals from reproductions (despite the fact that, paradoxically, the acceptance of the text of any document links one with the past moment when that document was produced). There is no need, however, to claim that everyone has or will have (or should have) an interest in primary records to make the point that such an interest must always exist, for some people will always have to turn to primary records, either because their temperament leads them to the study of the past or because their business requires them to locate the best evidence for a past

occurrence. There are other reasons, to be taken up below, for the importance of primary records. But the fact that they are "primary"—direct witnesses to the past and, thus, the ultimate sources against which the accuracy of any reproductions must be assessed—is enough reason for the permanent usefulness of all the records already produced and all those yet to be created.

FUTURE FORMS OF PRIMARY RECORDS

Speculations about the future, in any field, may be knowledgeable and shrewd, or ignorant and foolish, but they remain speculations nonetheless. Sometimes people engage in them through a desire to influence what happens and sometimes through disinterested intellectual curiosity. On the subject of records, the discussions in recent years have focused on an electronic future, with some discussions being eagerly receptive and others fearful or wary. Debates about whether printed books will, or should, continue to be produced have aroused strong feelings, on one side or the other, among large segments of the general public. This sort of controversy is natural enough at a time of significant change, and there is no doubt that the last part of the twentieth century and the early part of the twenty-first constitute such a time, with a proliferation of technological developments in the electronic manipulation and storage of texts. But these debates really have no relevance to the present topic.

Primary records, as defined here, will continue to be produced in some form and will continue to be important, regardless of their form. A concern with the future of primary records is not tied to any particular form but to whatever forms primary records take—the forms they have taken in the past and the forms they will take in the future. They have always taken multiple forms, and presumably they always will take a multiplicity of forms, though the dominant forms shift over time. Electronic forms are at the beginning of their ascendancy now, just as letterpress forms were (at least for some purposes) five centuries ago. Some people seem to believe that anyone arguing for the preservation of physical records from the past must be opposed to computers; and while of course some arguments may be motivated by a fear of change, the serious arguments for the retention of primary records imply no attitude, one way or the other, about the relative desirability of electronic forms. The electronic handling of texts offers so many advantages that it is hard to see why anyone would not welcome it. Be that as it may, one's welcoming it or not welcoming it has nothing to do with recognizing the importance of all primary records and understanding that the preservation of individual surviving electronic forms of texts will be just as imperative in the future as the preservation of handwritten and printed forms is at present.

Not only is the future form of new texts a matter of current discussion, so is the question of whether old texts should be repackaged in new forms. An awareness of the significance of primary records is not incompatible with a desire to see old texts converted to forms that make them amenable to the advantages of electronic access and searching. What it means, however, is a recognition that any converted form can never stand as a full substitute for the original record from which it derives. There is no reason not to use such a secondary record for convenience, so long as one understands its limitations as a source of documentary evidence; but to think, as some people do, that a converted form can replace the original is to disregard the role of primary evidence in pursuing the past. This issue is not new, for it has existed as long as people have been copying visible texts from one surface to another; but the electronic revolution is so pervasive at present that it sometimes seems to have produced the issue.

A useful illustration is the current conversion of many library card catalogs to electronic form, followed by the disposal of the cards. Some of the questions raised by these activities were brought to a large audience by the novelist Nicholson Baker's long, well-written, forceful article in *The New Yorker* of 4 April 1994.[6] Baker's defense of the card catalog was occasionally sentimental, but it enumerated some legitimate reasons for dissatisfaction with the conversions that have been taking place, notably the errors that result in even the best conversions and the fact that budgeting constraints have caused some library administrators, even in major research libraries, to ask for something less than the most sophisticated conversions available. It is hard to imagine, however, that these questions would have been the focus of a major article in a mass-circulation magazine if the computer had not been involved—if, that is, the problem had not been symbolic of the computer's many intrusions into familiar ways of doing things. (That the article touched a nerve is shown by the amount of discussion it engendered (e.g., see Barker,[7] Carpenter,[8] Douglas,[9] and Max[10]).) Yet, the real subject was not computerization but rather the relation of primary and secondary records. Although Baker chose not to say so, computerization was only the immediate occasion for taking up an old issue—old even in relation to library catalogs.

Retrospective conversions of card catalogs were, after all, undertaken in precomputer days as well. The National Union Catalog, for example, was once a card catalog in the Library of Congress, made up of copies of cards contributed by libraries throughout the United States and Canada. The process of turning it photographically into a book-form catalog, published as *National Union Catalog: Pre-1956 Imprints* between 1968 and 1981, involved hundreds of thousands of editorial judgments, such as deciding which cards could be eliminated (as duplicative) and replaced by library symbols added to other cards.[11,12]

Inevitably, errors were made, but there is now no way to check entries in the published catalog against the cards. One may not normally think of a union card catalog as a primary record, because the cards are not the books themselves, and even the cards are derived from the cards in other catalogs. But as a reference tool, as a particular grouping of references, the cards once housed in the Library of Congress were a primary record, for they constituted the original form of this tool. Any edited version of it is a derivative form, which despite its advantages still rests on the original for its authority. No computers were involved, but this conversion raised the same questions that Baker's article implicitly (if not explicitly) raised.

Another large card catalog, that of the New York Public Library, and the card catalogs of many special collections or specialized libraries have been similarly converted by photography into book-form catalogs. In these instances, the original catalogs have not uniformly been discarded, but the common tendency to think of the published catalogs as fully adequate replacements ignores the potentiality for defects in any reproduction. Publishing card catalogs in book form serves to reinforce the fact that the texts of such catalogs constitute reference works and that their reproduction, by whatever means, is analogous to the reproduction of other reference books, or other books of any kind. The conversion of card catalogs (whether by photography or by rekeyboarding) deserves no more, and no less, publicity than all other conversions of recorded texts. There is no reason to object to the conversions, if they are responsibly carried out at the highest level that current technology can offer. Indeed, it would be foolish not to take advantage of the benefits of new technology. But one can legitimately complain if the converted or reproduced form is thought to supplant the original and if the original is therefore not retained. (The fact that many libraries have an "official" and a shelf-list card catalog as well as a public one does not affect this point, for each of those catalogs is a separate record, and whichever one is used as the basis for a reproduction is the primary record for that purpose.) The future forms of primary records will be whatever they turn out to be; but, even though we may find an interim usefulness in converting many old texts to the new forms, those forms have no bearing on primary records of the past, the forms of which are historical facts.

USES OF PRIMARY RECORDS FROM THE PAST

There are many reasons for the retention of primary records as defined here, despite the usefulness that derived forms undeniably have for some purposes. It would not matter, however, whether there were any reasons other than the one already given: that primary records—the original physical objects—constitute the authority for judging every kind of copy. Occasions for questioning reproductions (in whatever form) occur continually. If the primary records from which the reproductions derive do not exist, those questions can only be speculated about, and any conclusions then drawn from the reproductions do not rest on as firm a foundation as if they had been based on the original artifacts. Whenever one settles for something other than the original (or has no choice but to do so), one is deprived, quite simply, of the best evidence.[13]

There are other reasons to use the originals, for they always contain unreproducible evidence. Every means of reproduction has its own characteristics, its own advantages and disadvantages; but whatever they are, they always leave some details unaccounted for and add new characteristics of their own. Electronic texts that have been freshly keyboarded, for example, have the advantage of being easily searchable for any given word or phrase; but they do not allow one—as photographed texts do—to see the typography (or handwriting) and lineation of the original. For this reason, electronic renderings of texts from the past, if they are to serve their readers well, should always be made up of a combination of keyboarded texts and scanned ("bitmap") images. But, even if texts reproduced in these ways were accurate as far as they can be (such accuracy to be determined, of course, by reference to the originals), there would still be important evidence that remains unaccessible, because reproductions do not give readers access, for instance, to the original paper, ink, and binding. "Accuracy" is clearly a relative matter, dependent on the details one is focusing on in a given instance. The common misconception that verbal texts can easily be extracted from their physical embodiments leads frequently to calling a reproduction "accurate" if the words and marks of punctuation are accurate. In addition, when the original typography or handwriting is reproduced, many people do not understand how the original is being misrepresented. Yet the fact that physical texts are our primary way of getting at intangible works means that the shape, feel, and structure of the objects conveying those texts—all the characteristics of the objects, in other words—constitute relevant evidence for assessing the texts and reconstructing the works (or, put more simply, for reading).

The physical evidence in books (or any other artifacts, for that matter) can be studied for two kinds of information: the light it sheds on how the objects were conceived and produced, and the insight it offers on how the objects have been responded to and treated since the time they left their producers' hands. Those who concentrate on the first of these in respect to printed books are often called analytical bibliographers.[14,15] Although the field of analytical bibliography was developed in connection with the study of fifteenth-, sixteenth-, and seventeenth-century books, especially the textual investigation of the plays of Shakespeare and his contemporaries, this kind of work has by now uncovered significant details about the manufacture of books of all periods. It has been particularly

associated with literary study, for analytical bibliographers have repeatedly demonstrated the way in which a detailed knowledge of the production history of a book is crucial for establishing the evolution and authority of the text printed in it.[16–20]

The amount of such analysis that can be undertaken with rekeyboardings or reproductions is extremely limited. One might at first think, for example, that the analysis of variant spelling and punctuation, which is useful in the attempt to distinguish portions of a text set by different typesetters, could be pursued with rekeyboarded texts (assuming their accuracy). But knowledge of the lineation of the original is essential for this purpose, because the spacing within a line and the position of the spelling or punctuation at issue are relevant to the interpretation of a typesetter's behavior. Photographic, xerographic, or electronic images of the originals are therefore necessary; but they, in turn, are insufficient for other kinds of typographical analysis. The identification of broken types, for instance, is a standard technique for working out the order in which pages were set and printed.[21] But such identification requires that one distinguish (often with the help of magnification) the traces of the typeface impression within the total ink smear, which can be affected by many factors; and reproductions never preserve this evidence. As Adrian Weiss, who has studied this matter intensively, said, "the nature of the typographical evidence present in reproductions renders them highly untrustworthy for absolute identifications, even in regard to those damaged types which seem obvious in a reproduction."[22]

If the failure of reproductions in this respect is surprising to some people, no one is startled by the fact that reproductions are useless for the analysis of paper, or of the way the type bites into the paper, or of the structure of the folded sheets in a book. Yet, such analysis reveals information important for printing history, literary history, and textual study. Identification of paper (through the study of its watermarks and chainlines or, if those features are lacking, as they are in many papers of the last two centuries, its texture, weight, and color) can be of assistance in dating a book, as in the celebrated instance of the *Missale speciale*.[23] It also helps one to detect cancel leaves or, more likely in later books, whole cancel gatherings (that is, leaves or gatherings inserted to replace others that had been removed). The indentations made in paper by the bite of the type can reveal the order in which the two sides of a sheet were printed, because the one printed second will be smoother.[21,24] And, the way in which the sheets were folded and sewn together can be established only by examining the paper and sewing, for the printed signatures that mark the early leaves of gatherings (in most books before 1900 and many afterward)—and that can thus be expected to show up in reproductions—cannot be relied on for this purpose. Signatures may accurately indicate the number of leaves in gatherings (as they usually do in the hand-press period), but they do not show whether the gatherings consist of folded single sheets, multiple sheets, or half sheets. It is not uncommon in nineteenth-century books for signatures to be unrelated to the actual gatherings.[25,26] These pieces of information, and others like them, retrievable through bibliographical analysis, are obviously relevant to printing history and, through their contribution to the story of how particular texts were made publicly available, to literary history. Their broader relevance to the concerns of readers comes through their role in textual criticism and scholarly editing. Knowing how a text was handled by the persons who printed and published it helps one to assess the relative responsibility of author, publisher's editor, typesetter, proofreader, and so on, for specific words or features of the text.

Furthermore, reproductions normally represent single copies; but there is no limit to the number of copies that are useful for textual collation and physical analysis. Differences among copies of the same editions exist in books of all periods, as a result of stop-press alterations, damage to type or plates during printing, changes or handling between printings, duplicate settings, cancellations and replacements of leaves or gatherings, and—in the era of edition binding—variations in the design and wording on bindings. Thus, no matter how many copies one has looked at, there is always the possibility that the examination of additional copies will disclose further variants. Although Charlton Hinman inspected in detail about two-thirds of the Folger Library's 80 copies of the Shakespeare First Folio,[17] new variants are still being found in other copies.[27] David L. Vander Meulen has learned new facts about the text of Pope's *Dunciad* in an ongoing investigation that by 1988 had encompassed some 800 copies of the early editions.[28] No period or kind of publication is exempt: there are significant differences, for example, among the so-called "editions" of nineteenth- and twentieth-century newspapers. And, the bibliographers of the famous Tauchnitz series of paperbacks (1841–1955), after examining a total of 56,000 copies and discovering thousands of previously undetected impressions and issues, can still say that, as additional copies are looked at, one in 60 is likely to be an unrecorded impression and one in 20 an unrecorded issue.[29] The ease with which electronic texts can be altered (both intentionally and inadvertently) is already a matter of concern to some readers seeking the primary records of writings that were originally transmitted in digital form. It is misleading, however, to contrast this instability with what one writer on the subject calls "the fixity of text in the print world",[30] for variations exist in printed editions of all periods. There is no means of textual transmission that is exempt from the possibility of alteration, and printing technologies have been a sophisticated step in the progressive development of easier ways to produce textual changes.

All of these uses of physical evidence for learning about the production history of printed books seem obvious enough, once they are pointed out, but most readers are not likely to be familiar with them. These approaches have been primarily employed by textual scholars, after all, and their impact on readers occurs through the effect they ultimately have on the texts of new editions. In contrast, the other large category of information dependent on physical evidence, the postproduction history of books, requires less explanation, for all readers are aware, from personal experience, that the reading of books is affected by their design, by the contexts into which verbal texts are placed. Although typographical arrangement can be seen in reproductions, its scale and placement on the page are not always evident, and the quality of the paper, the relation of ink and paper color, and the characteristics of the binding, endpapers, and jacket are of course not accessible in reproductions. Some authors have taken considerable pains with such matters, as Congreve did when preparing the three-volume octavo edition of his *Works* in 1710.[31] Whether the author or the publisher was responsible for format and layout, and whether or not one wishes to regard those features as part of the verbal work, they were often deliberately chosen to produce certain responses in readers, and they always produce responses, even if not necessarily the intended ones. The totality of a book's design constitutes a cultural message and is part of what the book offers for reading. D.F. McKenzie effectively demonstrated this point at the beginning of his centenary lecture to the Bibliographical Society, when he explored the meanings conveyed by the paper, format, and bulk of a blank book:[32] "every book," he observed, "tells a story quite apart from that recounted by its text." Historians are now charting, more intently than ever before, the role of book design in various times and places. The history of reading has become one of the most studied aspects of the history of books.[20] Scholars are not the only people who need access to artifactual evidence. Because the look and feel of books affect reading, all who wish to experience texts with as much historical understanding as possible require the objects that survive from particular past times.

These points are clearly valid for all varieties of printed matter, not just those with texts that can be classified as belles lettres; and they are applicable as well to all manuscript material. Scrutiny of the inks and papers in a manuscript is essential for drawing inferences about its production history—for working out stages of revision, for example, or simply determining which ink marks show through from the other side of the paper. And, whether the text consists of prose or of the entries in a business account, its physical setting plays just as important a role in understanding it as physical evidence does in the case of printed matter. The experience of reading an electronic text is also inevitably affected by its physical presentation.[33,34] The information conveyed by the physical object as a whole is what Ruth Perry called "embodied knowledge." In her eloquent statement at the Houghton

Library 50th anniversary symposium,[35] she said, "the object itself is part of the material culture of its own time, and carries with it something of the social context that produced it." For those interested in the past, there will always be uses for primary records, because their "content," their "meaning," can never be fully transferred to any other objects.

SURVIVAL AND ACCESSIBILITY OF PRIMARY RECORDS

Whether the primary records that now exist will survive and be available to serve these purposes in the future depends in part on the materials out of which they are made, in part on the unalterable vicissitudes they encounter, and in part (the largest part, in fact) on the attitudes people hold about them. Some of the destructive events that befall artifacts, whether caused by natural forces or human actions, are of course unpredictable or, in practical terms, unavoidable, but not all are inevitable, for human attitudes can often prevent them or alleviate their effects. Pre-nineteenth-century items are likely to be relatively safe, because the paper used in them is high in rag content and because they are widely perceived to be valuable in monetary terms. The voluminous stock of nineteenth- and twentieth-century materials, on the other hand, is certainly at risk, because many contain highly acidic wood-pulp paper that becomes brittle and because the vast majority are regarded as having insignificant market value. When these facts are combined with a belief that verbal content and physical form are distinct, the items considered important enough to be microfilmed or otherwise (as in electronic form) reproduced are in danger of being discarded afterward. And what is considered important or unimportant at one moment, it should be added, may not be so regarded at another.[36–38]

Considerable attention has fortunately been paid to the problem of books with brittle paper, and the pages of a great many books have been microfilmed as part of individual library programs or of the massive cooperative effort overseen by the Commission on Preservation and Access. As a general rule, there has been no concern with what happens to the artifacts after microfilming. In practice, most libraries have not kept them, regardless of the state of their deterioration or their mutilation by the microfilming process, and they have regularly been destroyed. Sometimes the point is made that items of "artifactual value" will be kept, as if it were logically possible for artifactual value (the value inherent in an artifact) not to be present in some artifacts.[39] Although no known treatment can return brittle paper to its original condition, there are deacidification processes (likely to become less expensive in the future) that can retard or stop the deterioration,[40] and whatever can be salvaged will be useful to future readers. Commonly, however, the existence of a microfilm or electronic copy of the text in a deteriorating book causes many people to believe that the artifact from which the copy was made is disposable. Although some pieces may be doomed to eventual destruction in any case, this notion serves to hasten their disappearance.

The question of the stability of the objects carrying texts has most frequently been discussed in relation to books containing acidic paper, but one must remember that other vehicles for textual transmission have limited life spans as well. As the *Scientific American* noted,[41] electronic documents are "far more fragile than paper." "The contents of most digital media," as stated in the article, "evaporate long before words written on high-quality paper." The text on a magnetic disk, for instance, can be completely erased by oxidation or stray magnetic fields. As more and more writings are initially produced in electronic form, the future problem of preserving primary records will be even more acute than the present one. (This problem is in addition to the difficulty of access resulting from the obsolescence of software and hardware).

Of course, the urge to make reproductions is not limited to instances in which physical deterioration of originals has been recognized. Texts of all periods are often reproduced, to save wear on the originals and to make the texts more accessible, even if the objects carrying them are not in danger of disintegrating or becoming otherwise unusable. When the reproductions take up less space than the originals, librarians sometimes prefer the reproductions and deaccession the originals. This practice may well increase, as the inventory of texts available in electronic form becomes ever larger. Certainly some library administrators have already predicted that book stack space can be diminished in the future. Although the books thus removed from stacks are not necessarily destroyed, they may wind up in less accessible locations. The accessibility of artifacts, not simply their survival, is of vital importance for the study of the past. When one understands the inseparability of texts and their transmitters, one sees that the phrase "preservation and access," often stated as the dual aim of textual reproduction, applies equally as the goal of a concern for textual artifacts. The uses of physical evidence, described above, imply, as far as printed books are concerned, the significance of multiple copies. A multiplicity of copies makes possible, even likely, a widespread distribution of copies. Whether one is looking at physical details as evidence of printing and textual history (in which case, every copy is a potential source of new information) or as an indication of a book's cultural milieu, access to copies is essential for the fullest kind of reading, where a physical text and its physical setting are read together. If the existence of electronic reproductions of old texts causes books to be moved from community and academic library stacks to less accessible (and perhaps noninstitutional) locations, the opportunities for this kind of reading are lessened. The idea that reproduced texts are replacements for the originals can thus affect not only the survival of artifacts but also the availability of those that survive.

Some of these points are well illustrated by recent events at the Kansas City Public Library, where the decision was made to dispose of the Rare Book Collection. This is not the place to debate whether the action was appropriate but only to note the reasoning that was considered adequate to justify it. The director of the library said that "it is the preservation of the ideas and information contained in the book, rather than the book itself, which the library preserves and makes available to the community."[42] This statement shows no awareness of the connections between text and artifact, or of the consequent usefulness of physical evidence to all readers, whether scholars or not. Indeed, the notion that so-called "rare books" are assembled only for scholars provides another of the arguments given for the deaccessioning: the director states that the "role of the public library is educational but not academic" and that its function is not the support of scholarly research. It is no doubt the case that most readers have not thought about the importance of artifacts in the reading process, but one can argue that a community library might appropriately undertake to educate them in this regard. Public libraries play an important role in bringing historical embodiments of texts, and the sense of the past they impart, to a wide readership. Still another argument for the decision is that the library has no climate-controlled storage space, as if "rare books" and books in the general stacks were somehow different in kind (if not in their physical makeup) and that the necessity for properly housing "rare books" does not extend to other books (any of which may be considered "rare" from a different viewpoint). If the flexibility of the line between "rare" and "nonrare" had been recognized, the additional argument that the Kansas City rare book collection had no focus might well have seemed irrelevant, because its "focus" would not then have been judged separately from that of the whole collection of the library. (It can be argued, as I have, that a library's entire book stack should be regarded as a "special collection" and treated as such.[35,43]) The director of the Kansas City Public Library should not be singled out here for special comment: his remarks could have been made by many other librarians. But for that reason, the remarks usefully point out a common misconception.

Its ubiquity is revealed by its presence in a great deal of the writing and speaking on the future of libraries. There has been no shortage of conferences, reports, and special issues of periodicals exploring the impact of digital technology on humanistic scholarship. In all of this commentary, there is scarcely any recognition of the role of artifactual evidence in reading, while many statements imply the replaceability of originals. For example, at the April 1990 meeting of the American Council of Learned Societies, which addressed the topic "Scholars and Research Libraries in the 21st Century," considerable emphasis was given to the idea that "access" will replace "ownership" as a goal of libraries—electronic access to texts, that is, in contrast to ownership of the objects that originally transmitted them. One speaker,[44] welcoming the new ways to "repackage" verbal works, saw the old system in terms of inefficient duplication ("multimillion volume collections...housed in massive buildings duplicated across the country at enormous expense"), overlooking the importance of multiple collections of artifacts for providing widespread access to physical evidence and to the historical insights that such evidence allows.

Two and a half years later, the Mellon Foundation's report, *University Libraries and Scholarly Communication*,[45] also made much of the opposition between ownership and access. It stated, in its third paragraph, that we have lived "with a world in which the technology of publication meant that access *required* ownership," but new technologies, it was stated, "allow the possibility of uncoupling ownership from access, the material object from its intellectual content." These comments led the authors to the question, "What is the viability of the traditional model of the library as a single-site comprehensive collection of printed materials?" Neither this question nor the more detailed discussion later in the report adequately recognizes that the concept of primary evidence is an essential ingredient of any useful response to the question. Indeed, the idea of "uncoupling...the material object from its intellectual content" logically involves rejection of the distinction between primary and derived documents. Even whenthe report turns to a future in which "the primary artifact is itself electronic," it does not pursue the implications introduced by the word "primary." It alludes, for instance, to changes that such artifacts will produce "in the relationship between interpretive works and the underlying data or primary texts on which they are based," as if that relationship could ever be different, regardless of the original form of the "primary texts."

The point is also made that "print products" will still have an "important role" to play in a world of electronic publishing. No note is taken of the fact that such products, when they are printouts of electronic texts, will be derived documents. What is ultimately missing from the discussion is an awareness of the immutable gap between intangible works and the tangible means of their transmission. The phrase "dematerialization of information" is used as a description of what the new technology is achieving. Actually, it describes what the process of reading has always accomplished, as readers extract works, or "information," from the physical details before them. Electronic documents offer a new set of physical details, but physical, nevertheless, and readers will still be in the position they have always been in. What is most basic for them, if they are historically minded, is not what the physical form happens to be but whether a given document is primary or derived.

The same misconceptions reappear continually in other reports. In the summary of the proceedings of the 1992 Irvine conference on "Technology, Scholarship, and the Humanities,"[46] for example, there are repeated references to an envisioned "national electronic library" or "digital library" of millions of volumes as a national priority, without any suggestion that having those volumes in this form (though unquestionably helpful) would not eliminate the need for reading them in their original forms. Indeed, the frequent linking of this project with "preservation" might seem to imply the opposite. The published report of the 1993 Bellagio conference on "Preserving the Intellectual Heritage," sponsored by the Commission on Preservation and Access,[47] also failed to address the question of primary evidence, even suggesting that the reason for scholars' resistance to microfilm is the "incredible force of custom and tradition." This report briefly noted that "some scholars make strong arguments for the conservation of the actual publication, the object itself." In response, it only suggests conserving samples or the "one best remaining copy" of "particularly important" works—an idea that shows no awareness of the nature of bibliographical evidence or of the need for broad access to it. (In the formal resolution that emerged from the conference, access to reproductions is not distinguished from access to originals for instance, the phrase "to promote more effective means of storage, conservation and preservation, to insure access in the future," in a context in which "preservation" refers to transferring texts to new physical objects).

Similarly, the Spring 1993 number of *Representations*, devoted to the subject "Future Libraries,"[48] contained no discussion of the future use of old books as primary evidence. Even Geoffrey Nunberg's thoughtful article on "The Places of Books in the Age of Electronic Reproduction" ignored this topic, though it includes a good description of the role of physical details in reading and briefly recognizes the distinction between texts that originally appeared in printed form and those that were initially disseminated in electronic form. Roger Chartier's contribution, "Libraries without Walls," asserted that, in the electronic age, "texts are no longer prisoners of their original physical material existence." But there was no indication of why such liberated texts are inappropriate for many purposes, despite Chartier's clear understanding, expressed in the next paragraph (and in many of his other distinguished writings), that a text "is no longer truly the same" when it is moved from codex to monitor screen, because the new "mechanisms" of transmission "modify the conditions of its reception and its comprehension." In the 1994 Cornell symposium on "Digital Imaging Technology for Preservation," sponsored by the Research Libraries Group, M. Stuart Lynn neglected artifactual evidence in his vision of the future in which "we convert back

and forth between the use of digital technologies for storage and transmission and analog technologies for human presentation and interaction."[49] What he called "paper facsimiles," produced from digital images of printed pages, can be, in his view, "reshelved for traditional forms of access," though the essence of the traditional process is not using paper but locating primary evidence.

Whatever else these various publications, and others like them, have accomplished (they contain much thoughtful comment), they do not build their arguments on a firm understanding (or at least an explicit acknowledgment) of the way historical study employs artifacts. Unfortunately, the level of sophistication in thinking about the physical book is frequently no higher among participants in conferences on the electronic future (many of whom think of themselves as "information specialists") than it is among the general public, or advertisers. The publisher Chadwyck-Healey's advertising brochure for its CD-ROM entitled *The English Poetry Full-Text Database* (1994) stated that "the texts are more accessible than any printed source and yet take up no shelf-space. There are no problems of conservation and security of rare volumes and no significant cataloging costs." There is obviously a built-in contradiction here. Why should "rare volumes" require "conservation and security" if the texts that are now made "more accessible" are the equals of the texts in those volumes? Despite the illogic of the statement, it will be persuasive to many people and thus reflects the popular perception of the situation.

One cannot entirely blame the public for this view, however, when the statements of prominent library administrators are similarly deficient. On 13 October 1994, the Librarian of Congress, James H. Billington, held a press conference to announce three donations, totaling $13 million, for the first phase of the creation of a National Digital Library. In his remarks, he spoke of making, through this project, a "mother lode" of "original" materials "accessible to people across America." He also predicted that the "user-friendly book will not disappear." By neglecting to say anything about the differences between originals and reproductions and by implying that the choice among presentations of texts is only a matter of personal preference, he was missing a significant opportunity for educating the public in the concept of primary evidence.[50,51] An earlier occasion on which Library of Congress officials spoke on this topic was the 10 March 1989 meeting of the Library's Council of Scholars. Although at that gathering Stephen R. Ostrow argued for a "collection-based institution" and made the distinction between primary and derivative documents, he was paired on the program with Robert Zich, who saw the interest in books as simply the "worship of original formats," which he designated as "idolatry" and "fanaticism."[52]

Zich is not alone in his view. For example, Michael Lesk took essentially the same position in his 1997 book *Practical Digital Libraries*.[53] As an administrator of the

Digital Library Initiative, he believed that libraries should, in general, replace books made of printed paper with electronic versions of the texts in them. The motivation for reproducing large quantities of texts is no longer simply to salvage them from objects thought to be disintegrating. Now, as Lesk and others see it, even the texts of books that are not deteriorating should be converted, because their electronic forms are searchable and take up (if on CD-ROMs) only a fraction of the space occupied by bound volumes or (if on the Internet) no space at all. This thinking lies behind several large projects, such as the Mellon Foundation's JSTOR, an Internet database of scholarly journals.[54] The searchable database that underlies the images unquestionably makes access to journal articles easier. But the idea that it also saves space (accepted by many of the subscribing libraries) ignores the fact that it cannot possibly render the originals unnecessary.

Just as Stanley Katz could observe at the 1992 Irvine conference[46] that adequate funding for the humanities and the arts will not come until "the public understands that it is in its interest to invest much more heavily" in them, so one can say that effective support for the retention of textual artifacts, and not just the texts, depends on a broad-based awareness of the fundamental role that such artifacts play in reading. The number of voices thus far raised to make this point is small compared to those championing reproductions. There is no reason, of course, for these two opinions to be thought of as opposed, or for those expressing them to think that both cannot be simultaneously embraced. An appreciation of the benefits conferred by reproductions—enormous benefits in the case of electronic texts—is not incompatible with an understanding of their limitations and of the irreplaceability of the originals.

Those who have spoken in defense of artifacts have usually expressed this comprehensive view. For some examples, one could turn to the published remarks of several speakers (Barker, Gundersheimer, McKitterick, Mason, Perry, and Tanselle) at the September 1992 Houghton Library symposium, a rare instance of a conference that repeatedly recognized the value of artifactual evidence.[35] (An earlier Harvard Library publication that recognized the importance of originals was the special issue of the *Harvard Library Bulletin* on "Preserving Harvard's Retrospective Collections."[55]) Another public occasion that included a particularly trenchant statement of the same kind was the October 1993 annual meeting of the Association for Documentary Editing, where Elizabeth Hall Witherell devoted her presidential address to this topic.[56] "I see," she said, "that the raw material that I need and that future editors and historians will need is in jeopardy"; the "threat is that, having been microfilmed, or digitized, or microfilmed and then digitized, the originals will be discarded with some relief by those making very hard decisions about allocating money and space."

Her main point is concisely and effectively phrased: "We cannot rely exclusively on copies, though we may begin our work with them, because they do not tell the whole story that we need to know."

One of the most powerfully expressed statements on the place of artifacts in reading was offered by D.F. McKenzie at the conclusion of a conference on "Scholarship and Technology in the Humanities" at Elvetham Hall, Hampshire, in May 1990.[57] Because books "encode the history of their production," he said, "It follows that to abstract a conceptual or verbal information content from them by representing them in another medium is to contradict the very assumption that the artefact is the product of a distinctive complex of materials, labour and mentality." To reproduce texts is "an impoverishment, a theft of evidence, a denial of more exact and immediate visual and tactile ways of knowing, a destruction of their quiddity as collaborative products under the varying historical conditions of their successive realizations." It is ironic, but not unexpected (given the usual approach to such matters), that the official "Resolutions" adopted by the conference (and printed only 10 pages after these sentences of McKenzie's) include the following: "Encouragement should be given to the conversion of printed texts to machine-readable formats and to the improved electronic transmission of such texts." (The only reference to conservation in the "Resolutions" failed to distinguish the use of originals from the use of reproductions: "In view of the rapid deterioration of printed materials, there should be national and international efforts towards their conservation and their reproduction in alternative forms.")

In recent years, there has been a growing interest in the artifactual evidence in printed books on the part of literary and cultural historians and those in the flourishing field of *histoire du livre*.[20] This interest has been reflected in the activities of the Modern Language Association of America (MLA). In June 1992, the executive director of that association, Phyllis Franklin, speaking at the American Library Association convention, reported on a survey she had taken of the views of scholars in the humanities.[58] Although, she said, they "respect the access photocopies and microfilms of the written and print records allow" and "welcome electronic databases of all kinds," looking forward to "the creation of electronic texts of publications that appeared originally in print," the majority also "argue that our society should maintain as complete a record of print as possible because such a record will continue to be essential to scholars who wish to study the print era." They felt that "saving a few copies of a book" is not sufficient. The following February, the MLA Council established an Ad Hoc Committee on the Future of the Print Record, consisting of eight scholars and librarians (Shelley Fisher Fishkin, Everette E. Larson, Philip Lewis, J. Hillis Miller, Ruth Perry, Alice Schreyer, Philip Stewart, and G. Thomas Tanselle, chair). Despite its name, the committee's purview was understood as textual artifacts of all kinds, not just printed ones. Its charge was to prepare an official MLA statement on the subject, to assist in disseminating it, and to engage in any related activities that would help to create public awareness of the issues. At the MLA's December 1994 convention in San Diego, the committee held three sessions, where, in addition to general discussion, 16 scholars and teachers reported instances in which primary records were crucial to their work.[59] The committee's statement explained the importance of retaining artifacts after the texts in them have been reproduced and also urged the establishment of standards for the creation and identification of reproductions.[60] Unfortunately, the effect of this statement was somewhat blunted by the appearance, four years later, of another MLA-endorsed statement, *Preserving Research Collections* by Jutta Reed-Scott,[61] which takes a step backward. It focuses on access through reproduction and does not recognize the value of physical details, except for items "that have scholarly value as artifacts," apparently unaware of the logical absurdity of that often-used phrase.

Another organization that was preparing a draft statement at the same time as the MLA is the American Institute for Conservation of Historic and Artistic Works (AIC). Its Library Collections Conservation Discussion Group (chaired by Maria Grandinette and Randy Silverman) wished to make more widely known the research value of publishers' bindings and the consequent importance of preserving them, using simple protective procedures or nondamaging conservation techniques.[62] (A survey of attitudes toward rebinding books, including those from the period before publishers' bindings, was offered in the spring of 1995 by Michèle Valerie Cloonan. She noted, "The current approach to conservation is to save as much of the original as possible in a rebind."[63]) Support for the preservation of artifacts has also come from a surprising source, BookLab, Inc., a firm that produces paper replacement copies of deteriorated books. In a series of pamphlets, this firm has promoted the idea that the originals should be regarded as "leaf masters" and retained as the sources for future reproductions.[64,65] Although the importance of access to physical evidence in reading is not sufficiently appreciated here, there is, nevertheless, a recognition that reproductions can be misleading and impermanent and that "a continuing role for originals"[64] exists, along with a corresponding need for facilities in which to house them. This concern with housing reminds one of a somewhat similar proposal, from the world of scholarly bibliography, for depositories in which books can be placed after microfilming or digitization.[66] The motivation of bibliographers is not the same as BookLab's, but both approaches share a disapproval of the widespread practice of discarding originals after reproduction.

Still another encouraging sign was the establishment in June 2000 of a Center for the Cultural Record at the Graduate School of Library and Information Science at the University of Texas at Austin. Its aim is to bring together, for mutual reinforcement, instruction in the fields of archives and records management, preservation and conservation, and museum studies. In the words of one of its initial statements, the center reflects a "growing convergence of interests" among these fields, which have "common foci" in that they are concerned with "managing the source original in a digital environment."[67] The act of treating verbal documents and museum objects under the same rubric is significant for its recognition of the essential role of artifacts in all approaches to the human cultural heritage, and one hopes that this action and its implications will be widely noticed.

Thus there have been some events to be applauded, but the primary credit for acquainting a broad public with the importance, and endangered position, of verbal artifacts belongs to Nicholson Baker. Following his card catalog article, he wrote, for *The New Yorker*, an exposé of the extensive book-discarding activity of the San Francisco Public Library, about which he had already raised public concern in San Francisco.[68] Then, in the summer of 2000, he published in *The New Yorker* an eloquent essay about the British Library's decision to dispose of a large part of its great collection of non-British newspapers.[69] Because most of the large American collections of American newspapers had already been decimated (on the grounds that space is scarce and that microfilms are an adequate substitute), many of the British Library runs of major American papers were the best surviving ones (and in some cases, probably unique). Baker's thoroughly informed piece made clear the tragedy of the British Library's action. And Baker announced that, in order to save at least some of the papers, he was using his own savings and raising additional money to establish a nonprofit American Newspaper Repository. His essay aroused a great deal of attention,[70,71] both favorable—such as H. R. Woudhuysen's article in the London *Times Literary Supplement*[72]—and unfavorable—such as an attempted defense of the British Library's action by its chief executive, Lynne Brindley.[73] Baker had already been working on a book dealing more broadly with the movement by libraries to replace printed matter on paper with space-saving reproductions. In the spring of 2001, he published *Double Fold: Libraries and the Assault on Paper*,[74] a remarkably researched account of the history and unfortunate consequences of library administrators' many schemes based on the misconception that reproduced texts are the equivalent of the originals. It is to be hoped that Baker's powerful and widely reviewed book will inaugurate a new period in the understanding of the nature of verbal artifacts.

Baker has, of course, focused on paper artifacts. Another task for the future is to confront the problems of identifying and preserving the originals of records that were first produced in electronic form. Fortunately, some people have made a start in thinking about this question.

There have, for example, been projects dealing with the subject at the University of Pittsburgh[75] and the University of British Columbia;[76] and the Council of Library and Information Resources established a Task Force on Archiving of Digital Information, which published a report in 1996[77] and held a conference on "Authenticity in a Digital Environment" on 24 January 2000.[78] Several of the speakers at this conference thoughtfully grappled, in a preliminary way, with the thorny issues of how to define a primary digital record and what role design features play in such documents. One tendency that must be recognized and counteracted, however, is to conflate the disparate concepts of authenticity, textual accuracy, and correctness of content. The mere fact that a text has been copied "accurately" (in terms of words and punctuation) from an original source does not make the new document (the text in a setting) authentic. Furthermore it does not signify that the wording and punctuation, and therefore the meaning, are what the author intended, to say nothing of being factually accurate. Clear thinking about digital texts, as about those on paper, demands vigilance in maintaining the distinctness of these concepts.

If other organizations and individuals endorse these positive activities and help to circulate the publications resulting from them, or undertake in their own ways to educate the public, the result will be a gradual increase in general awareness of the reasons for taking pains to protect verbal artifacts and to keep them in libraries of all kinds, community as well as academic. There will be a greater recognition that the choice between printed and electronic texts is not a question of personal preference but of primary evidence, and that the real issue is determining *which* printed text or *which* electronic text is the appropriate one for a given purpose. Obviously, some verbal artifacts, like some artifacts of every category, will be lost to the vagaries of time, chance, and human energy, and no one can realistically expect them all to survive. The realization that every one of them, however, has its role to play in the study of human culture provides a necessary grounding for thoughtful library decision making. Although the fallacious notion that texts are easily extractable from their physical embodiments is unlikely to be fully eradicated, there is the possibility of a considerably better informed public than has previously existed. Broad public understanding is a prerequisite for the demand, and in turn the funding, necessary to make preservation a goal fully compatible with conversion. Given sufficient public sensitivity to the issues, the two will be seen as complementary necessities, not competing alternatives.

The power exerted by the physical presentation of verbal texts is shown in many ways, such as the ease with which we remember page layouts as we recall certain passages of text, or the figurative use we make of specific book forms as embodiments of knowledge. Melville (in Chapter 32 of *Moby Dick*) used book formats to classify the varieties of whales, discussing the most imposing as "chapters" of the "Folio Whale" and then moving down to octavos and duodecimos (skipping quarto, because it "does not preserve the shape of the Folio volume" and hence would not be metaphorically appropriate). He later (Chapter 104) spoke of a fossilized Leviathan leaving "traces in the stereotype plates of nature," and thereby reinforced the idea of the world as a book. His frequent puncturing of pedantic commentary further suggests that there is no substitute for reading the book of nature in the original. Reading and writing are a part of life, however, and the objects that contain texts from the past are elements of our physical surroundings. At those times when it is our wish to examine the responses of other people to the world and to the writings they encountered, we must take care in locating the objects most appropriate to our purpose, for reading encompasses all aspects of the objects we choose. We learn something from the folio format (and something else from the quarto), and we learn from all the clues embedded in each set of stereotype plates (be they literal or metaphorical). Caught in a material world, we have no choice but to recognize that the most reliable evidence from the past comes to us in physical objects. The concept of primary sources cannot be separated from this fact. And the search for those sources, in whatever forms they happen to take, is a fundamental activity not only in the work of scholars, lawyers, and scientists, but also in the lives of all other thinking persons.

REFERENCES

1. Tanselle, G.T. Textual criticism and deconstruction. Stud. Bibliogr. **1990**, *43*, 1–33. Reprinted in his *Literature and Artifacts*; Bibliographical Society of the University of Virginia: Charlottesville, VA, 1998; 203–235.
2. Frieder, R. Building the future from the past: preservation at Northwestern University Library. Footnotes (Northwestern University Library Council) **1990**, *15*(3), 1–2.
3. Tanselle, G.T. *A Rationale of Textual Criticism*; University of Pennsylvania Press: Philadelphia, PA, 1989.
4. Matthiessen, F.O. *American Renaissance: Art and Expression in the Age of Emerson and Whitman*; Oxford University Press: New York, 1941; 392.
5. Nichol, J.W. Melville's "soiled" fish of the sea. Am. Lit. **1949–1950**, *21*, 338–339.
6. Baker, N. Discards. *New Yorker* April 4, **1994**, 64–70, 72–76, 78–86.
7. Barker, N. The catalogue and the card. Book Collect. **1994**, *43*, 320–350.
8. Carpenter, K.R. The great catalog-card to-do. Harv. Libr. Bull. **1994**, *n.s. 5*(1), 3–7.
9. Douglas, N.E. Debating "discards": a response to Nicholson Baker. Rare Books Manuscr. Libr. **1994**, *9*(1), 41–47.
10. Max, P.J. What's wrong with scrapping the card catalog?. Chron. High. Educ. June 29, **1994**, A44.
11. Cole, J.Y., Ed. *Celebration: The National Union Catalog, Pre-1956 Imprints*; Library of Congress: Washington, DC, 1981.

12. Smith, D.A. The national union catalog: pre-1956 imprints. Book Collect. **1982**, *31*, 445–462.

13. Tanselle, G.T. Reproductions and scholarship. Stud. Bibliogr. **1989**, *42*, 25–54. Reprinted in his *Literature and Artifacts*; Bibliographical Society of the University of Virginia: Charlottesville, VA, 1998; 59–88.

14. McKerrow, R.B. *An Introduction to Bibliography for Literary Students*; Clarendon Press: Oxford, U.K., 1927.

15. Gaskell, P. *A New Introduction to Bibliography*; Clarendon Press: Oxford, U.K., 1972.

16. Wilson, F.P. Shakespeare and the "new bibliography." In *The Bibliographical Society 1892–1942: Studies in Retrospect*; Bibliographical Society: London, U.K., 1945; 76–135. Reprinted as separate volume, Gardner, H., Ed.; Clarendon Press: Oxford, U.K., 1970.

17. Hinman, C. *The Printing and Proof-Reading of the First Folio of Shakespeare*; Clarendon Press: Oxford, U.K., 1963.

18. Blayney, P.W.M. *The Texts of "King Lear" and Their Origins*; Cambridge University Press: Cambridge, U.K., 1982.

19. Tanselle, G.T. Issues in bibliographical studies since 1942. In *The Book Encompassed: Studies in Twentieth-Century Bibliography*; Davison, P., Ed.; Cambridge University Press: Cambridge, U.K., 1992; 24–36.

20. Tanselle, G.T. *Introduction to Bibliography: Seminar Syllabus*, 5th Ed.; Book Arts Press: Charlottesville, VA, 2002.

21. Tanselle, G.T. The treatment of typesetting and presswork in bibliographical description. Stud. Bibliogr. **1999**, *52*, 1–57.

22. Weiss, A. Reproductions of early dramatic texts as a source of bibliographical evidence. Text **1988**, *4*, 237–268.

23. Stevenson, A. *The Problem of the Missale Speciale*; Bibliographical Society: London, U.K., 1967.

24. Povey, K. The optical identification of first formes. Stud. Bibliogr. **1960**, *13*, 189–190.

25. Nowell-Smith, S. Signatures in some nineteenth-century Massachusetts duodecimos. Library **1948**, *3*, 58–62; 5th series.

26. Melville, H. In *Clarel*; Hayford, H., Parker, H., Tanselle, G. T., Eds.; Northwestern University Press and Newberry Library: Evanston, IL, 1991; 678–679.

27. Werstine, P. More unrecorded states in the Folger Shakespeare Library's Collection of First Folios. Library **1989**, *6*(11), 47–51.

28. Vander Meulen, D.L. *Where Angels Fear to Tread: Descriptive Bibliography and Alexander Pope*; Library of Congress: Washington, DC, 1988; 24–27.

29. Todd, W.B.; Bowden, A. *Tauchnitz International Editions in English 1841–1955: A Bibliographical History*; Bibliographical Society of America: New York, 1988; x.

30. Graham, P.S. *Intellectual Preservation: Electronic Preservation of the Third Kind*; Commission on Preservation and Access: Washington, DC, 1994; 2.

31. McKenzie, D.F. Typography and Meaning: The Case of William Congreve. In *Buch und Buchhandel in Europa im Achtzehnten Jahrhundert*; Barber, G., Fabian, B., Eds.; Hauswedell: Hamburg, Germany, 1981; 81–125.

32. McKenzie, D.F. *"What's Past Is Prologue": The Bibliographical Society and History of the Book*, Hearthstone Publications: London, U.K., 1993; 8.

33. Lanham, R.A. *The Electronic Word*, University of Chicago Press: Chicago, IL, 1993.

34. Birkerts, S. *The Gutenberg Elegies: The Fate of Reading in an Electronic Culture*, Faber and Faber: Winchester, MA, 1994.

35. Wendorf, R., Ed. *Rare Book and Manuscript Libraries in the Twenty-First Century*; Harvard University Library: Cambridge, MA, 1993; 61. Also printed in Harvard Libr. Bull. **1993**, *n.s. 4*(1, 2).

36. Traister, D. What good is an old book? Rare Books Manuscr. Libr. **1992**, *7*, 26–42.

37. Traister, D. Condensed as garbage or treasure? The case for acquiring rare books. Chron. High. Educ. January 13, **1993**, A48.

38. Greenberg, D. Get out of the way if you can't lend a hand: the changing nature of scholarship and the significance of special collections. Biblion: Bull. N.Y. Public Libr. **1993**, *2*(1), 5–18.

39. Sullivan, J.; Johnson, J. The preservation directorate: saving the library's legacy. Libr. Congr. Inf. Bull. July 1, **1991**, 247–253.

40. Walls, D. Relative costs for three preservation modes. Abbey Newsl. **2000**, *24*(4), 75.

41. Rothenberg, J. Ensuring the longevity of digital documents. Sci. Am. **1995**, *272*(1), 42–47.

42. Bradbury, D.J. Barbarians within the gate: pillage of a rare book collection? Rare Books Manuscr. Libr. **1994**, *9*, 8–16.

43. Barker, N. Whither rare books? Book Collect. **1992**, *41*, 441–455.

44. Battin, P. Access to scholarly materials. In *Scholars and Research Libraries in the 21st Century*, Occasional Paper No. 14; American Council of Learned Societies: New York, 1990; 21–25.

45. Cummings, A.M.; Witte, M.L.; Bowen, W.G.; Lazarus, L.O.; Ekman, R.H. *University Libraries and Scholarly Communication: A Study Prepared for the Andrew W. Mellon Foundation*; Association of Research Libraries: New York, 1992; xv xxiii–xxv, 104.

46. Getty Art History Information Program. *Technology, Scholarship, and the Humanities: The Implications of Electronic Information*; American Council of Learned Societies and Getty Art History Information Program: New York, Santa Monica, CA, 1993; 21, 23, 26, 28, 37, 38.

47. The Commission on Preservation and Access. *Preserving the Intellectual Heritage: A Report of the Bellagio Conference*, June 7–10, 1993; Commission on Preservation and Access: Washington, DC, 1993; 15, 16, 27.

48. Bloch, R.H.; Hesse, C. Future libraries. Representations **1993**, *42*, 1–134.

49. Lynn, M.S. Digital preservation and access: liberals and conservatives. In *Digital Imaging Technology for Preservation*, Proceedings from an RLG Symposium Cornell University, Ithaca, NY, March 17 and 18, 1994; Elkington, N. E., Ed.; Research Libraries Group: Mountain View, CA, 1994; 1–9.

50. Billington, J.H. The librarian's remarks at the National Digital Library news conference. Libr. Congr. Inf. Bull. October 31, **1994**, 412, 413, 416.

51. Billington, J.H. The electronic library. Media Stud. J. **1994**, *8*(1), 109–112.

52. Cole, J.Y., Ed. *Research Collections in the Information Age: The Library of Congress Looks to the Future*; Library of Congress: Washington, DC, 1990.

53. Lesk, M. *Practical Digital Libraries: Books, Bytes and Bucks*, Morgan Kaufmann: San Francisco, CA, 1997.

54. Chepesiuk, R. JSTOR and electronic archiving. Am. Libr. **2000**, *December*, 46–48.

55. Preserving Harvard's retrospective collections. Harv. Libr. Bull. **1991**, *n.s. 2*(2), 1–80.

56. Witherell, E.H. ADE presidential address. Doc. Ed. **1994**, *16*(1), 1, 2, 20.

57. McKenzie, D.F. Computers and the humanities: a personal synthesis of conference issues. In *Scholarship and Technology in the Humanities*, Proceedings of a Conference, Elvetham Hall, Hampshire, U.K., May 9–12, 1990; Katzen, M., Ed.; Bowker-Saur: London, U.K., 1991; 157–169.

58. Franklin, P. Scholars, librarians, and the future of primary records. Coll. Res. Libr. **1993**, *54*, 397–406.

59. Significance of primary records. Profession 95 (MLA) **1995**, 29–50.

60. Tanselle, G.T. Statement on the significance of primary records. Profession 95 (MLA) **1995**, 27–28.

61. Reed-Scott, J. *Preserving Research Collections: A Collaboration Between Librarians and Scholars*; Association of Research Libraries, Modern Language Association, American Historical Association: Washington, DC, 1999.

62. *Checklist of Primary Bibliographical Evidence Contained in 19th and Early 20th Century Publishers' Bookbindings*; American Institute for Conservation of Historic and Artistic Works: Washington, DC, 1995.

63. Cloonan, M.V. Bookbinding, aesthetics, and conservation. Libr. Cult. **1995**, *30*, 137–152.

64. *Leaf Master*, BookLab BookNote; BookLab, Inc.: Austin, TX, 1993; Vol. 16.

65. *Change All Around Us*, BookLab BookNote; BookLab, Inc.: Austin, TX, 1994; Vol. 21.

66. Tanselle, G.T. The latest forms of book-burning. Common Knowl. **1993**, *2*(3), 172–177. Reprinted in his *Literature and Artifacts*; Bibliographical Society of the University of Virginia: Charlottesville, VA, 1998; 89–95.

67. Shaffer, R.I. Bringing things to the center: The Center for the Cultural Record of the Graduate School of Library and Information Science at the University of Texas at Austin. RBM: J. Rare Books Manuscr. Cult. Herit. **2000**, *1*, 136–144.

68. Baker, N. The author vs. the library. *New Yorker*, October 14, **1996**, 50–62.

69. Baker, N. Deadline. *New Yorker*, July 24, **2000**, 42–61.

70. McCrady, E. "Preserving" newspapers. Abbey Newsl. **2000**, *24*(4), 69–72.

71. McCrady, E. "Preserving" newspapers. Abbey Newsl. **2001**, *25*(1), 77, 80, 81.

72. Woudhuysen, H.R. Vandals of Colindale: why the British Library is discarding newspapers. Times Lit. Suppl. (Lond.) August 18, **2000**, 14–15.

73. Brindley, L. Pulp fiction about the BL. Times Lit. Suppl. (Lond.) November 17, **2000**, 15.

74. Baker, N. *Double Fold: Libraries and the Assault on Paper*; Random House: New York, 2001.

75. Duff, W. Ensuring the preservation of reliable evidence: a research project funded by the NHPRC. Archivaria **1996**, *42*, 28–45.

76. Duranti, L.; MacNeil, H. The protection of the integrity of electronic records: an overview of the UBS-MAS research project. Archivaria **1996**, *42*, 46–67.

77. *Preserving Digital Information: Report of the Task Force on Archiving of Digital Information*; Commission on Preservation and Access: Washington, DC, 1996.

78. Council on Library and Information Resources. *Authenticity in a Digital Environment*; Council on Library and Information Resources: Washington, DC, 2000.

Print on Demand

Steve Bosch
Administration Department, University of Arizona, Tucson, Arizona, U.S.A.

Abstract

Advances in digital printing have enabled print on demand to support major changes in book publishing and distribution. The ability to print small numbers of titles only when needed by consumers has allowed a huge increase in content to be made easily available in the marketplace. Print on demand has also impacted other areas especially art and artist book publishing as well as music publishing.

Advances in digital printing have enabled print-on-demand (POD) systems to support new channels of book publishing and distribution. The ability to print small numbers of titles only when needed by consumers has allowed a huge increase in content to be made easily available in the marketplace. POD has also impacted other areas of publishing, especially art and artist book publishing as well as music publishing.

POD is the process of creating print products using digital printing technology at the point when needed by customers. The POD process is based on the use of a digital image to directly feed a digital printer that can reproduce the image on the desired media. A single copy can be printed or large print runs can be produced all depending on the customer's need. The digital image can be a wide variety of objects including books, journals, art/photo reproductions, maps, sheet music, etc. Digital printing is also used in the commercial marketplace to produce packaging, brochures, and manuals at the point of need with the flexibility to make minor changes in the materials without reproducing a complete print run.

Based upon the technology first used in copying machines and then prevalent in desktop laser printers, digital printers have progressed far from their humble beginnings and now produce very-high-quality results across a broad spectrum of applications. Digital printing spans a huge variety of systems, from desktop printers for photos to large commercial presses used by companies like Ingrams' Lightning Source. The major differences between digital and other forms of printing are the lack of setup and cleanup required for the digital, enabling the process to produce works as needed. Digital printing has higher fixed costs per copy produced, so there are price points where digital printing is cheaper than offset, but if enough copies are printed, then the setup and clean-up costs are distributed across enough copies to make offset printing cheaper. Digital printing is not yet able to provide the very-high-quality results produced by letterpress printing, but the high expense of letterpress makes it attractive only to very specialized needs. For larger print runs, offset printing at this time remains the most economical approach, but for small print jobs digital printing has found its niche. It is precisely this ability to produce low-cost small printing jobs that makes POD an agent of change in the publishing industry.

POD impacts publishing in several ways. Foremost, POD enables publishers or authors to print books as needed, which means that books do not have to be printed in large batches and semipermanently warehoused, yet orders can still be fulfilled in a very short period of time. POD also cuts down on transactional overhead that adds costs to book distribution. Prior to POD, books moved through several intermediaries on their journey from the printer to the consumer. Books were shipped from the printer to publishers who then repacked and shipped the books to wholesalers or other intermediaries who then unpack and then repack the books for distribution to retailers, libraries, or consumers. At the retail level, books that do not sell are repacked and shipped back to the wholesaler and eventually publishers. POD removes most of these added transactional costs as only the required items are printed and shipped. Another important consideration, POD is a green technology. It only consumes paper and energy when a book is needed. It has a much lower carbon footprint as the book is shipped once, and by only printing what is needed it avoids pulping unused volumes, again an environmental plus. The digital file is sent from the creator/publisher to the POD supplier and the POD supplier can ship directly to the end customer. Larger POD suppliers can print orders and ship directly to customers within 24 hours of the order's receipt. Customers are provided with the item they want and are not frustrated by messages like, out of stock, back order only, title is out of print, etc. Without costs for added print runs and storage, books no longer have to go out of print. Backlists can produce sales without the added expense of

Encyclopedia of Library and Information Sciences, Fourth Edition DOI: 10.1081/E-EISA-120053598

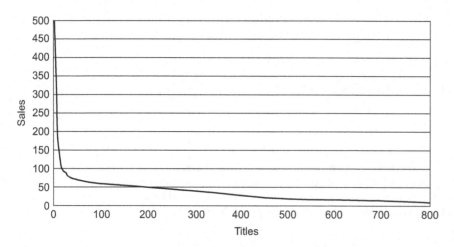

Fig. 1 Example of a long tail chart.

large prints runs and the need to warehouse the content. POD reduces the cost of book distribution and brings the long tail of publishing into the marketplace.

What is the long tail in publishing? Long tail is derived from the graphical representation of statistical data in which a small number of high-value data points dominates the left side of the graph while a high number of low-value data points dominate the right side of the graph. The chart in Fig. 1 is an example of what a long tail looks like as a graph. For publishing, this translates to a small number of titles produces very high sales while a huge number of titles sell but only at low volumes.

How long tail sales impact publishing has not been verified with quantifiable research, but there are some observable effects. Online retailers like Amazon have probably seen the most benefit from long tail sales. Although the exact sales breakdown between standard commercial titles and long tail sales are not available from Amazon, long tail sales make up a large portion of their commerce. Amazon, and similar online retailers, take metadata about books available for purchase from book data suppliers like Bowker and Nielsen, as well as metadata from wholesalers like Baker and Taylor, and Ingram and populate their online catalogs exposing huge amounts of content to customers. Changes in the industry like the development of POD and electronic books make it possible for retailers like Amazon to list huge amounts of content for sale as it can be easily delivered when ordered. Traditional book distribution systems could not support such a huge catalog as the transactional and storage costs would make it economically impossible to support based on the low volume of sales for the majority of titles in the catalog. POD changes that equation and makes it economically possible to sell huge numbers of titles in low-volume sales.

In addition to carrying other publishers' titles, Amazon provides a self-publishing service, CreateSpace, that assists authors with bringing their work to the marketplace without the need for a publisher. Self-published titles make up a large part of the long tail, and the area has seen huge growth over the past few years. CreateSpace provides a variety of services from simply printing a set of books, to assistance with the design, editing, marketing, and distribution of both print and electronic books. The service is not limited to book publishing but also provides similar services for music and video producers. Amazon not only profits from the sale of the self-published items, but also produces revenues on the front end by helping authors self-publish their works. CreateSpace is only one of many POD suppliers that can provide authors with a complete suite of services from printing to distribution.

How large is the long tail? In the summer of 2014, Bowker® released a report that describes the size of the U.S. book publishing industry and recent changes in output. The data are based on ISBNs registered. Bowker is the agency responsible for assigning and registering ISBNs. Ebooks are not included nor does the data pick up self-published books that do not register for an ISBN.

The data released for 2013 indicated that the number of titles reported for nontraditional publishing (e.g., self-published, the long tail) was nearly four times greater than the number of titles published by traditional publishers, 1,108,183 titles compared to 304,912. Bowker defines nontraditional publishing as reprint houses specializing in public domain works and presses catering to self-publishers and "micro-niche" publications with these producers marketing their titles almost exclusively on the web and printed on demand. Changes in web commerce and improvement in POD helped the long tail see explosive growth over the past decade. Traditional publishing grew by 27%, from 240,009 titles to 304,912, while nontraditional publishing grew by 4126% from 26,224 titles to 1,108,183. See the full report from Bowker.[1]

POD has led to some fundamental changes in the book industry. It is now far easier for authors to bypass traditional publishing, both commercial and vanity, and have their works produced and distributed at fairly low costs. Self-publishing has always been an option for authors. There are many great examples of authors who after being rejected multiple times by commercial publishers have taken the risk of printing a fairly large number of books and selling the titles themselves. The *Huffington Post* covered many of these success stories in a blog by Ronald Balson[2]. Amazon has a list of top-selling self-published books, and many of these titles were first self-published and then picked up by commercial publishers,[3] but POD lowers the required investment by huge factors and makes this an option for many authors as the risks are quite manageable.

Traditional publishers benefit from POD as they are able to make their mid and back lists easily available to consumers without having to maintain inventories. POD also reduces their transactional costs as items can be printed and shipped directly to consumers or bookshops without added handling. Traditional publishers can also risk underestimating initial print runs as POD could act as a stop gap, meeting immediate demand after the print run sells out while the publisher considers the need for another offset print run.

The growth in POD has also fueled growth in suppliers. Starting from a handful of suppliers just a few years ago, there are now hundreds of potential suppliers, far too numerous to discuss in a short article. There are websites that provide listings of POD suppliers, one being on the Bookmarket site.[4] Another site, *An Incomplete Guide to POD Publishers*, compared several of the major POD suppliers' costs and services.[5] Neither of these sites are complete by any means but they are good places to begin a review of suppliers. There are also many other websites that do comparisons of POD providers. Any good search tool can lead to a wealth of useful information. It is safe to say that practically any large-scale printing house will now offer some form of digital printing services to meet the needs of POD.

Although there are hundreds of POD suppliers and applications, there are some large players in the POD environment that should be discussed. One of the early adopters and one of largest POD suppliers is Lightning Source. Lightning Source, one part of the Ingram Content Group, provides POD services to the largest publishers as well as individual authors. According to the official website,[6] Lightning Source has more than six million titles in their inventory, processes 27,000 orders per day and prints 50,000 books per day. Lightning Source is an international operation with facilities in Australia, France, Germany, Italy, Spain, and the United Kingdom as well as the United States. As part of the Ingram Content Group, Lightning Source taps into the Ingram distribution chain and can distribute POD content to 38,000 booksellers and libraries including all of the major retailers like Amazon, and Barnes and Noble. Lightning Source is an industry leader and has demonstrated the viability of the POD process as a positive development in book distribution.

Another major player in the POD supply chain is on-demand books (ODB), distributor of the Espresso Book Machine (EBM). ODB does not market their services as a POD solution. They define themselves as digital to print sales channel that eliminates sales losses due to items being out of stock. Although their business model differentiates them from other POD suppliers, the basic service is still printing a digital object at the point in time needed by a customer. ODBs support a decentralized approach to supplying POD services. Their core business is the sale of the EBM to bookstores and libraries. The EBM is essentially a small stand-alone digital printing and binding installation. The technology is patented by ODB but the printers are actually supplied by Xerox. On demand at the point of sale, the EBM can print, bind, and trim a perfect bound library quality paperback book with four-color cover in a matter of minutes. The EBM cannot supply a full suite of print options, but it does bring POD directly to the end of the supply chain through a bookstore or library. ODBs maintain a catalog of over seven million titles that are available to be printed. ODB also provides software tool set to support self-publishing, and ODB makes it easy for authors to add their works to the online title list making an author's works available to all customers at EBM sites in a matter of minutes. ODB has a complex business model that distributes the proceeds from a book sale to the author, publisher, and EBM owner depending on who is involved with the transaction. Lightning Source does distribute many titles to ODB and also works with ODB self-publishing program to distribute that content through Ingram's digital network.[7]

Lightning Source and ODB are only two examples of the many POD suppliers that are active in the industry. This is not an endorsement of either company but merely a discussion of what a POD supplier looks like. Lightning Source was selected since they are probably the largest POD supplier. ODB was selected as they bring a unique model to the industry. There are many other quality providers available and information is abundant on the web.

Much of the discussion around POD has focused on book publishing but POD has had an impact in other types of publishing as well. As mentioned earlier, digital printing uses any digital image to directly feed a digital printer that then reproduces the image on the desired media at the point of need. The digital image can be practically any digital object. This could include maps, photographs, sheet music including scores, documents, art reproductions, posters, etc.

Art reproductions and artist books are areas that have seen changes due to the availability of POD. Very-high-end digital printers are capable of making excellent reproductions of artworks, photographs, and posters. In addition, the print jobs can be done in small batches and delivered in short periods of time. POD enables museums and galleries to tailor their printing needs to existing demand as opposed to having to pay to print 5,000 copies of an exhibition catalog and only needing 4,000. The same logic applies to other types of retail items that could be sold in connection with an exhibition, or any other need, including art reproductions, calendars, greeting cards, etc. These retail items can be ordered based on need, and consequently once demand dwindles, there is no over stock to deal with. POD enables museum and galleries to offer far more works to their customers since they avoid the costs of large print runs and storage of the items awaiting sales. Web commerce can expose the digital catalog to consumers, and at the point of sale, the item can be printed and sent to the buyer.

Artist books have been similarly impacted by the development of POD. In the late 1960s and early 1970s, artists were experimenting with creating books as works of art. Many of the artist's books were completely unique one-of-a-kind creations, and those are outside this discussion. However, many other artists' books were a fusion of text and graphics and these were printed and distributed. With traditional book distribution channels, creativity was hampered by the need to print fairly large amounts of books that had a very limited audience. With POD, artists, designers, architects, and photographers are now able to produce work at the scale needed, and in some areas like photography, new areas of creative work opened up. Nearly all weddings, or similar major social events, are now documented in books that accompany the photos of the event. The creation of senior portraits is seeing similar developments. The digital images are used to produce photos, books, and graduation announcements, all of these products enabled by POD. Traditional printing methods would be far too expensive to allow for a whole suite of customized products at a personal level. If anyone you know has recently been married, baptized, graduated from school, or you just happen to know a photo enthusiast, you probably have one of these books somewhere in your house—brought to you by POD.

Music publishing, like other areas, has seen new opportunities due to the availability of POD. Digital distribution of sheet music and scores has not become the standard distribution channel. It may be that trying to balance laptops or tablets on sheet music stands in the orchestral pit is not yet workable, and the killer app for sheet music has not come to market like the e-reader for ebooks. Music publishing like traditional book publishing has similar issues surrounding the warehousing and distribution of printed works. Works have been traditionally printed in fairly large runs and then distributed through channels to various retail outlets. Once a score goes out of print, the high cost of another print run frequently precludes a new printing and the score then becomes very hard to locate and acquire. A parallel exists between music and book publishing. Using POD and avoiding the costs for added print runs and storage, scores no longer have to go out of print. Music publishers' backlists can produce sales without the added expense of large prints runs and the need to warehouse the content. POD reduces the cost of music distribution and enables consumers to obtain sheet music and scores that were previously not available.

POD has created many opportunities for authors. There are now many entrance points to the marketplace and a variety of ways to have your work published without going through a commercial or vanity publisher. There is a huge spectrum of POD suppliers. Many will provide a minimal service and print whatever number of items you request. It may be 5 copies, it may be 500. Others suppliers will provide the author with a complete suite of services including editorial, design, and layout assistance, as well registration of the book to obtain the ISBN and provide marketing and distribution assistance. These added services all come with a price, but for many authors the price is worth getting their work to market. The major consideration for most self-publishing authors, there is no rejection notice from the POD provider. POD has opened up self-publishing, and consequently, there is now a huge number of books available for consumers to choose from.

Authors now have much to think about as they decide how to put their work forward. Do they go the route of a commercial press or publish on their own. If they got the route of the commercial press, they have to consider what rights they will sign away. Since their work may not go out of print, authors need to consider the impact of the terms of the agreement concerning the life of the work since for some titles, especially textbooks, authors may be asked to agree to not publish competing works. Similarly, authors have to be careful what they agree to as they sign self-publishing agreements. With the advances made in POD, authors and publishers now have many more choices about their product and the product's distribution than were available with traditional publishing and distribution systems.

POD is no longer a trendy new upstart. Many of the major businesses involved with book distribution have brought their version of POD services to market. The two major book retailers have POD services, Amazon supports CreateSpace and Barnes and Noble supports the Nook Press Program. Ingram launched Lightning Source and Baker and Taylor has textstream, which is a POD service delivered through a partnership with Bookmasters. Large printing houses like R.R. Donnelly have also launched POD/digital print services. In addition to these industry leaders' investment in POD, there are a huge numbers of smaller suppliers who offer competitive services to potential authors and small publishers. The nature of authorship is also changing. It is now common for significant social events to be recorded and "published" in books. The wedding album is fast becoming the wedding book. Even for those with no special skills, it is possible to take a series of digital photos, drop them into a template, add a few lines of description, and they have a book they can print and send to their friends and family. As long as consumers are interested in physical objects, there will be a market for printed objects. POD lowers the costs and entrance barriers to that market. The development of the on-demand supply chain goes together with the development of the long tail in retailing. They make each other possible.

POD opens up new market space for creators but who prospers in that market space remains to be seen.

REFERENCES

1. http://www.bowker.com/news/2014/Traditional-Print-Book-Production-Dipped-Slightly-in-2013.html (accessed April 27, 2015).

2. http://www.huffingtonpost.com/ronald-h-balson/bestseller-success-storie_b_4064574.html (accessed April 27, 2015).

3. http://www.amazon.com/Self-Published-Bestsellers/lm/R2U HB9O6LWN1QI (accessed April 27, 2015).

4. http://www.bookmarket.com/ondemand-l.htm (accessed April 27, 2015).

5. http://www.booksandtales.com/pod (accessed April 27, 2015).

6. https://www.lightningsource.com/# (accessed April 27, 2015).

7. http://ondemandbooks.com (accessed April 27, 2015).

Private Presses and Fine Printing [ELIS Classic]

Roderick Cave
Loughborough University, Loughborough, U.K.

Abstract

Cave, an expert on private presses, surveys several types of private presses, and includes a discussion of printing as a fine art.

—*ELIS Classic*, *from 1978*

INTRODUCTION

The term "private press" has been used by historians of printing from the mid-seventeenth century onward to describe a variety of printing or publishing establishments outside the normal run of printers active in the period or in the society in question.[a] In a totalitarian society, for example, any press not directly under state control might be regarded as a private press; but, this press, its raison d'être, and its publications will all be very different from those that are often (in the English-speaking world) regarded as the only private presses: those of the kind that regard the making of books as an art form.

One can trace the development of presses that are outside the normal pattern of printing and book production right back to the invention of printing from movable types in fifteenth-century Europe or even beyond: The manuscripts produced in the scriptorium of the Florentine scribe Vespasiano da Bisticci, for example, can, in more senses than one, be regarded as the ancestors of the modern "fine books" in the production of which the private press movement has played so large a part.

ORIGINS

After the invention of printing at Mainz, printers spread rapidly to the main mercantile and academic centers of Western European life. In the large centers, where the local demand was sufficient, printers could maintain themselves by their trade without outside assistance. But in smaller towns with a lesser local market, or in less settled parts of the world, there was insufficient work to keep a printer employed or to attract him there in the first place. In such circumstances, many presses that one must regard

as private grew up. In Chartres, for instance, a canon of the cathedral, named Pierre Plumé, in 1482 invited the Paris printer Jean du Pré to come to Chartres to produce a missal for the cathedral's use, and he installed du Pré and his equipment in the canon house while it was being printed. A Chartres Breviary was produced in the same way in the following year.[b]

THE QUASI-OFFICIAL PRESS

A distinct category of private press is to be found in those establishments financed and controlled by rulers and other wealthy patrons to produce work at their behest. Almost the first ruler to recognize the propaganda value of the printed book was the Holy Roman emperor Maximilian I. By appointing Johann Schönsperger the elder as court printer and by ordering the production of the emperor's prayerbook (1512–1513) and the *Theuerdank* (1517)—which glorified the exploits of the House of Habsburg in general and of Maximilian in particular—the emperor was controlling a press that was undoubtedly private. But it was also the forerunner for many prestige items produced by government printing houses, such as the Imprimerie Royale's *Médailles sur les principaux événements du règne du Louis le grand* (1702).

Rather similar in character were the presses that were established in less settled parts of the world. The introduction of printing into Iceland, for instance, followed the Chartres pattern closely when, in 1530, the last Catholic bishop of Hoolum organized the establishment of a press that produced a *Breviarium Nidarosiense* in the following year. That the press was not regarded as an undesirable eccentricity is shown by the fact that the bishop's Lutheran successor continued to give employment to his printer, Jon Matthiesen. Without such patronage, it is most unlikely that any printer would have set up in Iceland at

---

[a]The earliest writer to distinguish private presses was Bernard Mallinckrodt, in his *De ortu ac progressu artis typographicae dissertatio historica* (Cologne, 1639). The earliest extensive treatment of private presses was given by Adam Heinrich Lackman in *Annalium typographicorum* (Hamburg, 1740), of which a modern English version remains a desideratum in private press literature.

[b]The references for this and the later examples given in this article are to be found in Cave.[1]

Encyclopedia of Library and Information Sciences, Fourth Edition DOI: 10.1081/E-ELIS4-120009004

this early date. In many respects, the mission presses in Asia, Africa, and the South Seas—often as amateur in their operation as they were uncommercial in their aims—were the successors of this early variety of private press.

THE SCHOLARLY PRESS

A type of amateur press that has recurred time and time again is one that is established with the prime purpose of printing works of scholarship. This was, of course, sometimes undertaken by presses of the quasi-official or patron's kind—The production of the grat *Complutensian Polyglot Bible* at Alcalà in Spain is the best instance of this type of work, and it cost Cardinal Ximenes some 50,000 gold ducats (a sum roughly equivalent to $3–4 million dollars in today's terms).

Some of these scholarly presses were clearly filling the role that would later be taken by the typewriter and the mimeograph. Such was the production of a private edition of Archbishop Parker's *De antiquitate Britannicae ecclesiae*, which the Elizabethan printer John Day printed for him in Lambeth Palace so that the archbishop might always have a copy by him to amend the text as need arose. Cardinal du Perron is similarly credited with a press at his chateau de Bagnolet in France, which was used to print preliminary drafts of the cardinal's works. After these had been circulated (for comments and criticism) to a select group, the text would then be revised for general publication.

Most scholarly presses were not set up as aids to composition in this way, but rather to supply needs that the ordinary commercial printers could not handle. In the publication of astronomical work, for instance, where absolute accuracy is essential, it was not uncommon for the astronomer to have his work printed in his own house under his direct personal supervision: Regiomontanus, Hevelius, and (in particular) Tycho Brahe adopted this method for their books.

Tycho Brahe's press is particularly interesting. In 1576, he had been granted the island of Hveen by the king of Denmark and had built an impressive observatory there. Finding that Copenhagen printers could not meet his exacting requirements and that he was too remote from the better craftsmen in Germany to have his work produced there, he imported presses, type and other equipment, *and a printer*, and set up a printing office as an adjunct to his observatory. Subsequently, when paper supplies proved inadequate, he added a paper mill to his operations. With this equipment, some of the most significant work in the history of science was produced.

Another area of scholarship in which the normal commercial printer was often inadequate was in language studies. Many of the special typefaces needed for printing in exotic languages had their origin in private commissions.

The Anglo-Saxon type used for Elizabeth Elstob's *Anglo-Saxon Grammar* in 1715, and the type cut by Charles Wilkins for his *Grammar of the Sanskrita Language* (1808) are examples of such private typefounding, although in both cases the books were printed commercially. Another "linguistic" press was that operated in London by Prince Louis-Lucien Bonaparte in the 1850s. This printed texts from St. Matthew in a variety of Basque dialects, a specialized area of work in which the old advantages of having a printer under the scholar's direct control are obvious. But by that time, much of the need for a private scholarly printing house had disappeared: With the growth of academic publishing and of printing houses specializing in particular languages, it was perfectly possible for a scholar to have work printed, in Cambodian, Cree, Catalan, or what you will, without setting up a press of his own. Yet the private scholarly press is not dead, as will be seen below.

THE EDUCATIONAL PRESS

The advantages of a small printing establishment as an aid to education were widely recognized in ruling houses in Europe by the eighteenth century. Such did not call for a permanent establishment, of course a visit by the young Louis XIV to the newly established Imprimerie Royale in 1648, during which he "helped" with the production of an edition of the *Mémoires* of Phillippe de Commines, or the occasion on which, in 1731, the London printer Samuel Palmer set up a press in St. James's Palace so that the royal children could try setting up type—these are instances of the many occasions on which children of the ruling classes were exposed to the "black art." In a few cases, however, special permanent printing rooms were set up: Both Louis XV and Louis XVI as children had small presses on which they (with assistance) printed a few small books and no doubt more easily learned the texts they were setting up.

THE ARISTOCRATIC PLAYTHING

In the eighteenth century, printing also developed as a hobby among the wealthier and more leisured classes. Such had been advocated in England by the newspaper *The Craftsman* in reporting Palmer's work in St. James's Palace in 1731: "We could wish that our *Nobility* and *Gentry* would follow this Royal Example, and set up a *Printing Press* in their Houses; which. . .would be a much more polite as well as a more instructive Amusement for Themselves and their Heirs, than the modern fashionable Diversions of *Billiard Tables* and *Foxhunting*." Few of the English aristocracy took *The Craftsman*'s advice, though it was certainly known to Horace Walpole, owner of the Strawberry Hill Press (q.v.). During its 32 years of life, from 1757, the Strawberry Hill Press produced several books of real importance, as well as a good deal of ephemera (complimentary verses in honor of visitors, guides to the contents of the house, and the like). Walpole's comment that the Strawberry Hill books "have all the beautiful negligence of a gentleman" typifies the spirit of these presses.

On the continent, many such playthings existed. The duchesse de Bourbon-Condé had a press in the Palais de Bourbon in 1730; at Versailles, the duc de Bourgogne, Madame de Pompadour, and others were all printing in the 1760s and 1770s; while many of the aristocracy—the marquis de Lussay, the duc de Choseil, Président Saron, and others—had presses in their own chateaux from which they issued volumes of memoirs, family histories, and the like. Most of this work was of little general interest, but two exceptions must be noted. The press of Caperonnier de Gauffecourt in 1763 printed the first manual on bookbinding ever to be published separately, while, in the 1780s, Léorier de Lisle printed two books on papers made from nettles, mallow, and other fibers new to the papermaker's craft.

Far more substantial and serious in intent than most of these was the press "au donjon du château," which Frederick the Great of Prussia operated from 1748 until such things were brought to a halt by the outbreak of the Seven Years' War. As well as producing Frederick's own *OEuvres du Philosophe de Sans Souci* (1750), it printed Frederick's history of the House of Brandenburg, for which Voltaire acted as reader, and—unusual for such hobby-presses—a manual on military tactics for distribution to the Prussian general staff.

The French Revolution and the Napoleonic wars tended to dislocate, if not to stop, the activities of all private presses of this kind on the continent. In Britain, however, they gained a new lease on life from the fashion for book collecting, which went through a boom period in the early nineteenth century. Several collectors started presses with a more scholarly purpose than the playthings of the preceding century: to put into print manuscripts never before printed and to reprint very scarce works. Such presses as the Hafod Press of Colonel Thomas Johnes, or Sir Egerton Brydges's Lee Priory Press, or Sir Thomas Phillipps's Middle Hill Press served as forerunners to the publishing societies such as the Roxburghe Club and Hakluyt Society, whose work was to be important later in the century.

THE MIDDLE-CLASS HOBBY

Although the educational advantages of printing and the pleasure to be derived from it as a spare-time occupation were already clear in the eighteenth century, only persons with considerable means could afford the very heavy outlay involved in setting up a full-scale printing office. Until iron presses were developed at the beginning of the

nineteenth century, there was no really practicable way of miniaturizing printing equipment. Nearly all the private presses mentioned above were operated with the assistance of full-time paid personnel: Few indeed of the French aristocrats undertook the heavy work of operating their presses themselves. But in England, where the introduction of iron presses had been pioneered by Lord Stanhope in 1800, miniature printing outfits were being marketed from the 1830s onward for "the amusement and education of youth." In the United States, where the first press to cater specifically for the amateur market was introduced in 1857, the movement took a radically different form. The first advertisement of William A. Kelsey (whose firm at Meriden, Connecticut, still produces presses for the amateur market) emphasized its commercial advantages: "Business Men save expense and increase business by doing, their own printing and advertising. For boys, delightful *moneymaking* amusement."

Between Victorian high-mindedness and Yankee entrepreneurism, there was a very wide gulf, but between them was created a real craze for printing as a hobby. From Rudyard Kipling to Thomas Edison, from Robert Louis Stevenson to "Little Lord Fauntleroy" himself, one finds instances of people playing with printing. Most of these amateurs produced little of interest to other than their own immediate circle of friends (an exception being the Daniel Press, q.v.). By the end of the nineteenth century, the craze for printing had largely been superseded by other hobbies such as photography, and only those "back bedroom" amateurs who were following Kelsey's advertising and irritating the printing trade with their production of letterheads and other jobbing work at cut rates continued work.

THE AUTHOR AS PUBLISHER

This group fits uneasily into the categories of private presses already listed above. The man who buys a printing press in order to print his own work may do this (rather than employing commercial printers) because it is more rewarding financially: In Britain, a lawyer, Charles Viner, and a physician, John Hunter, both ran presses that were very profitable in the eighteenth century. More commonly, authors set up as their own publishers because they cannot sell their work to commercial publishers and cannot afford the rates charged by vanity presses. The supreme instance is of William Davy, a Devon clergyman who, between 1795 and 1807, printed his *A System of Divinity* in 26 thick octavo volumes. In its production, the only assistance he had was from his housemaid, whom he taught to set type.

In most cases, to get an author's texts into print was all that was required of such printing, no matter how badly it might be executed. But there were and are private presses operated by authors who choose this method for deliberate aesthetic reasons: where an author has felt that only by his personal design and decoration of the book that was to be the vehicle for his texts could the full intention of his work be realized. The exemplar for such work is to be found in the "illuminated" books printed by the artist/poet William Blake. Blake towers so far above most others who have attempted work of this kind that it is all too easy to forget that he *was* operating a private press—an extremely influential one. Among the enormous number of those inspired by his work and who have attempted work in the same tradition are a few that deserve mention, such as the Iona Press in the 1880s, or the work of Ralph Chubb from the 1930s to the 1950s, or today, Morris Cox's important Gogmagog Press in London.

CLANDESTINE PRESSES

Private printing establishments have, of course, flourished in secret ever since man discovered the power of the printed word, whenever there has been political, religious, or moral oppression. In Elizabethan England, for example, one finds instances of clandestine presses at both ends of the religious spectrum: in the work printed by the Catholic martyr Edmund Campion on the one hand, and in the Puritan "Martin Marprelate" tracts on the other. Or—to take another instance from a country with a long tradition of freedom of the press—the seizure of the private press operated by the English politician John Wilkes in London in 1763 (a seizure ostensibly on moral, but, in fact, on political grounds) is a classic case in British constitutional history.

Sometimes called "underground presses," such clandestine operations have occasionally been literally that, like that of the Abbé François Xavier de Feller at the end of the eighteenth century, which produced anti-Austrian propaganda from the bottom of a coal mine near Liège, while the police of the Austrian Netherlands vainly sought it. But normally "underground" refers only to the presses' clandestine status (and this has, in any case, been devalued as a descriptive phrase by its misapplication to presses espousing minority causes and an alternative society, which are not in danger of suppression at all). These clandestine presses flourished in Ireland during "the Troubles" and in prerevolutionary Russia (and since: the *samizdat* editions, which figure in contemporary Russia, are the direct descendents of earlier endeavors against censorship); and they were by no means the least important aspects of the resistance to Nazi occupation in Europe in World War II. In both France and the Netherlands—and only to a lesser extent in Poland, Denmark, and other occupied countries—there were extensive illicit printing enterprises carried on by amateurs in the 1940s.[c] Some of the work produced was of very high literary and typo-graphic quality, but with the twentieth-century development of easy photocopying and office duplicating methods, such illicit work is nowadays more often carried out by such simpler methods rather than by letterpress printing.

There are other private presses that are clandestine in their work for less high-minded reasons than those that inspire the operators of the presses named above. In the stricter moral climate of the past, the printing of erotica such as *Fanny Hill* was attended by such penalties that it tended to be produced by clandestine printers, as today hard-core pornography is still so produced. And for those who interpret the Kelsey Company's advertising slogan "Print—make money" too literally and turn to counterfeiting, the role of the clandestine printing plant is vital.

PRINTING AS A FINE ART

The twentieth-century private press movement and its association with the production of "fine books" is to be traced back to the establishment of William Morris's Kelmscott Press (q.v.), which was in turn inspired by a lecture given by Emery Walker (q.v.) to the Arts and Crafts Exhibition Society in 1888.

The work of such presses is discussed in the previously published, print version, of this encyclopedia (*see* Ashendene Press, Vol. 1, pp. 662–665; T.J. Cobden-Sanderson, Vol. 5, pp. 224–231; Daniel Press, Vol. 6, pp. 425–428; Doves Press, Eragny Press, Vol. 8, pp. 161–164; and Kelmscott Press, Vol. 13, pp. 407–415). Their function, so far as they understood it, was to reestablish sound principles of book *design*, which, during the nineteenth-century mechanization of the printing trade, had not kept pace with the technical advances of the period. These presses attempted it usually by returning to first principles: to the standards in design and execution to be found in the finest fifteenth-century Italian printing as a rule, although in some instances other models were adopted, for example, the Daniel Press's revival of seventeenth-century types.

With hindsight, it is possible to discern many mistaken routes taken in their quest for the "ideal book": the gothicising element in Kelmscott work, the frigid classicism of Cobden-Sanderson. By tying their work to the ideals of hand craftsmanship and "truth to materials," which were so important to those in the Arts and Crafts Movement, they did not form good examples for commercial book production. Those trade books that were produced early in the twentieth century under direct private press influence were not seldom ugly and ineffectual vehicles for an author's words. Nevertheless, the fact that work of Kelmscott, Doves, and other private presses was successful in redirecting attention toward book design—in making it a subject about which the ordinary educated

---

[c]cf. Dirk de Jong, *Het vrije boek in onvrije tijd* (Leiden, 1953); and "Vercors," in *Voices of Silence* (London, 1968).

man could be expected to be aware—was a major step forward.

During the years between the two world wars, the lesson of the private presses was successfully applied to trade book production. The work of professional typographers like Bruce Rogers, W.A. Dwiggins, and Stanley Morison (allied to the revivals of good type designs of the past by manufacturers of composing machines) was of particular importance in this respect. No less important were the publishing imprints, the Nonesuch Press and the Limited Editions Club, which showed that it was possible to produce books of excellent design and fully up to the standards of workmanship of the old private presses, while using the mechanized equipment of modern commercial printing houses. There was also the growth of small commercial printing houses that worked in the tradition and to the standards of the private presses. Such printers were to be found in many locations (a famous example being Will Carter's Rampant Lions Press in Cambridge, England); but these were to become a particular feature in California, where the work of such printers as the Grabhorn Press, the Plantin Press, and Ward Ritchie is justly of high reputation.

At the same time, many private presses much closer to the Kelmscott tradition continued to produce fine work, particularly in Germany, the United States, and in Britain. One may, for example, cite the Shakespeare Head Press, or the Golden Cockerel Press (q.v.), which was particularly important for the part it played in the revival of wood-engraved book illustration. In France, the influence of the arts and crafts movement had never been strong, and the French *livres d'artiste* were produced with different ideals in view from the private press credo, though similar in some respects to good private press work.

THE CONTEMPORARY PRIVATE PRESS SCENE

Although several of the important private presses continued operations in the 1940s (particularly, of the course, in the United States), World War II and the years of austerity that followed it in Europe almost destroyed the market for expensive books of the traditional "fine printing" kind. The era of the deluxe book seemed to be at an end, and obituary notices for the private press were commonplace in the early 1950s. However, just as the past quarter-century has seen the steady decline of commercial letterpress printing before the advances in offset lithography, so the same period has witnessed a recrudescence of private presses (most of which are devoted to letterpress work), so that today there are more amateur printers active than ever before.

The spirit that imbues the contemporary private printer is very different from that of the parlor printers of the nineteenth century. Today's amateurs are bibliographically well informed, being brought up on the typographic literature of D.B. Updike, Stanley Morison, and others, and, in consequence, they are able to practice their spare-time avocation with a taste and skill seldom possessed by their nineteenth-century predecessors.[d]

There are many private presses whose proprietors devote themselves mainly to amateur journalism, producing (sometimes as a collective venture) many hundreds of little magazines. Occasionally, these will print material of literary importance, but more usually their work is produced with a deliberately lighthearted ephemeral content, which renders it of limited interest outside their own immediate circle.

In contrast, one can, among today's private presses, distinguish many that work directly in the traditions of earlier varieties of the private press and that publish matter of much more weight and general interest. Their work, of which a substantial proportion is listed in the Private Libraries Association's annual bibliography *Private Press Books* (1959–), falls into several different (though not mutually exclusive) groups:

1. *The typographic presses*, which exist primarily to produce experiments in design, layout, and so forth. John Ryder's Miniature Press, or the Cuckoo Hill Press of David Chambers, or the Tuinwijkpers of Sem Hartz are good instances of such private presses. To an increasing extent, some of these are allied to a new hobby, that of the amateur typefounder. Such private printers as Paul Hayden Duensing at Kalamazoo, Michigan, have not only produced new castings of typefaces that have disappeared from the repertoires of commercial founders but have also originated some very effective new designs, some of which have been pirated for the commercial market in exactly the way that the Kelmscott Press's types were commercially imitated.

2. *The scholarly presses*, which print important texts of limited appeal, for which the normal commercial or academic publisher may not be well suited. In England, Geoffrey Wakeman's Plough Press—with its portfolio on *Nineteenth Century Illustration Processes* (1971), which was illustrated with leaves from nineteenth-century books that had used the processes described—is one example of the genre. In the United States, there are: Henry Morris's distinguished series of books on papermaking from his Bird and Bull Press; or from the Press of John Cumming in Mount Pleasant, Michigan, several substantial volumes of Michigan history; or from Charles Ingerman's Quixott Press in Doylestown, Pennsylvania, some studies on local Quaker history—these are representative of the valuable work published by contemporary amateurs.

---

[d]With the aid of such excellent manuals as Dobell[2] and Haas.[3]

3. *Fine art presses*: these are normally working directly in the tradition of William Morris and the private press movement in attempting to build books of typographic excellence as vehicles for worthy texts (though some, like the Allen Press in Kentfield, California, span the gap between the private presses and the French *livres d'artiste*). These range from Alan Tarling's modest "Poet and Printer" in Essex, England (which is content with unassuming texts for sale at a low price), through the severely classical and exquisitely produced work of the Nuns of Stanbrook Abbey Press (Worcester, England) and that of Kim Merker at the Stone Wall Press in Iowa City, through the less classical but equally splendid Janus Press books produced by Claire Van Vliet in Vermont, to the extraordinary work of Walter Hamady at the Perishable Press in Wisconsin. Perishable Press books, often printed on paper made at the press, have, at times, broken every typographic rule there is and are, at times, unsusceptible to adequate bibliographical description—yet they remain some of the liveliest and most exciting volumes of contemporary poetry.

Some presses transcend these categories, of course. In England, one of the most interesting private presses is that of Trevor Hickman, the Brewhouse Press in Leicestershire. Some of its books have been serious contributions to scholarly knowledge, whether typographic (*Typographia Naturalis*, a history of nature printing) or local history (*The Oakham Canal*); others are exercises in fine illustration (*The Pickworth Fragment*); yet other productions will be lighthearted ephemera or typographic experiments. This press is by no means unique in its range and styles of work; though producing more and often better work in the various fields in which it operates, it typifies much that is best in the private press of today.

The presses range as widely in equipment and scale of operations as in the types of work they issue. Some of them are virtually working museums, keeping in use presses built a century and more ago, and preserving techniques of craftsmanship that would otherwise be lost. Some, though still devoted to the use of the best materials, prefer to employ more modern presses in order to be able to produce long runs of high quality with less labor. Yet others will be very small indeed; a small flatbed press that can be stored under a bed, plus enough type to print a page at a time, will be the sum total of their equipment.

BIBLIOGRAPHICAL PRESSES

An interesting and significant development from the private presses has been the appearance of *bibliographical presses*.[4] Schools of art that teach courses in graphic design have, of course, for long had printing equipment on which student work was produced. Porter Garnett's famous Laboratory Press in Pittsburgh (1923–1935), and the Lion and Unicorn Press of the Royal College of Art in London are among the best known of these, and they have produced a considerable volume of important work prized by discerning collectors. The bibliographical presses, on the other hand, are working laboratories set up to assist the bibliographical student to an understanding of book production methods, through personal experience in setting, presswork, and so forth. Presses of this kind are to be found sometimes in university libraries (as at Bodley, McGill, or Sydney), sometimes in English departments, and often in schools of librarianship. In the nature of things, their productions tend to be slighter and more ephemeral, but they have also produced a generation of literary scholars and librarians whose understanding of the niceties of printing is much greater than a generation or two ago.

"LITTLE" PRESSES

The "little" presses may be regarded perhaps as an offshoot of, perhaps as a rival to the private press movement. These undertakings—the publishing industry of an alternative society—are not in general very much interested in typographical excellence: They exist in order to put into print works that their owners feel passionately *should* be published and that, for one reason or another, are unsuitable for the commercial publisher. Particularly active in the production of literary magazines, experimental poetry, and work of a kindred nature, they span the gap between the amateur and the full-scale publishing operation. At one end of the scale (because of their concern with the text rather than its presentation), they may produce their pamphlets by office duplicating processes; at the other, they may be semi-commercial publishing imprints having all their printing done for them by others. Advances in small offset litho printing have meant that many of these little presses will employ such techniques for their work rather than the letterpress printing favored by most other private printers. With a successful public response to their literary programs, they may become almost indistinguishable from the ordinary commercial publisher, with the important proviso that they remain more interested in producing what they think is good work than in maximizing profits (which is true of the better commercial publishers also, of course). The Unicorn Press in California and the Gaberbocchus Press of London are good examples of the species.

THE FUTURE OF THE PRIVATE PRESS

It is a commonplace that changes in the structure of the publishing industry, and in printing technology, have produced a situation in which the book that is of limited appeal or is a slow seller is much less likely to achieve publication than was formerly the case. In consequence, a book of merit, one that will appeal only to a minority group, will not in the future be published unless subsidized by a learned society or other body or if the amateur publisher takes an active role. To be sure, some unprofitable publishing areas will be catered for through the programs of scientific journals, publishing societies, and the like. But in the fields of imaginative literature and local history (in its widest sense), there is a distinct gap that can be filled only by the concerned group or individual enterprise.

The little presses can cater for some of society's needs in this way. Similarly, the traditional private press will continue to produce work for those who feel that the book can and should be more than just a vehicle for the texts they contain (or that on occasion the vehicle should be a Rolls-Royce rather than a Detroit production-line job). At present, there is too wide a gap between these two kinds of private press: though it may be unrealistic today to expect that private press ideals of craftsmanship can be carried over into normal commercial book production, many of these ideals could advantageously be applied by the little presses. In the same way, the little presses' concern for the texts they print would render more permanently valuable the work of those private printers who demonstrate great taste and skill in printing rather negligible texts.

CONCLUSION

There is no doubt that the increase in the number of amateurs producing books and literary magazines presents many problems for the librarian. A good deal of the work they print may technically not be published (in the legal sense) at all and so escape record in those national bibliographies that are based upon legal deposit. Being produced outside normal book trade channels, their work may not be listed in the standard trade bibliographies and will seldom be carried in the stocks of booksellers and library suppliers. In consequence, the librarian concerned with selection of stock will have difficulties in finding out about these publications. In addition to this barrier (which requires perseverance on the librarian's part to overcome), there is also, at times, a consumer resistance, on the librarian's part, to the purchase of material that may occasionally be very awkward to process, store, and make available to readers (how *does* one shelve a book that opens concertinawise? or one triangular in shape?). The puritan ethos that imbued many earlier librarians also made them reluctant to buy some of the rather luxurious (and expensive) private press work of the past. For these various reasons, one often finds that private presses' work is less widely distributed in public libraries than one might expect.

Some libraries deliberately cultivate good relations with those amateur printers/publishers active in the area they serve and build up an archive of the press's work (ephemera as well as books), which—although difficult to handle—has important long-term cultural significance. In addition, some research libraries built up substantial collections of private press material: the Eric Gill collections at University of California at Los Angeles, the Will Ransom collection in the Newberry Library, Chicago, and the Bodleian Library's collections are of particular importance in this way. But in general, professional librarianship's attitude to private press work has been one of lip service and little more: with the purchase of a few representative Kelmscott, Golden Cockerel, or Grabhorn books to grace the library's display cases, the librarian has assumed that he has performed his function adequately. But, given the increasing importance of much published by these amateur printers and publishers, unless librarians succeed in improving their coverage of private press work, posterity will judge their professional competence harshly.

REFERENCES

1. Cave, R. *The Private Press;* Faber: London, U.K., 1971;347–363.
2. Ryder, J. *Printing for Pleasure;* Phoenix House: London, U.K., 1955.
3. Allen, L. *Printing with the Handpress;* Van Nostrand: New York, 1969.
4. Gaskell, P. The bibliographical press movement. J. Print. Hist. Soc.**1965**,*1*, 1–13.

BIBLIOGRAPHY

Bibliographies of Private Presses and Their Literature

1. Association of Little Presses, *Little Press Books in Print;* A.L.P.: London, U.K., 1974.
2. Dobell, B. *Catalogue of Books Printed for Private Circulation;* Dobell: London, U.K., 1906.
3. Haas, I. *A Bibliography of Materials Relating to Private Presses;* Black Cat Press: Chicago, IL, 1937.
4. Manchester Public Library, *Catalogue of Private Press Books;* Manchester, England, 1959–60.
5. Martin, J. *A Bibliographical Catalogue of Books Privately Printed,* 1st Ed.; London, U.K., 1834.
6. Private Libraries Association, *Private Press Books;* an annual checklist edited by Roderick Cave [and others]. 1959–, P.L.A., Pinner, 1960–. Includes a section listing books and articles about private presses.

7. Ransom, W. *Private Presses and Their Books;* Bowker: New York, 1929.

8. Ransom, W. *Selective Check Lists of Press Books;* Duschnes: New York, 1945–1950.

9. Ridler, W. *British Modern Press Books;* Covent Garden Press: London, U.K., 1971.

10. Rodenberg, J. *Deutsche Pressen;* Amalthea-Verlag: Zurich, Switzerland, 1925.

11. Steele, R. *The Revival of Printing;* London, U.K., 1912.

12. Tomkinson, S.G. *A Select Bibliography of the Principal Modern Presses,* 1st Ed.; Club: London, U.K., 1928.

Histories and Critical Studies

1. Cave, R. *The Private Press;* Faber: London, U.K., 1971.

2. Franklin, C. *The Private Presses;* Studio-Vista: London, U.K., 1969.

3. Lucie-Smith, E. *The Little Press Movement in England and America;* Turret Books: London, U.K., 1968.

4. Standing, J. *The Private Press Today;* Brewhouse Press: Wymondham, England, 1967.

5. Turner, G. *The Private Press: Its Achievement and Influence;* Association of Assistant Librarians: London, U.K., 1954.

Provenance of Archival Materials

Shelley Sweeney
University of Manitoba, Winnipeg, Manitoba, Canada

Abstract

Historically, the principle of provenance was defined to mean that archivists must not mix the archival records of one person or organization with that of another. Sometimes this principle included respect for original order, which meant that records must be kept in the same order as maintained by the creator. In order to assign provenance, however, archivists needed to define the provenancial unit or the volume and level of records that would be described by provenance. This would be used as the basis for appraisal, acquisition, arrangement and description, retrieval, and reference. This definition was, and continues to be, problematic. Originally, the principle of provenance applied to both the physical and theoretical handling of records in an archives, but more recently archivists have suggested that provenance is a theoretical construct and that description based on provenance must capture all the myriad aspects of the origins of the records from the context of their use in the active record-keeping system to their transfer and handling in the archives. Since the inception of the principle of provenance, archivists have debated every aspect of it. The principle only gets more complex with time and the question becomes: how can these complex notions be applied in the real world?

INTRODUCTION

Provenance is considered to be a foundational principle of archival science, particularly in the Western world. It is the basis for acquiring, appraising, arranging, describing, and accessing archival records, or in other words, deciding what to acquire, how much to retain, whether to organize the records or leave them in their original order, how to describe the records, and how to find useful records. Provenance is also the means for establishing the authenticity of records and often can be used to date them. There is, however, disagreement among archivists and in the archival literature about what exactly constitutes provenance, how it can be attached to records, and how to apply provenance to various archival functions. Given this principle's importance to the practice of archival science and the complexity of its application, it is likely that the concept will continue to be further defined and refined in the future.

This entry covers the established definition of provenance, the origins and history of the development of the concept, the meaning of provenance, and the modern-day expansion of the principle. Readers will come to understand why, as French theorist Michel Duchein said, provenance "is easier to state than to define and easier to define than to put into practice."[1]

THE DEFINITION OF PROVENANCE

According to the International Council on Archives (ICA) *Multilingual Archival Terminology*, the word provenance is defined as being "the organization or individual that created, accumulated, and/or maintained and used RECORDS in the conduct of business prior to their transfer to a RECORDS CENTRE or ARCHIVES." The ICA Committee on Descriptive Standard's "Glossary of Terms Associated with General Rules" adds that it is also the relationship between records and the organizations or individuals that created, accumulated and/or maintained, and used them in the conduct of personal or corporate activity.[2] The principle of provenance means that "records/archives of the same provenance must not be intermingled with those of any other provenance."[3] There is an equivalent term for provenance: *respect des fonds*. The term *fonds* refers to the records created and accumulated by an individual, family, or organization in the conduct of their personal or corporate activity. So *respect des fonds* then means to respect these records by not intermingling them.

There is also the concomitant principle of original order, or *l'ordre primitif*, which according to the *Multilingual Archival Terminology* states that "archives of a single provenance should retain the arrangement (including the reference numbers) established by the creator in order to preserve existing relationships and evidential significance and the usefulness of finding aids of the creator.[4]

THE ORIGINS AND DEVELOPMENT OF THE CONCEPT

The Inclusion of Original Order and the Definition of the Provenancial Unit

The earliest documented origin of provenance was traced by Spanish archivist Rosana de Andres Diaz to the *Instruccion para el gobierno del Archivo de Simancas*

Encyclopedia of Library and Information Sciences, Fourth Edition DOI: 10.1081/E-ELIS4-120053423

published by Philip II in 1588, which applied the principle of provenance to the arrangement of title deeds.[5] E. Lodolini has traced the practice, if not the principle, back to the archives of Republican Rome.[6] American archivist Maynard Brichford brought to light the provenancial nature of the work of French Maurist scholar and Benedictine Dom Jean Mabillon. Mabillon's publication, *De re diplomatica libri sex*, published in 1681, established the science of diplomatics and paleography. His treatise on textual criticism and the authentication of documents directed attention to the source of records by employing detailed studies and comparisons of documents issued by the same chancellery.[7]

Mabillon's pioneering work was followed, Brichford noted, by diplomatic manuals employed by history professor Johann Gatterer at the historical institute that he founded in Göttingen, Germany, in 1764. These manuals similarly linked documents to the administrations that created them. According to Spanish archivist Antonia Heredia Herrera, archives were following the principle of *respect des fonds* in such diverse places as Halle (Saxony) in 1777, Denmark in 1791, and Naples in 1812.[8] Others have noted that the principle was legislated in the Grand Duchy of Tuscany in 1822 and the Papal State in 1839.[9]

These early forays into the theory and practice of provenance were supplanted in the nineteenth century by a new enthusiasm for subject arrangement. The practice of reorganizing records from different creators to fit subject classification schemes evolved into the principle of pertinence. There are many possible explanations for this interest in subject classification. Some of those employed in archives, such as Gottlieb Friedlaender, an archivist who worked in the Prussian State Archives from 1853 to 1873, were influenced by their library experience.[7] A number of authors have pointed out that during the European Enlightenment many scientists employed classification schemes to validate their pursuits and that this possibly provided a basis for the employment of such classification schemes in archives.[10]

But perhaps the most significant events that altered practices in archives were those where records associated with previous régimes were relegated to archives to fulfill scholarly interests rather than the interests of the state administration. This occurred in the Netherlands in 1795 and in France after the French Revolution in 1799. Instead of being working documents, these records became historical curiosities, and archivists began to cater to historians rather than to government officials. Subject classification only worked, however, if one could assign a classification to every document. As long as archivists did not have to manage any records of the current administration, they were able to assign such classification. While it was possible for them to classify each and every document when the amounts were very small, however, as time went on inevitably more current records began to enter the archives and as the volume of records grew it was no longer possible to treat records at the item level. The additional volumes began to affect the maintenance of a consistent classification scheme.

In addition to these reasons for abandoning subject classification for archival records, there was a growing realization that subject classification failed users in a number of important ways. For instance, subject classification physically assigned records to a single class. Further subject classification required a cross-reference system to be set up that linked the documents to other subjects, something that was extremely time-consuming for the significant amounts of individual documents that entered an archives. Yet records rarely provided information on only one or two topics, requiring a selection to be made as to which subjects were the most important. Organizing records classed by creator, however, gave unlimited points of entry, based on the activities and functions of that creator that could be captured globally for large numbers of documents tied together by their common provenance. Furthermore, there was a growing understanding that multiple relationships often existed between the records produced by one creator and that it was important to preserve these relationships. Later archival theorists would refer to this as the "organic" nature of records creation, reflecting the natural growth of records within a record-keeping system.

The French claim that they were responsible for reintroducing the notion of provenance when archivist, diplomatist, and historian Natalis de Wailly defined *respect des fonds* in a circular issued by the Minister of the Interior on April 24, 1841. In it, de Wailly stated that "all documents which come from a body, an establishment, a family, or individual form a *fonds*, and must be kept together." There is some debate about whether any consideration was given to original order. French archival theorist Michel Duchein maintained that *l'ordre primitif*, or original order, emerged shortly after de Wailly's original circular in France.[10] Canadian archival studies student Alain Giroux argued strongly that de Wailly's circular implied that *respect des fonds* was only to supplement pertinence, or the organization of records by subject, not to replace it and that original order emerged in Germany. Giroux noted that Johannes Papritz's "Verwaltungsstrukturprinzip" was used to classify records below the *fonds* level, employing administrative units of an organization in order to classify its records.[11]

In England, at about the same time de Wailly produced his circular in France, Sir Francis Palgrave, the first deputy keeper of public records, wrote in 1840 that archival records were to be placed in groups according to their provenance. Palgrave permitted a parallel "literary or theoretical classification" of records into subject groups to be registered on paper. This worthy attempt to establish the supremacy of *respect des fonds* was later supplanted by the physical rearrangement of records into different subjects or classes. In time however, Hilary Jenkinson, archivist and later deputy keeper of the British Public Records Office from 1906 to 1954, returned to the notion of provenance. The first step the archivist would make, Jenkinson declared, would be to determine which creators created and accumulated the different records in the archives. This practice would have reflected Jenkinson's own experience where records were disassociated from their creators. Only the records of an administration "complete in itself, capable of dealing independently, without any added or external authority, with every side of any business which could normally be presented to it" would warrant being kept together and these would be called an "archive group."[12] Once the creator was established, then the archivist was to study the history and organization of the administrations that produced the records, and to establish, or to reestablish as necessary, the original arrangement of the documents of the organization. However, as time went on and the volume of records increased, archivists abandoned Jenkinson's archive group and began to focus on the series or class level, a level that groups files or other physical units of related records together.[13]

Although we do not know how the notions of *respect des fonds* and original order spread, a number of countries developed these ideas shortly after de Wailly's circular. In Belgium, an Order in Council issued by Louis Prosper Gachard dated December 17, 1851, regulated the State archives in the provinces with instructions similar to de Wailly's.[14] In Italy, Francesco Bonaini developed the *metodo storico* in 1867, which included both *respect des fonds* and original order. This principle became state policy and was applied to all government records in Italy in 1875.[15] In Germany, the director of the Privy State Archives, Heinrich von Sybel, issued regulations employing provenance or *Provenienzprinzip* written by Max Lehmann on July 1, 1881. This principle was augmented by the registry principle or original order.[16] This principle made eminent sense in the context of the Prussian government because it was based on the central registry system used by the government bureaucracy. This system assigned designations to each document and then the designations were recorded in a central registry. It would have been exceedingly difficult for any archivist to try to tamper with such a rigid system once it was in place.

These developments, however, were eclipsed when the seminal *Handleiding voor het ordenen en beschrijven van archieven* or *Manual for the Arrangement and Description of Archives* by Dutch archivists Samuel Muller, Johan Feith, and Robert Fruin was published in the Netherlands in 1898.[17] It is pretty certain that this manual, which championed provenance or *herkomstbeginsel*, was influenced by developments in Germany and France. All three writers referred in their text to German and French manuals on diplomatics and to various French and German writers. In addition, Muller attended several lectures at the Écoles des Chartes, the archival studies school in

France, in 1873. It is also quite clear from studies made of the private papers left by the three authors that provenance included both *respect des fonds* and original order.[18] What made this development different from all the others across Europe was the influence the manual had on spreading and reinforcing these principles in other countries. The manual was published in German, Italian, French, and American editions in 1905, 1908, 1910, and 1940, respectively.

In their manual, Muller, Feith, and Fruin described the *fonds* or "archival collection" as "the whole of the written documents, drawings and printed matter, officially received or produced by an administrative body or one of its officials." Once the documents were placed in a repository, these collections were to be kept separate and in the same order that the organization that produced the records kept them in. The three authors felt that this order would correspond in the main to the organization of the administrative body.[17]

In 1910, the Conference of Librarians and Archivists held in Brussels gave international recognition to the principle of provenance when conference attendees formally endorsed the principle. Interestingly, although the conference actually used the word provenance, none of the early archival theorists or archivists, including the French, used that word, but most often referred to some variation of *respect des fonds*. The word provenance does not come into common use in English-speaking countries until much later in the twentieth century. British archivist Hilary Jenkinson wrote *A Manual of Archive Administration Including the Problems of War Archives and Archives Making* in 1922 and Italian archivist Eugenio Casanova published *Archivistica* in 1928.[19,20] These two manuals also helped publicize the ideas of *respect des fonds* and original order.

Waldo Gifford Leland, American historian and archivist, and New York State Archivist Arnold Johan Ferdinand Van Laer both attended the Congress in Brussels in 1910. Van Laer reported on the Brussels conference at a conference of archivists in Indianapolis in December of 1910, paving the way for the introduction of the principle of provenance to the United States. In a report to the Illinois State Education Building Commission in 1913, Leland outlined his understanding of the concept of provenance. He emphasized that the first activity of an archivist was to create a guide that outlined the various public offices and their functions. He felt that the records would clearly reflect the organization and functions that created them. These ideas were spread by annual meetings of the Public Archives Commission around the country. By the time the U.S. National Archives and Records Administration was founded in 1934, a number of state archivists were practicing the principle of provenance in their institutions.[21]

The employment of the principle took a sudden turn in 1941 when the committee set up to study the adequacy of finding aids at the National Archives introduced a variation of *respect des fonds*, which did not include original order and which established the "record group" as the unit of description. The record group was defined as "a major archival unit established somewhat arbitrarily with due regard for provenance and to the desirability of making the unit of convenient size and character for the work of arrangement and description and for the publication of inventories."[22] These record groups were themselves to be grouped into broad subject fields, such as defense or industry, or form, such as cartography or films, which it was hoped would aid in control. These groupings, however, were based in some cases on tenuous relationships, although the records continued to be identified by their creators. Commissions, for example, were all placed together even if they originated from different pieces of legislation to carry out completely different functions.

The reasons for the establishment of the record group were myriad. There were practical considerations to be made at the National Archives; archivists there had received 800,000 ft[3] of records *in a single decade* and were looking at even faster and larger accumulations in the years to come. According to American archivist Frank B. Evans, the lack of a strong tradition in methodical record-keeping, the absence of a fully developed registry system, the fluidity of administrative organization, the relatively late establishment of a national archival agency, the institutional autonomy and procedural diversity encouraged by a federal system of government, the strong influences exerted by the allied professions of the librarian and the manuscript curator, and the lack of a stable terminology all contributed to the development of this unique definition.[23] Whether the National Archives affected practices in other American archival repositories, or whether as American theorist Theodore Schellenberg supposed, the Library of Congress Manuscripts Division was responsible, Schellenberg discovered in 1942 that two-thirds of American repositories were arranging items chronologically and one-third were arranging material by subject, or using a combination of the two. In other words, almost no archives in the United States were employing the principle of provenance to arrange and describe their records.

Gradually, however, the ideas of *respect des fonds* and original order filtered down through the American archival community were strongly influenced by Schellenberg's seminal text *Modern Archives: Principles and Techniques* published in 1956 and reinforced by his second work *The Management of Archives*, which followed in 1965.[24,25] The archival community was also influenced by the writings of Schellenberg's compatriot Margaret Cross Norton who, often quoting Jenkinson, maintained that provenance was made up of both *respect des fonds* and original order.

In Canada, archivists were introduced to European archival theory in the 1950s through their colleagues in the United States. The then Public Archives of Canada followed the example of what became the National Archives and Records Administration by implementing a similar variation of provenance. In 1966, W. K. Lamb wrote in the journal *American Archivist* that the Public Archives of Canada used the word manuscripts to describe private papers and that this term enabled the archives to "organize the vast mass of miscellaneous papers into manuscript groups, each of which brings together collections that are alike in kind or in period or, occasionally, in subject matter."[26] The first Canadian essay on the principle of provenance was written by Robert Garon in Québec in 1969. However, it was not until 1977 that the attention of Québec archivists was drawn to the concept of *respect des fonds* by an article by French archivist Michel Duchein.[27,28] By the mid-1970s, Anglo-Canadian archivist Carl Vincent began to speak of using provenance theoretically on paper to define the record group, divorcing it from physical arrangement.[29]

The Consultative Group on Canadian Archives' report, published in 1980, established that archivists should employ the principle of provenance in order to provide the context of records. The group added what it called an extension of the principle that would become the first in a series of extensions of the concept. This extension was the principle of territoriality, which maintained that the locale or milieu of the records was part of their context. Allied to the principle of provenance was the principle of unbroken custody that stated that there needed to be a chain of continuous custody of the records in order to ensure their integrity. Thus, the group felt that archival materials "should be kept together, passed through as few hands as possible (at every stage with proper authority and continuity), and remain as close to their source as possible."[30] This report would be the foundation of the Bureau of Canadian Archivists' Planning Committee on Archival Descriptive Standards that chose the *fonds* as the basis of archival description in 1992. Finally, the translation of Michel Duchein's article into English in 1983 helped galvanize English-speaking archivists in Canada to apply the principle of provenance in their institutions.[1]

Australian archives employed provenance but in 1964 abandoned the record group in favor of the series. Peter J. Scott, an archivist at the National Archives of Australia, published an article in *The American Archivist* in 1966 that suggested that the record group was not capable of reflecting the variety of relationships that existed between records and government agencies. The lower level of the series was the only level that would allow records to be properly linked to all the various agencies that might have had responsibility for producing the records. As departments changed, as the names of departments changed, as their functions changed, as responsibilities for functions were split between departments, the records that arose from the same functions would be linked together. Peter Scott was the first to seriously challenge the level at which description would occur. After he fired the opening salvo in the battle over the level of the provenancial unit, there was a brief flurry of articles either supporting him and/or championing the status quo. Since Scott's application of provenance at the series level did not fit the records of private individuals very well, where series were ill defined and inconsistent, his system did not spread very far outside government archives in Australia. Several writers, including Australian Chris Hurley and Canadian Terry Cook, later noted that the real advancement that Scott made was not just linking records to multiple creators but more importantly breaking archival description away from the physical nature of the records. Scott in effect separated the description of the creator from the description of the records.[31]

HISTORIC DEVELOPMENTS IN THE MEANING OF PROVENANCE

While the definition of provenance, or what it was, changed over time, the meaning of the principle of provenance, or what it meant for archival practice, also changed. In Hilary Jenkinson's manual, for instance, he stated that papers that did not have the context provided by provenance would lack the qualities of *authenticity* and *impartiality*. Authenticity meant that the records were free from the suspicion of tampering; they were an authentic record of the person or organization that created them. Impartiality referred to the fact that records, by being drawn up in the course of daily activity, were an impartial testimony to the actions they represented. This was a very important point for Jenkinson. Archival records were not drawn up in the interests of posterity.

In the United States, Margaret Cross Norton felt that records were evidence and needed to be proven as authentic in order to be employed in a court of law and provenance was the tool to accomplish this. Theodore Schellenberg also saw records as evidence but, like Jenkinson, felt that they were evidence of actions. A birth certificate, for example, was the evidence of a government recognizing and documenting a birth; a diary was the evidence of persons recording their thoughts. This was the records' *evidential* value. But beyond the evidential value of records, Schellenberg felt that the contents of the records also held value and this was the records' *informational* value.

Based on the qualities of evidential and informational value, Schellenberg identified two uses for records. The *primary* use of a record was its usefulness to its creator. The *secondary* use of a record was its use to persons other than the creator. Schellenberg felt that records needed to be preserved for reasons beyond the creator's benefit in order to be considered archives, although the records might well be used by both the creator and others. Schellenberg felt that certain records would be preserved for their informational value only and not for their evidential value, and so records kept for that purpose could be

reorganized in an order that would best serve the needs of both scholars and government officials. Thus in that case, archivists would maintain the records by their creator but would not maintain original order.

French theorist Michel Duchein stressed the context of provenance, or the who, what, when, where, and why of records creation. He also talked about how to determine exactly what a *fonds* was, particularly the level of records creation. His *maximalist* level assigned the *fonds* at the highest level. Duchein pointed to Russia which treated the entire Russian country as forming a single *fonds*. Duchein's *minimalist* level would treat a department of a government as a *fonds*. When determining a *fonds*, the archivist would need to consider many qualities of the creator, such as a body having legal status, a structured, known organization regulated by an organizational chart, and so on. The *fonds* would be the basis for description.

Adolf Brenneke, the Director of the Prussian Privy Archives in Berlin, introduced in his lectures in the 1920s and 1930s the notion that provenance should reveal the functions of a business or government. It was the duty of the archivist to organize records to reflect how they were created. Researchers, he said, needed to know the structure of an organization, the organization's tasks and functions, and the structure of the records.[32] Brenneke was farsighted; many modern archivists have returned to this need for functional analysis of an organization either to produce a description of the record-keeping system or to appraise the value of records arising from these functions.

Thus, from the early archival theorists we can understand that keeping records by creator ensures that one can judge the authenticity of the record by answering such questions as who created these records for what purpose? In other words, are these documents what they purport to be? The context of the creation, under what conditions these records were created, is also critical to determining the value and reliability of the contents of the document. This becomes essential when one is caring for documents that ensure the rights of citizens for example. The legal values of records must be maintained in such cases. To use a modern-day example, knowing that a governmental office of vital statistics has recorded a death ensures that a will can be probated and heirs can inherit. By keeping records in their original order, where there is one, the archivist ensures that the functioning of the individual or organization is captured.

MODERN THINKING ABOUT PROVENANCE

In the early 1980s, there came a sea change in the understanding of provenance, propelled in part by both the urgent demand of electronic records and the possibilities offered by computer retrieval systems. In the United States, Richard Lytle reported on an experiment he conducted in comparing the results when archivists used provenance to retrieve archival materials versus when a computer system used content indexing methods of subject retrieval. He found that both methods had fairly similar retrieval results, but that provenance had its own strengths and could be improved.[33] In Canada, Gordon Dodds, addressing members of the Association of Canadian Archivists at their annual conference in 1982, entreated delegates to study provenance as a tool to tackle modern archival problems. His call to action was answered shortly after in an article by Terry Cook, who stated that archivists needed to shift from providing information from records to providing a contextual understanding of the provenance of the records.[34,35]

In the Winter 1985–1986 issue of Archivaria, Americans David Bearman and Richard Lytle wrote a prescient article that both consolidated thinking presented by earlier thinkers such as Scott and foreshadowed many later developments surrounding provenance. The two authors stated that archivists could make a unique contribution to information management by providing provenancial information about how organizations create, use, and discard information; provenance information about organizations (or creators) should be separate from descriptive data about the records themselves; archivists needed to capture organizational relationships in their provenance information; many-to-many relationships between creators and records also needed to be described; archivists should focus on the functions of organizations and the forms of their records to enhance the provenancial record; the authority record should include information about the history, structures, relationships, processes, and activities of records creating organizations; and such a record could show changes in particular functions or activities over time. Bearman and Lytle saw all of this enhanced provenancial information as providing a solid foundation for improved archival retrieval systems.[36] These first articles, combined with critical writings by Canadian Hugh Taylor a few years later, were the beginnings of a flowering of the notion of provenance.[37,38]

One of the new questions being asked was would provenance apply equally to both the physical and theoretical aspects of records? Although most assured the principle of provenance was meant to apply to the physical arrangement of archives in the repositories of the late eighteenth and nineteenth centuries, that slowly changed over time once more recent records began to enter archives. The volumes of these recently created archives increased exponentially, and many of the accumulated records remained open for further accruals. Archivists were no longer able to physically group together the total archival records of defunct administrations. Records typically began to be received and processed by archives in varying amounts referred to as accessions. Although there were still attempts at some sort of physical organization of records as late as the 1970s, eventually records were placed on shelves as they were received in whatever way made most

efficient use of space or eased retrieval and were assigned control numbers. There was no attempt to keep the records of a single department or person physically together. Archivists acknowledged that these accessions had to be maintained in order to preserve good physical and administrative control over the records. The accession would tell when the records were acquired, from whom and under what conditions. Archivists no longer used provenance in order to organize records physically in the archives but theoretically on paper.

With the advent of electronic records, the question was would provenance apply to such records, which often remained in situ, where they were created? The answer to the question of the application of provenance was fairly straightforward. As Terry Cook stated, "a world of relational databases, of complex software linkages, of electronic office systems, of hypermedia documents, of multilayered geographical information systems, is, when all the high-technology rhetoric is put aside, still a world of information relationships, of interconnections, of context, of evidence, of provenance."[39] Whether the records remained with the creator or were transferred into the archives, it would still be critical to know who was responsible for the creation of the records and the context of that creation and thus provenance would still be critically important to capture. Canadian Luciana Duranti emphasized that among other aspects, "an authentic electronic record is one the identity and integrity of which can be verified, that is, a record whose provenance and authorship are known at every time."[40]

At about the same time as Bearman and Lytle were writing of provenance in Archivaria, American Max Evans proposed the creation of authority control, or officially separating creator histories and linking them with all records associated with that body, which created a new relationship between provenance and original order.[41] Canadian Debra Barr expanded on Evans' idea, noting that inventories should demonstrate connections of records to as many creators *and other records* as was appropriate.[42,43] Chris Hurley added to this notion by suggesting that the context of records creation should expose multiple relationships based on formal functions.[44] Since then there has been major work on descriptive standards that would allow this separation of provenancial information from the descriptions of records, including the creation of the International Standard Archival Authority Record (Corporate Bodies, Persons, Families) or ISAAR (CPF). Australian Adrian Cunningham noted that the second iteration of ISAAR (CPF) added a new element to provenancial description: the relationships between creators and records. Michelle Light emphasized the importance of including all names or terms representing an entity as it changed over time.[45,46] David Bearman's desire to have functions recognized in provenancial descriptions came about with the development in 2007 of the ICA's International Standard For

Describing Functions, which provided guidance for describing the functions of corporate bodies associated with the creation and maintenance of archives, although the standard separates the description of functions from the description of provenance.[47]

Beyond these new considerations and developments, there has been a virtual explosion of writing on the subject, including proposals to radically expand the very notion of what constitutes provenance. Many of the authors have built on aspects of each other's work, adding new concepts and ideas. In analyzing provenance from a postmodern perspective, Terry Cook proposed a societal provenance that would acknowledge that records are authored and interpreted in a social context. This notion was seconded by Tom Nesmith who said this expanded view of provenance would contextualize the records more fully by providing information about the social circumstances that surrounded their creation. In this way, the provenance can never be fully known but is constantly emerging and evolving.[48,49] American Jeannette Bastian felt that creators of records and their acts of creation were tied to the actual spaces in which they engaged. This "provenance as place" suggested that there were multiple levels of provenance.[50] Lori Podolsky Nordland encouraged archivists to go beyond the surface interpretation of records to do the research and deconstruction of the records if necessary to add a "secondary provenance" to their description. She also noted that as records underwent what Hugh Taylor referred to as a "transmedia shift," the provenance of the record shifted or acquired new layers of meaning.[51] Joel Wurl proposed ethnicity as a form of archival provenance. This understanding of provenance would lead archivists to overcome a tendency toward excessive veneration in documenting ethnic groups, avoid oversimplified notions of cultural diversity, and would lead to the stewardship, instead of custodianship, of the records of ethnic communities. Chris Hurley stated that the provenancial context beyond that of the immediate creator should also be captured.[52,53] Emily Monks-Leeson also extended the coverage of provenance to new contexts created by new uses. "...As records take on new meetings and new contexts, understandings of provenance can shift to encompass not only the original contexts of creation (which should be preserved), but also those new contexts in which records come to belong."[54]

Other authors such as Canadian Laura Millar noted that while provenance was originally based on the concept of the *fonds*, the archival notion of the *fonds* was simply a theoretical construct. What came to the archives could never be the whole of the records created and accumulated by the creator, and what was preserved by the archives became an even smaller subset of the whole.[55] In Britain, Geoffrey Yeo agreed that the term fonds rarely describes the whole of the records of a single creator and furthermore, when those records are spread across a number of institutions, for each of those institutions to designate their part of a larger aggregation as a fonds is "misleading, if not erroneous."[56]

In applying provenance to personal records, Geoffrey Yeo said that conventional approaches to archival description used in capturing provenance did not do justice to the often complex histories of personal archives. Chris Hurley in Australia noted that all organizational records have both corporate and personal provenance.[56,57]

Laura Millar in recent years has suggested that provenance needs to capture three separate components: the creator context, the record-keeping context, and the custodial context. She based her definition of *creator context* on the definition by Terry Cook, stating that archivists should capture the functions and activities of the creator that produced the records. The *records-keeping context* would record the physical management and movement of the records over time and answer such questions as how the records were created and used, where the records moved to and why, and whether any records were lost, destroyed, enhanced, or altered and why, among others. The *custodial context* would document how the records came to be in the archives and how the archives managed the records over time.[55]

In terms of applying the principle of provenance to various archival functions, for Terry Cook , provenance was a tool for the appraisal of records, particularly the vast amounts of case files and records generated by government. Many other authors have agreed.[58] As for the role of the archivist in the principle of provenance, Emily Monks-Leeson in 2011 wrote that archivists and archival institutions contributed to the provenance of the records "through their acts of interpretation and inscription," and thus this also needed to be part of the description. Tom Nesmith noted "in their daily work archivists... make decisions about the origins of a record. For whatever reason, they focus on certain aspects of it which seem meaningful to them and omit much else which may or may not be knowable." He suggested that archivists may want to highlight different aspects of provenance depending on the records.[54,59] And finally, according to Jennifer Meehan in the United States, archivists should include information about their own maintenance, transmittal, and use of the records by all custodians, themselves included.[60]

Finally, regarding original order, in the Netherlands, Peter Horsman proposed in 2002 the principle of (virtual) provenance that would be a visualization through archival narratives that would describe "functional structures, both internal and external." Tom Nesmith stated that archivists should speak of the order the records are in when they arrive at an archives instead of original order.[61,62] As other postmodern archival scholars recognized, Canadian Heather MacNeil noted that the original order of a fonds is constructed, not found, by the archivist. She stated that "the arrangement of a body of records is not fixed at a single point in time. The survival and ongoing preservation of the records mean that they are in a continuous state of becoming as their physical and intellectual orders are shaped and reshaped, contextualized and recontextualized, initially by their creators and subsequently by their custodians." Archivists did not restore original order so much as construct and reconstruct it in accordance with their own biases and understandings. And finally, while archivists might understand the functions that created the records, they were also reminded that those records no longer carry out those functions. MacNeil called this "archivalterity."[63] When applying original order to personal records, Jennifer Meehan maintained that archivists could not use approaches that worked with organizational records but needed to focus attention on the relationships between records and activities whether there was a discernible order or not. Archivists should concentrate on the relationships between records and the activities that gave rise to them.[60]

CONCLUSION

The original conception of provenance was that it was the origin of archival records, and the notion that records of one creator must not be intermingled with those of another was the foundation of the principle of provenance. The corollary of this principle was the concept of original order that not only must records be identified by the person or organization that created or accumulated the records, but also the records should remain in the order in which they were originally kept. These two principles were born of necessity as European archivists struggled to gain physical control over records that had been passed from administration to administration. Depending on the unique situations of each country, different adaptations and interpretations of the concepts developed as they spread from Europe to other parts of the world. It is difficult to say whether countries outside the western tradition independently arrived at a similar principle (as only a small amount of archival literature from Asia, South America, the Middle East, etc., has been translated into English); this warrants further investigation.

Closely tied to this however has been the major struggle to identify the provenancial unit of control that formed the basis for arrangement, description, reference service, and so on. One could not identify the provenance of records unless one were able to determine the unit to which the identification would be attached. The advent of computers and the development of descriptive standards to take advantage of computer power only exacerbated the problem. Archivists began to take a renewed interest in provenance and original order and question the identification of the unit, the *fonds*, the archive group, the record group, or the series. It was only a matter of time before they began to reconsider every aspect of provenance and original order and their meaning for both archivists and researchers. Today the idea that provenance is simply the origin of archival records has been transformed into the idea that provenance captures the entire context of

the creation of records, everything from the identity of the person, persons, or organizations that created them, the system that supported them, and the conditions under which the records were created, to their movement from originator to archives, and the archivist or archivists who appraised chose and described them.

The principle of original order likewise changed to accommodate the postmodern realities that original order does not exist independent of the person who is describing it, and that it should reflect the relationships that exist between creators and records.

No doubt the future will bring further developments in thinking about the principles of provenance and original order. The changes these theoretical proposals have made to actual practice have been slow however, tempered by the awful reality of enormous twentieth-century backlogs of unprocessed records awaiting arrangement and description and the looming volume of physical records created from the Second World War on beginning to show up on archives' doors. A breakthrough that brings theory and practice together will require new thinking that concentrates on application.

ACKNOWLEDGMENTS

Thanks to the University of Manitoba for its support in completing this entry. Thanks also to Tom Nesmith, an acknowledged authority on the concept of provenance, for sharing his archival studies class reading list, and Mary Grace Golfo for tracking down further entries of interest. See also Shelley Sweeney, The ambiguous origins of the archival principle of 'provenance.' *Libraries Cultural Record* 2008, *43*, 193–215.

REFERENCES

1. Duchein, M. Theoretical principles and practical problems of *respect des fonds* in archival science. Archivaria **Summer 1983**, *16*, 64–82.
2. http://www.ciscra.org/mat/termdb/term/283 (accessed Oct 2014).
3. http://www.ciscra.org/mat/termdb/term/275 (accessed Oct 2014).
4. http://www.ciscra.org/mat/termdb/term/273 (accessed Oct 2014).
5. Andrés Díaz, R. The principle of provenance and the problems of authenticity regarding current records and their transfer from agency archives to other archives in the system. *The Principle of Provenance: Report from the First Stockholm Conference on Archival Theory and the Principle of Provenance*; Abukhanfusa, K., Sydbeck, J., Eds.; Centraltryckeriet: Borås, Sweden, 1994; 139–176.
6. Lodolini, E. Respect des fonds et principe de provenance: Histoire, theories, practiques. La Gazette des Arch. 1st trim **1995**, *168*, 210–212.

Print–Qualitative

7. Brichford, M. The provenance of provenance in Germanic areas. Provenance **1989**, 7, 54–70.

8. Herrera, A.H. *Archivística general: Teoría y práctica*, 5th Ed.; Publicaciones de la Exma, Diputación provincial de Sevilla: Seville, Spain, 1991.

9. Duranti, L. Origin and development of the concept of archival description. Archivaria **Spring 1993**, 35, 47–54.

10. Duchein, M. The history of European archives and the development of the archival profession in Europe. Am. Arch. **1992**, 55, 14–25.

11. Papritz, J. Méthodes modernes de classement d'archives: documentation écrite d'avant 1800. V congrès international des archives, Brussels, Belgium, Sept 1–5, 1964. Archives générales du royaume: Brussels, Belgium, 1964; 1–140; Quoted in Giroux, A. A theoretical and historical analysis of pertinence- and provenance-based concepts of classification of archives. MAS thesis, University of British Columbia, Vancouver, British Columbia, Canada, 1998.

12. Jenkinson, H. *A Manual of Archive Administration Including the Problems of War Archives and Archives Making*; Clarendon Press: Oxford, U.K., 1922; 84.

13. Roper, M. The development of the principles of provenance and respect for original order in the public record office. *The Archival Imagination: Essays in Honour of Hugh Taylor*; Craig, B., Ed.; Association of Canadian Archivists: Ottawa, Ontario, Canada, 1992; 134–154.

14. Geller, L.D.; Cuvelier, J. Belgian Archival Education and the First International Congress of Archivists, Brussels, 1910. Archivaria **Summer 1983**, 16, 26–34.

15. Lodolini, E. *Archivistica: Principie Problemi*; Franco Angeli: Milano, Italy, 1984; 129; Duchein, M. The history of European archives and the development of the archival profession in Europe. Am. Arch. **1992**, 55, 20.

16. Schellenberg, T.R. *Modern Archives: Principles and Techniques*; F.W. Cheshire: Melbourne, Victoria, Australia, 1956; 174.

17. Muller, S.; Feith, J.A.; Fruin, R. *Handleiding voor het ordenen en beschrijven van archiven (Manual for the Arrangement and Description of Archives)*; Erven B Van der Kamp: Groningen, the Netherlands, 1898; 13.

18. Horsman, P.; Ketelaar, E.; Thomassen, T. New respect for the old order: The context of the Dutch manual. Am. Arch. **Winter/Spring 2003**, 66, 249–270.

19. Jenkinson, H. *A Manual of Archive Administration Including the Problems of War Archives and Archives Making*; Clarendon Press: Oxford, U.K., 1922.

20. Casanova, E. *Archivistica*; Lazzeri: Siena, Italy, 1928.

21. Bartlett, N. France's archives: The library's counterpart. *Bibliographical Foundations of French Historical Studies*; McCrank, L.J., Ed.; Haworth Press: New York, 1991234.

22. Fenyo, M.D. The record group concept: A critique. Am. Arch. **1966**, 29 (2), 229–239.

23. Evans, F.B. Modern methods of arrangement of archives in the United States. Am. Arch. **1966**, 2 (2), 241–263.

24. Schellenberg, T.R. *Modern Archives: Principles and Techniques*; F.W. Cheshire: Melbourne, Victoria, Australia, 1956; 174.

25. Schellenberg, T.R. *The Management of Archives*; Columbia University Press: New York, 1965; 44.

26. Lamb, W.K. The changing role of the archivist. Am. Arch. **1966**, 29 (1), 9.

27. Garon, R. Le principe de provenance. Archives **1969**, 1 (2), 12–19.

28. Duchein, M. Le respect des fonds en archivistique: Principes théoriques et problèmes pratiques. La Gazette des archives **1977**, 97, 71–96.

29. Vincent, C. The record group: A concept in evolution. Archivaria **Winter 1976–1977**, 3, 3–16.

30. Report to the Social Sciences and Humanities Research Council of Canada by the Consultative Group on Canadian ArchivesCanadian Archives Social Sciences and Humanities Research Council of Canada: Ottawa, Ontario, Canada, 1980; 16.

31. Hurley, C. The Australian ('series') system: An exposition. *The Records Continuum Ian MacLean and Australian Archives: First Fifty Years*; McKemmish, S.; Pigott, M., Eds.; Ancora Press, 1994; 150–172; Cook, T. What is past is prologue: A history of archival ideas since 1898, and the future paradigm shift. Archivaria Spring **1997**, 43, 39.

32. Menne-Haritz, A. *Business Processes: An Archival Science Approach to Collaborative Decision Making, Records, and Knowledge Management*; Kluwer: Dordrecht, the Netherlands, 2004. http://books.google.com/books?id=4_PVoKNXzcC&pg=PA192&lpg=PA192&dq=Brenneke+Prussian+archives&source=web&ots=JKdTOpU7Il&sig=W8JlhWoZQR9Dur7GMZWo0xuNbcM&hl=en&sa=X&oi=book_result&resnum=7&ct=result(accessed Sept 3, 2008).

33. Lytle, R. Intellectual access to archives: I. Provenance and content indexing methods of subject retrieval. Am. Arch. **Winter 1980**, 43, 64–75; Intellectual access to archives: II. Report of an experiment comparing provenance and content indexing methods of subject retrieval. Am. Arch. Spring **1980**, 43, 191–207.

34. Dodds, G. What is an archivist? Unpublished manuscript1982; 1–2. Quoted in Nesmith, T. Introduction: Archival studies in English-speaking Canada and the North American rediscovery of provenance. In *Canadian Archival Studies and the Rediscovery of Provenance*; Nesmith, T., Ed.; The Scarecrow Press: Metuchen, NJ, 1993.

35. Cook, T. From information to knowledge: An intellectual paradigm for archives. Archivaria **Winter 1984–1985**, 19, 28–49.

36. Bearman, D.; Lytle, R. The power of the principle of provenance. Archivaria **Winter 1985–1986**, 21, 14–27.

37. Taylor, H. Transformation in the archives: Technological adjustment or paradigm shift. Archivaria **Winter 1987–1988**, 25, 12–28.

38. Taylor, H. 'My very act and deed': Some reflections on the role of textual records in the conduct of affairs. Am. Arch. **Fall 1988**, 51, 456–469.

39. Cook, T. What is past is prologue: A history of archival ideas since 1898, and the future paradigm shift. Archivaria **Spring 1997**, 43, 41.

40. Duranti, L. The impact of digital technology on archival science. Arch. Sci. **2001**, 1, 39–55.

41. Evans, M.J. Authority control: An alternative to the record group concept. Am. Arch. **1986**, 49, 249–261. Although in effect authority control had been part of Scott's solution on paper, most of his attention was placed on describing records at the series level.

42. Barr, D. The *fonds* concept in the working group on archival descriptive standards report. Archivaria **Winter 1987–1988**, *25*, 163–170.

43. Barr, D. Protecting provenance: Response to the report of the working group on description at the *fonds* level. Archivaria **Summer 1989**, *28*, 141–145.

44. Hurley, C. What, if anything, is a function. Arch. Manus. **Nov 1993**, *21*, 208–220.

45. Cunningham, A. Harnessing the power of provenance in archival description: An Australian perspective on the development of the second edition of ISAAR (CPF). J. Arc. Org. *5* (1–2), 15–31.

46. Light, M. Moving beyond the name: Defining corporate entities to support provenance-based access. J. Arc. Org. *5* (1–2), 49–74.

47. http://www.ica.org/10208/standards/isdf-international-standard-for-describing-functions.html (accessed Nov 2014).

48. Cook, T. Fashionable nonsense or professional rebirth: Postmodernism and the practice of archives. Archivaria **2001**, *51*, 14–39.

49. Nesmith, T. The concept of societal provenance and records of nineteenth-century Aboriginal-European relations in Western Canada: Implications for archival theory and practice. Arch. Sci. **2006**, *6*, 351–360.

50. Bastian, J.A. In a "house of memory": Discovering the provenance of place. Arch. Issues **2003–2004**, *28*, 9–19.

51. Podolsky Nordland, L. The concept of "secondary provenance": Re-interpreting Ac ko mok ki's map as evolving text. Archivaria **Fall 2004**, *58*, 147–159.

52. Wurl, J. Ethnicity as provenance: In search of values and principles for documenting the immigrant experience. Arch. Issues **2005**, *29*, 65–76.

53. Hurley, C. Ambient functions: Abandoned children to zoos. Archivaria **Fall 1995**, *40*, 21–39.

54. Monks-Leeson, E. Archives on the Internet: Representing contexts in provenance from repository to website. Am. Arch. **Spring/Summer 2011**, *74*, 44.

55. Millar, L. The Death of the fonds and the resurrection of provenance: Archival context in space and time. Archivaria **Spring 2002**, *53*, 312–345; An unnecessary complication: International perspectives on the record group, the series and the fonds. In Cunningham, A. Ed., The arrangement and description of archives amid administrative and technological change: Essays and reflections by and about Peter J. Scott, Australian Society of Archivists, 2010.

56. Yeo, G. Custodial history, provenance, and the description of personal records. Libr. Cult. Rec. **2009**, *44* (1), 50–64.

57. Hurley, C. Problems with provenance. Arch. Manus. **1995**, *23*, 234–259.

58. Cook, T. What is past is prologue: A history of archival ideas since 1898, and the future paradigm shift. Archivaria **Spring 1997**, *43*, 48.

59. Nesmith, T. Still fuzzy, but more accurate: Some thoughts on the "ghosts" of archival theory. Archivaria **Spring 1999**, *47*, 141.

60. Meehan, J. Rethinking original order and personal records. Archivaria **Fall 2010**, *70*, 27–44.

61. Horsman, P. The last dance of the phoenix, or the de-discovery of the archival fonds. Archivaria **Fall 2002**, *54*, 23.

62. Nesmith, T. Reopening archives: Bringing new contextualities into archival theory and practice. Archivaria **Fall 2005**, *60*, 259–74.

63. MacNeil, H. Archivalterity: Rethinking original order. Archivaria **Fall 2008**, *66*, 1–24.

BIBLIOGRAPHY

1. Barritt, M.R. Coming to America: Dutch *archivistiek* and American archival practice. Arch. Issues; **1993**, *18*, 43–54.

2. Berner, R.C. The power of provenance: A critique of David Bearman and Richard Lytle. Archivaria **Summer 1986**, *22*, 4–6.

3. Boles, F. Disrespecting original order. Am. Arch. **1982**, *4* (1), 26–32.

4. Collin, H. La mise en oeuvre du principe de respect des fonds: Réflexions sur l'état actuel. Archives **1990**, *22* (2), 3–8.

5. Cook, T. The concept of the archival fonds in the post-custodial era: Theory, problems and solutions. Archivaria **Spring 1993**, *35*, 24–37.

6. Green, K.A. The series: A specialized 'record group'? Arch. Manuscr. **1967**, *3* (2), 13–15.

7. Horsman, P. Dirty hands: A new perspective on the original order. Arch. Manuscr. **1999**, *27* (1), 42–53.

8. Hurley, C. The Australian ('series') system: An exposition. The Records Continuum; Piggott, M.; McKemmish, S., Eds.; Ancora Press: Melbourne, Victoria, Australia, 1994; 150–172.

9. Hurley, C. Problems with provenance. Arch. Manuscr. **1995**, *23* (2), 234–259.

10. Krawczyk, B. Cross reference heaven: the abandonment of the fonds as the primary level of arrangement for Ontario government records. Archivaria **Fall 1999**, *48*, 131–153.

11. Lodolini, E. *Archivistica. Principi e problemi*, 7th Ed.; Franco Agneli: Milano, Italy, 1995.

12. McCausland, S. Adapting the series system: A study of small archives applications. The Records Continuum; Piggott, M.; McKemmish, S., Eds.; Ancora Press: Melbourne, Victoria, Australia, 1994; 173–186.

13. Mulé, A. The Principle of provenance: Should it remain the bedrock of the profession. Archivum Proceedings of the 13th International Congress on Archives, Beijing, China, Sept 2–7, 1996; K.G. Saur: Munich, Germany, 1997; 233–256.

14. Polden, K.A. The record group—A matter of principle. Arch. Manuscr. **1968**, *3* (1), 3–7.

15. Rousseau, J. Le respect des fonds.- la quintessence de la discipline archivistique. Archives **1990**, *22* (2), 9–14.

16. Schellenberg, T.R. The principle of provenance and modern records in the United States. Am. Arch. **1965**, *28* (1), 39–41.

17. Smith, C. A case for abandonment of "respect" Arch. Manuscr. **1986**, *14* (2), 154–168. **1987**, *15*(1), 20–28.

18. Zelenyj, D. Linchpin imperilled: The functional interpretation of series and the principle of respect des fonds. Archivaria **Fall 1996**, *42*, 126–136.

Print–Qualitative

Provenance of Museum Objects

Layna White
San Francisco Museum of Modern Art, San Francisco, California, U.S.A.

Abstract

Museum professionals, museum supporters, and observers understand provenance to be the history and circumstances of an object's ownership and possession. Knowing the story of an object's ownership and possession may contribute to understanding the relative meanings and significances of that object to individuals, nations, groups, and locations and may improve understandings of legal rights, titles, and interests in objects. Museum professionals understand that ascertaining and sharing provenance information can further public trust and public service and build historical records for objects. However, the ability of museums of any type to ascertain provenance for objects is greatly dependent on the motivations and practices of past owners or possessors, and other interested parties, to document and share knowledge about ownership and possession. Discussions and actions within the last several years related to the history and practices surrounding twentieth- and twenty-first-century acquisitions of certain objects by museums have focused acute attention on the importance of studying, documenting, and revealing provenance.

INTRODUCTION

The meaning of provenance in a museum context is unambiguous. Museum professionals, museum supporters, and observers understand provenance to be the history and circumstances of an object's ownership or possession. While the definition of provenance may be commonly understood, the ability of museums of any type to ascertain provenance for objects is greatly dependent on the motivations and practices of past owners or possessors, and other interested parties, to document and share knowledge about ownership and possession.

Expressed stewardship mandates of museums commonly imply aspects of collecting, preserving, interpreting, and exhibiting objects. In museum parlance, *object* is used to describe very generically the fullest range of items conceivably collected, preserved, interpreted, and exhibited by museums, recognizing the flattening effect of using one term to denote items of potentially vastly different types and meanings, ranging, for instance, from works of fine art such as paintings and sculptures, and artifacts such as flags and masks to natural world specimens such as plants and shells. Distinctions might be drawn between definitions of *object* used here as a generic, equalizing term to describe products of humankind and nature, and *cultural property* used elsewhere to identify products of humankind and nature deemed by some to have special significance to the cultural heritage of a nation or group, or special significance to a location. This entry intends to review, under one umbrella, the meanings, roles, and practices around provenance information within the context of diverse types of museums, such as public, private, and governmental museums of art, cultural history, history, anthropology, natural history, and science.

The following provides an overview of topical issues facing museum professionals when studying, documenting, and sharing information about provenance, beginning with a general discussion of ownership and possession, and the relevance of such to museum policies, particularly reflecting on recent interest in the history and practices surrounding twentieth- and twenty-first-century acquisitions by museums of certain types of objects. The entry then considers sources for provenance information and explores the challenges of finding partial, conflicting, or otherwise not wholly complete and accurate information for an object, and the part museums may play in perpetuating the availability of only partial information.

While provenance research, documentation, and dissemination competes with other demands for museum resources, museum professionals understand that work around ascertaining and sharing provenance information can further public trust and public service and build historical records for objects. Within at least the last 40 years, motivations from within museums, and influences from without, have kept discussions of provenance related to museum objects active and passionate.

CUSTODIAL PATHS

The ownership and possession of an object is marked chiefly by place (location), time (duration), and purpose (circumstance). To determine and, ideally, ultimately, to share an object's provenance, museums must first map the path of ownership or possession, from the place and time of an object's origin through a maker, patron, or culture or from the time of an object's discovery at a findspot, through any subsequent points of rest and transactions,

Encyclopedia of Library and Information Sciences, Fourth Edition DOI: 10.1081/E-ELIS4-120053452

reaching the place and time of that same object's current or last known owner or possessor. The term *provenience* is used by archeologists to mean the original context of an object or, more precisely, to mean documentation of an object's original findspot, including description of its placement and interpretation of its situation relative to other objects found in the same place. This entry considers the findspot for an archeological object to be the starting point of its custodial path.

Custodial paths—marking points of rest and transactions—can vary in duration, purpose, and traceability, with some objects changing hands more frequently and more transparently than others. Objects might change hands through transfers of title, such as by gift, bequest, purchase, sale, or exchange. Ownership and possession might otherwise be defined by agreements for commissions, shared ownership, restitution, or repatriation. In theory (although unlikely in practice), an object might be transferred from the original owner, or location, through a hybrid and abbreviated combination of private, unknown, corporate, governmental, and museum collections, with the majority of transfers in ownership occurring at the private collection level (p. 269).[1] With familiar or longer-established media—such as paintings, decorative arts, coins—in layman's terms, owning an object is equated with having physical control of the object as property. Some contemporary artists are pressing understandings of what it means to own an object in that, in some cases, the original work of art may not have a primary, staid physicality. Observations about works created by the artist Tino Sehgal (born 1976, London; active Berlin) provide just one example:

Art can be defined, provocatively, as an intangible quantity that transforms an ordinary object—a urinal, a soup can, an unmade bed—into something worth many times more than its material value. Tino Sehgal seeks to isolate precisely that intangible quantity. His art is completely immaterial; it can be bought and sold without involving any objects whatsoever.[2]

In such cases, an owner may acquire from the artist a right to make new instances of the artist's original concept based on parameters agreed upon by the artist and the owner. Exercising a right to make new instances may or may not yield a physical object, and the outcome may vary, instance to instance, prompting questions about the object per se and what is actually being collected.

In other cases, simply possessing a physical object may not constitute legal or valid right, title, or interest in that object, as when, for example, a current owner consigns an object to an auction house in order for the auction house to promote the object, its maker, or past owner (e.g., someone of renown) when brokering the sale of that object to a new owner, or when authorities in a country at war give temporary custody of at-risk objects to a public museum located elsewhere for safekeeping until the objects can be returned to the country of origin. Provenance

information for an object should distinguish between those who have owned an object and those who have held the object transitionally.

Tracing the custodial path for an object is also intertwined with verifying that the information at hand about an object, its path, and caretakers is connected with the actual object under review. The concerns here include receipt of completely fabricated provenances or innocently inaccurate mix-ups that connect otherwise reliable details about provenance to the wrong object. Demonstrating verisimilitude between provenance information and an actual, or the original, object through place and time, however, might be predictably and acceptably variable. As noted, with some contemporary works of art, for example, a collector may acquire a right to use the artist's original concept, and any "object" resulting from exercising that right may or may not be the same as any previous instance. This kind of predictable, intended variability is distinguished from circumstances where caretakers take it upon themselves to change an object in ways unexpected and unintended by the artist/maker or culture, as when, for example, a medieval altarpiece has been radically restructured by division into parts for dispersal to different locations.

Rightful, Clear, or Good Title

Knowing the story of an object's custodial path may contribute to understanding the relative meanings and significances of that object to individuals, nations, groups, and locations, and the object's function within any intended and subsequent contexts. From legal and ethical perspectives, knowledge of provenance may improve understandings of rights, titles, and interests in objects. Ownership may be described as rightful, legitimate, legal, valid, clear, clean, good, and proper as in, having rightful, clear, or good title in objects. The means and requirements for acquiring rightful, clear, or good title in an object may differ under different nations' laws and may vary by type of object (e.g., requirements for acquiring a well-documented modern sculpture directly from the artist may be different from the level of diligence expected when acquiring a fragment of an ancient urn long removed from an archeological site).[3–5]

Depending on the types of objects and scopes of collections involved, the museum professional researching provenance will be aware that countries such as China, Egypt, Greece, Peru, and Turkey have modern patrimony laws that give the national government primary ownership rights and interests in some objects created or newly discovered in that nation's territories. Patrimony laws imply support for cultural nationalism, or a national cultural heritage view, which recognizes that certain objects have special significances to originating nations, groups, or locations, and privileges a nation's rights to possess and provide access to those objects over other ownership interests, in some cases, regardless of the perceived legitimacy of subsequent transfers in title or possession.[6] This position has been criticized as being retentionist and politically based.

The museum professional researching provenance will also be aware that some nations—including Australia, Canada, and the United States—have laws covering the possession and control of human remains and certain cultural materials. For example, the U.S. Native American Graves Protection and Repatriation Act of 1990 (http://www.nps.gov/nagpra) recognizes that descendants have primary rights to possess, control, and guide outcomes of ancestral remains, funerary and sacred objects, and cultural patrimony notwithstanding current possessions by nondescendants.[7,8]

Some museum professionals, museum supporters, and observers advocate cultural internationalism, or a world cultural heritage view, emphasizing the value of more open access to objects in furthering understandings of cultural heritage. Cultural internationalism holds that objects are common patrimony, belonging to all peoples, and assumes museums—depending on type, mission, and scope—need objects to move from location to location in order for museums to collect, preserve, interpret, and exhibit objects. This view foregrounds a belief in the contemporary museum as an impartial caretaker in providing objects, regardless of origin, with a good home, good care (such as curatorial, documentation, and conservation services), and good visibility through public display and discourse, an assertion reproached by others as elitist and encouraging destruction of original context.[9–11]

The "Elgin Marbles" (or the Parthenon sculptures) at the British Museum in London are a frequently cited example of a dispute over ownership, possession, and location.[6,12,13] In brief, the "Elgin Marbles" comprise a group of sculptures removed from the Parthenon on the Acropolis in Athens between 1801 and 1805 under the direction of Lord Elgin (an early-nineteenth-century British ambassador to the Ottoman Empire), with the assent of Ottoman Empire officials (then in control of Greece). Elgin transported the sculptures out of Greece to Britain; and in 1816 the sculptures were acquired by the UK Parliament from Elgin, and placed subsequently in the British Museum (https://www.britishmuseum.org/about_us/news_and_press/statements/parthenon_sculptures.aspx).

Some have argued that the "Elgin Marbles" in the British Museum should be returned to Greece because the sculptures are intrinsically Greek, therefore of utmost significance to Greece and the identity of the Greek people; this perhaps in addition to believing that the removal of the sculptures by Elgin was legally and ethically problematic. Taking this view, the sculptures should be returned and installed in the Acropolis Museum in Athens, opened in 2009 and located very near the Parthenon, providing an obvious place and time to reunite the sculptures removed

under Elgin's direction with those objects from the Parthenon still remaining in Athens. Counterarguments for keeping the sculptures at the British Museum consist of the perceived legitimacy of the transactions (to Elgin from Ottoman officials; to Britain by Elgin), as well as the bond the British people now have with the sculptures, and beliefs that the British Museum will continue to provide the sculptures with a good home, good care, and good visibility.

When questions about ownership or possession arise, an object's documented provenance may provide examiners and owners with key information. A previous owner may seek to recover an object when the modes of transfer surrounding later possessions are deemed problematic, a determination perhaps made partly after considering information (or lack thereof) about an object's path of ownership, possession, and location.[14] In some cases, the provenance secured by a current owner may be considered irrelevant when weighed alongside assertions that, for example, a nation holds primary rights to an object. Here, calls to right wrongful possessions may point to the special cultural, historical, archeological, religious, or spiritual significance of the physical object to a nation, group, or location (an argument put forth by both parties in the case of the "Elgin Marbles").

Interest in Provenance

Within at least the last 40 years [loosely marked by the 1970 United Nations Educational, Scientific and Cultural Organization (UNESCO) Convention described in the following text], governments, journalists, merchants (such as dealers and auction houses), and communities of museums, researchers, and descendants of object makers have focused acute attention on the importance of studying and revealing provenance. Much attention has been given to revealing information about aspects of ownership or possession that might suggest questionable transfers or, conversely, might provide evidence or convincing arguments to quash such suggestions. Discussions and actions are particularly heated around identifying and possibly returning to previous or rightful owners objects looted, seized, and/or illegally exported in the twentieth and twenty-first centuries such as antiquities, archaeological objects, and ethnographic materials taken clandestinely by individuals from historical structures and archeological sites located around the world and works of art and Judaica abandoned unwillingly by owners or taken forcefully in Europe during the Nazi era. DeAngelis poses the question, "…when can we ignore misdeeds of the past?" (p. 253);[15] see also Merryman[9] and Yeide et al.[16] for descriptions of pre-twentieth-century plundered objects finding their way into museum collections.

Museum organizations and international bodies such as the American Alliance of Museums (AAM, formerly the American Association of Museums), the Museums

Association in the United Kingdom, and UNESCO have campaigned to encourage museums to document and share, as widely as possible, images and descriptive information about objects in permanent collections, including information about known and incompletely known provenance. Calls for information sharing and transparency related to collecting activities often point to the public service and education goals of museums as reasons enough to make information about objects available through, for example, online collections catalogs, print publications, and on-site exhibitions.

MUSEUM POLICIES

Each type of museum may face, and certain objects may pose, distinct challenges relating to provenance. All museums, however, may consider a set of fundamental questions relating to ownership and possession when, for example, publishing descriptions of objects in collection or exhibition catalogs and borrowing objects from other collections for inclusion in temporary exhibitions. Questions about ownership and possession specifically comprise part of the diligence and care exercised by museums today when accepting or buying newly proposed objects for permanent collections.[17,18] Fundamental questions are considered concerning where an object has been, with whom, when, and under what circumstances. Contemporary museum policies for acquiring, preserving, interpreting, and exhibiting objects may acknowledge the importance of ascertaining as complete and accurate provenance information as possible in furtherance of good stewardship of objects (acquired for permanent collections or borrowed for temporary exhibitions), building historical records for objects, and sustaining public trust by demonstrating ethical practices.

It is not unusual, however, for museums to know imperfectly, at present, the full story of an object's ownership and possession, from place and time of origin to the current or last known owner or possessor. Museums will need and want to continue operating in the time between having partial, more than partial, and perhaps complete knowledge of provenance. In support of collecting activities in particular, a museum may establish parameters for accepting, buying, or rejecting proposed objects when provenance is, at the time of offer, known incompletely. For instance, a museum's acquisition policy might place the responsibility of judging and advocating the acquisition of objects with limitedly known, but not suspicious, provenances squarely in the hands of museum curators. See, for example, the British Museum's *Policy on Acquisitions*.[19]

Some believe, and museum acquisition policies may imply, that museums should be in positions to provide objects with good homes, good care, and good visibility. In other words, assuming objects are acquired properly and through open channels (e.g., reputable commercial markets), and absent evidence of problematic transfers, museums are in better positions than some to be repositories and advocates for objects with incompletely known provenances.[20] While a currently incompletely known provenance does not automatically or necessarily mean that something about an object's history of possession is problematic, others argue that by continuing to acquire objects (particularly those originating from historical structures and archeological sites) with incompletely known provenances, even good-faith donees or purchasers (who have conducted some form of due diligence and acquired objects properly), might inadvertently intensify the market for objects with problematic histories of possession and, further, encourage contemporary clandestine stripping of objects from historical structures and archeological sites, without regard to documentation or interpretation, resulting in loss of knowledge about contexts and meanings relative to a place, time, and people.[21]

The international agreement, the 1970 UNESCO Convention on the Means of Prohibiting and Preventing the Illicit Import, Export and Transfer of Ownership of Cultural Property (http://www.unesco.org), intends to protect objects from illicit removals and changes in possession, and protect nations from undue loss of cultural heritage. Many museum professionals, museum supporters, and observers have generally interpreted the principles and directives articulated in the Convention to mean that, to be acquired soundly and ethically today, certain types of objects must have been in proper circulation outside an originating nation before 1970 (using the date of the Convention as a marker), or have been legally exported from that nation and in proper circulation after 1970. Contemporary museum policies may refer to the Convention as one benchmark to apply when assessing the soundness of acquiring certain types of objects.[22,23] The literature includes passionate discussions about the implications of contemporary exporting and importing of objects, such as antiquities and ethnographic materials, with currently incompletely known ownership histories. It is generally agreed, however, that preventing illicit removals of objects from structures and sites should be a priority for the cultural heritage community.

MUSEUM PRACTICES

Beginning in the 1990s, many museums began making mostly modest portions of collections information available on institutional websites, including, to greater and lesser extents, some provenance information about objects. Ongoing moves by museums to share more collections information on websites, other digital platforms, and through linked open-data initiatives are in line with expectations of museum professionals, museum supporters, and observers that museums should share what they know or believe about artists/makers, the objects themselves, and the values, meanings, or functions associated with objects, and encourage discourse with museum audiences about objects and these contexts.

In this respect, provenance is one among several areas of interest in museums competing for research, documentation, and dissemination resources. Museums may need to prioritize which objects in a collection and which types of information will be the focus of research, documentation, and dissemination at a given time. Retrospective provenance research may be higher or lower in priority depending on the museum and its influences, such as the expressed interests of museum supporters (including museum audiences) and museum observers (including museum professional organizations and government agencies), as well as by work underway for contemporaneous museum activities (e.g., inventorying collections, making new acquisitions, exhibitions, publications, and conserving objects). Permanent professional positions focused solely on provenance research are uncommon in museums, excepting perhaps specialized positions created by some larger museums to speed sharing of provenance information. Provenance research is more likely part of a defined project, or folded into the routine information activities of staff with curatorial, registrarial, or documentation responsibilities.

Efforts to address issues related to some twentieth- and twenty-first-century acquisitions of antiquities, archeological objects, and ethnographic materials and looting of objects by the Nazis provide examples of expressed interests influencing museum prioritizations for research, documentation, and sharing of provenance. As a case in point, in 2000 the AAM, Association of Art Museum Directors, and the Presidential Advisory Commission on Holocaust Assets announced an agreement recognizing the commitment of U.S. museums to disclosing provenances for objects in permanent collections that might have changed hands in Europe during the Nazi Era (1933–1945).[24] In 2006 the Conference on Jewish Material Claims Against Germany sharply criticized U.S. museums for their slowness in making available provenance information for objects in accordance with the 2000 trilateral agreement. Today, the responsiveness and actions of U.S. and European museums in addressing matters of provenance for objects within this scope continue to garner international attention and concern.[25,26]

Museum Standards

Museums demonstrate differing practices for and commitments to sharing provenance information for all types of objects. Some museums may make available only the known and verified provenance for an object, which might include vague references to past owners (e.g., gift of an anonymous donor) and might exclude information for all but the most immediate past owner (i.e., excluding owners prior to the anonymous donor), and/or skim over known

gaps in the history of ownership or possession. Other museums may communicate, bluntly, in widely available online records that there are known gaps in the custodial path for a particular object. See, for example, efforts of U.K. museums to share information about objects with gaps in provenances covering the Nazi era: http://www.collectionstrust.org.uk/collections-link/cultural-property-advice/spoliation. For a chair made in France in 1925, for example, a museum might note that before acquisition by the museum in 2007, the chair was in the private collection of Jane and John Doe from 1940 to 2007, but the location of the chair from 1925–1939 is unknown. Putting consistently described provenance information in a shared online environment may increase access to that information, and help bring together distributed, related content, but its usefulness—to museum professionals, museum supporters and observers, previous owners, and descendants of object makers—will depend in some measure on the completeness, accuracy, and understandability of the information. For instance, the museum data standard Categories for the Description of Works of Art notes, "It should be possible, for example, to locate all the works in a particular collection, or to answer questions such as 'What works, now in American collections, were owned by the eighteenth-century Venetian collector Padre Resta?'"[27]

Museums keep provenance information, particularly about objects in permanent collections, in a combination of internal systems typically comprising a collections management system and documents (paper or digital) authored or collected by staff with curatorial, registrarial, or documentation responsibilities. Standards for museum object information reflect practices and certain expectations around provenance documentation and dissemination. A museum might refer to standards such as the Categories for the Description of Works of Art (CDWA) (http://www.getty.edu/research/publications/electronic_publications/cdwa/index.html), CIDOC Conceptual Resource Model (CIDOC CRM) (http://www.cidoc-crm.org/Version/version-6.2), and Spectrum (http://www.collectionstrust.org.uk/spectrum) when planning or vetting current systems for documentation. Each of these standards refers to ownership and possession, and each might offer museum professionals' part, or most, of what is needed to organize provenance information in, for example, a collections management system.

For example, the CDWA includes several data elements related to provenance:

- Ownership/collecting history—provenance description (e.g., prose description of the custodial path)
- Ownership/collecting history—owner/agent (e.g., Doe, Jane)
- Ownership/collecting history—transfer mode (e.g., gift, purchase)
- Ownership/collecting history—owner's credit line (e.g., Gift of Jane and John Doe)

- Current location—repository/geographic location—(e.g., City Art Museum, My Town)

The CDWA identifies just one provenance-related data element as a core category comprising a core record for an object: Current Location—Repository/Geographic Location. This category is intended to identify only the current or last known owner, a limitation that may well reflect practical experience in art museums in particular: namely, that it is not unusual for museums to know imperfectly the full story of an object's past ownerships and possessions; therefore, recording anything beyond current or last known owner may be highly recommended, but is optional.

The CIDOC CRM identifies two specific classes (or, loosely, elements) that are primed for data reflecting museum understandings of ownership and possession. The classes Acquisition and Transfer of Custody can be used to tease apart the state of having legal and valid right, title, and interest in an object (Acquisition) from that of having transitional custody (Transfer of Custody); both states, as noted earlier, are important for provenance research, documentation, and sharing.

Spectrum identifies units of information (or, loosely, elements) for recording an "owner's personal experience" with an object (such as personal meanings or relevancies) and an "owner's personal response" to an object (such as personal feelings about the object), in addition to identifying expected elements related to ownership history such as the Ownership Exchange Method (gift, purchase), Owner (City Art Museum), and Ownership Dates (1951–2007).

In terms of cataloging practices, several resources—including CDWA, the AAM Guide to Provenance Research,[16] and Cataloging Cultural Objects (CCO) (http://cco.vrafoundation.org/index.php/toolkit/cco_pdf_version/)—suggest basic principles and expectations for recording and communicating information about provenance: for example, be clear, specific, accurate, attempt to fully account for the history of ownership (to the extent possible), and cite information sources. Getting to the point where it is possible to record and communicate as complete and accurate provenance as possible can take time, diligence, and care. Museum professionals work—over periods of time and through changes in staffing—to reduce incompleteness or imperfections in provenance information to the extent possible, given that the information known and available to a museum at a particular time may be partial, conflicting, inaccurate, or otherwise not entirely satisfactory.

TIME, DILIGENCE, AND CARE

A museum's ability to secure provenance information will depend partly on the priority and standard for documentation and dissemination followed by each previous owner or possessor, and/or by those with professional or academic interests in objects, such as independent researchers. Each known collecting entity or interested party may have idiosyncratic motivations and practices for documenting and sharing knowledge about previous and current ownerships, possessions, and locations. Museums, for instance, may be motivated to share information in furtherance of public trust, public service, and building historical records for objects. (As noted, museums may have idiosyncratic practices and motivations for sharing provenance, and therefore may have a hand in perpetuating uncertainties.) Other owners may not feel bound or influenced by the same levels of accountability related to collecting activities and documentation expected of and by museums today.

Ascertaining provenance may be a simple exercise if the custodial path is well documented, trusted, and unbroken; as when a living artist sells one of her drawings directly to the first and remaining collector, and sufficient details about the transfer are known. As time passes, and objects change hands and information is exchanged (or not), ascertaining provenance can become complicated. Credible information may be readily available for some periods of ownership (e.g., ample knowledge of the immediate past owner), but the museum professional researching provenance may be challenged by a complete lack of information for other periods of ownership for the same object, and/or by the provision of partial, innocently inaccurate, or possibly manufactured information about still other periods, depending perhaps on the motivations of previous owners to share or withhold information. Museum professionals may need to identify and deal with any red herrings (no matter the source), such as fabricated provenances intended to mislead, or the perpetuation of informed best guesses about certain periods of ownership, or any innocently inaccurate bits of information that have cascaded through oral or written histories of ownership.

Finding Favored Sources

Ascertaining provenance requires familiarity with objects, collections, collectors, and documentation at all levels allowing the researcher to detect what information may be missing in sources and to parse good information from bad. Each successive owner must determine the levels of credibility, completeness, and accuracy of provenance information provided by sources, including information sought or inherited from previous owners. Sought sources for provenance will provide as specific, accurate, and complete information as is known or shareable by the source's author at a given time. A favored source will provide a cluster of credible information describing where, when, and from whom the object originated, and the circumstances surrounding any subsequent changes in ownership and possession.

Some of what is assumed or known about ownership comes from evidence left by previous owners or possessors. Art collectors, for example, use various methods to mark and communicate their ownership of works of art. Collectors might apply unique stamps, inscriptions, inventory or property numbers, or labels directly onto objects in their collections, or might signal ownership by lending objects (along with the owners' names) to exhibitions or by supporting references to objects in publications (e.g., exhibition catalogs and catalogues raisonné).

Some advise museums to get signed statements from sellers regarding provenance (when provenance is known),[5,17] an action that, if taken, serves museum goals for object documentation and furthering public trust (by helping to show good-faith purchases). Others caution that concerns for liability (as well as damaged reputations) may limit the extent to which sophisticated sellers (such as dealers and auction houses) will commit to statements about provenance, since what is known or understood at a given time about provenance may subsequently be proved inaccurate, if more pertinent information surfaces. Darraby notes, "Those who create a document entitling it 'provenance,' at least within the context of a mercantile transaction, do so at their own peril" (p. 86).[18]

Museum professionals researching provenance may encounter familiar research challenges related to information availability and accessibility; challenges such as chasing down and getting access to known materials distributed geographically, linguistically, and disciplinarily or discovering along the way that some materials have been lost or destroyed (as may be the case with records of dealers long gone out of business). Custodians of potentially useful materials may do nothing to document and publicize the existence of the materials in order to restrict access, or custodians may simply be unaware of the materials' potential value to anyone else. Not every object carries inscriptions or labels (trusted or not), has been studied, exhibited, or referenced in published or unpublished materials.

When researching provenance for proposed or acquired objects, for instance, museum professionals consult internal records (such as bills of sale, loan receipts, import and export documents, deeds of gift, and curatorial defenses) and may consult external records (personal and corporate papers, inventory lists, photographs, excavation field notes, and oral histories of previous collectors), as well as an array of generally available published materials, such as monographs, catalogues raisonné, journal and newspaper articles, catalogs and announcements related to exhibitions and auctions. The provenances for objects held in other collections sharing some ownership or possession-related context with an object under review by a museum might provide comparable information or clues about provenance, as when, for instance, some stretch of the custodial paths for a group of pendants, earrings, and lockets once held centrally in a private collection, and now dispersed among several collections, can be traced (backward and forward) through ancestors or descendants of the private collector.

Recent attention on the history and practices around twentieth- and twenty-first-century acquisition of antiquities, archeological objects, and ethnographic materials, and investigations into the custodial paths of objects possibly looted during the Nazi era, has in part fueled interest in maintaining centralized databases or other resources for information about sought objects and sought information, at least through specialized bibliographies, finding aids, and collection catalogs. See, for example, the subscription-based Art Loss Register for stolen objects (http://www.artloss.com/), the Object Registry (https://aamd.org/object-registry) where museums describe antiquities acquired with incomplete ownership histories, and two examples of freely available databases related to Nazi era looting: the Nazi-era Provenance Internet Portal (http://www.nepip.org/) and the earlier referenced database related to museums in the U.K. reporting gaps in provenances (http://www.collectionstrust.org.uk/collections-link/cultural-property-advice/spoliation). The AAM Guide to Provenance Research is an example of an existing print publication providing museum professionals with recommendations as well as extensive, annotated lists of resources for investigating changes in ownership or possessions specifically occurring during the Nazi era.

Centralized access to information, if described consistently and made freely available, might provide anyone with an interest in objects—including museum professionals, previous owners, descendants, researchers, lawyers, law enforcement agents—with starting points for investigation; starting points because sources may be in different states of completion and usefulness, with some offering extensive item-level access to needed documents, and others providing limited descriptions, leaving the option of travel to an archive, library, museum, or private collection for direct access to materials, unless restricted or restrictive.

TEMPERED SHARING

Even when information about ownership or possession is readily available, however, that information might be limited to only the most recent transactions or movements, depending on the venue for dissemination. Museum exhibitions and publications commonly identify the current owner of an object through credit lines accompanying object descriptions. A credit line for a drawing by an American artist might read, for instance, Collection Jane and John Doe. Credit lines for museum-owned objects are used, at the very least, to identify the current and immediate prior owner of an object and the means of transfer: for example, Collection City Art Museum, Gift of Jane and

John Doe. This does not tell the full story of an object's custodial path.

Museums, private collectors, dealers, auction houses, and independent researchers may create or perpetuate uncertainties about provenance by highlighting or, alternately, downplaying or suppressing some periods of ownership or possession over others. In the first of two extreme examples, a current owner may greatly value, and therefore want to emphasize, a perceived possession-related connection with a high-profile previous owner, perhaps because the position or reputation of that previous owner is intriguing (e.g., it may be fascinating and beneficial to know and promote the fact that an early-seventeenth-century painting once given to King Charles I of England is now in the collection of an American museum). By contrast, some owners or possessors may be less inclined to share details about previous owners or possessors who have earned notoriety through association with questionable modes of transfer (e.g., the Nazi art dealer Karl Haberstock).[16] Questionable possessions are equally important to document and share, as knowing each period of ownership or possession may contribute to collective awareness about an object, its custodial path, and caretakers.

Decisions to withhold some provenance information in some venues (e.g., exhibition wall labels or online collection catalogs) may be influenced by motivations to protect commercial interests (if in the business of trading objects) or commitments to respecting requests for confidentiality. Museums and auction houses, for example, are unlikely to freely disclose names of donors or consignors when anonymity is desired, and when no one has yet requested that information. Redacting known provenance information in some cases may be a response to past and continuing assumptions about what people want to know about objects; where it has been assumed that people are very interested in the "back story" for an object: for example, learning about the artist/maker or originating culture, the object itself, and the cultural, historical, archeological, religious, or spiritual significance of the object. Knowing about past owners and possessors may contribute to understanding these significances (and *Spectrum* includes elements for recording an "owner's personal experience" with an object and an "owner's personal response" to an object); however, many museums, previous owners, and other interested parties have demonstrated (and many still demonstrate) a lesser preoccupation with sharing known information about every past and intermediate owner and possessor of an object, at least in public venues like collection, exhibition, or auction catalogs.[14,15] A sinister assumption is that museums and other owners have in the past not asked about ownership, and not shared what they know, in order to skirt confronting dubious histories of ownership or possession.

One compounding effect of tempered sharing of known provenance—let alone not disclosing known gaps in provenance—is inheritance of light and possibly vague

documentation by subsequent owners and other interested parties and diminished abilities to fully know the story of an object's provenance; a state of awareness that may remain status quo for a long time or may change when information must be revealed, perhaps to comply with information disclosure requirements. More likely, as museums and other interested parties commit resources to researching provenance over time, partial or uncertain information provided by sources or inherited from previous owners might be fleshed out or corrected. Activities surrounding inventorying collections, making new acquisitions, exhibitions, publications, and conserving objects can present museums with ready opportunities and reasons to dig further into what is known about past ownerships and possessions, and to then share that information.

CONCLUSION

Recent calls for museums to share information about provenance more robustly have given profile to ascertaining as complete and accurate provenance as possible, even over time, as part of the diligence and care exercised when acquiring and managing objects. In a good scenario, a complete and accurate picture of the custodial path for an object will have credible, sourced information describing who has held the object in the past, when, where, and under what circumstances. Provenance information alone may not reveal the underlying motivations of an owner to give or accept, to sell, buy or to decline any proposed object. However, knowledge of provenance may improve (or help prove) understandings of rights, titles, and interests in objects from private property to national patrimony; understandings that serve museum goals for object documentation, education, and furthering public trust.

Further still, knowing the full story of an object's history of ownership and possession may contribute to understanding the relative meanings and significances of that object to individuals, nations, groups, and locations, and the object's function within any intended and subsequent contexts. The latter in particular jibes with the assumed interests of museum audiences to know the "back story" for an object, a natural complement to what is happening in museum research, documentation, and dissemination. The message sent in recent years to museums by supporters and observers is for museums to share more of what they know or believe about objects and contexts (including provenance), more widely and more quickly.

REFERENCES

1. Merryman, J.H. A licit international trade in cultural objects. In *Who Owns the Past? Cultural Policy, Cultural Property, and the Law*; Fitz Gibbon, K., Ed.; Rutgers University Press: New Brunswick, NJ, 2005.

2. Midgette, A. You can't hold it, but you can own it. The New York Times, November 25, 2007. http://www.nytimes.com/2007/11/25/arts/design/25midg.html?_r=1&oref=slogin (accessed December 29, 2014). See also Gleadell, C. Tino Sehgal: Invisible art worth £100k. The Telegraph, May 7, 2013. http://www.telegraph.co.uk/culture/art/art-news/10041272/Tino-Sehgal-Invisible-art-worth-100k.html (accessed December 29, 2014).

3. Fitz Gibbon, K. *Who Owns the Past? Cultural Policy, Cultural Property, and the Law*; Rutgers University Press: New Brunswick, NJ/London, U.K., 2005.

4. Malaro, M.C.; DeAngelis, I.P. *A Legal Primer on Managing Museum Collections*, 3rd Ed.; Smithsonian Books: Washington, DC, 2012.

5. Reyhan, P.Y. A chaotic palette: Conflict of laws in litigation between original owners and good-faith purchasers of stolen art. Duke Law J. **2001**, *50* (4), 955–1043. http://www.law.duke.edu/shell/cite.pl?50+Duke+L.+J.+955 (accessed December 29, 2014). See also Graefe, E.A. The conflicting obligations of museums possessing Nazi-looted art. Boston College Law Rev. **2010**, *51* (2), 473–515. http://lawdigitalcommons.bc.edu/cgi/viewcontent.cgi?article=3112&context=bclr (accessed December 29, 2014); and Brodie, N. Congenial bedfellows? The academy and the antiquities trade. J. Contemp. Crim. Justice **2011**, *27* (4), 408–437.

6. George, T.E. Using customary international law to identify "fetishistic" claims to cultural property. New York University School of Law, Law Rev. **2005**, *80* (4), 1207–1236. http://www.nyulawreview.org/sites/default/files/pdf/NYULawReview-80-4-George.pdf (accessed December 29, 2014). See also Fincham, D. The distinctiveness of property and heritage. Penn State Law Rev. **2010**, *115* (3), 641–684.

7. Grose, T.O. Reading the bones: Information content, value, and ownership issues raised by the Native American Graves Protection and Repatriation. Act.J. Am. Soc. Inform. Sci. **1996**, *47* (8), 624–631. See also Mashberg, T. Where words mean as much as objects: Apaches' dispute with American Museum of Natural History. The New York Times, August 19, 2013, http://www.nytimes.com/2013/08/20/arts/design/apaches-dispute-with-american-museum-of-natural-history.html?pagewanted=all&_r=0 (accessed December 29, 2014).

8. Sciolino, E. French dispute whether Maori head is body part or art. The New York Times, October 26, 2007. http://www.nytimes.com/2007/10/26/world/europe/26france.html (accessed December 29, 2014).

9. Merryman, J.H., *Imperialism, Art and Restitution*; Cambridge University Press: Cambridge, U.K., 2006.

10. Niedzielski-Eichner, N. Art historians and cultural property internationalism. Itl. J. Cult. Prop. **2005**, *12*, 183–200. [CrossRef].

11. Yasaitis, K.E. Collecting culture and the British museum. Curator **2006**, *49* (4), 449–462.

12. Committee on Culture, Media and Sport *Seventh Report, Cultural Property: Return and Illicit Trade I*; United Kingdom Parliament, House of Commons: United Kingdom, 2000. HC 371-I. http://www.publications.parliament.uk/pa/cm199900/cmselect/cmcumeds/371/37102.htm (accessed December 29, 2014).

13. Kennicott, P. Greeks go for all the marbles in effort to get back artifacts; a new museum's goal: To press the British to return Parthenon sculptures. The Washington Post, October 7, 2007. http://www.washingtonpost.com/wp-dyn/content/article/2007/10/05/AR2007100500162.html (accessed December 29, 2014). See also Beard, M. Lord Elgin–saviour or vandal? BBC History. February 17, 2011, http://www.bbc.co.uk/history/ancient/greeks/parthenon_debate_01.shtml (accessed December 29, 2014).

14. International Foundation for Art Research (IFAR) April 29, 2000, Provenance and due diligence: Proceedings of Workshop Conference. IFAR J. *3*(3 and 4), 2000.

15. DeAngelis, I.P. How much provenance is enough? Post-Schultz guidelines for art museum acquisition of archaeological materials and ancient art. In *Legal Problems of Museum Administration*; American Law Institute–American Bar Association Committee on Continuing Professional Education: Philadelphia, PA, 2005; 243–262.

16. Yeide, N.H.; Akinsha, K.; Walsh, A.L. *The AAM Guide to Provenance Research*; American Association of Museums: Washington, DC, 2001.

17. Department for Culture, Media and Sport, *Combating Illicit Trade: Due Diligence Guidelines for Museums, Libraries and Archives on Collecting and Borrowing Cultural Material*; United Kingdom Parliament, House of Commons: United Kingdom, October 2005. https://www.museumsassociation.org/download?id=17156 (accessed December 12, 2016).

18. Darraby, J.L. *Art, Artifact & Architecture Law*; Thomson West: Eagan, MN, 2007; 2007 Ed.

19. British Museum. Policy on acquisitions of objects for the collection. July 4, 2013. https://www.britishmuseum.org/pdf/Acquisitions%20policy%20July%202013%20FINAL.pdf (accessed December 29, 2014).

20. Cuno, J. View from the universal museum. In *Imperialism, Art and Restitution*; Merryman, J.H., Ed.; Cambridge University Press: Cambridge, U.K., 2006; 15–36.

21. Brodie, N.; Doole, J.; Watson, P. *Stealing History: The Illicit Trade in Cultural Material*; The McDonald Institute for Archaeological Research: Cambridge, U.K., 2000. https://www.museumsassociation.org/download?id=30258 (accessed December 12, 2016).

22. Anderson, M. Why Indianapolis will no longer buy unprovenanced antiquities. *The Art Newspaper*, April 30, 2007. See also Cooke, E. What should we do with "our" antiquities? US museum directors wrestle with the long-term consequences of artefacts acquired without watertight provenance. *The Art Newspaper*; November 17, 2011.

23. Museums Association, *Acquisition: Guidance on the Ethics and Practicalities of Acquisition*, 2nd Ed.; Ethical Guidelines, Number 1; Museums Association: London, U.K., 2004. http://www.museumsassociation.org/download?id=11114 (accessed December 29, 2014).

24. American Association of Museums *AAM Recommended Procedures for Providing Information to the Public about Objects Transferred in Europe during the Nazi Era*; American Association of Museums: Washington, DC, 2000. http://www.aam-us.org/docs/default-source/profes sional-resources/nepip-recommended-procedures (accessed December 29, 2014).

25. Claims Conference, Conference on Jewish Material Claims Against Germany; World Jewish Restitution Organization. Nazi-Era Stolen Art and U.S. Museums: A Survey, July 25, 2006. See also Thompson, E. Successes and failures of self-regulatory regimes governing museum holdings of Nazi-looted art and looted antiquities. The Columbia Journal of Law and the Arts **2014**, *37* (3), 379–404, http://lawandarts.org/wp-content/uploads/sites/4/2014/07/37.3-Thompson-Article.pdf (accessed December 29, 2014).

26. Kennedy, R. Museums' research on looting seen to lag. The New York Times, July 25, 2006. http://www.nytimes.com/2006/07/25/arts/design/25clai.html (accessed December 29, 2014). See also Cembalest, R. Tensions are rising between the restitution community and U.S. museums over the proper way to handle Holocaust art claims. ARTnews, October 2010, http://www.artnews.com/2010/10/01/claims-conflict/ (accessed December 29, 2014); and Cohan, W.D. The restitution struggle: Malaise, indifference, and frustration. ARTnews, September 2013, http://www.artnews.com/2013/09/11/the-restitution-struggle/ (accessed December 29, 2014).

27. Baca, M.; Harpring, P. Categories for the Description of Works of Art J. Paul Getty Trust and the College Art Association: Los Angeles, CA, 2014. http://www.getty.edu/research/publications/electronic_publications/cdwa/15ownership.html (accessed December 29, 2014).

Provenance of Rare Books

Marcia Reed
Getty Research Institute, Los Angeles, CA, U.S.A.

Abstract

Just as people have lives, so do books. Like identical twins who end their lives looking quite different, even the seemingly indistinguishable copies of twentieth-century trade books accumulate their own histories and physical characteristics over time from readers' habits and storage conditions. With regard to rare volumes, research on provenance seeks to describe not only books' origins but also their subsequent biblio-journeys as they are read, borrowed, sold, collected, and held by institutions. Unlike studies concerned with the subject matter or content of rare books, provenance investigates the specific histories of individual copies, either by themselves or in the context of larger collections.

A rare book's provenance is the history of its ownership, often elaborating its associations with libraries, private owners, or collections. A significant aspect of book collecting and the history of the printed record of cultural heritage, provenance concerns not only the initial origins of a book but also the ongoing connections to collectors and collections. Research and documentation of provenance deal with two categories of evidence that reveal the histories of individual books. Internal evidence, including marks, inscriptions, bookplates, and bindings, focuses on the physical components of volumes. External evidence, such as catalogs issued by publishers and booksellers and those compiled by libraries, dealers, and auction houses, documents the places and conditions of manufacture, subsequent sales, owners, and collections that held the volumes. Provenance research concerns primarily the authenticity and integrity of rare books; however, in recent decades its data can also be used to develop and write innovative histories of books' circulation, collecting, uses, and reading.

DEFINITION

In the English language, "provenance" refers to the origins of an object, particularly a work of art or an antique. The English and French words are spelled the same and have similar meanings. Both words derive from the Latin verb "provenire," to come forth. However, the root word reverses the direction of contemporary provenance studies that return or seek to go back as far as possible to the object's origins in order to discover proof or, in the best cases, documentation of past owners and locations from the time of an object's conception or production. In French, provenance has been used in commercial and legal contexts, as well as by art connoisseurs, bibliophiles, and book collectors, in the sense discussed in this entry. Provenience is a related term, often used in the same sense of provenance. Archaeologists use it to refer to the precise location or to find the spot of an excavated object.

A rare book's provenance is the history of its ownership, often elaborating its associations with libraries, private owners, or collections. As a significant aspect of book collecting and the history of the printed record of cultural heritage, provenance concerns not only the initial origins of a book but also the ongoing connections to collectors and collections. In the past, research on provenance was seen as an arcane area of interest limited to people who recorded and studied the history of books and collecting.

Those who researched and kept track of provenance were principally librarians and bookdealers, as well as collectors. Like aristocratic family backgrounds and high society connections, distinguished provenances pointing back to a famous collection or library have long been prized by collectors. This aspect of provenance is engagingly described in Frederick Adams' [1969] lecture with occasionally amusing vignettes of collectors among his tales from the world of books. As Adams points out, such "good" provenance affirms the present owners' and collectors' own taste and erudition. Booksellers recorded noteworthy provenances in their catalogs to enhance the interest or value of significant books and to encourage sales. Moving beyond marketing and commercial interests, today, the history of particular copies of books is central to research that seeks to reconstruct a collector's interests, scholarship, and collecting strategies. Provenance can help to define the importance of certain titles or the relationship among books and to create the social histories of reading and collecting.

In its broad contemporary sense, provenance concerns the original owners and all subsequent persons and institutions that acquired books by purchase, gift, inheritance, or legacy up to the present. Borrowed books were occasionally never returned to their owners and libraries. More dramatically, rare volumes were transported from collections in less savory or deliberately illegal ways including

Encyclopedia of Library and Information Sciences, Fourth Edition DOI: 10.1081/E-ELIS4-120053446

episodes of outright theft. Among other cultural artifacts, books were often taken as spoils; they have been looted during wars and civil unrest up to the present day. Extraordinary dispersals of books and destructions of entire libraries took place during the Reformation with the closure of monastic libraries, as well as during the French Revolution and World War II. Hence, much provenance information has been lost. Amid the disasters of wars, due to the prevalence of plunder and resulting devastation, it has always been the case that cultural conflicts and depredations wreak havoc with the clear views researchers seek to construct of books' and libraries' history.

Early Printed Books

From the invention of Western printing in the mid-fifteenth century to the present, books were printed in various editions or issues, sometimes on different papers. They were often sold in parts or fascicles, held in paper covers or boards. Books' owners frequently had volumes bound according to their own tastes; they and others wrote personal inscriptions denoting ownership (called an ex libris) on the inside front cover or on the first pages. Collectors pasted in their specially printed bookplates. Readers and scholars annotated the texts. Wealthy bibliophiles shelved their books in elegantly designed and decorated private libraries, binding the books in specially designed leather covers embellished with coats of arms and other collection-specific ornamentation. Other readers and librarians in religious or educational organizations housed books in less impressive ways. Books from these libraries and institutional collections also frequently bear ownership inscriptions, and they have characteristic (though more modest) bindings and shelf marks on the bindings or edges of pages. Some owners were less careful with their books, using them for professional purposes and/or scholarship. They may have kept books in places where dust, mold, and vermin had their own deleterious effects on the unstable and perishable materials from which books were made. However, such details of condition can sometimes be helpful in identifying books' past history.

As described in the section "Internal Evidence: Physical and Material Qualities," both the materials and physical condition of books can provide primary evidence about past history. Unfortunately for the present interest in provenance, it was not always deemed important for collectors and libraries to preserve the physical integrity of books. As Roger Stoddard writes in the preface to his 1984 catalog Marks in Books, up to modern times, binders reassembled books in the course of binding or refurbishing covers. Only rarely did they make a special effort to preserve historical evidence, especially when dealing with books in poor condition. Covers and endpapers were considered to be of little value and they were discarded, taking with them any past library indications and shelf marks,

ownership inscriptions, booksellers' notes and collations, and other annotations. According to Stoddard, "Typically, the only evidence of provenance is on covers and endpapers, so the whole history of the copy may be sacrificed," if indeed books have been restored or rebound.

Modern Editions

Provenance concerns not only early books but also twentieth-century trade books. Although they were published in editions of hundreds or sometimes thousands, these volumes sometimes contain original graphics and specially designed jackets or covers. Their present condition and the marks of provenance that they bear associate them with libraries and collectors in different locales. Signed copies of literary works, variants of book jackets, inserted pages or photos, special bindings, library stamps, collectors' signatures, and booksellers' notations all assist in establishing the history of ownership and location of specific copies. Recently, there is particular interest among collectors in books linked to authors and artists who were associated with twentieth-century avant-garde groups and circles. In turn, the libraries of well-known authors and historical figures can be tracked by their characteristic marks as well as by external documents such as library lists and sale catalogs.

THE STUDY OF PROVENANCE

Provenance research and documentation deal with two kinds of evidence that reveal the histories of individual books. Internal evidence concerns the physical components of volumes. External evidence documents the places and conditions of manufacture, subsequent sales, owners, and collections where the volumes were held.

Internal Evidence: Physical and Material Qualities

Specifics on places of production and means of manufacture provide essential clues that establish the authenticity of books and initiate the chain of provenance history and ownership. Early printed books have associations not only with printers but also with artists, illuminators, patrons, and other participants who played a role in accomplishing the finished volume. When books were offered for sale, printers' and booksellers' lists, in manuscript or printed versions, can provide information about where the books were marketed and where potential buyers lived and worked.

Types of paper and printing ink, page formats, and seemingly pedestrian elements such as folds and sewing styles can all reveal historical information about the place of production. Physical features and formats can indicate whether a book was initially valued highly, collected, and thus bound in an elaborate binding or rather printed for purposes of public information and record keeping, using less expensive materials and smaller formats. Other books, perhaps those used for educational purposes, were never bound but read and reread as indicated by tattered or heavily annotated copies. In rare but fortunate instances, heavily marked up and seemingly unattractive copies can be traced to historical figures or perhaps editors, sometimes indicating that the copy in hand was a proof copy and a witness of the publication process. Richard Rouse's detailed article on copy-specific features provides examples of marks, marginalia, and other kinds of evidence that he discovered in early books. These held clues that pointed back to early owners, libraries, and related works, which were either bound together as collected works or separated in the process of binding or by greedy dealers who made several books (and sales) from an early collected volume. Similarly, the very rare surviving copies of artists' model books depicting schematic figures and multipurpose decorations and ornaments for use by artists are frequently found with missing pages, cutouts, or pricks that indicate how artists made copies of the designs. In addition, such model books often have spots of paints or inkblots. These could seem to mar the beauty of the original book, yet collectors prize such marks as verifications of books' use by early artists.

All and any indications of ownership are central elements of provenance information that tell about the history of circulation and collection of books. Conveniently for the study of provenance, past owners frequently wrote their names in books, and they made reading notes and personal annotations as well. Collectors and libraries pasted a bookplate inside the front covers to identify their holdings. For locational purposes in their libraries, they affixed a spine label or wrote a shelf mark outside of the volume. These brief alphanumeric notations are found on books' spines or on the page edges if books are shelved on their sides.

Inscriptions: The most obvious evidence of ownership, highly useful to contemporary collectors, are inscriptions. These handwritten notations with full names or initials of owners, dedicatory or presentation phrases, or another mark (occasionally a cipher) most frequently appear on the book's initial pages, particularly the title page. In the simplest form, the owner writes her or his name, occasionally supplying the date when the book was acquired and its price. Several centuries later, such paleographic details can be difficult to read, and considerable research or expertise is needed to decipher them. In early printed books, owners' names were frequently written in their Latin form, with degrees, affiliations with educational institutions, and dedications to others in cases when the books were gifts. Some inscriptions, ciphers, and monograms combine initial letters in decorative calligraphic presentations. In addition, some book collectors inscribed favorite mottos that were related to their family heraldry, or of religious or emblematic significance. Although

inscriptions were frequently effaced as books passed through collections, twentieth-century science (e.g., black light) affords a way to read inscriptions no longer visible to the naked eye.

Bookplates: Owners' names, initials, and mottos may also be found on printed bookplates and labels, again most frequently on the book's initial leaves. The decorative designs of the bookplates comprise heraldic devices, emblemata, images drawn from family history, and, in recent centuries, vignettes that allude to libraries, books, and the practice of reading. Like inscriptions, in many instances, names or initials on bookplates are not immediately comprehensible but must be deciphered with the aid of reference works on bookplates, armorial designs, or initials—of which, fortunately, there are many published compilations. Pasted into the front cover or endpapers, bookplates are usually etched or engraved or printed in relief with woodblocks; occasionally, similar information has been applied with a stamp. Bookplates can be a study in themselves with a substantial literature and specific research strategies that overlap with the historical and art historical areas of genealogy, heraldry, emblems, and ciphers. These highly specialized works on paper (just a few collectors, such as the California bibliophile Estelle Doheny, have had leather bookplates) have been collected as a specific book-related genre for centuries.

Library marks and stamps: Institutional ownership of books was first recorded on the volumes themselves by way of handwritten inscriptions. These often accompanied shelf marks on the outside of each volume (occasionally, shelf marks are seen on the front pages of volumes also). Usually far simpler in their designs than private owners' marks, library marks gave the name of the institution and place. More recent kinds of library marks include embossed names as well as perforations. Although library stamps or deaccession marks of former owners and defunct collections could seem to be irrelevant and were sometimes erased or cut out to eradicate the past historical associations, this practice works against historical research, particularly provenance studies. In fact, marks of past institutional ownership serve to provide highly useful information for tracking provenance.

Heraldry: Marks of heraldry, such as coats of arms, special insignia, and devices associated with court collections and holdings of eminent families, can appear in many places on books but are most frequently found on covers and initial pages. As an important aspect of tracking collectibles, this is an essential element for provenance. Heraldry is an arcane field requiring special expertise because of the necessity for recognizing and deciphering the symbols used in the marks and understanding the protocols for their application.

Bindings: In addition to marks found on pages, book covers are bearers of considerable provenance-related evidence. Paper covers may carry the same types of inscriptions and stamps as the inner pages. Early books with leather bindings that had notable owners frequently have armorial ornaments or superlibros (ownership stamps on bindings), emblems, or initials applied with binding tools. Embellished by gold tooling with the words "IO. GROLIERII ET AMICORUM" (meaning that a volume belonged to Jean Grolier and his friends), the bindings on sixteenth-century French humanist's books are among the best known examples of collectors' bindings. On a grander scale, royal libraries such as those of the French court had characteristic styles of leather bindings marked with identifiable decorations that connected volumes with rulers and family members.

Conservation science: Recent advances in conservation techniques and material sciences not only serve to preserve books but also assist in the analysis of books' origins. In addition to aiding the identification of printers and publishers when these do not appear on the book itself, specifics on paper stock used for the text block, endpapers, and covers help to locate probable sites or regions of book production and binding. Analysis of paper and coloring also provides solid evidence that the copies of rare books are not recently constituted or newly colored. Further analysis of paper, pastes, bindings, and examination of past treatments assists in ascertaining the integrity of copies, insuring that no pages are inserts or facsimiles. The latter are made easily by means of digital photography and photocopy technology using blank sheets of old paper. Dealers, scholars, and collectors almost always desire complete copies of rare books with all pages intact. However, when books are fabricated from various incomplete volumes, considerations of provenance and bibliography are confounded. Indeed, these "restorations" obliterate books' history, since they are essentially new assemblages crafted from the spare parts of old or incomplete books.

External Evidence: Inventories and Library Catalogs, Auction Sales Catalogs, and Dealers' Catalogs

Manuscript inventories and printed lists can document conditions of manufacture, subsequent sales, owners, and collections holding rare books. Valuable accessory information concerning the persons who played roles in making the books (such as papermakers, typefounders and page designers, printers, publishers, and binders) are additional clues that provide historical verification relating to books' identification and biblio-history. Subscription lists enumerating future owners were printed for prospectuses and later insertions into the completed publications. In addition to collectors, businesses such as dealers and auction houses were central to books' circulation and, ultimately, to their survival. However, other institutions and social organizations, such as monasteries and missionary societies, were also crucial to the collection and transmission of books. As described in the following text, owners, dealers, and libraries all generate various kinds of lists and catalogs that provide specific information about individual copies of rare books, serving the study of provenance.

Inventories and library catalogs: Upon the owner's death, estate and house inventories were prepared that included art and furniture among other collectibles. Following this age-old practice, lists of book collections were first produced in manuscript versions. Early inventories are frequently organized in the order of rooms, according to the shelves and cabinets where books were kept. Arrangements of books in libraries were important elements in the process of creating a collection, and locations were subsequently recorded in catalogs. Sometimes lists and catalogs were organized by physical sizes, possibly relating to their storage or shelving orders, and booklists bear headings for octavos, folios, and portfolios. Within subject categorizations (such as history, religion, travel, festivals), early catalogs describe books briefly by authors and catch titles. Inconveniently for current researchers, the full form of a bibliographical citation (e.g., author, title, place, publisher, and date) by which books are identified according to current practice was almost never used in the early modern period. Therefore, it is often very difficult to identify specific copies or editions without further historical context or knowledge of the physical features of volumes, such as authors' signatures, bookplates, or bindings. Collocating the collector's printed works on paper, book catalogs often included prints and maps. Rather than single sheets, both maps and prints were frequently bound into albums for purposes of carriage and storage. Indeed, in the context of early modern collections, portfolios or albums of prints looked like books, although they lacked bibliographical features such as title pages. Given the brief mentions in early inventories and catalogs, it is often difficult to identify items exactly without the aid of further information from biographical, bibliographical, or historical sources.

According to their date of purchase, handwritten library catalogs were entered in ledger books in accession order. Fortunately, some meticulous bibliophiles did include details of their acquisitions, noting where, from whom, and how much the book costs. Parallel to the utility of booksellers' and dealers' catalogs that advertised books, when discovered, such documentary archives of collecting activity are mines of information that detail provenance, illuminating the history of book production and circulation. When a private library reached critical mass, collectors occasionally prepared owner's catalogs of their collections and had them privately printed. These were not intended for sale but rather for bibliophilic purposes, recognizing the collector's efforts, disseminating information about the collection, and publishing the collector's own scholarship and comments. Elaborating on the early lists and publications of private rare book collections and early museums, in later centuries, more comprehensive catalogs of libraries and collections of books on specialized subjects were produced. Beyond the utility of their bibliographic content, these described assemblages of books owned by a collector or held by an institution, and thus they are sometimes useful for determinations of provenance.

Auction sale catalogs and dealers' catalogs: Since the sixteenth century, auctions and dealers' sales have mediated the transfer of books among other collectibles, such as art and antiques, from former owners and estates to new ones. Using inventories or catalogs of collections as their basis, auction sale and dealers' catalogs provide valuable documentation on the contents of libraries and private collections, and specifics on individual books. For provenance, it is especially desirable to find dealers' and collectors' copies of catalogs interleaved with extra paper sheets inserted with notes giving the names of buyers and sale prices. Dealers and collectors routinely marked up their auction catalogs with information about the condition or physical characteristics of the book offered. All types of book inventories and catalogs can be studied not merely as lists but also as authentications of books' presence. They can indicate rarity or the availability of copies for readers. More generally, catalogs can provide an overarching view of the book business, the market for past publications, and genres of collecting.

THE USES AND VALUE OF PROVENANCE

Authentication: Most importantly, precise documentation of a rare book's history helps to establish that it is an authentic object, not a spurious work or facsimile. Careful examination of the material and collation of elements provides evidence of the work's integrity. Occasionally, incidents of war and theft, coupled with greed, conspire to obliterate books' provenance. This blurring of history opens doors for forgeries and fakes whose appearance is accompanied by a fictitious provenance. New owners do not realize the true identities of the works until they embark on research, seek to sell the book, and consult experts such as librarians, curators, or dealers. Ironically, in such cases, although the subject and content of a rare book are quite clear, its loss of provenance can amount to a decontextualized state of biblio-amnesia, like a person found wandering who has forgotten his name and address. On the positive side, books have long lives and can easily traverse national borders and cultural boundaries, passing from readers on to collectors through the centuries. For scholarship, however, the significance of a rare book is enhanced considerably by comprehension of its social meanings and contexts.

Association: For some collectors of art and books, the ability to link a particular work to its author, to a well-known patron, to an eminent collector, or to a prominent historic institution is a primary interest that has made certain books valuable and highly collectible. Book dealers and auction houses reliably stress "good

provenance," indicating that the rare book comes from a famous collection, such as those seen in current citations that track the diaspora of books emanating from the numerous sales of Sir Thomas Phillipp's collections in the nineteenth century. In other association copies, the volume was signed or annotated by a celebrity or a scholar. Noteworthy associations can become the reasons for present-day collectors' pursuits. Occasionally, association becomes the basis upon which a collection or a scholarly project is developed. Collectors like the Los Angeles doctor Elmer Belt sought to reconstruct the components of Leonardo da Vinci's library for the collection now held by UCLA, although it was not possible to do so with the specific volumes. In his scholarly quest of Horace Walpole's bibliographical milieu, Professor Wilmarth Sheldon Lewis at Yale University re-collected the collector's books and manuscripts, seeking volumes and related materials for the Lewis Walpole Library at Yale University, formerly owned by the eighteenth-century author and collector Walpole at Strawberry Hill in England. Conveying the aura of past collecting and taste, so-called association copies convey the pedigree of the collector along with the physical presentation of their rare books. Thus, present owners and libraries also associate themselves with a distinguished lineage of ownership and history of taste.

Book history: Past provenance research has focused on the history of a particular volume for purposes of ascertaining integrity and authentication. Viewed broadly, provenance research can also inform the history of collecting by identifying copies associated with specific readers, scholars, libraries, religious orders, and educational institutions. Inventories and catalogs can assist in identifying single copies and the contents of libraries. Similarly, information gathered in the course of provenance research itself provides data for constructing the history of scholarship and research techniques. It provides responses to specific questions such as "To what books and editions did historic figures have access?" and furnishing facts for histories of reading, research techniques and writing, and literary taste.

CATALOGING PROVENANCE INFORMATION

Until recently, information on previous owners of rare books was infrequently and somewhat erratically included in both dealers' catalogs and sales catalogs, as well as library catalog records. More often it was found in dealers' archives and in libraries' local files, recording physical characteristics of books such as heraldry, bindings, monograms, or embellishments such as fore-edge painting. The 1980s was a watershed for interest in provenance of rare books. Roger Stoddard introduced the topic visually in the innovative 1984 Houghton Library exhibition at Harvard University, *Marks in Books, Illustrated and Explained.* Published in 1985, the large format catalog was "devoted to those mysterious traces left in books by printer, binders, booksellers, librarians, and collectors." Stoddard's explanations are a useful guide to interpreting the often cryptic marks for purposes of identification of owners and readers of books.

In the last three decades, more detailed descriptions of specific copies and editions of rare books in bibliographic databases and in online book trade resources have made substantial contributions to the information now widely available on provenance. The advent of machine-readable cataloging and the proliferation and population of online catalogs not only afforded immediate access to bibliographic data but also provided a convenient venue for tracking ownership in specific volumes. Librarians and scholars realized that searches for provenance information, if data were entered in specific fields and in standard formats, could yield promising amounts of information on individual copies, rarity, past owners, and others who had documented relationships with particular books. Along with two other thesauri on rare publications and historical evidence (Printing and Publishing Evidence, 1986, and Binding Evidence, 1988), the ALA/ACRL Rare Books and Manuscripts Section Standards Committee published Provenance Evidence in 1988 (and it is now available online). These thesauri are intended to be used dynamically by catalogers for terms relating to evidence of provenance, and they contain a useful list of possibilities where provenance in rare books can be discovered.

Most helpfully, the term is "interpreted in its broadest sense to refer not only to former owners in the legal sense, but also to any who may have had temporary custody of the material (such as auction houses or library borrowers) and have left their mark in some way on it."

In 1997, the Bibliographical Society of America sponsored "Marks in Books," a conference for European and American researchers at Yale University that considered a range of perspectives on the uses of provenance information and the recording and organization of relevant information. Contributions to the conference were published the same year in the society's papers. Among these diverse reports on research projects, Paul Needham's article "Index Possessorum Incunabulorum" presents two simple rules gleaned from his records of provenance. The first and main principle is that "Unindexed provenance is lost provenance." The second is "Identification of ownerships should be based on definable and classifiable evidence." Present-day research and cataloging of provenance follow these two general but highly useful guidelines.

Reflecting recent developments in twenty-first-century book history, the Consortium of European Research Libraries (CERL) has put considerable effort into developing the Heritage of the Printed Book Database. Its records of rare books frequently include provenance information, and the CERL home page has a helpful link to its own resources on provenance. The CERL Thesaurus includes provenance records from a number of old and important German institutions as well as other European libraries. The CERL website also has a Provenance Information section, and some database records now include a digitized image of the ownership marks.

Recently, researchers from the Kislak Center for Special Collections, Rare Books, and Manuscripts at the University of Pennsylvania initiated the Provenance Online Project (POP). Digital images of provenance evidence contained in books, such as inscriptions, labels, bookplates, bindings, and other physical attributes indicating ownership, are available together with bibliographic and descriptive metadata about the books. POP is intended to create a collaborative international workspace and communication space to which librarians, researchers, and collectors can contribute information about the provenance images contained in POP. The goal is to capture and construct identifications of persons who can be associated with specific provenance marks, thus connecting individual copies of books and past owners. POP will ultimately create a network of provenance evidence and bibliographic information. Sparked by an initial group of 1200 images, the project's unique approach makes visual data easily accessible and enables an open community of users to contribute and exchange information. Although the database initially focused on works from the early modern period, the project is increasingly open to documenting books from any period. In addition, POP is currently expanding beyond Penn's collections to include images from other libraries' collections. POP is an innovative resource that demonstrates the growing significance of provenance evidence for research, which takes in book history and material culture, informing the study of past libraries, the uses of texts, and the cultural and geographic groups whose recorded history resides in books.

LEGAL IMPLICATIONS OF PROVENANCE

Insofar as provenance information provides documentation on books' past owners, their countries of residence, and the time span during which they owned the books, there are overlaps and intersections with national and international laws concerned with export and import. Accurate provenance information can be helpful for the determination of rightful ownership in instances of contention. According to the 1970 UNESCO Convention on the Means of Prohibiting and Preventing the Illicit Import, Export, and Transfer of Ownership of Cultural Property, rare books are included under the category of cultural property. Presently, the European Union defines a rare book as one that is more than 100 years old and valued at more than €50,000 (cf. Consolidated Text produced by the CONSLEG system of the Office for Official Publications of the European communities 1993L0007–July 30, 2001). If a rare book of this age and above this value not presently owned in the United States is acquired by a U.S.

collector or library, it must have an export license when it leaves the European country where it was sold. In addition, the U.S. Customs Service views rare books as cultural property [cf. "Rare manuscripts and incunabula, old books, documents and publications of special interest (historic, artistic, scientific, literary, etc.) singly or in collections" in Works of Art, Collector's Pieces, Antiques, and Other Cultural Property: An Informed Compliance Publication (February 2001); see also http://www.unesco.org/culture and http://www.unidroit.org for the 1995 UNIDROIT Convention on stolen or illegally exported cultural objects (not yet signed by the United States)]. Therefore, rare books entering the United States from abroad must have import documentation describing the item with the date of publication, price paid, and the country from which it was exported. Because of legal requirements for accuracy, all such information is of great use for identifying specific copies, owners, and institutional holders. In addition, security is enhanced by the detailed identifications of books in private and public collections. In cases of very rare books known in only a few copies, this can assist in establishing the authenticity of the volume. Similarly, although no documentation is usually required for books that have been in the United States for more than 5 years, it is very useful to extend the documentation of ownership back as far as possible in case there are questions concerning ownership similar to those asked about titles to any type of property. Throughout history, in times of war and oppression, looting and theft were widespread. Books frequently became booty or were seized by victors; thus, the entire contents of libraries and private collections were displaced. Likewise in times of peace, along with artworks, books are frequently pawns on political game boards and in legal debates concerning patrimony, cultural restoration, and ongoing attempts to preserve cultural artifacts from wanton destruction.

CONCLUSION: PROVENANCE AND BOOK HISTORY

Traditional rare book collecting has focused on a canon of important books or types (such as herbals and atlases) that chronicles the Western intellectual tradition, well described by bibliographies such as *Printing and the Mind of Man*. Volumes such as Shakespeare's *First Folio*, the *Nuremberg Chronicle*, Vesalius's *Anatomy*, and Newton's *Principia* have been highly collectible for centuries. This focus on a book's subject, particularly a book seen as a seminal work or turning point, provided secure avenues for collecting. More recently, historians and social and literary scholars have turned to studies of individual books as physical objects or artifacts. In this vein, provenance research can be used to identify a sequence of owners and readers who owned and used the books and their social contexts. These clusters of data provide substantial

evidence for rewritings of history that spotlight minor but revealing figures and shed light on less well-known contexts of book use (e.g., Carlo Ginzburg's tale of the sixteenth-century peasant's reading referenced in *The Cheese and the Worms*). Founded in history, the study of books' provenance itself creates innovative perspectives that define new genres hitherto seen as unimportant, describing environments of texts' availability, their communities of reading, and reasons for retention, often outlining less elevated versions of book collecting than were seen in country houses or royal libraries. Studies of particular libraries and collectors not only tell about the sources on which further research and book production is based but also supply a portrait of the world of knowledge in certain times and places. To date, provenance studies have not given much attention to non-American or non-European books and collectors. The increasingly global focus of advanced research in history, literature, and bibliography points toward a new avenue for scholarship that will shed light on cultural practices and cross-cultural exchanges in book history.

BIBLIOGRAPHY

1. Adams, F.B. *The Uses of Provenance*; School of Librarianship/School of Library Service, University of California: Berkeley/Los Angeles, CA, 1969.
2. Barker, N. Provenance. Book Collect. **1996**, *45* (2), 157–170.
3. Baurmeister, U. The recording of marks of provenance in the Bibliothèque Nationale de France and other French libraries. Pap. Bibliogr. Soc. Am. **1997**, *91* (4), 525–538.
4. Feigenbaum, G.; Reist, Inge *Provenance: An Alternative History of Art*; Getty Research Institute: Los Angeles, CA, 2012.
5. Gaskell, R. Provenance: The debate. In *British Rare Books Society*; George, F.H., Fletcher, H.G., Eds.; Gastorf & Lang: New York, 1979; 46–65. http://rarebooksociety.org/provenance.html Iacone, S.J. Inscribed books and literary scholarship. In A Miscellany for Book Collectors.
6. Jensen, K. Revolution and the Antiquarian Book: Reshaping the Past, 1780–1815 (Cambridge: Cambridge University Press, 2011) McKitterick, D. Institutional management of book stocks. Pap. Bibliogr. Soc. Am. **1997**, *91* (4), 477–483.
7. Needham, P. Index possessorum incunabulorum. Pap. Bibliogr. Soc. Am. **1997**, *91* (4), 539–555; Nikirk, R. Looking into provenance. In *A Miscellany for Book Collectors*; Fletcher, H.G., Ed.; Gastorf & Lang: New York, 1979; 15–45.
8. Thomas Tanselle, G. *Other People's Books: Association Copies and the Stories They Tell*; Caxton Club: Chicago, IL, 2011.
9. Oyens, F.B.M. ISTC and provenance. In *Bibliography and the Study of 15th-Century Civilisation*; Hellinga, L., Goldfinch, J., Eds.; British Library: London, U.K., 1987; 216–227.

10. Pearson, D. *Provenance Research in Book History: A Handbook*; The British Library: London, U.K., 1994.

11. Pearson, D. *Books as History: The Importance of Books beyond Their Texts*. London: British Library; British Library/Oak Knoll Press: London, U.K./New Castle, DW, 2008.

12. Provenance Evidence: Thesaurus for Use in Rare Book and Special Collections Cataloguing; Association of College and Research Libraries: Chicago, IL, 1988 (and updates). http://www.rbms.info/committees/bibliographic_standards/controlledvocabularies/.

13. Rouse, R. Copy specific features of the printed book: What to record and why. In *Bibliography and the Study of 15th-Century Civilisation*; Hellinga, L., Goldfinch, J., Eds.; British Library: London, U.K., 1987; 202–215.

14. Shaw, D. *Books and Their Owners: Provenance Information and the European Cultural Heritage*; CERL: London, U.K., 2005.

15. Stoddard, S. *Marks in Books*; Houghton Library, Harvard University: Cambridge, MA, 1985.

16. Taylor, A. *Book Catalogs: Their Varieties & Uses*; Newberry Library: Chicago, IL, 1957.

17. Woodfield, D. Marks of ownership of British and American book collectors. Pap. Bibliogr. Soc. Am. **1997**, *91* (4), 579–581.

Public Librarianship *[ELIS Classic]*

Kathleen de la Peña McCook
School of Library and Information Science, University of South Florida, Tampa, Florida, U.S.A.

Katharine J. Phenix
Northglenn Branch, Rangeview Library District, Northglenn, Colorado, U.S.A.

Abstract

Public librarians are the community's cultural support as providers of lifelong learning, reading, information provision, and a vibrant public sphere for people of all ages. Public librarians provide access to books and all varieties of media to meet the needs of people for education, information, and personal development. This entry focuses on public librarianship as it is practiced in the United States with a brief history of the field's development in two parts: beginnings to 1966 when the field used a national service model and 1966 to the present with a community-based focus. The education, certification, and working conditions of public librarians are reviewed. The philosophical and ethical worldview of practice with a human rights ethos is described. Finally, current (2009) issues in public librarianship are stated.

INTRODUCTION

The *Public Library Manifesto* as set forth by the International Federation of Library Associations and Institutions (IFLA) defines the public library as the local gateway to knowledge, which provides a basic condition for lifelong learning, independent decision-making, and cultural development of the individual and social groups.[1] Public librarianship as practiced in the twenty-first century is the occupation that provides access to books and all varieties of media to meet the needs of people for education, information, and personal development. This entry will focus on public librarianship as practiced in the United States, but the reader should be aware of the many varieties of public library practice due to the different level of public library development worldwide. At the time of this writing the Public Libraries Section, Standing Committee 2007–2009 of the International Federation of Library Associations and Institutions was comprised of representatives from 20 nations: Canada, Chile, China, Colombia, the Czech Republic, Denmark, Estonia, Finland, Germany, France, Iceland, Malaysia, Nigeria, Norway, the Russian Federation, South Africa, Spain, Sweden, the United Kingdom, the United States, and Uruguay.[2] The composition of this global committee demonstrates the great variety of nations that support public libraries today. We show here the development of the public library profession in the United States.

THE DEVELOPMENT OF U.S. PUBLIC LIBRARIANSHIP TO 1966

Tax-supported public libraries were established in the United States in mid-nineteenth century New England.[3] The documentation that provided the foundation for the Boston Public Library in 1852 demonstrates the earliest summary of the intended practice of public librarianship with a focus on developing the collection; support of learning beyond formal schooling; and the intellectual advancement of the whole community.[4]

Looking back on a century of library development, library historians Ditzion (1947)[5] and Shera (1949)[6] attributed the founding of public libraries to idealism and a societal commitment to education , while later historians such as Harris (1973),[7] Garrison (1979),[8] and Wiegand (1989),[9] took into consideration the element of societal control as crafted by the male gentry elite. As is true with much history, public librarianship was initially narrated through the biographies of men. Biographies of founders of the profession such as Justin Winsor (Boston Public Library, 1867–1877) or William Frederick Poole (Cincinnati Public Library, 1869–1873, Chicago Public Library, 1873–1887) were the backdrop to understanding the field of public librarianship during the first century of service.

But from the vantage point of the twenty-first century, the growth of public librarianship following the establishment of the American Library Association in 1876 is now

Encyclopedia of Library and Information Sciences, Fourth Edition DOI: 10.1081/E-ELIS4-120043804

more broadly understood in the context of a more progressive and humanitarian service style that owes much to the participation of women. Women comprise the majority of workers in public libraries—about 80% of public library workers are women. The historical evolution of the role of women in the field must be viewed as a reflection of the role of women in the larger society. It was not until the work of Weibel,[10] Maack,[11] and Hildenbrand[12] that the historical library past vis-à-vis women's central role began to be reclaimed. And it is only in the recent decades that the history of public librarianship has come to be understood against the backdrop of race, gender, and class as so cogently analyzed by Pawley.[13]

Many factors combined to increase the number of libraries established in the United States from 1876 to 1966. Prominent were 1) philanthropy including that of Andrew Carnegie; 2) the creation of new libraries often at the urging of women's clubs; 3) the establishment of state library commissions; 4) laws enabling tax-supported public libraries; and 5) national level legislation such as the Library Services Act (LSA, 1956). The LSA was designed to support rural library services. Successor legislation, the Library Services and Construction Act (LSCA, 1966), included support for all public libraries, and funded construction as well as services.[3,14–16]

As libraries began to be established in communities across the United States the scope of public librarianship as an occupation expanded. In addition to the administration, development and organization of collections specializations emerged. Three specializations that developed between 1876 and 1966 were adult education and services, service to youth, and service to special groups.

Adult education and service: The American Library Association was linked closely with the adult education movement in the first decades of the twentieth century. During the 1920s Learned's report to the Carnegie Corporation, *The American Public Library and the Diffusion of Knowledge*, and the ALA Commission on the Library and Adult Education report, *Libraries and Adult Education* provided philosophical rationales for the public library as an extension of public education.[3,17–20] In 1934 John Chancellor was appointed to the ALA headquarters staff to initiate a 10-year assessment of adult education and public libraries. Public librarians developed skills and techniques to accomplish adult education through readers' advisory, services to organizations, and establishment of discussion groups. With funding from the Ford Foundation, the ALA set up an Office for Adult Education from 1951 to 1961 for political education and Great Books discussion.[3,21,22] The role of public librarians as adult educators laid the basis for the ongoing support of public libraries as major contributors to lifelong learning and the preservation of cultural heritage. By the 1960s these ideas were challenged as librarians moved to community-based service provision.

Serving Youth: Public librarians serving youth have played an essential role in library development. While men dominated the administration of public libraries because of the public library's initial association with scholarship—a male sphere—a dedicated group of female librarians worked to develop books, magazines, and libraries for young people. Vandergrift has written the history of the first women who fought to establish and to expand service to young people in libraries, while developing a national and international presence for their philosophy and practices. Those interested in children's work in libraries came together in the Children's Librarians Club of ALA in 1900, which then became the Section for Library Work with Children. It was not until 1951 when the American Association of School Librarians (AASL) separated from what was then the Division of Libraries for Children and Young People that the missions of the two types of institutions became distinctly different.[23] Minerva Sanders, Lutie E. Stearns, Caroline Hewins, Anne Carroll Moore, and Effie Louise Power were pioneers of youth services in public libraries and their biographies provide insight into the development of services to children and young adults in the twentieth century.

Serving Immigrants and Minorities: Public librarians have also worked diligently to assist immigrants and minorities as a central part of their mission and librarians have developed expertise in working with underserved groups. In 1918 the American Library Association established the Committee on Work with the Foreign Born to address the needs of immigrants for library services, but also to assist with "Americanization."[24] This assimilation movement gradually became less of a rationale as librarians expanded their focus to work with people within the context of the adult education movement.[25]

Because the U.S. southern states did not permit African-Americans to use public libraries segregated facilities were established in some cities such as Charlotte, North Carolina; Houston, Texas; and Memphis, Tennessee. But very few libraries surveyed in 1922 employed African Americans or made special effort to serve this community. Although there were some notable exceptions such as the Harlem branch of the New York Public Library, few African-Americans had library services until the New Deal initiatives of the 1930s under President Franklin Roosevelt. By 1941 only four states had integrated library services for all.[26–29]

The Public Library Inquiry: "The Public Library Inquiry," a research and report initiative, shaped the way public librarianship was viewed as a profession following the Second World War. The publication of the series of volumes that comprised the "Public Library Inquiry" took place from 1947 to 1952 and are viewed by Raber as a professional legitimizing project and an exercise in identity creation that relied on public librarians viewing themselves as sustainers of democracy.[30]

The emphasis on the need to serve opinion leaders based on the assumption they constituted the library's "natural" and most likely audience—an assumption not entirely wrong—because they were educated and more likely to be readers as reported by the "Public Library Inquiry" authors became part of the long conversation throughout the 1950s that caused librarians to reconsider their practice and expand their methods of providing service to all people.[31]

COMMUNITY-BASED PUBLIC LIBRARIANSHIP— 1966 TO THE TWENTY-FIRST CENTURY

In the 1960s widespread recognition grew that U.S. society was split into a nation of rich and poor—that there was, indeed a "Other America." The "War on Poverty" declared by Lyndon B. Johnson in his State of the Union speech on January 8, 1964 affected the future of public library service and caused members of the American Library Association to launch a series of initiatives that responded to the reality of poverty and marginalization. The Social Responsibilities Round Table was begun within the ALA and a Coordinating Committee on Library Service to the Disadvantaged established. These new units within the national association provided context for public librarians' growing realization that the 1966 *Standards for Public Library Systems* did not clearly address the needs of all people.[32] The 1966 *Standards* were unacceptable to the field for many different reasons; including their perceived irrelevancy to emerging "modern" and evidenced-based management methods, i.e., output-driven effectiveness measures related to local conditions and goals. The 1966 *Standards* and the three prior sets of standards that had been issued by U.S. public librarians in 1933, 1943, and 1956 had defined public library services and staffing from a national perspective. After 1966 the Public Library Association launched a review of goals that resulted in a paradigmatic shift in the practice of public librarianship in the United States.[3]

Instead of top-down national standards public librarianship shifted to a planning model that sought input from library users. After 1966 public librarians no longer based service development on external guidelines, but worked collaboratively with their communities to analyze, set objectives, make decisions, and evaluate achievements. Pungitore has studied this innovation which resulted in community-based public librarianship based on the needs of the people rather than the standards formed by experts.[33] The core documents that were the foundation for the planning model of public library services were issued in two phases: 1) "Planning and Role Setting for Public Libraries" (1980–1995) based on *A Strategy for Public Library Change*;[34] and 2) the "New Planning for Results" approach (1995–present) based on the premise that resource allocation

decisions must be subordinate to and driven by the library's service priorities.[35] This signaled a major change of public librarianship's and the public librarian's identity; from humanitarian/scholarly to bureaucratic/manager practitioner. For lack of a better word, this represented a "paradigm" shift, although clearly the two identities still exist as opposing points of tension within librarianship's identity.

The practice of public librarianship in the twenty-first century United States as conceived by those involved in the development of the Public Library Association's "New Planning for Results" model is about managing change. The 2008 guide, *Strategic Planning for Results*, identified 18 service responses that were selected by public librarians through several years of meetings and interactive discussion. These 18 service responses will guide the practice of public librarianship in the United States for the next decade.[36,37] Each response defines a different specialization for public librarianship such as youth services, adult services, information technology, programming, community service, literacy educator, information services, collection development, and career guidance and planning.

The service responses set forth in *Strategic Planning for Results* are

1. "Be an Informed Citizen: Local, National and World Affairs."
2. "Build Successful Enterprises: Business and Non-profit Support."
3. "Celebrate Diversity: Cultural Awareness."
4. "Connect to the Online World: Public Internet Access."
5. "Create Young Readers: Early Literacy."
6. "Discover Your Roots: Genealogy and Local History."
7. "Express Creativity: Create and Share Content."
8. "Get Facts Fast: Ready Reference."
9. "Know Your Community: Community Resources and Services."
10. "Learn to Read and Write: Adults, Teens and Family Literature."
11. "Make Career Choices: Job and Career Development."
12. "Make Informed Decisions: Health, Wealth and Other Life Choices."
13. "Satisfy Curiosity: Lifelong Learning."
14. "Stimulate Imagination: Reading, Viewing and Listening for Pleasure."
15. "Succeed in School: Homework Help."
16. "Understand How to Find, Evaluate, and Use Information: Information Fluency."
17. "Visit a Comfortable Place: Physical and Virtual Spaces."
18. "Welcome to the United States: Services for New Immigrants."

In addition to this strategic planning model based on responses as promoted and developed at the national level, over 20 individual states have defined library services through state association standards.[38] Some states such as Wisconsin and Florida tie staffing to the state administrative code or statutes. An understanding of the working conditions of public librarianship requires reference to specific state standards and/or local level ordinances and civil service regulations as well as the national approach as outlined in the Public Library Association's *Strategic Planning for Results*.[37]

EDUCATION, CERTIFICATION, AND WORKING CONDITIONS OF PUBLIC LIBRARY WORKERS

The "librarian" designation generally refers to individuals who hold the master's degree in library and information science from a program accredited by the American Library association. Public libraries in the United States employed 140,000 paid full-time-equivalent (FTE) staff and "librarians" (staff with the credential from an accredited program) accounted for 33% of that total in the most recent government report (2008). Other library workers include library technicians, library assistants, clerks, and shelvers. These individuals worked at 9,208 public libraries (administrative entities) in the 50 states and the District of Columbia with 16,592 service stationary points (central libraries, branches) and 819 bookmobiles. They managed multiple materials in different formats as public libraries hold 807.2 million print materials, 42.6 million audio materials, and 43.9 million video materials, in their collections. They served people of all ages during 1.4 billion library visits—4.8 per capita. Serving youth was a special focus as circulation of material to children was 728.1 million items and 57.6 million children attended programs at public libraries. Provision of access to technology was a key service as 334 million uses were made at 196,000 Internet terminals available in public libraries nationwide.[39]

In 2005 the American Library Association-Allied Professional Association (ALA-APA) launched the Certified Public Library Administrator (CPLA) program, a voluntary post-MLS certification program for public librarians with 3 years or more of supervisory experience. The CPLA certification is intended to further professional education and development so that public librarians can move to a higher level of practical professional experience; improve career opportunities; demonstrate that the certified person has acquired a nationally and professionally recognized body of knowledge and expertise in public library administration; and improve the quality of library service through the provision of practical knowledge and skills essential to successful library management.[40]

The salaries of U.S. public librarians can be reviewed on the "Library Salary Database" maintained by the ALA-

APA. The 2007 median salaries for public librarians in 2007 were: Directors: $77,200; Associate Directors: $74,942; Department Heads: $60,327; Librarians who do not supervise: $47,772, and beginning public librarians: $41,334.[41]

There is no national union for public librarians. Instead local public libraries affiliate with unions like AFSCME (Boston Public Library, Brooklyn Public Library, Milwaukee Public Library, Los Angeles Public Library), SEIU (San Francisco Public Library, Orange County Florida), and various other unions such as the Civil Service Employee Association, United Public Employees of California, and the National Association of Government Employees.[42] Collective bargaining may be the library alone or in collaboration with a larger employee union. Union librarians earned an average of over 29% more than nonunion librarians in 2006.[43]

General advancement of the welfare of public librarians is addressed by national association such as the Public Library Association, and the ALA-APA as well as by local chapters/state associations that have annual workshops and programs for librarian development. The Public Library Association 2008 conference, for example, included the program, "How to Work Positively and Constructively in a Unionized Environment."

HUMAN RIGHTS: THE ETHICAL AND PHILOSOPHICAL WORLDVIEW OF PUBLIC LIBRARIANS IN THE TWENTY-FIRST CENTURY

Public librarians have developed philosophical and ethical statements and documents that guide daily practice. While there is little documentation as to underlying philosophies in these various guidelines and statements, we know that the profession has drawn from a variety of traditions of justice as ancient as the Code of Hammurabi (1780 B.C.) right on up to the *Universal Declaration of Human Rights* (1948) and subsequent treaties.

Many of librarianship's key statements and guidelines such as the *Code of Ethics of the American Library Association and* Library *Bill of Rights (LBR)* are shared by all librarians. The *LBR* was adopted in its current form by the Council of the American Library Association on June 18th, 1948 and is Policy 53.1 of the ALA *Policy Manual*.[44] 1961 the *LBR* was amended to include civil rights to ensure library rights are not denied because of race, religion, national origin, or political views. In 1980 and again in 1996, ALA reaffirmed these rights to persons of all ages. The final section on access in the *LBR* states: "A person's right to use a library should not be denied or abridged because of origin, age, background, or views."

In 1971 the American Library Association Office of Intellectual freedom collected Interpretations of the *Library Bill of Rights*. Political, social and technological history is reflected in these statements and a review demonstrates the convergence of technology and defense of freedom to read. For example, the 1951 statement against labeling arose during the McCarthy era to discourage labeling materials as subversive. It was revised in 1990 to address concerns regarding audiovisual rating guides (53.1.7). Contemporary pressures to limit intellectual freedom and human rights are reflected in statements about infringement of access through electronic filtering (53.1.16), invasion of privacy, which requires a distinction from confidentiality, and recognition of economic barriers (53.1.14).[45]

In 1991 the American Library Association endorsed the Universal *Right to Freedom of Expression* as set forth in the *Universal Declaration of Human Rights*, adopted by the United Nations General Assembly: "Everyone has the right to freedom of opinion and expression; this right includes freedom to hold opinions without interference and to seek, receive and impart information and ideas through any media and regardless of frontiers."

The Preamble to the *Universal Declaration* states that "...recognition of the inherent dignity and of the equal and inalienable rights of all members of the human family is the foundation of freedom, justice, and peace in the world...and...the advent of a world in which human beings shall enjoy freedom of speech and belief and freedom from fear and want has been proclaimed as the highest aspiration of the common people."

In 1997 the American Library Association passed the "Resolution on IFLA, Human Rights and Freedom of Expression" which committed the association to support of human rights and freedom of expression. Human rights values permeate library policies. As public librarians carry on their work it is inspirational to keep in mind the history of human rights advocacy, and note the work of librarians as essential to the commitment to foster an open society, a public space in the library where democracy lives.[46–48]

In the philosophical and ethical assessment of the field, *Librarianship and Human Rights: A Twenty-first Century Guide*, Samek has challenged librarians to act on human rights resolutions as a foundation for practice.[49] In keeping with this 21st mandate for public librarianship we provide three examples that illustrate the way public librarians serve human rights.[50] Increasingly the challenges and ethical situations public librarians face are given guidance by a human rights orientation for service.

Privacy

(*UDHR, Article 12: No one shall be subjected to arbitrary interference with his privacy, family, home or correspondence, nor to attacks upon his honour and reputation. Everyone has the right to the protection of the law against such interference or attacks.*)

Connecticut public librarians Peter Chase, George Christian, Janet Nocek, and Barbara Bailey in the *Doe v. Gonzales* case challenged the constitutionality of the nondisclosure provisions of the National Security Letters issued by the government under the USA Patriot Act in terrorist or other investigations. They won.[51]

People with Disabilities

(*UDHR. Article 21: Everyone has the right of equal access to public service in his country.*)

The Americans with Disabilities Act Assembly, a representational group administered by the Association of Specialized and Cooperative Library Agencies (ASCLA), a division of the American Library Association, developed the ALA Policy on "Library Services for People with Disabilities" that notes, "Libraries play a catalytic role in the lives of people with disabilities by facilitating their full participation in society. Libraries should use strategies based upon the principles of universal design to ensure that library policy, resources, and services meet the needs of all people."[52] Recognition that all people have a right to equal access to public service is underscored by public librarianship's commitment to universal libraries. Additionally, services such as the National Library Service for the Blind and Physically Handicapped require collaboration with librarians in community public libraries to activate service.[53]

Immigrants, People of Color

(*UDHR. Article 2: Everyone is entitled to all the rights and freedoms set forth in this Declaration, without distinction of any kind, such as race, colour, sex, language, religion, political or other opinion, national or social origin, property, birth or other status.*)

Public librarians have made great effort to work creatively with people of all backgrounds to deliver fair and equitable service. Library workers reflected on their role in the twenty-first century at the Joint Conference of Librarians of Color (JCLC) in October 2006. This transformative event connected librarians to over-arching societal issues and concerns such as war, economic injustice, environmental challenges, poverty, and racism. The event was a collaboration of the American Indian Library Association, the Asian/Pacific American Librarians Association, the Black Caucus of the American Library Association, the Chinese-American Librarians Association, and REFORMA (National Association to Promote Library Services to the Spanish Speaking). The participants shared experiences, best practices, research, and theory. They made new connections, and built and strengthened coalitions.[54]

In 2008 the report, *Serving Non-English Speakers in U.S. Public Libraries*, the first national study to consider the range of library services and programs developed for non-English speakers, including effectiveness of services, barriers to library use, most frequently used services and most successful library programs by language served was released. Researchers found that the most frequently used services by non-English speakers were special language collections (68.9%) and special programming (39.6%), including language-specific story hours and cultural programming.[55]

THE FUTURE OF PUBLIC LIBRARIANSHIP

As we wrote this entry we discussed the ideas in the air for public librarians in this winter 2009. Because public librarianship is ever changing in reflection of the nature of the communities served and because of the evolution of new technologies there is no static representation that we can use to describe the future. After attending the Public Library Association conference[56] in spring 2008 the topics that demonstrate the range of concerns that public librarians address today include community as in "One Book, One City";[57] adult and youth summer reading programs; cultural programming for libraries;[58] roving reference; serving homeless people;[59] electronic collections replacing paper; funding in times of fiscal austerity; political advocacy for library support; virtual reference;[60] fostering civic engagement; LEED certification for green libraries;[61] the economic impact of public libraries;[62] and the impact of new technologies; family places and early literacy environments in library space; home library services; and community services Web sites.

Public librarianship ranges from service in small communities where the library worker might take on multiple tasks from budgeting to story-telling to more focused service in large systems and highly specialized practice in local history, genealogy, service to different language users, or web development. The range of a public librarian's possible practice is as diverse as the communities where people live. Some public librarians will practice in sparsely populated rural counties, others in cities; in suburban communities; and still others on bookmobiles that take books and materials to people where they live. Regardless of the site of service public librarians act as the community's cultural support as advocates and providers of resources for lifelong learning, reading, information and the full-range of human capabilities.

REFERENCES

1. UNESCO. *The IFLA/UNESCO Public Library Manifesto.* 1994, http://www.ifla.org/VII/s8/unesco/eng.htm (accessed January 2009).
2. International Federation of Library Associations and Institutions (IFLA). Public Libraries Section, http://www.ifla.org/VII/s8/index.htm (accessed January 2009).
3. McCook, K. *Introduction to Public Librarianship;* Neal-Schuman Publishers: New York, 2004.
4. Boston Public Library. Report of the Trustees of the Public Library to the City of Boston; 1852.
5. Shera, J.H. *Foundations of the Public Library: The Origins of the Public Library Movement in New England, 1629–1855;* University of Chicago Press: Chicago, IL, 1949.
6. Ditzion, S.H. *Arsenals of a Democratic Culture: A Social History of the American Public Library Movement in New England and the Middle States from 1850–1900;* American Library Association: Chicago, IL, 1947.
7. Harris, M.H. The purpose of the American public library: A revisionist interpretation of history. Libr. J. September 15, **1973**, *98*, 2509–2514.
8. Garrison, D. *Apostles of Culture: The Public Librarian and American Society: 1876–1920;* University of Wisconsin Press: Madison, WI, [1979], 2003.
9. Wiegand, W.A. *The Politics of an Emerging Profession: The American Library Association, 1876–1917;* Greenwood Press: New York, 1986.
10. Weibel, K.; Heim, K.M.; Ellsworth, D.J. *The Status of Women in Librarianship, 1876–1976;* Oryx Press, Neal-Schuman: Phoenix, AZ, 1979.
11. Maack, M.N. Toward a history of women in librarianship: A critical analysis with suggestions for further research. J. Libr. Hist. **1982**, *17*, 164–185.
12. Hildenbrand, S. *Reclaiming the Library Past: Writing the Women In;* Ablex: Norwood, NJ, 2000.
13. Pawley, C. Reading *Apostles of Culture:* The Politics and Historiography of Library History. Foreword to reprint of *Apostles of Culture* by Dee Garrison; University of Wisconsin Press: Madison, WI, 2003.
14. Bobinski, G. *Carnegie Libraries: Their History and Impact on American Library Development;* American Library Association: Chicago, IL, 1969.
15. Watson, P.D. Valleys without sunsets: Women's clubs and traveling libraries. In *Libraries to the People: Histories of Outreach*; Freedman, R.S.; Hovde, D.M., Eds.; McFarland: Jefferson, NC, 2003; 73–95.
16. Fry, J.W. LSA and LSCA, 1956–1973: A Legislative history. Library Trends **July 1975**, *24*, 7–28.
17. Rose, A.D. Beyond the classroom walls: The Carnegie Corporation and the founding of the American Association for Adult Education. Adult Educ. Q. **Spring 1989**, *39*, 140–151.
18. Learned, W.S. *The American Public Library and the Diffusion of Knowledge;* Harcourt: New York, 1924.
19. American Library Association. *Libraries and Adult Education;* American Library Association: Chicago, IL, 1926.
20. Johnson, A. *The Public Library: A People's University;* American Association for Adult Education: New York, 1938.
21. Lyman, H.L. *Adult Education Activities in Public Libraries;* American Library Association: Chicago, IL, 1954.
22. Monroe, M.E. Library. *Adult Education: The Biography of an Idea;* Scarecrow Press: New York, 1963.
23. Vandergrift, K. Female advocacy and harmonious voices: A history of public library services and publishing for children in the United States. Library Trends **Spring 1996**, *44*, 683–718.

Print–Qualitative

24. Jones, P.A. Jr. *Libraries, Immigrants, and the American Experience;* Greenwood Press: Westport, CT, 1999.

25. Jones, P.A. Jr. *Still Struggling for Equality: American Public Library Services with Minorities;* Libraries Unlimited: Westport, CT, 2004.

26. Josey, E.J. *The Black Librarian in America;* Scarecrow: Metuchen, NJ, 1970.

27. Tucker, J.M. *Untold Stories: Civil Rights, Libraries and Black Librarianship;* University of Illinois: Urbana-Champaign, IL, 1998.

28. Dawson, A. Celebrating African- American Librarians and Librarianship. Library Trends **Summer 2000**, *49*, 49–87.

29. Battles, D.M. *The History of Public Library Access for African Americans in the South;* Lanham, Md.: Scarecrow Press: Metuchen, NJ, 2009.

30. Raber, D. *Librarianship and Legitimacy: The Ideology of the Public Library Inquiry;* Greenwood Press: Westport, CT, 1997.

31. McCook, K. Poverty, democracy and public libraries. In *Libraries and Democracy: The Cornerstones of Liberty*; Kranich, N., Ed.; American Library Association: Chicago, IL, 2001; 30–32.

32. Samek, T. *Intellectual Freedom and Social Responsibility in American Librarianship*, 1967–1974; American Library Association: Chicago, IL, Jefferson, NC.: McFarland & Co., 2001.

33. Pungitore, V.L. *Innovation and the Library: The Adoption of New Ideas in Public Libraries;* Greenwood Press: Westport, CT, 1995.

34. Martin, A. *A Strategy for Public Library Change: Proposed Public Library Goals Feasibility Study;* American Library Association: Chicago, IL, 1972.

35. Himmel, E.; Wilson, J.W. with the ReVision Committee of the Public Library Association. In *Planning for Results: A Public Library Transformation Process;* American Library Association: Chicago, IL, 1998.

36. Nelson, S.; Garcia, J. What are the core services offered by public libraries? PLA needs your help to define the unique role of public libraries today and into the future. Public Libr. **September/October 2006**, *45*, 48–51.

37. Nelson, S. *Strategic Planning for Results;* American Library Association: Chicago, IL, 2008.

38. Public Library Standards. WebJunction, http://ct.web junction.org/do/DisplayContent?id=8350 (accessed January 2009).

39. Miller, K.; Manjarrez, C.; Henderson, E.; Craig, T.; Dorinski, S.; Freeman, M.; Keng, J.; McKenzie, L.; O'Shea, P.; Ramsey, C.; Sheckells, C. *Public Libraries Survey: Fiscal Year 2006* (IMLS-2008– PLS-02); Institute of Museum and Library Services; Washington, DC, 2008. http://harvester.census.gov/imls/pubs/pls/pub_detail.asp? id=121# (accessed January 2009).

40. American Library Association-Allied Professional Association. Certified Public Library Administrator program, http://www.ala-apa.org/certification/cpla.html (accessed January 2009).

41. American Library Association-Allied Professional Association. *ALA-APA Salary Survey, 2007: A Survey of Public and Academic Library Positions Requiring an ALA-Accredited Masters Degree and ALA-APA Salary Survey, 2007: A Survey of Public and Academic Library Positions Not Requiring an ALA-Accredited Masters Degree.* Chicago, IL, 2007.

42. Union Librarian, http://unionlibrarian.blogspot.com/ (accessed January 2009).

43. AFL-CIO, Department of Professional Employees. Library workers: Facts and figures, 2007, http://www.dpeaflcio.org/ (accessed January 2009).

44. American Library Association. *Policy Manual,* http://www.ala.org/ala/aboutala/governance/policymanual/index.cfm (accessed January 2009).

45. American Library Association. Code of Ethics, http://www.ala.org/ala/aboutala/offices/oif/statementspols/codeofethics/codeethics.cfm (accessed January 2009).

46. McCook, K.; Phenix, K.J. Public libraries and human rights. Public Libr. Q. **2006**, *25* (1/2), 64–67.

47. Phenix, K.J.; McCook, K. Human rights and librarians. Ref. User Serv. Q. **Fall 2005**, *45*, 23–26.

48. American Library Association. Resolution on IFLA, Human Rights and Freedom of Expression, http://www.ala.org/ala/aboutala/offices/iro/awardsactivities/resolutionifla.cfm (accessed January 2009).

49. Samek, T. *Librarianship and Human Rights: A Twenty-First Century Guide;* Chandos: Oxford, U.K., 2007.

50. The United Nations. Universal Declaration of Human Rights, http://www.un.org/Overview/rights.html (accessed April 2008).

51. American Civil Liberties Union. ACLU to Honor Connecticut Librarians & John Doe during Seattle Conference. [Online] June 15, 2007. http://www.aclu.org/about/30137prs20070615.html (accessed January 2009).

52. American Library Association. Library Services for People with Disabilities Policy. 53.4.2, http://www.ala.org/ala/mgrps/divs/ascla/asclaissues/libraryservices.cfm (accessed January 2009).

53. National Library for the Blind and Physically Handicapped, http://www.loc.gov/nls/ (accessed January 2009).

54. Goodes, P.A. Historic gathering draws hundred to Dallas. Am. Libr. **2006**, *37*, (November), 20–21.

55. Koontz, C.M.; Jue, D. *Serving Non-English Speakers in U.S. Public Libraries: 2007 Analysis of Library Demographics, Services and Programs;* American Library Association: Chicago, IL, 2008.

56. Public Library Association Conference, March 25–29, 2008. http://www.placonference.org/ (accessed January 2009).

57. One Book One City, http://www.loc.gov/loc/cfbook/onebook/ (accessed January 2009).

58. Cultural Programming for Libraries, http://publicprograms.ala.org/orc/ (accessed January 2009).

59. Hunger, Homelessness & Poverty Task Force, http://www.hhptf.org/ (accessed January 2009).

60. Virtual reference. Wiki list of state supported networks of online reference done by public libraries, http://liswiki.org/wiki/Chat_reference_libraries (accessed January 2009).

61. LEED certification. U.S. Green Building Council, http://www.usgbc.org/DisplayPage.aspx?CategoryID=19 (accessed January 2009).

62. Economic Impact of Public Libraries, http://dpi.wi.gov/pld/econimpact.html (accessed January 2009).

Public Libraries [ELIS Classic]

Barbara H. Clubb
Ottawa Public Library, Ottawa, Ontario, Canada

Print–Qualitative

Abstract

This entry provides an introduction to public libraries throughout the world including an overview of the mission, roles, services, governance, legal and financial framework, collections, human resources, facilities, marketing and performance measurement. The trends, challenges, issues, and future of public libraries are also discussed. The entry is written from the perspective of informing a new library school student, legislators and decision makers, and/or someone looking to find basic information about the purpose and role of public libraries worldwide.

INTRODUCTION

The institution known universally as the public library is defined by the IFLA/UNESCO Public Library Manifesto as a local gateway to knowledge. It is an institution which provides a basic condition for lifelong learning, independent decision-making and cultural development of the individual and social groups.[1] It does this primarily through the provision of organized collections of books, documents, audio visual and other electronic and digital media, and related programs and services. Public libraries are a worldwide phenomenon and have existed in various forms for centuries. They occur in a variety of societies, in differing cultures and at different stages of development. Though no one body or institution is responsible for keeping global public library statistics it is estimated that there are over 251,324 public library locations worldwide including main libraries and branches. The United States and Canada respectively have 16,543[2] and 3100 public library buildings. Although the varied contexts in which public libraries operate inevitably result in differences in the services they provide and the way those services are delivered, public libraries the world over have many characteristics in common and all work toward making a contribution to the improvement of the lives of the citizens they serve and the societies in which they operate.

Since its inception the modern public library has been designed and aspired to be the local center of and access to information and ultimately knowledge. This initially was largely through the medium of print but libraries have always provided access to media in its multiple formats and that now includes digital content. Since their early days public libraries have also played multiple social roles (although book purveying has been a primary role). Public library services are usually provided free (or for a small charge) on the basis of supporting equality of access for all, regardless of age, race, sex or sexual preference, religion, nationality, language or social status or mental or physical

ability. They are funded primarily by local government, but often with assistance from regional/provincial, federal government authorities and established and increasingly supported by mandatory or permissive legislation.[3]

PURPOSE OF THE PUBLIC LIBRARY

The primary purposes of the public library are to provide facilities, resources, and services in a variety of media (print, audio, visual, electronic/digital) to meet the needs of individuals and groups for both formal and informal education, as well as for information and personal development which includes recreation and leisure. Public libraries have an important role in the development and maintenance of an open and democratic society by giving the individual access to a wide and varied range of knowledge, ideas, and opinions.[4] Public libraries are considered by many (but not all) citizens and parent governing bodies as essential or core public services which support civic engagement and economic development and which enhance the quality of life in a community.[5]

The IFLA/UNESCO Public Library Manifesto and Guidelines which were designed and redeveloped over the last 60 years to apply to public libraries worldwide, provide a succinct list of key missions or roles for the modern public library (Table 1). These roles relate to information, literacy, education, culture, and leisure. Of course cultural and political differences between states have significant implications for libraries and the actual meaning of these roles do vary. These key mission statements include creating and strengthening reading habits in children from an early age; supporting both individual and self-conducted education as well as formal education; providing opportunities for personal creative development; simulating the imagination and creativity of children and young people, promoting awareness of cultural heritage, appreciation of the arts, scientific achievements and

Encyclopedia of Library and Information Sciences, Fourth Edition DOI: 10.1081/E-ELIS4-120044295

Table 1 Mission and global ends Statements of Markham Public Library, Canada

The Markham Public Library (Markham, Ontario, Canada) is an example of a library that has developed a Mission, Vision and supporting Global ends policies

Vision: *Markham Public Library-the Place where Markham's communities come together to imagine, learn and grow.*

Mission: *We enrich the lives and empower people by providing a spectrum of resources and services that delight our diverse community. You will feel empowered at your library.*

Source: http://www.markhampubliclibrary.ca/about/mission.asp

Global Ends Policy: *The Markham Public Library exists to that people who live, work or study in Markham have lifelong, universal and equitable access to the information, and resources that support and contribute to an enriched community.*

- *The community is informed*
- *The community is inspired*
- *The community is empowered*
- *The community is linked*

Source: http://www.markhampubliclibrary.ca/docs/policies/board_policies.pdf

innovation; fostering inter-cultural dialogue and favoring cultural diversity; supporting the oral tradition; ensuring access for citizens to all sorts of community information, providing adequate information services to local enterprises, associations and interest groups; facilitating the development of information and computer literacy skills; and supporting and participating in literacy activities and programs for all age groups, and initiating such activities if necessary.[1]

Public libraries around the world have interpreted the IFLA Manifesto and Guidelines in different ways:

- In Singapore the stated mission of the National Library Board is to be "an inspiring beacon of lifelong learning, bringing knowledge alive, sparking imagination, and creating possibility for a vibrant and creative Singapore."[6]
- In South Africa, where many people particularly in rural areas have inadequate living space and no electricity to enable them to study, public libraries give a high priority to providing the basic facilities, light, tables, and chairs for their users to read and study[4] (Fig. 1).
- In the Barcelona province in Spain, some library services give support to distance learning students from the Open University in Catalonia.[4]
- In the state of Queensland, Australia, public libraries provide homework resources and support to upper primary and secondary school children through organized homework clubs in libraries. Electronic homework support is also available.[7]

In many respects the mandate and role of public libraries has remained timeless and universal throughout the years. However, in the last 30 years, public libraries as public institutions whether in developed countries or developing countries have experienced more change in terms of technology, format, approaches to customer service and democratization than in the previous 200 years. These changes are continuing into the twenty-first century at an accelerated and intensified pace as information and media goes increasingly digital and the way people use public libraries and their perceptions of public libraries continue to evolve.[8,9] These changing expectations have been

Fig. 1 Mpumalanga Township Library, Kwazulu Natal Province, South Africa.
Source: From Barbara Clubb (author).

documented in a number of studies about the perception and use of public libraries. In the OCLC study, *The Perceptions of Libraries and Information Resources*, researchers found that while libraries continue to be trusted information providers, users were not aware of the e-resources of the library, that the library brand (i.e., books) is dated, that users want more self-service and seamless access, and that libraries appear to be losing mindshare of the information-seeking public.[10] The study *Long Overdue* reported that public libraries get high marks from citizens for service, that computers and Internet access are priority service elements, that there is clear demand for more convenient hours and more service for teens, and that while there is strong community support for libraries, the public is generally unaware of how financially vulnerable libraries are becoming and finally that library representatives need to speak up and reach out if public libraries are to survive and thrive.[11]

New Roles for Public Libraries

In 2007 the Public Library Association, a division of the American Library Association completed a study to look at the unique roles of American public libraries and their core services today and into the future. The result has been the articulation of 18 new service responses for American public libraries services focusing on citizen outcomes:

- Be informed citizens: local, national, and world affairs.
- Build successful enterprises: business and non-profit support.
- Celebrate diversity: cultural awareness.
- Connect to the online world: public Internet access.
- Create young readers: early literacy.
- Discover your roots: genealogy and local history.
- Express creativity: create and share content.
- Get facts fast: ready reference.
- Know your community: community resources and services.
- Learn to read and write: adult, teen, and family literacy.
- Make career choices: job and career development.
- Make informed decisions: health, wealth, and other life choices.
- Satisfy curiosity: lifelong learning.
- Stimulate the imagination: reading viewing and listening for pleasure.
- Succeed in school: homework help.
- Understand how to find, evaluate, and use information: information fluency.
- Visit a comfortable place: physical and virtual spaces.
- Welcome to newcomers: services for new immigrants.

While these responses echo the IFLA/UNESCO Manifesto and Guidelines, they provide a more precise

definition of service as well as a more clearly stated relationship between the library and its customer within its political and civic environments. They also reflect the new environment in which many public libraries operate particularly with regard to rapidly changing technology and fiscal realities. For instance there is clear emphasis on the library's role to provide public Internet access and to help patrons use information technology and become fluent with new information. In this way, the Public Library Association (PLA) has performed a valuable service and provided a new tool for public libraries worldwide.[9]

LEGAL AND FINANCIAL FRAMEWORK OF PUBLIC LIBRARIES

To support the level of service proposed by the IFLA/UNESCO Manifesto and the concepts in the new PLA Public Library Responses, strong legislation and sustained funding is essential. Around the world there are a vast array of models which delineate the relationship between the public library and their governing and funding authorities. Depending on the country, the provinces, regions, states, or municipalities are either in whole or in part responsible for service. Usually it is the local municipal unit but often (e.g., some provinces in Canada) two or more levels of government provide a combination of sustained and special purpose funding. In some countries (e.g., Argentina) libraries are required to seek sustained funding from nongovernmental organizations, agencies and/or individuals. Even in developed countries, public libraries are becoming increasingly aggressive and sophisticated in their non-tax fund-raising activities largely from necessity as tax bases are stressed and service demands increase. In North America most public libraries are governed by appointed or elected boards. This is not common in the rest of the world.

The most important instrument for public library development is legislation at either the national and/or state/provincial level combined with provincial and/or national information policies, standards and guidelines. Public library legislation and related regulations vary greatly from country to country and within countries from state to state and region to region. Legislation can be simple or complex, mandatory or permissive, dictatorial or encouraging. Some examples of this variation include:

- Mexico and Venezuela have specific public library legislation whereas in Colombia and Brazil, legislation only includes references to public libraries.
- The Finnish Library Act of 1998, largely regarded as a model piece of legislation, stipulates that the public library should be provided by the municipality, either independently or in cooperation with other public libraries, that public libraries should cooperate with

other types of libraries and that the library should evaluate the library and information services that it provides.

- In Armenia, local authorities have responsibility for the financing and maintenance of public libraries. The Law on Local Self-Government, 1966, defines their obligations for maintaining and developing public libraries.

In addition to specific library legislation, the modern public library must respond increasingly to and/or be compliant with other legislation related to such issues as copyright, financial management, data protection, services for persons with disabilities, pay equity, health and safety, global trade negotiations, intellectual freedom, environmental protection and increasing requirements to develop environmentally supportive or "green" policies, practices and facilities.[4]

ELEMENTS OF THE PUBLIC LIBRARY

The IFLA/UNESCO Manifesto and the related Guidelines for Development provide a clear framework for understanding and defining public library service no matter what the local context. This entry has already touched upon role and purpose as well as the legal and financial framework. Within this organizational framework major elements of public library service include: meeting the needs of the users; collection development and access; the development of the library's human resources; the marketing of public libraries and their services and the physical facility—or library as place.

Meeting User Needs

Those responsible for public libraries have always recognized that they must know the size and characteristics of the current and potential user base, understand what these groups want from their public library, anticipate emerging needs, and make services and collections as accessible as possible. Needs assessments done by almost every public library finds that people want more books and resources, better hours, more and faster computers, and more parking (where public transportation is not available). More specific areas of need identified refer to serving people at all ages and stages of life as well as individuals and groups with special needs and institutions within the wider community network.[4] Because resources are always scarce, libraries have to carefully collect and analyze data that clearly identifies the needs and assists the library in putting them in a priority order that makes best sense in that particular community. Sometimes needs are deliberately underserved or not served at all because of resource

constraints or because another community agency has been able or has the mandate to address the needs. For example in a new community with many children, preschool programs and materials might be the library's highest priority, where a high seniors population would dictate different priorities in another community. In some locales assessing needs can be a simple enquiry to the community. In other instances, public libraries are using a wide range of research and information-seeking strategies to develop both qualitative and quantitative approaches to studying and planning for their community needs. This approach moves libraries away from strictly quantitative standards which may be inappropriate for an individual community. Quantitative standards may not be relevant to services or evaluation of their effectiveness yet still be politically important in the effort to raise or maintain revenue.

Once users needs have been identified, public libraries then have to plan to provide services to satisfy those needs often while eliminating or narrowing other areas of activity. In general the services include: loans of books and other media, provision of materials for use in the library, reference and information services, access to the public Internet and related technology, readers advisory services, information about the community, user education—in particular literacy including computer literacy, outreach services to those unable to physically access the library facilities, and a selection of materials, programs, and events for various age and ability groups.

Materials and Services for Children

Materials and services for children are a mainstay of the modern public library in all parts of the world. Libraries have embraced the role of helping children discover and experience the joy of reading and adapting to other media. They also work intensively with parents and caregivers as co-conspirators in the development of a literate youth population. Responding to these trends in 2008, the Danish Library Authority issued a report which recommended radical changes in the approach to library services for children. It is an encapsulation of how children's library services are responding to the complex digital world in which so many of our children live. The recommendations (translated from the Danish) take the form of 10 commandments and include: 1) New competencies create new activities in the library; 2) The library space must create surprise and inspiration; 3) Libraries must develop their net services (libraries create new frameworks and facilities by exploiting social technologies and using staff as hosts and resources in virtual networks for children); 4) Children play in the library; 5) The library gives children reading experiences and reading skills; 6) Create assets in new forms of cooperation between the school library and the public library; 7) The library creates community feeling—also for those outside (meaning children with special needs, handicapped, socially vulnerable and children with ethnic backgrounds other than Danish); 8) The library supports learning and cultural development; 9) The library must reach out to children; and 10) The library's management focuses on children.[12]

The range of programming for children in public libraries is rich with examples which illustrate the new Danish thinking. In Bucharest, Rumania, the city library offers summer programs, run by volunteers, aimed at children from 11 to 14 whose parents are at work. In Singapore, more than 40 children's libraries for children under 10 have been established in cooperation with grass roots organizations. These have over the years made way for larger public libraries complete with library services for children. During the war in Croatia, a step-by-step reading program was organized in Zagreb public library to aid the psycho-social recovery of children and adolescents through reading and literacy.[4] In Ottawa, Canada, the public library provides back-packs of high quality and popular children's materials for busy parents to grab on their way out the door of the library. In Fujian, China, the Xiamen Public Children's Library has established the Apple Tree Library aiming to promote English language competency. One of the newest service concepts is seen in the Library of 100 Talents in Heerhugowaard, the Netherlands. "In this library, the children are the librarians. The organization of the library reflects the way that children use information, create new contexts, and share this with other children. More than 250 children participated in the library's design; the multimedia collection is presented in a number of 'islands' of things to do: nature, the living room, me and the world and dreams." The Library is a successful attempt to move the library to be both linguistic and nonlinguistic in the discovery and learning experiences it offers its young clients.[13] Increasingly public libraries are creating early childhood learning and literacy centers in their children's departments. For instance these are being developed by the Toronto Public Library as substantial areas, as branches are renovated and have been trademarked as KidsStop™ (Fig. 2). This approach is built on research that proves that the higher the literacy rates in children and the earlier children are exposed to a positive reading and learning environment, the better chances they have for positive life-outcomes in such key areas as health, employment, and participation in the justice system.[14,15]

Materials and Services for Teens

Materials and services for teens have always been an important part of public library offerings. However, now many public libraries, such as the Jacksonville Public Library in Florida, United States, are placing increasing focus on the creation of separate physical teen spaces or teen zones (Fig. 3), specialized materials both print and digital, teen programming, and in particular the introduction of video/computer gaming as a form of both teaching, learning and building literacy and new social skills in young people.

In Hamburg, Germany, young adults help to select and buy media stock for the young adults' library in a project called EXIT. They select media reflecting their own cultural background and have organized and gained sponsorship for their own Internet café. In Singapore, a library aimed at people years 18–35 was established in the heart of the shopping area. Focus groups helped to define the profile of the collection and design the "library@orchard" which has been immensely popular and received 1.4 million visits per year. (It is currently closed for relocation in 2010.) In Queensland, Australia, public library staff

Fig. 2 Toronto Public Library, new KidsStop™ area in S. Walter Stewart Branch, Toronto, Ontario, Canada.
Source: From Ben Rahn/A-Frame, permission received.

Fig. 3 Jacksonville Public Library, Main Library Teen room, Jacksonville, Florida, United States.
Source: From Jacksonville Public Library, permission received.

receive specialist training in working with young adults. The training covers customer service, programming ideas, and how to run teenage advisory groups and homework clubs.

Services and Materials for Adults

Services and materials for adults in public libraries support lifelong learning, literacy, employment, health, recreation and reading, small business, literature and culture, settlement services, citizenship, civic engagement, and the strengthening of democracy. Again it is critical that the local library carefully analyze its community to determine the best place to invest limited resources and identify where networking with other institutions can leverage more service offerings for their clients.

Many public libraries support lifelong learning working with schools and other educational institutions to help students in both formal and informal educational settings. This often takes the form of support for literacy by supplying resources and facilities for students and trainers or actually being the primary provider of literacy programs themselves. In other libraries it means supporting distance education programs or providing invigilation services. For instance, the South Dublin County Library Service, Ireland provides self-learning facilities for adults, including computer-based learning and audio- and video-based language-learning materials.[4] The new central library in Salt Lake City welcomes all comers providing classes in English as a second language, meditation and Braille. Organizations such as Weight Watchers, to the Royal Court of the Golden Spike Empire, to No More Homeless Pets, have used the building for their meetings. Other groups such as Single Moms, the Utah Socialists and a group that reads to their dogs are also users of the library.[16]

Services for New-Comers, Immigrants, the Socially Excluded and Diverse Populations

Service for newcomers is not a new offering for many public libraries but increasing globalization and movement among countries has made this a new or higher service imperative for many public libraries particularly in countries that are experiencing high levels of immigration such as the United States, Canada, Australia, Great Britain, the Scandinavian and Benelux countries, and Germany. In the United States, the immigrant population has grown to 33.5 million or 12% of the population.[17] In Canada, according to the 2006 Census, one in five (19.8%) residents were born outside of Canada. Most newcomers settle in large urban centers. For example the Canadian metropolitan area of greater Toronto has a population of more than 5 million of which 45% were born in another country.[18]

Services for immigrants particularly in North America go back to library philanthropist Andrew Carnegie's desire to fund libraries as a place for immigrant self-education. For example, in 1910 the Minneapolis (United States) Public Library created a reading room for the unemployed most of whom were immigrants and in 1915 the Hibbing, Minnesota (United States) Public Library operated a library bus that served a clientele which included populations of Finnish, Irish, and Serbian immigrants.[19] Currently services range from collections in multiple languages, bilingual or multilingual staff, multilingual and newcomer sections of library Web sites (with both text and video) as well as library publications, computer services and training for newcomers often in a variety of languages, language and literacy training programs, multilingual conversation programs and book clubs, foreign language and bilingual workshops including book groups and literacy tutoring, heritage day celebrations, specialized outreach and program partnerships with a wide range of ethno-cultural organizations. Some examples include:

- In Nuremberg, Germany, there is a significant Russian immigrant population. The library provides print and audio visual material in Russian, language courses and books about Germany, specialized materials about career training and re-qualification. It also employs Russian speaking public service and technical services staff.[20]
- In Ottawa, Canada, the library Web site features a welcome to the library video in 17 different languages to supplement library settlement services in 9 of the 33 branch locations.[21]
- Public libraries also develop programs to foster intercultural harmony and understanding. In the public library in Malmo, Sweden and in some libraries in the United Kingdom and Canada, patrons can use the "living library" to borrow a living person for a 30 min chat. Two of the most popular individuals "borrowed" are immigrants such as a veiled Muslim woman and an imam.
- In Denmark, the growing number of immigrants and refugees is a relatively new experience for public libraries.[22] A major public library response published by the Danish Library Centre for Integration has been the creation, maintenance, and updating of FINFO a Web portal that gives local, national, and global information in the 11 most frequently used languages in Denmark.[23] The purpose of FINFO is to support integration of the minorities into Danish society.[24]
- In Queens, New York (United States), the public library has partnered with the Mayor's Office for Immigrant Affairs to provide computers and assistance for customers who wish to fill out the application for the Diversity (Green Card) Visa Lottery.

Susan Burke's research on public library resources used by immigrant households[25] found that newcomers were "less likely to use non-English language materials, attend library programs, for help finding a job or to search for information than the literature suggests. They were most likely to borrow books, tapes, and CDs, not specifically those in languages other than English, to pursue hobbies and entertainment, and use the library for educational pursuits." This suggests that the public library needs to carefully evaluate their newcomer services to ensure that they are reaching and meeting the needs of that specific target group.

In 2008, The Intergovernmental Council for UNESCO's "Information for All Programme," endorsed the IFLA/UNESCO Multicultural Library Manifesto.[26] This is a useful tool for public libraries to work with multicultural issues on the local, national, and international level. The three major pillars of the Manifesto states

that: libraries can play an important role in our globalized and multicultural world; respect for the diversity of cultures, tolerance, dialogue, and cooperation are among the best guarantees for international peace and security; and libraries promote and preserve cultural and linguistic heritage. This new Manifesto complements the IFLA/UNESCO Public Library Manifesto, the IFLA/UNESCO School Library Manifesto and the IFLA Internet Manifesto. It is also supported by the Guidelines for Libraries Serving Multicultural Populations.[27]

Services to diverse populations also take the form of many types of outreach programs including services to prisons, homeless and battered spouse shelters and residences, low-income communities, hospitals and persons confined to their homes for reasons of age or infirmity or both.[28] Libraries also provide on-site shelter and support for homeless and indigent populations and are often partners with social service agencies. This is particularly the case in large urban central libraries and branches in inner-city areas. Other libraries have developed specialties at specific branches which could include African-American history, genealogy and Aboriginal author, and oral history programs. Four major public libraries in Canada have recently concluded a multiyear project and produced a tool-kit called "Working Together" to assist libraries in reaching out to marginalized populations. More sophisticated market segmentation of communities is also revealing that the upwardly mobile middle and upper middle classes are also often underserved.[29]

Resource Collections

Collections are at the heart of all public libraries. They are never big enough or good enough. In 2008, there are several key external and internal issues and trends that are affecting collection management and the ability to provide client-focused service. The first of these is population including growth, continuing shifts from rural to urban centers and changing demographics. Demographic shifts, combined with limited budget increases, the relentless emergence of new formats and the increasing use of library collections mean that there could be fewer library materials for future users. In many developed countries like Germany and Sweden, an aging population, falling birth rates and new patterns of immigration are increasingly placing new and different demands on public library collections.

News media and many forms of entertainment continue to influence sales and demand for particular titles in a wide range of formats. Curiously, some libraries report that while there is an insatiable demand for new titles there is also sustaining customer interest in older publications at a time when publishers trend toward maintaining limited backlists. This can be attributed to the "long tail" effect where increased aggregation of titles and speedy access to the databases leads the library user away from best sellers and to the rest of what is available further afield.[30] It could also reflect the desire to find more, older works by authors (particularly novels) whose new or current works they have just discovered.

Social networks such as Facebook, Myspace, and Flickr are also having an influence on collections and services. Library customers of all ages, but particularly the young, use the Internet to stay tuned and connected. The February 19, 2007 issue of *Publishers Weekly* noted that,

> With kids now spending more time on the computer than they do in front of the TV or the printed page, publishers are trying to reach them where they live through online marketing campaigns, utilizing blogs, podcasts, instant messaging, video-sharing and social networking sites like MySpace which is a regular destination for 55% of teens according to a recent PEW survey.[31]

The history of public libraries shows that libraries have always, since their early days provided media in all its multiple formats. (p. 1)[32] Today, there is increasingly rapid change in all audio and visual formats. Library budgets must allocate larger percentages to film, television, and other performances available on an increasing variety of media formats, and the selection is becoming broader. In addition, DVD collections are increasingly reflecting libraries' expansion to world languages to better service newcomers to the community. The DVD has replaced the video as the format of choice for library users. Many library leaders and collection specialists believe that the DVD will soon give way to a faster, more compressed digital format.

Libraries are also registering usage declines in certain other and earlier formats. Many libraries have completely withdrawn their video-cassette collections and book tape collections are no longer being developed. For now CDs have become the format of choice for audio visual resources within the marketplace and within the library. This includes book CDs, downloadable audio books playable on computers, MP3 devices, and IPODs. In public libraries this is being expanded to music and video products. Digital rights management is coming more to the fore as producers work through the challenges of downloading and file sharing. Specialized resources for the print disabled are increasingly provided to libraries and clients using the Digital Accessible Information System (DAISY) format.

The growing range of resources in digital form is increasingly extending the Library's reach into the community providing registered customers with more convenient access to information and recreational materials. The majority of library catalogs have long been available via remote access on an almost 24/7 basis. Many libraries anticipate that electronic media will eventually become the norm for the delivery of spoken word and video

resources to customers and that these e-resources will replace books on tape, books CDs, MPS3 audio books, videos and DVDs. Electronic media is predicted to be the format of choice for language learning, test preparation, and career planning. E-book devices are becoming cheaper and easier to use. E-learning will increase. Best of all, unlike physical items, Web-based electronic products require no physical shelf space.

Public libraries are increasingly treating their collections of e-resources as another branch. Many public libraries subscribe to dozens if not hundreds of electronic databases. These are often provided through consortia or national, state, regional, or provincial licensing schemes. Library Web sites are being redesigned to draw the user in and keep them there. This is evident in the Vaughan Public Library's teen zone;[33] the Ottawa Public Library's Kids Site[21] and the Cleveland Public Library's island in Second Life virtual reality.[34] Other e-initiatives include online book clubs, online training, offerings such as NewspaperDirect PressDisplay which provides same day access to more than 230 newspapers from around the world with the text in the language of origin. As more vendors respond to new public needs, such digital resources as Home Repair Reference Centre, Small Engine Repair are becoming increasingly available in digital form.

The continuing migration from print to digital, especially in the area of reference tools, means that public libraries' print reference collections are now declining significantly particularly. In many library branches the print reference collection takes up no more than a few shelves.

However there is still the pull of print as Mattern states in *The New Downtown Library: Designing with Communities*:

> There is a materiality to particular media and artifacts and experiences that cannot be reproduced in a digital environment. There must be a place for this material knowledge—a place where people can feel the heft of a book, smell the ink of a newly printed magazine, turn gingerly the brittle pages of a worn manuscript, or dig through collections of yellowed historical photographs. (p. ix)[32]

And of course there must be a place where someone can go to get a book and settle in to read if she so desires.

Human Resources

The four pillars of public library services are books, buildings, bytes and bodies or in common parlance, materials, buildings, technology and staff, and other elements of human capital. The human resource element of the budget is usually the largest (between 60% and 80%+). Staff are required to lead, direct, manage, and plan for the future of the service, advocate for funding and resources, collect and organize the services and programs, provide direct services such as circulation and information services, function as the intermediary between the users and the resources and technology available, reach out to the un-served, develop service partnerships, work with professional colleagues of other systems and associations to plan for, leverage and advocate for service and funding improvements over larger units of service and governments. This is largely driven by the desire to provide as equitable a service to as many citizens as possible.

Categories of staff found in public libraries normally include directors and managers, qualified librarians, library assistants, technical staff and/or paraprofessionals, specialist staff, and a wide variety of support staff. Employees are either full time or part time in a variety of permanent, term, temporary, or casual status categories. Most public library workers are not unionized but most workers in large and/or urban library systems are either unionized or part of a staff association.

The public library workforce is currently under severe pressure. As public library service has become more complex so have the requirements for the skills and qualities of those working in them. Library service now requires confident, outgoing individuals at all levels of the organization who can communicate effectively with patrons, community groups, politicians, and fellow workers; understand and interpret their needs; and work effectively within a climate of cultural, ethnic and intergenerational diversity. Increasingly library staff are required to be innovative, flexible, entrepreneurial, imaginative and visionary, work as part of a team, and be able to respond to rapid change in both methods of service and professional practice. They are asked to be knowledgeable about building and maintaining facilities, computers, printers, photocopiers, scanners, digital environments, and social software while simultaneously developing and applying skills that some might see more appropriately assigned to a psychologist or social worker. And they work in institutions where only a few years ago the primary (but not only) reward system was too often driven by following the rules and getting the books back on the shelves. All public libraries are being asked to do more with less and to exploit technology to become more efficient and effective.

Libraries, like most public service institutions are now being charged with developing their workforce to reflect the community it services in terms of ethno-cultural and linguistic diversity. This is happening at a time when the library workforce is aging, there are insufficient recruits to fill all the vacancies, wages are not always competitive, there is increasing difficult in attracting professional librarians into the managerial ranks and an often blurred distinction between professionals and paraprofessionals.

One of the major challenges of the public library director is to provide an environment where staff have continuing opportunities for growth and development particularly in the areas of technology, networking, supervision, management and leadership skills development, budgeting and opportunities for special projects that provide an appropriate level of professional engagement. The IFLA Guidelines suggests that between 0.5% and 1.0% of the total library budget should be designated for training.[4]

Marketing the Service

Almost every public library needs assessments including the recent OCLC report on perceptions of libraries reveal that regardless of what new and innovative offerings libraries provide, the vast majority of users and potential users think of their public library as a place to get books and that they are unaware of the vast resources and connections available to them.[10] At the same time the *Long Overdue* study on public and leadership attitudes toward libraries reported that in America at least, people believe that their libraries are an important part of a healthy community; that libraries spend money well; that libraries need to provide information free of charge; that they expect a good supply of current books, reference materials, convenient hours, knowledgeable staff, and spaces for children and teenagers. Libraries are supported and given high marks for services by users but most users are unaware of the needs and pressures that libraries face in maintaining these services.[11] This was reinforced by the OCLC study *From Funding to Awareness* which reported that for many public libraries the need to grow awareness and mindshare is intensifying[35] as annual operating budgets fail to keep pace with the services and resources needed to meet the library's mission. The study reinforced that this lack of awareness is leading to reduced budgets staff, hours, and services in spite of increased circulation, library visits, and Internet use. The findings suggested that there is sufficient but latent support for increased library funding but that a large-scale library support campaign using brand segmentation and marketing is urgently needed. A further finding identified that the majority of elected officials while appreciative of the values and services of the public library and librarians are reluctant to support a tax increase for local services, including the public library.[35]

The IFLA Guidelines for public libraries state that libraries must continually promote their offerings to the public.[4] This requires a strategic vision plus communications, marketing and promotion policy, plans and strategies to tell the library story and engage both the user and potential user. Libraries worldwide have used an array of strategies including Web sites, print, electronic, and commercial media; displays and exhibits; friends of libraries and library foundations; celebrations of events, individuals and milestones; public speaking events; targeted activities to engage elected officials at the local, state and national levels; special campaigns such as one-city/one-book, library sign-ups and the use of well-known persons such as actors, astronauts, and authors to help link the library to the community.

Often staff, trustees (where they exist) and library friends and advocates receive special communications and media training to help them deliver the library message in a convincing and professional way to councils, groups, individuals, and potential funders. This activity is intensified at budget time but the most successful libraries employ these strategies on an ongoing basis. However, all studies indicate that these efforts are still not sufficient to get the message across or sustain the support needed.

Library as Place

Notwithstanding the above, public libraries continue to be regarded by many as relevant, vital public institutions (whether or not survey respondents use them). Now new forces are requiring and shaping library design and drawing users back. These forces include the proliferation of new media, the integration of non-media activities, new hours, the introduction of commercial elements such as coffee houses and other retail outlets, and the new view of libraries as economic generators as well as hubs of urban revitalization.

The library building is as much a part of public library service as the resources and the staff within. Increasingly, in many parts of the world the public library is becoming a third community place—apart from home and school or home and church—a community gathering place where there is no pressure to buy, consume, or perform as well as a place that provides encouragement for exploration, discovery, connection, and civility. Library space is becoming more and more important when so many other activities and services are increasingly offered in virtual form. From China, to Columbia to Australia to Slovenia to South Africa, new and beautifully designed libraries are becoming facilities of service, community congregation and human engagement, and a focus of civic pride.

When planning a library facility, the library staff, governing and funding bodies consider provisions for the range of functions of the library, the size of the library, designated spaces or zones, accessibility, way finding, ambience, information and computer technology, food services, meeting room space, heritage, genealogy, and archival functions.[4] Increasingly attention has to be paid to environmental sustainability and adhering to LEED (Leadership in Energy and Environmental Design) or equivalent standards, proximity or integration with public transportation hubs, group project and study space, catering facilities, prayer, meditation or quiet rooms, archival and heritage functional space, special and/or flexible spaces for groups such as newcomers, teens, children and seniors, and services for the alternately abled. In addition, the general public is increasingly being invited to participate in the planning and funding of these important

civic spaces which they pay for through their tax dollars or their participation in fund-raising and advocacy efforts.

At the same time, the ever adaptable public library still brings service to the people in many other forms. And so the concept of library as place also includes, bookmobiles, donkey libraries in Zimbabwe, camel library services in Kenya, subway and garden market library kiosks in Chile and floating libraries or library book boats in such diverse countries as Thailand and Norway. And making a debut are DIY (do-it-yourself) electronic kiosks libraries such as those in Roanoke, Virginia (United States), which are being located in community centers, transit stations, and commercial shopping malls as a way of extending service and keeping costs down in tight economic times. In these types of facilities, library staff are sometimes available through remote electronic access and the kiosks are restocked by non-public staff. But, everything that comes around, goes around. Allen Lane, founder of Penguin paperbacks, first established a "Penguincubator" in the mid-1930s in London, England—a slot machine that dispensed his paperbacks for a small fee of six pence—the price of a packet of cigarettes.[36]

In *The Library as Place*, Buschman and Leckie provide a collection of 14 original articles documenting the library as a place of immense cultural, symbolic, and intellectual meaning for users whether they are seeking pleasure, scholarship, or both.[37]

New Central Libraries

In the last 20 years, the building of significant new iconic central and/or national libraries has surged across the globe reinforcing the concept of third place beyond home, school, and work. The result has been such striking facilities as the Seattle Public Library by Rem Koolhausn (Fig. 4), the new Singapore National Library (Fig. 5), the Grande Bibliothèque du Quebec in Montreal by John Patkau (Fig. 6) as well as his renovation of the Winnipeg Public Library (Fig. 7), the Mitterand Library in Paris, the Amsterdam Public Library by Jo Coenen (Fig. 8), the Jacksonville Central Library in northern Florida, the Vancouver (Fig. 9) and Salt Lake City (Fig. 10) public libraries by Moshe Safdie and the Shanghai Library (Fig. 11) which with 83,000 m^2 is one of the 10 largest libraries in the world. In many situations including Seattle, Vancouver, Singapore, Jacksonville, and the Harold Washington Library Center in Chicago, the building of the central library has been part of a major redevelopment of existing branch libraries as well as the introduction of new service points throughout the city.

In building these massive facilities, library planners are having to balance the need for access while ensuring security, the provision of both public and commercial space, providing universal access within budget constraints, and an economical and efficient building.

Fig. 4 Seattle Public Library, new central library, "living room" area, Seattle, Washington, United States.
Source: From Paul Hussar, permission received.

Fig. 5 New Singapore National Library, Singapore.
Source: From Singapore National Library Board, 2009, permission received, All Rights Reserved.

Fig. 6 Bibliothèque et Archives du Quebec (Canada).
Source: BanQ, Bernard Fougères, permission received.

Fig. 7 Winnipeg Public Library, grand staircase, Winnipeg, Manitoba, Canada.
Source: From Winnipeg Public Library, permission received.

Notwithstanding the many significant central facilities that have been erected, the approval and funding process is often very difficult, challenging and always political. Many citizens, whether they are users or not, fear the reduction or elimination of beloved branch facilities in favor of a large downtown library. Sometimes the library capital scheme is bundled with other less attractive public sector projects. Some citizens and elected officials have concerns about the relevance of a large, expensive downtown facility in an increasingly digitized, decentralized, and privatized culture.[32] And a new downtown facility, indeed the whole library system always has to compete with other public service priorities such as police, schools, fire, and public housing. In many American cities, a major library project has to be put to a public vote. Once political and public approval is obtained most cities use an architectural competition to select its design team however the use of public–private partnerships is increasing and this sometimes affects the selection of architectural and design professionals. New central libraries must always be integrated into the life of the community whether there is a vibrant downtown to be nourished or the facility is part of a broader effort to revive life downtown.

MEASUREMENT AND EVALUATION OF PUBLIC LIBRARIES

Performance Measurement

Performance measurement has been used in libraries for many years. Originally libraries, library organizations and legislative bodies developed state, national, and international standards. In 1973 and 1977 IFLA issued *Standards for Public Libraries* which contained a range of quantitative standards including the recommended size of collection, size of administrative unit, opening hours, staffing levels and building standards. But beginning in 1986, IFLA took a different approach recognizing that worldwide resources and needs differed so significantly that there could be no common standards for service. Still

Fig. 8 New Amsterdam Public Library, Amsterdam, the Netherlands.
Source: From Ian Macredie, permission received.

Fig. 9 Vancouver Public Library, British Columbia, Canada.
Source: From Vancouver Public Library, permission received.

Fig. 10 Salt Lake City new central library (library pond), Salt Lake City, Utah, United States.
Source: From Dana Sohm, permission received.

Fig. 11 Shanghai Library, Shanghai, China.
Source: From Shanghai Library, permission received.

libraries, especially those in developing countries repeatedly asked for some type of levels or standards to assist them in their planning and development and in particular supporting the concepts of that public library services are provided without charge and without censorship. Therefore in developing the latest Guidelines for Development the planners decided to produce a set of guidelines with some standards that could be relevant at various points in a library's development, and to leave the development of specialist areas to the special sections of IFLA.[4]

Measuring the performance of libraries is increasingly a combination of quantitative and qualitative approaches. Measurement normally begins with identifying performance indicators to measure the resource input, as well as outputs or what is achieved as a result of the activity or service being carried out. For example, a lending service requires books and other resources, staff, space, delivery services, computers, and other equipment that can all be assigned a numeric and financial value. The output of this service could be described as the total number of books circulated, the cost per capita expended on resources, the number of first time check-outs and the number of renewals, the number of card-holders or users per capita, etc. Inputs and outputs are usually compared within an institution to determine changes over time and how effective the service is. They can also be benchmarked with results from other libraries of similar size and characteristics. These statistics are often required as a condition of funding from a parent body. They are often used to illustrate the role of the library in the community or to make a case for increased funding and support. State and national agencies and organizations usually provide statistical gathering support to individual libraries.

Increasingly libraries are being called on to provide detailed reports and statistics that present more and more qualitative assessment of library performance and to measure the outcomes or impact that a library has in addition to inputs and outputs. Some of the major qualitative indicators used by public libraries include results of user satisfaction surveys. For instance, many Canadian public libraries hire independent firms and/or use computerized survey instruments to obtain occasional or ongoing customer satisfaction ratings. On a municipal level, the city government often includes libraries in surveys of citizen satisfaction with a variety of municipal services. On a national level in Canada the "Citizens First" survey conducted every 4 years, measures a wide range of federal, provincial, and municipal services in both the private and public sectors.[38] The goal is to track improvement overtime. Repeatedly, public libraries have topped the list in service satisfaction usually exceeded only by the fire departments. Other quantitative measures have included prizes, honors, and awards won by the library and its staff and board; results of the library in citywide assessments of city departments making effective use of technology; the role of the library in scoring a city as a learning or smart

city. So important is the concept of consumer-centric service that one library administrator has even gone so far as to propose counting customer smiles per hour (on an occasional basis) as a proxy measure for customer satisfaction.

A new planning, measurement and political tool called A Library's Contribution to Your Community published by the Southern Ontario Library Services in Canada helps library boards and administrators measure their library's social and economic contributions to their community and society. It guides users through the development of a contribution strategy including selecting relevant library outcomes from among six contributions and 20 benefits through collecting and interpreting data and constructing the argument. The benefits include elements such as life-long learning, support for individuals in the education system, reading and numeracy skills, English as a second language, cultural awareness, information services to local business, tourism, career development, and search for employment. The contributions identified include: education and learning, literacy, culture and recreation, business and the economy, personal support and community development.[39] Rubin's publication Demonstrating Results: Using Outcome Measurement in Your Library (2006) is the sixth in a series of "results" publications that provide an integrated approach to planning, resource allocation outcome measurement and excellence that is defined locally rather than through a series of universal or national or state standards.[40]

The Value of Public Libraries

Identifying the economic role that public libraries play in communities is becoming more and more crucial to the funding, support and existence of libraries. Library authorities are now using tools from economics and political science to demonstrate, both qualitatively and quantitatively, the value of the public library to the community it serves.[41] While many of the studies are American, contributions also come from Canada, Hungary, and Great Britain. One of the most well-known economic impact studies is The Seattle Public Library Central Library: Economic Benefits Assessment 2007. The study included surveys and interviews with users, visitors, business owners, tourism operators and confirmed that the new central library which opened in 2004, was functioning as a highly effective gateway to public space and tourist destination and that it was a significant contributor to Seattle's economy, a catalyst for downtown revitalization and development and a new icon for the city. In particular, the study found that the new central library was associated with $16 million in net new spending outside of the library in its first year of operations.[42]

Increasingly citizens and political leaders are seeing that not only can new central libraries, like those in Vancouver, Denver, Vienna, Turin, Amsterdam, and Shanghai, demonstrate civic commitment to information, ideas, knowledge, and growth, but they can also be drivers of economic vitality, contribute to community character and liveability, and enhance the image and identity of the whole city area.

The seminal study by Griffith, King, and Harrington, *Taxpayer Return on Investment in Florida Public Libraries*, used a variety of approaches to assess taxpayer return on investment (ROI) in the state of Florida. The study showed substantial returns exceeding taxpayer investment and that over all public libraries return U.S. $6.75 for every U.S. $1.00 invested from all sources (federal, state, local, and other) and that the total impact of Florida's public libraries on the state economy was $6 billion/year. This impact included non-library job creation, increased gross regional product and income or wage increases.[43] Similarly, one of the earliest ROI studies of the St. Louis Public Library concluded that the users received $4.38 in benefits for every tax dollar spent.[44] A variety of other studies indicate that an overall ROI figure of between 3 and 6 is likely to result although there can be significant variation depending on the key factors relating to community needs, the actual services provided by the library and the evaluation methods used.

TRENDS AND CHALLENGES IN PUBLIC LIBRARY SERVICE

In 2008, in spite of dire predictions by some about the demise of the public library and the stiff competition offered by digitization in particular Google and the Internet, students and others are continuing to use public libraries in greater and greater numbers both physically and virtually. And with the near collapse of the global economic framework in the fall of 2008, it is likely, based on past experience in economic downturns, that public libraries will be busier than ever for the next few years.

Virtual Use

More and more frequently, patrons are accessing pubic-library services from remote locations. In a recent survey, more than half of American adults said they had visited a local public library in the past 12 months. And a survey conducted in 2006 by KRC Research and Consulting reported that 12% of the 1000 people interviewed "visited" their local library by phone and 12% visited by computer. Among those who visited by phone or computer 41% did so to renew a borrowed item, 48% to consult a librarian for help, 45% to check the library's online catalog and 42% to use other resources on the library's Web page.[45]

Gaming in Public Libraries

A new phenomenon in many public libraries is the introduction of computer or video gaming. This type of youth programming featuring such games as Guitar Hero and

Dance, Dance Revolution, was first initiated to attract teen-aged clients born in the age of the Internet and quite comfortable with conducting much of their lives in the virtual world. While this type of activity in libraries is not without its detractors, computer or video gaming is now used increasingly in intergenerational programming in libraries and other institutions such as seniors centers and long-term care facilities. In June 2008, the Verizon Foundation, the philanthropic arm of Verizon Communications, announced a $1 million grant to the American Library Association to study how gaming can be used to improve problem-solving and literacy skills.[46] Nicholson's study of the role of gaming states that 77% of libraries contacted have formal gaming programs ranging from video games to board games and other more traditional games like puzzles. Gaming he suggests, is a form of story telling and an activity that captures the imagination and creates a comfortable and inviting environment to encourage participants of all ages to enjoy spending time in the library.[47]

Technology and Access in the Public Library

Nothing has impacted on the role of the public library in the community more significantly in the last 20 years than the introduction of free public Internet access. This new service has changed staff roles and training, allocation of funding, design of facilities, and debates about intellectual freedom and censorship. Since 2006 the American Library Association has issued two major studies on public library funding and technology. Findings can apply to public libraries across the globe. The key highlights conclude that libraries play a strategic role in providing free access to networked information and related telecommunications services and that demand is increasing particularly for access to e-government, lifelong learning, and employment seeking. But the studies also document that funding for public technology access is volatile especially for small libraries; staffing levels to support access is not keeping pace with patron demand; the need for increased bandwidth is becoming critical given the types of information patrons are seeking; library online services (e.g., homework resources, e-books, audio and video, gaming) are growing dramatically but have corresponding impact on the library's public services and technology infrastructure. And finally, the reports' findings include that many library buildings, already inadequate in terms of space and infrastructure cannot support additional public access computers and technology infrastructure.[48]

This situation is in the context of the major report findings including: funding remains flat for many public libraries; staffing is at a standstill (inadequate staffing topped the list of library concerns); staff training needs outpace supply; ICT (information and communications technology) support is lagging whether supplied internally by the library or externally by another level of government; and connection speed is increasingly insufficient.

Internet services show double digit growth in the availability of a range of resources in five key online areas: audio content, video content, homework help, e-book availability, and digitized special collections. Buildings and infrastructure are being further stretched given that the majority of library buildings are 25–50 years old and 40% of library buildings are estimated to be in only fair to poor condition. While online services are growing everywhere and libraries are facing a growing strain to keep up with user demand for public access computing.

In keeping with the need to actively involve the user in public library service, more and more libraries are looking at and experimenting with using social software such as blogs, RRS feeds (really simple syndication), wikis, photo-sharing applications, chat reference, and electronic discussion forums. This is an example of Library 2.0, a term that is used to characterize the strategies that libraries should use to position themselves as relevant in a digital future.[49]

Bibliocommons is a new social discovery tool being developed for libraries by a Toronto (Canada) based company with support from two Canadian provinces and with strong potential to replace all user-facing functionality of the library online catalog and allowing for faceted searching, easier user commenting and tagging. It is being created to respond to the new inter-active world and to provide a platform for richer connections between users, content, and community. This is one development trend to watch closely.[50]

Public Library Funding

From a sample of 29 countries, the OCLC 2003 Environmental Scan estimated that library spending worldwide is approximately $31 billion/annum. This figure is approximate and likely understated as many countries such as China and Brazil do not regularly collect or report library expenditures.[16] While usage rates both physical and electronic continue to rise in public libraries, in general, financial support lags.[43] In most countries the majority of funding for public library services comes from the local level of government. Depending on the legal framework for library services, senior levels of government provide sustaining funding often to support resource development and sharing, and well as special grant funding often to stimulate and strengthen specific service responses e.g., literacy, service to business, public Internet access.

Without suitable and consistent levels of funding over the long-term, it is not possible to develop policies for service provision and make the most effective use of available resources.[4] Inadequate funding can result in a new library building without adequate funds to maintain it; collections with insufficient funds for new materials; computer systems and equipment not being replaced or upgraded. Most public libraries rely primarily on taxation at the local level. Additional sources of income include donations from private funding bodies or individuals; commercial activities e.g., book-sales; user fees; special related services e.g., photocopying and computer printing; sponsorships from and partnerships with other organizations e.g., Citizenship and Health departments; and lottery funds. Increasingly libraries are establishing their own separate charitable foundations to professionalize their fund-raising efforts and establishing formal friends of the library groups to both raise money and advocate for better funding from the parent body. Finally, to stretch the available funds most public libraries belong to one or more consortia or resource sharing schemes.

One of librarianship's oldest beliefs is that access to information should be free as a basic right of citizenship. The *IFLA/UNESCO Guidelines* state: "the public library shall in principle be free of charge."[4] Library membership in most countries is free with some special and supplementary services having associated fees. However in some countries small membership fees are permitted, e.g., Singapore; the province of Alberta, Canada. Many libraries, while not charging for membership, have found creative ways of increasing revenue with a variety of charges to users for such services as faster access to best sellers, printing and photocopying, replacement of lost membership fees, some types of business information services. A number of researchers such as Butterworth have demonstrated that many of these types of fees, but not all, can have a negative impact on borrowing and overall usage of the library, especially if they are combined with a real or perceived decline in service.[51] However, there is also evidence to indicate that it may not be the amount of money that libraries can raise with fees for service but the fact that they are trying to contribute to the operation of the library and easing the load on the primary tax base that is important.

Usually and especially in times of fiscal recession and constraint which is the situation in many parts of the world at the time of this writing, libraries are viewed as soft services and as targets for budget reductions particularly as replace funders and legislators may believe that the public library could be replaced by Google.

The 2008 OCLC report (*From Awareness to Funding*) studied funding to public libraries in the United States. It documented that while local taxpayers in the United States provided over U.S. $9 billion in 2004 to support the operations of their public libraries, in general library annual operating funds are not keeping pace with services and operations to meet their mission and that in 2005 over one-third of U.S. public libraries were operating with budgets that are declining and that many more were operating with budgets that are slightly ahead of inflation but significantly behind the current inflation rates for employee benefits, energy and materials. The result is that many libraries are being forced to reduce staff, cut hours, and reduce community services. The study demonstrated that it was possible to apply the latest marketing and advocacy techniques so successfully used in other venues to create funding awareness, drive action and ultimately increase funding for public libraries; that it was possible to position libraries along other critical hard services like fire and police; and that a national campaign could make a difference in funding. The study's findings strongly suggest that there is sufficient, but latent support for increased funding among the voting public in America. The study further suggested that the funding situation will not self-correct unless there is a major campaign to communicate the value of the public library to the public to funding sources to ensure they are considered for funding. This includes building market segmentation; identifying the drivers of library funding; understanding attitudes toward libraries and library funding among the most likely supporters and creating messaging to motivate the most likely supporters to action. The idea is that this would result in the creation of a brand which would make the library relevant for the twenty-first century; instill a sense of urgency and activate a community conversation about how the library is a vital part of the community's infrastructure and future. One of the most important findings was that positive perceptions of the librarian are highly related to support and that passionate librarians who are involved in the community make a major difference to a voter's willingness to fund the public library.[33]

In 2007, the American Library Association and the Bill and Melinda Gates Foundation joined forces to study public library funding and with particular emphasis on access to technology. The study revealed that public library infrastructure (staffing, space, and bandwidth) are stretched to capacity. Almost 73% of libraries reported that are the only source of free access to computers and the Internet in their communities; the funding sources to support this access is volatile; staffing levels are not keeping pace with patron demand and, while many libraries reported increased connection speeds to support use, the vast majority reported their wireless and desktop computers share the same network thus diminishing the effective speed of access to the Internet at the workstation. The study also reported that public access Internet services (including homework resources, e-books, audio and video) grew dramatically in the year since the previous study on the same topic and that many library buildings, inadequate in terms of space and infrastructure cannot support addition public access computers and technology infrastructure. Looking at funding over a 9-year period from 1996 to 2005 revealed that the average increase in operating funds was 4% but that there are decreases in both library expenditures and a shift of expenditures away from print collections and staff to other expenditures such as technology, utilities, and building maintenance. A trend to supporting staff salaries from soft funding such as fees, finds and special grants grew. For smaller libraries the shift of local revenue away from funding telecommunications, together with a growing reliance on soft funding

sources and state and federal support for these expenditures was also documented in the survey.[46]

CONCLUSION

The second decade of the twenty-first century will be very challenging for public libraries. The pressures will continue to come from the relentless march of technology, the competition and the opportunity of the Internet, the googlization of the world and the impact of social networking, the effects of the global recession on government and library budgets, the competition for well-trained, talented and representative staff, the demand of staff to have a balanced lifestyle, new copyright legislation, growing low literacy rates, the need to replace and redevelop aging infrastructure, the drive for libraries to become increasingly entrepreneurial while at the same time maintain a presence as an open, supportive public knowledge institution. Earlier encyclopedia articles on public libraries have all articulated the same concerns. However, public libraries have continually faced challenges of similar magnitudes and they have always come through with vitality, resiliency, and innovation. With history behind them and the support of their associations and advocates beside them they will continue do so. We are people of the book.

BIOGRAPHICAL NOTE

Barbara Clubb is the City Librarian and CEO of the Ottawa Public Library in the city of Ottawa, Ontario, Canada. Ottawa is the capital of Canada and has a population of more than 900,000.

Ms Clubb is a past president of the Canadian Library Association, past Chair of the IFLA Public Libraries Section and a current member of the IFLA Metropolitan Libraries Section Standing Committee. She is the 2009 winner of the ALA/PLA Allie Beth Martin Award for demonstrating a range and depth of knowledge about books and other materials and a distinguished ability to share that knowledge. She is also the recipient of the 2009 Outstanding Service to Librarianship awarded by the Canadian Library Association.

REFERENCES

1. International Federation of Library Associations and Institutions. *IFLA/UNESCO Public Library Manifesto, 1994,* IFLA Public Libraries Section: The Hague, the Netherlands, 1994. http://www.ifla.org/VII/s8/unesco/eng.htm (accessed October 2008).

2. American Library Association. *ALA Fact Sheet 1: Number of Libraries in the United States*, April 2009. http://www.ala.org/ala/aboutala/hqops/library/libraryfactsheet/alafactsheet1.cfm (accessed October 2008).

3. International Federation of Library Associations and Institutions. *FAIFE World Report 2007*. http://www.ifla.org/faife/report/world_report.htm (accessed November 2007).

4. International Federation of Library Associations and Institutions. *The Public Library Service: IFLA/UNESCO Guidelines for Development*. IFLA Publication #97. G.K. Saur: München, Germany, 2001. http://www.ifla.org/VII/s8/proj/publ97.pdf (accessed October 2008).

5. Putnam, R.D.; Feldstein, L.M. *Better Together: Restoring the American Community*. Simon and Schuster: New York, 2003; 34–54.

6. Singapore National Library Board. http://www.nlb.gov.sg/ (accessed October 2008).

7. State Library of Queensland, Australia. http://netlinks.slq.qld.gov.au (accessed October 2008).

8. Markham Public Library (Canada). http://www.markhampubliclibrary.ca/about/mission.asp and http://www.markhampubliclibrary.ca/docs/policies/board_policies.pdf (accessed October 2008).

9. Nelson, S. *Strategic Planning for Results: Sandra Nelson for the Public Library Association*; American Library Association: Chicago, IL, 2008.

10. OCLC, *Perceptions of Libraries and Information Resources*, A Report to the OCLC Membership: Dublin, OH, 2005. http://www.oclc.org/reports/2005perceptions.htm (accessed October 2008).

11. Public Agenda. *Long Overdue: A Fresh Look at Public and Leadership Attitudes About Libraries in the 21 Century*, Report Prepared with Support from Americans for Libraries Council and the Bill and Melinda Gates Foundation, New York, 2006, 5–13. http://www.publicagenda.org (accessed October 2008).

12. International Federation of Library Associations and Institutions. *Libraries for Children and Young Adult Section Newsletter*, June 2008, No. 68. http://www.ifla.org/VII/s10/pubs/s10-newsletter-June08.pdf (accessed October 2008).

13. *Library of 100 Talents*, Heerhugowaard, the Netherlands. http://www.debibliotheken.nl/content.jsp?objectid=20142 (accessed November 2008).

14. American Library Association. *Every Child Ready to Read*, Research Studies. http://www.ala.org/ala/mgrps/divs/alsc/ecrr/researcha/researchstudies/researchstudies.cfm (accessed October 2008).

15. Strickland, D.; Riley-Ayers, S. *Early Literacy: Policy and Practice in Preschool Years*. Reading Rockets, a project funded by a grant from the U.S. Department of Education, 2008, http://readingrockets.org/article/11375?theme = print (accessed October 2008).

16. OCLC. *2003 Environmental Scan*, A Report to the OCLC Membership: Dublin, OH, 2003, http://www.oclc.org/reports/escan/library/newroles.htm (accessed October 2008).

17. United States Citizen and Immigration Services (USCIS), *Library Services for Immigrants: A Report on Current Practices*, (Office of Citizenship), with the Institute of Museum and Library Services (USA), March 2006, http://www.uscis.gov/files/nativedocuments/G-1112.pdf (accessed October 2008).

18. Statistics Canada. *2006 Census: Immigration in Canada: A Portrait of Foreign-born Population, 2006 Census*. http://www12.statcan.english/census06/analyis/immcit/highlights.cfm (accessed October 2008).

19. Sisson, R.; Christian, K.Z.; Andrew, R.L.C. *The American Midwest: An Interpretive Encyclopedia*; Indiana University Press: Bloomington, IN, 2007; 567.

20. Schneehorst, S. *Library Services to Russian Speaking Immigrants in Germany*. Paper on Public Libraries and Multicultural Collections, Utrecht, the Netherlands, 2003, 1–5. http://www.sitegenerator.bibliotheek.nl/iflautrecht/img/docs/Schneehorst.pdf (accessed October 2008).

21. Ottawa Public Library, Ottawa, ON, Canada. http://www.biblioottawalibrary.ca (accessed November 2008).

22. International Federation of Library Associations and Institutions. *Library Services to Multicultural Populations-Newsletter*, June 2008. http://www.ifla.org/VII/s32/index.htm (accessed October 2008).

23. FINFO, http://www.finfo.dk (accessed October 2008).

24. Thorhauge, J. *Danish Strategies in Public Library Service to Ethnic Minorities*. Paper given at the IFLA World Library and Information Congress, Session #124, Berlin, Germany, August 1–9, 2003.

25. Burke, S.K. Public library resources used by immigrant households. Public Libr. July/August, **2008**, *47* (4), 32–34.

26. International Federation of Library Associations and Institutions. *IFLA/UNESCO Multicultural Library Manifesto*. IFLA Library Services to Multicultural Services Populations Section: The Hague, the Netherlands, 2008. http://www.ifla.org/VII/s32/index.htm (accessed November 2008).

27. International Federation of Library Associations and Institutions. *Guidelines for Libraries Serving Multicultural Populations*. Library Services to Multicultural Services Populations Section: The Hague, the Netherlands, 1998. http://www.ifla.org/VII/s32/pub/guide-e.htm (accessed November 2008).

28. Futterman, M. Finding the underserved. Libr. J. October 15 **2008**, 42–45.

29. *Working Together: Community-led Libraries Toolkit*. A project of the Halifax, Regina, Toronto, and Vancouver public libraries (Canada): funded by Human Resources and Social Development Canada, Ottawa, ON, Canada, 2008. http://www.librariesincommunities.ca/ (accessed November 2008).

30. Master Plan for Library Collections: One system, One collection 2006–2016 including update; Calgary Public Library: Calgary, AL, Canada, 2008.

31. Maughan, S. Way cool: Marketing and the Internet. *Publishers Weekly*, February 19, 2007. http://www.publishersweekly.com/article/CA417182.html (accessed November 2008).

32. Mattern, S. *The New Downtown Library: Designing with Communities*; University of Minnesota Press: Minneapolis, MN, 2007; 1, ix.

33. Vaughan Public Libraries, Vaughan, ON, Canada. http://www.vaughanpl.info/ (accessed October 2008).

34. Cleveland Public Library, Cleveland, OH, USA. http://www.cpl.org (accessed October 2008).

35. OCLC. From awareness to funding: A study of library support in America, Dublin, OH, 2008. http://www.oclc.org/us/en/reports/funding/ (accessed October 2008).

36. Willes, M. *Reading Matters: Five Centuries of Discovering Books*; Yale University Press: New Haven, CN and London, U.K., 2008; 245.

37. Buschman, J.E.; Leckie, G.J., Eds. *The Library as Place: History, Community and Culture*; Libraries Unlimited: Westport, CN, 2007.

38. Phase 5 Consulting. *Citizens First-4*; Institute for Citizen-Centred Service and the Institute of Public Administration of Canada: Toronto, ON, Canada, 2005.

39. dmA Planning and Management Services. *The Library's Contribution to Your Community: A Resource Manual*, 2nd Ed.; Southern Ontario Library Service: Toronto, ON, Canada, 2007.

40. Rubin, R.J. *Demonstrating Results: Using Outcome Measurement in Your Library*; American Library Association/Public Library Association: Chicago, IL, 2006.

41. Georgia Public Library Service. The Economic Value of Public Libraries: A Bibliography, July 2007. http://georgialibraries.org/lib/collection/econ_value.bib.php (accessed November 2008).

42. *The Seattle Public Library Central Library: Economic Benefits Assessment.* Prepared for the Seattle Public Library Foundation and the City of Seattle Office of Economic Development by Berk and Associates, Inc., 2005. http://www.spl.org/pdfs/SPLCentral_Library_Economic_Impacts.pdf (accessed October 2008).

43. Griffiths, J.-M. *Taxpayer Return on Investment in Florida Public Libraries: Summary Report.* State Library and Archives of Florida: Tallahassee, FL, 2004. http://dlis.dos.state.fl.us/bld/roi/pdfs/ROISummaryReport.pdf (accessed October 2008).

44. Holt, G.; Elliot, D. Proving your library's worth. Libr. J. *123* (18), 42–44.

45. American Library Association. *The State of America's Libraries*, A Report from the American Library Association; ALA: Chicago, IL, April 2008. http://www.ala.org/2008state (accessed November 2008).

46. American Library Association. *American Library Association Receives $1Million Grant from Verizon Foundation.* Media Release, June 28, 2008. http://www.ala.org/ala/pressreleases2008/june2008/ALA (accessed October 2008).

47. Nicholson, S. *The Role of Gaming in Libraries: Taking the Pulse*, 2007. http://boardgameswithscott.com/pulse2007.pdf (accessed October 2008).

48. American Library Association. *Libraries Connect Communities: Public Library Funding and Technology Access Study 2007–2008*; ALA: Chicago, IL, 2008. http://www.ala.org/ala/aboutala/offices/ors/plftas/0708report.cfm (accessed October 2008).

49. Rutherford, L.L. Building participative library services: the impact of social software use in public libraries. Libr. High Tech **2008**, *26* (3), 411–423.

50. Oder, N. BiblioCommons emerges. Libr. J. July 19, **2008**. http://www.libraryjournal.com/article/CA6579748.html?industryid = 4713 (accessed October 2008).

51. Butterworth, M. *The Entrepreneurial Public Library: The Policy and Practice of Fee-based Services.* ALIA (Australian Library and Information Association) Conference 2000. http://conferences.alia.org.au/alia2000/proceedings/margaret.butterworth.html (accessed October 2008).

BIBLIOGRAPHY

1. Ashton, R.J.; Millan, D. *Welcome Stranger: Public Libraries Build the Global Village*; Urban Libraries Council: Chicago, IL, 2008.

2. Christensen, K.; Levinson, D. *Heart of the Community: The Libraries We Love*; Berkshire Publishing Group: Great Barrington, MA, 2007.

3. D'Angelo, Ed. *Barbarians at the Gates of the Public Library*; Library Juice Press: Duluth, MN, 2006.

4. Durrance, J.C.; Fisher, K.E. Determining how libraries and librarians help. Libr. Trends. Spring **2003**, *31* (4), 305–334.

5. Elliot, D.S.; Holt, G.E.; Hayden, S.W.; Holt, L.E. *Measuring Your Library's Value: How to do a Cost-Benefit Analysis for your Public Library*; American Library Association: Chicago, IL, 2007.

6. Estabrook, L.; Evans, W.; Rainee, L. *Information Searches that Solve Problems: How People Use the Internet, Libraries and Government Agencies When They Need Help*; PEW Internet and American Life Project: Urbana, IL, 2007.

7. *The Future of Human Resources in Canadian Libraries.* Canadian Library Human Resource Study by the 8Rs Research Team/University of Alberta: Edmonton, Alberta, Canada, 2005.

8. Hoffert, B. Immigrant nation: How public libraries select materials for a growing population whose first language is not English. Libr. J. September 1, **2008**, *133* (14), 34–36.

9. Horrocks, N., Ed. *Perspectives, Insights and Priorities: 17 Leaders Speak Freely on Librarianship*; Scarecrow Press: Toronto, Canada, 2005.

10. American Library Association. *Libraries Prosper with Passion, Purpose and Persuasion: A PLA Toolkit for Success*; American Library Association, Public Library Association Division: Chicago, IL, 2007.

11. *Making Cities Stronger: Public Library Contributions to Local Economic Development.* Commissioned by the Urban Libraries Council, funded by the Bill and Melinda Gates and Geraldine R. Dodge Foundations: Chicago, IL, 2007.

12. McCabe, G.B.; Kennedy, J.R. *Planning the Modern Public Library*; Libraries Unlimited: Westport, CN, 2003.

13. McCook, K.P. *Introduction to Public Librarianship*; Neal-Schuman Publishers: New York, 2004.

14. The New Library Fad: Borrow a person. *TimesOnline*, April 22, 2009. http://women.timesonline.co.uk/tol/life_and_style/women/the_way_we_live/aarticle37903.

15. Newman, W. *Third Generation Public Libraries: Visionary Thinking and Service Development in Public Libraries (to 2020) and Potential Application in Ontario, Canada.* A Report for the Ontario Ministry of Culture: Toronto, Ontario, Canada, 2008. http://www.culture.gov.on.ca/english/library/newman_study.htm (accessed February 2009).

16. Nicholson, S. Reframing gaming. Am. Libr. August **2008**, *39* (7), 50–51.

17. OCLC. *Information Format Trends—Content not Containers*, A Report to the Membership, Dublin, OH, 2004.

18. Young, R.A. *The Library Reconsidered: Not Just a Place for Books Anymore*. Paper presented at the Annual Meeting of the Environmental Design Research Association, EDRA 36, Vancouver, BC, Canada, April 27–May 1, 2005. http://faculty.arch.utah.edu/young/RSCW.html.

Public Library Association (PLA)

Louisa Worthington
Public Library Association, Chicago, Illinois, U.S.A.

Kathleen Hughes
American Library Association, Chicago, Illinois, U.S.A.

Abstract

From its beginning in 1944 with only 1295 members, the Public Library Association (PLA), a division of the American Library Association (ALA), has grown to nearly 12,000 members today with the stated purpose "to strengthen public libraries and their contribution to the communities they serve." This mission positions PLA to: focus its efforts on serving the needs of its members; advocate for public libraries; and commit to quality public library services that benefit the general public. Based in Chicago and housed within ALA headquarters, PLA is a member-driven organization that exists to provide a diverse program of communication, publication, advocacy, continuing education, and programming for its members and others interested in the advancement of public library service.

INTRODUCTION

From its beginning in 1944 with only 1295 members, the Public Library Association (PLA), a division of the American Library Association (ALA), has grown to nearly 12,000 members today with the stated purpose "to strengthen public libraries and their contribution to the communities they serve." This mission positions PLA to: focus its efforts on serving the needs of its members; advocate for public libraries; and commit to quality public library services that benefit the general public. Based in Chicago and housed within ALA headquarters, PLA is a member-driven organization that exists to provide a diverse program of communication, publication, advocacy, continuing education, and programming for its members and others interested in the advancement of public library service.

OVERVIEW

The formation of the Division of Public Libraries of the ALA was approved by votes of the ALA Council in March and October 1944, following organizational meetings, filings of petitions by nearly 1200 members, and the adoption of a temporary constitution. It was decided that the purpose of the division would be to "advance public library interests and to cooperate in the promotion of library service in general." The dues were established as 20% of the dues paid to ALA, not to exceed $2.00. At that time the bylaws provided that "Any member of the American Library Association interested in public libraries may become a member of the Division of Public Libraries by

indicating the division and section when paying ALA dues." (from ALA Handbook December 1, 1944).

The first PLA president was Amy Winslow, Cuyahoga County (Ohio) Library. The first executive director was Julia Wright Merrill, an ALA staff member (from the ALA Handbook, December 1, 1945, and from Festschrift prepared by PLA staff for PLA's Fiftieth Anniversary).

At the time of its formation, PLA was composed of these eight special-interest sections:

Adult Education
Branch Librarians
Business and Technology
Lending
Librarians of Large Public Libraries
Order and Book Selection
Service Librarians
Small Libraries

Eventually, these sections evolved into the following six sections, which were in place until 1998:

Adult Lifelong Learning Section
Community Information Section
Marketing of Public Library Services Section
Metropolitan Libraries Section
Public Library Systems Section
Small and Medium-Sized Libraries Section

In the 1970s, public libraries were primarily planning and serving the traditional library users—educated, middle income, more women and children than men. PLA established three age-group task forces to examine goals, missions, and standards for public library services. The

Encyclopedia of Library and Information Sciences, Fourth Edition DOI: 10.1081/E-ELIS4-120044414

focus of these task forces was on what the public needed (not what was currently offered), and on moving from quantitative to qualitative measures for effective public library services. This led to the development of the first Planning Process for Public Libraries, published by ALA in 1980. There was still a difference in needs of public libraries serving small versus large communities, but marketing of public library services and outreach services had moved into new places of interest for all PLA members.

In the mid-1980s, articles reported that only 5% of America's public libraries were using computers for circulation. Debate was underway on whether mainframes or minicomputers would be the most effective method for automating libraries, and many libraries were experiencing difficulty convincing local officials that computers were needed. By the early 1990s, the impact of computers and the Internet had begun to forge changes in public library services. The PLA officers and members debated the pros and cons of the role of public libraries on the then-new "information superhighway." Few realized that, in less than 10 years, the Internet would become an essential and "natural" aspect of everyday life as well as public library services.

By 1996, the membership of the PLA, by a vote of 1477 (yes) to 539 (no), approved proposed bylaw changes in a special election. The bylaw changes, which replaced PLA's sections with special interest "clusters," took effect with the close of the 1998 ALA Annual Conference. The new clusters organized the work of the association into three key areas:

Library services cluster: Committees within this group focus on how public libraries and librarians can improve their services for library users, including service to children, the business community, literacy services, rural community, and homeschoolers.

Library development: Committees within this group focus on the working activities in which public librarians participate in their careers, such as those involving bibliography, continuing education, library collections, technology, and similar activities.

Issues and concerns: Committees within this group focus on activities that serve the library profession as a whole, such as those reviewing legislation, intellectual freedom, and research.

PLA's Priority Concerns identified in 1991 were given as:

- Adequate funding for public libraries.
- Improved management of public libraries.
- Recognition of the importance of all library staff in providing quality public service.
- Recruitment, education, training, and compensation of public librarians.
- Effective use of technology.
- Intellectual freedom.

- Improved access to library resources.
- Effective communication with the nonlibrary world.

In 2005, PLA approved a new strategic plan that outlined four organizational goals to help further strengthen public libraries and their contribution to the communities they serve:

Advocacy and recognition: Public libraries will be recognized as the destination for a wide variety of valuable services and their funding will be a community priority.

Literate nation: PLA will be a valued partner of public library initiatives to create a nation of readers.

Staffing and recruitment: Public libraries will be recognized as exciting places to work and will be staffed by skilled professionals who are recognized as the information experts, are competitively paid, and reflect the demographics of their communities.

Training and knowledge: PLA will be nationally recognized as the leading source for continuing education opportunities for public library staff and trustees.

In 2008, PLA's membership again voted 2731 to 163 to change the organization's bylaws, effectively reshaping the structure of the organization.

PLA members were given the opportunity to discuss and debate the proposed changes at the ALA 2008 Midwinter Meeting in Philadelphia, and again at member forums held during the 2008 PLA National Conference in Minneapolis, Minnesota. Major components of the bylaws changes include a reduction in the size of the PLA board, the disbandment of the PLA executive committee, and the transition from PLA committees to Communities of Practice. Communities of Practice are virtual groups that are interest-focused and member-driven. Members can create groups, as well as morph and/or disband them at their discretion. This will allow members, many of whom are unable to travel to in-person committee meetings, to get involved with the organization and the public library issues they care about most.

ORGANIZATION

The original officers of the PLA were the chairpersons of the original eight sections, president, first vice-president, second vice-president, treasurer, and executive secretary.

Through June 2008, the officers of this association are the immediate past-president; the president; the vice-president, who serves as president-elect; and the executive director. The executive director is chosen by the executive director of the ALA with the approval of the Board of Directors of the PLA.

With the bylaws change vote of 2008, the PLA Board of Directors changes. With the exception of the officer positions (president elect, president, past-president); and the ALA division councilor; and ALTA representative, PLA Board members are now all members-at-large. Board service is no longer tied to representing a specific Cluster of member committee. The Executive Committee has been eliminated. Through attrition, the Board will eventually be reduced in size from 24 to 12.

The new bylaws also changes board service requirements. The full Board of Directors will now meet four times a year instead of twice a year. The new meeting schedule consists of a fall board meeting held in conjunction with the ALA Executive Board meeting; a meeting held at the ALA Midwinter Meeting; a spring board meeting; and a meeting held at the ALA Annual Conference.

ACTIVITIES: PUBLICATIONS, CONFERENCES, AND SERVICES

Public Libraries Magazine

Public Libraries, as the official journal of the Public Library Division, commenced publication in January 1947. The editor at that time was Muriel E. Perry, Decatur Public Library, Decatur, Illinois (From the inaugural issue, *Public Libraries*, Vol. 1, Number 1, January, 1947). *Public Libraries* has since become an increasingly important benefit for members of PLA. In the fall of 1988, an editor was hired and paid a stipend, a change from the prior practice of only reimbursing the editor's expenses. This change was made because the board decided to increase the frequency of the magazine from quarterly to bimonthly. Upon the recommendation of the *Public Libraries* Advisory Board and the PLA Board of Directors, in 1990 the editorial responsibilities were divided with a PLA staff member assuming responsibilities as managing editor working with an outside feature editor. In 2006, the position of Editor became a full time PLA staff member position.

Notable PLA Publications

The PLA has developed several important publications in the management of public libraries. These titles focus on planning and measuring effective service to the community, including technology issues and services to children and young adults (see Table 1).

Preconferences and Workshops

PLA holds workshops as preconferences at the ALA Annual Conference, the PLA National Conferences, and the Spring Symposium, a group of five to six concurrent workshops held every other year. In addition, regional or special purpose events are developed in response to member needs.

Table 1 Key publications from PLA in chronological order

Public Library Data Service Statistical Report (PLA, published annually 1988–present).

Output Measures for Public Library Service to Children—A Manual of Standardized Procedures (ALA, PLA, Association for Library Service to Children, 1992).

PLA Handbook for Writers of Public Library Policies (PLA, 1993).

Bare Bones Young Adult Services: Tips for Public Library Generalists (ALA, 2000).

Latchkey Children in the Public Library (PLA, Association for Library Service to Children, 1988).

Unattended Children in the Public Library: A Resource Guide (PLA, Association for Library Service to Children, 2000).

Planning for Results—A Public Library Transformation Process (ALA, 1998).

Wired for the Future—Developing Your Library Technology Plan (ALA, 1999).

Managing for Results—Effective Resource Allocation for Public Libraries (ALA, 2000).

The New Planning for Results: A Streamlined Approach (ALA, 2001).

Libraries Prosper with Passion, Purpose and Persuasion: A PLA Toolkit for Success (PLA, 2007).

Field Guide to Emergency Response: A Vital Tool for Cultural Institutions (Heritage Preservation, 2006).

Public Library Service Responses 2007 (PLA, 2007).

Nursery Rhymes, Songs and Fingerplays: Rhyming Words Will Lead to Teaching Children How to Read! (PLA, 2007).

Defending Access with Confidence: A Practical Workshop on Intellectual Freedom (ALA, 2005).

Managing Facilities for Results: Optimizing Space for Services (ALA, 2007).

Creating Policies for Results from Chaos to Clarity (ALA, 2003).

Staffing for Results: A Guide to Working Smarter (ALA, 2002).

Strategic Planning for Results (ALA, 2008).

Public Library Data Service

The Public Library Data Service is a program of the division that consists of the collection of a set of statistics from a group of approximately 800 public libraries which participate voluntarily. These statistics are published in an annual publication, *The Public Library Data Service Statistical Report*. Don Napoli, Director of the St. Joseph County (Indiana) Public Library, originally collected and reported the statistics as a volunteer. In 1991, data collection was contracted out to the School of Library and Information Services at the University of Wisconsin, Madison; and in 1996 it was contracted out to the Library Research Center at the University of Illinois, Urbana-Champaign. In 2007, an interactive Public Library Data Service Statistical Report subscription database was made available for purchase, in addition to the print publication.

PLA National Conferences

The first PLA National Conference was held in Baltimore, Maryland, in 1983, and attracted 1706 paid registrants. For public librarians, friends of libraries, international visitors, educators, and politicians active in supporting libraries, the Baltimore conference provided opportunities to share ideas on current issues and trends in public librarianship and to hear colleagues and other experts in the field present a variety of educational programs. The format established at this first conference has been used for all subsequent PLA National Conferences. Subsequent PLA National Conferences were held in 1983, 1986, 1988, 1991, 1994, 1996, 1998, and 2000, 2002, 2004, 2006, 2008. These are events of great importance to PLA members and to librarians, trustees, friends, and others concerned with the development of public library services. Since the beginning, these conferences have grown steadily in all areas—attendance, exhibits, number of programs, and revenue. National conferences are currently held every two years, with the next conference scheduled for Portland, Oregon, in 2010 and Philadelphia, Pennsylvania, in 2012.

Certified Public Library Administrator (CPLA) Program

A joint committee with representatives from PLA, LLAMA (Library Leadership and Management Association), and ASCLA (Association of Specialized and Cooperative Library Agencies) was established to respond to the expressed need for education beyond the masters program that would lead to a recognized designation of achievement in public library administration. Begun in 2006, the CPLA program provides post-MLS/post-MIS participants, who complete an established curriculum of courses and demonstrate significant library experience and proof of related activities, the CPLA designation. PLA staff members are responsible for administering course offerings, contracts with presenters and organizers, promotion, registration, and financial management. These courses launched in conjunction with the ALA Allied Professional Association (APA) in summer 2007. The CPLA program is managed by the ALA-APA.

RECENT MAJOR PLA GRANT PROJECTS

The PLA has participated in grant projects related to association priorities. In 2007, the Bill & Melinda Gates Foundation awarded PLA a $7.7 million grant to develop and provide a national advocacy training program for public librarians from 2007 to 2009. PLA's training program provides librarians with the skills and resources necessary to seek increased funding, create community partnerships, and build alliances with local and regional decision makers. The training will support libraries that are eligible to receive Bill & Melinda Gates Foundation Opportunity Online hardware grants, which require grantees to match foundation funds with local dollars. It will also be available to non-grantees on a limited basis. Grantees will be encouraged to send teams of up to three people to the locally customized training where they will learn about and create advocacy plans grounded in the reality of their local, political, and economic environment. Each participant will also receive the *PLA publication Libraries Prosper with Passion, Purpose and Persuasion: A PLA Toolkit for Success*, which will provide them with step-by-step instructions for implementing their advocacy plan.

In addition, PLA has participated in grant projects related to association priorities. In 1995–1998, PLA was a partner in the Microsoft/Libraries Online project. Through Libraries Online, the Microsoft Corporation, the ALA/PLA, and the Technology Resource Institute joined forces to ensure that everyone has the chance to succeed in the information age. Libraries Online contributed computers, with the latest software and connections to the Internet, for public use and libraries and provided training for public library staff and patrons. Microsoft committed more than $15 million in grants and software to this project, in order to help build computer access at over 200 public libraries across the country. Key findings from this project included:

1. Libraries Online provided computers, training, and access to information for people in communities in need.
2. Participating libraries found innovative ways to support and maintain new technologies, even when additional staffing was not provided.
3. Once people were exposed to computing power, they became strong advocates—saying they would always want to have access through their libraries.

CONCLUSION

As the PLA continues to support the development of effective public library services, the focus of the organization will reflect changing conditions in our communities and our culture. Current trends in electronic information affect the development and delivery of information services; current research in early childhood development affects the content and presentation of public library programs for preschool children; growing diversity in our communities affects the development of particular services to meet language and cultural needs; changing lifestyles affect the time and location of the delivery of library services. The officers, members, and staff of the PLA will work together for the advancement of public library service.

APPENDIX: PUBLIC LIBRARY ASSOCIATION PRESIDENTS

PLA Presidents—Present back to 1970

Sari Feldman	(2009–2010)
Carol Sheffer	(2008–2009)
Jan Sanders	(2007–2008)
Susan Hildreth	(2006–2007)
Daniel L. Walters	(2005–2006)
Clara Nalli Bohrer	(2004–2005)
Luis Herrera	(2003–2004)
Jo Ann Pinder	(2002–2003)
Toni Garvey	(2001–2002)
Kay K. Runge	(2000–2001)
Harriet Henderson	(1999–2000)
Christine L. Hage	(1998–1999)
Ginnie Cooper	(1997–1998)
Linda Meilke	(1996–1997)
LaDonna Kienitz	(1995–1996)
Judy Drescher	(1994–1995)
Pat A. Woodrum	(1993–1994)
Elliot Shelkrot	(1992–1993)
June Garcia	(1991–1992)
Charles M. Brown	(1990–1991)
Sarah Ann Long	(1989–1990)
Melissa Buckingham	(1988–1989)
Susan S. Kent	(1987–1988)
Kathleen M. Balcom	(1986–1987)
Patrick O'Brien	(1985–1986)
Charles W. Robinson	(1984–1985)
Nancy M. Bolt	(1983–1984)
Donald J. Sager	(1982–1983)
Agnes M. Griffen	(1981–1982)
Robert Rohlf	(1980–1981)
Ronald A. Dubberly	(1978–1980)
Genevieve M. Casey	(1976–1978)
Dorothy M. Sinclair	(1974–1976)
Lewis C. Naylor	(1973–1974)
David Henington	(1972–1973)
Effie Lee Morris	(1971–1972)
Andrew Geddes	(1970–1971)

Qualitative Research Methods in Library and Information Science [ELIS Classic]

Brett Sutton
Aurora University, Aurora, Illinois, U.S.A.

Abstract

Sutton's essay is a masterpiece of concise, clear, and measured exposition on this difficult area of methodological theory and practice. As Sutton notes at the beginning: "What we call qualitative research out of convenience is actually a diverse collection of philosophies, historical traditions, discipline-specific concepts, and useful practices. One goal of this article is to articulate this diversity. Another is to demonstrate that the dualistic character that the methodological debate has sometimes taken, pitting qualitative against quantitative approaches, is unproductive, not to say unrealistic."

—*ELIS Classic, from 1998*

INTRODUCTION

Social scientists have practiced what is loosely called qualitative research in many forms for the better part of a century. The results have been both numerous and diverse, although some disciplines have found it better suited to their needs than others. Library and information science (LIS), after establishing a strong preference for quantitative approaches to research grounded in the epistemology of the natural sciences, has begun to develop a body of literature that explores nonquantitative methods of knowledge creation. This article seeks to contribute to this development by summarizing the principal features of qualitative research, reviewing its status in information studies, and exploring its potential for generating new research in the field. These tasks, not easy on their own terms, are made more difficult by the lack of precision of the term qualitative research and the absence of a clearly defined body of theory or practice conforming to such a concept. What we call qualitative research out of convenience is actually a diverse collection of philosophies, historical traditions, discipline-specific concepts, and useful practices. One goal of this article is to articulate this diversity. Another is to demonstrate that the dualistic character that the methodological debate has sometimes taken, pitting qualitative against quantitative approaches, is unproductive, not to say unrealistic. This article does not begin with a definition of the term qualitative research because definitions tend to conceal the very ambiguities and complexities that it hopes to capture. It is possible, however, to sketch the outlines of qualitative research by taking note of some of its identifying characteristics. Based on the published record, one might fairly say that qualitative research tends to emphasize interpretation rather than explanation, in-depth case studies rather than controlled multiple-case analyses, analytic description

rather than formal hypothesis testing, narrative reporting of results rather than the presentation of statistical analysis, acceptance of the investigator's subjective involvement rather than the cultivation of a neutral or objective attitude, attention to the uniqueness of the context in which research data are collected, and tolerance for diversity in claims to knowledge. This is not a complete list, however, and none of these factors can be said to be essential to the qualitative approach. Moreover, many real-world studies in the social sciences are hybrid in character, the product of both quantitative and qualitative techniques, so that attempting to isolate purely qualitative studies is something of an artificial exercise.

This article takes the term research rather broadly and nonrestrictively. It is not the goal here to prescribe a programmatic approach to qualitative analysis, but rather to suggest the variety of ways in which such an approach can be integrated into information studies, taking note of the risks as well as the benefits, suggesting the range of tools that are available, and linking these ideas at key points to the LIS literature. Although a number of studies are cited here by way of example, this is not a comprehensive account of the literature of qualitative methods, nor is it intended to serve as a tutorial in even the rudimentary sense. There are two reasons for this. First, the literature on the subject is too vast to summarize in the limited space available. Second and more important, it is not the particular techniques of qualitative research that play the greatest role in characterizing this research tradition, but the principles and theories that support them.

A central premise of this article is that LIS is a social science to which the entire range of research methods used in the social sciences is applicable. Another is that no single approach, however powerful and productive, can successfully solve all the problems in a field as diverse as LIS. There are several dimensions to this problem.

Encyclopedia of Library and Information Sciences, Fourth Edition DOI: 10.1081/E-ELIS4-120044785

A significant proportion of the research issues is LIS falls into the category of what are sometimes called the "human" sciences, in which researchers are, in an important sense, interpreting themselves rather than explaining an objective natural world. As Neill notes, "the dilemma in the area of research methods in information science is that information creation and use is complex, imprecise, and subjective".[1] The concept of information is so deeply part of the social and cultural experience of being human that the study of information cannot be easily detached from the very phenomena it seeks to investigate. This means that the research problems of LIS cannot be entirely captured by tools optimized for the natural sciences. An additional factor is that as an applied science LIS lends itself to a pragmatic handling of research methods. It is frequently the case that investigations in the field are not pursued merely in the interests of basic research but are also employed as tools for accomplishing practical goals, such as improved services to a user community, a better understanding of the research practices of a scholarly field, the design of new information technologies, or the development of public policy regarding access to information. A final complication is that LIS has in recent years allied itself in productive ways with fields ranging from literary criticism to cognitive science, and has taken up the research tools associated with those fields. All of these conditions lead to the necessity of a pluralistic methodology for LIS.

Before undertaking a discussion of the principles of qualitative methods, it is necessary to make two additional terminological clarifications, one involving the term qualitative and the other involving the term method. In the case of the former, the problem is that a false opposition between the terms quantitative and qualitative—implying, among other things, association with descriptions of phenomena that are numerical on the one hand and verbal on the other—threatens to undermine the more interesting and important aspects of the methodological questions under consideration here. Even a cursory examination of successful research illustrates that there are no social phenomena that are intrinsically unquantifiable, nor are there assertions based on quantification that can be articulately conveyed and interpreted without a verbal component. In Kaplan's words. "The point is that both quality and quantity are misconceived when they are taken to be antithetical or even alternative. Quantities are *of* qualities, and a measured quality *has* just the magnitude expressed in its measure. In a less metaphysical idiom, we could say that whether something is identified as a quality or as a quantity depends on how we choose to represent it in our symbolism" (p. 207).[2] We seem to be stuck with the terms, but it is wise to allow them to stand not as terms for types of data but as loose descriptors for a collection of concepts and reasoning procedures, and that is how they will be used here.

The other problematic term is method. The trouble here is that by focusing exclusively on method (in the sense of the means or procedures for accomplishing a task), we beg the question of theory and risk, missing some of the more important issues that any discussion of research should raise. It is possible, in fact, to identify at least three different levels of analysis of the research process: philosophy and theory, methods and techniques, and data. Debate over the relative advantages of various approaches to research has taken place within each of these domains. Philosophical questions address the epistemological foundations of scientific research and articulate hidden assumptions about the consequences of various forms of observation and inference. Theory, a natural extension of philosophy, encompasses investigator's goals in pursuing a particular line of research and their expectations about what that research is likely to yield. Although it is not necessary, nor even advisable, for investigators to begin every research report with a summary of the philosophical justifications behind their theoretical positions, it is nevertheless useful, some would say essential, for them to be able to articulate those principles. Methods, strictly speaking, are the systematic procedures that researches use to collect and process data in order to put their theories to the test, which in turn leads to the development of new theories. Aspects of method in this sense include research design, the selection and use of research tools and techniques, and the application of certain inferential procedures. Data and the reports that convey them are presented as the formal, tangible results of research and are a direct product of the theories and methods favored by the researchers. In this article the focus is primarily on theory, with some excursions into the area of methods as they relate to these theoretical principles.

QUALITATIVE RESEARCH AND THE LITERATURE OF LIBRARY AND INFORMATION SCIENCE

The literature on qualitative research is vast, ranging from essays on philosophical foundations to practical tutorials. Some of these works are general in nature, while others address the needs of particular disciplines. The methodological writing on research methods in LIS is small by comparison, and concentrates on quantitative approaches, but it is nevertheless worth reviewing, since it reflects the intellectual environment of the field and sheds light on the evolution toward qualitative approaches to research.

An appropriate starting point for this review is Charles C. Williamson's report to the Carnegie Commission on the state of library education in the 1920s. A central theme in Williamson's evaluation was not the quality of research in the field or the methods employed, but the virtual absence of research. He criticized librarians for their tendency to gain professional knowledge through trial and error, an attitude he criticized as "empirical."" Williamson's review of library education noted its prejudice against science: "I fear most teaching in library schools promotes rather than diminishes the empirical tendency. Quantitative studies are its greatest enemy, but probably not one librarian in a hundred has ever had training in quantitative methods".[3] Williamson's preference for quantitative research sounded a theme that was repeated by numerous later writers. For example, Pierce Butler, in a 1933 essay entitled "The Nature of Science," stated that "librarianship, in particular, will become scientific only as it conforms in essential to the habitual methods of thought in the modern temper," which for Butler included the scrutinization of "objective phenomena" with the "rigor of scientific observation," wherein "every possible device will be utilized for the isolation of activities and their quantitative measurements".[4] This positivistic formulation of library science research is important for its rejection of two concepts central to qualitative research: that human action must be understood not in isolation but in its sociocultural context, and that the forms of observation that do not rely on quantification are also useful.

In 1957 *Library Trends* published an issue devoted to research in librarianship. This collection of essays, however, concerned itself with the subject matter of LIS research and did not take up the issue of method. Only one article could be considered methodological, an essay by Leon Carnovsky supporting the pluralistic principle that the nature of an inquiry will properly determine the methods employed, and citing several approaches widely used by qualitatively oriented researchers—case study and historical analysis.[5] Carnovsky gives highest priority, however, to methods that yield statements on causality and discourages the use of narrative descriptions, which, although they can be difficult to work with, are important to qualitative researchers.

Seven years later. *Library Trends* returned again to the question of research, this time taking up more directly the question of research methods, with articles on many of the approaches currently in use at that time in the LIS community, including surveys, historical research, bibliographical research, and experimental research. Although there is no direct reference in this collection to qualitative methods as such, the collection does include an essay by Jesse Shera in which the author inscribes an inclusive circle of research in the field, avoiding the scientistic language of some of his predecessors. He noted, for example, in his review of approaches to research, the value of two fields closely linked to the development of qualitative methods, cultural anthropology, and philosophy.[6] Shera's characterization of research as a critical examination of relevant and reliable evidence and its use in producing valid and generalizable findings is broad enough to encompass qualitative as well as quantitative approaches.

Another volume of articles on research methods in LIS appeared in 1970, consisting largely of essays by noted experts in research outside the field.[7] Although once again qualitative research as an alternative to quantitative research was not explicitly addressed, the volume did contain articles on two methods widely used by qualitative researchers: participant observation and in-depth interviewing. Galvin's article the same year describes the use of case studies, but passes quickly over their application in research to concentrate on their utility as instructional tools.[8] In general, methodologists in LIS during this period continued to apply a quantitatively oriented model of research to information studies. In 1969 Herbert Goldhor, an influential theorist, researcher, and educator, wrote an introductory work whose purpose was to teach "how to do research in librarianship" (p. 2).[9] Although Goldhor's accounts of the general requirements of research—a well-formed hypothesis, accurate observation, attention to the validity of data collected—do not in themselves rule out qualitative approaches, his strong preference for the natural science approach is clear throughout. For example, he advocates the gathering of "evidence" (defined as accurately recorded data suitable for use with the scientific model of research), distinguishing it from "testimony" (subjective, unverifiable statements gathered under uncontrolled conditions; p. 18),[9] a form of observation that he considers unsuitable for scientific work. The problem with this distinction is the extent to which it dismisses the sort of subjective, ill-formed data that are of great value in qualitative research.

The search for rigor in library research continued in the 1970s with a strongly worded essay by Busha and Purcell that echoed Williamson's theme forty years earlier criticizing library researchers for engaging in too much description and bibliographical work with too little attention to generalization or theory construction.[10] The authors propose in this article a program for library science instruction that includes a minor role for qualitative research, but focuses almost entirely on techniques that have little or no relevance to qualitative work, including formal hypothesis testing and mathematical modeling. The article also makes a very strong case for impartiality and detachment, conditions that are at least problematic from the perspective of qualitative theory. Although the authors suggest that the ideal methods textbook for information studies should present both qualitative and quantitative approaches, they recommend that "heavy emphasis" be placed on the latter (p. 12).[10]

Several encyclopedia articles on methodology in LIS were published around this time. Busha's 1978 essay is devoted to quantitative methods and the natural science model, particularly statistics, and contains no references to the qualitative approach.[11] Similarly, Kaske and Rush focus almost entirely on mathematical, analytical, experimental, and statistical approaches, mentioning, of the more qualitative approaches, only historical research. Sounding a familiar theme, the authors note that "sound research is based chiefly upon the scientific method, which provides a framework within which hypothesis testing and inferential thought may be carried out in a disciplined manner," and suggest that because much LIS research has been unscientific, there is doubt about what has been learned.[12] A collection of essays published in 1981 addresses many aspects of research, but, outside the recurring exception of historical work, either ignores or criticizes approaches that are favored by qualitative researchers.[13] In his essay on error, for example, Katzer notes: "The weakest type of case is one based on the researcher's words rather than on the researcher's (or other researchers') deeds. The concerns for factual accuracy and generality still need to be considered, but their justification is limited to verbal arguments of what seems to be likely or plausible."[14] This statement, which is accurate for research in the natural science tradition, is incompatible with and in some critical ways undermines the value of interpretive approaches to research, which depend heavily on verbal arguments.

In 1984 *Library Trends* published another collection of essays on research in information studies. Although consistent with earlier compendiums, many of the articles in this collection were not directed toward methodological issues, and when methods were addressed, the highest priority continued to be placed on the model of the natural sciences. In the introductory essay to this volume. Lynch develops a distinction between "scientific" research, which seeks to create new knowledge, and "scholarly" research, in which the data are collected from books rather than nature" (p. 369).[15] The author goes on to suggest that the preference among humanists for the scholarly type of research in conjunction with the affinity of humanists for librarianship accounts for the field's prejudice against scientific research in library education (p. 371).[15] Although this argument does place what are now frequently called qualitative methods in a rather unfavorable light, the analysis is nevertheless accurate in its characterization of such methods, which have in fact frequently been inspired—and are often practiced—by humanities scholars. The approach taken in this and most previous essays on the subject—that natural science is the ideal to which research in LIS should aim—was reiterated by a number of other works published in the 1980s.[16–19]

The preference for quantitative research models in information studies has not gone unchallenged in information studies. There are, among the methodological writings of the field, occasional statements expressing reservations about the mainstream position on research, such as Shiflett's comment in the 1984 *Library Trends* collection that historians did not usually have the opportunity to perform statistical tests and sought to convince their readers "not by elaborate numerology" but by facts and persuasive argument,[20] the latter phrase being of

some significance for its recognition of the role of language in scientific research. Occasionally, however, these arguments took the form of sharply worded theoretical statements that can be viewed as part of the larger debate over the identity (and even the name) of the field. Among these are Curtis Wright's philosophically oriented discussions of library research, key to which is his explicit separation of librarianship from natural science, the exact opposite of the position taken by the mainstream methodologists of LIS, and his skepticism about the appropriateness and utility of the scientific model in the field. Characterizing librarianship as metaphysics rather than physics, and invoking the literature discrediting the positivistic philosophy (unrecognized or unacknowledged by the earlier authors) on which the scientific model is based, Wright notes that "librarians do indeed invert the world of science, because librarianship is the mirror obverse of science as a knowledge system; it is a technology of knowing based on philosophy, not a scientific technology of action."[21] Similarly, Michael Harris, in a review of the 1984 methods issue of *Library Trends*, criticized the identification of librarianship with natural science and expressed concern about "the extent to which this profession has systematically isolated itself from contact with significant empirical and theoretical developments in the social sciences."[22] Harris was explicit in his criticism of the field for its commitment to varieties of positivism that were in the process of being abandoned in other social sciences, and directed the debate toward the larger question of whether there can be a library "science" at all.[23] Relevant in this context is Radford's epistemological critique of the field, which does not explicitly take up the matter of research, but argues, along with Wright and Harris, that the modern conception of the library has been grounded in a positivistic commitment to neutrality and objectivity, values that have figured significantly in the methodological writing in LIS.[24]

A small number of writers have invoked the social science literature to defend qualitative approaches to knowledge. Several have voiced the need for a broader range of methods in information studies and for research designs that do not in principle reject particular approaches but rather attempt to fit the tool to the task.[25–27] Others have argued for the use of interpretive methods based on principles derived from hermeneutics and the "human sciences."[28,29] In recent years, rising interest in the qualitative approach has produced extended works examining the application of these methods in LIS.[30–32]

Taken as a whole, this corpus of methodological literature, with some notable and mostly recent exceptions, clearly takes the model of quantitative techniques and the natural sciences to be the best (and in some cases the only) method for use in information studies. It is important to acknowledge the significance and historical purpose of this work, which has not only helped to improve the rigor and the generalizability of LIS research, but has served the function of encouraging a field rooted in practice to take up a more research-oriented, theoretically driven professional posture, a movement that has helped to increase its credibility among scholars in other fields. This literature reveals very little awareness of qualitative methods, however, and the articulation of a research program that draws on qualitative, interpretive, and naturalistic approaches to research has yet to occur. This is of some interest, since these methods have been practiced for decades in other social sciences, in which lively and productive debates over methodology are commonplace. The remainder of this article briefly surveys some of the principles on which qualitative research is based and discusses the associated techniques that have proved useful in information studies.

THE PRINCIPLES OF QUALITATIVE RESEARCH

Although it is possible to generate data by applying the techniques of social science research without reference to the philosophical principles on which those techniques are based, it is difficult for researchers to build useful theory out of those data without some understanding of those principles. Research is not so much a matter of gathering up data that already exist, but a process of making successive observations and inferences during which data are not merely gathered but in some sense created according to the theoretical assumptions that drive the researcher's approach. As the authors of a recent methodological essay have pointed out, "The various happenings, objects and people of the world are not data until made relevant within a framework which constitutes them as evidential materials for some purpose."[33] This in turn suggests that to gain an effective command of a research method is more than just mastering certain skills and tools, but also entails cultivating an understanding of the epistemological implications that drive them. There is no canonical list of the theoretical propositions on which qualitative research is based, but the paragraphs that follow summarize some of the more significant ones evident in the qualitative research of the social sciences.

Most methodologists, whatever their orientation, would agree that *empiricism*, the principle that knowledge is based on observations of the world rather than the imagination, is fundamental to any kind of scientific research. Although Williamson, as noted above, accused librarians of harboring an "empirical tendency" that was an impediment to doing useful research, it is clear that there can be no research in the usual sense of the term without the use of the senses. Quantitative and qualitative researchers differ, however, on the role of the observer. The former tend to argue that scientific observations of the world must be achieved with minimal personal involvement, and lean toward the positivistic position that the most secure form of knowledge is produced by observations that can be

verified by any observer. From this perspective, the researcher is a data-gathering instrument. Qualitatively oriented researchers, on the other hand, without sacrificing their scientific goals, find it not only difficult but a source of error to overlook the interpretive role of the observer. This view is a result of the recognition by qualitative researchers of the role of the knowing subject, a concept that can be traced in the philosophical literature to Kant's break with Cartesian dualism, particularly as articulated in the work of philosophers such as Wilhelm Dilthey and Alfred Schutz. Qualitative researchers, nevertheless, do not believe that their recognition of the role of the observer undermines the claims of qualitative research to being empirical or even scientific, and include in their methods a commitment to basic principles such as validity, reliability, falsifiability, and the proper use of inductive thinking. The key difference is that the researcher is taken to be an interpretive rather than merely a recording instrument. At the risk of oversimplification, one might even say that quantitative research tends to seek to repress the subjective, while qualitative research accepts and even exploits it.

Qualitative research is often associated with *naturalism*, which in this context refers to the avoidance of abstract or reductionist forms of data collecting and analysis and the construction of any explanatory apparatus that is at odds with the subjects' own experience of the phenomenon under study.[34,35] Naturalistic researchers thus tend to focus on the ongoing multidimensional character of the social world, an approach that tends to increase the proximity of researchers to their subjects, and to report their understandings of this world in ways that respect its irreducibility. Practitioners of the naturalistic approach are generally more interesting in discovery and insight than in establishing laws through formal hypothesis testing (although what is discovered may later be confirmed using quantitative procedures), and tend to seek understanding of phenomena in a way that reflects their interrelatedness and complexity. Thus, observation in naturalistic research sometimes takes the form of complex, detailed descriptions rather than the isolation of discrete variables. One particularly interesting feature of naturalistic research is its tolerance of ambiguity and incompleteness. Quantitative approaches are frequently designed to reduce ambiguity by focusing exclusively on those observations that can be objectively confirmed. Qualitative research recognizes complications that call confirmability into question, including politics (people involved in competition over power don't always say everything that they know) and the subconscious (people don't always say everything that is true, whatever they may happen to believe), and looks for ways to operate within these constraints.

Many forms of qualitative research are based on the principles of *constructivism*, a term that refers to the social processes by which humans create a meaningful world. A central assumption of this approach is that meaning (such as the utility of an information source for a user, the relevance of a fact to a need, or the cultural role of a library) is not an inherent attribute or phenomenon, but is continuously created and recreated by the human participants in that world. Qualitative, interpretive methods provide the tools for understanding and explaining this process. A landmark account of this way of examining the social world is Berger and Luckman's *The Social Construction of Reality*,[36] a work that has had a major influence on social science research in many disciplines. Constructivism places a great deal of emphasis on the observer and on the process of interpretation. From the perspective of information studies, constructivism is concerned with the processes by which knowledge is made and how it is identified as knowledge. Social studies of science, which examine the details of the settings in which scientific knowledge is created, fall into this category.[37] Recent applications of constructionist theory in educational evaluation, a subdiscipline that is of particular relevance to LIS, have been explored by Guba and Lincoln.[38]

One form of constructivist research is *symbolic interactionism*, a term that is applicable both to a theoretical approach as well as to a collection of research techniques. Chief among its philosophical founders is George Herbert Mead.[39] According to Herbert Blumer, a sociologist who has given Mead's theory methodological form, the three principles of symbolic interactionism are first, that humans act toward the things of the world on the basis of the meanings those things have for them; second, that meaning is derived from social interaction; and third, that meanings are managed through an ongoing interpretive process.[40] Understanding social reality from the perspective of symbolic interactionism thus requires not just the gathering of objective data, but the negotiation of a complex network of the processes through which meaning is constructed.[41]

Central to both constructivism and interactionism is the principle of the interconnectedness of social phenomena. One of the concerns that qualitative researchers tend to have about formal data-gathering instruments such as surveys forms, particularly when used alone, is that they are too effective in filtering out the surrounding social environment. Qualitative research is often designed more to explore the relationships between the phenomenon under investigation and its entire environment than to decompose a research question into parts, an approach sometimes referred to as *holism*. Diesing describes the concept as follows: "The holist standpoint includes the belief that human systems tend to develop a characteristic wholeness or integrity. They are not simply a loose collection of traits or wants or reflexes or variables of any sort: they have a unity that manifests itself in nearly every part" (p. 137).[42] Moreover, the concepts used to capture this holistic quality must be relatively concrete and particularized, close to the

real system being described, rather than abstract mathematical concepts developed in some other science and imposed on the subject matter a priori or concepts that grow out of a testing instrument and get their meaning from the instrument. As many of the concepts as possible should be derived from the subject matter itself, from the thinking of the people being studied: and the other concepts should at least not be foreign to their way of thinking (p. 139).[42]

Qualitative researchers, whatever their particular research goals or techniques, are usually interested in the meaning of natural human contexts in this holistic sense, which requires attention to more than just the object under examination. This has important methodological ramifications for the qualitative researcher, favoring an "immersion" approach in which the observer is present in the research setting for extended periods of time, a labor-intensive but data-rich way to discover the multiple dimensions of the subject under study that would drop out of many more formalistic, quantitative approaches.

Another way to characterize qualitative research is to say that it emphasizes *discovery* over explanation. This approach to research problems has yet to be broadly practiced in information studies, which historically have tended to focus on the problems of causality, prediction, and control. Pierce Butler, for example, in a discussion of scientific research, noted that "so far as they are possible, explanations will be formulated in chains of immediate causes."[4] Qualitative methods do not lend themselves easily to these sorts of research goals, but are grounded in the recognition that for symbol-making human beings, "causes" often take the form of articulations of meaning rather than objective accounts of sequences of events (pp. 140–142).[34] It is not immediate causes that interest qualitative researchers, but frameworks of significance.

The recognition of the significance of subjectivity and contextuality in the human sciences leads to the twin issues of *relativism* and *pluralism*. Relativism refers to the principle that the standards of what passes for truth are not the same in every human community and therefore that each community must be understood in its own terms, while pluralism in the corresponding recognition that the social world cannot be reduced to a single paradigm or system of explanations. These principles have implications not only for the understanding of how people view their own environments and experiences, but also how researchers view those people as subjects of research. Most important, they suggest that the scientific observer's role, particularly in the human sciences, is never purely objective, but is conditioned by values and expectations. The unity of knowledge as a total, well-integrated system that is posited by natural science is not feasible according to this view. It follows that if knowledge has pluralistic aspects then the methods use to produce it must be equally diverse.

In this vein, some theorists have taken as a subject of analysis science itself and identified the possibility of multiple forms of scientific knowledge, distinguishing, for example, traditional science from a "feminist" science.[43,44] A pluralistic view of knowledge necessarily admits natural science, but does not necessarily accord it a privileged position.

The key to accommodation among paradigms is rejection of the "queen science" viewpoint that philosophical first principles must determine methodology. Once one begins to look at what researchers do, the walls between paradigms start to break down. In practice, researchers use a variety of imperfect approaches to enhance the credibility of their arguments that require complex trade-offs among precision, generalization, and existential reality.[45]

This assertion, that there are no clear standards against which to measure knowledge, is possibly one of the most disturbing and challenging aspects of the interpretivist approach to research, but it has the advantage of accommodating a wide range of research practices, a situation of considerable benefit to a multidisciplinary field such as library and information studies.

Another problematic aspect of qualitative research is its accommodation of *subjectivity*, a concept with two linked aspects: the subjectivity of the targets of research and the subjectivity of the researcher. The first refers to the recognition that those persons whose behavior social science attempts to understand and explain possess a subjectively constructed view of the world that may not only be concealed from the scientific observer but also may not be easily articulated even by those who possess it. Human behavior is a complexity that is highly resistant to being untangled by outsiders in a way that accurately reflects its meaning for insiders. While this may not be a serious problem when the subjects of the investigation are members of the researchers' own culture (often the case in information studies), it can lead to invalid results if the researcher and subject do not share common assumptions and the researcher's methods are poorly chosen. Some of the most interesting methodological solutions to this problem have been devised by anthropologists, who more than any other social scientists face the challenge of comprehending world views radically different from their own and who have developed ethnographic tools to achieve this goal. But it is clear that similar difficulties are present even when the subjects of research are not members of other cultures. For example, concerns about possible disjunctions between the assumptions of information professionals and their users is a significant issue in information studies, and the application of qualitative approaches to observation and analysis opens the way for new strategies for developing more responsive and effective information systems. Well known among the research addressing this problem is Dervin's approach to the problem of user needs, which takes into account the users' own environment and their subjective adaptation to it.[46–48]

The second key aspect of the subjectivity question focuses on the subjective role of the observer, which can be managed in qualitative research but in principle never neutralized. The principles of constructivism and relativism mean that no human observer can be wholly detached from the research setting, and many qualitative approaches to social research recognize this condition. Research performed under the constraints of subjectivism can be viewed as an attempt to link the perceptions of the observer and the observed by achieving some degree of common understanding, not always an easy task. Norman Denzin has noted that "being a scientist reflects a continual attempt to lift one's own idiosyncratic experiences to the level of the consensual and the shared meaning. It is in this context that the research method becomes the major means of acting on the symbolic environment and making those actions consensual in the broader community of sociologists" (p. 12).[49] The use of participant observation, for example, provides an opportunity for researchers to experience firsthand the phenomena under investigation from a perspective similar to the other actors, an approach that forces recognition of the observer's own role in the research setting. A notable example is Janice Radaway's ethnographic study of women who read romance novels, a work that concentrates not on the texts themselves but on the meaning they have for their readers. As the author notes, the construction of meaning in this project involved the observer as well as the observed: "It is essential to point out here that in formulating a hypothesis about the significance of romance reading as an act, that hypothesis inevitably will be a critic's construction of the reader's construction of the import of her reading behavior."[50]

This characterization of social behavior contrasts with quantitative approaches that make an attempt to isolate certain unwanted forms of meaning, which are sometimes described as bias, from other forms that are described as fact. Qualitative theory does not accept so quickly the characterization of bias as "noise" that must be eliminated; rather, it recognizes that all observations are biased in the sense that they reflect the observer's intentions and ways of knowing and are inevitably accompanied by unstated assumptions. The task is not to eliminate bias, but to examine it and determine the degree to which it can be controlled. Linked to the issue of the researcher's subjectivity are questions regarding the truth value of published research results. Qualitative research reports are sometimes essentially first-person descriptive reports of these experiences, a situation that has led to considerable debate over the role of the researcher's own narrative voice in social science reporting.[51,52] Acknowledging one's limitations as an observer, of course, has its risks. It would be a mistake to equate the limitations on the role of the observer with a complete lack of objectivity, and successful qualitative research still requires that the observer maintain a certain balance between detached analysis on the one hand and sympathetic participation on the other, so as to avoid, for example, the dangers of interpreting events as more patterned than they actually are or "going native" by becoming completely absorbed by the setting and losing the analytic perspective of the researcher.

An interesting and important result of the acknowledgment of observer subjectivity in qualitative research is a heightened sensitivity to issues of *values* and *ethics*. To recognize that the researcher is also an actor is the research setting may raise serious moral and political issues.[53,54] Qualitative researchers, because of the involving nature of their work, frequently find themselves handling privileged information, falling into moral dilemmas, gaining knowledge of immoral or even illegal acts, becoming entangled in power conflicts, and in other ways being forced out of their roles as neutral observers. Qualitative researchers also face ethical questions when they presume to speak for silent or powerless individuals, particularly when those expressions have the power to influence others' lives positively or negatively. It is but a short step from a researcher's acknowledgment that social research cannot be value-free (as natural science has sometimes claimed to be), to the adoption of an activist approach to research whose goal is not merely knowledge, but social change. The perspectives of the "critical theorists," inspired by the work of writers such as Theodore Adorno, Herbert Marcuse, and Michel Foucault, have drawn the attention of qualitative researchers to these issues.[55] Recognition of the role of libraries as agents for social change has a lengthy history in LIS, and although this aspect of the field has not inspired a large number of research efforts, there have been attempts to develop these ideas in the LIS literature. Examples include Berman's revealing juxtaposition of Library of Congress subject headings with facts and commentaries from a variety of other sources, exposing the value-laden nature of the former.[56] Buschman and Carbone's application of new theories of education to LIS,[57] and Frohmann's critique of the limitations of the "cognitive viewpoint" in LIS.[58]

METHODS AND TOOLS

As noted above, although a primary purpose of research is to gather data, it is clear that research is more than "fact finding." No observation, whether recorded as words, numbers, images, or something else, is inherently "factual," nor do data occur naturally, but rather are the product of observations, which are themselves conditioned by theory. In this sense constructionist principles apply not only to the objects of research, but to the research process as well. Neither theory without data nor data without theory can lay a claim to being research. The process of moving from theory to data is a difficult one, and it is in this relationship that the essence of qualitative research lies. Quantitative researchers use the term *operationalize* to describe the process by which a hypothesis or research question is embodied by some form of data, and

qualitative researchers must pass through a similar stage. This section contains descriptions of some of the higher-level methodological approaches that are used to realize the theoretical goals of qualitative research. Details on the numerous tools and techniques that are appropriate to each of these approaches are described in the handbooks listed in the bibliography at the end of this article.

The *historical* approach to the analysis of human society and culture is sometimes overlooked as a member of the family of qualitative approaches to research, but it is one that embodies many of the attributes described above, and has the added distinction of being used continuously in information studies longer than any other qualitative approach.[59] Although not every form of historical writing can be considered qualitative, or even research in the social scientific sense, the data-gathering and analytical processes used by historians share a number of important features with other forms of qualitative work, with the close examination of documentary evidence taking the place of direct observation of the social world.[60] One might argue that some forms of historical writing are examples of ethnographic analysis practiced in remote time frames. Included in this category are biographical works that seek an understanding of the history of libraries and information systems by examining the life and work of individuals who have played pivotal roles in their development, the historical equivalent of the life history method that is widely used in anthropology.

The task of historians is to overcome the analytical limitations of examining phenomena through indirect means. Most forms of qualitative work, however, are designed to avoid having to resort to indirect measurements of human behavior and instead place the researcher as close as possible to the events under examination. These practices are often referred to collectively as *ethnographic* methods. Many entail some form of *participant observation*, in which the researcher, rather than taking up the position of a detached observer, makes an effort to take part in the phenomena under investigation, and in doing so is in a position to perceive complexities of the setting that might otherwise escape attention. "Participation" might be as simple as a series of informal discussions with a subject or as complex as an extended period of full-time residence in the community under examination. Being able to interact with the research subjects in a continuous way, to observe directly the complexities and uniqueness of individual behavior, and to follow the patterns of changing events, are all benefits of this approach. Perhaps most important, participant observation makes it possible to gather data on the subtle and unpredictable events of normal human environment. To give a simple example, the author of this article was sitting in a meeting of librarians, listening to a serious discussion of proposed changes to the library's mission statement, when one of the staff members passed over a scrap of paper on which were written the words "You'll note a certain 'Alice in

Wonderland' character to these discussions." This impromptu act, small as it was, revealed aspects of the organization's culture that staff had not up to that point articulated in more formal interview settings. In a similar way. Forsythe used participant observation to study the work of knowledge engineers, achieving an understanding of their perception of human knowledge and how this perception dramatized the contrast between belief and practice that might have otherwise remain concealed.[61]

Engaging in ethnographic work and participant observation does entail certain trade-offs. Although these methods are capable of producing richly detailed, highly accurate depictions of social phenomena, they possess certain disadvantages. One is that they tend to generate massive amounts of data, which may include extensive field notes, charts and tables, photographs, transcribed recordings, documents, artifacts, and even quantitative data sets. The higher the volume of data, the more complex the analysis and the greater the time and effort required to move from the planning stages of a research project to the finished report. Qualitative researchers have found their work more difficult than the tasks typically associated with quantitative research to the extent that they have not had the same efficient tools for data processing that are available to quantitative researchers (although the availability of new computer tools for organizing and analyzing qualitative data is changing that). A second class of disadvantages is a consequence of the highly contextualized level at which qualitative research tends to occur. The findings of ethnographic field studies, for example, do not lead as easily to predictive models of behavior, and are not as easily generalized beyond the setting in which they were produced. Moreover, ethnographic approaches can place greater personal stress on the researcher, resulting from difficulties in entering into and maintaining relationships in an unfamiliar social environment.

Compared to the work produced in sociology, anthropology, and education, LIS has not produced large numbers of ethnographic studies. One effort worthy of mention is the High John project, an ambitious experiment in which library students from the University of Maryland collaboratively developed and staffed a public library in an economically disadvantaged minority community.[62] Although this project had more to do with library development and education than research, it possessed many of the attributes of ethnographic field work (extended participatory involvement in an unfamiliar community, close attention to process, a case-study concentration on a single setting), and serves as an indicator of the kinds of opportunities that exist for field-oriented studies in LIS. Examples of the use of ethnographic research methods in information studies are Chatman's study of the information needs and practices of elderly women[63] and Tanner's account of the role of ministers as information providers.[64] Another ethnographic study relevant to the concerns of LIS is Heath's field-based comparative analysis of speech, reading, and writing in socioeconomically contrasting communities.[65] Heath's work is just one example of an expanding body of work that examines the sociocultural aspects of reading.[66] Zuboff's study of the role of information technology in a changing workplace is another useful implementation of ethnographic methods.[67] The rapidly developing area of the sociology of science has also produced ethnographic studies that provide insights into the ways that scientists produce knowledge and the social dynamics of the writing and publishing process.[68,37]

Field-based ethnographic research is the classic form of qualitative research, but it is not as much of a "method" as it is a setting in which a wide variety of particular methods might be employed. One of the most common ethnographic tools is *interviewing*, a technique based in large part on conversation, arguably the most natural of all forms of human communication. The subject of interviewing, which is addressed in nearly every handbook of qualitative methods, has long been recognized in sociology for its ability to generate the kind of data that are useful to qualitative analysis.[69] For researchers unable to actually live or work as participant observers in the community under study, interviewing is one of the most effective ways of collecting qualitative data. Interviewing takes many forms; it may be more or less structured, brief or extended, individual or group-oriented. Researchers may confine their attention to a single cooperative informant, or they may employ sampling procedures to interview a large number of people. Within an interview, the researcher may engage in a variety of tasks: establish rapport in the community, collect life-history accounts, administer open-ended surveys, probe for explanations to questions raised by other aspects of the research process, or conduct psychological tests. Interviewing may be employed, in fact, as a high-yield method for collecting closed-response survey data, and used as such is not really a qualitative method at all. Often in interviewing it is important to gather the subject's responses verbatim, which requires either very careful note taking or recording. This not only facilitates later analysis, but it protects researchers from their tendency to project meaning unintended by the speaker when recording the events in the form of field notes. A disadvantage of interviewing is that it is not entirely a natural setting, and the subjects' awareness of the interviewer's role and purposes may lead them to modify what they say, but this problem can be compensated for by interviewing a large number of subjects, or the same subject a large number of times.

Much qualitative research is based on the *case-study* model, the basis of which is an in-depth understanding of a single event or setting. Typically, in case-study analysis, "the emphasis is on the individuality or uniqueness of the system, its wholeness or boundedness, and the ways it maintains its individuality" (p. 5).[42] Detailed case studies have limited use in quantitative approaches in which the goal is the identification of regularities over multiple cases, but they are ideally suited to the goals of qualitative work, in which the recording of contextual detail is a high priority and the researcher can focus on what Denzin calls the "situated aspects" of human conduct (p. 10).[49] Case studies are often narrative in their final form, but they may be constructed using a variety of data types, a strategy that increases the richness and also the validity of the study. Cases may be reported individually, but gain value when they are juxtaposed with additional similar cases, yielding a comparative case study capable of highlighting not only what is unique about each case, but what they have in common.[70] In LIS the case method has been used productively in the longitudinal analysis of attitudes and behaviors of information system users, incorporating participant journals and logs, interviews, observational analysis, relevance judgments, and citation analysis, and combining all the elements in a detailed contextual account of the user's experience.[71,72]

Qualitative approaches to research tend to be less regularized and structured than quantitative approaches. It would be difficult in fact to demonstrate that qualitative research constituted a particular "system" or set of linked procedures, a characteristic that makes qualitative methods difficult to master. Methodologists, however have succeeded in developing qualitative research approaches that have a certain systematic character. One that has been widely studied and applied is the *grounded theory* approach, as articulated by Glazer and Strauss.[73,74] The principal purpose of this method is the inductive generation of theory from data through a disciplined application of observation and interpretation. The developers of this approach note that theory is said to be properly grounded when it fits the data used to generate it, is understandable to both the researcher and the subjects of the research, remains abstract enough that it can be usefully applied in other settings, and offers the researcher sufficient tools to exercise some control over its application in subsequent situations (pp. 237–249).[73] Grounded theory is more than an interesting intellectual construct; it is a practical tool for building useful knowledge about social settings. Its focus on utility and application makes it well suited to a professional field such as LIS, where it has seen some use in recent years.[75,76]

Another systematic qualitative approach is *ethnomethodology*, which can be briefly described as the study of commonplace behaviors in natural contexts, with particular emphasis on how individuals organize and make sense of their environments.[77,78] Ethnomethodology is inspired by phenomenological philosophy, which takes up the question of the semantic organization of the social world and is also closely linked to the principles of constructivism. Of particular interest to ethnomethodologists is the use of language, especially the forms of speech that ethnomethodologists call "indexical expressions," utterances whose meaning cannot be determined apart from the

context of their use. Paying attention to what people normally take for granted, asking how it is that those commonplace perceptions are created, and investigating the procedures by which these meanings are conveyed is the work of ethnomethodology. This approach seeks not only to account for humans' understanding of their social environments, but also social processes by which that understanding is negotiated and maintained. Ethnomethodological approaches have been applied to several problems in information studies. Relevant to the field of user studies, for example, is Whalen and Zimmerman's analysis of telephone requests to dispatchers of emergency assistance, a study that elucidates how callers use their knowledge of the conversational situation and how they make their purposes evident.[79] An influential study with ethnomethodological components is Suchman's exploration of the complex ways that humans react to machines. A principal theme of this work is to demonstrate that insofar as actions are always situated in particular social and physical circumstances the situation is crucial to the actor's interpretation."[80] This understanding has important theoretical implications for sociologists, but it also has practical consequences for the designers of information systems, who must learn to anticipate the complex and not always predictable ways that users respond to the tools that they use.

As some of these examples have already suggested, there is no form of data more important in qualitative research than language, and the methods used in qualitative work are often designed to elicit, organize, process, and analyze both written and spoken language. Working with words poses certain problems not encountered with numbers, however. Their meaning is in part a consequence of the context in which they appear and changes over time. They are difficult to record and process, and they possess an interpretive openness that complicates analysis. As noted above, quantitative methodologists have on occasion looked for ways to avoid the entanglements of interpretive language altogether, considering it a contaminating force in scientific research, but for qualitative theorists, the role of language in structuring human experience is an essential feature of the research setting, which neither the subjects of research nor the researchers themselves can avoid. Clearly this raises many problems in analyzing linguistic data collected from informants, but those problems also extend to the researcher's own use of words in reporting the results of research. This is a pattern that holds true, qualitative theorists are eager to point out, even for positivistically oriented researchers. For example, in a critique of the quantitative orthodoxy of economics, Donald McCloskey defends the role of words: "If science is to cohere it must use the art of argument; and if it is to be agreed upon by free people it must be argued persuasively. In English the words 'science' and 'rhetoric' quarrel childishly."[81] An interesting body of literature on the rhetorical character of science that is of particular relevance to LIS are sociological studies of the verbal strategies employed by scientists in reporting their work.[82]

One class of useful qualitative research techniques that draw on the centrality of language view human settings as "texts" that observers may examine in order to extract their meaning and come to an understanding of the processes that drive them. Semiotics, for example, the study of signs and their significance, is a branch of linguistics that has been widely applied as a research tool in many disciplines, including communications, anthropology, and literary criticism. Warner has suggested incorporating semiotics into LIS as a way to extend the dimensions of the latter field beyond its customary alignment with the physical sciences and technology.[83] Other examples of the use of literary studies in LIS are those that draw on the characteristically human tendency to organize experience as narrative or story. One example is Urquhart and Crane's use of narrative vignettes drawn from the professional literature as a way to elicit in a realistic way data about the information skills of nurses.[84] A similar strategy is the use of protocol analysis by the builders of expert systems as a method of capturing the elusive knowledge of human experts. This technique involves asking subjects to perform a task while simultaneously producing a narrative account of that task, which can then be used to derive formalized accounts of that knowledge.[85,86] Another study in which language plays a key role is Myer's contextual analysis of scientists' progressive revisions of patent applications, examining the social conditions that affect the articulation of new knowledge.[87] Also attracting some interest in information studies is "reader-response criticism," a type of literary analysis based on the proposition that the meaning of a text resides not in the words, but in the reader's reaction to those words.[88] Radaway's study of romance readers is one notable contribution to this literature.[50] Such studies, when used to determine the effect of literature on various communities of readers, are tools that can be used by libraries to help the solve the always difficult task of understanding what their communities want, and has practical consequences for collection development.

CONCLUSION

This article, although brief has traversed a rather wide range of territory. Even as a special topic within the social sciences, qualitative methods lacks distinct boundaries, and any discussion that attempts to summarize this approach runs the risk of granting to the topic a false degree of concreteness. In that regard it is useful to conclude with two related points of a cautionary nature. The first is to clarify that it is not the purpose of this article to impose an authoritarian or prescriptive character to the subject of qualitative methods, but to present a representative range of issues and techniques. This is in keeping with the spirit of the qualitative approach, which is useful in complex or rapidly changing settings precisely because of its open-ended and adaptable nature. It is unlikely, in fact, that any abstract analysis can really do justice to the topic. Although for reasons already stated this article has taken a somewhat theoretical approach, neither this nor any other similar treatment of the subject is more effective in conveying the essence of the qualitative approach to students of method than a patient examination of the published research literature, and readers interested in learning to use these tools are encouraged to seek out the best examples of qualitative research, not just in LIS but in related fields as well. By extension, just as reading about the principles of research cannot replace reading actual research reports, reading published reports cannot take the place of firsthand field experience. To apply the tools of qualitative research to real research questions and to struggle with the problems of data collecting and analysis using qualitative paradigms is one of the most effective ways of coming to terms with their utility and significance.

The second (and related) point is that any set of research tools must ultimately be measured by the effectiveness of those tools in producing the kinds of understanding that significantly advance the field of study in which they are used. Reflective methodologists are familiar with the danger that a particular set of research tools, once widely used, may become entrenched, and rather than serving the cause of creating new knowledge, may come to dominate it by limiting the kinds of questions that are asked and the kinds of answers that are judged acceptable. According to Abraham Kaplan, who named this condition "the law of the instrument," what is objectionable about this situation "is not that some techniques are pushed to the utmost, but that others, in consequence, are denied the name of science" (p. 29).[2] One of the main contributions of qualitative research methods to information studies is their role in increasing the variety of the contents of the researcher's toolkit, and consequently in expanding the range of what can be learned. This is of particular significance in a field as diverse and rapidly changing as LIS.

REFERENCES

1. Neill, S.D. The dilemma of method for information research: Is information science a science, a social science, or humanity?. In *Dilemmas in the Study of Information: Exploring the Boundaries of Information Science*; Greenwood Press: New York, 1992, 141.

2. Kaplan, A. *The Structure of Inquiry: Methodology for Behavioral Science*; Chandler, Scranton, PA, 1974.

3. Williamson, C.C. *The Williamson Reports of 1921 and 1923*; Scarecrow Press: Metuchen, NJ, 1931; 8.

4. Butler, P. *An Introduction to Library Science*; University of Chicago Press: Chicago, IL, 1993; 25.

5. Carnovsky, L. Methodology in research and applications. Libr. Trends **1957**, *6* (2), 243–246.

6. Shera, J. Darwin, Bacon, and research in librarianship. Libr. Trends **1964**, *13* (1), 141–149.

7. Bundy, M. L.; Wasserman, P., Eds. *Reader in Research Methods for Librarianship*; Microcard Editions: Dayton, OH, 1970.

8. Galvin, T. Case studies and case method. In *Encyclopedia of Library and Information Science*; Kent, A., Lancour, H., Eds.; Marcel Dekker. New York, 1970; Vol. vol. 4, 214–219.

9. Goldhor, H. *An Introduction to Scientific Research in Librarianship*; U.S. Department of Health, Education and Welfare: Washington, DC, 1969.

10. Busha, C.H.; Purcell, R. A textual approach for promoting rigorous research in librarianship. J. Educ. Libr. **1973**, *14* (1), 3–15.

11. Busha, C. H. Research methods. In *Encyclopedia of Library and Information Science*; Kent, A., Lancour, H., Daily, J.E., Eds.; Marcel Dekker: New York, 1978; Vol. vol. 25, 254–393.

12. Kaske, N.K.; Rush, J.E. Library and information science research. In *ALA World Encyclopedia of Library and Information Science*; American Library Association, Chicago, IL, 1980; 318.

13. Busha, C.H., Ed. *A Library Science Research Reader and Bibliographic Guide*; Libraries Unlimited: Littleton, CO, 1981.

14. Katzer, J. Understanding the research process: An analysis of error. In *A Library Science Research Reader and Bibliographic Guide*; Busha, C.H., Ed.; Libraries Unlimited: Littleton, CO, 1981; 52.

15. Lynch, M.J. Research and librarianship: An uneasy connection. Libr. Trends. **1984**, *32*(4).

16. Swisher, R.; McClure, C.R. *Research for Decision Making: Methods for Librarians*; American Library Association: Chicago, IL, 1984.

17. Busha, C.H.; Harter, S.P. *Research Methods in Librarianship: Techniques and Interpretation*; Academic Press: Orlando, FL, 1980.

18. Powell, R.R. *Basic Research Methods for Librarians*; Ablex: Norwood, NJ, 1985.

19. Davis, C.H.; Rush, J.E. Library and information science research. In *ALA World Encyclopedia of Information Services*, 3rd Ed.; American Library Association: Chicago, IL, 1993; 464–465.

20. Shiflett, O.L. Clio's claim: The role of historical research in library and information science. Libr. Trends **1984**, *32* (4), 385–406.

21. Curtis Wright, H. Inquiry in science and librarianship. J. Libr. Hist. **1978**, *13* (3), 252.

22. Harris, M.H. Review of "Research in Librarianship." Libr. Inform. Sci. Res. **1986**, *8* (1), 109.

23. Harris, M.H. The dialectic to defeat: Antinomies in research in library and information science. Libr. Trends **1986**, *23* (3), 515–531.

24. Radford, G.P. Positivism, foucault, and the fantasia of the library: Conceptions of knowledge and the modern library experience." Libr. Q. **1992**, *64* (4), 408–424.

25. Grover, R.; Glazier, J. Implications for applications of qualitative methods to library and information science research. Libr. Inform. Sci. Res. **1985**, *7* (3), 247–260.

26. Maguire, C. What qualifies as research in librarianship? In *Research and the Practice of Librarianship: An International Symposium*; Allen, G.G., Exon, F.C.A., Eds.; Western Australian Institute of Technology: Perth, Western Australia, Australia, 1986, 6.

27. Bradley, J.; Sutton, B. Reframing the paradigm debate. Libr. Q. **1993**, *63* (4), 405–410.

28. Benediktsson, D. Hermeneutics: Dimensions toward LIS thinking. Libr. Inform. Sci. Res. **1989**, *11* (3), 210–234.

29. Natoli, J. Librarianship as a human science: Theory, method, and application. Libr. Res. **1989**, *4* (2), 163–174.

30. Mellon, C. *Naturalistic Inquiry for Library Sciences*; Greenwood: New York, 1990.

31. Glazier, J.D.; Powell, R.R., Eds. *Qualitative Research in Information Management*; Libraries Unlimited: Englewood, CO, 1992.

32. Bradley, J.; Sutton, B.Guest, Eds. *Symposium on Qualitative Research: Theory, Methods, and Applications*, special issue of. Libr. Q. **1999**, *63* (4).

33. Ackroyd, S.; Hughes, J. A. *Data Collection in Context*, 2nd Ed.; Longman: London, U.K., 1992; 3.

34. Lincoln, Y.S.; Guba, E.G. *Naturalistic Inquiry*; Sage: Newbury Park, CA, 1985.

35. Guba, E.G. *Toward a Methodology of Naturalistic Inquiry in Educational Evaluation*; UCLS Graduate School of Education: Los Angeles, CA, 1978; 12–17.

36. Berger, P.; Luckman, T. *The Social Construction of Reality*; Doubleday: New York, 1966.

37. Knorr-Cetina, K. *The Manufacture of Knowledge: An Essay in the Constructivist and Contextual Nature of Science*; Pergamon, New York, 1981.

38. Guba, E.G.; Lincoln, Y.S. *Fourth Generation Education*; Sage: Newbury Park, CA, 1989.

39. Mead, G.H. *Mind, Self, and Society*; University of Chicago Press: Chicago, IL, 1934.

40. Blumer, H. *Symbolic Interactionism: Perspective and Method*; University of California Press: Berkeley, CA, 1969.

41. Fine, G.A. The Sad Demise. Mysterious disappearance, and glorious triumph of symbolic internactionism. Ann. Rev. Social., Annual Reviews, Inc., Palo Alto, CA, 1993; 61–87.

42. Diesing, P. *Patterns of Discovery in the Social Sciences*; Aldine: Chicago, IL, 1971.

43. Harding, S., Ed. *Feminism and Methodology*; Indiana University Press: Bloomingtom, IN, 1987.

44. Bleier, R., Ed. *Feminist Approaches to Science*; Pergamon Press: New York, 1986.

45. Firestone, W.A. Accommodation: Toward a paradigm-praxis dialectic. In *The Paradigm Dialog*; Guba, E.G., Ed.; Sage: Newbury Park, CA, 1990; 122–123.

46. Dervin, B. Information as a user construct: The relevance of perceived information needs to synthesis and interpretation. In *Knowledge Structure and Use: Implications for Synthesis and Interpretation*; Ward, S.A., Reed, L.J., Eds.; Temple University Press: Philadelphia, PA, 1983; 153–183.

47. Dervin, B.; Nilan, M. Information Needs and Uses. In *Annual Review of Library and Information Science*;

Knowledge Industry Publications. Inc., White Plains: NY, 1986; vol. 21.

48. Savolainen, R. The sense-making theory: Reviewing the interests of a user-centered approach to information seeking and use. Inform. Proc. Mgm. **1993**, *29* (1), 13–28.

49. Denzin, N. *The Research Act: A Theoretical Introduction to Sociological Methods*; Butterworth: London, U.K., 1970.

50. Radaway, J.A. *Reading the Romance: Women, Patriarchy, and Popular Literature*; University of North Carolina Press: Chapel Hill, NC, 1984.

51. Van Mannen, J. *Tales of the Field: On Writing Ethnography*; University of Chicago Press: Chicago, IL, 1988.

52. Clifford, J.; Marcus, G.E., Eds. *Writing Culture: The Poetics and Politics of Ethnography*; University of California Press: Berkeley, CA, 1986.

53. Punch, M. Politics and ethics in qualitative research. In *Handbook of Qualitative Research*; Denzin, N.K., Lincoln, Y.S., Eds.; Sage: Thousand Oaks, CA, 1994; 83–98.

54. Lee, R.M. *Doing Research on Sensitive Topics*; Sage: Newbury Park, CA, 1993.

55. Kincheloe, J.L.; McLaren, P.L. Rethinking critical theory and qualitative research. In *Handbook of Qualitative Research*; Denzin, N.K., Lincoln, Y.S., Eds.; Sage: Thousand Oaks, CA, 1994; 138–157.

56. Berman, S. *Prejudices and Antipathies: A Tract on the Library of Congress Subject Headings Concinnity People*; McFarland: Jefferson, NC, 1993.

57. Buschman, J.; Carbone, M. A critical inquiry into librarianship: Applications of the new sociology of education. Libr. Q. **1991**, *61* (1), 15–40.

58. Frohman, B. The power of images: A discourse analysis of the cognitive viewpoint. J. Doc. **1992**, *48* (4), 365–386.

59. Davis, D.G., Jr.; Tucket, J.M. *American Library History: A Comprehensive Guide to the Literature*; ABC-CLIO: Santa Barbara, CA, 1989.

60. Tuchman, G. Historical social science: methodologies, methods, and meanings. In *Handbook of Qualitative Research*; Denzin, N.K., Lincoln, Y.S., Eds.; Sage: Thousand Oaks, CA, 1994; 306–323.

61. Forsythe, D.E. Engineering knowledge: The construction of knowledge in artificial intelligence. Soc. Stud. Sci. **1993**, *23* (3), 445–77.

62. Moses, R. The training of librarians to serve the unserved: The 'high john' project. In *Library Service to the Unserved*; Sherrill, L.L., Ed.; Bowker: New York, 1970; 71–78.

63. Chatman, E.A. *The Information World of Retired Women*; Greenwood Press: Westport, CT, 1992.

64. Tanner, T.M. *What Ministers Know: A Qualitative Study of Pastors as Information Professionals*; American Theological Library Assn. and Scarecrow Press: Metuchen, NJ, 1994.

65. Heath, S.B. *Ways with Words: Language, Life, and Work in Communities and Classrooms*; Cambridge University Press: New York, 1983.

66. Boyarin, J., Ed. *The Ethnography of Reading*; University of California Press: Berkely, CA, 1993.

67. Zuboff, S. *In the Age of the Smart Machine: The Future of Work and Power*; Basic Books: New York, 1988.

68. Latour, B.; Woolgar, S. *Laboratory Life: The Social Construction of Scientific Facts*; Princeton University Press: Princeton, NJ, 1979.

69. Merton, R.; Fiske, M.; Kendall, P. *The Focused Interview: A Manual of Problems and Procedures*, 2nd Ed.; Free Press: New York, 1956.

70. Sutton, B. *Public Library Planning: Case Studies for Management*; Greenwood Press: Westport, CT, 1995.

71. Kuhlthau, C.C. Inside the search process: Information seeking from the user's perspective. JASIS **1991**, *42* (3), 362–371.

72. Smithson, S. Information retrieval evaluation in practice: A case study approach. Inform. Proc. Mgmt. **1994**, *30* (2), 205–221.

73. Glaser, B.G.; Strauss, A.L. *The Discovery of Grounded Theory: Strategies for Qualitative Research*; Aldine De Gruyter: New York, 1967.

74. Strauss, A.; Corbin, J. *Basis of Qualitative Research: Grounded Theory Procedures and Techniques*; Sage: Newbury Park, CA, 1990.

75. Ellis, D. Modeling the information-seeking patterns of academic researchers: A grounded theory approach. Libr. Q. **1993**, *63* (4), 469–486.

76. Mellon, C.A. Library anxiety: A grounded theory and its development. College Res. Libr. **1986**, *47* (2), 160–165.

77. Garfinkle, H. *Studies in Ethnomethodology*; Prentice-Hall: Englewood Cliffs, NJ, 1967.

78. Maynard, D.W.; Clayman, S.E. The diversity of ethnomethodology. In *Annual Review of Sociology*; Annual Reviews, Inc.: Palo Alto, CA, 1991; 385–418.

79. Whalen, M.R.; Zimmerman, D.H. Sequential and institutional contexts in calls for help. Soc. Psych. Q. **1987**, *50* (2), 172–185.

80. Suchman, L.A. *Plans and Situated Actions: The Problem of Human-Machine Communication*; Cambridge University Press: Cambridge, U.K., 1987.

81. McCloskey, D.N. *The Rhetoric of Economics*; University of Wisconsin Press: Madison, WI, 1985, 4.

82. Latour, B. *Science in Action*; Harvard University Press: Cambridge, MA, 1988.

83. Warner, J. Semiotics: Information science, documents, and computers. J. Doc. **1990**, *46* (1), 16–32.

84. Urquhart, C.; Crane, S. Nurses' information-seeking skills and perceptions of information sources: Assessment using vignettes. J. Inform. Sci. **1994**, *20* (4), 237–246.

85. Ericsson, K.A.; Simon, H.A. *Protocol Analysis: Verbal Reports as Data*, rev. Ed.; MIT Press: Cambridge, MA, 1993.

86. Kidd, A.L., Ed. *Knowledge Acquisition for Expert Systems: A Practical Handbook*; Plenum: New York, 1987.

87. Myers, G. From discovery to invention: The writing and rewriting of two patents. Soc. Stud. Sci. **1995**, *24* (1), 57–105.

88. Tompkins, J.P., Ed. *Reader-Response Criticism from Formalism to Post-Structuralism*; Johns Hopkins University Press: Baltimore, MD, 1980.

BIBLIOGRAPHY

The literature of qualitative research is large and continues to grow. The items listed below have been selected because of their comprehensive treatment of the subject, recency of publication, extensive bibliographies, and relevance to library and information science..

1. Bogdan, R.; Biklen, S.K. *Qualitative Research in Education: An Introduction to Theory and Methods*, 2nd Ed.; Allyn and Bacon: Boston, MA, 1992.
2. Bradley, J.; Sutton, B., Eds. Symposium on Qualitative Research: Theory, Methods, and Applications. Special issue of Libr. Q., **1993**, *63* (4).
3. Bryman, A. *Quantity and Quality in Social Research*; Unwin Hyman: London, U.K., 1988.
4. Denzin, N. *The Research Act: A Theoretical Introduction to Sociological Methods*; Butterworth: London, U.K., 1970.
5. Denzin, N.K.; Lincoln, Y.S., Eds. *Handbook of Qualitative Research*; Sage: Thousand Oaks, CA, 1994.
6. Diesing, P. *Patterns of Discovery in the Social Sciences*; Routledge & Kegan Paul: London, U.K., 1972.
7. Diesing, P. *How Does Social Science Work? Reflections on Practice*; University of Pittsburgh Press: Pittsburgh, PA, 1991.
8. Eisner, E.W.; Peskin, A. *Qualitative Inquiry in Education: The Continuing Debate*; Teachers College Press: New York, 1990.
9. Fidel, R. Qualitative Research in Information Management. Libr. Inform. Sci. Res. **1993**, *15* (3), 219–247.
10. Glazier, J.D.; Powell, R.R. *Qualitative Research in Information Management*; Libraries Unlimited: Englewood, CO, 1992.
11. Guba, E.G. *The Paradigm Dialog*; Sage: Newbury Park, CA, 1990.
12. Hughes, J. *The Philosophy of Social Research*, 2nd Ed.; Longman: London, U.K., 1990.
13. Lancy, D.; Lancy, F. *Qualitative Research in Education: An Introduction to the Major Traditions*; Longman: New York, 1993.
14. LeCompte, M.D.; Millroy, W.L.; Preissle, J. *The Handbook of Qualitative Research in Education*; Academic Press: San Diego, CA, 1992.
15. Lincoln, Y.S.; Guba, E.G. *Naturalistic Inquiry*; Sage: Newbury Park, CA, 1985.
16. Lofland, J.; Lofland, L.H. *Analyzing Social Settings: A Guide to Qualitative Observation and Analysis*; Wadsworth: Belmont, CA, 1984.
17. Mellon, C. *Naturalistic Inquiry for Library Science*; Greenwood: New York, 1990.
18. Miles, M.B.; Huberman, M.A. *Qualitative Data Analysis: A Sourcebook of New Methods*; Sage: Newbury Park, CA, 1984.
19. Patton, M.Q. *Qualitative Evaluation Methods*, 2nd Ed.; Sage: Beverly Hills, CA, 1990.
20. Schwartz, H.; Jacobs, J. *Qualitative Sociology: A Method to the Madness*; Free Press: New York, 1979.
21. Taylor, S.J.; Bogdan, R. *An Introduction to Qualitative Research Methods: The Search for Meanings*, 2nd Ed.; Wiley: New York, 1984.
22. Tesch, R. *Qualitative Research: Analysis, Types and Software Tools*; Falmer: New York, 1990.
23. Weitzman, E.A.; Miles, M.B. *Computer Programs for Qualitative Data Analysis: A Software Sourcebook*; Sage: Thousands Oaks, CA, 1995.
24. Westrook, L. *Qualitative Evaluation Methods for Reference Services: An Introductory Manual*; Office of Management Services. Association of Research Libraries: Washington, DC, 1989.

Rare Book Collections

Andrew J. Berner
University Club of New York, New York, New York, U.S.A.

Abstract

This entry presents a history and definition of rare book collections, as well as a description of how they are formed and maintained. There are two major responsibilities that rare book librarians face in their role as stewards of these collections: collections must be made available for use, and at the same time, care must be taken to ensure that delicate, and often unique, materials are preserved to ensure their availability in the future as well.

INTRODUCTION

The identification of rare books as such and their segregation as distinct parts of general library collections are relatively recent phenomena. The origins of modern rare book collections are largely to be found in the eighteenth and nineteenth centuries, a time when book collecting came into its own as a private endeavor and when the antiquarian book trade developed to meet the needs of those private collectors and to create new demand for rare books. This led to an increased awareness of rare books as a separate entity within the general world of books and manuscripts, although certain book rarities had long been considered worthy of collecting. Incunabula—books printed in the period from the appearance of movable metal type (ca. 1455) until the end of the year 1500—were highly sought by collectors, as were other books and manuscripts whose age and other factors made them significant. Although the existence of collections of books had been in place for centuries in institutional settings, these were not rare book collections per se.

The earliest interest in establishing collections of rare books (i.e., books collected for their rarity) came primarily from individuals and particularly those individuals whose wealth and/or social standing made it possible for them to devote time and funds to such an activity and to relish the intellectual cachet that a fine collection provided. At the same time that the overall awareness of rare books was increasing, the identification of significant volumes, worthy of being collected, was made easier by the rise of modern scholarship and the modern system of academic training. These worked to create a body of knowledge of what constituted the key works in most fields of study, many of which fell into the category of rare books. In addition, research, which had long been recognized as a part of scientific work, came to be accepted as a necessary component of study in other fields as well. To support this

research, viable collections of source materials needed to exist, and again it was rare books and manuscripts that offered some of the best resources.

On the institutional level, the movement to segregate rare books and manuscripts into distinct collections, or even into separate libraries, developed most strongly in the United States, coming somewhat later to Europe and other areas. Perhaps this was because the age of the libraries involved was a major factor in the ease with which the segregation of these materials could take place. In Europe, for example, where many libraries had been developing their collections for hundreds of years, older volumes and volumes that were considered "significant," tended to have long been incorporated into general collections. Identifying them, locating them, and physically moving them was no easy task. In the United States, with so many collections being started and so many libraries being organized—particularly in the nineteenth century—it was easier to identify and segregate the rare materials where they were present or to work with the newly active antiquarian book trade to purchase works specifically to establish or expand a rare book collection; this was true particularly in academic settings, where such collections came to be seen as an important adjunct to the educational mission of the parent institution.

It was also in the United States that the term "special collections" first came into use to describe a particular type of institutional collection. This term has always suffered from an imprecision of meaning, a problem that is compounded by the fact that its definition has evolved over the years. Originally, a special collection was simply one that had a specific subject focus and was, thereby, "specialized." This topical focus remained important, although additional factors came into play over the years, such as the depth of the collection and the extent to which it included what might be considered the primary source materials within its given topic. Rare books would often

Encyclopedia of Library and Information Sciences, Fourth Edition DOI: 10.1081/E-ELIS4-120008780

be part of such collections, but the collections included much else as well. Additional formats might include, for example, photographs, ephemera, manuscripts, prints, drawings, and various forms of realia. To add to the confusion, the term "special collection" is, at times, used synonymously with the term "rare book collection, " or they are used jointly, as in "rare books and special collections." Generally speaking, all rare book collections are special collections, but the converse is not true. That is, not all special collections are rare book collections. In all cases, the two—rare book collections and other special collections—form a complementary whole as a resource for scholarship and as a section of the library's collections that, compared with general library collections, is treated in a special manner for such standard library practices as acquisition, cataloging, processing, storage, security, conservation/preservation, and use.

WHAT CONSTITUTES A RARE BOOK?

In its purest sense, the word "rare" means existing in limited numbers, and this is certainly true of rare books as well. But although the number of copies of a particular book may be one factor in determining if it qualifies as rare, it is certainly not the only factor, and, indeed, it is probably not the most important one. The determination of whether a book qualifies as rare (i.e., whether it merits placement in a collection of rare books) is, in some ways, one of the purest applications of the law of supply and demand. Not only should there be a relatively small number of copies of a work, but it should be in high demand as well. As noted bibliographer A.W. Pollard wrote in his entry on "book-collecting" in the famed 11th edition of *The Encyclædia Britannica*, "...the rarity of a book devoid of interest is a matter of no concern."[1] The demand for a particular book, then, is determined by the level of interest or desirability it engenders, and that, in turn, is determined by numerous factors.

Laypeople often think that age alone makes a book desirable, and therefore rare, but this is not the case. Many fine press books of the twentieth century are considerably more desirable than are certain books of earlier centuries. Whatever their age, early editions of important works are generally considered desirable, as are works that brought to the world new discoveries and new ways of looking at things, whether geographic, philosophic, economic, scientific, or artistic. Illustrations can often affect the desirability of a book, particularly if they are early examples of a specific technique, if they are especially fine in quality, or if they were done by a noted artist. Controversial works tend to be desirable and are often to be found in small numbers if they were the subject of censorship when they were first issued. Even the place of publication of a particular work can affect its desirability. Early examples of imprints from a particular location tend to be sought,

although if the location is of relative unimportance, the desirability of its early imprints is likely to be only local. There are times when factors other than those intrinsic in the book itself have a great effect on its desirability. Provenance, for example, is a major factor. Books that were owned by famous people or were demonstrably parts of famous private collections have an increased cachet. Related to provenance are books containing notes or marginalia by famous people, particularly if they are commenting on a controversial or significant work. Presentation copies (i.e., books that have been presented to someone by the author and bear the author's signature) are desirable, the more so if the author is particularly famous, if the book is noteworthy, or if the person to whom it was presented is prominent. Many other factors go into determining desirability as well, including special bindings, limited editions or special printings, and, of course, the condition of the book. Clearly, there is more to determining if a book is rare than simply the number of copies that exist.

Because the determination of rarity involves the application of the law of supply and demand, it is not surprising that the monetary value of a book also plays a part in the decision whether to segregate it in a rare book collection. Here, however, we must tread carefully. Value is less a factor in determining a book's desirability than it is the product of that desirability coupled with the number of copies available. Still, because the value of a book is generally influenced directly by the aforementioned factors, value is often used as one of the primary guidelines in determining what books will be segregated. This can lead to difficulties as prices for mainstream books continue to rise. Although particularly expensive mainstream books may need to be segregated in some way to make them more secure, they are not necessarily rare and do not necessarily merit inclusion in a rare book collection. In addition, it is not unusual for all books of a certain age (e.g., eighteenth century or earlier) to be segregated into rare book collections, whether they have a monetary value commensurate with other materials deemed rare. Because there are no hard-and-fast rules about what should or should not be segregated and because "local" considerations often come into play, what is deemed to constitute a rare book in one collection may not be deemed so in another.

Whatever factors are used to determine whether a book should be segregated into a rare book collection, the fact remains that this determination is not a one-time event; it must be an ongoing process. Changing tastes and changing demand lead to a constant shift in what is considered rare. Occasionally, works previously considered rare are no longer thought to be so, having, perhaps, been discredited in some way or having been added to the rare book collection in error. Far more common, however, is for works previously considered mainstream to be shifted into the category of rare books. New subjects become popular for collectors, making previously unsought volumes more desirable, thereby increasing their value and making it more likely that they should be segregated. Because much of the decision making on segregating rare volumes is done on the basis of hindsight (i.e., identifying volumes that have already been deemed rare) the greatest challenge comes in recognizing what will constitute the next generation of rare books. This is a difficult—some would say impossible—task.

WHERE ARE RARE BOOK COLLECTIONS FOUND?

Generally speaking, rare book collections exist either as private collections owned by individuals or as institutional collections (or departments within institutional collections) in a variety of settings. Within these settings, collections of rare books can be of almost any extent, depending on the size and scope of the parent institution, the means through which the rare books were originally acquired (i.e., through purchase or as the result of the donation of a large discrete collection), and whether there is in place a program for the ongoing expansion of the rare book collection. Among the institutions in which significant rare book collections are likely to be found are national libraries, university libraries, public libraries, museum libraries, the libraries of learned societies, occasional special libraries, and independent research libraries.

National libraries invariably will have some form of rare book collection, as well as other special collections, generally quite large and with a depth that makes them of great importance as research collections. Not infrequently, significant parts of these rare book collections originated in the donation of important private collections. The British Library (http://www.bl.uk), for example, has been the recipient of numerous fine collections, including those of both King George II and King George III. The National Széchényi Library of Hungary (http://www.oszk.hu/eng), takes its name from the fact that it was founded with the collections of Count Ferenc Széchényi, and in the United States, the Library of Congress (http://www.loc.gov), was reformed after its destruction in the War of 1812, with the personal collection of Thomas Jefferson. Many more examples exist.

Colleges and universities have traditionally been the sites of a broad variety of special collections, including rare book collections, in part because they exist to promote scholarship and learning but also because they are the natural beneficiaries of the largesse of alumni collectors. Major rare book collections are to be found in most great universities, although occasionally these are actually independent research libraries that are affiliated with the university. Some of the most important rare book collections in the United States (and elsewhere) are to be found in university settings, including the Beinecke Rare Book

and Manuscript Library at Yale University (http://www.library.yale.edu/beinecke), the Houghton Library at Harvard University (http://hcl.harvard.edu/houghton), the John Carter Brown Library at Brown University (http://www.brown.edu/Facilities/John_Carter_Brown_Library), the Lilly Library at Indiana University (http://www.indiana.edu/~liblilly), and the Bancroft Library at the University of California, Berkeley (http://www.lib.berkeley.edu/BANC), to name a few.

Significant rare book collections are also to be found in many large public libraries where, again, they have often originated as private collections and are maintained and expanded as a means of serving the scholarly community. At times, public libraries have benefited from the involuntary transfer of collections as well. In France, for example, many public municipal libraries throughout the country boast fine rare book collections, the result of the confiscation of private collections and the collections of religious institutions during the French Revolution and the redistribution of those collections to public libraries where they could be made available to all. In Russia, Eastern Europe, and many other areas, similar redistributions of collections from private to public hands have taken place, although the decline of Communism in some areas has led to the return of some collections to their original owners or their descendants.

Independent rare book libraries are generally based on the collection of a particular individual, who creates a foundation or similar apparatus for the purpose of continuing and maintaining the collection for the future. Many years ago, Randolph G. Adams referred to this as "the wistful desire of the collector, great or small, to want his collecting work preserved," and further noted, "If a collector wants his scholarly work of collecting, as well as his books, conserved, he must look around and find, or erect, an institution in which that can be done."[2] In this way, private collections built over the course of a lifetime can be retained unaltered or even expanded. A few examples of such independent rare book and research libraries include the Pierpont Morgan Library in New York City (http://www.morganlibrary.org), the Folger Shakespeare Library in Washington, D.C. (http://www.folger.edu), the Huntington Library in San Marino, California (http://www.huntington.org/LibraryDiv/Library Home.html), and the Bibliotheca Bodmeriana, near Geneva, Switzerland (http://www.ville.ge.ch/geneve/culture/offre_culturelle/musees/musees_ca/bodmer/bodmer.html).

Although the above represents some of the types of institutions in which large and significant rare book collections are likely to be found, the fact is that small collections of rare books may be found in almost any institution with a library. Individual volumes or small collections of value and significance may be donated to smaller libraries, sometimes because donors believe that these "lesser" donations would simply be lost in a major library setting. Such donations can be problematic for an institution not prepared to deal with them adequately, and some small libraries will choose to sell rare book gifts rather than face the issue of properly securing, housing, and preserving them while making them available for use. Such a decision is problematic at best, because it ensures that the library will not be considered for donations—small or large—in the future.

A DELICATE BALANCE

Although the owners of personal collections of rare books may or may not make their collections available to the public as they see fit, those who work with public or quasi-public collections face an odd dilemma. There are two major responsibilities that rare book librarians face in their role as stewards of these collections, and, unfortunately, these responsibilities can sometimes be in direct conflict. Collections must be made available for use, and at the same time, care must be taken to ensure that delicate, and often unique, materials are preserved to ensure their availability in the future as well. The difficulty of this dichotomy may best be understood if we try to imagine a museum in which visitors are permitted to handle the exhibitions while curators are charged with ensuring that the objects remain intact for future use. To be sure, rare books are not simply museum objects; they are important for their content as well, yet they have much to tell of a nontextual nature (through paper, bindings, ink, endpapers, etc.), and this involves their being preserved in as close to their original state as possible. No matter how open one may wish to make access to rare books (and this desire differs greatly from country to country and from institution to institution), the fact remains that use and preservation are conflicting goals, and therein lies the quandary that stands at the core of rare book collections.

The variety of settings in which rare book collections are found makes it difficult to generalize about how such collections are handled, but it can be said that in virtually all rare book collections some restrictions on use are in place. Primary among these restrictions is that the materials consulted do not circulate. Also virtually universal are restrictions such as identification of readers, use only in a restricted and observable area, note taking only in pencil or using a laptop computer or personal digital assistant, and restricted photocopying. In some libraries, restrictions go well beyond these, and potential readers may be required to demonstrate a clear need to see the materials in question and to explain the purpose of their use—questions that would be anathema to most general collection users and librarians in countries that have a history of promoting open access to books and information in public or quasi-public hands.

The range of opinion on the efficacy of various restrictions on use is broad to say the least. At one end of the spectrum, we have those who say that serious restrictions are necessary to ensure that materials will be available in the future and who posit that librarians who are not vigilant in applying such restrictions on the use of rare books are performing a disservice to their profession. At the opposite end, are some mavericks who claim that such restrictions are outdated and call for the open use of all library materials on more or less the same basis as general materials, particularly in academic settings. Librarians who do not allow such access—who squirrel away collections to preserve them for the future while restricting use by current readers—are, they say, marginalizing the importance of such collections and are making it more difficult to justify the ongoing expense of maintaining and expanding those collections. In other words, they too are charged with performing a disservice to their profession. As with most such issues, the best path seems to lie between the two extremes, with policies reviewed to ensure that restrictions are not more severe than necessary but with some restrictions remaining in place to ensure the preservation of materials for future use. The "delicate balance" between access and preservation must be maintained, but it must be truly in balance, swinging too far in neither direction.

GROWTH OF COLLECTIONS: PURCHASE

The growth of a personal collection of rare books relies solely on the desire of the owner. Where expansion takes place, it is almost always the result of a direct purchase of materials from antiquarian book dealers and/or auction houses. The relationship between collector and dealer has long been a strong one and a special one, and this is true whether the collector is an individual or an institution, for institutions also use purchase as one of the primary ways in which rare book collections are expanded. It is not unusual for individuals or institutions to establish close working relationships with one or more dealers, who are made familiar with collecting needs and who use their web of contacts and connections to meet those needs.

In recent years, another web—the Internet—has altered the way in which some individuals and institutions make purchases for their collections. In part, this involves the relative immediacy and ease of e-mail contact with dealers and the ability to peruse the web sites of individual dealers, on which they have listed some, if not all, of their holdings. Of greater significance, however, are the multidealer sites in which one can peruse the stock of an international array of hundreds or thousands of antiquarian and second-hand book dealers with a single query. In theory, such sites make it possible for a potential purchaser to see, together, numerous listings for the same title (assuming that it is available from more than one dealer) and to compare prices. Unfortunately, with little standardization in entries, comparisons are not always easy, because the amount and quality of information provided differs from dealer to dealer. Nonetheless, with the Internet, determining the availability of an item—a process that could take days, weeks, or months in the past—and purchasing that item become issues that can be settled within seconds by just a few keystrokes.

The quantity of material listed is vast, but we must not assume that these listings will suddenly make it possible to find any item that one might desire for a collection. True rarities (i.e., items that exist in only a small number of copies, most of which already reside in institutional collections) will continue to be elusive. As Eric Holzenberg has written, "Although the Internet has certainly brought masses of hitherto obscure and unregarded material to light, and to some extent fostered a market for such material, traditionally scarce and desirable materials have not become more common: the Internet has not brought to light unrecorded copies of the Bay Psalm Book."[3]

Relationships with dealers will continue to be significant in the purchase of materials for rare book collections. The Internet—however, sophisticated it may become, and however successful may be attempts to impose standards on descriptions and condition statements to make them more useful—is still just a tool. Rare books cannot be purchased from the Internet. They are purchased from dealers who use the Internet as a means of reaching potential buyers in a more efficient way than through catalogs or storefronts alone. The number of dealers with whom a purchaser can interact is increased vastly through the Internet, and its use has already had a great effect on the ability to gather information on rare books and to make purchases. But for many purchasers, the establishment of a special relationship with a relatively small number of dealers will remain as another method for securing works to be purchased for rare book collections.

GROWTH OF COLLECTIONS: GIFTS

Purchase is not the only means by which rare book collections grow. Gifts are another major source of materials for collection development; indeed, in some cases, they may be the primary source of such materials. Gifts may be of money or they be in kind (i.e., gifts of individual rare books or rare book collections). Monetary gifts may—depending on the wishes of the donor—be used to expand a collection through purchase, as described above. Gifts in kind provide a more direct means of expanding collections, but there are issues involved in accepting such gifts.

Ideally, only unrestricted gifts (gifts that the library can accept and then is free to use or dispose of as it wishes) would be offered and accepted. The fact is, however, that potential gifts often come with at least some connected restrictions. Indeed, even when restrictions are not explicitly stated, it should be assumed that they exist. Most potential donors have at least a tacit understanding that

their donation will be added to the collection and preserved for the future. If this is not to be the case, it is important that the donor be so informed before the gift is accepted. Donors may agree to allow the sale of items that are not suitable for the collection to allow for the purchase of more fitting items. Nonetheless, they should be aware that such a sale, or the transfer of their gift to another institution, is a possibility (if, indeed, it is) before the gift is accepted.

When collections are offered, it is not unusual for there to be at least some explicitly stated restrictions. This is particularly true if the donor is the person who has amassed the collection. Such restrictions may be nothing more than desiring a plaque in the library, or having a collection shelved separately from other materials, or naming the collection for the donor. Sometimes, however, more onerous restrictions are included. In all cases, a determination must be made about whether the importance of the collection is such that restrictions will be accepted or if the donation should be refused. The latter is not an easy course to follow. It requires a great deal of tact and diplomacy, but under no circumstances should a gift be accepted with restrictions if there is no intention of adhering to them.

One useful tool in the gift process is a written gift policy. The gift policies of many libraries and special collections can be found on the Web. These can provide good examples and a framework for creating such a policy, though each institution's policy will need to reflect the specific needs of that collection. This should address such issues as the criteria that the library applies to the acceptance of gifts, the particular strengths of the collection, the areas in which the library is most seeking to expand the collection, the nature of unrestricted gifts and how they might be disposed of, and contact information for potential donors. Under no circumstances should the librarian, or anyone directly connected with the institution, which is to receive the gift, act as an appraiser. This must be done by the donor and at the expense of the donor to avoid the possibility of a conflict of interest.[4] This also should be clearly stated in a gift policy.

With a clearly defined policy, gifts need not become the minefield that they sometimes do but, rather, can be a major means of allowing for the expansion of rare book collections. For most collections, purchase and gifts will be the two primary avenues of growth, but for collections that are part of a larger library, there is a third means through which this takes place, and that is through the transfer of materials, which previously have been part of the general collection.

GROWTH OF COLLECTIONS: TRANSFERS

Although the first two methods for expanding a collection involve the purchase or acceptance of books known to be rare, this last involves the identification of materials that were not considered rare at the time they were acquired. The evolution of rarity is an ongoing process. Various factors cause the desirability of a certain work to grow, or this may happen as the result of the passage of time, the development of new scholarship, or the emergence of new fields. Accordingly, review of the general collection is called for on an ongoing basis. Unfortunately, this is a task that is extraordinarily labor intensive and ideally requires a level of expertise in the subject field involved as well as some expertise in rare books management. This alone makes it difficult or impossible for many libraries to undertake a comprehensive review and forces them to adopt alternative approaches.

For example, limited reviews can be undertaken for subject areas in which it is known that materials have greatly increased in value (i.e., desirability). It is also possible for records that are in machine-readable form to be scanned to locate those that meet a particular criterion or set of criteria. This is particularly useful in cases where books printed before a particular date are being sought, because such specific information is readily identified and isolated.

Alternatively, attempts can be made to educate general library staff about the types of materials that are likely to be candidates for transfer, in the hope that they will identify such materials in the course of the day-to-day operations of the general library. This also can be a daunting task, because there are numerous library operations during which such materials might come to light. These include circulation, cataloging, copy services, conservation, interlibrary loan, exhibitions, shelf-reading, retrospective conversion, and weeding. In large libraries, the number of staff who would have to be trained could prove a stumbling block. Nonetheless, where it is possible for "consciousness raising" to be undertaken with general library staff, such staff can be an invaluable resource in identifying materials for possible transfer to the rare book collection or other special collections. In any event, no matter what method is undertaken, in a rare book collection, which is part of, or affiliated with, a larger general collection, it must be understood that there may well be important works worthy of transfer that are to be found in the general stacks.[5]

DEACCESSIONING

The growth of collections, whether through purchase, gift, or transfer, is a vital factor in keeping such collections viable and active. There are times, however, when these ends can also be accomplished, in part, by the removal of certain materials from the collections. The deaccessioning of rare books is perfectly legitimate under certain circumstances. Most collections, no matter how focused they may be, end up with at least some materials that are

beyond the scope of the collection. In fact, the more focused the collection, the easier it is to identify such materials. In other cases, materials not previously out-of-scope may be deemed to be so if the institution has redefined its mission or focus to better serve users. To retain such materials would be a disservice, because they would no doubt receive the lowest priority in issues such as conservation or housing.

It is perfectly acceptable to deaccession materials under such circumstances, once it has been determined that to do so would not violate any prior agreements or restrictions that have been placed on such an activity by donors. If such restrictions are in place, legal action may be required before deaccessioning can take place, or it may simply be deemed unwise to pursue the issue. In any case, it should be kept in mind that the deaccessioning of materials—and especially rare materials—by a library is a process fraught with dangers and potential public relations disasters, and these should all be considered before a decision is made.

Efforts should always be made to ensure that those involved (and in public institutions that includes the public) are kept informed and are aware of the reasons for the deaccessioning, and the legitimacy of undertaking it as a means of strengthening the collection by eliminating materials marginal to the core mission of the library. Unfortunately, there may be times when institutions decide to sell all or part of their rare book collections to raise money for other purposes or to meet financial obligations in difficult economic times. This is a far less defensible undertaking and one that ensures only that the said institution will never again be considered to be the recipient of future largesse in this area. Nonetheless, it is a scenario that unfolds at times, particularly with institutions that have small rare book collections that have come largely as a result of gifts, rather than having been built through purchase. Having said that, when deaccessioning is done for the correct reasons and when it is handled properly, it can be a part of maintaining, and even strengthening, a viable rare book collection.

PROVIDING ACCESS POINTS

In any library, books are not simply acquired and placed on the shelves. In addition to the physical processing of the materials, they are analyzed or cataloged to provide access points that will enable potential readers to identify them when the need arises. Rare book collections are best served by specialized analysis and cataloging, which establishes standard access points describing content and publication while also offering detailed descriptive analysis of the books themselves. This recognizes that rare books are often studied as objects as well as for their content and that their physical attributes may be deemed significant to a scholar. Thus, the analysis of a rare book will often include access points for things such as bindings, typography, illustration technique, paper, provenance, significant associations, inscriptions, marginalia, and any number of additional copy-specific identifiers, depending on the knowledge and skill of the cataloger and on the importance, which the institution places on such in-depth analysis.

Remote access to resources and records worldwide is becoming greatly enhanced by the conversion of library catalogs to on-line systems, digitization projects, and the power of the Internet and World Wide Web to assist in finding and sharing such information. Standards being developed, such as the Dublin Core set of machine-readable descriptors (http://dublincore.org) and Encoded Archival Description (EAD) Document Type Definition (DTD) (http://lcweb.loc.gov/ead) address the uniform coding of metadata to facilitate Internet/WWW searching of information resources. Although these were not created with rare book collections in mind, metadata schemes such as Dublin Core and EAD have the potential, through standardization and rich description standards, to vastly increase the accessibility of information about materials in rare book collections.

ENVIRONMENTAL ISSUES

Although it is to be hoped that all library collections—general or rare—are housed in suitable environments, it would be naïve to assume that this is the case. Heat, light, and moisture are the primary enemies of books, and the control of these three elements is essential to the preservation of collections. Virtually all serious rare book collections address these and other environmental issues in determining proper housing for those collections. Smaller collections do what they can to provide a suitable environment, but all collections—personal and institutional regardless of size—should strive to meet certain basic criteria.

We have become aware, in recent years, of the problems inherent in the papers used in books printed after the mid-nineteenth century; papers made with wood pulp and chemicals react with moisture in the air and become brittle. The existence of this problem, undeniable though it may be, has become so all-consuming that it has led some to think that there are no problems with earlier books. This is decidedly not the case. All natural materials deteriorate, and books are made up of natural materials: paper, leather, cloth, vellum, parchment, ink, wood, sewing thread, glue; all of these elements of books are made (or have been made) of organic materials, which deteriorate over time.

Generally speaking, the lower the temperature the slower the deterioration, but it must also be kept in mind that rapid fluctuations of temperature are most damaging. It is usually accepted that temperatures of 68–72°F are best for books that are being kept in areas where people are also present, with temperatures as low as 60°F favored

for books that are kept in storage. Fluctuations of no more than 5° are considered acceptable.

Humidity, too, is a major factor in the deterioration of books, because fluctuations in moisture content cause natural materials to shrink and expand, thereby weakening their structure. For rare books, a relative humidity within the range of 40–55% is generally considered acceptable, although with both humidity and temperature, photographic materials have different requirements and should be dealt with separately from other rare books.

Everyone has seen the faded spines of books that have been on shelves where they are exposed to the sun. This is a clear demonstration of the destructive nature of ultraviolet light, and this same destructive nature is found in light that originates in sources other than the sun, such as fluorescent bulbs. If rooms with windows are used to house rare books, draperies or blinds should be used to eliminate direct sunlight, and ultraviolet filtered glass should also be considered. If rare books are in storage rooms, from which they are retrieved, lighting in these rooms should be activated on an "as-needed" basis and should not be kept on unnecessarily. Where fluorescent bulbs are used, steps should be taken to minimize ultraviolet exposure.

Other factors affect the deterioration of rare books and should be taken into account when deciding on storage and shelving options for such works. Glass or metal shelves that are properly treated to avoid harmful gases are generally preferable to wooden shelves. Air filters help to reduce the amount of dust and airborne particulates, which work their way into books and cause abrasion and other damage. Food, of course, should always be kept away from rare books, not only because of the direct damage that it might cause but because of the pests and vermin that it might attract. Mice, roaches, silverfish, and the like can cause major damage to rare books. We cannot eliminate all of the forces of decay, but we can minimize them, and if we cannot provide true immortality to our rare books, we should at least ensure that they last as long as possible.

SECURITY

Although not every rare book collection will be housed in a perfect environment, it is likely that virtually all rare book collections—where books that are recognized as rare have been segregated from the remainder of a larger collection or where rare books constitute the full collection—have been secured in some way. This may be anything from a small locked cabinet near the librarian's desk to elaborate vaults in which the treasures of major rare book collections are protected. Both personal collections and institutional collections face problems with security. Because personal collections are not necessarily heavily used by other than the owner, some form of physical security for the collection as a whole may suffice (depending on the size and value of the collection, more extensive measures may be required). In an institutional setting, however, there is always more to security than simply placing collections under lock and key.

Some of the previously mentioned restrictions that rare book libraries place on use are for security purposes. For example, identification of users and the use of rare materials only in specific areas and under observation by library staff are significant deterrents to theft. To assume, however, that any measure is completely reliable in preventing the theft of rare books from libraries would be foolish. Accordingly, any viable security program must address both the issue of prevention and the issue of recovery in the event of a theft.

If a theft occurs, the library must have means by which the stolen item or items can be identified. It has already been noted that the extensive analysis of a book is helpful to users in locating the specific work they need. Such detailed descriptive cataloging can also be useful in identifying stolen items. The inclusion in catalog records of unique, copy-specific identifiers can be most helpful. These would include such things as inscriptions, marginalia, extra illustrations, special bindings, or the presence of additional or tipped-in materials. The existence of such a detailed record can be a powerful tool in proving ownership should the need arise.

Copy-specific cataloging alone, however, is not sufficient, and other means are also used to establish ownership of specific materials. Generally, this includes one or more means of placing ownership markings on the book itself. Although curatorial practice frowns on any form of permanent marking, it is often seen as an acceptable compromise, given the difficulty of proving ownership of unmarked books. Bookplates alone are usually not considered sufficient, because they are readily removed. Markings should be permanent but should use archival materials. Special inks are available for this purpose, both commercially and—for U.S. libraries, archives, and museums—through the Library of Congress (http://lcweb.loc.gov/preserv/inks.html). Two types of markings are best used, one which is obvious and readily observable and another which is more difficult to detect. To maximize effectiveness, markings should be on a part of the book, the removal of which would significantly reduce the value of the book. This, again, is an issue that must be discussed with curatorial staff.

As with so many aspects of administering a rare book collection, it is best to have a written policy laying out guidelines for security and stating specific actions to be taken in the event of a theft. Security, though, involves more than protection from theft, it involves protection from damage as well. As with theft, preventive measures against damage are important, but it is equally important to be prepared in the event that damage threatens or actually occurs. To this end, a written disaster plan is essential.

Such a plan needs to address a broad range of issues relating both to disaster preparedness and to disaster response. Potential disasters may include fire, water damage (resulting from flood, leaks, or fire-fighting activities), earthquake, tornado, hurricane, physical collapse, and more. Because disasters, by their nature, require swift response, it is imperative that the plan be in place to ensure that decisions are not made under the pressure of the moment. The same is true of a good security plan. Hopefully, the reaction part of each will never have to be put into effect, but having these plans, being familiar with them, and ensuring that staff is also familiar with them and with the roles they are expected to play will go a long way toward guaranteeing the overall safety of the rare book collection, and ensuring that response—when needed—will be swift and proper. The website of the Rare Books and Manuscripts Section of the Association of College and Research Libraries (http://www.rbms.nd.edu) contains standards and guidelines relating to security and theft, as well as a variety of additional issues important to rare book collections. It also includes numerous links to relevant Internet sites of use to rare books librarians, scholars, and archivists. Among the topics covered are preservation issues, security, associations and organization, book dealers, digitization, newsletters and E-journals. Many of these, in turn, will lead to further links.

OUTREACH

As with most aspects of life, institutional support for the maintenance and expansion of rare book collections is cyclical in nature. In flush economic times, such support is more readily available than during an economic downturn. In addition, there are times when the intellectual pursuits supported by such collections are more highly valued than at other times. In periods in which support is difficult to come by, the administrators of rare book collections may be called on to justify the expense of these collections. It is unfortunate that concrete measurements, such as return on investment, are often considered inadequate to justify rare book collections, particularly when using the statistics most often quoted by libraries. There is no doubt that by normal standards of library use, rare book collections are expensive. The materials usually cost more to acquire than general library materials, they require specially trained staff and more exacting care and protection, and they are used less frequently than general collections. Research in the humanities and the social sciences—the type of research often supported by rare book collections—does not generally bring the kind of "breakthrough" or lifesaving results that scientific or medical research can yield and is, thereby, more likely to be questioned in terms of expense.

To counteract the difficulty that sometimes exists in presenting statistical justifications for rare book collections, the administrators of such collections should not be shy about taking advantage of what one might call the "mystique of rare books." There is a long history of rare book collections being seen as enhancing the prestige of the individual or institution to whom they belong. Particularly in academic settings, a rare book collection large enough and of sufficient depth to support research in a variety of subjects has often been thought to credentialize the institution and to demonstrate that the institution is able to provide the intellectual framework necessary for serious academic study and learning.

Another means of exploiting this mystique comes through various forms of outreach—methods for bringing rare books to the attention of the institution's users and potential users and subtly educating them about the importance of these collections. This is most often accomplished through a schedule of some type of exhibitions, although other forms of outreach exist, including educational programs, publications, special events, and anything else that demonstrates to the collection's "public" the significance of the materials to be found in that collection.

In recent years, another form of outreach has become possible. Through the technology of digitization, the content of some rare books can be made available to a vast audience via the World Wide Web. For many—particularly scholars and bibliographers—such images can never replace the actual object, nor are they meant to. But for those for whom the content of the rare book is more important than its artifactual presence, digitization offers a means of making the text available without causing additional wear to the original object each time it is examined. Although there are numerous issues involved in the issue of digitization, there seems little doubt that it adds one more potential tool to the outreach arsenal that rare book librarians will need to put into use to demonstrate the significance of their collections, in an effort to ensure the continued survival of those collections.

THE FUTURE OF RARE BOOK COLLECTIONS

Personal collections of rare books will exist as long as there are bibliophiles with sufficient disposable income to allow them to engage their passion for such collections. As the rarest materials find their way into institutional collections—and particularly large, wealthy institutional collections where they are likely to remain indefinitely—collectors may have to turn to "new" subjects on which to focus their collections. Incunabula in the traditional sense may no longer be a viable focus for one starting a collection on a limited budget, but the incunabula (i.e., the earliest books) of specific subjects may prove more attainable. Early writings on computers, television, the Internet, perhaps even the earliest e-books,

are likely someday to be the "stuff" of which rare book collections are made.

Although in the future, the actual hardware and software of our current technology may be the focus of collections of their own, at this point, they are tools—and increasingly important tools—in the maintenance and administration of rare book collections. Electronic and digital media allow for easy access to records; the Internet provides an additional source of acquisitions and also provides for the ready exchange of information on all aspects of rare books and collections; digitization offers a means of making rare materials available to a broader audience; technological advances even make it easier to control environmental issues. All of these technologies are going to continue to evolve, as will the effect that they will have on rare book collections, and new technologies are likely to emerge that will also have such an effect. Change is inevitable, not only with regard to technology but in relation to the overall concept of the rare book collection.

As that change occurs, specific rare book collections may not remain intact, and specific institutions or individuals may choose to divest themselves of these collections for a variety of reasons. In the case of institutions, those reasons are most frequently economic. Some smaller institutions may decide to divest themselves of collections that seem burdensome to maintain, with the materials dispersed through sale to larger institutions or to individuals. The collections of private individuals will continue to be offered for sale on a regular basis until such time as bibliophiles find a way to ensure that their heirs share their passion for rare books. The books from these collections—both personal and institutional—will not simply disappear. They will find their way, by purchase or as gifts, into other collections, again both personal and institutional.

Rare book collections in general are likely to exist for as long as there are those who understand the importance of preserving—both as objects and for content—materials that help to tell us about who we are, what we do, what we think, and why we think it. If those involved with rare book collections—whether as administrators, librarians, scholars, bibliophiles, or in any other capacity—help to spread such understanding, there is every reason to believe that these monuments to the endeavors of humanity throughout the centuries, these active and vital sources of knowledge, these essential aids to research, which are our rare book collections, will continue, effectively, forever.

REFERENCES

1. Pollard, A.W. Book-collecting. In *The Encyclopedia Britannica*, 11th Ed.; Cambridge University Press: Cambridge, England, 1910; Vol. 4, 221–225.

2. Adams, R.G. Librarians as enemies of books. Libr. Quart. **1937**. Available at http://www.people.virginia.edu/~pm9k/libsci/enemy.html) (accessed September 2001).
3. Holzenberg, E. Second-hand and antiquarian books on the internet. RBM: J. Rare Books, Manuscr. Cult. Herit. **2001**, 2(1), 35–46.
4. Association of College and Research Libraries. *Standards for Ethical Conduct for Rare Book, Manuscript, and Special Collections Librarians...*; American Library Association, 1992. Available at http://www.ala.org/acrl/guides/rarethic.html (accessed September 2001).
5. Association of College and Research Libraries. *Guidelines on the Selection of General Collection Materials for Transfer to Special Collections*; American Library Association, 1999. Available at http://www.ala.org/acrl/guides/sel-tran.html (accessed September 2001).

Reading and Reading Acquisition

Brian Byrne
Discipline of Psychology, School of Behavioural, Cognitive and Social Sciences, University of New England, Armidale, New South Wales, Australia; Australian Research Council Centre of Excellence in Cognition and its Disorder, Australia; National Health and Medical Research Council Centre of Research Excellence in Twin Research, Australia

Abstract

The role of written language and therefore of reading in society and in the individual is examined. This is in part achieved by an examination of the historical emergence of writing systems, which in turn is used to suggest parallels with the acquisition of literacy by the child. The hypothesized parallels are tested against empirical evidence on the normal trajectory of reading acquisition. Failures of acquisition (developmental dyslexia) are also discussed. Turning attention to skilled reading, some abiding issues, such as speed reading, eye movements, and the role of "inner speech," are canvassed. Modern computer-based models of reading are also introduced, models that are bringing the study of reading to new levels of scientific rigor and promise.

INTRODUCTION

Written language as an information source, with "reading" the name of the way we extract the information, is an integral part of the modern world. Instruments of social order (laws), agreements among individuals and groups (contracts), accumulated knowledge of the physical and social worlds (scholarship), and novels (creative works) are examples of the information and ideas stored and broadcast in written form. Thus writing and reading run deeply and broadly through modern social life. In this entry, I consider the status of written language in society and in the individual human mind. I trace how humans moved from oracy to literacy, considering as I do so the various solutions that have been adopted for how to record speech. I then draw some lessons from the history of writing for the processes that a child must go through in learning to read, and go on to summarize recent research on learning to read and on how this acquisition process might go awry. I then consider some of the salient features of skilled reading and the computer models being developed to account for those features. Among other goals, these models are being used to help illuminate why some children and adults remain so unskilled that their educational and economic opportunities are hampered.

THE LITERATE MIND

As pointed out earlier, the operation of many societies is now heavily dependent on print and reading—that much is beyond doubt. But we can also ask how profoundly written language influences the mind of the individual. How different would our processes of thought be without having a graphic form to capture spoken language?

One thing that we can assert with confidence is that mental operations that are close to the interface of written and spoken language are jointly shaped by both forms. The "interface" is where graphic symbols map onto the sound system of language (to be described in more detail later). We have clear evidence of tight integration of print and speech. For example, even though speech is the primary form of language for humans, both in evolutionary and ontogenetic terms, it can be shown that when literate people think about spoken words, they automatically (and often unconsciously) invoke the printed forms. Likewise, when literate people think about printed words, they invoke their spoken counterparts. Ask someone to tell you if there are more sounds in "pitch" than "rich" and chances are they will say "yes," an erroneous response that shows that spelling, the addition of "t" in pitch, influences conceptions of pronunciation. This influence is evident early in children's development as readers.[1] In other classic findings, adults are slower to acknowledge rhyme in spoken pairs with different spelling patterns, like "make" and "ache," than in pairs like "make" and "cake."[2] Adults are also slower to notice that words with similar spellings, like *paid* and *said*, do not rhyme than they are for words with different spellings, like *paid* and *head*.[3] They are also slower to agree that *rough* and *cough* share a spelling pattern than they are for *rough* and *tough*, showing the influence of phonology (pronunciation) on judgments of orthography (spelling patterns). There is even (anecdotal) evidence that orthography can override phonology and the consequent link to meaning. A regional airline that serves my town is called Rex (a contraction of Regional Express). It is indeed fortunate for the airline's proprietors that passengers do not "hear" another rendering of Rex, as "wrecks." Finally, and at a more scientific level, compelling evidence for the obligatory invocation of orthography

Encyclopedia of Library and Information Sciences, Fourth Edition DOI: 10.1081/E-ELIS4-120053433

in the mental machinery of literate people comes from the famous Stroop effect, whereby people asked to name the color of the ink in which a word is printed are massively disrupted if the word in question is itself the name of a color, such as when the word *green* is printed in red ink and the correct response is "red." This automatic triggering of the reading response appears in children as young as first graders.[1] All the evidence, then, points to a tight mental bond between speech and print, and to the easy facilitation of the act of reading even when it is not required, or worse, when it is actually disruptive.

So becoming literate alters mental operations. But how broad in scope are the effects of literacy in the mind? To get an answer to this question, we need to compare groups of people who are literate with those who are not but are in other ways similar, no easy assignment in the modern world with widespread literacy. But there are two well-known sets of studies that have achieved this goal, and the broad picture they paint is that being able to read and write does not have extensive effects on mental processes beyond the print–speech interface. A Belgian group has compared Portuguese-speaking adults who became literate later in life with some who have not had the advantage of reading and writing lessons, with both groups denied early literacy instruction for much the same reasons.[4] The data are too extensive to do justice to here, but the overall picture is that becoming literate stimulates an awareness of the phonological structure of language, such as becoming aware of how many individual sounds make up a spoken word, and has positive effects on lexical (vocabulary) skills, probably through the very act of reading. But there is little direct effect on other linguistic capacities, or indeed on cognitive processing more generally.

The second study is the classic volume of Scribner and Cole.[5] They studied the Vai people of Liberia, some of whom were unschooled, others literate in the Vai script, a syllabic one, and some in Arabic, an alphabet. The book is valuable on many levels, including its survey of the range of ideas concerning how, or whether, literacy "changes minds," on methodological issues such as disentangling the effects of schooling from the effects of literacy per se, and its empirical results. Abbreviated summaries of such works never do justice to their contributions, but here are some of their own words: "Reading and writing the [Vai] script was associated with specific skills in synthesizing spoken Vai…, in using graphic symbols to represent language…, in using language as a means of instruction…, and in talking about correct Vai speech…" (p. 244). But "our results are in direct conflict with persistent claims that 'deep psychological differences' divide literate and nonliterate populations.…On no task—logic, abstraction, memory, communication—did we find all illiterates performing at lower levels than all literates. Even on tasks closely related to script activities, such as reading or writing with pictures, some nonliterates did as well as those with school or literacy experiences" (p. 251).

Thus, the available evidence points to clear effects of becoming literate on mental processes relatively close to script, such as conceptualizing the sound structure of the language, and perhaps to some mental activities a little further removed from script, such as vocabulary enrichment through reading and the mechanics of teaching. But profound changes in human cognition do not seem to attend learning to read and write, despite the liberating consequences of having a substitute for oral memory in maintaining a society's sense of itself and gaining the facility to communicate across space and time.

A final comment in this section: Presumably, the bonds between written and spoken language exhibited by skilled readers are built on what neuroscientists refer to as the massive interconnectivity of the human brain, with approximately 60 trillion synaptic connections in the cortex. But the fact that tight bonds between speech and print do form, and do so with only a year or two's exposure to written language, does not mean that the two forms of language are cut from the same cloth. Indeed, all the evidence points to the primacy of speech over writing, and it is to this idea that we turn as we trace the development of literacy, within society and within the individual mind.

SPEECH AND WRITING

The human species is characteristically singled out not only for its intellectual powers but also for its language, the most complex and precise of all animal signaling systems. Note, however, that in evolutionary terms speech preceded writing by a vast margin, perhaps by as much as 100,000 years. Given the value of written language in modern societies, we can ask how humans got on so long and so well without it and why it took so long to emerge. We can also ask whether there are lessons to be learned from the historical emergence of writing and reading for the individual development of literacy in the child.

Preliterate Society

A society without literacy must, by definition, depend on oracy for the maintenance and transmission of laws, contracts, the accumulated knowledge of the physical and social world, and linguistic creations. At the core, feats of memorization needed to stand in place of written records, and they did. History sometimes affords opportunities to capture the changeover from oracy to literacy in mid-flight, as it were, and with thoughtful reconstruction, Ancient Greece presents us with one such opportunity. In his entertaining and scholarly treatise on the origins of the alphabet, Man[6] summarizes a case for the first alphabetic works, Homer's Iliad and Odyssey, being written versions of pre-existing recited epics. Man suggests that "they were more than after-dinner entertainment. They were works of genius, designed to tell listeners where their roots lay and what made them what they were. To do this, they included vast amounts of information, so much that Eric Havelock called them 'tribal encyclopaedias'" (p. 215). The tradition of "oral literature," a term that could be applied to pre-Homeric recitations and to any number of modern equivalents such as the Balkan bards of the 1930s observed by Milman Parry,[7] encompasses not only astounding acts of memory but degrees of improvisation set in an agreed metrical form. But once these performances were turned into writing, as began to happen as the alphabet took hold of Greek society, they became fixed. As Man puts it: "A living thing had been captured, and one world sacrificed to create another" (p. 228). The new world included what is now commonplace, the transmission of culture beyond the bounds of person-to-person contact.

Not everyone greeted this transformation with enthusiasm or even equanimity. Socrates famously objected to the emergence of writing on the grounds that it more or less froze language, drained the life out of words, and therefore doomed the dialog that was at the heart of the "examined life."[8] He also regretted what he saw as the destruction of memory, which in turn, by the discipline needed to build it, contributed to the examination of knowledge. And perhaps bizarrely to our conceptions of social opportunity, he saw writing as making knowledge available to people who were ill-prepared to use it appropriately. Maryanne Wolf's entertaining account of the history (and science) of written language[8] tells us that other scholars around the world had worries similar to Socrates, but that the advantages of the written word overcame these objections to see it spread worldwide.

The facility with which culture could be taught and preserved through face-to-face means, attested to in Greek and many other cultures, may itself have been a reason for the late emergence of script. The U.S. Census Bureau[9] provides estimates of the world's population at various points of time, and at 8000 BC, before anything recognizable as writing existed, estimates put the number of people on earth at 5 million. Scattered across Africa, Europe, Asia and the Americas, this allows for groupings of modest size, within the limit suggested by Aristotle as the ideal maximum of about 5,000 citizens (or 25,000 people) that could be "addressed by a single herald."[6] Population growth remained slow over the next 4000 years, reaching perhaps 7 million in 4000 BC, but increased to 14 million just a 1000 years later and 50 million by 1000 BC. These latter years were periods of high activity in the development of writing systems, perhaps no coincidence as pressure built for other means of preserving social identity with larger numbers aggregating in single locations.

Another reason for the long period of human history in which people spoke but did not write may have been human psychology in the sense of what comes naturally to human consciousness and what does not. We will return

to this theme in more detail when we consider theories of reading acquisition, but a sense of what is meant emerges already in the historical development of writing systems, to which we now briefly turn.

The Emergence of Writing

There are several classic and more recent sources on the history and comparative natures of writing systems, and readers are referred to two under Bibliography. Here, we consider aspects of the developmental progression that might illuminate the act of reading, and in particular its acquisition.

Sampson[10] provides the classification of writing systems of Fig. 1. The division between semasiographic and glottographic captures the difference between the direct versus language-mediated representation of ideas. Universal symbols valuable for the tourist trade, such as signs for male and female toilets, passport control, bus stations, taxi ranks, and the like, can be understood by people unfamiliar with the language of the country. They are not always entirely transparent in meaning, as a veridical painting would be, because their interpretations do depend on a degree of enculturation—a picture of a stylized woman could in principle signal many affordances other than toilet facilities, and when it comes to a red bar across an object depicted in a red circle, such as a cigarette, the social learning involved is considerable. But systems that were basically semasiographic did exist, and, as the aforementioned examples demonstrate, still do as elements of communication.

The distinction between direct and language-mediated representation of ideas is a broad-brush one in the context of more-or-less pictorial signs versus ones that stand for speech. But it is a distinction that appears in finer form within glottographic systems for they too vary in how directly the graphic elements map onto units of meaning.

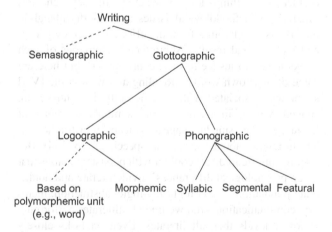

Fig. 1 Sampson's analysis of writing forms. Dashed lines represent forms whose inclusion as writing is open to doubt.
Source: From Byrne,[11] Figure 2.1, p. 28.

In a logographic system, should one exist in pure form, the graphic elements stand in for the words of the language, with no lower-level correspondences. To illustrate, consider logographic elements of English such as &, $, =, and the numbers, 3, 14, 26 (versus three, fourteen, twenty-six). These symbols appear in running text, but only as elements that do not decompose into a more basic currency of representation—thus, while *and* represents the three phonemes of the word "and," & does not. Nor do we typically think of them as standing for "sounds." If we did, as Sampson points out, we might be happy to accept *&rew* and *l&* for "Andrew" and "land." So such symbols are close to meaning in the sense that they represent the words of a language and not its sounds.

Phonographic systems do stand in for sound, and the phonology of language offers several possible sites for mapping graphic symbols onto phonological constituents. Fig. 1 shows syllables (basically a vowel surrounded optionally by one or more consonants), segments (or more commonly, phonemes, the individual vowels and consonants), and features (the building blocks of phonemes, such as the place in the vocal tract where an occlusion occurs in producing a consonant, the height and position of the tongue in producing a vowel). (We will not consider feature-based systems further except to note that features form part of the basis of the Pittman shorthand, and that the Japanese syllabaries represent the voicing feature with diacritics; other manifestations are very rare.) The election to use syllables or phonemes is probably not an arbitrary one available for languages on a whim. Some languages, like English, have a high number of syllables because they permit complex syllables, ones with several consonants on either margin of the vowel, like "strand." Others, like Japanese, are more or less restricted to single consonant-vowel sequences, like "ma," with consequently a modest number of total syllables possible. Hence, assuming each syllable gets its own grapheme, one would need thousands for English but less than 200 for Japanese.

As units of sound, syllables are no closer to meaning than are phonemes. But there appears to be a psychological difference in their accessibility to consciousness. There is a substantial research tradition demonstrating that young children can detect rhyme, a syllabic property of words, well before they can detect shared phonemes across words. Thus a child can tell you that "hot" and "pot" rhyme well before they can tell you that "hot" and "cat" end with the same phoneme, or even that "hot" and "hip" start the same.[11]

It appears therefore that humans possess a hierarchy of self-awareness about language. It proceeds from meaning to words to sound, and within sound, from the large-scale units of syllables to the small-scale ones of phonemes. This hierarchy matches the historic development of writing systems. The earliest graphic systems, those of the Sumerians and Egyptians which were flourishing around 4000 BC, were close to meaning in that they initially employed pictorial representations. With time, and with the demands of transcription by stylus into wet clay, the symbols became stylized, the pictorial origins obscured. At the same time, and with the aid of insights from the rebus principle, the new logographic signs came to represent first the words (rather than their meanings) and then fragments of the words' sounds, typically syllables. Syllabic writing gave way to phonemic in the supportive linguistic context of the Semitic language of the Phoenicians, where vowels were fairly predictable from the consonantal frames and the contextual support of meaning, so that symbols needed to stand for consonants only. The Greeks, perhaps around 800 BC, adopted the Phoenician consonantal alphabet. They also adapted it to a language where vowels were not conditioned by the words' meanings-in-context, and so where vowels needed their own symbols. A mismatch in phonology between the languages also meant that there were "spare" signs, such as the first Phoenician letter, alep, which stood for the glottal stop, absent in Greek. It became the letter for the vowel "a." Thus was born the complete alphabet, wrought to represent the full range of phonemes, a device that spread from that beginning to become the modal writing system around the globe.

Gleitman and Rozin[12] neatly capture the psychological progression that this history embodies:

> The history of writing… involves the use of successively more analytic units of language to correspond to the squiggles on the page (or rock). Change has always been in this direction: from the representation of ideas or meanings, to the representation of words and morphemes, thence to syllables, and then to the smaller alphabetic units of vowels and consonants…popularly called phonemes. No revisionists are recorded in history. Nostalgia for bygone scripts and more global units has been absent from the history of writing… (p. 21).

Not that all modern systems are alphabetic. Chinese, for instance, uses characters that basically stand in for the morphemes of the language, though semantics and phonetics figure in the design of the characters through radical-phonetic compounds (see Fig. 2 for examples). Japanese employs characters, originating with Chinese, along with two forms of syllabary.

Finally, within alphabets, different languages vary in how consistently they represent the phonology of the language. English is notorious for its unruly nature, with such historical relics as *debt* and *knight*, and traces of the dominance of meaning over sound with such features as the use of "s" to represent the plurals of both *cats* and *dogs*, even though the last sound in "dogs" is "z" and we have a perfectly good letter for that sound. Finnish is an example of a highly regular script, largely with one letter for one sound, and French is an intermediate case. These comparative properties also have implications for the course of reading acquisition, as described later.

Rare–Reference

Character based on a pictograph:

羊　　pronounced *yáng*, means sheep

Some characters that share the same phonetic:

蛘　　insect radical 虫 with *yang* phonetic 羊: pronounced *yáng*, means *"a kind of Weevil found in rice, etc"*

養　　eating radical 食 with *yang* phonetic 羊: pronounced *yǎng*, means *raise (livestock, children, flowers etc)*

洋　　water radical 氵 with *yang* phonetic 羊: pronounced *yáng*, means *ocean*

氧　　gas radical 气 with *yang* phonetic 羊: pronounced *yǎng*, means *oxygen*

痒　　sickness radical 疒 with *yang* phonetic 羊: pronounced *yǎng*, means *to itch*

Some characters that share the same radical:

洋　　water radical 氵 with *yang* phonetic 羊: pronounced *yáng*, means *ocean*

汗　　water radical 氵 with *gan* phonetic 干: pronounced *hàn*, means *sweat*

淌　　water radical 氵 with *shang* phonetic 尚: pronounced *tǎng*, means *drip* or *shed tears*

油　　water radical 氵 with *you* phonetic 由: pronounced *yóu*, means *oil*

海　　water radical 氵 with *měi* as phonetic: pronounced *hǎi*, means *sea*

湖　　water radical 氵 with *hu* phonetic 胡: pronounced *hú*, means *lake*

河　　water radical 氵 with *ke* phonetic 可: pronounced *hé*, means *river*

Notes:

1. Not all Chinese characters are of the "radical + phonetic compound" character type. There are also ideographs, simple and compound pictographs, borrowings, etc.

2. Both the radical and the phonetic component are guides only; sometimes the connection between the radical and the character's meaning is obscure; and sometimes geographical and historical variation mean that the phonetic component is quite far removed from the pronunciation of a character in present-day Mandarin.

Fig. 2　Examples showing components of Chinese radical-phonetic compound character types.

LEARNING TO READ

Lessons from the History of Writing

Following is a series of observations from the history of writing accompanied by implications for the child's emergence as a reader, with supporting research where appropriate.

Observation 1: The long period of human existence prior to the emergence of written versions of language shows that humans by nature talk and listen but do not write and read. In contrast to speech, written language is an invention, not an inheritance. Thus, a child will not know, by nature, that written language is possible. This needs to be taught. Parents who encourage their children to understand that print tracks speech are doing the children a service, laying a foundation for the growth of literacy.

Observation 2: Humans have invented several ways to write. Thus, when children do come to understand that language can be written, it cannot be assumed that they know how their language is written. This, too, needs to be taught, as evidence under Observations 3, 4, and 5 indicates.

Observation 3: Writing progressed, historically, from direct representation of meaning, pictorially based symbols, to indirect representation, language-based symbols. This progression may re-occur within the individual. The celebrated Mexican educationist, Emilia Ferreiro,[13] observed children who think that when one reads, one "reads" the pictures. A child's early attempts to write are often replete with pictographic elements, such as choosing to use a lot of letters to represent a large object like an elephant, and few to represent a small object like an ant, even when the words' lengths are the opposite (in Hebrew elephant is pil and ant is nemala[14]).

Observation 4: Glottographic systems first developed as representing the meaning units of words and morphemes. Once children accept that writing is language-based, they may assume that symbols stand in for elements of meaning, not sound. The present author[15] conducted experiments in which preliterate children, aged four and five, were taught to discriminate printed word pairs like *small* and *smaller* and associate them with the spoken forms. The young "readers" could correctly select which said "*cold*" and which said "*colder*" when challenged with a new pair (cold and colder) that preserved the morphemic relation of an adjective with its comparative. But with pairs in which the "er" represented a sound, not a morpheme, like *corn* and *corner*, they failed. That is, in learning that the letter group "er" discriminated the two training words, the children's focus was on its morphemic, not phonological, value.

The failure to understand the phonographic nature of writing can undermine reading growth, as self-reports from adults suffering from marked reading disability attest.[16]

> I had learned symbols...1 and 2 and 3...so I wanted that for five-letter words...I had this idea that...I was going to know just by looking...But there's no way you could possibly take all the words in the dictionary and just learn them by sight (p. 157).

This man believed that written words were related to their speech counterparts just as numerals are related to theirs, as unanalyzed wholes. His hypothesis obviously remained entrenched long enough for him to abandon that way of learning, but for one reason or another, he could not replace it with the more systematic alphabetic method.

Observation 5: The alphabet was the last writing system to appear, and has only been invented once, following a long period in which syllables were the speech unit of choice. We might conclude from this that syllables are more prominent linguistic objects and that the insight into the organization of the speech stream necessary for the alphabet's invention does not come readily to the human mind.

Two kinds of evidence support the idea that these aspects of history duplicate themselves in reading and writing development in the child. The first is that children's initial guesses about phonographic script appear to be syllabic. Once children abandon the idea that a single letter can stand for an entire word, their next strategy is to use as many letters as there are syllables in a word.[13]

The second kind of evidence is the voluminous research on what has come to be termed phonemic awareness. Starting with work cited earlier,[11] which showed that children are sensitive to the large-scale phonological unit of the syllable before the small-scale one of the phoneme, an overwhelming case has been made for the importance of the child's grasp of how speech is composed of segments, like the three in "and" or the four in "mist." This understanding is tested in a variety of ways, such as asking children to affirm that "mist" and "man" begin the same, or to say "fall" without saying "f." Preliterate children are generally incapable of succeeding with such assignments. Phonemic awareness as a variable measured on the cusp of learning to read predicts later reading growth, and measured during childhood and even adulthood correlates substantially with reading skill[11]).

A theoretical basis for the difficulty in becoming aware of the phonemic structure of the speech stream has been offered by speech scientists at the Haskins Speech Laboratories in New Haven. Starting with the observation that individual phonemes are integrated into words by a process known as coarticulation, such that the identity of each "sound" is smeared across the word rather than appearing as a discrete block of acoustic energy (see Fig. 3 for an example), Liberman and Liberman draw out the consequences for perception as follows:[17]

> Coarticulation...folds into a single segment of sound information about several successive phonemes.... This produces a very complex relation between the sounds and the phonological structure it conveys, but this considerable complication causes the listener no trouble; he or she has only to listen, for the phonological specialisation parses the signal automatically recovering the several coarticulated gestures that produced it...Given the automaticity of that specialization, the constituent phonemes do not ordinarily rise to the level of consciousness (p. 351).

This account, built on the motor theory of speech perception, so named because under it the true units of speech perception are the motoric gestures that produce speech, is advanced as explaining how we can be expert talkers and listeners without needing to be consciously aware of the

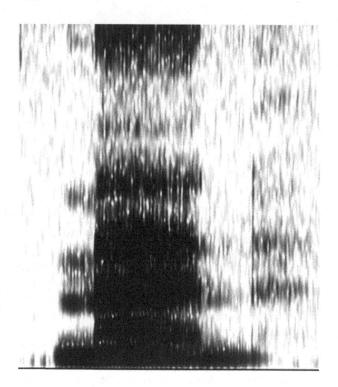

Fig. 3 Spectrogram of the word "man." Time is on the horizontal axis, frequency is on the vertical axis. The dark horizontal bars show concentrations of energy at particular frequencies.

phonemes that, linguistically, are the units from which words are constructed. Thus the child needs to have the existence of these units brought to conscious attention if they are to make sense of an orthography that exploits them, namely an alphabet.

Two other lines of evidence support the phonemic awareness hypothesis: One is that adults who have grown up without having been taught to read an alphabet are normally unable to perform tasks that reveal phonemic awareness such as deleting a phoneme from a word.[4] The second is that instruction designed to foster phonemic awareness in preliterate children has been shown in turn to foster early reading development, and indeed to leave traces of a reading advantage well into middle school.[18]

BEYOND THE ALPHABETIC PRINCIPLE

There is more to becoming a skilled reader in an alphabetical language than understanding the alphabetic principle and learning letter-sound mappings. That allows one to compute the pronunciation of printed words by blending the individual phonemes represented by the letters into whole words, as in "f" + "i" + "g" = "fig." But if that were all there was to it, reading would be a very tedious business. Further, users of highly consistent languages, such as Finnish, would all be perfectly adequate readers, yet they are not. (As an aside, there is evidence that during the formative stages of reading development, linguistic

consistency is a variable that affects progress. For example, one estimate has it that English-speaking children need nearly twice as many years of learning to establish basic decoding functions as do readers of other European languages.[19]) What is needed beyond basic decoding, for all readers, is a high degree of automaticity in the ability to recognize the words on a page such that reading speed can rise to a level where the reader can understand the text without diverting their energies into laborious decoding. At this level of skill, for example, a person should be able to read number words like *three* and *forty* as rapidly as *3* and *40*. This facility comes with increasing exposure to written words, although some children require more exposure to reach an appropriate level than do others, and it now appears that this difference among learners has a partial genetic basis.[20] We return to the genetics of reading acquisition later.

Much of the available research on the growth of "sight word reading," as this kind of automatized reading is often called, is summarized by Ehri,[1] who distils the evidence into a coherent and appealing theory of the phases children go through in achieving mature levels. They are, in brief: the pre-alphabetic phase, in which a child will form connections between print and words that are arbitrary, often based on some prominent feature of the print sequence, such as the large M in McDonalds; the partial alphabetic phase, in which a child can use some alphabetic knowledge to link print and speech, such as the names of letters to create spellings like LFN for "elephant"; the full alphabetic phase, in which the child can exploit letter knowledge to fully decode new words; the consolidated alphabetic phase, corresponding to what was described earlier as skilled reading, where words are recognized more or less as wholes, or if too long for that, on the basis of familiar sequences such as ing, str, and est.

Failures of the basic insight into the nature of alphabetic script, leading to low levels of accuracy in decoding letter sequences, and failures to achieve automaticity, leading to accurate but slow word identification, are presented as two causes of reading disability in the double-deficit model.[21] Wolf and colleagues identified verbal fluency, the speed at which a child or adult can reel off the names of a sequence of repeated items such as pictures of familiar objects, as a marker of the ability underlying the development of automaticity, and one separate from decoding skill. If decoding accuracy and automaticity are indeed governed by partially independent processes, we can see how there could be marked reading disability in highly consistent languages like Finnish, where accuracy is barely an issue, even in young children.

It should be emphasized that the issue of reading growth and reading disability across different languages is more complex than suggested so far. For one thing, it appears that there is a common core of cognitive deficiencies present to some degree in children suffering dyslexia whatever their language; deficits in phonological awareness, verbal short-term memory, and verbal fluency.[22] Despite this, there may be differences, such that, for example, children taught to read Chinese by rote may depend more on visual abilities than children learning alphabetic languages. But, as Caravolas says, "the study of dyslexia in languages other than English is relatively recent, and many questions remain."[22]

INDIVIDUAL DIFFERENCES

The Role of Genes

In discussing dyslexia, the focus has shifted from factors that are at work in learners of literacy in general, which I have argued are mirrored in the historical emergence of writing systems, to factors that generate differences among learners in how well and/or how quickly they master the skill of reading. Here the elephant in the room is genetics. Whether one contemplates cases of severe reading difficulties or variation among readers in speed and/or accuracy of reading within what could be called the "normal range," genetic differences play a major role. We know this largely from the study of twins, who are informative when it comes to distinguishing between environmental and genetic factors in determining variation in human traits. In the case of reading, this distinction is necessary because reading difficulties "run in families," and families share both environments and genes. Insofar as genes are the major determining factor, identical twins, who share the same genetic code, will be more alike than fraternal twins, who share, on average, half their segregating genes (genes that make people different). Statistical estimates of the role of genes from twin studies suggest that they contribute around 50–80% of the variability in reading skill, including the propensity for severe reading problems, with family-based and individual experiences contributing the rest of the variability. There are accessible and economic summaries of this research.[23,24]

Some of the genes that affect literacy growth have been tentatively identified, and a recent summary is available.[25] But relatively little is known about the paths from DNA to variability in reading, making the search for these paths a vital one for the future.

The Role of the Environment

The facts that learners bring their own genetic endowment to the task of learning to read and that these endowments are important do not mean that teaching practices are unimportant. If some new and revolutionary method of instruction were found that lifted the average reading performance by 50% but still left differences among readers, then genes would probably determine most of those remaining differences. Apart from this matter of principle, evidence indicates that early and intensive intervention to prevent and/or overcome reading problems can be effective for many if not all children.[18] This intervention often includes explicit training to foster phonemic awareness and the alphabetic principle. But evidence is accumulating that an early boost does not routinely translate into effective long-term improvement, and researchers are beginning to highlight the need for longer-term support designed to encourage children to keep engaging in reading.[26]

Differences among children in learning to read can thus be attributed to teaching practices to a degree, though apparently less convincingly than to genetic variability. They can also be attributed to some extent to the home and/or aspects of the school environment, which in twin research forms part of what is called "shared environment" because twins share the home and, for the most part, the school. In one such study, estimates of shared environment on tests of literacy skills in Grade 2 ranged from just 0.03 to 0.07, meaning that between 3% and 7% of the variability among children could be attributed to variability in factors that come under the heading of shared environment, such as home literacy and school attended.[27] Other research has put these estimates higher, especially where literacy instruction is quite varied within an educational jurisdiction; to put it the opposite way, genetic variation matters more when environmental variation is restricted through more uniform teaching practices.[28] Some of the effective aspects of the (modest) home environment influences are understood, such as the practice of engaging the child while reading to him or her, but so far these factors have not been fully elucidated.

Differences in Comprehension: Reading and "Higher" Language Processes

The goal of reading is not to pronounce the words on the page but to understand the meaning of the text. If a child fails to understand something he or she is reading, the problem may lie not in printed word identification but in the language itself. That is, failure might also attend just listening to the same words—there may be deficiencies in vocabulary, in parsing the words syntactically, in concentrating long enough to extract the gist, and so on. The interplay of printed word identification (call it D for decoding) and more general language processes (call it L for listening comprehension) is neatly captured in the Simple View of Reading,[29] which has at its heart the formula R (reading comprehension) = D × L. This multiplicative relationship between the more mechanistic aspects of reading and the "higher-level" linguistic aspects has proven to be robust in the face of substantial research.

Differences in semantic and syntactic processes are beyond the scope of this essay. However, reading researchers are alive to the need to integrate the investigation of the factors contributing to decoding with those contributing to higher levels of language in order to build up a complete picture of the psychology of reading.

SKILLED READING

Some Perennial Questions

Eye movements

> I took a speed-reading course and read War and Peace in twenty minutes. It involves Russia.
>
> —*Woody Allen*

This celebrated quotation successfully lampoons extreme claims about speed reading. There are, however, people who class themselves as speed readers, and who may read at a rate of around 600–700 words per minute, about twice as high as "normal" skilled readers. When they are studied in detail, it appears that these readers are capable of extracting the gist of text but rather poor at answering questions of detail, particularly in regions of text that they had not fixated. Normal readers asked to "skim" text exhibit eye movements and comprehension patterns similar to speed readers, so there appears to be no great mystery about, and no great feats involved in, speed reading.[30]

Eye movements in reading have been studied extensively. In reading English, skilled adults tend to fixate on a place in the text for about a quarter of a second, to fixate on most words (94 fixations per 100 words), and to regress (move their eyes back) around 14% of total eye movements. In a single fixation readers can process around 3–4 letters to the left of the fixation point and up to 15 to the right, although in Hebrew, which is read right to left, the asymmetry is reversed. In Chinese, where each character contains more information than each letter in an alphabet, the span is around 1 and 3 characters from fixation. Foveal vision, where acuity is high, subtends about 2° of visual angle, the parafovea extending out about 5° on either side of fixation point. Some information is gained from the letters included in the parafoveal range, though the further out in the periphery the less information—mostly just word length.

Between fixations, eye movements, known as saccades, suppress visual information. They tend to occur across 7–8 letter spaces on average (though with a large range of 1 to around 25 letters), and take between 20 and 40 ms (thousandths of a second). When words are skipped, they are mostly function words (articles, prepositions, and the like) rather than content words (nouns, verbs, adjectives), because function words tend to be shorter and more predictable.

During literacy development, fixation duration, number of fixations per 100 words, and proportion of regressions all drop with increasing age and therefore reading skill, as would be expected. Abnormal patterns of eye movements can be observed in dyslexia (longer and more frequent fixations, shorter saccades, and more regressions), but these appear to be more a consequence than a cause of reading disability as the dyslexic person struggles with word identification and text comprehension. For a recent, extended summary of much of this eye movement research, see Rayner et al.[31]

Phonology and reading

Another abiding issue is whether during reading the progression is from print to inner speech to meaning, or if meaning can be accessed directly from print. For 100 years imaginative experimental techniques have been created and harnessed to support either the mediated or direct accounts of word recognition from print, with no compelling conclusion. Most recently, the question has been finessed to some extent by the proposal that in skilled readers orthography, phonology, and semantics (word meanings) are integrated into a fully interactive system, with automatic feedback among them once one is activated (e.g., orthography by the act of reading, or phonology by the act of listening). The massive interconnectivity of the human brain, mentioned previously, allows for such a system to develop. If this is an accurate description of how things work, then it is not a matter of a causal chain in one direction (e.g., orthography to phonology to meaning) but an almost simultaneous activation of all three systems. Empirical evidence indicates that this can happen very quickly, with the phonological code for a word coming into play within about 20 ms of seeing its printed form. Recall also the evidence presented earlier for the influence of spelling on conceptions of the sound of words (e.g., that there are more sounds in "pitch" than "rich"), evidence that is consistent with this multiple activation model. On the other side of the coin, there is evidence that reading aloud a word with multiple pronunciations, such as tear, is slower than reading one with a single pronunciation, such as bear, indicating that the existence of competing pronunciations interferes with reading the word aloud.[32]

COMPUTER MODELS OF SKILLED READING

In much of modern psychology computers are being used to model human behavior, and reading is no exception. The goal of this endeavor is not to replace human with computer reading (though text-to-speech programs do have that facility), but to understand the act of reading better. There are several widely agreed virtues of trying to model reading with a computer program.[33] First, a theory of how reading proceeds must be very explicit if it is to be successfully turned into a program—and trying to do so will expose any parts of the theory that are not sufficiently precise. Second, once such a program has been written, its performance can be compared with that of humans, and adjusted to make it conform better if the match is poor. Third, as often happens, more than one simulation can be written that successfully mimics the behavior. This in turn should stimulate more refined descriptions of the behavior so that the models can be adjudicated.

Another advantage is that variation in reading skill can be modeled to test ideas about the origins of reading disability, including developmental dyslexia, encountered during reading acquisition, and acquired dyslexia, reading and spelling difficulties consequent upon brain injury or disease. Typically, this is accomplished by "damaging" one or more of the components of the models in ways that capture deficiencies hypothesized to underlie the acquired dyslexia in question and examining the new output for how faithfully it reproduces the reading profile of the dyslexic. For example, the models might be underpowered by reducing the number of "units" in the learning algorithm, or random noise might be added to mimic phonological imprecision.[34]

In this short essay there is not the space to summarize and evaluate current models. Suffice it to say that models with different computational architectures have been developed and tested. Some are connectionist. In these, connections are physically real objects created in an attempt to be "biologically plausible" and in which neural-net learning algorithms are typically employed—see examples for English[33] and French.[35] Others are nonconnectionist. They use programming codes with symbolic rules but similarly attempt to achieve biological plausibility by, for example, having excitatory and inhibitory connections between elements, just as the nervous system does.[33]

CONCLUSIONS

We began in prehistory and ended in the computer age. The uniting theme was literacy in human society and mind. Humans listened and talked before they read and wrote, and so do modern children. There are interesting parallels between the emergence of literate, historical societies and of literate, modern children such that the latter recapitulates the former. At the very least, the temporal primacy of spoken over written language at the social and personal levels should alert us to the fact that children are not born into literacy in the same way as they are born into speech, and that instruction needs to acknowledge this in practical ways.

Once literate, however, the structure of the human brain appears to guarantee a tight bond between written and spoken language, a bond which manifests itself primarily as mutual arousal of the two codes even in activities where only one is required. In normal reading, this bond serves the reader well, if for no other reason than that

mutual activation is fast, allowing reading to proceed with the efficiency and accuracy of speech. Modern models of reading exploit this bond, and are taking the study of reading to new levels, characterized by precision, testability, and clinical significance. Given the value of the skill of reading, and the personal and social burden of lacking it, continued scientific interest in the underlying biological and cognitive machinery can only be applauded.

ACKNOWLEDGMENTS

Helen Fraser, Richard Olson, and Jeff Siegel supplied helpful comments on a draft of this entry. Isabel Tasker created Fig. 2. I am grateful to all four.

REFERENCES

1. Ehri, L.C. Development of sight words: phases and findings. In *The Science of Reading: A Handbook*; Snowling, M., Hulme, C., Eds.; Blackwell: Oxford, U.K., 2005; 135–154.
2. Seidenberg, M.S.; Tanenhaus, M.K. Orthographic effects on rhyme monitoring. J. Exp. Psychol. Hum. Learn. Mem. **1979**, *5* (6), 546–554.
3. Polich, J.; McCarthy, G.; Wang, W.S.; Donchin, E. When words collide: orthographic and phonological interference during word processing. Biol. Psychol. **1983**, *16* (3–4), 155–180.
4. Morais, J.; Kolinsky, R. Literacy and cognitive change. In *The Science of Reading: A Handbook*; Snowling, M., Hulme, C., Eds.; Blackwell: Oxford, U.K., 2005; 188–203.
5. Scribner, S.; Cole, M. *The Psychology of Literacy*; Harvard University Press: Cambridge, MA, 1981.
6. Man, M. *Alpha Beta: How the Alphabet Changed the Western World*; Headline Book Publishing: London, U.K., 2000.
7. Parry, A. *The Making of Homeric Verse: The Collected Papers of Milman Parry*; Oxford University Press: Oxford, U.K., 1971.
8. Wolf, M. *Proust and the Squid: The Story and Science of the Reading Brain*; Harper: New York, 2008.
9. Wikipedia. World population. https://en.wikipedia.org/wiki/World_population (accessed March 2016).
10. Sampson, G. *Writing Systems: A Linguistic Introduction*; Hutchinson: London, U.K., 1985.
11. Byrne, B. *The Foundation of Literacy: The Child's Acquisition of the Alphabetic Principle*; Psychology Press: Hove, U.K., 1998.
12. Gleitman, L.R.; Rozin, P. The structure and acquisition of reading 1: Relations between orthographies and the structure of language. In *Toward a Psychology of Reading*; Reber, A.S., Scarborough, D.L., Eds.; Lawrence Erlbaum Associates: Hillsdale, NJ, 1977; 1–53.
13. Ferreiro, E. The interplay between information and assimilation in beginning literacy. In *Emergent Literacy: Writing and Reading*; Teale, W.H., Sulzby, E., Eds.; Ablex: Norwood, NJ, 1986.

Rare–Reference

14. Levin, I.; Tolchinsky Landsmann, I. Becoming literate: referential and phonetic strategies in early reading and writing. Int. J. Behav. Dev. **1989**, *12* (3), 369–384.

15. Byrne, B. The learnability of the alphabetic principle: children's initial hypotheses about how print represents spoken language. Appl. Psycholinguist. **1996**, *17* (4), 401–426.

16. Johnston, P.H. Understanding reading disability. Harvard Educ. Rev. **1985**, *55* (2), 153–177.

17. Liberman, I.Y.; Liberman, A.M. Whole language versus code emphasis: underlying assumptions and their implications for reading instruction. In *Reading Acquisition*; Gough, P.B., Ehri, L.C., Treiman, R., Eds.; Lawrence Erlbaum: Hillsdale, NJ, 1992; 343–366.

18. Byrne, B.; Fielding-Barnsley, R.; Ashley, L. Effects of preschool phoneme identity training after six years: outcome level distinguished from rate of response. J. Educ. Psychol. **2000**, *92* (4), 659–667.

19. Seymour, P.H.K. Early reading development in European orthographies. In *The Science of Reading: A Handbook*; Snowling, M., Hulme, C., Eds.; Blackwell: Oxford, U.K., 2005; 296–315.

20. Byrne, B.; Wadsworth, S.; Boehme, K.; Talk, A.; Coventry, W.; Olson, R.; Samuelsson, S.; Corley, R. Multivariate genetic analysis of learning and early reading development. Sci. Stud. Read. **2013**, *17* (3), 224–242.

21. Wolf, M.; Bowers, P. The double deficit hypothesis for the developmental dyslexias. J. Educ. Psychol. **1999**, *91* (3), 415–438.

22. Caravolas , M. The nature and causes of dyslexia in different languages. In *The Science of Reading: A Handbook*; Snowling, M., Hulme, C., Eds.; Blackwell: Oxford, U.K., 2005; 336–355.

23. Pennington, B.F.; Olson, R.K. Genetics of dyslexia. In *The Science of Reading: A Handbook*; Snowling, M., Hulme, C., Eds.; Blackwell: Oxford, U.K., 2005; 453–472.

24. Olson, R.K.; Byrne, B. Genetic and environmental influences on reading and language ability and disability. In *The Connections Between Language and Reading Disabilities*; Catts, H.W., Kamhi, A.G., Eds.; Lawrence Erlbaum Associates: Mahwah, NJ, 2005; 173–200.

25. Buitelaar, J.; Franke, B.; Pauls, D.; Poelmans, G. A theoretical molecular network for dyslexia: integrating available genetic findings. Mol. Psychiatry **2011**, *16* (4), 365–382.

26. Hurry, J.; Sylva, K. Long-term outcomes of early reading intervention. J. Res. Read. **2007**, *30* (3), 227–248.

27. Byrne, B.; Coventry, W.; Olson, R.; Samuelsson, S.; Corley, R.; Willcutt, E.; Wadsworth, S.; DeFries, J. Genetic and environmental influences of aspects of literacy and language in early childhood: continuity and change from preschool to Grade 2. J. Neurolinguist. **2009**, *22* (3), 219–236.

28. Samuelsson, S.; Byrne, B.; Olson, R.; Hulslander, J.; Wadsworth, S.; Corley, R.; Willcutt, E.; DeFries, J. Response to early literacy instruction in the United States, Australia, and Scandinavia: A behavioral-genetic analysis. Learn. Individ. Differ. **2008**, *18* (3), 289–295.

29. Hoover, W.A.; Gough, P.B. The simple view of reading. Read. Writ.: An Interdiscip. J. **1990**, *2* (2), 127–160.

30. Rayner, K. Eye movements in reading and information processing: 20 years of research. Psychol. Bull. **1998**, *124* (3), 372–422.

31. Rayner, K.; Juhasz, B.J.; Pollatsek, A. Eye movements during reading. In *The Science of Reading: A Handbook*; Snowling, M., Hulme, C., Eds.; Blackwell: Oxford, U.K., 2005; 79–97.

32. Van Orden, G.C.; Kloos, H. The question of phonology and reading. In *The Science of Reading: A Handbook*; Snowling, M., Hulme, C., Eds.; Blackwell: Oxford, U.K., 2005; 61–78.

33. Coltheart, M. Modeling reading: the dual-route approach. In *The Science of Reading: A Handbook*; Snowling, M., Hulme, C., Eds.; Blackwell: Oxford, U.K., 2005; 6–23.

34. Plaut, D.C. Connectionist approaches to reading. In *The Science of Reading: A Handbook*; Snowling, M., Hulme, C., Eds.; Blackwell: Oxford, U.K., 2005; 24–38.

35. Ans, B.; Carbonnel, S.; Valdois, S. A connectionist multiple-trace memory model for polysyllabic word reading. Psychol. Rev. **1998**, *195* (4), 678–723.

BIBLIOGRAPHY

1. Gelb, I.J. *A Study of Writing*; Chicago University Press: Chicago, IL, 1963.

2. Rogers, H. *Writing Systems: A Linguistic Approach*; Blackwell: Oxford, U.K., 2005.

3. Snowling, M.; Hulme, C. *The Science of Reading: A Handbook*; Blackwell: Oxford, U.K., 2005.

Reading Disorders

H.L. Swanson
GSOE, University of California, Riverside, California, U.S.A.

Abstract
This entry summarizes current research on reading disorders. Historical trends along with the most recent perspectives on the definitions, subgroup classifications, and causes of the problems related to reading are reviewed. This entry also provides an analysis of interventions to improve reading skills and types of interventions resulting in successful outcomes. This entry concludes by examining the main issues in the field of reading disabilities.

INTRODUCTION

The goal of this entry is to review literature on reading disorders and problems associated with poor reading skills. First, the variety of terminology and definitions are examined and the current definitions of the disorder and the classifications are provided.

Next, a more detailed description of the processes involved in good reading and possible causes of problems in reading are explored. Among these potential causes are impairments associated with basic processes related to word recognition, language processes, naming speed, and memory. The neurological basis of reading problems and some possible genetic factors to account for reading deficits are also discussed. Then we proceed to examining various scientifically based interventions and factors that are related to successful intervention outcomes. Finally, the chapter concludes by reviewing controversial and problematic issues in the field of reading disabilities.

The term reading disorders has been used interchangeably in literature with the term dyslexia, learning-disabled readers, specific reading disabilities, learning disabilities in reading, learning disorders in reading, or reading disabilities. For simplicity, we will use the term reading disabilities. Children or adults with reading disabilities have an unexpected failure in reading, but otherwise possess average intelligence and motivation in schooling considered necessary for accurate fluent reading. Reading disabilities are among the most common neurological-based disorders affecting children with prevalence rates of 5%–10% in clinics and about 17% in unselected population-based samples.[1] These incidence figures and the review of research reflected in this entry are primarily based on children who are having difficulty learning to read alphabetic language. There has been little consensus on the incidence of reading disabilities in nonalphabetic languages. Reading disabilities is a persistent chronic condition that does not represent a transient developmental lag. Depending on the definition, the incidence of children with reading disabilities in special education classes is conservatively estimated to reflect 2%–5% of the public school population. It is also the largest category of children served within the context of the label learning disabilities, and children with learning disabilities are the largest diagnostic group of children served in special education.

By definition, children and adults classified as having reading disabilities are those individuals with normal intelligence, but who suffer mental information processing difficulties. Children or adults with reading disabilities are a subgroup of a larger diagnostic category known as learning disabilities. The terms are used interchangeably because approximately 80% of the intervention research on learning disabilities focuses on reading.[2] Several definitions refer to reading disabilities as reflecting a heterogeneous group of individuals with "intrinsic" disorders that are manifested by specific difficulties in the acquisition and use of listening, speaking, reading, and writing. Most definitions of reading disabilities assume that the difficulties of such individuals are

1. *Not* due to inadequate opportunity to learn, to general intelligence, or to significant physical or emotional disorders, but to *basic* disorders in specific psychological processes (such as remembering the association between sounds and letters).
2. *Not* due to poor instruction, but to specific psychological processing problems. These problems have a neurological, constitutional, and/or biological base.
3. *Not* manifested in all aspects of learning. Such individuals' psychological processing deficits depress only a limited aspect of academic behavior. For example, such individuals suffer problems in reading, but not necessarily arithmetic.

Before discussing the causes and issues related to reading disabilities, a brief historical review is necessary.

Encyclopedia of Library and Information Sciences, Fourth Edition DOI: 10.1081/E-ELIS4-120053426

HISTORICAL TRENDS

In 1877, Kussmaul called attention to a disorder he referred to as word blindness, which was characterized as an inability to read, although vision, intellect, and speech were normal. Following Kussmaul's contribution, several cases of reading difficulties acquired by adults due to cerebral lesions, mostly involving the angular gyri of the left hemisphere, were reported (see Hinshelwood[3] for a review). In one important case study, published by Morgan,[4] a 14-year-old boy of normal intelligence had difficulty recalling letters of the alphabet. He also had difficulty recalling written words, which seemed to convey "no impression to this mind." That case study was important because word blindness did not appear to occur as a result of a cerebral lesion. After Morgan's description of this condition, designated as a specific reading disability, research was expanded to include children of normal intelligence who exhibited difficulties in reading. Hinshelwood's[3] classic monograph presents a number of case studies describing reading disabilities in children of normal intelligence. On the basis of those observations, Hinshelwood inferred that reading problems of those children were related to a "pathological condition of the visual memory center" (p. 21).

Researchers from the 1900s to the 1940s generally viewed reading difficulties as being associated with structural damage to portions of the brain that supported visual memory (e.g., see Geschwind[5] for a review; also see Monroe[6]). A contrasting position was provided by Orton,[7,8] who suggested that reading disabilities were reflective of a neurological maturational lag resulting from a delayed lateral cerebral dominance for language. Orton described the phenomenon of a selective loss or diminished capacity to remember words as strephosymbolia (twisted symbols). Orton[8] noted that "although these children show many more errors of a wide variety of kinds it is clear that their difficulty is not in hearing and not in speech mechanism, but in recalling words previously heard again or used in speech, and that one of the outstanding obstacles to such recall is remembering all of the sounds in their proper order" (p. 147).

Orton stated that such children with reading disabilities had major difficulties in "recalling the printed word in terms of its spatial sequence of proper order in space" (p. 148). Thus, for Orton, reading difficulties in children with reading disabilities were seen as reflecting spatial sequences in visual memory or temporal sequences in auditory memory. However, it is important to note the conceptual foundation for much of Orton's research was challenged in the 1970s (see Vellutino).[9] Today reading difficulties are viewed primarily as language problems and memory difficulties (e.g., see Stanovich and Siegel).[10] Memory difficulties are popularly conceptualized in terms of difficulties in language processes.

SUBGROUPS OF READING DISABILITIES

The heterogeneity of performance of individuals with reading problems has led to some confusion in the field and has prompted researchers to theorize the existence of distinct subtypes of reading disabilities.[11–13] In their recent examination of the current state and perspectives on learning disabilities, Fletcher et al.[11] proposed the existence of three types of reading disability. The first type is associated with problems in word recognition and spelling. The second form refers to difficulties in reading comprehension. Finally, the third type includes individuals who experience difficulty in reading fluency and poor automaticity of word reading.

The largest number of students with reading disabilities demonstrates problems on word level recognition. It is the most common and best understood form of reading disability and is associated with deficits in phonological awareness (the ability to hear and manipulate sounds in words and understand the sound structure of language), automatized rapid naming, and verbal working memory. However, a subset of students with reading disabilities who have intact word recognition skills show deficits in reading comprehension. This type of disability is related to problems in oral language and working memory. (Working memory is the capacity to integrate new information with old information when high demands are made on attention.) Finally, a group of students with average word decoding skills differ in reading fluency. These individuals have average word recognition accuracy but a slow reading rate.

A prominent study by Morris and colleagues[12] explored the variability of reading disability subtypes in a large group of 7–9-year-old children with reading problems. Based on the results of their study, several reading subtypes emerged: two subtypes without reading disability, five subtypes with specific reading disability, and two as "globally deficient," in the sense that performance across all measures was very low. Five specific reading disability subgroups varied with regard to phonological (working) memory and rapid naming. Six of the reading disability groups exhibited deficits in phonological awareness skills. The authors concluded that children with reading disabilities could be differentiated from the "garden variety" poor readers on the basis of their vocabulary level, which was in the average range for children with specific reading disabilities.

Overall, Morris and colleagues' work on subtyping reading disabilities is consistent with the phonological processing hypothesis, which postulates that problems in the phonological domain account for reading difficulties. These phonological problems either occur in isolation or co-occur with problems in other cognitive domains.

Other subtype studies tested whether good and poor readers could be differentiated on their performance on memory-related measures. For instance, Swanson[13] examined individual differences in several forms of memory of students with and without reading disabilities. Although several subgroups with different profiles emerged, the results indicated that children with reading disabilities had low performance on memory tasks not because of reading, but rather due to inefficient working memory. Swanson concluded that "connections between reading and WM operate on a continuum of independence to dependence as reading becomes more skilled" (p.327).

ADULTS WITH READING DISABILITIES

Reading disability persists through the life span, and children with reading disabilities grow up and become adults with reading disabilities. As these young adults transition to a new stage of their lives, they encounter new problems and challenges at home, at work, and in the community. In adulthood, the implications of having a reading problem are different and not that obvious. Unfortunately, the general population today is still unaware of the specifics of reading disability, and because it is "invisible," the behavior of these individuals is often misinterpreted and not understood by people with whom they interact in the beyond-school world. Less research has been conducted with adults with reading disabilities than with school-age children and adolescents. The majority of research on adults with reading disabilities has focused largely on examining their social and emotional development, vocational training, transition to postsecondary education, and issues related to employment.

The Individuals with Disabilities Education Act of 2004 (IDEA 2004), the Americans with Disabilities Act (ADA), and Section 504 of the Rehabilitation Act define the rights of people with learning problems, including reading disability. Individuals with learning disabilities in reading are legally entitled to receive special services and appropriate instruction to help them cope with and overcome their learning problems and to adapt to the new environment. Such services may include workplace accommodations, extended time on tests and exams, or use and provision of assistive technology.

READING DISABILITIES AS A SUBCATEGORY OF LEARNING DISABILITIES

As mentioned earlier, a great deal of research on reading disabilities has been linked to a larger diagnostic category known as learning disabilities. The term learning disabilities was first coined in a speech by Samuel Kirk delivered in 1963 at the Chicago Conference on Children with Perceptual Handicaps. Clinical studies prior to 1963 showed that a group of children who suffered perceptual, memory, and attention difficulties related to their poor academic (i.e., reading) performance, but who were not intellectually

retarded, were not being adequately served in the educational context. Wiederholt,[14] in reviewing the history of the learning disabilities field, said that its unique focus was on identifying and remediating specific psychological processing difficulties. Popular intervention approaches during the 1960s and 1970s focused on visual–motor, auditory sequencing, or visual perception training exercises. Several criticisms were directed at these particular interventions on methodological and theoretical grounds.

By the late 1970s, dissatisfaction with a processing orientation to remediation of learning disabilities, as well as the influence of federal regulations in the United States (Public Law 94-142), remediation programs focused primarily on teaching the basic skills of reading, such as phonics and sight word identification. The focus on basic skills rather than psychological processes was referred to as direct instruction. The mid-1980s witnessed a shift from the more remedial academic approach of teaching to instruction that included both basic skills in reading and cognitive strategies (ways to better learn new information and efficiently access information from long-term memory). Children with learning disabilities, primarily in the area of reading, were viewed as experiencing difficulty in "regulating" their learning performance, especially on reading comprehension tasks. An instructional emphasis was placed on teaching students to check, plan, monitor, test, revise, and evaluate their learning during their attempts to learn or solve problems.

The early 1990s witnessed a resurgence of direct instruction intervention studies, primarily influenced by reading research, which suggested that a primary focus of intervention should be directed to phonological skills. The rationale was that because a large majority of children with learning disabilities suffer problems in reading, some of these children's reading problems are exacerbated due to a lack of systematic instruction in processes related to phonological awareness. This view gave rise to several interventions, which focused heavily on phonics instruction and intense individual one-to-one tutoring to improve children's phonological awareness of word structures and sequences.

From the turn of the twenty-first century to the present, assessments of reading disabilities have been linked to intervention. A method of identifying school-aged students with reading disabilities known as response to intervention (RTI) first establishes low academic performance and then determines if a disability is present. The RTI model is partially based on intervention programs that have distinguished children experiencing academic difficulty due to instructional deficits from those with disability-related deficits.[15] Federal regulations in the United States regarding the Individuals with Disabilities Education Act of 2004 have influenced the use of RTI by supporting a child's response to scientific, research-based intervention as a process for learning disabilities identification. In general, the RTI model identifies whether a student's current skill level is substantially lower than the instructional level (based on predetermined criteria: e.g., below the 25th percentile). Low academic performance is established using standardized, norm-referenced and/or curriculum-based measurements. After establishing low performance, empirically based interventions are implemented to determine if a disability is present. Student progress is monitored during the intervention. When a student does not respond to high quality intervention, the student may have a reading disability.

CAUSES OF READING DISABILITIES

Before discussing the possible causes of reading disabilities, it is necessary to highlight what good reading entails and some of the processes (when not operating properly) that may underlie or contribute to reading disabilities. Written words are symbolized representations of the spoken word. The ability to read depends on the acquisition of a variety of different types of knowledge and skills. Good reading ability assumes adequate language comprehension and fluent word identification. Most models of reading suggest that information is stored in our mind (referred to as coding) and can be transformed into units of spoken/written language. This stored information allows us to acquire information related to the spoken and written language. The storing and retrieving of language information is referred to as linguistic coding. Some aspects of linguistic coding involve speech codes or our ability to represent information in the form of words and word parts. This is referred to as phonological coding. There are other types of coding processes that are related to reading. Some of these codes relate to semantic coding that relates to our ability to store information about the meaning of concepts represented by words and word parts (e.g., -ing, -ed) and syntactic coding that is the ability to store word rules that set constraints on how words are organized in sentences. There is also pragmatic coding that is the ability to store information about conventions governing the use of language and how we communicate (in terms of changes in volume, pitch, intensity of spoken language). Linguistic and visual processes together also facilitate the establishment of associations of printed words. Visual coding refers to sensory or high level visualization processes that facilitate storage or representations of written words or graphic symbols.

Proficiency in reading would require the child to actively engage in all of the aforementioned coding processes. There is an "awareness" feature to the coding process, for example, *phonological awareness*, which refers to a child's ability to conceptually understand and have an explicit awareness of spoken words that consist of individual speech sounds (phonemes) and that are combinations of speech sounds (syllables). Such knowledge is viewed as very important in learning letters and converting the alphabet symbols to sounds. There is also *orthographic*

awareness, which refers to the child's sensitivity to how letters or words are organized.

Given all these particular coding process, several models of reading disabilities have emerged. Vellutino et al.[16] provide an overview of research on specific reading disabilities across four decades. They conclude that adequate facility in word identification, due to basic deficits in phonological coding (converting written letters and words into sounds, skills of segmenting and blending sounds associated with letters—what is generally referred to as phonics knowledge), underlie reading disabilities. These deficits in phonological coding are defined as an inability to use speech codes to represent information in the form of words and parts of words. In short, these individuals have an inability to represent sound units in one's mind. Based on the review by Vellutino et al.,[16] most cases of reading disabilities are due to phonological coding deficiencies rather than more basic deficits such as visual, semantic, and syntactic processing of information. There are some studies that have suggested that there may be some general language deficits in this population. Some of these general problems have been related to difficulties in attention, making association between sounds and visual shapes, processing verbal to auditory information or transfer, and working memory. We will briefly review some of the research programs that seek to determine the causes of reading disabilities.

Basic Processes Related to Word Recognition

Linda Siegel and her colleagues at the University of British Columbia have conducted several studies on basic processes related to reading disabilities (see Siegel and Mazabel,[17] Siegel[18] for a review). Her studies define reading disabilities in terms of word recognition skills that "all" children with reading problems have. A significant contribution of Siegel's program is her definition of reading disabilities. She suggests that the focus of definition should be at the reading recognition level and suggests that a cutoff below the 25th percentile or 20th percentile should contribute to the operationalization of reading disabilities. This work is based on the assumption that there is no reliable evidence to indicate that IQ plays a cognitive role in the development of reading skills. Reading-disabled children at all IQ levels have equal difficulty in phonological processing tasks, such as recognizing the visual forms of pseudo words, and pseudo word spelling. Work by Siegel indicates there are five possible processes that underlie the development of reading skills in the English language. These processes involve phonology, syntax, working memory, semantics, and orthography. Most of this research shows that difficulties in phonological processing are fundamental problems for children with reading disabilities, and these problems continue to adulthood. Three processes are critical in the analysis of reading disabilities: those related to phonological processing, syntax, and working memory.

Language Processes

Virginia Mann at the University of California at Irvine has focused on language processes and their relationship to reading disabilities (e.g., see Mann).[19] Her studies on language processing skills and reading problems indicate that poor readers have problems with phonemic awareness, with morpheme awareness, and with three aspects of language skill: 1) speech perception under difficult listening conditions; 2) vocabulary, especially in terms of naming ability; and 3) use of the phonetic representation in linguistic short-term memory. Several of these process share a common core related to phonological coding, which concerns the sound pattern of language. Based on comparative studies (e.g., American and German instruction), her research suggests that awareness of phonemes is enhanced by methods of instruction that direct a child's attention to phonetic structures of words. Instructional experiences alone are not the only factors that account for failure to achieve phoneme awareness. Some other factors are related to speech perception (i.e., the awareness of rhyme), working memory, and problems with morphology.

Naming Speed

Several studies by Maryanne Wolf[20,21] have found a connection between rapid naming of letters, numbers, and objects and reading disabilities. Slow naming speed marks a core deficit associated with reading disabilities. Her work has found strong relationships between rapid naming of letters and sound deletion (phonological awareness task). Rapid naming is associated not only with initial reading fluency but also whether there are any fluency gains after practice. Some research has investigated the role of rapid naming and reading achievement in languages other than English. The research suggests that slow naming speed is somewhat distinct from phonological awareness. Some of Wolf's work has focused on subtyping by strengths and weaknesses in rapid naming as well as phonological awareness. That research suggests a double deficit hypothesis, in which children can vary in terms of difficulty on phonological skills, rapid naming skills, or both of those skills. Georgiou and Parrila's[22] comprehensive review of the research on rapid automatized naming (RAN) and reading suggests that the factors that underlie the connection are unclear. Some researchers have attributed RAN to the coordination of attention, perception, memory, and lexical processes, whereas others have viewed it as accessing phonological information in long-term memory.

Memory

Lee Swanson and his colleagues[23] have researched reading disabilities by primarily focusing on short-term memory, working memory, and their distinction. Deficits in reading comprehension and problem solving experienced by children with reading disabilities are related to memory problems in a speech-based storage system and/ or memory problems related to specific aspects of a general executive system of working memory. The executive system focuses on the monitoring of information, focusing and switching attention, and activating representations from long-term memory. Problems in the executive system of children with reading disabilities are related to the inefficient mental allocation of attention and the poor inhibition of irrelevant information. Problems in executive processing are described in terms of limitations in attentional capacity rather than processing strategies. Because short-term memory has minimal application to complex academic tasks, the majority of his research on reading disabilities focuses on the relationship between working memory and complex cognition (reading comprehension, word problems).

Neurological Basis

Evidence from this neurological data suggests the disruption of the neurological system for language in individuals with reading disabilities.[1] Brain-based research in reading disabilities has focused on the planum temporale, gyral morphology of the perisylvian region, corpus callosum, and cortical abnormalities of the temporoparietal region. Although at this point in time it is difficult to summarize this research, the neural biological codes believed to underlie cognitive deficits in the reading-disabled seemed to be centered on the left temporoparietal region. Differences in the asymmetry of the planum temporale have consistently been found in association with reading disabilities. Specifically, asymmetry of the planum temporale is due to a larger right planum. A reversal of normal pattern of left greater than right asymmetry has been found in individuals with developmental dyslexia.

Recent studies by Sally Shaywitz and Bennett Shaywitz[1] at Yale University have found differences in the temporoparieto-occipital brain regions between reading-disabled and non-impaired readers. The converging evidence using functional brain imaging in adult reading-disabled readers shows a failure in the left hemisphere posterior brain system to function properly during reading. Some brain imaging studies show differences in brain activation in frontal regions in reading-disabled compared to non-impaired readers. The majority of this research has focused on the brain regions where previous research has implicated reading and language. The research shows clear activation patterns related to phonological analysis. For example, on non-word-rhyming tasks, reading-disabled readers experience a disruption of the posterior system that involves activation of the posterior superior temporal gyrus (also known as Wernicke's area, the angular gyrus, and the striate cortex). The research demonstrates a persistent nature of a functional disruption in the left hemispheric neural systems and indicates that this disorder is lifelong.

Genetic Factors

Several studies have addressed genetic influences on reading disabilities. This research suggests that phonological coding abilities have a genetic etiology. The Colorado twin studies support the existence of major gene effects on reading disabilities, although the precise information about the mode of inheritance is less clear. Some of the literature (see Svensson et al.[24] for a review) has found the localization of dyslexic gene sites (some of the gene sites have been attributed to chromosome 1, 2, 6, 15, and 18). Some research suggests that genes that contributed to nonword repetition also account for the genetic basis of memory span score. Petrill[25] reviews recent research showing that both genetic and environmental influences are important in understanding reading disabilities. The presence of significant genetic factors among is viewed as a starting point for addressing some of the important theoretical questions concerning the genetic and environmental contributions to reading disabilities. Petrill discusses a fundamental issue referred to as the "missing heritability paradox." He suggests that a considerable proportion of the genetic variants that influence learning disabilities (reading and math) may be genes that are infrequent within the particular population. Petrill's research team suggests that there are multiple genetic pathways and routes through which abilities and disabilities emerge.

SCIENTIFICALLY BASED INTERVENTIONS

In the field of reading disabilities, the term treatment or intervention is defined as the direct manipulation (usually assigned at will by the experimenter) of variables (e.g., instruction) for the purposes of assessing learning: 1) efficiency; 2) accuracy; and 3) understanding. Swanson et al.[2] have provided the most comprehensive analysis of the experimental intervention literature on learning disabilities, and specifically reading disabilities to date. Interventions were analyzed at three levels: general models of instruction, tactics used to convey information, and components that were most important to the instructional success.

In terms of general models, their synthesis of methodologically sound studies (those studies with well-defined control groups and clearly identified samples) found that positive outcomes in remediation reading were directly related to a combination of direct and strategic instructional models. These models included a graduated sequence of steps with multiple opportunities for learning over the content and skills, cumulative

review routines, mass practice, and teaching of all component skills to a level that showed mastery. The interventions involved: 1) teaching a few concepts and strategies in depth rather than superficially; 2) teaching students to monitor their performance; 3) teaching students when and where to use the strategy in order to enhance generalization; 4) teaching strategies as an integrated part of an existing curriculum, and 5) providing teaching that included a great deal of supervised student feedback and practice.

In terms of tactics, Swanson[26] divided studies into eight models based on key instruction tactics: direct instruction (a focus on sequencing and segmentation of skills), explicit strategy training, monitoring (teaching children strategies), individualized and remedial tutoring, small interactive group instruction, teacher-indirect instruction (teacher makes use of homework and peers' help for instruction), verbal questioning/attribution instruction (asking children key questions during the learning phase and whether they thought what they were learning would transfer), and technology (using computers to present concepts). The results indicated that explicit strategy instruction (explicit practice, elaboration, strategy cuing) and small group interactive settings best improved the magnitude of intervention outcomes. Explicit strategy instruction included two key components. One component included strategy cues. These studies included instructional components related to reminders to use strategies or multisteps, the teacher verbalizing steps or procedures to solve problems, and use of "think aloud" models. The other component of strategy instruction was elaboration. These studies included instructional components related to providing additional information or explanations about concepts and/or providing redundant text or repetition within text.

What makes an intervention effective regardless of its theoretical orientation or approach? Swanson[26] analyzed interventions at the component level to address this question. He and his colleagues[26] found that effective instructional models follow a *sequence of events*:

1. State the learning objectives and orient the students to what they will be learning and what performance will be expected of them.
2. Review the skills necessary to understand the concept.
3. Present the information, give examples, and demonstrate the concepts/materials.
4. Pose questions (probes) to students and assess their level of understanding and correct misconceptions.
5. Provide group instruction and independent practice. Give students an opportunity to demonstrate new skills and learn the new information on their own.
6. Assess performance and provide feedback. Review the independent work and give a quiz. Give feedback for correct answers and reteach skills if answers are incorrect.
7. Provide distributed practice and review.

They also found that some instructional components were far more important than others. For reading comprehension, those key instructional components that contributed in significantly improving the magnitude of outcomes were as follows:

1. *Directed response/questioning*: Interventions related to dialectic or Socratic teaching, the teacher directing students to ask questions, the teacher and a student or students engaging in reciprocal dialog.
2. *Control difficulty or processing demands of a task*: Interventions that included short activities, level of difficulty controlled, teacher providing necessary assistance, teacher providing simplified demonstration, tasks sequenced from easy to difficult, and/or task analysis.
3. *Elaboration*: Interventions that included additional information or explanation provided about concepts, procedures or steps, and/or redundant text or repetition within text.
4. *Modeling by the teacher of steps*: Interventions that included modeling by the teacher in terms of demonstration of processes and/or steps the students are to follow to solve the problem.
5. *Small group instruction*: Interventions that included descriptions about instruction in a small group and/or verbal interaction occurring in a small group with students and/or teacher.
6. *Strategy cues*: Interventions that included reminders to use strategies or multisteps, use of "think aloud models," and/or teacher presenting the benefits of strategy use or procedures.

In contrast, the important instructional components that increased the effect sizes for word recognition were the following:

1. *Sequencing*: Interventions included a focus on breaking down the task, fading of prompts or cues, sequencing short activities, and/or using step-by-step prompts.
2. *Segmentation*: Interventions included a focus on breaking down the targeted skill into smaller units, breaking into component parts, segmenting and/or synthesizing component parts.
3. *Advanced organizers*: Interventions included a focus on directing children to look over material prior to instruction, directing children to focus on particular information, providing prior information about a task, and/or the teacher stating objectives of instruction prior to commencing.

The importance of these findings is that only a few components from a broad array of activities were found to enhance intervention outcomes.

Two very important instructional components emerged in Swanson's analysis of interventions for children with reading disabilities. One component was explicit practice that included activities related to distributed review and practice, repeated practice, sequenced reviews, daily feedback, and/or weekly reviews. The other component was advanced organizers that included: 1) directing children to focus on a specific material or information prior to instruction; 2) directing children about task concepts or events before beginning; and/or 3) the teacher stating the objectives of the instruction.

Issues in the Field of Reading Disabilities

Fundamental problems of definition have severely affected the field of reading disabilities within the public school context. This is because considerable latitude exists among psychologists in defining reading disabilities. This latitude is influenced by social/political trends as well as nonoperational definitions of reading problems. The field of study is further exacerbated because the number of individuals classified with reading disabilities has increased dramatically over the last twenty years. Unfortunately, without reliable and valid definitions of reading disabilities, very little progress in terms of theory development will emerge.

A related impediment to advances in the field is whether students with reading disabilities perform any different than low achievers. Traditionally, studies that have studied children with reading disabilities have relied primarily on uncovering a significant discrepancy between achievement in a particular academic domain and general intellectual ability. The implicit assumption for using discrepancy scores is that individuals who experience reading problems, unaccompanied by a low IQ, are distinct in cognitive processing from slow or low achievers. This assumption is equivocal. A plethora of studies have compared children with discrepancies between IQ and reading with children who are nondiscrepantly defined poor achievers (i.e., children whose IQ scores are in the same low range as their reading scores). These studies found that the two groups were more similar in processing difficulties than different.[27,28] As a result, some researchers state that current procedures to identify children with reading disabilities are invalid.[29] They have suggested dropping the requirement of average intelligence, in favor of a view where children with reading problems are best conceptualized as existing at the extreme end of a continuum from poor to good readers. In addition, some researchers have argued that IQ is irrelevant to the definition of reading disabilities and that poor readers share similar cognitive deficits, irrespective of general cognitive abilities.

In contrast to the argument that children with reading disabilities look no different than other poor readers in cognitive functioning or intervention outcome, Hoskyn and Swanson[27] found in a synthesis of the literature that although children with reading disabilities and poor readers share some deficits in phonological processing and automaticity (naming speed), performance by children with reading disabilities was superior to poor readers on measures of syntactic knowledge, lexical knowledge, and spatial ability. Another important finding was that cognitive differences between the two ability groups were more obvious in the earlier grades. Perhaps more important, Swanson and Hoskyn[30] found that students with reading disabilities and low achievers differed in the magnitude of their responsiveness to intervention. After reviewing several intervention studies, the results showed that students who had low reading scores (25th percentile) but average IQ scores were less responsive to interventions than children whose reading and IQ scores were in the same low range (25th percentile) (also see Swanson and Hoskyn,[31] pp. 300–301).

One of the practical difficulties within the field is that students who are identified by a political notion of reading disabilities have very little resemblance to the description offered within the scientific discipline. Thus, in contrast to the arguments presented related to the validity of reading disabilities as a field, most researchers who study the processing difficulties of children with reading disabilities do not use the discrepancy criteria. The majority of researchers rely on cutoff scores on standardized measures that are above a certain criterion of general intelligence measures (e.g., standard score > 85) and cutoff scores below a certain criterion (standard score < 85) on primary academic domains (e.g., reading or mathematics). Researchers distinguish individuals with reading disabilities from other general handicapping conditions, such as mental retardation and visual and hearing impairments. Further specification is made that socioeconomic status, being bilingual, and conventional instructional opportunity do not account for depressed achievement scores. Such specification allows the scientists to infer that the learning problems are intrinsic to the individual.

CONCLUSION

Children and adults with reading disabilities have normal intelligence but have difficulties in phonological processing, syntax, and working memory. These problems manifest themselves by poor performance on word recognition and reading comprehension tasks. Poor performance is defined as reading scores below at least the 25th percentile on a norm-referenced reading test. There is a biological basis to reading disabilities that causes lifelong difficulties in reading. Effective intervention programs focus on the explicit teaching of word recognition and comprehension skills.

REFERENCES

1. Shaywitz, S.E.; Shaywitz, B.A. Making a hidden disability visible: What has been learned from neurological studies of dyslexia. In *Handbook of Learning Disabilities*; Swanson, H.L., Harris, K.R., Graham, S., Eds.; Guilford Press: New York, 2014; 643–657.

2. Swanson, H.L.; Hoskyn, M.; Lee, C. *Interventions for Students with Learning Disabilities: A Meta-Analysis of Treatment Outcomes*; Guilford: New York, 1999.

3. Hinshelwood, J. *Congenital Word Blindness*; Lewis: London, U.K., 1917.

4. Morgan, W.P. A case of congenital word blindness. Brit. Med. J. **1896**, *2*, 1378–1379.

5. Geschwind, N. The anatomy of acquired disorders of reading. In *Reading Disability: Progress and Research Needs in Dyslexia*; Money, J., Ed.; Johns Hopkins Press: Baltimore, MA, 1962; 115–129.

6. Monroe, M. *Children Who Cannot Read*; University of Chicago Press: Chicago, IL, 1932.

7. Orton, S.T. "Word-blindness" in school children. Arch. Neurol. Psychiatry **1925**, *14*, 581–615.

8. Orton, S.T. *Reading, Writing, and Speech Problems in Children*; Norton: New York, 1937.

9. Vellutino, F.R. *Dyslexia: Theory and Research*; MIT Press: Cambridge, MA, 1979.

10. Stanovich, K.; Siegel, L.S. Phenotypic performance profile of children with reading disabilities: A regression-based test of the phonological-core variable-difference model. J. Educat. Psychol. **1994**, *86*, 24–53.

11. Fletcher, J.M.; Lyon, G.R.; Fuchs, L.S.; Barnes, M.A. *Learning Disabilities: From Identification to Intervention*; Guilford Press: New York, 2007.

12. Morris, R.D.; Stuebing, K.K.; Fletcher, J.M.; Shaywitz, S.E.; Lyon, G.R.; Shankweiler, D.P. et al. Subtypes of reading disability: Variability around a phonological core. J. Educat. Psychol. **1998**, *90*, 347–373.

13. Swanson, H.L. Individual differences in working memory: a model testing and subgroup analysis of learning-disabled and skilled readers. Intelligence **1993**, *17*, 285–332.

14. Weiderholt, L. Historical perspective on the education of the learning disabled. In *The Second Review of Special Education*; Mann, L., Sabatino, D., Eds.; Pro-Ed: Austin, TX, 1974; 103–152.

15. Vellutino, F.R.; Scanlon, D.M.; Sipay, E.R.; Small, S.G.; Pratt, A.; Chen, R. et al. Cognitive profiles of difficult-to-remediate and readily remediated poor readers: Early intervention as a vehicle for distinguishing between cognitive and experimental deficits as basic causes of specific reading disability. J. Educat. Psychol. **1996**, *88*, 601–638.

16. Vellutino, F.R.; Fletcher, J.M.; Snowling, M.J.; Scanlon, D.M. Specific reading disabilities (dyslexia): What have we learned in the past four decades? J. Child Psychol. Psychiatry **2004**, *45*, 2–40.

17. Siegel, L.S.; Mazabel, S. Basic cognitive processes and reading disabilities. In *Handbook of Learning Disabilities*; Swanson, H.L., Harris, K.R., Graham, S., Eds.; Guilford Press: New York, 2014; 186–214.

18. Siegel, L.S. IQ-discrepancy definitions and the diagnosis of LD: Introduction to the special issue. J. Learn. Disabil. **2003**, *36*, 2–3.

19. Mann, V.A. Language processes: Keys to reading disability. In *Handbook of Learning Disabilities*; Swanson, H.L., Harris, K.R., Graham, S., Eds.; Guilford Press: New York, 2003; 213–228.

Rare-Reference

20. Wolf, M.; Bowers, P.G.; Biddle, K. Naming-speed processes, timing, and reading: A conceptual review. J. Learn. Disabil. **2000**, *33*, 387–407.

21. Wolf, M.; O'Rourke, A.; Gidney, C.; Lovett, M.; Cirino, P.; Morris, R. The second deficit: An investigation of the independence of phonological and naming-speed deficits in developmental dyslexia. Read. Writ. **2002**, *15*, 43–72.

22. Georgiou, G.K.; Parrila, R. Rapid automatized naming and reading: A review. In *Handbook of Learning Disabilities*; Swanson, H.L., Harris, K.R., Graham, S., Eds.; Guilford Press: New York, 2014; 155–169.

23. Swanson, H.L.; Zheng, X. Memory difficulties in children and adults with learning disabilities. In *Handbook of Learning Disabilities*; Swanson, H.L., Harris, K.R., Graham, S., Eds.; Guilford Press: New York, 2014; 214–239.

24. Svensson, I.; Nilsson, S.; Wahlstrom, J. Familial dyslexia in a large Swedish family: A whole genome linkage scan. Behav. Genet. **2011**, *41*, 43–49.

25. Petrill, S.A. Behavioral genetics, learning abilities, and disabilities. In *Handbook of Learning Disabilities*; Swanson, H.L., Harris, K.R., Graham, S., Eds.; Guilford Press: New York, 2014; 307–328.

26. Swanson, H.L. Searching for the best model for instructing students with LD: A component and composite analysis. Educat. Child Psychol. **2000**, *17*, 101–121.

27. Hoskyn, M.; Swanson, H.L. Cognitive processing of low achievers and children with reading disabilities: A selective review of the published literature. School Psychol. Rev. **2000**, *29*, 102–119.

28. Stuebing, K.K.; Fletcher, J.M.; LeDoux, J.M.; Lyon, G.R.; Shaywitz, S.E.; Shaywitz, B.A. Validity of IQ-discrepancy classifications of reading disabilities: A meta-analysis. Am. Educat. Res. J. **2002**, *39*, 469–518.

29. Fletcher, J.M.; Stuebing, K.K.; Morris, R.D.; Lyon, G.R. Classification and definition of learning disabilities: A hybrid model. In *Handbook of Learning Disabilities*; Swanson, H.L., Harris, K.R., Graham, S., Eds.; Guilford Press: New York, 2014; 33–51.

30. Swanson, H.L.; Hoskyn, M. Definition x treatment interactions for students with learning disabilities. School Psychol. Rev. **1999**, *28*, 644–658.

31. Swanson, H.L.; Hoskyn, M. Experimental intervention research on students with learning disabilities: A meta-analysis of treatment outcomes. Rev. Educat. Res. **1998**, *68*, 277–321.

FURTHER READING

1. Fletcher, J.M.; Lyon, G.R.; Fuchs, L.S.; Barnes, M.A. *Learning Disabilities from Identification to Intervention*; Guilford Press: New York, 2007.

Rare-Reference

Reading Interests

Catherine Sheldrick Ross
Faculty of Information and Media Studies, University of Western Ontario, London, Ontario, Canada

Abstract

"Reading interests" refers variously to the following: an individual's interest in doing reading itself, as demonstrated by the amount of actual reading done; what a reader wants to read "about" as expressed by a list of topics or subject areas or genres that the reader reads by preference; or the elements in a text, sometimes referred to as appeal factors, that engage a particular reader with a text. Apart from examining bestseller lists and circulation records, two of the most direct ways to find out about reading interests are to ask the readers themselves and to ask the writers who have demonstrated their ability to interest readers by writing popular, bestselling books. Research on reading interests foregrounds the individual reader, whose interests, choices, tastes, reading behaviors, reading competencies, opportunities, frustrations, and pleasures in reading are given a starring role.

INTRODUCTION

Like the related terms "reading habits" and "reading motivation," the term "reading interests" has the appearance of a stable trait—reading interests shows up in the titles of numerous research studies and has achieved the status of subject descriptor in indexes. Depending on who is asking the question, reading interests refers variously to the following: an individual's interest in doing reading itself, as measured by the amount of reading actually done; what a reader wants to read "about" as expressed by a list of topics or subject areas or genres that the reader reads by preference; or the elements within a text, sometimes referred to as "appeal factors," that engage a particular reader with a text. Reading comprehension, though a different concept, is nevertheless related to reading interests. Whatever else it may mean, reading interest entails a necessary element of engagement, as the reader makes meaning from the black marks on the page.

Apart from examining bestseller lists and circulation records, two of the most direct ways to find out about reading interests are to ask the readers themselves and to ask the writers who have demonstrated their ability to interest readers by writing popular, bestselling books. Wilkie Collins, friend of Charles Dickens and popular nineteenth century novelist, said that the secret was to "Make 'em cry, make 'em laugh, make 'em wait." By the early 1970s, there was already a substantial body of scholarship on reading interests summarized in Alan Purves and Richard Beach's *Literature and the Reader*. Purves and Beach[1] sort research on reading interests into three categories: 1) the reading interests themselves, which are broken down to include "interests in content, interests in form, amount of reading and interests, book difficulty and interests, and literary quality and interests; 2) personal

determinants of interests which are taken to be "age, sex, intelligence, reading ability, attitude, and psychological needs"; and 3) institutional determination of interests which are taken to be "availability of books, socioeconomic and ethnic determinants, peer, parent, and teacher influences, and television and movies as determinants."

On examination, concepts such as reading interests/habits/attitudes/motivation/choices/preferences are hard to pin down and hard to distinguish. One thing we can say is that research on reading interests and cognate areas foregrounds the individual reader, whose interests, choices, tastes, reading behaviors, reading competencies, opportunities, frustrations, and pleasures in reading are given a starring role. In a nutshell, this field of research is reader-centered, in contrast with text-centered approaches that focus on the literary work or with structural approaches that focus on the social milieu in which the text is produced, distributed, taken up, and used. It puts the spotlight on reading itself within the broader communication circuit that includes the text, the author, the publisher, bookstores, and libraries, as well as social and technological factors such as copyright regimes, censorship, educational institutions, and technologies of printing and distribution.[2] It privileges the cognitive and emotional responses of readers themselves and pays special attention to voluntary reading rather than to required or assigned reading. It is interested in the "why" and "how" of reading as well as in the "who" and "what."

Why be concerned about reading interests? One answer lies in the link between reading interests, literacy acquisition and the demands for enhanced literacy in citizens of knowledge-based economies and societies. From studies of literacy acquisition, we know that readers learn to read by doing a lot of reading.[3] And what keeps beginning readers reading through the thousands and thousands of

Encyclopedia of Library and Information Sciences, Fourth Edition DOI: 10.1081/E-ELIS4-120043679

hours it takes to become a practiced reader? It's the pleasure of the experience itself—what some researchers call "intrinsic motivation." So in the field of education and literacy studies as well as in the field of librarianship, there is the desire to know what factors motivate people to want to read, help them acquire the reading habit, and keep them reading across the lifespan. The term reading interests points to a key question: what kinds of reading materials/types of stories/kinds of experiences give people sufficient pleasure that they choose to continue reading rather than put the reading material down in favor of some competing activity?

But almost from the beginning reading interests turned out to be a surprisingly complex phenomenon to tease out from other factors and pin down. In the first heyday of library-based, scientific studies of reading, centered at the Graduate Library School at the University of Chicago in the 1930s under the leadership of Douglas Waples, reading interests tended to be thought of as something that preexisted—a causal factor that preceded reading. Researchers asked people to indicate their interests from a set of topics such as history, biology, economics, politics, government, personal hygiene, etc. that could be satisfied by reading nonfiction books on the topic[4] and that therefore predicted (or ought to predict) reading choices. In more recent reading research, especially in the field of Library and Information Science, reading interest is more apt to be seen as the positive engagement that occurs during a reading transaction when there is an appropriate match between reader and text. This appropriate match often involves a number of intersecting considerations, including the amount of background knowledge needed by the reader to comprehend the text. It turns out that for some readers, the topic is key—there are readers who will read almost anything written about flying or about cooking or about sailing. But for many others, topic turns out to be one factor among many, some others being the feel of the book (upbeat and life-affirming or ironic and critical), pacing (a quick read or a dense, detailed text), setting (similar to the reader's everyday experience or very different), and the demands on the reader made by the language and literary conventions used.[5]

While studies of reading interests foreground the active role of the reader in making choices and acting on preferences, it has also been recognized for a long time that there is an interplay between the interests and choices of individual readers and the availability of reading material that reaches readers through the various gatekeeping channels provided by intermediaries—e.g., publishers' choices of what to publish and later to advertise as well as the decisions of bookstores and libraries of what to stock and make available. As early as the 1930s, landmark studies by Douglas Waples and Leon A. Carnovsky explored the relationship between expressed reading interests and actual reading as part of a larger research agenda on reading and libraries summarized helpfully by

Stephen Karetsky.[6] Carnovsky's *Library Quarterly* article, "A Study of the Relationship Between Reading Interest and Actual Reading,"[7] for example, reports that book readers tend to read most in areas in which they have previously reported most interest, but only when such books are as accessible, as well-advertised, and as readable as other books. In other words, availability and accessibility can trump interest.

RESEARCH APPROACHES TO STUDYING READING INTERESTS

A problem for researchers of course is that reading interests cannot be observed directly. They can, however, be inferred from what people *say* about reading in letters, diaries, and Web-postings and in response to surveys, questionnaires, and interviews as well as from what they *do* through their book-buying, book-borrowing, and participation in book clubs and reading groups. Each of these research approaches is partial and has its own limitations. Bestseller lists and circulation statistics tell us what is sold or borrowed, not what is read or how it is read. Autobiographies, diaries, letters, and to some extent even marginalia are composed with an audience in mind of future readers by whom the writer hopes to be viewed in a favorable light. Small case studies based on interviews or ethnographic observation of individual readers may be idiosyncratic and not representative of general patterns. Large scale questionnaires using national samples are generalizable but tell us only about averages and not about any actual reader. Nevertheless, taken together, a growing body of research using different research methods from different disciplines, including education, sociology, history, psychology, literary history, and library and information science has achieved considerable understanding of the reading interests of readers of the past and present.

Historians and literary scholars have taken the lead in studying readers from periods before the twentieth century. Literary historians have paid most attention to the reading interests of elite readers, in particular of canonical authors. They examine these authors' texts for evidence of literary borrowings and verbal echoes and they track down the books held in authors' personal libraries in the hope of finding underlinings of significant passages and marginalia indicating reader response. Bibliophile Nicholas A. Basbanes[8] has written entertainingly on studies that examine the "silent witnesses" to reading provided by library collections such as Leon Edel and Adeline R. Tintner's *The Library of Henry James*[9] or that focus on marginalia, such as the six volumes of Coleridge's marginalia published as part of a Princeton University Press project to publish all of Coleridge's writings.

The burgeoning field of history of the book, or "*histoire du livre*," has expanded our understanding of the reading interests and experiences of ordinary readers from various historical periods and geographical areas. In her introduction to a theme issue in *Library Quarterly* on retrieving the reading experiences of ordinary readers by means of library records, Christine Pawley[10] observed, "Still, some readers are more difficult to recover than others. Especially hard to access are the reading choices and practices of millions of 'common readers,' those with relatively anonymous lives and whom archival collections tend to ignore." Using census records, library catalogs and circulation records, subscription lists, estate inventories, advertisements, printing and transportation records, autobiographies, diaries, letters and other traces, book historians have tried to recreate a detailed picture of the what and how of reading of people in various different times and places. A notable example is William Gilmore's *Reading Becomes a Necessity of Life*,[11] which examines transformations in reading in rural New England from 1780 to 1835, as reading materials in the home grew from a Bible and Farmers' Almanac to an expanded mix of newspapers, periodicals and books, including fiction. Readers' letters to authors and to publishers have also proved a fruitful source of evidence of reading experience and reception. For example, Robert Darnton[12] reconstructed the Rousseauistic reading of Jean Ranson, an eighteenth century provincial French merchant, by examining his letters to the Societé Typographique de Neufchatel, a Swiss publisher of French books. Similarly, James Smith Allen's study[13] of fiction reading in France was based in part on voluminous archives of letters sent by a privileged readership of acquaintances to 10 French authors.

Marginalia has proved an unexpectedly rich resource for investigating ordinary reading. Cathy Davidson's account of nineteenth century American novel readers was based, among other sources, on the marginalia inscribed in copies of early American novels. About well-used books, she notes, "Broken boards, turned-down pages, and abounding marginalia . . . reveal patterns of reading, patterns of use, the surviving traces of an interpretive community long-since gone" through which "some of the early readers remain surprisingly vivid even after nearly two centuries."[14] English Professor Heather Jackson, in particular, has been a seeker-out of marginalia of all kinds, by exceptional celebrated readers and by common anonymous readers alike. An editor of the Coleridge project, she confesses, "Coleridge's marginalia converted me to writing in books."[15] In *Marginalia*, she examined some 3000 books annotated in English by various readers from 1700 to 2000 and made the claim that marginalia can contribute to the history of reading by revealing codes of reading of the period as well as by recovering the experiences of individual readers.

As we move to the twentieth century, an expanded array of research methods has become available to investigate contemporary reading interests. Using tools developed for surveys and polling, a large body of work focuses on the *what* of reading interests, often with the help of checklists,

reading inventories, or questionnaires. Survey research uncovers broad patterns by correlating various aspects of reading (amount of reading in various formats, preferred genres, reasons for reading, and source of reading materials) with demographic variables of sex, age, educational level, or occupational group. In contrast, ethnographic research based on in-depth interviews or case studies of individual readers provide a fine-grained picture of reading interests in the context of the reader's life. A notable example is Janice Radway's *Reading the Romance*, which used a combination of individual and group interviews and questionnaires to understand the reading experiences of romance readers. Although the term reading interests is nowhere to be found in the index, the entire book in fact explores the special satisfaction that romance reading provides to romance fans. Radway says, "This theme of romance reading as a special gift a woman gives herself dominated most of the interviews."[16] Also using interviews with readers, in *Children Talk About Books*,[17] Donald Fry presents vivid case studies of six child readers as the grounded starting point for discussing familiar themes relating to reading interests: why readers choose to repeat the experience through many rereadings of a favorite book; the role of strong topical interest in motivating a reader to stretch beyond his usual comfort level; the attraction of series books such as those by Enid Blyton; the enjoyment of story; the popularity of genre fiction such as horror stories; and the move from children's fiction into adult books.

Talking to actual readers, rather than generalizing from one's own experience, is especially important in the case of children and young adults. As Holly Virginia Blackford notes in *Out of this World*:[18] "How children themselves produce meaning is a particularly crucial area of study because child readers are, by definition, colonial subjects of a genre that is controlled by layers of adults and adult institutions (writers, publishers, marketers, critics, bookstores, libraries, educators, parents, and producers and marketers of commercial products and multimedia adaptations)." Blackford herself interviewed 33 girls, ages 8–16, from California and New Jersey, expecting to find that young female readers do identity work by reading fictional representations of characters like themselves and identifying with the protagonists. To her surprise, she found that despite "differences in race, class, age, family circumstances, reading preferences, and reading abilities, the girls' reading practices reveal a consistent pattern. They read for a good story, and a good story means one that they are *not* living—that actually looks *nothing* like the life they know."[18]

From an accumulating body of research, certain generalizations have been robust. Almost everyone in westernized countries *can* read—95% or more of young adults are proficient at basic reading tasks;[19] the problem is that too few readers are proficient at the more demanding reading tasks that are increasingly required in a knowledge-based society. Despite widespread belief that literacy skills are falling from some earlier golden age of reading, performance on literacy tests tell a different story. For example, the Canadian *Reading the Future*[20] found that there is an enormous improvement in literacy for those educated after World War II in comparison with those who completed their education before the war. Studies conducted over the last 50 years have been remarkably consistent in showing that the vast majority of the population reads something, about half the population reads books, and about 10–15% are avid readers. Occupation group and educational level are more important than age when it comes to predicting whether or not a person is a book reader. Younger people tend to read more than those over age 50; college-educated people and people with higher annual incomes tend to read more than those without a college education or with lower incomes; whites read more than nonwhites.[21]

Gender makes a difference at all ages: girls and women have reading histories different from those of boys and men. Researchers report that from as young as 2 years old boys and girls display different preferences, with boys preferring scary fairytales and girls preferring romantic ones—preferences that extended into adulthood where men read more westerns, adventure, and science fiction and women read more romance. Boys enjoy information books, humor, action stories, and science fiction, with Harry Potter books enjoying phenomenal success, even among those who normally don't enjoy reading.[22] Summarizing research on gender and literacy, Smith and Wilhelm[23] note, among other things, that girls understand narrative texts and most expository texts significantly better than boys do; that boys value reading as an activity less than do girls; and significantly more boys than girls call themselves nonreaders. To build guy-friendly school library collections, Patrick Jones and his colleagues[24] recommend spending a little less on novels and investing in magazines, graphic novels, comics, joke books, newspapers, books with colored illustrations, and nonfiction in areas of high interest such as sports, vehicles, etc. On average, girls learn to read sooner than boys and with more facility; they read more and they are more apt than boys to report that they enjoy reading for pleasure. As school age readers get older, there is a steady decline in the percentages of both boys and girls who say they enjoy reading and do it voluntarily for fun, with an accelerated drop-off around age 12 or 13. Among adult readers, women read more than men, particularly more fiction. Women are much more likely than men to belong to reading groups or book clubs: Jenny Hartley found that about 65% of reading groups are women, 28% mixed, and 6% men only.[25] Elizabeth Long's booklength study of white women's reading groups in Houston, Texas[26] suggests that, for these women, reading is fundamentally a social activity and book club participation a way of reflecting on the meaning of their lives in relation to others.

Reading preferences are idiosyncratic and individualistic, emerging from what Ruth Strang[27] has called "a central core or radix" that determines any individual's

pattern of reading. Popular fiction, particularly detective fiction/mystery, science fiction/fantasy, and romance, accounts for a large proportion of what people say they like reading as well as what they actually do buy and borrow. An interest in reading materials is positioned within a larger network of media consumption and for many readers is stimulated or reinforced by tie-ins with comics, music, movies, television, or videogames.[28] Readers develop an awareness of popular literary genres by paying attention to the craft of storytelling across media, learning how, say, fantasy works by experiencing instances of the fantasy genre in books, films, television shows, and videogames.[29] Although we may think of reading as a solitary activity, social elements are powerful influences. Relationships with family, teachers, and friends are important factors in fostering reading and in influencing what materials are read.[30] Studies of reading interests of students of all ages repeatedly have found a disconnect between reader interests and the traditional canon entrenched in the high school literature curriculum in U.S. schools[31,32] where *To Kill a Mockingbird*, *Huckleberry Finn* and *The Scarlet Letter* remain common choices. Not surprisingly, readers are more likely to find books which they have chosen themselves more interesting than they find assigned reading; furthermore high interest increases ease of comprehension.[33]

Because so much of the research on reading interests has depended on a questionnaire or checklist, it is worth taking a look in more detail at the types of instruments used. Typically researchers elicit basic demographic information (including grade level for school age subjects), ask for the title of the last book read in whole or in part, and ask respondents to complete a checklist or reading interest inventory. "When given the opportunity to read any kind of book you choose, what kind of books do you read. Chose one" (or sometimes two or three):

1. science fiction;
2. fantasy;
3. horror;
4. mystery/thrillers;
5. adventure;
6. western;
7. romance/love stories;
8. biography/autobiography;
9. literary fiction;
10. sports;
11. true life;
12. historical;
13. humor;
14. other (please explain).

Such research based on self-reports is subject to all the usual problems of inexact memory and a lack of shared understanding of the meaning of terms. Is "true life" on this checklist intended as a synonym for nonfiction or does it mean a realistic novel, set in a familiar setting and focused on real life problems? Does "historical" include historical fiction such as regency romances or war stories or does it refer only to nonfictional historical accounts? As noted by Purves and Beach,[33] "*Adventure* as a category may have a number of interpretations (action, suspense, violence, faraway places, and manliness), and the researcher's conception of adventure may be far from the respondents' and one respondent's from another." These typical problems of survey research are exacerbated in the case of reading by biases introduced by the value society places on certain kinds of sanctioned reading and denies to other kinds of reading which are denigrated if not out and out forbidden. Often the only format asked about is books. Reading magazines, newspapers, fanzines, comics, manga, or Web sites does not count as real reading in most of these studies, although we know that, especially for adolescent boys, these formats are preferred sources of reading pleasure.[34,35] Research that compiles lists of favorite books or recently read books is likely, especially in the case of students, to reflect the composition of readily available sources of books, such as school-sponsored book clubs and accessible school library or classroom collections.

READING ENGAGEMENT, BOREDOM, AND COMPREHENSION

The flip side of reading interest is reading boredom. In *On Being Literate*, Margaret Meek[36] says that we need to pay more attention to what beginning readers think they are doing when they read: "Here, again, their boredom is a clue because it manifests itself in their disinclination to continue. When they are bored they shut the book." Boredom, argues Meek,[36] is frequently the result of a misalignment between the reader and the text or the learner and the task; boring texts are usually either too difficult or too easy for the reader. Texts can be too hard when they require preliminary knowledge that the reader doesn't have—either knowledge of the way stories work or of the way the world works—because making meaning out of texts involves fitting what is read into the pattern of what is already known. In any case, what is missing when readers describe books as boring is the element of engagement.

Victor Nell[37] used the experimental methods of cognitive psychology to investigate the conditions of reader engagement, using terms like "arousal," "reading involvement," and "entrancement" to describe the experience of the engaged reader. Experimental subjects who read for pleasure (ludic readers) were asked to read in a laboratory setting an enjoyable book that they chose themselves. Meanwhile subjects were attached to electrodes that recorded heart rate, muscle activity, skin response, and breathing—the variables measured as indicators of

arousal. Among other findings, Nell discovered that levels of arousal were higher during ludic reading than during work reading, despite the fact that the readers themselves experienced the pleasure reading as effortless. The paradox of ludic reading is that deep engagement and high physiological arousal go hand-in-hand with the reader's sense of effortlessness, where the words on the page drops from consciousness as the reader is absorbed into the world of the book.

The interesting–boring continuum turns out to be a key theme in understanding frustrated readers who have trouble "getting into" a book. When Anne Reeves set out to understand resistant student readers who did not share her own sense of reading as a joyful activity, she conducted in-depth interviews with 25 adolescent readers in grades 9–12 and developed fine-grained case studies of five of these readers. Asked what comes to mind when they hear "reading," most said the literature studied in English class. These resistant readers all insisted that 1) they could read and 2) that they did read when they were interested in the text. Since most school reading did not interest them, they had developed more or less successful strategies to avoid it, including watching the film, asking someone to tell them what happened in a novel on the English curriculum, or using Cliff notes. The most common advice from her 25 interviewees to teachers was "Choose interesting stuff. Don't try to make us read boring stuff."[38] As Reeves notes, these students view interest as a stable commodity that resides in a text, something that the author can choose either to include or to leave out. They thought of interestingness as something "outside over there," not as a product of their own relationship with the text and dependent on their own activity.

Reeves found that readers call a book boring when it requires them to take risks, when the readers' sense of competence is called into question by a reading task that is too challenging, when the world represented in the book is threatening or painful, or when readers don't have the necessary background knowledge to make sense of the text. Similarly, in their study of 49 adolescent boys, Smith and Wilhelm[34] emphasize the crucial importance for readers to have a sense of competence and control in reading; when the boys in their study felt "overmatched" by the reading task, they stopped reading. "Boring" turns out to be a catchall term to describe a negative reading experience, however produced. For example, in Reeves's study, Duke, a 17-year-old high school senior, described as "boring" the YA book *Go Ask Alice* (1971), which was assigned in one of his English classes. Duke explained: "I don't like readin' depressin' stuff. Her life just started gettin' worse and worse. ... It's bringing me down."[39] In the same study, Joel, a 15-year-old student in grade 10, chose to read Stephen King's *Cujo* (1994) for an English class assignment. He picked *Cujo* because he had heard that King is interesting and because the book itself is "not too long." However, *Cujo* did not live up to its promise:

Joel found himself at sea because of King's strategy of introducing multiple sets of characters in small introductory scenes, switching rapidly to new scenes and new sets of characters who are apparently unrelated to previously presented ones: "It's just he goes on from one thing, you start reading, and it's like switch to a different thing, and I just kinda got lost about what was going on."[39] Joel had not read enough complex fiction to have learned that when it's not clear how scenes, characters, or events fit together, you don't start over again at the beginning and read more slowly; you press on because you know the pattern of significance will eventually be revealed. Successful reading of prose fiction depends on knowing what Peter Rabinowitz has called the "rules of reading": these rules "serve as a kind of assumed contract between author and reader—they specify the grounds on which the intended reading should take place."[40] And how do readers learn these rules of engagement with texts? Most often through reading texts themselves, starting with highly patterned fictions such as fairy tales, series books, and genre books that make the design clear.

READING INTERESTS: HIGH AND LOW

Some scholars have been disheartened by one seemingly intractable fact about reading interests: a majority of readers, when given the chance to choose, prefers a good story told in an accessible style to a literary classic. There are more readers for Harlequin romances than for *Middlemarch* and more readers for thrillers than for serious poetry. When transformations in the technology of printing and distribution, the power-driven cylinder press, new paper-making machinery, cheap postal rates, and a new railway system dramatically lowered costs and made reading materials affordable to a mass audience in the second-half of the nineteenth century in North America, people turned out to want to read cheap popular fiction, a fact that worried some observers. In *The Intellectual Life of the British Working Classes*, Jonathan Rose[41] notes, "In the late nineteenth and early twentieth centuries, the penny dreadful (cheap crime and horror literature for boys) created something approaching panic among middle-class observers, who were certain that it encouraged juvenile delinquency." A great deal was written at the time and following on the theme of cheap books, trash, rubbish, penny dreadfuls, and sensation novels, some commentators saying that such materials are harmful because they instill "false views of life" and displace better reading while others said that they are beneficial because they introduce readers to the love of reading.

The field of librarianship itself has provided a terrain for a more than century-long contest between two opposed views on what to do about people's reading interests. Should libraries cater to these interests or try to change them by improving reading tastes and inculcating a desire

for something better? Advocates of libraries as a place to serve leisure and recreational readers have recommended finding out more about readers' interests in order to provide reading materials that satisfy these interests. From this perspective, understanding reader interests provides a foundation for building collections of popular materials and for effective readers' advisory service. Advocates of the purely educational function of libraries have criticized this catering to readers' interests as a "Give 'em what they want" approach that undermines the library's educational mandate and produce impoverished "drug store" collections.

Esther Jane Carrier's book *Fiction in Public Libraries 1876–1900*[42] provides a well-documented account of how these opposing arguments played out during the formative years of public librarianship in North America. With generous quotes from her nineteenth-century sources, Carrier examines what eminent librarians said at the time on such topics as "What is trash?," "High Quality," and "Reading Improvement." During the nineteenth century, there was a strongly held sense of a natural hierarchy of quality in books in themselves. At the bottom were materials whose very names signaled trashiness: penny dreadfuls, dime books, series books, sensational fiction, and popular romances. Further up were solid works of literary fiction as well as nonfiction works that tell a story such as history, biography, or travel books. At the top were serious, nonnarrative forms such as philosophy and theology.

The goal for librarians was to push the reader up the reading ladder from recreational reading to educational reading.[43] William M. Stevenson,[44] librarian of the Carnegie Free Library of Allegheny, Pennsylvania, stirred up controversy when he removed from the library books he deemed too low on the reading ladder: books by Horatio Alger, Bertha M. Clay, May Agnes Fleming, Martha Finley (the Elsie Books), E.P. Roe, Mrs. E.D.E.N. Southworth and other popular fiction catering to a taste for "recreation and entertainment only." In his 1896 and 1897 annual reports, he acknowledged that, since "devotees of this class of literature will read nothing else," it was inevitable that overall library circulation figures would drop, but he justified his decision by stating that it is the unswerving duty of libraries to supply "nothing but good books" and set a "high standard for reading in a community." In Stevenson's view, "As a rule the people who care for reading nothing but the latest sensational novel cannot be reached beneficially by the public library. It is a waste of time and money to try." (Quoted in Carrier[45]). More than a century later, a strong endorsement of the public library's educational function can be found elaborated in Dilevko and Magowan's *Readers' Advisory Service in North American Public Libraries, 1870–2005*. The authors lament the erosion of an earlier age's commitment to a central mission of "meaningful education through serious and purposeful learning."[46] Regrettably, in their view, public libraries have become increasingly infiltrated by "a mindset in which the reading of books, no matter their intrinsic quality, is construed as good and where discretionary reading becomes commodified and disposable entertainment, as manifested principally in genre fiction and genre nonfiction (genre titles), bestsellers, celebrity-authored books, and prize-winning titles."[46]

READING THE GENRES

Opponents of this hierarchical view of books and reading deny that it is useful to open up too wide a gulf between "high" texts and "low," between high art and "mass" literature. They point to historical instabilities in the evaluation of genres, one century's bestselling popular authors such as Dickens and Wilkie Collins becoming canonical works in the next. They argue instead that valuable texts are to be found in all media and in many different genres. Successful reading begins with situating the text: asking what kind of text this is and what qualities and effects do we normally expect to find in texts of this type. The publication of Betty Rosenberg's *Genreflecting: A Guide to Reading Interests in Genre Fiction*[47,48] can be seen as a watershed event within the library and information science (LIS) field that legitimized a nonhierarchical way of looking at texts. Rosenberg's First Law of Reading, "Never apologize for your reading tastes," included in all six editions of *Genreflecting*, shifts the emphasis to the tastes and reading interests of the reader.

In a simple breakthrough, *Genreflecting* solved for librarians the intractable problem of trying to find a single ladder of quality on which all books can be arranged. Instead *Genreflecting* takes the approach of helping readers situate a given text within its own literary genre, so that comparisons of quality are made *within* a genre not between types of literature that aim at quite different effects. The western is about facing death in an environment stripped down to its bare essentials; the horror story is about scaring the reader; the speculative science fiction story is about "What if?"; the romance is about the developing love relationship of two central characters and the guaranteed happy ending; the mystery story is about uncovering a secret. Since each genre attempts to provide different satisfactions, comparisons are more useful within a genre than across genres. The helpful questions to ask about a particular work become: what are the qualities, effects, and literary conventions that distinguish this particular genre? who are the outstanding exemplars of the craft of writing in this genre? what is it about these exemplars that appeal so strongly to readers who enjoy this genre? how well does this particular work compare with the best examples of the genre in delivering these satisfactions?

An approach to understanding reading interests by studying popular genres has gathered momentum. Robert Scholes defines a literary genre as "a sort of template, used by both writers and readers, to allow for relatively rapid composition and comprehension. That is, a writer composing a text in a recognized genre begins with a template, a preexisting form, that leaves certain blanks to be filled in."[49] This template includes a set of formal qualities that we recognize as typical of the genre and that together work to provide the reader with a predictable experience of pleasure. These formal qualities are like the elements of what Wittgenstein called "family resemblance"—features such as a high-bridged nose or wide-set eyes or red hair that show up in generations of family portraits even though one does not need to find that nose or any other particular feature to identify a portrait as belong to the family. In the case of the Western, for example, the set of stock features, as described by John Cawelti[50] and Jane Tompkins,[51] are as formalized as those of the *commedia del arte* or the Petrarchan sonnet. These features include the frontier setting in big sky country of desert, prairie, or mountain; characters such as good and bad gunmen, the solitary outsider who rides into town, the schoolmarm, plucky widow, and saloon girl, the saloon owner, broken-down doctor, cowboy, cattle baron, cavalry officer, scout, Indian, and of course the horse; and plot devices such as betrayal, revenge, retaliatory violence, Indian captivity, the chase, lynching, train robbery, range war, and the show-down or shoot-out.

Blackford[52] reports that the girls in her study are so familiar with generic conventions "that they identify those conventions as 'rules': 'Now, there's . . . certain rules that you have to have in horror stories, like whenever you turn around there's always somebody there, it always has to be nighttime in a thunderstorm, and something scary happens.' " The genre book, when it is successful, embodies the familiar elements but in a new way, providing the reader with a satisfying mix of the familiar and the unexpected. Joyce G. Saricks's *The Readers' Advisory Guide to Genre Fiction*[53] provides a very helpful overview of 15 different genres and their characteristic appeal, including for each genre five exemplary authors and titles that are good starting points for exploring the genre. Libraries Unlimited have followed up their wildly successful *Genreflecting* with a series of guides to reading interests, edited by Diana Tixier Herald, that focus specifically on particular genres such as fantasy, mystery, horror, adventure/suspense, historical fiction, romance, or mainstream fiction. Another useful form of introduction to rules governing popular literary genres come from bestselling writers themselves who provide an insider's view of the genre and its appeal to readers, for example, Sue Grafton's edited collection of essays on writing mysteries,[54] Jayne Ann Krentz's edited collection *Dangerous Men and Adventurous Women: Romance Writers on the Appeal of Romance*,[55] and Orson Scott Card's guide to writing science fiction and fantasy.[56]

As Scholes points out, the genre template serves the needs of writers by providing a ready-made structure and serves the needs of readers by helping them find their bearings in a book, once reading has begun. Readers use their familiarity with the rules of genre fiction to predict what could possibly happen in a new book they pick up—whether it will scare them or reassure them or amaze them or present them with a mystery to be solved. And of course publishers, who know that readers use genre as a filter in choosing books to read, package books in covers that provide strong generic cues including color-coded covers in green for fantasy, sandy gold for westerns, shades of pink for romance, and black for horror.

Some cultural theorists argue that genre readers are dupes of corporate publishing interests, which provide only the appearance of choice while selling a standardized, mass-produced, cheap commodity that relies on spurious gratifications and emotional appeals. The test case has been the romance, which is the most denigrated of all the genres. Romance accounts for a huge percentage of book sales—one-quarter of all books sold and 40% of mass paperback sales, according to the Romance Writers of America Web site.[57] The Romance Writers of America website notes that in 2006 there were approximately 6400 romance titles released, generating 1.37 billion in estimated revenue. In her introduction to *Dangerous Men and Adventurous Women*, Krentz describes romance as a fantasy of female empowerment in which the woman always wins: "In romance the success of an individual author is . . . [based] on how compellingly she can create her fantasy and on how many readers discover they can step into it with her for a couple of hours." Krentz argues that readers have no difficulty distinguishing the inevitably happy endings of the fantasy from the reality of their everyday experience. They *choose* to enter the romance world for a couple of hours to experience a reaffirmation of hope and the importance of loving human relationships.

READERS' ADVISORY AND APPEAL FACTORS

Understanding reading interests has been considered foundational for readers' advisory work as it has been practiced in public libraries since the early 1980s. Melanie Kimball's chapter on the history of readers' advisory in the sixth edition of *Genreflecting*[58] describes what she calls a "complete overhaul" of readers' advisory service. She identifies several significant milestones in the formation of the new breed of readers' advisor as someone who understands reading interests and can "recommend fiction reading, particularly genre fiction." Among these milestones were the already-mentioned first edition of *Genreflecting*, Joyce Saricks and Nancy Brown's *Readers' Advisory Service in the Public Library*,[59] Ted Balcom's *Book Discussion Guide for Adults: A Leader's Guide*,[60] and the formation of the Adult Reading Round Table in

Chicago in 1984, a group of librarians who met to foster the study of reading interests and popular genres of fiction. Because fiction accounts for such a large share of popular reading, readers' advisory work focused initially on popular genres of fiction and their appeal factors. By the 1990s, however, the scope of readers' advisory service was expanding to include popular nonfiction which can be read for pleasure, specifically those nonfiction works with a strong sense of story, such as travel, biography, history, true accounts of crime, adventure, or sports. Robert Burgin's *Nonfiction Readers' Advisory*[61] is an edited collection of articles that argue that the concepts of genre and appeal factors used for fiction can also be used effectively to serve nonfiction reading interests.

Appeal factor is a concept introduced by Saricks and Brown in the first edition and elaborated in Saricks's third edition of *Readers' Advisory Service in the Public Library*. Thinking about a book's appeal factors takes us beyond subject headings or a bare plot summary. It is a way of helping readers' advisors identify textual elements in a book that satisfy a reader's desire for a particular reading experience. On the basis of many years of front-line work with public library users, Saricks[62] reported, "We have found that most [leisure] readers are not looking for a book on a certain subject. They want a book with a particular 'feel.' . . . Appeal elements describe more accurately [than subject headings alone] the 'feel' of a book." Readers provide clues about the appeal factors they prefer when they talk about a book read recently and enjoyed. Does the reader use terms like "compelling" and "fast-paced" or does the reader praise the book's leisurely unfolding? Is the reader looking for something that is heartwarming and comforting or challenging and edgy? Following deep listening to what readers say they look for in a good book, readers' advisors try to match a reader's interests with a book's appeal factors, namely pacing, characterization, storyline, and frame (i.e., the book's particular atmosphere or tone).

IN CONCLUSION

As fine-grained case studies of individual readers accumulate, they have confirmed Ruth Strang's 1942 finding that reading interests and preferences, in all their individuality, emerge from a central core or radix that determines any individual's pattern of reading. Correlations of demographic factors to reading choices—e.g., men read nonfiction; women read novels; men prefer science fiction and action adventure; women prefer fantasy and romance—these generalizations can be useful in predicting trends in sales and borrowing but don't help much in understanding any particular reader, whose reading preferences are as individual as a fingerprint. For some librarians and readers' advisors, the next step in understanding readers is writing a reader profile, starting with themselves. As

Joyce Saricks notes about the process of reflecting on our own reading interests, "When we see the variety of books we enjoy, we begin to understand that other readers feel the same way."[63]

REFERENCES

1. Purves, A.C.; Beach, R. *Literature and the Reader: Research in Response to Literature, Reading Interests, and the Teaching of Literature*; National Council of Teachers of English: Urbana, IL, 1972; 61–144.
2. Darnton, R. What is the history of books?. Daedalus **1982**, Summer 65–83.
3. Krashen, S.D. *The Power of Reading: Insights from the Research*, 2nd Ed.; Libraries Unlimited: Westport, CT, 2004.
4. Waples, D.; Tyler, R.W. *What People Want to Read About: A Study of Group Interests and a Survey of Problems in Adult Reading*; American Library Association and the University of Chicago Press: Chicago, IL, 1931.
5. Ross, C.S. Making choices: What readers say about choosing books for pleasure. Readers, Reading, and Librarians (Theme issue edited by Katz, B. Acquis. Libr. **2001**, *25*, 5–21).
6. Karetzky, S. *Reading Research and Librarianship to 1940: A History and Analysis*; Greenwood Press: Westport, CT, 1982.
7. Carnovsky, L.A. Study of the relationship between reading interest and actual reading. Libr. Quart. **1934**, January *4*, 76–110.
8. Basbanes, N.A. *Every Book Its reader: The Power of the Printed Word to Stir the World*; HarperCollins: New York, 2005.
9. Edel, L.; Tintner, A.R. *The Library of Henry James*; UMI Research Press: Ann Arbor, MI, 1987.
10. Pawley, C. Retrieving readers: library experiences. Libr. Quart **2006**, *76*(4), 379–387.
11. Gilmore, W. *Reading Becomes a Necessity of Life: Material and Cultural Life in Rural New England, 1790–1835*; University of Tennessee Press: Knoxville, TN, 1989.
12. Darnton, R. Readers respond to Rousseau: The fabrication of romantic sensitivity. In *The Great Cat Massacre and Other Episodes in French Cultural History*, Penguin: New York, 1984; 209–249.
13. Allen, J.S. *In the Public Eye: A History of Reading in Modern France, 1800–1940*; Princeton University Press: Princeton, NJ, 1991.
14. Davidson, C.N. *Revolution and the Word: The Rise of the Novel in America*; Oxford University Press: New York, Oxford, 1986; 79.
15. Jackson, H.J. *Marginalia: Readers Writing in Books*; Yale University Press: New Haven, CT, 2001; 234 2001.
16. Radway, J. *Reading the Romance: Women, Patriarchy and Popular Literature*; University of North Carolina Press: Chapel Hill, NC, 1984; 91.
17. Fry, D. *Children Talk About Books: Seeing Themselves as Readers*; Open University Press: Milton Keynes, U.K., 1985.
18. Blackford, H.V. *Out of this World: Why Literature Matters to Girls*; Teachers College Press, Columbia University: New York, 2004; 3–6 London, U.K.
19. Stedman, L.C.; Kaestle, C.F. Literacy and reading performance in the United States from 1880 to the present. In *Literacy in the United States: Readers and Reading since 1880*; Kaestle, C.F., Damon-Moore, H., Stedman, L.C., Tinsley, K., Trollinger, W.V., Jr., Eds.; Yale University Press: New Haven, CT, 1991; 99; London, U.K.
20. Statistics Canada. *Reading the Future: A Portrait of Literacy in Canada*; The Canadian Report of the International Adult Literacy Survey (IALS), 1996; Available at http://www.statscan.ca/english/freepub/89F0093XIE/free.htm (accessed October 2007).
21. Ross, C.S.; McKechnie, L.(E.F.); Rothbauer, P.M. *Reading Matters: What the Research Reveals about Reading, Libraries, and Community*; Libraries Unlimited: Westport, CT, London, 2006; 133 U.K.
22. Ross, C.S.; McKechnie, L.(E.F.); Rothbauer, P.M. The Boy Problem. In *Reading Matters: What the Research Reveals about Reading, Libraries, and Community*; Libraries Unlimited: Westport, CT 87–97 London, U.K.
23. Smith, M.W.; Wilhelm, J.D. *"Reading Don't Fix No Chevys": Literacy in the Lives of Young Men*; Heinemann: Portsmouth, NH, 2002; 10.
24. Jones, P.; Fiorelli, D.C.; Bowen, M.H. Overcoming the obstacle course: teenage boys and reading. Teach. Libr **2003**, *30*(3), 9–13.
25. Hartley, J. *Reading Groups*; Oxford University Press: Oxford, U.K., 2001; 25.
26. Long, E. *Book Clubs: Women and the Uses of Reading in Everyday Life*; University of Chicago Press: Chicago, IL, 2003.
27. Strang, R. *Explorations in Reading Patterns*; University of Chicago Press: Chicago, IL, 1942; 5.
28. Cavazos-Kottke, S. Five readers browsing: the reading interests of talented middle school boys. Gifted Child Quart **2006**, *50*(2), 132–147.
29. Blackford, H.V. *Out of this World: Why Literature Matters to Girls*; Teachers College Press, Columbia University: New York; London, U.K., 2004; 42.
30. Smith, M.W.; Wilhelm, J.D. *"Reading Don't Fix no Chevys": Literacy in the Lives of Young Men*; Heinemann: Portsmouth, NH, 2002; 142.
31. Applebee, A.N. Stability and change in the high-school Canon. Engl. J. **1992**, September 27–32.
32. Sarland, C. *Young People Reading: Culture and Response*; Open University Press: Buckingham, U.K., 1991.
33. Purves, A.C.; Beach, R. *Literature and the Reader: Research in Response to Literature, Reading Interests, and the Teaching of Literature*; National Council of Teachers of English: Urbana, IL, 1972; 87 69.
34. Smith, M.W.; Wilhelm, J.D. *"Reading Don't Fix no Chevys": Literacy in the Lives of Young Men*; Heinemann: Portsmouth, NH, 2002.
35. Bergin, M. Who is reading manga?. Young Adult Libr. Serv **2005**, *3*(4), 25–26.
36. Meek, M. *On Being Literate*; The Bodley Head: London, U.K., 1991; 198–199; 172.
37. Nell, V. *Lost in a Book: The Psychology of Reading for Pleasure*; Yale University Press: New Haven, CT/London, U.K, 1988.

38. Reeves, A.R. *Adolescents Talk About Reading: Exploring Resistance to and Engagement with Text*; International Reading Association: Newark, DE, 2004; 243.

39. Reeves, A.R. *Adolescents Talk About Reading: Exploring Resistance to and Engagement with Text*; International Reading Association: Newark, DE, 2004; 82 201.

40. Rabinowitz, P. *Before Reading: Narrative Conventions and the Politics of Interpretation*; Cornell University Press: Ithaca, NY/London, U.K., 1987; 43.

41. Rose, J. *The Intellectual Life of the British Working Classes*; Yale University Press: New Haven, CT/London, U.K., 2001; 367.

42. Carrier, E.J. *Fiction in Public Libraries l876–1900*; The Scarecrow Press: New York/London, U.K., 1965.

43. Ross, C.S. Metaphors of reading. J. Libr. Hist. Philos. **1987**, *22*(2), 147–163.

44. Stevenson, W.M. Weeding out fiction in the Carnegie Free Library of Allegheny. Pa. Libr. J. **1897**, March 22, 133–135.

45. Carrier, E.J. *Fiction in Public Libraries l876–1900*; The Scarecrow Press: New York, 1965; 258–259; Quoted in Carrier, London, U.K.

46. Dilevko, J.; Magowan, C.F.C. *Readers' Advisory Service in North American Public Libraries, 1870–2005: A History and Critical Analysis*; McFarland and Co: Jefferson, NC, 2007; 50, 9 London, U.K.

47. Rosenberg, B. *Genreflecting: A Guide to Reading Interests in Genre Fiction*, 1st Ed.; Libraries Unlimited: Englewood, CO, 1982.

48. Herald, D.T. *Genreflecting: A Guide to Popular Reading Interests*, 6th Ed.; Libraries Unlimited: Westport, CT, 2006.

49. Scholes, R. *The Crafty Reader*; Yale University Press: New Haven, CT, 2001; 143–146 London, U.K.

50. Cawelti, J. *Adventure, Mystery and Romance: Formula Stories as Art and Popular Culture*; University of Chicago Press: Chicago, IL, 1976.

51. Tompkins, J. *West of Everything: The Inner Life of Westerns*; Oxford University Press: New York; Oxford, U.K., 1992.

52. Blackford, H.V. *Out of this World: Why Literature Matters to Girls;* Teachers College Press, Columbia University: New York/London, U.K., 2004; 71 .

53. Saricks, J.G. *The Readers' Advisory Guide to Genre Fiction*; ALA Editions: Chicago, IL, 2001.

54. Grafton, S., Ed. *Writing Mysteries: A Handbook by the Mystery Writers of America*; Writers Digest Books: Cincinnati, OH, 2002.

55. Krentz, J.A., Ed. *Dangerous Men and Adventurous Women: Romance Writers on the Appeal of Romance*; The University of Pennsylvania Press: Philadelphia, PA, 1992.

56. Card, O.S. *How to Write Science Fiction and Fantasy*; Writer's Digest Books: Cincinnati, OH, 2001.

57. http://www.rwanational.org/cs/home Romance Writers of America Website.

58. Kimball, M.; A brief history of readers' advisory. *Genreflecting: A Guide to Popular Reading Interests*, 6th Ed.; Herald, D.T., Ed.; Libraries Unlimited: Westport, CT/London, U.K., 2006; 15–23.

59. Saricks, J.G. Brown, N. *Readers' Advisory Service in the Public Library*, 1st Ed.; American Library Association: Chicago, IL, 1989.

60. Balcom, T., Ed. *Book Discussion Guide for Adults: A Leader's Guide*; American Library Association: Chicago, IL, 1992.

61. Burgin, R., Ed. *Nonfiction Readers' Advisory*; Libraries Unlimited: Westport, CT, 2004; London, U.K.

62. Saricks, J.G. *Readers' Advisory Service in the Public Library*, 3rd Ed.; American Library Association: Chicago, IL, 2005; 40–41 London, U.K.

63. Saricks, J. Writing a reader profile; or, what I like and why. Booklist **2005**, October 1 *102*(3), 35.

BIBLIOGRAPHY

1. Carlsen, G.R.; Sherrill, A. *Voices of Readers: How We Come to Love Books*; National Council of Teachers of English: Urbana, IL, 1988.

2. Karetzky, S. *Reading Research and Librarianship to 1940: A History and Analysis*; Greenwood Press: Westport, CT, 1982.

3. Korda, M. *Making the List: A Cultural History of the American Bestseller 1900–1999*; Barnes & Noble: New York, 2001.

4. National Endowment for the Arts. *Reading at risk: A survey of literary reading in America; Research Division Report #46*, Washington, DC, 2004; Available at http://www.nea.gov/news/news04/ReadingAtRisk.html (accessed October 2007).

5. Radway, J. Beyond Mary Bailey and Old Maid Librarians: Reimagining readers and rethinking reading. J. Educ. Libr. Inf. Sci **1994**, *4*(35), 275–296.

6. Radway, J.A. *A Feeling for Books: The Book-of-the-Month Club, Literary Taste, and Middle-Class Desire*; The University of North Carolina Press: Chapel Hill, NC/London, U.K, 1997.

Recommender Systems and Expert Locators

Derek L. Hansen
University of Maryland, College Park, Maryland, U.S.A.

Tapan Khopkar
University of Michigan, Ann Arbor, Michigan, U.S.A.

Jun Zhang
Pitney Bowes, Shelton, Connecticut, U.S.A.

Abstract

This entry describes two important classes of systems that facilitate the sharing of recommendations and expertise. Recommender systems suggest items of potential interest to individuals who do not have personal experience with the items. Expert locator systems, an important subset of recommender systems, help find people with the appropriate skills, knowledge, or expertise to meet a particular need. Research related to each of these systems is relatively new and extremely active. The use of these systems is likely to continue increasing as more and more activity is implicitly captured online, making it possible to automatically identify experts, and capture preferences that can be used to recommend items.

INTRODUCTION

Despite the abundance of recorded information, many information seekers turn to other humans for advice and recommendations. Humans, after all, can be quite adept at identifying and solving problems, summarizing relevant content, generating new ideas, and personalizing information. In addition, for some, interacting with other humans is far more socially enjoyable than interacting with static content. Thus, it is no surprise that the Internet is as much a platform for social interaction as it is a document repository.

System designers have taken advantage of the fact that so much social action is captured online by creating systems that extend traditional word-of-mouth exchanges. This entry discusses two such systems: *recommender systems* that provide personalized recommendations (e.g., movie suggestions) for items of potential interest, and *expert locator systems* that automatically identify experts on a particular topic of interest making it possible to obtain personalized advice from knowledgeable individuals outside of one's immediate social network. Expert locator systems can be thought of as a subset of recommender systems where experts are the "items" being recommended. We treat them separately in this entry because in practice there are often important distinctions between recommending items and people. The remainder of the entry defines these two types of systems, outlines their key characteristics, provides some historical and current examples, and identifies the key research questions related to them. It concludes with a discussion about the importance and potential of these

techniques given the increased amount of activity that can be digitally captured.

RECOMMENDER SYSTEMS

People are often confronted with situations where they need to assess the potential value of something that they have never experienced before. We need to find a new book to read, choose a doctor, and know which business is credible. When confronted with these situations, we often turn to experts or peers for recommendations. Increasingly, people receive recommendations from automated tools called recommender systems. For example, people browsing a book at Amazon are presented with a list of related books of potential interest. The related books (listed under the "People who bought this book also bought" header) are identified by a recommender system that relies upon the historical purchasing patterns of Amazon customers. More generally, recommender systems suggest items of potential interest to individuals who do not have personal experience with the items.

Though recommender systems have gained visibility with the spread of the Internet, they are not confined to the Web. Better Business Bureaus, Zagat's restaurant reviews, and The Times Book Review are some examples of recommender systems that predate the Web. Two things make Web-based recommender systems fundamentally different. First, they are able to provide personalized recommendations tailored to individuals. In contrast to The Times Book Review that provides the same recommendations to every reader, recommender systems can recommend a book based

Encyclopedia of Library and Information Sciences, Fourth Edition DOI: 10.1081/E-ELIS4-120044532

on the other books you personally enjoy, while not recommending it to others with different tastes. Second, recommender systems are able to base recommendations on the data from the masses, not just a handful of reviewers and editors. The online environment has also made it easier to efficiently capture people's preferences and easily distribute recommendations.

Broadly speaking, recommender systems can be classified into two types: collaborative and content-based. Collaborative recommender systems make recommendations based on the prior experience of other users, while content-based systems make recommendations based on features or descriptions of the items themselves. There are also hybrid recommender systems that mix these two approaches. For simplicity, we present them independently in the following sections.

Collaborative Systems

Collaborative recommender systems draw on the historical experience, or preferences of some users to make recommendations to other users. These systems are also called "Collaborative Filters" or "Social Filters" and have been used in a variety of settings to recommend newsgroup articles (e.g., GroupLens), books (e.g., Amazon's "People who bought this also bought" feature), movies (e.g., MovieLens), music (e.g., Last.fm), and even people (e.g., eBay's feedback system and other expert locators systems discussed in the following section).

Last.fm is a good example of a collaborative recommender system that offers many different recommendations. The site is a music portal that allows users to listen to music, find new music they are likely to enjoy, and find people with similar music tastes. When a user logs into the site, he can enter in his favorite songs and bands and add them to his "playlist," one of the components of his user profile. The system then compares the user's profile with the profiles of other Last.fm users. This comparison makes it possible to identify users who have similar tastes (e.g., people who like and dislike the same music). These individuals are shown as "neighbors" and a user is presented with opportunities to view their music lists. In this way, the system recommends people based on the similarity of user profiles. The system also provides a user with the option of hearing songs that his neighbors as a collective enjoy. Furthermore, when visiting an artist's home page a user can have songs by "similar" artists recommended, where similarity is based on the collective preferences of people who listen to that artist.

To make recommendations like those at Last.fm, a collaborative recommender system must perform the following tasks:

1. Elicit Preferences: Learn about the users' preferences and store them in user profiles.

2. Compute Predictions: Predict how well a user would like an unfamiliar item based on the data from the user profiles.
3. Make Recommendations: Use the predictions to make recommendations.

Fig. 1 provides a schematic representation of a recommender system, showing how these tasks relate to one another. Different recommender systems use different approaches to perform each of these tasks. We now discuss each of the tasks in turn.

Elicit preferences

Recommender system can learn about the users' preferences by explicitly asking them to rate certain items; or by using implicit measures such as purchase history, search history, or time spent browsing an article. Most recommender systems that use the explicit method ask users to rate items in the database that they have experienced in the past. The systems use these ratings to form and periodically update a model of the user's preferences. Some recommender systems employ an alternative approach where they ask all users to rate items from the same "gauge" data set and model their preferences based on these ratings.[1]

Recommender systems can vary in the amount of detail that is captured with the ratings and the scale used to capture them (i.e., the dimensionality and granularity of ratings). A recommender system could obtain detailed ratings along multiple dimensions (e.g., quality and timeliness) or it could ask for a one-dimensional rating (e.g., overall satisfaction). Ratings could be on an all positive scale, all negative scale, or a positive and negative scale. The ratings can also vary on granularity. They may use a 1

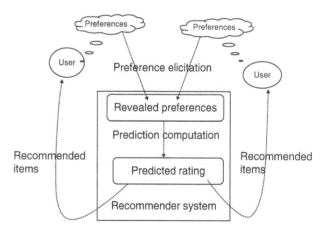

Fig. 1 Schematic representation of a collaborative recommender system.

to 5 scale like Amazon.com or a "thumbs up" and "thumbs down" scale like Digg. Each of these design choices has different implications for the accuracy of recommendations and also a user's privacy and the ease of entering ratings. They will also influence which prediction algorithms are possible to use.

Compute predictions

Several alternative algorithms are used to make predictions and thus recommendations. Improving the accuracy of predictions is an area of active research, which has received additional impetus through Netflix's announcement in late 2006 of a $1 million prize for the first team that improves the predictions of Netflix's recommender algorithm by 10%.

Recommender algorithms can be classified into two types: (1) memory-based and (2) model-based.[2] Memory-based algorithms use data from all users to make predictions directly, while model-based algorithms use data from all users to formulate a single model of user preferences, and then use this model to make predictions. Recommender algorithms can also be classified based on whether they use correlations between users or between items.

In the user-user approach, correlation between two users is computed based on the scores of items that are rated (or used if the recommender system uses implicit measures) by both the users. The recommender system computes correlations between all such user pairs, which can be used in a variety of ways. One of the popular approaches is to use these correlations as weights when making predictions by taking a weighted average over the opinions of other users who have rated an item. Another approach is to use the user–user correlations to divide the user population into clusters of users, where users in the same cluster are considered to have similar preferences. Predictions for a user's hitherto unrated item are made by averaging the opinions of the other users in her cluster. Other approaches use statistical techniques such as Principal Component Analysis or Singular Value Decomposition and seek to identify latent factors in the data and make predictions based on those.

In systems that use the item–item approach (e.g., Amazon.com's "Users who bought this book also bought" feature), correlations between item pairs are computed instead of correlations between user pairs. Correlation between two items is computed using ratings of all the users who have rated both items. The system recommends items that are highly correlated with the items that are highly rated (or used) by the user.

When computing predictions, recommender algorithms usually perform some sort of normalization in order to account for systematic differences in the way people choose ratings. For example, if a person's average rating is 4.5 out of 5 and they give something a 3, the 3 rating is pretty bad. On the other hand, if a person has an average rating of 2.5 out of 5, a 3 rating is pretty good.

Make recommendations

The objective of a recommender system is to present each user with items she is most likely to enjoy. To this effect, a recommender system can use the predictions in a variety of ways. As illustrated in the Last.fm example, the user can choose to have recommended songs play based on similar artists, neighbors, or her entire history.

System designers need to make several important design decisions in this phase. Besides the obvious design decisions about the interface, the system designer needs to determine what is the maximum permissible error. The error could be an error of commission (incorrectly recommending an item) or an error of omission (not recommending an item that should be recommended). The margin of permissible error for either type depends on the benefit of a correct recommendation and the cost of an incorrect recommendation. Consider a hypothetical Web site where medical treatment in discussed and recommended. Here a good recommendation not made or an incorrectly made recommendation could affect the health of a user. For video sharing, Web sites like YouTube, a recommendation is unlikely to have such important ramifications for the user, but it is still an important decision for the service provider. The service provider has an incentive to provide more recommendations if it leads to increased usage (or sale). At the same time the reduced usability due to poor recommendations may result in the user opting out of the system altogether, so there is still a need for an appropriate threshold.

The system designer needs to consider these issues when deciding the metrics for evaluating the predictions and the magnitude of permissible error. A good recommender system should continually seek feedback from the user and evaluate the accuracy of its predictions. Root Mean Square Error (RMSE) and Mean Absolute Error are some of the evaluation metrics commonly used in recommender systems. The Netflix prize requires a 10% RMSE improvement in the predictions of Netflix's algorithm.

Content-Based Systems

Content-based systems recommend items based on features of the items themselves. Unlike collaborative systems, there is no need for data from other individuals. For a content-based system to work, a representation of each item must be generated. This can be done automatically, as when all of the words in a book or article are indexed. Or, it can be done manually as when a human cataloger associates a particular genre (i.e., romance) or subject heading to a book. An example of a very simple content-based system would be a news aggregation Web site that displays "related" articles that are textually "similar" to the one that a user is currently reading.

Many content-based systems provide personalized recommendations. In addition to having a representation of each item, this requires that individuals have a user profile that includes data about a user's likes and dislikes. As with collaborative systems, data for a content-based user profile can be explicitly entered or implicitly captured based on behavior (e.g., purchasing patterns).

This user profile is then compared with the representations of potential items and those that match closely are recommended. A variety of different techniques (i.e., algorithms) are used to compare user profiles and item representations in order to predict which items a user will like. These differ from those used in collaborative systems because the comparison is not between different ratings; it is between a user's profile and the representations of items. Common techniques are the use of information retrieval and machine learning algorithms (Hinshelwood[3] for a more complete list with examples).

Pandora is an example of a content-based system that recommends music. In contrast to Last.fm, it does not rely on any other user recommendations. Instead, it is based on a representation of each song, called a Music Genome, which is created automatically by a special software tool. A song's Music Genome consists of hundreds of musical attributes that describe qualities of melody, harmony, rhythm, form, composition, and lyrics. When a user enters a favorite song, Pandora recommends other songs with a similar Music Genome. Over time, users are presented with new songs which they rate. A user profile is automatically created that keeps track of the user's likes and dislikes. Additional songs are recommended taking into consideration the entire user profile.

Challenges of Recommender Systems

Designers and managers of recommender systems face several challenges. Some of these are dependent on the type of recommender system.

Content-based systems face two primary challenges:

1. Creating representations of certain items can be costly and time intensive. Although full-text, digital documents lend themselves well to automatic indexing, other items such as physical objects, small textual items such as quotes, and movies are difficult to automatically index in a satisfactory way.
2. Even when representations of items are available, they may not represent the characteristics that are most important to the user's enjoyment of the item. Jokes are a good example of this. While one could index the words used in a joke, the user's enjoyment of the joke has far less to do with the words than it does with the humor. In other words, knowing that a

joke is about a chicken doesn't help a user know if she would enjoy the joke. One potential strategy for overcome this problem would be to add meta-data to items. However, for items like jokes or poems the meta-data would be so subjective that it would not likely produce accurate predictions for any particular user.[3]

Since collaborative systems are not based on the representation of an item, they can work for items that are costly or difficult to accurately represent, such as physical objects or jokes. However, they have their own set of challenges:

1. Eliciting enough user ratings to generate accurate predictions for all items is a constant source of concern for the designers and managers of recommender systems. Users need to be provided with sufficient incentives to participate.
2. New users and new items both suffer from the "cold-start" problem. New users do not get good recommendations until they have rated a sufficient number of items; and new items rarely get recommended until a sufficient number of users have rated (or used) them.
3. There may be entities that have an interest in manipulating the recommender system in order to promote certain items. An example of such a manipulation scheme called "sybil attack" or "shilling attack" involves creating a number of spurious users and providing ratings such that certain items get recommended more often. Preventing such manipulations or limiting the damage they cause, is an important consideration for recommender system designers and an active area of research.

To overcome some of these challenges, recommender systems may use a combined approach (both content-based and collaborative) or provide tools that allow people to use preexisting data (e.g., upload iTunes playlists all at once).

Recommender System Research

Online recommender systems have been developed and studied since the mid-1990s. Two related systems were simultaneously developed in the mid-1990s and were instrumental in showing the value of collaborative recommender systems:

1. GroupLens—a net news collaborative recommender system created by Resnick et al.[4] Resnick continued to study recommender systems as an editor for a special issue of *Communications of the Association for Computing Machinery (ACM)* on the topic in 1997[5] and as a contributor to numerous articles on the subject. Reidl has also remained highly active in recommender system research with his colleagues at the

GroupLens research lab at the University of Minnesota. They have performed a number of studies of MovieLens, a recommender system for movies. Their Web site[6] is a good starting point for potential researchers with its list of publications and downloadable datasets.

2. Ringo—a music collaborative recommender system developed at MIT by Shardanand and Maes.[7] It was later made into a commercial product called Firefly, which was eventually bought out by Microsoft. Music recommender systems are now common and among the most advanced and popular (e.g., Last.fm, Pandora).

Research on recommender systems has continued to grow and doesn't show any signs of slowing down. Several special issues of well-respected journals have focused on recommender systems including the *Communications of the ACM*,[5] *ACM Transactions on Information Systems*,[8] *ACM Transactions on Computer-Human Interaction*,[9] and *IEEE Intelligent Systems*.[10] Research can also be found in conferences like ACM Special Interest Group on Information Retrieval, ACM Computer-Human Interaction, and ACM Electronic Commerce. Numerous workshops have been held over the years, and in 2007, the first annual ACM Recommender Systems[11] conference was held. Current research focuses on nearly every aspect of recommender systems from the recommendation algorithms, to interfaces design, to security, and privacy issues.

Summary

Recommender Systems are a powerful tool for recommending new items to individuals either based on content (content-based systems) or other users' experiences (collaborative systems). It is a highly active area of research that epitomizes the current social computing trends. While there are challenges with recommender systems (e.g., needing sufficient numbers of people and items rated before it works), they have already become widely used by corporations such as Amazon, NetFlix, Pandora, TiVo, Google, and others.

EXPERT LOCATOR SYSTEMS

Turning to experts for help is nothing new. We are all familiar with the ability of experts to diagnose a complex problem, clarify an issue, identify hidden structure, point us to a hard-to-locate resource, and perform a task that requires significant skill. Although some expert knowledge can be made explicit in the form of books, videos, diagrams, and knowledge-base entries, other knowledge is implicit and difficult to codify. Thus, it is often preferable to gain access to the source of the knowledge, the expert, in order to obtain the full benefit of the expertise. Unfortunately, it is not always easy to identify experts, especially within large organizations or distributed communities. Recently, systems have been developed to help locate individuals with needed expertise. These expert locator systems go by many names including expertise finders, expertise location engines, expert locators, and enterprise expertise management systems.

An expert locator system is a collection of technologies and social practices designed to help an individual find someone with the appropriate skills, knowledge, or expertise to meet a particular need. Some are stand-alone systems, but most are integrated into a more comprehensive knowledge management solution. While a basic organizational chart or an informal friendship-based network may be considered an expert locator system in the broadest sense, the term typically refers to more advanced systems that use implicitly or explicitly provided data to identify experts.

Researchers and practitioners have developed and examined expert locator systems since the early 1990s. Most empirical studies have taken place within large corporate settings, although more recent work has looked at expertise location among peer groups and virtual help-based communities. The most active research communities currently examining expert locator systems are the Computer Supported Cooperative Work (CSCW) and Knowledge Management communities. As a result, research on the topic is often published in conference proceedings in these areas (e.g., ACM–CSCW, ACM Conference on Information and Knowledge Management, ACM International Conference on Knowledge Discovery and Data Mining, ACM Recommender Systems) and information systems journals such as CSCW and KES (Knowledge-Based and Intelligent Engineering Systems). However, a considerable amount of research is scattered throughout publications on topics such as artificial intelligence, algorithms, Web personalization, and information systems more generally.

The following sections describe different subtypes of expert locator systems. The area is new enough that the vocabulary around them has not yet solidified. We group the systems into the following categories: *expert databases*, *automatic expertise finders*, *expertise recommenders*, and *expert referral systems*.

Expert Databases

Early expert locator systems were usually called expertise databases, knowledge directories, yellow pages, or knowledge maps. These systems consist of a searchable database of individuals along with data about their prior experience, expertise, organizational role, and contact information. Typical systems include Microsoft SPUD, HP CONNEX, and the NASA expertseeker. These systems are usually designed for identifying experts to help solve technical problems or to match employee competencies with company positions.

Inputting accurate and detailed enough data into these databases can be a significant challenge. Some organizations rely upon assessment interviews, skill inventories, and extensive surveys of employees, but such methods can be costly and labor intensive. In other cases, individual employees are expected to enter information about themselves. Although individuals are the most qualified to describe their own expertise, they often lack motivation to add content—an activity that has few immediate rewards. Furthermore, they may not recognize the potential value of some of their less obvious skills and fail to report them. No matter who contributes the data, expert database entries can suffer from being over-simplified, one-dimensional assessments of expertise that are not informative enough to help direct the fine-grained, context specific questions that lead people to seek out experts. Finally, some systems rely on taxonomies to describe and catalog people's knowledge and skills. While this may encourage consistency and point out areas that may not have been considered, developing, and implementing taxonomies requires considerable effort and are likely to be misapplied if individuals are entering their own data.

Another related challenge is maintaining content over time. People leave, new skills are developed, positions change. For those who rarely use expert locator systems, keeping their data current is not on their top list of priorities. As a result, some expert databases quickly become obsolete. Additionally, organizations may not initially recognize the full investment required to maintain these systems once they are created.

Automatic Expertise Finders

As more and more activity occurs in the digital environment, it has become possible to profile individuals' expertise based on their conversations (e.g., in discussion forums and e-mail exchanges) and the documents associated with them (e.g., publications). An *automatic expertise finder* is a type of expert locator system that takes advantage of the implicit data left behind in the form of digital traces and documents. Such systems typically build expertise profiles from the implicit data by using information retrieval techniques (e.g., indexing). A person's expertise is usually described as a term vector and is used later for matching expertise queries using standard IR techniques. This allows people to search for a relevant expert in much the same way that they might search for a relevant document.

Well-known systems in this category include Who-Knows,[12] ContactFinder,[13] and MITRE MII Expert Finder.[14] Who-Knows identifies experts across an organization by using Latent Semantic Indexing techniques on the project documents people produce. ContactFinder identifies experts based on their participation patterns and message content. Expert Finder identifies experts based on documents people produce, as well as some experience-related information including basic employment information (e.g., positions held) and projects in which they participated.

These systems solve many of the challenges of expert databases since there is no need to manually contribute and maintain expertise information, and the automatically generated profiles are considerably more developed than the simple keyword-based profiles. However, these systems also have limitations. First, some individuals have expertise that is not yet represented in their digital traces. This is particularly true of new employees, as well as individuals who rely primarily on telephone and face-to-face meetings. Second, from the technical perspective, we still need to improve ways of selecting and integrating different sources and types of data to better reflect people's expertise. We also need to improve the ways of matching information seekers' fine-grained information needs with the large and amorphous expertise profiles. These are active areas of research, and we can expect improvements in the techniques that are used.

Finally, and perhaps most importantly, these systems largely do not consider the social perspectives of expertise sharing. For instance, their results are usually ranked purely based on the computed information similarity between the query and profiles. However, there are many other criteria that people use to select experts in real life and many other social factors that contribute to individual's willingness to share information and have meaningful interactions. The following section discusses systems that were designed with these social considerations in mind.

Expertise Recommenders

Rooted in the field of CSCW, Ackerman and other researchers developed a series of systems that address both social and technical issues related to expertise location and sharing. In contrast to systems that only identify experts based on content overlap, these systems attempt to create a social and technical environment that encourages information sharing and recognizes the importance of social context.

Answer Garden (AG) is a system designed to help in situations like technical support, where there is a continuing stream of questions, many of which occur repeatedly, but some of which have never been seen before.[15] It has a branching network of diagnostic questions that helps users find answers. If there is no available answer, it automatically routes the question to the appropriate expert who can answer the user and record the answer into the branching network for future users. The design of AG addresses two important social issues in expertise finding. First, askers are anonymous to the experts. This decreases the asker's social costs related to status implications and the need for reciprocity, although it also loses some of the potentially helpful contextual information. Second, by continually adding questions and answers into the corpus, it decreases the expert's workload in answering the same questions repeatedly and grows the organizational memory incrementally.

Field studies of AG showed mixed results. Questioners appreciated the anonymity, but many of the answers they received were not at the appropriate level (e.g., an answer was too technical and lengthy). This finding suggests that expertise locator systems should route organizational members to individuals with the right level of expertise, not just to experts with the highest level of expertise. A future field study of an AG-like system highlighted some of the limitations of the system including frustration due to incomplete data and continually changing classification schemes.[16] The study also found that the AG approach is subject to the impact of the given division of labor and organizational micro-politics.

A new version of AG, AG2 was developed to overcome some of the original limitations.[17] Unlike AG, where the expert location occurred manually, an expertise location engine was developed for AG2. Various computer-mediated communication mechanisms are also added. One important social innovation was the fact that the AG2 expert locator algorithm prefers to "stay local" when selecting expertise to allow contextualization, a concept that was found useful in later systems as well. If a local expert is unavailable, the system supports an escalation process whereby the query is sent on to others until an answer is provided. Thus, the system helps gracefully overcome failures with initial expert recommendations. Another interesting change to AG2 is that the system tends to blur the dichotomy between experts and seekers, recognizing that individuals may be novices in some areas and experts in other areas.

Expertise Recommender (ER) is another system developed by McDonald and Ackerman in order to address issues identified from a field study of AG2.[18] The major contribution of this system is that it can select experts based on a range of social factors such as organizational closeness and workload, not just level of expertise. As more data about our actions and relationships become available online, many new possibilities for identifying an *appropriate* expert become viable.

It is important to recognize that the systems discussed in this section are research prototype systems that are not as widely used as those previously discussed. Although a framework for including additional factors into the expert identification algorithms has been developed, few modules have been implemented. Future research examining the social factors that should be considered (e.g., privacy considerations and motivational issues) when recommending experts seems promising. It short, this research shows that finding an expert is not enough. One must also understand the other social factors related to

their willingness to participate and have enough contextual knowledge to help.

Expert Referral Systems

Another approach to identifying experts is to use a referral process, where an individual has his colleagues and friends introduce, or refer, an expert. This referral method has been used throughout time. However, as more information about our social relationships is made available in digital form, systems have been developed to augment our ability to get high quality referrals from our peers. We call these *expert referral systems*.

ReferralWeb was the first well-known system that utilized social network information to help individuals find and be introduced to experts on a particular topic.[19] In ReferralWeb, people's expertise are indexed based on individuals' publications. Social network information is extracted from the coauthorships or co-appearances in their Web pages. Experts are identified via traditional information retrieval techniques (as described in the *automatic expertise finders* section). Once identified, the information seeker is presented with visualizations of the network structure, and a list of referral chains that can be taken to get from your known peers to the desired expert. For example, it might show that my friend John knows Lucy who knows the expert Jack; likewise it would show other paths to Jack through different friends who know him.

Although not designed specifically for the purpose of finding experts, Yenta[20] helps individuals find others with similar interests—individuals who may be in the best position to provide expert advice. Yenta acts like a personal agent. It creates people's personal interest profiles by mining documents in their local machines. The profile is stored locally and uses inter-agent communication to find people who have information similar to the query, all the while protecting the actual content from being shared with others. Yenta also clusters people based on their shared interests to built social coalitions and provides tools to communicate with others in the same cluster. Thus, Yenta can be thought of as a recommender system as described earlier in this article. Other related systems include MARS[21] and SWIM.[22] Recently, with the advancement of social network theory research, there are increasing number of peer-to-peer applications designed to share knowledge and resources (e.g., files and contacts) through social networks, as well as commercial social network systems (e.g., spoke and visiblepath) that are designed to help people share contact information. As social networking sites such as Facebook and LinkedIn become ubiquitous, expert referral systems will be a natural fit.

These expert referral systems have several advantages and disadvantages. They support the age-old practice of finding information through social contacts that is familiar to all of us and socially acceptable. They provide added motivation for individuals to help those who seek them out; after all, an expert is more likely to provide help if they have been introduced by a mutual friend or perhaps even an automatic agent that has identified some hidden similarity. These systems are relatively easy to implement using basic peer-to-peer and information retrieval techniques. They also can provide contextual information about individuals based on their social network relationships, helping expert seekers make more educated decisions about whether or not it is worth contacting a particular expert. Unfortunately, systems like ReferralWeb increase the amount of time required to contact an expert; not only the information seeker's time but also the friends that are part of the referral chain. They may also decrease the pool of experts who are reachable in practice, since referral chains that are too long (or nonexistent) discourage contact with the expert. There is a need for more empirical studies of these systems to help reveal additional advantages and disadvantages.

Summary

In this section we have outlined a variety of different expert locator systems including expert databases, automatic expertise finders, ERs, and expert referral systems. Additional systems are described in Ackerman et al.[23] Because research on expert locator systems is still in its infancy, the specific terminology and categorization we provide is tentative and likely to change as new techniques are developed and integrated with other knowledge management and social software programs. However, many of the key principles, trends, and design considerations discussed above are enduring. In this summary, we address two of the most prominent.

One common trend is the use of implicit data rather than explicitly entered data in expert locator systems. This trend is likely to continue as more and more of our activities are recorded in a digital environment and can potentially be used to identify our expertise domains, our social network ties, and other factors of interest (e.g., availability). For instance, Zhang et al.[24] explored ways of using people's asking-answering histories in online forums to infer expertise levels. Further developing tools to integrate these various data sources will be vital to improving expert locator systems. These issues are also important for designing recommender systems more generally.

Another common theme is the need to consider the social implications of expert locator systems. The *expertise recommenders* and the *expert referral systems* emphasize that locating the most knowledgeable individual on a topic is not enough. After all, the most knowledgeable individual may not be able to present information at the right level for the information seeker or may be too far removed from the local context to be of benefit. Furthermore, the most knowledgeable individuals may not have sufficient incentives to participate, especially if they are bombarded with questions from strangers. Systems that take into consideration these social factors and align the incentives of the various parties are far more likely to succeed in the long run. In this sense, expert locator systems may be better labeled expertise sharing systems.

CONCLUSION

In this entry we have discussed two types of systems that facilitate learning from other people in a highly personal way. Recommender systems provide personalized recommendations for individuals about items that they have not yet experienced for themselves. Expert locators help identify people who are knowledgeable on a topic, so they can personally engage with those who seek their expertise. These systems provide nice alternatives and complements to traditional information retrieval techniques. When finding a relevant document is not enough, expert locators provide access to individuals with expertise and recommender systems provide additional pointers to resources that may not have been considered in the original search query. Research on these topics is growing rapidly and the methods for performing them are improving as a result. In addition, as more and more activity is implicitly captured online, it is increasingly possible to improve these tools and apply them in new domains.

REFERENCES

1. Goldberg, K.; Roeder, T.; Gupta, D.; Perkins, C. Eigentaste: A constant time collaborative filtering algorithm. Inform. Ret. **2001**, *4* (2), 133–151.
2. Breese, J.; Heckerman, D.; Kadie, C. Empirical analysis of predictive algorithms for collaborative filtering. In *Proceedings of the 14th Conference on Uncertainty in Artificial Intelligence*, Uncertainty in Artificial Intelligence, Madison, WI, July 24–26, 1998; Cooper, G.; Moral, S., Eds.; Morgan Kaufman: San Francisco, CA, 1998; 43–52.
3. Pazzani, M.J.; Billsus, D. Content-based Recommendation Systems. In *The Adaptive Web*; Brusilovsky, P., Kobsa, A., Nejdl, W., Eds.; Springer: Berlin/Heidelberg, Germany, 2007; 325–341. http://www.springerlink.com/content/qq35wt68l6774261/ for all info) .
4. Resnick, P.; Iacovou, N.; Suchak, M.; Bergstrom, P.; Riedl, J. GroupLens: An open architecture for collaborative filtering of netnews. In *Proceedings of the 1994 ACM Conference on Computer Supported Cooperative Work*, Computer Supported Cooperative Work, Chapel Hill, NC, October 22–26, 1994; ACM Press: New York, 1994; 175–186.
5. Crawford, D., Ed. Commun. ACM **1997**, *40* (3).
6. http://www.grouplens.org/ (accessed February 2008).
7. Shardanand, U.; Maes, P. Social information filtering: Algorithms for automating "word of mouth". In *Proceedings of the SIGCHI Conference on Human Factors in Computing Systems*, Conference on Human Factors in

Computing Systems, Denver, CO, May, 7–11, 1995; Association for Computing Machinery/Addison-Wesley: New York, 1995; 210–217.

8. Konstan, J.A., Ed.; Introduction to recommender systems: Algorithms and Evaluation. ACM Trans. Inform. Syst. (TOIS) **2004**, *22* (1), 1–4.

9. Riedl, J.; Dourish, P. Introduction to the special section on recommender systems. ACM Trans. Comput.-Hum. Interact. (TOCHI) **2005**, *12* (3), 371–373.

10. Felfernig, A.; Friedrich, G.; Schmidt-Thieme, L. Guest editors'. Introduction: Recommender systems. IEEE Intell. Syst. **2007**, *22* (3), 18–21, doi: 10.1109/MIS.2007.52.

11. *Proceedings of the 2007 ACM Conference on Recommender Systems*, RecSys'07, Minneapolis, MN, October 19–20, 2007; ACM Press: New York, 2007.

12. Streeter, L.; Lochbaum, K. Who knows: A system based on automatic representation of semantic structure. In *Proceedings of the Conference on Computer-Assisted Information Retrieval*, RIAO'88 Program Conference, Cambridge, MA, March, 21–24, 1988; CID: Paris, 1988; 380–388.

13. Krulwich, B.; Burkey, C. Contactfinder agent: Answering bulletin board questions with referrals. In *Proceedings of the13th National Conference on Artificial Intelligence*, AAAI National Conference, Portland, OR, August 4–8, 1996; AAAI Press: Menlo Park, CA, 1996; 10–15.

14. Maybury, M.; D'Amore, R.; House, D. Automated discovery and mapping of expertise. In *Sharing Expertise: Beyond Knowledge Management*; Ackerman, M.S., Pipek, V., Wulf, V., Eds.; MIT Press: Cambridge, MA, 2003; 359–382.

15. Ackerman, M.S. Answer garden: A tool for growing organizational memory. Wirtschaftsinformatik **1995**, *37* (3), 320–321.

16. Pipek, V.; Wulf, V. Pruning the answer garden: Knowledge sharing in maintenance engineering. In *ECSCW 2003: Proceedings of the Eighth European Conference on Computer Supported Cooperative Work*, Computer Supported Cooperative Work, Helsinki, Finland, September 14–18, 2003; Kuutti, K., Karsten, E.H., Fitzpatrick, G., Dourish, P., Schmidt, K., Eds.; Kluwer Academic: Dordrecht, the Netherlands, 2003; 1–20.

17. Ackerman, M.S.; McDonald, D.W. Answer garden 2: Merging organizational memory with collaborative help. In *Proceedings of the 1996 ACM Conference on Computer Supported Cooperative Work*, Computer Supported Cooperative Work, Boston, MA, November 16–20, 1996; ACM Press: New York, 1996; 97–105.

18. McDonald, D.W.; Ackerman, M.S. Expertise recommender: A flexible recommendation system and architecture. In *Proceedings of the 2000 ACM Conference on Computer Supported Cooperative Work*, Computer Supported Cooperative Work, Philadelphia, PA, December 2–6, 2000; ACM Press: New York, 2000; 231–240.

19. Kautz, H.; Selman, B.; Shah, M. Referral web: Combining social networks and collaborative filtering. Commun. ACM **1997**, *40* (3), 63–65.

20. Foner, L.N. Yenta: A multi-agent, referral-based matchmaking system. In *Proceedings of the 1st International Conference on Autonomous Agents*, International Conference on Autonomous Agents, Marina del Rey, CA, February, 5–8, 1997; ACM Press: New York, 1997; 301–307.

21. Yu, B.; Singh, M.P. Searching social networks. In *Proceedings of the 2nd International Joint Conference on Autonomous Agents and Multiagent Systems*, International Conference on Autonomous Agents, Melbourne, Australia, July, 14–18, 2003; ACM Press: New York, 2003; 65–72.

22. Zhang, J.; Van Alstyne, M. SWIM: Fostering social network based information search. In *CHI '04 Extended Abstracts on Human Factors in Computing Systems*, Conference on Human Factors in Computing Systems, Vienna, Austria, April 24–29, 2004; ACM Press: New York, 2004; 1568.

23. Ackerman, M.; Pipek, V.; Wulf, V., Eds. *Sharing Expertise: Beyond Knowledge Management*; MIT Press: Cambridge, MA, 2002.

24. Zhang, J.; Ackerman, M.S.; Adamic, L. Expertise networks in online communities: Structure and algorithms. In *Proceedings of the 16th International Conference on World Wide Web*, International World Wide Web Conference, Banff, Canada, May 8–12, 2007; ACM Press: New York, 2007; 221–230.

BIBLIOGRAPHY

1. Ackerman, M.S.; Halverson, C.A. Sharing expertise: The next step for knowledge management. In *Social Capital and Information Technology*; Huysman, M., Wulf, V., Eds.; MIT Press: Cambridge, MA, 2004; 273–300.

2. Ackerman, M.; Pipek, V.; Wulf, V., Eds. *Sharing Expertise: Beyond Knowledge Management*; MIT Press: Cambridge, MA, 2002.

3. Adomavicius, G.; Tuzhilin, A. Toward the next generation of recommender systems: A survey of the state-of-the-art and possible extensions. IEEE T. Knowl. Data. En., **2005**, *17* (6), 734–749.

4. http://www.grouplens.org/ (accessed February 2008).

5. *Proceedings of the 2007 ACM Conference on Recommender Systems*, RecSys'07, Minneapolis, MN, October 19–20, 2007; ACM Press: New York, 2007.

6. Resnick, P.; Varian, H.R. Recommender systems. Comm. ACM **1997**, *40* (3), 56–58.

7. Riedl, J.; Konstan, J. *Word of Mouse: The Marketing Power of Collaborative Filtering*; Warner Books: New York, 2002.

8. Terveen, L.; Hill, W. Beyond recommender systems: Helping people help each other. In *HCI in the New Millennium*; Carroll, J., Ed.; Addison Wesley: Boston, MA, 2001.

Records Compliance and Risk Management

Bradley J. Wiles
Hill Memorial Library, Louisiana State University, Baton Rouge, Louisiana, U.S.A.

Abstract

This entry considers *records compliance* and *risk management* in the context of archives and records administration. It provides a definition of these terms as separate concepts and examines them in combination.

INTRODUCTION

The concepts of *compliance* and *risk management* have been applied to various methods and strategies of business operations in a wide variety of industries over the past several decades.[1] This entry identifies banking, investment firms, and insurance companies as being particularly sensitive to managing risk and maintaining compliance to ensure sound business management. Minimizing risk and meeting various levels of statutory obligations are consistently perceived as necessary for stability, growth, and longevity. This is particularly relevant in the *archives and records administration* field, where securing the human record depends on evolving legal requirements, professional norms, and institutional standards. This entry will examine the place of compliance and risk management within the context of archives and records administration. It will provide separate definitions of each concept and evaluate these as related and complementary aspects of the creation, capture, and use of records.

Perhaps first it would be useful to provide a comprehensive definition for records management, simply because the principles it encompasses are generally applicable to a wide array of records and information activities. Records management is,

a professional discipline that is primarily concerned with the management of document-based information systems. The application of systematic and scientific controls to recorded information required in the operation of an organization's business. The systematic control of all organizational records during the various stages of their life cycle, from their creation or receipt, through their processing, distribution, maintenance, and use, to their ultimate disposition.[2]

The purpose of records management is, "to promote economies and efficiencies in recordkeeping, to assure that useless records are systematically destroyed while valuable information is protected and maintained in a manner that facilitates its access and use."[2]

Records management is also concerned with the analysis of any and all recorded information created, received, maintained, or used by an organization in accordance with its mission, operations, and activities.[3] Furthermore, records management deals with records regardless of age, type, or format, and is often an enterprise-wide undertaking that relies on cooperation at all levels of an organization.[4] Present-day records management is an outgrowth of traditional archival practice, but typically deals with contemporary recorded information and documents.[4] In the mid-twentieth century, a distinction was made between "historical" and "modern" documents, mostly because of the deluge of records flowing into traditional archives following World War II.[4] However, this distinction is no longer prevalent, and records management principles are applied to records produced by corporations, businesses, and governmental units (organizations using and retaining documents in the course of regular business), as well as those kept by historical societies, manuscript libraries, and other cultural institutions (organizations who hold collections for reasons of scholarship or posterity). In nearly all instances, the concepts of compliance and risk management factor significantly into the modern practice of archives and records administration.

RECORDS COMPLIANCE

It is somewhat difficult to comprehensively define compliance in the context of archives and records administration, simply because compliance measures are constantly in flux. In most instances, recordkeeping and reporting are part and parcel of other core compliance areas within organizations. These might include promoting fair and ethical business conduct, requiring proper environmental, health, and safety policies, or ensuring consumer protection,[5] and may or may not have a records component.

Encyclopedia of Library and Information Sciences, Fourth Edition DOI: 10.1081/E-ELIS4-120044624

In general, records compliance requirements derive from legislation, regulatory standards, codes of best practices, or community expectations (p.10).[4] These requirements exist at all social, political, and organizational levels, might be explicit or implied, and incorporate any number or combination of requirements (pp. 38–39).[4] For example, explicit legal requirements for the creation and management of records in a particular industry could mandate the extended retention of certain types of records created in particular operational contexts. It might also dictate the form in which these records should be maintained, the rights of individuals or corporate bodies to have access to those records, and the protection of the intellectual property that the records contain (p. 38).[4]

Compliance requirements affect records at all stages throughout their life cycle and can be subject to multiple legal jurisdictions. A significant amount of legal research is often necessary for organizations to determine the legal requirements for retention, destruction, discovery, and disclosure. The first step is to verify which authoritative entities the organization falls under. The degree of regulation varies by the type of industry and while the majority of businesses and organizations are not subject to any recordkeeping guidelines, those that are (e.g., financial services and pharmaceuticals) tend to be heavily regulated by multiple entities.[6] In particular, those responsible for an organization's legal and regulatory records compliance in the United States should be familiar with the Uniform Rules of Evidence (which apply to state courts), the Federal Rules of Evidence (which apply to federal courts), the National Conference of Commissioners on Uniform State Laws (which helps interpret and standardize laws across jurisdictions), the Uniform Commercial Code, the Uniform Electronic Transactions Act, the Photographic Copies as Evidence Act, the Federal Paperwork Reduction Act, the Code of Federal Regulations, and the statutes of the National Archives and Records Administration.[6]

The notion of accountability factors heavily into an organization's need to maintain compliance with strictures set forth by internal and external forces. In order to support accountability the records management department or representative must initiate a multilateral assessment of business needs, evidentiary requirements, legal obligations, and recognized best practices (pp. 155, 158).[4] This will enable ready response to legal challenges, grievances, and complaints from within and outside of the organization. Typically, compliance is checked—and accountability is fostered—through any number of internal and external inspections and audits, which often consist of a close physical examination of an organization's recordkeeping system measured against whatever compliance issues are at hand (p. 159).[4] The most effective audit procedures are ones established at the founding of the vital records management program and that remain sensitive to changing compliance regulations (pp. 75–76).[3] Audits best support accountability through regular scheduling that matches other organizational troubleshooting efforts and through designating proper authority to carry out inspections, make assessments, and implement recommendations. Though records retention audits typically only consist of a sampling of an organization's records series, this is usually sufficient to determine that organization's appropriate level of need for records security, storage, duplication, and destruction (pp. 75–76).[3]

RISK MANAGEMENT

According to the Association of Records Managers and Administrators, or ARMA International, risk management is a process that ensures an organization does not assume an unacceptable level of risk and includes both risk analysis and risk assessment procedures as key components.[7] The level of risk is determined by the importance of the record. All records have relative value, but vital records—ones that are unique and irreplaceable—tend to take precedence over those that can be recreated or those that are not essential to normal business operations (p. 73).[2] Risk analysis involves the evaluation of exposure of vital records to specific risks and provides a basis for protection planning by identifying threats and vulnerabilities (p. 133).[3] There are several broad categories of threats, which include destruction, loss, corruption, and improper disclosure of records and information (p. 133).[3]

In any organization it is imperative to discern acceptable levels of risk and typically this is accomplished through qualitative or quantitative risk assessment. The qualitative approach is most useful at identifying and categorizing physical security problems and other vulnerabilities such as malicious destruction, warfare, terrorist attacks, civil insurrections, purposeful sabotage, vandalism, and theft, as well as natural disasters or man-made accidents, errors, negligence, and incompetence (pp. 133, 136).[3] Quantitative risk assessment is based on methodologies developed for product safety analysis and computer security applications (p. 136).[3] It initially relies on qualitative measures such as site visits, and focuses on group discussions, but also uses numeric calculations to determine the annualized loss expectancy of a given institution (p. 136).[3] This dollar amount is estimated by figuring the probability of a particular event (or events) occurring over a given time span (p. 137).[3] Ultimately, it factors in the cost of record or information restoration, the loss of business as a result of not being able to perform specific business functions, and the costs of any litigation that might ensue (p. 137).[3] Upon completion of the analysis and assessment, risk can be managed through a series of controls, protections, and preventative measures that include strategic location (or relocation) of facilities, limiting access to vital records storage areas, stringent personnel screening and training, effective physical and electronic security, maintenance of multiple copies of vital records and information, initiating disaster recovery and business continuity plans, and developing a system of internal audits to ensure structural integrity (pp. 138–141).[3]

Though risk management largely addresses the prospect of lost business or capital, it would be insufficient to consider records risk management strictly in financial terms. One of the main tools of managing risk is the development of records retention policies and schedules. A records retention plan helps prioritize value by determining the risks involved in not keeping or destroying a set of records against the costs of maintaining them (p. 161).[4] However, this often represents a convergence of competing interests between internal and external factors, which are not always financial. For example, cultural institutions such as archives repositories or special research libraries might feel justified spending an inordinate amount of resources to keep a certain records collection because of its social or historical importance, or because of the prestige it confers on the institution. Likewise, organizations that do not use records expressly for their scholarly or cultural value still might justify the expense of maintaining an historical archive because of its potential to provide materials for advertising, marketing, public relations, and in support of corporate memory (pp. 158–159).[4] The length and quality of any retention program can be radically contingent among the various types of organizations that use records and the functions that those records fulfill.[8] This entry identifies the traditional retention schedules as following along departmental and functional lines, which can cause a tremendous amount of overlap and duplication. It recommends a process-based retention schedule that documents the work flow and follows legal retention requirements and business needs. This duration is based on the operational needs of the institution and the multiple levels of risk that accompanies those needs.

Though risk management procedures are partially based on what *might* happen—the worst-case scenario, the probability of disaster—it also involves active management of records and information assets from the earliest stages of production. Increasingly this means following a legally viable records retention policy, after taking steps to ensure authenticity in the production of records and information to meet all legal and regulatory requirements (p. 103).[4] The possibility of litigation has emerged as a primary concern in the creation and capture of records, particularly in the digital age when most documents are not necessarily created, stored, and disseminated in static formats.[9] The types of records that withstand legal challenges are those created as part of a transaction (as opposed to those created *ad hoc* or retroactively) during the regular course of business and that comply with legal

guidelines for content, medium, or layout (pp. 103–104).[4] Indeed, the landscape of records management, and thus the tools and procedures for managing risk, currently operate under a hyper-regulated atmosphere of compliance.

RECORDS COMPLIANCE AND RISK MANAGEMENT IN COMBINATION

According to a recent article in a financial services publication,

> In recent years... risk management and compliance have begun to converge in a new paradigm. In what amounts to a subtle but important shift in mindset, compliance requirements are now considered a major source of risk... Such thinking leads to a natural prioritization of compliance initiatives: Those risks that pose the greatest threat... are highest on the list. Strategies to eliminate and/or manage such risks become the primary focus of the compliance function. Since compliance requirements that relate to protecting client interests pose some of the greatest risks... taking a risk-oriented approach to compliance naturally aligns the firm's interests with client interests.[10]

The relationship of records compliance and risk management in archives and records administration is often one of reciprocity. The identification and management of risk is usually dictated by compliance measures that exist within and outside of an organization. Compliance measures—through legislation, best-practices initiatives, or organizational rules—are sensitive to business needs and generally reflect standards determined by industry-wide risk assessment. This reciprocal relationship is perhaps most fully embodied in the Australian National Archives, which adopted the Australian Standards for Records Management (AS-4390) in 1996.[11] AS-4390 approaches government records from a risk management perspective and seeks to ensure impartiality and accountability among the creators and keepers of state records.[11] AS-4390 also provides for a system of compliance audits and continual monitoring of documentary integrity (pp. 171–172).[4] In this sense, AS-4390 demonstrates how, when applied to an organization, the principles of risk management and compliance are interrelated and complementary. In 2001, it was adapted by the International Organization for Standardization (ISO 15489-1:2001) as the preferred model for electronic records produced and maintained by governmental bodies (pp. 27, 249).[4] The authors note that ISO 15489–1:2001 standard for sustainable records management is based on AS-4390, and these provide the "benchmark against which records management programmes and systems can be measured."

In some instances the confluence of risk management and compliance complicates the rubric under which an organization operate's. Risk often accompanies reward and sometimes the benefit of partial or noncompliance is perceived as outweighing the cost. For example, a multi-national company may have branches in several jurisdictions that all require different retention periods for vital records. To keep all vital records in every jurisdiction for the longest possible period to cover all bases may be cost prohibitive. To irregularly schedule and follow several retention plans may be logistically impossible. In this instance, the organization will likely turn to whatever cost/benefit analysis its risk and compliance cohorts have formulated. They would consider which records were most abundant and valuable, where these records were located, and exactly what compliance requirements it was absolutely necessary to fulfill. In the event that the compliance measures did not specifically address records, the organization would factor in limitations on legal recourse against any action they might carry out (p. 159).[4] From there, it could be decided that the risk of less than full compliance of certain records (of relatively low value) in certain jurisdictions (with less punitive measures and enforcement) is acceptable. The likelihood of getting caught and receiving a fine, or of losing business and prestige, might be considered less than the cost of full compliance.

Though this may not present an ideal scenario, realistically the level of compliance becomes a matter of how an institution chooses to allocate its resources, particularly in a regulation-heavy climate.[12] This entry asserts that despite the billions of dollars spent to accommodate laws like Sarbanes-Oxley and HIPPA, one hundred percent compliance is "fundamentally impossible." However, compliance and risk management are increasingly no longer viewed as necessary evils or impediments to profitable business operations. More and more records are considered assets, whether they are used in everyday business transactions or for academic and cultural reasons. As a result, risk management and compliance are increasingly perceived as core operational functions, integral to the solvency and growth of an organization. In the wake of far-reaching banking, investment, and corporate accounting scandals of this decade, risk management and compliance in records administration should further gain cachet as necessary systemic enhancements. They should no longer merely serve as corrective measures only used after an organization gets caught doing something illegal or unethical.

CONCLUSION

This entry has attempted to identify the key elements of risk management and compliance in archives and records administration, both as individual concepts and as complementary components of recordkeeping. It should be reiterated that the management of risk requires an enterprise-wide assessment of threats and vulnerabilities increasingly

aimed at securing dynamic documentary formats. As a result of greater reliance on digital mediums, the move toward more stringent regulation and standardization has found both support and controversy in the archives and records management world. It could safely be assumed that as governments, businesses, cultural institutions, and other organizations become more fully digitized, risk management and compliance will become even more closely connected.

ACKNOWLEDGMENTS

The author would like to thank the following: Dr. Ciaran Trace and Dr. Louise Robbins at the University of Wisconsin School of Library and Information Studies, and Dr. Peter Gottlieb at the Wisconsin Historical Society.

REFERENCES

1. Ludwick, K. Tackling risk-based compliance. J. Invest. Compl. **2006**, *7* (4), 61.
2. Robek, M.; Brown, G.; Stephens, D., Eds. *Information and Records Management: Document-Based Information Systems*, 4th Ed.; Glencoe/McGraw-Hill, Inc.: Woodland Hills, CA, 1995; 585.
3. Saffady, W. *Records and Information Management: Fundamentals of Professional Practice*; ARMA International: Lenexa, KS, 2004.
4. Shepherd, E.; Yeo, G. *Managing Records: A Handbook of Principles and Practice*; Facet Publishing: London, U.K., 2003.
5. Cellini, R.J. Compliance risk: A top-10 list. Directors Boards **2007**, *31*, 52–53.
6. Cogar, R.N. Legal 101 for RIM Professionals. Inform. Manag. J. **2005**, *39* (6), 49–56.
7. ARMA International, *Vital Records: Identifying, Managing, and Recovering Business-Critical Records*; ANSI/ARMA International: Lenexa, KS, 2003; 6.
8. Torres, T. Creating a process-focused retention schedule. Inform. Manag. J. **2006**, *40* (5), 62–69.
9. Arnold, J.R. We're not in Kansas anymore. AIIM E-doc Mag. **2007**, *21* (1), 50–54.
10. Martin, D.; Manley, M.R. Linking compliance, risk management. Pensions Investments **2006**, *34* (18), 12.
11. Boles, F. *Selecting and Appraising Archives and Manuscripts*; Society of American Archivists: Chicago, IL, 2005; 31–32.
12. Gincel, R. The awful truth about compliance. InfoWorld **2005**, *27* (50), 29.

BIBLIOGRAPHY

1. Allman, T.Y. Fostering a compliance culture: The role of the Sedona guidelines. Inform. Manag. J. **2005**, *39* (2), 54–61.

2. Kahn, R.A. Records management and compliance: Making the connection. Inform. Manag. J. **2004**, *18* (3), 28–35.

3. Lemieux, V.L. *Managing Risks for Records and Information*; ARMA International: Lenexa, KS, 2004.

4. Montana, J.C.; Dietel, J.E.; Martins, C.S. *Sarbanes-Oxley Act: Implications for Records Management*; ARMA International: Lenexa, KS, 2003.

5. St. Germain, R. Information security management best practice based on ISO/IEC 17799. Inform. Manag. J. **2005**, *39* (4), 60–66.

6. Swartz, N. Enterprise-wide records training: Key to compliance success. Inform. Manag. J. **2006**, *40* (5), 34–44.

Records Continuum Model

Sue McKemmish
Franklyn Herbert Upward
Centre for Organisational and Social Informatics, Monash University, Melbourne, Victoria, Australia

Barbara Reed
Recordkeeping Innovation, Sydney, New South Wales, Australia

Abstract

The entry begins with general statements on records continuum concepts. It then briefly outlines the evolution of records continuum thinking and practice in Australia because that Australian background helps explain the records continuum model and its points of entry into international discourse. It explores key continuum concepts and provides a detailed exposition of the records continuum model. The use of the model in teaching and research, and its application to professional practice are discussed. The entry also explains how the records continuum model connects to the broader discourses of postmodernism, philosophy and sociology. The entry concludes with a brief discussion of possible future uses and applications of the model.

INTRODUCTION

The records continuum concept of records encompasses records of continuing value (archives) and records in any form. Continuum ideas therefore challenge understandings which differentiate "archives" from "records" on the basis of selection for permanent preservation in archival custody, and definitions of records as physical artifacts in terms of their format or media. Adopting a pluralist view of recorded information, continuum thinking characterizes records as logical objects, belonging to a special genre of recorded information made up of the documentary traces of social and organizational activity. They are accumulated and managed by recordkeeping and archiving processes as record, archive and archives.

All transactions can leave archival traces. They become records when they are stored and managed by recordkeeping and archiving processes. Beyond the immediate business and social contexts which surround records they are transformed into a corporate or personal archive by recordkeeping and archiving processes that "place" records into frameworks for the social and business activities and functions of an organization, group or individual, and manage them in ways that enable them to function as individual, group, or corporate memory. And beyond the boundaries of organizations and individuals, recordkeeping and archiving processes transform the individual or corporate archive by "placing" it into a larger archival framework that enables it to function as accessible collective memory.

Recordkeeping is "a" form of witnessing and memory making, a particular way of evidencing and memorializing individual and collective lives. Records have multiple purposes in terms of their continuing relevance to an individual, organization, or society. They are vehicles of communication and interaction, facilitators of decision-making, enablers of continuity, consistency and effectiveness in human action, memory stores, identity shapers, repositories of experience, evidence of rights and obligations. On a darker note, they can also be instruments of repression and abuse of power. Whatever function they are performing, their usefulness as evidence is bound up with how they have been created, how they have been captured in recorded form, how they have been organized for distribution and recall, and how widely accessible they are on a continuing basis beyond the confines of the systems managed by records creating agents and their successors. Can records be trusted as accurate, complete, reliable, and authentic sources of information? Can they be recalled and disseminated when needed and do they have integrity? Can users of records be assured that they have not been altered or tampered with? Is information available about related documents, the acts and events which they document, and does it provide links in some way to the wider context of social and organizational activity, and the people and organizations involved?

In records continuum professional discourse and practice, the differences between records on the one hand, and other forms of recorded information on the other, rest on their evidential qualities, purposes, and functionality. From this perspective, the recordkeeping profession and archival institutions in our society are charged with the mission of building and managing frameworks and systems which assure the preservation and accessibility of

Encyclopedia of Library and Information Sciences, Fourth Edition DOI: 10.1081/E-ELIS4-120043719

accurate, complete, reliable, and authentic records "in" and "through" time and space. The accountability of the recordkeeping profession and archival institutions is therefore a critical issue in democratic societies.

Records continuum thinking takes a multidimensional view of the creation of documents as part of our activities (proto record-as-trace), their capture into records systems (record-as-evidence), their organization within the framework of a personal or organizational archive (record-as-personal/corporate memory), and their pluralization as collective archives (record-as-collective memory). This view is captured in the records continuum model developed by Frank Upward in the mid-1990s. Before discussing that model, the following section trace the evolution of continuum thinking and practice in Australia.

THE EVOLUTION OF CONTINUUM THINKING IN AUSTRALIA

A records continuum approach shares many things with other archival approaches where connections are made between current and historical recordkeeping processes, although sometimes its vocabulary is deliberately provocative in an attempt to disturb preconceptions. For example, a book published in Australia in 1993 used the term "archival documents" in its title as a term to cover both current and historical records, a standard enough usage in some countries perhaps, but relatively rare in Australia. In the opening paragraphs of the book (p. 1), it was noted that:

> The effective creation and management of archival documents are critical to their use and the role they play in governing relationships in society over time and space. Their effective creation and management are also preconditions of an information-rich society and underpin the public accountability of government and non-government organisations, freedom of information and privacy legislation, protection of people's rights and entitlements, and the quality of the archival heritage, made up of documents of continuing value. The concept of the archival document can provide a framework for a greater shared understanding of the nature of recorded information, and of the importance of transactional records to the continuing functioning of a society.[1]

The book explored a unifying concept of records which is inclusive of archives and encompasses records in any form. It also addressed a key concern of the recordkeeping and archiving communities in the twentieth century in many countries, the recordkeeping-accountability nexus, linked to an emphasis on records as evidence of social and organizational activity. While concerns relating to recordkeeping and accountability are shared by professional recordkeeping communities, the book argued that the divisions in the communities militated against developing recordkeeping professional practice that could meet

society's accountability needs. The unifying concept of archival documents was intended to be provocative, to challenge the archival and records management divide.

The use of the term recordkeeping by continuum archivists is also provocative. The term is widely used in North America in relation to electronic communications, but is interpreted narrowly in relation to paper based systems and is not inclusive of archiving processes. As used in continuum writings, recordkeeping is broad and inclusive, a form of witnessing, remembering, and forgetting. It encompasses a range of intertwined recordkeeping and archiving processes and activities carried out by records managers and archivists for current, regulatory, and historical recordkeeping purposes. These purposes include the roles that recordkeeping plays in and through space and time in governance and accountability, remembering and forgetting, shaping identity and providing value-added sources of information. In classificatory terms "recordkeeping" in this usage subsumes records management and archival administration. It also encompasses the personal and corporate recordkeeping activities undertaken by individuals in their everyday lives, in families, work or community groups, and in organizations of all kinds. In classificatory terms, recordkeeping runs through records management and archival administration in recurring and equally present fashion. It cannot simply be subsumed as a subordinate activity within either area of activity. The continuum approach tries to avoid the threat posed to recordkeeping and archiving processes if the professional drive of archivists and records managers to separate their disciplines is allowed to override the recordkeeping and archiving needs of particular systems and situations.

Gene Pool

The first clear examples of continuum-based practice in Australia were in the Commonwealth Archives Office in the 1960s. Ian Maclean, the Chief Archivist, noted retrospectively that a hallmark of the Office's operation was its drive to seek a "continuum of (public) records administration" from administrative efficiency through recordkeeping to the safe keeping of a "cultural end-product."[2] MacLean's reference to the continuum is far from the *Shorter Oxford English Dictionary* definition:

> A continuing thing, quantity, or substance; a continuous series of elements passing into each other.

However his approach had genuine continuum-based components. He provided Australian archivists with a topology, a continuing logic for the study of the formation of archives in any place, in any time, and in whatever form, emphasizing three key elements—the characteristics of recorded information, classification processes and recordkeeping systems. The characteristics of recorded information of most interest to archivists are authenticity and reliability as the basis for evidence-based decision making and public accountability. Classification is the basis for records construction as well as retrieval, and is based on knowledge of organizational functions, activities and processes. Maclean's recordkeeping system emphasis was grounded in the registry tradition and also reflected the organizational and methods approaches of the time.

Maclean's proto-continuum implementation model challenged emerging professional differences between archivists and records managers. He argued that the archival profession has three branches. One branch, registrars, worked in government departments designing record-keeping systems and maintaining survey data about where records were being created and kept. Members of this branch in his mind were the "true archivists" because they were the ones most directly involved in the archival formation process. Another branch, described as historical recordkeepers, worked in archival institutions. A third branch liaised between the current managers of record-keeping processes and the historical recordkeepers. The three branches brought recordkeeping and archiving processes together into a style of records continuum management.[3] One of Maclean's colleagues, Peter Scott, provided the final element in continuum management in the CRS (Commonwealth Record Series) or series system, an archival system of registration that could control recordkeeping objects at any point in time from creation in agencies through to custody in government archives.

In the 1970s this system was at its peak. A strong evidence-based recordkeeping culture had emerged in the Commonwealth Archives Office. Staff engaged in the evolution and implementation of Scott's CRS system developed rich understandings of the web of multiple social, functional, provenancial, and documentary relationships established during the ongoing creation, management and use of records. For a number of reasons including changing technologies, and changes in management emphasis within the Commonwealth Archives Office (known as Australian Archives from 1984), the approach began to wane in the 1980s. New managerial approaches moved away from reliance on registry systems which tightly controlled and integrated business and recordkeeping processes, and downplayed the ethical responsibility of public servants to document their actions.

The Second Generation

In the1990s when archivists in Australia were challenged by electronic recordkeeping issues, there was a renewed interest in the proto-continuum implementation models of Maclean and Scott. As was being discovered simultaneously by both Australian and North American archivists, in electronic recordkeeping environments, authenticity and reliability issues could not be addressed at the desktop—they needed to be dealt with through systems design and implementation tactics.

Authenticity and reliability issues were also a particular concern in Australia in the early 1990s. At that time the findings of a number of Royal Commissions and major inquiries into a series of accountability crises in government and the corporate sector in the 1980s were released. They focused attention on the role of recordkeeping in supporting democratic and corporate accountability. Complementary questions included: what constitutes accountable recordkeeping, what types of organizational and societal risks are associated with failures in recordkeeping, how can recordkeeping professionals demonstrate the causal links between poor or negligent recordkeeping, and failures in accountability, how can recordkeeping professionals play a part in addressing the need for evidence based decision-making in all spheres of life, and how can the role of public archival authorities as accountability players in democratic societies be safeguarded?

Emerging continuum-based frameworks for the management of electronic records and understandings stemming from preoccupation with the recordkeeping-accountability nexus drove the development of standards for accountable corporate recordkeeping regimes within the Australian community during the mid-1990s, in particular AS 4390, the *Australian Standard: Records Management*.[4] They also fed into reviews of archival law and the dual role of public archival authorities at national and state level in managing accountable public recordkeeping and the archival heritage. The University of Pittsburgh's "Functional Requirements for Evidence in Recordkeeping Project," in particular Bearman's formulation of a mix of policy, standards, system design, and implementation tactics to satisfy them,[5] also significantly influenced the Australian standard. AS 4390, elements of which were later picked up in an International Standard (ISO 15849), continued the Australian practice of being transactionally focused, emphasizing the links between activities and functions and related records, but did so in a media independent fashion. The Australian recordkeeping profession is still taking a lead role in developing recordkeeping standards, including standards that link recordkeeping to business processes as part of the formation of archives, e. g. standards relating to work process analysis, functional analysis, and organizational analysis. There was a particular synergy between the work of Bearman,[6] understandings of recordkeeping systems derived from the registry tradition in Australia, and Maclean's legacy. In continuum practice, recordkeeping system requirements are specified in terms of capturing the content of documents, representing their structure, and linking related documents together. The information content and structure of records at their point of creation needs to be retained in reconstructible relationships. A cumulating history of events documenting the subsequent, management, access and use of records is essential. As more archival traces are incorporated into the record, more documentary and contextual links and relationships need to be captured and documented. Recordkeeping systems thereby enable records to be retrieved at a later date in a form that represents their original content and structure, exposes their documentary relationships, and reflects their multiple contexts of creation, ongoing management and use, thus preserving their evidentiary nature.

By the early 1990s the use of the term records continuum was becoming ubiquitous in Australia. This usage followed the publication of Atherton's groundbreaking article that showed how the life cycle stages that records supposedly underwent were in fact a series of recurring and reverberating activities within both archives and records management.[7] At the same time records continuum literature[8–12] began to expand and engage in discourse across archival boundaries, both geographical in terms of the archival profession, and professional in terms of cognate disciplines. In particular, continuum writers engaged with the writings of Duranti on European archival theory and diplomatics,[13] and of Hedstrom,[14] McDonald,[15] and Hofman[16] relating to the early implementation of electronic recordkeeping policies and strategic approaches in New York State, Canada, and the Netherlands respectively. Cook's writings on postcustodialism and appraisal, grounded in Canadian re-conceptualizations of provenance, also provided a touchstone for Australian records continuum thinkers.[17,18] As did Ketelaar's writing in relation to societal and cultural frameworks.[19]

Records continuum approaches to building holistic, multidimensional frameworks for integrated recordkeeping and archiving processes were informed by the synergies between these discourses. Australian understandings of the nature of records as evidence, and the integrated recordkeeping and workflow processes associated with registry systems were also significant inputs. As were the concepts of multiple provenance and the rich and dynamic views of records present in the CRS system, as further developed and refined in the work of Chris Hurley.[20]

THE MODEL

The records continuum is most commonly represented in the seminal model form (Fig. 1) developed by Frank Upward with input from colleagues Sue McKemmish and Livia Iacovino and first published in 1996. As indicated in the preceding sections, the model is representative of a more complex body of thought which came before it and has continued to develop since its publication.

Of key importance in understanding the model, and the continuum approach embedded within it, is the notion of transactionality. In continuum thinking it is defined in terms of the many forms of human interaction and relationships that are documented in records at all levels of aggregation. It encompasses individual acts of communication, and social and business transactions of all kinds, the social and business activities or processes of which they are a part, the social and business functions they fulfill, and the social purposes they serve.

> The archival document [record] can be conceptualised as recorded information arising from transactions. It is created as a by-product of social and organisational activity in the course of transacting business of any kind, whether by governments, businesses, community organisations or private individuals. ...The documentation of transactions may be in any storage media and is increasingly an electronic process. In Australia and North America, the use of the terms "records" and "archives", to refer to current

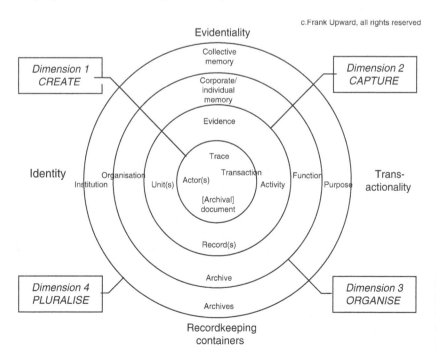

Fig. 1 The records continuum model.
Source: Structuring the records continuum, Part One: Post custodial principles and properties, by F. Upward. In Arch. Manuscripts **1996**, *24*(2), 268–285.

archival documents and archival documents selected for preservation respectively, has created a distracting division within the recordkeeping profession between records managers and archivists. The unifying concept of the archival document encompasses both records and archives. It directs attention to the continuum of processes involved in managing the record of a transaction so that it retains its evidentiary quality... (p. 1).[1]

The model is explained below using a dimensional (circles) then an axial (lines and points) view. The explanation works from the first dimension outwards to the fourth dimension, but it could equally be written from the fourth to the first dimension. The records continuum is not linear, although for the purposes of explanation it might sometimes seem to be.

The Dimensions of the Records Continuum

This explanation draws substantially from an article by Reed.[21] Table 1 summarizes the dimensions of the records continuum.

The first "create" dimension of the records continuum model represents the locus of all action, including representations of actions in documents. This dimension provides a perspective on things that are in the process of formation, may exist in versions or as partial expressions. The document has the potential to move beyond the locus of creation, but as yet this potential is nascent—all the elements required for robustness are present but not explicit. Until the connections are explicit, the document cannot be managed as a record.

The beginnings of that journey to robustness occur with transition into the second "capture" dimension when the document is communicated or connected through relationships with other documents, with sequences of action. With characteristics from the second dimension, records, now attest to action and are able to be distributed, accessed and understood by others involved in business activities. The transition to the second dimension may be formal or informal, may involve a deliberate act of registration in organizational systems, or may be an intention represented by placement or grouping. Here contextualizing metadata elements are added and the record is able to be referenced or drawn upon by others. The first and second dimensions of the model can be thought of as the immediate zones of interaction and the recording of that action.

The third dimension, the "organize" dimension, represents an aggregation above individual instances of sequences of actions, investing the record with explicit elements needed to ensure that it is available over time and beyond the immediate environments of action. Here, a record joins multiple other records deriving from multiple sequences of actions undertaken for multiple purposes. This is the dimension of the "archive" or the "fonds," the whole, extant or potential, of all of the records of an organization or individual cumulating to form organizational or personal memory. At an implementation level, this is the dimension of policy or rule establishment which will affect the "create" and "capture" dimensions.

The fourth or "pluralize" dimension represents societal perspectives on recordkeeping—the cultural, legal, and regulatory environment of recordkeeping, which is different for every society and in every period. Recordkeeping does not occur in a social, cultural or political void. The environment of recordkeeping external to a specific locus of records action, and the memory and evidence paradigms of a particular time and place, critically determine the nature of the record. The fourth dimension also represents the capacity of a record to exist beyond the boundaries of creating entities, to meet the needs of those not involved with the actions precipitating records creation, capture, and organization. Pluralization processes enable records to be reviewed, accessed and analyzed beyond an organization or individual life, for multiple external accountability and memory purposes in and through time and space.

The Points in the Records Continuum

The words in the model should be thought of as points around which many other words and definitions can cluster, revealing an increasingly complex array of issues of critical concern to recordkeeping, rather than as prescriptive signifiers. The points can be connected in a multiplicity of ways to represent the dynamic relationships between records and their rich, complex and multilayered social, functional, provenancial, and documentary contexts of creation, management, and use in and through space and time. In the records continuum model these concepts find expression in a range of continua described in Table 2. In the original representation of the model, the points were plotted along four axes, but later versions represent only the points, not the lines.

A records continuum approach acknowledges the need to discuss and describe recordkeeping objects in conventional ways, but tries to put that discussion and description into relational contact with other concepts and with the functioning of systems that create, capture, organize, and pluralize the objects. Records can be described with the assistance of different points in the continuum, including memory as it is contained in records, the way they are managed and classified in accordance with the identities of those involved in activities, and their connections with transactions that are the subject of recordkeeping processes.

The evidential continuum opens up many questions for records managers, archivists and others. Does a recordkeeping object provide a trace of action, can it testify to the events it documents (in many different places, not just courtrooms), and what does it witness? Even more

Table 1 The dimensions of the records continuum model.

Dimensions	Concerns addressed in the dimension
Dimension 1: Create [archival] documents-as-trace *The first dimension encompasses the **actors** who carry out the act (decisions, communications, acts), the **acts** themselves, the **documents** which record the acts, and the **trace**, the representation of the acts.*	In the first dimension, acts, communications and decisions are documented. Document creation and control processes are implemented which: • capture structure (documentary form) • order and place documents in their immediate context of action and facilitate their retrieval • store documents and provide for their security.
Dimension 2: Capture records-as-evidence *The second dimension encompasses the personal and corporate recordkeeping systems which capture **records** (documents in their contexts of action) in ways which support their capacity to act as **evidence** of the social and business **activities** of the **units** responsible for the activities.*	In the second dimension, recordkeeping processes and systems are implemented in accordance with the design requirements, standards and best practice models set up in the third and fourth dimensions. Implemented processes and systems: • capture records at specified points in business processes (when predetermined "boundaries" are crossed) • capture and maintain the metadata required to assure their quality as records of business and social activity (i.e. metadata that places them in relation to other records and links them to their context of activity), and to manage their usability (completeness, accuracy, and reliability) and accessibility through time • deliver records for use through time according to relevant access permissions, and user views • store and secure records through time.
Dimension 3: Organize records-as-corporate memory *The third dimension encompasses the organization of recordkeeping processes. It is concerned with the manner in which a corporate body, **organization** or **individual** defines it/her/his recordkeeping regime and in so doing constitutes/forms the **archive** as **memory** of its/her/his business or social **functions**.*	In the third dimension, recordkeeping concerns involve: • identifying personal and corporate requirements for essential evidence to function as personal/corporate memory • establishing recordkeeping regimes in the personal or corporate domain • developing organizational knowledge bases and classification schemes that represent the personal and corporate contexts of recordkeeping • putting in place storage and migration strategies that carry records through the life of an organization or a person • developing access strategies that manage access according to the rules of a particular personal or corporate domain.
Dimension 4: Pluralize records-as-collective memory *The fourth dimension concerns the manner in which the **archives** are brought into an encompassing (ambient) framework in order to provide a **collective** social, historical, and cultural **memory** of the **institutionalized** social purposes and roles of individuals and corporate bodies*	In the fourth dimension, recordkeeping concerns involve: • identifying social and cultural mandates for essential evidence to function as collective memory • establishing recordkeeping regimes that can carry records beyond the life of an organization or person • developing knowledge bases and classification schemes that represent the broadest structural and functional contexts of record keeping • putting in place storage and migration strategies that carry records beyond the life of an organization or a person • developing access strategies that manage access across jurisdictions.

The words in italics in the first column are cited from an article by Upward[22] and those in the second column from an article by McKemmish.[23]

tantalizingly difficult to ascertain, how heavily is it memorialized—inscribed into individual psyches, used by groups and organizations? And most dynamic of all, is it fighting with or fitting into other forms of individual, corporate or collectively accessible memory?

The continuum of transactionality raises many professional recordkeeping issues, with the points providing different levels of analysis for such matters as appraisal, metadata, and classification schemes.

The continuum of identity raises general questions about how we see ourselves and how we relate to the groups, organizations and wider societies to which we belong. Significant issues relating to privacy and openness are brought into play. In a more pragmatic sense, for

Table 2 The points in the records continuum model.

Points	Explanation
Continuum of recordkeeping objects: [archival] documents, records, the corporate and individual archive, and the collective archives	Represents recordkeeping objects—the [archival] document, i.e., the documentary form in which it is created, the records system in which it is captured, the individual or corporate archive and the "plural" (collective) archives.
Evidential continuum: trace, evidence, corporate, and individual [whole of person] memory, collective memory	Represents the quality of recordness, the role that the record plays as trace, evidence, organizational/individual memory, and encompassing collective memory—in informing, witnessing and memorializing.
Continuum of transactionality: act, activity, function, purpose	Here the act (decision, communication, act) forms part of a business or social activity or process, which in turn is part of a business or social function which is an aspect of a higher-level social purpose or ambient function.
Continuum of identity: actor, work group/unit, organization/corporate body, and institution	Represents the actor, the unit (person or group with the corporate or socially assigned authority or power to undertake an activity or play a role in relationship to other units), the organization (a corporate body established to perform certain functions or an individual acting as a legal entity) and the institution (the broad social domain, jurisdiction or competence with reference to which the authority may be exercised or the role played).

The words in the second column are drawn from an article by Upward.[22]

archivists, identity is significant for purposes of representation, recall and dissemination. Does the data kept about recorded information include and utilize information about the actor, the unit, the organization and the institution? How effectively is that data garnered and used by recordkeeping systems?

The Model in the Broader Intellectual Discourse

The construction of the records continuum model had some grounding in the broader philosophical and sociological discourses of the time. For example four French academics—Jacques Lacan, Michel Foucault, Jacques Derrida, and Jean-François Lyotard—were in vogue in academies in English speaking countries and the model has a genetic connection to all of them.

To Lacan[24] the model owes its determination to find an accurate and useful topology, a logical structure for the stretching of information and data into different recordkeeping objects. The circles in the model represent the changing shapes of the documentary objects in information stores, a very Lacanian depiction of through-time stretching processes that he sees as part of personality formation, but in the continuum relate to archives formation. Lacan's famous metaphor for this process in psychoanalysis is the doughnut and the needle, the shapes of the female and the male. At conception we all have the shape of the female, and the needle in fact retains that shape but in apparently different form.

The circles of the model can also be read as thresholds that might or might not be crossed in the manner of Foucault's thresholds for the process of knowledge formation.[25] He writes of the irregular manner by which discursive formations build across the thresholds of "positivity" (positive statements about something),

"epistemologization" (arrangement within dominant groupings of statements), "scientificity" (the making of laws for the construction and testing of statements), and "formalization" (when the laws become axiomatic, existing as starting points for statements and shutting out other statements). This view helps explain why Gilles Deleuze at the time this book was published called Foucault the "new archivist." He placed considerable importance on the way a discursive archive builds up control over discussion by the manner in which participants in it file documents as monuments in a multidimensional, controlled, and controlling manner.

The model's development also involved a technique for deconstruction which can be called post-Derridan in that the intention is to derail the ingrained habit so common in modern thinking of defining words in terms of the pairing of imagined opposites.[26] Whenever you have a discourse settling in to dualisms such as archives and records, interpolate a third point into the discussion and relate the other terms to it. Using that technique many pairs of words that are defined in opposition to each other suddenly reveal a wealth of similarities and differences. The interpolation of third points can also be called continuum mathematics, and in the model this grew into interpolating other points, establishing a multiplicity of relationships. The model as a tool can also be linked more directly to Derridan thinking by pausing on words, their use in different places and times, and the spaces that surround them (Derrida's work, Archive Fever: A Freudian Impression[27] was being drafted in the same time frame as the model itself and therefore had no impact on the development of the model).

Groundings of this type were part of the play of ideas involved in the model's construction, and no tight academic connections are being claimed. When the model was first presented in print, however, attention was drawn to Lyotard's[28] recommendation to use the following approaches to challenging settled discourses:

- Think problems through from every possible direction using conventional analytical techniques (analysis)
- Accept new shapes for our thinking (anamorphosis)
- Sometimes accept solutions because they feel right (anagogy – for Lyotard, for example, it was beyond debate that society's memory banks should serve justice even if we will never achieve consensus about what justice means)
- Be willing to accept that some forgetting needs to be part of the process (anamnesis).

While one can develop transcendental readings of the model relating to aspirations for future professional practice, the model will always provide a critical way of assessing what is actually being done. This capacity for different readings is what makes the model an open one. Continuum philosophies are monistic, offering single explanations, but paradoxically their monadic nature deliberately encompasses diversity. They provide a single metanarrative, but never exclude other metanarratives. This postmodern position, a form of relativism first put by the philosopher Samuel Alexander in 1920 in his epic treatise, *Space, Time and Deity*, has been subject to inconclusive debate in philosophy ever since. Indeed the perpetually postmodern aspect of continuum theory means that debate on it will always be inconclusive.

Attempts to address the metaphysics of the spacetime continuum are taking place across many disciplines, but one of particular relevance to archivists given the close connection between the formation of archives and the modes of operation and survival of social groups, is sociology. One of the most widely read sociologists of the last quarter century, Anthony Giddens, explores spacetime issues at great length and depth.[29] Giddens' structuration theory deals with the ongoing relationship between our actions and the structures in which they take place. It is a time space theory dealing with the transmutation of structures, the reproduction of social systems, and, most significantly for archivists, the role of recorded information in these processes. In particular, Giddens' ideas suggest that recordkeeping and archiving professionals should be concerned with both the fixity and the mutability of records, and with the persistent and the contingent nature of recordkeeping. The records continuum will always be with us but to the professionally functioning archivist, it does not present itself in the same way in different times and places. At present it is not being managed well. Evidence based decision-making systems are collapsing and many people are suffering as a result. To appreciate this, consider those retirees whose superannuation depended upon the shares of the failed company Enron, or the citizens of Iraq invaded, it was said, because of the existence of weapons of mass destruction. In these examples the expanding complexity of the spacetime continuum have led to complex changes to corporate operations and the conduct of foreign affairs and war, and these changes have outstripped our capacity to manage the records continuum in matching complex ways.

USES OF THE MODEL

Rather than allowing us to think in convenient pairs or binaries, the model encourages consideration of the multiple potential points of recordkeeping intervention and actions. It brings much more complex layers of implicit and explicit meanings to the fore, and importantly enables exploration of the space revealed between the points, opening out a range of possibilities. The model allows what is actually occurring in different environments to be brought in to the discussion. All its spaces and silences make it a very democratic and global instrument inviting anyone to relate to the points in the continuum from any perspective and to enter into a discussion irrespective of their cultural background or professional experiences. Alternatively, and equally, those with sophisticated understandings can convey their developed ideas easily and quickly:

> The critical importance of the continuum rests on five factors: 1) its conceptual interaction of the sixteen levels and axes too often viewed in archival circles as separate and static; 2) its insight that these complex relationships are fluid, multiple, and simultaneous across time and space, not sequential and fixed; 3) its reconciliation (with some adjustments as suggested) of evidence and memory; 4) its potential for imaginatively incorporating private-sector manuscripts with institutional archives; and 5) its assertion through pluralization that societal and thus cultural values will influence appraisal and, indeed, all aspects of record-keeping.[30]

The model is at its most useful when it is made to dance as the Australian archivist, Chris Hurley, once observed. Those who cannot or do not want to make it dance see only circles and words with spaces in between them. But choreographing its dimensions and points reveals complex relationships which are "fluid, multiple, and simultaneous across time and space,"[30] not sequential and fixed. Relationships between evidence and memory between the private and the corporate, between the archive as an instrument of restriction and the archives as a liberating force can be discussed within its framework in both practical and speculative fashion.

CURRENT USE OF THE MODEL

The records continuum model can serve as metaphor, as a topological model to repattern archival knowledge and reshape professional practice, and as a topographical or implementation model.

Rare–Reference

As metaphor, for example, it turns the recursivity of action represented in Atherton's continuum insight into a constant return to the moment in time when action occurs. The notion of recursiveness unlocks many different perspectives on recordkeeping processes through spacetime. Examples of the model's use as a topological model are provided below, including its application as a teaching and training tool, and research instrument, and its role in reshaping professional practice in Australia. The proto-continuum implementation models of Maclean and Scott are discussed in the first part of this entry. Their legacy and the use of the Upward model as a topographical model are exemplified in Australia in the development of recordkeeping standards, metadata entity-relationship models and schemas, and best practice guidelines for the design of recordkeeping systems and appraisal programs.

Teaching Tool

The model has been successful as a teaching tool, spreading into educational and training programs worldwide. As a pedagogical tool it provides a framework for interpreting records and archives thinking and practice. For example, the international and national records management standards, developed to serve plural frameworks (the fourth dimension of the model), establish compliance requirements and community expectations for accountable corporate recordkeeping and archiving regimes which need to be implemented in ways that take into account the creating, capturing, and organizing recordkeeping processes (the other three dimensions of the model).

Scott's CRS of series system provides a fourth dimension framework for processes implemented throughout all the dimensions for carrying records beyond the life of an individual or organization. It does so by enabling the representation of the broader structural, functional, and documentary contexts of records' creation, management, and use. The Canadian Total Archives Concept and function-based macro appraisal strategies provide a fourth dimension framework for the incorporation of personal and corporate archive(s) from all sectors of society into the collective archives, enabling them to function as the collective memory of the whole nation.

The records continuum model is also widely used as a training tool opening up discussion about positioning the participants' practice and potential action strategies. Many continuum-based case studies have been developed to explore records continuum practice, the ubiquity of recordkeeping in society and community expectations for recordkeeping.

Research Instrument

Particularly noteworthy is the model's use as a conceptual model and an analytical research tool by researchers around the globe in archival and records management studies. For example it has been used as a conceptual framework and analytical tool in the development of the Australian Recordkeeping Metadata Schema (ARKMS) as part of a collaborative research project involving Monash University, the National Archives of Australia and State Records NSW.[31] The records continuum model played a similar role in the development of the US Inter PARES metadata schema and archival descriptive standards registry, MADRAS,[32] and the Australian Clever Recordkeeping Metadata Project.[33] Iacovino used the model to analyze the recordkeeping-law nexus[34] and to explore complex cross-organizational electronic transaction systems.[35] Oliver employed it, and its sibling the information continuum model, as a research instrument to analyze and present her findings on the influence of national culture on information management in Australia, Germany, and Hong Kong.[36] Outside Australasia Dunbar has proposed using it as part of opening up Critical Race Theory issues[37] and it is being used in a number of Northern European informatics research projects.

Reshaping Professional Practice

The model is a Rorschach test, allowing practitioners to understand, think about, and implement recordkeeping and archiving actions. It provides a concise way to express concerns in a shared framework, opening up further thinking and action. It challenges recordkeeping professionals to rethink recordkeeping and archiving processes as recursive actions imparting the characteristics of recordness on any object, in any format, which needs to function as a record-as-evidence or record-as-memory.

Appraisal ceases to be about evaluating the value of a record for evidential and informational purposes from an archival perspective. Rather it becomes a multifaceted, recursive process which begins with defining what should be created (first dimension), what should be captured and managed as record (second dimension), what should be managed as a part of individual or organizational memory (third dimension) and what should be pluralized beyond organizational or individual memory (fourth dimension). Appreciating that records are constructs rather than physical realities, we can begin to see that records can have many manifestations, equally valid over time, in multiple different sequences of action, each of which creates individual records out of potentially the same record object. This understanding of appraisal has been incorporated into Australian practice through implementation of the national and international records management standards, AS4390 and AS/ISO15489,[38] the development of the DIRKS (Design and Implementation of Recordkeeping Systems) methodology, and the appraisal programs of the National Archives and state archival institutions. The DIRKS methodology was developed by the State Records Office of NSW for use in that State, and is now also mandated for use in Commonwealth government agencies by the National Archives of Australia.

Description is no longer a post hoc archival process applied within the walls of an archival repository, but one which is continuously building connectors between business transactions, activities and functions as the record is formalized for sharing in wider spaces and across longer periods of time. This process commences as a record is first created (first dimension), becoming more formalized at the first point of capture of a record (second dimension), continuing to occur as records are shared beyond the initial process that created them, within the organization (third dimension) and beyond the organization (fourth dimension). It is undertaken by multiple applications of recordkeeping metadata to maintain the connections to the creating business actions the records evidence and memorialize. This continuum view of description informs the development of national and international metadata standards and schema. The model Australian Recordkeeping Metadata Schema was implemented in standards developed by State Records NSW[39] and the South Australian Archives,[40] and more recently in work undertaken by Standards Australia which was adopted as Part 2 of the new International Standard for recordkeeping metadata, ISO 23081.[41] The ARKMS continuum-based metadata model was also used as a conceptual framework in Part 1 of ISO 23081.[42]

Preservation cannot be left until records are within a protective custodial space. Archives are increasingly virtual, perhaps never existing as a physical place. Records must be built to withstand the pressures that sustaining them will bring. In electronic systems this implies attention to formats, documenting links with other records, people and processes in ways that will be sustainable over time, and enabling the management of objects independently from the software that created them. Preservation becomes multiple recurring actions designed to provide flexibility for different ways of maintaining records and their authenticity in a world where no ultimate archiving solution does, or ever will, exist. This continuum view of preservation can be seen in increasing attention to migration processes and standard formats for storage in records management functional specifications emerging in Australasian jurisdictions. It is also reflected in organizational concern over continuing support for older proprietary software formats. Records continuum thinking is particularly relevant to the digital preservation community as it increasingly turns its attention to managing digital objects from their point of creation. New digital technologies can enable captured records to be stored simultaneously in multiple physical domains—and thus in both business and archival contexts. Projects such as VERS (the Victorian Electronic Records initiative) extend models of custodial preservation into an active collaborative approach consistent with records continuum practice.

Socially the concept of access to records has undergone the most significant restructuring of all our recordkeeping processes. It has evolved from being a tightly controlled and monitored archival process of permission to use records to being a process continually negotiated and renegotiated depending on what, why, and when access to records is sought. On the one hand, notions of transparency and accountability have shifted the locus of access and security to different implementation points in the continuum. On the other, social and community interests still protect and define rights associated with use which are highly dependent on circumstances—think of the response to accessing government information post 9/11 or increasing individual rights over access to and use of our personal information. Emerging records continuum approaches to access can be seen in increasing attention to modeling access and security permissions in current records systems, an increasingly complex process in the face of decontextualized digital identities. The beginnings of more formalized articulation of access permissions as a component of recordkeeping in all contexts can be seen in the ISO 15489-2 recommendations for creating formalized instruments for such purposes. Tagging of records as available for public access from the time of their creation is now a reasonably commonplace workplace reality.

CONCLUSION

In discussing the nature and uses of the model we have indirectly indicated that as a way of analyzing recordkeeping systems the model can be given a forensic focus (looking over the past to find records, relationships and meaning), a clinical focus (for example, assessing whether appropriate records are being created and maintained) or a speculative focus to identify imminent changes or transcendental views of the future (for example thinking about recordkeeping in emerging technological environments). In other words it can claim to be a genuine continuum model in that it can be used to address the past, the present, and the future. It can also be used to analyze the relationship between particular issues and archiving and recordkeeping processes, as the research examples above indicated. Each style of analysis has its place in knowledge formation and in working out what skills are required for particular tasks. These uses will continue into the future, but two areas of use are likely to have particularly strong future relevance. Those relate to archival informatics, and to paradigms for forming knowledge about archiving processes.

The records continuum model was designed to open up thinking about the formation of archives and the way documents are shaped, stretched, and re-created into different archival forms within different technologies. Thus it copes comfortably with an increasing emphasis upon informatics, an emerging science dealing with the application of technologies across our activities. In any era and place this will always include the technologies used in creating documents, capturing them and other information objects as records, organizing them into individual bodies of records (the archive), and bringing the archives together in plural holdings. These "stretching" processes have been occurring in some way or another ever since people began to dance, sing, paint, and carve in ways that recorded transactions and passed on ways of doing things through generations. The record within the continuum is "always in a process of becoming," and also of dissolving.[43] In a twentieth century filing system, for example, they might be stretched into new shapes and structures during the filing and aggregating processes that form them. In emerging service oriented approaches, recordkeeping is being disaggregated into component functionality, operating on logical objects at multiple points and in recursive ways, stretching them into new configurations constructed through multiple relationships. Disposal and new administrative patterns can alter their physicality and the control and attention that they receive, and disposition is never final. Records no longer extant or moved elsewhere can still be observed in the place they once occupied through data about their life history or their connection with events. They have multiple lives in spacetime as their use and control alter and open up new threads of action, reshaping and renewing their creation and disposition.

The model can provide a take-off point for visualizing different multidimensional and interconnected topographies. The four interconnected processing dimensions, creation, capture, organization, and pluralization, are always going to be present in any worthwhile informatics project, albeit within a transdisciplinary framework involving many more points to pause upon than the records continuum model itself provides. The difference between archival informatics and archival science is that, whereas the latter concentrates on archival functions as understood by archivists over the ages, archival informatics is still something of a clean slate. From a continuum perspective it involves the application of technology to recordkeeping and archiving processes in and from any era and will lead to a large-scale reconstruction of archival activities.

In modern systems, depending upon the requirements and analysis of the specific technologies involved, the functionality of system selection and deployment can be directed at achieving multiple recordkeeping ends. Building regimes for managing records in such environments involves consideration of every dimension of the records continuum model, and often a rethinking of our professional recordkeeping processes. Ways and means will differ but the aim is still to create appropriate documents in the first place (first dimension), store them as reliable and accessible records in ways that link to the fluidity and ongoing nature of our activities (second dimension), store them as an archive at organizational or personal archive levels (third dimension) and enable cross organizational and personal connections and workings, as well as allowing for multiple patterns of access (fourth

dimension). We happen to be on the threshold of archives formation within the multidimensional places of inscription and consignment provided by Internet and web-browser technologies. We need to seize the opportunities present in our emerging technologies to form archives in continuum fashion.

As a paradigm the continuum provides a way of thinking based on the ongoing and expansionary states of being (more strictly speaking of becoming). The records continuum model is meant to be paradigmatic in this largest of ways, moving from notions of the archives as an end product to an emphasis upon the never-ending process of archiving, with particular emphasis upon recordkeeping and the maintenance of records about our actions. If archivists are to play a real-world role in the construction of the archives in the future, they need to repattern their professional practice with reference to the ways organizations and individuals build their stores of knowledge (their archive), the processes of recordkeeping and archiving, and the role recordkeeping professionals play in these processes. The battles between fixity and fluidity, between traditional views of the record and modern views of free floating information are no longer meaningful. Our technologies can manage both fixity and fluidity and give both characteristics to our recorded information in many locales, including electronic reading rooms and desktops. A focus on "becoming" reveals ways of managing an end product that more of us can now see was never actually an end product anyway.

The need for transmission of recorded information about our actions into different times and spaces is a survival issue for our species, not just a faddish endeavor. To support survival—and that is what is at stake in the formation of archives—information professionals involved in recordkeeping and archiving processes need to be diverse in their approaches, capable of undertaking different styles of analysis, and work within robust and inclusive paradigms for knowledge formation. They need to operate using the technologies of their times and places allied to an understanding of the technology of the eras they happen to specialize in, including present eras and places. As indicated above, the records continuum model opens up perspectives on all these things. Like many schematic drawings, however, it is a tool that is only of value when it is being used.

REFERENCES

1. McKemmish, S.; Upward, F., Eds. *Archival Documents: Providing Accountability Through Recordkeeping*; Ancora Press: Melbourne, Australia, 1993.
2. Maclean, I. Obituary notice for Sir Harold White. Arch. Manuscripts **1992**, *20*(2), 196.
3. Maclean, I. Australian experience in records and archives management. Am. Arch. **1959**, *22*(4), 383–418.

4. Standards Australia, *AS 4390-1996 Australian Standard: Records Management*; Standards Australia: Homebush, Sydney, Australia, 1996.

5. Bearman, D. Record-keeping systems. Archivaria **1993**, *36*, 16–37.

6. Bearman, D. *Electronic Evidence: Strategies for Managing Records in Contemporary Organizations*; Archives and Museum Informatics: Pittsburgh, PA, 1994.

7. Atherton, J. From life cycle to continuum: Some thoughts on the records management-archives relationship. Archivaria **1985–1986**, *21*, 43–51.

8. Acland, G. Managing the record rather than the relic. Arch. Manuscripts **1992**, *20*(1), 57–63.

9. McKemmish, S.; Piggott, M., Eds. *The Records Continuum: Ian Maclean and Australian Archives First Fifty Years*; Ancora Press in association with Australian Archives: Melbourne, Australia, 1994.

10. O'Shea, G.; Roberts, D. Living in a digital world: recognizing the electronic and post-custodial realities. Arch. Manuscripts **1996**, *24*(2), 286–311.

11. Reed, B. Electronic records management in transition. Arch. Manuscripts **1994**, *22*(1), 164–171.

12. Upward, F.; McKemmish, S. Somewhere beyond custody. Arch. Manuscripts **1994**, *22*(1), 138–149.

13. Duranti, L. *Diplomatics: New Uses for an Old Science*, SAA and ACA in association with Scarecrow Press: Lanham, 1998; Reprints of the series of five articles originally published under the same title in successive issues of Archivaria in 1989–91.

14. Hedstrom, M., Ed. *Electronic Records Management Program Strategies*; Archives and Museum Informatics: Pittsburgh, 1993.

15. McDonald, J. Managing records in the modern office: taming the wild frontier. Archivaria **1995**, *39*, 70–79.

16. Hofman, H. Off the beaten track: the Archivist exploring the outback of electronic records. In *Playing For Keeps*, Proceedings of an Electronic Records Management Conference hosted by the Australian Archives Canberra, Australia November, 8–10, 1994 Australian Archives: Canberra, 1995; 68–83.

17. Cook, T. Mind over matter: towards a new theory of archival appraisal. In *The Archival Imagination: Essays in Honour of Hugh A. Taylor*; Craig, B., Ed.; Association of Canadian Archivists: Ottawa, Canada, 1992; 38–70.

18. Cook, T. Electronic records, paper minds: the revolution in information management and archives in the post-custodial and post-modern era. Arch. Manuscript **1994**, *22*(2), 300–329.

19. Ketelaar, E. The difference best postponed? Cultures and comparative archival science. Archivaria **1997**, *44*, 142–147.

20. Hurley, C. The Australian (Series) System: an exposition. In *The Records Continuum: Ian Maclean and Australian Archives first fifty years*; McKemmish, S., Piggott, M., Eds.; Ancora Press in association with Australian Archives: Melbourne, Australia, 1994; 150–172.

21. Reed, B. Reading the records continuum: interpretations and expectations. Arch. Manuscripts **2005**, *33*(1), 18–43.

22. Upward, F. Structuring the records continuum, Part one: Postcustodial principles and properties. Arch. Manuscripts **1996**, *24*(2), 268–285.

23. McKemmish, S. Yesterday, today and tomorrow: A continuum of responsibility. *Preserving Yesterday, Managing Today, Challenging Tomorrow*, RMAA 14th National Convention Perth, Australia Sept, 15–17, 1997 RMAA: Perth, 1997; 18–36.

24. Hill, P. *Lacan for Beginners*; Writers and Readers: London, UK, 1997; 139–151.

25. Foucault, M. *The Archaeology of Knowledge*; Tavistock Publications: London, UK, 1972; 186–187.

26. Collins, J.; Mayblin, W. *Derrida for Beginners*; Icon Books: Cambridge, 2006; 18–22.

27. Derrrida, J. *Archive Fever: A Freudian Impression*; University of Chicago Press: Chicago, IL/London, UK, 1996.

28. Lyotard, J-F. *The Postmodern Explained to Children: Correspondence 1982–1985*; Power Publications: Sydney, Australia, 1992.

29. Giddens, A. *The Constitution of Society: Outline of the Theory of Structuration*; Polity Press: Cambridge, UK, 1984.

30. Cook, T. Beyond the screen: The records continuum and archival cultural heritage. In *Beyond the Screen: Capturing Corporate and Social Memory*, Proceedings of the Australian Society of Archivists National Conference Melbourne, Australia August, 18, 2000 Australian Society of Archivists: Canberra, Australia, 2000; Presented at the Australian Society of Archivists National Conference. Available at http://www.archivists.org.au/.

31. McKemmish, S.; Acland, G.; Ward, N.; Reed, B. Describing records in context in the continuum: The Australian recordkeeping metadata schema. Archivaria **1999**, *48*, 3–43.

32. Anne Gilliland-Swetland, A.; Rouche, N.; Lindberg, L.; Evans, J. Towards a twenty-first century metadata infrastructure supporting the creation, preservation and use of trustworthy records: Developing the InterPARES 2 Metadata Schema Registry. Arch. Sci. **2005**, *5*(1), 43–78.

33. Evans, J.; McKemmish, S.; Bhoday, K. Create once, use many times: the clever use of recordkeeping metadata for multiple archival purposes. Arch. Sci. **2005**, *5*(1), 17–42.

34. Iacovino, L. Multi-method interdisciplinary research in archival science: the case of recordkeeping, ethics and law. Arch. Sci. **2004**, *4*(34), 267–286.

35. Iacovino, L.; Reed, B. Trustworthy electronic health records: recordkeeping research tools in a multi-disciplinary context for cross-jurisdictional information systems. Arch. Sci. **2008**, *8*(1), 37–68.

36. Oliver, G. Investigating information culture: a comparative case study of research design and methods. Arch. Sci. **2004**, *4*(3–4), 287–314.

37. Dunbar, A. Introducing critical race theory to archival discourse: getting the conversation started. Arch. Sci. **2006**, *6*(1), 109–129.

38. International Standards Organisation, *Information and documentation—Records Management (ISO 15489-1:2001)*, ISO: Geneva, Switzerland, 2001.

39. State Records Authority of NSW, *NSW Recordkeeping Metadata Standard*, SRANSW: Sydney, Australia, 2000.

40. State Records of South Australia, *Recordkeeping Metadata Standard*, SRSA: Adelaide, Australia, 2003.

41. International Standards Organisation, *Records Management Processes—Metadata for Records—Part 2: Conceptual and*

Implementation Issues, Technical Specification (ISO 23081.2), ISO: Geneva, 2007.

42. International Standards Organisation, *Information and Documentation—Records Management Processes—Metadata for Records, Part1: Principles*, (ISO 23081.1) ISO: Geneva, 2004.

43. McKemmish, S. Are records ever actual?. In *The Records Continuum*; McKemmish, S., Piggott, M., Eds.; Ancora Press: Melbourne, 1994; 187–203.

BIBLIOGRAPHY

1. McKemmish, S. Placing records continuum theory and practice. Arch. Sci. **2001**, *1*(4), 333–359.

2. McKemmish, S.; Piggott, M.; Reed, B.; Upward, F. *Archives: Recordkeeping in Society*, Centre for Information Studies, Charles Sturt University: Wagga Wagga, Australia, 2005.

3. Reed, B. Reading the records continuum: interpretations and expectations. Arch. Manuscripts **2005**, *33*(1), 18–43.

4. Upward, F. Structuring the records continuum, Part Two: postcustodial principles and properties. Arch. Manuscripts **1996**, *24*(2), 268–285.

5. Upward, F.; McKemmish, S. In search of the lost tiger by way of Saint-Beuve: reconstructing the possibilities in "Evidence of me...". Arch. Manuscripts **2001**, *29*(1), 22–43.

Records Organization and Access

Sue Myburgh
School of Communication, University of South Australia, Adelaide, South Australia, Australia

Abstract

Records, as documents which provide evidence of business transactions that have taken place, are collected and preserved for as long as they are useful to the organization, or as is demanded by law. In order to be useful, however, they must be organized in such a way that they can easily be identified, located, accessed, and used, for whatever purpose. First, the records must be described by identifying the most useful salient characteristics; then, they are categorized in various ways, according to their age, function, level of confidentiality, privacy and security, and access to them controlled according to these categories. Records may be arranged by one of several ordinal systems, usually involving letters and numbers, but also color: these symbolically represent the characteristics that are considered as important descriptors. Thus, records can be accessed (or protected from access) by their category; they can be located by correspondence between terms (which may be words or numbers) used to describe characteristics and terms used in searching for particular records or records series. These principles apply to both physical and virtual records.

INTRODUCTION AND BACKGROUND

The work of records management comprises capturing the records produced by an organization by distinguishing them from documents, and describing them; ensuring that they are disseminated to those who require them for action; providing access to them while at the same time keeping them private and secure as necessary; discarding them when they are no longer required, or passing those with historical value to the archives for long-term preservation once their value has been appraised. Records are usually organized by some element of description; access takes place both through the organizational systems as well as constraints, and processes suggested by law or administrative purpose.

The International Organization for Standardization (ISO), in their standard ISO 15489: 2001, defines a record as "information created, received, and maintained as evidence and information by an organization or person, in pursuance of legal obligations, or in the transaction of business." Typically, this information is contained in a document of some kind, of whatever medium or format. The important characteristic of a record that differentiates it from other documents is that it provides evidence of a business transaction. This is usually interpreted by records managers as the ability of a record to provide evidence by the mere fact of its existence. However, besides providing evidence, records are also the documents used (primarily for the information they contain) in order to conduct the business of an enterprise, thus, records are closely associated with general document management strategies with an organization, as well as workflow processes, as they facilitate the work of the organization. There is increasing interest, however, in the informational qualities of records from the strategic information management point of view. Records are valuable, therefore, for three reasons:

1. Their existence provides evidence of transactions undertaken (or not);
2. They facilitate the work—processes, procedures, and communication—of an organization (both internally and externally);
3. They contain valuable information which can be used to increase competitive advantage.

When records are no longer actively used in any of these fundamental ways, most of them are discarded and destroyed. However, there will certainly be a group of records which are considered to have an historical value, and these will, in due course, be managed in an archives.

It is worth noting that there are different records management traditions internationally. In the United States, for example, there is a clear distinction between records managers and archivists and their work, while in Australia there has been considerable movement towards uniting the two professions, largely through the enunciation of continuum theory.[1,2] In Europe, there is a focus on archival work and preservation, with not much attention being paid to current records, although there is increasing interest in such issues. Work is still required to reconcile the various approaches, in spite of the existence of an international standard, and some of these differences are articulated in various organization and access arrangements. However, archival organization, arrangement, and access (such as

Encyclopedia of Library and Information Sciences, Fourth Edition DOI: 10.1081/E-ELIS4-120044299

fonds, original order, and provenance) are excluded here. Also excluded is discussion of metadata for records, except insofar as it is related to organization, arrangement, and access.

RECORDS ORGANIZATION

One of the major functions of records management is to describe and organize records. Good organization of records is vital: ISO 15489 recommends, "The higher the level of accountability and/or public scrutiny, the greater the need for accuracy, and speed in locating individual records." [This applies to all three of the essential functions of records: as evidence, as information, and as tools to facilitate the work of the organization. In particular, good organization is required if records are to be acceptable as evidence in a court of law: the system must be consistently implemented, for example, and each record must be complete, identifiable, coherent, accessible, and available (amongst other criteria)].

It is possible to organize records in many ways. One way which seems obvious is to arrange records by the structure of the organization or by the subject with which the record deals. However, both of these methods are subject to a number of problems, particularly because the organizational structure or nomenclature might change. Overall, a functional approach is most commonly adopted. This method of categorization is predicated upon the processes that are identified as critical to the mission and tasks of an enterprise, incorporating the tasks required to perform them. The categories therefore reflect the functions of the organization, which may be, for example, the following:

- General administration.
- Establishing policy.
- Accounting.
- Budgeting.
- Managing contracts and agreements.
- Information and communication technology support.
- Human resources management.
- Manufacturing.
- Goods and services procurement and supply.
- Arranging travel.

In this way, records can be grouped by activity and will relate to the work undertaken by each department. There are several advantages to this approach.

1. Analysis of individual documents (or document series) is avoided, as the principle of division becomes the functions and workflows of the organization;
2. The business context of the record is more-or-less self-evident, often clarifying issues of privacy and security;

3. There is a logical coherence to this style of organization which assists in eliminating duplication;
4. Within each function, file series can be more easily identified and, once these have been approached, disposal of such files is more easily managed as a whole file can be discarded at once, avoiding the need to examine each document within a file.

RECORDS SERIES

The notion of functional classification or organization of records is associated with the concept of "records series." A records series is a group of related records (such as the minutes of a particular committee) which can be filed as a unit. The records in a series are usually uniform in both form and function, and often cover a particular unit of time (e.g., a financial year or a decade). They can also be appraised as a unit and scheduled for disposition—which makes such tasks simpler. So, there is a logical and useful connection between the categorization, filing, accessing, evaluating, and scheduling activities of the records manager. Functional organization, based on records series, is used in both analog and digital environments.

Classification and Indexing

Records classification occurs after business functions and activities have been identified and categorised, according to the standard structures, procedures, and processes of theorganization. The thesaurus provides common administrative support terms, rather than terms that describe core business functions in organizations. This means that the record is classified according to why it exists and where it was created, rather than its information content, which may only be suggested by organizational functions and processes. This differentiates records from other documents, such as monographs or journal articles, which are primarily categorised and indexed according to the subject of their content.

As previously suggested, a classification scheme, based on organizational functions, assists in the other records management activities of appraisal, disposition, security, privacy, and so forth. At the same time, the classification scheme will indicate the location of specific documents, and connect physical and electronic documents that are functionally linked. The process is otherwise similar to the classification and indexing processes undertaken in libraries and other document management centers.

There remains the problem, however, of how to deal with files and folders (and indeed, individual records) at finer levels of granularity and specificity. For these purposes, classification schemes are developed, which can use either alphabetical or numerical notations (and often both—for different purposes). A classification scheme suggests that similar things can be grouped together in categories, and any relationships between categories are indicated, such as in a hierarchy. Before the classification scheme can be finalised, however, a taxonomy must be created, which articulates the topics and subject categories, as well as their structure. After this, each category can be briefly described through use of notation—which could be words, letters of the alphabet, or numbers. These elements in turn can be used as a basis for the filing arrangement.

Deciding on the appropriate word or code to assign a particular record, or series is guided by the vocabulary selections made in a thesaurus, which controls how the records are classified or indexed. The thesaurus must first, of course, be constructed: this can be a time-consuming process. It involves an analysis of business hierarchies and functions, interviews in order to determine terminology, selecting and developing the terminology, and ensuring its consistency. It is essential that the thesaurus reflects the requirements of the organization and its staff. Once the terminology has been selected and approved, this controlled indexing language is recorded in the thesaurus, ensuring that terms are used consistently, and in the same manner.

A records management thesaurus pays little attention to the information content of a record, however; as noted, it is more important for these purposes to classify the record according to its context and why it was created, rather than what it is about, even though the information content of records can be valuable for strategic purposes. There is nonetheless increasing interest into systems that reveal the subject of such documents as well as meeting the more traditional requirements of records management, so that organizations can compete more successfully.

In Australia, the State Records Authority of New South Wales developed a Keyword AAA Thesaurus intended for use by all agencies of government, as it contains terminology common to the business functions and activities of most enterprises. In this way, records that are common across the state, but found in a range of agencies, will all be described in the same way. Indeed, it has been found to have such general applicability that it has been used, either in its entirety or as a basis for other thesauri, throughout Australia and internationally. It is intended to be used with a functional thesaurus that specifically deals with the functions, activities, and procedures of a particular office or agency—thus, extending its flexibility of use.

All business classification schemes, as recorded in a thesaurus, must include all the functions of the particular enterprise, but not be related to various departments; the terminology should be widely used and familiar to all staff; ideally should be hierarchical (proceeding from broad categories to specific items); and should be constantly maintained. It can then be used by all staff to index the records they create and receive.

Indexing

Using the thesaurus as a guide, the record can be described, identifying the document as well as providing the mechanism for arrangement, retrieval, and disposition. Increasingly, electronic records management systems allow for the storage, retention, and searching of the complete, full-text document, which to some extent assists in access but is not helpful for retention and disposal purposes. That records are managed primarily for their evidential properties must never be forgotten.

Filing and Arrangement

The arrangement of records or files—whatever their medium—should be kept as simple as possible, so that all can understand it. This helps at all stages of locating and returning records. Deciding on a filing system, first of all requires determining what descriptor will constitute the filing element: will it be the indexing term, a sequential numbering system, the name of the department from which the record originates, or the surname of the action officer? What must also be borne in mind is how the filing system will identify linked files if they occur in a variety of media and formats, and so are not all found together in the same place.

A most useful work which explains filing in great detail is Suzanne Gill's *File Management for Information Retrieval Systems: A Manual for Managers and Technicians* (1993).[3] This comprehensive work, now in its third edition, includes how and why various filing systems might be chosen and used. She includes alphabetical filing (and the differences that various filing rules can make, either letter-by-letter or word-by-word); numerical filing—including serial, middle digit, and terminal number; chronological (subject and alphabetical); alphabetical subject and hierarchical subject; phonetic filing, geographical filing, and color-coded filing.

Records Access

Records must, of course, be made accessible to the employees of an enterprise to enable them to do their work. In a physical, or paper-based environment, the record will be sent to an action officer who can perform the work required by the document; the action officer might also need to access records which have already been dealt with—perhaps only partially—and will recover these either from the records center or by the records management system. The records manager keeps a close account of where all records are at any particular time—as well as who the record might be passed on to prior to returning to the file. This process is known as tracking, and this can be either manual (like a circulation system) or automated (often through the use of bar codes).

Generally speaking, the question of access is associated with controlling the distribution or circulation of physical records within an organization. Access management systems are usually designed to work with records series rather as individual documents. It is, however, necessary to ensure that rights of access to records and to functions are granted to authorized individuals and groups and withheld from unauthorized individuals and groups. Access management aims to strengthen privacy and security while facilitating information sharing.

Access to records can, however, be differentiated in a number of ways. For example, there are different issues and procedures related to access to physical records, as opposed to digital or electronic records. There are also different ways to manage access to active, semiactive, or inactive records. Other dimensions of access include the ease with which an individual can understand the descriptions of records, and how they have been arranged, so that the correct record can be identified and located without the constant intervention of the records manager. In addition, there is the issue is that of controlling access, so that records remain uncorrupted by unauthorized amendments or deletions.

The information that records contain, which, as previously noted, has largely been ignored by records managers for the most part, is clearly a concern here, as it is the information (rather than the physical artifact) that must be protected from violations of privacy and security. These issues are covered by a number of international laws and regulations (so much so that some records managers feel that their more appropriate title should be "compliance officer"!). On the other hand, there are also laws that specifically permit access to records about people (such as Freedom of information legislation) and governments, after certain periods of time have expired. Yet, another issue that controls access to records is that of intellectual property, as many companies would not wish to have their information (as intellectual capital) made widely available. There are additionally specific issues of records access management and control related to particular industry sectors, such as health, nuclear power, the military, and chemical industries.

Access, security, and privacy

Many systems that provide access to information permit only selected persons to exercise access. It is frequently the case that some records may never be allowed to leave the organization; some may only be seen by certain individuals or certain categories of staff, for a range of reasons, such as privacy, organizational or national security, industrial espionage, and so forth. These restrictions may be put in place either manually or electronically. Records contain evidence of business transactions and many activities that must remain confidential, and may also possess personal, commercial, or other sensitive information. It will be necessary to manage access to these records to

ensure compliance with the regulatory environment and corporate policy, and in accordance with the organization's security policy. With reference to access, the main areas to be considered are freedom of information, privacy, security, and intellectual property (which includes copyright, trademarks, and patents).

Freedom of information legislation has to do with providing citizens access to information (particularly about themselves) which is held by government bodies. Each country has its own suite of legislation which controls these aspects. In the United Kingdom, for example, there are Public Records Acts and a Code of Practice on Records Management for Freedom of Information; in the United States there is the 1966 Freedom of Information Act, and the 1996 Electronic Freedom of Information Act Amendments.

Privacy laws seek to control potential misuse of personal information. The European Community, in 1995, issued the European Directive on Protection of Personal Data, and in the United States there is the Code of Fair Information Practice issued by the Office of Technology Assessment. Privacy in the United States is also controlled by the Health Insurance Portability and Accountability Act (1996), the Fair Credit Reporting Act, and the Electronic Communication Privacy Act. Security of information continues to be an issue, as instances of identity theft rise, as well as the possibility that trade or other secrets might be stolen and used inappropriately. Authentication (by either security framework or by some kind of electronic signature) is increasingly required, and the transaction—the request for access to a particular record or record series—can be recorded.

Access to physical records

Active records (in other words, records that are still being used by action officers on a regular basis) can be controlled through a tracking system, as the location of a file or document must be known at any time (One of the great disadvantages of the physical artifact is that it can only be at one place at a time, and this has led, rather dangerously sometimes, to many duplicate copies being made, which may fall into the wrong hands as they are difficult to control). Tracking systems can be manual or automated. Some examples of manual systems are:

1. File movement book registers, which are hopelessly inefficient and have mostly been replaced.
2. Separate file movement card for each file, held in one sequence. These are a little better, but they are held outside the file which means users must make an effort to sign them.
3. File movement markers—placed into the file storage area in place of a file when that file is taken by a user. This is widely used.

However, all of these systems rely on the users providing the necessary information. Automate tracking systems offer much better control over materials and are easier to use (especially by the action officers). They work in the following way.

- Each user is allocated a borrower's code.
- The electronic recording of file movements may be centrally controlled or may be done at remote workstations by departmental users.
- Remote recording of file movements can eliminate the need for other usually inefficient methods of informing records staff that a document or file has been handed on to someone else.
- Many systems incorporate bar code tracking of documents and/or files. This works like the library's circulation system. A portable bar code reader can also be used to carry out a file census. The records staff member enters each office, passes the reader over the user's bar code, and then over each file in the office.

Resubmit systems allow files to be returned to users (action officers) on a predetermined date for follow-up action. This is necessary when, for example, annual reminders need to be sent out. Users can book a file to be sent (or submitted) to them by a particular date.

Once records become semiactive or inactive, they are usually moved to a "records center," which is a central storage area where inactive records are kept. This could be on-site, which is common for small or medium size companies, but more commonly such records are moved off-site, which may be managed by the company itself or by a commercial records management center. The choice can be determined by, inter alia, costs of leasing or purchase, insurance, power and other overheads, staffing retrieval times, protection against the elements and disasters, security, growth rate, and general convenience.

Access to electronic records

More and more work is done in digital format only, in both public and private enterprises. Part of the notion of an "information society" is that of "e-government" or "e-democracy," in which governments at all levels—local, state, and federal—are encouraged and obliged to make their documents easily available to the public at large. Electronic records can be easily transmitted using information and communication technologies, and this makes them more vulnerable to modification and destruction. There also remain a number of uncertainties with regard to the long-term preservation of digital documents.

CONCLUSIONS

As long as paper is used, questions of physical organization, arrangement, and filing will be important. How to

identify and locate individual records or records series is an important issue in records management. A great deal of work is currently being undertaken to protect and preserve electronic documents and records, and this will continue, as will increased interest in using the information contained by records for competitive advantage.

REFERENCES

1. Upward, F.; McKemmish, S. Search of the lost tiger, by way of Sainte-Beuve: reconstructing the possibilities in 'Evidence of Me...'. Archi. Manus. **2001**, *29* (1), 22–43. http://www.mybestdocs.com/mckemmish-s-upward-f-ontiger-w.htm (accessed October 2008).
2. McKemmish, S. Placing records continuum theory and practice. Arch. Sci. **1987**, *1* (4), 333–359.
3. Gill, S. *File Management and Information Retrieval Systems: A Manual for Managers and Technicians*, 3rd Ed.; Libraries Unlimited: Englewood, CO, 1993.

BIBLIOGRAPHY

1. Bilotto, A.; Maria, G. The management of corporate records in Italy: traditional practice and methods and digital environment. Rec. Manage. J. **2003**, *13* (3), 136–146.
2. Gill, S. *File Management and Information Retrieval Systems: A Manual for Managers and Technicians*, 3rd Ed.; Libraries Unlimited: Englewood, CO, 1993.
3. Hurley, C. What if anything, is a function? Arch. Manus. **1993**, *21* (2), 208–220.
4. Kennedy, J.; Schauder, C.; Rosenthal, M. *Records Management: An Introduction to Principles and Practices*; Royal Melbourne Institute of Technology: Melbourne, Victoria, Australia, 1991.
5. McKemmish, S. Placing records continuum theory and practice. Arch. Sci. **1987**, *1* (4), 333–359.
6. Mordel, A. Breaking arms won't change human nature. Rec. Manage. Q. **1990**, *24* (1), 36–39.
7. National Archives of Australia, *Developing a Functions Thesaurus*; 2003. http://www.naa.gov.au/Images/developing-a-thesaurus_tcm2-916.pdf (accessed October 2008).
8. State Records Authority of New South Wales, Guidelines for Developing and Implementing a Keyword Thesaurus, 2003. http://www.records.nsw.gov.au/recordkeeping/keyword_aaa_424.asp (accessed October 2008).
9. State Records Authority of New South Wales, Guideline 15: Developing and Implementing a Keyword Thesaurus. 2003. http://www.records.nsw.gov.au/recordkeeping/guideline_15_keyword_thesaurus_7273.asp (accessed October 2008).
10. Upward, F.; McKemmish, S. Search of the lost tiger, by way of Sainte-Beuve: reconstructing the possibilities in 'Evidence of Me...'. Archi. Manus. **2001**, *29* (1), 22–43. http://www.mybestdocs.com/mckemmish-s-upward-f-ontiger-w.htm (accessed October 2008).

Records Retention Schedules

Barbara E. Nye
Ictus Consulting, LLC, Pasadena, California, U.S.A.

Abstract
Records retention is managed within an organization by developing and implementing a records retention schedule. A records retention schedule is a list of records maintained by an organization and the length of time that the records must be retained. It is a policy document that states the organization's intent to maintain its records for defined time periods and to disposition them systematically once the time period is reached. Thus the retention schedule supports compliance activities within the organization, promotes transparency and good "corporate" governance.

The purpose of the retention schedule is to manage each records series throughout its "life cycle"—the creation or receipt of the record through its disposition. Proper management of each records series ensures that the growth of records is controlled; that is, records are available as long as they are required to support the business need or to comply with a statutory or regulatory requirement and they are dispositioned when they have met these two requirements. Thus, records do not accumulate unnecessarily, and the organization does not incur the costs of maintaining obsolete records. Additionally, removing obsolete records routinely and systematically helps the organization to avoid the appearance of willful destruction, obstruction of justice (in the event of a pending legal action) and thus serves to limit the organization's legal liability.

INTRODUCTION

Records retention is a key element of a comprehensive records management program. It consists of determining how long to retain a record (the retention period), maintaining that record so that it is retrievable and useable over the defined time period, and when the retention period has been met, destroying the record or—if it has historical value—transferring it to an archive. The process of records destruction or transfer to an archive is called "dispositioning."

Records retention is managed within an organization by developing and implementing a records retention schedule. A records retention schedule is a list of records maintained by an organization and the length of time that the records must be retained. It is a policy document that states the organization's intent to maintain its records for defined time periods (or, in some cases, until an event occurs) and to disposition them systematically once the time period is reached or the event occurs. Thus the retention schedule supports compliance activities within the organization and promotes transparency and good "corporate" governance.

The records retention schedule is the basic tool used in performing records retention activities and an appropriate records management tool for all organizations: private enterprise, government agencies, cultural institutions, or non-profit groups.

The schedule is typically organized by "records series," a group of related records that are maintained or used as a unit and that can be evaluated as a unit for retention purposes.[1] The time period for maintaining each records series is called the "retention period."

A comprehensive retention schedule includes all records in all stored formats, including, for example, paper-based, electronic, and photographic records, as well as physical objects (e.g., soil or water samples, scale models, etc.) that are determined to be records.

Records retention schedules must be customized specifically for an organization. There are no "generic" records retention schedules that can be used "as is."[2] Although organizations may produce many similar type records, especially for those functions such as accounting or human resources management that are common to most organizations, the differences in industry regulations, geographic locations, legal jurisdictions, and especially the "corporate culture" are all factors in determining how long an organization is prepared to maintain records, or conversely, at what point in time the organization is comfortable destroying records deemed obsolete.

PURPOSE

The purpose of the retention schedule is to manage each records series throughout its "life cycle"—the creation or receipt of the record through its disposition. Proper management of each records series ensures that the growth of records is controlled; that is, records are available as long as they are required to support the business need or to

Encyclopedia of Library and Information Sciences, Fourth Edition DOI: 10.1081/E-ELIS4-120043549

comply with a statutory or regulatory requirement and they are dispositioned when they have met these two requirements. Thus, records do not accumulate unnecessarily, and the organization does not incur the costs of maintaining obsolete records.

Additionally, removing obsolete records routinely and systematically helps the organization to avoid the appearance of willful destruction or obstruction of justice (in the event of a pending legal action) and thus serves to limit the organization's legal liability.

RETENTION SCHEDULE TYPES

There are two basic retention schedule models based on the method for organizing the records series—the "departmental" model and the "functional" model. Other types of retention schedules, such as "process-based" or "large aggregation" schedules are a variation on the functional model. There are advantages and disadvantages to the development and maintenance of each model.

A records series is a group of files or documents kept together (either physically or intellectually) because they relate to a particular subject or function, result from the same activity, document a specific type of transaction, take a particular physical form, or have some other relationship arising out of their creation, receipt, maintenance, or use.[3]

Departmental Retention Schedules

Traditionally, records retention schedules have been organized by the business unit (department) where the records were identified during the records inventory process. Therefore, the "departmental" retention schedule organizes the record series alphabetically by the business unit (department, division, or section) in which the records are maintained and to which responsibility for maintenance is assigned. This type of retention schedule is also called the "detailed retention schedule" because it generally has a greater number of records series (more "detail") than a functional schedule. Departmental retention schedules are still in wide use because they are relatively easy to develop. The business unit uses its own terminology for the records series name, sets an operating retention period to meet the business unit's needs, and there is no need to classify the records series.

A disadvantage in using departmental retention schedules is that they require maintaining not only multiple schedules per organization (one for each business unit) but also significantly more records series, as the same records series is often maintained by many business units in an organization. For example, contracts, expense reports, and some personnel records may be maintained in many different business units and thus must appear on many schedules. It is not unusual for an organization

maintaining multiple departmental retention schedules to identify and maintain hundreds or perhaps thousands of records series. Different business units may assign conflicting retention periods to the same records series, which can be a liability when trying to defend retention practices. An additional requirement is that the departmental retention schedules must be revised each time there is a re-organization.

Functional Retention Schedules

The "functional" retention schedule classifies each records series by the "function," or purpose, that the records series serves. Schellenberg[4] defines functions as "the responsibilities assigned to an agency to accomplish the broad purposes for which it was established." Within each function the records series are listed alphabetically.

The functional retention schedule approach eliminates tracking of duplicate records series, as each series is listed only once, associated with the appropriate function. Thus the functional schedule generally contains significantly fewer records series. Skupsky[5] states, "The typical functional retention schedule for even a large organization will contain under 100 different retention categories. . . ."

In addition, the functional retention schedule does not have to be significantly revised each time there is a re-organization; only the ownership information, or "office of record," may require revising. However, developing a functional retention schedule requires collaboration from each business unit to agree on the naming conventions for the records series, on the retention period, and on the "owner" or "office of record"—the unit that is responsible for maintaining and dispositioning the records series. An additional step is required in developing a functional retention schedule as the records series must also be classified into the appropriate function. As with any classification initiative, functional retention schedule development is part art and part science.

Large Aggregation Retention Schedules

A more recent development in records retention schedule theory is the so-called "big bucket" or large aggregation approach to developing records retention schedules. This approach is based on the theory that maintaining fewer records series promotes more efficient and more accurate classification of records into the proper records series and thus promotes compliance. The U.S. National Archives and Records Administration (NARA), which provides records management expertise to federal agencies, has embraced this approach to ease the perceived burden of using and maintaining the traditional retention schedule.[3] This approach is somewhat controversial and has not been widely adopted.[6]

Records management software application vendors are strong proponents of this approach. To support successful implementation of an electronic document management system, an enterprise content management system, or other automated recordkeeping system, vendors urge their customers to simplify retention requirements.[7] The users of that system must select the appropriate category (records series) to classify records, in order that the system can automatically impose retention times and systematically disposition the electronic records.

As the volume of records created and maintained steadily increases (due to the ease of creating and distributing electronic records) and as the burden for classifying records by records series is increasingly placed on individual employees, the manual application of the retention periods becomes extremely labor-intensive and time-consuming. If there are too many records series "choices," the user has difficulty accurately and consistently classifying the record. Thus there is pressure to reduce the number of "places" where users can classify their documents.

In developing a large aggregation retention schedule what defines a records series changes. Instead of being "a group of related records that are maintained or used as a unit and that can be evaluated as a unit for retention purposes," large aggregation retention schedules are organized by very broad functional categories containing many records series or, in some instances, by the retention period.

For example, multiple records series classified into the "Accounting" function on a typical functional retention schedule (e.g., accounts payable, accounts receivable, and general ledger records), are combined into one big bucket, "Accounting" records series. The longest retention period of the various accounting records series that have been classified into the new larger "bucket" is assigned to the entire group. The disadvantage to this approach is the risk that many records will be maintained much longer than is strictly necessary. Another strategy is to establish the organizing principle for the "bucket" as the retention period. A few retention periods are selected (e.g., one-year, five-year, ten-year, and "permanent" time frames), and all records are classified into the "buckets" by time period rather than by record subject matter or function.[6]

A disadvantage to this strategy, in addition to maintaining many records beyond the time they are useful is that it does not accommodate the application of events in considering how long to keep the records. Rather this strategy relies on a fixed time frame for calculating retention which may not adequately span the time until the event occurs.

Report format

There are also different retention schedule report formats. For example, schedules can be presented as simple alphabetical lists of record names, in a descriptive paragraph format, or in a table format.

Traditionally the records retention schedule has been maintained as a "stand-alone" document published and distributed by the records management group within an organization. More recently, database technology has been used to maintain retention schedule data and to publish the retention schedule report as a hardcopy report or as a file posted on an organization's intranet site.

Report content

In addition to the records series name and retention period, schedules may also include descriptive information about the records series. For example, schedules can contain:

- The office of record—the group within the organization that is assigned responsibility for maintaining the records series.
- The basis for the assigned retention period—an administrative or operating requirement, a legal statute, or agency regulation.
- Separate time periods for retaining the records series "onsite," for transferring records "offsite," for destroying records, and for duplicate copies.
- Records storage formats (e.g., paper, microfilm, digital).
- Records destruction requirements (e.g., shredding).
- Access, preservation, or security requirements (e.g., records are "confidential"—access must be restricted; or "historical"—records have research or social importance beyond the business and legal need; or "vital"—records must be available to respond to an emergency or disaster).
- Notes or comments.

RETENTION PERIODS

A retention period is the length of time, usually stated in terms of the number of years, that records must be maintained to meet operating, legal or fiscal requirements of the organization.[1] Many records series must be maintained until a certain event has transpired. In some instances retention periods are a combination of the event plus a set number of years.

A retention period based on a finite time period (such as a certain number of years) is used when it is known that the records will not be needed past that time frame. A retention period that is based on an event is used when the retention time that the record is required is based on the occurrence of an event or on a circumstance whose date cannot be predicted. For example, for the records series, "Personnel Files," the retention period would be governed by the event that was the end of employment, or "termination" (the event). The termination date of employment cannot be accurately predicted. Therefore Personnel Files would have a retention period of "Termination," or a number of years after that event (e.g., "Termination plus 5 years").

The retention period is sometimes further delineated into the time period to retain the records in the working environment (e.g., office, workstation, online), a time period for retaining records in a lower-cost storage area (e.g., a warehouse for paper-based records, a climate-controlled vault for photographs or microfilm, or off-line storage on tape for digital records), and a total retention time.

DEVELOPMENT

In order to manage its records, the organization needs to understand what records are maintained and how they are used. The information needed to have this understanding is collected during the development of the retention schedule in a process known as the "records inventory."

The first step in creating the retention schedule is to prepare a plan that describes the strategy for the retention schedule. This strategy should include determining:

- The scope of the retention schedule—which parts of the organization will be inventoried (e.g., all operations, domestic operations only, headquarters office only), what storage formats are used for records (e.g., hardcopy only, electronic, photographic)
- The type of retention schedule to be developed—departmental or functional
- The type of information to be collected
- The records inventory method to be used—detailed physical inventory, high-level survey approach, or questionnaire
- The resources needed to develop the retention schedule—in-house staff, outside consultants, or a combination
- A project schedule for development
- The type of approval—the level of internal management, external counsel, or board of directors approval required
- The method of implementing the retention schedule—for example, one business unit at a time or one location at a time

Records retention schedules can be developed using one of several methods: a detailed physical inventory, a questionnaire, a high-level overview or "survey," analysis of business processes, questionnaires, or a combination of these methods. Regardless of the type of retention schedule and the exact method of schedule development, the basic need is to understand what records exist and how long they must be retained.

The inventory process collects information about the records that can be determined by a visual inspection (e.g., the volume of records stored, and their physical condition) and by interviewing knowledgeable individuals in each business unit (e.g., concerning records usage, electronic records creation or maintenance, government reporting requirements, if any, and litigation history). The type of data collected varies depending on decisions made during the development of the records retention schedule strategy. It can include, for example:

- Names of the files and documents
- Storage location
- Storage equipment
- Volume of records
- Date range
- Condition of the records
- Storage format (paper, microfilm, electronic, photographic)

The interview process collects information about the use of records, frequency of reference, computer applications that create or store electronic records, problems encountered with finding or storing records, government regulatory requirements for preparing, reporting, or maintaining records, and the records required to respond to legal actions.

The inventory and interview data are analyzed to develop records series, the building blocks of the retention schedule. Once the draft version of the retention schedule is complete, the following activities complete the schedule development process.

Legal Research

It is necessary to establish the legal jurisdictions that apply to the organization in order to understand which recordkeeping statutes and agency regulations must be followed. The records management function of the organization can research these requirements as well as consult with legal counsel to establish what the legal recordkeeping requirements are, if any. Not all records are governed by statutes or regulations. The retention period for the majority of records series is determined by the business need to refer to the record (sometimes referred to as the "operating" need). The legal requirements are considered with the business need and the longer of the two time periods is selected.

Review and Approval

Once the first draft of the retention schedule is completed, it is issued to the business units and to legal counsel for review and comment. The retention schedule is then revised based on the comments received and then issued to the appropriate group within the organization for approval (executive office, legal department, or governing board).

Implementation

Once approved, the records management function within the organization applies it to the organization's records, matching the record series to the physical or electronic records maintained and culling obsolete records from their stored locations. This begins the systematic process of destroying obsolete records (those records whose retention period has been met).

Maintenance

Periodically the records management function of the organization completes the retention schedule review and update process to incorporate new record series and new legal requirements, to add in changes that have occurred in the organizational structure affecting the responsible department (office of record), and to delete record series which are no longer maintained. The frequency of update will vary from one organization to another depending on the frequency of change to governing statutes and regulations and to the internal business practices.

CONCLUSION

Records retention has been called "...the defining responsibility of records management as a business discipline."[8] The primary tool used in records retention activities is the records retention schedule. Developing and implementing the retention schedule are fundamental activities of a records management program.

The retention schedule is the official policy that allows an organization to effectively manage its records and it is the primary building block upon which other program components are constructed.

The retention schedule categorizes and describes the organization's records and how long they must be kept. Maintaining a comprehensive retention schedule is key to managing records to ensure that they are available for use as long as they are needed, and are destroyed (or transferred to an archives, if historical) when no longer needed, thereby avoiding costs associated with uncontrolled records growth, limiting legal liabilities, and promoting operational efficiencies.

REFERENCES

1. ARMA International. *Glossary of Records and Information Management Terms*, 2nd Ed., ARMA International: Prairie Village, KS, 2000.
2. Robek, M.F.; Brown, G.F.; Stephens, D.O. *Information and Record Management: Document-based Information Systems*, 4th Ed.; Glencoe/McGraw-Hill, Inc.: Woodland Hills, CA, 1995; 45.
3. NARA Bulletin 2008-04, Guidance for Flexible scheduling, April 30, 2008.
4. Schellenberg, T.R. *Modern Archives: Principles and Techniques*; Society of American Archivists: Chicago, IL, 2002.
5. Skupsky, D.S. *Records Retention Procedures: Your Guide to Determine How Long to Keep Your Records and How to Safely Destroy Them!*; Information Requirements Clearinghouse: Denver, CO, 1991; 65.
6. Cisco, S. How to Win the Compliance Battle Using 'Big Buckets.' Inform. Manag. J. **2008**, *42* (4), 30–38.
7. Cisco, S. Big Buckets for Simplifying Records Retention Schedules. Hottopic Supplement, Inform. Manag. J. **2008**, *42* (5), 3–6.
8. Saffady, W. *Records and Information Management: Fundamentals of Professional Practice*; ARMA International: Lenexa, KS, 2004; 9.

BIBLIOGRAPHY

1. Choksy, C.E.B. *Domesticating Information: Managing Documents inside the Organization*; Rowman and Littlefield Publishers, Inc.: Lanham, MD, 2006.
2. International Organization for Standardization (ISO). *ISO 15489-1:2001, Information and documentation—Records management—Part 1: General*; ISO: Geneva, Switzerland, 2001.
3. Robek, M.F.; Brown, G.F.; Stephens, D.O. *Information and Records Management: Document-based Information Systems*, 4th Ed.; Glencoe/McGraw-Hill, Inc.: Woodland Hills, CA, 1995.
4. Shepherd, E.; Yeo, G. *Managing Records: A Handbook of Principles and Practice*; Facet Publishing: London, U.K., 2003.

Reference and Informational Genres

Thomas Mann
Library of Congress, Washington, District of Columbia, U.S.A.

Abstract

In order to reduce the problems of information overload, librarians and indexers have created systems of categorization that allow large numbers of individual books or articles to be perceived initially through smaller numbers of categories of literature. These categories can be either subject or format groupings. Format designations are particularly useful in segregating reference works from larger collections or retrievals. The distinctive nature, and the purposes and uses of reference works ("tertiary literature" composed of 60% or more of files or lists, as opposed to "primary" or "secondary" literature) are discussed. The mechanisms for finding such works via *Library of Congress Subject Headings*, or via the peculiarities of their shelving in either the Library of Congress Classification or the Dewey Decimal Classification, are explained. "Publication types" and "document type" searches within databases covering formats other than books are also treated.

The phrase "reference and informational genres" refers to types of literature that are distinctively formatted in such a way as to expedite the discovery of particular kinds of information. Such genres include almanacs, atlases, chronologies, dictionaries, encyclopedias, and so on, that usually present informational content in brief, segmented displays, rather than in connected narratives or continuous expositions.

The need for such genres arises from the fact that efficient research cannot be done in large, unsorted collections of resources, whether printed or electronic. Some kind of categorization of the material is necessary to prevent information overload. While the mind cannot grasp huge numbers of individual items in relationship to each other, it can more easily discern relationships among broader—and fewer—*categories* into which the items may be sorted or assigned.

In book literature, for example, one can get a better sense of what is or is not contained within the category of works on "Afghanistan—history" if one can readily see that subdividing categories other than "history" per se have been created for country's "antiquities," "boundaries," "civilization," "economic conditions," "foreign relations," "geography," "intellectual life," "politics and government," "social life and customs," and so on. That is, one can more readily discern what may be contained within a "history" of Afghanistan category by being able to note, quickly, the relationship of this category itself to an array of all the other subject-aspects that impinge on "history" without being included by it. (These particular categorizations are all formal terms within the *Library of Congress Subject Headings* system.)

The segregation of large collections of resources into smaller and more manageable "chunks," however, is not solely accomplished by the creation of *subject* groupings; it is also brought about by *format* and *genre* categorizations. In the same example, a researcher interested in "Afghanistan—history" may, in a large research library, still be overwhelmed by too much material within that subject itself; but further subdivisions of the topic into types of literature such as "Afghanistan—history—bibliography," "—chronology," "—dictionaries," "—encyclopedias," can provide the additional options needed to make the various aspects of the "Afghanistan—history" group more perceptible and manageable.

Format and genre groupings thus allow very useful discriminations to be made on a basis other than subject content: on the one hand, they enable immediate focus to be directed toward some particular types of relevant resources "within" a subject; on the other, they enable whole groups of irrelevant sources to be immediately excluded, which would otherwise remain as cluttering elements if only subject (rather than format/genre) categories were available to choose from. In this same example, still other format designations ("personal narratives," "pictorial works," "registers of dead," "songs and music," and so on) may appear as subdivisions of "Afghanistan" directly—e.g., "Afghanistan—pictorial works" rather than "Afghanistan—history—pictorial works," thus allowing other relevant *genre* categories to be recognized in the same roster in which *subject* subdivisions appear.

The major types of format and genre categorizations used in the library field were initially developed as mechanisms to sort and characterize literature contained in books; but similar or analogous types of category designations have been created to prevent, in comparable ways, the retrieval of "too much" information within other kinds of knowledge records. (For example, within journal literature it is possible to focus on, or filter out, letters-to-the editor, book reviews, editorials, etc. from conventional

Encyclopedia of Library and Information Sciences, Fourth Edition DOI: 10.1081/E-ELIS4-120043707

"articles"—points that will be discussed below.) The present entry therefore starts with a consideration of mechanisms for sorting book collections, and then moves on to consider nonbook resources.

Several key formats and genres within book literature are traditionally distinguished:

Almanacs. These contain miscellaneous data and information for quick look-up purposes. They are good sources for information concerned with statistics, awards, historical dates and anniversaries, geography (i.e., basic data on countries, states, large cities, and natural features such as mountains, rivers, volcanoes), sports records, flags, lists of governmental agencies and officials, directory information for consumers, information on national or world figures, brief chronologies or overviews of world historical events, astronomical data and calendars, postal information, basic world maps, and so on. Almanacs are particularly useful for answering questions having to do with *who*, *what*, *when*, and *where* when only brief, objective information is required.

Atlases. These are usually compendiums of maps that display information graphically and spatially. Maps can show not just national or political relationships but also data on atmosphere and weather, temperature and rainfall, climate variations, crop production, vegetation, soil conditions, biodiversity, ecological changes, mineral concentrations or distributions, geologic processes, fishing patterns, military power balances, wars and conflicts, status of women, literacy levels, technological levels, population trends, occupational distributions, trade patterns, spread of diseases, health levels, standards of living, area histories, and the like. Many atlases also include representations of astronomical information on stars and constellations, the solar system, planets, moons, comets, and so on. (The term *atlases* is also sometimes used in an older sense, referring to compilations of statistical tables rather than maps.)

Bibliographies. These are compilations of citations to books, journal articles, conference papers, dissertations, reports, and so on. They may be *enumerative* (listing works from a country or other locale, from an author, or from a printer), *descriptive* (providing details of the physical characteristics of published works), or *subject* compilations. The latter are usually assembled by experts who have specialized knowledge of the topic, and so the listings in subject bibliographies are often annotated with descriptive summaries or evaluative notes on the intellectual content of the works cited. A particularly valuable feature is that these bibliographies may include many sources that lie beyond the range of database indexing. They serve to provide overviews, often comprehensive, of the extent of literature on a topic; and, being compiled by human scholars rather than machine algorithms, they often provide readers with a better survey of research options than computer printouts can supply. They usually have some arrangement or categorization of entries reflecting something of the internal structure or chronological development of the topic itself, an overall mapping of parts or aspects of the subject that cannot be captured or conveyed by automated term-weighting. Frequently subject bibliographies have detailed indexes revealing additional connections among the citations that are not apparent from the structured order of the listings within the body of the bibliography. Bibliographies compiled by experts, in short, are often much better than databases in providing starting points for research, or initial overview listings of resources. They are especially important in historical and literary research.

Catalogs. Catalogs provide listings of objects rather than bibliographic citations; the objects may be merchandise, art objects, equipment, machine parts, professional or art/craft supplies, and so forth, that are located at particular places or that are available for sale. Catalogs, like bibliographies, may also list publications; but catalog listings are usually for publications as physical objects residing in a particular place. Catalogs often provide descriptive details, technical specifications, and prices of the listed objects.

Chronologies. These present historical facts arranged by the time sequence of their occurrence. Some chronologies present parallel listings that display the developments within different areas of interest (e.g., politics, arts, technology, and religion) simultaneously, so that a reader may correlate the events of one area with contemporaneous, earlier, or later developments in other subject areas.

Concordances. These are alphabetical lists of individual words derived from particular texts (usually literary or philosophical classics) that enable researchers to determine exactly where any particular word or words appear within the text.

Dictionaries. These provide an alphabetically arranged list of words with their definitions, pronunciations, etymology, scope of usage, variant forms or spellings, and so on. Often they contain biographical and geographical names. Their scope may vary from coverage of an entire language to a focus on only the technical terms or jargon of a particular subject area. The term "dictionary" is often synonymous with "encyclopedia," referring simply to an alphabetical (rather than a systematic) arrangement of entries, regardless of whether the entries are brief and factual or lengthy and expository.

Directories. Directories are sources for identifying and locating individual people, organizations, or institutions; they list persons or corporate bodies that are situated in certain geographical areas, or that are related by thematic, professional, commercial, or subject concerns. Nowadays they usually list names, addresses, telephone and fax numbers, e-mail addresses, Web home pages, or other contact data; and they may provide basic information about an individual's qualifications and background, or an institution's purposes, history, and internal structure. Directories may be arranged alphabetically, geographically, or numerically (e.g., by telephone numbers or street addresses).

Encyclopedias. Encyclopedias are usually compilations of information in expository form in articles arranged alphabetically. The articles are generally intended to provide concise (rather than exhaustive) overview-summaries of the basic facts on a subject, written for an audience of nonspecialists who do not start with any prior knowledge of the subject or its technical jargon. Encyclopedia articles, too, usually provide brief bibliographies of basic works rather than exhaustive lists of all relevant sources. The aim of an encyclopedia, as a whole, is to summarize established or objective knowledge at a level comprehensible by lay people, and to provide a starting point for more extensive or in-depth research. The scope of individual encyclopedias may vary from attempting to survey all knowledge in all fields to focusing on particular subject areas or academic disciplines. (Note that encyclopedias specialized in a particular *subject area* still tend to be written with a nonspecialist *audience* in mind.) Subject encyclopedias, as a form, may be contrasted to treatises, which also attempt to survey entire subjects, but which do so exhaustively (rather than concisely) in both their texts and bibliographies, in a systematic (rather than alphabetical) order of presentation, and at a level of detail appropriate to specialists. Encyclopedias often include cross-references among articles, and frequently have detailed indexes that reveal specific data and interrelationships not discoverable by the alphabetical arrangement of the articles themselves.

Gazetteers. These are alphabetical dictionaries of geographic place-names; entries often include brief descriptions of the history, population, economic characteristics, and natural resources of the places listed. Gazetteers are also useful for identifying the larger geopolitical units in which a smaller locale is included (e.g., an entry on a town name will also designate the county, state, or other larger district of which it is part).

Handbooks and manuals. These are a type of information source intended to be easily transportable for actual use "in the field" rather than just in libraries. They are related to encyclopedias and treatises in that they try to provide the principles and important facts of a subject area, and in that they can be arranged either alphabetically or systematically. Their major distinction from these other forms is their emphasis on practice, procedures, and other "how to" directions for producing actual results or specific identifications of natural objects (plants, birds, botanical specimens, etc.), rather than just broad intellectual understanding. Also, they tend to be much more concisely written, as well as formatted in smaller-sized volumes, so as to be more easily carried about in field situations.

Newsletters. These are sources for current information in fields that develop or change rapidly. In print form, they appear daily, weekly, or monthly.

Sourcebooks. These are compilations of primary sources relevant to a particular topic or subject area. They conveniently assemble in one place original documents important to an understanding of the history or development of the subject, often with introductions that provide context and point out relationships not apparent from the texts themselves.

Union lists. These are location devices; they enable researchers who have already identified specific sources to determine which libraries (or other repositories) actually own a copy of the desired works. They are like catalogs in that they list physical objects; but the items recorded in union lists are drawn from multiple institutions in different locales.

Yearbooks. This type of literature seeks to provide a record of the year's developments in a particular field, often with evaluative commentary on what has transpired. Such annuals are often cumulations of the updating information contained in newsletters, but with more structured arrangement, additional introductory material, and better indexing; they are also usually produced as hardbound volumes to serve as permanent replacements for the ephemeral newsletter formats they may cumulate or supersede.

Many other formats and genres have also been customarily distinguished within book-format literatures. The *Library of Congress Subject Headings* roster provides numerous standardized form categories; note that in each instance in the following list, as with the above roster, the particular *subject* of the work to which these designations can be given is not relevant. (One obvious qualification is in order, however, some format and genre designations do have defined subject *scope ranges*—i.e., a form designation such as "description and travel" may have wide applicability within works on geographical topics, but not be appropriate at all for works in biology or physics.) Among the many traditional form and genre subdivisions, in addition to the above list, are

Abstracts
Archival resources
Bio-bibliography
Case studies
Charts, diagrams, etc.
Correspondence
Criticism and interpretation
Cross-cultural studies
Description and travel
Diaries
Discography
Fiction
Film catalogs
Guidebooks
History
Indexes
Interviews
Inventories

Manuscripts—catalogs
Microform catalogs
Patents
Periodicals—bibliography
Personal narratives
Photograph collections
Pictorial works
Portraits
Quotations
Registers
Problems, exercises
Sermons
Statistics
Tables
Textbooks

A practical problem for librarians arises in distinguishing *reference* genres within the larger roster of all form and genre designations. That is, within the entirety of a library's book collection, librarians need to create subcollections of *reference books* segregated from the general collections, and located in close proximity to the reference staff whose job is to provide quick information on some topics, and overall guidance into the larger collections not immediately at hand.

Although every book may be said to contain information, not every one qualifies as a *reference book* on its topic. Format and genre considerations come into play here, although not *all* format and genre considerations. "diaries" and "correspondence," for example, are labels indicating formats (rather than subjects), but not formats that would be considered appropriate for assignment to a reference collection. The "history" label is less clear cut. In one sense, "history" is a subject in itself (as distinguished from, say, "anthropology" or "religion"). In another, however, "history" is indeed a format designation, indicating a presentation of information in connected narrative sequence, as opposed to other presentation possibilities ("encyclopedias," "quotations," and "pictorial works"). Even if "history" is regarded as a form, however, all histories cannot possibly be shelved in working reference collections, which have particular space limitations.

How then can librarians make practical distinctions of reference genres from other informational genres? Two considerations are generally useful. The first is the distinction among *levels* of literature: primary, secondary, and tertiary. *Primary literature* is generated by participants in a particular activity or event, recording their original impressions, experiences, observations, experiments, or creative expressions. *Secondary literature* is generally comprised of either popularizations or scholarly analyses of the primary literature; it is based on surveys of, or research into, primary sources. *Tertiary literature* consists of works that identify, point out, summarize, abstract, compile, or repackage the information provided by the

other two levels. As Ranganathan[1] has pointed out, they are works intended to be consulted for one or more of their parts, rather than read through consecutively and completely. Reference works, such as almanacs, dictionaries, chronologies, and encyclopedias, are usually at this third level.

A second distinction between reference genres and others is provided by a particularly insightful analysis by Bates.[2] "Reference books," she writes, "have traditionally been defined administratively (e.g., as books that are noncirculating) or functionally (e.g., as books used for reference), rather than descriptively (i.e., in terms of the essential characteristics that distinguish reference books from other books)." She then provides a very useful definition of reference books based on their organizational structure: they are

> books that contain a substantial percentage of their length—operationally defined... as 60 percent or more in pages—in files and/or lists. Files are sets of records ordered according to a readily recognizable ordering principle [e.g., alphabetical order, chronological date, geographic continent/country relation, biological phylum/species relationship, etc.], and lists are sets of records ordered in the same manner as [an] author's idiosyncratic ordering of the contents of a book.

The best example of an author's "idiosyncratic ordering" of material would be, exactly, the *table of contents* of his or her book, which is likely to show an arrangement or conceptual structure other than that of an alphabetical, ordinal, geographic, or other immediately-recognizable sequence (as in a "file"). If the actual book itself, however—i.e., the *content* of the book that follows the *table* of contents—is primarily composed of discrete informational units or entries that "can stand alone" (i.e., rather than being integrated in continuous expository or narrative text), and if these discrete units could have been "arranged in different orders with respect to each other without harming their meaning or use," then such an idiosyncratic order is designated a "list" rather than a "file." "Reference books," again, are defined as those having 60% of more of their pages made up of files or lists. Thus not all genre or form designations (e.g., "case studies," correspondence," "diaries," "personal narratives") are *reference* genres.

Bates's theoretical distinctions were backed by an empirical study of the characteristics of actual books in the reference collections of three libraries, in comparison to the "stacks" books of the same libraries. Nearly 90% of the volumes designated "reference" books did indeed have "60% or more of their pages made up of files or lists." One notable exception was discovered: "canonical texts" are frequently included in reference collections although they are not made up primarily of files or lists. Such texts are things like standard treatises on particular subjects; compilations of laws and regulations; collections of standards and specifications; or literary, religious, and other authoritative texts (e.g., the *Bible*, the *Qu'ran*, or an indexed set of *Great Books*).

The primary virtue of having form and genre designations, in addition to subject groupings of material, to work with is that these categorizations greatly facilitate research for certain kinds of information *within* any subject area. The fact that the reference literature of any topic can be expected to fall into bibliographies, chronologies, dictionaries, directories, encyclopedias, and so on, provides a predictability factor to research that enables immediate attention to be directed toward some sources rather than others. Without the existence of predictable *formats* of literature being available, much time would be wasted—i.e., some questions are immediately answerable by directories, whereas regular monographs or dictionaries or chronologies within the same subject area would be irrelevant; others are best answered by encyclopedias, where monographic or atlas-format sources would only get in the way if they showed up in the same retrievals.

If one has a foreknowledge of the existence, as well as of the range and functions of the different reference formats available within *any* subject area, one can immediately think in terms of those categories, and thereby channel one's search efforts right from the start to only those resources whose format characteristics are appropriate to the question, while bypassing the others. For example, if one wishes to get brief overview knowledge of the Muslim historian Ibn Khaldun—his dates, his most important writings, his key ideas, and so forth—without having to read through hundreds of full-length books on him, one's search time and effort will be greatly reduced if one knows enough to anticipate the likely existence of an "encyclopedia" format reference source within the field of Islamic studies. In this case, the *Encyclopedia of Islam* (E.J. Brill, 1960–2002) provides a seven-page article that provides just the overview desired. Similarly, a researcher looking for an overview of the extensive literature on the British essayists Addison and Steele would be well served by first looking for a "bibliography" on the topic, such as Charles A. Knight's *Joseph Addison and Richard Steele: A Reference Guide, 1730–1991* (Prentice Hall, 1994), a 561-page annotated listing of 2006 directly relevant books, editions, articles, and doctoral dissertations—*none* of which have "the right keywords in the wrong contexts," the bane of Internet type searches. The important point here is that searchers who can frame their questions in terms of predictably existing *reference formats* may, even without having any prior *subject* knowledge of the field in question, be much more efficient in finding desired information about a topic, without any wasted effort, than even full professors who have subject expertise but who lack an understanding of the predictability of various formats.

The same predictability of genre formats facilitates not just research itself but also the teaching of how to do it. Many courses in library research methodology use texts that are themselves structured by formats or types of literature. Such texts may seek to provide the means of searching, via reference formats, within all subjects across the board[3]; or they may confine themselves to research within a specific discipline. An example of the latter is C. D. Hurt's *Information Sources in Science and Technology*[4]; the first three sections of its contents are structured as follows:

MULTIDISCIPLINARY SOURCES OF INFORMATIONS

1. Multidisciplinary sources of information
    Guides to the literature
    Bibliographies
    Abstracts and indexes
    Encyclopedias
    Dictionaries
    Handbooks
    Serials
    Directories
    Biographical directories
    Theses and dissertations
    Meetings
    Translations
    Copyrights and patents
    Government documents and technical reports
    Internet guides
    Web sites

THE BIOLOGICAL SCIENCES

2. Biology
    History
    Guides to the literature
    Abstracts and indexes
    Encyclopedias
    Dictionaries
    Handbooks
    Treatises
    Directories
    Web sites
3. Botany
    Guides to the literature
    Bibliographies
    Abstracts and indexes
    Encyclopedias
    Dictionaries
    Handbooks
    Directories
    Web sites

Essentially, the same few format breakdowns are used in 21 different subject areas (zoology, astronomy, chemistry, environmental sciences, general engineering, civil engineering, health sciences, etc.) It is, again, *predictable* that such reference genres can be found within *any* subject. While no one can remember the 1542 individual sources described in Hurt's book, anyone with a bit of training can remember the much smaller number of *types* of literature that can be expected to exist, no matter what subject is being researched. The predictability of this format structure within any topic area, once more, allows many inquiries to be much more immediately focused, with fewer wasted steps, and accomplished without the searcher having to wade through massive retrievals of term-weighted irrelevancies. (The phrase "relevance ranking"—*term weighting* is more accurate—is misleading in more ways than one. Not only does such algorithmic weighting fail to bring about the conceptual categorization of relevant sources, no matter what keywords [or languages] the sources themselves use; it also fails to bring about format categorizations that allow immediate focus to one's search efforts.)

One drawback in reliance on reference-format materials to pursue inquiries should be noted: a foreknowledge of the various types of literature enables a researcher to zero in quickly on reference sources relevant to a topic—i.e., those made up essentially of 60% or more of files or lists—but it does not enable the searcher to see "regular" books that are written in connected narrative or expository form. In terms of the distinction made earlier, not all primary literature or secondary literature is adequately covered by the tertiary literature of reference works. Direct access to the former levels, unconstrained and unchanneled by access through listings in reference sources, is still imperative. To gain this direct access (at least in research libraries in the English-speaking world) one must also know how to use the *Library of Congress Subject Headings* (*LCSH*) system within the library's general catalog; and one must also be aware of the trade-offs between searching via standardized conceptual and format categories (determined by *LCSH* terms) versus searching by keywords, no matter how the words are term-weighted by computer algorithms. Research instruction classes, in other words, need to cover more ground than a survey of reference-types of literature alone; they must also cover additional methods of searching (e.g., via controlled vocabularies [such as *LCSH*], via keywords, via citation links [showing which articles cite a known source], via related record links [showing which articles have footnotes in common with a known source], via bookstacks-browsing [exploiting LC or Dewey classification shelving arrangements], etc.). The predictable availability of this larger array of search methods (for gaining access to primary and secondary literature) is just as useful in focusing some searches as is the predictable availability of certain reference formats (for gaining access to tertiary literature) in focusing other inquiries.[5]

Form and genre designations are primarily useful within library catalogs or subject bibliographies, as mechanisms for *subdividing* larger categories of items that are themselves created on the basis of subject similarities. (Again, the subject "Afghanistan" is subdivided by the formats "bibliography," "encyclopedias," "gazetteers," etc.). To a lesser extent, format considerations also play a role in library classification schemes, in determining how physical book volumes may be shelved in relation to each other. The Library of Congress Classification (LCC) scheme, for example, is primarily structured according to subject categorizations (e.g., Class E books for American History, Class L for education, R for medicine, etc.). These groupings are further subdivided primarily by other subject considerations—but also, in some cases, by considerations of literature formats. A structured order of these subgroupings was largely standardized by Charles Martel, one of the architects of the LCC system in the early years of the twentieth century. As Immroth[6] has noted, "The order of entries or foci within a class or subclass or individual subject is another unifying feature of LC classification. This order is called the General Principle of Arrangement within the Classes or 'Martel's Seven Points' as Martel is said to have instructed the subject specialists to follow this order as appropriate in the development of any section of the classification." That order is as follows:

1. General form divisions
    Periodicals
    Societies
    Collections
    Dictionaries
    Encyclopedias
    Congresses
    Exhibitions
    Museums
    Yearbooks
    Documents
    Directories
2. Theory, philosophy
3. History
4. Treatises, general works
5. Law, regulation, state relations
6. Study and teaching
7. Special subjects and subdivisions

As Immroth further notes, "Usually the general form divisions that are applied [within any subject class] precede any other divisions. There is no absolute internal order for the general form divisions."

An example of the form subdivisions within Martel's structure may be found within the N (Visual Arts) class in the current LCC schedule:

N	(Visual arts)
N1–N8.Z	Periodicals
N9.A1–N9.9.Z	Yearbooks
N10–N17.Z	Societies
N21	Congresses
N25–N27	Collected writings (serial)
N31	Encyclopedias
N33	Dictionaries
N34	Terminology
N40–N44.Z	Biography
N45	Artists's marks and monograms
N50–N55.Z	Directories

The clustering of distinctive formats at the beginning of a class arrangement may be found in the Dewey Decimal Classification (DDC) system as well as in LCC. In Dewey, several form subdivisions are indicated by standard numerical designations that subdivide many different subject-classes at the same numerical position within each. Thus the 100s group in DDC (i.e., classes 100 through 199), representing the subjects "philosophy, parapsychology and occultism, pyschology," has several form clusters at its start:

103	Dictionaries, encyclopedias, concordances of philosophy
105	Serial publications of philosophy
106	Organizations and management of philosophy (roughly corresponding to "societies" in Martel's Seven Points within LCC)

The designations -03 for dictionaries, -05 for serial publications, and -06 for organizations show up in the same positions within other topical classes, for example, 403 for dictionaries, 405 for serial publications, and 406 for organizations within the overall 400s (language) class.

The clustering of forms—particularly reference forms—at the beginning of any new class area, in either LCC or DDC, facilitates reference work for those who know what to look for. To begin with, the appearance of long runs of volumes of the same height, and having uniform bindings, immediately signals the presence of serial publications within a library's book stacks. Since "periodicals" (LCC) or "serial publications" (DDC) always appear at the beginning of any new subject-class area, such visual markers indicate transitions on the bookshelves from one major subject-category to the next. But then, because of Martel's Seven Points, a stacks-browser in an LCC library who notices a clustering of uniform serial volumes will also be able to predict that reference formats such as yearbooks, encyclopedias, dictionaries, and directories will *follow* the bound journals in reasonably close proximity. In a DDC library, the browser who spots the serial runs will similarly be able to predict that dictionaries, encyclopedias, and

concordances will immediately *precede* the cluster of journal volumes. The classes in both systems were designed by practicing librarians who, more than a century ago, did not have the array of databases and full text electronic sources that we take for granted today; for them, the arrangement of the books themselves, in the stacks, was structured to enable reasonably efficient access even in the absence of a card (or other) catalog of the collection. Even today, the structure of that arrangement retains a practical utility for reference work that cannot be matched by any system of mere "mark it and park it" inventory control shelving, in which neither subject nor format relationships of volumes determine the order of their arrangement.

Format considerations also show up the LCC in other significant ways, beyond Martel's use of them as structuring elements within individual classes. Specifically, large parts of two entire classes (A and Z) are mainly composed of nothing but reference format material. Class A (General Works), right at the start of the entire LCC sequence, brings about some very useful groupings of reference genres. "General," here, means "not discipline-specific"; for example, the *Encyclopaedia Britannica* seeks to cover all areas of knowledge; and a standard index to journals, *Readers' Guide to Periodical Literature*, similarly covers articles in all subject areas. The various subdivisions of Class A deliberately bring together such "initial overview" sources:

AE	Encyclopedias
	For example: *Encyclopaedia Britannica* [AE5], *La Grande Encyclopedie* [AE25], *Brockhaus Enzyklopadie* [AE27], *Enciclopedia Universal Ilustrada* [AE61]
AG	Dictionaries and other general reference works
	For example: *The Columbia Encyclopedia* [AG5], *Famous First Facts* [AG5], *The New York Public Library Desk Reference* [AG6], *Guinness World Records* [AG243]
AI	Indexes
	For example: *Readers' Guide to Periodical Literature* [AI3], *Essay and General Literature Index* [AI3], *Poole's Index to Periodical Literature* [AI3], *New York Times Index* [AI21]
AP	Periodicals (general or multi-topical, not discipline-specific)
AS	Academies and learned societies
	For example: *Gale Directory of Learning Worldwide* [AS2], *The Europa World of Learning* [AS2], *Encyclopedia of Associations* [AS22], *The Foundation Directory* [AS911]
AY	Yearbooks, almanacs, directories
	For example: *World Almanac* [AY67], *Whitacker's Almanack* [AY754]

One of the overall purposes of Class A as a whole is thus to serve as a kind of "table of contents" to all of the other classes (B through Z1199). Works shelved here tend to provide introductory-level information—wide in scope but not very deep in coverage, providing a kind of overview mapping of the terrain that will be covered in greater depth, in its various parts, within each of the following classes. Thus the general encyclopedias in Class AE provide articles that are very brief (compared to full books) in all subject areas; and their articles also usually have concise bibliographies of the most important "starting place" sources for further reading (rather than exhaustive listings of all relevant sources). In a similar way, the periodical indexes in Class AI provide access to general magazines and newspapers; the articles contained therein may be on any topic, but they do not match the depth of subject penetration provided by whole books and specialized journals, which will be shelved in the subsequent classes starting with B. Class A, then, is a mixture of categorizations created by both "general" subject and reference-format characteristics, but it is especially laden with the latter.

The DDC has somewhat analogous clusters of general encyclopedia-format material near its beginning, in Class 000 (computer science, information, general works): Class 030 consists of "general encyclopedic works." Bringing all of the general encyclopedias to the front of the entire scheme here, too, provides a kind of introductory overview mapping of subjects that are covered in much greater detail within the whole books and specialized journals shelved in the subject categorizations to follow (100 through 999).

Whereas Class A in the LCC system serves as the "table of contents" to the classes which follow, Class Z at the very end serves much like the "index volume" at the end of a large encyclopedia. The Z (bibliography and library science) grouping has two major parts: Z4 through the Z1100s are classes mainly composed of monographs and serials about books, publishing, and library science as subjects in themselves; the Z1200s and above are clusters of actual reference-format bibliographies covering *all* subject areas (i.e., not limited to bibliographies about books, publishing, and libraries).

The noteworthy point is that these subject bibliographies (covering particular subjects or geographic regions *as* subjects, in depth) are not shelved with the regular books on their corresponding topics. For example, regular monographs on Indians of North America tend to be classed in E51–E59 (pre-Columbian America and Indians of North America), but bibliographies on the same subject are classed in Z1209–Z1210. Similarly, monographs on President Millard Fillmore tend to be classed in E426–E430 (United States—Revolution to the Civil War); but bibliographies on him are in Z8295.9.

As mentioned earlier, in most instances in either the *LCSH* system (in the library catalog) or the LCC system (in the bookstacks), format considerations are used to subdivide subject groupings, rather than vice versa. The subdivisions of the "index volume" bibliographies at the end of Class Z, however, are an exception. The material

in this range is all of a particular reference format—bibliographies—to begin with; the arrangement of the bibliographies' sequence is then subdivided by topical considerations, in three large clusters:

Z1201–Z4890	Geographically localized subject bibliographies (by continent, country, state, county, etc.) arranged in the order of North America, South America, Europe, Asia, Africa, Australia, and Oceania, with narrower localized subdivisions within each continent.

For example:

North America	Z1201–
The United States	Z1201–1363
Alaska	Z1255–1256
Arizona	Z1257–1258
Canada	Z1365–1401
Mexico	Z1411–1431
Central America	Z1437–
Belize	Z1441–1449
Costa Rica	Z1451–1459
South America	Z1601–

Z5000–Z7999	Subject bibliographies (usually lacking geographical limitations or focus, arranged alphabetically by subject).

For example:

Agriculture	Z5071–5076
Anthropology	Z5111–5119
Astronomy	Z5151–5156
Bees and bee culture	Z5256
Biology	Z5319–5323

Z8000–Z8999	Personal bibliographies (on individual people, usually literary authors or historical figures), arranged alphabetically by the surname of the subject.

For example:

Adams, Henry	Z8015.3
Austen, Jane	Z8048
Burton, Sir R.F.	Z8136.2
Chesterton, G.K.	Z8166.5

The use of simple and easily remembered ordering mechanisms (continent/country, alphabet) for these unusually important reference-format materials once again enables stacks-browsers to recognize where they are in relation to the whole scheme, even in the absence of a separate catalog of the collection. The class scheme thus increases the predictability of finding bibliographies on any topic—i.e., even if one does not know in advance that a bibliography actually exists on a particular subject, the arrangement of the Z classes gives an informed searcher a foreknowledge of which niches within the overall system are likely to contain such works, since the existence of the geographical and alphabetical niches is itself predictable, even if their specific contents are not.

The clustering together of all subject bibliographies, on all topics, at the very end of the LCC scheme also enables them to be browsed in relation to each other, as reference sources, without the cluttering presence of millions of non-reference works on the same subjects. This gives the bibliographies a cumulative utility that would be dissipated if each one were shelved with the monographs on its topic, in the regular B through Z1100s subject classes. (For example, the ability to see whole shelves of hundreds of subject bibliographies on women's studies, in Z7961 through Z7965, gives searchers in this subject area the capability of seeing relationships, and paths of access into the relevant literature, that could not otherwise be noticed.) The aggregation of reference sources at the end of the LCC scheme, again, enables them to serve as a kind of "index" to material to be found in all of the other classes. Whereas Class A provides relatively superficial "overview" access to all subjects, Class Z provides corresponding in-depth access to each of them. These functions are brought about primarily by the respective clustering of different *reference formats*, in strategic beginning and ending positions in the overall LCC sequence, which placements serve the different purposes.

The DDC system has a class analogous to LCC's Z1200–Z8999 for grouping together all subject bibliographies; but Dewey puts its "index volume" class at the beginning of its sequence, in Class 016 (Bibliographies and catalogs of works on specific subjects or in specific disciplines) within the 000s, rather than at the end, in the 900s.

Libraries must collect or provide access not just to conventional monographic books, but to other kinds of knowledge records as well. Journals, periodicals, and magazines have always been sought for research collections; but, as a rule, their individual articles are not indexed within a library's own catalog. Further, although journals do receive classification numbers in both LCC and DDC systems, the shelving of all volumes of the same journal in one location does little to indicate to a shelf-browser the particular subject content of any particular article(s) contained within the extensive runs of issues. Thus, neither the designations of reference formats in the library's catalog through form subdivisions of LCSH headings (e.g., Philosophy—encyclopedias, France—history—chronology), nor the classification schemes' various clusterings of reference formats (i.e., via Martel's arrangements within classes, or via the A and Z groupings) reveal the content of individual journal articles in the way that the catalog and the class scheme reveal *books'* content. The various printed indexes themselves are indeed clustered intelligibly within the A and Z classes in LCC (or 016 in DDC); but this placement also separates the indexes from physical (and browsable) proximity to the hundreds of journals, shelved throughout the entire classification scheme, whose contents they index.

Although libraries catalog and classify the indexes that provide access to individual journal articles, they do not usually create such indexes to begin with; with the exception of some few special libraries' catalogs that do cover articles,[7] this matter has largely been left to commercial publishers. Of course computerized versions of such indexes are the norm today; and many databases now provide full text access to journals, too; but these databases as well are generally created by commercial services rather than by libraries themselves. (Research libraries, all with chronic budget limitations, have always found it less expensive to subscribe to the indexing work done by private industry than to duplicate such costly labor on their own.)

But here, too, format and genre designations come into play, in ways analogous to their functions in the realm of book collections—i.e., journal articles, like books, may often be indexed not just according to their subjects, but also according to their various formats. And some of these journal formats are unusually important as reference genres. For example, the commercially-produced database *RILM Abstracts of Music Literature*, from the National Information Service Corporation, is not simply a subject index to thousands of journals (also books, conference papers, dissertations, etc.); it also enables users to search or limit by formats and genres. Specifically, it provides a search box allowing access by "publication type," including all of the following:

> All
> Article in a collection of essays
> Article in a dictionary of a related discipline
> Article in a newspaper
> Article in a periodical or yearbook
> Article in a symposium proceedings or Congress report
> Article in a volume of essays printed as a Festschrift
> Article in translation
> Book division or chapter
> Book in facsimile or reprint form
> Book in translation
> Book of collected essays, letters, or documents
> Book of essays printed as a Festschrift

Book of symposium proceedings or a Congress report
Book, monograph, or pamphlet
Book: periodical as a whole
Commentary accompanying a recording
Commentary printed in the program of a concert or opera
Commentary printed within an edition of music
Commentary, printed separately, on an edition of music
Dissertation, doctoral
Dissertation, master's or other non-doctoral thesis
Electronic resource
Motion picture
Music recording, sound recording
Review of a book, monograph, or pamphlet
Review of a dissertation
Review of a facsimile or reprint edition
Review of a new edition or music other than scholarly
Review of a periodical or yearbook
Review of a recording or film
Review of a scholarly edition of music
Review of a symposium proceedings or Congress report
Review of a translation
Review of a volume of collected essays
Review of a volume of essays printed as a Festschrift
Review of an article
Review of an opera or concert
Review of electronic resource
Review of motion picture (video)
Technical drawing of a musical instrument

Similarly, the *ISI Web of Science* database, from the Institute for Scientific Information (a subsidiary of The Thomson Corporation) is an index to 9000 scholarly journals in all subject fields (including social sciences and humanities, not just sciences); and it allows searches to be limited to a variety of "document types":

All document types
Article
Abstract of published item
Art exhibit review
Bibliography
Biographical item
Book review
Chronology
Correction
Correction, addition
Dance performance review
Database review
Discussion
Editorial material
Excerpt
Fiction, creative prose
Film review
Hardware review
Item about an individual
Letter

Meeting abstract
Meeting summary
Music performance review
Music score
Music score review
News item
Note
Poetry
Record review
Reprint
Review (i.e., literature survey articles)
Script
Software review
TV review, radio review, video
Theater review

Many other commercial databases offer such "publication type" or "document types" search features. Several of these literature types—especially "reviews" of various sorts—are unusually important for reference work. Reviews are not easy to find within books; but such format-search capabilities in journal databases make them quite easy to zero in on, without burying them within much larger keyword retrievals—and it is within journals that most reviews appear in any event. As with the reference formats distinguished within book collections, such types of literature here, too, are not dependent on particular *subjects* (although there are sometimes *scope ranges* involved, as with the various formats connected to music—i.e., document types such as "dance performance review" or "music score review" will obviously not be found within journals devoted to subjects such as linguistics or nursing). The fact that most of these nonbook reference formats will predictably appear within multiple journals, usually regardless of the overall subject area of the journals, similarly enables many searches to be done much more efficiently, quickly, and precisely, than they could be if only subject (or keyword) searching were possible.

The predictability of reference formats, and their use in narrowing and focusing searches that would otherwise result in information overload, is, on the whole, still lacking in Internet search environments. Although it is now possible to limit Net searches to some large format-segments of sites—e.g., blogs, images, games, maps, news stories, patents, videos—the range of such types of sites is noticeably limited compared to the wider variety and greater specificity of format options available within library catalogs and commercially produced index databases. A major reason for the difference lies in most search engines' reliance primarily on automated computer algorithms to bring about the sorting of retrieved results; and term-weighting of keywords, designed mainly to cut down the clutter of sites irrelevant by subject, is not adequate either to make important distinctions among, or to clearly segregate, formats of records. Cataloging or indexing according to document types, especially the subset of types that are reference formats, has up to now been successfully accomplished only by human beings. Whether it can be accomplished in the future by machine algorithms is a question not yet answered.

In any event, whether human-created or machine-generated, reference form and genre designations play an increasingly important role in research today: the greater the size of any subject retrieval, the more necessary are filtering mechanisms that sort, categorize, and subdivide the results in ways that prevent information overload and allow searches to be efficiently focused on only the most appropriate sources. In addressing this need, form categorizations are equally as important as subject groupings.

REFERENCES

1. Ranganathan, S.R. *Reference Service*, 2nd Ed.; Asia publication House: London, 1961; 257.
2. Bates, M.J. What is a reference book? "A theoretical and empirical analysis". RQ **1986**, *26*(1), 37–57.
3. Katz, W.A. *Introduction to Reference Work*, 8th Ed.; McGraw-Hill: Boston, MA, 2002.
4. Hurt, C.D. *Information Sources in Science and Technology*, 3rd Ed.; Libraries Unlimited: Englewood, CO, 1998.
5. Mann, T. *The Oxford Guide to Library Research*, 3rd Ed.; Oxford University Press: New York, 2005.
6. Immroth, J.P. Library of congress classification. In *Encyclopedia of Library and Information Science*; Marcel Dekker: New York, 1975; Vol. 15, 93–200.
7. Nelson, B.R. *A Guide to Published Library Catalogs*; Scarecrow Press: Metuchen, NJ, 1982.

BIBLIOGRAPHY

1. Chan, L.M. *A Guide to Library of Congress Classification*, 5th Ed.; Libraries Unlimited: Englewood, CO, 1999.
2. Intner, S.S.; Weihs, J. *Standard Cataloging for School and Public Libraries*, 4th Ed.; Libraries Unlimited: Westport, CT, 2007.
3. Mann, T. *Library Research Models*; Oxford University Press: New York, 1993.
4. Miksa, F. The development of classification at the Library of Congress. 1984; 164 University of Illinois, Graduate School of Library and Information Science, Occasional Papers.

Reference and User Services Association (RUSA)

Barbara A. Macikas
American Library Association, Chicago, Illinois, U.S.A.

Abstract
The Reference and User Services Association (RUSA), a division of the American Library Association (ALA), has the following mission: RUSA is responsible for stimulating and supporting in every type of library the delivery of reference/information services to all groups, regardless of age, and of general library services and materials to adults.

INTRODUCTION

The Reference and User Services Association (RUSA), a division of the American Library Association (ALA), has the following mission: RUSA is responsible for stimulating and supporting in every type of library the delivery of reference/information services to all groups, regardless of age, and of general library services and materials to adults. At the 2000 ALA midwinter meeting, the RUSA Board of Directors adopted the following vision statement: The RUSA is the foremost organization of reference and information professionals who make the connections between people and the information sources and services they need.

Also at the 2000 ALA midwinter meeting, the RUSA Board of Directors adopted the following statement of values:

- We believe in universal access to information in a wide variety of formats.
- We value collections and information sources of the highest possible quality.
- We believe in reading as fundamental to quality of life and value all activities that promote it.
- We value the provision of innovative services and programs that meet the changing information needs of diverse populations.
- We value continuous evaluation and improvement in the management and delivery of collections and services to users.
- We value the professional growth and development of reference and user services staff.
- We value the role of reference and user services staff as educators in creating lifelong learners and critical thinkers.
- We value the unique contributions that human beings bring to the process of connecting users with the information they need.

MEMBERSHIP

The RUSA has a membership of over 5000, including both personal and organizational members. Personal members of RUSA work in all types of libraries and the publishing and information industry. Past studies of the membership have shown that about one-half of the membership works in academic libraries, one-fourth in public libraries, and the remainder in school libraries, networks, library education, and publishing. Members of RUSA are reference librarians, bibliographers, administrators, adult services librarians, collection development specialists, readers' advisers, public service librarians, and individuals working in the publishing and information industry.

NAME CHANGE

The RUSA was previously named the Reference and Adult Services Division (RASD). The RASD was formed in 1972 when two ALA divisions, which had been created in 1957, merged—the Reference Services Division (RSD) and the Adult Services Division (ASD). In 1995, the RASD Board of Directors considered changing the name of the organization. During their deliberations, they indicated their interest in including the word "association" in the name to clearly indicate that the organization was an association in its own right in addition to being one of the component parts of the ALA. By this time all of the other ALA divisions had already changed the word "division" in their names to "association." The Board of Directors was also concerned that the name "Reference and Adult Services Division" did not adequately reflect the mission of the organization, since the name did not mention reference services to children. Lastly, the board also wanted a name with a pronounceable acronym. After it was approved by the membership in the spring of 1996, the change from RASD to RUSA took effect in September 1996.

Encyclopedia of Library and Information Sciences, Fourth Edition DOI: 10.1081/E-ELIS4-120044402

ORGANIZATION

The RUSA is organized into six membership sections: Business Reference and Services Section (BRASS), Collection Development and Evaluation Section (CODES), History Section (HS), Machine-Assisted Reference Section (MARS), Reference Services Section (RSS), and Sharing and Transforming Access to Resources (STARS). Each section offers members committee and discussion group opportunities. The BRASS has committees on business reference in academic and public libraries, as well as a committee that reviews business reference sources. The CODES sponsors the Notable Books Council, a group that selects the best fiction, poetry and nonfiction for adults, as well as committees on readers' advisory, collection development and evaluation, and a committee that selects the year's best reference sources. In 2007, CODES created a genre fiction booklist award, the Reading List. The Reading List Council highlights outstanding genre fiction in eight categories including: Adrenaline titles (suspense, thrillers, and action adventure); Fantasy; Historical Fiction; Horror; Mystery; Romance; Science Fiction and Women's Fiction. The History Section sponsors groups that focus on genealogical research, historical events and historical bibliographies. The MARS has committees on management of electronic services, local systems and services, and user access to services. The RSS represents all aspects of reference and information services including delivery, management, and evaluation, with committees focusing on services to specific populations such as the aging, Spanish-speaking, and adults, as well as those concerned with research, marketing and information literacy. The STARS focuses on interlibrary loan, document delivery, remote circulation, access services, cooperative reference, cooperative collection development, remote storage, and other shared library services.

PUBLICATIONS

The RUSA publishes *Reference and User Services Quarterly (RUSQ)*, a scholarly journal with referred articles, regular columns and reviews of reference sources, professional materials, and electronic resources. Previously named *RQ*, the journal's name change took effect with Volume 37, Number 1 in 1997. The association also publishes *RUSA Update*, a quarterly electronic newsletter containing news of division activities. In addition to these periodical publications, the association publishes monographs and an occasional paper series. Recent titles include *Key Business Sources of the U.S. Government*; *Adult Programming: A Manual for Libraries*; *Towards a New Vision of Reference: Kaleidoscopic Collections and Real Librarians*; and *Collection Evaluation Techniques: A Short, Selective, Practical, Current Annotated Bibliography*.

AWARDS

The RUSA has an active award program to recognize outstanding achievement by members of the library profession. The division sponsors the following awards:

- Isadore Gilbert Mudge—Gale Cengage Learning Award (established 1958): $5000 and a citation to an individual who has made a distinguished contribution to reference librarianship.
- Dartmouth Medal (established 1974): A medal and honorable mention certificate that honors the creation of reference works of outstanding quality and significance.
- John Sessions Memorial Award (established 1980): A plaque given to a library or library system to honor significant work with the labor community and to recognize the history and contributions of the labor movement toward the development of this country.
- Margaret E. Monroe Library Adult Services Award (established 1985): A citation to honor a librarian who has made significant contributions to library adult services.
- Reference Service Press Award (established 1985): $2500 and a plaque presented to recognize the most outstanding article published in *RUSQ* during the preceding two-volume year.
- Gale Cengage Learning Award for Excellence in Business Librarianship (established 1989): $3000 and a citation to an individual who has made a significant contribution to business librarianship.
- Gale Cengage Learning Award For Excellence in Reference and Adult Library Services (established 1990): $3000 and a citation to a library or library system for development of an imaginative and unique resource to meet patron's reference needs.
- Louis Shores—Greenwood Publishing Group Award (established 1990): $3000 and a citation to an individual reviewer, group, editor, review medium or organization to recognize excellence in book reviewing and other media for libraries.
- BRASS/Gale Cengage Learning Student Travel Award (established 1992): $1000 award given to a student enrolled in an ALA accredited master's degree program to attend the ALA Annual Conference.
- Genealogical Publishing Company Award (established 1992): $1500 and a citation awarded to a librarian, library, or publisher to encourage professional achievement in historical reference and research librarianship.
- Virginia Boucher—OCLC Distinguished ILL Librarian Award (established 1999): $2000 and a citation recognizing a librarian for outstanding professional achievement, leadership, and contributions to interlibrary loan and document delivery.

- Dun & Bradstreet Public Librarian Support Award (established 1999): A citation and $1000 to support the attendance at the annual conference for a public librarian who has performed outstanding business reference service and who requires financial assistance to attend the ALA annual conference.
- Dun & Bradstreet Award for Outstanding Service to Minority Business Communities (established 1999): $2000 and a citation that recognizes one librarian who, or library that has created an innovative service for a minority business community, or has been recognized by that community as an outstanding service provider.
- ABC-CLIO Online History Award (established 2005): Every other year beginning in 2005, $3000 and a citation recognizing a person or a group of people producing a freely available online historical collection, or an online tool tailored for the purpose of finding historical materials, or an online teaching aid stimulating creative historical scholarship.
- Emerald Research Grant Award (established 2006): $5000 and a citation to individuals seeking support to conduct research in business librarianship.
- STARS-Atlas Systems Mentoring Award (established 2006): $1000 to a library practitioner who is new to the field of interlibrary loan/document delivery or electronic reserves, for travel, registration, and membership at ALA Annual Conference.

CONTINUING EDUCATION OPPORTUNITIES

The RUSA offers its members many continuing education opportunities. At each ALA annual conference, the division sponsors programs on a broad range of topics such as readers' advisory services, best practices in reference and user services, collection development, the use of electronic journals, and the dynamics of print vs. online reference sources. Before the ALA annual conferences, the division also offers full-day workshops on topics such as business reference, emerging electronic reference sources, genealogical research, and resource sharing. RUSA also offers a variety of online electronic courses on topics including the reference interview, reader's advisory and genealogy.

GUIDELINES

The association establishes guidelines to serve as authoritative documents offering suggested levels of performance for the profession. Guidelines in the following categories have been established:

Electronic Services

- Guidelines for Implementing and Maintain Virtual Reference Services, 2004.
- Guidelines for the Introduction of Electronic Information Resources to Users, 2006.

Genealogy, History

- Guidelines for Developing Beginning Genealogical Collections and Services, 1999.
- Guidelines for a Unit or Course of Instruction in Genealogical Research at Schools of Library and Information Science, 1996.
- Guidelines for Establishing Local History Collections (2006).

Interlibrary Loan

- Interlibrary Loan Code, for the United States and Explanatory Supplement, 2001.

Reference/Information Services

- Guidelines for Behavioral Performance of Reference and Information Service Providers, 2004.
- Guidelines for Cooperative Reference Services, 2006.
- Guidelines for Implementing and Maintaining Virtual Reference Services, 2004.
- Guidelines for Information Services, 2000.
- Guidelines for Liaison Work in Managing Collections and Services, 2001.
- Guidelines for Medical, Legal and Business Responses at General Reference Desks, 2001.
- Professional Competencies for Reference and User Services Librarians, 2003.
- Definition of a Reference Transaction, 2008.

User Populations

- Guidelines for the Development and Promotion of Multilingual Collections and Services, 2007.
- Guidelines for Library Services to Older Adults, 1999.
- Guidelines for Library Services to Spanish-Speaking Library Users, 2007.

PROBLEMS AND ISSUES

Concerns of RUSA members mirror those of many of the ALA's other divisions: recruitment, professional development, and library school education. But RUSA members are also concerned about issues focused on reference librarianship, particularly the development of reference services in a digital age, and the diminishing value that information seekers place on more traditional library reference services.

To respond to these concerns, RUSA's strategic focus is on the future of reference and users services, with a goal to recast the provision of reference service to meet the needs of twenty-first century users. In particular this means positioning reference librarians to serve as consultants to help patrons evaluate and select quality information amid a rising sea of information presented in ever increasing formats and technologies and encouraging reference librarians to more than ever serve as resources and teachers of new technologies, information and research skills to increasingly diverse populations with a wide range of needs and skill levels.

Another challenge facing RUSA membership is that while demand for electronic resources and collections continues to grow, concerns persist about costs, coverage, availability, and access. Reference librarians constantly strive to provide accurate and current information to their users, but are often stymied when database coverage changes or license changes curtail access. Future access to database information could also be in jeopardy as database companies change ownership or discontinue a product.

Although many libraries have reported a decline in the number of reference transactions, the length of the reference encounter seems to be on the rise. The decline has been attributed to more people using the Internet to find the information they need. The reason for the longer encounter time is also the Internet. Reference librarians are increasing the amount of time they are taking to teach patrons how to design effective search strategies and then evaluate the search results. Although some have predicted that Internet search engines will put reference librarians out of business in 10 years, reference librarians know this is unlikely. In fact, they believe that reference and user services will become the library's core service. The key to this, however, is how well we can reinvent our services to match the changing needs of our clients. The RUSA will be there to help reference librarians in this endeavor.

NOTES

More information on the RUSA, including the full-text of guidelines, *RUSQ*, *RUSA Update*, lists of best reference websites, bibliographies, and information on the organization is available on the RUSA Web site at http://rusa.ala.org.

Reference Services

Linda C. Smith
School of Information Sciences, University of Illinois at Urbana-Champaign, Champaign, Illinois, U.S.A.

Abstract
This entry provides an overview of reference services and the impact of technology on reference sources and services. Following a brief overview of the history of reference services, the types and scope of reference services are explained. Features of the reference interview and factors contributing to its success are considered, followed by a discussion of the various types of reference sources and the development of reference collections. An outline of the impact of technology on new forms of service delivery includes an explanation of both asynchronous and synchronous approaches. The ways in which reference ethics and reference policies guide services are reviewed, and the role of evaluation in assessing effectiveness of reference services is explored. This entry concludes with indications of future trends in reference services.

INTRODUCTION

To mediate between a library user's information needs and the information resources accessible to that user through the library, libraries offer reference services. The provision of reference services in libraries dates from the late 1800s. As noted by Margaret Hutchins in 1944, "Reference work includes the direct, personal aid within a library to persons in search of information for whatever purpose, and also various library activities especially aimed at making information as easily available as possible."[1] Reference services continue to exist in libraries because the many means of access to and use of information resources are not intuitively self-evident. Reference services may range from a minimal level of aid to users in locating their own information to the actual delivery of information to users. Librarians may also offer assistance to users in deciding which materials to read for pleasure or study.

Prior to initiating a search in response to a question, the reference librarian conducts a reference interview to develop a more complete understanding of the user's information need. Successful reference interactions require a variety of skills in addition to effective questioning. Librarians should have a genuine interest in users' information needs, an ability to establish trust and confidence, flexibility in developing search strategies, and knowledge of reference sources. Reference sources can be divided into two main classes: compilations that furnish information directly and compilations that refer to other sources by indicating places in which the information sought may be found. The work of reference librarians includes selection of an adequate and suitable collection of reference sources and arrangement and maintenance of the collection so that it can be used easily and conveniently.

Developments in telecommunications and computer technology have impacted both reference work and reference sources. Users need no longer come to the library to ask questions; instead they may use the telephone, e-mail, web forms, or instant messaging. Physical reference collections housed in reference rooms in libraries are now supplemented by licensed databases and freely available authoritative web resources.

In their work reference librarians are guided by ethical principles as expressed in professional codes of ethics and by their own library's reference policies. The continuing improvement of reference services depends on regular evaluation of service effectiveness.

HISTORY OF REFERENCE SERVICES

The generally recognized starting point for the history of reference services is the 1876 paper by Samuel Swett Green of the Worcester Public Library on *Personal Relations between Librarians and Readers*.[2] Green identified four components of reference services: (1) instruct the reader on how to use the library and its resources; (2) answer readers' questions; (3) aid the reader in the selection of good works; and (4) promote the library within the community. The concept of reference services emerged in the United States in first public and then academic libraries as the result of a number of factors—increasing urbanization, growing immigrant populations, the rise of public education, and changing modes of instruction in American colleges and universities.[3] In a growing number of libraries, this led to the designation of one or more library staff members to fill the reference function, the creation of reference rooms, and the establishment of distinct reference collections. Beginning in the early 1900s, the special

Encyclopedia of Library and Information Sciences, Fourth Edition DOI: 10.1081/E-ELIS4-120053428

library movement in business, industry, government, and research settings placed an emphasis on more in-depth information services to the clientele of those organizations. To better prepare library staff for this emerging role, courses in reference work were introduced in library schools, and the first text, Alice Bertha Kroeger's *Guide to the Study and Use of Reference Books*,[4] was published in 1902. Over the next century, reference services continued to develop as library collections grew and library organizations became more departmentalized. In larger libraries, specialization could occur by subject (e.g., business), clientele served (e.g., children), form of material (e.g., government documents), or function (e.g., interlibrary loan). Throughout the same period, developments in technology, from the telephone to the Internet, had a significant influence on the emergence of new approaches to reference services. The maturing of reference services as an area of specialization is also reflected in the establishment of the Reference Services Division within the American Library Association (ALA) in 1957. This became the Reference and Adult Services Division in 1972, renamed the Reference and User Services Association (RUSA) in 1996.[5] An important function of RUSA is the development of guidelines for various aspects of professional practice.

Beginning in the 1970s, reference services transitioned from a period of certainty regarding roles, resources, and methods to a period of change and challenge,[6] driven in large part by developments in computer and communications technology. In his 1984 article "What's wrong with reference," William Miller called for a reexamination and reorganization of reference services.[7] This led to a period of "rethinking reference" that included exploring alternative staffing models, experimentation with newer technologies, and a focus on patron-centered service. Nevertheless, most libraries kept their reference desks as the focal point of reference services. The emergence of the World Wide Web and search engines resulted in a dramatic shift beginning in the 1990s. The proliferation of high-speed campus networks, broadband access from homes, and wireless access in public spaces highlighted the inadequacy of a building-centered model for delivery of reference services.

CHANGING CONTEXT FOR REFERENCE SERVICES

Trends in technology impact the extent to which the reference librarian is needed as an intermediary between the user and resources in digital form. Digital databases were initially accessible through telecommunications networks beginning in the 1970s. Reference librarians searched these resources on behalf of users because of the expertise required to search effectively and the cost associated with access. When databases on CD-ROM later became

available on computer workstations housed in the library, the era of "end-user searching" began.

With the emergence of the World Wide Web, it has become much easier for users to find information on their own. Mobile communication devices have led to the diffusion of access into a wide range of work, school, and leisure activities. In this information-rich world, information can be sought anytime, anywhere. Now users have alternatives that are more convenient than coming to a physical library at set hours to consult with a reference librarian. As a result, reference librarians have to find ways to respond to contemporary users' values and expectations of immediacy, interactivity, personalization, and mobility. If reference services are to be used, attention must be given to minimizing the time, the effort, and the difficulty of use.

While the intermediary role of the librarian may now sometimes involve doing some searching on behalf of the user, it is more likely to emphasize guidance in choosing among and using available resources, both print and digital. Reference librarians need to raise user awareness that the resources freely available through Internet search engines are only a portion of what could be helpful in meeting their information needs. Library print collections still contain centuries of accumulated knowledge not yet in digital form (although mass-digitization projects by organizations such as Google and the Open Content Alliance are shifting that balance) and libraries subscribe to databases because they provide information not available elsewhere. Because users can answer simple questions themselves, the types of question handled by reference librarians have become more complex.

Another trend to which reference librarians have to respond is the increasing diversity in populations served. Users of libraries in the United States today come from all over the world and speak many different languages. Library users can also vary in such dimensions as age (e.g., children, teens, adults, senior citizens) or disability (e.g., physical, mental). Success in providing reference service depends on flexibility, cultural competence, openness, and empathy toward the many diverse users.

SCOPE OF REFERENCE SERVICES

Definitions

The contemporary role of the reference librarian is reflected in two definitions approved in 2008 by RUSA:[8]

> *Reference transactions* are information consultations in which library staff recommend, interpret, evaluate, and/or use information resources to help others to meet particular information needs. Reference transactions do not include formal instruction or

exchanges that provide assistance with locations, schedules, equipment, supplies, or policy statements.

Reference work includes reference transactions and other activities that involve the creation, management, and assessment of information or research resources, tools, and services.

In the second definition, creation and management of information resources includes the development and maintenance of resources that can be used independently, either in-house or remotely, to satisfy information needs. Assessment activities include the measurement and evaluation of reference resources and services. These definitions emphasize the informational dimension of reference work. In many libraries, reference services also include responsibilities for both instruction (formal or informal) and guidance (the readers' advisory role). The relative emphasis among information, instruction, and guidance depends on the library's mission and users' needs. While the definition of reference transaction excludes "exchanges that provide assistance with locations, schedules, equipment, supplies, or policy statements," users do need assistance in such activities as getting oriented to the library building, working with computers and printers, and understanding circulation policies. Either reference librarians also answer these questions or some type of tiered service is implemented, with reference assistants answering basic questions and referring more complex questions to the reference librarians.

Types of Reference Service

Some common types of reference service include readers' advisory, ready reference, research consulting, bibliographic verification and interlibrary loan, and instruction. Some reference librarians may be involved in all of these activities, while others may specialize in areas such as readers' advisory services or instruction. Marketing is needed so that users are made aware of the range of services available from the library.

Readers' advisory is the process of recommending sources to library users. A successful readers' advisory service is one in which knowledgeable staff help fiction and nonfiction readers with their leisure-reading needs. Readers' advisors see themselves as links between readers and books, just as reference librarians are the connections between users and informational materials.[9]

Ready reference is the provision of short, factual answers to highly specific questions. A wide array of reference sources, such as directories, dictionaries, and encyclopedias, are useful in answering ready reference questions. In the past, reference librarians did more ready reference simply because the sources required to answer such questions were in library collections and not available to users. With the increasing volume of authoritative

content made accessible through a library's website or search engines such as Google, many users now have the tools to find this type of information on their own. As a result, there is less need to consult a librarian for ready reference. With the decline in ready reference has come an increase in emphasis on research consulting. In this case, the librarian may suggest sources, search terms, and strategies that will lead to material related to the user's information need.

Given the increasing volume and complexity of information sources in both print and digital form, reference librarians are often called on for bibliographic verification, determining full and accurate bibliographic information for a sought document and its location. If the document is not available as part of the library's collection or freely available on the web, then the librarian can assist the user in securing a copy through interlibrary loan.

Instruction can take two forms: direct and indirect. Direct instruction is characterized by the librarian communicating directly with the user. This may occur one-on-one with the librarian teaching the user as they work together to locate information or it may be done in a group environment in workshops or classes. Indirect instruction is provided in anticipation of user needs and involves development of instructional tools. These may include guides that describe how to use the catalog, a database, or a specific reference source. Other guides may focus on a specific discipline, highlighting relevant and authoritative print and digital sources.

While some users will discover the range of available reference services unaided, many will need to have the services promoted to them before they will be aware of what modern reference services have to offer. Marketing is the activity through which librarians develop the needed services, decide how to deliver the services, determine how best to communicate their value, and then promote the services relevant to each group of users. Reference librarians are often central to a library's marketing efforts.

Approaches to Reference Service

In the late nineteenth century, the reference desk was established as the central point of library services and patron interaction. For over a century, it remained largely unchallenged, but the reference desk is now just one of many avenues by which users can receive assistance. Any location in the library can be served by a roving reference librarian. The roving method is distinguished by the fact that the librarian is the one who initiates the reference transaction by approaching the potential user. Tiered service enables staff with varying levels of expertise to answer questions at different levels of difficulty. Paraprofessionals or student assistants staff an information desk and answer directional questions and basic ready reference or library holdings questions, freeing up reference librarians to answer more challenging research-level questions.

In contrast to these models that require that the user be physically in the library building in order to receive assistance, there is now increasing emphasis on serving users at a distance. This may involve "embedded" librarians, spending time where the users are, such as in a student union or academic department on a college campus. Alternatively virtual (also called digital or electronic) reference uses available technologies such as e-mail, instant messaging, or web-based forms to enable users at a distance to submit questions and receive responses from reference librarians. Technologies on the horizon for enhanced interactivity include Skype and videoconferencing.

The impact of technology on reference is best seen as a continuum rather than as primarily a phenomenon of the recent past. For several decades, many libraries have provided some question answering over the telephone. Increasingly, the attitude among reference librarians in all types of libraries is to support whatever means possible for responding to users' information needs, within staffing and budgetary constraints. This can mean having a virtual presence where users are, whether in online courseware, social networking sites such as Facebook, or virtual worlds such as Second Life. E-mail, text chat or instant messaging, and web-based forms have come into wide use as a way for reference librarians and users to communicate.

REFERENCE INTERVIEW

Purpose of the Interview

A reference transaction is initiated by a reference interview. The user's initial question often has to be clarified. The purpose of the interview is to elicit from the user sufficient information about the user's information need to enable the librarian to understand it enough to begin searching. Some reference questions are straightforward and do not require a high degree of interaction between the reference librarian and the user to be successful. Others require a great deal of negotiation. Questioning during the reference interview may elicit information about what the user wants to know; how the user plans to use the information; what level of detail would be useful; what format of information is preferred; and any other restrictions, such as whether there are time limits or deadlines. After determining a more complete understanding of the information need, the librarian must match that need with the information sources available, whether in print or digital form.

Communication Techniques

The reference interview has been the subject of much research and analysis, demonstrating that the quality of the interaction that the user has with the librarian is important to a successful outcome of the transaction. As a result, guidelines have been developed with the goal of enhancing communication effectiveness.[10] These guidelines outline in a linear way the elements of best practice in reference interviewing, including visibility/approachability, interest, listening/inquiring, searching, and follow-up. These guidelines have been updated to encompass both face-to-face and remote encounters by telephone, e-mail, chat, and so on, where traditional visual and nonverbal cues do not exist. However, since the reference interview is a process, with steps repeated and returned to as necessary, the guidelines alone do not give a complete picture.

The questioning process seeks to: (1) elicit the user's question in his or her own words; (2) make information available that the librarian needs to enable effective searching and accurate provision of information; and (3) verify that the librarian and user share the same understanding of the information need. There are several communication strategies that can be used during question negotiation, including the judicious use of open and closed questions. Open questions encourage users to talk about the information need using their own terms (e.g., We have a number of books/articles about [TOPIC]. Was there something in particular you were looking for?). Closed questions ask for a "yes" or "no" response or present the user with options from which to choose (e.g., Do you want advanced material or something basic?).

It is important not to start searching too early in the interview process. Once the search process has been started, the librarian can continue to ask questions, refining the search strategy accordingly. When providing information, it is important to cite the source and verify that the answer matches the scope of the user's question and that the level or amount of information given is what was desired. The end of the reference interview should leave open the opportunity for the user to request further assistance if needed.

Increasingly, reference interviews are taking place virtually rather than face-to-face. The two basic modes of virtual service, asynchronous and synchronous, differ substantially in their immediacy and interactivity. Asynchronous services based on e-mail and web-based forms offer the advantage of a medium familiar to nearly all users of the Internet. Though it is possible to engage in a reference interview through a series of e-mail exchanges and clarifications, e-mail is best suited for straightforward questions. Some libraries attempt to overcome the limitations of unstructured and potentially incomplete e-mail questions by utilizing a web-based form in an effort to elicit enough information and context to provide a useful response. In contrast to the asynchronous communication mode of e-mail, synchronous reference service using the telephone and now chat or instant messaging has the potential to enhance communication effectiveness through real-time collaboration between the user and the librarian.

Librarians are justifiably concerned with the quality of the user's virtual experience when compared with face-to-face transactions. RUSA Guidelines for Implementing and Maintaining Virtual Reference Services provide librarians with things to consider as they prepare for and provide such services.[11] Libraries are extending their participation in resource sharing to include sharing reference expertise as an extension of virtual reference services. For example, the QuestionPoint service of OCLC Online Computer Library Center (OCLC) provides libraries with access to a growing collaborative network of reference librarians in the United States and around the world.

REFERENCE SOURCES AND REFERENCE COLLECTIONS

Reference Sources

Reference librarians must be able to respond to a wide variety of questions, depending on the needs expressed by library users. Increasingly, the concept of a reference collection made up of reference books is an inadequate characterization of the resources most frequently used by reference librarians. Although print materials continue to be used, they are supplemented by authoritative digital resources. With the availability of a growing number of freely available resources on the web, it is limiting to think of the reference collection as only those materials that are purchased or licensed by the library. As more and more information has become available in digital form, libraries are finding that the use of print reference collections has decreased substantially.

It is possible to divide reference sources into two main classes: compilations that furnish information directly and compilations that refer to other sources containing information. In practice, this distinction becomes blurred because sources of the first type often refer to others for fuller information, and those of the second type are adequate for answering some questions. Sources of the first type include encyclopedias, dictionaries, almanacs, handbooks, yearbooks, biographical sources, directories, atlases, and gazetteers; sources of the second type include catalogs, bibliographies, and indexes.

While some indexes and abstracts have been available in digital form for nearly 50 years, the digital availability of other categories of reference sources, such as specialized subject encyclopedias and handbooks, is much more recent. The last decade has seen a rapid increase in the availability of reference titles in digital form, the aggregation of multiple titles into virtual reference collections, and the emergence of new forms of collection that go beyond a simple aggregation of the contents of individual print titles. An example of a resource that aggregates content from multiple publishers is Credo Reference. As of

2016, this web-based collection included hundreds of titles from more than 100 publishers.

This proliferation of digital products has allowed librarians to access content they may not have been able to collect in print, but there are potential drawbacks. Rather than having the flexibility to select individual reference volumes from many different publishers, librarians increasingly have to select one aggregated package over another. This can have the effect of increasing the range and depth of a reference collection while also decreasing the flexibility to customize the collection to reflect the interests of the library's specific user community. An additional concern is that digital content is often licensed rather than purchased, meaning that such titles are not permanently added to the collection.

Reference Collection Development and Maintenance

The work of reference librarians includes selection of an adequate and suitable collection of reference sources and arrangement and maintenance of the collection so that it can be used easily and conveniently. Increased costs of reference sources and proliferation of formats and titles have focused attention on the importance of a systematic approach to reference collection development. Decisions in collection development include whether to buy newly published titles, buy new editions of titles already in the collection, cancel a title that is now freely accessible on the web, continue serials such as indexes, or license access to a newly published web-based resource. A written collection development policy can provide guidance in making these decisions and will help in establishing and maintaining an effective reference collection.

Just as different libraries have somewhat different sets of titles making up their reference collections, there are different possible arrangements of titles. One possibility is to maintain a classified arrangement regardless of type. An alternative is to group types of sources together, creating sections for encyclopedias, biographical sources, directories, indexes, and so forth. Most collections designate a portion of the titles as ready reference, kept at or near the reference desk. With the increasing availability of resources in digital form, reference librarians are often involved in projects to design the interface or gateway to orient library users to available digital resources and aid in their selection. There must be a systematic basis for weeding and for adding new titles to the collection. A growing number of libraries are weeding and reducing the size of their print reference collections, reflecting the decreasing use of print resources as more materials become available in digital form.

In building the reference collection, the librarian must evaluate the quality of individual sources and their suitability for inclusion in the library's reference collection. Selection criteria can include format, content, authority, and cost. Added considerations of digital resources include such factors as the user interface and possibilities for customization. The Internet has facilitated new forms of collaborative authorship that make it more difficult to judge the authority and accuracy of the resulting product. For example, Wikipedia is written and edited by numerous volunteers, who can continuously change and add articles.[12] Reference librarians need to exercise the same type of selectivity that they do in building physical reference collections when developing virtual collections. The Library of Congress Virtual Reference Shelf[13] is an example of a virtual reference collection. As the emphasis on building digital collections grows, guidelines are being developed to inform their design.[14]

REFERENCE ETHICS AND EVALUATION OF SERVICES

Reference Ethics

Reference services are guided by both reference policies at the institutional level and the Code of Ethics of the American Library Association.[15] The Code consists of eight principles. Those with particular relevance to reference services include Items I, II, III, IV, VII, and VIII.

Principle I expresses the responsibility for providing courteous, accurate, unbiased, and equitable service (drawing on a strong collection of resources): "We provide the highest level of service to all library users through appropriate and usefully organized resources; equitable service policies; equitable access; and accurate, unbiased, and courteous responses to all requests." Principle VIII addresses the need for the reference librarian to stay up-to-date with the field and continually expand one's knowledge: "We strive for excellence in the profession by maintaining and enhancing our own knowledge and skills. . . ."

Principle III speaks to the need to respect user privacy and confidentiality in the context of reference transactions: "We protect each library user's right to privacy and confidentiality with respect to information sought or received and resources consulted, borrowed, acquired or transmitted." Principles II and VII emphasize the need to uphold intellectual freedom in building strong, balanced reference collections and providing users the information they seek: "We uphold the principles of intellectual freedom and resist all efforts to censor library resources" and "We distinguish between our personal convictions and professional duties and do not allow our personal beliefs to interfere with . . . the provision of access to . . . information resources." Finally, the provision of reference services needs to conform to authors' and publishers' intellectual property rights as outlined in Principle IV: "We respect intellectual property rights and advocate

balance between the interests of information users and rights holders."

Expectations for reference librarians are further elaborated in the RUSA Professional Competencies for Reference and User Services Librarians that describe the activities of a reference librarian performing ethically.[16] Reference librarians also need to be aware of necessary limits on question answering, especially as they relate to medical, legal, and business questions where librarians must be careful to be of assistance without offering advice.[17]

Ethical issues such as confidentiality and privacy are also relevant in the digital environment, where it is possible to track a record of an individual's questions. Such records should be treated with the same respect for confidentiality and privacy as library circulation records. There is also the ethical issue of availability of and access to digital reference services. If librarians devote more and more of their resources and time to digital reference, then service to those who do not have Internet access could be negatively affected.

Evaluation of Services

Principle I of the ALA Code of Ethics indicates that librarians should provide "the highest level of service to all library users." In order to gauge the effectiveness of references services, evaluations must be undertaken. At the individual level, evaluation can be continual self-assessment of the effectiveness of the reference interview and the quality of answers given. A more formal evaluation of reference services in a library can focus primarily on inputs to the reference process, such as assessing the quality of the reference collections, whether physical or virtual. Or evaluation can emphasize the process of the interaction between the librarian and the user. In a virtual reference transaction, this can include reviewing the text of e-mail exchanges or chat session transcripts. Finally, evaluation may focus primarily on the outputs or outcomes of the transaction—was the user satisfied with the process and/or the information received. Evaluation data can be gathered through surveys and questionnaires, observation, or focus groups and interviews. As libraries face increasing pressures to demonstrate value to their parent organizations, methods to determine return on investment in reference services need to be developed.[18]

CONCLUSION

Reference services have changed considerably since Green first proposed the core concept. As Robert Kieft observes, "The service edifice built by reference librarians beginning in the late nineteenth century does not so much threaten to collapse as to be reborn in ways that we are still groping to discern."[19] Reference librarians are now providing "personal assistance to readers" both within the library and far beyond library walls and embracing new technologies as they retain traditional values. Rapid changes in technology will likely continue and those changes will affect the ways in which users seek and manage information. Those changes in user behavior will, in turn, continue to challenge the ways that reference librarians offer their services. As the popular perception that "everything is on the web" grows, reference librarians must find ways to show which types of information resources answer which questions best. As reference librarians develop and work with hybrid collections of purchased, licensed, and freely available web resources, a better understanding of the questions most easily answered by each will emerge. The volume and diversity of information available on the web opens new possibilities to both reference librarians and users, but both must continue to keep in mind that at present it can be hard to find the information sought; once found, such information may later disappear (or at least move); and the accuracy of information found may be difficult to assess. Recalling the definition of "reference work" cited earlier as "reference transactions and other activities that involve the creation, management, and assessment of information or research resources, tools, and services," it seems likely that more attention will be given to those other activities in order to enable users to serve themselves. To fully realize the promise of reference service in the digital environment, Michael Buckland argues that the objective should be to empower the user, developing organization and access mechanisms using digital technology and attentive to user needs and preferred modes of use.[20]

REFERENCES

1. Hutchins, M. *Introduction to Reference Work*; American Library Association: Chicago, IL, 1944; 10.
2. Green, S.S. Personal relations between librarians and readers. Am. Libr. J. **November 30, 1876**, *1*, 74–81.
3. Rothstein, S. The development of the concept of reference service in American Libraries, 1850–1900. Libr. Quart. **1953**, *23* (1), 1–15.
4. Kroeger, A.B. *Guide to the Study and Use of Reference Books: A Manual for Librarians, Teachers and Students*; American Library Association: Boston, MA, 1902.
5. Bourdon, C. Reference and User Services Association, *Encyclopedia of Library and Information Science*, 2nd edn.; Drake, M.A., Ed.; Marcel Dekker: New York, 2003; *4*, 2475–2478.
6. Rettig, J. Reference service: From certainty to uncertainty. Adv. Libr. **2006**, *30*, 105–143.
7. Miller, W. What's wrong with reference: Coping with success and failure at the reference desk. Am. Libr. **1984**, *15* (5), 303–306. 321–322.
8. Reference and User Services Association. Definitions of reference. January 14 2008. http://www.ala.org/rusa/ resources/guidelines/definitionsreference (accessed December 2016).
9. Saricks, J.G. *Readers' Advisory Service in the Public Library*, 3rd edn., American Library Association: Chicago, IL, 2005.
10. Reference and User Services Association. Guidelines for behavioral performance of reference and information service providers. May 28, 2013. http://www.ala.org/ rusa/resources/guidelines/guidelinesbehavioral (accessed December 2016).
11. Reference and User Services Association. Guidelines for implementing and maintaining virtual reference services. March 2010. http://www.ala.org/rusa/sites/ala.org.rusa/ files/content/resources/guidelines/virtual-reference-se.pdf (accessed December 2016).
12. Ayers, P. Wikipedia, user-generated content, and the future of reference sources. In *Reimagining Reference in the 21st Century*; Tyckoson, D.A., Dove, J.G., Eds.; Purdue University Press: West Lafayette, IN, 2015; 103–117.
13. Library of Congress. Virtual reference shelf, http://www. loc.gov/rr/askalib/virtualref.html (accessed December 2016).
14. NISO Framework Working Group. *A Framework of Guidance for Building Good Digital Collections*, 3rd Ed; National Information Standards Organization: Baltimore, MD, 2007. http://www.niso.org/publications/rp/frame work3.pdf (accessed December 2016).
15. American Library Association. Code of Ethics. Adopted at the 1939 Midwinter Meeting by the ALA Council; amended June 30, 1981; June 28, 1995; and January 22, 2008. http://www.ala.org/advocacy/proethics/codeofethics/ codeethics (accessed December 2016).
16. Reference and User Services Association. Professional competencies for reference and user services librarians; January 26, 2003. http://www.ala.org/rusa/resources/guide lines/professional (accessed December 2016).
17. Reference and User Services Association. Guidelines for business information responses; May 28, 2013. http:// www.ala.org/rusa/resources/guidelines/business; Health and Medical Reference Guidelines; June 2015. http:// www.ala.org/rusa/resources/guidelines/guidelinesmedical (accessed December 2016).
18. Kaufman, P.; Watstein, S.B. Library value (return on investment, ROI) and the challenge of placing a value on public services. Ref. Ser. Rev. **2008**, *36* (3), 226–231.
19. Kieft, R.H. The return of the Guide to Reference (Books). Ref. User Serv. Quart. **2008**, *48* (1), 6.
20. Buckland, M.K. Reference library service in the digital environment. Libr. Inform. Sci. Res. **2008**, *30* (1), 81–85.

BIBLIOGRAPHY

1. Cassell, K.A.; Hiremath, U. *Reference and Information Services: An Introduction*, 3rd edn.; Neal-Schuman: Chicago, IL, 2013.
2. Harmeyer, D. *The Reference Interview Today: Negotiating and Answering Questions Face to Face, on the Phone, and Virtually*; Rowman & Littlefield: Lanham, MD, 2014.
3. Mulac, C. *Fundamentals of Reference*; American Library Association: Chicago, IL, 2012.

4. Ross, C.S.; Nilsen, K.; Radford, M.L. *Conducting the Reference Interview: A How-To-Do-It Manual for Librarians*, 2nd edn.; Neal-Schuman Publishers: New York, 2009.

5. Saunders, L.; Rozaklis, L.; Abels, E.G. *Repositioning Reference: New Methods and New Services for a New Age*; Rowman & Littlefield: Lanham, MD, 2015.

6. Singer, C.A. *Fundamentals of Managing Reference Collections*; American Library Association: Chicago, IL, 2012.

7. Thomsett-Scott, B.C. *Implementing Virtual Reference Services: A LITA Guide*; American Library Association: Chicago, IL, 2013.

8. Tyckoson, D.A.; Dove, J.G. *Reimagining Reference in the 21st Century*; Purdue University Press: West Lafayette, IN, 2015.

9. Smith, L.C.; Wong, M.A., Eds. *Reference and Information Services: An Introduction*, 5th edn; Libraries Unlimited: Santa Barbara, CA, 2016.

Rare–Reference

Regional Library Networks: United States

Catherine C. Wilt
PALINET, Philadelphia, Pennsylvania, U.S.A.

Abstract

The U.S. Regional Library Networks (RLNs) are a loosely federated system of 15 membership organizations of libraries and related cultural organizations, established in the 20th century to facilitate access to information through resource sharing and cooperation among members. Created by librarians, the RLNs support their members through an array of services (predominately technology based) and provide a formal structure by which their members can work cooperatively to create programs members could not create individually. From as early as the 1930s, the RLNs have served as change agents and facilitators for the introduction and implementation of innovations into their members' operations, including the integration of large-scale technological systems such as Online Computer Library Center (OCLC). In the example of the RLNs' collaboration with OCLC, the result is a highly organized, now international, network of the world's bibliographic information, constituting a cooperative database development model that is unparalleled.

DEFINITION OF "REGIONAL LIBRARY NETWORK"

Because the term "network" is used to describe a variety of infrastructures and activities in the library and information industry, its use in describing a library service organization can be confusing. The formal definition of "network" implies a technical connection or system with numerous users. Within the library field, the term has been "a catch-all for a broad range of cooperative activities."[1] The American Library Association (ALA) Glossary defines library network as "a specialized type of library cooperation for centralized development of cooperative programs and services, including the use of computers and telecommunications, and requiring the establishment of a central office and a staff to accomplish network programs rather than merely coordinate them." In contrast, library consortium is "a formal association of libraries, usually restricted to a geographic area, number of libraries, type of library, or subject interest, which is established to develop and implement resource sharing among the members and thereby improve the library services and resources available to their respective target groups."[2]

Cooperation among libraries, librarians, and researchers has been a major force defining the nature and structure of library service programs for much of the 20th century. The benefits of working cooperatively and sharing resources toward collective achievements greater than the sum of individual achievements have been successfully demonstrated repeatedly. That success has resulted in one of the most organized models of cooperation within any industry in the United States.

An important, if not the most important, aspect of the RLNs is their social networking role, which is inherent in the term "consortium." Librarians created the RLNs to support each member's library programs symbiotically through information and resource sharing, continuing professional development and support, research and development, and collaboration. The distinction between RLNs and consortia has become less clear in recent years, as their organizational structures and the services they offer are very similar. In fact, several long-standing RLNs have begun to refer to themselves as consortia or cooperatives.

HISTORY

The beginning of the individual RLNs in the United States is quite varied. The oldest RLNs are the Bibliographical Center for Research (BCR) and PALINET. These Networks were created as resource centers to facilitate interlibrary lending. Both received grant support from private foundations and the federal Works Progress Administration (WPA) to create union catalogs of library holdings to aid researchers in locating materials.

As a specific example, PALINET started in 1933 as the Union Library Catalog of the Philadelphia Metropolitan Area. A small group of Philadelphia historians, tired of the difficulties they encountered locating books in the numerous and scattered area libraries, issued a prospectus for the proposed union catalog. Ultimately housed at the University of Pennsylvania, the massive union card catalog was created, serving as the centralized resource for locating materials. Over time, this catalog became the tool that enabled interlibrary loan activities to commence among the participating libraries. Other related services naturally followed, such as the Duplicate Book Exchange, where

Encyclopedia of Library and Information Sciences, Fourth Edition DOI: 10.1081/E-ELIS4-120008782

not needed duplicates were made available to other libraries.

Library networking drew much interest and attention in the 1970s. The ALA and the U.S. Office of Education cosponsored the landmark National Conference on Interlibrary Communications and Information Networks in 1970 to explore the library network concept and recommend a plan of action. This conference grew out of discussions acknowledging the enormous value of the nation's library resources and the need to develop interinstitutional networks among libraries for effective, affordable access to these resources. Recommendations from the conference included a call for the newly established National Commission on Library and Information Science to ensure financial support for developing network programs and to provide a broad base of public and legislative understanding of the need for a national network of libraries and information centers.[3]

Much federal funding and standards development since that conference have supported the growth of library networks, library systems, and consortia to the point that now over 425 such organizations are listed in the American Library Directory.[4]

One of the most important developments in library cooperation was OCLC. Founded by the visionary presidents and librarians of the Ohio College Association, OCLC's mission was to reduce libraries' costs by sharing cataloging records through a centralized database.[5] This enabled libraries to use cataloging records already entered by other libraries and to add original records that did not yet exist in the database.

In many cases, the first computers in libraries were OCLC terminals. Often they were also the first computers used within the libraries' parent organizations, e.g., campuses, school districts, municipalities. Libraries were positioned as technology leaders for computing within their institutions.

A leader in U.S. network development, Barbara Markuson, formerly Executive Director of INCOLSA, noted, "Library networks developed primarily as a mechanism to allow rapid technology transfer in the U.S. library system."[1] "Networking provides unparalleled opportunities for a dramatic restructuring of the library as an operational unit and for an astounding array of new information services better designed to meet the needs of an increasingly complex user community."[1]

REGIONAL LIBRARY NETWORKS TODAY

There are 15 independent library service organizations in the United States known collectively as the RLNs (see Table 1). They are a diverse group of organizations providing many unique programs and services, with OCLC the key service offered by all these organizations. Even though the RLNs are not exactly alike, commitment to cooperation, exceptional customer service, and innovative programs are common among them. Each RLN is a

Table 1 U.S. regional library networks.

Official name	Founding date	Primary service area
Amigos Library Services, Inc. (Amigos)	1978	Arizona, Arkansas, New Mexico, Oklahoma, Texas
Bibliographical Center for Research (BCR)	1935	Colorado, Iowa, Kansas, Nevada, Utah, Wyoming
Federal Library and Information Network (FEDLINK)[a]	1976	U.S. federal agencies in any state or country
ILLINET/OCLC Services (ILLINET)[b]	1977	Illinois
Indiana Cooperative Library Services Authority (INCOLSA)[b]	1974	Indiana
MINITEX Library Information Network (MINITEX)[b]	1968	Minnesota, North Dakota, South Dakota
Michigan Library Consortium (MLC)	1974	Michigan
Missouri Library Network Corporation (MLNC)	1981	Missouri
Nebraska Library Commission (NEBASE)[b]	1976	Nebraska
NELINET, Inc. (NELINET)	1978	Connecticut, Maine, Massachusetts, New Hampshire, Rhode Island, Vermont
Nylink[b]	1973	New York
OHIONET	1977	Ohio
PALINET & the Union Library Catalogue of Pennsylvania, Inc. (PALINET)	1936	Delaware, Maryland, New Jersey, Pennsylvania, and West Virginia
Southeastern Library Network, Inc. (SOLINET)	1973	Alabama, Louisiana, Mississippi, Kentucky, Tennessee, Virginia, North Carolina, South Carolina, Georgia, Florida, Puerto Rico, and U.S. Virgin Islands
Wisconsin Library Service (WiLS)	1972	Wisconsin

Networks are independent 501(c)3 organizations except as noted:
[a]Federal agency.
[b]State agency or state-affiliated.
Source: Networks and Service Centers: An OCLC Members Council Directory, 85–86.

separate entity with its own unique mission and characteristics. Some RLNs are federal or state agencies, e.g., FEDLINK and NEBASE; most are independent 501(c) 3 not-for-profit organizations, e.g., Amigos and SOLINET. Many Networks serve libraries in a single state, e.g., MLC (Michigan) and WiLS (Wisconsin); others serve members in a multistate region, e.g., NELINET and BCR.[6]

Governance

The staff at the member organizations of RLNs are active participants in the governance of their respective Network. The RLNs are governed by Boards of Trustees/Directors or similar advisory groups, elected from and representing the membership. Some Networks' Board positions are designated to represent certain segments of the membership, e.g., type of library or state. Some have public, at-large Board members, people outside the membership and from the community at large with an interest in libraries and the Network. Two Networks, MLC and PALINET, now facilitate their Board elections electronically.

The Networks host annual membership meetings and conferences, some over multiple days. They facilitate the work of numerous advisory committees and user groups within the Network, including the work of their OCLC Members Council delegates.

Support

The RLNs employ nearly 500 staff to support their programs. In 2003, nearly 17,000 libraries are served by the RLNs. Communication with members is facilitated through numerous means: newsletters, technical bulletins, training catalogs, electronic lists, e-mail, and web sites. Most communications and publications are now distributed electronically.

Many Networks have "support" or "help desks" through which they provide member support. They are beginning to use chat and instant messaging as additional ways to communicate with members.

The web sites of the RLNs offer extensive information about their unique governance and membership structures, as well as detailed descriptions of their programs and services (see Table 2).

Alliance of Library Service Networks

In the 1980s, the RLNs founded the Alliance of Library Service Networks. Originally, an informal forum for RLNs to discuss issues of mutual concern, the Alliance has become an effective means by which the RLNs implement cooperative ventures. Of note are the recent national negotiations with LexisNexis® led by SOLINET and with the Oxford University Press led by NELINET and Nylink. These programs dramatically reduced the cost of database access to these electronic resources for member libraries,

Table 2 Web sites of the U.S. regional library networks.

Network	Web site
Amigos	http://www.amigos.org/
BCR	http://www.bcr.org/
FEDLINK	http://lcweb.loc.gov/flicc/
ILLINET	http://www.cyberdriveillinois.com/ departments/ library/who_we_are/ OCLC/home.html
INCOLSA	http://www.incolsa.net/
MINITEX	http://www.minitex.umn.edu/
MLC	http://www.mlcnet.org/
MLNC	http://www.mlnc.org/
NEBASE	http://www.nlc.state.ne.us/netserv/nebase/nebserv. html
NELINET	http://www.nelinet.net/
Nylink	http://nylink.suny.edu/
OHIONET	http://www.ohionet.org/
PALINET	http://www.palinet.org/
SOLINET	http://www.solinet.net/
WiLS	http://www.wils.wisc.edu/

Source: Networks and Service Centers: An OCLC Members Council Directory, 85–86.

many of which could never have financially afforded access to these resources. Thus, the Alliance has become a means by which the RLNs can reduce costs through collaborative partnerships with each other and with vendor partners to serve the entire U.S. library community: a model "network of the networks," as envisioned in the 1970s.

RELATIONSHIP WITH OCLC

A primary service provided by all RLN's is access to and support of OCLC, the international membership organization (http://www.oclc.org/) that originally developed and currently manages a shared cataloging and interlibrary loan system, which has become the de facto U.S. national bibliographic database. The ability of OCLC to operate outside of Ohio is due largely to the work of the RLNs nationwide in promoting the benefits of OCLC in their respective regions and providing OCLC-related technical support and training for their members.

The RLNs' relationship with OCLC started in 1970 with the Pittsburgh Regional Library Center (now part of PALINET), a year before the on-line shared cataloging system was introduced. Some Networks existed prior to the founding of OCLC, e.g., BCR and PALINET, as previously described. Others came into existence to provide OCLC support for libraries in their region, e.g., SOLINET and Amigos. In some cases, state libraries established service programs to support OCLC services in their state, e.g., ILLINET and NEBASE.

Initially, in determining how shared cataloging functionality would be provided for libraries outside of Ohio, some regional Networks proceeded to replicate the OCLC database for their regions, e.g., NELINET, Amigos, and

SOLINET, reflecting a distributed national catalog model. After study and testing, it was quickly determined that the more favorable means by which to provide this service was through the centralized OCLC system accessible via propriety telecommunications lines. OCLC telecommunications hubs were housed and managed by several of the RLNs.

Of the U.S. libraries participating with OCLC 99.9% do so through an independent RLN- or OCLC-owned Service Center. Reciprocally, libraries have a direct role in the governance of OCLC through their RLN or OCLC Service Center. The RLNs and OCLC Service Centers comprise the membership of OCLC's Members Council, a 66-person advisory group responsible for providing advice to OCLC on service development and for the election of 6 of its 15 Board members. Networks also facilitate the work and communication of their OCLC Members Council delegation. For more information on the OCLC Members Council, see http://oclc.org/memberscouncil/default.htm/.

As of September 2003, nearly 17,000 libraries were members of the RLN's. This represents 90% of the U.S. libraries participating in OCLC. The remaining 10% of U. S. libraries receive support and training from two OCLC-owned and operated Service Centers: the OCLC CAPCON and the OCLC Western Service Centers.

To participate in OCLC, libraries typically join the RLN or OCLC Service Center serving their geographic area, but may choose to join any RLN or OCLC Service Center of their choice. A map illustrating the geographic service areas for the RLN's and OCLC Service Centers is located at http://oclc.org/contacts/regional/default.htm.

In-depth information on the RLN's and OCLC Service Centers is available in *Networks and Service Centers: An OCLC Members Council Directory* at http://oclc.org/memberscouncil/documents/directory.pdf.

GROWTH OF REGIONAL LIBRARY NETWORK SERVICES

The array of services provided by RLNs has grown dramatically over the years and continues a rapid evolution as the needs of their members evolve and innovative technological solutions become available. Services include, but are by no means limited to, training and continuing education, access to electronic databases (full-text, and abstracting and indexing services), consulting, technical support, preservation, digitization, retrospective conversion, union listing, web site development and hosting, courier/delivery services, remote storage facilities, and electronic publishing.

In the 1980s, RLNs were among the first suppliers of e-mail and then internet access to their members. This is another example of how Networks facilitate the broad adoption of new technologies by libraries through their extensive technical support and training infrastructure.

The RLNs have a long-standing role in advocacy on behalf of their members through national and international groups. Several RLNs are active participants in policy and standards organizations like the National Information Standards Organization, the Coalition for Networked Information, and the International Consortium of Library Consortia. Networks also work with regional and local groups to promote the role and needs of libraries.

Educational Programs

RLNs are well known and highly regarded for their training and continuing education programs. Thousands of library staff receive training in hundreds of classes offered by Networks annually.

Traditionally, training has consisted of instructor-led, in-person workshops held at the Network offices and at sites throughout each Network's specific region. In the past, self-paced courses were available in the form of workbooks, audio courses, and computer-based training. Recently, RLNs have made significant advances in the application of distance learning technologies to their training programs, bringing educational opportunities to broader audiences: those unable to travel and those who prefer a self-paced approach. The distance learning technologies implemented include videoconferencing, Web-based interactive workshops, and Web-based self-paced courses. Some Networks are beginning to include streaming video technology in their distance learning workshops.

Several RLNs have entered into cooperative training agreements with their Network colleagues. Still in the developmental stages, these programs now permit libraries to attend the training programs of other Networks at reduced cost. These alliances have the potential to expand greatly libraries' access to training.

As a natural extension of training, several RLNs offer custom consulting services. Consulting projects include, but are not limited to, workflow analysis of library operations and process reengineering, technology needs assessment, automation system selection, human resources development, web site design, facilities and buildings, database negotiation, collection development, and management of regional consortia.

Electronic Resources

Another primary service offered by most RLNs is access to electronic information resources. From the early years, the RLNs have provided access to traditional abstracting and indexing services such as Dialog and BRS. Electronic services have evolved dramatically to include full-text and image databases. The RLNs have effectively negotiated significant group discounts with hundreds of database providers, resulting in substantial cost savings to their members. Each RLN will typically negotiate with each database vendor separately. There have been, however, examples of some excellent national discounts for databases, facilitated through the Alliance of Library Service Networks, e.g., LexisNexis® and the Oxford University Press electronic resources.

Amigos and Nylink have embarked on promising new electronic publishing ventures, supporting the electronic publication of intellectual property held in educational institutions and learned societies. Amigos is the American (United States and Canada) distributor for BioOne®, a collaborative project founded by the American Institute of Biological Sciences, the Scholarly Publishing & Academic Resources (SPARC), The University of Kansas, the Greater Western Library Alliance, and Allen Press, to provide electronic access to biological resources. Nylink has a similar alliance with Cornell University for Project Euclid, a nonprofit venture developed by Cornell University. These models have been instrumental in making journals from independent publishers and learned societies available electronically while preserving the publishers' intellectual and economic identities. These and related electronic publishing ventures bear continued examination as a means of keeping electronic resources affordable and the control of the intellectual property within the academy.

Unique Programs

The list of services provided by the RLNs is extensive. The following are a few examples of unique projects developed and managed by Networks:

- SOLINET and Amigos, with the support of the National Endowment for the Humanities, manage regional preservation education and support programs. As participants in a national network of regional preservation programs, they offer training in preservation treatment, needs assessment and disaster recovery, and preparedness.
- Several RLNs facilitate the development of digital resource collections. One example is Virtually Missouri, managed by MLNC and a collaborative project with the Missouri State Library.
- Amigos, Nylink, and MINITEX manage interlibrary delivery services for their members, enabling the rapid shipment of materials between libraries at reduced cost. These services are typically supported in part by the state libraries and like groups within individual RLN service areas.
- NELINET operates the New England Regional Depository, a remote storage facility. Members with limited space for collections may choose to store low-use materials at this facility and retrieve the materials as needed via delivery service.

CONCLUSIONS

Regional Library Networks in the Future

The RLNs have a long and successful history of assisting libraries with the integration of technology into their operations. The cost savings for libraries have been astounding, and the task of supporting and training so many libraries has been monumental.

As services mature and become mainstream, those services are often replicated by other consortia. With the recent increase in the number of consortia, many offering services competing with those offered by the RLNs, library administrators are faced with the dilemma of choosing between organizations with which to be affiliated. Those affiliations require staff resources to manage, and at some point, the duplicative relationships are no longer cost-effective. This has led to a waning in libraries' long-standing loyalty to their regional Network to the point that their choice to participate in any group is based solely on which has the lowest price for a specific service.

Therefore, the RLNs continue to be challenged to find the next set of innovative services to offer their members. To address this challenge, some RLNs have established research and development units within their organizations to identify the next areas in which they can provide value for their members. These units, coupled with the widespread assessment of member needs and satisfaction, position RLNs for the successful continuation of their role as leader organizations for libraries.

Susan Martin stated recently in "The Transformation of Library Networks," "Library networks are changing in character and concept in order to address changing technological, economic, and social needs of libraries and their patrons. Any idea that the network has gone away as a force in our environment is inaccurate. Rather, librarians need to recognize the strength the cooperative alliances have in shaping their future, and align their organization to deal effectively with these critically important partnerships."[7]

ACKNOWLEDGMENTS

My thanks go to Susan Olson and Suzanne Lauer from OCLC for securing my prepublication access to *Networks and Service Centers: An OCLC Members Council Directory*, and to Paul Vasquez for his editorial assistance.

REFERENCES

1. Markuson, B.E. Revolution and evolution: critical issues in library network development. In *Networks for Networkers: Critical Issues in Cooperative Library Development*;

Markuson, B.E., Woolls, B., Eds.; Neal-Schuman Publishers: New York, 1980; Vol. 4.

2. Young, H. *The ALA Glossary of Library and Information Science*; American Library Association: Chicago, IL, 1983; 131.

3. Hayes, R.M. Library networks. In *Encyclopedia of Library and Information Science*, 1st Ed.; Kent, A., Lancour, H., Eds.; Marcel Dekker: New York, 1968; 367–370.

4. Networks, Consortia & Other Cooperative Library Organizations. *American Library Directory: A Classified List of Libraries in the United States and Canada with Personnel and Statistical Data, Plus a Selected List of Libraries Around the World*, 56th Ed.; Information Today: Medford, NJ, 2003; 2411–2440.

5. Maciuszko, K.L. *OCLC: A Decade of Development, 1967–1977*; Libraries Unlimited, Inc.: Littleton, CO, 1984; 1–8.

6. Carver, D.; Seal, R.; Cornette, R.; Lauer, S.; Olson, S.; Van Orden, R. *Networks and Service Centers: An OCLC Members Council Directory*, 6th revision; OCLC: Dublin, OH, 2003; v Regional Networks, Service Centers.

7. Martin, S.K. The transformation of library networks. Portal Libr. Acad. **2002**, 2 (2), 1–3.

Relevance in Theory

Howard D. White
College of Information Science and Technology, Drexel University, Philadelphia, Pennsylvania, U.S.A.

Abstract

Relevance is the central concept in information science because of its salience in designing and evaluating literature-based answering systems. It is salient when users seek information through human intermediaries, such as reference librarians, but becomes even more so when systems are automated and users must navigate them on their own. Designers of classic precomputer systems of the nineteenth and twentieth centuries appear to have been no less concerned with relevance than the information scientists of today. The concept has, however, proved difficult to define and operationalize. A common belief is that it is a relation between a user's request for information and the documents the system retrieves in response. Documents might be considered retrieval-worthy because they: 1) constitute evidence for or against a claim; 2) answer a question; or 3) simply match the request in topic. In practice, literature-based answering makes use of term-matching technology, and most evaluation of relevance has involved topical match as the primary criterion for acceptability. The standard table for evaluating the relation of retrieved documents to a request has only the values "relevant" and "not relevant," yet many analysts hold that relevance admits of degrees. Moreover, many analysts hold that users decide relevance on more dimensions than topical match. Who then can validly judge relevance? Is it only the person who put the request and who can evaluate a document on multiple dimensions? Or can surrogate judges perform this function on the basis of topicality? Such questions arise in a longstanding debate on whether relevance is objective or subjective. One proposal has been to reframe the debate in terms of relevance theory (imported from linguistic pragmatics), which makes relevance increase with a document's valuable cognitive effects and decrease with the effort needed to process it. This notion allows degree of topical match to contribute to relevance but allows other considerations to contribute as well. Since both cognitive effects and processing effort will differ across users, they can be taken as subjective, but users' decisions can also be objectively evaluated if the logic behind them is made explicit. Relevance seems problematical because the considerations that lead people to accept documents in literature searches, or to use them later in contexts such as citation, are seldom fully revealed. Once they are revealed, relevance may be seen as not only multidimensional and dynamic, but also understandable.

DEFINING RELEVANCE

Relevance is widely held to be the central concept in information science (IS). Discussions of it abound in the discipline, but there are so many conflicting accounts that some reviewers believe the term cannot be defined. Among the majority who believe otherwise, Rebecca Green's formulation of 1995[1] captures something like the standard view: "Relevance is the property of a text's being potentially helpful to a user in the resolution of a need." Patrick Wilson in 1978[2] was more succinct. Applied to a document retrieved by a query, "relevant" means "retrieval-worthy." What Wilson calls "the chief evaluative term in information retrieval" is simply the discipline's specialized form of the word *acceptable* or *good*. But where information retrieval (IR) systems are concerned, the acceptability or goodness of retrieved documents is a prediction, not a guarantee.

When IR systems are formally evaluated, judges decide the goodness of fit between documents and the sense of the query that elicited them. In everyday life we constantly do the same thing less formally when we search the Web. Relevance is thus a variable; in judgments of documents it can take at least two values, "Relevant" and "Not Relevant," and many IR system evaluators have used scales that allow values in between.

Goodness of fit is most commonly based on the degree to which a document matches the *topic* implied by the query. However, for many years critics in IS have protested that relevance is not solely a matter of topical match, because a document need not be on a pre-expressed topic to be useful or helpful. For example, a passage in a document could count as evidence for or against a claim without matching the claim in topic. In like fashion, authors often cite documents that are topically unlike what they are writing about; a mathematical textbook, for example, could be relevant to articles in vastly different areas, from measuring the size of the Internet to estimating global warming. Conversely, a document that perfectly matched the topic

Encyclopedia of Library and Information Sciences, Fourth Edition DOI: 10.1081/E-ELIS4-120043266

of a query could still be judged irrelevant because the potential user had already read it or had other grounds for rejecting it.

Despite these complexities, topical match remains the most important component of relevance as it is understood in IS. That is because topical match is something that IR system designers can design for, whereas other considerations, such as the novelty of the document to the user, are beyond their control.

This chapter explores these and other notions of relevance in IS theory and practice, including the long-running debate on whether it is subjective or objective or both. While relevance in IR is the main focus, there is some discussion of the concept as it motivates citers to link their documents to other documents. The chapter ends by suggesting that relevance, despite its complex and contested nature, is now reasonably well understood.

LITERATURE-BASED SYSTEMS

Although we may put our questions more readily to other people, we also want the powers that answers from literatures can give. When IS is defined as *the study of literature-based answering*, much else falls into place, including the oft-repeated claim that relevance is the central concern of IS.

"Literature-based answering" grounds *IR*, a traditional IS concern, in bodies of related writings such as are studied in *bibliometrics*. The phrase thus suggests the two main subfields of IS. "Answering" implies human questioners, since literatures cannot query themselves. And since they cannot respond by themselves either, it also implies that literatures must communicate through a system or systems of some kind. A questioning person and an answering system (and not pairs of persons) are the main dyad in IS. The strategically ambiguous term "information" in IS connotes both the answers that questioners want and the literatures (aka documents, writings, Web pages, material texts) that provide them. In Michael Buckland's formulation,[3] answers can be construed as messages expected to produce cognitive change on the human side (his "information as process"), and literatures can be construed as sources of that change on the system side (his "information as thing").

While the questioner–answerer pairing implies a dialog, the pairing in this case is unusual in that one of the participants is human and the other, artificial. But dialogs between persons remain the point of reference, especially where implicit expectations are concerned, because that is humanity's default setting. Answers from literatures, that is, will be held to much the same standards as answers from persons. For example, just as we rarely want persons to lie to us or be mistaken in what they say, we do not, as a rule, want to be presented with lies or errors from literatures. We want *truthful* answers,

which Patrick Wilson[2] defines as information in the strong sense, as opposed to misinformation or disinformation. At the same time, we want *relevant* answers—answers appropriate to *what we meant* by our questions as put. In practice, this usually includes their being on topic or relatable to the topic by inference. Wilson characterizes literature-based answers that are topically appropriate but of uncertain truth value as information in the weak sense or "content." Information in his strong sense is *what is known* about a matter; in his weak sense, *what has been said* about it.

Notoriously, systems can also deliver answers that miss the intended topic altogether. This is annoying, especially if such answers are numerous. The more dangerous possibility, however, is the system-supplied answer that is highly relevant but *false*. Imagine that your happiness depends on your catching a certain train, but the timetable you trusted—surely a relevant text—is outdated and the train no longer runs. Or imagine entrusting your eternal fate to scriptures that, although applicable to your case, happen to be wrong. If "information" is taken in Wilson's strong sense, these are examples of literature-based answering but not of IR. Indeed, much of what is called IR is content retrieval at best. IR that *consistently* informs in any domain is still science fiction.

In their standard textbook,[4] Ricardo Baeza-Yates and Berthier Rebeiro-Neto distinguish IR from *data* retrieval. In the latter, likely questions and appropriate answers are foreseeable, and systems can meet strict standards of relevance. Such systems are often databases that accept regimented language in limited domains—for example, telephone directories, personnel files, flight monitors in airports, dictionaries, topographical maps, stock price listings, and theater pages. Relevance is not a major issue in judging the performance of these nonbibliographic systems (and IS has had little to say about them), because the ability to match query statements with answer statements in them is seldom problematic. (Flight monitors, a boarding pass, and signs at the gate all answer the airline passenger's predictable question, "Where's my plane?") In contrast, the literature-based systems of IR are portals to relatively unstructured full-text writings that may or may not speak to inquirers' real questions, and relevance *is* problematic in judging their outputs.

When systems deliver multiple possible answers, we apparently screen first for relevance and only then for truthfulness; the truth value of what we filter out remains a matter of indifference. But we make other judgments as well. In our dialogs with systems no less than people, an invisible meter is running, and we want answers that are both timely and of acceptable length. Qualitatively, they should convey neither more nor less than we want to know, and they should not merely repeat what we know already. These latter requirements may be seen as components of relevance along with topical appropriateness.

INTERMEDIARIES AND DISINTERMEDIATION

A major way of obtaining true and relevant answers from systems has been to rely on human intermediaries who can connect questioners with the right parts of literatures because they understand both explicit and implicit criteria for what is wanted. (By giving answers from writings rather than from their own heads, they act as mouthpieces for systems rather than as communicators in their own right.) While the obvious example is reference librarians, anyone with sufficient expertise can play this role. With writings, however, neither sentences nor passages nor entire texts are marked as to truth value, which means that intermediaries will frequently be unable to guarantee the truthfulness of the answers they supply. At best they can retrieve one or more texts that have passed through society's (and perhaps their own) mechanisms for establishing veracity—crude editorial filters that may nevertheless screen out the blatantly false. As for relevance, intermediaries may be able to guarantee topically appropriate content because, given sufficient conversation, they can pick their way through the homonyms, synonyms, pronouns, and other complexities of natural language to understand what questioners mean. They can disambiguate what they hear and respond in a way that, in the dictionary definition of relevance, "bears on the matter at hand."

Even so, the problem that has always most interested information scientists, including those of precomputer times, is how to make writings respond to questioners in these ways *without benefit of human intermediaries.* IS explores disintermediation in the sense of replacing workers in libraries and bibliographic publishing houses with devices and machines. ("Library automation" is a historical synonym of IS.) Unlike people, bundles of selected texts can be made universally and perpetually available. But can they be induced to perform like a helpful human agent? Can they be made as easy to query as a person? Can they be turned into something that forestalls the need for endless exploratory reading by responding truthfully and to the point and in real time?

The only reply at present is, *sometimes.* We still lack, and are not likely to have soon, systems that understand language like a human conversationalist. What we have instead, and have always had, are systems that match the words in people's questions with words in texts that may yield good answers or at least cater to interests. The premise in many of these systems is that users' words will be mapped onto text-words through intervening vocabularies—that is, through indexing. But, as noted earlier, the truthfulness of textual statements is not explicitly marked—not indexed—and so no metadata exist for word-matching technologies to operate on. The problems of supplying information in the strong sense must be addressed through publishers' quality-control measures, such as peer review of scientific articles or periodic updating of reference works, that IS has always more or less taken for granted. That leaves word-matching systems to address the other major requirement in dialogs—that answers be relevant to questions. Human beings have a natural gift for relevance in verbal exchanges, but our best attempts to duplicate this gift artificially are as yet far from wholly successful. All that can be said is that, through schemes developed over centuries, we have some chance of matching people's question-texts with appropriate answer-texts from literatures. It is relevance in this sense that preoccupies information scientists, who have long foregrounded the problems involved. A concern with relevance is central to the study of human communication in general, but it becomes acute in IS, where systems can respond only through artificial substitutes for human capacities, such as computer programs and indexed stores of writings.

What IS really deals with, then, are system-supplied answers that may or may not be truthful and that may or may not be relevant to users' real questions. Exactly the same may be said of answers from people, of course, but we want our information systems to avoid or minimize human imperfections. Ironically, the study of user–system dialogs in IS has shown that limitations of users for which systems cannot compensate are in no small part the source of failures of performance. On their side of the dialog, users do not know (and are often too impatient to learn) how to put queries so as to get the answers they want. On the opposite side, designers still cannot cope with all the complexities of natural language (let alone people's unspoken expectations) and so routinely turn out systems that either overwhelm users with irrelevant answers or produce no answers at all. This is not to say that successes are not also frequent; merely that attempts to communicate with literatures meet with barriers not easily removed.

SOME HISTORICAL PRECEDENTS

It is worth noting that systems for delivering relevant answers from literatures without human mediation appeared long before the computer. For example, Melvil Dewey's widely used decimal classification system, which dates from 1876, underpins an attempt to build an answering device out of library books themselves. The word-bearing bookspines are shelved in standardized subject classes to curb the unconstrained vocabularies of authors and to respond relevantly to inquirers facing them. One might even see in these massed books an incipient artificial intelligence possessing some of the characteristics of a person. In any case, the system anticipates how we will ask for items of interest to us and suggests, through proximity, other items of potential interest. It is, in today's lingo, a "recommender system."

Complementing it, Dewey's "Relativ Index" (thus spelled) alphabetizes thousands of terms both in and not in the classification schedules and maps them onto the decimal classes. Thus people can look up noun phrases in their questions alphabetically and find the corresponding Dewey classes (often more than one) without knowing the nonintuitive decimal order. This easing of the mapping process may be seen as Dewey's move to make his scheme more responsive—more relevant—to users.

The full-scale alphabetical index that was added to Peter Mark Roget's *Thesaurus* in 1879 is a close analog. The *Thesaurus* was first published in 1852 as a list of words in classified order. According to David Crystal (p. 158),[5] "Roget assumed that his readers would be able to find their way through the Thesaurus by working intuitively down through his classifications. He added a short alphabetical index, but it was left to his son, John Lewis Roget, to develop this in the 1879 edition into a major feature of the book." Again we see an attempt to make a less-than-intuitive system respond more relevantly in user-system dialogs. As confirmation in this case, the son's index contributed to increased sales and became almost everyone's doorway into the *Thesaurus*.

Another nineteenth-century example of designing for relevance is the subject cataloging system devised by Charles A. Cutter. Francis Miksa[6] relates that Cutter, in his *Rules for a Dictionary Catalogue* (first edition 1875; fourth edition 1904), advocated entering books under *the most specific* subject heading that matched their entire scope (e.g., he would put a book on cats under "Cats" not "Domestic Animals"). In making headings for complex topics without established subject names, he preferred *concrete individual nouns* to *concrete general nouns*, and the latter to *abstract general nouns* (e.g., he would put a book on the ornithology of Massachusetts under "Massachusetts" with a cross-reference from "Ornithology"). These principles derive from Cutter's faith in the psychology of mental faculties advanced by eighteenth-century Scottish philosophers such as Thomas Reid. That faith was probably misplaced, but there can be no doubt that Cutter was trying to increase the relevance of subject cataloging—and hence library collections—to users by designing headings that conformed to what he took to be laws of human thought. In this, he was acting much like Peter Roget before him and the designers of search engines today.

Cutter's work anticipates twentieth-century thesauri that predate the computer—for instance, the Library of Congress Subject Headings (LCSH) for books and the Medical Subject Headings (MeSH) of the National Library of Medicine for journal articles. Such tools contain controlled vocabularies for building verbal bridges between writings and users. A look at what "control" means in them sheds additional light on how relevance is sought in literature-based answering.

The vocabularies make explicit certain abilities of an answering person, who, though absent, serves both indexers and literature searchers. The ability to understand that different expressions have a common underlying meaning is imitated by establishing a preferred expression and linking synonyms to it with *See* or *Use* references—for example, "Attorneys, *See* Lawyers." The ability to connect an expression with its nonsynonymous conceptual neighbors is imitated by *See Also* or *Related Term* references—for example, "Lawyers, *See Also* Judges." For hierarchical neighbors, *Broader Term* or *Narrower Term* references are added—for example, in the "Guns" hierarchy, "Weapons" is *Broader* and "Pistols" is *Narrower*. The ability to discriminate among homonyms is imitated by attaching indicators of sense—for example, "Interest (Monetary)" versus "Interest (Psychological)." Finer shadings of word-knowledge can be imitated by full-sentence scope notes, as when "Bibliometrics" is differentiated from "Scientometrics" or "Informetrics."

While all of these aspects of vocabulary control may seem old hat, they in fact serve as ways of inducing relevance that Google and several other search engines now lack. These engines process not indexers' controlled vocabulary but authors' and users' natural language to provide near-instantaneous answers from a very wide range of writings. The answers returned, sometimes numbering in the thousands, are algorithmically ranked high to low by predicted relevance to the query. Identification of the *best* answer, if it exists, is left to users. But the lack of vocabulary control as a screening device guarantees the frequent appearance of answers that are largely or entirely irrelevant. At the same time, other potentially relevant answers are not returned because they do not match users' input terms.

RELEVANCE IN SYSTEMS EVALUATION

The example just given implicitly pits natural-language retrieval against controlled-vocabulary retrieval, or perhaps Google against a search engine built with different algorithms. Which is better? The answer leads us back to why the concept of relevance is central to IS. A major historical reason is that, from the 1950s onward, it has been central to the most challenging practical enterprise in IS—the design and evaluation of IR systems. The intent is always to discover explicit operations on explicit bodies of texts that designers can use to improve system performance. Toward that end, researchers have recruited people to judge the goodness of retrievals in experimental trials because they thought this would eventually show the most effective techniques for retrieving relevant answers and blocking irrelevant answers.

The thinking goes something like this. Given a large collection of documents containing wide-ranging discourse, the goal of an IR system is to retrieve documents that satisfy unforeseen requests: those that adequately answer a question or that speak appropriately to an interest. At the same time, the IR system should screen out documents that fail to do these things. For any query put to the system, there is a set of documents that *should* be retrieved because they meet the specifications of the request—in the words of IR evaluators, are relevant to it. Assuming that these documents can be retrieved in comparable ways, such as by natural language or by controlled vocabulary, one can set up retrieval trials to see how many of these documents are in fact retrieved by each competing mode, and how many are missed. One can also see how many documents each mode retrieves that in fact *should not* have been: they are somehow unsuitable, even though their indexing matches the language of the input request. Finally, one can relate these counts to the size of the entire collection from which retrievals are made.

There is a persistent technical problem in determining the total number of documents in a collection that are relevant to a request. Either the entire collection must be examined to find them, or, if that is impracticable, the total must be estimated. Examining collections for relevant documents query by query is highly laborious, but it can be done: some documents are prejudged as relevant, and then various competing means are used to retrieve them. The alternative is to take each query, perform a retrieval, have a judge identify relevant and irrelevant items, and then try to estimate through additional searches or sampling techniques the relevant documents that the first search missed.

In the pioneering days of IR experiments, relatively small test-bed collections of documents were used to compare the effects of different forms and levels of indexing and different search strategies. Since the 1970s, larger operational collections have been similarly evaluated. Regardless of size, the standard summary measures for individual tests are computed from data partitioned as in Table 1. The cells are filled in as follows: a, a count of documents that should have been retrieved and were—the hits; b, a count of documents that should not have been retrieved but were—the junk (also called noise, false alarms, false positives); c, a count of documents that should have been retrieved but were not—the misses (also called false negatives); and d, a count of the remaining collection correctly dodged in the retrieval.

Once these numbers are known, common summary measures for evaluation—precision, recall, and fallout—can be computed. Precision is the proportion of retrieved

documents that are relevant: $a/(a + b)$, the higher the better. (In systems that rank documents by relevance, the upper ranks should have higher precision than the lower.) Recall is the proportion of all relevant documents that are retrieved: $a/(a + c)$, also the higher the better (except when reading is to be minimized, or the *absence* of hits is desired, as in some patent searches). Fallout is the proportion of all irrelevant documents that are retrieved: $b/(b + d)$, the lower the better. (With large collections, one wants a relatively tiny fraction broken out.)

Further interpretations and refinements of these summary measures need not detain us here. The key point is that the measures depend crucially on what documents have been declared relevant. "[I]n using recall and precision ratios," writes Cyril Cleverdon (p. 171),[7] leader of the classic IR evaluation studies at the Cranfield Institute of Technology in England, "it is not relevance which is being measured, but the decisions regarding relevance that have already been made." If those decisions are often faulty across retrieval trials, then comparative evaluations of IR systems are neither reliable nor valid. For half a century there has been a battle in IS over whether relevance can be objectively determined, as it must be if tables like Table 1 are to be believed. Naysayers hold either that relevance is altogether subjective or that it has both objective and subjective sides, and that the latter is more important.[8–10]

In the culture of Cranfield-style IR evaluation, relevance is presumed to be objective. It is like a "beep" that only certain documents emit (perhaps in varying strengths) when matched against the user's input terms. Table 1 is in fact historically related to tables in the field called signal detection theory (SDT). Indeed, one of the creators of SDT, John A. Swets, applied it to the results from three large-scale IR evaluation studies of the 1960s.[11] But, as noted, critical information scientists have long argued that the "borrowed toolbox" from SDT is not right for evaluating IR systems. These critics doubt that *relevance to a request* is a good criterion for judging documents and filling in the cells of Table 1, because the concept has not been well operationalized. It has not resulted in quick, reliable agreements on what is at issue, and some would say it cannot.

As input, SDT uses data on people's ability to discriminate between signal (noteworthy items) and noise (unnoteworthy items) under conditions of uncertainty. However, in typical SDT studies the phenomena from which signal and noise emerge are well defined and could be readily agreed on by judges. For example, if enemy planes are the signal and friendly planes are the noise, military spotters might misjudge some enemy planes as friends, or some friendly planes as enemies, but they would not be in doubt as to what they were monitoring. An analogous case involves faces. In an STD study described on the Web, people were asked to memorize faces from a pictured set. They were then shown pictures

Table 1 Table for computing standard IR evaluation measures.

	Relevant	Not relevant	
Retrieved	a	b	$a + b$
	Hits	Junk	Hits + Junk
Not retrieved	c	d	$c + d$
	Misses	Dodged	Misses + Dodged
	$a + c$	$b + d$	$a + b + c + d$
	Hits + Misses	Junk + Dodged	Total collection

of individual faces and asked whether each was one they had seen earlier. Their correct and erroneous responses can be captured in four cells just like those for relevance judgments in Table 1. But, unlike the abstract and protean relation called relevance, it is easy enough to say what they were judging. Swets himself noted that relevance is a thorny problem in IR and sidestepped defining it himself, although he based his large-scale statistical analysis on data involving relevance judgments that others might consider suspect.

OBJECTIVE RELEVANCE

Of the various grounds for deciding a document is relevant to a request, three seem most likely to be considered objective. The first is that a document constitutes evidence for or against an inquirer's claim. The second is that a document acceptably answers an inquirer's question. The third is that a document is on (or about) the inquirer's stated topic of interest. To comment briefly on these possibilities in turn:

Evidentiary relevance. That something counts as evidence for or against a claim is the *definition* of relevance, according to many dictionaries. The objective quality of such evidence can be tested when claims are made public in, for example, science, scholarship, or courts of law. But bringing evidence to bear is a creative act. Just as documents are not indexed by their truth value, so they are not indexed by their evidentiary value in strengthening or weakening an assumption or a case. If they are not already known, they cannot be retrieved simply by entering a claim (or topical noun phrases from a claim) in an IR system. (Citation indexes might sometimes lead to them, but only if they have already been used and cited by another author.) As a result, IR evaluation tests do not involve judgments on the value of documents as evidence for claims.

Question relevance. Questions and proper answers are logically related. Don R. Swanson writes (p. 392):[12] "The idea of objective relevance is perhaps clearest in the case of requests that leave little room for subjective interpretation—for example, requests that entail questions about the physical world. A document that gives the vapor pressure of mercury at ten different temperatures is objectively relevant to the question, How does the vapor pressure of mercury depend on temperature?" William Cooper shows that, in pairings of this type, objective logic guarantees the relevance of certain answers to questions.[13] Similarly, objective logic makes proofs relevant to theorems in mathematics (even if relatively few persons can follow them). "In such cases," Patrick Wilson writes (p. 458),[14] "we presume the existence of a relationship that holds whether or not it is noticed, one about whose presence or absence we can be mistaken, and one that can be investigated by other than purely psychological

means." Swanson and Wilson view objective relevance as arguable in principle; it can be intersubjectively determined if it meets standards of criticism (such as the possibility of being proven wrong).

Topical relevance. IR studies involving topics are more common than studies involving questions. Questions are sentences, whose syntax clarifies their meaning. By contrast, statements of topics are usually only noun phrases, not all of whose possible meanings were intended by the person submitting them. Moreover, even when disambiguated, topics lack sharp cognitive boundaries. While judgments on them are far from wholly subjective, the notion of a document's being on (or about) a topic depends on judges' interpretations, which vary. (Different indexers are likewise known to vary in how they index the same document.) Sometimes most or even all judges agree that a document matches the sense of a given topical request. Other times, they do not. For example, Swanson recalls a well-known clash between judges from two organizations in 1953 (p. 390):[12] "After each team had reviewed all of the retrieved documents, they jointly agreed that 1390 documents were relevant to the ninety-eight requests, but there were an additional 1577 documents that were considered relevant by one team but irrelevant by the other, a rather large arena of disagreement." Studies rarely if ever make the reasons for such disagreements explicit (a point to be further considered below).

DEGREES OF RELEVANCE

Like goodness, relevance for most information scientists admits of degrees. Some researchers have asked judges to measure it on nine- or seven-point scales or by marking an unmarked line representing a continuum (no relevance at left, complete relevance at right). Other researchers have called for simple binary judgments. Table 2, which reproduces instructions to judges on using a five-point, a three-point, and a binary scale, shows how researchers have operationalized the measurement of relevance in three major studies from the past 40 years.[15–17] They treat it as if judges can assess the retrieval-worthiness of documents without a great deal of explanation.

Also admitting of degrees is the *focus* of an inquiry, which ranges from a specific question with a definite answer to a broad and nebulous interest that any number of documents might satisfy. The study by Saracevic and others[16] used five-point scales to capture the range of specificity, as well as clarity and complexity, in questions. The 1966 Cranfield study (pp. 185–200)[15] illustrates something of this range in the questions that were used in retrieval tests in aeronautics. Very specific: "How do interference-free longitudinal stability measurements (made using free-flight models) compare with similar measurements made in a low-blockage wind tunnel?"

Table 2 Scales and instructions for judging relevance in three studies.

Instructions to Relevance Judges, Aslib Cranford Research Project

Mark as (1)	References which are a complete answer to the question. Presumably this would only apply to supplementary questions. . .since if they applied to the main question, there would have been no necessity for the research to be done.[a]
Mark as (2)	References of a high degree of relevance, the lack of which either would have made the research impracticable or would have resulted in a considerable amount of extra work.
Mark as (3)	References which were useful, either as general background to the work or as suggesting methods of tackling certain aspects of the work.
Mark as (4)	References of minimum interest, for example, those that have been included from a historical viewpoint.
Mark as (5)	References of no interest.

Source: Cleverdon, C.; Mills, J.; Keen, M. *Factors Determining the Performance of Indexing Systems. Volume 1. Design. Part 2. Appendices*; College of Aeronautics: Cranfield, England, 1966. (p. 129).[15]

[a]The judges were aeronautical engineers who were scoring the relevance of (a) papers they cited in their own works to (b) questions they themselves created for the study. Those are the "supplementary questions" referred to; the "main question" was the one their own works answered—HDW.

Instructions to Relevance Judges, A Study of Information Seeking and Retrieving

The following definitions have been provided to users for judging the answers (i.e., abstracts):

"Each abstract should be evaluated according to its degree of relevance to the question you submitted for searching. The degree of relevance should be determined using the following three-point scale:

Relevant—Any document which on the basis of the information it conveys is considered to be related to your question, even if the information is outdated or already familiar to you.

Partially Relevant—Any document which on the basis of the information it conveys is considered only somewhat or in some part related to your question or to any part of your question.

Nonrelevant—Any document which on the basis of the information it conveys is not at all related to your question."

Source: A study of information seeking and retrieving. I. Background and methodology by T. Saracevic, P. Kantor, A.Y. Chamis, D. Trivison, *J. Am. Soc. Inform. Sci.* 1988, *39* (3), 161–176. (p. 169).[16]

Instructions to Relevance Judges, Text Retrieval Conference (TREC)

Relevance judgments, or the "right answers," are a vital part of a test collection. TREC uses the following working definition of relevance: If you were writing a report on the subject of the topic and would use the information contained in the document in the report, then the document is relevant. Only binary judgments ("relevant" or "not relevant") are made, and a document is judged relevant if any piece of it is relevant (regardless of how small the piece is in relation to the rest of the document).

Source: National Institute of Standards and Technology. Data—English retrieval judgments, 2000. http://trec.nist.gov/data/reljudge_eng.html.[17]

Quite general: "[I want] papers on pressure and force distributions on wings."

Reflecting similar differences in scope decades later, the Text REtrieval Conference sponsors "tracks" in which researchers compete not only in retrieving entire documents but in algorithmic answering of specific questions from TREC test collections. The question–answering track,[18] whose test collections are drawn from large corpora of news articles, is "designed to take a step closer to IR rather than document retrieval." For example, an actual TREC question is:[19] "What is the relationship between poverty and disease?" TREC's gloss on acceptable answers (supplied for all questions) states: "Documents that do not link poverty to diseases directly but mention a link between poverty and health care are relevant. Documents that simply mention poverty and disease but do not draw a connection are not relevant."

In daily life, questions are put constantly, and everyone routinely judges the degree to which answers are relevant. (To "Where's our flight?" the answer "Gate B9" is both relevant and *more* relevant than "Somewhere in Terminal B.") While the questions in the TREC question–answering trials are the special kind asked at reference desks, the cognitive skills required to judge the answers for relevance (if not truth-value) are the same ones people use successfully every day. It therefore should be easy enough to score answers, especially with the glosses TREC provides. For example, millions of people could judge answers to the request for articles on the relationship between poverty and disease. Many of them could at least *recognize* apparent answers to the technical Cranfield question about longitudinal stability measurements in aircraft, even if they were unfamiliar with the aeronautical vocabulary. Moreover, people would probably agree on what documents contained answers, as opposed to those that did not, even if they did not always agree on the *best* answer.

However, these are examples of inquiries at the specific-question end of the scale. When the focus is broadened from specific questions to interests expressed as topics, people tend to agree less on what literature-based answers are relevant. They read different things into noun phrases expressing topicality (such as the request in the Cranfield study for "papers on pressure and force distributions on wings") and produce inconsistent results.

As noted above, such inconsistencies have prompted the claim that relevance on the user side is subjective or that relevance has an objective component (documents that match the stated topical request) and a subjective component (documents that for any other reason are retrieval-worthy). Swanson writes (p. 397),[12] "For the most part, bibliographic retrieval systems are topic oriented, and topics are presumed to be objectively defined and applied. However, the question of whether a document is or is not about some topic can depend on the observer's point of view, and so a subjective element may intrude into a topic-oriented relevance judgment." In *Information Retrieval*, an influential textbook in the Cranfield tradition, C. J. van Rijsbergen states flatly that relevance is subjective (p. 146).[20] However, he seems to have in mind something like Swanson's mixture, since he, like other Cranfield-style researchers, thinks there is enough agreement among judges for IR evaluation tests to be successfully conducted.

Contributing to the supposedly subjective component are factors such as the user's expertise, situation, work task, cognitive style, and stage of searching; the amount of information provided about the document; and the conditions under which judgments are made. Linda Schamber extracted from IS studies some 80 variables that supposedly affect relevance judgments (p. 11),[21] and her unprioritized list is not exhaustive.

WHOSE SUBJECTIVITY COUNTS?

Surrogates, such as students, librarians, or subject experts, have replaced end users as judges in many retrieval evaluation tests. In the limited time periods of the tests, what can they reasonably be expected to do? Can they judge whether short, specific answers adequately respond to a set of short, specific questions? Yes. Can they compare a set of retrieved citations plus abstracts with a request and decide whether each has the same sense as the request? Yes again. Crucially, however, such judges lack a stake in the information they are given because they lack real needs generated by real projects. The only criterion by which they can reasonably be asked to evaluate retrievals is whether a retrieved document answers a question or matches a topic. Since this tells us little about the relevance of the document (or passage or phrase or image) to the person who asked for it, they cannot judge documents validly, and—so goes the critique—it is fatuous to base system evaluations on their opinions.

By this light, the only judge of relevance worth considering is the person who requested the information. Consider again Green's definition: "Relevance is the property of a text's being potentially helpful to a user in the resolution of a need." Her wording allows surrogate judges to judge relevance by topicality, because any document they deem to be on topic—even mistakenly—is at least *potentially* helpful. But for evaluations to be convincing—again, according to the critique—relevance should depend on whether a text *actually* helped an end user resolve a need.

Only end users can decide whether they benefited cognitively from seeing a particular system-supplied document. Only they can connect documents with ideas material to their projects. Only they can know how well documents capture the *intended sense* of their search terms, despite literally matching them.

Consider further that systems can respond to user needs only as they are expressed in language the systems can accept. That means that the needs must be couched in words that explicitly match either controlled vocabulary or authors' natural language. However, neither type of indexing permits easy matches on pieces of unknown text that users might find *extremely* relevant: evidence for their new claims, original appearances of a concept, good examples of some phenomenon, ways of putting a complex matter in a nutshell, critiques not labeled as such, interesting analogies, lucid popularizations, fruitful metaphors, anecdotes appropriate to a context, linkages between hitherto unlinked ideas, better methodologies than those already used, arguments paralleling one's own, discussions of terms as terms, and so on.

While another person could help find these desiderata, more often they can be found only by creative reading over time. They are not quickly retrievable through an IR system because they cannot be adequately expressed in any language known to IR. They depend on interactions with full texts, not indexing. Given enough time, readers do find them, but they are not generally available as criteria to judges in IR evaluation tests.

So, if one cannot ask for the inexpressible, what *can* be expressed to IR systems? Other than bibliographic data such as titles, authors, and journals, what can be entered as search terms? Practically speaking, the answer turns out to be: phrases representing topics and phrases representing questions. This would seem to put users and surrogate judges back in the same boat as they decide on the goodness of document retrievals. According to many information scientists, however, it does not. For them, "objective system relevance" as achieved by term-matching goes out the window, to be replaced by something like Buckland's "information as process."

The judges in Cranfield-style evaluations must regard requests to the system as indicators of a fixed user need, to which the documents retrieved by the request are a fixed response, complete in itself. Even if searches are revised to take user feedback into account, it is assumed that the underlying need does not change. In sharp contrast, the needs of real-world users and the requests they lead to are constantly changing, sometimes over long periods. Such users draw on IR systems progressively, taking in new information to reach new conclusions or revise old ones. This fact prompted Stephen Harter to argue that "user need" should not be equated with the *initial* state of consciousness that led to a request but with the dynamic *current* state (p. 606).[22] It prompted Marcia Bates to advocate a "berrypicking" model of literature retrieval over the classic Cranfield model. In her words (p. 421):[23] 1) typical search queries are not static but rather evolve; 2) searchers commonly gather information in bits and pieces [like berries] instead of in one grand best retrieved set; 3) searchers use a wide variety of search techniques which extend beyond those commonly associated with bibliographic databases; and 4) searchers use a wide variety of sources other than bibliographic databases.

RELEVANCE THEORY APPLIED

Opposition to static topicality as the sole basis for relevance judgments is now commonplace among information scientists. In making his case against it, Harter[22] adapted Dan Sperber and Deirdre Wilson's relevance theory (RT) from linguistic pragmatics. He was attracted to their ideas because, although their book[24] deals mainly with talk between persons, they treat relevance at a level of psychological complexity appropriate to serious users of literatures (e.g., writers who cite for many reasons) and not merely as a verdict on topical matches.

In briefest summary, RT says that the relevance of any communication varies directly with its cognitive effects in a context and inversely with the effort it takes to process—that is, Relevance = Cognitive effects/Processing effort. (The more pronounced the effects and the smaller the effort, the greater is the relevance.) Human beings experience communications by means of this ratio automatically. Cognitive effects are the new inferences drawn when a new message interacts with a person's existing assumptions in a context. In general, the new inferences add to, cancel, or strengthen or weaken the existing assumptions. Such effects can be ordered by degree although they cannot be precisely measured. Processing effort serves as a brake on the potentially endless multiplication of cognitive effects; whatever inferences are *easiest* to draw are the ones we stop at. Possible effects that are harder to process are eliminated.

Extrapolating from RT, Harter argues that if a document produces little or no cognitive effect after it has been read, the fact that it is on topic does not matter; it is not relevant. Conversely, if, upon reading, the document does have a cognitive impact, it *is* relevant, even if it misses one's expressed topic of interest. The issue becomes, did a document, for whatever reason, prove informative? Did exposure to it yield valuable new inferences? The document's novelty and whether its appearance is well-timed (given one's current cognitive state) may also contribute to its impact. Other components of relevance mentioned earlier, such as whether a document is acceptable in length and neither under- nor over-informative, can now be seen as related to processing effort.

The addition of processing effort to the concept of relevance improves IS theory. Following RT, we may infer that the harder a communication is to process, the more likely it will be rejected or ignored; it literally becomes *less relevant*. This goes for entire IR systems as well as individual messages. (Recall that Dewey, J. L. Roget, and Cutter all acted to reduce the effort of using their systems, so as to increase their perceived relevance to users.) Reviews by Herbert Poole[25] and Thomas Mann[26] show that, when people interact with information systems, they tend to attain relevance not by seeking high cognitive effects but by minimizing processing effort. (George Zipf's phrase, the "principle of least effort," is often adduced in this regard,[27] and Herbert Simon's notion of "satisficing"[28] is also related.) Yet, over the years, the least-effort studies and the copious writings on relevance in IS have generally been separate streams of analysis. The RT formula for relevance has rich implications for uniting the two streams, as Howard White argues.[29],[30] The numerous variables seen in the IS literature on relevance (such as many of those tabulated in Schamber's review) become more meaningful and less miscellaneous if they are organized as either cognitive effects or as determiners of processing effort.

This line of reasoning from RT further allows that a document's being on topic may indeed contribute to its cognitive effect and hence its relevance. Harter dwells more on the point that people *create* relevance by seeing connections across topics, a point Swanson also makes.[12] But while topical relevance is far from being the only kind, it remains a very important kind, as Kelly Maglaughlin and Diane Sonnenwald found.[31] (We want neither our conversational partners nor our IR systems to be constantly changing the subject.) Relevance theory's inclusion of processing effort in the relevance formula leads to insight here: topical match is an important component of relevance because it depends on explicit language and is *relatively easy to see*. Harter calls it "weak relevance" (i.e., subject to quick negation), which resembles Green's calling a document "potentially helpful." Thus, we can better understand why surrogate judges are used in IR evaluation tests: it is because they can recognize weak relevance (as potential helpfulness) in documents. They can stand in for end users because they share this ability with them (and are often more convenient to work with). Judgments on topical match, in other words, have high, although far from perfect, intersubjectivity.

It nevertheless remains true that judges cannot accurately take into account all the other factors that affect the relevance judgments of actual users—implicit factors that only the latter perceive. What is hard or impossible for judges to evaluate may be easy for users with project-driven needs.

Harter's criterion for a relevant document[22] is whether it produced in him a desirable cognitive effect, regardless of where, how, why, or when the document was obtained. This cognitive effect ("psychological relevance" for him; "subjective relevance" for Swanson) exists only for the end user who *wants to create new knowledge*. The experience of surrogate judges in IR tests is not comparable, and to assign relevance judgments to them is considered a serious error by Swanson. Swanson (p. 139)[32] says, "We therefore infer that a consensus as to whether a particular document is relevant to some request is meaningless, for this notion of relevance has meaning only in the mind of the one person whose information need gave rise to the request." If consensus with other judges is nevertheless sought and reached, it can only be on the relatively trivial grounds of topic match. The Harter-Swanson critique vitiates Cranfield-style tests of particular IR systems, and in fact Harter writes (p. 612):[22] "I no longer believe that there is a valid interpretation of the meaning and results of such tests."

A key consideration for Harter is *whether the document is read*. All the valuable "finds" mentioned earlier, such as evidence for claims, interesting analogies, good examples, and arguments paralleling one's own, are discoverable only by someone interested enough to read documents at length. Surrogate judges cannot be presumed to have interests this strong, and they are generally asked to read only brief forms of documents, such as a citation plus abstract.

Users, too, of course, need not read a document to form some opinion of it, and a glance will tell them more than its subject matter. According to a study by Carol Barry,[33] they go also by their impressions of authors, the quality of a journal or publisher, the apparent specificity or generality of what is discussed, the apparent difficulty of the exposition, and about 20 other implicit criteria. Even so, lists such as Barry's merely complement topical relevance; they do not invalidate it. Judy Bateman (p. 30)[34] shows that students rate topic-match highest among the criteria in their literature searches. Moreover, if one looks at the documents that professionals cite, one finds that their choices tend to conform to their own main topics. For example, writers on relevance such as Barry, Harter, Schamber, Swanson, and the present author frequently cite other writings on relevance.

This account bears as well on surrogate judges' *disagreements* about topical relevance. Judges, like users, may be swayed by implicit criteria that go beyond topicality in the strict sense. Even with only a citation plus abstract, a judge might declare a document relevant to a request because, for instance, she makes a connection not readily apparent to others or lets the name of an author or journal tip the scales in the document's favor. The judge here is acting creatively, like an end user (although not necessarily as a real user would), and disagrees with judges who are more literal-minded. When the inferences behind such creativity are hidden, judgments seem bewilderingly subjective. In the language of RT, undercommunicated chains of reasoning increase others' processing effort, which makes claims of relevance based on them problematic.

Courts of law have a procedure for standoffs like this: a lawyer who, in arguing a case, is charged with irrelevance by opposing counsel ("Objection, Your Honor!") must clarify his or her reasoning to the satisfaction of the court. IR evaluation trials being less grave, differences are seldom ironed out so that relevance judgments reach a higher level of intersubjective agreement. If judges in retrieval tests could be induced to reveal the logic by which they reached controversial conclusions on relevance, their assumptions—including possible mistakes—*could* be objectively evaluated, and this would dispel the mystery of disagreements. (This resembles getting coders in content analysis to resolve their differences so as to improve intercoder reliability.) But time and energy are too short for such additional labor to be likely.

OBJECTIFYING SUBJECTIVITY

The RT formula permits a new approach to the vexed question of whether there are two kinds of relevance, objective and subjective, in IS. Following RT, we may want to dispense with the objective/subjective split altogether and simply conclude that people differ in the assumptions they bring to documents, which affects their processing effort, which affects the cognitive effects the documents have.

To say that something is RT-relevant implies that its cognitive effects were not zero. Communications that produce no effect—no change in one's assumptions—are irrelevant even though the effort to process them may be very low (e.g., weather reports from most places on earth). Communications may also produce no effect and hence be irrelevant because the effort required to process them is too high (e.g., for many persons, mathematical models of weather patterns).

In both cases, a person's mind is always the context in which communications are evaluated and effects occur. People differ widely in the cognitive contexts they embody (e.g., for some, mathematical models of weather patterns are child's play). But they do not differ on *kinds* of relevance, objective versus subjective, they perceive within these contexts. As their powers of inference operate, they simply experience a communication's greater or lesser cognitive effects. In that sense, perceived relevance is unitary. It does not require switches between, say, one capability that knows a question has been answered, a second that realizes a line in a play is funny, a third that takes "I want a divorce" more seriously than "I want a snack," and a fourth that sees a hitherto unseen connection between two documents or between a document and a request.

What does seem to vary across people, given the cognitive context each sets, is processing effort. Some communications are relatively easy for many people to process. They produce cognitive effects with little need for explanations or new thought. Many communications called "objectively relevant" in IS would seem to be of this sort. It is not that they are necessarily popular in content, like sitcom dialog. It is that most people can follow their underlying logic by using the same inferential abilities they bring to content of all kinds. By this line of reasoning, "subjective" relevance in IS may mean no more than "as yet obscure, as yet hard to follow."

The notion of subjective relevance has two main uses in IS, both having to do with topical relevance. First, it is invoked in IR tests when surrogate judges *disagree* on whether a document matches a topical request. (Their agreements are taken as signs of objective relevance.) Second, it is invoked when actual end users (the persons who put the requests) use criteria *in addition to* topical relevance in judging documents, because no topical statement can capture the full, dynamic complexity of their information needs. Such end users might *agree* that a document matches the topic of their requests, yet still reject it on other grounds often called subjective.

Swanson and other information scientists treat subjective relevance as if it results from a flash of insight during an IR experiment—a moment of creativity that then remains mysterious. It is true that judges in IR tests usually score documents without explanation, so that, if they go beyond topic matching, their reasons are hidden from others. But such tests are too artificial to be a suitable base for a general psychology of information needs and uses. In life, a person who wants credit for linking topics across documents cannot leave the linkage unexplained. What started as subjective creativity—unique cognitive effects—must be communicated so that others can understand it. It must be recontextualized from private to public— more plainly, explained by writing and citing. As a result, it moves toward objective relevance, or at least much higher intersubjectivity.

This is not to say that claims of relevance will always be convincing. When explained under standards of criticism, they may turn out to be feeble or wrong. Rather, it is to say that the "subjectivity" of relevance judgments has roots in the way IR tests are administered: researchers want to avoid saddling judges with processing effort beyond filling out simple forms. The whole subjective–objective muddle in IS results from attempts to derive user psychology from the narrow world of Cranfield-style evaluation, where relevance judgments typically have little explanatory context.

If, moreover, end users are the only ones whose judgments should count, why not ask them what they *did* with the citations plus abstracts in some period after a search? For example, was an item obtained in full-text? Was it filed but never looked at? Was it read? Assigned to students? Cited in the preparation of a new work? Surveys of this sort would replace users' subjective judgments with reasonably objective behavioral measures. (Their original hit-lists might be quite altered in the process.)

Judy Bateman[34] and Peiling Wang[35] have initiated research along these lines that would seem to offer a more valid account of the retrieval-worthiness of documents than the snap judgments of IR tests. But longitudinal studies go contrary to the ethos of the Cranfield tradition, where, to this day, the emphasis is on getting quick counts for the various evaluation ratios.

While purists may want to reserve the term "objective relevance" for relations of logical entailment,[13] that seems overfastidious in the messy world of IS. There are relations other than entailment that are admissible as instances of relevance—for example, the relations of analogy or illustration or historical continuity. In any case, what Swanson and others in IS call "subjective relevance" can be taken as a set of effects that are temporarily hard for others to process because their justification has not yet been shared. For example, since one of Swanson's favorite philosophers, Karl Popper, never wrote specifically on IR, the bare assertion that he is relevant to IR would puzzle the uninitiated. Yet readers can easily see Popper's relevance once they read Swanson's bridging accounts (p. 138).[32] Popper has also been adapted and cited by other information scientists, which heightens the sense of intersubjectivity with Swanson.

RELEVANCE AND CITATION

As we have seen, Swanson and Harter are leading underminers of topical relevance as the sole basis for evaluating IR systems. Swanson's claim that end users create relevance across topics is elaborated at length by Harter,[22] who shows how nine IS papers not strictly on his stated interest (which is "empirical research on how people do online searches") can in fact be brought to bear on it through theoretical conjectures. "Thus," Harter writes (p. 612),[22] "we come to the perhaps surprising conclusion that, in IR, *references on the topic may be less important than relevant references not on the topic*— references that allow the making of new intellectual connections or cause other cognitive change" (italics his).

We come also to a practical question: how does one search for relevant references not on the topic? How, for instance, did Harter find his nine stimulating papers? Using the standard noun-phrases of topical retrieval, neither he nor anyone else can frame the idea, *items not on the topic but relevant to it*. Granted, if he had already guessed that online search behavior might be related to another topic, he could search on the latter. But that strategy is likely to produce few hits (or far too many). The most probable assumption is that Harter did not assemble the nine papers through deliberate search; they had simply found their way into his personal collection from various sources over the years, and now he was able to exploit them. In other words, he was putting the fruits of long-term berrypicking to new use.

Could Cranfield-style tests be replaced by the berry-picking model as a means of evaluating IR systems? The latter is certainly a more realistic model of human–literature interactions. On reflection, however, they could not. Berrypicking includes, but is more complex than, literature searches by topic and so is incommensurable with them.

Harter discusses another possibility (p. 614).[22] That is for information scientists to link theorizing on relevance to citation analysis. Citations are to relevance judgments what fossils are to paleontology—objective evidence of what has gone before—and the prose around them feeds interpretations of their functions and of citer motives. Several studies reveal that writings tied to a document through citation have little overlap with writings tied to the same document through subject indexing. These studies confirm, with data from end users rather than surrogate judges, that relevance relations go beyond topicality. Citation indexes in fact answer the question asked above: how does one search for relevant references not on the topic? Google Scholar, Scopus, and the Web of Science allow this by enabling a searcher to retrieve later documents that cite an earlier one for *any* reason, whether they match it in topic or not. According to White's nonexhaustive list of reasons (p. 595),[30] a citer might cite an earlier document to recognize topical similarity, but also to point out an analogy, establish a causal connection, acknowledge use of a research method, provide evidence or examples, borrow rhetoric, or discuss terminology.

So, why not base evaluation of IR systems on some form of citation data rather than judges' opinions? Actually, Cleverdon, Mills, and Keen in England and Gerard Salton in America did experiment with citation links, as opposed to subject headings, in their project (pp. 106–112).[36] But they used straight citation matches (e.g., bibliographic coupling) without embellishment. To go further requires additional processing effort. Citations do not come tagged with the metadata needed for more refined IR evaluations. For instance, they lack labels such as "provided an analogy" "provided historical background," or "provided a method." This deficiency was noted by (among others) Swanson (p. 145):[32] "[W]hat is lacking in present systems is any convenient and rapid method for discovering the *nature* of the relevance link which the citing author has established. This can be discerned only by studying the citing article" (italics his).

Interestingly, the five-point Cranfield scale shown in Table 2 was a bit of early citation analysis, though not billed as such. It called for citers to rank the relevance of their own citations to particular research questions—in Swanson's phrase, "to show the *nature* of the relevance link." Quotes from those citers indicate they thought the task difficult (pp. 29–31).[36] The Cranfield project took place more than 40 years ago, yet little has changed today. It is utopian to think that citers will ever enrich their citations with metadata, as proposed by Swanson (pp.

145–146),[32] among others. Several bibliometricians have added metadata to others' citations by hand, in the style of old-fashioned content analysis, but that is very slow. The best hope lies in *automated* enrichment of citations with explicit pieces of language around them, such as tagging citations in a scientific paper with the headings of sections in which they occur. For example, one would expect citations from *Methodology* sections to refer to methods papers, but citations from *Introduction* sections to refer to earlier substantive findings or theory. As data increased over time, citations would come to be typified by their tags, and this information depending on the nature of the relevance links could be exploited to increase the precision of retrievals in citation databases. Experimental analysis of full-texts along these lines is ongoing.[37]

CONCLUSION

Writers on relevance in IS often observe that the concept is not well understood and call for further research to clarify and ultimately measure it. The conclusions here are that, on the contrary, we understand relevance quite well (thanks in part to explications such as those cited here), and that it will always be measured only crudely (ordinally at best, according to Sperber and Wilson). What is relevance in IS? In an RT-flavored sentence, it is the ability of a document to produce in the mind of a user *valuable cognitive effects without undue processing effort*. This way of putting it can be made compatible with the definitions of Rebecca Green and Patrick Wilson in the first paragraph and with those of many other information scientists. The debates of the past seem increasingly passé.

The Cranfield tradition of evaluation lives on—for example, in the TREC competitions—but it is hard to believe such tests will dramatically improve IR systems, at least during the shelf-life of this *Encyclopedia*. The early researchers in IR assumed that systems could and should be designed to serve demanding people with fixed information needs, expressed through well-chosen noun phrases. Hence the idea of the IR system as a fine-tuned robot—one that applied the best algorithms to the best indexing so as to deliver all relevant documents in a collection and only those. That idea died long ago. In its place, we have systems that simply recommend more or less plausible items and facilitate exploration by trial and error. They work because people are so adept at creating relevance as they go, especially by intuitive manipulations of their own processing effort.

Undeniably, current systems such as Google need improvement, but it is not likely to come about through tests of recall and precision. One evident need is for better disambiguation of search terms. Systems in which natural language has replaced controlled vocabulary produce countless "false drops"—false not in nuance but in major differences of sense. For example, Google at present cannot tell whether the phrase "shoulder of mutton" means a cut of meat or an English pub. (Human beings can almost always tell from the context.) A few search engines do cluster their retrievals by sense (on the basis of words that frequently co-occur with the search term). They can separate, for example, recipes for meat dishes from ads for pubs, so that requesters can choose the cluster they meant rather than having to scroll through a long mixture of items. But Google and Yahoo, to name only the giants as of 2008, lack that ability. To say they need better precision ratios is a roundabout way of stating the obvious. They need the ability to detect various search-term senses and group documents accordingly. Less effort means greater relevance for users.

As a provocation, however, suppose that the future brings *no* improvements in IR systems—that we simply cope with what we have today. There is no reason to think human communication would suffer much. People have always had ways of compensating for the defects in their literature-based answering systems. For example, designers of computerized IR systems have probably never relied on their own systems to find most of what they themselves read and cite. They berrypick. Their friends and assistants hand them things. Rumor has it that Stephen Harter came across Sperber and Wilson's *Relevance* while browsing in an airport bookstore. Even if that is biographically false, it is true as a parable. No one can complain that, because systems do not find all relevant documents, or only relevant documents, too little of value is written.

REFERENCES

1. Green, R. Topical relevance relationships. I. Why topic matching fails. J. Am. Soc. Inform. Sci. **1995**, *46*(9), 646–653.
2. Wilson, P. Some fundamental concepts of information retrieval. Drexel Libr. Quart. **1978**, *14*(2), 10–24.
3. Buckland, M.K. Information as thing. J. Am. Soc. Inform. Sci. **1991**, *42*(5), 351–360.
4. Baeza-Yates, R.; Ribeiro-Neto, B. *Modern Information Retrieval*; Addison-Wesley: New York, 1999.
5. Crystal, D. The thesaurus. In *The Cambridge Encyclopedia of the English Language*; Cambridge University Press: Cambridge, England, 1995; 158–159.
6. Miksa, F. Subjects as subjects alone. In *The Subject in the Dictionary Catalog from Cutter to the Present*; American Library Association: Chicago, IL, 1983; 24–44.
7. Cleverdon, C.W. User evaluation of information retrieval systems. J. Doc. **1974**, *30*(2), 170–180.
8. Ellis, D. The dilemma of measurement in information retrieval research. J. Am. Soc. Inform. Sci. **1996**, *47*(1), 23–36.
9. Harter, S.P. Variations in relevance assessments and the measurement of retrieval effectiveness. J. Am. Soc. Inform. Sci. **1996**, *47*(1), 37–49.
10. Borlund, P. The concept of relevance in IR. J. Am. Soc. Inform. Sci. Technol. **2003**, *54*(10), 913–925.
11. Swets, J.A. Effectiveness of information retrieval methods. Am. Doc. **1969**, *20*(1), 72–89.
12. Swanson, D.R. Subjective versus objective relevance in bibliographic retrieval systems. Libr. Quart. **1986**, *56*(4), 389–398.
13. Cooper, W.S. A definition of relevance for information retrieval. Inform. Storage Ret. **1971**, *7*(1), 19–37.
14. Wilson, P. Situational relevance. Inform. Storage Ret. **1973**, *9*(8), 457–471.
15. Cleverdon, C.; Mills, J.; Keen, M. *Factors Determining the Performance of Indexing Systems. Volume 1. Design. Part 2. Appendices*; College of Aeronautics: Cranfield, England, 1966.
16. Saracevic, T.; Kantor, P.; Chamis, A.Y.; Trivison, D. A study of information seeking and retrieving. I. Background and methodology. J. Am. Soc. Inform. Sci. **1988**, *39*(3), 161–176.
17. National Institute of Standards and Technology. In *Data—English retrieval judgments*; 2000. Available at http://trec.nist.gov/data/reljudge_eng.html.
18. National Institute of Standards and Technology. In *TREC tracks*; 2008. Available at http://trec.nist.gov/tracks.html.
19. National Institute of Standards and Technology. In *Data—English test questions (topics)*; 2000. Available at http://trec.nist.gov/data/testq_eng.html.
20. Van Rijsbergen, C.J. Evaluation. In *Information Retrieval*, 2nd Ed.; Butterworths: London, 1999; 144–183. Available at http://www.dcs.gla.ac.uk/~iain/keith/.
21. Schamber, L. Relevance and information behavior. Ann. Rev. Inform. Sci. Technol. **1994**, *29*, 3–48.
22. Harter, S.P. Psychological relevance and information science. J. Am. Soc. Inform. Sci. **1992**, *43*(9), 602–615.
23. Bates, M.J. The design of browsing and berrypicking techniques for the online search interface. Online Rev. **1989**, *13*(5), 407–424.
24. Sperber, D.; Wilson, D. *Relevance: Communication and Cognition*; Harvard University Press: Cambridge, MA, 1986.
25. Poole, H. *Theories of the Middle Range*, Ablex: Norwood, NJ, 1985.
26. Mann, T. The principle of least effort. In *Library Research Models: A Guide to Classification, Cataloging, and Computers*; Oxford University Press: New York, 1993; 91–102.
27. Zipf, G.K. *Human Behavior and the Principle of Least Effort: An Introduction to Human Ecology*; Addison-Wesley: Cambridge, MA, 1949.
28. Simon, H. *Administrative Behavior: A Study of Decision-Making Processes in Administrative Organization*, 3rd Ed.; MIT Press: Cambridge, MA, 1976.
29. White, H.D. Combining bibliometrics, information retrieval, and relevance theory: Part 1. First examples of a synthesis. J. Am. Soc. Inform. Sci. Technol. **2007**, *58*(4), 536–559.
30. White, H.D. Combining bibliometrics, information retrieval, and relevance theory: Part 2. Implications for information science. J. Am. Soc. Inform. Sci. Technol. **2007**, *58*(4), 583–605.
31. Maglaughlin, K.L.; Sonnenwald, D.H. User perspectives on relevance criteria: A comparison among relevant, partially relevant, and not-relevant judgments. J. Am. Soc. Inform. Sci. Technol. **2002**, *53*(5), 327–342.

32. Swanson, D.R. Information retrieval as a trial-and-error process. Libr. Quart **1977**, *47*(2), 128–148.
33. Barry, C.L. User-defined relevance criteria: An exploratory study. J. Am. Soc. Inform. Sci. **1994**, *45*(3), 149–159.
34. Bateman, J. Changes in relevance criteria: A longitudinal study. Proceedings of the 61st Annual Meeting of the American Society for Information Science **1998**, *35*, 23–32.
35. Wang, P.; White, M.D. A cognitive model of document use during a research project. Study II. Decisions at the reading and citing stages. J. Am. Soc. Inform. Sci. **1999**, *50*(2), 98–114.
36. Cleverdon, C.; Mills, J.; Keen, M. *Factors Determining the Performance of Indexing Systems. Volume 1. Design. Part 1. Text*; College of Aeronautics: Cranfield, England, 1966.
37. Teuful, S.; Moens, M. Summarizing scientific articles—Experiments with relevance and rhetorical status. Comput. Linguist. **2002**, *28*(4), 409–445.

BIBLIOGRAPHY

1. Cosijn, E.; Ingwersen, P. Dimensions of relevance. Inform. Process. Manage. **2000**, *36*(4), 533–550.
2. Froehlich, T.J. Relevance reconsidered—Towards an agenda for the 21st century: Introduction. J. Am. Soc. Inform. Sci. **1994**, *45*(3), 124–133 (The entire issue is devoted to articles on relevance research.).
3. Mizzaro, S. Relevance: The whole history. J. Am. Soc. Inform. Sci. **1997**, *48*(9), 810–832.
4. Ruthven, I.; Baillie, M.; Elsweiler, D. The relative effects of knowledge, interest and confidence in assessing relevance. J. Doc. **2006**, *63*(4), 482–504.
5. Saracevic, T. Relevance: a review of the literature and a framework for thinking on the notion in information science. J. Am. Soc. Inform. Sci. **1975**, *26*(6), 321–343.
6. Saracevic, T. Relevance: a review of the literature and a framework for thinking on the notion in information science. Part II. Nature and manifestations of relevance. J. Am. Soc. Inform. Sci. Technol. **2007**, *58*(13), 1915–1933.
7. Saracevic, T. Relevance: a review of the literature and a framework for thinking on the notion in information science. Part III. Behavior and effects of relevance. J. Am. Soc. Inform. Sci. Technol. **2007**, *58*(13), 2126–2144.

Relevance Judgments and Measurements

Erica Cosijn
Department of Information Science, University of Pretoria, Pretoria, South Africa

Abstract
Users intuitively know which documents are relevant when they see them. Formal relevance assessment, however, is a complex issue. In this entry relevance assessment are described both from a human perspective and a systems perspective. Humans *judge* relevance in terms of the relation between the documents retrieved and the way in which these documents are understood and used. This is a subjective and personal judgment and is called *user relevance*. Systems compute a function between the query and the document features that the systems builders believe will cause documents to be ranked by the likelihood that a user will find the documents relevant. This is an objective *measurement* of relevance in terms of relations between the query and the documents retrieved—this is called *system relevance* (or sometimes similarity).

INTRODUCTION

One of the main objectives of information science as a discipline is to retrieve relevant information, and as such the concept of relevance is regarded as a central notion in the field. The concept of relevance has changed substantially over the years and it is now realized that relevance implies a relation, has many dimensions, various manifestations, can either be judged in absolute or relative terms, is dynamic, and is very difficult to define.

The idea of quantifying relevance is a very complex issue, and one that has been studied for many years with varying degrees of success. A user very often intuitively knows whether a retrieved document is relevant or not and relevance is mostly understood in the fuzzy sense of "I will know it if I see it." On the other hand, an information retrieval system (IRS) may confidently rate a document as 100% relevant to the query used to retrieve it, while the user does not judge it as relevant at all.

It is already clear that there are at various interpretations of the term "relevance." In systems approaches to information retrieval (IR), relevance is considered to be a property of the relation between the content of the document and the system's search criteria. In user-oriented and cognitive approaches to IR, relevance has to do with the cognitive processes of the users and their changing knowledge and needs regarding information, within or stimulated by the context.[1] Context hence implies the socio-organizational environment as well as the systems and information objects involved and surrounding the actual user.

It is widely accepted that IR comprises three elements or role players—systems, users, and the environment.

- The system involves documents or information objects (represented in various ways), which are then organized in some way and, through a given algorithm, prepared for matching a query via an interface mechanism.
- The user typically has a problem to solve, a work task to perform, or an interest to satisfy, and a derived information need which has to be apparent to a certain degree to the user. For example, it might be verbalized before it can be transformed into a query that is acceptable to the system algorithm.
- The socio-organizational environment provides the context or situational framework influencing the activities of the user. This can include anything from the definition of the work task, to the choice of retrieval system, the type of information available, etc.

The process of information seeking and retrieval clearly consists of many aspects that may influence the role players, the steps followed to find and use information and the iterations of the processes as various circumstances change over time (e.g., the manner in which the user understands the problem, the work task, the situation). Perhaps the easiest way to understand the complexity of the process is by means of the following example: A chef works at an embassy and receives notice that he/she has to prepare a dish for a dinner meeting where an important trade agreement might be signed. The chef identifies keywords and selects an appropriate database to look for a suitable recipe. In this scenario, the following role players may be identified:

- The chef is the *human user*.
- The preparation of the dish is the *work task*.
- The meeting is the *situation* for which the information retrieved will be utilized.
- The embassy and the guests at the meeting are the user's *socio-organizational environment*.

Encyclopedia of Library and Information Sciences, Fourth Edition DOI: 10.1081/E-ELIS4-120044537

- The database and search engine is the *IRS*.
- The keywords combined by logical operators is the *query* that is input into the IRS.
- The recipe is the *document* that will be retrieved.

Once the user realizes that his/her state of knowledge is incomplete and decides that an IRS has to be used to find documents that will satisfy the information need, the process of information seeking and retrieval starts and typically consists of the following stages:

- A question (in natural language) has to be reformulated as a query to be input into the IRS.
- Documents are retrieved, measured, and ranked according to relevance by the IRS.
- The relevance of the documents are then judged by the human user in terms of his/her own cognition, in terms of the work task that has to be executed, in terms of this situation for which the information is to be utilized, and also within the socio-organizational environment in which the information is presented (in the latter case not necessarily by the user himself/herself).
- Depending on a variety of factors, the documents that were retrieved are then either rejected or used.
- The entire process of seeking and retrieval is iterative—any of the stages may be repeated if the outcome is not satisfactory.

The example illustrates that there are many factors involved when we deal with the issue of relevance. In each of the stages from the definition of the work task to the outcome of the meeting, relevance was measured or judged.

Whether relevance is measured objectively by an IRS or subjectively judged by a human user, ultimately it is a *relation* that has to be evaluated. Mizzaro[2,3] stated that relevance may be viewed in terms of a relation between two groups of entities:

- The first group of entities deals with the information and information objects as such—documents, document surrogates, or the information which the user perceives when reading the document or surrogate.
- The second group of entities deals with the work task (the problem that has to be solved, the task that has to be fulfilled, or the interest that has to be satisfied), the information need resulting from the work task (this is a representation of the problem in the mind of a user), the request that is formulated on the basis of the information need (a representation of the information need in human language), and the query (a representation of the information need in a format that can be processed by an IRS).

Relevance can be viewed as a relation between any of two entities, one from each group. Each of these entities may

be divided further into three components: *topic* (subject area), *task* (activity that will be executed when documents are retrieved), and *context* (other factors, excluding topic and task that will influence the information behavior).

In addition to these components within the relationships, there is yet another dimension, namely that of time. The information-seeking situation takes place over time and the user's cognition of his/her work task changes over time. An overview document that was highly relevant at the beginning of a research project (perhaps because the user did not understand the problem) may no longer be relevant at the end of the project, because the user then knows the background, and that same document is then viewed as too elementary. The same argument goes for a user whose problem has changed over a period of time.

Mizzaro[2] also discusses the issue of "who judges what?" and this can happen in any of the following five dimensions: the kind of relevance judged; the kind of judge (user or nonuser); the physical entity the judge can use (document, surrogate, information) for making his/her relevance judgment; what the judge can use (query, request, information need, or problem) for expressing his/her information need; and the time at which the judgment is expressed.

For the purpose of this entry we will make a distinction between *relevance judgments* and *relevance measurements* (these should not be read as formal definitions of the terms):

- *Relevance judgments* can be seen as a subjective process where the human user decides on the relevance of retrieved documents in relation to the work task that he/she has to fulfill. Humans judge the relevance of information objects in terms of a variety of factors, some of which are very subjective and individualized. Furthermore, it is acknowledged that as a user's cognition changes over time, his/her judgment of relevance (even of the same documents) also changes. This is called *user relevance*.
- *Relevance measurement* is an objective method where the process of retrieval can be quantified in terms of its outcome. The term measurement implies objective criteria, physical entities, and quantification. When a query is entered into an IRS, the user is presented with a ranked or sorted list of documents. These documents are those that have been assessed as relevant based on the degree of similarity between the query and the documents. This is an objective measurement of relevance and is called *system relevance*, sometimes also called *similarity*.

RELEVANCE JUDGMENTS

The judgment of the relevance of a document is the evaluation of a relation. These relations are always between the document (or information object) on the one hand and some aspect of the seeking process on the other—for example the request, the information need, the underlying situation. Furthermore, these relations change over time.

User Relevance Criteria

Longitudinal studies show that users have a wide variety of factors that can affect judgments of the relevance of an information object. Two of the major longitudinal studies where responses were elicited from the users themselves are those by Barry and Schamber[4] and Vakkari and Hakala.[5]

Barry and Schamber[4] combined the results of two separate studies on relevance criteria in order to establish whether there is a "finite array" of user relevance criteria. The result of the study indicated that this array does indeed exist and is also finite, and that it is applied consistently across types of information users, problem situations, and source environments. The list below shows the criteria by which users judge the relevance of information objects:

- Depth/Scope/Specificity: Focused, specific to user's needs, sufficient detail or depth, interpretation, etc.
- Accuracy/Validity: Accuracy, correctness, and validity of information.
- Clarity: Presentation of information in a clear or well-organized manner.
- Currency: Current, recent, up-to-date, timely.
- Tangibility: Extent to which information relates to real, tangible issues, proven information, hard data, actual numbers.
- Quality of sources: General standards of quality, reliability.
- Accessibility: Effort and costs.
- Availability: Availability of information/sources of information.
- Verification: Consistent with or supported by other information in the field. Agreement with the user's point of view.
- Affectiveness: Affective or emotional response to information (e.g., pleasure, enjoyment, or entertainment).
- Effectiveness: The extent to which a procedure that is presented is effective or successful.
- Consensus within the field: Consensus or agreement in the field relating to the information being evaluated.
- Time constraints: Whether time constraints or deadlines are a factor in deciding to pursue information.
- Relationship with author: User's personal or professional relationship with author.
- Background/experience and ability to understand: User's background and experience helps to judge quality, reliability, or understanding of the issues.

- Novelty: Document novelty, source novelty, and content novelty.
- Geographic proximity: Geographic location covered in document may not be relevant to user's situation.
- Dynamism: Presentation of information: live or dynamic. Can user manipulate the presentation of information.
- Presentation quality (excluding entertainment value): Format or style of presentation.

The aim of the Vakkari and Hakala[5] study was to analyze how changes in relevance criteria are related to changes in the problem stages during task performance processes and it was concluded that the user's relevance criteria are (partially) dependent on the stage of the task performance process. The list below shows the relevance criteria users identified, and the subcategories of each criterion:

- Information content: topicality, point of view, recency, discipline, geographical area, references, examples, clarity, research approach.
- Sources of documents: person's relation to sources, source type, author.
- Document as physical entity: availability, length.
- User's situation: time constraints, stage of the process.
- User's experience and preferences: ability to understand, language, interest, novelty, saturation.
- Information types: general information, specific information, theories, methods, empirical results.

From the two studies above it is clear that users judge the relevance of an information object on much more than simply the relationship between the query and the documents—the manner in which systems measure relevance. It would seem that in some cases, users do not even take the content of the document into account when they judge the relevance of these—there are many other factors that play a role.

Subjective Relevance Types

In 1996 Saracevic (and expanded in 2007)[6–8] produced a stratified model that deals specifically and comprehensively with interactive communicative aspects of interactive IR. The model described five increasingly subjective types of relevance:

- Algorithmic relevance is objectively measured through an algorithm and results in a sorted or ranked list of documents. These objective measurements will be described in the next section.
- Topicality or topical relevance is the assessment of the aboutness of the query as compared to the aboutness of a document.

- Cognitive relevance or pertinence is the judgment of the content of the information object and the information need as perceived by the user at a given point in time.
- Situational relevance is the judgment of the document in terms of the work task situation as perceived by the user.
- Motivational or affective relevance is an emotional or intentional type of judgment that is highly individualized.

It was argued by Cosijn and Ingwersen[9] that this emotional/intentional type of relevance is included in all the subjective relevance types. They also argue that another type of relevance should be defined, namely:

- Socio-cognitive relevance that refers to domain, context, and collective situational preferences.

Each of the subjective relevance types will be discussed in more detail below, with specific reference to what relations are evaluated and how the measurement or judgment is made. The example used in the introductory section will also be used to illustrate the complexity of the subjective relevance judgments.

Topical relevance judgments

When a user has a work task to fulfill and realizes that he/she has to use an IRS to find information, he/she first has to find the focus of the problem. The information need is typically verbalized, but this "question" has to be reformulated as a query in order to be processed by an IRS. If we return to the example of the chef in the introduction, the information need is the need for a recipe that fulfils the requirements of the situation. In order to find a recipe, the chef has to identify appropriate search terms, combine them with logical operators, input this query into an IRS, and retrieve a set of information objects.

Topical relevance may be defined as the relation between the *topic* of the query and the *topic* of the retrieved information objects, and is assessed in terms of the aboutness of the information objects. If the chef used the query "lobster AND fish," he/she might retrieve several documents: some are recipes having lobster and fish as ingredients; others are recipes having lobster and fish only as terms in the description of the recipe (e.g., a novelty birthday cake in the shape of an aquarium). In this case, only the first group of recipes will be relevant in terms of the topic of the query (being ingredients in a recipe) and the topic on the retrieved information objects.

The assumption is that both query and the objects may be assessed by a cognitive agent as being about the same or a similar topic. This assumption implies a degree of subjectivity on the user side. The subjectivity is compounded if the information objects are represented by human-indexed terms.

Pertinence or Cognitive Relevance Judgments

Pertinence is measured in terms of the relation between the state of knowledge, or cognitive information need of the user, and the information objects as interpreted by that user. The criteria by which pertinence are inferred are cognitive correspondence, informativeness, authorship, information preferences, currency, and adequacy of form. For instance, a paper may be topically relevant but repeating what the user already knows. In the example of the chef now having retrieved several recipes with "lobster" and "fish" as ingredients, and having judged this subset of documents relevant on a topical level, it may be that he/she already has knowledge of some of these recipes, but for some reason did not deem these as relevant to the task at hand. Other recipes are new to him/her, and these are judged as pertinent (or cognitively relevant).

In the case of an intrinsically ill-defined information need at a given point in time, the user may not be able to assess pertinence.[10] One may say that if the user has insufficient knowledge and does not have a good grasp of the structure of the task, he/she will not have the necessary cognition to understand the problem. Cognitive relevance can therefore be described as the ability to connect a task to prior knowledge.[5]

This type of relevance is also extensively described by Barry[11] during an empirical study to define the criteria mentioned in users' evaluations of the information within documents as it is related to their need situations. The study showed that users included tangible features as well as subjective qualities, together with affective and situational factors.

Situational relevance judgments

Situational relevance[12,13] describes the relationship between the perceived situation, work task, or problem at hand and the usefulness of the information objects as perceived by the user. The criteria by which situational relevance is inferred are usefulness in decision-making, appropriateness of information in problem solving, and the reduction of uncertainty. In the example of the chef, he/she now has a subset of recipes which are topically as well as cognitively relevant. From this subset of documents the chef has to assess each in terms of suitability within the situation (a very important dinner where a trade agreement is dependent on the outcome). Unusual recipes, both looking and tasting good, may be judged as situationally relevant.

The judgment of situational relevance is deemed not only the evaluation by a user of whether a given information object is capable of satisfying the information need. It offers the additional potential of creating new knowledge which may motivate change in the decision maker's cognitive structures. In turn, this change may lead to a modification of the perception of the situation and the succeeding relevance judgment, and in an update of the information need.[14]

Socio-cognitive relevance judgments

Socio-cognitive relevance describes the relationship between the situation, the work task or problem at hand in a given socio-cultural context on the one hand, and the information objects on the other, as perceived by one or more cognitive agents. The social or organizational domain, or cultural context in which the individual finds himself is defined by a paradigm or tradition, which dictates what problem explanations may be found to be acceptable.

The relevance judgments within a particular context are not necessarily made by the user of the information objects. Returning to the example of the chef, we can summarize the process of finding and using relevant information as follows: the user has an information need derived from a particular context. The user perceives the work task in a certain way, states his/her information need, formulates a suitable request, translates the request into a query, inputs the query into an IRS, and retrieves a set of information objects which are measured as relevant by the system (algorithmic or system relevance measurement). The user judges the set of retrieved documents firstly on a topical level (topical relevance judgment) and then within his/her own knowledge of the topic (pertinence or cognitive relevance judgment). The user then decides whether the use of these documents will be suitable within a particular situation (situational relevance judgment). However, the result of this process will ultimately be judged, not by the chef, but by the dinner guests and the outcome of the dinner. If the trade agreement was signed, the documents were relevant, but if the chef was not aware that the some of the key guests were vegetarians (thereby adversely affecting the attitude of these guests by serving fish) and the agreement was thus not signed, then the documents were not relevant within the context (socio-cognitive relevance judgment).

Affective relevance

Affective relevance is described in terms of the relation between the goals, intents, and motivations of the user and the information objects. Affective relevance should not be seen as the ultimate subjective relevance in a scale of relevances, but rather as another dimension of relevance judgments that may be associated with the other subjective types of relevance. A user may, for example, decline to use a document that is judged as topically, cognitively, as well as situationally relevant because it goes against his/her moral principles.

Based on the discussion above, it is clear that when a user judges the relevance of a document (or other information object) there are many factors at play. Some of these factors can be relatively objective (e.g., whether the document is dealing with the right topic or not), and some are very subjective, personal, or even emotional.

Algorithmic relevance

Algorithmic relevance as defined by Saracevic[6] is another synonym for system relevance or similarity. This type of relevance is objectively measured through an algorithm and results in a sorted or ranked list of documents. The following example once again illustrates the difference between system relevance and user relevance. When two users use a particular IRS and input identical queries, they will retrieve identical sets of documents. This is because system relevance is a computed similarity function and as such is an objective measurement as opposed to the subjective judgments, i.e., user relevance. Once these two users have retrieved a set of (systemically) relevant documents from an IRS, they can peruse the documents and know whether a particular document is relevant or not in terms of their own information needs. These two different users may have exactly the same work task (e.g., a class assignment) to fulfill and yet one may judge a particular document relevant while the other may not (perhaps because she already knows the content of that particular document). The complexities of the process of user relevance judgments of information objects have been discussed above. The next section will deal will various aspects of system relevance measurements.

RELEVANCE MEASUREMENTS

System or algorithmic relevance is measured in terms of the comparative effectiveness of logical or statistical similarity of features inferring relevance.[6] This is system-oriented to a very large extent, as it depends on the degree of similarity between the features of the *query* and the features of the *document*. It is not influenced by the user, nor is it related to any subjective information need the user may have.

Historically, research into the evaluation and improvement of system relevance relied largely on the so-called laboratory model of information retrieval. In the laboratory model there is a test collection (a database of documents), a well-defined set of topical queries and a set of relevance assessments to identify the documents that are topically relevant to the query. The assessments are often (but not always) binary in nature. The results of the assessments are then usually expressed in terms of precision and average recall (see discussion below).

Recently, however, the laboratory model has been challenged by developments in research on relevance and information seeking. One of the main thrusts in this line of research is the importance of user interaction and involvement during the retrieval process and assessment of the retrieved documents in terms of subjective information needs. For a comprehensive discussion of these issues see Ingwersen and Järvelin.[12] This section deals mainly with assessment of system relevance within the laboratory model, but ends with a recommendation that the laboratory model be reviewed and extended to also include users and their context.

The laboratory model has its origins in the so-called Cranfield experiments (1957–1968) by Cyril Cleverdon et al.[15] These experiments entailed comparing several alternative indexing languages. The results of the performance of the different indexing languages were quantified in terms of precision and recall—evaluation measures that calculate the proportion of retrieved documents that are relevant (precision) and the proportion of relevant documents that are retrieved (recall).

In a closed system such as this, we can then use a matrix to evaluate the retrieval of documents in relation to a query:

Precision (P) is defined as the proportion of retrieved

	Retrieved	Not retrieved	
Relevant	a	b	$n_1 = a + b$
Not relevant	c	d	
	$n_2 = a + c$		$N = a + b + c + d$

documents that are relevant:

$$P = \frac{a}{(a+c)} = \frac{a}{n_2}$$

Precision can alternatively be defined as

$$P = \frac{|\{\text{relevant documents}\} \cap \{\text{document sretrieved}\}|}{|\{\text{document sretrieved}\}|}$$

Recall (R) is defined as the proportion of relevant documents that are retrieved:

$$R = \frac{a}{(a+b)} = \frac{a}{n_1}$$

Recall can alternatively be defined as

$$R = \frac{|\{\text{relevant documents}\} \cap \{\text{document sretrieved}\}|}{|\{\text{relevant documents}\}|}$$

Both precision and recall have a maximum value of 1 and a minimum value of 0.

For each query that is submitted to an IRS, a precision-recall value can be calculated. Each precision-recall value is denoted by an ordered pair (P_n, R_n) where P denotes

Fig. 1 The precision-recall graphs for two separate queries.

precision; R denotes recall and n a parameter (e.g., rank position). A graph can be plotted (see Fig.1) utilizing the set of ordered pairs for a particular query. In practice and on average, the relationship between precision and recall tends to be inversely proportional—as recall increases, precision will tend to decrease, and vice versa.

Other measures related to precision and recall are fall-out and generality:

Fallout (F) measures how well an IRS filters out nonrelevant documents during the retrieval process and is defined as the proportion of nonrelevant documents that are retrieved:

$$F = \frac{c}{c+d} = \frac{c}{N - n_1}$$

Generality (G) is the proportion of relevant documents within the entire collection:

$$G = \frac{a+b}{(a+b+c+d)} = \frac{n_1}{N}$$

The relative performance of an IRS may be expressed in terms of the measures above:

$$\frac{R}{F} = \frac{P/(1-P)}{G/(1-G)}$$

It should be noted that fallout and generality are not used anymore as measures of retrieval system effectiveness in the context of test collections. Fallout is not used because it is generally uninformative. In a collection of any reasonable size the vast majority of the document collection is not relevant to a particular query and thus almost none of the nonrelevant documents are retrieved (even by systems that are grossly ineffective). Generality is not used because test collections can only be used to compare systems' performance on that given collection, and generality is a constant across systems for a particular collection.

There are many problems related to using recall and precision as a measure of retrieval effectiveness (for a more detailed discussion, see Korfhage[16] and Baeza-Yates and Ribeiro-Neto)[17]:

- In a closed test collection, both recall and precision can be calculated with some accuracy. In a real-world situation, however, recall cannot be determined, since this would require knowledge of all the documents in the collection.
- Although precision and recall are related to each other, each in isolation does not give a good indication of retrieval effectiveness.

An alternative measure combining precision and recall into a single measure is the Harmonic Mean.[17]

The *Harmonic Mean* (F) of recall and precision is calculated as

$$F = \frac{2 \times \left(\text{Recall} \times \text{Precision} \right)}{\text{Recall} \times \text{Precision}}$$

This is also called the F_1 measure, since recall and precision are evenly weighted. The generalized F-measure is defined as

$$F_\beta = \frac{\left(1 + \beta^2 \right) \times \left(\text{Precision} \times \text{Recall} \right)}{\left(\beta^2 \times \text{Precision} \right) + \text{Recall}}$$

where F_β "measures the effectiveness of retrieval with respect to a user who attaches β times as much importance to recall as precision."[18] The F_2 measure thus weights recall twice as much as precision, while the $F_{0.5}$ measure weights precision twice as much as recall.

Precision and recall are based on the entire set of documents retrieved by the system related to a query. The *Mean Average Precision* (MAP) (also referred to as the mean non-interpolated average precision) is a mean calculated over a set of queries. The average precision is calculated after every retrieved relevant document (zero is used as the precision for not-retrieved relevant documents). The average precision is then calculated over the total number of relevant documents retrieved for a query:[19]

$$AveP = \frac{\sum_{r=1}^{N} \left(P(r) \times \text{rel}(r) \right)}{\text{Number of relevant documents}}$$

where r is the rank, N the number of documents retrieved, rel() a binary function on the relevance of a given rank, and $P()$ precision at a given cut-off rank.

In an ordered list of retrieved documents, the *bpref measure* (binary preference) measures the number of faulty orderings (e.g., where a nonrelevant document is ranked before a relevant document):[19]

$$bpref = \frac{1}{\text{ard}} \sum_{r=1}^{\text{ard}} \left(1 - \frac{\text{nn}_r}{\text{nn}} \right)$$

where nn_r is the number of nonrelevant documents in the results list up to the position of the rth relevant document, nn is the number of nonrelevant documents in the results list, and ard is the number of relevant documents in the results list.

Laboratory experiments related to relevance measurements have also started to change from predominantly using binary relevance assessments to using graded relevance assessments by means of N-ary measures (e.g., a three-point scale: not relevant, partially relevant, relevant or a four point scale: not relevant, marginally relevant, fairly relevant, highly relevant). A higher value for N will increase expressiveness of assessment, but will decrease the consistency of assessments.

Normalized Discounted Cumulative Gain (NDCG) is a relatively new measure that utilizes multipoint scales (as opposed to binary). This means that a particular document "gains" according to the level of relevance. The overall utility of N documents are measured by the sum of the gain of each relevant document ("cumulative"). The gain of a low-ranked document is "discounted" so that a highly ranked document will count more toward the gain. "Normalized" means that an ideal ranking is used to calculate an upper limit and the actual gain value is then normalized against this limit.[20]

In the measurements described in the section above, relevance is a function of the system—the absolute relationship between the query and the document is measured. The assumptions are that relevance depends on static topical similarity and that relevance is a binary (or at least based on discrete values) assessment. It does not take into account that different users may have different cognitive interpretations and information needs.

The process of user relevance judgment starts when the user is confronted with a set of documents for use in the work task. This set of documents (or other information objects) might be a set retrieved through an IRS and was defined as (systemically) relevant, it might be a set of documents gathered through manual effort, or it might even be a set of documents supplied by an intermediary. At this stage, it is dependent on the user to judge the relevance of these documents in terms of his/her own information needs. If the documents were retrieved through an IRS, the relevance of the retrieved set has been measured objectively as a relationship between the query and the documents retrieved. Once the user starts perusing the documents, their relevance is judged in different terms. User relevance is subjective and individualized, based on a variety of factors.

This multidimensionality of relevance would suggest that the computing of system relevance is but one aspect of the process of Information Seeking and Retrieval. Ingwersen and Järvelin[12] argue that the laboratory model of IR evaluation has been challenged due to its lack of realism and proposes two alternative approaches to traditional laboratory model—one is to extend IR research to take the user and his/her context into account, and the other is to extend Information Seeking research toward the context of the task as well as toward the technology.

CONCLUSION

Users know intuitively if a document is relevant or not. The formal assessment of relevance and the associated theory, however, is a much more complex issue. Relevance can be assessed in one of two ways. Relevance can be measured through an algorithm in terms of the relation between the query and the information objects retrieved by the query. When a query is entered into an IRS, the user is presented with a ranked or sorted list of documents. These documents are those that have been assessed as relevant based on the degree of similarity between the query and the documents. This is an objective measurement of relevance, and is not necessarily in agreement with what the user perceives to be relevant.

Humans judge the relevance of information objects in terms of a variety of factors, some of which are very subjective and individualized. Users judge documents in terms of their own perception of the problem or work task, in terms of the complexity of their own situation, in terms of the context that they operate in, as well as other subjective and affective factors which are not always clearly verbalized. Furthermore, it is acknowledged that as the user's cognition changes over time, the judgment of relevance (even of the same documents) also changes.

REFERENCES

1. Ingwersen, P.; Borlund, P. Information transfer viewed as interactive cognitive processes. In *Information Science: Integration in Perspective*; Ingwersen, P.; Pors, N.O., Eds.; Royal School of Library and Information Science: Copenhagen, 1996; 219–232.

2. Mizzaro, S. Relevance: The whole history. J. Am. Soc. Inform. Sci. **1997**, *48* (9), 810–832.

3. Mizzaro, S. How many relevances in information retrieval? Interact. Comput. **1998**, *10*, 305–322.

4. Barry, C.L.; Schamber, L. User's criteria for relevance evaluation: A cross-situational comparison. Inform. Process. Manage. **1998**, *34* (2/3), 219–236.

5. Vakkari, P.; Hakala, N. Changes in relevance criteria and problem stages in task performance. J. Doc. **2000**, *56* (5), 540–562.

6. Saracevic, T. Relevance reconsidered '96. In *Information Science: Integration in Perspective*; Ingwersen, P.; Pors, N.O., Eds.; Royal School of Library and Information Science: Copenhagen, 1996; 201–218.

7. Saracevic, T. Relevance: A review of the literature and a framework for thinking on the notion in information science. Part II: Nature and manifestations of relevance. JASIST **2007**, *58* (13), 1915–1933.

8. Saracevic, T. Relevance: A review of the literature and a framework for thinking on the notion in information science. Part III: Behavior and effects of relevance. JASIST **2007**, *58* (13), 2126–2144.

9. Cosijn, E.; Ingwersen, P. Dimensions of relevance. Inform. Process. Manage. **2000**, *36* (4), 533–550.

10. Ingwersen, P. *Information Retrieval Interaction*; Taylor Graham: London, 1992.

11. Barry, C.L. User-defined relevance criteria: An exploratory study. J. Am. Soc. Inform. Sci. **1994**, *45* (3), 149–159.

12. Ingwersen, P.; Järvelin, K. *The Turn: Integration of Information Seeking and Retrieval in Context*; Springer: Dordrecht, 2005.

13. Schamber, L.; Eisenberg, M.B.; Nilan, M.S. A re-examination of relevance: Toward a dynamic, situational definition. Inform. Process. Manage. **1990**, *26* (6), 755–776.

14. Borlund, P. *Evaluation of Interactive Information Retrieval Systems*; Doctoral dissertation, Åbo Akademi University Press: Åbo, 2000.

15. Cleverdon, C.W. The Cranfield tests on index language devices. In *Readings in Information Retrieval*; Sparck, Jones, K., Willett, P., Eds.; Morgan Kaufman Publishers: Amsterdam, 1997; 47–59.

16. Korfhage, R.R. *Information Storage and Retrieval*; Wiley Interscience: New York, 1997.

17. Baeza-Yates, R.; Ribeiro-Neto, B. *Modern Information Retrieval*; ACM Press: New York, 1999.

18. Van Rijsbergen, C.J. *Information Retrieval*, 2nd Ed.; Butterworths: London, 1979.

19. Voorhees, E.; Buckley, C. The effect of topic set size on retrieval experiment error. *Annual ACM Conference on Research and Development in Information Retrieval*, Proceedings of the 25th Annual International ACM SIGIR Conference on Research and Development in Information Retrieval, Tampere, 2002; 316–323.

20. Järvelin, K.; Kekäläinen, J. Cumulated gain-based evaluation of IR techniques. ACM Trans. Inform. Syst. **2002**, *20* (4), 422–446.

Regional–School

Renaissance Libraries [ELIS Classic]

Lawrence S. Thompson
University of Kentucky, Lexington, Kentucky, U.S.A.

Abstract

The author surveys the history of libraries during the Renaissance and the Reformation in several European countries.

—ELIS Classic, from 1983

INTRODUCTION

To define the Renaissance in broadly acceptable terms or to set limits for its beginning and end and its geographical scope is all but impossible.[1,2] One aspect, perhaps the central one, is beyond any dispute: The book—its collecting, preservation, reproduction, and exploitation for new ideas—was the key to the break with medieval tradition. While there are early and late manifestations of the spirit of the Renaissance, the role of books and libraries in the revival of learning begins, roughly, in the mid-fourteenth century and may be said to continue into the latter sixteenth century when classical scholarship began to take full advantage of the revival of ancient learning and its application to contemporary culture. The library of the seventeenth century is in a direct continuum from those of the previous two centuries; and, as far as modern libraries are concerned, the institutions we know today took shape in the seventeenth and eighteenth centuries.

The humanists found in the book something permanent, over and above its specific service in perpetuating the traditions of classical antiquity.[3] Thus, they viewed libraries, the basic tool for preserving books, as the most important servants of scholarship. When Cardinal Bessarion gave 746 manuscripts to the Venetian Republic in 1468, the origin of the Marciana, it was "ad communem hominum utilitatem."[4] Time and again, we have expressions of confidence in libraries as the one indispensable tool of scholarship.[5,6] A legend was created that endures today, sometimes to the detriment of scholarship in the reverence for the printed book, much as the respect for the manuscript affected the acceptance of the printed book in the fifteenth century.

ITALY

Francesco Petrarca (Petrarch; 1304–1374) stands at the head of the roll of Italian humanists.[a] He must have been an impassioned bibliophile at an early age. In 1337, he prepared a list of "libri mei," and he was well on his way to developing the first great humanistic library. He copied Cicero's letters, discovered in the Verona Cathedral library in 1345; and after he found a manuscript of Vergil, now in the Ambrosian Library in Milan, he always took it on his extensive travels despite its size. In 1362, Petrarch left Milan on account of an epidemic; he went to Padua and then to Venice, where he made an arrangement to deposit his books in Saint Mark's. He was in Venice for five years, must have left some books there (a sorry remainder was discovered two and a half centuries later), and then went to Arquà (near Padua), with whose master, Francesco da Carrara, he was acquainted. Petrarch's will of 1370 does not mention his library, and it has been assumed that most went to Carrara. The latter's library was seized by the Visconti of Pavia in 1388, and, in 1500, it was taken by Louis XII with other bibliological booty and shipped to Blois, then removed in 1544 to Fontainebleau. Twenty-six manuscripts from Petrarch's library are in the Bibliothèque Nationale today, a few others in other places. While Petrarch's library did not survive intact, it was the prototype of the Renaissance book collection, in the method of acquisition, in content, and in its intended use. His notion about a library in Venice for scholars was an enduring one among later humanists.

If Petrarch or his friend Giovanni Boccaccio had never contributed a line to creative literature, they would still be major personalities of the Italian Renaissance on account of their dedication to collecting books for the revival of learning.[6,14–16] Boccaccio, unlike Petrarch, had limited means and copied most of the manuscripts he found. His most famous discovery was the Tacitus (*Annales*, XI–XVI, and *Historiae*, I–V) at Monte Cassino, whose library he described in some detail for the neglect it had suffered—possibly an excuse to justify removal of the manuscript.[b] The Tacitus manuscript fell into the hands of Niccolò dei Niccoli (1363–1437; infra), who allowed

---

[a]Of the extensive Petrarch bibliography, only the following may be noted here. See Ullman.[7]–de Nolhac.[13]

[b]Now Laurentianus 68, II. It also contained the *Agricola*, perhaps more, when the monk Petrus Diaconus used it for his life of Saint Severus about 1135. See Bloch[17] and Pralle.[18]

Encyclopedia of Library and Information Sciences, Fourth Edition DOI: 10.1081/E-ELIS4-120009030

Poggio Bracciolini ("Florentinus," 1380–1459; infra) to copy it; and it ended in the Marciana after Niccoli's death. In 1374, Boccaccio wrote a will bequeathing his collection of over 200 volumes to his confessor, the Augustinian Martino da Signa, after whose death it went to the monastery of San Spirito in Florence with the understanding that it be generally available. Niccoli heard about the neglected books and had a cabinet made for them, but after the remodeling of the monastery in 1560, most were lost. Fortunately, we do know titles from an inventory of 107 items preserved in Ashburnham 1897 of the Laurentian Library.[19] Of these, 10 have been found in the Laurentian and the Riccardiana in Florence, of which 2 were copied in whole or in part by Boccaccio. A third has notes in his hand.

Coluccio Salutati (1331–1406) did not attain the literary renown of Petrarch and Boccaccio, but his services as a manuscript collector are no less significant.[20–22] He held high civil office in Florence, and his position enabled him to identify and acquire many valuable manuscripts, notably Cicero's *Epistolae ad familiares* (now in the Laurentian) and Cato's *De agricultura*. He had a copy made of the Catullus manuscript in Verona (Petrarch had done it earlier), and he also possessed a Tibulus manuscript (Ambros. R 26 sup.). Salutati did not plan to found a library, but the purchase of his books by Giovanni de' Medici had the same effect.

Petrarch, Boccaccio, Niccoli, and Salutati placed much heavier emphasis on Latin than on Greek literature; but when Antonio Corbinelli (ca. 1370 to 1375–1425) left his collection to the Abbey of Santa Maria in Florence, it included 194 Latin and 79 Greek manuscripts, with 105 Latin and 65 Greek authors.[23] Many of the latter were not known by the humanists of the time, and there were basic things such as an eleventh-century Thucydides, a manuscript of Sophocles and Euripides (now Cod. Laur. C.S.71), and an *Odyssey* (Cod. Laur. C.S.52).

The most famous of all manuscript collectors of the Renaissance was Poggio, prototype of the book hunter down to the age of Lyman Copeland Draper and Herbert Hoover.[24] Salutati took Poggio into his service when the latter was barely 20 years old and introduced him to his circle, which included Niccoli. In 1403, Salutati arranged for Poggio to secure a position in the Roman Curia, where he was able to intensify his work in copying manuscripts. His great opportunity came when he went to the Council of Constance as a secretary (1414–1418), even though he lost his job when the first John XXIII lost his. He probably spent much of his time poking around monasteries looking for manuscripts, and he was as shocked by the condition of their collections as Boccaccio was by the situation at Monte Cassino. His most significant discovery was the first known complete text of Quintilian's *Institutio oratoria*. Subsequently, he found other texts, lost up to that time, in monastic libraries of Switzerland, Germany, and France: notably three and a half books on Valerius Flaccu's *Argonautica*, Asconius Pedanius's commentary of five speeches of Cicero, Lucretius, Silius Italicus, Ammianus Marcellinus, Tacitus, Plautus, Columella, Tertullian, and others. Poggio collected more for others than for himself, since only 95 manuscripts appeared in the inventory taken after his death. His sons and nephew inherited them, but today there are only 5 in the Laurentian, 1 in the Vatican, and 1 in the Riccardiana. But Poggio's service to scholarship in locating, copying, and preserving classical manuscripts will be remembered long after schoolboys stop snickering over his amusing but naughty *Facetiae*.

The concentration of early humanists in Florence and presence of the wealthy and influential family of Medici[25–30] were decisive elements in making Florence a major cultural center with incomparable art collections and libraries. Cosimo the Elder (1389–1464) established a firm position and a fortune for his family after he became the acknowledged head of the Florentine state in 1434. He established a Platonic academy headed by Marsilio Ficino,[31] but directly pertinent here is that Niccolò dei Niccoli was his adviser in matters relating to books.[32] Niccoli collected some 800 volumes, which he wanted to be available to scholars in the Camaldolese monastery of Santa Maria degli Angioli in Florence; but, on account of his debts, he changed this decision shortly before his death and left the disposition of his collection to a committee of 16 fellow humanists. Happily, Cosimo assumed responsibility for these liabilities and acquired 200 manuscripts for his personal collection (*la Medicea privata*); he also placed some 400 in the Dominican monastery of San Marco in 1441 in the handsome hall designed by Michelozzo and still basically intact, the first public library in Italy (*la Medicea pubblica*). The librarian, Giuliano Lapaccini, was allowed to draw on the Medici bank for new acquisitions.

Cosimo also rehabilitated the library of the Abbey of Fiesole (the Badia) and provided it with a corps of copyists under the supervision of Vespasiano da Bisticci (1421–1498), who produced some 200 manuscripts in less than 2 years. Along with the collection placed in San Marco, it is the oldest part of the modern Medicea–Laurenziana. The *Medicea privata* was housed in San Lorenzo and was rather modest until Cosimo's grandson, Lorenzo il Magnifico (1449–1492)[29,33,34] assumed leadership of the family and of Florence in 1469. Especially constructive was his concern for the acquisition of Greek manuscripts and the effective support of his agent, Andreas Janos Laskaris (ca. 1445–1535), in the Levant.[35] The library was used by such humanists as Politian, Pico della Mirandola, and Marsilio Ficino. From the expulsion of the Medici in 1494, the library was subject to many vicissitudes (and losses), taken to Rome by Lorenzo's youngest son (Leo X after 1513), and finally returned to Florence by Clement VII (Giulio de' Medici) in 1532.

Clement had commissioned Michelangelo in 1525 to design and construct a library building in the upper cloisters of the basilica of San Lorenzo, but it was not opened until 1571, seven years after Michelangelo's death. The magnificent structure is recognized generally as the finest of all Renaissance library buildings.[c] The collection in San Marco (the Marciana) was combined with the Laurenziana in 1808 when monastic property was secularized. The Medicea–Laurenziana has survived wars and political changes, but of its subsequent history, we may note only the acquisition of 1,903 Ashburnham manuscripts in 1885.

When Petrarch left Milan on account of the plaque in 1362, he went to Venice, where he gave part of his collection to San Marco in return for personal housing in the Palazzo di Due Torri; but, as we have noted, it did not develop into the public library for scholars that Petrarch probably envisioned. It remained for Basilios Bessarion (1395–1472) of Trebizond—bishop of Nicea and later a Roman cardinal (1439) in the movement for reconciliation—to establish a scholarly library in Venice.[4] In Italy, with the authority of a cardinal, he collected and copied zealously, and, after the fall of Constantinople (1453), he made a special effort to protect remnants of Greek culture by acquiring manuscripts. His young associate, Niccolò Perotti, who traveled as far as Trebizond, was particularly successful.[37] Further, his connections with Giovanni Aurispa and Francesco Filelfo, two prominent humanists who had been in Constantinople and acquired manuscripts there, must have been productive.[38–40] In 1423, Aurispa brought back 238 volumes of Greek classics, including the basic collective volume with the plays of Aeschylus and Sophocles and the *Argonautica* of Apollonius Rhodius.

On May 31, 1468, Bessarion presented his library of 482 Greek and 264 Latin manuscripts of the Republic of Venice.[4,41] In the humanistic tradition, he expressed, in the document of transmission, his concept of books as the best companions of the scholar. The collection was originally destined for the Benedictine monastery of San Giorgio Maggiore, but San Marco was substituted on May 14, 1468. The library was not adequately housed, and, consequently it was not used to full advantage in the beginning. Finally, in the period 1536–1553, Jacopo Sansovino constructed the magnificent quarters for the library long admired as one of the great architectural achievements of Renaissance Italy.[42,43] Over the last five centuries, the library has had various homes and made important acquisitions,[44] but most significant are the tradition of Bessarion and his contributions to the preservation of ancient Greek culture.

Outside of Florence and Venice, there were other collections in princely residences. The Visconti and the Sforza had an impressive library in Pavia, in which 988 manuscripts were recorded in 1426,[45,46] when the Medici and Niccoli had no comparable collections. But, unlike the Medici, the Visconti and the Sforza and their courtiers had no passion for learning comparable to that of the Medici. Florence and, somewhat later, Venice had stature and influence in Renaissance Italy that grew from men who knew how to use books as well as how to collect them.

In Ferrara, the house of Este owned a library that had origins at least in the fourteenth century.[47–49] A catalog of 1436 recorded 279 manuscripts, mostly Latin but with some Italian and French, and, in 1495, there was a record of 512 manuscripts, with only 2 Greek titles. After Clement VIII claimed Ferrara as a papal fief in 1597, Duke Caesar took the library to Modena in 1598, where it survives today in association with the university (founded 1772). There are remarkable illuminations, bindings,[50] and vernacular works (Dante, Tasso, Provençal, among others), in all some 9,000 manuscripts in addition to important printed works acquired during the librarianships of Muratori, Tiraboschi, and other competent bookmen.

The Aragonese kings of Naples were diligent bibliophiles and patrons of scholarship, in particular Alfonso V, who assumed power in 1435. He was not only deeply concerned for the development of his library but also entertained such brilliant personalities as Lorenzo Valla.[51–54] His son, Ferdinand, had less personal interest but continued to add to the collection, particularly with confiscated collections, until his death in 1494. A decade later Naples became a viceroyalty of the Spanish crown, and the noble library was broken up, part going to France and another part to Valladolid. Much of both portions survives.

Perhaps most famous of all the libraries in the smaller residences was that of Federigo da Montefeltro (1410 or 1411–1482), duke of Urbino. Primarily a politician and an effective condottieri chieftan, Federigo nevertheless made strong and successful efforts to furnish his seat with books and works of art. He was not well informed about literature, but he was wise enough to entrust Vespasiano da Bisticci with his buying. He kept a corps of some 30–40 copyists busy in Urbino. An inventory taken after Federigo's death recorded 1,120 volumes.[55–58] In 1658, Alexander VII bought the collection and turned over the manuscripts (1,767 Latin and Italian, 165 Greek, and 128 Oriental) to the Vatican Library, but he gave the printed books to the library he had recently established for the University of Rome (henceforth called the "Biblioteca Alessandrina").

The Gonzaga family assumed power in Mantua in 1328. During the next century, Gianfranco and Lodovico III were personally concerned about the development of their book collections. In 1407, there were some 300 volumes, including some important Greek manuscripts.[59]

---

[c]The libraries and library rooms of the Renaissance in Venice (the Marciana), Siena (in the cathedral), Urbino (in the castle), and elsewhere are noteworthy more for their architectural significance than for any advances in coordinating physical facilities with readers' needs. See von Stegmann.[36]

THE VATICAN LIBRARY

The Vatican Library was destined to be the most important of all Renaissance libraries and to hold a leading position through the centuries.[60] From very early periods there had been archives in the Holy See, and there were major collections in the fourteenth century at Avignon, now partially surviving in the Bibliothèque Nationale in Paris and in the Borghese Collection, which finally came into the possession of the Holy See in 1902. The real founder of the modern Vatican Library was Tommaso Parentucelli (1397–1455), who held the pontificate as Nicholas V for the last eight years of his life.[61] As a young man, he established a respected position for himself among the Florentine humanists and was an eager collector. Bisticci recorded him as a bibliophile whose appetite for books excelled his means.[62] When Cosimo was developing the library of San Marco, he entrusted Parentucelli with the chore of drawing up a list of desiderata.[63]

The modest collection of some 350 manuscripts that Nicholas inherited from his predecessor, Eugene IV, was increased by every possible means through agents in Constantinople and book centers in Italy. He accepted only the best copies in fine bindings. His librarian, Giovanni Tortelli, a competent humanist in his own right, did much to promote Nicholas's objective to make the papal library the world's greatest scholarly collection. In 1455, there were some 1,200 important manuscripts, of which about 800 were in Latin. At Nicholas's death it was the largest library of its time.

Calixtus III (1455–1458) was not a bibliophile and scholar of the same stamp, and it was only in the papacy of Sixtus IV (1471–1484), of the della Rovere family, that the library began to thrive again. In 1481, there is a record of 3,499 volumes. Sixtus's first librarian was Giovanni Andrea dei Bussi,[64,65] succeeded at his death in 1475 by another distinguished humanist, Bartolomeo Platina. In the same year, a budget was provided for the library, and it was increased in 1477. Adequate housing was provided in handsomely decorated quarters, executed by Domenico, David Ghirlandaio, and Melozzo da Forli. The standards of service in the Vatican Library were superior for the age.

Two Medici popes whom we have already encounted, Leo X and Clement VII, were active patrons of the library. Under Paul III, a new catalog of manuscripts was prepared by Cardinals Marcello Cervini and Jacopo Sadoleto. During the sack of Rome by imperial forces in 1527, the library, now with over 4,000 manuscripts, was probably saved because Philibert of Orange had headquarters in the papal palace, a situation that probably made it immune to looting. It cannot be overlooked that the Vatican itself was the beneficiary of two of the greatest loots of libraries of all time; first, when Tilly captured Heidelberg in 1622 and Duke Maximilian of Bavaria gave the great collection of the Palatina to Gregory XV; and second, when the apostate queen of Sweden, Christina, took to Rome the handsome collection made up largely of the spoils from her father's campaigns in Poland and the Germanies. The latter was bought by Alexander VII in 1690. The subsequent history of the Vatican Library and some of its great acquisitions belongs to the world history of scholarship, but the policies of Nicholas V have had an abiding influence.

FRANCE

It is ironical that France benefited enormously from the productive activities of Italian collectors and scholars, and yet there were few counterparts of the Italian Renaissance bibliophiles. The remnants of some of the great princely collections such as those in Pavia and Naples found a home in Paris, and rulers of the land promoted the Bibliothèque du Roi. While France produced a collector of the stature of Jean Grolier de Servin (1479–1565), private book collecting in France did not reach the proportions it had attained in Italy in the quattrocento until the age of Richelieu.

There had been a royal library in the Louvre, but as the Hundred Years' War waned, about 1430, a new collection began to take shape in Blois.[d] Here the collections brought from Naples by Charles VIII and from Pavia by Louis XII found a home. The first French monarch to perform bibliologically in the style of the Medici was Francis I (1494–1547). He founded a library in Fontainebleau,[70–73] which included the family collection of his own house (Angoulême), and, in 1544, he combined the Bibliothèque du Roi in Blois with it. After Laskaris acquired important Greek manuscripts for Lorenzo il Magnifico, he rendered the same service to Francis. Francis invested Guillaume Budé (1467–1540) with the office of *maître de librairie,* and this great humanist was lifelong adviser to the king.[74] Although Francis preferred the manuscript to the printed book, he initiated legal deposit when, in 1536, he gave the librarian at Blois, Mellin de Saint-Gelais, the right to claim a copy of every book printed in France.[75] Henri II (1547–1559) was an aficionado of fine bindings (as was Francis), and his monograms were an *H* combined with a *D* (his mistress, Diane de Poitiers; 1499–1566) or a *C* (his wife, Catherine de Médicis; 1519–1589).

Catherine was completely imbued with the bibliophilic tradition of her family.[76] She had a library of some 4,000–5,000 ancient and modern texts in the

---

[d]Of the extensive literature on the origins and history of the Bibliothèque Nationale, see Vallée[66]–Serrurier.[69]

Château of Saint Maur, supervised by her confessor, Benciveni, abbé de Bellebranche. It was the collection of a great *femme bibliophile* as well as of an avid reader. Her most noteworthy acquisition was the collection of some 800 manuscripts held by Marshal Pietro Strozzi after he fell at Thionville in 1558. She claimed it as Medici property. After her death, her creditors claimed the Strozzi collection, but it was saved by J.-A. de Thou for only 5,400 écus put up by Henri IV, and most of the collection is in the Bibliothéque Nationale today. The beautiful Diane's collection remained in the Château d'Anet until it was auctioned in 1724 after the death of Anna of Bavaria, who had inherited the castle in 1718.[6] J.B. Guyon de Sardière bought most of the books, and they ultimately went with his collection to the Duc de La Vallière.[e]

EASTERN EUROPE, ENGLAND, AND SPAIN

In the Germanies, the late arrival of humanism was to coincide with the early proliferation of printing and, later, with the Reformation, and to lend a peculiarly national character to the development of libraries and of private and princely collections. Elsewhere, the Renaissance collector appeared sporadically although occasionally in brilliant instances. Most famous was the great collection of King Matthias Corvinus (Hunyadi; 1458–1490) of Hungary.[78–82] His chancellor, John Vitéz, had studied in Italy, knew the humanists of his day, and was a zealous collector of manuscripts; and his nephew, John Pannonius, followed in his steps. The Hunyadi had had relations with the Visconti and the Sforza, and, in 1476, Matthias married Beatrice of Aragon, daughter of King Ferdinand of Naples. With the help of Bisticci and others, he put together a library in Buda that any Italian prince might have envied. His preference was for handsomely decorated manuscripts from Italian artists, and he was not greatly concerned with the importance of texts. The fame of the Corviniana created exaggerated rumors about its quantity, but there may well have been up to 3,000 titles. His early death, Beatrice's return to Italy, and the indifference of Matthias's successors hastened the dispersion of the collection. After the crushing defeat of the Hungarians at Moháczin 1526, the Turks took what had survived (finally restored in part to the University of Budapest by the Osmanli sultan in 1877). There are other remnants all over the Western Hemisphere.[83]

Hungary's northern neighbor, Poland, had a major intellectual center in Cracow, where the university had been founded in 1364 and was to acquire distinction, particularly in mathematics and astronomy, culminating in the work of Italian-trained Copernicus a century and a half

later. Gregory Sanok, a *magister* at Cracow, was a zealous humanist and book collector, and the Jagiellonian University owes much to him.[84]

Humanism found its way to England by the end of the fifteenth century with scholars of the stature of William Grocyn and Thomas Linacre, but neither they nor others were collectors in the tradition of the Italians. Thomas Wotton (1521–1587), a sort of an English Grolier who inscribed his Italianate bindings "Thomas Wottoni et amicorum," was the closest to a Renaissance collector that England had.[85] Sir William Pickering (1516–1575) had similar tastes. His daughter married Sir Edward Wotton, Thomas's son. The combined library came to the Stanhope (Chesterfield) family, and the collection survived until 1920 when it was sold at Sotheby's.

Spain had a distinguished collector in the son of the admiral, Don Fernando Colón (1488–1539), who assembled an important library of some 12,000 volumes and deposited it in the Dominican monastery of San Pablo in Seville, but it was neglected and plundered.[86] The library of San Lorenzo del Escorial was a commitment by Philip II after the battle of Saint Quentin in 1557, established formally in 1565.[87] Both contained rich collections on Renaissance culture from the beginning, but neither were collected or administered in the same spirit, or for the same purpose as were the libraries of the Medici or of the Holy See of Nicholas V.

THE GERMANIES

Humanism first touched German-speaking territories when Cola di Rienzi, friend and confidant of Petrarch, pleaded with Charles IV in Prague for regeneration of the church. Petrarch himself corresponded with the imperial court. But humanism came north slowly. In 1417 and 1418, Poggio was actively engaged in his constructive carpetbagging in German-speaking areas. Poggio rescued many a basic manuscript; but another brilliant contemporary, Enea Silvio Piccolomini (1405–1464), Pius II after 1458, was the most effective representative of humanism north of the Alps when he served as secretary in the chancellery of Friedrich III.[88] Thus, in the University of Vienna, and later in other institutions, interest in classical studies began to expand slowly. There is only slight evidence of the acquisition of classical manuscripts by the existing collections in universities, city halls, and monasteries. Most important were private collectors whose inventories reflected the penetration of the new learning. Nikolaus von Cues, Albrecht von Eyb, Hartmann Schedel, and the Fuggers were among the prominent early collectors inspired by Italian humanism.

Nikolaus von Cues (1401–1464), latinized as Cusa or Cusanus, cardinal after 1448, had become a doctor of both laws in Padua and was influenced not only by

---

[e]For the subsequent history of the La Vallière and other important collections, mentioned here see Bogeng, Bogeng[6] and Thompson.[77]

German mysticism but also by Neoplatonism and humanism.[18,89–91] He recognized significant classical manuscripts in Fulda and probably took a basic Plautus manuscript (now Vat. Lat. 3870) from there to Rome. He also discovered Tacitus manuscripts and may have been the first German in modern times to know the *Germania*. He read Greek and had the opportunity to collect in Constantinople. A significant fact is that, in 1459, his long-time friend Enea Silvio appointed him papal vicar-general. Cues willed his property, including philosophical apparatus and books, to a hospital in his home town of Bernkastel–Kues on the Mosel, and 314 manuscripts (270 from his own collection) are still there, although much has been removed over the centuries (e.g., more than 30 are now in the British Library).

Albrecht von Eyb (1420–1475), Franconian baron, spent 13 years in the south and was a zealous collector.[92,93] He translated Plautus, and two of his manuscripts of this author are in Augsburg today. His library, including printed books, went to the Eichstätt Cathedral, but it was dispersed without any accurate record. About 20 pieces have been identified in modern German libraries.

Hermann Schedel (1410–1485) and his cousin Hartmann Schedel (1440–1514) both studied medicine in Padua and brought humanism to their native Nuremberg.[94,95] Hermann's library was inherited by Hartmann, famous for his *Weltchronik*. The latter had studied Greek, as well as medicine, in Padua. While he owned important manuscripts, he also collected printed books. The catalog shows 632 titles. The collection was sold in 1552 to Hans Jakob Fugger, and it contained some 400 collective manuscript volumes and 700 printed books. It was acquired in 1571 by Duke Albrecht V of Bavaria, the founder of the Munich Hofbibliothek (now Bayerische Staatsbibliothek). About 360 manuscripts belonging to Hartmann Schedel have been identified in the modern collections.

Johann von Dalberg (1455–1503) spent most of his productive life in Heidelberg, where he was chancellor of the university from 1480 to 1497.[96] He was closely associated with humanists of the stature of Rudolf Agricola, Johannes Reuchlin, and Dietrich von Plenningen, and he also collected a significant library. He bought manscripts in Italy and, back home, commissioned the Strassburg printer and bookseller Adolf Rusch to buy classical texts at the Frankfurt Fair. His librarian, Johannes Vigilius, professor of law, also bought for him at the fair. After Dalberg fell out with the Palatine elector in 1497, he retired to Worms where he was bishop. Presumably, his collection remained in the episcopal see but was gravely neglected. Fewer than 20 titles from this once great collection can be identified today, mainly in various German libraries.

Maximilian I, emperor from 1493 to 1519, had a library as archduke and acquired a vastly greater treasure of books in the dowry of Marie of Burgundy.[97,98] He was a romantic ("the last knight") but may well have listened to

Enea Silvio in Vienna. Certainly, his confidence in Konrad Celtis (1459–1508) indicated his inclination to humanism.[6] Celtis was entrusted with the custody of part of Maximilian's collection, inherited from his father, Friedrich III, and left in the residence of Wiener Neustadt (the more valuable part was moved to Castle Ambros near Innsbruck). In 1497, Celtis was appointed by Maximilian to the chair of poetry and eloquence at the University of Vienna, and it became an important center of humanistic activity with men such as Celtis, the versatile Joachim von Watt (Vadianus; infra), and the historian Johannes Cuspinianus. The latter built a handsome collection that was acquired in 1530 by the Vienna bishop Johannes Faber (died 1541), whose collection of 2,162 items passed to the University Library. The collections in Innsbruck were not always given the best care, but ultimately most of these (with subsequent additions) and the material in Wiener Neustadt found a home in the Austrian National Library.

One of the most spectacular events in Celtis's career was the discovery of a map of Roman military roads, 34 centimeters by 7 meters in length, in Worms. It was to have been edited by Konrad Peutinger (1455–1547), but it disappeared until 1714 when Prince Eugene of Savoy discovered it and later willed it to the Hofbibliothek in Vienna. The *Tabula Peutingeriana* is famous enough,[99] but the role of Peutinger, an Augsburg patrician, in German humanism is even more important.[100] Today his collection of over 2,000 works, a good proportion reflecting Peutinger's humanistic interests, has been scattered, with less than 100 items identified (happily, 36 went to the Augsburg Stadtbibliothek in 1810). Peutinger did compile two catalogs, a rich source for our knowledge of humanistic book collecting in Germany.

In Nuremberg, the patrician Willibald Pirckheimer (1470–1550) was the central figure in the humanistic movement.[6,101,102] After study in Pavia and Padua, he assumed a respected position in his native city. He was a friend not only of Celtis but also of Reuchlin and Erasmus. An indefatigable collector, he boasted, in 1504, in a letter to Celtis, that he owned every Greek book printed in Italy. Pirckheimer's library remained in the family for over a century after his death and was sold to Thomas Howard, earl of Arundel, in 1636. It was donated by Henry Howard to the Royal Society in 1667, and, in 1831, the manuscripts (except the Oriental ones) were sold to the British Museum.

Schlettstadt in Alsatia produced two major humanists, Jakob Wimpheling (1450–1528)[103,104] and Beatus Rhenanus (1485–1547).[105] We know almost nothing about Wimpheling's library, although he gave books regularly to the church library there. Today the rich old Stadtbibliothek of Schlettstadt has two manuscripts and three printed books that once belonged to Wimpheling. His literary production is well known, but his interest in book collecting is equally meaningful. In 1496, he and Johannes Vigilius (supra) visited Johannes Trithemius (or Tritheim; 1462–1516), abbot of the Benedictine monastery in Sponheim.[106–108] Trithemius's collection of over 2,000 works included many Greek works and others of obvious humanistic interest. It was a victim of secularization in 1564, and only about 30 pieces are identifiable in various repositories today. Rhenanus, a competent historian, critic, and philologist, was associated with the great Basel printers Amerbach and Froben (Erasmus's intimate) and had a collection of over 900 volumes, which he willed to his native city. Neglected for centuries, it finally was given a suitable home in 1889.

Ulrich von Hutten (1488–1523), famous for his participation in the second part of the *Epistolae obscurorum vivorum* (1515–1517) in defense of Reuchlin's cause, led too turbulent and itinerant a life to have gathered a substantial library.[109,110] Yet he did have a collection probably useful at least for reference. It was with his friend Franz von Sickingen on the Ebernburg when the latter fell at the end of the Knight's War in 1523 and was captured and sold in Heidelberg by the imperial forces. Most curious about Hutten's bibliological interests is the rather strong evidence that he stole books from Fulda.[111,112]

In Münster, the canon Rudolf von Langen (ca. 1438–1519) had traveled in Italy in 1466 and most probably acquired books.[113] The cathedral library received them as a legacy, but virtually all were destroyed in the Anabaptist disturbances of 1534. More important was a protégé of Langen and a friend of Hutten and Reuchlin, Hermann von dem Busche, or Pasiphilus (1468–1534), best known for his *Vallum humanitatis* (1518). Langen urged him to travel in Italy, and he was later at various German universities, always defending Lutheran principles. He collected a small but choice library, which he willed to the Münster Cathedral; but a friend, Rotger Schmising, himself the master of a library, took the books to protect them from the violence of the Anabaptists. The latter carried out his friend's wishes and willed them to the cathedral upon his death in 1547. Most passed, about 1589, to the Jesuits, whose library became the basis of the University of Münster Library. Some 20 books, mostly Venetian editions of Greek and Roman authors, have been identified as Busche's original property.

The greatest of the German humanists, Johannes Reuchlin (1455–1522), was also one of the most zealous book collectors of his age.[114–119] He began to collect books as a student in Paris under his famous master, Johannes Heynlin vom Stein,[f] and he constantly acquired books during his Italian trips of 1482, 1490, and 1498. He knew Aldus Manutius and corresponded with him about book acquisitions. Latin, Greek, and Hebrew books fell

within the scope of his interest. Active in a troubled era and the central figure of all sorts of political issues and controversies about church policy, Reuchlin left an enduring legacy to subsequent ages in his dedication to seeking historical accuracy through sound texts. When the converted Jew Johann Pfefferkorn proposed the destruction of all books in Hebrew, Reuchlin replied that only books that were antagonistic to Christendom should be removed from the shelves, and that the Jews should be compelled to furnish books for the universities and set up chairs of Hebrew in all of them. Reuchlin was vigorously supported by the humanists, above all in the *Epistolae obscurorum vivorum* (supra; first part most probably largely by Crotus Rubianus and the second most probably largely by Ulrich von Hutten), a satire in purposely bad Latin reinforcing the *Epistolae clarorum vivorum* (1514) issued by Reuchlin's friends. Toward the end of his life, he encountered grave problems about the disposition of his books. The larger part of his collection went first to the church in Pforzheim and ultimately to the Landesbibliothek in Karlsruhe, but there are also a few in other major libraries of western Europe.[5,121,122]

Desiderius Erasmus (1466 or 1469–1536) was the most influential of the humanists, north or south; and it was inevitable that his prestige, his intimacy with Aldus Manutius, his position as an authoritative consultant of Johannes Froben, and his stature in the world of learning resulted in a major private collection.[g] In the years 1524–1526, a young Polish nobleman, Johannes Laski, lived with Erasmus in Basel. The latter, feeling the need of funds to live in the style he desired, sold his books to Laski on the condition that he keep them and have the use of them in his lifetime. At the time of Erasmus's death, there was a sketchy checklist of 413 titles. The new owner, who had held a high position in the church in his native Poland, forsook his old faith in 1538 and dedicated himself to promotion of Protestantism in North Germany, Denmark, the Low Countries, and England. He sold the books piecemeal, and today only 15 can be identified, scattered from England to Cracow.

REFORMATION LIBRARIES

A major emphasis of the Reformation leaders—above all, of Luther himself and of Philipp Melanchthon (1497–1560), the "Preceptor Germaniae" and great-nephew of Reuchlin—was on the utility of books and libraries for the new faith and for popular culture in general.[5,129,130] An immediate result was the incorporation of policies for church libraries in the organizational documents of individual congregations. The oldest (1528) and one of the most important policy statements is that of Johannes

---

[f]Heynlin died in the Carthusian monastery in Basel and left his collection to this institution. The books have been in the University of Basel Library since the Reformation. See Heusler.[120]

[g]Of the voluminous Erasmus literature, one might start with Bömer[5] and Smith[123]–ter Horst.[128]

Bugenhagen for the church of Saint Andreas in Braunschweig, but the collection of 336 volumes willed to the church in 1495 by Gerwin von Hameln was reported in 1587 to have been sadly neglected.[131,132] Bugenhagen drew up similar policy statements for churches in Hamburg, Lübeck, and his native Pommerania, where he visited all libraries and archives in the province on the order of Duke Bogislaus X. We know something about at least nine newly founded church libraries at Melanchton's death in 1560.

The libraries depended on gifts and secularization of Roman establishments for their growth. Just as in England, they would have been vastly richer had not biblioclasm accompanied the dissolution of monasteries. A ducal order in Pommerania in 1552 directed that unsuitable (i.e., "popish") books from monasteries be sold for scrap. More serious was the violence in the Peasants' War of 1524–1526.[133] In Thuringia alone, 70 monasteries and their contents were destroyed, and reports from other places are staggering. Libraries of secular nobility and high church officials also suffered.

Luther's insistence on the development of education resulted in a number of new schools with libraries. Some 40 such institutions, which had libraries, survived into the twentieth century, and one might guess that in the sixteenth century, there were probably as many more for which we have no firm evidence of the presence of libraries. Even more significant was the effect of the Reformation on the universities, both the older ones and those founded at this time (Marburg, Königsberg, and Jena).

In Leipzig, there was no general university library, only faculty collections, until 1543.[134] Thanks to the secularization of three monasteries in Leipzig and seven others in Saxony, the university library was enriched by about 1,500 manuscripts and 4,000 printed books. The real founder of the library, Kaspar Börner, left his collection to it upon his death in 1547. Melanchthon's friend Joachim Camerarius was librarian until his death in 1574. After 1550, the library was open for two hours every week.

In Basel, the puny university library received a major impulse forward in 1535 when the rector, Bonifatius Amerbach, persuaded all shops in this major center of printing to deliver one copy of each book to the university.[120] In 1559, the university acquired the holdings of the Dominican monastery and of the cathedral. The catalog of Heinrich Pantaleon, the librarian, shows a *bibliotheca antiqua* (to 1583: 150 manuscripts and 243 printed books) and *bibliotheca nova* (810 volumes, excluding 190 works donated by Professor Martin Borrhus in 1564).

In Tübingen, there was provision for a library, in 1477, when the university was founded.[135,136] There were faculty libraries and also a Bibliotheca Publica as early as 1501, but the latter was most likely destroyed with the burning of the *Sapienzhaus*. It was just about the same time that the Reformation reached Tübingen, and a new general library was put together and housed in a recently constructed university building, where it remained until 1819.

Elector Frederick ("the Wise"; 1486–1525) founded the University of Wittenberg in 1502, where humanism was welcomed from the beginning; and, in less than two decades, the Reformation was to find there an intellectual stronghold.[137–139] The first sure evidence of the founding of a library at Wittenberg is from December 1512 when the elector wrote to Aldus Manutius asking him for a list of available titles, most probably on the advice of his secretary, the humanist and reformer Georg Spalatin (born Burckhardt; 1484–1545). A catalog of Spalatin's personal library in the Gotha Landesbibliothek also contains invoices for other books purchased on behalf of the elector. Under Elector John Frederick ("the Magnanimous"; 1532–1547), Spalatin again became librarian and had an annual appropriation of 100 guilders after 1534. We know a good deal about Spalatin's administration of the Electoral Library,[140] and we know that the library served the faculty and that Luther and Melanchthon used it.[141] Some pieces from Luther's personal library can be identified,[142] but of Melanchthon's collection, we know only a volume in the Halle University Library and perhaps one in the Vatican.[143]

Margrave Phillip I ("the Generous"; 1509–1567) of Hessia founded the University of Marburg in 1527, and its library was established on the basis of secularized monasteries.[144] About 1532, the library was moved from the castle to the Discalced monastery, but it grew slowly despite a regular appropriation. We know a good deal about the administration of the library. Medieval traditions (e.g., chaining of books in the 1564 regulations) persisted. The professor of logic, Heidericus Theophilus Leonicerus, supervised the library from 1564 to 1581, and he prepared a catalog (not preserved) in 1578. The collections were increased substantially in 1605 with about 650 volumes from the collection of Count Christoph Ernest zu Diez, but the library did not thrive for two centuries, what with the division of holdings with Giessen in 1650. A major impulse forward came in 1748 when Marburg acquired the collection of the lawyer Johann Georg Estor.

Elector John Frederick I of Saxony ("the Magnanimous") was finally defeated in the Schmalkaldic War at Mühlberg in 1547, and the gymnasium founded at Jena in 1548 received his library, the "Electoralis." A decade later, the school became the University of Jena.[145–147] The "Electoralis" was extraordinarily rich in manuscripts and printed books, altogether about 3,100 pieces, relating to the Reformation, and it remains today one of the major resources for the study of the origin and early development of Lutheranism.

There was a library in the University of Heidelberg soon after its founding in 1386,[148] but it was the incomparable Palatina that served the university for three-quarters of a century until it was sent to Rome by Duke Maximilian of Bavaria (supra).[149-151] It was actually founded by Elector Philipp ("the Honest"; 1476–1508), patron of Chancellor Johann von Dalberg (supra), but it was developed by Ottheinrich (1502–1559; elector 1556–1559). He not only promoted the Reformation vigorously but also had the laudable ambition to develop a library comparable to those of the Italian Renaissance princes. He purchased books from all over Europe, incorporated into his collection that of the famous old monastery at Lorsch, and conveniently forgot to return manuscripts borrowed from the Mainz Cathedral. The library from his seat at Neuburg and the Electoral Library were housed with a collection in the Church of the Holy Spirit, and it is clear from various sources that Ottheinrich meant for the collection to be used by the members of the university along with other books that had been at their disposal. One of the most noteworthy additions came to the library in 1584 upon the death of Ulrich Fugger, the only Protestant in this distinguished Augsburg patrician family. He left his collection to the Palatina in gratitude for the hospitality of Elector Frederick III (1553–1576). As we have noted in connection with the Vatican Library, the catastrophe came in 1622 when Tilly directed the greatest bibliological loot in history. Except for the partial restoration of 1816, the modern University of Heidelberg Library dates from 1706.

The situation was somewhat similar in Königsberg, where there was a court library (Schlossbibliothek) available to the university and also a university library.[152,153] The last grand master of the Teutonic Order, Albrecht von Brandenburg, became a Protestant in 1525 and made the old lands of the order a hereditary duchy of Prussia. He soon began to acquire books with Lukas Cranach and his own secretary, Crotus Rubianus (supra), as his agents. After Crotus left Königsberg, a Dutchman, the ex-Carthusian Felix König, became Albrecht's librarian and conducted his office vigorously,[154] as did Heinrich Zell, librarian from 1557 to 1564. Over the years, the library was reasonably well cataloged and available to scholars. When Albrecht founded the university in 1544 he provided it with its own library, and ultimately, in 1827, the Schlossbibliothek and the University Library were combined as the Königliche (Staats-) und Universitätsbibliothek, a great library, which disappeared in 1945. Albrecht had his private collection, famous for the 20 volumes of his "Silver Library" books bound in finely wrought silver covers, most executed in Königsberg, as were the more conventional bindings.[155,156]

There were princely libraries elsewhere in Germany (notably in Dresden, Wolfenbüttel, Dessau, and Kassel) that were significant into our own times, but these generally pushed beyond the immediate objectives of Renaissance and Reformation. In Switzerland, the university libraries in Bern, Lausanne, and Geneva (originally based in part on Calvin's collection) have roots in the Reformation. A particularly noteworthy monument of the period is the collection of Joachim von Watt, or Vadianus (1483 or 1484–1551; supra), humanist and reformer of Saint Gall, now in the local municipal library (Stadtbibliothek).[157-159]

CONCLUSION

Perhaps with the founding of the University of Leiden in 1575, Renaissance, humanism, and Reformation had run their destined courses, and libraries began to serve scholars in a gradually evolving tradition of analytical scholarship with meticulous attention to detail. The resources had been provided by the great collectors of the previous two centuries; the methods and standards, by scholars with the insight and discipline of Erasmus and Reuchlin.

REFERENCES

1. Burckhardt, J. *Die Cultur der Renaissance in Italien: Ein Versuch*; von Ludwig Geiger, D.A., Ed.; E.A. Seemann: Leipzig, 1899; Vol. 7, 2 vols. (translated by S.G.C. Middlemore, The Civilization of the Renaissance in Italy, Allen and Unwin, London, 1937).
2. Symonds, J.A. *Renaissance in Italy*; Modern Library: New York, 1935; 22 vols. Both works have appeared in other editions.
3. Bracciolini, P. Opera. In *Strassburg*; Preface, 1513.
4. Mohler, L. *Kardinal Bessarion als Theologe, Humanist und Staatsmann*; Quellen und Forschungen aus dem Gebiete der Geschichte, 20, 22, and 24; F. Schoningh: Paderborn, 1923–1942; Vol. 1, 408–415, 3 vols.
5. Bömer, A. Von der Renaissance bis zum Beginn der Aufklärung. In *Handbuch der Bibliothekswissenschaft*; 2nd Ed.; Leyh, G., Ed.; Otto Harrassowitz: Wiesbaden, 1952–1957; Vol. 3, 502–503. Revised by Hans Widmann; 3 vols.; Part 1; 269, 499–584; The motivations and the genius of Italian Renaissance book collectors are effectively summarized.
6. Bogeng, G.A.E *Die grossen Bibliophilen: Geschichte der Büchersammler und ihrer Sammlungen*; E.A. Seemann: Leipzig, 1922; Vol. 1, 39–86. 3 vols.; covering Italy; 93, 94, 135, 234, 237; Celtis's personal collection went to the Hofbibliothek at his death.
7. Ullman, B.L. Petrarch's favorite books. Trans. Proc. Am. Philol. Assoc. **1923**, *54*, 25–38.
8. Tatham, E.H.R. The library of petrarch. Fort. Rev. **1908**, *79*, 1056–1067. n.s.
9. Morf, H. Die Bibliothek Petrarcas. In *Aus Dichtung und Sprache der Romanen*; K.J. Trübner: Strassburg, 1903–1922; Vol. 1, 172–184. 3 vols.
10. Schneider, K. Die bibliothek petrarcas und ihre schicksale. Z. Bücherfreunde **1909/1910**, *1*, 157–160. n.s.
11. Eppelsheimer, H.W. Petrarca und seine bücher. Jahrb. Dtsch. Bibliophilen **1925–1926**, *12/13*, 9–16.

12. Arrigoni, L. *Notice Historique et Bibliographique sur Vingt-cinq Manuscrits ... Ayant Fait Partie de François Pétrarque*; Firenze, Tipografia dell'arte della stampa: Milan, 1883.

13. de Nolhac, P. *Petrarch and the Ancient World*; Merrymount Press: Boston, 1907, Part 2, "Petrarch's Library."

14. Hecker, O. Die schicksale der bibliothek boccaccios. Z. Bücherfreunde **1897–1898**, *1*, 183–186.

15. *Boccaccio-Funde, Stücke aus der Bislang Verschollenen Bibliothek des Dichters*; G. Westermann: Braunschweig, 1902.

16. Rostagno, E. La libreria del boccaccio. Riv. Bibl. **1905**, *14*, 93–94.

17. Bloch, H. A manuscript of Tacitus' Agricola. Classical Philol. **1941**, *36*, 183–187.

18. Pralle, L. *Die Wiederentdeckung des Tacitus: Ein Beitrag zur Geistesgeschichte Fuldas und zur Biographie des jungen Cusanus*; Quellen und Abhandlungen zur Geschichte der Abtei und der Diözese Fulda; Verlag Parzeller: Fulda, 1952; Vol. 17.

19. Goldmann, A. Drei italienische handschriftenkataloge. Zent. Bl. Bibl. Wes. **1887**, *4*, 137–155.

20. von Martin, A.W.O. *Coluccio Salutati und das Humanistische Lebensideal*; Beiträge zur Kulturgeschichte des Mittelalters und der Renaissance, No. 23; B. G. Teubner: Leipzig, 1916.

21. Ullmann, B.L. *The Humanism of Coluccio Salutati*; Medievo e Umanesimo, Editrice Antenore: Padua, 1963; Vol. 4.

22. Petrucci, A. *Coluccio Salutati*; Bibliotheca Biographica, No. 7, Istituto della Enciclopedia Italiana: Rome, 1972.

23. Blum, R. *La Biblioteca della Badia Fiorentina e i codici di Antonio Corbinelli*; Studi e Testi, Biblioteca Apostolica Vaticana: The Vatican, 1951; Vol. 155.

24. Walser, E. *Poggius Florentinus, Leben und Werke*; Beiträge zur Kultur des Mittelalters und der Renaissance, No. 14, B. G. Teubner: Leipzig, 1914.

25. Castelnau, A. *Les Médicis*; Calmann Lévy: Paris, 1879, 2 vols.

26. Young, G.F. *The Medici*; J. Murray: London, 1909, 2 vols.

27. Collison-Morley, L. *The Early Medici*; G. Routledge: London, 1935.

28. Schevill, F. *The Medici*; Harcourt: Brace, New York, 1949.

29. Bizzari, E. *Il Magnifico Lorenzo*; Mondadori: Milan, 1950.

30. Acton, H.M.M. *The Last Medici*, rev. ed.; St. Martin's Press: New York, 1959.

31. Kristaller, P.O. *The Philosopy Marsilio Ficino*; Columbia Studies in Philosophy; Columbia University Press: New York, 1943; 6.

32. Zippel, G. *Niccolò Niccoli, Contributo alla Storia Dell' Umanesimo*; Florence, 1890.

33. Macina, L.G. *La vita e l'opera di Lorenzo il Magnifico*; Felice Le Monnier: Florence, 1927(Luigi di San Giusto, pseud.).

34. Palmarocchi, R. *Lorenzo de' Medici*, Grandi Italiani, Collana di Biografie; Unione Tipografico-Editrice Torinese: Turin, 1941; 5.

35. Müller, K.K. Neue mittheilungen über janos laskaris und die mediceische bibliothek. Zent.Bl. Bibl.Wes. **1884**, *1*, 333–412.

36. von Stegmann, C.M.; von Geymüller, H. *Die Architektur der Renaissance in Toscana*; F. Bruckmann: Munich, 1885–1908; Vol. 2, 11 vols., passim.

37. Mercati, G. *Per la Cronologia Della Vita e Degli Scritti di Niccolò Perotti, Arcivesco di Siponta*; Studi e Testi, Biblioteca Apostolica Vaticana: Rome, 1925; 44.

38. Sabbadini, R. *Biografia Documentata di Giovanni Aurispa*; F. Zammit: Noto, 1890.

39. *Carteggio di Giovanni Ausripa*; Fonti Per la Storia d'Italia: Epistolari, Secolo XV, Tipografia del Senato: Rome, 1931; Vol. 70.

40. Calderini, A. Ricerche intorno alla biblioteca e alla cultura greca di Francesco Filelfo. Studi ital. filol. clas. **1913**, *20*, 204.

41. Omont, H.A. Inventaire des manuscrits grecs et latines donnés à Saint Marc de Vanise par le Cardinal Bessarion en 1468. Kvtu. Szle **1894**, *4*, 129–187.

42. Lorenzetti, G. La libreria sansoviniana di venezia. Accad. Bibl. **1929**, *2*, 75–98.

43. Lorenzetti, G. La libreria sansoviniana di venezia. Accad. Bibl. (**1929–1930**), *3*, 22–36.

44. Pittoni, L. *La Libreria di San Marco, cenni storici*; Tipo-lito di G. Flori: Pistoia, 1903.

45. d'Adda, G. *Indagini Storiche, Artistiche e Bibliografiche Sulla Libreria Visconteo-Sforzesca del Castello di Pavia, I*; G. Brigola: Milan, 1875, Appendice, 1879.

46. Schmidt, O.E. Die visconti und ihre bibliothek zu pavia. Z. Gesch. Polit. **1888**, *5*, 444.

47. Capelli, A. La biblioteca estense nella prima metà del secolo XV. G. Stor. Lett. Ital. **1889**, *14*, 1–30.

48. Bertoni, G. *La Biblioteca Estense e la Coltura Ferrarese ai Tempi del Duca Ercole I (1471–1505)*; E. Loescher: Turin, 1903.

49. Fava, D. *La Biblioteca Estense nel suo Sviluppo Storico*; G. T. Vincenzi e Nipoti di D. Cavallotti: Modena, 1925.

50. Fumagalli, G. *L'arte della Legatura alle Corte Degli Estensi a Ferrara e a Modena dal Secolo XV al XIX, col Catalogo delle Legature Pregevoli della Biblioteca Estense di Modena*; Tammaro de Marinis: Florence, 1913.

51. Mazzatinti, G. *La Biblioteca dei re d'Aragona in Napoli*; L. Capelli: Rocca S. Casciano, 1897.

52. de Marinis, T. *Per la Storia della Biblioteca Dei re d'Aragona in Napoli*; Stab. tip. Aldino: Florence, 1909.

53. *La biblioteca Napoletana dei re d'Aragona*; Hoepi: Milan, 1947–1952, 4 vols.

54. Omont, H.A. Inventaire de la bibliothèque de Ferdinand I d'Aragone, roi de naples (1418). Bibl. Ec. Chartes **1909**, *70*, 456–470.

55. Stornajolo, C. *Codices Urbanates graeci Bibliothecae Vaticanae I*; Ex Typograpeo Vaticano: Rome, 1895, containing a substantial proportion of the original collection.

56. Bombe, W. La biblioteca di Federigo da Montefeltro. Rass. Marchig. **1929–1930**, *8*, 235–246.

57. Guasti, C. Inventario della libreria urbinate compilato nel secolo XV da Federigo veterano. G. Stor. Arch. Toscani **1862**, *6*, 134–147.

58. Guasti, C. Inventario della libreria urbinate compilato nel secolo XV da Federigo veterano. G. Stor. Arch. Toscani **1863**, 745–55, 130–154.

59. Girotta, P. La biblioteca di Francesco Gonzaga secondo l'inventario del 1407. Atti Mem. Accad. Virgiliana di Mantova **1921–1923**, *14–16*, 60–72. n.s.

60. Müntz, E.; Fabre, P. *La Bibliothèque du Vatican au xve siècle, d'après des documents inèdits*; Bibliothèque des Ècoles Françaises d'Athènes et de Rome; E. Thorin: Paris, 1887; 48.

61. Pastor, L. *Geschichte der Päpste seit dem Ausgang des Mittelalters*; Herder: Freiburg im Breisgau, 1866–1938; Vol. 1, 562–570, 21 vols.

62. Lucchesi, A. Der buchhändler des cosimo de' Medici: Aus den erinnerungen des vespasino da bisticci. Philobiblon **1939**, *11*, 292–305.

63. Sforza, G. *La Patria, la Famiglia e la Giovinezza di Papa Niccolò v, Ricerche Storiche*; Giusti: Lucca, 1884; 359–384.

64. Hartlich, O. Giovanni Andrea dei Bussi, der erste bibliothekar der Vaticana. Philologische Wochenschrift **1939**, *59*, 327–336, 364–368, 395–399.

65. Haebler, K. *Die Deutschen Buchdrucker des XV. Jahrhunderts im Auslande*; J. Rosenthal: Munich, 1924; 13.

66. Vallée, L. *La Bibliothèque Nationale: Choix de Documents Pour Servir à l'histoire de l'établissement et de ses Collections*; É. Terquem: Paris, 1894.

67. Franklin, A. *Précis de l'histoire de la Bibliothèque du Roi*, 2nd Ed.; L. Willem: Paris, 1875.

68. Esdaile, A.J.K. *National Libraries of the World*; Grafton: London, 1934; 61–92.

69. Serrurier, C. *Bibliothèque de France*; M. Nijhoff: La Haye, 1946.

70. Bauchart, E.Q. *La Bibliothèque de Fontainebleau et les Livres des Derniers Valois à la Bibliothèque Nationale (1551–1589)*; L. Huard et Guillemin: Paris, 1891.

71. Lhuillier, T. *La Bibli-othèque et les Bibliothécaires du Château de Fontainebleau*; Meaux, 1878.

72. Michelant, H.V. *Catalogue de la Bibliothèque de François Ier à Blois en 1518*; Frank: Paris, 1863.

73. Omont, H.A. *Catalogues des Manuscrits Grecs de Fontainebleau sous François Ier et Henri II*; Imprimerie Nationale: Paris, 1889.

74. Hamel, F. The libraries of the royal library at Fontainebleau. Library **1903**, *3* (Ser. 1), 190–199.

75. Lamaître, H. *Histoire du Dépôt Légal: I. France*; A. Picard et fils: Paris, 1910.

76. Le Roux de Lincy, A.J.V. *Notice sur la Bibliothèque de Cathérine de Médicis Avec des Extraits de l'inventaire de Cette Bibliothèque*; Extrait du Bulletin du Bibliophile, Mai 1858, 13e Serie, J. Techener: Paris, 1858.

77. Thompson, L.S. Private Libraries. In *Encyclopedia of Library and Information Science*; Kent, A.; Lancour, H., Daily, J.E., Eds.; Dekker: New York, 1978; Vol. 24, 125–192. The history of many of the great libraries of our time is inextricably tied to the story of great private collections of the Renaissance.

78. Gulyás, P. *Matyás Király Könyvtára*; Franklin-társulat: Budapest, 1916.

79. de Hevesy, A. *La Bibliothèque du roi Matthias Corvinus*; Pour les membres de la Société Française de Reproductions de Manuscrits à Peintures: Paris, 1923.

80. Karl, L. Le roi Matthias de Hunyad, mécène et bibliophile. La Bibliofilia **1934**, *36*, 370–382.

81. Weinberger, W. *Beiträge zur Handschriftenkunde: I. Die Biblioteca Corvina*; Sitzungsberichte der Akademie der Wissenschaften in Wien, Philosophisch-historische Klasse, 159, 1908, Abh. 6, A; Hölder: Vienna, 1908.

82. Fitz, J.; Zolnai, K. *Bibliographia Bibliothecae Regis Mathiae Corvini*; Az Orszáagos Széchényi Könyvtar Kiadvanyai, No. 10, Budapest, 1942.

83. Löffler, K.; Ruf, P. Allgemeine Handschriftenkunde. In *Handbuch der Bibliothekswissenschaft*; Leyh, G., Ed.; Refs. [5,6], Vol. 1, 120–123, provides an adequate résumé of the dissipation of the Corviniana and present whereabouts of the pitiful remnants.

84. Barycz, H.K. *Historja Uniwersitetu Jagiellońskiego w epoce humanizmu*; Nakl. Uniwersytetu Jagiellońskiego: Krakow, 1935; 659–712.

85. Duff, E.G. The bindings of Thomas Wotton. Library **1910**, *1* (3rd ser.), 337–350.

86. Harrisse, H. *Grandeur et Décadence de la Colombine*, 2nd Ed.; Chez Tous les Marchands de Nouveautés, Paris; Impr. Protat Frères: Macon, 1885. The Colombina issued a Catálogo de sus libros impresos, bajo la inmediata dirección de su bibliotecario Servando Arboli y Faraudo, con notas bibliográficas del Dr. D. Simón de la Rosa y López, Impr. de E. Rasco, Seville, 1888–1948, 7 vols. See also Catalogue of the Library of Ferdinand Columbus: Reproduced in Facsimile from the Unique Manuscript in the Columbine Library of Seville, Archer M. Huntington, New York, 1905.

87. Antolin, G. *La Real Biblioteca de El Escorial*; Impr. del Real Monasterio del Escorial: Escorial, 1921. A number of catalogs of the Escorial manuscripts have been printed, notably the Latin (1910–1916), Greek (1936), Spanish (1924–1929), Catalan (1932), and French and Provençal (1933), all recorded and described under Escorial, Biblioteca, in the National Union Catalog.

88. Buyken, T. *Enea Silvio Piccolomini: Sein Leben und Werden bis zum Episkopat*; L. Röhrscheid: Bonn, 1931 (part of a Cologne dissertation).

89. Volkmann-Schluck, K.H. *Nicolaus Cusanus: Die Philosophie im Übergang vom Mittelalter zur Neuzeit*; V. Klostermann: Frankfurt am Main, 1957.

90. Meuthen, E. *Die Letzten Jahre des Nikolaus von Kues*; Wissenschaftliche Abhandlungen der Arbeitsgemeinschaft für Forschung des Landes Nordrhein-Westfalen; Westdeutscher Verlag: Cologne, 1958; 3.

91. Rotta, P. La biblioteca del cusano. Riv. Filos. Neo-scolast. **1927**, *19*, 22–47.

92. Herrmann, M. *Albrecht von Eyb und die Frühzeit des Deutschen Humanismus*; Weidmann: Berlin, 1893.

93. Thompson, L.S. German translations of the classics between 1450 and 1550. J. Engl. Ger. Philol. **1943**, *42*, 343–363.

94. Schottenloher, K. Hartmann schedel (1440–1514): Ein gedenkblatt zum 400. [i.e., 500] geburtstag des nürnberger humanisten. Philobiblon **1940**, *12*, 279–291.

95. Stauber, R. *Die Schedelsche Bibliothek* Hrsg. von Otto Hartig, Studien und Darstellungen aus dem Gebiete der Geschichte; Herder: Freiburg im Breisgau, 1908; 6, Heft 2–3.

96. Morneweg, K. *Johann von Dalberg, ein Deutscher Humanist und Bischof*; C. Winter: Heidelberg, 1887.

97. Ulmann, H. *Kaiser Maximilian I auf Urkundlicher Grundlage Dargestellt*; J. G. Cotta: Stuttgart, 1884–1891, 2 vols.

98. Gottlieb, T. *Die Büchersammlung Kaiser Maximilian I: Miteiner Einleitung über Älteren Bücherbesitz im Hause*

Habsburg; Die Ambraser Handschriften, Beitrag Geschichte der Wiener Hofbibliothek; M. Spirgatis: Leipzig, 1900; 1.

99. Miller, K. *Die Konrad Peutinger'sche Tafel order Weltkarte des Castorius*, 2nd Ed.; Strecker und Schröder: Stuttgart, 1929.

100. König, E. *Peutingerstudien*; Studien und Darstellungen aus dem Gebiete der Geschichte, Herder: Freiburg im Breisgau, 1914; 9. Heft 1–2.

101. Reicke, E. *Willibald Pirckheimer: Leben, Familie und Persönlichkeit, Deutsche Volkheit*; E. Diederichs: Jena, 1930; 75.

102. Offenbacher, E. La bibliothéque de Willibald Pirckheimer. La Bibliofilia **1938**, *40*, 241–265.

103. Knepper, J. *Jakob Wimpheling (1450–1528): Sein Leben und seine Werke*; Erläuterungen und Ergänzungen zu Janssens Geschichte des Deutschen Volkes, Herder: Freiburg im Breisgau, 1902; 3. Heft 2–4.

104. Newald, R. *Elsässische Charakterköpfe aus dem Zeitalter des Humanismus*; Alsatia Verlag: Kolmar, 1944.

105. Knod, G.C. *Aus der Bibliothek des Beatus Rhenanus: Ein Beitrag zur Geschichte des Humanismus*; O. Harrassowitz: Leipzig, 1889.

106. Schneegans, W. *Abt Johannes Trithemius und das Kloster Sponheim*; R. Schmithals: Kreuznanch, 1882.

107. Fischer, J. Der nachlass des abtes Johannes Tritheims. Arch. Hist. Ver. Unterfrank. **1928**, *67*, 41.

108. Lehmann, P. *Johannes Sichardus und die von ihm Benutzten Bibliotheken und Handschriften*; Quellen und Untersuchungen zur Lateinischen Philologie des Mittelalters; C. H. Beck: Munich, 1911; 4, 176–179. Heft 1; This latter work deals with Johannes Sichardus (1499–1552), who studied church and monastic libraries; in 1526–1530 he published 24 different texts he found in Fulda and Lorsch.

109. Strauss, D.F. *Ulrich von Hutten: His Life and Times*; Daldy, Isbister, and Company: London, 1874.

110. Benzing, J. Ulrich von Hutten und seine Drucker. In *Beiträge zum Buch- und Bibliothekswesen*; O. Harrassowitz: Wiesbaden, 1956; 6.

111. Clemen, O. Ulrich von hutten—ein bücherdieb? Arch. Reformationschich. **1926**, *23*, 150–155.

112. Kalkoff, P. Huttens Bücherraub. Arch. Reformationschich. **1926**, *23*, 300–306.

113. Detmer, H. Zur geschichte der münsterschen dombibliothek. Westdeutsche Zeitschrift **1895**, *14*, 203–229.

114. Burger, H.O. *Renaissance, Humanismus, Reformation: Deutsche Literatur im Europäischen Kontext*; Frankfurter Beiträge zur Germanistik; Gehlen: Bad Homburg, 1969; 7.

115. Brod, M. *Johannes Reuchlin und sein Kampf*; Kohlhammer: Stuttgar, 1965.

116. Secret, F. *Les Kabbalistes Chrétiens de la Renaissance*; Collection Sigma; Dunod: Paris, 1964; 5.

117. Reuchlin, J. Briefwechsel. In *Hrsg. von Ludwig Geiger, Bibliothek des Litterarischen Vereins in Stuttgart, No. 126*; Litterarischer Verien in Stuttgart: Tübingen, 1875 (reprinted, Olms, Hildesheim, 1962).

118. *Festschrift der Stadt Pforzheim zur Erinnerung an den 400. Todestag Johannes Reuchlins*; Sonderdruck aus der Zeitschrift für die Geschichte des Oberrheins; O. Riecker: Pforzheim, 1922; 37. n.s. Heft 3.

119. Willms, J. *Bürcherfreunde, Büchernarren, Entwurf zur Archäogie einer Leidenschaft*; Eine Deutsche Humannistenbibliothek—Die Bibiliotheca Reuchliniana; Harrassowitz: Wiesbaden, 1978; 61–77.

120. Heusler, A. *Geschichte der öffentlichen Bibliothek der Universität Basel*; Universitätsbuchdruckerei von F. Reinart: Basel, 1896. (1834–1921).

121. Brambach, W. *Die Grossherzogliche Hof- und Landesbibliothek in Karlsruhe*; A Spaarmann: Oberhausen, 1875.

122. Christ, K. *Die Bibliothek Reuchlins in Pforzheim*; Beiheft zum Zentralblatt für Bibliothekswesen; O. Harrassowitz: Leipzig, 1924; 52.

123. Smith, P. *Erasmus: A Study of His Life, Ideals, and Place in History*; Harper: New York, 1923.

124. Oelrich, K.H. *Der Späte Erasmus und die Reformation*, Reformationsgeschichtliche Studien und Texte; Aschendorf: Münsterfs, 1961; 86.

125. Kohls, E.W. Die Theologie des Erasmus Theologische Zeitschrift, "Sonderband," No. 1; F. Reinhardt: Basel, 1966. 2 vols.

126. *Opus Epistularum Desiderii Erasmi*; Allen, P.S., Ed.; Typographeo Clarendoniano: Oxonii, 1906–1947, 12 vols.

127. Husner, F. Die Bibliothek des Erasmus. In *Gedenkschrift zum 400. Todestage des Erasmus von Rotterdam*; Braus-Riggenbach: Basel, 1936; 228–259.

128. ter Horst, J.H. Nog enkele aanteeningen over de bibliotheek van Erasmus. Het Boek **1937**, *24*, 229.

129. Radlach, O. *Bibliothekswesen*, 3rd Ed.Realencyklopä-die für Protestantische Theologie und Kirche; Hinrichs: Leipzig, 1896–1913; Vol. 3, 187–192, 24 vols.

130. Kohfeldt, G. Zur geschichte der büchersammlungen und des bücherbesitzes in Deutschland. Z. Kulturgeschichte **1900**, *7*, 354–375.

131. Hering, H. Doctor Pomeranus, Johannes Bugenhagen. In *Schriften des Vereins für Reformationsgeschichte*; Verein fü Reformationsgeschichte: Halle, 1888; 6, Stück 1, Nr. 22.

132. Herbst, H. Die bibliothek der St. Andreaskirche zu Braunschweig. Zent.Bl. Bibl.Wes. **1941**, *58*, 301–338.

133. Schottenloher, K. Schicksale von Büchern und bibliotheken im bauernkrieg. Z. Bücherfreunde **1908–1909**, *11*, 396–408.

134. Friedberg, E.A. *Die Universität Leipzig in Vergangenheit und Gegenwart*; Veit and Company: Leipzig, 1898. 29; 54.

135. Klüpfel, K.A. *Die Universität Tübingen in ihrer Vergangenheit und Gegenwart*; Fues's Verlag [R. Reisland]: Leipzig, 1877.

136. Zoepf, L. Aus der geschichte der tübinger universitäts-biblithek (1477–1607). Zent.Bl. Bibl.Wes. **1935**, *52*, 471–485.

137. Steinmetz, M. Die Universität Wittenberg und der Humanismus (1502–1521). In *450 Jahre Martin Luther-Universität Halle-Wittenberg*; Martin Luther-Universität: Halle, 1952; Vol. 1, 103–109. 3 vols.

138. Weissenborn, B. Die Wittenberger Universitätsbibliothek (1547–1817). In *450 Jahre Martin Luther-Universität Halle-Wittenberg*; Martin Luther-Universität: Halle, 1952; Vol. 1, 355–376. 3 vols.

139. Hildebrandt, E. Die kurfürstliche schloss- und universi-tätsbibliothek zu Wittenberg 1512–1547: Beiträge zu ihrer Geschichte. Z. Büchherkunde **1925**, *2*, 34–42, 109–129, 157–188.

140. Buchwald, G. Zu spalatins reisen insbesondere nach Witten-berg in angelegenheit der kurfürstlichen bibliothek. Arch. Bibliographie, B- Bibliothekswesen **1928–1929**, *2*, 92.

141. Brandis, C.G. Luther und Melachthon als benutzer der Wittenberger bibliothek. Theol. Stud. Krit. **1917**, *90*, 206–221.

142. Luther, J. Review of Max Herrmann, ein feste burg ist unser gott. Zent.Bl. Bibl.Wes. **1906**, *23*, 128.

143. Göber, W. Aus melanchthons bibliothek. Zent.Bl. Bibl. Wes. **1928**, *45*, 297–302.

144. Zedler, G. *Geschichte der universitätsbibliothek zu Mar-burg von 1527–1887*; N. G. Elwert: Marburg, 1896.

145. Müller, K.K. Geschichte der universitätsbibliothek jena. Zent.Bl. Bibl.Wes. **1902**, *19*, 380–384.

146. Willkomm, B. Die bedeutung der jenaer universitätsbi-bliothek für die reformationsgeschichtliche forschung. Zent.Bl. Bibl.Wes. **1915**, *30*, 245–261.

147. Koch, H. Die 'electoralis'. Zent.Bl. Bibl.Wes. **1952**, *66*, 345–358.

148. Thompson, L.S. University Libraries, Medieval. In *Ency-clopedia of Library and Information Science*; Kent, A., Lancour, H., Daily, E., Eds.; Dekker: New York, 1981; Vol. 32, 169.

149. Wilken, F. *Geschichte de Bildung, Beraubung und Vernichtung der alten heidelbergischen Büchersammlungen: Ein Beitrag zur Literärgeschichte vornehmlich des fünfzehnten und Sechszehnten Jahrhunderts; Nebst Einem Meist Beschreibenden Verzeichnis der im Jahre 1816 von dem Pabst Pius VII. der Universität Heidelberg Zurückgegebenen Handschriften, und Einigen Schriftproben*; A. Oswald: Heidelberg, 1817.

150. Wille, J. Aus alter und neurer zeit der heidelberger bibliothek. Neue Heidelb. Jahrb. **1906**, *14*.

151. Schottenloher, K. *Pfalzgraf Ottheinrich und das Buch: Ein Beitrag zur Geschichte der Evangelischen Publizistik*; Reformationsgeschichtliche Studien und Texte, 50, 51; Aschendorf: Munster, 1927.

152. Kuhnert, E. *Die Königliche und Universitätsbibliothek zu Königsburg in Preussen*; Hartungsche Buchdruckerei: Königsberg, 1901.

153. *Geschichte der Staats- und Universitätsbibliothek zu Königsberg*; K.W. Hiersemann: Leipzig, 1926. Band 1, "Von ihrer Begründung bis zum Jahre 1810."

154. Förstemann, J. Felix König (Rex), erster bibliothekar des herzogs Albrecht von Preussen. Zent.Bl. Bibl.Wes. **1899**, *16*, 306–314.

155. Schwenke, P.; von Lange, K. *Die Silberbibliothek Herzog Albrechts von Preussen und Seiner Gemahlin Anna Maria*; K. W. Hiersemann: Leipzig, 1894.

156. Rohde, A. *Die Silberbibliothek des Herzogs Albrecht in Königsberg*; Bilderhefte des Deutschen Ostens; Gräfe und Unzer: Königsberg, 1928; 4.

157. Ruland, A. Die vadianische bibliothek in St. Gallen. Serapeum **1865**, *26*, 1–12, 17–23.

158. Näf, W. *Vadian und Seine Stadt St. Gallen: I. Bis 1518. Humanist in Wien*, Fehr'sche Buchhandlung: St. Gallen, 1944–1957. 2 vols.

159. *Vaiannische Analekten* Vadian-Studien: Untersuchungen und Texte; Fehr'sche Buchhandlung: St. Gallen, 1945; 1.

160. *Lexikon des Gesamten Buchwesens*, Löffler, K., Kirchner, J., Eds.; Hiersemann: Leipzig, 1935–1937, 3 vols. (New edition is in preparation).

Resource Description Framework (RDF)

Nicholas Gibbins
Nigel Shadbolt
School of Electronics and Computer Science, University of Southampton, Southampton, U.K.

Abstract

The Resource Description Framework (RDF) is the standard knowledge representation language for the Semantic Web, an evolution of the World Wide Web that aims to provide a well-founded infrastructure for publishing, sharing and querying structured data. This entry provides an introduction to RDF and its related vocabulary definition language RDF Schema, and explains its relationship with the OWL Web Ontology Language. Finally, it provides an overview of the historical development of RDF and related languages for Web metadata.

INTRODUCTION

The Resource Description Framework,[1] or RDF, is a knowledge representation language for the Semantic Web,[2,3] and is used to express knowledge about things both on and off the Web; RDF can be used to write metadata about web pages and to describe real-world objects with equal facility. RDF is a key language in the technical architecture of the Semantic Web, being both a format for describing instance data, and the foundation for the vocabulary definition languages RDF Schema[4] and OWL.[5]

The Semantic Web is a development of the World Wide Web that aims to provide an infrastructure for machine-understandable information on the Web. By expressing information in a form that makes the meaning, or semantics, accessible to machines, the goal of the Semantic Web is to create a next-generation Web in which information can be mediated by software agents on behalf of and without intervention from their users. At present, information on the World Wide Web is predominantly textual and requires human understanding to interpret it; the meaning of such natural language information must be made explicit if a machine is to be able to make sense of it. In artificial intelligence, the long-standing discipline of knowledge representation has developed a variety of approaches for expressing information to facilitate reasoning; these knowledge representation languages are of varying degrees of complexity and expressivity, but they share the common feature that they encode information as structures that can be formally interpreted to give some sense of their meaning.

By itself, RDF provides a domain-neutral framework for information interchange that must be augmented with terms to meet the requirements of a specific application domain. For example, a bibliographic application needs to be able to talk about works and authors, while an e-commerce application needs to be able to talk about orders and prices. This orientation to a particular application domain or domains is accomplished by means of one or more domain vocabularies, or *ontologies*.[6] In Computer Science, an ontology is a formal description of a domain of knowledge. Gruber[7] defines an ontology as "a specification of a conceptualization"; in other words, a formal account of an abstract model of some application domain which includes, but is not limited to, the classes of entity that exist within the domain, and the relations that link those entities.

RDF has two accompanying ontology languages, RDF Schema[4] and the Web Ontology Language OWL.[5] RDF Schema is the simpler of the two, and provides a small set of modeling constructs for defining classes, properties and certain global constraints on those properties. OWL is more expressive (and correspondingly more complex to reason with), and provides a larger set of modeling constructs that allows an ontology designer to more richly specify classes in terms of the necessary and sufficient conditions for membership of those classes. An in-depth treatment of OWL is beyond the scope of this entry; we refer the reader to[8,9] for further information.

In addition to these languages for defining RDF vocabularies, the World Wide Web Consortium (W3C) has also published an SQL-like query language for interrogating RDF graphs, known as the SPARQL Protocol and RDF Query Language[10,11] (or more simply as SPARQL).

THE TRIPLE MODEL

The information presented on the Semantic Web can be viewed as a directed, labeled graph in which the nodes stand for things and values, and the edges (with their labels) are the properties that relate nodes to one other.

Encyclopedia of Library and Information Sciences, Fourth Edition DOI: 10.1081/E-ELIS4-120043688

Regional–School

The fundamental unit of knowledge representation is the triple, a directed edge that represents a binary relationship between two nodes. Customarily, the components of this triple are referred to as the subject, the predicate and the object: the subject is the node that the directed edge leaves, the object is the node that it enters, and the predicate is the type of the edge. Alternatively, a triple could be considered to be a statement that a particular entity (the subject) has a property (the predicate) with a particular value (the object); this corresponds closely to object-oriented[12] or frame-based[13] models of knowledge representation.

The nodes in an RDF graph denote resources, which are things in the domain of discourse. Nodes may be Uniform Resource Identifiers (URIs),[14] literals, or blank nodes. URIs are used to denote things with identity, such as web pages, organizations, people, or books. Literals are values such as character strings, numbers or dates, which do not have identity; a (plain) literal is considered to denote itself, so two literals with the same value are treated as if they were the same literal. Finally, blank nodes are used to indicate the existence of a thing, without saying anything about the name of that thing.

With the careful use of URIs, RDF allows machines to unambiguously identify entities and vocabulary terms; each URI identifies a single thing, even though it is expected that there may be multiple URIs that identify the same thing (effectively synonyms for the thing). Adapting an example from the RDF Primer,[15] we can represent the statement (that a particular web page was created by John Smith) as a triple with:

- a subject, http://www.example.org/index.html
- a predicate, http://purl.org/dc/terms/creator
- and an object, http://www.example.org/staffid/85740

In this example, we refer to the web page using its URI: http://www.example.org/index.html. We also use URIs to refer to John Smith (http://www.example.org/staffed/85740), and to the creator relation (http://purl.org/dc/terms/creator), taken from the Dublin Core vocabulary.[16] Presented graphically, this statement forms a graph containing two nodes with a single directed edge between them, as shown in Fig. 1.

This triple can also be written as:

<http://www.example.org/index.html>   <http://purl.org/dc/terms/creator>   <http://www.example.org/staffid/85740>

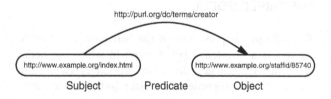

Fig. 1   An RDF graph containing a single triple.

This example uses a syntax based on the Notation 3 syntax for RDF[17] (discussed in more depth below), in which terms in angle brackets denote resources identified by URIs. In the order written, the three terms are the subject, predicate and object of the triple, and the completed triple is followed by a period.

COMPARING XML AND RDF

The relationship between RDF and the eXtensible Markup Language (XML)[18] warrants further explanation. Both are used to represent structured information on the Web, and XML is used as the standard syntax for RDF, but the two languages are distinct and have different characteristics.

The most fundamental difference between XML and RDF is in the way in which they structure information. As described above, RDF structures information as a labeled, directed graph, whereas XML is limited to tree structures, which has consequences in the way that data from different sources can be merged. Merging two RDF files can be accomplished by taking the union of the underlying graphs; this operation does not require any knowledge of the vocabularies (schemas) that are used in these graphs. In contrast, merging two XML files that use different schemas is a more difficult operation, because the resulting file will not validate using either schema, but rather a new schema that combines the two original schemas must be used instead.

An XML document can be parsed to give an unambiguous structure, but this structure has no innate meaning; the meanings of XML schemas must be agreed between the relevant parties on a case-by-case basis. RDF differs from XML in that the triples that are created when an RDF file is parsed have a well-defined semantics, which facilitates further information exchange by providing a basic set of rules for manipulating the information while preserving its knowledge content. Together with the ease of merging RDF files, these formal semantics mean that RDF has considerable advantages for information interchange over XML, and can be used to facilitate interoperability between heterogeneous systems.

Finally, RDF uses URIs to refer to objects in the domain of discourse. This has been used to promote what is known as the linked data model of publishing.[19,20] Given that the resources in an RDF graph may be represented by URIs, the aim of the linked data model is that it should be possible to dereference those URIs and by doing so retrieve a description of the resources that they represent. In effect, linked data results from the hypertextual foundations of the World Wide Web (and so of the Semantic Web); users of the Web follow links to obtain human-readable information in the form of web pages, so Semantic Web agents should be able to do likewise. Linked data may be implemented using several different

Web technologies; a general overview of the more common approaches is given in Sauermann,[21] and a summary of the best practices for publishing ontologies as linked data is given in Berrueta.[22]

FEATURE SUMMARY

RDF defines the triple model of data and a standard syntax for expressing those triples (RDF/XML), but does not constrain the vocabulary used in those triples: the URIs denoting categories and relations that we might wish to use in our descriptions. RDF Schema defines a basic vocabulary for use with RDF that lets users represent and define vocabularies that are specific to their problem domains. This basic vocabulary supports the following primitive modeling constructs:

- Named classes and explicit hierarchies of classes
- Named properties and explicit hierarchies of properties
- Global ranges and domains of properties
- A reification vocabulary for using triples to describe other triples
- Containers and collections, two methods for representing information about groups of resources
- A set of ancillary properties for providing human-readable documentation and links to further information

All of the vocabulary terms defined in RDF Schema are assigned URIs from one of two namespaces, rdf and rdfs (for largely historical reasons that originate with the first version of RDF, the terms defined in RDF Schema are divided across two different namescapes). For clarity, we will write rdf:XXX as a shorthand for http://www.w3.org/1999/02/22-rdf-syntax-ns#XXX, and rdfs:YYY as a shorthand for http://www.w3.org/2000/01/rdf-schema#YYY. This abbreviation style, whereby a lengthy URI is reduced to a short string consisting of a namespace abbreviation (representing a URI prefix), a separating colon, and a name defined in that namespace (which is to be appended to the URI prefix), is known as a Qualified Name or QName.[23,24]

Classes

RDF Schema defines the property rdf:type that allows a user to indicate that a resource is an instance of a particular class. For example, if we wished to indicate that John Smith (denoted by the URI http://www.example.org/staffid/85740) was an instance of the Person class defined in the FOAF (Friend of a Friend) ontology,[25] we would write the triple:

<http://www.example.org/staffid/85740> rdf:type <http://xmlns.com/foaf/0.1/Person>.

In this example, rdf:type is a QName which represents the "type" from the rdf namespace; the QName is expanded to the URI http://www.w3.org/1999/02/22-rdf-syntax-ns#type as described above. We can define a resource to be a class by declaring it to have an rdf:type of rdfs:Class. For example, to define a class of documents (represented by the URI http://example.org/ontology#Document), we would write:

<http://example.org/ontology#Document> rdf:type rdfs:Class.

These classes may be arranged into an explicit hierarchy by stating that a class is a subclass of another class, using the rdfs:subClassOf property:

<http://example.org/ontology#Newspaper> rdfs:subClassOf <http://example.org/ontology#Document>.

In this example, we have stated that the class Newspaper is a subclass of the class Document, which is equivalent to saying that every newspaper is also a document (or to put it a third way, that the set of newspapers is a subset of the set of documents).

Properties

In the same way that classes are defined in RDF Schema, properties may be defined by declaring a resource to be of rdf:type, rdf:Property. Properties may be arranged into hierarchies to represent the specialization and generalization of relationships. For example, an "employed by" property might be considered to be a specialization of an "affiliated with" property. A property can be declared to be a specialization of another property by stating that it is rdfs:subPropertyOf the other.

<http://example.org/ontology#employedBy> rdfs:subPropertyOf <http://example.org/ontology#affiliatedWith>.

Properties can be further described by defining their domain and range using the rdfs:domain and rdfs:range properties. The domain of a property is the class of objects that it runs from. For example, the "employed by" property might run from a class Person (being the class of people). The range of a property is the class of objects that it runs to; the range of "employed by" might be the class of organizations. These constraints on properties permit a reasoner to make inferences about the types of objects that are involved in a relationship.

<http://example.org/ontology#employedBy> rdfs:domain <http://example.org/ontology#Person>.

<http://example.org/ontology#employedBy> rdfs:range <http://example.org/ontology#Organisation>.

Containers and Collections

RDF Schema provides two different mechanisms for defining groups of objects, each with separate properties. The first of these, RDF containers, represents a group of objects with a resource which may be typed to informally indicate the intended semantics of the group; a group of type rdf:Bag is unordered, one of type rdf:Seq is an ordered sequence, and one of type rdf:Alt is a set of alternatives from which a single member should be selected (in practice, rdf:Alt is rarely used). The vocabulary pertaining to containers includes a countably infinite set of special properties (the ordinal container membership properties rdf:_1, rdf:_2 and so on), which indicate both the membership of a resource in the group, and for the ordered rdf:Seq, the position of a member within the group.

A sequence of three resources (for example, three email addresses) would be represented as follows:

<http://example.org/data#seq1> rdf:type rdf:Seq.

<http://example.org/data#seq1> rdf:_1 <mailto:groucho@example.org>. <http://example.org/data#seq1> rdf:_2 <mailto:chico@example.org>.

<http://example.org/data#seq1> rdf:_3 <mailto:harpo@example.org>.

The container vocabulary has the disadvantage that it produces groups that are open and mutable. There is no way to state that a group is closed, that is that the stated members of a group are the only members; a third party could assert that the above sequence has an extra member by adding the following triple:

<http://example.org/data#seq1> rdf:_4 <mailto:karl@example.org>.

The collection vocabulary addresses this by supporting the definition of closed groups that can have no further members. A collection is a recursive data structure that defines a group as a resource of type rdf:List, which consists of the first object in the group (indicated using the rdf:first property), and another rdf:List which contains the remainder of the group (indicated using the rdf:rest property). This second rdf:List contains the second element of the collection, and another rdf:List with the remainder of the collection, and so on. This recursion is terminated by the term rdf:nil, which represents an empty list. The example above could be represented in the container vocabulary as follows:

<http://example.org/data#list1> rdf:type rdf:List.

<http://example.org/data#list1> rdf:first <mailto:groucho@example.org>.

<http://example.org/data#list1> rdf:rest <http://example.org/data#list2>.

<http://example.org/data#list2> rdf:type rdf:List.

<http://example.org/data#list2> rdf:first <mailto:chico@example.org>.

<http://example.org/data#list2> rdf:rest <http://example.org/data#list3>.

<http://example.org/data#list3> rdf:type rdf:List.

<http://example.org/data#list3> rdf:first <mailto:harpo@example.org>.

<http://example.org/data#list3> rdf:rest rdf:nil.

As can be seen, an RDF collection requires more triples to represent the same group of objects than does a container, but it has the property that an attempt to tamper with the collection by adding extra members will result in an ill-formed data structure in which one of the component rdf:Lists has more than one rdf:first or rdf:rest property.

Reification

Reification is a mechanism for treating triples as first-class objects about which other assertions can be made (that is, as resources which can be referred to as the subjects or objects of other triples). The reification vocabulary in RDF Schema introduces the class rdf:Statement, which represents triples, and the properties rdf:subject, rdf:predicate and rdf:object, which represent the three components of a triple.

If we were to reify our original example (that a web page was written by John Smith), we would construct a small RDF graph containing four triples: one to represent the type of the reified statement, and one for each of the three components.

<http://example.org/data#stmt1> rdf:type rdf:Statement.

<http://example.org/data#stmt1> rdf:subject <http://www.example.org/index.html>.

<http://example.org/data#stmt1> rdf:predicate <http://purl.org/dc/terms/creator>.

<http://example.org/data#stmt1> rdf:object <http://www.example.org/staffid/85740>.

In this example, the statement itself is represented by the URI http://example.org/data#stmt1; this may be used in other triples to express information about the statement. For example, if John Smith wanted to assert that he was the author of the statement, he could write:

<http://example.org/data#stmt1> <http://purl.org/dc/terms/creator> <http://www.example.org/staffid/85740>.

The reification vocabulary provides a simple framework that supports the expression of fine-grained (triple level) provenance information about Semantic Web data. However, RDF reification is rarely used in practice, with many RDF practitioners preferring to use named graphs (a set of triples that is identified by a URI) to achieve the same ends, that of making assertions about other assertions.

Ancillary Properties

Finally, RDF Schema contains a number of properties that are not used to define ontology concepts, but to provide human-readable documentation, or to link to related information. The rdfs:label property is used to attach a human-readable label to a resource (necessary, given that URIs may be verbose), while rdfs:comment is used to add a comment (a natural language definition or rationale, perhaps). The rdfs:seeAlso property is used to indicate another resource which contains further information about a given resource; this is specialized by the rdfs:isDefinedBy property, which can be used to indicate the Web resource that defines a particular resource (for example, an ontology).

SYNTAX

The standard (normative) syntax for serializing RDF graphs for storage or transmission is RDF/XML.[24] This syntax is defined by a set of rules for transforming an XML document into an RDF graph;[18] element names, element contents, attribute names and attribute values are turned into resources, predicates and literals. While this syntax builds on the availability of high-quality XML tools, it tends to verbose serializations; in situations where RDF is to be read (and written) by people rather than machines, other non-XML syntaxes are preferred by many practitioners.

The best known of these alternative syntaxes is Notation 3 (N3),[17] a non-XML format that produces easy-to-understand serializations that can be quickly written by hand (or reproduced compactly in printed materials). Although it is well-known, N3 is a work in progress and subject to change, and has ambitious design goals; the expressivity of N3 goes beyond that of both RDF and OWL, so an arbitrary document written in N3 might contain constructs that cannot be translated into RDF/XML. For this reason, a number of N3 variants have evolved. N-Triples[26] is the simplest of these, and represents triples with no abbreviations such as QNames. Turtle[27] includes the QName-based namespace and abbreviation mechanism used by N3, but restricts the expressivity of the language to match that of RDF/XML.

Finally, there are two different approaches to serializing RDF graphs by embedding them within XHTML documents; the intent with both is to expose the structured data in ordinary web pages in such a way that Semantic Web agents can recognize and extract that data for their own use. The first of these, RDFa[28] defines a convention for expressing triples using the attributes on the elements in an XHTML document. A SW agent, on receiving a document containing RDFa markup, would first parse it as XML to obtain an intermediate representation, such as that provided by the Document Object Model (DOM), then parse this intermediate representation to obtain the encoded triples. GRDDL,[29] the second technique, provides a method for attaching a transformation to an XML document; this transformation, typically written in the eXtensible Stylesheet Language (XSLT),[30] can be used to extract selected information from the XML document and turn it into an RDF/XML document which can then be parsed to yield the RDF triples.

All of these RDF syntaxes have the feature that they do not define a canonical way in which an RDF graph can be written to a flat file for storage (a process known as serialization). Because a graph has no beginning or end, and no order to the edges, two implementations of the same serialization algorithm may process the triples in the graph in different orders, producing two different sequences of characters in the flat file. This complicates the process of comparing RDF data; comparison must be performed on the graphs themselves, rather than on their serializations.

SEMANTICS

RDF has a formal semantics[31] that defines the meaning of RDF statements by means of a model theory, an abstract, mathematical account based on the truth or falsity of statements. The goal of a model theory is that it enables the determination of the soundness and completeness of an inference process.[32]

The RDF semantics permit certain new triples to be inferred from those in an RDF graph. The following list of inferences is not comprehensive, but rather an indicative list of the sorts of inference that RDF permits:

- Transitivity of the rdfs:subClassOf relation
  — (if A is a subclass of B, and B is a subclass of C, then A is a subclass of C)
- Transitivity of the rdfs:subPropertyOf relation
  — (if A is a subproperty of B, and B is a subproperty of C, then A is a subproperty of C)
- Inferring general properties from more specific properties
  — (if two resources are related by a property, and there is a generalization of that property, then the resources are related by the superproperty)
- Inferring membership of general classes from membership of more specific classes
  — (if a resource is an instance of a class A, and A is a subclass of B, then the resource must also be a instance of class B)
- Inferring membership of classes from domain and range constraints.
  — (if a resource has a property whose domain is B, then the resource must be an instance of B)

Comparison of RDF Schema and OWL

RDF Schema and OWL both fulfill similar roles within the architecture of the Semantic Web, in that they both support the definition of formal vocabularies for classifying entities and specifying the natures of their interrelations. The key difference between the two approaches is one of expressiveness; RDF Schema provides a concise set of primitives that are familiar to users of object-oriented modeling methodologies, but these primitives are limited to expressing explicit subclass and superclass relationships between classes and properties.

The OWL language extends the modeling capabilities of RDF Schema using a family of formal logic known as description logics[33] in order to produce a more expressive ontology language that allows the user to specify the nature of a class in terms of the necessary and sufficient conditions that must be met by members of that class. Necessary conditions are those which must be satisfied by all resources that are members of a class, while sufficient conditions allow an OWL reasoner to infer that a resource that satisfies them must be a member of a the class. For example, "is an animal with four legs" is a necessary condition for the class Horse (if an entity is a horse, we can infer that it is an animal and that it has four legs), but not a sufficient condition (if an entity is an animal and has four legs, we cannot be certain that it is a horse, because things other than horses will satisfy those conditions).

If classes are defined in terms of their necessary and sufficient conditions for membership, it is possible to identify the implicit subclass hierarchies that must naturally follow from these definitions. For example, if the class Quadruped is defined with the sufficient condition that it is an animal with four legs (that is, if we have a four-legged animal, then we can infer that it is a quadruped), then we could infer that Horse is a subclass of Quadruped (every Horse is a Quadruped), even though this relationship has not been explicitly stated in our ontology.

HISTORY

RDF and RDF Schema have a strong lineage which draws on the knowledge representation formalisms developed over the past 40 years. The graph-oriented triple model resembles the approaches made by network knowledge representation techniques (principally semantic networks[34] and conceptual graphs).[35] Although the simple class and property model of RDF Schema owes much to object-oriented approaches to software engineering, which in turn were derived in part from Minsky's frames,[36] RDF Schema is a purely declarative representation (unlike object-oriented models with member functions on objects, or frames with demons attached to slots). There is a further difference between the approach taken by RDF, and that taken by traditional object-oriented languages such as C++ or Java. The former is a property-centric approach, in that classes are associated with properties by defining the global range and domain constraints on the properties, while the latter is more class-centric, and defines classes in terms of the properties that may appear on objects of that category. This is largely a difference of emphasis rather than of the fundamental underlying logic, however. It should be noted that OWL takes an approach closer to that of the frame-based systems, in that classes are defined in terms of the necessary and sufficient properties that their instances must have.

The lineage of RDF in the context of Web-based knowledge representation and metadata languages dates back to the mid-1990s, with the publication of the Meta Content Framework (MCF) and the Platform for Internet Content Selection (PICS). The two languages prepared the way for RDF, by introducing a key use case (web page

description) and the notion of a triple. The first version of RDF was published as a W3C Recommendation in 1999, and this version was deprecated by a revision in 2004 which sought to provide a formal foundation for the more expressive ontology language OWL; the description of RDF in this entry is based on the 2004 standard.

PICS

PICS[37,38] is a W3C Recommendation that was designed as a means for attaching machine-readable ratings to web pages in order to inform filtering software of the nature of the content of the web pages, with the intent that such filtering software would better be able to control the content displayed to users.

The technology emerged in part as a response to the U. S. Communications Decency Act of 1996 (Sec. 502), which effectively sought to place censorship restrictions on material distributed via the Internet. Rather than place the onus for removing unacceptable material on the publisher, PICS proposed a model whereby a potential consumer of such material could obtain an accurate description of the material that would enable them to decide whether or not they wished to view the material. The descriptions, known as content labels, consisted of values taken from some rating system, where a rating system comprised a set of independent dimensions on which an Internet resource could be evaluated. Such rating systems can be considered to be more complex versions of those used for film classification (for example, the film ratings G, PG, PG-13, R and NC-17 specified by the Motion Picture Association of America); the commonly used ICRA system[39] specified by the Family Online Safety Institute classifies works on seven different scales: nudity, sexual material, violence, language, potentially harmful activities, user-generated content, and context.

PICS originally used a non-XML (Lisp-like) syntax for expressing content labels, with specific ratings represented by numeric values; a rating system might specify a rating category (dimension) for language, with ratings for "slang" given the value 0, "mild expletives" the value 1, "expletives" the value 2, "obscene gestures" the value 3, and so on. A content label also included information about the party that had generated the metadata, and could be digitally signed to support the verification of the identity of the rating party.

Although the practice of attaching PICS metadata to web pages was never widespread, several Web browsers implemented the standard, including Internet Explorer (from version 3.0 onwards). The principle of a standard syntax for Web metadata was a key step towards the advent of the Semantic Web, even if PICS was too tightly coupled to its application domain to serve well as a general-purpose metadata language. In 2000, W3C published a proposal for the use of RDF as the underlying syntax for content labels, which specified an RDF Schema vocabulary for expressing both content labels and rating systems.[40]

MCF

MCF[41] originated at Apple Computer Inc. in 1995 as a metadata format for representing the content and structure of Web sites, and was used by the HotSauce web navigation system (a browser that allowed a user to fly through a 3D map of a Web site). The author of MCF, Ramanathan V. Guha, moved from Apple to the Netscape Communications Corporation in 1997, and reimplemented MCF as an application of the emerging XML dialect of SGML. This XML syntax for MCF has been an important influence on the development of RDF, and introduced a number of features that persist in the most recent version of RDF and its XML syntax.

The underlying model of an MCF description is a directed labeled graph much like that of RDF. The nodes in the graph can represent both literal values and objects with identity (which could be either web objects or real-world objects), and are linked by typed binary relations. Unlike RDF, it assumes that only Web-addressable objects have URLs; real-world objects are identified by non-URI strings.

RDF (1999 Version)

The original 1999 specifications of RDF[42] and RDF Schema[43] differ from the versions described above in three main ways. First, they do not contain a formal account of the semantics of the languages that would be suitable for reasoning. The 1999 RDF specification contains a definition of a triple and an explanation of the entailed triples produced by reification, and the RDF Schema specification informally defines rdfs:subClassOf and rdfs:subPropertyOf as transitive properties, but there is no model-theoretic account of the sort that would be needed to verify the soundness and completeness of a reasoning engine.

Secondly, they contain a number of features that were deprecated in the 2004 specification because they could not be given an unambiguous meaning. Chief amongst these features is the ability to express statements about the members of a container. Given an rdf:Bag containing a number of resources, it was possible to write a single triple which applied to each member of the Bag by using the rdf:aboutEach attribute instead of the rdf:about attribute to indicate the subject of the triple. While this could be seen as a convenient shorthand for expressing repetitive information, there is an unfortunate interaction with the non-closed nature of RDF containers. In the absence of a framework for provenance, it is possible for a third party to state that a container has extra members; it thus becomes possible to make the original claim about the

members of the container apply to more resources than were intended. A similar construct, rdf:aboutEachPrefix, allowed an author to express statements that would hold for all resources whose URIs began with a particular string. The set of triples entailed by this could not be determined without detailed knowledge of all the URIs with a particular prefix, and so the construct would therefore have unpredictable consequences as web pages were created and deleted over time. These two constructs, rdf:aboutEach and rdf:aboutEachPrefix, were included in the 1999 specification in order to support certain functionality provided by PICS, and in doing so to facilitate the transition from PICS to RDF. The 2004 specification also clarified the formal basis for reification; while the reification vocabulary remains part of the language, a triple does not entail its reification, nor vice versa.

Finally, the 2004 specifications contain a number of new constructs that were intended to bolster those constructs of RDF-1999 that were felt to have awkward consequences, but which were too widely used to be deprecated; the RDF container vocabulary was considered to be such, and was supplemented with the collection construct which enforced a well-formedness criterion on closed lists.

The RDF revision in 2004 aimed to make a number of corrections and improvements following feedback from implementers, and to complete the work on RDF Schema, which had previously only reached the state of W3C Candidate Recommendation. This new version of RDF was developed contemporaneously with the OWL Web Ontology Language, and so there was a close dialogue between the relevant W3C working groups in order to ensure that the revised form of RDF would form a suitable foundation for OWL; the earlier language DAML+OIL,[44] from which OWL was derived, used RDF/XML as a serialization syntax but disregarded its semantics (or lack thereof) and adopted a conventional description logic semantics.[33] An aim of the collaboration between these working groups was therefore to develop a semantics for RDF and RDF Schema that would be compatible with the semantics of OWL.

CONCLUSION

The RDF is a versatile knowledge representation language that can be used to express information about both Web resources and real-world objects. In conjunction with the vocabulary description languages RDF Schema and OWL, both of which are built on RDF, it can be used to create complex descriptions of application domains that a computer may use to infer new knowledge. The role played by RDF in the development of the Semantic Web is crucial; it integrates with the existing Web architecture to provide a common infrastructure for the creation and publication of structured data.

REFERENCES

1. Klyne, G.; Carroll, J.J.; McBride, B. Resource Description Framework (RDF): Concepts and abstract syntax, World Wide Web Consortium; 2004, http://www.w3.org/TR/rdf-concepts/ (accessed February 2008).

2. Berners-Lee, T.; Hendler, J.; Lassila, O. The Semantic Web. Sci. Am. May **2001**, 29–37.

3. Shadbolt, N.; Hall, W.; Berners-Lee, T. The Semantic Web revisited, IEEE Intell. Syst. May/June **2006**, 96–101.

4. Brickley, D.; Guha, R.V. RDF vocabulary description language 1.0: RDF Schema, World Wide Web Consortium, 2004, http://www.w3.org/TR/rdf-schema/ (accessed February 2008).

5. McGuinness, D.L.; van Harmelen, F. OWL Web Ontology Language overview, World Wide Web Consortium, 2004, http://www.w3.org/TR/owl-features/ (accessed February 2008).

6. Staab, S.; Studer, R., Eds. *Handbook on Ontologies*, 2nd Ed.; Springer: Berlin, 2009.

7. Gruber, T.R. A translation approach to portable ontology specifications. Knowl. Acquis. **1993**, *5* (2), 199–220.

8. Dean, M.; Schreiber, G.; Bechhofer, S.; van Harmelen, F.; Hendler, J.; Horrocks, I.; McGuinness, D.L.; Patel-Schneider, P.F.; Stein, L.A. OWL Web Ontology Language reference, World Wide Web Consortium, 2004, http://www.w3.org/TR/owl-ref/ (accessed February 2008).

9. Horrocks, I.; Patel-Schneider, P.F.; van Harmelen, F. From SHIQ and RDF to OWL: The making of a Web Ontology Language. Web Semantics: Science, Services and Agents on the World Wide Web **2003**, *1*, 7–26.

10. Prud'hommeaux, E.; Seaborne, A. SPARQL query language for RDF, World Wide Web Consortium, 2008, http://www.w3.org/TR/rdf-sparql-query/ (accessed February 2008).

11. Clark, K.G.; Feigenbaum, L.; Torres, E. SPARQL protocol for RDF, World Wide Web Consortium; 2008, http://www.w3.org/TR/rdf-sparql-protocol/ (accessed February 2008).

12. Information technology—open distributed processing—unified modelling language (UML) Version 1.4.2, ISO/IEC 19501:2005.

13. Minsky, M. A framework for representing knowledge. In *The Psychology of Computer Vision*; Winston, P.H., Ed.; McGraw-Hill: New York, 1975; 211–277.

14. Berners-Lee, T.; Fielding, R.; Masinter, L. Uniform Resource Identifier (URI): Generic Syntax, RFC3986, Internet Engineering Task Force, 2005, http://www.ietf.org/rfc/rfc3986.txt (accessed February 2008).

15. Manola, F.; Miller, E. RDF primer, World Wide Web Consortium, 2004, http://www.w3.org/TR/rdf-primer/ (accessed February 2008).

16. DCMI metadata terms; 2008. http://dublincore.org/documents/dcmi-terms/ (accessed February 2008).

17. Berners-Lee, T. Notation 3, 2006, http://www.w3.org/DesignIssues/Notation3.html (accessed February 2008).

18. Bray, T.; Paoli, J.; Sperberg-McQueen, C.M.; Maler, E.; Yergeau, F. Extensible markup language (XML) 1.0 (Fourth Edition), World Wide Web Consortium, 2006, http://www.w3.org/TR/xml (accessed February 2008).

19. Berners-Lee, T. Linked Data, 2007, http://www.w3.org/DesignIssues/LinkedData.html (accessed February 2008).

20. Bizer, C.; Heath, T.; Idehen, K.; Berners-Lee, T. Linked data on the web. In *Proceedings of the 17th International World Wide Web Conference (WWW2008)*, Beijing, China, April, 21–25, 2008; Association of Computing Machinery: New York, 2008.

21. Sauermann, L.; Cyganiak, R.; Ayers, D.; Völkel, M. Cool URIs for the Semantic Web, World Wide Web Consortium, 2008, http://www.w3.org/TR/cooluris/ (accessed April 2008).

22. Berrueta, D.; Phipps, J. Best practice recipes for publishing RDF vocabularies World Wide Web Consortium, 2008, http://www.w3.org/TR/swbp-vocab-pub/ (accessed February 2008).

23. Bray, T.; Hollander, D.; Layman, A.; Tobin, R. Namespaces in XML 1.0, World Wide Web Consortium, 2006, http://www.w3.org/TR/REC-xml-names/ (accessed February 2008).

24. Beckett, D. RDF/XML syntax specification (revised), World Wide Web Consortium, 2004, http://www.w3.org/TR/rdf-syntax-grammar/ (accessed February 2008).

25. Brickley, D.; Miller, L. FOAF vocabulary specification, 2007, http://xmlns.com/foaf/spec/ (accessed February 2008).

26. Grant, J.; Beckett, D. RDF test cases, World Wide Web Consortium, 2004, http://www.w3.org/TR/rdf-testcases/ (accessed February 2008).

27. Beckett, D.; Berners-Lee, T. Turtle—terse RDF triple language, World Wide Web Consortium, 2008, http://www.w3.org/TeamSubmission/turtle/ (accessed February 2008).

28. Adida, B.; Birbeck, M. RDFa primer: Embedding structured data in web pages, working draft, World Wide Web Consortium, 2007, http://www.w3.org/TR/xhtml-rdfa-primer (accessed February 2008).

29. Connolly, D. Gleaning resource descriptions from dialects of languages (GRDDL), World Wide Web Consortium, 2007, http://www.w3.org/TR/grddl/ (accessed February 2008).

30. Clark, J. XSL transformations (XSLT) version 1.0, World Wide Web Consortium, 1999, http://www.w3.org/TR/xslt (accessed February 2008).

31. Hayes, P. RDF semantics, World Wide Web Consortium, 2004, http://www.w3.org/TR/rdf-mt/ (accessed February 2008).

32. Hunter, G. *Metalogic: An Introduction to the Metatheory of Standard First Order Logic*; University of California Press: Berkeley, CA, 1973.

33. Baader, F.; Nutt, W. Basic description logics. In *The Description Logic Handbook: Theory, Implementation and Applications*; 2nd Ed.; Baader, F., Calvanese, D., McGuinness, D.L., Nardi, D., Patel-Schneider, P.F., Eds.; Cambridge University Press: Cambridge, U.K., 2007, 47–104.

34. Quillian, M.R. Word concepts: A theory and simulation of some basic semantic capabilities. Behav. Sci. **1967**, *12*, 410–430.

35. Sowa, J.F. *Knowledge Representation: Logical, Philosophical, and Computational Foundations*; Brooks Cole Publishing Co.: Pacific Grove, CA, 2000.

36. Minsky, M. A framework for representing knowledge. In *Readings in Cognitive Science*; Collins, A.; Smith, E.E., Eds.; Morgan-Kaufmann: San Francisco, CA, 1992.

37. Resnick, P. Filtering information on the Internet. Sci. Am. **1997**, *276* (3), 62–64.

38. Miller, J.; Resnick, P.; Singer, D. Rating services and rating systems (and their machine readable descriptions), World Wide Web Consortium, 1996, http://www.w3.org/TR/REC-PICS-services (accessed February 2008).

39. The ICRA vocabulary http://www.icra.org/vocabulary/ (accessed February 2008).

40. Brickley, D.; Swick, R. PICS rating vocabularies in XML/RDF, World Wide Web Consortium, 2000, http://www.w3.org/TR/rdf-pics (accessed February 2008).

41. Guha, R.V.; Bray, T. Meta content framework using XML, World Wide Web Consortium, 1997, http://www.w3.org/TR/NOTE-MCF-XML/ (accessed February 2008).

42. Lassila, O.; Swick, R. Resource description framework (RDF) model and syntax specification, World Wide Web Consortium, 1999, http://www.w3.org/TR/1999/REC-rdf-syntax-19990222/ (accessed February 2008).

43. Brickley, D.; Guha, R.V. Resource description framework (RDF) schema specification, World Wide Web Consortium, 1999, http://www.w3.org/TR/1999/PR-rdf-schema-19990303/ (accessed February 2008).

44. Connolly, D.; van Harmelen, F.; Horrocks, I.; McGuinness, D.L.; Patel-Schneider, P.F.; Stein, L.A. DAML+OIL reference description, World Wide Web Consortium, 2001, http://www.w3.org/TR/daml+oil-reference (accessed February 2008).

BIBLIOGRAPHY

1. Antoniou, G.; van Harmelen, F. *A Semantic Web Primer*, 2nd Ed.; MIT Press: Cambridge, MA, 2008.

2. Berners-Lee, T. *Weaving the Web: the Past, Present and Future of the World Wide Web by Its Inventor*; Texere Publishing: London, U.K., 1999.

3. Fensel, D. *Ontologies: A Silver Bullet for Knowledge Management and Electronic Commerce*, 2nd Ed.; Springer: Berlin, Germany, 2004.

4. Fensel, D.; Hendler, J.; Lieberman, H.; Wahlster, W. *Spinning the Semantic Web: bringing the World Wide Web to its full potential*; MIT Press: Cambridge, MA, 2003.

Regional–School

Saudi Arabia: Libraries, Archives, and Museums

Ayman Shabana
International Institute, University of California, Los Angeles, Los Angeles, California, U.S.A.

Abstract

This entry surveys the history of libraries and librarianship in Saudi Arabia. It traces the development of librarianship from a branch under the Ministry of Education into an independent field that has become closely tied with the Information Industry. It also briefly touches on museums, archival institutions, and library professional associations in Saudi Arabia.

INTRODUCTION

Ever since the time of Prophet Muhammad (d. 632), the region which had been known as the Arabian Peninsula acquired a lasting symbolic significance not only for its residents but also for Muslims all over the world. For the purpose of simplification, the Arabic diacritics were not used for the letters *hamzah*, <*ayn* as well as the long vowels å, í, or ú. It not only comprises the holiest sites of Islam and the places that witnessed the early formative period of the Islamic past, but its importance is reinforced continuously into the present as Muslims face the direction of the Kabah in the city of Makkah during their prayers at least five times a day. The two cities of Makkah, where the Prophet was born, and Madinah, where he died and where he established his religious and political authority, are particularly important due to their connection with the two holy shrines. In recognition of their spiritual significance, King Fahd Ibn Abd al-Aziz (d. 2005) acquired the primary title of Custodian of the two Holy Shrines.

The two shrines have always been recognized as major seats of Islamic learning. Apart from being destinations for the annual pilgrimage of all Muslims, they served as major centers of Islamic education. It was a common practice for any scholar of repute to spend some time in their vicinity to communicate with the leading authorities in the different branches of Islamic knowledge. These constant and vibrant scholarly activities have always facilitated the contact of Arabia with the outside world and also the circulation of the most important educational and cultural commodity: the book. While the political history of the region witnessed many discontinuities, disruptions and dramatic turning points, the two shrines continued to enjoy their prestige due to their strong association with the two major institutions of pilgrimage and Islamic learning.

COUNTRY PROFILE

Saudi Arabia occupies the larger part of the Arabian Peninsula, about four-fifths, in south-western Asia with a total area of about 1.24 million mi^2 (2 million km^2). It is situated between the Red sea and the Arabian Gulf and it is bordered by Jordan, Iraq, and Kuwait to the north, by Yemen to the South and East, and by Qatar and the United Arab Emirates to the north east. The country's longer western coastline on the Red Sea faces Egypt, Sudan and Eritrea and shorter eastern coastline on the Arabian Gulf between Kuwait and Qatar faces Iran. The larger part of the Kingdom of Saudi Arabia is arid desert. The average summer temperature in coastal areas ranges from 38°C to 49°C with high humidity. The average annual rainfall is between 100 mm and 200 mm. Arabic is the official language which is spoken by almost all the population which according to the estimates for 2007 was 24.3 million. Islam is the official religion and almost all the inhabitants are Muslims where about 85% of the population are Sunni and the remaining 15% are Shia, largely in the eastern part of the country. The capital is Riyadh.[1] The gross national income per capita is $22,300. The adult literacy rate for both sexes is 84% (male 88.6% and female 78.4%). Saudi Arabia is an absolute monarchy which was established by the family of Al-Saud and the current king is Abd Allah Ibn Abd al-Aziz Al-Saud. The legal system is based on Shariah-inspired Islamic law (Fig. 1).

HISTORICAL BACKGROUND

The history of the current Kingdom of Saudi Arabia goes back to 1932 when King Abd al-Aziz Al-Saud succeeded in subjugating the competing tribal rulers of the different regions and thereby bringing the entire Arabia under his rule after 30 years of constant struggle between 1902 and 1932.[3] The claim of Al-Saud family to the rule of the region goes back to their leading ancestor Muhammad Ibn Saud (d. 1765) who consolidated his political influence by adopting the reformative teachings of Muhammad Ibn Abd al-Wahhab (d. 1792) and consequently established the first Saudi state in the Diriyah province of the central region of Najd (1744–1818). The appeal of the Wahhabi

Encyclopedia of Library and Information Sciences, Fourth Edition DOI: 10.1081/E-ELIS4-120045401

Fig. 1 Map of Saudi Arabia.
Source: From CIA The World Factbook.[2]

teachings was largely due to its emphasis on purifying the Islamic creed from the later accretions that crept into its basic monotheistic message. The Saudi forces were able to subdue most of the regions of Arabia and they also repeatedly attacked the border regions of Iraq and Syria. The steady advances of the Saudi forces eventually incurred the anger of the Ottoman sultan who instructed the Egyptian ruler Muhammad Ali to send his troops to subdue the Saudi-Wahhabi movement. Under the leadership of Ibrahim Pasha (Muhammad Ali's son), a strong army marched towards the Saudi strongholds and managed to defeat the Saudi forces and destroy the Diriyah. This event signaled the end of the first Saudi state. As the Egyptian forces retreated, the Saudi leaders attempted to restore their rule and eventually succeeded in establishing the second Saudi state under the leadership of Faysal (d. 1865) son of Turki (d. 1834). The second Saudi state, however, did not fare well due to the internal strife among the family of Al-Saud which led to their defeat by Al-Rashid forces. It was not until 1902 when Abd al-Aziz returned from his exile in Kuwait and defeated the al-Rashid forces, an event which marked the beginning of the third and current Saudi State. King Abd al-Aziz

(d. 1953) was succeeded by his sons Saud (abdicated 1964 and died 1969), Faysal (d. 1975), Khalid (d. 1982), Fahd (d. 2005), and Abd Allah (current King).

The political stability achieved by the unification of the region under the rule of King Abd al-Aziz facilitated the task of modern nation building. The discovery of oil during the 1930s brought the wealth that made this task possible. The oil revenues rose from $13.5 million in 1946 to around $212 million in 1952.[3] During the reign of King Faysal the oil revenues reached the all time high of 92.2 billion Saudi Riyals in 1975.[3]

LIBRARIES AND BOOKS IN THE ARABIC AND ISLAMIC CULTURE

Written manuscripts have always enjoyed outstanding prestige within the Islamic culture. Muslims were inspired by the teachings of the Quran and the instructions of their Prophet to gain knowledge which in itself was considered an act of devotion and a means of drawing near to God. Throughout Islamic history, the transmission of knowledge relied first and foremost on the communities of learned authorities and certification was given after direct personal training under these authorities. Classical bibliographical works describe in detail the high level of sophistication that this culture of learning reached. For the larger part of the Islamic history, the various educational activities took place either inside a mosque or in a school that was attached to one. Big mosques, therefore, often consisted of compounds that comprised various educational institutions. These compounds traditionally included schools for children, schools for the general public as well as specialized centers especially for the advanced study of Islamic law and theology. Libraries or Book Houses as they were called, also started as one of these institutions that were attached to mosques. Grand mosques such as the two shrines in Makkah and Madinah, al-Azhar in Cairo, Umawi mosque in Damascus as well as other famous mosques across major Islamic cities have always comprised large libraries with rich collections. In addition to mosque libraries, schools often had large libraries that served the needs of its faculty and students.[4]

Moreover, many Muslim rulers developed great interest in books and some of them built famous libraries that commemorated their legacy for centuries after their death. Many of these libraries started as private libraries and later turned into either public libraries or major research centers. Three institutions in particular were quite reputable: *Bayt al-Hikmah* (House of Wisdom) of Baghdad, *Dar al-Ilm* (House of Knowledge) of Cairo and the Library of Qurtubah.[5]

Bayt al-Hikmah was founded by caliph Harun al-Rashid (d. 786). It is considered by far the first public library and academy in the Muslim World. During the reign of al-Rashid's son al-Mamun, it became the most important educational institution in the world. It was particularly famous for being the center for the translation movement sponsored and led by the Abbasid caliphs. It was geared towards translating the major works of the classical Greek, Roman, Persian and Indian thought. *Dar al-Ilm* was founded by the Fatimid caliph al-Hakim in 1004 as a rival to the *Bayt al-Hikmah* of Baghdad. The holdings of this major institution was estimated around 2,200,000 volumes which was unmatched by any other library in the world at that time. Following the example of the major libraries and learning institutions in the eastern part of the Muslim world, the caliph al-Mustansir (d. 976) founded the Library of Qurtubah in Muslim Spain which was famous for its rich and rare collection and whose index consisted of 44 big volumes.

PLANNING/LEGISLATION IN MODERN SAUDI ARABIA

With the establishment of the Central Planning Organization (1965), later Ministry of Planning (1975), the kingdom started its five-year development plans, the first of which was during the period of 1970–1975. The early development plans focused on the development of the basic infrastructure such as the construction of roads, airports, ports, electrical and telecommunication projects. Expenditure on public education rose steadily as the allocations to the Ministry of Education (established 1953) and Ministry of Higher Education (established 1975) increased incrementally.[6] For example the total number of students in all general and higher education stages increased from about 547,000 in 1969 to about 4.9 million in 2001. In addition to the libraries within the educational institutions (both general education and higher education), the development plans provided allocations for public libraries as well.[7] For example, the first development plan (1970) emphasized the role of library and museum systems for the enhancement of the various educational and cultural services:

> In providing for the cultural development of the Kingdom, the public library system is to be expanded and improved with priority given to enlarging the book collections and periodical sections, and providing libraries with the necessary furniture and equipment. In view of the cultural importance of archeological finds and the educational value of museums, the plan proposes to expand the activities of the Ministry of Education in this area. An annual program of archeological missions is planned for field surveys, site investigations, and site registrations. An acquisition and maintenance program has been designed to assure that buildings and landmarks of historical significance are not lost.[8]

The plan for the Ministry of Education also provided some provisions on the public library system and archeology.

> The ten general public libraries are to be expanded and improved, with priority given to enlarging the book collections and periodical sections and to providing the necessary additional furniture and equipment. A photographic department is to be established at the Riyadh Library to record documents and publications. Five of the libraries that now occupy rented facilities are to be provided with appropriate buildings through a phased construction program, and a new library is to be established in Tayf . . . . In view of the cultural importance of archeological finds and the educational value of museums, the plan includes provisions for the establishment of an archeological museum and library.

The second development plan (1975–1980) provided more specific details about the projects that pertain to the sector of libraries and museums which included the establishment of a national museum system and the development of the facilities and activities of the King Abd al-Aziz Research and Cultural institute as a major library, research, publishing, and cultural center. It also provided for the establishment of: biography center, 10 new general libraries (increasing the number of public libraries from

22 to 32 by the end of the plan), six regional museums, two Islamic museums and four specialized museums.[8]

The third development plan (1980–[5]) continued with the expansion of the national library and museum systems.[8] It also provided for carrying out a preinvestment study for a National Central Library.[8] The increased economic surplus from the oil revenues facilitated the execution of the consecutive development plans. Eventually, the transformation of life styles created more demand for cultural and recreational activities which meant among other things increased need for a robust library and museum systems as clearly manifested in the fourth development.[8] The subsequent development plans continued to emphasize the important role that both libraries and museums play in the enhancement of the national educational system and culture in general. They also continued to highlight the need to facilitate the integration of the modern technological applications within the national library system in the light of the increasing connection between library and information sectors.[8]

MAJOR INSTITUTIONS

King Fahd National Library

Planning for the establishment of a central national library for the Kingdom of Saudi Arabia started many years before the project finally materialized. Several proposals were made based on both theoretical and field research.[9] Eventually, the Council of Ministers issued the resolution no. 80 on December 19, 1990 approving the statute of the King Fahd National Library and its administrative structure. The resolution was ratified by the Royal Decree no. M/9 on December 26, 1990.[10] The articles of the Statute explained the objectives and the functions of the library. The first article provides that:

- King Fahd Library shall become the national Library of the Kingdom of Saudi Arabia and its name shall become King Fahd National Library.
- The library shall exist as an independent body.
- The library shall be linked administratively to the Presidency of the Council of Ministers.
- The headquarters of the library shall be in Riyadh.
- The library may establish branches in the Kingdom.

The second article explains the main functions of the library to be: collecting, organizing, documenting, and publicizing the intellectual and cultural output of the country. This includes, for example, collecting materials published in or about Saudi Arabia, materials published by Saudi nationals outside the Kingdom, materials of interest from outside the Kingdom, materials from outside the Kingdom that will facilitate research, study and understanding of the human culture in all its facets, and also collecting old and rare books, manuscripts, documents, and illustrated materials, especially those that are related to Arabic and Islamic civilization. The library also carries out a wide array of activities such as:

- Processing the acquired/deposited materials according to professional standards.
- Publishing national bibliographies, union catalogs, and other documentations.
- Conducting reference studies for the Government departments and commissions.
- Providing reference and borrowing services to individuals, government departments, and the private sector.
- Organizing and hosting conferences, symposia, and book fairs.
- Representing the Kingdom in international meetings and conferences related to the objectives and functions of the library.
- Exchanging books and information with other libraries and cooperating with international organizations and associations.
- Providing leadership for the development of library services and information centers by active participation in:
  1. Preparing a national plan for the development of library and information services in cooperation with the concerned bodies.
  2. Developing national bibliographical standards and specifications in cooperation with the relevant bodies.
  3. Encouraging libraries and information centers to adopt and implement those standards.
  4. Encouraging and developing programs for investment of resources in the field of information including the establishment of an information network of libraries and information centers.
  5. Participating in the preparation and publishing of research studies, guides, directories in the field of library and information services and other areas.[10]

In addition to its large collection of printed books and modern information resources, the National Library devotes special attention to rare items, historical documents, manuscripts, and numismatics.[10] According to the Library's Web site, the total number of its holding until 2006 is 1,205,482. The library also contains around 30 special collections and private libraries of prominent scholars and famous personalities that include, in addition to rare books, a diverse collection of unpublished manuscripts. Some examples of these private library collections are:

- The Library of Ihsan Abbas with a collection of 8390 books.
- The library of Sheikh Muhammad Ibn Abd al-Aziz al-Mani with a collection of 5480 books.

- The library of Sheikh Abd Allah Ibn Muhammad Ibn Khamis with a collection of 7740 books.
- The library of Sheikh Uthman Ibn Hamad Al-Haqil with a collection of 17,400 books.
- The library of Sheikh Muhammad Husayn Zaydan with a collection of 4420 books.
- The library of Fawzan Ibn Abd al-Aziz al-Fawzan with a collection of 4470 books.
- The library of Dr. Yusuf Ibrahim al-Sallum with a collection of 4890 books.
- The library of the late painter Muhammad Musa al-Salim.
- The library of Sheikh Muhammad Mansur al-Shaqha with a collection of 8960 books.
- The library of Sheikh Abd Allah Abd al-Aziz al-Anqari.
- The library of Sheikh Abd Allah Ibn Umar Al-Sheikh.
- The library of Sheikh Abd Allah Ibn Muhammad al-Nasban.
- The library of Sheikh Husayn Ibn Abd Allah al-Jarisi with a collection of 4400 books.

King Abd al-Aziz Public Library in Riyadh

In addition to King Fahd National Library, there is also a number of independent educational and cultural institutions that promote libraries and librarianship. One of the most important institutions in this regard is King Abd al-Aziz Public Library in Riyadh. It was established in 1987 by the current King Abd Allah Ibn Abd al-Aziz.[11] Its holdings include a total number of 150,000 information resources. The library functions as a major cultural center that provides a variety of services and promotes a number of educational and cultural activities especially in the areas of publishing and translation.[11]

ACADEMIC AND RESEARCH LIBRARIES

The Saudi Ministry of Higher Education was established in 1975 to regulate and oversee university system of the Kingdom.[6] The system comprises seven universities:

- King Saud University in Riyadh, established in 1957.
- The Islamic University in Madinah, established in 1967.
- King Abd al-Aziz University in Jeddah, established in 1967.
- The Islamic University of Imam Muhammad Ibn Saud in Riyadh, established in 1974.
- King Fahd University for Petroleum and Minerals in Zahran, established in 1965.
- King Faysal University in Dammam, established in 1975.
- University of Umm al-Qura in Makkah, established in 1987.

The organizational structure of the Saudi Universities Administration includes four main sectors: the teaching sector, the educational support and services sector, the graduate studies and research sector, and the administrative and financial affairs sector.[6] Academic librarianship is regulated by the educational support and services sector. Each of the universities houses a central library, the largest of which is the one at King Saud University which consists of a central library and nine branches.[9] Each university has a dean of library affairs who oversees the affairs of the university library system. Each library is run by a library director to whom department librarians report and who in turn reports to the dean of library affairs.[9] Only the libraries of King Faysal University and King Fahd University for Petroleum and Minerals use the classification of the Library of Congress while the rest of the universities use the Dewey Decimal Classification (DDC) system.

According to a survey conducted in the late 1990s, the total number of volumes in the collections of the seven universities was 2,684,837, out of which 913,312 were in Arabic and 1,771,525 were in English. The non-Arabic collection included books in French, German, Spanish, Urdu and Hindi. Some of the problems that were found to obstruct collection development included: lack of collection building plans, managerial problems, insufficient financial support, and absence of interlibrary loan and online searching facilities.[12] Ongoing efforts are being made to enhance the services and utilize the different Information Technology applications in the day-to-day operations of the academic libraries.[13]

In addition to the university library system under the Ministry of Higher Education, there is also a number of higher education institutions that are affiliated with other government sectors such as:

- The Presidency for Girls' Education
- Ministry of Education
- Ministry of Health
- General Institution for Technical Education and Vocational Training[6]

PUBLIC LIBRARIES

Libraries, archives and museums play an important role in preserving a nation's cultural heritage as well as shaping its collective memory and consciousness. This is the reason why governments often give special attention to these institutions. Modern librarianship, as an integral part of the modern educational systems, started with the foundation of modern nation states in most of the Muslim world during the first half of the twentieth century. In the case of Saudi Arabia it started with the formal foundation of the Kingdom of Saudi Arabia by King Abd al-Aziz (Ibn Saud) in 1932. Al-Nahari dates the beginning of modern libraries back to 1945, with the establishment of the library of the college of Islamic Law in Makkah.[6] This library was annexed to the library of the College of Education which became the central library of the King Abd al-Aziz University in Makkah, later acquired the name of the University of Umm al-Qura in 1980.

The first public library was founded in Riyadh in 1950 as the Saudi Library in Riyadh and the first modern library was established as a part of King Saud University (Riyadh) which was the largest library in the country with a collection of 398,551 multilingual volumes, 3896 serials subscription, and a large collection of rare books and manuscripts. Gradually with the tangible development of the educational system, the need for a modern system of public libraries was felt and consequently King Faysal signed a Ministerial Decree to establish the Directorate General of Public Libraries within the Ministry of Education in 1959 with the objective of fostering the development of public libraries in the country.[6] The Directorate consisted of several departments for administration, public libraries, library services, binding, storage, photocopying and microfilming.[14]

Researchers who trace the history of libraries in Saudi Arabia often refer to the libraries that were established by notable individuals either before or after the foundation of the Kingdom. Most of these libraries were attached to major mosques especially the two Holy Shrines in Makkah and Madinah.[9,14] Examples of these libraries include the libraries of Sheikh Abd al-Rahman al-Sadi (1940) and Prince Musaid ibn Abd al-Rahman (1944). They also include the libraries that were established by collective communal efforts such as the libraries of al-Riyadh (1951), Shaqra (1952), al-Hariq (1953) and Hawtat Bani Tamim (1956).

The Ministry of Education's Directorate General of Public Libraries is one of the main five supervisory bodies that regulate and oversee the activities of public libraries in the Kingdom. It supervises 68 public libraries throughout the country with an average of one library in each city with the exception of Riyadh which has three public libraries. The Directorate is the major supervisory agency.

It oversees 80% of the public libraries in the Kingdom and provides the technical services for all of them including acquisition and cataloging. The collections in these libraries are classified according to the 17th edition of the DDC after its modification to suit Arabic libraries. The total holdings of these libraries exceed one million volumes (Table 1).[14]

The second major supervisory body is the Ministry of Islamic Affairs, Endowments, Religious Preaching, and Mentoring. Some of the main libraries under its supervision are:

One of the most important libraries that are currently under the supervision of the Ministry of Islamic Affairs, Endowments, Religious Preaching, and Mentoring is the Library of Holy City of Makkah (*Maktabat Makkah al-Mukarramah*). Administratively it was under the supervision of the Ministry of Information, and then the Ministry of Pilgrimage before it finally came under the supervision of the Ministry of Islamic Affairs, Endowments, Religious Preaching, and Mentoring in 1993.[4] This library enjoys a particular historical and symbolic significance because it was established on the birthplace of the Prophet after King Abd al-Aziz issued a royal decree for this purpose in 1951.[15]

The third major supervisory body is the Presidency of Religious Research and Legal Responses. It supervises the Saudi Library of Riyadh which was established in (1944). Its holdings include 45,000 volumes. The fourth supervisory body is the Presidency of the Affairs of the Two Holy Shrines. It supervises the two libraries in the two Holy Shrines. The fifth supervisory body is the Darah (house) of King Abd al-Aziz. It is an independent governmental organization established by the Royal Decree no. M/45 in Riyadh in 1972. Its holdings include 29,734 volumes in Arabic and 3316 in other languages which are all classified according to a modified DDC system.

Given their symbolic importance for Muslims all over the world, the two Holy Shrines mosques in Makkah and Madinah have always received special attention from the different Muslim rulers and dignitaries across history. Because these two mosques were considered major centers of Islamic education, they have always comprised rich

Table 1 Public libraries in Saudi Arabia.

Name of library	Founder	Year	Place	Holdings
Arif	Sheikh Arif Hikmat al-Husayni	1852	Madinah	7045 printed volumes, 4373 manuscripts, and 630 miscellaneous
Mahmudiyah	Sultan Mahmud II	1855	King A. Aziz Library, Madinah	4391 printed volumes and 3314 manuscripts
Abd Allah B. Al-Abbas Mosque	Ottoman ruler of Hijaz Rushdi al-Sharwani	1874	Taif	10,000 volumes and 450 manuscripts
King Abd al-Aziz	N/A	1983	Madinah	45,000 volumes
Public Library in Madinah	N/A	1962	Madinah	4200 volumes and 178 manuscripts
Salihiyah	Muhammad ibn Uthman al-Qadi	1919, annexed to the Ministry in 1977	Unayzah	N/A

Source: From Al-Dubayan, *Itlalah Tarikhiyah*, 28.[14]

Regional–School

collections of books and manuscripts. Historians often speak of the different collections that were donated, bequeathed or offered to these two mosques. The Library of the Holy Shrine in Makkah was first established in 1095. Some of these collections that once existed include the collection of the Sharabiya Madrasah (founded 1233), the collection of Qaytbay Madrasah (founded 1477), the Sharawani Library (late nineteenth century), the Faydiya Library. The most famous library to be established in the Holy Shrine of Makkah was the Sulaymaniyah which was founded by the Ottoman sultan Abd al-Majid (1823–1861). Following the damage that was caused by the violent floods of 1861, the salvaged books were housed in what came to be known as the Shrine Library (*Maktabat al-Haram*). From that moment on the collection of the Shrine Library continued to grow with the continuous donations it received.[16] The current holdings are estimated to be about 65,535 volumes and 6500 manuscripts.[16]

Similarly, the Holy Shrine mosque in Madinah received many book collections throughout history. Some of them include the Persian collection (1184), the Ashrafiyah collection, the Mahmudiyah Library, the Hamidiyah Library, and Bashir Agha collection. Most of these collections were included in the central library that was established in 1933 and became known as the Prophetic Shrine Library (*Maktabat al-Haram al-Nabawi*). Its current holdings are estimated to be about 18,000 volumes and 2000 manuscripts.

Apart from the major governmental supervisory bodies, there are also several nongovernmental organizations that provide similar services and whose organizational structure resemble, to some extent, that of King Abd al-Aziz Library. These include:

- Dar al-Jawf established by Sheikh Abd al-Rahman Ahmad al-Sudayri in 1984. It comprises two libraries, one for men and one for women. The total number of their combined holdings is 47,063 and 103 serials.
- King Faysal Center for Research and Islamic Studies in Riyadh. It comprises two libraries. The adults' library was established in 1983 and its holdings include 37,765 volumes and 280 serials. The children library was established in 1987. Its holdings include 16,384 volumes.
- The Salihiyah Philanthropic Organization in Unayzah. It was established in 1987 and its holdings include 7145 volumes organized according to the modified DDC system.
- Library of the Cultural Center of Salih ibn Salih (for women). It was established in 1959 and its holdings include 13,685 volumes.

SCHOOL LIBRARIES

School libraries started as a division under the General Administration for Research, Curricula, and Instructional

Resources in the Ministry of Education in 1970.[16] Prior to the creation of this administrative body, school libraries were affiliated to their regional public libraries. The bylaws of the administration states that it aims to:

- Provide the books, reference materials, audiovisual aides that serve the educational curricula as well as all aspects of educational and cultural activities.
- Encourage students to pursue the free reading and research which is appropriate for their age and aptitude.
- Train students to acquire the necessary library skills that enable them to benefit from the library resources.
- Help achieve the goals of school curricula.
- Develop literary and artistic appreciation and encourage useful entertainment.
- Serve the environment by extending the service hours to meet the needs of the students and their families.[9]

The Administration serves as a central supervisory and executive body for all the schools under the supervision and control of the Ministry of Education. The management of the school libraries follows the local and regional administrative hierarchy of the Ministry of Education. Each library is run by the school librarian who reports to the school principal. Regional Education Districts include a body of library supervisors who oversee the activities of the libraries under their mandate and who report to the superintendent and to the Ministry. They are also responsible for conducting regular assessment and evaluation of the activities and performance of the library personnel. The books are organized according to a modified DDC System. Collection development is carried out by the central administration which undertakes the purchase and acquisition of materials and examines them before dispatching them to the regional districts. Although some of the public libraries are administratively under the Ministry of Education, the two systems (school libraries and public libraries) remain entirely independent from each other.[9]

Special Libraries

According to a study that was undertaken in 1984,[17] there were about 9 special libraries with collections of more than 5000 volumes. There were the libraries of ARAMCO in Dhahran, Institute of Public Administration in Riyadh, Saudi Arabia Consulting House in Riyadh, Educational Data Center in Riyadh, Industrial Studies and Development Center in Riyadh, Ministry of Planning in Riyadh, Saudi Arabia Airlines in Jeddah, King Abd al-Aziz Research Center in Riyadh and Information Center at the Ministry of Finance in Riyadh. In addition to these libraries, there were other small government and corporate libraries such as: The Department of Investigation and Public Security, 738 books and 8 serials; Saudi

Arabia Industries Corporation, 700 books and 80 serials; General Organization for Social Insurance, 598 books and 5 serials; Chamber of Commerce and Industry, 586 books and 26 serials; Ministry of Public Works and Housing, 520 books and 195 serials. All these libraries are in Riyadh. The three libraries of Jeddah Broadcasting, Ministry of Petroleum and Minerals in Riyadh, as well as Saudi Arabia Standards Organization use the Universal Decimal Classification system. The other libraries use the DDC system.

LIBRARY EDUCATION AND TRAINING

Library Education in Saudi Arabia started its first program in the academic year of 1973–1974 in the department of Library and Information Science in the Faculty of Arts—King Abd al-Aziz University.[17] This program offers bachelor, master, and Ph.D. degrees. It started as a regular department but later adopted the credit hours (semester) system.[18] Undergraduate students need to successfully complete 134 credit hours in order to receive their degree in four years of full-time enrollment divided as follows:

- University compulsory requirements (14 hr)
- College compulsory requirements (11 hr)
- College selective requirements (15 hr)
- Department compulsory requirements (38 hr)
- Department selective requirements (40 hr)
- Other departments compulsory requirements (10 hr)
- Other departments selective requirements (6 hr)

After finishing the bachelor's degree, students can enroll in the masters program after taking an entrance exam. Students with B.A. in library science are required to finish 36 credit hours and students from other fields are required to finish 46 credit hours. Out of the total credit hours, 6 hr are designated for the master's thesis. Upon successful completion of the M.A. degree, students are eligible for admission into the Ph.D. program which requires a total of 47 credit hours out of which 20 are designated for the Ph. D. dissertation.[17]

The second program started in the academic year 1974–1975 with the establishment of Library and Information Sciences Department at Imam Muhammad Ibn Saud University. In addition to its focus on general library education, the program offers special training in manuscripts and other heritage-related literature. The program offers a bachelor degree of arts in library science for which students have to complete 174 credit hours divided as follows:

- Library science courses (118 hr)
- Religion, language, education and other courses (56 hr)

The department offers also a postgraduate diploma in library and information science for which students have to complete 20 credit hours and recently started also M.A. and Ph.D. programs.[18]

The third academic program started in 1986–1987 with the establishment of the Library and Information Science in the College of Arts at King Saud University. The program offers two main specializations upon the completion of the program's core courses: library science and information science. The department's bachelor of arts degree requires the completion of 120 credit hours divided as follows:

- University compulsory requirements (15 hr)
- College compulsory requirements (13 hr)
- Elective compulsory requirements (6 hr)
- Departments compulsory requirements (27 hr)
- Specialization compulsory requirements (47 hr)
- Minor field compulsory requirements (12 hr)

The fourth academic program started in 1987–1988 with the establishment of the Library and Information Science Department in the College of Social Studies at Umm al-Qura University. For the bachelor degree, students have to complete 130 credit hours divided as follows:

- University compulsory requirements (18 hr)
- College compulsory requirements (12 hr)
- Elective compulsory requirements (12 hr)
- Departments compulsory requirements (40 hr)
- Specialization compulsory requirements (30 hr)
- Minor field compulsory requirements (18 hr)[17]

The fifth academic program is in the department of Library and Information Studies at the Girls College of Arts. The bachelor degree requires 190 credit hours divided as follows:

- Library science courses (107 hr)
- Religion, language, education and other courses (83 hr)

In addition to these five academic programs, there are other institutions that offer training programs in librarianship. The most important program is offered by the Institute of Public Administration. The program consists of two-year training leading to a diploma in library. Similar long-term and short-term programs are offered at the College of Education of King Saud University as well as the Central Library in Riyadh.

Although these programs produce hundreds of graduates every year, recent surveys indicated that the overall quality of the programs is not up to the desired level. These programs were found lacking in many critical areas mainly because they were not updated for many years. They do not offer ongoing training or training in modern trends in the field due to shortage of adequate resources and facilities.[19] Many institutions started offering continuing education in the form of courses, workshops, short courses, seminars, conferences and online support in order to help library professionals keep up with users' needs, demands and expectations in a rapidly changing information landscape.

Despite the numerous constraints that the library and information science training faces in Saudi Arabia[9,17] efforts are being made to modernize the system and cope with the fast-paced changes in the field. For more information about the Arabic Union Catalog, see the Web site of King Abd al-Aziz Public Library in Riyadh.[20] Special attention is devoted to create a robust education system which is indispensable for producing a well-trained and highly qualified manpower for the country. Most early Saudi library professionals and faculty received training abroad, especially in the United States, Britain and Egypt respectively. See the deliberations and the minutes of the establishing meeting of the Federation that took place in Qayrawan, Tunisia, January 19, 1986.[21]

ASSOCIATIONS AND JOINT PROJECTS

Arabic Union Catalog

The project of Arabic Union Catalog was launched by King Abd al-Aziz Library in November 2006. It aims to create a unified cataloging system that serves as a platform for all the Arabic-speaking countries in the areas of cataloging and bibliographical standards. The Union seeks to perform the functions of projects such as OCLC or WorldCat but on a regional level. The project aims to:

- Include all the Arabic information resources in a single standardized database.
- Unify the efforts in the area of Arabic cataloging and share a single catalog by all the professionals.
- Reduce the cost of cataloging and bibliographical duplications.
- Promote cooperation and collective initiatives in publishing and circulating Arabic information resources both regionally and internationally.
- Support the Arab researchers.
- Encourage and Facilitate scientific research.
- Facilitate the process of collection development in the Arabic libraries.

Currently, the project includes more than four million bibliographic records that has been prepared according to the most up-to-date standards and that can be easily shared or downloaded by the any of the participating institutions. The project has more than 40 participating institutions most of them are located in Saudi Arabia. The project also includes other participating institutions that are based in

United Arab Emirates, Kuwait, Oman, Qatar, Lebanon, Jordan, Algeria, Morocco, and France. Most of these institutions are University libraries but there are also a number of public libraries as well as research organizations.[21]

The Arab Federation for Libraries and Information

The Arab Federation for Libraries and Information (AFLI) was founded in 1986 and has members from 20 Arab countries.[22] Among other things, the association aims at strengthening the ties between the national libraries organizations and preserving the written, oral and visual heritage of the Arab world. The Federation publishes a newsletter, *Sada al-Ittihad* (the echo of the federation), in Tunisia which started its first issue in June 1995. The Federation also started a new scholarly journal which is published in collaboration with King Abd al-Aziz Public Library *Ialam* whose first issue was published in October 2007.[8]

Arabian Gulf Chapter of the Special Library Association

It was established with the goal of providing an opportunity for Library and Information professionals in the Gulf area to interact and share professional knowledge and experience. More than 150 professionals participated in the inaugural conference that was held in January 1994.

ARCHIVES AND ARCHIVAL INSTITUTIONS

One of the most prominent themes that have been emphasized in the different national development plans is the "desire to maintain a national Saudi identity rooted in Arab and Islamic civilization."[23] The plans also seek to take advantage of the modern advances in science and technology in all fields. These two goals capture the tension that the Saudi government, like other Arab and Islamic governments, has to contend with. It seeks to preserve its cultural heritage without falling behind the rest of the world. The fifth development plan speaks about heritage as "the authenticity deriving from the security of firmly established cultural roots, which in the case of Saudi context, are founded on Arab and Islamic civilization giving our contemporary culture its own unique identity and endowing it with an ability to withstand attack or undesirable influences."[24]

One of the important ways to maintain this heritage and to preserve this cultural and historical identity is through museums and archives. Although the plans do not provide specific details on these institutions or their activities, they include however general statements that reflect the government's support for these activities. They also speak about the importance of cooperation between the government and the private sector in this area. For example, the

Fifth Development Plan recognizes the efforts of organizations such as King Faisal Center for Islamic Research and Studies as well as King Fahd Library and museums.

The National Center for Documents and Archives is the formal archival institution in Saudi Arabia. It was founded by the Royal Decree no. (M/55) in 1989. Administratively, it is affiliated to the Council of Ministers and is supervised by its chairman.[24] The center aims to collect, classify, and store documents and to facilitate their retrieval. The center drafts the policies that regulate the preservation and the circulation of all types of government documents. It coordinates the preservation activities among the different government agencies inside the country and cooperates with similar institutions on the international level.

One of the most important archival institutions in Saudi Arabia is King Abd al-Aziz Foundation for Research and Archives. It aims to preserve and document the history, geography, as well as the literary and cultural heritage of the Kingdom of Saudi Arabia and other Arab and Islamic countries. The foundation was established by the Royal Decree no. (M/45) in 1972. For more information, see the Web site of the Foundation[25] Other than the library, it includes many different departments for renovation and preservation of historical items, public affairs, research and publication, journal of the foundation, archive for photographs and documentaries, geographical information systems, manuscripts, documentation of the history of the Saudi Royal family, historical Documents and oral History.

Its documentation center is one of the most important historical and archival institutions in the country. It collects and preserves all types of documents that relate to the history of Saudi Arabia. It holds a rare collection of original as well as copies of important historical documents that include correspondences, deeds, contracts, formal letters, decrees, statements, and reports. The collection includes more than 1,400,000 national and regional documents. It also includes other important documents from foreign archives that deal with the history of Saudi Arabia such as the Ottoman, American, British, French, Dutch, German, Indian, Russian, and Italian archives. The center collaborates with major international organizations in the area of renovation and preservation of rare historical documents such as the Library of Congress, the International Council on Archives, the International Federation of Library Associations, and the UNSCO.

MUSEUMS

According to the directory issued by the Undersecretariat of Archaeology and Museums in the Saudi Ministry of Education, there are more than 50 museums in different regions of the Kingdom (Table 2).[26] For the museums in Jeddah see the directory posted on the municipality's Web site.[27] These museums can be classified into five main categories: archaeological and historical museums, educational and academic museums, scientific museums, popular and cultural museums and private museums. They range from large state-of-the-art museums to small-scale local and private museums. Some of the important museums listed in this directory are:

The most important museum in Saudi Arabia is of course the Saudi National Museum in Riyadh which was inaugurated in 1999. It is located at the eastern side of King Abd al-Aziz historical compound. It is built on an area of 17,000 m^2 and the total area of its two story structure is 28,000 m^2. In addition to places for exhibits and shows, the museum includes 8 main halls which display various objects and artifacts that represent the different historical stages of Saudi Arabia. The general themes for these halls are: man and the universe, ancient Arabian kingdoms, Pre-Islamic phase, early Islamic phase, Islam and Arabian Peninsula, 1st and 2nd Saudi states, Unification of Saudi Arabia, Pilgrimage and the two Holy Shrines.[26]

Another important museum which is also located in the city of Riyadh is the citadel of al-Masmak which was turned into a museum in 1995. It has special historical significance for its connection with the events that influenced the rise of the Saudi state. The capture of the citadel by the young emir Abd al-Aziz Ibn Abd al-Rahman in January 1902 marked the reestablishment of the supremacy of the Al-Saud family over the city of Riyadh. It includes several exhibit halls that depict the different stages of the Saudi family history and recounts the story of the unification of the Kingdom under King Abd al-Aziz.[28]

The Museum of the Two Holy Shrines in Makkah illustrates the history of the two holy sites. It includes seven main halls with each focusing on one general theme as follows: The Hall of the Entrance, The Hall of Holy Mosque of Makkah, The Hall of Kabah, the Hall of Photographic Pictures, The Hall of Manuscripts, The Hall of Zamzam Well and The Hall of the Holy Mosque of Madinah. It includes numerous collections of old and recent large-scale photos as well as maquettes of the Two Holy Shrines. It also includes many items and artifacts from these sites across the different historical eras.[28]

CONCLUSION

The successive Development Plans continued to both reflect and drive the steady advances in the different sectors of the Saudi economy. The growing economic surplus from the oil revenues has facilitated the implementation of these successive Development Plans. Librarianship aided by the modern applications of the Information Technology has made great strides. The demand for libraries and other cultural institutions such as museums and archives is increasingly on the rise because of the remarkable

Regional–School

Table 2 Museums in Saudi Arabia.

Name	Type	Region
National Museum	Historical	Riyadh
Masmak Museum	Historical	Riyadh
King Fahd Library Museum	National	Riyadh
Numismatics Museum	Historical	Riyadh
Postal Museum	National/historical	Riyadh
Zoology Museum	Scientific/academic	King Saud University
Archeology Museum	Historical/academic	King Saud University
Folklore Museum	Historical/academic	King Saud University
Pharmacology Museum	Scientific/academic	King Saud University
Anatomy Museum	Scientific/academic	King Saud University
Geological Museum	Scientific/academic	King Saud University
King Fahd Security College Museum	Academic	Riyadh
King Abd al-Aziz Military Museum	Military	Riyadh
Sheikh Muhammad Abd al-Rahman al-Duwayhi Museum	Historical	Riyadh
Sheikh Sad Ibn Abd Allah Al-Muhaymid Museum	Historical	Shaqra
The Two Shrines Museum	Religious/historical	Makkah
Jiddah Regional Folklore Museum	Historical	Jeddah
Ta'if Regional Folklore Museum	Historical	Ta'if
Ocean Museum	Scientific/academic	King A. al-Aziz University
Earth Sciences Museum	Scientific/academic	King A. al-Aziz University
Jiddah Museum	Historical	Jeddah
A. Ra'uf H. Khalil Museum	Historical/private	Jeddah
Al-Khujah Museum	Historical	Makkah
Waqdani Museum	Historical/private	Makkah
Ukaz Museum	Historical/private	Makkah
Al-Madinah Museum	Historical	Madinah
Al-Ula Archeological Museum	Historical	Al-Ula
Royal Association Museum	Historical	Madinah
Buraydah Museum	Historical	Al-Qasim
Al-Dammam Regional Museum	Historical	Al-Sharqiyah
Al-Ahsa Regional Museum	Historical	Al-Sharqiyah

Source: From *Dalil al-Matahif fi al-mamlakah al-Arabiyah al-Saudiyah*, Wakalat al-Athar wa al-Matahif, Riyadh, 2000.[26]

demographic changes that the country has witnessed in the past few decades. For example, the number of schools and colleges has increased from 3283 in 1969–1970 to 22,770 in 1999–2000. Consequently, the total number of teachers increased from 231,000 to 3,548,000 and the total number of enrolled students in the different educational institutions increased from 547,000 to 4.8 million during the same period. Also, the number of students who completed their university degrees both at home and abroad rose from 808 to 42,950 during the same period.

Like many other Muslim countries, Saudi Arabia is striving to preserve its historical heritage but also to catch up with modern education and technology. In the modern period and with the initiation of national development plans, librarianship has initially been attached to the Ministry of Education but gradually it has been developing its independent identity. Many national organizations such as King Fahd National Library and King Abd al-Aziz Foundation for Research and Archives are actively engaged in the process of shaping this identity. Through national, regional, and international programs they are striving to further enhance the field. The early Saudi Information professionals received their education and training abroad but with the establishment of academic programs in national universities much of the undergraduate and even graduate education is currently being provided at home. As many researchers already observed, the field still faces many challenges that often accompany the localization of technology and standardization procedures.

ACKNOWLEDGMENTS

I would like to thank Prof. Mary Maack for her insights and useful feedback. I would like also to thank Mr. David Hirsch for his helpful comments.

REFERENCES

1. Saudi Arabia, *The Europa World Year Book 2008*, 49th Ed. Routledge: London, 2008; Vol. 2, 3874.
2. CIA The World Factbook—Saudi Arabia. https://www.cia.gov/library/publications/the-world-factbook/geos/sa.html.
3. Al-Rasheed, M. *A History of Saudi Arabia*; Cambridge University Press: New York, 2002; 120; 4, 94.

4. Sibai, M. *Mosque Libraries: An Historical Study*; Mansell Publishing Limited: London, 1987.

5. Hamadah, M. *al-Maktabat fi al-Islam*; Muassasat al-Risalah: Beirut, Lebanon, 1978; 54.

6. *National Report on Higher Education*, King Saud University Press: Riyadh, 1998; 68 42, 22, 32, 67.

7. Abbas, H. *al-Rakaiz al-Asasiyah lil Nizam al-Watani lil Maktabat al-Ammah bi al-Mamlakah al-Arabiyah al-Saudiyah*; Matbuat Maktabat al-Malik Fahd al-Wataniyah: Riyadh, 1993; 38.

8. *The Development Plans of the GCC States, Saudi Arabia*, Oxford, 1994; Archive Ed. Vol. 1, 26, Vol. 3, 352–355, Vol. 5, 338–340, 318, Vol. 7, 354–355, 352–353, Vol. 9, 323.

9. Al-Nahari, A. *The Role of National Libraries in Developing Countries with Special Reference to Saudi Arabia*; Mansell Publishing Limited: London, 1984; Vol. 123, 74, 69, 73, 76.

10. *King Fahd National Library*, King Fahd National Library: Riyadh, 1992; Vol. 9, 35.

11. Yusuf, M. *Maktabat al-Malik Abd al-Aziz al-Ammah*; King and al-Aziz Public Library Press: Riyadh, 1999; Vol. 58, 328.

12. Siddiqui, M. Academic libraries in Saudi Arabia: A survey report. Ref. Libr. **1998**, *60*, 167–168.

13. Siddiqui, M. The use of information technology in academic libraries in Saudi Arabia. J. Libr. Inform. Sci. **1997**, *29* (December), 195–203.

14. Al-Dubayan, S. *Itlalah Tarikhiyah ala al-Maktabat al-Ammah fi al-Mamlakah maa Dalil Shamil laha*, Maktabat al-Malik Fahd al-Wataniyah: Riyadh, 1994; 26, 25, 28.

15. Abu Sulayman, A. *Maktabat Makkah al-Mukarramah*; King Fahd National Library Press: Riyadh, 1995; 29.

16. Al-Sallum, H. *al-Talim al-Amm fi al-Mamlakah al-Arabiyah al-Saudiyah*; Washington, DC, 1991; 395–400.

17. Siddiqui, M. Library and information science education in Saudi Arabia. Educ. Inform. **1996**, *14* (October), 198–201.

18. Khurshid, Z. Continuing education for catalogers in Saudi Arabia. Catalog. Classif. Quart. **2006**, *41* (3/4), 463.

19. Alsereihy, H. The status of LIS education in Saudi Arabia. J. Educ. Libr. Inform. Sci. **1998**, *4*, 334–338.

20. http://www.kapl.org.sa (accessed October 2008), http://www.aruc.org.

21. Qaddurah, W., Ed. *al-Takshif wa al-Tasnif fi Marakiz al-Malumat al-Arabiyah*; King Fahd National Library Press: Riyadh, 1993; 211–270.

22. http://www.afli.info/Detail.asp?InServiceID=4&InTemplateKey=MainPage.

23. *Achievements of the Development Plans Facts and Figures*; Ministry of Planning: Riyadh, 2001; 183; 19th issue (1390-1421/1970-2001).

24. http://www.ncda.gov.sa/Detail.asp?InSectionID=1706&InNewsItemID=132646.

25. http://www.darah.org.sa.

26. *Dalil al-Matahif fi al-mamlakah al-Arabiyah al-Saudiyah*; Wakalat al-Athar wa al-Matahif: Riyadh, 2000.

27. http://www.jeddah.gov.sa/directories/entertainment/museums.php.

28. *Achievements of the Development Plans Facts and Figures*; Ministry of Planning: Riyadh, 2002; 156, 162; 18th issue (1390–1420/1970–2000).

Scholarly and Trade Publishing [ELIS Classic]

Richard Abel
Portland, Oregon, U.S.A.

Abstract

Richard Abel developed vast experience in the publishing and library communities, and brings great perspicuity to his discussion of the publishing industry. In 2008 he received the Jack D. Rittenhouse Award from the Publishers Association of the West. An announcement of the award states: "Richard worked in a bookstore, became a bookstore owner, started a private press for limited edition books, founded a company that grew into an international library distributor, founded a book marketing and distribution company, started a trade publishing company that has grown into a well respected mid-sized publisher, and is the author of numerous articles and a forthcoming book." [http://www.against-the-grain.com/d/taxonomy/term/26]

—ELIS Classic, from 2005

INTRODUCTION

This entry is intended to focus on the place of the "trade" in the transmission and dissemination of knowledge, literature, and information in the society. The term the "trade" has long been the shorthand referent to book and journal publishers, book wholesalers, journal agents, retail bookstores, specialist booksellers to libraries, and out-of-print (OP) dealers. Various elements of the trade are integral partners with libraries as the originators and/or suppliers of books, periodicals, and related services. Book and journal publishers are the key players in the trade as they first produce the books and journals, which come to rest on the shelves or in the computers of libraries. As the originators of the knowledge/literature/information packages stored and circulated by libraries publishers stand at the beginning of the process, which results in the dissemination of the material embodiments of ideas, bodies of knowledge, and research findings. (Some may argue, and in substantial measure correctly, that authors stand at the beginning of this creative process, but such commentators fail to understand the role that publishers play in not simply providing the means for authors to make their work available in the marketplace of ideas but in seeking out, stimulating, encouraging, assisting in the writing, and editing their work to get it to and make it most useful to readers.) By virtue of this role of origination in the intellectual and creative process of knowledge and information formation, the present standing and condition of publishing is of substantial interest to librarians and information specialists. This entry does not have as its burden an explanation of the processes and practices of the publishing trade. Rather, its intention is to inform readers of the present trends and problems faced by publishers internationally and how the present state of publishing may affect libraries.

Any effort to provide a statistical portrait of the trade is so marred by inaccuracies as to make such a representation virtually meaningless. The wide differences in the numbers provided by various agencies for a specific year in a specific country not only befuddle veterans of the trade but also simply confuse outside observers. It is a matter of some irony that a trade dedicated to the origination and dissemination of knowledge and information possesses so little information about itself. Probably the most reliable source of statistical information about the U.S. book trade is the Book Industry Study Group. They estimate the total dollar sales of books in the United States is $26,000,000,000. The reader will quickly note that the individual sales of any number of large corporations exceed the total of sales of all classes of books published by all publishers in the United States. To use a boxing metaphor: "The trade punches above its weight" in terms of setting the cultural agenda of the United States.

THE MAJOR PRESENT TRENDS MARKING PUBLISHING

Several worldwide trends mark, and have marked, the book and journal publishing trade in recent decades. The first is the continuing increase in the number of new titles issued. This trend is really only a continuation of the trend, which began with the invention of printing and has continued ever since, save for the occasional short periods of leveling off attributable to major wars. However, since World War II the rate of increase virtually the globe around has accelerated to an incrementally higher annual rate. In earlier centuries, this secular growth in new book titles could be attributed to the roughly parallel increases in literacy—first in Europe and North America and

Encyclopedia of Library and Information Sciences, Fourth Edition DOI: 10.1081/E-ELIS4-120008948

subsequently in the other major regions of the world. Indeed, increases in literacy quite closely track increased economic well-being across entire countries and regions. Economic well-being, in turn, generally correlates with not only increased personal income beyond sheer creature needs and increased leisure but job markets depending upon ever larger percentages of more highly skilled jobs. All these consequences, of course, contribute to the desire and need to allocate increased percentages of wealth to reading for increased comprehension, augmenting skills, and filling leisure time in a satisfying way.

Inextricably linked to this growth in book readership is the second observable major trend. That is the globalization of reading interests. This is to say that some titles come to enjoy a near-global readership. This concentrating of readers' taste is served not only through the sale by the original publisher of coeditions to publishers in other countries employing the same language or through the sale of translation rights, but also by the globalization of publishing firms. Although the sale of coeditions and translation rights is a universal practice, and the numbers of titles involved is rapidly growing, the largest fraction of such transactions involve titles published by English-language publishers.

In parallel with this widespread interest in writings originating in English-language countries, the English language has become the principal language of scientific, technical, and medical (STM) writing/publishing, as well as the language of much other scholarly writing/publishing, throughout the world. STM publishing represents about 10% of total book sales in the advanced countries but markedly less in developing countries.

Globalization of reading taste and subject interest based in significant measure on English language writings coupled with the near-universal use of the English language in STM publications and, to a lesser degree, in other scholarly writing/publishing, has led to the third major trend in international publishing. That is the economic concentration of the publishing trade, particularly in the advanced countries. The need to be able to successfully market a substantial fraction of any publisher's list to copublishers, translation partners, and in the case of STM and scholarly books to readers/users worldwide virtually dictates that publishers establish a presence in those countries that constitute their major markets, usually by means of acquiring existing publishers in those countries. The firms involved must possess the financial resources necessary to maintain staffs of a size consistent with the nature of such markets; the management skills to operate such geographically dispersed organizations successfully; and the financial integrity to assure partners of their capacity to fulfill the various agreements into which they enter—almost exclusively on trust, for international contracts and agreements are but at best scarcely enforceable in any way other than moral integrity. Furthermore, such firms typically seek a presence in the countries that

represent their major markets, not only in terms of the sale of the bulk of their titles but in terms of the editorial content and list-building by the acquisition of titles from writers in the countries in which they are domiciled.

The almost inevitable outcome of this concentration produces the fourth major trend, again most marked in the advanced countries where the consequences of increased economic complexity are most clearly being played out. That is the almost exponential growth of small publishers publishing exclusively in narrowly defined subject matter fields and serving fairly readily defined reader audiences. In the United States alone over 50,000 small publishing firms have been formed as documented by R.R. Bowker and *Publishers Weekly*. Such publishers are often styled "niche publishers" reflecting the quite definite outlines of subject matter and audience that they have rigorously focused on. The large, economically concentrated publishers, compelled to support a large and highly specialized staff, must necessarily seek out "big-name" authors, whether writers of fiction or writers of dense scholarly syntheses and every kind of book between these extremes. The large publishers are no longer in a position to gamble heavily on unknown authors or run many of the risks incident to the new, and often novel, hypotheses and syntheses continually being advanced in the various realms of scholarship by young scholars. Therefore, the niche publishers, often founded by editors exiting the world of the large concentrated houses, have identified a multitude of subject matter/audience interests/markets in which they can make genuine cultural contributions as well as reasonable livelihoods. Audiences are typically reached by specialized marketing programs designed to apprise niche audiences of the availability of books devoted to their subject-matter interests. To reach beyond their domestic market for their titles, they typically develop a network of other niche or small publishers in the other major markets for books suited to the specialized subject matter involved. Much trading of coeditions and translation rights is ultimately conducted within these networks. By carefully developing and employing these networks, the niche publisher can reach virtually the entire universe of authors and readers concerned with the subject matter or writings defining such niche networks.

It should be clearly articulated here that the titles classified as "trade" books and marketed by and large through the "trade" channels of retail bookstores constitute not only the most highly visible aspect of the book trade but roughly one-fourth of total book sales. The book-reviewing media and the associated publicity and "smart" talk in literary circles fundamentally turn on trade books. The world of trade books is almost entirely dominated by a handful of large, publishing conglomerates, which are usually international in scale. The same observation can be made of the small contingent of STM book and journal publishers, save only that STM books are not marketed through retail bookstores in any significant numbers. STM marketing more closely resembles that pursued by niche publishers. It bears repeating that the trade book world, which is what the general public construes as the entire world of books, constitutes but roughly 25% of the total sales of books in most countries. (Of this 25% about one quarter are children's books.) The remaining 75% will be dealt with below.

The fifth major trend is still largely confined to the publishing trades of the advanced countries. That is the leveling off of the sale of units of books. This is to say that the total number of books purchased in the advanced countries has become virtually flat, in year-on-year comparisons, since the last few years of the last century. Given that the total number of titles continues to increase while the number of book units purchased has largely flattened out, the obvious consequence is that the sales of most titles has been declining over the past decade. The book trade economist, Fritz Machlup, first identified this trend in the late 1978.[1] In a major review of book publishing *The Economist* noted, ". . . the overall amount of money that the public spends on books is no longer rising."[2] As this trend continues, the consequences thereof, in terms of book prices, publisher economic viability, etc. have only been ameliorated by the appearance of short-run printing and print-on-demand technologies. The most likely explanation for this phenomenon is, first, that the increasing affluence of the citizens of the advanced countries has led to the formation and articulation of a markedly increased number of more narrowly and selective personal interests.

Second, as Curtis Benjamin pointed out some years ago, virtually all scholarly fields have in recent decades demonstrated what he styled a "twigging effect." This is to say that what were in the early 20th century fairly coherent bodies of knowledge, the content of which most of the scholars in those fields were presumed to have mastered and about which they were in a position to teach both the general public and new recruits to the field, have divided and redivided into increasingly narrow subfields. As the apparent pace of discovery quickened, such generalists became fewer while the numbers of "specialists" who were on the cutting edges of the newly defined subfields increased. In short, these specialties "twigged" off the trunk of the general field. These specialists spent much of their professional lives increasingly narrowly focused on narrow and specialized subfields. As they did so, entirely new subdisciplines arose bringing in their stead specialized books and journals. These specialists, in turn, concentrated most of their attention on these specialized publications to the exclusion of those in other specialties. Thus, while the number of new titles published in the general field increased the specialists mostly purchased titles in their field, thereby increasing the number of titles associated with each general field. They outcome, of course, was fewer copies of most titles sold despite the increase in the numbers of titles published.

A third factor also contributed to this outcome. Libraries have long formed a dependable and major market for books—the public libraries for "trade" books, the school libraries for supplementary "textbooks", and the university and research libraries for scholarly books. But demands on library budgets to offer an ever wider array of materials/ services, most notably periodical literature; electronic products, and Internet access have increased very rapidly. The costs of traditional purchases plus this increased demand for other products/services have outstripped available funding. The inevitable outcome, of course, is that library book purchases have been held steady or reduced and so contributed to the reduction in numbers of copies sold of a larger number of titles being published.

Substantial increases in the purchasing of books remain to be realized in second and, more notably, in third world countries. Realization of these increases will depend on both economic development and the retreat of governmental command-and-control authorities from the publishing trade—just as had to occur earlier in the development of the advanced countries to free the public square for open debate occasioned by the increasing complexity of advancing societies.

The sixth major and worldwide trend affecting publishing is the explosion of electronic products and the extension of the Internet to public access, not simply in the United States but worldwide. Much has been made in recent decades of the repeatedly prophesized demise of the printed codex and the replacement of the book by first one and then another electronic product whether as stand-alone devices or some kind of Internet download. A steady stream of fiascoes and exploded hopes and the loss of quite substantial sums of money have failed to diminish widespread enthusiasm for such notions; several celebrity figures in the world of publishing have kept up the drumbeat for such alternatives.

Outcomes such as those associated with the attempted mechanization of the codex have not attended all efforts to provide electronic access to formerly printed material. A brief glance at these successful ventures and the character thereof will, in all likelihood, identify the nature of the kinds of intellectual material that can satisfactorily transit to electronic means of transmission. The most obvious and successful kind of electronic presentation of formerly printed material has proved to be the "encyclopedia" and similar "reference" materials. In short, the electronic transmission and presentation of information (think discrete bits and pieces of data) seems to work quite well for a number of users and uses. Related thereto is the still emerging electronic transmission of more complex forms of information in the shape of research reports and journal articles communicating new discoveries of discrete data. (Many libraries now prefer to receive journal subscriptions in electronic form.) What has become thoroughly evident in the last three to four decades is that information/data transits relatively readily to electronic forms.

Electronic technology has proved, on the other hand, a major boon to book publishers in the "backroom" functions of the publishing cycle. The typical journey of a writing from author to a printed book is now conducted almost entirely electronically. Writing, editing, peer-reviewing, designing, preparing electronic input for the printer, and control of the presses in the printers shop is now largely done on computers. Additionally, all warehousing billing, shipping, accounting, etc. within the publishing house is computer controlled.

Thus, book publishers are well acquainted with electronic procedures and practices. However, their repeated efforts to replace, or offer an electronic alternative to, the printed book have proved fruitless. A brief look at the nature of the book provides the obvious answer to these repeated fizzles. The difference between the miscellany of any assemblage of information/data (think encyclopedias, dictionaries, law reports, an issue of a journal, etc.) and the coherent body of knowledge or the sustained discourse of a fiction writing is a matter of human epistemology and the quite different purposes mental processes served by each. A book of knowledge or a fiction depend for their meaning and use on an extended discourse or narrative—readers must be presented with an often extensive body of evidence or the development of a story, all configured in a logical and coherent way to acquire, in at least some measure, the sense the author intended. Information gathering, by way of contrast, commonly involves simply finding a datum to serve a particular purpose defined by the immediate needs of a mental process engaged by the seeker (think a telephone number or a dictionary word or a brief chronology of the development of the computer or a library catalog entry, etc.). The discursive discourses demanded by the exposition of a knowledge concept, an ethical precept or the telling of a story are not well handled in terms of human epistemological requirements by digital devices. An entirely different epistemological process is involved in the acquisition of a datum or a body of data than is called for in the following of the line(s) of thinking involved in the transfer of knowledge concepts and precepts or the development of a story line inherent to the construction of fiction.

To cast this profound intellectual difference in an entirely other way: a base of knowledge is an absolute prerequisite not only for intelligently seeking information but is equally necessary to the rational understanding of whatever data bits are located. By way of example: imagine an intelligent person who is utterly unacquainted with financial markets. Seat this person before three networked computer screens displaying real-time financial data. The ignorant subject of this thought experiment placed in this situation will prove utterly unable to make any sense of these masses of data, despite the fact that financial data is probably the most complete and accurate body of information/data presently in existence. Only a broad and deep knowledge of financial markets and the economics

underlying them will permit a viewer to decipher this information and put it into understandable and usable form. The same thought experiment could be employed with any body of data resulting in precisely the same outcome of incomprehensibility for the unknowledgeable. In short, the epistemological realities of the human mind must needs deal with knowledge and information in quite different ways. Therefore, the successful migration of information books to electronic forms is perfectly consistent with the functioning of the human mind. The operation of the human mind equally well explains the repeated failures to adapt books of knowledge and fiction to electronic forms.

An exception to this general formulation may occur when a reader requires but a limited portion—a chapter or several pages—of a longer discursive writing. In such cases, electronic access may prove as useful as access to the printed form of the text.

The seventh major trend in publishing again relates to another player in the wider world of books, in this case booksellers. Again this trend has been most clearly played out in the advanced countries enjoying maximum retailing freedom. This retailing trend is being played out in two forms. Both forms take as their base operational objective the immediate supply of the widest possible range of titles. This trend first became evident in the form of the "super bookstore" chains. The huge bookstore stocking 150,000 to 250,000 discrete titles has been the occasional feature of a limited number of major cities for some years. However, such stores were not readily accessible to a large fraction of the population of any country. (This fact also explains the dramatic growth of direct-mail book clubs of all descriptions in the 1930s to the 1940s—they offered most of the citizenry both some information on current publishing output and the opportunity to easily purchase titles of interest.) The radical change in bookselling, which the chain superstores inaugurated, was to place well-stocked stores (75,000 to 200,000 individual titles) in all manner of market locations—even some in which small-scale, "mom and pop" bookstores had failed. The opportunities offered the reader to personally examine hands-on a broad range of books for suitability and immediately acquire any of interest were almost overnight geometrically increased. The advent of the chain superstores has provided a much larger number of readers with a service well beyond that previously available. And not surprisingly, the committed independent booksellers undertook to match the competition created by the chain superstores in virtually every aspect, from increasing the number of titles immediately in stock to providing seating and other amenities for browsers—which has, in turn, benefited readers.

The emergence of the bookstore chains has led to some quite unsustainable conclusions about their impact on publishing. Probable the most common is that the chains have furthered the purported homogenization of taste and interest among readers and, thereby, narrowed the range of subject matters open to authors and publishers and/or lowered the levels of sophistication to which books have to be tailored. Either one or both of two lines of argument are advanced to support this cluster of related conclusions. The first, and most egregious, is that the buyers/management of the large chains exercise greater or lesser control over the publishing programs of the trade publishers. The fact of the matter is that the opinion of chain bookstore staff is occasionally solicited, e.g., when a publisher harbors some concerns with respect to the size of print run to order or again, as approximations of the quantity of a title that might be purchased when advertising and promotion budgets are being formulated. However, such inquiries are light-years apart from editorial control.

The other common causative factor advanced in support of the notion of the progressive homogenization of public taste and interest attributable to the chain bookstores is that the centralized buying employed fails to offer the full range of subject matters and writings that are available. The obvious assumption is that the chain booksellers are appealing to only the lowest common denominator and thereby lowering and narrowing the literary and cultural horizons of the reading public. The general taste and interest of the reading interests of the vast numbers of readers as documented over the centuries apparently is insufficient evidence of the fact that the chain booksellers, in step with the stocking practices of the independent booksellers, is to stock books that seem to have the potential for enjoying a reasonable sale. In short, the chain buyers are simply doing what they insist they are doing—stocking those titles that in their opinion will find a reasonable audience, even one numbering but one or two copies in most of the chain's stores.

In every age litterateurs, authors, and some publishers have found fault with the taste and interests of the general book-buying public. Thus, it is hardly surprising that the same players are leveling identical complaints but falsely attributing them to the emergence of a class of retail bookseller they instinctively dislike.

This new means of providing rapid access to a stupendous range of books in large numbers of physical locations created by the chain superstores and their independent competitors was then translated to Internet bookselling. So, it is now possible for the readers to learn of and then order books of interest from the precincts of their own home and expect, in most cases, to have the books delivered to the front door three or four days later. The databases of book titles now maintained by the largest of the Internet booksellers are, for all practical purposes, identical to the books in print of one or several countries. These large Internet booksellers have now gone a step beyond the provision of in-print titles to conducting out-of-print searches in cooperation with hundreds of out-of-print book dealers. So, the acquisition of an out-of-print title has now become nearly as routine as the acquisition of an in-print title. Additionally, universities and other vendors have digitized a large number of out-of-print titles, most of which can be downloaded and printed out. The world of hard-to-find titles has been radically reduced.

The eighth major trend, which has emerged only in the last few years, is the extensive reprinting of titles using print-on-demand technology (POD). The POD grew out of the joining of the photocopying and computer technologies. Like all such new technologies, POD migrated through about a 20-year period of rapid, successive marginal improvements paralleled by a widening body of buyers thereby progressively reducing costs. The technology is now so effective and cheap that it can successfully compete with conventional presswork for editions of up to about 500 copies. However, perhaps more importantly, it can be economically employed for editions of 10 or so copies, assuming the original text exists in a suitable digital format. As the POD technology has been progressively improved, it has become virtually impossible to distinguish a POD volume from a printed volume. The obvious consequence is that publishers are now in a position to keep much larger and increasing fractions of their backlist in print and within the bounds of an acceptable list price. Some of the more farsighted publishers—largely niche and STM firms—are now producing a significant number of their new titles employing POD. By so doing they cannot only print quantities from digitized manuscripts more closely approximating estimated short-term forward sales but reprint in very small quantities, from the same digital format, as demand dictates.

The second largest single class of books in terms of sales is that of textbooks—typically representing 25% of total book sales in advanced countries and larger percentages in developing countries. Textbooks have a history almost as long as that of the book, whether in scroll or codex form. Indeed, Albert Kapr, presently regarded as the leading authority on Gutenberg, opines that the first book printed from movable type was the standard Latin grammar and dictionary textbook used throughout the Middle Ages and early Renaissance for instruction in the universal language of that period, the 27-line Aelius Donatus *Ars Minor* printed in Strasbourg.[3] Since that day textbooks became an increasingly important and profitable element in almost every publisher's list. Neither the growth of literacy or learning is comprehensible save in the context of an appreciation of the central role the textbook has played in the evolution and present prominence of the culture of the West. The textbook and related supplementary readings continue today to be the principal educational tools in the shaping of the minds of the young and their induction into the mainstream of their culture, now throughout the world.

The textbook, despite its critical role in education, has for much of its history been the lightning rod of cultural conflict, thanks to this very criticality of its role—both within the West and between the West and the balance of the world. As a consequence, the publishing of textbooks is far from the static, seemingly benign activity it is commonly thought to be. The textbook has always been the target of all manner of special interest groups seeking to impose their various agendas on education—and thereby, on the shaping of the minds of the oncoming generations. While these conflicts over the contents of textbooks erupt on occasion into the view of the larger society—one thinks, e.g., of the contests over the control of schools and textbooks, in the centuries following the Reformation—they are usually confined to the immediate and, in many ways, inbred circle of the educationists. Textbook publishers have long since seen themselves and been considered by other segments of the educational establishment as members in good standing thereof. The textbook publishers, therefore, have chosen, by and large, to accommodate these differences by steering a middle course between contending special interest groups, which often results in a quite bland editorial substance, which in turn proves of questionable educative value.

Textbook publishers, particularly those publishing college and university-level textbooks have turned to alternative forms of publishing over the past two or three decades. The first radical departure from the standard textbook was the "course pack." The course pack is a collection of chapters from two or more textbooks all focused on a usually narrower subset of the topics typically treated in a textbook, but also commonly derived from the fashion in which professors wish to structure their instructional approach. In the most recent and radical departures from the traditional print textbook, entire textbooks and course packs are now being offered for sale in digital form as CD-ROMs or for downloading from publishers' Internet sites.

Whatever the periodic lapses by some textbook publishers from contemporaneous best standards of knowledge content, the textbook and its publishers are so central to the passing along and maintenance of the received cultural heritage that they will continue to represent a significant and critical element in the world of publishing.

The next largest class of publishers is the STM publishers. As the name implies their editorial foci are oriented to related worlds of pure and applied science. The STM publishers range in size from international conglomerates publishing widely across the spectrum of the sciences and their applied practices to highly specialized niche publishers. Many also devote a considerable amount of capital and editorial effort to the publishing of journals in some or all of the specialties in which they publish.

Related to STM publishing, and often conducted by STM publishers, is the publishing of professional literature. As the name implies, this publishing sector serves the needs of the growing army of professionals—lawyers, accountants, and the like—and the even faster growing battalions of "experts" of all kinds, both private and public. The political, economic, and social structures and

practices of modern society, and particularly that of the advanced countries, have become so complex that all manner of specialized knowledge is now required to negotiate the tortuous corridors often imposed on the citizen by this complexity. Of necessity, the citizenry has been compelled to turn such experts for help whenever compelled to navigate these uncertain waters. So, the professional publishing sector has arisen and expanded in parallel with this growth of experts. One of the most obvious of these specialized fields is that of management to which a multitude of books are now oriented every year. At a somewhat lower and more common level are the numerous books aimed at serving those seeking entrée to and subsequently maintaining currency in one or another of the numerous skilled vocations that have accompanied the increased complexity incident to the modernization project.

The last major class of books published is that serving a religious orientation. These range from the texts of the sacred texts of the world's religions to devotional tracts. This class represents about 10% of total book sales in the developed countries and probably larger percentages in some regions of strong religious belief elsewhere in the world. Religious publishing, while remarkably difficult to track and quantify, seems from several accounts to be enjoying a significant upsurge in numbers of publications and in terms of sales at the present writing.

In addition to the major categories of books dealt with above, there is a large and generally unquantified body of publishing conducted across the globe every year. This transient body of publishing is commonly referred to as "ephemeral literature." The publishing of ephemera serves a multitude of purposes usually confined to the narrow, self-contained objectives of a vast array of small, special interest groups. These groups appear to be endemic to every region of the world, save the poorest and/or most remote portions thereof, and are particularly committed to the use of publication to articulate, advance, and sustain their particular interests.

PRESENT PROBLEMS

Although a shallow backwater in financial terms the publishing trade exerts political, economic, social, scientific, and, more broadly, a cultural impact of the first rank—an influence greatly in excess of its fiscal stature. This disproportionate importance in cultural consequence imposes on the trade in general, and publishers and editors in particular, an enormous professional cultural responsibility. Shabby publishing inevitably and invariably leads to shabby long-term cultural outcomes, as has been agonizingly evident and with alarming frequency in past centuries. It is all too easy for publishers and editors to seek short-term financial relief or wealth by trolling for the lowest common denominator. At least as culpable is the knowing publication of books that advance untrue or ethically impoverished propositions. Such resorts to the dissemination of populist or dubious goods are not simply contemptible in terms of the critical role that the finest publishing tradition fulfills but culturally corrosive.

Perhaps the gravest problem presented by present publishing trends, second to the continuing extent of shabby publishing, is a fundamental cultural epistemological problem. It arises out of the growing imbalance between the increasing volumes of raw data/information published in journal or electronic form and the comparatively slighter fraction thereof being synthesized/reduced to knowledge concepts published in coherent book form. Random bits and pieces of data/information are of no intrinsic intellectual value save as they can be integrated/synthesized by savants into knowledge concepts. Individual bits of data are absolutely essential and of the utmost importance to the prepared mind, but they possess no meaning and, hence, value to a mind not well stocked with knowledge concepts or working hypotheses into which they can be fitted to support or refute a knowledge hypothesis. There are in a number of subject-matter fields of genuine importance imbalances between the numbers of research people digging out/discovering new data/information and the numbers of people involved in synthesizing these data into hypotheses, thereby weaving some form of coherent knowledge concept out of these data and integrating these concepts/hypotheses into existing bodies of knowledge. Authentic book publishers can play an enormously useful cultural role, as they have in the past, by closely and continually monitoring these imbalances and then identifying and seeking out potential synthesizers and to then encourage them to imbed their works of synthesis into a book for broad circulation—and possible falsification.

In all likelihood, the next most serious problem faced by book publishers is the continuing attrition of library budgets. Two significant deleterious consequences arise from these budgetary constraints. First, libraries are able to acquire a constantly declining percentage of the print output resulting from the still increasing output flowing from research and synthesis. These progressively diminishing budgets are additionally being expected to acquire a far wider range of materials, most notably but not confined to electronic forms. The outcome is that libraries are acquiring a diminishing fraction of an increasing intellectual output—both print and electronic. Consequently, publishers are being increasingly constrained in the performance of their cultural function. Second, libraries have traditionally been not only an indispensable support of serious publishing but a necessary and useful partner in the larger cultural "peer-review process." In the latter role, they have long been looked to endeavor to not only weed out the culturally mediocre but to promote the dissemination of the culturally sound. Both the preservation of the good and weeding out of the mediocre are at the very best very difficult and subject to real abuse.

Obviously, the acquisition of a declining proportion of the books and journals published in both print and electronic form limits to a greater or lesser degree the effective discharge of both of these two vital cultural functions. Possibly as great a harmful consequence of the throttling of library material budgets and the resulting reduced capacity to bring books into library holdings is either increased book prices for all buyers or, in the more acute cases, the choking off of book manuscripts in publishers' offices induced by uncertainties about viable markets.

A continuing publishing problem remains that of copyright protection—intellectual property protection. This problem is most acute in the case of STM books and textbooks. While the problem is worldwide, it is especially acute in the underdeveloped regions of the world. The books involved are most commonly those published in the English language. Although Western publishers have over the years made all manner of concessionary exceptions for the underdeveloped countries, the problem continues to evade solution. However, this problem is not confined to underdeveloped countries; the unauthorized use of the intellectual and literary efforts of others is widespread in developed countries. Since the widespread acceptance of the Internet, an increasing volume of piracy in the form of downloading intellectual property has developed in this channel as well. The consequence of these alternative methods of acquiring intellectual property yields the unintended consequences of higher prices for all books and journals for the ethical users as well as a proportional reduction in the property owner's income.

Another of the seemingly intractable international publishing problems is the matter of publishing in languages of limited usage. The common remedy invoked to solve the publishers' problem is to look for government subsidies to publishers. This, as any reader of John Milton's *Areopagitica* knows, is a dangerous game at best. The continuing history of governmental intervention in the publishers' workshop since Milton's time simply confirms the wisdom codified by him and provides a continuing sorry account of the unintended consequences resulting from this rent-seeking solution of government subventions. A far better solution to not only this problem but opening a far larger perspective to the citizenry of such minor-language countries as well would seem to be intensive and sustained instruction in one of the world's major languages. The economic benefits resulting from such an educational investment would likely recover the costs involved many times over.

THE FUTURE

Turning from the disconcerting matter of the problems confronting the publishing trade to the equally dangerous enterprise of trying to make some sense of the present trends in the world of culture, knowledge maintenance and formation, and authentic publishing some of the following observations may be useful in orienting the planning exercises of librarians and information specialists.

In all likelihood the most important trend that will greatly impact the future of publishing is the continuing increase in the financial support of research, both private and public. One of the major conclusions that can be drawn from the history of the scholarship of the last half century is that the extent of our ignorance not just of our world and our natures but of the history that landed us on the shores we presently occupy is dauntingly large. While the totality of our knowledge is impressive indeed, it still falls short of that level of understanding with which all can feel intellectually and ethically relatively comfortable. This realization has driven the continued increases in support and the inevitable increased publication, as it has in the past. It seems almost certain, therefore, that the number of new book titles being published can only increase. This increase is the inescapable consequence of not simply the synthesizing of new knowledge concepts and the integration of these new concepts into the bodies of existing knowledge. It will also follow from the necessary and continuing falsifying of older, unsupportable knowledge hypotheses in light of the new knowledge hypotheses that emerge or the contradictions that appear as these new hypotheses find their place in existing bodies of knowledge. Book publishers and editors will play a crucial role in this knowledge-building process.

Preceding the falsifying of unsustainable hypotheses and the synthesizing of new hypotheses in books containing coherent bodies of knowledge is the discovery/uncovering of data/information resulting from this continued vigorous support of research. The third likely future outcome is quite how these research results will likely enter into the larger public square of discourse and debate. On present trends, this process of dissemination seems a highly uncertain matter. Traditionally, research results have been made public in the form of journal articles and research reports. The rapidly emerging technology of electronic transmission has radically altered the likely future channels of dissemination.

To come to grips with this seeming conundrum some of the leading characteristics of the uses of the journal and of the nature of the thing in itself at the opening of the new century must be noted. First, as is well understood the cutting edge of research in virtually every subject-area field is dominated by a tiny handful of key players. These key players seldom look to the journal literature for cognitive purposes for they know most of the other members of their respective invisible college as well as the avenues of research/discovery/hypothesis formation being pursued or advanced by their peers. This elite rather employs the journal for several other purposes. First, journals are used to establish priorities of discovery in the highly competitive environment of work at research frontiers. Second, the elite uses journal papers to signal to others in the invisible

college the marking off of future research avenues in an effort to foreclose competition. And lastly, of course, these movers and shakers still intend to communicate their results to the vast bulk of others in the subject field who use these results to maintain currency for the discharge of their pedagogical responsibilities.

These latter preponderant pedagogical members use the journal for quite other purposes. As noted above they use journals to maintain subject currency for instructional purposes. They are, however, also faced with the "publish or perish" employment mandate. Consequently, they tend to publish that 75% to 80% of the papers that make no contribution to the information base of their particular subject area field or are essentially meaningless. This is also the group that uses the journal literature maintaining currency in the intellectual content of their field and for verification purposes.

Turning to the journal itself the principal observation to be made is that it is, and always has been, a miscellaneous gathering of papers. As such any specific issue possesses no substantial coherence for any particular reader. Thus, the vast percentage of papers contained therein is remote from the intellectual interests of most readers. (Notable exceptions are such high-status, general-purpose journals, such as *Science* and *Nature*.)

The second, major characteristic of the journal is that it remains, in essence, a print product and as such is conceived in terms of an issue and for commercial purposes as a subscription for all the issues published within a defined period, usually a year—this for historic reason that the first journals were published as a member benefit by learned societies and so, tied to yearly dues. Thus, the present thinking remains tied to yearly subscriptions to a specific journal title. (Historically, reports are spin-offs, for they did and do not fit the journal format well.) However, the retention of this association with a yearly subscription cycle is becoming increasingly dysfunctional for the publication of research results and that of related forms of information/data as the volume of the latter continues its recent increase.

It seems probable, in light of the recent development of massive computer capacity and the escalating sophistication of management software for enormous databases, that information/data will increasingly be made available by highly defined systems, akin to the approval plan system for books and tailored to the specific needs of individual users. The ongoing operational costs of such a system will prove sufficiently small that such individual profiles can be maintained and serviced directly to subscribers' desktop computers at a very reasonable cost to the individual subscribers.

If this trend is realized an entirely new journal/report infrastructure must be created. Subscribers to such a system will probably be served by newly formed organizations serving as middlemen between publishers and users. Libraries will continue to have a role in information/data dissemination as the middleman between publishers and occasional users, i.e., those users whose information/data needs do not warrant signing up for a sustained service.

It also seems likely that libraries, operating as stakeholders in some kind of consortium arrangement, will be responsible for warehousing/archiving these vast bodies of raw information/data until various chunks of it are reduced to knowledge concepts by library scholars. The latter are scholars devoted not to uncovering new information/data working in a research setting, but scholars working in libraries on the already discovered information/data literature to reduce it to some kind of comprehensible form—knowledge concepts and ethical precepts—which can be incorporated into existing bodies of knowledge.

The latter role of knowledge concept and ethical precept formulation/synthesis will become increasingly important as the society more fully recognizes the unsustainable disparity between information/data discovery and knowledge formation/synthesis. Consequently, librarians will be called on to play an increasingly critical role as partners in marshalling of information/data for the utilization of the library scholars who will be virtual habitués of libraries.

All of this intellectual work of synthesizing new knowledge concepts and integrating them into existing bodies of knowledge will, of course, be disseminated to the broader public in the form of sustained discourses. Manifestly, so doing will result in a marked increase in the number of books published.

All of which brings us back to library as the cultural warehouse of the culture or the memory of the species—all those seemingly old-fashioned and presently disdained descriptions of the cultural place and function of the library. It brings us back, as well, to where this entry began. The number of book titles published yearly will continue to grow as humankind seeks to better come to grips with the true and the good.

CONCLUSION

Substantial clouds of uncertainty surround publishing at this writing. The principal cloud is economic resulting from the flattening of sales and the other problems noted above. All of this uncertainty is further complicated by the yet unknown consequences of the digital revolution. Publishers have, however, had to perform their cultural role through all manner of difficulties and uncertainties. So, at the end of the day they will continue to originate books and journals as the cultural need for knowledge, literature, and information is not likely to disappear.

ACKNOWLEDGMENTS

Much of the material included here is recast from *Scholarly Publishing: Books, Journals, Publishers, and Libraries in the Twentieth Century*, 2002, edited by Richard Abel and Lyman Newlin, New York, John Wiley & Sons, Inc. I wish to thank the various contributors to that volume for their help in preparing this entry. Any errors or shortcomings in this entry are the author's, not that of these contributors.

REFERENCES

1. Machlup, F.; Leeson, K.; et al. *Information through the Printed Word: The Dissemination of Scholarly, Scientific, and Intellectual Knowledge*; New York University: New York, NY, March 15, 1978.
2. Book publishing: the discontinuities of scale. Economist. April 7, **1990**, 25–28.
3. Kapr, A. *Johann Gutenberg: The Man and His Work*; Scolar Press: Aldershot, England, 1996; 88.

School Librarianship

Blanche Woolls
iSchool, San Jose State University, San Jose, California, U.S.A.

Abstract

Professional school librarians have served schools in the United States for just over 100 years. They are certified or licensed to teach in schools as a part of the education rules and regulations established state by state. Their role is to provide access to information for students and teachers, to help teachers teach and students learn. They collaborate with teachers to build curriculum and they expand the use of technology in their schools to help others navigate through the mass of information on the Internet. Studies have shown a strong relationship between the presence of a professional school librarian and a school library, which are factors in the achievement of students.

INTRODUCTION

Over the past century, the role of school librarians evolved from keepers of a book collection to providing multimedia resources, teaching information literacy in all its formats, providing electronic access to the world's information, and offering professional development to colleagues in the use of technologies and the implementation of the Common Core State Standards. Collaborating with teachers, school librarians share the responsibility of educating their students from preschool through high school, ages 4–18. Through computer access and other electronic devices, they offer training in the finding and use of information for administrators, teachers, students, and sometimes parents and the community. While school librarians continue to encourage reading and help students find books for recreational reading, they now collaborate with teachers to improve teaching and learning, helping to plan the teaching of curricular units and to evaluate student responses to the assignments. They collect data to show how school libraries are used to help improve student academic achievement. Their history is short, and many challenges remain to be overcome.

HISTORY OF SCHOOL LIBRARIANSHIP

The first trained school librarian, Mary Kingsbury,[1] began work at Erasmus Hall in 1900. In 1903, Mary E. Hall was named to the Girl's High School in Brooklyn, and she described her library

> ...to realize what we mean by a "modern school library" one must see it in action... To have as your visitors each day, from 500 to 700 boys and girls of all nationalities and all stations in life, to see them come eagerly crowding in, 100 or more every 40 minutes, and to realize that for four of the most important years of their lives, it is the opportunity of the library to have a real and lasting influence upon each individual boy and girl, gives the librarian a feeling that her calling is one of high privilege and great responsibility.[2]

Providing school libraries and librarians had slow growth over the years until regional accrediting agencies began requiring a trained school librarian in each school. Since few districts accredited their elementary schools, it was not until the mid-1960s and the passage of The Great Society Funding with ESEA Title II dedicated to the creation and improvement of school libraries, that elementary schools created libraries and added professional staff. During this time of expansion, multimedia formats were added to the book collection.

To better describe the role, the American Association of School Librarians (AASL) through its publication of new standards changed the name to school library media specialist, but it reversed this decision in the new century. Today, some states are beginning to adopt a term used in Australia and Canada, *teacher librarian*, to emphasize the teaching role of school librarians.

The numbers of school libraries under the direction of a certified school librarian continue to grow and lessen depending upon the nation's economy. At the beginning of the second decade of the new century, the numbers are declining with some libraries closed and others run by technicians or parents. As parents and school staff become aware of the need for someone to help students become lifelong learners able to access and use information that is accurate and useful, the pendulum should swing again.

Regional–School

Encyclopedia of Library and Information Sciences, Fourth Edition DOI: 10.1081/E-ELIS4-120053097

PREPARATION OF SCHOOL LIBRARIANS

In 2013, the National Council on the Accreditation of Teacher Education (NCATE) merged with the Teacher Education Council (TEAC) to become the Council for the Accreditation of Educator Preparation (CAEP). Programs in schools of library and information science accredited by the American Library Association's (ALA) Committee on Accreditation, also accepted by the CAEP. School librarians differ from their colleagues preparing for positions in other types of libraries and information agencies because of the focus on teaching and working to improve learning. The degree from an ALA program is the license for public and academic librarians throughout the United States. The school library certificate is unique to each of the 50 states because the education of children is the responsibility of each state's board of education.

Requirements for the school library certificate or credential vary; in many states, school librarians are considered to be "teachers," and they must meet the established requirements or competencies for certification to be eligible to teach in a classroom as well as meet library certification. This means they hold a teaching credential for either multi-subjects in an elementary or high school-specific subject areas. Competencies vary according to the level of student being taught so that elementary teachers may meet one set, while secondary teachers follow a different course.

In other states, a person may be certified only as a school librarian who is not required to be certified as teacher for elementary school or a subject area in a secondary school. In this case, teachers are considered to be "special" teachers—teachers of art, music, and physical education; librarians; and guidance counselors, and they are usually certified for K-12. Persons holding this specialty may not be able to remain when the specialty is no longer considered a necessity.

Moving from one state to another can require a school librarian to take additional courses. Many states allow the first credential to be given at the undergraduate level, whereas other states may require a master's degree. Further, some education agencies insist that all teachers complete a course on that state's history, whereas others may ask the person to complete requirements to teach in elementary or high school if they only hold a school library credential.

The actual certification process for most states employs one of the following three methods: passing a test, certification through the state education agency, or designated teacher training institutions. In the first method, interested applicants sit for a test designed to confirm their eligibility for the credential, and when they pass the test, they are granted the credential. If the state department is responsible, the applicant submits the required documentation directly to the appropriate state department office. Either personnel in that office or their designated evaluators match this information to the state requirements and grant the certificate or point out the deficiencies. In the last method,

a process of program approval is granted to institutions of higher education within the state. The state education agency establishes standards, guidelines, and competencies required by those who will be teaching, and each training program supplies a plan to confirm the competencies are covered in the curriculum. State agencies then send teams of evaluators to the program to confirm that they are, indeed, able to graduate school librarians who have those skills. Continued periodic evaluation ensures that the quality of education programs within the state is maintained.

Most certification programs for school librarians require courses or demonstrated competencies in reference, management, cataloging, and technology. Students must complete courses introducing them to literature for children and young adults, both fiction and nonfiction. A curriculum integration course may be required or this may be interwoven into all courses. If a student has had no classroom teaching experience, this may be required, and most programs require a school library practicum experience, working in a school library with an exceptionally good school librarian for a designated period of time. In many states, a teacher may begin work as a school librarian on a emergency certificate while finishing the requirements for the credential. Also in some states, all teachers, including school librarians, must take additional courses to keep their credentials current with regular, confirmed professional development in college courses or other experiences.

In 2001, the U.S. National Board for Professional Teaching Standards completed Library Media Standards (for teachers of students ages 3–18+). Performance-based assessment procedures have been developed, including a portfolio of practice during a school year and summer "assessment center activities." School librarians who meet the competencies determined by these procedures will become National Board Certified and as such may not only receive recognition for their accomplishments, but their salary also increases. In some states, funding is allocated to teachers to encourage their participation.

The Working Environment

The role of the school librarian may be affected by the educational requirements of the school. No Child Left Behind (NCLB) Public Law 107–110 was first proposed during the Bush administration and put in place by President Obama. It was a part of the reauthorization Title I of the Elementary and Secondary Education Act. Each state was required to develop assessments of basic skills if they were going to continue to receive federal funding. These assessments were conducted yearly at select grade levels to determine the students' annual progress in academic programs. This new emphasis on testing with some of the results tied to teacher salaries has turned education in the second decade of the new century into a test environment, leaving little time for anything but testing. Teachers are reluctant to have their students spend any time on any activity that does not apply directly to the tests they will be taking. This has further isolated the school librarian and other teachers from offering experiences for students.

In most schools, the school librarian works alone or with an aide. In only the largest schools will a second or third professional be in place. For this reason, they are often solely responsible for the activities going on in the school library, and unless they are able to have classes come to the library under a flexible schedule, collaborating with teachers for curriculum integration is very difficult. Flexible scheduling allows the teachers and the school librarian to determine when classes, students in small groups, or even individual students may visit the library. In other cases, and particularly at the elementary level, classes are scheduled into the library to provide the requisite preparation period for the teacher.

With the downturn in the economy, some school librarians are assigned to multiple schools. An aide may be in the school when the librarian is off-campus, or the library may be closed.

School librarians may have a great deal of autonomy partially because a few in the school or district understand the role of the school librarian. In larger districts, a supervisor of the school library program may work in a central office to oversee programs. However, authority and responsibility for all teachers including the school librarian belong to the school principal. School librarians often spend a great deal of their time educating both principals and teachers on the role of school librarians.

When school librarians are technology leaders in their school, they become responsible for professional development to assure teachers are making the best use of all available technologies. The use of social media by students has made this format a challenge to teachers who can, if prepared, turn these devices into a learning environment rather than a nuisance. School librarians can help teachers prepare for this new educational opportunity.

The Librarian's Responsibility for Teaching and Helping Teachers Teach

While school librarians have been, for many years, teaching students how to locate information in the school library, the 1998 publication of *Information Power* described the new role of the school librarian to include information literacy.

> Information literacy—the ability to find and use information—is the keystone of lifelong learning. Creating a foundation for lifelong learning is at the heart of the school library media program. Just as the school library media center has moved far beyond a room with books to become an active, technology-rich learning environment with an array of information resources, the school library media specialist today focuses on the process of learning rather than dissemination of learning.[3]

This role moves beyond information literacy to the myriad of other literacies that have surfaced including business, computer, health, media, technology, and visual among others.[4] An even more recent addition is digital literacy. All of these are a part of much that is being taught in classrooms and collaboration between teacher and librarian effectively increases the ability for students to become literate in each.

The role of the school librarian has expanded with the ever-changing technologies in the school, and with the changes in curriculum that have come into schools with programs such as the Common Core State Standards. These were developed in 2009 by David Coleman who was employed by the National Governor's Association to write curriculum standards for literacy, now English language arts, and mathematics. While these standards have not been adopted by every state, where they are in effect, teachers need some assistance in meeting the requirements. This provides school librarians with an excellent means to help teachers teach.

The Librarian's Responsibility for Teaching and Helping Students Learn

School librarians teach students how to find resources to help them learn to become information literate. When school librarians collaborate with teachers, this becomes inquiry learning and provides the student with the skills to become lifelong learners. This responsibility includes making sure those resources are available for their students and that all students have the ability and the freedom to access these resources. The ability specifies their access to technologies needed to search online; and the freedom means the librarian supports and protects the students' intellectual freedom rights. One of those restrictions, filtering, is discussed later in this entry. However, here, the selection of materials and the protection of those choices from censorship by members of the community mean the librarian has a selection policy in place and the process to follow when someone questions any item in the collection.

School Library Standards and Guidelines

Standards for school libraries were published in 1919, 1920, and 1948. It was not until 1960 that the AASL published its own *Standards for School Library Programs*. These standards and those published in 1969 and 1975 were based on quantitative numbers such as professional librarians hired for so many students and so many books per student.

In 1988, *Information Power*[3] changed the focus from quantitative guidelines to the role of school librarians. School librarians were expected to be leaders and links between students, teachers, administrators, parents, and community, as well as providing information resources.

School librarians were assigned the responsibility for collaborating with teachers to improve teaching and learning.

The newest, *Standards for the 21st Century Learner*, continues the traditional role stating "Reading is a window to the world" as one of the nine common beliefs. The rest focuses on how learners will use skills, resources, and tools. The school librarian functions as someone who will make sure students have the key abilities needed for understanding (skills), ongoing beliefs and attitudes that guide thinking (dispositions in action), common behaviors used by independent learners in researching (responsibilities), and self-analysis strategies.[5]

FUNCTIONS AND SKILLS OF SCHOOL LIBRARIANS

A key document to describe school librarians is found in the ALA/AASL Standards for Initial Preparation of School Librarians (2010). This document is available at http://www.ala.org/aasl/sites/ala.org.aasl/files/content/aasl education/schoollibrary/2010_standards_with rubics_and_ statements_1-31-11.pdf.

Because school librarians usually work alone, they are responsible for all activities, programs, and services including management, cataloging, acquisition, reference, and readers' advisory. As mentioned earlier, school librarians are the managers of their libraries. While most of their books may come to them from the vendor with the electronic records needed for the online public access catalog, not everything comes from a vendor, so some knowledge of cataloging is required.

Teachers, students, and even parents may make suggestions for purchases for the library; but the final purchase orders are generated by the school librarian. Also, while school librarians strive to help teachers and students learn how to use online references and keep them current as new online resources arrive, this is a skill requiring constant practice and school librarians have the opportunity to use their skills regularly, making them effective reference librarians.

Another skill is that of helping their students choose books that will interest them so that they become lifelong readers. Readers' advisory takes many approaches including book talking books for students, developing reading lists for teachers, and simply suggesting an interesting title to a student who seems to be having trouble finding something to read. To be truly successful, the school librarian must be an effective communicator, keeping current on new technologies, and being able to make sure their students have open access to information, a truly great challenge, and they must also be ready to change, learn, and grow so that their program and activities respond to the best resources for teachers to teach and students to learn. Once that program is in place, it is imperative that what is offered and what is being consumed be reported to the people who are important in the continued support of school libraries.

Effective Communication

The first major audience for communication is the student. This may be translated into maintaining good discipline in the library to allow students to learn what they have available for them and a place to exercise their critical thinking skills. It is also being able to talk to students about their lives. In this way, they can learn of problems they may be having with their school work and how information in the library may help them overcome these problems. Because teachers have students in a classroom within a specific time frame, little opportunity may be available for students with problems to share them with their teachers. The relative freedom of the library environment often makes it possible for the school librarians to find out what is troubling students and to help them find the persons or information for the solution of that problem. The next, and perhaps in many instances, teachers must learn what services are offered and how the librarian can collaborate in making sure students learn effective critical thinking skills, becoming literate, and setting them on the path to being lifelong learners. When two professionals are working together to provide curriculum, it doubles the number of persons working with students for a single period of time. They must learn how the librarian is able to help them enhance their teaching and evaluate what students are accomplishing.

Effective communication with the principal means regular reports of interesting activities going on in the library. This can be done with written reports, but even more effective are demonstrations by students. Showing what students are achieving in their use of the library draws the school board and the community into continuing support for school libraries and school librarians. Another important service for both administrators and teachers is keeping them informed about trends in teaching and learning, the results of research reports of methods that could be implemented in their schools, and other ideas to make teaching and learning more effective. Culling the education literature to provide the best will take time, but will also point out most effectively the role of the school librarian in providing information for all.

All of these, administrators, teachers, and students can become effective advocates for the program. Showing members of local social clubs and other community groups what is going on in school libraries allows them to see the value of the school library in the lives of students. Students, teachers, and parents who visit local, state, and national government officials can explain what happens in school libraries and how their school librarian is essential in the learning environment.

Use of Technology

School librarians have been on the cutting edge of the implementation of technology in their schools. In 1915, Mary Hall reported having lantern slides, and "for the English work and indeed for German and French, a Victrola with records which make it possible for students to hear the English."[2] Funding in the 1960s found new media and the equipment to play and project these on the library shelves. School librarians began adding computers to the services offered in the early 1980s. The first use was for word processing and management of the collection, cataloging and circulation, closely followed by reference materials on CD-ROMs. These became quickly obsolete with access to online resources from vendors. Computers moved into the library, sometimes in a separate room, in the reference area, and where the card catalog used to stand. Students used computers in the library to write and print their papers.

Student use of computers has become so essential that some schools are providing for laptops and electronic notebooks either for a year or semester assignment or at least checkout for a time from the library. This means that no students are handicapped because their families cannot provide them with computer technology.

School librarians have been responsible for interconnecting classrooms to libraries and providing the electronic resources in the library to be shared beyond classrooms to the student's home. When school and public librarians have a cooperative relationship, this interconnectivity may be between the public library, school, and homes. This means school librarians have become computer savvy and able to select, install, and use new technologies.

School librarians recognize the constant need to upgrade computers. With every change in software, hardware must have additional storage and a faster response time. As the hardware expands beyond the computer itself to printers, scanners, and copy and fax machines, these also must be upgraded. It is not a situation that will become easier. Also, with the expansion of the Internet, school librarians had an additional challenge of how to keep information one would not choose to have in the library, out of the library.

The Challenge of the Internet: Filtering the Internet

The opening of the Internet has provided a myriad of opportunities to search for information on the World Wide Web (WWW). With this, access to online resources expanded beyond the ability of the school librarian to monitor what information came into the school library. It was possible for students to locate pornography, hate messages, and other information that a school librarian would not select for users. Information on the Internet may be somewhat more difficult to spot than a student with an issue of an "adult" magazine tucked into a notebook which could be permanently removed by confiscating the magazine. Websites on the Internet are much more difficult to monitor and stop their being used on a school library computer. One solution to the challenge is a filtering system for library computers.

Filters that review information being received via the Internet are available. They have several problems, one of which is that filters often keep important information from coming through; another is that a clever student can easily circumvent them. Other solutions seem to work as well or better. One is to have students and parents or caregivers sign a contract concerning the use of the Internet in the library. Not abiding by this contract can mean the student cannot use the library's computers or access the library's other resources. Another solution is to establish links to acceptable websites that will provide students with information that is relevant to their needs.

Even greater challenges are present with the Internet and access to the WWW: misinformation, students who find too many sources and choose irrelevant information, and those students who simply copy information. If students are looking at a screen filled with pornography, it is instantly recognizable for what it is, but the greater problem is the misinformation that can be found on the Web. Unless the librarian is seated with the student and reading what they are reading, the misinformation may go undetected until it is being corrected by a teacher.

Helping students to learn how to find the relevant, accurate, useful information from the overwhelming quantities available on the Web is another responsibility. So much information is available that it is difficult to help students sort through it all to select what they need for their research. School librarians can help students by doing some of the first searching and providing links to relevant information. This does not stop the student from simply copying what is found.

It is also far too easy to download information and reposition it within a report without thinking through the information and adding to it or taking away from it or analyzing it to create new information. At no time has the ability to plagiarize been greater. It takes strong collaboration with teachers to make sure students use their critical thinking skills to determine appropriate information and to use that information to analyze a situation and propose a solution by repackaging the information.

Perhaps the greatest challenge of all is how to help teachers learn how to physically use new electronic resources and how to integrate them into their courses. The constantly changing hardware and software, as well as the constantly changing access to new databases, can be confusing to the school librarian who works with them daily. It is even more distressing to the classroom teacher who is not so close to the situation. This means that the school librarian serves as teacher of teachers to make sure that they also keep up to date.

Ability to Change, Learn, and Grow

Changes in educational theory and methodology for teaching dictate much of what happens in schools. School librarians take responsibility for learning about new trends and methodologies and share these with their principals and their teachers. They constantly demonstrate their ability to change, learn, and grow, and this is most evident in their awareness of the constant upgrading of technologies and their willingness to teach their colleagues how to use each new technology as it becomes available. The advent of the new social media creates a challenge to teachers who do not wish to have their students use cell phones and text during class. While confiscating all cell phones may provide a temporary fix, making an educational application for these technologies so dear to all students can be a more effective solution.

Collaboration with Teachers

The school librarian has moved from the support role of providing resources for teachers and students to one of collaborating with teachers to increase student learning. School librarians plan with teachers, actively helping with the development of curriculum units. As an expert in information resources, learning styles and patterns for students, and teaching styles of all the teachers, the school librarian suggests the best methods for implementing curriculum. Expanding the classroom into the wider world of information, the librarian integrates research skills into the students' everyday questioning, helping students to learn how to judge which materials to use in their research reports, helping students with inquiry skills and increasing their critical thinking skills.

Helping teachers make the best use of the opportunities provided by the new technologies their students have readily adopted is essential. From e-mail and cell phones to texting, Tumblr, Instagram, and blogging are the ways students communicate. These will not go away because teachers ignore them or, worse still, try to forbid their use. Rather, the school librarian helps them make effective uses of these technologies.

The collaboration role does not end with helping match resources to the curriculum, the school librarian helps assess student learning. An active participant in the building of units of instruction, the collaboration continues through the evaluation process and design for the next group of students. This role is not automatic nor is it an easy one. Whenever education moves into a paper and pencil test to ascertain if children are learning, teachers move back to teaching to the test and are reluctant to take time for students to learn in ways other than rote memorization. This makes it very difficult for collaboration until the pendulum swings back and students can learn through a collaborative process which makes their learning based in the real world.

Assessment and Evaluation

School librarians have learned of the need to measure the effectiveness of their services. Many studies[6–9] have been completed in several states showing the relationship between academic achievement and the presence of a school librarian and an adequate collection of materials.

Workshops at conferences or in the online environment suggest to school librarians that they should conduct their own research to show the value of their libraries in the educational lives of students. Articles in school library periodicals offer many ideas for how to carry out such projects. It is never easy with the demands of the school year; nevertheless, some school librarians do small studies and report the results to their school and even to the district administrators and the members of the school board.

Advocacy

School librarians remain relevant in the school when they are able to "sell" their program and resources. This begins with the development of a website for the library where new arrivals in the library or new activities may be listed. Teachers post assignments and homework with links to the library's resources as well as safe websites and databases available to complete the assignment.

It is both an education and a survival process. In the education mode, school librarians encourage teachers and students to make use of the collection to further their research and learning. New materials and new technologies available in the library itself or virtually through the library increase its importance. School librarians make presentations of new products in the library at meetings of department staff or in teachers' meetings. They provide effective bulletin boards in the library to encourage students to "buy" the products offered. They send lists of new materials to classrooms.

In the survival mode, the use of the school library must be shared with the broad community. School librarians send monthly reports of the activities in the library to their principals. They write columns in both the school newspaper, and whenever possible to the local news media. They plan and implement programs such as inviting a book author, a local politician, or a state or national legislator to the school to bring attention to the library. School librarians singly may ask their principals to invite district administrators and school board members to the school to observe an effective program outcome, or, as a group, they make yearly presentations to their school boards and provide programs about school library initiatives to their communities through their service organizations. All of this serves to help present the role of the school librarian to audiences, most of whom are truly unaware of what they should expect from their school librarian.

The Leadership Role of School Librarians

The traditional role of the person who shares books with students encouraging them to read both for information and enjoyment remains and provides resources for teachers on special subjects being taught continues to be important, but a wider role has opened.

Responsibility for audio-visual materials purchased for the library meant school librarians began to take a leadership role in integrating these new items into the curriculum. Their role expanded from helping find appropriate resources to showing teachers how to use the equipment needed to play or project those materials and even how to create new teaching aids. When computer technology became available to schools, online information became a large part of the library collection, and school librarians accepted the responsibility for teaching both teachers and students how to find information available on a variety of databases.

Today, school librarians continue to lead by presenting new uses of the Internet. They build websites where information about the school library is posted. Working with teachers, homework assignments are available for students and their parents, and the accompanying resources are linked there through bookmarked websites. Keeping up with the trends and suggesting educational uses of each new technology leads teachers into turning what might be considered a distraction into a learning tool.

As the single teacher in any school who works with all of the students, all of the teachers, and all of the curriculum all of the time, school librarians are in a unique position to help build an atmosphere of sharing across the school. When the focus is on something other than testing to determine if students are learning, teachers in all areas of the curriculum are able to work as a team to offer learning experiences which are more closely related to real life than the total separation of school tasks from the student's daily experiences. At that point, school librarians lead teachers in blending all areas of the curriculum, social studies, literature, science, math, art, music, and the others.

Compensation and Unionization

In public educational systems within the United States, school librarians are considered teachers, and as such, are on a salary scale comparable to teachers. These salaries are usually based upon years of service, coursework taken, and degrees completed. Additional stipends are paid for additional work such as staying for one or more weeks at the end of the school year to close the library and coming early to open it in the fall. A school librarian who played soccer in college may be asked to coach the girls' soccer team and receive a stipend for that.

In the second half of the twentieth century, the National Education Association (NEA) began to be challenged by the American Federation of Teachers to represent teachers in labor relations; and the era of teacher negotiation began. One central issue was preparation time for teachers. At the elementary level, this translated into special teachers providing release time for the classroom teacher. Thus, classroom teachers walked with their students to the door of the music room, the art room, the gymnasium, and the school library, and departed. Some administrators solved this dilemma by having teachers assigned their preparation period either before the school day begins or after it ends. If no such remedy is available, school librarians can suggest a different approach.

One possibility to open the library has been using flexible scheduling, where teachers and the school librarian determine the needs of the students in use of the library and time in the library, or time for the school librarian to come to the classroom. When the school librarian has the opportunity to collaborate with teachers and the time in the library has been carefully designed, children are more interested in finding and sharing information, increasing their critical thinking skills, and setting the stage to become lifelong learners. When the release time for classroom teachers is a union requirement, alternatives must be found.

Another solution might be to have two classes in the library at the same time for book exchange and recreational reading, thereby freeing the same amount of time for planned curriculum integration. This, as with flexible scheduling, means that librarians are no longer required to provide library lessons with no relationship to what is being taught in the classroom.

For school librarians to be considered within the union contract negotiations, the most effective way to do this is to have a school librarian a member of the union negotiating team. Someone must become political enough to win an election to the union board. This will add to an already busy life, but it will be a great benefit to all school librarians in a district.

Performance Evaluation

Many states have created forms for the evaluation of teachers within that state. These have been approved by the teacher's union. They are often difficult to apply in the situation of the school librarian who is not just responsible for teaching but also responsible for managing the inventory of books and equipment found in the school library.

Tenure

As teachers, school librarians fall under the same rules as teachers. In some states, tenure cannot be granted until a teacher has a certain level of education. In others, it is a matter of being certified in a teaching area and a certain number of years of successful teaching, often as few as three.

The yearly evaluation process of teaching is a part of this tenure process. In most cases, the evaluation is done by the building principal, although a teacher or the school librarian might be visited by someone from the central district office with expertise in a particular area. Finally, tenure is granted by the governing Board of Education for the district.

Professional Development

For most school librarians as with most teachers, professional development is offered at the district level through staff development programs offered by the school district. These are effective when they are planned to meet established needs for those who will be in the audience. School librarians, with their knowledge of trends and issues in the world of education can be helpful to the principal or anyone else planning these events. Their research skills can locate experts in the field and determine the cost of the speaker. Often these district-wide sessions are directly related to curriculum content and are less related to librarianship. While many school librarians would like to attend other types of learning sessions, most have a difficult time being released to go to programs during the school day. They are seldom compensated for travel, housing, or daily expenses, and therefore do not feel they can participate. School librarians are well aware and make use of many online opportunities for them to engage in staff development without leaving their homes.

Professional Associations

School librarians have their choices of several professional associations in both the education community and librarianship and at local, state, national, and international areas. In the education world, many school librarians, as teachers, must join either the NEA or the American Federation of Teachers (AFT) through their local and state organizations. One of these will serve as the bargaining unit for the school district or the schools in the state.

Other organizations include the Association for Supervision and Curriculum Development (ASCD) and the International Society for Technology in Education (ISTE). ASCD allows school librarians to attend conferences and meet superintendents, principals, and other administrators and advocate for school libraries. ISTE offers leadership to improve teaching and learning through effective use of technology. Both ASCD and ISTE have members worldwide.

The American Educational Research Association (AERA) has a Special Interest Group (SIG), "Research, Education, Information and School Libraries." The SIG welcomes the posting of research conducted in and about school libraries.

In the library world, divisions of the American Library Association that would be of interest are the AASL, the Association for Library Service to Children (ALSC), and Young Adult Service Association (YALSA). AASL aims to provide a national audience for school librarians, and it holds a national conference every other year. Both ALSC and YALSA serve librarians working in public libraries, but many school librarians are also members of these two. Because these are national associations, travel to conferences is a greater challenge than travel to a state conference.

School librarians choose to join their state associations which are affiliates of AASL, although in some states, New Mexico, New York, and Texas, the library associations include all types of libraries. Conferences are held within the state making travel to the meeting and perhaps the registration a little less costly; yet hotels and meals will be about the same. School librarians need to join professional library associations and attend conferences whenever possible so they have these more applicable staff development opportunities.

Local groups of information professionals may have loosely organized meetings. If public or special librarians meet, school librarians should try to join them to gain support for information services for all. School librarians in a regional area who meet at least twice a year can be better able to see the challenges from one district to another. Because administrators meet regularly and learn of cost-cutting trends that may affect school librarians, the regular meeting of all school librarians in an area can serve as a warning of what may be facing them and allow for the development of ways to counteract negative actions.

SCHOOL LIBRARIANS IN THE GLOBAL COMMUNITY

Because our students are living in a global community, school librarians can help them meet their peers in other parts of the world. Students can ask their fellow students to share cultural events such as celebration of holidays, types of food, recreational activities, and their environment as a beginning. It is very easy to establish these relationships when the school librarian is a member of an international professional association.

Two international professional library associations have school librarians as members from across the globe. The International Federation of Library Associations and Institutions (IFLA) represents information professionals from all types of library associations as well as libraries and institutions. The American Library Association is an association member of IFLA while institutional membership is held by national, city, and governmental libraries, and schools of library and information science. Very few individuals join as personal members because they have no voting privileges. Rather, they choose to be considered a member of IFLA because they are a member of one of the library associations or work in a member library. The School Library Section of IFLA is directly related to school librarians. IFLA holds its yearly meetings in different countries each year.

The International Association of School Librarians (IASL) is a smaller organization, but programming and publications are directly related to school librarians. Their activities are open to school children and how to become a part is available on the IASL website. This organization also meets yearly in countries across the globe.

School libraries with personnel, facilities, and collections are more likely to exist in the global community in those countries with the designation, "developed," and less likely to be more than a small collection of books in a locked cupboard in the developing nations. A series of vignettes of a day in the life of a school librarian were published in the publication of the International School Librarians Association, *School Libraries Worldwide*.[10] Longer articles provide glimpses of the duties of school librarians in Israel, Canada, South Africa, United Kingdom, Namibia, Botswana, and Australia. A series of shorter explanations are found under "International School Library Day."

Joining an international association provides a global picture for the school librarian who can, in turn, share activities and other suggestions with teachers and students. The cost is small unless one wishes to become more active and attend conferences, but opportunities to travel to another country may just become a vacation opportunity as well as a professional development experience.

Closing

School librarians must be leaders in their schools so that when curriculum or teaching methods change and new technologies become available, they can help their colleagues make the changes needed. The role of school librarians continues to evolve. They continue to monitor the provision of information available from resources around the world and teach both their teachers and their students how to find the best possible materials to meet their needs. School librarians navigate the Internet and research databases as well as use print resources to provide access to information. School librarians will continue to learn and grow to make sure they provide the best information available for the teachers and students and that these users know how to use the resources. School librarians are critical members of the school's teachers if all students are going to have access to information, to have higher achievement scores, and if they are going to become lifelong users of information. Beginning more than 100 hundred years ago, school librarians provide "the opportunity of the library to have a real and lasting influence upon each individual boy and girl,"[2] because this role is "one of high privilege and great responsibility."[2]

REFERENCES

1. Clark, M.B. Pioneer portrait. Wilson Libr. Bull. **1951**, *26*, 26.
2. Hall, M.E. The development of the Modern High School library. Libr. J. **September 1915**, *40*, 627.
3. American Association of School Librarians and Association for Educational Communications and Technology. *Information Power: Guidelines for School Library Media Programs*; American Library Association: Chicago, IL, 1988.
4. Thomas, M.J.K. *Redesigning the High School Library for the Forgotten Half*; Libraries Unlimited: Westport, CT, 2008; 48.
5. American Association of School Librarians. *Standards for the 21st Century Learner*; American Library Association: Chicago, IL, 2007; 8.
6. Lance, K.C.; Loertscher, D.V. *Powering Achievement: School Library Media Programs Make a Difference: The Evidence*; Hi Willow Research and Publishing: San Jose, CA, 2001.
7. Lance, K.C.; Rodney, M.J.; Hamilton-Pennell, C. *How School Librarians Help Kids Achieve Standards: The Second Colorado Study*; Hi Willow Research and Publishing: San Jose, CA, 2002.
8. Lance, K.C.; Hamilton-Pennell, C.; Rodney, M.J.; Peterson, L.; Sitter, C. *Information Empowered: The School Librarian as an Agent of Academic Achievement in Alaska Schools*; Alaska State Library: Juneau, AK, 2000.
9. Lance, K.C.; Rodney, M.J.; Hamilton-Pennell, C. *Measuring up to Standards: The Impact of School Library Programs & Information Literacy on Pennsylvania Schools*; Pennsylvania Citizens for Better Libraries: Greensburg, PA, 2000.
10. Sch. Libr. Worldw. January 2000, *6*, entire issue.

School Libraries

Blanche Woolls
iSchool, San Jose State University, San Jose, California, U.S.A.

Abstract

School libraries have a comparatively short history, but their importance in the achievement of elementary, middle, and high school students and their role in providing access to the ever-increasing information available worldwide makes them an essential component on the education scene. School libraries are essential because students need free access to information, but not all students have access to the technologies away from school and this makes information unavailable to them online. Standards and guidelines that help define the school library are presented, the effect of changes in the school environment is discussed, and an introduction is given to the research pointing out the importance of the role of the school library in student achievement. Finally, the relationship between the school library and the public library is given. While most of the focus for this entry is the United States, brief mention is made of the international perspective of school libraries in other parts of the world.

HISTORICAL CONTEXT

From the earliest published reports, school libraries were poorly funded with "… any funding allocated for school libraries was limited and sporadic and given without providing for State aid, or supervision of the selections of books."[1] Usually disinterested in a second assignment beyond their classrooms, teachers were placed in charge of any collection of books located in schools, allowing the so-called libraries "to sink into neglect and contempt through failure to provide regular supplies of fresh reading."[1]

Although book collections, perhaps identified as a school library, existed prior to 1900, it was not until then that Mary E. Kingsbury, the first professionally prepared school librarian, was appointed to Erasmus Hall in Brooklyn, New York, and professional services began.[2] The number of school libraries grew slowly until accreditation of schools began. "Regional accrediting agencies specified a high school librarian with a trained librarian as a requirement for all schools seeking to be accredited by their association."[5] Certainly, two world wars and the Great Depression affected the development of school libraries until the mid-twentieth century.

The launching of *Spudnik* in the 1950s confirmed the superiority of the space program in the USSR and made the United States focus on what were considered to be serious national problems with foreign language, science, and math. Congress passed the National Defense Education Act (NDEA) that provided matching funds to school districts to purchase materials to improve these areas of the curriculum. Later, these funds could be spent for almost any materials in the school library as well as all types of multimedia and the equipment to play or project these. When schools had a library and a professional school librarian, many of these materials became part of the library collection and the library moved beyond a collection of books.

In the 1960s, a concerted effort was made to point out the lack of facilities, collections, and personnel in school libraries. Mary Helen Mahar's 1964 national report on the status of school libraries pointed out that "46.3 percent of the public schools of the survey had centralized libraries in 1960–1961. Of the school grade levels, elementary schools had the lowest percentage with centralized libraries—31.2%."[3]

With the concentrated efforts of school librarians nationwide, Congress provided one part of the Great Society Funding for ESEA, Title II. With this dedicated funding for the purchase of library materials for school libraries, school districts began to hire professional staff to manage libraries, to remodel or expand existing facilities, and to select new resources such as multimedia. Children at all levels now had access to information in their schools, and school librarians could work to meet standards and guidelines.

The expansion of school libraries continued until the 1980s when the downturn in the economy saw much of the steady growth come to an end, and, in some cases, losses in funds for collection building as well as losses of staff and professional positions. The development of microcomputer technology while increasing access to information and providing new management tools placed an additional burden on the school librarian who saw the limited funding previously allocated for library materials being diverted into the purchase of this new technology.

At the end of the twentieth century, the introduction of affordable computing for library management saw the creation of networks and consortia, especially in the creation of online access catalogs. These databases expanded the sharing of resources through interlibrary loan.

Encyclopedia of Library and Information Sciences, Fourth Edition DOI: 10.1081/E-ELIS4-120053098

The use of a variety of technologies affordable to schools, including scanners, fax machines, and the Internet allows the transmission of information electronically and seamlessly making the school library an essential part of each student's school life and is critical for those students who do not have access to these technologies away from school. School districts may provide notebooks or laptop computers for each student to take home or in other schools, students must depend upon finding these in their school libraries.

STANDARDS AND GUIDELINES

School library standards and guidelines provide models for developing programs, services, and facilities. The first guidelines[4] for school library services were developed in 1919 by a committee of the National Education Association. They outlined staffing, collection, and facilities for high schools. The companion standards for elementary school were published in 1925.[5] Both differentiated between the services offered in a public library and the role of the school library within a school.

The 1945 standards,[6] the first published by the American Library Association (ALA), were not given much attention as school districts faced the challenge of providing classrooms and teachers to accommodate the large number of children entering schools. However, they did help to create the foundations for those new guidelines that followed.

In 1951, the members of the Children's Services Division of the ALA who worked in schools began the American Association of School Librarians (AASL) as a separate organization. This newer division within the ALA, published their first *Standards for School Library Programs*[7] in 1960, helping to launch a decade of development made possible with the increased funding.

During the unprecedented growth period of the 1960s, the AASL published their second *Standards for School Media Programs*,[8] in 1969. The next guidelines, *Media Programs*: *District and School*,[9] were published in 1975. All three documents used quantitative requirements for all aspects of the library. By 1975, the new standards were given little attention because redirection of federal funds and the reduction of local funding for schools found school library positions and collections in jeopardy.

Members of the AASL had hoped to produce new standards every 5 years. However, it took them almost 15 years to produce the next edition. In 1988, *Information Power*[10] changed the focus from quantitative guidelines to a statement of the role of the school library from the standpoint of the building level program. Rather than using what appeared to be an arbitrary establishment of quantities to what constituted an adequate number of staff, collection, facilities, and equipment, a survey of actual school libraries allowed the standards committee to use information gathered from exemplary elementary, middle/junior high schools, and high schools. School personnel could now match their programs to real-life situations and see how closely their programs met or exceeded those reported in the high-service programs using the results as an indication of their own level of achieving excellence.

The 1998 publication of *Information Power*[11] came after a decade of change in both educational systems and the school library program. Students began to look for information beyond what they could learn in the classroom, and the school library was able to provide access to the constantly increasing wealth of knowledge. "*Information Power* approached this twofold growth by advocating the creation of a community of lifelong learners. Information literacy - understanding how to access and use information - is at the core of lifelong learning."[11] These standards included nine information literacy standards defining the student who is information literate, the student who is an independent learner, how the student who is an independent learner is information literate, and how the student who contributes positively to the learning community and to society is information literate.

In 2008, new standards were developed for school libraries and the focus is entirely on the student and what the student can learn. *Standards for the 21st Century Learner* will ask school librarians to help "learners use skills, resources, & tools to:

- Inquire, think critically, and gain knowledge.
- Draw conclusions, make informed decisions, apply knowledge to new situations, and create new knowledge.
- Share knowledge and participate ethically and productively as members of our democratic society.
- Pursue personal and aesthetic growth."[12]

The final document described the learner's skills, dispositions in action, responsibilities, and self-assessment strategies. They are based upon nine common beliefs:

- Reading is a window to the world.
- Inquiry provides a framework for learning.
- Ethical behavior in the use of information must be taught.
- Technology skills are crucial for future employment needs.
- Equitable access is a key component for education.
- The definition of information literacy has become more complex as resources and technologies have changed.
- The continuing expansion of information demands that all individuals acquire the thinking skills that will enable them to learn on their own.
- Learning has a social context.
- School libraries are essential to the development of learning skills.

When standards and guidelines such as these are developed by professional organizations rather than government agencies, their implementation remains voluntary. It remains the responsibility of school librarians and supporters in the school and community to gather support for them. The new AASL standards explain a philosophy and place the responsibility for implementation on the school librarian working with teachers and are written to have an increasing impact on the education of students.

Government agencies in individual states may publish official standards and they are, in effect, laws. Because of this, these agencies are aware that they will be asked to provide adequate funds if such regulations are expected to be met. Therefore, those standards usually have such low numbers so that most schools can meet them.

Government agencies may also state the number of school librarians per school or per number of students. Again, these often place responsibility upon school districts that have inadequate sources of funds to hire the number or personnel. Most regulations have clauses that allow school districts to use a different route to providing overseeing of school library programs.

CHANGES IN EDUCATION THEORY AND PRACTICE: EFFECT ON SCHOOL LIBRARIES

Constant efforts to improve the education of students result in continual restructuring of schools, rearranging the school day, week, and even year, all under definition of educational improvements sometimes within the curriculum offerings. Changes are implemented, often without adequate research or testing. Prophets gather disciples who accept the pedagogy espoused and put it into practice, sometimes reporting that this change is successful with little or no concrete evidence. The process is similar to a small flame in dry grass; a little wind moves the fire through the land with incredible speed, often leaving behind an utter wasteland. One example of this was the new math movement in the last century. In-service sessions were provided and school teachers were required to attend. At the elementary level, teachers who were weak in math often did not understand the concepts. Parents could no longer help their students with homework, and it slowly faded away. Some of these have more direct effect upon the school librarian. The rearrangement of the school day, week, and semester reflects some of these attempts to improve learning.

With block scheduling of classes, teachers and students move from the pattern of 45-minute daily classes into longer periods of time each day for single subjects and a different pattern of subjects throughout the week. When teachers have a longer time with a single group, it provides the opportunity to work with the librarian to schedule and monitor the research process. Furthermore, students who want to conduct research have a longer time to work in the library without interruption.

Year-round schooling is another innovation, and this varies in choosing how to schedule the year. Sometimes, teachers and students attend on a rotation with different students and teachers occupying the same classrooms depending on the schedule. In others, the school remains closed when students and teachers are not in class. Another model has been to schedule the number of weeks in attendance throughout the year with longer breaks between each school term. In the first case, rotation of teachers and students means the need for additional staffing in the school library.

Changes in practice may come from organizations related to education, and this sometimes has government support supplying further initiatives and implications. Efforts by educators to implement the national program, No Child Left Behind, have turned teaching into total focus on test results. Because salary increases for teachers and funding for schools may be unduly influenced by test scores, teachers now teach students only things that will help them achieve high test scores. It has made a serious impact on the relationship between teachers and the school library and upon the use of the school library as a learning environment. When teachers revert to teaching only what they understand will be on the test, they are not willing to spend any time on research in a school library.

Another innovation has been the Common Core State Standards (CCSS). In 2009, David Coleman was employed by the National Governor's Association to write curriculum standards for literacy, now English-language arts, and mathematics. These have not been accepted by all states, and some states have only adopted some of the standards. The stated purpose of this initiative "is to provide a consistent, clear understanding of what students are expected to learn, so teachers and parents know what they need to do to help them."[13]

> The CCSS Initiative is a state-led effort coordinated by National Governors Association Center for Best Practices (NGA Center) and the Council of Chief State School Officers (CCSSO). The standards were developed in collaboration with teachers, school administrators, and experts, to provide a clear and consistent framework to prepare our children for college and the workforce.[13]

The CCSS initiative has provided an opportunity for school librarians and the library to offer support to teachers who do not understand the concept or who seem unable to move into the requirements. School librarians can be very helpful in conducting professional development to help understand the program and to work with teachers to build the school curriculum.

NEW TRENDS: LEARNING COMMONS AND MAKERSPACES

One of the newest trends has been the remodeling of the library space into a more open area. As reliance on digital information increases, the need for book shelving has decreased allowing for repurposing use. In some cases, it became a newly created space. Most often through the efforts of one or two school librarians, a new concept is being integrated in many school districts: the recreation of the school library into a learning commons. In this setting, the school library becomes the true center of the school with new and expanded virtual services. When this is implemented fully, a central location in the school is designed to provide the space for teachers who teach other than in a formal classroom. Art, music, guidance counselors, and even school nurses are housed in this central location encouraging collaboration among all the teachers in planning experiences for students and providing the space to carry out this planning.

Another area being created within the school library is a place where students can gather to think, build, create, and produce their ideas and solutions to problems, a makerspace. Designed to promote creativity in students, it has all sorts of tools and equipment and such new technologies as the 3-D printer. If the library is heavily used for other purposes, the components of makerspaces can be placed on a book truck and moved from the library to classroom. The truly creative school librarian can offer much with little output and can engage the community to get them to volunteer to mentor students with their projects.

TECHNOLOGY AND THE SCHOOL LIBRARY

While some technologies were found in libraries before the mid-twentieth century, it was the influx of funding with NDEA and ESEA that provided for audiovisual resources and the accompanying hardware. Libraries were expanded to provide space for listening and viewing, as well as for housing and use of these multimedia resources. They were added to the library card catalog and systems were designed for check out and return. Perhaps two greater challenges came with the need for sufficient electrical outlets and a way to darken the library when the materials were being used.

This new media required a new approach to working with students and teachers, as well as many new skills beyond storage and retrieval. Demonstrating both the effective integration of audiovisual materials into the curriculum and the actual use of the equipment followed the new approaches to acquisition and organization of these, and a new role for the librarian who was suddenly thrust into the role of a teacher-trainer. This continues with available microcomputer technology and all the new formats of social media.

At the present time, librarians continue to demonstrate the appropriate use of the databases available and select appropriate websites and other information from the ever-increasing amount found on the Internet. They help teachers understand the best uses of social media for their

assignments and keep everyone apprised of new technologies.

The school library is the center for learning about the resources found on the Internet and how to use the available databases for teachers and students. Learning how to use new software whether for word processing or other applications happens in the school library. The librarian now trains both teachers and students in finding and using information, making the library the professional development center for the school.

ADVOCACY AND THE SCHOOL LIBRARIAN

The perception of many educators that the school library is no longer a needed part of a school and the consequence of loss of positions for school librarians is a constant threat to student access to information. The support of students, teachers, and members of the community who recognize the value of the information found in and through the library is essential. Readers of Levitov's book, *Activism and the School Librarian*, will "learn the theoretical foundation for activism, how to move from advocacy to activism, how to create a culture of advocacy in terms of working with parents, community groups, and local businesses."[14]

This advocacy must move beyond the local community and reach legislators at the state and national levels. Kaaland and Kachel suggest that "school library *legislation* advocacy begins with the development of a relationship between school library advocates—librarians an beyond—and legislative decision makers."[15] School librarians need to convince their students, teachers, and parents to help lobby for school libraries if these programs are to survive.

RELATIONSHIP WITH PUBLIC LIBRARIES

From the beginning, the relationship between schools and public libraries is one of constant change. In the early days of the United States, children did not attend school for long and libraries were only for the wealthy. As the country grew and as it became apparent that it would take informed citizenry to protect the new democracy, state governments began to fund public schools. As the townspeople built their public libraries, they looked at the school funding and wished that they had a similar mechanism for building an adequate budget. This resulted in some public libraries being a part of the school district funding, a model that exists at the present time in some cities.

Although early in education in the U.S. state legislatures were funding school districts, school libraries were not necessarily a part of this plan. Public librarians, looking at the dismal state of libraries at the elementary level, began sending classroom collections to the schools so that children would have literature to read. The public library also provided the collection and often a librarian in the high school.

In the mid-twentieth century when this began to change particularly when elementary school libraries began to be developed and expanded, school librarians were hired. They could meet with their public library counterparts and true cooperation began. Some of the traditional ways that school and public librarians cooperate include the following:

- Public librarians come to schools to give book talks.
- School librarians collect any book left for students to read and return them after students have finished reading them.
- School librarians share homework assignments with the local public library using fax and e-mail to facilitate the process.
- School librarians invite the public librarian to come to school to explain the summer reading program and to encourage students to participate.
- Librarians invite each other to their staff meetings.
- Public librarians invite teachers to bring their students to the public library. School librarians promote these visits and even accompany teachers and students during the visit.
- Librarians can share the costs of author visits to their libraries, sure that they will attract students.

Cooperation is made easier when public and school librarians are active members of local librarians' groups. Again, newer technologies allow the establishment of e-mail lists to communicate. When cooperation is alive and well between school and public librarians, joint proposals can be written for funding.

With great regularity, as budgets for both schools and public libraries shrink, library and school administrators continue to seek ways to control funding for library services. Although the research shows that combining these two agencies does not result in budget savings,[16–19] joint facilities continue to be viewed as a measure to cut costs. Little recent research has been conducted, but the factors in place for the earlier research have not changed enough to change those results. None were shown that actually saved money without cutting services.

Successful cooperative efforts that have been cost cutting have been the statewide efforts to provide digital collections, crossing all types of libraries and bringing information equity to everyone within a community. Joining networks that encourage the sharing of resources is a win-win situation. Opening electronic access to information opens access to children at school and to the community, not only when the public or school library is open, but also every day since homes with Internet access will have constant access to online resources. While public libraries offer access to the Internet, getting to the public library may be difficult for children and for those who live in homes without Internet access, the school library may be their only access to the digital world.

MEASURING THE EFFECTIVENESS OF SCHOOL LIBRARIES

With the funding for the development of school libraries in the twentieth century, the need for professional school librarians increased. Academic programs needed full-time faculty to teach, and a greater number of persons joined doctoral programs to prepare for open positions. The increase in dissertation research added to the body of research. As these new faculty members worked for tenure, they had to continue their research output.

School librarians and faculty teaching school library courses in library and information science programs were eligible for competitive research from the Institute for Museums and Library Services and the Association for Library and Information Science Educators. Smaller grants were available through professional associations, and some vendors offered small grants. Moreover, professional journals featuring research results began providing a venue to share findings.

Research studies served to point out student success when schools had libraries, librarians, and resources. Gaver's landmark study showed the effect of centralized library services in elementary schools.[20]

In 1989, David Loertscher, then Chair of the AASL Research Committee, and Phil Turner organized the first Treasure Mountain Research Retreat. The school library field was asked "What research questions should be answered by the time the next guidelines are written?" Seventeen research questions emerged, and research reviewers were asked to respond to the following:

- Analyze and synthesize the major research studies dealing with the topic.
- Describe the implications of these studies for practitioners.
- Identify research needs in the topic area for the next decade.
- Discuss the best approaches to use in designing and carrying out this research.
- Describe the infrastructure that must be present.[21]

Fifty participants discussed the entries developed for this retreat. Subsequently, regular Treasure Mountain retreats have been held usually before the biannual AASL meetings. The results are published and available to help both practitioners and researchers understand what is needed in this field, how to go about collecting the data, and of even more importance, the reporting of this data to a wide audience.

Regional–School

At one Treasure Mountain session, school librarians met Stephen Krashen and discussed reading research, Krashen's *Power of Reading*[22] (a second edition is available). In spite of the deluge of technology, reading was and is an integral part of the school librarians' assignment. Both Krashen and McQuillan[23] continue to point out the role of the school library in providing opportunities for students to learn to read. Krashen suggests that few people in the United States are illiterate, it is just that they do not read or write very well. His solution is free voluntary reading, access to quantities of books and other materials that students will want to read, and time allocated so they can read. McQuillan suggests:

> Many students attend schools where the level of print access is abysmal, creating a true crisis in reading performance.... I do *not* wish to argue that simply providing books is all that is needed for schools to succeed.... Teaching is much more than physical resources, and no progress can be made without qualified and sensitive teachers. But just as we would not ask a doctor to heal without medicine, so we should not ask teachers and schools to teach without the materials to do so. Reading material is basic to all education, and providing a rich supply of reading matter to children of all ages, as well as a place and time to read, is the first step to bridging the gap between poor and good readers. This means that school libraries must be stocked with interesting and appealing materials and appropriately staffed; students need to be given time to read silently books of their own choosing.[23]

By the mid-1990s, the leader in the movement to show that well-stocked and well-staffed school libraries were keys to academic achievement, Keith Curry Lance, completed the first study of school libraries in Colorado.[24] He patterned his federally funded study after one done by School Match, an independent company.[25,26] This group had been hired to help real estate agents point out the best school systems for persons moving into the area. In his first study and three among many that followed, Pennsylvania, Alaska, and the second Colorado study, the same results prevailed. What the results of all these studies show is that to increase student achievement, a school community should do two things:

First, they create a quality information-rich and technology-rich environment easily accessible by students and teachers. That is, the school library now extends beyond its walls delivering quality information into the classrooms and into the homes of every learner 24 hours a day, 7 days a week. Learners flourish when quality information is close at home.

Second, they employ a staff of both professional and support personnel in the library center who provide leadership and tireless partnering with the teachers to deliver quality learning experiences. Achievement is affected by the two teaching partners using the best information technology and learning strategies.[27–30]

School library research continues with individuals in more and more states conducting studies that use or modify the Lance methodology. All these studies report the effects of the library program on the education of children in schools today. The research confirms the importance of such a facility for preparing students to become lifelong learners.

THE VIRTUAL SCHOOL LIBRARY

Much has been written about the school without a library. The argument is that everything anyone needs is available electronically, which means that a school librarian in a book-filled library is no longer required. Certainly, the use of a reference book collection in a school has become obsolete because that type of reference is readily available online, and the speed to find answers is a plus. As evidence of this, watch what happens when someone poses a question about an actor as they are going into a movie. Cell phones appear and fingers click away until someone finds the answer.

As speedy and efficient as this seems, students and teachers need to know where to find accurate information. Students need to be able to use critical thinking skills to determine what information they need to find, to develop questions to guide their research, to evaluate what they find, and to report it in a variety of formats. Students also still need to be taught to read and to be discriminating readers, to sort out what is fact versus what someone would like to be perceived as a fact. As more and more becomes available electronically, it becomes even more important to have the information professional, the school librarian, select the best from these resources for students to use and to teach them how to use them. This is essential if they are going to learn to separate fact from misinformation. In some cases, it is essential that relevant resources be made available through selection by the librarian and links made so students do not drown in the wealth available to them. As the library moves from shelves and shelves of books to access through electronic devices, the school librarian is there to make sure all students have the devices and access to information no matter the economic status of their parents.

The school library remains the bastion to free access to information. Further, students must be encouraged to become lifelong learners if they are to accept their responsibility as citizens in a democracy.

AN INTERNATIONAL PERSPECTIVE

School libraries worldwide are better developed in the countries in the category of "developed" nations and found less often in those countries considered "developing." In the poorest nations, books of any kind are limited from textbooks to reference books and recreational reading. In some countries, the librarian is totally responsible for the collection and must pay for any books lost. This does not encourage free exchange of materials even if there are books available.

Cell phone technology is becoming available to students throughout the globe. It is only a matter of time until these students will be able to access information. With the speed with which translating software is being developed, this information will be available to them in their native language.

Two international organizations foster school library development. The International Association of School Librarianship (IASL) has almost 800 members in more than 60 countries. The group holds a meeting each year in a host country, publishes a quarterly online and print newsletter, and offers their excellent research journal, *School Libraries Worldwide* online. Furthermore, IASL maintains a website for its members and an electronic list for communication.

The School Library section of the International Federation of Library Associations and Institutions (IFLA) also focuses on the development of school libraries internationally. The IFLA also meets in a different country each year. The difference between this association and the IASL is that one joins the IASL directly, whereas one is a member of the IFLA through its member associations. That is, all IASL members may attend the IFLA as a member of the IFLA because the IASL is an association member. The IASL and IFLA's School Library section have been able to work together on projects that will further development of school libraries worldwide, the latest being the development of international school library standards. More information about both these organizations may be found on their websites:

IASL: www.iasl-online.mlanet.org/
IFLA: www.ifla.org/

CONCLUSION

The future of school library services in schools has a challenge at the current time. The explosion of information that seemed overwhelming before the advent of the computers with their great storage capacities, coupled with the advent of the Internet and the introduction of the world's knowledge in a teacher's or student's home, has increased the need for a location and an information expert who can help to sort through the myriad of resources available. It is up to school librarians to convince administrators, teachers, and the community to make sure students in today's schools have open access to information.

REFERENCES

1. U.S. Bureau of Education. *Public Libraries in the United States of America their History, Condition, and Management: Special Report*; Government Printing Office: Washington, DC, 1876; 38.
2. Clark, M.B. Pioneer portrait. Wilson Libr. Bull. **1951**, *26*, 26.
3. Mahar, M.H. *Statistics of Public School Libraries, 1960–61: Part II. Analysis and Interpretation*; U.S. Department of Health, Education and Welfare: Washington, DC, 1962; 1.
4. Committee on Library Organization and Equipment of the National Education Association and of the North Central Association of Colleges and Secondary Schools. *Standard Library Organization and Equipment for Secondary Schools of Different Sizes*; American Library Association: Chicago, IL, 1920.
5. Certain, C.C. *Elementary School Standards. Prepared Under the supervision of a Joint Committee of the National Education Association and the American Library Association*; American Library Association: Chicago, IL, 1925.
6. Committee on Post-War Planning of the American Library Association. *School Libraries for Today and Tomorrow: Functions and Standards*; American Library Association: Chicago, IL, 1945.
7. American Association of School Librarians. *Standards for School Library Programs*; American Library Association: Chicago, IL, 1960.
8. American Association of School Librarians and Association; Department of Audiovisual Instruction of the National Education. *Standards for School Media Programs*; American Library Association: Chicago, IL/National Education Association: Washington, DC, 1969.
9. American Association of School Librarians and Technology; Association for Education for Educational Communications. *Media Programs: District and School*; American Library Association: Chicago, IL, 1975.
10. American Association of School Librarians; Association for Educational Communications and Technology. *Information Power: Guidelines for School Library*; American Library Association: Chicago, IL, 1988.
11. American Association of Librarians, Association for Educational and Technology. *Information Power: Building Partnerships for Learning*; American Library Association: Chicago, IL, 1998, Vol. 1, vii.
12. American Association of School Librarians. *Standards for the 21st Century Learner American Library Association*; American Library Association: Chicago, IL, 2007.
13. Common Core State Standards Initiative: Preparing American Students for College and Career. *Process*. www.corestandards.org (accessed March 5, 2015).
14. Woolls, B.; Weeks, A.C.; Coatney, S. *The School Library Manager*, 5th Ed.; Libraries Unlimited: Santa Barbara, CA, 2014; 223.
15. Kaaland, C.; Kachel, D.E. School Library Legislative Advocacy defined. In *Activism and the School Librarian: Tools for Advocacy and Survival*; Levitov, D., Ed.; Libraries Unlimited: Santa Barbara, CA, 2012; 57.
16. Aaron, S.L. *A Study of the Combined School Public Library*; State Library of Florida: Tallahassee, FL, 1978.

17. Aaron, S.L.; Smith, S.O. *Study of the Combined School Public Library*; Phase I, Florida State University: Tallahassee, FL, 1977; Phase II, 1978; Phase III, 1978.

18. Jaffee, L.L. Collection development and resource sharing in the combined school/public library. In *Collection Management for School Library Media Centers*; White, B.H., Ed.; Haworth Press: New York, 1986.

19. Bauer, P.T. Factors affecting the operation of a combined school/public library: a qualitative. PhD dissertation, Florida State University, Tallahassee, FL, 1995.

20. Gaver, M.V. *Effectiveness of Centralized Library Service in Elementary Schools*, 2nd Ed.; Rutgers University Press: New Brunswick, NJ, 1963.

21. Woolls, B. *The Research of School Library Media Centers: Papers of the Treasure Mountain Research Retreat, Park City, UT, October 17–18, 1989*; Hi Willow Research and Publishing: Castle Rock, CO, 1990.

22. Krashen, S. *The Power of Reading: Insights from the Research*; Libraries Unlimited: Englewood, CO, 1993.

23. McQuillan, J. *The Literary Crisis: False Claims, Real Solutions*; Heinemann Press: Portsmouth, NH, 1998; 86.

24. Lance, K.C.; Welborn, L.; Hamilton-Pennell, C. *The Impact of School Library Media Centers on Academic Achievement*; Hi Willow Research and Publishing: Castle Rock, CO, 1993.

25. American Library Association. Pupil success firmly linked to school library funding. Am. Libr. **1987**, *18*, 632–633.

26. Lynch, M.J.; Weeks, A. School match revisited. Am. Libr. **1988**, *19*, 459–460.

27. Lance, K.C.; Loertscher, D.V. *Powering Achievement: School Library Media Programs Make a Difference: The Evidence*; Hi Willow Research and Publishing: San Jose, CA, 2001.

28. Lance, K.C.; Rodney, M.J.; Hamilton-Pennell, C. *How School Librarians Help Kids Achieve Standards: The Second Colorado Study*; Hi Willow Research and Publishing: San Jose, CA, 2000.

29. Lance, K.C.; Hamilton-Pennell, C.; Rodney, M.J.; Peterson, L.; Sitter, C. *Information Empowered: The School Librarian as an Agent of Academic Achievement in Alaska Schools*, Rev. Ed.; Alaska State Library: Juneau, AK, 2000.

30. Lance, K.C.; Rodney, M.J.; Hamilton-Pennell, C. *Measuring up to Standards: The Impact of School Library Programs and Information Literacy on Pennsylvania Schools*; Pennsylvania Citizens for Better Libraries: Greensburg, PA, 2000.

Science and Engineering Librarianship

Margaret Ann Mellinger
OSU Libraries & Press, Oregon State University, Corvallis, Oregon, U.S.A.

Abstract
Science and engineering librarianship is an integral part of a broad range of theoretical and applied scientific fields; it provides access to current and cutting-edge research and preserves access to the historic scientific record. Science and engineering librarians work in organizations of all sizes ranging from solo operations and small libraries, to corporate research centers and research libraries of large universities. To interact successfully with their clientele, librarians must understand the scientific method, the structure of the scientific literature, and the communication patterns of scientists and engineers.

INTRODUCTION

Science and engineering librarianship has its roots in the specialized subject collections early scientific societies assembled for their members. Connections between scientific research and industrial progress fueled the need for science and engineering libraries and for establishing collections of scientific literature in university, public, and governmental libraries. The number of scientific societies and industrial organizations with libraries grew rapidly in the late 1800s and early 1900s, especially in Great Britain and the United States.[1] Ranganathan attributes the rise of such specialized libraries, in part, to a change in focus from the macroscopic, or book level, to the microscopic, or article level.[2] Scientists and engineers in research and industry recognized their need for collections of periodical literature and for librarians to organize those collections. Science and engineering librarianship provided documentation of the growing universe of scientific periodical literature through selection, acquisition, cataloging, indexing and abstracting, and tracking translations of the international science literature. Some of the major indexes of engineering and scientific information began in the late nineteenth century (e.g., *Index Medicus* and *Engineering Index*) or early twentieth century (e.g., *Chemical Abstracts* and *Biological Abstracts*).

Much of the literature on science and engineering librarianship from the 1920s to the 1970s focuses on the physical layout and management of the ideal library, training of staff, delivery of services, and the collection and organization of scientific literature. Scientific research and funding boomed in the period after World War II until the late 1970s, particularly in the United States, and there was a corresponding growth in libraries. The role of the librarian was to optimize the selection, acquisition, organization, and delivery of scientific information for the use of scientists, engineers, faculty, researchers, students, legislators, and the public.

Improvements in information technology led to new formats for library collections and new roles for librarians. Science and engineering libraries subscribed to online systems, purchased CD-ROM counterparts to print indexes, and offered mediated search services for early online systems and full-text databases. As the World Wide Web became predominant in the late 1990s, librarians no longer needed to mediate online database searches; library users could do those searches themselves. Librarians took on new roles to address issues related to electronic resources, such as licensing, managing subscriptions, devising new funding models, cataloging, user instruction, outreach, and promotion. In addition, librarians and researchers continued to conduct research on the information-seeking behaviors of scientists and engineers to learn how libraries could best facilitate information retrieval.[3,4] Librarians began to offer value-added services such as literature searching, market research, patent searching, and materials properties searching.

Roles for science and engineering librarians shift and change as the information technology environment grows and changes. As access to scientific information and data becomes more ubiquitous, librarians can focus more on fundamental of the profession such as ensuring equitable access to information, providing safe spaces for learning and inquiry, and connecting learners to the skills and information they need to create knowledge. Rather than merely serving as custodians of scientific literature, twenty-first-century science and engineering librarians participate in the scientific process, help educate future researchers, and advocate for fair and equitable access to the scientific record.

SCIENCE AND ENGINEERING LIBRARY SETTINGS

Science and engineering libraries range in size from solo operations and branches of public libraries to settings in

Encyclopedia of Library and Information Sciences, Fourth Edition DOI: 10.1081/E-EISA-120053514

Science–Semantic

very large corporations and universities. Public libraries, college and university libraries, corporate research centers, hospitals and medical libraries, and other special and technical libraries employ science and engineering librarians. Science and engineering librarians may also work as self-employed information researchers, in information brokerages, in government agencies, in museums, zoos, and aquariums, or for scientific, technical, and medical (STM) publishers and database providers.

Academic

Many science and engineering librarians work in college or university libraries. Depending on the type of academic institution, their duties can include core library functions such as reference, instruction, collection development, outreach, and, for tenure-track positions, research and writing. Some universities have separate libraries for various science disciplines. For example, the University of Wisconsin has science libraries covering agriculture and veterinary medicine, astronomy, biology, chemistry, engineering, health sciences, geology and geophysics, plant sciences, and physics.[5] Other academic libraries provide science and engineering materials from a single science library, still others from a unified central library.

Public

Larger public libraries often have significant science and engineering collections, although they may not be housed in a separate library, as they are in the Science, Industry and Business Library of the New York Public Library[6] or in the Los Angeles Public Library's Science, Technology & Patents Department.[7] Investors, inventors, students, and entrepreneurs can access specialized collections of books, databases, and patent literature, and receive expert research help from highly trained librarians. Another example of a large public library dedicated to science and technology is the Linda Hall Library, an independent public library of science, engineering, and technology in Kansas City, Missouri.[8] Linda Hall Library has an extensive collection of materials and librarians offer a suite of fee-based research and document delivery services to companies, academic institutions, and individuals throughout the world.

Corporate

Access to scientific and technical information is essential to scientists and engineers developing and designing industrial products. Special libraries in industrial or corporate settings employ science and engineering librarians to facilitate the research needed to bring new products to market. Some information centers or technical libraries can be centralized and large, while others serve smaller segments of corporate organizations. Sometimes, technical libraries are in the research and development arm of the company. In response to the availability of online resources and materials, many corporate libraries have reduced the physical footprint of the library and moved to a virtual model of desktop delivery of information critical to the daily work of their clientele. Some corporations have closed their research centers in favor of the virtual library. Examples of corporations where science and engineering librarians work are Ford Motor Company, Intel, and Nike.

Government

U.S. federal government agencies run special or technical libraries such as those in the Environmental Protection Agency,[9] the United States Forest Service,[10] and NASA.[11] Science and engineering librarians may work in major federal government libraries such as the Science Technology and Business Division of the Library of Congress,[12] the National Library of Medicine,[13] National Institutes of Health Library,[14] and the National Agricultural Library.[15] Some science librarians work directly with legislators, for example, at the national level in the Resources Science and Industry Division of the Congressional Research Service,[16] or within state libraries. They also work on digital libraries and information initiatives such as the National Center for Biotechnology Information,[17] and the databases Medline and Agricola.

Other examples of governmental technical libraries are those in the National Laboratories including Los Alamos National Laboratory[18] and the Oak Ridge National Laboratory where librarians "help researchers compete for and carry out research of national importance."[19] Public users may not be able to visit these technical libraries because of the sensitive nature of the work in the national laboratories and the locations of the libraries within them. An exception is the Hanford Technical Library, run by the Pacific Northwest National Laboratories, which is open to the public and shares a building with a Washington State University branch campus library and a United States Department of Energy Reading Room.[20] Whether or not the physical libraries of national labs are open to the public, an increasing number of technical reports and unclassified documents from those libraries are available online. An example of such an online collection is SciTech Connect, administered by the Office of Science and Technology Information where thousands of United States Department of Energy documents can be searched and downloaded for free.[21]

National Science Libraries

Many of the national libraries worldwide have collections or separate libraries dedicated to science and technology. Examples include the British Library's Science Technology and Medicine Collections,[22] the *Bibliothèque Nationale*

Science–Semantic

de France Département Sciences et Techniques,[23] the Russian Academy of Sciences,[24] the German National Library of Science and Technology,[25] the Japan Advanced Institute of Science and Technology Library,[26] and the United States Library of Congress Science Reference Services.[27]

Medical

Hospitals, government agencies, pharmaceutical companies, and other medical-related corporations are the settings for many medical libraries. There are also health sciences or medical libraries within teaching institutions offering programs in medicine, nursing, veterinary medicine, pharmacy, or allied health. The National Library of Medicine supports the dissemination of biomedical information in the United States, through the National Network of Libraries of Medicine (NN/LM®). Eight Regional Medical Libraries of the NN/LM® work to "improve the supporting infrastructure for health sciences librarians."[28] Another resource for medical librarians is the Medical Library Association.

Solo

Sometimes, there is only one science or engineering librarian in a company or institution. Solo librarians are "most likely found in a small library without extensive holdings or resources. Solos are expected to do it all—ordering, cataloging, reference, bibliographic instruction, online searching, filing, budgeting—everything."[29] Solo librarians can be found in marine science centers, or observatories.[30] Professional organizations such as the Solo Librarian Division of the Special Libraries Association connect solo librarians to share resources, expertise, and provide continuing education opportunities.[31]

Other Settings

Museums, aquariums, and zoos may have science libraries to support staff as they conduct research, build exhibits, and manage those institutions. Outside researchers and the public also use these libraries.[32]

Other employment options for science and engineering librarians are to work as information brokers, to subcontract with governmental or corporate science and technical libraries, or to work for publishers. Information brokers are information professionals who provide as-needed or contract-based services to clients. Some information brokers are librarians with scientific backgrounds specializing in information collection and analysis. They may have skills in patent searching, engineering, chemistry, or computer programming and software design, for example. Information brokers may be self-employed or work in an information brokerage. They may be subcontractors

working with government or corporate clients, other research firms, or for individuals.[33]

STM publishers and database producers employ librarians with science and engineering backgrounds to construct controlled vocabularies, perform indexing and abstracting services, and to interact with science and technology libraries and other clients for sales and training.

JOB REQUIREMENTS

Education

A master's degree in library and information studies from an accredited program[34] is required for most science and engineering librarian positions in public, academic, special, and federal government libraries.[35] Some positions require qualified candidates to have an undergraduate science or engineering background or to hold a second master's in a scientific field. There are distinct advantages to having a degree in the sciences, including enhanced subject knowledge, understanding the culture of the field, and increased credibility with clientele.[36] Librarians with science degrees may also be better equipped to work in such specialized subfields as health, bioinformatics, chemistry, data services, or geographic information systems (GIS). To fill these specialized roles, some libraries hire candidates with advanced degrees in relevant scientific fields rather than degree holders in library and information sciences.

Skills

Science and engineering librarians need the same core skills that all librarians require—grounding in the philosophy and techniques of library service, knowledge of library materials and resources, and facility with computers, the Internet and commercially available library software.[37] A study of job descriptions for science and engineering positions showed that the most frequently required qualifications were not specific to science or technology.[38] Communication skills, computer and technology literacy, reference experience, teaching experience, and a team orientation were the most commonly required qualifications.

There are some science-related preferred qualifications for prospective science and engineering librarians. Employers may prefer candidates with a science and technology background, which can be coursework in science, a bachelor's degree in science, a library science course in science librarianship, an internship or practicum, or experience in a science library. Additional preferred qualifications are familiarity with the organization and structure of science and technology literature and knowledge of the scientific method as a process of discovery and invention. Some positions require specialized software skills, such as the ability to work with and teach GIS software. Other jobs require expertise in searching chemical or molecular structures. The Medical Library Association has defined competencies for lifelong learning and professional success that include understanding of the health-care environment, the ability to manage health information resources in a broad range of formats, and understanding of scientific research methods.[39]

Libraries are changing, and candidates who thrive in changing environments have an edge. Many of the preferred qualifications found in position advertisements are attitudinal. Candidates should exhibit innovation, creativity, curiosity, vision, optimism, integrity, and the ability to work well with a team.[40] Another aspect of change in libraries is the focus on computer technology—technological skills and aptitude, web design skills, understanding of database structure and design, and searching expertise are examples of preferred qualifications for science librarians.

RECRUITMENT AND CONTINUING EDUCATION

Recruitment continues to be an issue in science and engineering librarianship. Administrators use a number of approaches to recruit librarians, one of which is to relax the requirement for a second degree in a science discipline. Many science librarians with social science or humanities backgrounds have learned science or engineering librarianship on the job. A 2000 survey of science and engineering librarians found that over half of the respondents came into their positions without a science background.[41] One approach is to recruit promising students from science and engineering majors into library and information science degree programs. Many science or engineering students are unaware of the career opportunities in librarianship. Another approach is for libraries to fill specialty roles by hiring candidates without the library degree who have advanced science degrees and experience in areas like GIS, bioinformatics, statistics, or data collection and analysis.

Continuing education is important as many people come into science and engineering librarianship without a science background (or are assigned to areas outside of their science background), and because new roles are emerging. In some settings (e.g., medical libraries), continuing education credits are required. Professional organizations, library and information science programs, and conferences are venues for updating skills and learning about new areas. Training may be face-to-face, online, or a hybrid and may take place over a few days or a few months. An example of a successful face-to-face continuing education event is the Science Boot Camp for Librarians, which was developed in 2009 by science librarians in New England to help librarians learn about topic areas in science.[42] This annual regional event has been duplicated

in regions across the United States and Canada. Another example is the Data Carpentry Workshop, which provides data skills training especially useful to librarians who provide research data services (RDS).[43] Additional examples of selected professional development, conference, and continuing education resources have been compiled by the Science and Technology Section of the Association of College and Research Libraries Division of the American Library Association.[44]

PROFESSIONAL RESPONSIBILITIES

Science and engineering librarianship includes reference, instruction, cataloging, collection development, and outreach or liaison. Beyond these traditional professional responsibilities, as previously noted, new roles are emerging in response to an ever-changing information environment. The importance of ensuring access to scientific literature spurred librarians to develop expertise in scholarly communication issues, including open access advocacy. Health sciences librarians may provide support for systematic reviews or serve as an embedded librarian in a research term, or as an informationist in a clinical or public health setting.[45] RDS are increasingly offered to help students, faculty, and staff meet funding agency mandates and, more importantly, to encourage researchers in planning for the whole research lifecycle.

Reference and Consultation

Writing in 1994, C.D. Hurt asserted that "good reference service is predicated on three elements: 1) knowledge of the user, 2) knowledge of the literature, and 3) knowledge of the sources."[46] Librarians still need these three elements, but there are now many more channels for interaction with library users. Library clientele may now contact reference librarians 24 hours a day. To cover more hours of virtual reference service, librarians collaborate within their institutions and through networks of colleagues across time zones. Librarians interact with clients by using software tools for virtual reference, instant messaging, video-conferencing or video chat, and even in online game environments. Transactions can take place in real time or asynchronously. Librarians in special libraries provide value-added services along with reference consultations. They may synthesize the research on a particular problem or question, mine the literature for solutions to a problem, and write summaries for clients.

Many science and engineering librarians are skilled in searching highly specialized online databases, as well as standard print reference sources. Chemistry librarians track down chemical information using tools like *SciFinder Scholar (Chemical Abstracts)*, *Beilstein*, and patent literature search engines. Genetics and molecular structure databases such as *GenBank*[47] and *BLAST*[48] are important tools for biology and bioinformatics librarians.[17] Geosciences and map librarians can develop reference and instruction services around GIS software. Engineering librarians can be part of courses where students are learning engineering design principles and need to gather information for their projects throughout the term.[49]

Health sciences librarians integrate reference services into their clients' workflow in a number of ways. One way is to deliver content to mobile devices. Students in evidence-based medicine classes work with librarians to identify best evidence for treatment plans. In the Vanderbilt University Medical Center, the Research Informatics Consult Service (RICS) offers "... training, grant assistance, access to electronic resources, database searching and information filtering."[50] Librarians make rounds, or house calls to deliver reference services directly to researchers and practitioners in the hospital.[51]

Instruction

Science and engineering librarians teach people to create productive search strategies, as well as how to use subject-related periodical databases. Librarians train clientele to use powerful search tools for retrieving scientific information, such as those used in bioinformatics.[52] Science and engineering librarians instruct users one-on-one, in workshops or classes, in stand-alone college courses, as well as through online tutorials. Academic librarians teach students information literacy skills and promote information literacy and science literacy concepts with faculty. They advise instructors constructing research assignments. Ideally, they are building relationships in which they can convey the tenets of information literacy to those who teach in the disciplines, as well as to students. Scientists and engineers need information literacy skills to succeed in their coursework, but also to develop lifelong information skills to help them succeed in their careers. Librarians have developed information literacy standards for science and engineering[53] based on the Association of College and Research Libraries (ACRL) Information Literacy Competency Standards for Higher Education.[54]

Science and engineering librarians use technology to deliver instruction to distance learning courses or distributed teams. Librarians increasingly depend on web page design, interface and tool design, online tutorials, blogs and wikis to deliver library content and services to users.

Collections

To work effectively with the scientists and public they serve, science and engineering librarians must understand the structure of scientific communication and develop a strong background in the specialized literature of their particular fields. This includes digital content. Librarians

manage access to digital resources such as online bibliographic, full-text, or fact-based databases. Online access issues, pricing, and license negotiations can be part of the collection development role for science and engineering librarians, especially those in smaller institutions. One of the challenges for libraries is that with online reference sources come yearly subscription or maintenance fees. Another aspect of the collection development role is collection analysis and evaluation in a hybrid print and electronic environment.

Science and engineering librarians select the same formats of materials most librarians select, for example, books, periodicals, reference materials, and multimedia. For many disciplines, the journal is the most important vehicle for scientific communication and it represents the historical scientific record.[55] Online access to the periodical literature is critical to scientists and engineers, and librarians dedicate a lot of energy to the process of providing it. Many libraries have canceled print journals in favor of electronic journals and purchase online back files as a way to preserve access. Other types of periodicals that can be useful for science and engineering are product and trade catalogs and trade journals.

To further support and enhance access to the scientific record, librarians build institutional repositories and develop and manage digital libraries comprising born-digital and digitized information. There are nearly 2000 institutional repositories tracked by the Webometrics organization.[56] Science librarians identify unique information sources for digitization and submission to institutional repositories. One example of this is the Technical Report Archive and Image Library, a collaborative project of the Greater Western Library Alliance and the Center for Research Libraries.[57] On a broader scale, the National Science Digital Library "provides high quality online educational resources for teaching and learning, with current emphasis on the sciences, technology, engineering, and mathematics (STEM) disciplines—both formal and informal, institutional and individual, in local, state, national, and international educational settings."[58]

Librarians require a working knowledge of formats that are particularly important in science and engineering librarianship: patents, standards and specifications, technical reports, conference papers, preprints and e-prints, maps, and data. Any of these formats can be "gray literature." Gray literature is "produced on all levels of government, academics, business and industry in print and electronic format, not controlled by commercial publishers."[59] It is especially important in applied fields such as forestry and engineering.

The following is a superficial overview of some of the types of information sources particular to science or engineering. To gain understanding of the structure of science and engineering literatures, new or prospective librarians should consult the many secondary guides that are available.[60]

Patents

The patent literature is a rich source of scientific and engineering information. While there are free online sources for patent searching (United States Patent Office Database, Google Patents, eSpace.net), librarians should be aware of more powerful subscription patent search engines and to understand when to refer library clientele to expert patent searchers.

Standards and specifications

Standards and specifications guide the design, production, and testing of goods and services. Each industry has many standards-developing organizations. Some of the major standards organizations are the National Institute of Standards and Technology, the International Standards Organization, and the American National Standards Institute. Librarians continually track the best ways for accessing standards and specifications. While some libraries still have print collections of standards, many libraries have moved to online subscription packages that provide access to standards when needed. Library users sometimes need historic standards for academic or legal research.

Technical reports

Technical reports are important in rapidly changing fields such as computer science and engineering where it is important to keep up with the latest techniques and innovations. Technical reports can result from grants, or contracts, and as such, are not subject to the same type of prepublication peer review as journal articles. Scientists and engineers can quickly disseminate their methodology, data, and results for others to review.[61] Science and engineering librarians support the digitization of technical reports that increases discoverability and access.

Conference proceedings

Because conference proceedings introduce new ideas in a timely manner, the conference paper is the most important type of literature for much of computer science and engineering. Researchers in rapidly changing fields such as computer science and electrical engineering keep up with changes by tracking conference papers. Proceedings from very small or international conferences are sometimes difficult for librarians to collect. Some sponsoring organizations publish proceedings erratically.

Preprints and e-Prints

Preprint means prepublication print. Preprints gained widespread use in the field of high-energy physics after World War II.[62] Physicists were also early adopters of online dissemination of preprints, known as electronic preprints or e-prints. The High Energy Physics e-print archive, known as arXiv, was developed by Paul Ginsparg at Los Alamos National Laboratories and went online in August 1991.[63] The arXiv, now at Cornell, contains over half a million documents covering physics, mathematics, nonlinear science, computer science, and quantitative biology. E-prints continue to thrive in physics and other scientific fields such as computer science and astronomy.

Handbooks and data sources

Handbook information is critical for science and engineering research and practice. Handbooks can contain information on anything from materials properties to spectral data, to biological and genetic data. Handbooks, data sources, and other types of reference sources are increasingly available in digital format. Online access to handbooks and data sources is advantageous to users in laboratories and off-campus.

Maps

Maps are core resources in astronomy, geomorphology, physical geology, and other geosciences, and are widely used in other disciplines such as the agricultural and biological sciences.[64] Identifying, acquiring, cataloging, storing, and preserving maps is a complex group of tasks. Digital maps and their preservation add another level of complexity to map librarianship.

Data sets

Data Sets are used in geosciences, environmental sciences, health sciences, astronomy, and many other disciplines. Librarians assist investigators to discover and locate appropriate data sets for research and to identify data sets that can be curated for future use. The Registry of Research Data Repositories is a useful starting place.[65] RDS in libraries range from simple reference (finding and citing data sets) to consulting with students, faculty, or staff on data management plans or metadata standards, to providing technical support and preparing data for repositories.[66]

Translations

Scientific research is increasingly global. In addition, while English is currently the primary language for scientific publishing, this has not always been the case. Science librarians should be aware of translation services and of sources for translated scientific and technical literature.

Management, Marketing, and Promotion

Science and technical library managers establish strategic goals to align with the institution. They recruit, interview, hire, manage, and evaluate and support the career development of library staff. Managers may also determine appropriate funding sources and financial management practices, and assess and communicate the value of the library to the broader organization.

Marketing and promotion are especially important in corporate libraries, where librarians must regularly demonstrate the value of the information center to the parent organization. Special libraries have developed means to measure the value of librarians and library services and to communicate the value to clients. Studying the needs of their potential internal customers, librarians focus services on the most critical needs of the organization or clients. The Special Libraries Association conducts research and collects information on the value of the information center.[67] Marketing, promotion, and measuring the value of library services are increasingly important in academic and public libraries, as well. There have been a number of studies of return on investment for academic libraries.[68]

Research and Writing

Writing is a vital part of science and engineering librarianship, whether it is composing content for web pages and pathfinders, analyzing and summarizing background information for an engineering client, crafting a press release, or compiling a grant proposal. Tenure-track academic librarians conduct research about all aspects of libraries and services, and communicate those results to the profession. All librarians need excellent research and communication skills and to keep up with new research and best practices in librarianship by reading journals such as *Issues in Science and Technology Libraries* and *Science and Technology Libraries*, by reading magazines such as *Information Outlook*, by following discussion lists and blogs, and by attending conferences and giving presentations.

Web Technologies

Web technologies continue to shape science and engineering librarianship. Science and engineering librarians use the capabilities of the participatory Web to deliver library content and services via blogs, wikis, RSS feeds, podcasts, streaming video, and instant messaging. They teach users to organize, manage, track, and share research using online tools such as EndNote, Zotero, or Mendeley. Librarians have an online presence on social networking websites and online communities. As stated in the revised *Competencies for Information Professionals of the 21st Century,* the successful science and engineering librarian "maintains current awareness of emerging technologies that may not be currently relevant but may become relevant tools of future information resources, services or applications."[69]

Scholarly Communication

Science and engineering librarianship has had a close relationship with the universe of scientific periodical literature from the beginning. *The World List of Scientific Periodicals published in the years 1900–1921*[70] contained in two volumes the titles of 24,028 periodicals. Some estimates suggest that the number of scientific periodical titles doubles every 9 years.[71] The journal literature is pivotal for scientists and engineers, and librarians have been actively tackling the complex issues surrounding scholarly communication for some time. These issues include publishing and subscription costs, copyright, and maintaining equitable access to scientific information in the digital environment. Journal subscription rates have escalated for many years, greatly outpacing the rate of inflation. Science and technology journals generally have the highest subscription rates as well as the highest annual price increases, which raises serious concerns about the sustainability of the current system of scientific communication.[72] The scientific process builds on prior and related research, much of which is reported in peer-reviewed articles; decreased access to journals puts scientific researchers at a disadvantage.

Science and engineering librarians disseminate information about the crisis, and advocate for publishers and vendors to adopt more sustainable business models. Productive and close relationships with publishers and vendors give librarians a venue to communicate library issues. One example is the *Punch List of Best Practices for Electronic Resources*.[73] This list, compiled by the Scholarly Communication Committee of the Engineering Libraries Division of the American Society for Engineering Educators, offers librarians and vendors a starting point for conversations. Librarians are active in SPARC®, the Scholarly Publishing and Academic Resources Coalition (SPARC), "an international alliance of academic and research libraries working to correct imbalances in the scholarly publishing system."[74]

Science and engineering librarians support a number of practices that improve access to scientific articles, including alternative publishing and pricing models, open access journals, and the development of institutional repositories. One early example of an alternative publishing model is how the SPARC collaborated with small societies and noncommercial publishers to build *BioOne*, a cost-effective online journal collection supporting biological, ecological, and environmental sciences.[75] Another example of science librarians taking the lead is SHERPA, a UK consortium of research universities and industry partners that runs a number of projects supporting the development of open access repositories and researching scholarly communication issues.[76]

Open Access

Science and engineering librarians have long championed open access as a means to address the serials crisis and to ensure access to the scientific literature. One way to do this is to support open access publishing. The *Directory of Open Access Journals* includes journals in scientific and scholarly subject areas published in any language.[77] *BioMedCentral* is an open access publisher with over 270 peer-reviewed journals.[78] *PubMed Central (PMC)* is the U.S. National Institutes of Health (NIH) free digital archive of biomedical and life sciences journal literature.[79] The Public Library of Science (PLOS) is a nonprofit publisher of a number of free, high-impact, open access journals supported by pay-to-publish fees, including the largest journal in current publication, *PLOS ONE*.[80]

Global access to scientific information is an issue of great importance in science and engineering librarianship. Researchers, doctors, and scientists in developing countries are at a disadvantage because they lack access to scientific literature. Partnerships between major publishers of scientific information and three United Nations organizations are making medical, agricultural, and environmental sciences journals available for free or very low cost to local not-for-profit institutions in the developing world.[81] The World Health Organization and six major publishers[82] introduced the Health InterNetwork Access to Research Initiative in 2002. In 2003, the Food and Agriculture Organization and publisher partners initiated Access to Global Online Research in Agriculture.[83] Online Access to Research in the Environment was launched in 2006 by a partnership of the United Nations Environment Programme, Yale University, and major publishers of environmental science information.[84] These three programs will likely continue until 2015 as part of the United Nations' Millennial Plan.

E-Science

An enormous amount of scientific data is generated from satellites, telescopes, lasers, sensors, experiments, and simulations, giving scientists unprecedented access to large sets of networked scientific data. Computational power in conjunction with large data sets is driving a new research methodology called e-Science.[85] E-Science, or cyber infrastructure, as it has been known in the United States, is a set of technologies that enable people to collaborate: to share computing, data, and the use of remote instruments. In other words, e-Science encompasses the technologies that allow networked, distributed, collaborative, multidisciplinary science. As libraries continue to define roles in collecting, preserving, and disseminating research derived from these large data sets, new areas of focus have emerged for science librarians, including data curation and digital preservation.

Data Management Plans and Research Data Services

A related role for librarians is to offer RDS to researchers and students. One of those services is to consult with and

guide scientific investigators proposing grants to the NIH and the National Science Foundation (NSF). In 2009, the NIH Public Access Policy required investigators funded by the NIH to submit an electronic version of their final peer-reviewed manuscripts within 12 months after publication.[86] Beginning in January 2011, proposals submitted to the NSF were required to include a Data Management Plan (DMP), a document of two pages describing how research data will be stored and shared.[87] Public access policies for government-funded scientific research are continuing to be instituted in agencies across Europe, the United Kingdom, Canada, and the United States.[74] Librarians are in a good position to track these requirements and to offer assistance with open access publishing and data management plans to facilitate compliance. Communities and organizations have formed around supporting various aspects of data management. DataOne has developed the Data Management Planning Tool to give investigators templates for writing their own plans.[88] DataCite is an organization that supports the standards for identifying and citing data.[89]

Citizen Science

Citizen science is a term used to describe "public participation and collaboration in scientific research to increase scientific knowledge."[90] While scientists have partnered with amateurs to conduct research for years, the Internet, digital media, and mobile devices equipped with geographic positioning units have increased the opportunities for public involvement in the scientific process. Librarians can support citizen science in many ways; by connecting library users with science researchers and by providing services for citizen science, such as data curation and technology training, and by capturing and preserving the formal and informal outputs of citizen science.[91]

Makerspaces

Makerspaces are places where people meet to share resources like knowledge, skills, tools, and technologies in order to work on their own projects and creations. The focus is on community and sharing—values libraries share. For this reason, many public and academic libraries have developed spaces and programs that support "do-it-yourself" or "do-it-with others activities." Public libraries large and small employ technology loving librarians and volunteers to run spaces like the TechCentral in the Cleveland Public Library and TekVenture in Indiana's Allen County Public Library.[92] Librarians at the DeLaMare Engineering Science and Engineering Library at the University of Nevada, Reno offer a makerspace with 3D printers, 3D scanners, and laser cutters.[93] They also circulate equipment such as electronics and robotics kits that students can use in their own projects.

PROFESSIONAL ORGANIZATIONS

Engineering Librarianship. Science and engineering librarians can be active in a variety of national and international professional organizations, depending upon subject specialty, library setting, and personal interests. The following are some key organizations of particular interest.

American Library Association (ALA) Science and Technology Section (STS)

http://www.ala.org/ala/acrl/aboutacrl/acrlsections/science tech/sts.cfm

The Science and Technology Section (STS) is in the ACRL Division of the American Library Association. Established in 1961, as the Agricultural and Biological Sciences Subsection of ACRL, the organization later changed its name to reflect the subject specialties of its members. STS offers its over 1700 members conference programming and continuing education opportunities. Publications of the section include the STS-L discussion list, the STS-Signal newsletter, and a peer-reviewed online journal, *Issues in Science and Technology Librarianship.*

American Society for Engineering Education, Engineering Libraries Division (ASEE/ELD)

http://eld.lib.ucdavis.edu/

Engineering Library Division members are librarians and information professionals interested in promoting the role of the library as an integral part of engineering education. ELDNET-L is the open electronic discussion list for the division.

Special Libraries Association (SLA)

http://www.sla.org/

The Special Libraries Association began in 1909 "to promote the collection, organization and dissemination of information in specialized fields and to improve the usefulness of special libraries and information services.[94]" Several Special Libraries Association Divisions are related to science and engineering. They are the Science and Technology Division, the Physics, Astronomy and Mathematics Division, the Chemistry Division, the Engineering Division, the Biomedical and Life Sciences Division, the Environment and Resource Management Division, and the Food, Agriculture and Nutrition Division.

Medical Library Association (MLA)

http://www.mlanet.org/

The Medical Library Association was founded in 1898 and has members worldwide.[95] The MLA focuses on the unique issues faced by health sciences information professionals as they deliver critical medical information to physicians, health practitioners, and patients. Several types of publications meet MLA members' needs: the peer-reviewed *Journal of the Medical Library Association;* newsletters MLA-Focus and MLA News; books; standards; reports; and other documents. MLA offers continuing education courses and delivers medical information training around the word through the Librarians without Borders[SM] program.

International Federation of Library Associations and Institutions (IFLA)

http://www.ifla.org/index.htm

IFLA's Science and Technology Libraries Section (Special Libraries Division) was formed in 1978. The section supports science and engineering librarianship worldwide, through programming at the IFLA Annual Conference, by conducting research projects on topics of global interest, and by collaborating with other library associations to address issues pertaining to the access and dissemination of scientific literature. Members share information through the section newsletter and the STL-SC discussion list.

International Association of Aquatic and Marine Science Libraries and Information Centers (IAMSLIC)

http://www.iamslic.org/

IAMSLIC directs the Aquatic Commons, an open access repository for literature on natural marine, estuarine/brackish, and freshwater environments. Its purpose "is to promote such cooperation and sharing of resources among libraries and information centers which specialize in any aspect of aquatic science—freshwater, brackish and marine."[96]

There are also smaller organizations that focus particular fields of librarianship. In addition, many science and engineering librarians join organizations related to their subject domain. These are a few examples:

Association of Independent Information Professionals (AIIP): http://www.aiip.org/index.html

American Association of Physics Teacher (AAPT): http://www.aapt.org/

The American Chemical Society (ACS) Division of Chemical Information: http://www.acscinf.org/

American Society for Information Science and Technology (ASIST) Scientific and Technical Information Science (STI) Interest Group: http://www.asis.org/SIG/SIGSTI/sti.html

Geoscience Information Society: http://www.geoinfo. org/

International Association of Agricultural Librarians and Documentalists (IAALD): http://www.iaald. org/

International Association of Technological University Libraries (IATUL): http://www.iatul.org/

United States Agricultural Information Network (USAIN): http://usain.org/

CONCLUSION

For over a century, science and engineering librarianship has been instrumental in the advance of modern theoretical and applied science and technology. To remain relevant, future science and engineering librarians will need a keen understanding of the interplay between the information needs of scientists and engineers, and the technologies, economics, and politics that influence access to critical data and information. Librarians alone will not be able to solve the information challenges that a new era of science will bring; a greater degree of collaboration with other professionals will be essential. As Web technologies mature, librarians will require the knowledge and skills to employ them to improve information retrieval and to facilitate research that will be increasingly global, collaborative, and interdisciplinary. Science and engineering librarianship has clearly evolved in the twentieth century in response to changes in information technology and shifts in scientific research, and the pace of change is unlikely to slow. The future of science and engineering librarianship is not in responding to change, but in facing change by participating fully in it.

REFERENCES

1. Gomme, A. Scientific and technical libraries. In *The Uses of Libraries*; Baker, E.A., Ed.; University of London Press: London, U.K., 1927; 128–130.

2. Ranganathan, S.R. Special librarianship—What it connotes. Spec. Libr. **1949**, *40* (9), 364.

3. Tenopir, C.; King, D. *Communications Patterns of Engineers*; IEEE Press: Piscataway, NJ, 2004.

4. Hemminger, B.M.; Lu, D.; Vaughan, K.T.L.; Adams, S.J. Information seeking behavior of academic scientists. J. Am. Soc. Inf. Sci. Technol. **2007**, *58* (14), 2205–2225.

5. University of Wisconsin-Madison Libraries. Campus Libraries. n.d. http://www.library.wisc.edu/libraries (accessed July 2016).

6. New York Public Library. Science, Industry and Business Library (SIBL). n.d. https://www.nypl.org/locations/sibl (accessed July 2016).

7. Los Angeles Public Library. Departments and Services – Central Library. n.d. http://www.lapl.org/branches/central-library/departments (accessed July 2016).

8. Linda Hall Library, Science, Engineering & Technology Information for the World. n.d. http://www.lindahall.org (accessed July 2016).

9. United States Environmental Protection Agency. EPA National Library Network. n.d. https://www.epa.gov/libraries (accessed July 2016).

10. United States Department of Agriculture Forest Service. National Forest Service Library. n.d. http://www.fs.fed. library (accessed July 2016).

11. National Aeronautics and Space Administration. NASA HQ Library. n.d http://www.hq.nasa.gov/office/hqlibrary (accessed July 2016).

12. United States Library of Congress. Science Technology & Business. n.d. https://www.loc.gov/topics/science (accessed July 2016).

13. United States National Institutes of Health (NIH). National Library of Medicine (NLM). n.d. http://www.nlm.nih.gov (accessed July 2016).

14. United States National Institutes of Health, Office of Management, Office of Research Services. NIH Library Home. n.d. http://www.nihlibrary.nih.gov (accessed July 2016).

15. United States Department of Agriculture. National Agricultural Library. n.d http://www.nal.usda.gov (accessed July 2016).

16. United States Library of Congress. Resources Science and Industry Division. n.d http://www.loc.gov/crsinfo/research/div-rsi.html (accessed July 2016).

17. National Center for Biotechnology Information (NCBI). Welcome to NCBI. n.d. http://www.ncbi.nlm.nih.gov (accessed July 2016).

18. Los Alamos National Laboratory. Research Library. n.d. http://www.lanl.gov/library (accessed July 2016).

19. Oak Ridge National Laboratory. Research Library. n.d. https://www.ornl.gov/content/research-library (accessed July 2016).

20. Washington State University Tri-Cities Information Service Consolidated Libraries. About the Libraries. n.d. (accessed February 2016). http://www.tricity.wsu.edu/dis/consolidated (accessed July 2016).

21. United States Department of Energy Office of Science and Technical Information. SciTech Connect. n.d. http://www.osti.gov/scitech (accessed July 2016).

22. British Library. Science. n.d. http://www.bl.uk/subjects/science (accessed July 2016).

23. Bibliothèque Nationale de France. Science & Technology Department. http://www.bnf.fr/en/bnf/dpt_sct_eng.html (accessed July 2016).

24. National Library of Russia. n.d. http://www.nlr.ru/eng (accessed July 2016).

25. Technische Informationsbibliothek (TIB). n.d. https://www.tib.eu/en/ (accessed July 2016).

26. The Library of Japan Advanced Institute of Science and Technology (JAIST). n.d. http://www.jaist.ac.jp/library/english (accessed July 2016).

27. Library of Congress, Science Technology & Business Division. Science Reference Services. n.d. http://www.loc.gov/rr/scitech (accessed July 2016).

28. United States National Library of Medicine. National Network of Libraries of Medicine Fact Sheet. n.d. https://www.nlm.nih.gov/pubs/factsheets/nnlm.html (accessed July 2016).

29. Siess, Judith, A. Flying solo: librarian, manage thyself. Am. Libr. **1999**, *30* (2), 32–34.

30. Mizzy, D. Observations of an observatory librarian. Coll. Res. Libr. News **2003**, *65* (7), 458–459.

31. Special Libraries Association (SLA), Divisions. n.d. https://www.sla.org/get-involved/divisions (accessed July 2016).

32. Mount, E., Ed. Sci-tech libraries in museums and aquariums. Sci. Technol. Libr. **1985**, *6* (1/2).

33. Association of Independent Information Professionals, Inc. The Independent Information Professional, 2000. http://www.aiip.org/resources/Documents/Public/IIPWhitePaper.pdf (accessed July 2016).

34. American Library Association. Directory of ALA-Accredited and Candidate Programs in Library and Information Studies. 1996-2016. http://www.ala.org/accreditedprograms/directory (accessed July 2016).

35. United States Bureau of Labor Statistics. Librarians. In *Occupational Outlook Handbook*; United States Department of Labor: Washington, DC, 2015. http://www.bls.gov/ooh/education-training-and-library/librarians.htm (accessed July 2016).

36. Hallmark, J.; Lembo, M.F. Leaving science for LIS: interviews and a survey of librarians with scientific and technical degrees. Issue Sci. Technol. Librariansh. **Spring 2003**, http://www.istl.org/03-spring/refereed1.html (accessed February 2016).

37. American Library Association. What librarians need to know. 1996-2016. http://www.ala.org/educationcareers/careers/librarycareerssite/whatyouneedlibrarian (accessed July 2016).

38. Baker Jones, M.L.; Lembo, M.F.; Manasco, J.E. Recruiting entry-level sci-tech librarians: an analysis of job advertisements and outcome of searches. Sci-Tech. News **2002**, *56* (2), 12–16.

39. Medical Library Association Professional Development. Professional Competencies for Health Sciences Librarians. 2016. http://www.mlanet.org/p/cm/ld/fid=39 (accessed July 2016).

40. Mitchell, Victoria S. The top ten things a new sci/tech librarian should know: developing core competencies. Issues Sci. Technol. Librariansh. **Winter 2004**, http://www.istl.org/04-winter/conf1.html (accessed February 2016).

41. Hackenberg, J.M. Who chooses sci-tech librarianship? Coll. Res. Libr. September **2000**, *61* (5), 448.

42. Schmidt, M.; Reznik-Zellin, R. *Science boot camp for librarians: CPD on a shoestring*; International Federation of Library Associations and Institutions: San Juan, PR, May 2011. http://conference.ifla.org/past-wlic/2011/200-schmidt-en.pdf (accessed February 2016).

43. Data Carpentry. Building Communities Teaching Universal Data Literacy. n.d http://www.datacarpentry.org (accessed July 2016).

44. Association of College & Research Libraries Science & Technology Section, Professional Development Committee. A Guide to Professional Development Resources for Science and Technology librarians, 2016. http://www.ala.org/acrl/aboutacrl/directoryofleadership/sections/sts/stswebsite/committees/stscontinuing (accessed July 2016).

45. Crum, J.A.; Cooper, I.D. Emerging roles for biomedical librarians: a survey of current practices, challenges and changes. J. Med. Libr. Assoc. **2013**, *101* (4), 278–286.

46. Hurt, C.D. *Information Sources in Science and Technology*, 2nd Ed.; Libraries Unlimited: Englewood, CO, 1994.

47. National Center for Biotechnology Information. GenBank. n.d. http://www.ncbi.nlm.nih.gov/genbank (accessed July 2016).

48. National Center for Biotechnology Information. Basic Local Alignment Search Tool (BLAST). n.d. http://blast.ncbi.nlm.nih.gov/Blast.cgi (accessed July 2016).

49. Weiner, S.T. Librarians as teaching team members in a mechanical engineering senior design course. Sci. Technol. Libr. **1996**, *16* (1), 3–10.

50. 50.Vanderbilt University Medical Center, Center for Knowledge Management. Evidence-based services – Research Informatics Consult Service, 2016. https://www.mc.vanderbilt.edu/km/ebm/rics (accessed July 2016).

51. Mizzy, D. Informationists: making rounds makes a difference. Coll. Res. Libr. News **2003**, *64* (3), 176–177.

52. Alpi, K. Bioinformatics training by librarians and for librarians: developing the skills needed to support molecular biology and clinical genetics information instruction. Issues Sci. Technol. Librariansh, **Spring 2003**, http://www.istl.org/03-spring/article1.html (accessed February 2016).

53. ALA/ACRL/STS Task Force on Information Literacy for Science and Technology. Information literacy standards for science and engineering/technology, n.d. http://www.ala.org/acrl/standards/infolitscitech (accessed July 2016).

54. ALA/ACRL, Guidelines, Standards and Frameworks. Information Literacy Competency Standards for Higher Education, (rescinded June 25, 2016). http://www.ala.org/acrl/standards/informationliteracycompetency (accessed July 2016).

55. Walker, R.D.; Hurt, C.D. *Scientific and Technical Literature: An Introduction to Forms of Communication*; American Library Association: Chicago, IL, 1990.

56. Cybermetrics Lab. Ranking Web of World Repositories. http://repositories.webometrics.info (accessed July 2016).

57. Technical Report Archive & Image Gallery (TRAIL). n.d. http://www.technicalreports.org/trail/search/ (accessed July 2016).

58. National Science Digital Library, Overview. n.d. https://nsdl.oercommons.org/nsdl-overview (accessed July 2016).

59. Auger, C.P. *Information Sources in Grey Literature*, 3rd Ed.; Bowker-Saur: London, U.K., 1994.

60. Balay, R., Ed. At the broad level, start with the Science, Technology and Medicine section of. In *Guide to Reference Books*; American Library Association: Chicago, IL, 1996.

61. Library of Congress Science, Technology & Business Division, Science Reference Services. Technical reports and standards. n.d. http://www.loc.gov/rr/scitech/trs/trswhatare.html (accessed July 2016).

62. Tompson, S.R. A tale of two worlds: high energy physics preprints in the 1990s. Sci. Technol. Libr. **2001**, *19* (2), 43–51, 44.

63. Cornell University Library, arXiv. General information about arXiv. n.d. http://arxiv.org/help/general (accessed July 2016).

64. Walker, R.D.; Hurt, C.D. *Scientific and Technical Literature: An Introduction to Forms of Communication*; American Library Association: Chicago, IL, 1990; 181.

65. Re3data.org. Registry of Research Data Repositories. n.d. http://www.re3data.org (accessed July 2016).

66. Tenopir, C.; Sandusky, R.J.; Allard, S.; Birch, B. Research data management services in academic libraries and perceptions of librarians. Libr. Inf. Sci. Res. **2014**, *36* (2), 84–90.

67. Mayes, R.; Baker, G. ROI—Return on investment. Special Libraries Association Future Ready 365 blog. http://futureready365.sla.org/04/29/roi-return-on-investment/ (accessed February 2016).

68. Luther, J. University investment in the library: what's the return?: a case study at the University of Illinois at Urbana–Champaign. *Library Connect White Paper #1*; Elsevier: San Diego, CA, 2008. https://libraryconnect.elsevier.com/articles/university-investment-library-what-s-return-case-study-university-illinois-urbana-champaign (accessed July 2016).

69. Abels, E.; Jones, R.; Latham, J.; Magnoni, D.; Gard Marshall, J. *Competencies for Information Professionals of the 21st Century*, Rev. Ed.; Special Libraries Association: Washington, DC, June 2003. http://sla.org/wp-content/uploads/2013/01/0_LRNCompetencies2003_revised.pdf (accessed February 2016).

70. Smith, W.A.; Sheppard, L.A.; Wharton, L.C.; Pollard, A.W.; Mitchell, P.C. *A World List of Scientific Periodicals Published in the Years 1900–1921*; Oxford University Press, H. Milford: London, U.K., 1925.

71. Van Noorden, R. Global scientific output doubles every nine years. Nature News Blog, **2014**, http://blogs.nature.com/news/2014/05/global-scientific-output-doubles-every-nine-years.html (accessed February 2016).

72. Van Orsdel, L.C.; Born, K. Serial wars. Libr. J. **2007**, *132* (7), 43–48. http://lj.libraryjournal.com/2007/04/ljarchives/periodicals-price-survey-2007-serial-wars/ (accessed July 2016).

73. ASEE, Engineering Library Division. Punch list of best practices for electronic resources. 2005. http://depts.washington.edu/englib/eld/punchlist/PunchlistRevision2005.pdf (accessed February 2016).

74. Scholarly Publishing and Academic Resources Coalition (SPARC). Policy and Advocacy. n.d. http://sparcopen.org/what-we-do/active-policy (accessed July 2016).

75. BioOne. 2016. http://www.bioone.org (accessed July 2016).

76. University of Nottingham. SHERPA. 2006. http://www.sherpa.ac.uk (accessed July 2016).

77. Directory of Open Access Journals (DOAJ). 2016. https://doaj.org (accessed July 2016).

78. BioMed Central. About. n.d. http://www.biomedcentral.com/about (accessed July 2016).

79. United States National Library of Medicine, National Institutes of Health. PubMed Central. n.d. http://www.ncbi.nlm.nih.gov/pmc (accessed July 2016).

80. Public Library of Science (PLOS). n.d. https://www.plos.org (accessed July 2016).

81. World Health Organization, Hinari, Oare, Agora Leaflet. http://www.oaresciences.org/publicity/Hinari-Oare-Agora_Leaflet.pdf (accessed July 2016).

82. World Health Organization, Hinari. Hinari Access to Research for Health programme. n.d. http://www.who.int/hinari/en (accessed July 2016).

83. Food and Agriculture Organization of the United Nations. AGORA, Access to Global Online Research in Agriculture. n.d. http://www.fao.org/agora/en (accessed July 2016).

84. United Nations Environment Programme. OARE, Research in the Environment. n.d. http://www.unep.org/oare (accessed July 2016).

85. Hey, T.; Trefethen, A. The data deluge: an e-science perspective. UK eScience Core Programme. http://eprints.soton.ac.uk/257648/1/The_Data_Deluge.pdf (accessed February 2016).

86. National Institutes of Health. NIH Public Policy Details. Last updated March 25, 2016. http://publicaccess.nih.gov/policy.htm (accessed July 2016).

87. National Science Foundation. NSF ENG Data Management Plan Requirements. n.d. http://www.nsf.gov/eng/general/dmp.jsp (accessed July 2016).

88. University of California Curation Center, California Digital Library. Data Management Planning Tool (DMPT). n.d. https://dmptool.org (accessed July 2016).

89. DataCite. n.d. https://www.datacite.org (accessed July 2016).

90. National Geographic Society, Education Encylopedic Entry, Citizen Science. n.d. http://nationalgeographic.org/encyclopedia/citizen-science (accessed July 2016).

91. Cohen, C.M.; Cheney, L.; Duong, K.; Lea, B.; Unno, Z.P. Identifying opportunities in citizen science for academic libraries. Issues Sci. Technol. Librariansh. **Winter 2015**, http://www.istl.org/15-winter/article1.html (accessed February 2016).

92. American Libraries. Manufacturing Makerspaces. Am. Libr. Mag. **2013**, http://www.americanlibrariesmagazine.org/article/manufacturing-makerspaces (accessed February 2016).

93. University of Nevada Reno, DeLaMare Science & Engineering Library. n.d. http://www.delamare.unr.edu/default.aspx (accessed July 2016).

94. Mitchell, A.C., Ed. *Special Libraries Association, Its first 50 years 1909–1959*; Special Libraries Association: New York, NY, 1959.

95. Medical Library Association. MLA Milestones. n.d. http://www.mlanet.org/p/cm/ld/fid=334 (accessed July 2016).

96. The International Association of Aquatic and Marine Science Libraries and Information Centers (IAMSLIC). About. http://www.iamslic.org/about-us/faq (accessed July 2016).

Science and Technology Studies

Sanna Talja
Department of Information Studies and Interactive Media, University of Tampere, Tampere, Finland

Abstract

This entry introduces theories of technology developed within the interdisciplinary field of science and technology studies (STS). Theories of technology within STS are conventionally divided into the social shaping of technology (SST) perspective, the social construction of technology (SCOT) perspective, actor-network theory (ANT), and gender and technology studies. The practice theory is emerging as a distinct line of thought and analysis.

INTRODUCTION: THEORIES OF TECHNOLOGY AND INFORMATION SCIENCE

This entry introduces theories of technology developed within the interdisciplinary field of science and technology studies (STS). Theories of technology within STS are conventionally divided into the social shaping of technology (SST) perspective, the social construction of technology (SCOT) perspective, actor-network theory (ANT), and gender and technology studies. The practice theory is emerging as a distinct line of thought and analysis.

Theories of technology developed within STS are important from the viewpoint of information science. Theories and assumptions of what technologies are, how they emerge, and how humans and technologies interact, are important for many research areas in information science. In fact, regardless of whether researchers explicitly define and expose their viewpoint on technology, such views are always present and influence research aims and questions in information science, a field that is concerned with the interaction between information/documents, technologies, and users.

Within information science, STS theories are applied in research fields such as knowledge organization, scholarly communication, citation studies, scientometrics, social informatics, digital libraries, and knowledge management. Some scholars have argued, however, that STS and information science should not be seen as separate fields of study. According to this view, theories developed within STS are the core theories that empirical research programs in information science should draw on. In fact, three different views exist on the relationship between the interdisciplinary fields of STS and information science. Some scholars see these fields as overlapping, that is, as having shared theoretical foundations and research interests. Some scholars see that there is partial overlap between STS and information science in theoretical constructs and research interests. According to a third view, STS and information science are separate research fields—there is only little or no overlap in research topics and interests. Research areas in information science where STS theories have traditionally been less cited and applied are, for example, everyday life information seeking research and information literacy research.

Regardless of whether STS and information science are seen as unified in their interests and theories, to some extent overlapping, or as separate domains, information science and STS are cognate research fields. Their research interests increasingly cross since information, media, and technology are in current digital environments more and more intertwined. Examples of such integrated information, media, and technology environments are, for example, social media applications such as wikis, blogs, social networking, and social bookmarking services.

This entry proceeds by first briefly introducing STS. After presenting some antecedents to theories of technology in STS, this entry introduces the theoretical perspectives of SST, ANT, SCOT, gender and technology studies, and practice theory of technology. This entry ends by briefly discussing the relationships between STS theories, and the relationship between information science theories and theories of technology.

THE ROOTS OF SCIENCE AND TECHNOLOGY STUDIES

Science and technology studies has roots in the sociology of scientific knowledge and in the social constructivist movement in the study of scientific knowledge production, the "empirical programme of relativism."[1] This movement consisted of historical and sociological analyses of the processes which lead to the acceptance of new scientific knowledge. Empirical "laboratory studies" of the mundane everyday practices of scientific work conducted in the late 1970s and 1980s sought to show

Encyclopedia of Library and Information Sciences, Fourth Edition DOI: 10.1081/E-ELIS4-120043529

how scientific facts are socially constituted and negotiated.[2–4] A central insight was the indecisiveness of experimental data taken by themselves. Results from scientific experiments are rarely self-evidencing, and initially allow for a degree of interpretative flexibility, that is, alternative interpretations of the empirical evidence. Such ambivalences and potential controversies must for practical reasons at some stage be closed down, since the results must be presented in a clear and non-ambivalent manner in the form of reports and journal articles. The detailed empirical analyses of the contingencies involved in the construction of scientific facts showed how like any work practice, scientific knowledge production involves not only purely cognitive factors but a complex configuration of technological tools, work organization, professional norms and skills as well as formal and informal communication practices. The empirical programme of relativism was influential for the development of the STS research field.[5] It brought about the understanding that it is fruitful to view technology and technological practices as built through processes of social construction and negotiation in the same way as scientific knowledge.

Science and technology studies were also preceded by sociotechnical studies of computerization in organizations conducted in the 1970s (for a review, see Kling[6]). These studies stressed that technologies are tightly interwoven with the overall organization of work, the nature of work tasks, social relations at the workplace, and the very conditions and experience of work. This insight led to a more general understanding that a work task mediated by a new technology does not remain the same. New technologies require new intellectual and bodily moves and skills. As a consequence, new needs, meanings, practices, and purposes arise in the work. The concepts of "reskilling" and "deskilling" were used in early studies of computerization and social and organizational change to describe these changes. Later, these concepts were replaced by a more general understanding that any work task involves a combination of physical objects, knowledge and skills, social interactions, and routinized ways of doing things.

Theories of technology in the STS field also developed as contests to technological determinism. Technological determinism is an influential way of thinking about the relationship between individuals, technology, and society—or, more explicitly, the "information society." It is based on the implicit assumption that technologies are developed through series of innovations undertaken in attempts to overcome the weaknesses and shortcomings of earlier technologies, and that new technologies straightforwardly represent progress and outdate earlier technologies. This perspective constructs technologies as tools with fixed meanings whose uses are known (i.e., immediately identifiable and clear), and defined by the original aims of their designers.

Technological determinism has also been called the technology independence assumption.[7] According to this assumption, technology and social relationships each are constituted and evolve independent of one another. Within STS, technologies are not understood solely as tools used for practical purposes. The assumption is that technologies are more pervasive in nature: social and power relations are encoded into technologies, and technologies also embody social relations and aspirations in concrete and powerful ways.

Another central idea in STS is that technologies are the products of "heterogeneous engineering"[8] which refers to how they are emergent rather than stable phenomena. Whatever may have been the system designers' original plan, what actually gets produced and reproduced does not fully follow a single fixed plan or strategy. What happens depends on the strategies of a whole range of actors. The "technical features" of technologies are not fully controlled and regulated by any single group of actors. Neither are the consequences, opportunities, and constraints of technologies stable across contexts.

SOCIAL SHAPING OF TECHNOLOGY

The SST perspective emphasizes the mutually shaping relationship between the technical and the social.[9] The relationship between technology and society is described as "a seamless web"[10] meaning that technological, social, and cultural worlds and practices are interrelated and inextricably linked.

Social shaping of technology posits that the formation of technologies cannot be explained through a single rationality or imperative: economic (market demands), political (social power relations), technological or material conditions for innovations, or the social interests and desires of particular groups. It seeks to open up the "black box" of technology production by a detailed analysis of how the social, organizational, cultural, and political environment in which a technology originally was created fundamentally shaped the technical characteristics of the artifact.[11] In its interest of going back in history to study how technologies developed, SST is closely related to historical studies of technology.

Central concepts in SST are "interpretative flexibility," "relevant social groups," and "closure." These concepts contest the notion that technology develops autonomously and according to an inner logic. The concept of interpretative flexibility refers to a core assumption in SST that every stage in the generation and implementation of new technologies involves a set of choices between different options. The initial openness means that choices could always have been different. Each technology could have been constructed based on a different set of premises and decisions. The choices eventually made are not dictated solely by technological considerations. A range of social and contextual factors affect which options are eventually selected.

"Closure" means that the openness to alternative solutions and interpretations present at earlier stages must at some point become regarded as closed, and potential disagreements related to design decisions and their consequences resolved. Such decisions are seen to be guided by alliances between "relevant social groups" and the coming together of their interests. For instance, when a technology moves from planning stages to selling and marketing stages, the representations concerning its content, functions, meanings, and uses become relatively stable.

Ruth Schwartz Cowan's "How the refrigerator got its hum"[12] is one influential study in the SST perspective. The study showed that technical qualities, in terms of energy-saving and silent machinery, did not explain the type of refrigerator technology that came to dominate the market—a better technology lost the competition. Analyzing the processes of innovation, patenting, production, and marketing, she came to the conclusion that many interrelated factors explained the outcome of the process and the type of technology that gained market dominance.

Studies conducted from the SST perspective seek to track down all possible proposed solutions by relevant players that were available in the design context in the formative time period, regardless of whether the solutions later turned out to be successes or costly mistakes.[13] Such historical investigations shed light on why some artifacts succeed and others fail. Both historical and organizational case studies have lead to a deeper understanding of typical causes for failure and conditions that must be filled for a technology to succeed.

The assumption in SST is that a technology is eventually stabilized through getting rooted in stable organizational arrangements. But whatever the system designers may have had in mind and wished to do is not the only factor explaining the outcome. What actually takes form depends on the actions, interests, and strategies of a range of other actors as well. There is a network of varying interests and strategies at play, and technological closure means that these reach some kind of accommodation. Closure in technology does not mean, however, that both designers and users would eventually agree on the content, purposes, and uses of the technology. The notion of interpretative flexibility also means that differences continue to exist between different social groups in how they come to see and experience a particular technical artifact. Not only is there a great deal of flexibility in how an artifact is designed, the process of redesign continues throughout its marketing, implementation, and use.

ACTOR-NETWORK THEORY

The ANT was developed by Michel Callon,[14] Bruno Latour,[15] and John Law[8] as an attempt to more fully incorporate technical artifacts as actors in accounts of human action. Latour[15] termed nonhumans as the "missing masses" in sociological accounts. He argued that the orderliness of everyday life to a great extent relies on a distribution of tasks between human and nonhumans. Tasks performed by humans can be delegated to nonhumans, as when a policeman guiding traffic is replaced by traffic lights. The function of traffic lights is to guarantee orderly behavior. Even more generally, argues Latour,[16] when nonhumans are delegated human tasks, nonhumans shape human action in that they "prescribe" certain kinds of action. Prescription is what a device anticipates, allows, or forbids a human actor to do. There is morality in such prescriptions, termed by Akrich[17] as the "affordances" of a technology. Traffic lights aim at permitting some actions and inhibiting others. This does not mean that a real human actor would necessarily follow the action guidelines of the prescribed, inbuilt user. Latour's[15,16] main point is that nonhumans deserve full consideration as social actors. As prescriptions are encoded in machines or devices, they are delegated not only duties but also values and ethics that greatly add to the overall orderliness of societies.

In a similar vein, Law[18] argued that "the social is not purely social at all," since the social world would not hang together if the natural, the corporeal, the technological, and the textual were taken away. What we usually call technical is partly social, since in practice nothing is purely technical. And what appears to be the social is partly technical; scraping the social surface we will find that it is composed of networks of heterogeneous materials (p. 10).[18]

The first version of ANT had much in common with the SST approach. It was developed to avoid explanations of single influences, interests, or background factors—social, economic, or technical-guiding the development of technical artifacts.[19] ANT posits that the background "interests" formative in technology development are in themselves achievements which depend on a coming together of many conditions: creative, material, financial, legal, markets, and so on.

Within information science, ANT has been applied, for example, by Rob Kling and his colleagues. Kling, McKim, and King analyzed Electronic Scholarly Communication Forums (e-SCFs) such as e-journals, digital libraries, and collaboratories, as sociotechnical interaction networks (STINs).[20] Kling and colleagues (p. 48)[20] defined an e-SCF as a network that includes people/organizations, equipment, data, diverse resources (such as money, skills, status), documents and messages, legal arrangements, enforcement mechanisms, and resource flows. There are social, economic, and political factors that enable the interactions that sustain such a network. Attempts to analyze the success or failure of an e-SCF also must take into account the interactions between different technical systems, both large-scale global technological systems and local technologies-in-use.

ANT studies focus on exploring how actor-networks get formed, hold themselves together, or fall apart.[21]

Kling and his colleagues[20] conducted insightful analyses of why a technology that on the surface is essentially the same technology—a pure e-journal—can gain momentum in one context and fail in another. Kling and colleagues[20] showed that if a single network element differs across contexts, the innovation simply no longer is the same. Their empirical studies on the successes and failures of pure e-journal and preprint archive initiatives in some disciplines explained under what kinds of circumstances some components of the STIN will offer resistance (termed by Latour as "antiprograms)."[16]

ANT case studies have been criticized by Latour, Callon, and Law[22] themselves as being merely descriptive. Others have criticized ANT studies for the preference for historical analyses of the formation of actor-networks rather than tackling contemporary technologically mediated social life-forms. Kling and colleagues[20] argued, however, that STIN modeling could be conducted before implementation, which would help in predicting the success of e-SCF design initiatives.

Latour,[15] in turn, preferred to describe ANT as purely sociological analysis, the "sociology of translation." In his view, the purpose of ANT research is to "follow the actors" that constitute a sociotechnical actor-network. The study of the constitution of an actor-network is not to study a process of straightforward acceptance or rejection of an innovation, it means following the process of its transformation. "Translation" implies that one technology may stand for another thing in a different context. Actor-network theory analyses show how keeping an innovation functional and achieving its intended effects is a constant struggle with no guaranteed outcomes. Actor-network theory also assumes that social groups encountering a new technology can in fact be deeply transformed by the innovation. Actors and technologies hence coproduce each other, and the interest in ANT is in how these coevolve.

One of the best known studies based on ANT's concept of translation is by Star and Griesemer[23] who examined the early development of a natural history research museum (a museum not open to general public), the Museum of Vertebrate Zoology at the University of California, Berkeley. Star and Griesemer focused on how scientific work, conducted as the cooperation between diverse groups (humans, nonhumans, scientists, and non-scientists), inhabiting and participating in different social worlds, was achieved and managed. Objects such as species and subspecies of mammals and birds carried different meanings in these different worlds. Actors wishing to cooperate faced the task of developing tools for reconciling these meanings and for maintaining effective collecting and information-keeping practices. Star and Griesemer[23] found that developing methods for standardization and the creation and management of "boundary objects" were the main means for disciplining the joint activities.

The analytical concept boundary object, having its roots in ANT, has become widely used both in STS and many other research domains, including knowledge organization research. Star and Griesemer likened boundary objects to "road maps" whereby concrete objects such as field notes are turned into abstract objects for the purposes of standardizing work practices. Boundary objects thus guide and inform the translation work required for successful collaboration between diverse groups. Boundary objects reconcile differences in interests between groups, differences in degrees of abstraction in the description of objects, and differences in units of analyses. A standard indexing scheme is one example of a boundary object. It does not accurately describe the details of any one object or thing. It is, however, able to serve as a means of communication across diverse lifeworlds. It conveys standard information and reconciles multiple viewpoints. It satisfies the minimum informational demands of all concerned parties in describing and capturing properties of objects (e.g., data or documents) that fall within the minimally acceptable consensus range.[24]

Geoffrey Bowker and Susan Leigh Star's[24] well-known work on classification systems also draws from ANT. Bowker and Star showed how in many types of work, classification systems and recordkeeping technologies form the infrastructure that allows the ongoing reproduction of relevant practices and historically constituted order of things. They showed how classification and recordkeeping technologies are a fundamental aspect of the practical management of everyday activity. The interest in document work and recordkeeping practices has continued to occupy a central position in practice-oriented studies of work and technology. Many practice-oriented studies focus on organizational practices of documentation and recordkeeping and analyze them in a detailed manner. The assumption is that organizational records are central for the ongoing accomplishment of mutually intelligible concerted action and function as ordering devices for organizational accountability.[25,26]

From the viewpoint of information science, ANT has been particularly influential in two ways. First, it teases apart the common notion that it is meaningful to make a division between "people-centered research" and "system-centered research." Actor-network theory takes the analytical stance that it is not tenable to start from the notion that people are special, and divide people and technologies into two separate heaps.[21] From the ANT lens, a copy machine, for instance, is a network of interacting technical materials but also entails roles played by human actors such as operators and repair-persons. Human actors are also generated in networks of heterogenous social relations and technical materials. This is because human actors assume specific roles and have special attributes in diverse STINs. The concept of affordance, central in ANT, posits that there exists no sharp division people and technology and thus mandates research designs bridging existing divides between people-centered studies and system-centered studies.

SOCIAL CONSTRUCTION OF TECHNOLOGY

The SCOT perspective is embedded in the linguistic turn in the human and social sciences. Social constructionism emphasizes the role of language in the construction of social reality. The basic assumption in social constructionism is that language is not merely a tool for expressing ideas, rather, language sets the boundaries for expressing emotions, knowledge, and views. Studies in the SCOT perspective focus on "representations" of technology and users. Keith Grint and Steve Woolgar (p. 32)[27] defined the object of research in SCOT as "the regimes of truth which surround, uphold, impale, and represent technology." The SCOT perspective defines technologies as texts that are written and read. Although technologies are, naturally, also concrete and material, for the purposes of analysis, it is fruitful to adopt a counterintuitive way of thinking about technologies as texts. This makes it possible to see that technologies do not exist independently of human interpretation. Capabilities are attributed to technologies by humans.

The emphasis on the textuality of technology is based on the insight that any attempt to study the "impacts" of new technologies inevitably represents a specific discourse. Descriptions of the large-scale effects of technological change or impacts of new technologies tend to get trapped in either positive (utopian) or negative (dystopian) discourses.[28] Grint and Woolgar[27] argued that impact studies are implicitly based on the assumption that there are some inherent static properties in technologies which account for their impacts on work and everyday lives. In SCOT, technologies are unstable and indeterminate artifacts whose significance is negotiated and interpreted but never settled. According to the SCOT theory, since we have no access to reality other than through our social constructions of it, we always have to hold a question mark over what the significant constraints or enablers of a technology are.

According to Foucauldian, thinking concerning the relationship between power and knowledge, not every representation of the nature of a new technology carries equal authority. Some interpretations appear as more credible and objective than others. According to Grint and Woolgar,[27] in analyzing accounts and representations of technology, the important question to ask is "why do we believe some people's accounts but not others?" and "What is the work that discourses of technology perform in different communities and contexts?"

Talja[29] applied the SCOT approach to analyze the implications of discourses concerning information technology users and IT skills. She emphasized that neither standardized tests of skills nor self-assessments of computer skills represent the truth about IT competencies. The variables tested such as computer attitudes, computer self-efficacy, or computer anxiety, are in themselves parts of large-scale discursive formations. They are based on specific lenses on what are the "core" properties of information and communication technologies and what constitutes competent IT use. In addition, people's self-assessments of their own computing skills are context-dependent communicative constructs. They are dialogic, situational, perspective-dependent, variable, and multilayered entities. When IT and IT skills are described and approached from different angles, different aspects and truths concerning computing come into view. However, the discourses generally used in society to describe IT competencies shape users' interpretations of their own IT expertise. General notions of IT expertise and of the groups that possess IT expertise may leave ordinary technology users with a conception of their competencies as limited or elementary.[29] In dominant discourses, computing expertise is not described as something that is always situated, work task and domain-related.

In advocating the SCOT perspective, Grint and Woolgar[27] contested both ANT and SST case studies. Such case studies in their view typically bring out only one version of "what happened in reality," and posit their stories as objective facts. They also criticized the innovation-centeredness of SST, the focus of studies on early stages of technology development at the expense of analyzing prevailing technology discourses that have a profound influence on IT policies and initiatives and IT training.

GENDER AND TECHNOLOGY STUDIES

Gender and technology studies foreground the ways in which technology, expertise, and gender are intertwined and mutually shaped. Feminist scholars such as Cynthia Cockburn[30] and Judy Wajcman[31,32] emphasized that the way technologies are designed and implemented contain specific ideas of what is the logical and desired way of performing work tasks. In gender and technology studies the notion of "interpretive flexibility" loses some of its credibility. Whenever an artifact is designed, theories of about users and their behavior, assumptions concerning their activities and their social contexts, notions of what is simple, pleasurable or aesthetically satisfying, specific ideas about knowledge and rationality, come into play. Women and also men, having their own practices and experiences, may in fact experience technologies as highly inflexible.[33]

As technologies and technological languages highlight certain expectations of use and qualities of users, they also implicitly tell people what sort of people they are. A central interest in gender and technology studies is how information technology intertwines with our thinking, acting, and identities. Donna Haraway's[34] famous cyborg concept conveys an idea that the boundaries between humans and machines, natural and artifactual are leaky; all people are hybrids of machines and living organisms. The cyborg image presents technology as an aspect of our embodiment: it is inbuilt in us. Gender and technology studies mandate that technology needs to be subjected to discerning and critical examination both from the viewpoint of subjects' bodily and historical experiences and from the viewpoint of larger (macro)social and discursive orders.

The emphasis on the situated nature of knowledge is the major difference between SCOT and gender and technology studies. The SCOT perspective has often been criticized of extreme relativism. Some critics view especially the argument posed by Woolgar that every sociological explanation ends up positing a final truth when the final truth cannot by any means be captured, as "deconstruction gone mad." Gender and technology studies start from the assumption that knowledge is site-specific and relative to human agents in specific settings. Knowledge is also embodied, that is, deeply rooted in specific practices and experiences.[34] This notion does not mean that "agency" would be limited to human actors, only that technologies cannot be understood or studied independently of everyday experiences and practices which constitute people as specific kinds of people. Gender and technology studies are interested in how the intertwining of the self and technology takes place in concrete everyday life settings.[35]

Empirical studies within the gender and technology studies tradition do not claim to be nonpolitical, neutral, or objective. Gender and technology studies adopt an analytic stance called strong objectivity. This stance is based on the standpoint epistemology developed by Sandra Harding,[36] Donna Haraway's[34] concept of situated knowledge, and Karen Barad's[37] theory of agential realism. All these theorists stress that knowledge is always positioned; it is produced from a particular standpoint and can only represent a partial perspective. Acknowledging this, the important question is from whose viewpoint is the social world examined and described. Haraway's[34] concept of situated knowledge embraces a view that a degree of partial objectivity can be reached if the analyst explains her position as clearly as possible. Haraway[34] argues for the replacement of various forms of unlocatable, and hence irresponsible, knowledge claims with a practice of objectivity that privileges especially marginalized and excluded voices, in the hope for transformations in technological systems, systems of knowledge, and ways of seeing. Gender and technology studies mandate accepting responsibility for the kinds of representations produced and attentiveness to the way that scientific accounts take action in the ongoing reproduction of phenomena.

Gender and technology studies contest the notion of technological systems and environments as gender-neutral. Historically, technology and especially information technology, has been developed mainly by men. Information technology has carried and invisibly still carries strong connotations and images of male expertise.[32]

Studies of technologies in home environments have shown that girls' and boys' computing activities tend to be perceived differently.[38] Studies have for instance shown that girls' computing activities such as chatting and online shopping are more often constructed as forms of entertainment, casual leisure, or consumption. Boys' activities such as gaming and downloading free software are more often perceived as expertise-building and expertise-requiring activities. In a study of IT in Finnish homes and families, Nieminen-Sundell[38] discovered that computers in families were often placed in boys' own rooms and surrounded by objects related to the boys' interests in computing. There is a strong connotation between computing and male expertise. The families in Nieminen-Sundell's study regarded boys' interest and engagement in computing as more than natural and something to be encouraged. In the Finnish families studied by Nieminen-Sundell,[38] the mothers often had extensive work-related experience of computing. Yet, in family interviews, mothers' computing skills were often downplayed or even joked about. Even the mothers themselves often described themselves as incompetent and as needing their sons' help and advice in matters related to computers. Regardless of the real breadth and depth of the computing expertise of mothers or their sons, the cultural expectation is that young boys perform well with computers. Computing can also have deep symbolic and ritual meanings. Young girls may avoid getting too much involved in computing whereas as regards boys, mastery of computing may culturally be unconsciously perceived as part of the growth into manhood.[38]

Ethnographic studies of the domestication of new technologies have reached interesting findings concerning the status of diverse technologies at homes. This is not reflected only in the physical placement of technological artifacts at the home and or the domestic patterns of their use.

Nieminen-Sundell[39] asked married couples to name the technologies they have in their homes. Alarm systems, computers, and digital cameras were typically named and classified as representing technology. Hair dryers, vacuum cleaners, and cooking stoves, in turn, were not typically mentioned or counted as technology. What represented technology was related to the relative novelty of the technology and to whether they were used mainly by men or women.[39] What represents "smart" technology or even technology thus changes with both the domestication of technologies and gendered patterns of their use.

PRACTICE THEORY OF TECHNOLOGY

Anthropological studies of technology conducted since the 1970s at the Xerox Palo Alto Research Campus (PARC) (e.g., Wynn–Whalen[40–42]) directed attention to technologies as they are used in everyday work tasks. Xerox researchers conducted detailed studies on the use and role of technologies in the practical accomplishment of work activities. Through studying workers' activities and interactions, they described how the workers themselves in practice produce the functionality of tools and technologies.[43] Studies of the fine details of situated work practices proved to be productive for gaining guidelines for technology development. In addition to naturalistic workplace studies, Lucy Suchman's book *Plans and Situated Actions*[44] had a major influence in the emergence of the practice theory.

Suchman[44] argued that the formal plan-based models of work task performance which guided studies in artificial intelligence (AI) and cognitive science had failed to consider the immediate context of work activities. Plans, cognitive schemas, scripts, and rules are not static but dependent on the situations in which they are invoked. These do not determine conduct but provide a resource through which people orient in diverse situations and interpret their action and the conduct of others. Suchman argued that formal models of work tasks disregard the contingencies which inevitably arise in real-life problem-solving and ignore the improvisational, interactive, and situational character of individuals' reasoning. This is nevertheless what accounts for the successful execution of work tasks.[44]

The fundamental assumption in practice theory is that practices are always social. Even when people seemingly work alone and do not belong to any specific group, they rely on a complex body of socially shared skills and understandings.[43] Views of what constitutes competent practice develop among a community of practitioners.[45] Practices are therefore always organized in relation to significant others, who may be coworkers, coproducers, recipients, or customers. In this view, all work is collaborative, and the accomplishment of work requires some form of collaborative interaction.[43]

The term practice refers to recurrent mundane activities through which individuals in situ become skilled workers or learners. Practice theorists define practices as embodied, materially mediated arrays of human activity centrally organized around a shared practical understanding.[45] The practice approach is not oriented solely toward linguistic representations, since knowledge and expertise are taken to be both implicit, embodied in ways of performing work tasks, and explicit, formed in and through documents and face-to-face interactions. Practice theorists argue that conventional approaches to technical design have tended to underestimate the importance of the socially organized competencies and reasoning on which workers rely in using technologies as part of their daily work. Consequently, system designers miss important aspects of how the work is done that are critical for fitting and integrating technology into work processes.[46,47]

Practice-based studies focus on the "work practice–artifacts/technology/material objects–human interactions" triangle. Assumption is that it only makes sense to study these in concert, that these are not isolatable. The practice theory of technology is first and foremost a theory of technology-in-action. Studies adopting a practice approach are oriented toward gaining a detailed understanding of how groups organize their work practices through interacting with texts, coworkers, technologies, and other material objects. Consequently, the practical accomplishment of work activities is usually analyzed in its moment-by-moment emergence.

As observed earlier, many studies in this tradition focus on practices of producing, preserving, using, coding, categorizing, and filing documents for the purposes of work and in the course of work. Studies have placed equal importance on affordances of paper documents and affordances of electronic documents.[48,49] The attention paid to the role of documentation and documents in the organization of work is exemplified by studies focusing on the production of medical records[26,49] and practices of indexing of documents in a law office.[25]

CONCLUSION

The ANT, SST, SCOT perspective, gender and technology studies and practice theories focus on different aspects of sociotechnical practices and processes. While the SST and early studies within the ANT focused more on historical studies and the early stages technology development, the SCOT perspective, gender and technology studies, and practice-oriented studies focus more on current practices.

Each STS theory has opened up new insights into the interplay between technologies and social practices. STS theories have introduced concepts that have enabled the taking of distance to everyday "natural" assumptions regarding technology. Concepts such as "heterogeneous engineering" typically function as labels designed to enable the effective transport of complicated ideas. However, STS theories and studies have often been criticized of heavy use of jargon and of having adopted a complicated style of writing. According to critics, this is an obstacle for a more widespread application of STS theories.

Compared to many theories of human information behavior within information science, STS theories contain a distinctly different view of what is problematic and what is not. The formulation of problems requiring study can be likened to the choice of languages and vocabularies for talking. Most of the time, we do not consciously choose the language or vocabulary we use but just do what comes naturally, use the language of our community. Information science languages and communities are many, however. As observed in the beginning of this entry, some information science topics are also STS topics and commonly approached and studied using the vocabularies that also STS communities deploy. Examples of such topics are classification, documentation, and recordkeeping practices. In some areas information science and STS concerns and research programs overlap, whereas in some research areas, languages and problem definitions do not overlap.

Within information documents, theories have been developed around the concept of information. Technology, in turn, has not been viewed as an equally important concept and object for theoretical work. STS theories extend the scope of theory building to the nature and affordances of technical artifacts. At the heart of STS is the idea that the social and the technical interact and mutually shape one another, leading to the notion that human–information interaction cannot be meaningfully studied as disconnected from technological systems. Another core idea in STS is that technological systems must be conceived very broadly as consisting of technologies-in-use, working practices, social relationships, and larger social/textual and technoscientific orders and processes.

Studies in STS have shown how technologies take shape through conflicts, negotiations, and alternative interpretations. STS theories allow seeing technologies as less closed, fixed, and stable. Looking at technologies as more indeterminate and open to reinterpretation encourages an active critical involvement in interpretative work and the recreation of understandings of how technologies could or should be redeveloped.

REFERENCES

1. Collins, H.M. Stages in the empirical programme of relativism. Soc. Stud. Sci. **1981**, *11*(1), 3–10.
2. Latour, B.; Woolgar, S. *Laboratory Life: The Social Construction of Scientific Facts*; Sage: London, 1979.
3. Knorr-Cetina, K. *The Manufacture of Knowledge: An Essay on the Constructivist and Contextual Nature of Science*; Pergamon Press: Oxford, U.K., 1981.
4. Latour, B. *Science in Action: How to Follow Scientists and Engineers Through Society*; Harvard University Press: Cambridge, MA, 1987.
5. Pinch, T.; Bijker, W. The social construction of facts and artifacts: Or how the sociology of science and the sociology of technology might benefit each other. In *The Social Construction of Technological Systems: New Directions in the Sociology and History of Technology*; Bijker, W.E., Hughes, T.P., Pinch, T.J., Eds.; The MIT Press: Cambridge, MA, 1987; 17–50.
6. Kling, R. Social analyses of computing: Theoretical perspectives in recent empirical research. Comp. Surv. **1980**, *12*(1), 61–110.
7. Bruce, B.C. Technology as social practice. Educ. Found. **1997**, *10*(4), 51–58.
8. Law, J. Technology and heterogeneous engineering: The case of Portuguese expansion. In *The Social Construction of Technological Systems: New Directions in the Sociology and History of Technology*; Bijker, W.E., Hughes, T.P., Pinch, T.J., Eds.; The MIT Press: Cambridge, MA, 1987; 111–134.
9. Hughes, T.P. The evolution of large technical systems. In *The Social Construction of Technological Systems: New Directions in the Sociology and History of Technology*; Bijker, W.E., Hughes, T.P., Pinch, T.J., Eds.; The MIT Press: Cambridge, MA, 1987; 51–82.
10. In *The Social Shaping of Technology*; Mackenzie, D.A., Wajcman, J., Eds.; Open University Press: Milton Keynes, U.K, 1985.
11. Williams, R.; Edge, D. What is the social shaping of technology?. Res. Pol. **1996**, *25*(6), 856–899.
12. Schwartz Cowan, R. How the refrigerator got its hum. In *The Social Shaping of Technology: How the Refrigerator Got Its Hum*; MacKenzie, D., Wajcman, J., Eds.; Open University Press: Milton Keynes, U.K., 1985; 202–218.
13. Schwartz Cowan, R. The consumption junction: A proposal for research strategies in the sociology of technology. In *The Social Construction of Technological Systems: New Directions in the Sociology and History of Technology*; Bijker, W.E., Hughes, T.P., Pinch, T.J., Eds.; The MIT Press: Cambridge, MA, 1987; 261–280.
14. Callon, M. Struggles and negotiations to define what is problematic and what is not. The socio-logic of translation. In *The Social Process of Scientific Investigation: Sociology of the Sciences Yearbook*; Knorr-Cetina, K.D., Krohn, R., Whitley, R.D., Eds.; Reidel: Dordrecht, 1980; 197–221.
15. Latour, B. Where are the missing masses? A sociology of a few mundane artifacts. In *Shaping Technology—Building Society: Studies in Sociotechnical Change*; Bijker, W.E., Law, J., Eds.; The MIT Press: Cambridge, MA, 1992; 225–258.
16. Latour, B. Technology is society made durable. In *A Sociology of Monsters: Essays on Power, Technology and Domination*; Law, J., Ed.; Routledge: London, 1991; 103–131.
17. Akrich, M. The description of technical objects. In *Shaping Technology—Building Society: Studies in Sociotechnical Change*; Bijker, W.E., Law, J., Eds.; The MIT Press: Cambridge, MA, 1992; 205–224.
18. Law, J. Introduction: Monsters, machines and sociotechnical relations. In *A Sociology of Monsters: Essays on Power, Technology and Domination*; Law, J., Ed.; Routledge: London, 1991; 1–25.
19. Callon, M. Technoeconomic networks and irreversibility. In *A Sociology of Monsters: Essays on Power, Technology and Domination*; Law, J., Ed.; Routledge: London, 1991; 132–161.
20. Kling, R.; McKim, G.; King, A. A bit more to IT: Scholarly communication forums as socio-technical interaction networks. J. Am. Soc. Inform. Sci. Tech. **2003**, *54*(1), 47–67.
21. Law, J. *Notes on the Theory of the Actor Network: Ordering, Strategy and Heterogeneity*, Centre for Science Studies, Lancaster University: Lancaster, 1992. Available at http://www.comp.lancs.ac.uk/sciology/papers/law-notes-on-Ant.pdf (accessed May 2007).
22. In *Actor Network Theory and After*; Law, J., Hassard, J., Eds.; Blackwell: Oxford, U.K., 1999.
23. Star, S.L.; Griesemer, J.R. Institutional ecology, "translations" and boundary objects: Amateurs and professionals in Berkeley's Museum of Vertebrate Zoology, 1907–39. Soc. Stud. Sci. **1989**, *19*(3), 387–420.
24. Bowker, G.; Star, S.L. *Sorting Things Out: Classification and Its Consequences*; The MIT Press: Cambridge, MA, 1999.

25. Suchman, L. Making a case: "Knowledge" and "routine" work in document production. In *Workplace Studies: Recovering Work Practice and Informing System Design*; Luff, P., Hindmarsh, J., Heath, C., Eds.; Cambridge University Press: Cambridge, U.K., 2000; 29–45.

26. Berg, M. Practices of reading and writing: The constitutive role of the patient record in medical work. Sociol. Health Ill. **1996**, *18*(4), 499–524.

27. Grint, K.; Woolgar, S. *The Machine at Work: Technology, Work and Organization*; Polity Press: Cambridge, U.K., 1997.

28. Kling, R. Reading all about computerization: How genre conventions shape non-fiction social analysis. Inform. Soc. **1994**, *10*(3), 147–172.

29. Talja, S. The social and discursive construction of computing skills. J. Am. Soc. Inform. Sci. Tech. **2005**, *56*(1), 13–22.

30. Cockburn, C. *Brothers, Male Dominance and Technological Change*; Pluto Press: London, 1983.

31. Wajcman, J. *Feminism Confronts Technology*; Polity Press: Cambridge, 1991.

32. Wajcman, J. *TechnoFeminism*; Polity Press: Cambridge, U.K., 2004.

33. Lie, M. *Computer Dialogues: Technology, Gender and Change*; Norges teknisk-naturvetenskapelige universitet NTNU, Senter for kvinneforskning: Dragvoll, 1998.

34. Haraway, D.J. *Simians, Cyborgs, and Women: The Reinvention of Nature*; Routledge: New York, 1991.

35. Vehviläinen, M. Gendered agency in information society: on located politics of technology. In *Women and Everyday Uses of the Internet: Agency and Identity*; Consalvo, M., Paasonen, S., Eds.; Peter Lang Publishing: New York, 2002; 275–291.

36. Harding, S. *The Science Question in Feminism*; Cornell University Press: Ithaca, NY, 1986.

37. Barad, K. Getting real: Technoscientific practices and the materialization of reality. Differences. J. Femin. Cult. Stud. **1998**, *10*(2), 88–128.

38. Nieminen-Sundell, R. Tietokonepoika—kuinka tuotetaan sukupuolittuneita käytäntöjä, koneita ja ihmisiä [The computer boy—the production of gendered practices, machines,

and humans]. In *Tietotekniikkasuhteet: Kulttuurinen näkökulma [Relationships with Computers: A Cultural Viewpoint]*; Talja, S., Tuuva, S., Eds.; The Finnish Literature Society: Helsinki, 2003; 41–55.

39. Nieminen-Sundell, R. *Is hair dryer technical? Gender and household technology*; Department of Sociology, University of Tampere: Tampere, 1999; Unpublished master's thesis.

40. Wynn, E. *Office conversation as an information medium*; University of California: Berkeley, CA, 1979; Unpublished doctoral dissertation.

41. Orr, J. *Talking About Machines: An Ethnography of a Modern Job*; Cornell University Press: Ithaca, NY, 1996.

42. Whalen, J. Expert systems vs. systems for experts: Computer-aided dispatch as a support system in real-world environments. In *The Social and Interactional Dimension of Human-Computer Interfaces*; Thomas, P., Ed.; Cambridge University Press: Cambridge, U.K., 1995; 161–183.

43. Heath, C.; Knoblauch, H.; Luff, P. Technology and social interaction: The emergence of workplace studies. Br. J. Sociol. **2000**, *51*(2), 299–320.

44. Suchman, L. *Plans and Situated Actions: The Problem of Human-Machine Communication*; Cambridge University Press: New York, 1987.

45. Schatzki, T.R. Introduction: practice theory. In *The Practice Turn in Contemporary Theory*; Schatzki, T.R., Knorr Cetina, K., Savigny, E. von, Eds.; Routledge: London, 2001; 1–14.

46. Heath, C.; Luff, P. *Technology in Action*; Cambridge University Press: Cambridge, 2000.

47. In *Workplace Studies: Recovering Work Practice and Informing System Design*; Luff, P., Hindmarsh, J., Heath, C., Eds.; Cambridge University Press: Cambridge, U.K., 2000.

48. Harper, R. *Inside the IMF: An Ethnography of Documents, Technology and Organisational Action*; Academic Press: London, 1998.

49. Heath, C.; Luff, P. Documents and professional practice: "bad" organisational reasons for "good" clinical records. Proceedings of Computer Supported Cooperative Work '96, Cambridge, MA, 1996; 354–363.

Search Engine Optimization

Nicholas Carroll
Hastings Research, Inc., Las Vegas, Nevada, U.S.A.

Abstract
Search engine optimization (SEO) is the craft of elevating Web sites or individual Web site pages to higher rankings on search engines through programming, marketing, or content acumen. This section covers the origins of SEO, strategies and tactics, history and trends, and the evolution of user behavior in online searching.

INTRODUCTION

Search engine optimization (SEO) is the craft of elevating Web sites or individual Web site pages to higher rankings on World Wide Web (WWW) search engines through programming, marketing, or content acumen. The definition often includes specifications for increased traffic to a given Web site, improved quality of traffic, increased profits, or brand awareness.

In a typical online search on a topic, anywhere from hundreds to millions of articles may be extracted and ranked by probability of relevance on a search engine results page (SERP). From the earliest appearance of Web search engines, creators of Web sites realized that ranking high was vital for visits to their Web sites, since users seldom look on even second or third screens of rankings, let alone the hundredth screen. The numbers of Web sites on the Web increased so rapidly from the beginning that the competition for the most desirable top positions developed rapidly.

In this entry, we move through several key aspects of SEO. First, we define "rankings," and review the origins and history of SEO. Then we discuss what is known as "Black Hat" and "White Hat" SEO, as the competition for rankings can lead to distortions and misleading rankings, depending on what techniques are used.

The heart of the entry concerns SEO methods. We review keyword selection and then attend to various aspects of the content of the Web pages, such as keyword density, placement, and consistency. We then go on to the technical aspects and review techniques such as keyword stuffing, meta tags, and cloaking, as well as strategies for boosting page rank through links from and to other Web sites, with brief discussion of combined strategies and the analytic methods applied to track results.

The entry expands into more general issues such as broad vs. narrow targeting, page longevity and rank, geographic targeting, and increasing competition. Trends in SEO practices are described from early to present time, as are external trends affecting SEO.

We conclude with a description of SEO regulation, mostly in the form of search engines policing their listings, and an overview of typical behavior patterns of search engine users.

All the methods described have been or continue to be effective SEO to some degree. Changes in search engine indexing protocols as well as their methods for displaying search results mean that no strict description of the best method or methods can remain entirely accurate indefinitely. This entry does not cover pay-per-click, other forms of online advertising, or the resale of Web site traffic or links.

Because the discipline originated in the mid-1990s, terminology is still in flux. General references at the end of this entry point to the more authoritative Web sites and definitions.

DEFINITION OF HIGHER RANKINGS

"Higher rankings" in the popular press or lay discussion generally equates with the goal of having a Web page appear in the first 10 or 20 search records for a particular search term, as it is broadly established by tracking that few search engine users will click through to any link beyond the 20th record. SEO professionals usually discuss rankings in terms of SERP position (Fig. 1).

Before search engines accepted paid advertisements, SEO was considered a unique form of promotion, radically different from all traditional forms of advertising. It is now more often considered a subset of search engine marketing (SEM), and is sometimes referred to as "organic search" or "natural SEM," as opposed to paid advertisements placed on the pages of search engines or their affiliates.

Online commerce was the originating force behind search engine promotion and remains the primary driving force behind SEO. Nonprofits and government bodies apply some SEO methods but tend to rely on their unique identity to assure them a prominent SERP position,

Encyclopedia of Library and Information Sciences, Fourth Edition DOI: 10.1081/E-ELIS4-120043453

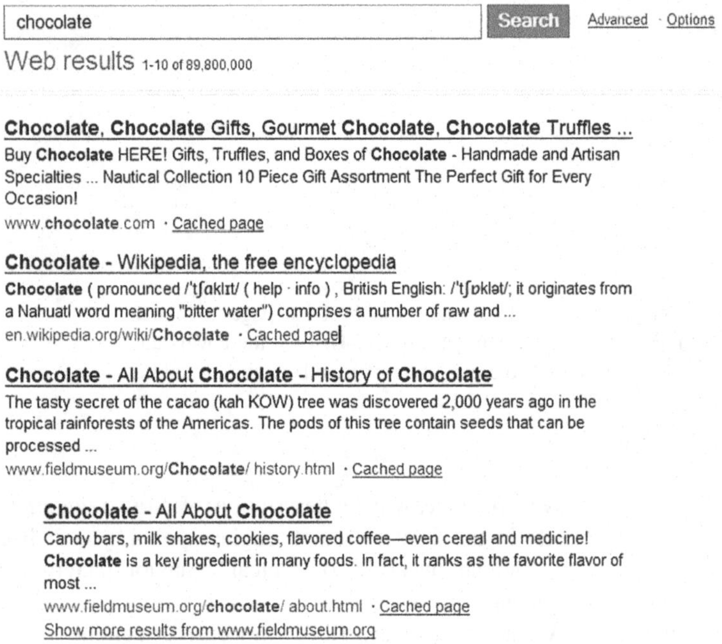

Science–Semantic

Fig. 1 Typical SERP in search for chocolate, showing the first four results.

e.g., the Red Cross, Amnesty International, the Vatican, the New York Department of Motor Vehicles, or the Peoria Public Library.

ORIGINS AND HISTORY OF SEO

The term "search engine optimization" came into popular use in 1997–1998 and is frequently attributed to Danny Sullivan,[1] then operating "Search Engine Watch," though Sullivan states he is uncertain who coined it. Previous terms included "search engine placement," "search engine ranking," "search engine positioning," and "search engine promotion," the latter attributed to Jim Rhodes,[2] author of "The Art of Search Engine Promotion." Predecessors such as Heath[3] in his 1995 article "Pointers on how to create business Web sites that work" did not have a formal name for SEO.

The period from the mid-1990s to about 2000 was characterized by broad experimentation on the part of both search engines seeking a business model and Web site creators intent on promoting themselves. Search engines were relatively under-powered and minimally staffed; their primary focus was on keeping pace with the growth in new Web sites. SEO quickly became part of the American "wild, wild Web" metaphor, with more active Web site owners engaging in a huge variety of methods to gain higher rankings, as described in "SEO Methods." In a period when many multinational organizations did not have Web sites at all, smaller and more nimble organizations and individuals aggressively practiced SEO to establish a beachhead on the WWW.

The early days of search engines were in some ways a struggle against pornography. Visitors who started using search engines after 2000 have little conception of how pervasive the online sex industry was at one time, with their records appearing among search results for cooking, art, quilting, travel, and other innocuous subjects.

As search engines have grown and become more sophisticated, and the number of Web sites has increased more than tenfold, aggressive maneuvering to rank well in the SERPs has to some extent given way to a focus on ranking well in particular niches, and executing well on fundamentals rather than exercising brilliance in manipulating search engines.[4]

PRACTITIONERS AND SOFTWARE

Early Search Engine Promoters and Reporters

Early SEO innovation was an individualistic endeavor, primarily developed by small-to-midsize businesses ranging from small hotels to makers of custom sports equipment. Several such niche and popular products were financially successful, demonstrating that SEO was a path to profit.

Web sites with forums for exchange of SEO strategies began to appear by 1996, including still-existing Web sites such as http://virtualpromote.com, http://www.searchengineforums.com, and the archived http://www.deadlock.com/promote.

Web sites reporting on search engines and optimization began about the same time, including http://www.

wilsonweb.com, http://www.searchenginewatch.com, and http://www.webmasterworld.com. More recent additions include http://www.seobook.com/blog, http://www.searchengineland.com, and http://www.toprankblog.com/search-marketing-blogs.

The Current SEO Industry

Whether offered as a subset of SEM services or sold alone as organic search, SEO has become a niche industry with its own sales forces and conventions. The service may be sold as a one-time audit or on an ongoing basis with monthly billing and performance reporting.

Pure SEO consulting firms now number in the thousands, primarily concentrated in North America and the United Kingdom. Tens of thousands more Web designers and developers offer the service as ancillary to building Web sites, and an unknown number of Webmasters and Web site owners apply SEO methods to their own Web sites.

Gross expenditures on SEO in 2006 were estimated at over USD one billion, with steady annual growth anticipated. This figure describes organic search and does not include paid advertising or most in-house work in smaller companies.[5]

SEO Software (Automating the Process)

Automated Web page submission tools came into being in the mid-1990s soon after search engines began indexing the WWW. For some years, they were a vital part of SEO strategy for large Web sites, as manually entering thousands of URLs into the submission pages of a dozen search engines was extremely time-consuming. Submission tools fell into disuse as search engines became more adept at "deep crawling" (following links into the lower levels of Web sites' file hierarchies). The ones currently in use typically offer additional features such as help in choosing keywords and automated reporting on SERP positions.

Web analytics tools move beyond automated reporting to features such as tracking visitors' paths through Web sites, and integrating the data with financials.[6]

Most content management systems, originally focused on intranets, now include management features for Web sites, and many are programmed to allow a significant modification of variables important to SEO.[7] Likewise most blogging software includes features that encourage users to add keywords to the title tags, the Web page body, and the filename of a given Web page.

SEO Worldwide

While search engines are now used worldwide, most SEO reporting is about the United States, Canada, and the United Kingdom. Activity in other countries must be inferred. Australia, Ireland, and Russia in particular have significant indications of entrepreneurial SEO, including blogs on the subject.[8]

BLACK HAT VS. WHITE HAT SEO

"White Hat" SEO typically refers to strategies and tactics that are in concordance with the policies of online search engines, in a loose tacit agreement to provide Web surfers with "relevant content." "Black Hat" SEO describes tactics that ignore generally accepted conventions of ethical WWW behavior to advance an agenda or commercial interest. The focus on search engine policies before other interests flows from the pervasive position of search engines, at the mid-point in the process of aggregating Web page data and delivering it to users. The tilted point of view is buttressed by the oligopoly of major search engines, with a small number of them processing the vast majority of searches, while millions of Web sites vie for high rankings.

Technically sophisticated tactics are often equated with Black Hat SEO, and a focus on high-quality content with White Hat SEO. However, there is substantial overlap; few if any tactics can be inherently classified as good or evil. From the perspective of a user, the main criteria of legitimate SEO is whether a given search return is relevant to their interests, regardless of how it achieved its ranking. Most experienced SEO practitioners consider intent to be the defining factor.

Typically, methods considered Black Hat SEO develop high page rankings faster, while those known as White Hat SEO tend to create longer-lasting rankings. A preference for one approach or the other is not entirely a matter of the SEO practitioner's personal preferences; it also depends on the business model. Web sites or pages promoting products and services with short life cycles are suited to Black Hat methods, as they do not suffer from being "burned," meaning they have drawn the attention of search engine administrators and been banned from that search engine's index entirely. (This has also happened to sites of long-view organizations such as auto manufacturers when SEO subcontractors acted with an excess of zeal.)

White Hat SEO is better suited to Web sites that offer products with long life cycles. It is also suited to academic or government Web sites, where there is likely to be a consistent focus over decades—such Web sites often gain high and enduring SERP rankings simply by publishing high-quality content about a particular subject.

SEO METHODS

In describing SEO it is necessary to distinguish between automated search engines and manually created directories such as Yahoo! Directory (http://dir.yahoo.com) or the Open Directory Project (ODP) (http://www.dmoz.org), where listings are added by human editors rather than automated protocols.

SEO describes strategies and tactics for influencing page rank on search engines that use "robots" (http://www.robotstxt.org/wc/faq.html) or "spiders" to "crawl" Web pages, traveling from page to page through hyperlinks, and indexing those pages by algorithms and protocols. While directories such as the original Yahoo! Directory can be searched from within Yahoo!, and the ODP pages can frequently be found in SERPs, it is the manner of creating the index that differentiates search engines and directories.

Elements of a Web Page to Be Optimized

The following example of HTML (Hypertext Markup Language) is referred to throughout this entry. The markup language and page structure used are explained in Table 1 below the example. (Web page structure can be viewed in almost all Web browsers by selecting the "View > Source" or "View > Page Source" option.)[9]

```
<html>
<head>
<title>ELIS—Encyclopedia of Library and Information Sciences 2008–2009</title>
<meta name="description" content="The definitive reference to library and information sciences.">
<meta name="keywords" content="encyclopedia, marcia, bates, mary, niles, maack, mack, optimise">
</head>
<body>
<h1>ELIS—Encyclopedia of Library and Information Sciences</h1>
<img src="images/ELIS-cover.gif" alt="ELIS encyclopedia cover" />
```

<p>Body content written for SEO is rich in keywords and also readable. Proper nouns such as "encyclopedia" are used instead of pronouns. Initializations such as "SEO"

Table 1 Tags and text in a simple Web page

Tags and text in a simple Web page, as seen through an HTML editing tool	Explanation of HTML tags and structure
<html>	Flag to user's browser: Begin parsing for HyperText Markup Language
<head>	Begin the head content (which is not visible in a browser)
<title>ELIS: Encyclopedia of Library and Information Sciences</title>	The page title is the single most important part of Web page text for search engine ranking. While not shown in the body text in a Web browser, it can be seen in the title bar at the top, and is shown as the title of the Web page in almost all search engine listings
<meta name="description" content="The definitive reference to library and information sciences.">	Most search engines will use the meta description as the default description in SERPs. SEO practitioners consider this tag a minor influence on SERP position, and usually orient the text towards readers rather than search engines
<meta name="keywords" content="encyclopedia, marcia, bates, mary, niles, maack, mack, optimise">	The meta keywords tag, originally intended as a field for general metadata, was widely abused by SEO practitioners and is now a minor or irrelevant element of SEO
</head>	End of the Head section
<body>	Begin the text visible in a browser
<h1>ELIS: Encyclopedia of Library and Information Sciences</h1>	Headings tags, from H1 down to H6, are the equivalent of chapter and section headings in books, and are usually considered influential in SEO
<img src="images/ELIS-cover.gif" alt="ELIS encyclopedia cover" />	IMG tags define what image to display as part of a Web page. The "alt" attribute is used to store a brief description, typically keywords
<p>Body content written for SEO is rich in keywords... [etc.]"</p>	The paragraph tag is the fundamental "container" for body content
<h2>Resources</h2>	The second-level heading tag may have influence on SERP position, as well as significance for metadata and document readability
<p>See the <a href="http://informationr.net/ir/12-4/colis/colis29.html">encyclopedia description</a> for further information on ELIS.</p>	An outbound link where the "anchor text" contains the relevant keyword "encyclopedia"
<p>Keywords: encyclopaedia, taylor, francis, marcia, bates, mary, niles, maack, mack, optimise</p>	This is an unsightly but often necessary addition to the body content, displaying related keywords in the body text, where the search engines will read and index them. This practice evolved when search engines stopped indexing meta keywords
</body>	End of the body element
</html>	Flag to user's browser: end of HTML file

Further information on HTML is available at http://www.w3.org/MarkUp/Guide/.

are spelled out as "search engine optimization," both to include alternate search terms and to increase keyword density in the Web page. To target both sophisticated and lay searchers, common terms such as "acronym" are used in addition to precise terms such as "initialization." Concepts are described by all likely variants, such as "SERP," "search engine position," or "ranking."</p>

<h2>Further Encyclopedia Resources</h2>
<p>See the <a href="http://informationr.net/ir/12–4/colis/colis29.html">encyclopedia description</a> for further information on ELIS.</p>
<p><font size="-1">Keywords: encyclopaedia, taylor, francis, marcia, bates, mary, niles, maack, mack, optimise</font></p>
</body>
</html>

Choosing Keywords to Target—The Core of SEO

Regardless of preferred methods, White Hat or Black Hat, content or technical, the most critical part of effective SEO is deciding which keywords to target for high rankings. While search engines continually work to improve their ranking algorithms, they are not clairvoyant; targeting the right keywords is still the foundation of reaching the right audience.[10]

A self-centric viewpoint will usually lead an organization to aim at high rankings for its own name, services, agendas, or products. For example, the Raffles Hotel or the band U2 might focus on targeting searches for their own name, in a reasonable belief that most potential customers are specifically seeking them, rather than hotels in Singapore or rock music in general.

While this may be a successful strategy for broadly known organizations or people, it is considered poor-quality SEO when an unknown product, service, or agenda is being advanced. Products and agendas without name recognition are better served by targeting a generic search term such as "stainless steel ball bearings" than a term like "Smith Ball Bearing Company." A multinational company such as General Electric or Hitachi—that manufactures a huge variety of products—might likewise target searches for the products rather than its own company name.

Regardless of whether the focus is on the organization or the products, SEO can fail when names are chosen without forethought to online search, particularly when they compete with long-established names. Two examples:

- Any product named "Guardian" must compete in the SERPs with dozens of well-established newspapers throughout the English-speaking world.
- Organizations using initializations that might be unique in a local telephone directory frequently face obscurity when competing for recognition in a global medium—"ABC" is not only an initialization for the American Broadcasting Company, but hundreds or thousands of other organizations throughout nations that use the Roman alphabet.

This leads to a fundamental truth about the limits of SEO as a promotional avenue: it can only succeed if people are searching for relevant keywords. If an idea or product is beyond the public's conception, it cannot be promoted through search engines—in contrast to promotion through traditional untargeted media such as radio, TV, or print. This usually makes SEO a poor method for promoting radically new ideas. For example, "anti-gravity belts" is a search only used by 10-year-old boys.

When possible, experienced SEO practitioners perform keyword analysis before a Web site is built, expanded, or redesigned, using paid or free online tools such as http://www.keyworddiscovery.com, http://www.wordtracker.com, http://inventory.overture.com/d/searchinventory/suggestion/ or https://adwords.google.com/select/KeywordToolExternal to view aggregated searches conducted on search engines.

Content

At its simplest, the content-focused approach to SEO is to tell the story thoroughly and precisely, in hopes that the words (content) will find a fit with search engine indexing algorithms, and rise in the rankings for particular search terms. The presumption in this strategy is that the writer's words will also find harmony with the terms used by searchers, and if the writer does have the same interests—and frame of reference—as the target audience, this by itself can result in highly successful SEO. (Conversely, Web pages written in ignorance of either subject matter or audience may achieve high SERP positions, but not necessarily for the keywords that draw the desired audience.)[11]

A highly content-oriented strategy is often seen in Web sites that were conceived and designed by an individual or small group. Content-oriented Web sites or sub-sites may also come into being in an organization with no SEO strategy at all, such as a department of a university, where the authors are discussing the same or related subjects.

Density

Keyword density receives attention because it is easy to understand and simple to calculate through online density-checkers such as http://www.keyworddensity.com. (Such tools are easily found through search engines with the term "keyword density analyzer.")

Though the effectiveness of intentionally repeating keywords throughout a Web page is debated by SEO practitioners, a search for highly promoted products such as "loans," "chocolate," or "discount shoes" will return numerous high-ranking Web pages with the core keyword repeated dozens of times, and keyword densities reaching up to 7% or higher of the page's content. (However, exceptionally high-density pages can suddenly plummet in the

SERPs or be dropped from the index entirely if search engines classify them as examples of "keyword spamming," described in the Technical strategies section below.)

Conversely, using a set of keywords only once in a Web page usually results in SERP obscurity, even if the set is extremely precise. For example, even "dodo bird nesting" returns tens of thousands of Web pages, and of the first few dozen search engine records, almost all will have the three keywords used several times.

Many SEO practitioners and analysts favor well-written content over keyword density, as search engines become better at differentiating between conventional prose and deliberately enhanced Web pages. This school of thought says that content should be primarily aimed at humans, not search engines, and that good writing not only entices users to read and act, but is better search engine bait in the first place. The belief is often expressed as "Content is king."

Placement

The placement of keywords in a Web page is a significant factor in SEO, since search engine algorithms accord more weight to certain positions, whether visible or within tags (see Table 1). Notable areas for placement include:

Visible in Web page
Inside heading tags <h1, h2, h3. . . .>
Placed at the beginning (top) of a Web page.
Within outbound links, i.e., "anchor text" (example in Table 1).
Placed NEAR other keywords (generally within 10 words).
Visible in SERPs and browser title bar
Inside the HTML <title> tag.
As part of the URL

Competition over search terms and SERP positions has expanded the use of keywords to the point that they are now routinely made part of file names (e.g., http://www.mysite.com/used-software-for-sale.html), or may even form the domain name itself, e.g., http://www.usedsoftwareforsale.com.

The title tag is almost universally agreed to be highly important by SEO practitioners. Most other placements are debated. The <meta="keywords"> tag is largely considered of no importance. The "alt" content in image tags <img src alt="[image description]"> is considered significant in image SERPs, less so in the overall ranking of a Web page.[12]

Inclusion of related keywords

Due to the unpredictability of user search behavior, many SEO practitioners include synonyms, cognates, tangential terms, and misspellings in Web pages. In the mid-1990s, SEO practitioners placed such related keywords in the meta keywords field (see Table 1), but massive abuse and misuse

of that field led virtually all search engines to stop indexing meta keywords. As a result, SEO practitioners reluctantly turned to placing them as a visible footer on the Web page, though this compromises the esthetics of page design. Some examples of keyword (or "tags") line listings:

Synonyms, cognates, and closely related terms for a medical page about trigeminal neuralgia, formerly called tic douloureux:
"Keywords: tic douloureux, neuropathy, facial pain, face pain."
Tangential terms (statistical outliers) for a site on vegetarian diet:
"Keywords: low sodium, low fat, organic."
Variants on the author's name for a Web page written by Jon Smythe:
"Keywords: John, Smith, Smyth."
Common misspellings for a travel Web site about Colombia:
"Keywords: accommodation, Columbia."
(However, when a keyword tag is used to repeat words already in the body content, it simply becomes "keyword stuffing"—see "Keyword Loading" below.)

Consistency

Building a Web site with a consistent pattern of clearly related keywords is commonly known as creating a "theme."[13] A Web site with a clear theme stays on a single topic or closely related topics throughout its pages (barring such standard pages as "Contact Us"). This strategy builds the overall ranking of the Web site and, as a consequence, the SERP positions of the individual Web pages.

The concept "clearly related" restricts thematic rank-building to keyword relationships that search engines are capable of recognizing. Where "ship" and "marina" might begin to build a theme relating to recreational sailing, search engines would be less likely to recognize a theme in a Web page with the separate keywords "ship" and "space." Once combined into the more specific keyword "spaceship," the page becomes identifiable as related to science fiction or space exploration, and if the Web site also contains the words "galaxy" and "parsec," a theme begins to build.

The interest in themes peaked around 2004, alarmists suggesting that Web sites without a keyword theme would plummet in the SERPs.[14] However, there are exceptions to the rule: newspapers, encyclopedias, and many news blogs will never have a clear theme, yet they still can reach high SERP positions for a variety of keywords, based on meeting search engine criteria other than consistency of subject matter.

Technical

A technically oriented SEO strategy emphasizes programming skill or ingenuity over command of language, familiarity with the target audience, or interweaving related content. Tactics vary from the simple, which can be executed by anyone familiar with HTML, to the sophisticated, which require knowledge of programming, Web site servers, or WWW and Internet protocols.

Keyword loading, stuffing, and spamming

Keyword density can be taken to an extreme. Efforts to increase keyword density or variety that involve excessive or awkward repetition are known as "keyword loading." An example would be replacing every instance of "it" in a page with the noun in question.

When this repetition reaches the level of incoherence, with the same word or words used dozens of times in the body, title, or tags of a Web page, it is usually called "keyword stuffing" (a.k.a. "cramming"), "spamming the index" ("index" referring to the search engines' databases of Web pages), or "spamdexing." One of the earliest SEO tactics, it began with simply repeating keywords hundreds of times, generally at the bottom of the page, and frequently with the font color the same as the background color, thus rendering the text invisible to humans. As search engine algorithms began to discount this tactic, keyword spamming evolved into a more precise metering of keyword density. This obsolete technique periodically sees a resurgence as search engine administrators let down their guard.

The meta keywords tag

Located in the head section of a Web page's HTML (see Table 1) and invisible to users viewing a Web page in a browser, the meta keywords tag was created purely for metadata.

In the mid to late 1990s meta keywords were highly popular as a quick path to higher rankings, and indeed stuffing the meta keywords field showed some success when only a few million pages were being indexed. By the time the tactic became broadly known—with "keyword-jacking" lawsuits over copyright and trademark infringement—search engines were on their way to down-ranking the meta keywords tag contents, and usually not indexing the keywords in the field at all.

Entry pages

"Entry page" is the broadest descriptor for the strategy of creating particular pages to rank well with search engines, sometimes finely tuned to rank well with a particular search engine. "Doorway page" and "gateway page" imply that a page contains some relevant content that has been tuned for high SERP position. "Bridge page" or "jump page" imply that a page may be little more than an uninformative landing page that either urges the visitor to click through to the rest of the Web site, automatically redirects them to the rest of the Web site, or redirects them

to an entirely different Web site.[15] Most media coverage of such pages classifies them as Black Hat SEO. However, there is no clear agreement on the definition of these pages or their relative level of deception. Many SEO practitioners observe that while bridge and jump pages may be technical and possibly Black Hat as well, all pages visible to search engines are in a real sense entry pages.

Cloaking

"Cloaking" is used to describe a broad range of tactics. The common element is that the human visitor and the search engine spiders "see" different content when visiting a Web page. In the simplest form, the SEO practitioner creates a page tuned for high SERP position, and replaces it with a human-readable page after the page has been indexed by search engines (of course the artificially high ranking only lasts until search engine spiders visit the page again).

Two of the more technical methods, which attempt to deceive search engines on a continuing basis:

- *User-agent-specific page delivery*, in which the Web page server "sniffs" the incoming page request, extracts the data that identifies what browser the visitor is running (e.g., "googlebot" or "msnbot"), and delivers a special Web page tuned to gain higher SERP on that SE.
- *IP-specific page delivery*, in which the Web page server delivers a special Web page based on the visitor's Internet Protocol address (e.g., "127.0.0.1").

Cloaking is broadly considered one of the most aggressive and sophisticated forms of Black Hat SEO, but search engine analysts point out that even cloaking has legitimate purposes, as when a Web site is migrating to a new domain name; the owners may want to keep the old Web site available to the public until the new one becomes established in SERPs.[16]

Linking

Links have become such an important determinant of SERP position that under some circumstances they may override all other elements of ranking, and catapult a Web page of little or no relevance to a top SERP position.

Link-weighting fundamentals

Since the mid-1990s, search engines have routinely tracked the links from (and to) Web sites, often assigning a relative value based on the links' source or destination. Links pointing to a Web site are generally called "inbound links," and links pointing to other Web sites "outbound links." (Inbound links are frequently called "backlinks," though the term has other technical meanings in computing.)[17]

"Link-weighting" is frequently described as "link popularity" or even "popularity" measurements by popular media. More accurately, search engine link analysis algorithms attempt to infer the value of a Web page or entire Web site based on four factors:

1. The number of inbound links.
2. The "quality" of the inbound links, based on the quality of the originating Web site. Assessing the quality of Web sites is where link-weighting moves into more sophisticated and sometimes arcane mathematics.[18,19] In simple terms, an inbound link from a major university has more value than a link from an obscure small business, and has a greater beneficial effect on SERP position.
3. The "relevance" of the inbound link. A Web site about a baseball team benefits more by inbound links from other baseball-oriented Web sites than by links from the personal pages of fans.
4. The keywords contained within inbound links (the linked text visible in a browser), known as "anchor text." The most famous example was the 2003 link manipulation of Google SERPs (known as "Google bombing") in which hundreds or more Web site owners inserted the link <a href="http://www.whitehouse.gov/president/gwbbio.html">Miserable Failure</a> into their pages, causing the U.S. White House biography of George W. Bush to rise to the top ranking for the term "miserable failure."[20] (The gwbbio.html page rose to #1 ranking on Google for that term even though it did not contain either of the keywords in question.)

The cumulative importance of these factors in SERP position has led to naming the collective effect of inbound links "link juice" (American "slang definition of" "juice": influence, clout, http://www.m-w.com.)

Web sites with many relevant or high-quality links pointing to them (inbound links) are known as "authority" Web sites; those with many links pointing to other relevant Web sites (outbound links) as "expert" or "hub" Web sites. The presumption built into the search engine algorithms is that a Web site with many inbound links from high-quality Web pages is an authoritative source, and that pages with many outbound links to authority Web sites serve as a WWW resource. (The mathematics can become circular and even self-reinforcing, as when http://www.wikipedia.org Web pages briefly started to dominate #1 SERPs positions for thousands of subjects.)

Strategies for leveraging links

Link-weighting was implemented to in effect create a weighted voting scheme and take some of the control of rankings away from a Web site's designer. Since weighting means that not all inbound links are of equal value to SERP position, the methodology also opened the door to SEO opportunities of bewildering complexity, in which Web sites buy, sell, and trade links to and from their Web sites in order to improve their SERP positions.

Always a factor in SEO, "link building" is now broadly considered a core element of strategy, and in some schools of thought the most important element.[21] Increasing media attention brought linking as a SERP ranking factor to the attention of Web site owners and the quickly growing number of SEO practitioners, and today organizations spend substantial time and effort on link building aimed at high rankings.

Non-reciprocal links (a.k.a. "generosity links") were the first evolution, in the mid-1990s. At that time Web site creators linked to almost any remotely related Web site, including their competitors. By the late 1990s "reciprocal links" had become the standard, though the exchange was offered with a view to a direct increase in traffic rather than SERP position.

Soliciting inbound links, at first done casually, now often means assigning employees or subcontractors to solicit links from high-ranking Web sites. The return on investment is questionable—high-ranking Web sites have little to gain by giving an outbound link, and the site owners may be concerned that linking to a low-quality Web site will harm their own rankings. (Soliciting links should not be equated with link building, a broader term that covers all strategies for gaining inbound links.)[22]

The practice of posting links in discussion groups also originated with the goal of direct traffic rather than influencing SERP positions. "FFAs" (Free For All Web sites), "link farms," and "link rings" were crude early link-exchange schemes, most variants indiscriminately exchanging thousands of links without regard to relevance. While such sites are still active, their value in SEO has largely been eliminated by increasing sophistication of search engine ranking protocols. Most SEO practitioners today consider participating in them to be useless at best, and at worst, possibly injurious to a Web site's SERP positions.

"Paid links"—inbound links that have been purchased, sometimes masking as editorial recommendations—existed before the WWW on Internet bulletin boards, always with the intent of publicity or direct financial gain. With the broadening awareness of SEO, using paid links to influence SERP position has become both a business strategy and a source of contention between Web site owners and search engines.

Good content, the oldest link-building strategy of all, is a somewhat indirect way to build links. Coupled with even a modest amount of self-promotion beyond good SEO—or occasionally just with good content that perfectly targets a popular search—competent writing on a particular subject can generate hundreds or thousands of inbound links to a given Web page, often without any communication at all with the Web sites that are giving the links. Because content-inspired linking may produce results slowly (in months or years), and is often difficult to quantify, few organizations devote serious effort to the method.

Web Site and Web Page Structure

The directory (folder) structure of an SE-friendly Web site looks similar to a clearly and logically organized hard drive on a personal computer, with the additional proviso that every document is directly or indirectly linked from the home page or some other prominent Web page. Ideally the structure is "shallow" (three or fewer sub-directory levels), to make it easier for search engines to spider, though that has become less important as all major search engines now perform deep crawling.

Actual page structure of HTML pages is in theory dictated by an adherence to W3C standards. In practice, Web sites use almost any markup code that can be rendered by a Web browser and leave the difficulties of indexing to the search engines.

There are drawbacks to unorthodoxy where search engine rankings are concerned. Use of highly irregular Web site structure, page structure, or file naming conventions can seriously harm SERP position. In extreme cases, search engines simply do not add a Web site to their indexes; poor Web site structure can be as destructive to Web site rankings as the most extreme Black Hat tactics, and "site maps" generated specifically to aid search engines in indexing a Web site are not a substitute for logical Web site structure.[23]

Despite a broad disregard for standards among Web site owners, most SEO practitioners consider disciplined site and page structure fundamental good practice, though these are seen as a foundation for SEO rather than an SEO strategy in themselves.

Web Analytics

The most thorough SEO practitioners use "Web analytics" to analyze Web site traffic for patterns that can lead to enhanced SEO. While the term embraces areas more concerned with usability and user behavior while on a Web site, analytics sweeps in SEO functions such as keyword analysis and SERP position monitoring.

Data can be collected by "tagging" individual Web pages with Javascript and other programming, or by placing cookies on visitors' browsers.

"Keyword analysis" is often initiated at the server level through "log analysis." Because WWW communications protocols usually pass the full URL of the previously visited page to the destination Web site, the headers can be processed for search terms, and those terms then organized and further analyzed.

In either case, data is then analyzed manually, or with in-house programming, or with one of the many commercial Web analytics programs.

The data below is a sample of some of the information that can be extracted from Web site server logs: visitor's ISP, visitor's IP address, number of pages visited, time and date, visitor's browser and operating system, the Web site the visitor came from, the search terms they used, and the landing page.

A visitor from "dynamic.dsl.com" (88.104.65.226) was logged twice, starting at 12:46:36 on Sunday, October 14, 2007.

The initial browser was Firefox/2.0.0.7 (Windows XP; en).

This visitor first arrived from http://www.google.co.uk while searching "ecommerce business models 1–10" and visited "digitalenterprise.org/models/models.html."

There has been a general shift in Web analytics from log analysis to page tagging, in part due to the limits of log information compared with information gained by tagging, and in part driven by vendors of analytics software.

Combining Content, Technical, and Linking SEO

Strategies that combine all three forms of SEO may be the most effective in gaining high SERP positions. Combined strategies are uncommon because Web sites are normally designed without regard to SEO (although the most effective SEO is begun at the conceptual level), and because Web site owners and managers rarely allow significant changes to the structure or content of their Web sites after they are built and online.

An alternate way of viewing SEO is "on page" or "off page" SEO, the former being methods applied directly to Web sites and pages, the latter focusing on methods external to a Web site, such as link strategies.[24]

BROAD ISSUES IN SEO

A number of strategic issues that may affect a Web site go beyond fundamental SEO tactics or current "best practices."

Building Downwards vs. Outwards

Large or growing organizations face the question of whether to house all their Web pages under a single WWW domain, or to establish separate Web sites for different services, product lines, or agendas. An established organization with a strong brand will usually lean keyword targeting towards its own brand name in SERP positions, and thus benefit from housing all its Web pages under a single domain, whereas a newer organization with separate divisions would be more likely to establish separate Web sites for each product line or goal.

Science—Semantic

This is not strictly a business issue; a university establishing a new campus in a different city would probably create a new Web site for that campus, just as a business that sells to both architects and game designers might choose to divide its product lines into two separate Web sites. The university would certainly link its two Web sites for the link-weighting benefits; the company selling unrelated products might not link its Web sites at all.

Broad vs. Narrow Targeting and Long-Tail Terms

The potential benefits in targeting highly specific searches were known to SEO practitioners by 1995–1996. Bed and breakfasts were one of the earliest and most evident examples, showing how highly specific keywords (e.g., "bed breakfast Ireland Kilkenny") could reach precisely the right audience.

Since the Web was still sparsely populated, the more skilled practitioners were able to gain high SERP rankings for broad searches at the same time as they targeted narrow niches. For example, in 1997, it was possible for an Irish bed and breakfast's Web site to gain a high SERP position for both its own locale and Irish B&Bs in general. That grew more difficult with increasing competition, and today a search for "bed breakfast Ireland" will generally return a SERP dominated by bed and breakfast directories and associations.

The changing situation became somewhat better understood in 2003, when Zipfian distributions were mentioned in an article by Clay Shirky about "power laws" as applied to blogs.[25] Power laws were later popularized as "The Long Tail" by an article in *Wired* magazine.[26] With use of the term growing, many clients and SEO practitioners now refer to any three- to four-word term as a "long-tail term"; others use the description more correctly to describe an uncommon search term.

There are now indications that the pendulum of interest has swung too far towards uncommon terms, and that organizations are targeting long-tail terms without a clear view towards long-term benefits such as memberships or profits.[27]

Balancing Targeting and Serendipity

While some organizations have only one easily described product or agenda, for most organizations SEO can be too successful when it targets particular search terms so tightly that their Web pages can be found by little else. When virtually all traffic to a Web site comes from a small number of terms, analyzing incoming search terms becomes an exercise in analyzing what one already knows. Ideally, improvements in SEO create an increase in targeted traffic along with an increase in unanticipated search terms. While this can be analyzed in terms of Zipfian distributions, in proactive marketing it is better represented by the APUPA (Alien–Penumbral–Umbral–Penumbral–Alien) bell curve (Fig. 2).

SEO can also be too successful when a Web page captures a high SERP position on a major search engine for an extremely broad term like "health." Where this might be satisfactory to a large organization like the U.S. National Institutes of Health, an organization focusing on a particular niche of health could be swamped with masses of unwanted Web site visitors and e-mail.[28] Web sites deluged by unwanted traffic sometimes convert a liability to an asset by "reselling" the traffic or the entire Web site.

Lead Time and Longevity

Search engines rarely assign top rankings to newly indexed Web pages. A Web site can take months or even

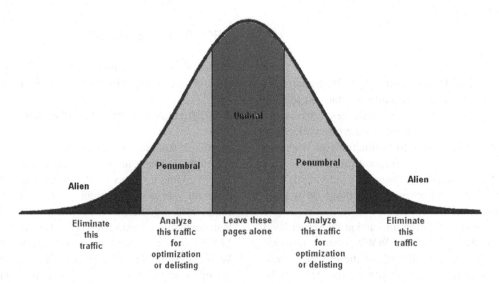

Fig. 2 APUPA chart expressed in SEO terms.
Source: © Hastings Research, 2005.

years to reach its "natural" position in SERPs. This is sometimes called the "sandbox," referring to the period a new Web site may wait for a good SERP position or even to be listed at all by a search engine.

Equally, search engines assign value to longevity, and older well-ranked Web sites dating from the 1990s can be notoriously difficult to dislodge from their SERP positions by new competitors.

Geographic Targeting

Geographic targeting through SEO had limited success through the mid-00s. Few early Web site designers made a diligent attempt to anticipate all the geographic keywords searchers might use, and those who did target searches with geographic keywords often used so many keywords (e.g., "London," "Pimlico," "Knightsbridge," "Belgravia," "Dulwich," "Stratford," "Paddington," "Fleet Street"—and every other village and neighboring town) that the pages were treated as index spam by search engines, and down-ranked to obscurity. Other designers created dozens or even thousands of "mirror pages" (pages with substantially similar content), each targeting a particular locale, with the result that the pages were down-ranked for "duplicate content."

In a cause-and-effect loop, users learned that searching by locale was nearly useless, and abandoned the effort (with the exception of specific travel destinations), leading most SEO practitioners to abandon their efforts at geographic targeting.

With the now-growing success of geographic targeting efforts by search engines—typically displaying maps showing physical locations—users have again started searching geographically, and most SEO practitioners advise making some effort to target searches containing geographic keywords, even though geographic searches may be defined by commercial databases rather than SEO efforts.

SEO Source Tracking

The wealth of data that accompanied visitors to Web sites led many ecommerce pioneers to think the perfection of marketing analysis had arrived. While this sometimes bordered on true for new businesses that were entirely WWW-based, the opposite turned out to be the case for large, established organizations already being marketed through advertising, mail, public relations, and retail outlets; the WWW added another layer of complexity to their market tracking. Due to its 24-hr availability, the WWW also creates a "smoothing" effect on response to promotional efforts, which can hinder analysis of event-driven spikes in visitor traffic.

Refinements in Web analytics have not entirely compensated for these factors, and in many ways Web site traffic source analysis remains less precise than that of traditional promotion and advertising.

Increased Competition

The continuing growth in the number of Web sites and Web pages means newly created Web sites have increasing difficulty gaining rankings for common keywords, so their approach is often to use a fanciful domain name and drive Web traffic via social networking or publicity instead of SEO.

Aside from the natural growth in Web sites, huge numbers of "made for ads" (MFA) Web sites have been created for no purpose other than to make money by hosting online advertisements—they have no products, services, or agendas of their own. Because advertising revenue indirectly comes from organizations that pay for online ads, MFA Web sites often specifically target keywords used by existing organizations. Nonprofit informational Web sites such as Wikipedia (http://www.wikipedia.org/) also compete directly for many search terms, often gaining very high search rankings.

Search Engines Only Index Words

While search engines are often technically capable of distilling words when they are represented in images, and in theory from audio tracks, in practice they index words from readable text documents, file names, or metadata attached to other forms of electronic files. There is a persistent failure to understand this aspect of SEO, with many Web site owners believing that if the human eye can read the words or grasp the meaning, the search engines will correctly index the files.

Further restricting SEO, search engines by choice index only certain types of text documents or metadata. At one time that meant pure text or HTML only. Most search engines are now willing to crawl and index file formats such as PDF (Portable Document Format), Microsoft Word and Excel, and in some cases Flash.

TRENDS

Fading Trends

"Meta keyword tags" were the first major chimera in SEO ("The meta keywords tag" earlier) They have been followed by other imaginary fast-tracks to high SERP position, all beginning with a grain of truth then blown out of proportion.

"Google PageRank" has been one of the most persistent areas of focus in SEO. Because of media attention and the easy access to the publicly visible PageRank via the Google Toolbar, the scale has commanded a great deal of interest from Web site owners, many of whom consider the published PageRank a practical scale for performance-based SEO contracts. Most SEO professionals now consider public PageRank in itself a minor factor in a Web site's actual SERP positions, more an effect than a cause. The latter opinion is to some extent corroborated by Google, Inc.[29] Over the course of 2007, countless Web sites saw their Google public PageRank drop significantly, which may further diminish interest in the measurement. ("PageRank" in popular usage should not be confused with "pagerank," an internal Google term.)

Web site "traffic"—whether measured in "hits" (requests for individual files, whether pages or images), "page views," "unique visitors," or the dot-com measure of "more eyeballs"—is slowly losing its popular connection to rankings, as organizations focus on conversion rate of users' visits to desired actions. (In extreme cases, traffic volume will have greater influence on SERP positions than relevance; however, this is uncommon and often results from a situation such as a major news event, where the boost in rankings may be due to a proliferation of inbound links, rather than traffic volume itself.)

Current Trends

Link building previously described in "Link-weighting fundamentals"
   Pursuing "long-tail" searches (previously described in "Broad vs. Narrow Targeting and Long-Tail Terms")
   Bringing SEO in-house: Major companies in North America and Europe are increasingly bringing SEO in-house as their online sales grow to (USD) millions or hundreds of millions. Companies are hiring in consultants, training current employees, or both.[30]
   Using best practices: Clients and employers are now commonly asking that practitioners follow "best practices." For SEO, the term describes such basic practices as prioritizing meta titles and heading tags, including keywords, and avoiding discredited (Black Hat) tactics.[31]
   Tuning metadata for search engine interfaces: Increasingly, practitioners structure Web pages so that titles, descriptions, and filenames are presented appealingly on SERPs. Eye-tracking studies, where eye motion is represented by printed "heat maps," are currently the basis for most decisions in tuning metadata.[32]
   Tagging Web pages: adding keywords or allowing visitors to add keywords to the visible text—is common on many social networking Web sites and some ecommerce and media Web sites, but has shown mixed results in improving SERP positions, possibly due to the indiscriminately chosen keywords selected by lay users, Web site owners, and bloggers. Tagging may benefit SERP position most for Web sites that encourage commentators to use "controlled vocabularies."[33] It may also boost SERP positions for "long-tail" search terms.
   Web 2.0 designs: Web 2.0 methods have been criticized as being detrimental to SEO. This criticism has arisen with

each evolution in Web site development, from "dynamic page delivery" (assembling Web pages from databases "on the fly") through Cascading Style Sheets and PDF files. In most previous instances, organizations' design preferences have won out over SEO considerations, and eventually the major search engines have adapted their protocols to classify new Web page structures and document formats.

Since search engines do not immediately retool for new forms of Web page markup and structure, Web sites that employ Web 2.0 methods such as AJAX (Asynchronous Javascript and XML) or that stream together content from different sources ("mashups") may drop in SERP positions until search engines decide how to interpret these new document structures.

Trends Affecting SEO

New search engine presentation methods

Clusters of search records such as those displayed by http://www.clusty.com or http://www.ask.com are likely to continue improving in relevance; if they increase in popularity, each cluster link will constitute a second-tier SERP, and SEO may begin targeting particular clusters.

Drop-down *contextual search suggestions* are now offered at http://www.ask.com and http://www.yahoo.com. Because users see contextual suggestions as they type, even before seeing the first SERP, "contextual position" may become a sought-after goal of SEO. Since contextual suggestions are all displayed on the first screen of a search engine's Web site, without the need for scrolling down, position is not likely to be as critical as SERP position, and "contextual inclusion" may prove to be the desired goal. (Contextual search flows from a given search engine's database of "most likely" requests; it should not be confused with the URL suggestions that Web browsers make by accessing a user's own search history.) (Fig. 3)

With exceptions, such as the European search engine Kartoo (http://www.kartoo.com), interfaces such as topic maps and link maps show little sign of entering the mainstream of WWW search, and thus do not affect SEO.

Blended search—the blending into the primary WWW SERPs of news, images, maps, videos, and other types of records once considered niche searches—have now been instituted by major search engines.[34] This presents

Fig. 3   Example of drop-down contextual search suggestions.

opportunities to the more aggressive SEO practitioners, some of whom are attempting to dominate blended SERPs with a mix of varied data formats. (Blended search has also been called "universal search.")

Specialized searches

Specialized searches have been offered for decades through pre-Web online information providers. They are often called "vertical searches" (i.e., niche search). Specialized search could disrupt current SEO strategies, whether it is offered by major search engines or niche suppliers. First, if niche searches or tools proliferate in the GYM group (Google, Yahoo, Microsoft)—each with its own classification protocols—they may dilute the value of SEO methods that address the GYM standard algorithms. Second, niche search engines such as http://www.vivisimo.com have entered the search race, and others such as http://www.northernlight.com (founded 1996) are reentering public search; these specialized search engines are usually less susceptible to technical methods, as they tend to use proportionately more human editing than broad reach search engines. Either trend could diminish the importance of technical- or link-based SEO.

"Personal search" has been a holy grail of the Internet industry since the mid-1990s. Early attempts at personal search included Yahoo! personalization features and numerous failures in "push technology" (Push technology: A means of automatically delivering information via the Internet to subscribers based on their choices for customized news, etc. *Webster's New Millennium Dictionary of English*, 2007. Described by H.P. Luhn as "SDI" (Selective Dissemination System), http://www.ischool.utexas.edu/~ssoy/organizing/l391d2c.htm, accessed February 2009). The current trend is towards analyzing individual users' search requests in the context of their previous searches (remembered by the server) and delivering customized results. Taken to an extreme, this could theoretically filter out a majority of available Web pages regardless of the SEO efforts invested, as search engines "learn" to focus on individual users' core interests.

"Local search" (geographic search) has become a serious goal for search engines. However other than travel destinations, few small retail businesses have Web sites, so search engines cannot easily find data for them by crawling the WWW. The primary solution to date has been to buy or barter for data such as traditional telephone book databases. Other new local search companies are aggregating local data for search engines, often crawling online local directories for source data search engines themselves are encouraging data entry from local organizations. Some trades with guilds such as law or medicine have niche Web sites with search functions; as yet few are comprehensive. Trades without guild organizations such as auto repair or beauty services may depend entirely on the success of aggregation if they are to be located through broad search. In few of these cases do current SEO

methods provide a clear path into SERPs, and paid listings may vie with SEO in creating online exposure for local businesses.[35]

Alternate search channels

Alternate search channels could have an even more dramatic effect on SEO practices than blended or niche search services:

SEO for mobile communications devices: Analysis of users' WWW search behaviors on mobile devices has shown an emphasis on local retail search followed by entertainment. Coupling mobile search with GPS navigation feedback opens the prospect of delivering content or ads raises the prospect of directing mobile users to the nearest restaurant or a movie showing, thus both of these searches are potentially lucrative advertising venues—search engines are pursuing them, and SEO will follow. It is not yet certain whether search engines will convert conventional Web pages to mobile-friendly formats, or whether organizations will have to create new pages specifically targeting mobile devices.[36,37]

SMO (Social Media Optimization): It is arguable how much SMO involves "search" in the sense of users searching by keywords, because the spread of information on social networking Web sites is largely viral (self-promotion coupled with word-of-mouth). SMO is currently practiced by creating profiles on popular social media sharing and news Web sites, building a large base of "friends" and contributing unique promotional content with the option for other community members to vote in favor or against. Popular content that goes "hot" is placed on the high traffic home pages of the social media sharing and news sites, sometimes generating tremendous amounts of exposure, direct traffic, and secondary effect inbound links from bloggers that post about the content. SMO also involves using software to make posts automatically, this latter method being simply spamming. There may be a growing synergy between SEO and SMO, and SMO may become a parallel profession lumped under the umbrella of SEM.[38,39]

STANDARDS AND REGULATION IN SEO

The practice of SEO is marked by the absence of standards, other than those imposed by the willingness of major search engines to index Web pages, their level of effort in returning the most relevant Web pages, and punitive actions (down-ranking or de-listing) taken against what search engine administrators consider unacceptable manipulation of SERP positions.

HTML

Standard Web pages (HTML) are in theory defined by W3C standards—which are largely ignored by both Web developers and amateurs. Other formats now being indexed by search engines—including PDF, Microsoft Word and Excel, and still images and videos—follow even fewer standards.

Certification

Certification is in beginning stages. Some businesses have begun offering SEO credentials, and accredited colleges are now beginning to offer courses in SEO.

SEO Industry

The SEO industry may be loosely divided into SEO professionals of varying ability; Web designers and programmers who know the rudiments; and a much more visible group of low-cost SEO companies that operate through advertising and e-mail marketing.[40]

While there are no formal standards or regulation, informal standards are slowly evolving through consensus of trade associations and Web sites reporting on SEO. (See "Bibliography" at the end of this entry.)

Search Engines

Because it is difficult to mathematically determine whether a given Web page's content accurately reflects the page's relevance to visitors (much less the creator's true agenda), search engines have faced and continue to face an impossible task in down-ranking deceptive pages without penalizing legitimate ones. (In the classic if now simplistic example, a medical Web site can unwittingly trigger an algorithm aimed at filtering out pornography pages.)

Attempts to "game" (manipulate) search engine rankings have been so relentless, from the first significant appearance of online search engines, that many experts consider search engine administration to be equally a process of excluding Black Hat pages and elevating relevant pages.[41] While penalizing irrelevant content faces the same problem as returning relevant content—a struggle to develop artificial intelligence—most search engines strongly downgrade Web sites that are found to be using the more technically complex SEO tactics such as IP-specific page delivery (see "Cloaking" earlier).

This issue of controlling Black Hat SEO without penalizing White Hat SEO is a continued source of tension between search engine administrators and SEO practitioners. Search engines selling advertising space on their own SERPs has exacerbated the tension by raising the issue that pursues traditional media, of whether there is a true division between editorial and advertising departments (or search relevance and advertising, in the case of search engines).

Like the evolution of military tactics, regulation is a game of innovation and counter-measure. The counter-measures may make a given tactic so ineffective that it is completely forgotten by both attackers and defenders, at which point it may be reintroduced by the attackers. (A medical analogy would be the mutation of microorganisms in reaction to new antibiotics, accompanied by the resurgence of forgotten diseases when society no longer guards against them.)

Government Regulation

At present there is no hint of SEO regulation. As subcontractors, SEO consultancies are in a position similar to advertising agencies—with no actual control over organizations or distribution channels—so any government regulation is likely to flow indirectly from regulation of Web sites themselves (trade practices) or of search engines (particularly in the United States, where antitrust law may affect conglomeration of major search engines with software, hardware, or media companies).

USER BEHAVIORS IN SEARCH

User behavior while searching online shows more consistency than change in the period from 1995 to 2008. This section will briefly address the consistent behaviors and available research on the course of changes.

Users' search behavior has a strong effect on SEO, since many users click the first listing in a SERP. On the other hand, gaining a #1 SERP position for a particular search term does not guarantee that a user will click that link; they might click the #2 link or the #10 link if those page titles, descriptions, or URLs are more compelling.

In the same vein, there is no clear evidence that users who click the first record will take further action; many SEO practitioners believe the more motivated users will scan an entire SERP before deciding which link to click. Regardless, user behavior while visiting SERPs affects SEO decisions as well as the search engines' goal of relevance.

Research into specific behaviors has revealed a great deal about what users do in the specific environment of a search engine interface when tested in a laboratory setting. It leaves unanswered many questions about why users search the way they do—in part because most research has focused on what users do when looking at a SERP, without inquiring how or why they arrived at that particular SERP, or what actions they take after clicking a particular link. More research is required to develop consistent conclusions. Substantial research from information science has yet to be incorporated in SEO; when it is, it may transform strategies and tactics.

Variables that affect user search behavior:

- Users' level of subject knowledge.
- Improvements in results returned by search engines.
- Users' confidence in the quality of search results.

- Degree of users' sophistication in search.
- Presentation style of individual search results (title, description, URL, etc.).
- Motivation/curiosity/laziness.
- Habituation among users (hardening behaviors).
- Search engine interface design.
- Number of search engines available.

Basic Behaviors

Few users methodically click search results in sequential order, from the first result to the bottom of the page. Typically they skip over unappealing titles or URLs, and may bounce back and forth between organic search listings and paid listings. (Depending on SERP design, users may not always know the difference between paid and organic listings.) If a relevant Web page is not found quickly, users may change search engines, change their search term, or migrate to a general information Web site such as a dictionary, encyclopedia, or user-fed Q&A Web site.

Searching Popular Subjects

Patterns of search seen on Wordtracker, Yahoo! search tool, or KeywordDiscovery continue to show a preponderance of searches for celebrities and popular news, as described since 1999 in the weekly "Lycos 50" listing of the most popular topical searches (http://50.lycos.com/archives.asp) with written analysis and opinion. Google Trends (http://www.google.com/trends), which shows the number of searches for chosen terms in chart format, is well-suited to display spikes in interest, relative interest in different subjects, or seasonal patterns in popular searches; like the Lycos 50, it demonstrates that a huge proportion of Web searches are for popular subjects rather than niche information.

Use of Boolean Syntax

In the 1990s, WWW search engines typically limited the use of search syntax to Boolean AND, OR, and NOT, with OR as the default. (With AND or NOT typically applied by +/− symbols.) Initially these options were only available by typing them into the search term entry box. HotBot search engine was one of the earliest to offer Boolean logic to untrained users, with the addition of a drop-down box offering AND as well as "exact phrase" options, but the options were rarely used.

In the late 1990s, search engines moved towards a default (or forced) Boolean AND; by early 2003, it was the default on all major search engines search engines.[42] Although this change narrowed search results, it also hugely increased the relevance of results, and, at the same time, reduced the average user's motivation to learn Boolean syntax. Some data samples suggest that Boolean search skills are known to a smaller percentage of users today than in 1997, though it is uncertain whether the decrease is due to a loss of interest in search syntax or an influx of less sophisticated users.[43]

Search Engine Loyalty

Available statistics strongly indicate that users are now more likely to refine or expand their search term than switch to another search engine.[44] The disinclination to switch is often called "loyalty" in a broad sense; motivating factors could be the generally improved quality of search returns over the last few years, or users' increased recognition of the value of using precise search terms. In terms of user behavior, this could be described as a slight shift from "berrypicking" (wandering about and collecting bits of information) to more linear search behaviors.[45]

Hardened User Behaviors

Users' search behavior search engines may have become "hardened," or fixed, by their expectations, in particular in the United States and Canada, because the majority of popular search engines have presented returns as linear lists since the mid-1990s. Current SEO is predicated on the idea that users type keywords into a box, click a "Search" button, and scan a list from top to bottom.[46] Because they represent a large conceptual shift, interfaces that present information in clusters, topic maps, or relationship maps face an entry barrier.

User Behavior Worldwide

Patterns of user behavior outside the United States and Canada do not show identical evolution. While less analysis has been done, in regions as disparate as England and China users are apparently more willing to examine entire SERP pages, as well as second and third pages, and less likely to click on the first or first few SERP positions.

CONCLUSION

Beginning in the mid-1990s, SEO evolved from placing random keywords in all possible parts of Web pages, to more focused doorway page strategies targeting particular keywords. By 2000, improvements in search engines were rendering most of such tactics obsolete, and SEO practitioners moved on to the integration of overall Web site structure, and then on to establishing a Web site's relationship with the WWW as a whole through linking.[47] For most, the reluctant and secondary focus of SEO was on users or quality of content. For others, a focus on user experience as well as SEO provided long term, sustainable results throughout the evolution.

SEO now faces broad changes in search and user behavior. The growth of online information is outpacing the indexing rates of all search engines. Search engines are struggling to deal with that overload, and in the process changing their strategies about what information to present and how to present it. Hardware—notably mobile communications devices—is redefining the technical limits of information presentation and also creating niches in user search behaviors.

ACKNOWLEDGMENT

With thanks to Jim Rhodes, Jim Heath, Lee Odden, Guy Shalev, Paula Sheil, and Kelly Bryan.

REFERENCES

1. Sullivan, D. http://forums.searchenginewatch.com/show thread.php?t=78 (accessed February 2009).
2. Rhodes, J. Art of search engine promotion, 1997. http://www.deadlock.com/promote/search-engines (accessed February 2009).
3. Heath, J. *Pointers on How to Create Business Websites That Work*, Published online, 1995. Earliest available version at http://www.viacorp.com/pointers1995.html (accessed February 2009).
4. November 2006 Web Server Survey Netcraft **2006**, http://news.netcraft.com/archives/2006/11/01/november_2006_web_server_survey.html (accessed February 2009).
5. Search Engine Marketing Professional Organization (SEMPO), *The State of Search Engine Marketing 2006: Survey of Advertisers and Agencies*, 5. Search Engine Marketing Professional Organization (SEMPO): Wakefield, MA, 2007.
6. Web Analytics Association, http://www.webanalyticsassociation.org (accessed February 2009).
7. CMSWatch, http://www.cmswatch.com (accessed February 2009).
8. Wilsdon, N., Ed.; Global Search Report 2007, E3internet, 2007. http://www.multilingual-search.com/global-search-report-2007-released-free-pdf/15/10/2007 (accessed February 2009).
9. The Global Structure of an HTML Document, http://www.w3.org/TR/html401/struct/global.html (accessed February 2009).
10. Grappone, J.; Couzin, G. *Search Engine Optimization: An Hour A Day*; Sybex: Hoboken, NJ, June 2006; 46–47. 101. http://www.yourseoplan.com/book-inside-contents.html (accessed February 2009).
11. Whalen, J. Avoiding clueless-is as clueless-does SEO, http://searchengineland.com/070927–071933.php (accessed February 2009).
12. Stamoulis, N. The top 8 SEO techniques (A dispute), http://www.searchengineoptimizationjournal.com/2007/09/17/the-top-8-seo-techniques-a-dispute (accessed February 2009).
13. Seda, C. *How to Win Sales & Influence Spiders*; New Riders: Berkeley, CA, February 2007, 5.
14. Bradley, S. Using keyword themes to structure your site content, 2006, http://www.vanseodesign.com/blog/seo/keyword-themes-for-site-structure/ (accessed February 2009).
15. Sullivan, D. *What Are Doorway Pages?* Published online, 2007, http://www.searchenginewatch.com/showPage.html?page=2167831 (accessed February 2009).
16. Sherman, C. *In Defense of Search Engine Cloaking*; Published online, 2001, http://www.searchenginewatch.com/showPage.html?page=2157261 (accessed February 2009).
17. Nelson, T.H. *Literary Machines*; Mindful Press: Sausalito, CA, 1982. (This is the earliest specification of the term hyperlinking, ca. 1965.)
18. Langville, A.; Meyer, C. *Google PageRank and Beyond: The Science of Search Engine Rankings*; Princeton University Press: Princeton, NJ, 2006.
19. Kleinberg, J. *Authoritative Sources in a Hyperlinked Environment*. Proceedings of the 9th ACM–SIAM Symposium on Discrete Algorithms, San Francisco, CA, 1998. Extended version in J. ACM **1999**, *46*. Also appears as IBM Research Report RJ 10076, May 1997, http://www.cs.cornell.edu/home/kleinber/auth.pdf (accessed February 2009).
20. Sullivan, D. Google kills Bush's miserable failure search & other Google bombs; 2007. http://searchengineland.com/070125–230048.php (accessed February 2009).
21. Wall, A. *The SEObook*; 2007, 197–199. http://www.seobook.com.
22. Bodden, L. Making sense of linking and site promotion; 2007. http://www.toprankblog.com/2007/09/linking-site-promotion/ (accessed February 2009).
23. Thurow, S. The right way to think about site maps; 2007. http://searchengineland.com/070809–091501.php (accessed February 2009).
24. Off Page Optimisation VS On Page Optimisation, http://www.directtraffic.org/on_page_optimisation.htm (accessed February 2009).
25. Shirky, C. Power laws, weblogs, and inequality; 2003. http://www.shirky.com/writings/powerlaw_weblog.html (accessed February 2009).
26. Anderson, C. The long tail. Wired Mag. **2004**. http://www.wired.com/wired/archive/12.10/tail.html (accessed February 2009).
27. Brynjolfsson, E.; Hu, Y.; Smith, M.D. From niches to riches: the anatomy of the long tail. Sloan Manage. Rev. **2006**.
28. Carroll, N. The anti-thesaurus: A proposal for improving internet search while reducing unnecessary traffic loads; 2001. http://www.hastingsresearch.com/net/06-anti-thesaurus.shtml (accessed February 2009).
29. http://www.google.com/corporate/tech.html (accessed February 2009).
30. *Search Marketing Benchmark Guide 2008*, 2008, 43–50. http://www.sherpastore.com/Search-Marketing-Benchmark-2008.html (accessed February 2009).
31. Fusco, P.J. SEO Best Practices: 20 Questions; 2007, http://www.clickz.com/showPage.html?page=3624560 (accessed February 2009).
32. Whitepapers and videos on user eye tracking, http://www.enquiroresearch.com/ (accessed February 2009).

33. Tagging advisory from DailyKos.com political blog, http://www.dkosopedia.com/wiki/Standard_Tags_-_alpha_list (accessed February 2009).

34. Sullivan, D. Search 3.0: The Blended & Vertical Search Revolution, http://searchengineland.com/071127–091128.php (accessed February 2009).

35. Guide on how to get your business listed on major local search engines, yellow pages sites and social local networks. http://www.locallytype.com/pages/submit.htm (accessed February 2009).

36. Carroll, N.; McGraw, M.; Brahms, S.; Rodgers, D. Wireless usability 2001–2002 report, http://www.hastings-research.com/reports/62-wap-2001.shtml (accessed February 2009).

37. Holahan, C. The battle for mobile search. BusinessWeek **2007**, http://www.businessweek.com/technology/content/feb2007/tc20070220_828216.htm (accessed February 2009).

38. Bhargava, R. 5 Rules of Social Media Optimization (SMO), 2006. http://rohitbhargava.typepad.com/weblog/2006/08/5_rules_of_soci.html (accessed February 2009).

39. Seda, C. *How to Win Sales & Influence Spiders*; New Riders: Berkeley, CA, 2007; 58–74.

40. Seda, C. *How to Win Sales & Influence Spiders*; New Riders: Berkeley, CA, 2007; 16–22.

41. Price, G. Personal communication about gaming search engines, http://www.resourceshelf.com (accessed February 2009).

42. Sullivan, D. *Search Features Chart*; 2001, http://searchenginewatch.com/showPage.html?page=2155981 (accessed February 2009).

43. Hastings Research proprietary databases of real-time searches and web server logs, 1995–2008.

44. Search Marketing Benchmark Guide 2008, 2007, 135, http://www.sherpastore.com/Search-Marketing-Benchmark-2008.html.

45. Bates, M.J. The Design Of Browsing And Berrypicking Techniques For The Online Search Interface, 1989, http://www.gseis.ucla.edu/faculty/bates/berrypicking.html (accessed February 2009).

46. Nielsen, J. Mental models for search are getting firmer, 2005, http://www.useit.com/alertbox/20050509.html (accessed February 2009).

47. Rhodes, J. Personal communication on early SEO practices.

BIBLIOGRAPHY

1. A timeline of SEO. http://blog.searchenginewatch.com/blog/060417-130526 (accessed February 2009).

2. http://www.searchengineland.com (accessed February 2009).

3. http://www.searchenginewatch.com (accessed February 2009).

4. http://www.seopros.org (accessed February 2009).

5. http://www.sempo.org/learning_center (accessed February 2009).

6. http://www.sempo.org/learning_center/sem_glossary (accessed February 2009).

Users section

1. Mezei, C. Website and search engine user behavior analysis, 2006, http://www.searchnewz.com/latestsearch/senews/sn-4-20061101WebsiteandSearchEngineUserBehavior-Analysis.html (accessed February 2009).

2. Search Engine User Behavior Study, iProspect, 2006, http://www.iprospect.com/about/whitepaper_seuserbehavior_apr06.htm (accessed February 2009).

Search Engines

Randolph Hock
Online Strategies, Annapolis, Maryland, U.S.A.

Abstract

This entry provides an overview of Web search engines, looking at the definition, components, leading engines, searching capabilities, and types of engines. It examines the components that make up a search engine and briefly discusses the process involved in identifying content for the engines' databases and the indexing of that content. Typical search options are reviewed and the major Web search engines are identified and described. Also identified and described are various specialty search engines, such as those for special content such as video and images, and engines that take significantly different approaches to the search problem, such as visualization engines and metasearch engines.

INTRODUCTION

Web search engines, for the public at large, have come to be perhaps the most frequently used computer services for locating information. To some degree, the same is true for many researchers, information professionals, and others. To most effectively and efficiently utilize these services, some understanding of the structure, makeup, content, features, and variety and breadth of these services is essential. This entry addresses those various aspects including just what is meant by "search engines," the components of a search engine, and typical search features, and it provides a profile of the major general Web search engines and a look at specialty search engines, visualization engines, and metasearch engines.

WHAT IS MEANT BY "SEARCH ENGINES"?

The term "search engines" can have a variety of meanings, in the broadest sense referring to any computer program that facilitates the searching of a database. In the context of library and information science, however, the term has come to primarily refer to "Web search engines," that is, those services on the Web that allow searching of a large database of Web pages and other Web content by word, phrase, and other criteria. (For this discussion, hereafter, "search engines" will be taken to refer to "Web search engines.") A certain level of ambiguity becomes apparent, however, when it is realized that what is often referred to as a "search engine" is often a reference to the overall service that is provided, beyond just a search of websites. ("Google" is thought of not as just the searching part of the Google enterprise, but the many added features and content as well.) It is often impossible and unproductive to discuss the narrower "searching" part without discussing the broader range of services. That ambiguity in terminology is a result and artifact of the history of search engines, but recognition of the ambiguity is necessary for an understanding of the current nature of such services.

Search engines vary in a number of ways and most could be considered to fall into one of four categories: general Web search engines (which have the purpose of searching a large portion of all pages that exist on the Web), specialty search engines (which focus on searching a specific kind of document, file type, or sources from a particular subject or geographic region), visualization search engines (which furnish diagrams, images, or other "visuals" to show relationships among the items in a particular set of retrieved items), and metasearch engines (which gather together the search results on a specific topic from multiple search engines).

COMPONENTS OF A SEARCH ENGINE

General Web search engines and specialty search engines can be considered to have four major components that correspond to the steps required to create the service: 1) the identification and gathering of the material (Web pages, etc.) to be included in the engine's database; 2) an indexing program and the corresponding generated indexes; 3) the searching and ranking algorithms; and 4) the user interface. In understanding the history and the capabilities of search engines, it is important to note the rapidly increasing role played by artificial intelligence and related areas such as natural language processing (NLP) in the development of these components.

Identifying Material to Be Included

Search engines identify those Web pages (and other items) to be included in the service's database by two means: "crawling" and submissions of pages. The first,

Encyclopedia of Library and Information Sciences, Fourth Edition DOI: 10.1081/E-ELIS4-120053699

"crawling" consists of having programs ("crawlers" or "spiders") that on an ongoing basis scan the Internet to identify new sites or sites that have changed, gather information from those sites, and feed that information to the search engine's indexing mechanism. The crawlers start by examining pages that the service already knows about and looking there for "new" links (links that the service does not already know about). When such links are identified, the pages to which the links led are likewise examined for "new" links, and so on. More popular websites (such as those that have lots of links to them) may be crawled more thoroughly and more frequently than less popular sites.

The second way search engines identify new items to be added to the database is by having website owners (or others) "submit" sites or pages. Most engines provide a form by which this can be done. Search services maintain their own policies as to whether submitted (or for that matter, pages identified by crawling) will indeed be added to the database, particularly looking to exclude unacceptable content (spam, sexually explicit material, etc.)

Search Engine's Index and Indexing Program

After a new or changed page is identified by the search engine's crawler, the page will typically be indexed under virtually every word on the page (up to some usually undisclosed limit). In addition to text words, other parts or characteristics of the page may also be indexed, including the URL (uniform resource locator, the "Web address"), parts of the URL, links, metadata found in the "head" of the document, the URLs of links on the page, image filenames, and words in linked text. By identifying and indexing these pieces of data (pieces or characteristics of the Web page or other type of indexed document, such as an Excel file), they become searchable "fields," thereby allowing users to use those fields to increase the quality of their search. The search system may also "derive" additional fields, such as language, by analysis of the document. Analysis of the document utilizing NLP techniques also allows the indexing of the document under other terms not necessarily found in the document (but implied by the text) and also allows more precise indexing by identifying specific "entities" (people, places, companies, etc.)

The Search Engine's Retrieval and Ranking Algorithms

By narrow definition, the actual search "engine" is the search service's retrieval program, that is, the program that identifies (retrieves) those pages in the database that match the criteria indicated by a user's query. That identification function is necessarily supplemented by another important and more challenging program that is used to determine the order in which the retrieved records should

be displayed, based on measures that try to identify which retrieved records (pages, etc.) are likely to have the highest relevance in respect to the user's query.

This "relevance-ranking" algorithm usually takes many factors into account.

Exactly what factors go into the relevance-ranking process varies, but they include the use of keywords in titles, text, headings, etc., popularity of the sites (how many and which sites link to the site), words used in anchors (clickable text), internal links (how many and what kind of links within the larger site point to the page). Google led the field (and to a significant degree gained its reputation for high relevance) by putting high emphasis on "links", particularly on the "popularity" of a page based on how many pages linked to the site and the popularity of the sites that were linking to the page. Increasingly, the use of artificial intelligence has become a major factor in determining ranking. Ranking of results is determined to some degree (often a very high degree) by "who" is searching—the user's location, search history, etc.

The success or the failure of the relevance-ranking algorithm is critical to the user's perception of the search engine, the user's continued use of that system, and the commercial success of the engine.

The Interface Presented to the User for Gathering Queries

This interface the user typically sees includes the home page of the search service and other pages (such as an advanced search page) that present search options to the users and accept the users' search queries, as well as the search results page. The search service can choose to have their page focus almost exclusively on "search" (as with Google) or be a more general, wide-reaching "portal" page, providing much more than just searching capabilities. (The "portal" dilemma for search services will be discussed in more detail later.)

Regardless of what other services and information are provided on the service's home page (or mobile app), the "searching" part usually consists of a single search box plus links to other searchable databases that are made available by the service (images, video, news, etc.). Usually, there are also links to "help" screens, etc. While the simplicity of a single search box appeals to the less experienced user, the search box also usually provides substantial, but not obvious, capabilities for extensive searching sophistication, such as the potential for using Boolean logic and "prefixes" (e.g., "title:") to perform field searching and other functions. An advanced search page may also be provided, which can much more explicitly lay out the possibilities to the user, providing a menu-based approach to utilization of features.

While the most basic element of the search engine interface (a search box into which users enter their queries) remained very much the same for most of search engine history, that has also changed with the proliferation of "mobile" devices (smartphones, tablets, and wearable computers). Voice input has become not only possible, but the *preferred* interface for an increasing number of users.

The Portal Dilemma

From the early days of search engines, search engine providers have wrestled with the decision as to whether to make their home page one that focuses almost exclusively on "search" or one that provides a variety of added services, such as news and weather; the latter approach often referred to as a "portal." From its beginning, before it was even a "search engine" and was just a directory, Yahoo! preferred the portal approach. AltaVista, a leading search engine in the 1990s, went back and forth between the two extremes, a situation that may have contributed to its demise. Google was, from the beginning, almost purely a "search engine," and the simplicity of its interface was undoubtedly one factor in its rapid rise in popularity. Search services may "cover their bets," however, by providing alternatives. For example, Yahoo! has provided a Google-like option at search.yahoo.com and Google at one point provided a "portal" version interface (iGoogle).

Searching Options Typically Provided

Search engines may provide a range of user accessible options that permit the user to modify their search queries in ways that can improve both the precision and the recall of their search results. Which specific options are provided varies from engine to engine. The most notable options include Boolean operations, phrase searching, language specification, and specifying that only those pages are retrieved for which the search term appears in a particular part (field) of the record such as the title or URL. Since engines usually cover other document types beyond just pages written in hypertext markup language (HTML), with some engines, users can also narrow their search to a specific file format (Web pages, Adobe Acrobat files, Excel files, etc.). Engines also provide an option to filter "adult content" material.

Up until the early 2010s, most search engines provided two ways for a user to take advantage of these options, syntax applied to search terms or an advanced search page. "Syntax" includes such things as explicitly including Boolean operators, such as "OR" in a search query and inserting a prefix in front of a search term. An example of the latter would be entering *intitle:malaria* in a search statement to specify that only items where the word *malaria* appears in the title should be retrieved.

Boolean logic

In the context of Web searching, "Boolean logic" refers to the process of identifying those items found in the database that contain a particular combination of search terms. It is used to indicate that a particular group of terms must all be present (the Boolean "AND"), that any of a particular group of terms is acceptable (the Boolean "OR"), or that if a particular term is present, the item is rejected (the Boolean "NOT"). (See the entry, Boolean Algebras [*ELIS Classic*], p. xxx.)

Engines may provide two different ways to qualify a query with Boolean operations:[1] the option of applying a syntax directly to what is entered in the search box and[2] menu options on an advanced search page. Using the menus can be thought of as "simplified Boolean" and, depending upon the structure of the advanced search page, may or may not provide the precision achievable by the use of syntax in the main search box. (For example, the ability to apply "OR"s to more than one of the concepts included in the query may be done in the main search box but may not be allowed for on the advanced search page.)

The exact syntax used varies with the search engine. All major engines currently automatically apply an "AND" between your terms, so when the following is entered, *prague economics tourism*, what will be retrieved is what more traditionally would have been expressed as *prague AND economics AND tourism*.

Very precise search requirements can be expressed using combinations of the operators along with parentheses to indicate the order of operations. For example, (grain OR corn OR wheat) *(production OR harvest) oklahoma 1997*.

At various times, search engines have allowed the use of symbols (+, &, −, etc.) instead of words (AND, OR, NOT), and indeed, for the "NOT," search engines typically suggest the use of a minus sign in front of the term. Some search engines require the use of parentheses around "nested" (OR'ed) terms, and some do not.

For details on Boolean syntax for any search engine, the help pages for that engine should be consulted. There are also websites that summarize the syntax (and other features) for all major engines.

The alternative to using syntax to apply Boolean is the use of menus on an advanced search page. There, for example, you may find a pull-down menu, where, if you choose the "all the words" option, you are requesting the Boolean AND. If you choose the "any of the words" option from such a menu, you are specifying an OR. There is usually also a box for excluding terms ("NOT").

Phrase searching

Phrase searching is an option that is available in virtually every search engine, and almost always uses the same syntax, the use of quotation marks around the phrase. For example, searching on "*Red River*" (with the quotation marks) will assure that you get only those pages that contain the word "red" immediately in front of the word "river." Of all search engine techniques, this is widely regarded as one of the most useful and easiest for achieving higher precision in a Web search. It is also useful for such things as identifying quotations and identifying plagiarism.

Title searching

Title searching, that is, limiting your retrieval to only those items (pages) that have a particular term or combination of terms in their title, is one example of "field searching," as referred to earlier. It is also another example of a technique that can yield very high precision in a search. Some search engines use the "intitle:" prefix and/or the "allintitle:" prefix for the syntax for title searching. ("allintitle:" allows specifying that more than one term be included in the title, not necessarily in any particular order.)

URL, site, and domain searching

A search engine may index Web pages (and other document types) by both the overall URL and the segments of the URL. This facilitates the finding of any document that comes from a particular domain or part of a domain (also a specific site or part of a site). Doing a search in which results are limited to a specific site allows one, in effect, to perform a search of that site. Even for sites that have a "site search" box on their home page, more complete results can often be found by using this technique than by using the site's own search feature. "inurl:," "allinurl:," and "site:" are the prefixes commonly used.

The term "domain searching" is sometimes used to refer to the process mentioned earlier, and the use of the term "domain" points out that this approach can be used to limit retrieval to sites having a particular top-level domain, such as gov, edu, uk, ca, or fr. This could be used, for example, to identify only Canadian sites that mention tariffs or to only get educational sites that mention biodiversity.

Language searching

A search engine may allow limiting retrieval to pages written in a given language with perhaps the 40 or so most common languages specifiable. Though some engines have provided a prefix option for searching for languages, more typically one would go to the engine's advanced search page to narrow to a language.

Date searching

Searching by the date of Web pages is an obviously desirable option, and most major engines provide such an option. Unfortunately, because of the lack of clear or reliable information on a page regarding when the page itself was initially created, the date on which the content of the page was created, or even when the content on the page was significantly modified, it is often impossible for a search engine to assign a truly "reliable" date to a Web page. As a "work-around," engines may take the date when the page was last modified or may assign a date based on when the page was last crawled by the engine. For searching Web pages, users should be aware of this approximation and its effect on precision when using the date searching option that is offered by most search engines (usually on their advanced search page). (On the other hand, for some of the other databases an engine may provide, such as news, the date searching may be very precise.)

Searching by file type

For most of the 1990s, most search engines only indexed and allowed searching of regular HTML pages. In the crawling process (or for submitted pages) when the engine's indexing program encountered a link that led to another type of document, such as an Adobe Acrobat (pdf), or Excel (xls) file, the link was ignored. Starting with Adobe Acrobat files, other file types were fairly rapidly added to the corpus of "indexable" pages. This not only increased the breadth of resources available to the searcher but also provided the capability for the searcher to limit retrieval by type of file. Limiting to Adobe Acrobat files provides documents more suited to printing. Narrowing to PowerPoint files can provide convenient summaries of a topic. Limiting to Excel files can often enable a greater focus on statistics.

Natural language queries

In the early days of search engines, users could (and often did) enter "natural language" queries, such as *What is the capital of Bulgaria?* Engines would typically ignore the smaller, more common words and simply apply the Boolean "AND" to the remaining words. This often did provide users with an acceptable answer. At present, search services are extensively applying Natural Language Processing NLP) both to the interpretation of the user's query and to the analysis of the documents being searched, consequently making natural language queries much more effective and efficient. This became particularly important in light of the greatly increased availability and accessibility of search engines as "apps" on smartphones and tablets, NLP is also central to the utility and effectiveness of the voice input technologies for these devices, for example for Apple's Siri, Google's "Google Now", and Microsoft's Cortana, The importance of search engines' NLP and voice input technologies likewise applies to smart home devices such as Amazon's Alexa and Google's Google Home.

Search Results Pages

As well as providing enhanced searching capabilities, search engines also enhance the content of results pages, beyond presenting just a listing of the Web page results that match the user's query. At the same time, they search their Web database, they may automatically search the other databases they have, such as news, images, and video, and on search pages may automatically provide links to the matching items from those additional databases. Some search engines may search additional "reference" resources, such as dictionaries, encyclopedias, and maps, and likewise display matching content from those sources and may also provide, "on the fly", a consolidated collection of facts on certain search topics such as places, people, companies, etc.

As well as displaying such supplemental content on results pages, search engines may also provide suggestions for ways in which the user might further qualify search criteria. This is done by suggesting related, narrower, or broader topics. Some engines also provide links to narrow the search by file type, language, or other criteria.

Specific options may also be offered on results pages for each individual retrieved item. Some engines keep a copy of each page they have indexed and provide a link to that "cached" page. This is particularly useful if, in the time since the page was indexed, the page was removed, is not available because of a server problem, or has changed in a way such that the term the user searched for is no longer on the page.

With records for pages that are not in the language of the search engine interface, there may be an option to translate the record (e.g., if the user is using an English language version of Google and a page is in French or if the user is using the French version and the page is in English). Click on the "translate" link to receive a machine translation of the page. As with other machine translations, what you get may not be a "good" translation, but it may be an "adequate" translation, adequate in that it will give you a good idea of what the page is talking about.

One feature offered on search results pages by all of the major engines is a spell-checker. If you misspelled a word, or the search engine thinks you might have, it graciously asks something like "Did you mean?" and gives you a likely alternative. If it was indeed a mistake, just click on the suggested alternative to correct the problem.

In many searches, search results pages will display links labeled as "ads," "Sponsor Results," "Sponsored Links," etc.—these are ads for websites and are there because a company or other organization has paid to have the ad appear on the search engine's results pages. Searchers should remain aware that it is the presence of these ads that makes the existence of search engines possible.

The Search Engine Leaders in the Second Decade of the Twenty-First Century

Popularity of various search engines can change fairly quickly. In the early and mid-1990s, a list of the most popular engines included, among others, AltaVista, HotBot, Excite, InfoSeek, and Lycos (Yahoo! was still primarily a directory, and though it had a search engine function, for that function it made use of, at various times, AltaVista's and Google's databases).

By the late-2010s, for the U.S. search marketplace, the search engine leaders were Google, Bing, and Yahoo! (in that order). Those three search engines represented 96% of all U.S. (desktop) searches.[2] (Brief profiles of the engines just mentioned are given in the following text.) Outside the United States, in terms of market size and reputation, the leaders are Baidu (China) and Yandex (Russia).

Google

Google, which emerged as a company in 1998, grew very rapidly; its growth attributed largely to the simplicity of its interface, the lack of advertisements on the home page, and the quality of its relevance ranking (that fact significantly affected by Google's patented PageRank program).[3] Google rather quickly went beyond "search" and began providing additional features and content, some of the enhancements emerging from within the Google organization and some (such as its e-mail service, Gmail) being patterned after such services already offered by its competitors. By the late 2000s, Google claimed more of the search market than all of its competitors combined and was offering a broad range of search services and a number of services not directly related to search.

For its Web search offerings, Google provides all of the typical search options (Boolean, field searching, etc.) plus some unique searching features, the latter including numeric range searching (e.g., *china history 1850..1890*). As well as the searching of Web pages, Google also offers searches of databases of images, maps, news, shopping, books (Google Books), journal articles (Google Scholar), etc. Some of these search offerings are very similar to corresponding services offered by Google's competitors, and some, such as "Google Books," were original and regarded by many as "groundbreaking." (Google Books is a major book digitalization project, in cooperation with major publishers and libraries.) The search features provided with each of these databases are typically tailored to the specific nature of that kind of content.

Many of Google's Web search features are features that were already found on other search engines, but for which Google provided significant enhancements. One example is Google Translate. Many search engines have provided a translation option that allows retrieved items from a number of non-English languages to be translated, using programs such as SYSTRAN's Babelfish. In 2007, Google enhanced its own translation feature by allowing the user not just to translate a specific result, but to input a search in the user's own language, then have Google automatically translate the search terms, perform the search, and then deliver results in both languages. Translations are done using Google's own statistical translation technology. Google Translate also epitomizes another Google characteristic, rapid changeability. By 2015, Google Translate features had been pared down and though still regarded by many as the best translation tool on the Web, the direct integration of search with translation had been greatly diminished.

As it grew, Google rather rapidly redefined itself to be much more than a "search engine," adding services that went beyond "search" and even beyond usual website content. Some services had a direct relationship to "search," such as Google News Alerts, Google's financial portal ("Google Finance"), and Google's own Web browser ("Chrome"). Some of the services Google began to offer included types of things that already existed as "portal" features in other search services. These offerings included Gmail (a Web-based e-mail service), Google Earth (imagery and related geospatial content for the entire Earth, as well as the Moon and the sky), and Google Calendar. Google Drive (formerly Google Docs) offers a collaborative spreadsheet, word processor, presentations, form generator, drawing programs and "cloud" storage.

Bing

Microsoft has made several attempts since the mid-1990s to produce a Web search engine that is competitive with Google and Yahoo!. The attempts have gone by a variety of names, including Microsoft Search, MSN Search, Windows Live, Live Search, and, most recently, Bing. Search features have varied considerably and have at times been less robust than those of its competitors. Live Search presented some innovative features such as a design that allowed continuous scrolling through search results, but it, like some other features in the MSN Search products, was short lived. The 2008 version provided the typical Boolean and field searching options, plus some additional options such as "prefer:" by which the user could adjust the ranking weight for search terms and "feed:" and "hasfeed:" that identify websites that contain RSS links on the user's chosen topic.

In 2009, MSN further enhanced its engine and renamed it as "Bing." Bing has a different look and feel than the older versions, with a main page that has the now-usual minimalist search engine interface but with a large, attractive photographic background image. Bing enhances its search results with useful "facts," gathered from selected websites. Regarding search features, Bing search features are also somewhat minimalist, with no advanced search page and very few filters. However, Bing does maintain a large number of prefix search options.

In addition to the search for Web pages, Bing also offers searches for images, video, news, and maps.

Yahoo!

Yahoo! was among the earliest websites that had the purpose of leading users to a specific content on the Web. In the beginning, Yahoo! was exclusively a "Web directory," a categorized list of selected websites. By 2000, however, it had begun a transformation to a portal site, having, in addition to the directory, over three dozen links to news, services, and other resources provided by Yahoo! and its affiliates, including pages for shopping, auctions, phone numbers, and a calendar. From its earliest days, the Yahoo! home page contained a search box, but results for that search came from a search of the directory, and later a search of Web databases from other search providers.

Yahoo!'s directory function became less and less central, and in 2004 Yahoo! created its own database of Web pages. Though emphasis on "search" continued to increase and the emphasis on the directory declined significantly, Yahoo!'s main image continued to be that of a portal, with the emphasis on the wide range of other services provided by Yahoo! and its partners, including Yahoo!'s highly popular e-mail service and its sections on autos, finance, games, groups, health, job listings, maps, real estate, travel, and over 20 other extensive content areas.

As of mid-2010, Yahoo! no longer provides a Web search technology or a Web database of its own. Yahoo!'s Web, image, and video searches were subsequently "powered by" at first by Bing. More recently, Yahoo's search technology, databases, and ads have been powered by combinations of Google, Bing, and Yahoo!s own resources.

In addition to Web search, Yahoo! offers searching of the following databases: news, video, maps, businesses, shopping, sports, and more.

Non-U.S. general search engines

At various points, a number of other search engines have appeared in various countries. Two in particular have become successful in terms of international attention, extensive usage, and longevity: Baidu and Yandex. Baidu, from the People's Republic of China, was incorporated in 2000 and is used almost exclusively within China. It provides Web, images, and video searches. It may actually be best known because throughout its history, it has been the subject of widespread and extensive reports of government censorship. Yandex, from the Russian Federation, also first appeared in 2000. It provides searches for Web pages, images, video, and maps and also offers e-mail and translation services. Interfaces are available in Russian, English, and Indonesian.

Specialty Search Engines

Over the years, a variety of search engines have appeared that could be classified as "specialty" search engines. Among these, there have been attempts to create search engines that focus on a particular topic or geographic location. In most cases, an examination of these showed that what was provided was more of a "directory" of selected sites than a broad ranging crawler-based search of Web pages for the specific topic or locality. On the other hand, there have been many successful attempts to produce search engines that provide searching for a particular format or type of document, such as images, video, blogs, and forums.

News

Searching of news databases is available from all of the general Web search engines. There are numerous other websites that specialize in searching news content. Each of these has varying degrees of searchability, and from the research perspective, it is important to note that the coverage can vary significantly, especially in regard to the number of news sources included, the time span for the content of the database, and the languages covered. Among the better-known news search engines are NewsNow, Silobreaker, and News Explorer.

Images

The most commonly encountered image search engines are those that are included within the general Web search engines, including Google, Yahoo!, and Bing. As well as subject searching, most of these engines allow for Boolean, and narrowing by size, coloration, site, and adult-content filtering. On Google's advanced image search page, you can also narrow to photos that appear to contain faces. Flickr (flicker.com), an image-sharing website, has also gained extensive popularity as an image search engine. The extensive tagging of photos by Flickr users makes millions of images searchable. Picsearch provides an extensive collection of images from the Web and, in addition to the search criteria mentioned, also allows narrowing to animated images. There are also image search engines such as Corbis, Fotosearch, and Stock. XCHNG which enable users (for a fee) to use photos from commercial photographers and photo archives.

Image searching technology has made major advances since 2010. Earlier, images were indexed for searching almost entirely based on text found near the image (captions, other text near the image, file names, etc.) Since then, the major search engines and other organizations and researchers have utilized technologies such as NLP,

entity identification, and machine learning to be able to identify specific people, places, things, and a very wide range of other characteristics of an image. Once these "entities" and other characteristics are identified, all of them can be used as search terms or selectable categories, allowing image search engines to accomplish far more precise and complete results than in earlier years.

Video

As with image searching, searching for video is available from major search engines, including Google, Yahoo!, and Bing. Extensive searching of videos produced by individuals, as well as commercial video, is available from YouTube, the leading video-sharing site. Depending upon the search engine, options are provided for searching by Boolean, language, duration, domain/site/source, format, popularity, aspect ratio, and resolution, plus filtering for adult-content. Some video search engines specialize in video from TV, including news programs and interviews. These include TV News Archive (from Internet Archive, archive.org) and TVEyes (fee based).

Forums

Content found in forums (discussion groups, groups, newsgroups, etc.) can be utilized for a number of applications, ranging from hobbies to tracking terrorist activities, and there are search engines that specialize in finding this category of document. Though at one point there were multiple engines specifically for searching forums, by 2017 the only remaining one that was well-known was BoardReader. (There are a number of other places where groups can be searched, such as Google, Yahoo!, and Delphi Forums, but those sites focus on searching only the content that is hosted on their own websites.)

Other specialty search engines

There are still other categories of specialty search engines, including those for searching podcasts (e.g., podcastdirectory.com), and for searching for information on people (e.g., pipl, Infobel, Intelius, PeopleFinders).

Visualization Engines

Visualization search engines are websites (or programs) that provide a very different "look" (literally) at search results. Instead of the traditional linear, textual list of retrieved items, results are shown on a map that spatially shows conceptual connections. Most visualization engines have not utilized a database of their own but have borrowed one from other engines (Google, Yahoo!) or other sites such as Amazon.com. Visualization has been, and continues to be, an area of extensive research, and there have been several sites for demonstrating various visualization approaches. The type of conceptual and visual mapping done by these sites can be especially useful for quickly exploring the concept possibilities, directions, and terminology for a particular search. It presents a "connect the dots" approach, enabling understanding relationships among the concepts found in various search results. Some such engines have appeared but are now gone, particularly Kartoo and Grokker. Still extant are TouchGraph and Quintura, the latter as a downloadable program. Visualization technologies are used within a number of websites, including news search engines such as SiloBreaker and EMM NewsExplorer.

Metasearch Engines

The term "metasearch engine" (or "metasearch site") usually refers to websites that search multiple search engines in a single search. The degree of overlap (or lack thereof) between search engine results is something that professional searchers frequently consider and allow for as they search, and searching more than one engine is a widely encouraged technique. Metasearch engines have been available since the 1990s and include sites such as Dogpile, and Clusty. Each of these may provide additional benefits beyond just a compilation of results from more than one engine, for example, the "clustering" (categorization) of retrieved results, a feature that may not be provided by the target engines themselves. However, users should be aware of several shortcomings that may be encountered with these tools: 1) most of the current metasearch engines have not included results the largest major engines, particularly Google and Yahoo!, which tend to block queries from metasearch engines; 2) metasearch engines typically only return the first 10–20 results from any of the "target" engines; 3) metasearch engine results often discard useful and search-relevant information found on the actual search engine's results pages; 4) metasearch sites, even if they do cover the largest engines, may be required by those engines to show paid listings first; and 5) metasearch engines typically do not allow application of many of the search features available in the target engines themselves.

CONCLUSION

Web search engines have evolved extensively since they were first introduced in the early 1990s. The basic concept has remained the same, but the quality of results, the size of their databases, and the types of material that they have included increased dramatically. The total number of general Web search engines "in the race" has decreased and at present is dominated by one service, Google. What has evolved even more dramatically is the "mission" of search services, which, particularly in the case of Google, has gone far beyond "search." With advancing technologies, increasing interactiveness of the Web, and a more and more Internet-centered society, users can expect continued, fast-paced innovation.

REFERENCES

1. Sullivan, D. How Google Measures the Authority of Web Pages. searchengineland.com/google-authority-metric-274231. Accessed May 2017.
2. Latest Rankings—Search. ComScore, Inc. www.comscore.com/Insights/Rankings. Accessed May 2017.
3. Vise, D.; Malseed, M. *The Google Story*; Bantam Dell: New York, 2005; 37–40.

Self-Publishing Online

Caryn Wesner-Early
ASRC Aerospace & Defense, US Patent & Trademark Office, Alexandria, Virginia, USA

Abstract
Over the past 10 years, self-publishing on the Internet has taken off and presents problems and opportunities for both authors and libraries. Tasks involved in self-publishing are reviewed, and current issues and future trends are discussed.

INTRODUCTION

Until the advent of the Internet, self-publishing (also known as vanity or subsidy publishing) had very little impact on the library world. Without mechanisms for marketing, reviews, and library distribution, vanity press publications were invisible to librarians and library users. Since vanity publishers required up-front payment by authors, their publications carried a stigma, and the widespread belief was that if an author could not persuade a reputable publisher to buy a book, it was not up to library standards.

In the 1980s, however, the development of desktop publishing made it possible for authors to print their works without necessarily having to go through a publisher. These efforts were often amateurish, and the available printer speeds kept production down. There were still few ways to publicize and market such a book, and the products were unattractive. Authors were beginning, though, to realize the power of self-publishing.

Since the mid-1990s, the Internet, and especially the World Wide Web, has become the medium of choice for self-publishers. Some self-publishing is informal in the extreme; according to many, if a person mounts a web page of any kind, they have self-published on the Internet.[1] Many web users post in message boards or newsgroups, contribute articles to e-newsletters, write fan fiction based on literary or television characters, or maintain "blogs" (weblogs of interesting sites), which may also be considered online self-publishing. For the purposes of this entry, however, self-publishing online will be defined somewhat more formally.

DEFINITION OF SELF-PUBLISHING ONLINE

The *Oxford Companion to the Book* defines an e-book as an electronic book (variously: e-book, eBook, e-Book, ebook, digital book, or even e-edition) is a book-length publication in digital form, consisting of text, images, or both, readable on computers or other electronic devices.[2]

Electronic publishing usually takes one of three forms: commercial, subsidy (vanity), or self-publishing.[3] Subsidy e-publishers operate as the traditional vanity press, publishing an author's work for a fee. When self-publishing, the author is responsible for all aspects of the book. Rather than a clear delineation between vanity publishing and self-publishing, there is now a continuum, from a flat fee for all services, as in traditional vanity publishing, through the author investing very little out of pocket and doing all work himself or herself. In between are myriad systems whereby authors can decide which publishing tasks to do and which to outsource to publishing services.

For the purpose of this entry, then "Self-Publishing Online" will be defined as "Electronic content that is transmitted and/or displayed on a device or system to be read by the viewer similar in experience to reading a book, with technical publication tasks performed or contracted out by the author."

TECHNOLOGIES FOR E-PUBLISHING

While online publishing can be as simple as a HTML web page, that is not the ideal format for many publications. There are a number of e-book formats vying for attention, and it is too early to tell which will become a standard. Many people believed that e-books would not become popular until they could pass the "Four B" test: ability to be carried comfortably to the beach, the bathroom, the bus, and the bedroom.[4] To this end, several portable formats are in use, many for the cell phones and tablets people already use. Some devices use unique display software, so that an e-book cannot be published in all formats simultaneously. There are also dedicated e-book readers that are often called e-books themselves; although with the rise of smartphones and tablets, they are already becoming rarer.[5] They do nothing but read e-books (rather than including web-surfing capabilities or printing) and include the Amazon Kindle (original version).

Industry organizations are at work trying to frame standards that will allow interoperability among the devices

Encyclopedia of Library and Information Sciences, Fourth Edition DOI: 10.1081/E-ELIS4-120053491

Science–Semantic

and their software. The International Digital Publishing Forum (formerly The Open eBook Forum) released version 3.0.1 of the EPUB® specification, "a distribution and interchange format standard for digital publications and documents," in October 2011.[6] It and Adobe Acrobat are the most widely used open standards for electronic publishing. EPUB can be read on many platforms, including the Sony Reader and the Barnes & Noble Nook, but in order to be used on a Kindle, files must still be converted to their proprietary format.[7] Another popular e-book platform, iBooks (for use on iPad and related readers), also has its own format.[8]

Still, eventually standards may enable a manufacturer to produce a device that will read a number of formats. There is historical precedent for this: In 1947, an industry-wide agreement allowed manufacturers of phonographs to include both 33 and 45 rpm speeds on their turntables, making possible the huge popularity of phonograph records in the 1950s and 1960s.[9]

A variation on electronic publishing is print on demand (POD), which allows books to be stored electronically but printed in book form when a reader wants one. This service is offered by many electronic publishers and favored by some authors. Like pure electronic publication, POD does not require large sales volume in order to be profitable. There is also interest in using it to bring back out-of-print titles for which rights have reverted to the author.[10] POD can be offered as a choice along with electronic means of publication for e-books.[11]

TECHNICAL PUBLICATION TASKS

There is a wide variety of tasks that have been traditionally performed by publishers but are now being done by authors who self-publish. Some of these tasks are the same as they have always been (e.g., editing and design of cover art), while some are peculiar to e-publishing (such as converting files to e-book formats and setting up a website for the publication). The more of these tasks that the author elects to perform, the more control the author will have, but the more labor-intensive the project will be. Many authors find that a hybrid approach, contracting out some tasks and performing others, works well. Tasks that must be performed, either by the author or by a publisher or publishing service, include[12]

- *Editing*: Most authors have trouble changing their work, so this task is often outsourced to a professional editor.
- *Layout and design*: For most text-only books, this can be done using a computer, by either the author or a professional design service. If the book is very visual, however (e.g., an art book), this may be done largely by the author.

- *File conversion*: It is necessary to convert the file format to forms that are readable by the various e-book devices discussed earlier.
- *Web presence*: In order for something to be published online, it must have an online presence; in most cases, a web page. A web host must be found and contracted for, a URL must be decided on and purchased, a website must be designed, and then the site must be maintained to make sure it does not go out of date. Even if the book is published in a portable e-book reader format, there must still be a web page from which purchasers can download it.
- *Cover illustration*: Many authors new to online publishing do not realize that a cover is still important, even for an electronic publication. The web is a visual medium, and customers are likely to pay more attention to a well-designed cover than to a plain title listing.[13]
- *International Standard Book Number* (*ISBN*): If the author wishes to list the e-book in *Books in Print*, *Forthcoming Books*, and other such directories, or to distribute it through online bookstores, an ISBN is necessary. ISBNs can be bought individually, or in blocks of ten or 100. A different ISBN is needed for each format, so if the author expects to create several different versions of the book (for instance, more than one electronic format), purchasing ten or more would be most economical.[14]
- *Publicity, marketing, and listing with online bookstores*: A book must be promoted to its prospective audience, or there will be no customers. Websites that attract the people who would be interested in the book must be contacted with offers of a free review copy or an entry for the site.[15] Reviews, interviews, radio or television appearances, and other publicity events must be planned. If the author wishes to distribute the work through online bookstores, listing must be arranged with the bookstores.

A new method of publicity and marketing is being pioneered by author Seth Godin, among others. Instead of writing the book and then marketing it, Godin builds what he calls "tribes" via his website and blog, then funds it with a Kickstarter campaign.[16] This has the advantage of investing his readers in the book before publication, so that they already know what they're going to get when they buy it, and are eager to read it. This requires intensive effort on the part of the author, though, to build the emotional connection with readers that will make them want to be a part of the enterprise.

- *Sales and order processing*: There are a number of models for pricing and collecting payment. If payment is to be received via credit cards, a merchant account must be set up, either directly through a bank or indirectly through merchant account providers.[17] Once payment is arranged, one method of delivering e-books is to load a few entries onto the web for customers to read for free, then charge for the rest. The balance of the book can also be on the web, but under password protection; the file can be transferred to the buyer's computer/reader; or it can be downloaded to disk or printed.[18] Some sites that host self-published works will also keep track of the number of times an item is downloaded and pay the author a certain amount of money per download. Another part of the transaction can be the collection of information from customers so that future e-books can be marketed to them. An e-mail address is particularly important for reaching customers with news.[19]

- *Copyright*: It is no secret that copyright of materials on the Internet is a thorny problem. Technically, anything published, whether in print or on the Internet, is considered copyrighted as of publication.[20] However, enforcing a copyright is often more difficult and is the province of digital rights management (DRM). Usually, people speak of "A" copyright, but it is legally "generally considered to be a bundle of legal rights that accompany the physical creative product... [and] which can be assigned or retained in whole or in part."[21] Rights under copyright include film rights, serial rights, foreign publishing rights, and more.

- *Security and DRM*: Since it is extremely easy for anyone to download an item from the Internet, and to plagiarize it or quote it out of context,[22] DRM is an important consideration for electronic publications. DRM has been defined as "effective rights management and protection of digital content across the entire value chain - from creators [and] distributors to customers."[23] Its purpose is to enforce copyright while maintaining as much interoperability as possible among different e-publishing systems. Opinions differ as to how much of a problem e-book piracy is. On the one hand, there are websites that deal in pirated e-books [24] and may be losing publishers and authors' untold amounts of money. On the other hand, DRM may not actually be preventing piracy, instead causing a loss of goodwill on the part of the customers.[25] Publisher's Weekly discovered that it is actually a sales-killer, harming sales "at any price point."[26] Whether or not to use it is one of the decisions which an author must make.

- *Print on Demand fulfillment, if desired*: The author may not wish to provide access to the e-book via POD, but if it is desired, a method for high-speed printing, as well as shipping the physical item, must be considered.

- *Metadata, if desired*: In early 2000, Guidelines for ONline Information eXchange (ONIX) were published by the Association of American Publishers establishing a set of over 200 elements that will describe every aspect of a book in detail. (The current edition of these guidelines is ONIX 3.0, published in April 2009)[27] These elements, tagged for the Internet using eXtensible Markup Language (XML), are searchable online, providing more ways of discovering or finding e-books. Many of the elements are the kinds of information often found on the book jacket of a printed book, such as an author biography or an excerpt, as well as "kernel" data such as author, title, and ISBN. This can increase sales of an e-book as much as eight times those of an e-book without this metadata.[28]

SELF-PUBLISHING USING A PUBLISHER OR E-PUBLISHING SERVICE

Electronic self-publishing can be done in a way that is close to the old vanity press model. The author can negotiate a contract, pay a fee, and submit a manuscript for publication. However, instead of clear delineation between self-publishing and vanity publishing, it can be seen that there is a continuum from total self-publishing, through contracting some or all of the services above, to actual vanity or subsidy publishing. E-publishing services can do any or all of the tasks listed above for set fees.[29] The Internet has made the demarcation between publishers and publishing services, like many others, more vague. Publishers may even, in the words of Barnes and Noble's Steve Riggio, "become ... unnecessary [middlemen] in the distribution of electronic content...."[30] An alternative to this is that publishers may "change from being producers of commodities (books) to being creators of a suite of content-based services"[31]—in other words, publishing services.

A new profession has arisen to help with any or all of the tasks mentioned earlier but in a more personal way than a traditional publisher might. It goes by a variety of titles, including book shepherd, book coach, publishing strategist,[32] book consultant, book coach, book doctor, book midwife, book birther, and more.[33] A book shepherd can help with everything from determining the potential audience and creating platforms, through connecting the author with printers, agents, and other team members, to making sure everything works smoothly throughout the project.[34] Like the role of the author itself, the role of the book shepherd is fluid, depending on what the author needs and what kind of budget is available.

PROS AND CONS OF SELF-PUBLISHING ONLINE

There are many advantages to self-publishing online, as opposed to more traditional publishing methods.

One of the most obvious reasons is to make more money per copy. Rather than the 6%–10% of the sale price in royalties that traditional printed books bring in, self-published books can pay 35%,[35] and with far less overhead for print costs and the like, electronically self-published books could pay even more. The profit margin on electronic publishing is much higher than on traditional publishing; low costs for manufacturing and distribution mean that it may take only a few hundred books to make a profit.[36] The advantages of speed and full author control are also appealing.[37]

Noncommercial works, such as "novella"-length fiction, can be published electronically with more success than by traditional means. One of the earliest self-e-publishing projects, Stephen King's "The Plant," was of this length. Publication of that story was halted before it was finished because the honor-system pay arrangement did not work, with fewer than half of the downloads paid for.[38] Newer funding processes are being worked out now, many using social media or crowdfunding sites such as Kickstarter. Seth Godin may be one of the best-known self-publishers and has used the Kickstarter model, in which the author builds interest and gathers seed money before publishing the work.[39]

"Niche" publications, which appeal to a sufficiently narrow audience that sales are not expected to be large, can also benefit from this model, as can crossover books which span more than one genre (e.g., such as a science-fiction mystery).[40]

Authors whose works have previously been published traditionally but have gone out of print are using online self-publishing to bring back out-of-print books. When a traditional book goes out of print, rights revert to the author, and authors whose books have become popular several years after publication (because of a movie, for instance) find that they can make new profit by publishing them on their own, on the Internet.[41,42] Some authors may prefer to self-publish online so that they never lose their copyright at all.[43] Authors may also be able to serialize long works, as was frequently done through magazines in the nineteenth and twentieth centuries.[44]

Electronic publishing also offers quick, easy updating of information that changes frequently, as well as interactivity and the convenience of hyperlinks to other parts of the same publication or others on the web.[45]

There are, however, many disadvantages to this publishing model as well. One is the lack of standards; now that anyone can publish, there will inevitably be many substandard publications. Walt Crawford, of the Research Libraries Group, quotes Sturgeon's Law: "90 percent of everything is crap." It is possible that, without standards or gatekeepers, the bad books will crowd out the good ones.[46] Also, good publications may have no credibility because they have not been subjected to the editorial and critical review that has been the norm.[47]

Production values are often amateurish, since authors are not accustomed to performing the technical tasks of publishing an e-book. Similar problems arise with promotion, marketing, and distribution.[48] In fact, MightyWords.com, a company that worked with authors to publish books electronically, discontinued many of their self-publishing efforts because "As a company, we can't do a perfect job promoting self-published titles... the authors didn't do enough to participate in the process of marketing and promoting their titles themselves."[49] (In 2001, MightyWords closed down, citing insufficient demand for virtual content.[50]) Unless a book is publicized and marketed, it can hardly be considered to have been published at all.

Copyright, as noted earlier, also presents unique challenges to electronic publications. DRM is becoming big business; according to the Dutch firm GfK, "only 10% of all eBooks on devices were actually paid for, with most of the digital books being pirated."[51] Since there is a widespread perception that anything on the Internet is free for the taking, anyone can change and/or repost electronically published material, and finding, proving, and prosecuting such misuse is, so far, very difficult.[52] The lack of standards and interoperability of e-book devices, mentioned earlier, also contributes to the difficulty of reading and publishing electronically. Archiving of electronic content, with the related problem of the ability of the actual owner of the work (not the person or institution leasing it) to change content in e-books previously "bought," presents very serious ethical considerations for both individuals and libraries.[53]

IMPACT OF SELF-PUBLISHING ONLINE ON LIBRARIES AND LIBRARIANS

The impact of electronic publishing in general has been felt in libraries for some years now. Librarians are already dealing with problems of cataloging and bibliographic control, contracts for multiple users, and devices and formats. Adding virtual publications to library collections, monitoring use by library patrons, and deciding on which readers and software to invest in will occupy librarians for years to come. Electronic publishers can help librarians in this by making sure the metadata on their publications conforms to a standard such as ONIX, described earlier, or the Dublin Core (a separate metadata system being developed by librarians).[54]

Libraries are now "buying" (actually, leasing) more and more e-books, as patrons with reading devices demand them.[55] The problems of dealing with publisher limits on a number of loans and ridiculously high costs for libraries' (as opposed to individuals') downloads of e-books are well known in the library field.[56] There are a number of distributors, such as OverDrive and Freading, but they can cause new problems, with different requirements for libraries and readers making the borrowing experience more complicated than it is with paper books.[57] These are problems whether the e-books are self-published or not. Offering self-published books can bring additional concerns.

Science-Semantic

One of the big problems with offering self-published books, whether electronic or not, has been the difficulty of finding reviews, but with new sources of reviews available, this may not have as much influence as previously.[58–60] Even such heavyweights as Kirkus Reviews and Publishers Weekly, through their programs Kirkus Discoveries and PW Select, have begun reviewing self-published works.[61] Another problem has been that the large distributors (such as Overdrive) have not handled self-published books, but that is also starting to change. In May, 2014, Overdrive and Smashwords, one of the largest self-publishing platforms, made a deal to offer Smashwords books to libraries via Overdrive.[62] Some of the walls are beginning to come down, and libraries will almost certainly be able to offer more and more self-published e-books in the future.

But checking self-published e-books out to patrons is not the only way libraries are interacting with them. Libraries may become centers for authors who wish to publish electronically. Mark Coker, owner of e-publishing platform Smashwords, has developed a series of seminars for libraries to use to help their own users become self-publishing authors,[63] and has worked with libraries to organize contests for electronic authors,[64] offering the prize of Smashwords' help in publishing their books. An exciting opportunity for librarians in online self-publishing is the ability for libraries to publish their own resources on the web. Many librarians already count web publishing as part of their jobs, as libraries publish their own unique bibliographies and other home-grown resources to the world via the web.[65] Thus, items that have been relatively inaccessible to anyone outside the immediate library community can become accessible to a broad audience.

FUTURE TRENDS

As electronic self-publishers become more successful, traditional publishers are moving into this new area in order to preserve their leadership. For instance, Penguin Books purchased a self-publishing platform called Author Solutions in 2012,[66] German publishing group Verlagsgruppe Georg von Holtzbrinck now owns self-publishing platform epubli,[67] and Simon & Schuster has its own self-publishing platform, Archway Publishing.[68] However, some data suggests that this may not be working for them: major publishers charge more per book than self-publishers, but tend to get lower reader reviews. They are also losing ground quickly, with major publishers selling almost the same number of units as self-publishers (based on Amazon sales of "top five" publishers' e-books).[69] There are several areas in which electronically published books (whether self-published or put out by more traditional publishers) are expected to grow quickly. Quoting a Bowker report, Francine Fialkoff says that most self-

publishers polled "plan to bring fiction to market, followed by inspirational or spiritual works, books for children, and biographies."[70]

New technologies are also expected to have an effect on online publishing. Electronic ink is a new digital paper substitute. Display screens are already 30% lighter and thinner than LCDs, and the goal is to make them thin enough to be rolled or folded like paper.[71] But even with current readers, a person can carry one book, the text of which can be changed or updated at will wirelessly.[72] The ethical considerations alone of such an innovation are dizzying.

CONCLUSION

After a decade or so of very little growth, self-publishing on the web has exploded since the introduction of convenient readers and tablets like Kindle and Nook,[73] which pass the "Four Bs": ability to be carried comfortably to the beach, the bathroom, the bus, and the bedroom. People are reading more e-books, and a surprising number of them are self-published. This field is even more volatile than the Internet upon which it depends, and changes will be happening dynamically for the foreseeable future.

REFERENCES

1. NetLingo definition of Electronic Publishing. http://www.netlingo.com/right.cfm?term=electronic%20publishing (accessed Nov 13, 2014).
2. Gardiner, E.; Musto, R.G. The electronic book. *The Oxford Companion to the Book*; Suarez, M.F., Woudhuysen, H.R., Eds.; Oxford University Press: Oxford, U.K., 2010; 164 (quoted in Wikipedia entry "E-book," accessed Nov 17, 2014).
3. Palmer, P. The e-book revolution: Self-publishing goes high-tech. Black Enterprise **2001**, *31* (9), 49–50.
4. Pack, T. E-publishing: Revolution or virtual vanity press. EContent **2000**, *23* (2), 52–56. [Web of Science (r)], [CSA].
5. Tablets Gain on Dedicated E-Readers, Says New BISG Study: Kindle Fire users read, while iPad users surf the Web and catch up on e-mail (Press release for BISG's Consumer Attitudes Toward E-Book Reading survey 2012) http://www.bowker.com/en-US/aboutus/press_room/2012/pr_11142012.shtml (accessed Nov 17, 2014).
6. EPUB 3 Overview. http://www.idpf.org/epub/301/spec/epub-overview.html (accessed Nov 17, 2014).
7. The Publication Standards Project. The Publication Standards Project: Learn. Web. http://pubstandards.org/learn.html (accessed Nov 23, 2014).
8. Webb, J.; McCoy, B.The Give and Take between E-publishing Standards and Innovation. O'Reilly TOC: Tools of Change for Publishing. O'Reilly Media, Inc.,

March 20, 2012. [http://cdn.oreillystatic.com/en/assets/1/event/73/KF8 and iBooks Author_ Up and Running Presentation.pdf] (accessed Nov 23, 2014).

9. Hilts The wait for an E-book format. Pub. Wkly. **2000**, *274* (45), 55–56.

10. Costello, M.WarrenAdler.com, digital D.I.Y: Author W. Adler sells his own books in electronic format via his website. Publ. Wkly. **2001**, *248* (23), 31.

11. Costello, M. POD, E-books drive great unpublished. Publ. Wkly. **2001**, *248* (33), 29.

12. Van Buren, C.; Cogswell, J. *Getting your E-book published and sold. Poor Richard's Creating E-Books: How Authors, Publishers, and Corporations Get into Digital Print*; Top Floor Publishing: Lakewood, CO, 2001; 115–118.

13. Adair-Hoy, A. How to create an E-book. *How to Publish and Promote Online*; Rose, M.J.; Adair-Hoy, A., Eds.; Martin's Griffin : New York, 200114.

14. Bowker Identifier services. https://www.myidentifiers.com/ (accessed Nov 30, 2014).

15. Adair-Hoy, A. People won't read your book if you don't market it. *How to Publish and Promote Online*; Rose, M.J.; Adair-Hoy, A., Eds.; Martin's Griffin: New York, 2001; 108.

16. Schawbel, D. Seth Godin used Kickstarter to fund his next book raising over $130,000. Forbes. *Forbes Magazine*, June 8, 2012. http://www.forbes.com/sites/dans chawbel/2012/06/18/seth-godin-uses-kickstarter-to-fund-his-next-book/ (accessed Dec 7, 2014).

17. Adair-Hoy, A. People won't read your book if you don't market it. *How to Publish and Promote Online*; Rose, M.J.; Adair-Hoy, A., Eds.; Martin's Griffin: New York, 2001; 31.

18. Ibid.

19. Rosenborg, V. *Distributing your eBook*; ePublishing for Dummies; IDG Books Worldwide, Inc.: Foster City, CA, 2001; 236.

20. Pike, G.H. A book is a book is E-book. Info. Today **2001**, *18* (7), 19.

21. Ibid.

22. Sowards, S.W. Novas, Niches, and Icebergs: Practical lessons for small-scale web publishers. J. Electr. Publ. **1995**, *5*(2), http://quod.lib.umich.edu/j/jep/3336451.0005.201/–novas-niches-and-icebergs-practical-lessons-for-small-scale?rgn=main;view=fulltext;q1=novas+niches (accessed Nov 11, 2014).

23. Gandee, B. XrML: The language for digital rights management. In *Technology Day 2001: A Knowledge Odyssey October*. Laurel, MD, October 15, 2001.

24. Kozlowski, M.Ebook piracy becomes a top concern. Good Ereader Digital and Ebook Publishing News RSS. Sept 22, 2014. http//goodereader.com/blog/e-book-news/ebook-piracy-becomes-a-top-concern. (accessed November 30, 2014).

25. Pogue, D.The E-Book Piracy Debate, Revisited. Pogues Posts. *The New York Times*, May 9, 2013. http://pogue.blogs.nytimes.com/2013/05/09/the-e-book-piracy-debate-revisited/ (accessed December 14, 2014).

26. Sargent, B.K. Surprising self-publishing statistics. PublishersWeekly.com. *Publisher's Weekly*, July 28, 2014. http://www.publishersweekly.com/pw/by-topic/authors/pw-select/article/63455-surprising-self-publishing-statistics.html (accessed December 14, 2014).

27. About Release 3.0. ONYX. EDItEUR, April 1, 2009. http://www.editeur.org/12/About-Release-3.0/ (accessed Nov 30, 2014).

28. Hilts, P. AAP unveils E-retail guidelines. Publ. Wkly. **2000**, *247* (4), 170.

29. Hane, P.J. E-publishing competition heats up: Recent developments have squeezed traditional publishers. Info. Today **2001**, *18*(2), http://www.infotoday.com/IT/feb01/hane2.htm (accessed Nov 13, 2014).

30. Lichtenberg, J. What can publishers learn from librarians? Publ. Wkly. **2001**, *248* (12), 17.

31. Poynter, D. Your publishing options: Why you should consider self-publishing. In *The Self-Publishing Manual: How to Write, Print and Sell Your Own Book*, 9th Ed.; Para Publishing: Santa Barbara, CA, 1996; 27.

32. King, J. What Is the Work of a Book Coach or Book Shepherd? Book Publishing Inspirations and Explanations. Jan B. King, Mar 4, 2010.http://janbking.wordpress.com/2013/03/17/what-is-the-work-of-a-book-coach-or-book-shepherd/ (accessed Dec 7, 2014).

33. Alexander, L. An Author's Guide to Book Birthers, Book Shepherds and Other Consultants. The Book Designer RSS. Joel Friedlander, July 20, 2011. http://www.thebookdesigner.com/2011/07/an-authors-guide-to-book-birthers-book-shepherds-and-other-consultants/ (accessed Dec 7, 2014).

34. Briles, J. How Book Shepherding Works. The Book Shepherd. The Book Shepherd, Nov 27, 2013. http://thebookshepherd.com/judith-services/how-book-shepherding-works.html (accessed Dec 7, 2014).

35. Curtis, R. The flight to quantity. Publ. Wkly. **2000**, *247* (42), 26.

36. Jensen, M. The appropriateness matrix (sidebar to cost recovery and destiny). J. Electr. Publ. **1998**, *4*(1), http://quod.lib.umich.edu/j/jep/3336451.0004.101/–cost-recovery-and-destiny-developing-the-appropriateness?rgn=main;view=fulltext;q1=appropriateness+matrix (accessed November 13, 2014).

37. McCrary, V.R. Convergent technologies: E-Books. In *Technology Day 2001: A Knowledge Odyssey*. Laurel, MD, October 15, 2001.

38. Rosenborg, V. *Working with an ePublisher*; ePublishing for Dummies; IDG Books Worldwide, Inc.: Foster City, CA, 2001; 262.

39. Schawbel, D. Seth Godin Used Kickstarter to Fund His Next Book Raising Over $130,000. Forbes. Forbes Magazine, Jun 8, 2012. http://www.forbes.com/sites/danschawbel/2012/06/18/seth-godin-uses-kickstarter-to-fund-his-next-book/ (accessed Dec 7, 2014).

40. Pack, T. E-Publishing: Revolution or virtual vanity press. EContent **2000**, *2*, 52–56.

41. Costello, M.WarrenAdler.com, digital D.I.Y: Author W. Adler sells his own books in electronic format via his website. Publ. Wkly. **2001**, *248* (23), 31.

42. Ortman, M. Five reasons to self-publish. In *A Simple Guide to Self-Publishing: A Step-by-Step Handbook to Prepare, Print, Distribute & Promote Your Own Book*, 3rd Ed.; Wise Owl Books: Bellingham, WA, 2000; 8.

43. Pack, T. E-Publishing: Revolution or virtual vanity press. EContent **2000**, *23* (2), 52–56.

44. Day, R.A. The Internet and the world wide web. *How to Write and Publish a Scientific Paper*, 5th Ed.; Oryx Press: Phoenix, AZ, 1998; 148–149.

45. Pack, T. E-Publishing: Revolution or virtual vanity press. EContent **2000**, *23* (2), 52–56.

46. Crawford, W. Universal self-publishing. In *Being Analog: Creating Tomorrow's Libraries*. American Library Association: Chicago, IL, 1999; 158–159. http://www.netLibrary. com/ebook_info.asp?product_id=45140&piclist=22188 (accessed Jun 28, 2007) (subscription to NetLibrary required for access).

47. Day, R.A. The Internet and the world wide web. *How to Write and Publish a Scientific Paper*, 5th Ed.; Oryx Press: Phoenix, AZ, 1998; 148–149.

48. Jensen, M. The appropriateness matrix (sidebar to cost recovery and destiny). J. Electr. Publ. **1998**, *4*(1), http:// quod.lib.umich.edu/j/jep/3336451.0004.101/–cost-recovery-and-destiny-developing-the-appropriateness?rgn=main;view= fulltext;q1=appropriateness+matrix (accessed Dec 10, 2014).

49. Pack, T. E-Publishing: Revolution or virtual vanity press. EContent **2000**, *23* (2), 52–56.

50. Nawotka, E. MightyWords closes down: Little demand for digitally delivered content cited as reason for shutdown. Publ. Wkly. **Dec 17, 2001**, *248* (51), http://www. publishersweekly.com/pw/print/20011217/31524-mighty words-closes-down.html (accessed Dec 10, 2014).

51. Kozlowski, M. EBook Piracy Becomes a Top Concern. Good EReader EBook and Digital Publishing News RSS. 22 Sept. 2014. http://goodereader.com/blog/e-book-news/ ebook-piracy-becomes-a-top-concern (accessed Nov 30, 2014).

52. Losowsky, A. Library.nu, Book Downloading Site, Targeted in injunctions requested by 17 Publishers. The Huffington Post. TheHuffingtonPost.com, 15 Feb. 2012. http://www. huffingtonpost.com/2012/02/15/librarynu-book-downloading-injunction_n_1280383.html (accessed Dec 10, 2014).

53. Hamaker, C. Ebooks on fire: Controversies surrounding Ebooks in libraries. SEARCHER Magazine Info Today. http://www.infotoday.com/searcher/dec11/Hamaker.shtml (accessed Dec 10, 2014).

54. Jantz, R.C. Providing access to unique information sources: A reusable platform for publishing bibliographic databases on the Web. Libr. Hi Tech. **2000**, *18* (1), 28–36.

55. Vaccaro, A. Why it's difficult for your Library to Stock Ebooks. Boston.com. Boston Globe Media Partners, LLC, 27 June 2014. http://www.boston.com/business/technology/ 2014/06/27/why-difficult-for-your-library-stock-ebooks/rrl4 64TPxDaYmDnJewOmzH/story.html (accessed Dec 10, 2014).

56. Brodsky, A. The Abomination of Ebooks: They Price People Out of Reading | WIRED. Wired.com. Conde Nast Digital, September 30, 2013. http://www.wired.com/ 2013/10/how-ebook-pricing-hurts-us-in-more-ways-than-you-think/(accessed Dec 10, 2014).

57. Ellis, J.; Cook, K. Building a Community of Readers: Social Reading and an Aggregated EBook Reading App for Libraries. Building a Community of Readers. In the Library with a Lead Pipe, March 20, 2013 Web. http:// www.inthelibrarywiththeleadpipe.org/2013/building-a-community-of-readers-social-reading-and-an-aggregated-ebook-reading-app-for-libraries/ (accessed Dec 10, 2014).

58. Sclf-Publishing Review Professional Book Reviews, Editing Services. Self-publishing review. http://www. selfpublishingreview.com/ (accessed Dec 10, 2014).

59. Library Journal Launches Self-Publishing Partnership with BiblioBoard [news]. *School Library Journal*. New York: Media Source, May 21, 2014. http://www.slj.com/2014/05/ books-media/ebooks/library-journal-launches-self-publishing-partnership-with-biblioboard/#_ (accessed Dec 10, 2014).

60. Vinjamuri, D. Publishing is broken, We're drowning In Indie Books—And that's a good thing forbes. *Forbes Magazine*. August 15, 2012. http://www.forbes. com/sites/davidvinjamuri/2012/08/15/publishing-is-broken-were-drowning-in-indie-books-and-thats-a-good-thing/6/ (accessed Dec 14, 2014).

61. Bradley, J.; Bruce, F.; Marlene, H.; Katherine, A.P. *Non-Traditional Book Publishing: First Monday:Peer-Reviewed Journal on the Internet*; University of Illinois at Chicago University Library: Chicago, IL, Aug 1, 2011. http://firstmonday.org/ojs/index.php/fm/article/view/3353/ 3030#p7 (accessed Dec 12, 2014).

62. OverDrive and smashwords ink deal to distribute Indie Author Ebooks to Libraries [Press Release]. In Digital Book World; FW Media: New York, May 20, 2014. http://www. digitalbookworld.com/2014/overdrive-and-smashwords-ink-deal-to-distribute-indie-author-ebooks-to-libraries/ (accessed Dec 10, 2014).

63. Coker, M. Libraries to become community publishing portals. *The Huffington Post*. TheHuffingtonPost.com, Mar 28, 2013. http://www.huffingtonpost.com/mark-coker/library-ebooks_b_2951953.html (accessed Dec 10, 2014).

64. Catalano, F. *How the Seattle Public Library is Helping Authors Overcome the Internet's Big Lie*; GeekWire: Seattle, WA, August 3, 2014. http://www.geekwire.com/2014/seattle-public-library-internet/ (accessed December 10, 2014).

65. Results for 'au:library' [WorldCat.org]. "Results for 'au: library' [WorldCat.org]. WorldCat. https://www.worldcat. org/search?q=au:library&fq=x0:book + x4:digital&qt=advanced&dblist=638 (accessed Dec 10, 2014).

66. Greenfield, J. Penguin buys self-publishing platform Author solutions for $116 Million. In *Digital Book World*. New York:F W Media, July 19, 2012. http://www. digitalbookworld.com/2012/penguin-buys-self-publishing-platform-author-solutions-for-116-million/ (accessed Dec 12, 2014).

67. Global Publishing Leaders 2014: Holtzbrinck. Publishers Weekly. Publisher's Weekly, June 27, 2014. http://www. publishersweekly.com/pw/by-topic/industry-news/publisher-news/article/63083-global-publishing-leaders-2014-holtz brinck.html(accessed Dec 12, 2014).

68. Archway Publishing, Self-Publishing Company from Simon & Schuster. Simon & Schuster, 2014. http://www. archwaypublishing.com/Default.aspx (accessed Dec 14, 2014).

69. Howery, H. The 7k Report. Author Earnings. Hugh Howey, February 12, 2014. http://authorearnings.com/report/the-report/ (accessed Dec 14, 2014).

70. Fialkoff, F. Self-publishing Skyrockets|PubCrawl. Libr. J. Nov 22, 2013. http://lj.libraryjournal.com/2013/11/publishing/ pubcrawl/self-publishing-skyrockets-pubcrawl/#_ (accessed Dec 14, 2014).

71. Flexible Displays. E Ink: Technology: E Ink Holdings, Inc. 2014. http://www.eink.com/flexible.html (accessed Dec 14, 2014).

72. Fisher, K. Why Amazon Went Big Brother on Some Kindle E-books. Ars Technica. Conde Nast, July 17, 2009. http://arstechnica.com/gadgets/2009/07/amazon-sold-pirated-books-raided-some-kindles/ (accessed Dec 14, 2014).

73. Finder, A. The joys and hazards of self-publishing on the web. *The New York Times*. Aug 15, 2012. http://www.nytimes.com/2012/08/16/technology/personaltech/ins-and-outs-of-publishing-your-book-via-the-web.html?pagewanted=all&_r=0 (accessed Dec 14, 2014).

Science-Semantic

Semantic Interoperability

Marcia Lei Zeng
School of Library and Information Science, Kent State University, Kent, Ohio, U.S.A.

Lois Mai Chan
School of Library and Information Science, University of Kentucky, Lexington, Kentucky, U.S.A.

Abstract

This entry discusses the importance of semantic interoperability in the networked environment, introduces various approaches contributing to semantic interoperability, and summarizes different methodologies used in current projects that are focused on achieving semantic interoperability. It is intended to inform readers about the fundamentals and mechanisms that have been experimented with, or implemented, that strive to ensure and achieve semantic interoperability in the current networked environment.

INTRODUCTION

Semantic interoperability, which is defined as the ability of different agents, services, and applications to communicate (in the form of transfer, exchange, transformation, mediation, migration, integration, etc.) data, information, and knowledge—while ensuring accuracy and preserving the meaning of that same data, information, and knowledge—is central to the effective management, sharing, and retrieval of information in an open environment. Within the spectrum of different perspectives on interoperability, semantic interoperability lies at the heart of all matters. It deals with the language and vocabulary used in communication (human and machine) and facilitates information retrieval and resource sharing by users through whatever language or vocabulary they choose to use (often across language and cultural barriers). This entry is intended to inform readers about the fundamentals and mechanisms that have been experimented upon, or implemented, that strive to ensure and achieve semantic interoperability in the current networked environment.

Related standards such as the Resource Description Framework (RDF),[1] RDF Schema,[2] Web Ontology Language (OWL),[3] and Simple Knowledge Organization Systems (SKOS),[4] developed under the auspices of the World Wide Web Consortium (W3C), and the theoretical basis of semantics, are not discussed in detail here; these topics are covered in separate entries elsewhere.

SEMANTIC CONFLICTS AND AGREEMENTS

The ability to exchange services and data with and among components of large-scale distributed systems is contingent on agreements between requesters and providers. Those agreements may be based on e.g., message-passing protocols, procedure names, error codes, and argument types. This means that these exchanges must make sense—that the requester and the provider have a common understanding of the meanings of the requested services and data.[5] When multiple pieces of information are being exchanged, however, correct interpretation of some or all fractions of that information may be considered either partially or perfectly interoperable semantically.

We shall consider the example of the sequence "071210," which can be literally transferred from one system to another; however, its meaning may be interpreted in any number of different ways. We might ask:

1. Is it a string or an integer?
2. If it is a string, does it represent a date, a phone number, an area code, or a hexadecimal number representing a color?
3. If it specifies a date, what date is it: a person's birth date, a publication's issuing date, or an archaeological site's discovery date?
4. If it represents a date associated with a historical monument, what date is it indicating: the creation date, the restoration date, or the alteration date?
5. If "071210" represents a date in the twentieth century, which format does it represent: yy-mm-dd (i.e., 1907, December 10), mm-dd-yy (i.e., July 12, 1910), mm-yy-dd (i.e., July 1912, 10), or dd-mm-yy (i.e., 07 December, 1910)?
6. If information about *start-time* and *duration* is provided in a system, will the values be equal to the *earliest-date* and *latest-date* (derived by adding duration to the start-time) that are modeled on another system?
7. If "1912" is the value of a year in a system, how could this be mapped to the terms representing the same time period but from different perspectives? For example, in a Dublin Core (DC) record, this value associated with *dc.coverage* could be "Republic of

Encyclopedia of Library and Information Sciences, Fourth Edition DOI: 10.1081/E-ELIS4-120043711

China 1st Year (民国元年),"[6] or in a MAchine-Readable Cataloging (MARC) record, in field 260, it could appear as "min kuo 1 [1912]."

8. If the value of the year "1912" from one system is to be mapped to a value defined by another system, how should the non-one-to-one correlation be reconciled? For example, when applying the Library of Congress Subject Headings (LCSH) in subject-related fields in many metadata records, the closest match to "1912" might be a longer time period (e.g., "Nineteen Tens"), especially in the context of historical events, e.g., "Qing dynasty, 1644–1912" or "United States—History—1865–1921."

9. If a system was designed to generate a second value from a value, e.g., "date < 1920," which should result in the corresponding value "class = unclassified" (in terms of document release status), will another system be able to interpret the aggregated value?

Indeed, the number could represent almost any of millions of types of quantitative measure, and the strings could be mapped to constructed expressions in many different systems. Questions such as those above illustrate just some of the many possible *semantic conflicts*.

Interpretation of the meanings carried by the string depends strictly on the circumstances of transmission according to the *agreements* among systems. One study[7] states that the goal of interoperability is to build coherent services for users from components that are technically different and managed by different organizations. This requires cooperative agreements at three levels:

• Technical agreements cover, among other things: formats, protocols, and security systems so that messages can be exchanged.
• Content agreements cover data and metadata and include semantic agreements on the interpretation of information.
• Organizational agreements cover group rules for access, preservation of collections and services, payment, authentication, and so on.

Semantic agreements require the involvement of people (users, designers, and developers) who associate semantics with data structure, data content, and data values. The impact could be at any of the implementation levels such as procedure names, type definitions and type hierarchies, screen layouts, and report formats (e.g., titles, column and row headings, dates, units of measures, sort order, or footnotes). These and many other types of semantic information might be *implicit* in application codes, in diagrams, and in the local "oral tradition."[5]

Experience has shown that interoperability through comprehensive standardization is hard to achieve.[7] There is a need to maximize the amount of semantics that can be utilized and to make it increasingly *explicit*.[8] Making

semantics explicit in metadata would allow people to detect mismatched assumptions and to create the required mappings to overcome them, despite the still extraordinary difficulties.[5]

DIMENSIONS OF INTEROPERABILITY

There have been many attempts at defining the concept of *interoperability*. Stressing a result-oriented definition, *Understanding Metadata* states that "[i]nteroperability is the ability of multiple systems with different hardware and software platforms, data structures, and interfaces to exchange data with minimal loss of content and functionality."[9] Other groups emphasize a process-oriented definition: "Interoperability is the ability of two or more systems or components to exchange information and use the exchanged information without special effort on either system"[10] "Interoperability: The compatibility of two or more systems such that they can exchange information and data and can use the exchanged information and data without any special manipulation."[11]

It should be apparent that merely having the ability of two or more systems or components to exchange data does not ensure correct interpretation of an integer or string. Interoperability issues must be addressed not only at the syntactic and functional levels, but also at the semantic level.[12] Without *syntactic interoperability*, data and information cannot be handled properly with regard to formats, encodings, properties, values, and data types; and therefore, they can neither be merged nor exchanged. Without *semantic interoperability*, the meaning of the language, terminology, and metadata values used cannot be negotiated or correctly understood.[13] Varying degrees of semantic expressivity can be matched with different levels of interoperability: low at syntactic interoperability, medium at structural interoperability, and high/very high at semantic interoperability.[14]

Ouksel and Sheth[15] identify four types of heterogeneity which correspond to four types of potential interoperability issues:

• System: incompatibilities between hardware and operating systems.
• Syntactic: differences in encodings and representation.
• Structural: variances in data models, data structures, and schemas.
• Semantic: inconsistencies in terminology and meanings.

Obrst,[14,16] on the other hand, intertwines six levels (object, component, application, system, enterprise, and community) of interoperability with three kinds of integration (syntactic, structural, and semantic). According to

Obrst, semantics is fundamentally interpretation within a particular context and from a particular point of view. Semantic interoperability/integration is fundamentally driven by the communication of coherent purpose.

Pollock and Hodgson[17] consider data to be the foundation of all information sharing programs and believe that next-generation systems rest upon an expanded view of the dialectic of data—information. This view is illustrated in a pyramid in which the interface-level integration, method-level integration, and process-level integration all have developed on top of a foundation of data. With semantic interoperability, the expanded notion of data includes *semantics* and *context*, which thereby transforms data into information. This transition both broadens and deepens the foundation for all other integration approaches, blending semantic interoperability within various levels of interoperability:

1. Semantic interoperability of *data* enables data to maintain original meaning across multiple business contexts, data structures, and schema types.
2. Semantic interoperability of *process* enables specific business processes to be expressed in terms of another by: 1) inferring meaning from the process models and contextual metadata; and 2) applying it in a different process model elsewhere or outside the organization.
3. Semantic interoperability of *services/interface* enables a service to look up, bind, and meaningfully communicate with a new service.
4. Semantic interoperability of *applications* enables platform-independent interactions between heterogeneous software applications.
5. Semantic interoperability of *taxonomy* enables correct expression of all categories (including the definitions and relations with other categories) between different taxonomy systems.
6. Semantic interoperability of *policies and rules* enables businesses to protect valuable resources.
7. Semantic interoperability of *social networks* enables people in different communities of interest to network, make inferences, and discover meaningful connections.[17]

In general, interoperability, no matter at what level, is concerned with the capability of different information systems to communicate with one another. This communication may take various forms such as the transfer, exchange, transformation, mediation, migration, or integration of information. Therefore, as stated at the outset, we may define semantic interoperability as the capacity for different agents, services, and applications to communicate data, information, and knowledge while ensuring accuracy and preserving the meaning of that data, information, and knowledge.

PERSPECTIVES ON THE CONSTITUENTS OF SEMANTIC INTEROPERABILITY

Semantic interoperability has been a topic discussed in information processing and exchange communities since long before the World Wide Web emerged. However, the issue has never been so critical or of such great concern among so many communities as today. Although the Web is an information resource with virtually unlimited potential, this potential is relatively untapped because it is difficult for machines to process and integrate this information meaningfully.[18] Components that contribute to achieving semantic interoperability have been proposed by researchers from a number of diverse perspectives.

Semantic Interoperability in Different Processes

In a report entitled *Semantic Interoperability in Digital Library Systems* prepared by Patel, Koch, Doerr, and Tsinaraki at UKOLN, a research organization that is based at the University of Bath, U.K.,[19] semantic interoperability is characterized by the capability of different information systems to communicate information consistent with the intended meaning of the encoded information (as it is intended by the creators or maintainers of the information system). It involves: 1) the processing of the shared information so that it is consistent with the intended meaning; and 2) the encoding of queries and presentation of information so that it conforms to the intended meaning regardless of the source of information.

Seligman and Rosenthal[20] categorize information interoperability according to two principal types of processes. For information exchange, a provider responds to a request, and the information is transformed to suit the requester's needs. For information integration, in addition to being transformed, information from multiple sources is also correlated and fused. Integration requires that four levels be addressed: Level 1—Overcome geographic distribution and infrastructure heterogeneity; Level 2—Match semantically compatible attributes; Level 3—Mediate between diverse representations; Level 4—Merge instances from multiple sources. Information interoperability is required both in the information exchange and information transfer processes.

Obrst[14] has suggested that semantic interoperability could be enabled through: 1) establishing base semantic representation via ontologies (class level) and their knowledge bases (instance level); 2) defining semantic mappings and transformations among ontologies; and 3) defining algorithms that can determine semantic similarity by employing their output in a semantic mapping facility that uses ontologies.

In many cases, mapping and integration are conducted on top of existing systems that might have been created without considering integration with other systems. Addressing semantic interoperability in different processes helps to identify related problems and methodologies and then resolve those (and other) issues.

Semantic Interoperability at Different Levels

The UKOLN report on *Semantic Interoperability in Digital Library Systems* distinguishes three levels of information that are treated in a distinct manner to address semantic interoperability[19]: 1) *data structures*, be they metadata, content data, collection management data, or service description data; 2) *categorical data*—data that refer to universals, such as classification, typologies, and general subjects; and 3) *factual data*—data that refer to particulars, such as people, items, or places. It might be expected that the treatment of data structures and factual data would achieve a high level of semantic agreements; however, this correlation is not guaranteed when dealing with categorical data. Whereas the local degree of standardization of categorical data may be very high, the global one may be poor.

Slightly different from the perspectives above is a differentiation based on *data structure*, *data content*, *data values*, and *data communication* in metadata practices. The most notable practice is in the cultural heritage community, which has developed a set of comprehensive standards and guidelines for describing cultural objects. The conceptual reference model (CRM) produced by the International Committee for Documentation (CIDOC) of the International Council of Museums (ICOM) provides definitions and a formal structure for describing the implicit and explicit concepts and relationships used in cultural heritage documentation. Semantic interoperability is defined as the capability of different information systems to communicate information that is consistent with intended meaning (see also the "Semantic Interoperability in Different Processes" section). More precisely, the intended meaning encompasses: 1) the data structure elements involved; 2) the terminology appearing as data; and 3) the identifiers used in the data for factual items such as places, people, objects, etc.[21] In the museum and visual resources community, agreements have been reached on these constructs to ensure the creation of sharable and high-quality metadata. Categories for the Description of Works of Art (CDWA)[22] defines a *data structure* which "enumerates a set of categories or metadata elements that can be used to create a structure for a fielded format in a database."[23] Cataloging Cultural Objects (CCO)[23] is a *data content* standard that guides the choice of terms and defines the order, syntax, and form in which data values may be entered into a data structure. Examples of standards for *data values* in the form of controlled vocabularies include the Art and Architecture Thesaurus (AAT),[24] the Thesaurus for Graphic Materials (TGM),[25] the Union List of Artist Names (ULAN),[26] and the Getty Thesaurus of Geographic Names (TGN).[27] Data content and data

value standards must be used in conjunction with an agreed-upon data structure.

Chung and Moen's two-dimensional approach for investigating issues of semantic interoperability in digital libraries[28] is related to the two perspectives above. The *data-attribute* area defines the names, labels, semantics, and granularity of metadata elements and database fields. The *data-value* area addresses the data or information provided in an element or database field. In this approach, the deduction that the data-attribute dimension's components are *semantics* and *content* was based on another discussion about metadata interoperability by the authors of this entry.[29] In that paper, the *semantics* aspect is understood to constrain the attributes (metadata elements and their refinements and relationships) according to agreed-upon meanings. The *content* aspect is defined as the declarations or instructions of what and how data values should be assigned to the metadata element.

Addressing semantic interoperability at different levels leads to improved standardization in related communities and the correct implementation of standards at each level. Following all agreements, metadata produced are intended to be shareable from day one.

Conceptualizing Underlying Models

As early as 1923, Ogden and Richard published their famous *triangle of meaning* which illustrates the relationship between language, thought content, and referent.[30] The graph implies that the referent of an expression (a word or another sign or symbol) is relative to different language users. The model was also adopted by researchers in library and information science as the basis for building knowledge organization systems (KOS).[31] A working group of the International Federation of Library Associations and Institutions (IFLA) Functional Requirements for Subject Authority Records (FRSAR)[32] has recently proposed a conceptual model that contains thema and nomen entities related to the *aboutness* of works in the bibliographic universe.[33] In this instance *thema* means anything that can be the subject of a work. *Nomen* is any alphanumeric, aural, and visual (etc.) symbol or combination of symbols by which a thema is known, referred to, or addressed. The importance of this model for the subject authority data is to separate and distinguish the concepts (or topics and subjects) from how they are designated or represented. In different efforts to achieve global sharing and use of subject authority data, some have focused on nomen (e.g., a translated metadata vocabulary, a symmetrical multilingual thesaurus, or a multi-access index to a vocabulary). However, the majority of projects have concentrated on the thema level, e.g., mapping the concepts between two thesauri or between a thesaurus and a taxonomy. These concept-centric efforts usually encounter far greater challenges because they are concerned not only with the concepts as such, but the relationships among them as well.

This thema–nomen conceptual model matches well with encoding languages such as SKOS, OWL, and more general encoding that uses RDF with Uniform Resource Identifiers (URIs) as the basis of a mechanism for identifying subjects, predicates, and objects in statements. SKOS defines classes and properties sufficient to represent the common features found in a standard thesaurus and is an example of the concept-centric view of vocabulary where primitive objects are not terms but abstract concepts represented by terms/labels. Each SKOS concept is defined as an RDF resource, and each concept can have RDF properties attached, which include: one or more preferred terms (at most one in each natural language); alternative terms or synonyms; and, definitions and notes with specification of their language.[34] Established semantic relationships are expressed in SKOS and intended to emphasize concepts rather than terms/labels.

When the DCMI Abstract Model[35] became a DCMI Recommendation in 2007, its one-to-one principle (i.e., each DC metadata description describes one, and only one, resource) was recognized or followed by more metadata standards (e.g., the newly released VRA Core 4.0).[36] Under the one-to-one principle, a record can contain more than one *description set*. A description set contain *descriptions* composed of *statements* which use property–value pairs. The results are data which can then be processed, exchanged, referred to, and linked to at the statement level. At implementation, when a record contains descriptions of the resource, the individual descriptions also can be linked to the authority data that manages the *values* associated with those properties (e.g., the subject authority data, the property name authority data, and the geographic authority data). Such an information model is independent of any particular encoding syntax and facilitates the development of better mappings and cross-syntax translations.[35] The conceptual model proposed by the FRSAR group corresponds to this abstract model because it allows any thema to be independent of any nomen, including any syntax that a nomen may use. This results in facilitating the sharing and reuse of subject authority data among not only the subject vocabularies themselves, but also among metadata resources.

SEMANTIC INTEROPERABILITY ACTIVITIES

The researchers at UKOLN (see the section "Semantic Interoperability in Different Processes")[19] proposed a list of the information life cycle activities in which the creators/authors, publishers, information systems managers, service providers, and end users are all involved. These activities include: 1) creation and modification; 2) publication; 3) acquisition, selection, storage, system and collection building; 4) cataloging (metadata, identification/ naming, registration), indexing, knowledge organization, knowledge representation, and modeling; 5) integration, brokering, linking, syntactic and semantic interoperability engineering; 6) mediation (e.g., user interfaces, personalization, reference, recommendation, and transfer); 7) access, search, and discovery; 8) use, shared application/ collaboration, scholarly communication, annotation, evaluation, reuse, and work environments; 9) maintenance; and 10) archiving and preservation. While semantic interoperability issues seem to be relevant in each part of the information life cycle, they are paramount in activities 4 (cataloging), 5 (integration), and 6 (access).

In this section, we will narrow our focus to the activities concerned with metadata and KOS because they are the two areas of most interoperability efforts. In reports on data exchange and integration, data values in metadata records appear to lead to increased scrutiny with regard to the semantics of semantic interoperability. This is because most of the concerns are related to terms or codes controlled by some form of KOS. It is our observation, however, that in addition to providing controlled terms, names, and codes for metadata value spaces, KOS have a more important function: to model the underlying semantic structure of a domain and to provide semantics, navigation, translation through labels, definitions, typing, relationships, and properties for concepts.[37,38]

KOS Interoperability

Knowledge organization systems have been recognized as the prerequisites to enhanced semantic interoperability.[19] The term KOS is intended to encompass all types of schemes for organizing information and promoting knowledge management, including classification schemes, gazetteers, lexical databases, taxonomies, thesauri, and ontologies.[39] Embodied as Web services, they facilitate resource discovery and retrieval by acting as semantic road maps, thereby making a common orientation possible for indexers and future users, either human or machine.[38] Thus the term KOS refers to controlled vocabularies as well as to systems/tools/services developed to organize knowledge and to present the organized interpretation of knowledge structures.

Establishing and improving semantic interoperability in the whole information life cycle always requires the use of KOS.[40] Sometimes new vocabularies need to be created (or extracted) first; in other cases, existing vocabularies need to be transformed, mapped, or merged.[19] This is especially important—and challenging—if existing KOS are different with regard to structure, domain, language, or granularity. In a project conducted by the authors,[41] over 40 KOS were found to have been involved in interoperability projects between 1980 and 2004. The sizes of differing KOS ranged from less than 100 to nearly one-quarter million terms depending on individual system requirements. Several of the projects comprise different vocabularies, ranging from a dozen, e.g., the Renardus project[42] and H.W. Wilson's combined heading list,[43] to over one hundred, e.g., the Unified Medical Language System (UMLS),[44] and many are multilingual. During the transforming, mapping, and merging of concept equivalencies, specific term representations formed with definite syntax are sought. Different types of equivalencies have been defined by various standards organizations. The complex requirements and processes for matching terms, which are often imprecise, may have a significant impact on the following aspects of vocabulary mapping: browsing structure, display, depth, nontopical classes, and the balance between consistency, accuracy, and usability. Various levels of mapping/linking can coexist in the same project, such as those identified by the Multilingual Access to Subjects (MACS) project:[45] terminological level (subject heading), semantic level (authority record), and syntactic level (application).[46]

Special challenges and controversial opinions have always overshadowed the projects that have attempted to map multilingual vocabularies. For example, equivalence correlation must be dealt with not only within each original language (intra-language equivalence), but also among the different languages (inter-language equivalence) involved. Intra-language homonymy and inter-language homonymy are also problematic semantic issues.[47]

Taking a different view, Gilreath[48] suggests that there are four basic requirements that must be harmonized in terminology work: concepts, concept systems, definitions, and terms. Further complications arise when perspectives of different cultures need to be integrated. With the assumption that all languages are equal in a crosswalk table, the central question is whether the unique qualities of a particular culture expressed through a controlled vocabulary—or classification—can be appropriately transferred during the mapping process.

In addition to language and cultural variants, KOS have different microstructures and macrostructures: they represent different subject domains or have different scope and coverage; they have semantic differences caused by variations in conceptual structuring; their degrees of specificity and use of terminology vary; and, the syntactic features (such as word order of terms and the use of inverted headings) are also different.

Metadata Interoperability

Metadata is also an extensively discussed topic within the domain of information exchange and integration activities. Metadata are structured, encoded data that describe characteristics of information-bearing entities (e.g., individual objects, collections, or systems) to aid in the identification, discovery, assessment, management, and preservation of the described entities. Metadata is often simply defined as "data about data" or "information about information."[9] In the literature, the words

"schema" and "element set" have been used interchangeably to refer to metadata standards. In practice, metadata element sets are standards for data structures and semantics. An element set is a group of elements useful for describing resources of a particular type, or for a particular purpose. Examples are the 15-element DC Metadata Element Set (DCMES)[49] and DC Metadata Terms (an extended element set which complements the DCMES).[50] The word "schema" usually refers to an entity that includes the semantic and content components of the element set(s) as well as the encoding of the elements with a markup language such as Extensible Markup Language (XML). Examples include the XML schemas for simple and qualified DC. In this discussion, when the term "schema" is used, it refers to a metadata standard, although the major focus is often on the semantics and content of the schema rather than the encoding.

The rapid growth of Internet resources and digital collections has been accompanied by a concurrent proliferation of metadata standards, each of which was designed to be based on the requirements of particular user communities, intended users, types of materials, subject domains, project needs, and much more. Problems arise in the creation of large digital libraries or repositories when metadata records are prepared according to so many diverse standards.

In recent years numerous projects have been undertaken by the many players and stakeholders in the information community toward achieving interoperability among different metadata standards and their applications. Ideally, a uniform standard approach would ensure maximum interoperability among resource collections. If all participants of a consortium or repository were required to use the same data structure standards, such as the MARC21 format[51] or DCMES, a high level of consistency would be created and therefore maintained. This, of course, has been the approach in the library community for over a century and is the optimal solution to the interoperability problem. The uniform standardization method is only viable in the early stages of building a digital library or repository, before different schemas have been adopted by the participants. Although conceptually a simple solution, it is not always feasible. This is especially true in heterogeneous environments serving different user communities where components or collections contain different types of resources already described by particular, specialized schemas. Therefore, other mechanisms of achieving interoperability must be adopted. Implementing interoperability may be considered at different methodological levels:

1. Structure and semantics level—Efforts are focused on the structure and semantics of metadata elements, independent of any applications. Outcomes include derived element sets or encoded schemas, crosswalks, application profiles, and element registries.

Science–Semantic

2. Record level—Efforts are intended to integrate meta-data records through the mapping of elements according to semantic meanings of the elements. Common results include converted records and new records resulting from combining values of existing records.

3. Repository level—With harvested records from varying sources, efforts at this level focus on mapping value strings associated with particular elements (e.g., terms associated with "subject" or "format" elements). The result enables cross-collection searching.[52]

Common Methodologies

Knowledge organization systems and metadata interoperability efforts have implemented similar methodologies. In the following analysis, we use *vocabulary* to refer to both KOS vocabulary and metadata vocabulary (metadata element set). The projects mentioned in this section are examples only (see also longer discussions).[29][41][52]

Derivation

A new vocabulary may be derived from an existing vocabulary which is seen as a "source" or "model" vocabulary. This ensures a similar basic structure and contents, while allowing different components to vary in both depth and detail for the individual vocabularies. Specific derivation methods include adaptation, modification, expansion, partial adaptation, and translation. In each case, the new vocabulary is dependent upon the source vocabulary (see Fig. 1). A current example is the Faceted Application of Subject Terminology (FAST)[53] vocabulary which derives subject terms from the LCSH and modifies the syntax to enable a post-coordinate mechanism.[54] Among the metadata standards, a significant number of lighter element sets (e.g., Text Encoding Initiative (TEI) Lite,[55] MARC Lite,[56] CDWA Lite)[57] and various formats or different encoded schemas have been derived from comprehensive ones. Derivation can also occur in the encoding format (e.g., MARCXML,[58] CDWA Lite), but the basic original content elements are retained. Many

derivations can be regarded as occurring inside a family, as with the MARC family which includes MARC21, MARCXML, Metadata Object Description Schema (MODS),[59] and MARC Lite. A derived vocabulary could also become the source of a new vocabulary (as in the case of some translated vocabularies). Another variation might include the adaptation of an existing vocabulary, with slight modifications to accommodate local or specific needs. The degree of modification is relatively low in contrast to specially localized vocabularies such as application profiles (Fig. 1).

Localization and expansion

Even within a particular information community, there are different user requirements and distinctive local needs. The details provided in a particular vocabulary may not meet the needs of all user groups.

Based on the premise that metadata standards are necessarily localized and optimized for specific contents, the emergent concept of *application profiles* is typical for considering individual needs.[60] While existing element sets are used as the basis for description in a unique digital library or repository, individual needs are met through a set of specific application guidelines or policies established for interest or user groups. Application profiles generally consist of metadata elements drawn from one or more metadata element sets that are combined into a single compound structure and encoded in a schema by implementers, and then optimized for a specialized local application.[61,62] It should be noted that the DCMI community has recently developed a framework application profiles[63] based on the DCMI Abstract Model,[35] that emphasizes the *machine-processable* application profiles which encode metadata elements in machine-processable schemas employing markup languages.

An application profile may also be based on a single element set and then tailored to different user communities. For example, the DC-Library Application Profile (DC-Lib) elucidates the use of the DC metadata element sets in libraries and library-related specific applications and projects.[64] In practice, the development of an application profile often involves the following steps: 1) selecting a "base" metadata namespace; 2) selecting elements from other metadata namespaces; 3) defining local metadata elements and declaring new elements' namespaces; and 4) enforcing application of the elements (including cardinality enforcement, value space restriction, and relationship and dependency specification)[62,65] (Fig. 2).

In thesaurus and classification development, a method known as *leaf nodes* has been used in which extended schemes for subtopics are presented as the nodes of a tree structure in an upper vocabulary. When a leaf node in one thesaurus is linked to a high level (e.g., "wetlands"), and more specific subtopics of that concept exist in a specialized vocabulary or classification system (e.g., "wetlands

Derivation of new vocabularies from a source vocabulary

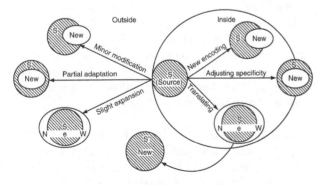

Fig. 1 Derivation of new vocabularies from a source vocabulary.

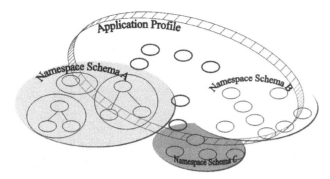

Fig. 2 An application profile consisting of elements drawn from one or more metadata element sets.

classification scheme"), then the leaf node can refer to that specialized scheme.[41] As with the application profile approach, a new vocabulary can be built on the basis of more than one existing vocabulary. A major task of the developers is to not be unnecessarily redundant. Rather, their primary role is to extend from nodes and grow localized vocabulary leaves (see Fig. 3).

With careful collaboration and management, *satellite vocabularies* can be developed around a superstructure in order to meet the needs of managing specialized materials or areas. The superstructure can exist physically (e.g., LCSH) or virtually (e.g., Getty's Vocabulary Database).[66] LCSH-based thesauri include the Legislative Indexing Vocabulary (LIV),[67] the Thesaurus for Graphic Materials (TGM),[25] and the Global Legal Information Network (GLIN).[68] The English Heritage Project's National Monuments Thesauri[69] are composed of several separate online thesauri for monument types: archaeological objects, building materials, defense, evidence, maritime cargo, craft type, place name, and so on. These thesauri are displayed in an integrated space through a frame-based Web site. Terms are grouped by classes rather than by broadest terms (Top Term) and are cross-linked (Fig. 3).

Satellites under a superstructure are usually developed deliberately as an integrated unit and require top-down collaboration for management. An alternative approach, though apparently similar in terms of processes, is to plug-in different pieces to an existing *open umbrella structure*. The reason is that, in the example of ontology development, the upper level of an ontology (i.e., the more general concepts) is more fundamental for information integration. Automatic methods may be used for the semantic organization of lower-level terminology.[70] The responsibility of ensuring interoperability is that of the developers who will create the plug-ins to coordinate under the umbrella. Patel et al.[19] identify a three-tier structure of upper-core-domain ontologies: 1) *upper ontologies* define basic, domain-independent concepts as well as relationships among them (e.g., CYC Ontology[71] and WordNet);[72] 2) *core (or intermediate) ontologies* are essentially the upper ontologies for broad application domains (e.g., the audiovisual domain); and 3) *domain ontologies* in which concepts and relationships used in specific application domains are defined (e.g., a "goal" in the soccer video domain). The core ontologies comprise concepts and relationships that are classified as basic in the broad application domain context, e.g., an event in the audiovisual domain. The concepts defined in domain ontologies correspond to the concepts and relationships established in both upper and core ontologies, which may be extended with the addition of domain knowledge (Fig. 4).

The *Digital Curation Center's Digital Curation Manual: Installment on "Ontologies"*[70] recommends that the editors of KOS first agree on a common upper-level ontology across disciplines in order to guarantee interoperability at the fundamental and functional levels. On the other hand, it is important to fully grasp the conditions and cost-benefit ratio of connecting an upper ontology and domain KOS: 1) the intended purpose—indexing and retrieval vs. automatic inferencing; 2) the alignment of the ontology and domain KOS; 3) the number of different KOS intended to be modeled; and 4) the use cases to be supported.[73]

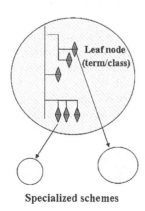

Specialized schemes

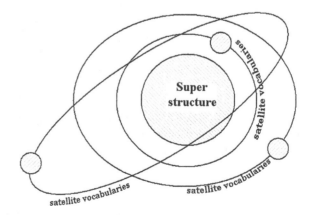

Fig. 3 Leaf node linking and satellites.

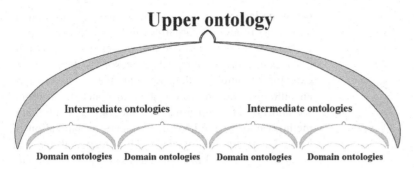

Fig. 4 Intermediate and domain vocabularies plugged-in under an open umbrella structure.

Mapping, crosswalking, and data conversion

The process of mapping essentially consists of establishing equivalencies between terms in different controlled vocabularies and between metadata element sets. In both cases the vocabulary may be presented in verbal terms and/or notation numbers in a scheme. Depending on the number of schemes involved in the process, two different models may be considered.

In *direct mapping*, one-to-one mapping is usually applied when two (or a limited few) schemes are involved. Almost all metadata standards have mapped their elements to the DC 15 elements defined by ISO 15836-2003.[74] The MACS project mapped subject headings in three monolingual lists: Schlagwortnormdatei/Regeln für den Schlagwortkatalog (SWD/RSWK), Répertoire d'autorité-matière encyclopédique et alphabétique unifié (Rameau), and LCSH.[46] Nevertheless, when using the direct mapping model, four schemes would require twelve (or six pairs of) mapping processes. This not only is extremely tedious and labor intensive, but also requires enormous intellectual exertion.

Cross-switching is another kind of model usually applied to reconcile multiple schemes. In this model, one of the schemes is used as the switching mechanism between the multiple schemes. Instead of mapping between every pair in the group, each scheme is mapped to the switching scheme only. Such a switching system can be a new system (e.g., the UMLS' Metathesaurus)[75] or an existing system (e.g., the Dewey Decimal Classification (DDC)). Another example is Getty's crosswalk which allows multiple metadata schemas to all crosswalk to CDWA.[76] For KOS and subject directories, this is the approach adopted by Renardus and a number of other projects. The Renardus project maps local class schemes to a common scheme: the DDC. Each DDC class that Renardus presents links to "related collections" which enables the user to then jump to the mapped classes in the participating local gateways while continuing to browse in the local classification structure. In addition, a virtual browsing feature allows the merging of all local related records from all mapped classes into one common Renardus result set[77] (Fig. 5).

In the metadata community, the word *crosswalk* is established and commonly used among practitioners. Previously this format was also referred to as a *concordance* when subject headings were mapped and stored. A metadata crosswalk is "a mapping of the elements, semantics, and syntax from one metadata scheme to those of another."[9] The mechanism used in crosswalks is usually a chart or table that represents the semantic mapping of data elements in one data standard (source) to those in another standard (target) based on similarity of function or meaning of the elements.[78] According to the NISO document, *Issues in Crosswalking Content Metadata Standards*, common properties may include a semantic definition of each metadata element and other issues including:

- Whether a metadata element is mandatory or optional based on certain conditions.
- Whether a metadata element may occur once or multiple times within the same record.
- Constraints as to the organization of metadata elements relative to each other, (e.g., hierarchical parent–child relationships).
- Constraints imposed on the value of an element (e.g., free text, numeric range, date, or a controlled vocabulary).
- Optional support for locally defined metadata elements.[79]

Major efforts in metadata mapping have produced a substantial number of crosswalks. Almost all schemas have created crosswalks to widely applied schemas such as DC, MARC, or Learning Object Metadata (LOM).[80] Metadata specifications may also include crosswalks to a previous version of a schema as well as to other metadata schemas, e.g., the VRA Core 3.0[81] and 4.0.[36]

Two approaches have emerged in crosswalking practice. The *absolute crosswalking* approach requires exact mapping between involved elements (e.g., vra. title → dc.title) of a source schema (e.g., VRA Core) and a target schema (e.g., DC). Where there is no exact equivalence, there is no crosswalking (e.g., vra. technique → [empty space]). Absolute crosswalking ensures the equivalency (or closely equivalent

Cross-Switching

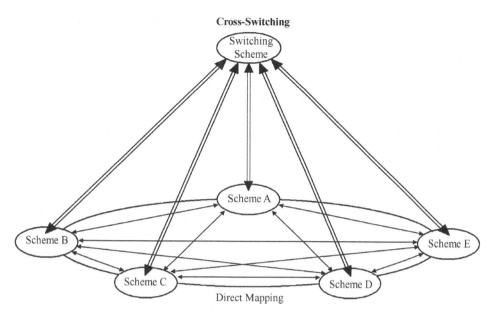

Fig. 5   Direct mapping and cross-switching.

matches) of elements, but does not work well for data conversion. The problem is the data values that cannot possibly be mapped, particularly when a source schema has a richer structure than that of the target schema. To overcome this problem, an alternative approach, *relative crosswalking*, is used to map all elements in a source schema to at least one element of a target schema, regardless of whether the two elements are semantically equivalent or not (e.g., vra. technique → dc.format). The relative crosswalking approach appears to work better when mapping from a complex to a simple (or basic) schema (e.g., MARC to DC), than the reverse.

Functionally, crosswalks should allow systems to effectively convert data and enable heterogeneous collections to be searched simultaneously with a single query as if within a single database. The reality is that crosswalks constructed from real data conversion may be very different from those based on metadata specifications. The major challenge in *converting records* prepared according to a particular metadata schema into records based on another schema is how to minimize loss, or distortion, of data. In studies by Zeng and colleagues,[82,83] it was found that when data values were involved, converting may become imprecise and conversion tasks become more complicated. When the target schema is more inclusive and has defined elements and sub-elements with greater detail than the source schema, the values in a source metadata record may need to be broken down into smaller units (e.g., from DC elements to MARC records subfields). As mentioned above, the risk is that data values may be lost when converting from a complex to a simple structure in absolute crosswalking. Equally, granularity may be lost when

converting from a complex to a simple structure in relative crosswalking. Other vexing problems include converting value strings associated with certain elements that have rules for required, mandatory, or optional usage (in addition to the decisions about which controlled vocabularies are selected). Detailed explanations should be provided for as many contingencies that can be foreseen. Regrettably, most crosswalks focus only on element mappings that are based on *metadata specifications*, and not on *real data conversion results*. A recent study on metadata quality provides strong evidence for the impact of crosswalks on quality when converting large amounts of data.[83] The most serious difficulties include misrepresented data values, important data values lost, incorrectly mapped elements and data values, and, missing elements. It is understood that collaborative approaches are needed in order to solve these problems. Zeng and Shreve recommend a set of approaches to correct many of the errors found in a metadata repository regarding data conversion:

1. Recreating and improving crosswalks.
2. Reharvesting records if quality reviews indicate the need.
3. Sponsoring and enforcing comprehensive standards and best practice guidelines for all elements.
4. Enriching data—both pre- and post-harvest—by automatic processes.
5. Supplying consistent mapping tables to past, present, and future data providers when harvesting is to be conducted.
6. Encouraging and ensuring active collaboration and open communication between repositories and local collection groups.

Co-occurrence mapping is similar to what was done in the MACS project where values in the subject fields of a record from different vocabularies are treated as equivalents. When a metadata record includes terms from multiple controlled vocabularies, co-occurrence of subject terms allows for an automatic, loose mapping between vocabularies. As a group, these loosely mapped terms can answer a particular search query or a group of questions. Existing metadata standards and best practice guides have provided the opportunity to maximize the co-occurrence mapping method. A good example is the VRA Core Categories versions 3.0 and 4.0, which recommend the use of AAT, LCSH, Thesaurus of Graphic Materials (TGM), ICONCLASS,[84] and the Sears List of Subject Headings[85] for culture and subject elements. Also, a Feature Class field of the gazetteer of the Alexandria Digital Library[86] includes terms from two controlled vocabularies (ADL Feature Thesaurus and GNS Feature Classes) in one record.[87] Additionally, metadata records often include both controlled terms and uncontrolled keywords. Mapped subject terms can be used as access points that lead to full metadata records. These *fielded-in* value strings associated with multiple sources may be integrated to enrich metadata records through automatic processes. As more co-occurrence types of mapping are widely applied, loosely mapped values will become very useful in productive searching with highly relevant results.

Crosswalking services mark a further stage of crosswalk development toward meeting the challenge of ensuring consistency in large databases that are built on records from multiple sources. Efforts to establish a crosswalking service at OCLC have indicated the need for robust systems that can handle validation, enhancement, multiple character encodings, and allow human guidance of the translation process.[88] The OCLC researchers developed a model that associates three pieces of information: 1) crosswalk; 2) source metadata standard; and 3) target metadata standard. Researchers at the National Science Digital Library (NSDL)[89] have also included a crosswalking service in their sequence of metadata enhancement services. These crosswalking services are a type of metadata augmentation operation that generates new fielded metadata values that are based on crosswalking from a source (schema or vocabulary) to a target (schema or vocabulary). The operation can be performed on either controlled or uncontrolled vocabulary value strings associated with specific elements.[90] Both element-based and value-based crosswalking services assist in achieving semantic interoperability and improve the reusability of metadata in a variety of knowledge domains.

Registries, repositories, and web services

Registries and repositories for metadata and KOS vocabularies, powered by semantic technologies such as RDF,

SKOS, and OWL, have emerged in recent years. Their primary functions include registering, publishing, managing diverse vocabularies and schemas, as well as ensuring they are crosslinked, crosswalked, and searchable. Their presence promotes the wider adoption, standardization, and overall interoperability of metadata by facilitating its discovery, reuse, harmonization, and synergy across diverse disciplines and communities of practice.[91]

The purpose of *metadata registries* is fairly straightforward: to collect data related to metadata schemas. Since the reuse of existing metadata terms is essential to achieving interoperability among metadata element sets, the identification of existing terms becomes a precondition of any new metadata schema development process. Metadata registries are expected to provide the means to identify and refer to established schemas and application profiles, as well as the means to crosswalk and map among different schemas.[62] The importance of the management and disclosure roles of registries will increase as more metadata and application profile schemas are developed.

The basic components of a metadata registry include identification of data models, elements, element sets, encoding schemes, application profiles, element usage information, and element crosswalks. In addition to these common components, each registry usually has a specific scope and range. Registries can be categorized as:

- Cross-domain and cross-schema registries, e.g., UKOLN's SCHEMAS Registry.[92]
- Domain-specific, cross-schema registries, e.g., UKOLN's MEG (Metadata for Education Group) Registry.[93]
- Project-specific registries, e.g., The European Library (TEL) metadata registry[94] whose purpose is recording all metadata activities associated with TEL.
- Standard-specific registries, e.g., DCMI Metadata Registry.[91]

Metadata standards often specify vocabulary encoding schemes (such as controlled term lists, subject heading lists, name authority files, and thesauri) for use in value spaces associated with certain metadata elements or fields. Consequently, metadata registries may also contain, or link to, terms and codes from these schemes (e.g., DCMI Registry also includes the DCMI Type Vocabulary). Thus the term "metadata registry" could also refer to an integrated structure housing both metadata and terminologies.

At a minimal level, *terminology registries* hold *scheme information*, and list, describe, identify, and point to sets of KOS and other types of vocabularies (e.g., dictionaries) available for use in information systems and services. At a higher level, a terminology registry can comprise the *member* terms, classes, concepts, and relationships contained in a vocabulary (either monolingual or multilingual). Related to the terminology registries are *services*, which may also be listed in a terminology registry or separately hosted in a *service registry*. These services, based on terminology, are used for automatic classification, term expansion, disambiguation, translation, and semantic reasoning.[95] When registering member terms and classes, the scale of the vocabularies becomes significant, often containing hundreds and thousands of entries, along with the complicated relationships among them.

Efforts to register KOS begin with the set of common attributes that describe them. In 1998, researchers belonging to an informal interest group Networked Knowledge Organization Systems/Services (NKOS)[96] began developing a set of elements for a registry for thesauri and other subject vocabularies. A taxonomy of KOS was developed so as to better differentiate the types and functions of subject vocabularies.[97] In 2001, the registry reference document was extended to cover more types of KOS in the second version renamed the NKOS Registry.[98] It includes two blocks of elements. The first block of elements, *KOS Title* through *Rights*, closely corresponds to the Dublin Core Element Set and is intended for creating metadata descriptions that will facilitate the discovery of KOS resources. The second block of elements is intended for the recording of specific characteristics of a KOS resource which will facilitate evaluation of the resource for a particular application or use. Another work, Vocabulary Markup Language: Metacode strawman DTD, was also proposed in 2001[99] and has been an area of ongoing research by NKOS members.

The National Science Digital Library (NSDL) Registry project, funded by the National Science Foundation in 2005, was commissioned to develop and deploy an NSDL Registry to complement the existing NSDL Central Metadata Repository. The Registry is designed to conform to the DCMI Registry application, and so enables multiple diverse collection providers as well as other NSDL projects to identify, declare, and publish their metadata schemas (element/property sets) and encoding schemes (controlled vocabularies). Further, the project intends to provide support for registration of vocabulary encoding schemes and metadata schemas for use by human and machine agents, as well as to support machine mapping of relationships among terms and concepts in those schemas (semantic mappings) and schemas (crosswalks).

It is one of the production deployments of SKOS.[100] The functions of the registry serve across metadata, terminology, and services.

Over the past several years, an eXtended MetaData Registry project has been jointly sponsored by several major government agencies[101] and is currently hosted by the Lawrence Berkeley National Laboratory at the University of California. This project was initiated with the intent of developing improved standards and technology for storing and retrieving semantics of data elements, terminologies, and concept structures in registries. It plans to propose extensions of the ISO/IEC 11179 Metadata Registry (MDR)[102] standards, create a prototype extended metadata registry, and load selected KOS into the prototype. The diverse types of complex semantic metadata (i. e., concepts), are registered in more formal, systematic ways (e.g., description logic) to facilitate machine processing of semantics in order to: 1) link together data elements and terms across multiple systems; 2) discover relationships among data elements, terms, and concepts; 3) create and manage names, definitions, terms, etc.; and 4) support software inference, aggregation, and agent services.[103] This last function leads to what we will discuss next: *terminology services* (Fig. 6).

Terminology services are usually related to or include a registry, but are not limited to registering vocabularies. A terminology service can be defined as a group of *services* that present and apply vocabularies, member concepts, terms, classes, relationships, and detailed explanations of terms which facilitate semantic interoperability. The goals are ambitious: to enable searching, browsing, discovery, translation, mapping, semantic reasoning, automatic classification and indexing, harvesting, and alerting. Terminology services can be machine-to-machine or interactive; user-interfacing services can also be applied at all stages of the search process. For example, in supporting the needs of searching for concepts and the terms representing the concepts, the services can assist in resolving search terms, disambiguation, browsing access, and mapping between vocabularies. As a search support for queries, the services facilitate query expansion, query reformulation, and combined browsing and search. These can be applied as immediate elements of the end user

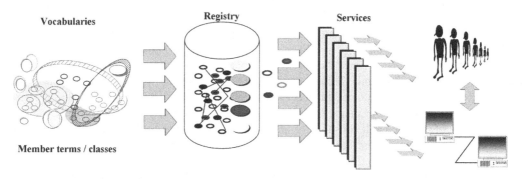

Fig. 6 Terms from metadata and KOS vocabularies registered and used/reused through Web services.

interface, or they can act in underpinning services behind the scenes, depending upon the context.[104] Technologically, they use Web services to interact with controlled vocabularies, and this represents an entirely new dimension in KOS research and development.

A relevant example is OCLC's Terminology Services project.[105] As of June 2008, mappings had been made for eight knowledge organization resources through direct mapping (associations between equivalent terms) and co-occurrence mapping (associations based on the co-occurrence of terms from different schemes in the same metadata or catalog record). Co-occurrence mappings are considered to be mapped more loosely than direct mappings, and usually have an intellectual review component.[106] These services have made records accessible to users through a browser and to machines via the OAI-PMH Web services mechanisms.[107] OCLC immediately began in 2007 to offer its Terminologies Service™ (more than 10 controlled vocabularies served through a single interface thus far) to its thousands of member institutions throughout the world. In addition to the ability of searching descriptions of controlled vocabularies and their member terms/headings, finding single terms/headings by their identifiers, and viewing term relationships, users can retrieve terms/headings in multiple representations such as HTML, MARC XML, SKOS, and Zthes specifications for thesaurus representation, access, and navigation.[108]

The High Level Thesaurus (HILT) projects[109]—a series of research projects funded by the U.K. Joint Information Systems Committee (JISC)—demonstrate a different approach. HILT is concerned with facilitating subject-based access across the broad spectrum of JISC collections that is combined with the automated discovery of relevant collections. HILT has investigated pilot terminology services in collaboration with OCLC Research and Wordmap. DDC was chosen as the central spine for mapping among major vocabularies such as DDC, LCSH, UNESCO Thesaurus,[110] Medical Subject Headings (MeSH),[111] and AAT. HILT Phase 3 focuses on developing a machine-to-machine demonstrator based on Web services, the Search/Retrieve Web Service (SRW) protocol,[112] SKOS Core, and SKOS-type concept URIs. It is being designed so that end users will not access HILT directly; rather, they will be routed through Web-based user services.[19,113]

Other current operational and experimental terminology services have been reviewed in detail in a report entitled *Terminology Services and Technology* prepared for JISC by Tudhope, Koch, and Heery in 2006.[104] Since then, more projects have been initiated. The Semantic Technologies for Archaeological Resources (STAR) project, funded by the British Arts & Humanities Research Council (AHRC), is based at the University of Glamorgan. It aims to develop new methods for linking digital archive databases, vocabularies (and associated gray literature), and to exploit the potential of a high-level, core ontology, and natural language processing techniques.[114] In collaboration with

English Heritage,[115] a set of extensions to the CIDOC CRM[21] core ontology have been produced as RDF files. Thesaurus data received from the English Heritage National Monuments Record Centre was converted into the standard SKOS RDF format for use in the project.[116] The project has developed an initial set of Web services that are based on SKOS representations. The designed function calls can be integrated into a textual- or metadata-based search system. In addition to search and browse concepts in a thesaurus, the service supports semantic expansion of concepts for purposes of query expansion. By an automatic traversal of SKOS relationships, it yields a ranked list of semantically close concepts.[73]

Another new UKOLN project, Terminology Registries and Services (TRSS), is examining how a registry might support the development of terminology and other services within the context of a service-oriented environment. In particular, it is analyzing issues related to the potential delivery of a Terminology Registry as a shared infrastructure service within the JISC Information Environment.[95]

Although there is no official recognition or definition regarding the relationships between KOS and ontologies (particularly formal ontologies), there are *ontology repositories* that host formal ontologies, thesauri, and taxonomies together. Practically speaking, artifacts on the ontology spectrum are considered to have not only the OWL ontologies and axiomatized logical theories, but also include traditional and new structures/schemes, from controlled vocabularies, taxonomies, and thesauri to folksonomies, and from KOS schemes to data schema and data models.[117]

An ontology repository is a facility where ontologies and related information artifacts can be stored, retrieved, and managed. One example is BioPortal,[118] an open-source repository of ontologies, terminologies, and thesauri that is relevant to biomedicine, developed by the U.S. National Center for Biomedical Ontology. As of June 2008, users may access the BioPortal content (over 100 ontologies) interactively via Web browsers or programmatically via Web services. Downloading, searching, and visualizing are three basic functions of these OWL or Protégé ontologies. Users can search for content within a specific ontology, a group of ontologies, or across all ontologies in the library by: Class/Type Name, Class ID, and other attributes such as definitions and synonyms.

An Open Ontology Repository (OOR)[119] initiative planning meeting was conducted in January 2008 by ONTOLOG,[120] an open, international, virtual community of practice. OOR discussions have progressed through a series of mini-conferences that have culminated in the Ontology Summit. With the word "open" added, the ontology repository aims at implementation via open access and compliance with open standards: open technology (with open source), open knowledge (open content), open collaboration (with transparent community process), and open integration with "non-open" repositories through an open interface.[121] The project mission and charter of OOR are to

1. establish a hosted registry-repository.
2. enable and facilitate open, federated, collaborative ontology repositories.
3. establish best practices for expressing interoperable ontology and taxonomy work in registry-repositories.[119,122]

Some current ontology registries/repositories do not provide concept-based mapping. Consequently, most results are based on terms representing concepts, for example, a search for "aging" in an ontology repository may find classes such as "biological im*aging* methods," "im*aging* device," and so forth that are not relevant to the query. The development of concept-based mapping will be a major and much-needed service, and it will also bring in its wake new challenges for ontology repositories.

CONCLUSION

Semantic interoperability plays a central role in information communication; it has a direct impact on a whole range of interoperability issues. This entry has discussed the importance of semantic interoperability in the networked environment, introduced various approaches contributing to semantic interoperability, and summarized different methodologies used in current projects that are focused on achieving semantic interoperability. The proliferation of repositories, interfaces, metadata models, and semantic technologies accentuates the need for semantic interoperability. The open, networked environment encompasses multiple user communities that employ a plethora of standards for describing and providing access to digital resources. To enable federated searches and to facilitate metadata sharing and management, many efforts have been initiated to address interoperability issues, to overcome numerous obstacles, and to address problems encountered along the way. Nevertheless, new and unforeseen interoperability difficulties continue to emerge. The complexity of interoperability does not stop at the international or industry standards level. Guidelines, rules, measurements, and certification are indispensable at the implementation level to ensure that available standards and technologies are optimized. The foundation of all of these requirements is global collaboration. It should be obvious that in order to build the true Semantic Web, not only must existing issues be addressed, but semantic problems of the future also need to be anticipated where possible.

Interoperability requires commonly agreed-upon standards and protocols at different levels for different levels of interoperability. The prospect is emerging for a broad set of standards across different aspects of terminology

services: persistent identifiers, representation of vocabularies, protocols for programmatic access, and vocabulary-level metadata in repositories.[19] XML, RDF, RDFS, OWL, and SKOS are the high-level standards that will enable the achievement of semantic interoperability in the networked environment.

ACKNOWLEDGMENTS

The authors would like to thank Mr. Wm Joseph Robertson, Ms. Sarah Osinsky, and Mr. Haiqing Lin for their assistance in preparing this manuscript, and Dr. Doug Tudhope for sharing his internal reports.

REFERENCES

1. Resource Description Framework (RDF), A general-purpose language for representing information in the Web; http://www.w3.org/RDF/ (accessed July 2008).
2. RDF Vocabulary Description Language 1.0: RDF Schema, W3C Recommendation, 2004. RDF Schema is a standard which describes how to use RDF to describe RDF vocabularies on the Web; http://www.w3.org/TR/rdf-schema/ (accessed July 2008).
3. Web Ontology Language (OWL), A language for defining and instantiating Web ontologies; http://www.w3.org/TR/owl-features/ (accessed July 2008).
4. Simple Knowledge Organization System (SKOS) Reference. W3C Candidate Recommendation 17 March 2009; http://www.w3.org/TR/2009/CR-skos-reference-20090317/ (accessed July 2009).
5. Heiler, S. Semantic interoperability. ACM Comput. Surv. **1995**, *27* (2), 271–273.
6. An era name could only be declared by the emperor before the Republic of China was established. The Republic of China retains the era system, and uses the name "Republic" (民國) for its official dating. The 1st year of the "Republic Era" was 1912. The system is still used in Taiwan.
7. Arms, W.Y.; Hillmann, D.; Lagoze, C.; Krafft, D.; Marisa, R.; Saylor, J.; Terrizzi, C.; Van de Sompel, H. A spectrum of interoperability: The site for science prototype for the NSDL. D-Lib Mag. **2002**, *8* (1), http://www.dlib.org/dlib/january02/arms/01arms.html (accessed July 2008).
8. Obrst, L. Ontologies for semantically interoperable systems. In *Proceedings of the Twelfth ACM International Conference on Information and Knowledge Management (CIKM 2003)*, New Orleans, LA, November 3–8, 2003; Frieder, O., Hammer, J., Quershi, S., Seligman, L., Eds.; ACM Press: New York, 2003; 366–369.
9. NISO, *Understanding Metadata*; NISO Press: Bethesda, MD, 2004; http://www.niso.org/publications/press/Understanding Metadata.pdf (accessed July 2008).
10. CC:DA Task Force on Metadata: Final Report. Association for Library Collections and Technical Services (ALCTS)—Committee on Cataloging: Description & Access (CC:DA), June 16, 2000; http://www.libraries.psu.edu/tas/jca/ccda/tf-meta6.html.

11. Taylor, A. *The Organization of Information*, 2nd Ed.; Libraries Unlimited: Westport, CN, 2004; 369.

12. Moen, W. Mapping the interoperability landscape for networked information retrieval. In Proceedings of 1st ACM/IEEE-CS Joint Conference on Digital Libraries, Roanoke, VA, ACM Press: New York, 2001; 50–51.

13. Koch, T. Electronic thesis and dissertation services: Semantic interoperability, subject access, multilinguality. In E-Thesis Workshop, Amsterdam, 2006-01-19/20; http://www.ukoln.ac.uk/ukoln/staff/t.koch/publ/e-thesis-200601.html (accessed July 2008).

14. Obrst, L. Ontologies and the semantic web for semantic interoperability 2007. (updated 2008); http://web-services.gov/OntologiesSemanticWebSemInteropSICOP909-Obrst.ppt (accessed July 2008).

15. Ouksel, A.M.; Sheth, A. Semantic interoperability in global information systems. ACM SIGMOD Rec. **1999**, *28* (1), 5–12.

16. Obrst, L. Ontologies and the semantic web for semantic interoperability 2007. (updated 2008); http://web-services.gov/OntologiesSemanticWebSemInteropSICOP909-Obrst.ppt (accessed July 2008).

17. Pollock, J.; Hodgson, R. The promise of adaptive information. In *Adaptive Information: Improving Business through Semantic Interoperability, Grid Computing, and Enterprise Integration*; Wiley-Interscience: New York, 2004; Chapter 3, 259–346.

18. Hefline, J. Towards the semantic web: Knowledge representation in a dynamic distributed environment; University of Maryland: College Park, MD, 2001; http://www.cs.umd.edu/projects/plus/SHOE/pubs/#heflin-thesis (accessed July 2008).

19. Patel, M.; Koch, T.; Doerr, M.; Tsinaraki, C. Semantic interoperability in digital library systems. DELOS Network of Excellence on Digital Libraries, European Union, Sixth Framework Programme. Deliverable D5.3.1, 2005; http://www.ukoln.ac.uk/ukoln/staff/t.koch/publ/SI-in-DLs.doc (accessed July 2008).

20. Seligman, L.; Rosenthal, A. A framework for information interoperability. Inform. Interoperability Issues **2004**, *8*(1), http://www.mitre.org/news/the_edge/summer_04/seligman.html (accessed July 2008).

21. CIDOC Conceptual Reference Model, Version 4.2. Produced by ICOM/CIDOC Data Standards Working Group and continued by CRM Special Interest Group. Crofts, N., Doerr, M., Gill, T., Stead, S., Stiff, M., Eds. 2005; http://cidoc.ics.forth.gr/docs/cidoc_crm_version_4.2.pdf (accessed July 2008).

22. Categories for the Description of Works of Art (CDWA); Baca, M.; Harpring, P., Eds. *The J. Paul Getty Trust and College Art Association*, revised 2006. Los Angeles: J. Paul Getty Trust, Getty Research Institute, 2000. http://www.getty.edu/research/conducting_research/standards/cdwa/index.html (accessed July 2008).

23. Baca, M.; Harpring, P.; Lanzi, E.; McRae, L.; Whiteside, A., Eds. *Cataloging Cultural Objects: A Guide to Describing Cultural Works and Their Images*; American Library Association: Chicago, IL, 2006; xi.

24. Art and Architecture Thesaurus (AAT), J. Paul Getty Trust: Los Angeles; http://www.getty.edu/research/conducting_research/vocabularies/aat/index.html (accessed July 2008).

25. Thesaurus for Graphic Materials (TGM), Library of Congress. Online version at: http://www.loc.gov/lexico/servlet/lexico/tgm1/brsearch.html (accessed July 2008).

26. Union List of Artist Names (ULAN), J. Paul Getty Trust: Los Angeles; http://www.getty.edu/research/conducting_research/vocabularies/ulan/ (accessed July 2008).

27. Getty Thesaurus of Geographic Names (TGN), J. Paul Getty Trust: Los Angeles; http://www.getty.edu/research/conducting_research/vocabularies/tgn/ (accessed July 2008).

28. Chung, E.; Moen, W. The semantics of semantic interoperability: A two-dimensional approach for investigating issues of semantic interoperability in digital libraries. In Proceedings of the 69th ASIS&T Annual Meeting, Milwaukee, WI, 2007; http://www.asis.org/Conferences/AM07/posters/35.html (accessed July 2008).

29. Chan, L.M.; Zeng, M.L. Metadata interoperability and standardization—A study of methodology. Part I: Achieving interoperability at the schema level. D-Lib Mag. **2006**, *12* (6). doi:10.1045/june2006-chan; http://www.dlib.org/dlib/june06/chan/06chan.html (accessed July 2008).

30. Ogden, C.K.; Richards, I.A. *The Meaning of Meaning: A Study of the Influence of Language upon Thought and of the Science of Symbolism*; Constable, J., Ed.; Routledge & Kegan Paul: London, U.K., 2001; 11.

31. Dahlberg, I. Knowledge organization and terminology: Philosophical and linguistic bases. Int. Classif. **1992**, *19*, 65–71.

32. Functional Requirements for Subject Authority Records (FRSAR) Working Group, established by International Federation of Library Associations and Institutions (IFLA) Division IV. Bibliographic Control, 2005; http://www.ifla.org/VII/s29/wgfrsar.htm (accessed July 2008).

33. Zumer, M.; Salaba, A.; Zeng, M.L. Functional requirements for subject authority records (FRSAR): A conceptual model of aboutness. In *The 10th International Conference on Asian Digital Libraries (ICADL)*, Hanoi, Vietnam, December, 10–13, 2007.

34. Simple Knowledge Organization System (SKOS) Primer. W3C Working Draft 21, February 2008; http://www.w3.org/TR/skos-primer/ (accessed July 2008).

35. Powell, A.; Nilsson, M.; Naeve, A.; Johnston, P.; Baker, T. DCMI Abstract Model. Dublin Core Metadata Initiative; 2007; http://dublincore.org/documents/abstract-model/ (accessed July 2008).

36. Visual Resource Association Core Categories (VRA Core) 4.0, 2007; http://www.vraweb.org/projects/vracore4/index.html (accessed July 2008).

37. Hill, L.; Buchel, O.; Janee, G.; Zeng, M.L. Integration of knowledge organization systems into digital library architectures. In *Advances of Classification Research*, Vol. 13, Proceedings of the 13th ASIST SIG/CR Workshop, Philadelphia, PA, November, 17, 2002; Jens-Erik, M., Ed.; Learned Information: Medford, NJ, 2002; 62–68.

38. Koch, T.; Tudhope, D. New applications of knowledge organization systems: Call for papers, 2003; http://jodi.tamu.edu/calls/newnkos.html (accessed July 2008).

39. Hodge, G. *Systems of Knowledge Organization for Digital Libraries: Beyond Traditional Authority Files*; The Digital Library Federation, Council on Library and Information Resources: Washington, DC, 2000, CLIR Pub91; http://www.clir.org/pubs/reports/pub91/pub91.pdf (accessed July 2008).

40. Tudhope, D.; Binding, C. A case study of a faceted approach to knowledge organisation and retrieval in the cultural heritage sector. Resource Discovery Technologies for the Heritage Sector. DigiCULT Thematic Issue **2004**, *6*, 28–33; http://www.digicult.info/downloads/digicult_thematic_issue_6_lores.pdf (accessed July 2008).

41. Zeng, M.L.; Chan, L.M. Trends and issues in establishing interoperability among knowledge organization systems. J. Am. Soc. Inform. Sci. Technol. **2004**, *55* (5), 377–395.

42. Renardus, An EU project for subject searching across European subject gateways; http://renardus.sub.uni-goettingen.de/ (accessed July 2008).

43. Wilson OmniFile Full Text, Mega Edition. http://www.hwwilson.com/Databases/omnifile.htm.

44. Unified Medical Language System® (UMLS), Developed by the National Library of Medicine, USA; http://www.nlm.nih.gov/pubs/factsheets/umls.html (accessed July 2008).

45. Multilingual Access to Subjects (MACS), An European project for searching across cataloging databases of the partner libraries in different languages (English, French, and German); https://macs.vub.ac.be/pub/ (accessed July 2008).

46. Freyre, E.; Naudi, M. MACS: Subject access across languages and networks: Subject retrieval in a networked environment. Proceedings of the IFLA Satellite Meeting, Dublin, OH, August, 14–16, 2001; McIlwaine, I.C., Ed. K. G. Saur: München, 2003; 3–10.

47. Guidelines for Multilingual Thesauri (Draft). IFLA Classification and Indexing Section, 2005; http://www.ifla.org/VII/s29/pubs/Draft-multilingualthesauri.pdf (accessed July 2008).

48. Gilreath, C.T. Harmonization of terminology—An overview of principles. Int. Classif. **1992**, *19*, 135–139.

49. Dublin Core Metadata Element Set (DC), version 1.1. Dublin Core Metadata Initiative, 2006; http://dublincore.org/documents/dces/ (accessed July 2008).

50. DCMI Metadata Terms. DCMI Usage Board, 2008; http://dublincore.org/documents/dcmi-terms/ (accessed July 2008).

51. The MARC formats are standards for the representation and communication of bibliographic and related information in machine-readable form, developed by the Library of Congress, USA; http://www.loc.gov/marc/ (accessed July 2008).

52. Zeng, M.L.; Chan, L.M. Metadata interoperability and standardization—A study of methodology. Part II: Achieving interoperability at the record and repository levels. D-Lib Mag. **2006**, *12*(6); doi:10.1045/june2006-zeng; http://www.dlib.org/dlib/june06/zeng/06zeng.html (accessed July 2008).

53. Faceted Application of Subject Terminology (FAST); http://www.oclc.org/research/projects/fast/ (accessed July 2008).

54. Chan, L.M.; Childress, E.; Dean, R.; O'Neill, E.T.; Vizine-Goetz, D. A faceted approach to subject data in the Dublin Core metadata record. J. Internet Catalog **2001**, *4*, 35–47.

55. Text Encoding Initiative (TEI) Lite, A manageable subset of the full TEI encoding scheme; http://www.tei-c.org/Lite/ (accessed July 2008).

56. MARC 21 LITE Bibliographic Format, A subset of the markup defined in the full MARC 21 Bibliographic Format; http://www.loc.gov/marc/bibliographic/lite/ (accessed July 2008).

57. CDWA Lite, An XML schema to describe core records for works of art and material culture based on the Categories for the Description of Works of Art (CDWA) and Cataloging Cultural Object (CCO); http://www.getty.edu/research/conducting_research/standards/cdwa/cdwalite.html (accessed July 2008).

58. MARC 21 XML schema (MARCXML), Developed by the Library of Congress; http://www.loc.gov/standards/marcxml/ (accessed July 2008).

59. Metadata Object Description Schema (MODS), Developed by the Library of Congress; http://www.loc.gov/standards/mods/ (accessed July 2008).

60. Johnston, P. Metadata and interoperability in a complex world. Ariadne **2003**, *37*, http://www.ariadne.ac.uk/issue37/dc-2003-rpt (accessed July 2008).

61. Heery, R.; Patel, M. Application profiles: mixing and matching metadata schemas. Ariadne **2000**, *25*, http://www.ariadne.ac.uk/issue25/app-profiles/ (accessed July 2008).

62. Duval, E.; Hodgins, W.; Sutton, S.; Weibel, S.L. Metadata principles and practicalities. D-Lib Mag. **2002**, *8* (4), http://www.dlib.org/dlib/april02/weibel/04weibel.html doi:10.1045/april2002-weibel (accessed July 2008).

63. Nilsson, M.; Baker, T.; Johnston, P. The Singapore Framework for Dublin Core Application Profiles; 2008. http://dublincore.org/documents/2008/01/14/singapore-framework/ (accessed July 2008).

64. Library Application Profile (DC-Lib), DCMI-Libraries Working Group, 2004; http://dublincore.org/documents/library-application-profile/ (accessed July 2008).

65. Zhang, X. Tutorial on metadata. *Tutorials, 7th International Conference of Asian Digital Libraries (ICADL)*, Shanghai, China, December 13–17, 2004; Shanghai Jiaotong University Library: Shanghai, 2004; 107–136.

66. Getty Vocabulary Databases, Getty Vocabulary Program; http://www.getty.edu/research/conducting_research/vocabularies/ (accessed July 2008).

67. Legislative Indexing Vocabulary (LIV), Library of Congress; http://www.loc.gov/lexico/servlet/lexico?usr = pub-236:0&op = frames&db = LIV (accessed July 2008).

68. Thesaurus for Global Legal Information Network (GLIN); Library of Congress; http://www.glin.gov/subjectTerm Index.action (accessed July 2008).

69. National Monuments Record Thesaurus, National Monuments Record Centre, English Heritage, 1999; http://www.english-heritage.org.uk/thesaurus/thes_splash.htm (accessed July 2008).

70. Doerr, M. DCC Digital Curation Manual: Installment on "Ontologies," 2008; http://www.dcc.ac.uk/resource/curation-manual/chapters/ontologies/ (accessed July 2008).

71. CYC Ontology, Cycorp: Austin, TX; http://www.cyc.com/ (accessed July 2008).

72. WordNet, A semantic lexicon for the English language developed by Princeton University Cognitive Science Laboratory; http://wordnet.princeton.edu/ (accessed July 2008).

73. Tudhope, D.; Binding, C. Machine understandable knowledge organization systems. DELOS Network of Excellence on Digital Libraries, Project no. 507618 report, 2008.

Science–Semantic

74. ISO Information and documentation—The Dublin Core metadata element set. ISO Standard 15836-2003 2003; http://dublincore.org/documents/dces/ (accessed July 2008).

75. UMLS Metathesaurus, A multi-lingual vocabulary database developed by the National Library of Medicine, USA; http://www.nlm.nih.gov/pubs/factsheets/umlsmeta. html (accessed July 2008).

76. Metadata Standards Crosswalks. Harpring, P.; Woodley, M.; Gilliland-Swetland, A.; Baca, M., Eds.; http://www. getty.edu/research/conducting_research/standards/intrometa data/metadata_element_sets.html (accessed July 2008).

77. Koch, T.; Neuroth, H.; Day, M. Renardus: Cross-browsing European subject gateways via a common classification system (DDC). In *Subject Retrieval in a Networked Environment*. Proceedings of the IFLA Satellite Meeting, Dublin, OH, August, 14–16, 2001; McIlwaine, I.C., Ed.; K. G. Saur: München, Germany, 2003; 25–33.

78. Baca, M.; Gill, T.; Gilliland, A.J.; Woodley, M.S. Introduction to Metadata: Pathway to Digital Information, Online edition, Version 2.1. 2000; Glossary; http://www.getty. edu/research/conducting_research/standards/intrometadata/ glossary.html (accessed July 2008).

79. St. Pierre, M.; LaPlantJr., W.P. *Issues in Crosswalking Content Metadata Standards*; NISO Press: Bethesda, MD, 1998; http://www.niso.org/publications/white_papers/ crosswalk/ (accessed July 2008).

80. Learning Object Metadata (LOM), Developed by IEEE Learning Technology Standards Committee; http://ltsc. ieee.org/wg12/index.html (accessed July 2008).

81. Visual Resource Association Core Categories (VRA Core) 3.0; http://www.vraweb.org/projects/vracore3/index.html (accessed July 2008).

82. Zeng, M.L.; Xiao, L. Mapping metadata elements of different format. In *E-Libraries 2001*, Proceedings, New York, May, 15–17, 2001; Information Today: Medford, NJ, 2001; 91–99.

83. Zeng, M.L.; Shreve, G. Quality Analysis of Metadata Records in the NSDL Metadata Repository, 2007; A research report submitted to the National Science Foundation.

84. ICONCLASS, An international classification system for iconographic research and the documentation of images; http://www.iconclass.nl/ (accessed July 2008).

85. Sears List of Subject Headings, 18th Ed.; H.W. Wilson Company: New York, 2003.

86. The Alexandria Digital Library (ADL), A digital library with collections of georeferenced materials; http://www. alexandria.ucsb.edu/ (accessed July 2008).

87. See Ref. 52; Figures 2 and 3.

88. Godby, C.J.; Young, J.A.; Childress, E. A repository of metadata crosswalks. D-Lib Mag. **2004**, *10* (12), http:// www.dlib.org/dlib/december04/godby/12godby.html; doi:10.1045/december2004-godby (accessed July 2008).

89. National Science Digital Library (NSDL), An online library for education and research in science, technology, engineering and mathematics, funded by the National Science Foundation from 2003 to 2006; http://nsdl.org/ (accessed July 2008).

90. Phipps, J.; Hillmann, D.I.; Paynter, G. Orchestrating metadata enhancement services: Introducing Lenny. In Proceedings of the International Conference on Dublin Core and Metadata Applications, Madrid, Spain, September, 2005; 57–66. http://arxiv.org/ftp/cs/papers/0501/0501083.pdf (accessed July 2008).

91. Dublin Core Metadata Registry. OCLC Research; DCMI Registry Working Group Ed., 2005; http://dcmi.kc. tsukuba.ac.jp/dcregistry/ (accessed July 2008).

92. SCHEMAS Registry, UKLON; http://www.schemas-forum. org/registry/ (accessed July 2008). Now used in CORES project; http://cores.dsd.sztaki.hu/ (accessed July 2008).

93. Metadata for Education Group (MEG). Registry, UKOLN; Facilitates schema registration within the educational domain; http://www.ukoln.ac.uk/metadata/education/registry/contents.html (accessed July 2008).

94. The European Library (TEL), http://www.theeuropean library.org/portal/index.html metadata registry.

95. Terminology Registry Scoping Study, UKOLN; http:// www.ukoln.ac.uk/projects/trss/ (accessed July 2008).

96. NKOS (Networked Knowledge Organization Systems/ Services); http://nkos.slis.kent.edu/ (accessed July 2008).

97. Hodge, G.M. Taxonomy of Knowledge Organization Sources/Systems, 2000; http://nkos.slis.kent.edu/KOS_ taxonomy.htm (accessed July 2008).

98. NKOS Registry-Reference Document for Data Elements, 2001; http://staff.oclc.org/~vizine/NKOS/Thesaurus_Registry_version3_rev.htm (accessed July 2008).

99. Busch, J.A. Vocabulary ML: Metacode strawman DTD, 2001.

100. Collaborative project: An NSDL Registry, NSDL Award 0532828, 2005; http://nsdl.org/about/index.php?pager = projects&this_sort = start_date&keyword = &project_id = 0532828 (accessed July 2008).

101. eXtended MetaData Registry (XMDR), Hosted at the Lawrence Berkeley National Laboratory at University of California, 2005; http://www.xmdr.org/ (accessed July 2008).

102. ISO/IEC 11179, Information Technology—Metadata Registries (MDR); http://metadata-stds.org/11179/ (accessed July 2008).

103. McCarthy, J.L. A standard & prototype starting point foran open ontology repository: The extended metadata registry project. In *Presentation at An Open Ontology Repository: Rationale, Expectations & Requirements*, Joint OpenOntologyRepository-OntologySummit2008 Panel Discussion Session, March, 27, 2008; http://ontolog. cim3.net/file/work/OpenOntologyRepository/Requirements-Panel/XMDR-for-OOR–JohnLMcCarthy_20080327.ppt (accessed July 2008).

104. Tudhope, D.; Koch, T.; Heery, R. Terminology Services and Technology. JISC State of the Art Review **2006**; http://www.ukoln.ac.uk/terminology/JISC-review2006. html (accessed July 2008).

105. Vizine-Goetz, D. Terminology services: Making knowledge organization schemes more accessible to people and computers. OCLC Newslett. **2004**, 266; http://www.oclc. org/news/publications/newsletters/oclc/2004/266/research. html (accessed July 2008).

106. Terminology Services homepage. OCLC Research; http:// www.oclc.org/research/projects/termservices/ (accessed July 2008).

107. The Open Archives Initiative Protocol for Metadata Harvesting (OAI-PMH) Version 2.0, 2002; http:// www.openarchives.org/OAI/openarchivesprotocol.html (accessed July 2008).

108. The Zthes specifications for thesaurus representation, access and navigation, 2006; http://zthes.z3950.org/ (accessed July 2008).

109. High Level Thesaurus (HILT) project; now in Phase IV; http://hilt.cdlr.strath.ac.uk/ (accessed July 2008).

110. UNESCO Thesaurus, 1995; http://www2.ulcc.ac.uk/unesco/index.htm (accessed July 2008).

111. Medical Subject Headings (MeSH), The National Library of Medicine, USA; http://www.nlm.nih.gov/mesh/meshhome.html (accessed July 2008).

112. Search and Retrieve URL/Web Service (SRU/SRW); Web services for search and retrieval based on Z39.50 semantics developed at the Library of Congress, USA; http://www.loc.gov/standards/sru/ (accessed July 2008).

113. Nicholson, D.; Shiri, A.; McCulloch, E. HILT: High-Level Thesaurus project phase II, A Terminologies server for the JISC information environment—final report to JISC, 2003; http://hilt.cdlr.strath.ac.uk/hilt2web/finalreport.htm (accessed July 2008).

114. Semantic Technologies for Archaeological Resources (STAR), University of Glamorgan Hypermedia Research Unit; http://hypermedia.research.glam.ac.uk/kos/star/ (accessed July 2008).

115. English Heritage; http://www.english-heritage.org.uk/ (accessed July 2008).

116. Semantic Technologies for Archaeological Resources (STAR), AHRC ICT Methods Network, 2007; http://www.methodsnetwork.ac.uk/resources/casestudy13.html (accessed July 2008).

117. Baclawski, K.; Duggar, V.Ontology Summit 2007 Assessment Report; http://ontolog.cim3.net/file/work/Ontology Summit2007/Assessment/ (accessed July 2008).

118. BioPortal; The National Center for Biomedical Ontology; http://bioportal.bioontology.org (accessed July 2008).

119. Open Ontology Repository (OOR) Initiative; http://ontolog.cim3.net/cgi-bin/wiki.pl?OpenOntologyRepository (accessed July 2008).

120. ONTOLOG—Collaborative work environment; http://ontolog.cim3.net/ (accessed July 2008).

121. Baclawski, K. Open Ontology Repository: User Needs & Requirements. In *Open Ontology Repository SessionOOR-Team Presentation*. Ontology Summit 2008, Gaithersburg, MD, April, 29, 2008; http://ontolog.cim3.net/file/work/OOR/OOR-presentation_20080429/OOR-Presentation–Mike Dean-LeoObrst-PeterYim_draft_20080429h.ppt (accessed July 2008).

122. Open Ontology Repository (OOR) Goals & a Mission Statement; http://ontolog.cim3.net/cgi-bin/wiki.pl?Conference Call_2008_01_03#nid16PN (accessed July 2008).

Semantic Web

Kieron O'Hara
Wendy Hall
Intelligence, Agents, Multimedia Group, University of Southampton, Southampton, U.K.

Abstract

The "semantic web (SW)" is a vision of a web of linked data, allowing querying, integration, and sharing of data from distributed sources in heterogeneous formats, using ontologies to provide an associated and explicit semantic interpretation. This entry describes the series of layered formalisms and standards that underlie this vision, and chronicles their historical and ongoing development. A number of applications, scientific and otherwise, academic and commercial, are reviewed. The SW has often been a controversial enterprise, and some of the controversies are reviewed, and misconceptions defused.

INTRODUCTION

The semantic web (SW) is an extension, in progress, to the World Wide Web (WWW), designed to allow software processes, in particular artificial agents, as well as human readers, to acquire, share, and reason about information. Whereas the WWW consists largely of documents, which are generally created for human consumption, the SW will be a web of data, making them more amenable for computers to process.[1] The data will be processed by computer via semantic theories for interpreting the symbols (hence: *semantic* web). In any particular application, the semantic theory will connect terms within a distributed document set logically, and thereby aid interoperability.

For instance, people use a lot of data in daily interactions, viewing bank statements, or digital photographs, or using diaries or calendars. But this does not constitute a web of data, because the data are neither exported from the applications in which they are stored or were created, nor linked to other relevant data. In a genuine web of data, such data could be used seamlessly in a number of applications. For example, one could view one's photographs (which will contain a time stamp) in one's calendar, which would then act as a prompt to suggest what one was doing when they were taken. The data which one uses would be to some extent freed from the constraints of particular applications, and instead could be interlinked and reused creatively.

As another example, Web services can currently be accessed and executed via the Web, but because the Web does not provide much information-processing support, services must be specified using semiformal languages and as with information retrieval humans need to be kept in the loop. Web services described using SW techniques should provide support for autonomous agents and automatic systems.[2]

The world of linked information is a very unstructured, "scruffy" environment. The amounts of information that systems need to deal with are very large indeed. Furthermore, systems must pull together information from distributed sources, where representation schemes can be expected to be highly heterogeneous, information quality variable, and trust in information's provenance hard to establish. SW technology needs to be based on standards that can operate in this heterogenous information world.

The SW therefore requires two types of information standard to operate. First, it requires common formats for integrating information from these diverse sources. And second, it needs a language to express the mapping between the data and objects in the real world, in order to allow a seamless understanding of a distributed set of databases. Hence, for instance, we could signal that a database containing a column *zip code* and another database with a column labeled *ZC*, were actually both referring to the same concept with their different labels, and by creating such a semantic link, we could then start to reason over both databases in an integrated fashion. Such semantic links are often obvious to humans, but not to computers. A key formalism here is the *ontology*, which defines the concepts and relationships that we use in particular applications. Ontologies are central to the SW vision, as providing the chief means by which the terms used in data are understood in the wider context.[1,3]

THE AIM OF THE SEMANTIC WEB

The aim of the SW is to shift the emphasis of reasoning from documents to data, for three reasons. First, it will facilitate data reuse, often in new and unexpected contexts. Second, it will help reduce the amount of relatively expensive human information processing. Third, it will release the large quantity of information, not currently accessible, that is stored in relational databases (RDBs) by making it directly machine-processable.[4]

Encyclopedia of Library and Information Sciences, Fourth Edition DOI: 10.1081/E-ELIS4-120043686

This implies that RDB objects must be exported to the Web as first-class objects, which in practice entails mapping them onto a consistent system of resource identifiers—called Universal Resource Identifiers (URIs—see below). The SW itself is a suite of languages and formalisms designed to enable the interrogation and manipulation of representations which make use of URIs.[1]

It is hoped that the SW will exhibit the same *network effects* that promoted the growth of the WWW. Network effects are positive feedback effects connected with *Metcalfe's Law* that the value of a network is proportional to the square of the number of users/members. The more people share data that can be mapped onto URIs, the more valuable that data is. As value increases, more agents join the network to get the benefits, and include information that they own in the network which further increases its value. This, like the WWW model, is radically different from other models of the value of information, wherein value is dictated by *scarcity* (copyright, intellectual property restrictions, etc). In decentralized networks like the Web the value of information is dictated by *abundance*, so it can be placed in new contexts, and reused in unanticipated ways.

This is the dynamic that enabled the WWW to spread, when the value of Web documents was seen to be greater in information-rich contexts. One initiative to support the development of the SW is the creation of a discipline of *web science*, which is intended to exploit study of both technical and social issues to predict such matters with more accuracy.[5,6]

If the SW is to grow in an analogous way, more data has to be exposed to the Web that can be mapped onto URIs. In practice, this means that the data must be exposed in the resource description framework (RDF), an agreed international standard whose role in the SW is described below[7]; in particular, it can be used not only to assert a link between two resources, but also to name (and therefore make explicit) the relationship that links them. RDF is the language of choice for reuse, because it is a relatively inexpressive language compared to other formalisms used in the SW (see Fig. 1 for a pictorial representation of the layers of formalisms required for the SW vision—expressivity increases as we ascend the diagram). The importance of RDF in this model is dictated by the so-called principle of least power, which states that the less expressive the representation language, the more reusable the data.[8]

The importance of growth is such that a stage can be reached when reuse of data—one's own or that of other people—is facilitated. There would ideally be so much information exposed in RDF that the contexts into which one's own data can be placed would be rich enough and numerous enough to increase its value significantly. RDF (as described below) represents information as a subject–predicate–object triple each of whose component parts is a URI. If the objects, resources, or representations referred

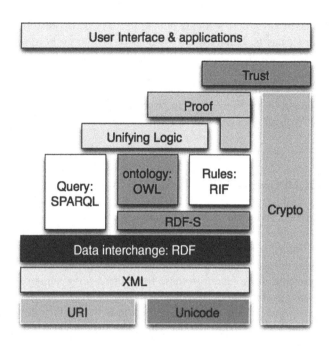

Fig. 1   The layered view of the semantic web.
Source: From A framework for Web Science, by T. Berners-Lee, W. Hall, J.A.; Hendler, K; O'Hara, N.; Shadbolt, D.J. Weitzner, Found. Trends Web Sci. 2006, *1* (1), 1–134.[6]

to by the URIs are defined in ontologies, then this enables the interoperability at which the SW aims.

Hence another vital component in the SW is the development and maintenance of ontologies. These must be endorsed by the communities that use them, whether they are large-scale, expensive ontologies developed as a result of a major research effort, or relatively ad hoc creations intended to support small-scale collaboration.

Ontologies can also play an important role in bringing (representatives of) two or more communities together for a common purpose, by expressing a common vocabulary for their collaboration, onto which the terms of each discipline can be mapped. Such collaborative efforts are extremely important for reuse of content.[3]

This is not to say that search and retrieval on the current Web is not of high quality; the methods pioneered by Google and others work very well. Nevertheless, keyword-based search techniques are vulnerable to a number of well-known flaws. Individual words can be ambiguous. A document can refer to a topic of interest without using the keyword. Keywords are language-dependent. Information distributed across several documents cannot be amalgamated by keyword search. And even though PageRank and related algorithms for search produce impressive results, the user still needs to read manually through the ordered list of retrieved pages, and inspect their content to determine relevance to his/her inquiry. This involvement of the user is a hindrance to scalability.

The SW should make more accurate querying possible, using ontologies to help with problems of ambiguity and unused keywords, and data linking to query across distributed datasets. Furthermore, it should be able to go beyond current search with respect to the three issues of reuse, automation, and exploitation of RDBs. And as well as search and retrieval, the addition of information processing support to the Web will help promote other functions such as Web services and knowledge management.

COMPONENTS OF THE SEMANTIC WEB

At one level, the SW is a complex of formalisms and languages each doing a different job in the representation of information, as shown in Fig. 1. Each formalism is an internationally agreed standard (see below), and the composition of the functions these formalisms serve supports semantically enabled reasoning on data.

At the bottom of this diagram stands the URIs which identify the resources about which the SW provides reasoning capabilities.[9] The universality of URIs is extremely important—i.e., it is vital that whatever naming convention is used for URIs is adopted globally, so as to create the network effects that allow the SW to add value. Interpretation of URIs must also be consistent across contexts. In other words, when we *dereference* URIs (i.e., when we locate the resource to which the URI refers), we should always get the same object. If these conditions about URI naming schemes are met, then making an association between a URI and a resource means that different people can refer or link to it consistently in their conversations. The other basic formalism, Unicode, is an industry standard that allows computers to represent text in different writing systems.

The next layer up, eXtensible Markup Language (XML), is a language to mark up documents, and a uniform data exchange format between applications.[10] It allows the insertion of user-defined tags into documents that provide information about the role that the content plays. So, for instance, XML allows one to write a document describing a book, and also to *annotate* the document with machine-readable *metadata* to indicate e.g., who the authors of the book are.

RDF[7] is a very minimal knowledge representation framework for the Web, which uses a basic subject–predicate–object structure, with the twist that it assigns specific URIs to its individual fields—including in the predicate position, thereby identifying a relationship between the entities identified by the connected nodes. This use of URIs allows us to reason not only about objects but also about the relationships between them. XML is a metalanguage that provides a uniform framework for markup, but it does not provide any way of getting at the *semantics* of data; RDF is the first step toward semantics.

The resource description framework schema (RDFS, sometimes known as RDF(S)[11]) gives greater scope for sharing information about individual domains; whereas

RDF is a data interchange language that lets users describe resources using their own vocabularies, and makes no assumptions about the domains in question, RDFS provides a basic set of tools for producing structured vocabularies that allow different users to agree on particular uses of terms. An extension of RDF, it adds a few modeling primitives with a fixed meaning (such as class, subclass and property relations, and domain and range restriction).

A key component for SW applications is the *ontology*. Ontologies[3] are shared conceptualizations of a domain which are intended to facilitate knowledge and information sharing by coordinating vocabulary and allowing basic inference of inheritance and attributes of objects. Several initiatives are developing ontologies, particularly in a number of sciences, which means that the scientists are likely to be among the important early adopters of SW technology (see below). RDFS is an important step toward the SW vision, as the addition of modeling primitives makes it a basic ontology representation language.

However, greater expressivity is likely to be required in the development of more complex ontologies, and the World Wide Web Consortium (W3C) has issued a Web Ontology Language (OWL[12]) in multiple versions that allows ontologies to be not only represented but also checked for logical properties such as consistency. The three species of OWL are: 1) OWL Full, containing all the OWL primitives, allowing arbitrary combination of those primitives with RDF and RDFS (allowing changes in meaning even of predefined OWL or RDF primitives), but also providing so much expressive power as to make the language undecidable (i.e., it cannot be guaranteed that a computation using the full expressive power of OWL Full will be completed in a finite time); 2) OWL DL, which restricts application of OWL's constructors to each other, and corresponds to a decidable *description logic*, but which is not fully compatible with RDF; and 3) OWL Lite, which sacrifices even more expressive power to facilitate implementation and reasoning.[12] This set of relations affects the downward compatibility of the SW layer diagram—the only version of OWL that is downward compatible with RDF and RDFS (i.e., so that any processor for that version of OWL will also provide correct interpretations of RDFS) is OWL Full, which is undecidable (pp.113–115).[13,14]

All varieties of OWL use RDF for their syntax, and use the linking capabilities of RDF to allow ontologies to be distributed—ontologies can refer to terms in other ontologies. Such distributivity is a key property for an ontology language designed for the SW.[15]

OWL supports some kinds of inference, such as subsumption and classification, but a greater variety of rules and inference is needed. Hence, work is currently ongoing on the Rule Interchange Format (RIF), which is intended to allow a variety of rule-based formalisms, including Horn-clause logics, higher order logics, and production systems, to be used.[16] Various insights from Artificial

Intelligence (AI) have also been adapted for use for the SW, including temporal (time-based) logic, causal logic, and probabilistic logics.[1]

Having represented data using RDF and ontologies, and provided for inference, it is also important to provide reliable, standardized access to data held in RDF. To that end, a special query language SPARQL (pronounced "sparkle"), which became a W3C recommendation in January 2008, has been designed.[17] Logic and proof systems are envisaged to sit on top of these formalisms, to manipulate the information in deployed systems.[1]

A very important layer is that of *trust*.[18] If information is being gathered from heterogeneous sources and inferred over, then it is important that users are able to trust such sources. The extent of trust will of course depend on the criticality of the inferences—trust entails risk, and a risk-averse user will naturally trust fewer sources.[19,20] Measuring trust, however, is a complex issue.[21] A key parameter is that of provenance, a statement of: 1) the conditions under which; 2) the methods with which; and 3) the organization by which, data were produced. Methods are appearing to enable provenance to be established, but relatively little is known about how information spreads across the Web.[22]

Related issues include respect for intellectual property, and the privacy of data subjects. In each case the reasoning abilities of the SW can be of value, and initiatives are currently under way to try to exploit them.[23] Creative commons[24] is a way of representing copyright policies and preferences based on RDF to promote reuse where possible (current standard copyright assumptions are more restrictive with respect to reuse). And research into the policy aware web is attempting to develop protocols to allow users to express their own privacy policies, and to enable those who wish to use information to reason about those policies.[25] Cryptography protocols to protect information will also play an important role, as shown in Fig. 1.

ADDITIONAL FACTORS IN SEMANTIC WEB DEVELOPMENT

Infrastructure

Another important part of SW development is the infrastructure that supports it. In particular, if data is to be routinely published to the Web in RDF format, there must be information repositories that can store RDF and RDFS. These *triple stores* (so-called because they store the RDF triples) must provide reasoning capabilities as well as retrieval mechanisms, but importantly must be *scalable*. Examples of triple stores include JENA,[26] 3store,[27,28] and Oracle 11*g*.[29] OWLIM is a repository which works as a storage and inference layer for the Sesame RDF database, providing reasoning support for some of the more

expressive languages of the SW, RDFS, and a limited version of OWL Lite.[30,31]

Reasoners

As representation in the SW is more complex than in previous technologies, so is reasoning. The area of SW reasoning has been the focus of much research, in order to infer the consequences of a set of assertions interpreted via an ontology. In such a context, inference rules need clear semantics, and need to be able to cope with the diverse and distributed nature of the SW.

There are a number of important issues of relevance in this area: 1) Under what conditions is negation monotonic (i.e., the addition of new facts does not change the derivation of not-p), or nonmonotonic (including negation as failure, deriving not-p from the failure to prove p)?; 2) How should we handle conflicts when merging rule-sets?; 3) "Truth" on the Web is often dependent on context—how should a reasoner represent that dependence?; 4) How should scalability be balanced against expressivity?; 5) Logic often assumes a static world of given "facts," but how should it be adapted to the SW, a much more dynamic space where propositions are asserted and withdrawn all the time?; and 6) The heterogeneous nature of the SW means that data in the SW is of varying trustworthiness; how should a reasoner deal with variable reliability? None of these questions has a "correct" answer, but any SW reasoning system needs to address them.

There has been a lot of research on SW reasoning, but an important desideratum is that a reasoner should support the W3C recommended formalisms, in particular supporting OWL entailment at as high a level as possible, and SPARQL querying. Examples include: Jena, an open source SW framework for Java, with a rule-based inference engine;[32] Pellet, a sound and complete OWL-DL reasoner;[33] and KAON2, an infrastructure for managing ontologies written in OWL-DL and other SW rule languages.[34] For a short review of the problems and prospects for SW reasoning, see Fensel.[35]

Bootstrapping

Bootstrapping content for the SW is one more important issue. Sufficient content is required for the hoped-for network effects to appear. There are initiatives to generate data in RDF and to expose it on the Web as a vital first step. The DBpedia[36] is based on the Web 2.0 community-created encyclopedia Wikipedia, and is intended to extract structured information from Wikipedia allowing much more sophisticated querying. Sample queries given on the DPpedia Web site include a list of people influenced by Friedrich Nietzsche, and the set of images of American guitarists. DBpedia uses RDF, and is also interlinked with other data sources on the Web. When accessed in late 2007, the DBpedia dataset consisted of

Science–Semantic

103 million RDF triples. Other examples of linked data applications include the DBLP bibliography of scientific papers,[37] and the GeoNames database which gives descriptions of millions of geographical features in RDF.[38]

Even if RDF began to be published routinely, there is still a great deal of legacy content on the Web, and to make this accessible to SW technology some automation of the translation process is required. Gleaning Resource Descriptions from Dialects of Languages (GRDDL) allows the extraction of RDF from XML documents using transformations expressed in Extensible Stylesheet Language Transformations (XSLT) an extensible stylesheet language based on XML. It is hoped that such extraction could allow bootstrapping of some of the hoped-for SW network effects.[39]

Annotating documents and data with metadata about content, provenance, and other useful dimensions (even including relevant emotional reactions to content[40]) is also important for the effort to bring more content into the range of SW technologies.[41] Multimedia documents, such as images, particularly benefit from such annotation.[42] Again, given the quantities of both legacy data, and new data being created, methods of automating annotation have been investigated by a number of research teams in order to increase the quantity of annotated data available without excessive expenditure of resources.[41,43,44]

The Social Context: Web Science

The SW vision has been delineated with some care by the W3C, and as has been seen involves an intricate set of connections between a number of formalisms, each of which is designed to do a certain job. As we will describe in the next section, that vision has altered and gained complexity over time.

In general, there are severe complications in the mapping between the microlevel engineering of Web protocols, and the macrolevel social effects that result from large-scale use of the Web. The combination of scales, effects, and phenomena involved is too large to be easily covered by a single discipline, even computer science. The social interactions enabled by the Web place demands on the Web applications underlying them, which in turn put requirements on the Web's infrastructure. However, these multiple requirements are not currently well-understood.[45] Social studies tend to regard the Web as a given, whereas the Web is rather a world changeable by alterations to the protocols underlying it. Furthermore, the Web changes at a rate that is at least equal and may be faster than our ability to observe and analyze it.

The SW is a development bringing the Web vision to a new level of abstraction, yet the current state of our knowledge of the Web and its relation to off-line society leaves a number of questions unanswered about how it will impact at a large scale. In particular, it is unknown what social consequences there might be of the greater public exposure

and sharing of information that is currently locked in databases. Understanding these consequences is important partly because the developers of the SW want to build a technology that is not harmful to society thanks to emergent social effects, and partly because it is important that the SW goes with the grain of society, in order that it be effective in real-world situations.[5]

To this end, in 2006 the Web Science Research Initiative (WSRI) was set up as a joint venture by the Massachusetts Institute of Technology and the University of Southampton to foster the interdisciplinary study of the Web in its social and technical context. WSRI's role includes crafting a curriculum for study across the various relevant disciplines; Berners-Lee.[6] is a detailed review of the wide range of scientific and social-scientific research that is likely to be relevant, including graph and network theory, computer science, economics, complexity theory, psychology, law, etc.

HISTORY AND INTELLECTUAL BACKGROUND

The vision of a web of data was always implicit in the ideas underlying the development of the WWW, and was articulated by Sir Tim Berners-Lee at the first WWW conference in 1994. Berners-Lee is well known as the inventor of the WWW in 1989–1991, and has been a leading figure in the development of the SW. As well as holding chairs at the Massachusetts Institute of Technology, United States, and the University of Southampton, United Kingdom, Berners-Lee is the director of the W3C, which he founded in 1994.

A key moment in the development, and public perception, of the SW was an entry written for *Scientific American* by Berners-Lee, James A. Hendler, and Ora Lassila in 2001.[46] This entry postulated the next stage of the WWW explicitly as one where data and information, as well as documents, are processed automatically, and envisaged a world where intelligent agents were able to access information (e.g., from calendars, gazetteers, and business organizations) in order to undertake tasks and planning for their owners.

This vision of automation of a series of routine information processing tasks has not emerged at the time of writing (2008). The article's agent-oriented vision distracted attention from the main point of the SW, the potential of a web of linked *data* (as opposed to documents) with shared semantics. Hence, in 2006, Berners-Lee, together with Nigel Shadbolt and Wendy Hall, published another article in the IEEE journal *Intelligent Systems*, which made that point explicitly, and argued that the agent-based vision would only flourish with well-established data standards.[1]

The *Scientific American* article painted a very enticing picture, but its key message was less to do with the agents and more to do with the semantic information infrastructure that Berners-Lee et al. were advocating. Indeed, the infrastructure will be used for many knowledge management purposes, not only in allowing agents to communicate. The agent-focused rhetoric of the article has prompted some to argue that the SW is a restatement of the program of AI in the 1960s and 1970s, and will share its perceived failures. We address this question below, in the section entitled "Controversies."

In 2001 (and before), the conceptualization of the various formal layers of the SW was as shown in Fig. 2, with a fairly straightforward cascade up from URIs to XML and namespaces, to RDF and RDFS, through ontologies to rules, logic, proof and trust (the diagram has been widely distributed, but see e.g., Berners-Lee).[47] Comparison with Fig. 1 shows how the details of the SW layers have had to be amended over time as implementation has continued. The requirements for expression of ontology-related information has led to an extra complexity from that envisaged in 2001, while the criticism of the SW vision based on the *Scientific American* article has led to a realization that not only the expressive formalisms need to be in place, but also tools and methods need to be created to allow use of SW technologies to integrate smoothly into organizations' standard information workflows (e.g., Shadbolt, Vargas-Vera, Golbeck and Alani[1,44,48,49]). This led to a top layer, User Interface, being added to the Fig. 2 structure at a later date.

Where intelligent agency has appeared—and there are currently several applications, including shopbots and auction bots—it has tended to be handcrafted and unable to interact with heterogeneous information types. This is largely because of a lack of well-established scalable standards for information sharing; however, progress is being made toward that goal, especially via the painstaking committee-based standards development processes instituted by the W3C. These standards are crucial for the SW to "take off," and for the hoped-for network effects of a large number of users to emerge.[1]

The SW vision has been implemented by standard bodies, such as the Internet Engineering Task Force (IETF) as well as the W3C (the W3C is responsible for standards specific to the WWW), which have orchestrated efforts together with the user community to develop the languages at various levels to share meaning. Once standards are set by the W3C, they are called *recommendations*, acknowledging the reality that with the decentralization of the Web, and a lack of a central authority, standards cannot be enforced. The first RDF standard was specified in 1997 and became a W3C recommendation in 1999, thereby providing a minimal knowledge representation language for the Web with the clear backing of the nascent SW community.

Fixed standards for expressing ontologies appeared later in the process, with RDFS and OWL becoming recommendations in 2004. OWL evolved from other ontology language efforts, including Ontology Inference Layer (OIL)[50] and DARPA Agent Markup Language (DAML)[51] whose merged product, DAML+OIL, was the most important predecessor to OWL.[52] In January 2008, the query language SPARQL became a W3C recommendation, while the RIF was under development in mid-2008.

Fig. 3, created in 2003, illustrates Berners-Lee's vision of the pattern of SW development using the visual metaphor of a tide flowing onto a beach (this diagram is widely available, but see Connolly).[53] From top to bottom in the diagram are the various layers of the SW diagram, from trust and proof down to data exchange and markup. From left to right come the various stages in a rough lifecycle from research to deployment: the first stage is a blue-sky research project; the second is the production of a stable system or formalism that is not a standard; the best aspects of these systems are then used as the bases for W3C standards, and the final stage is one of wide deployment. Hence, for instance, early ontology efforts like Cyc and description logics led to efforts such as DAML and OIL, which in turn helped create OWL. Wide deployment of OWL then results in a so-called web of meaning.

The "sea" of research and deployment approaches from the bottom left of Fig. 3 to the top right, as the "tide" comes in. Hence in 1998, various formalisms were in place for all the various levels of representation of the SW, but only XML was a Web standard and beginning to be used widely. By 2003, OWL and RDFS were close to their final forms, and RDF was beginning to be used widely for cross-application interoperability. At the time of writing, the "tide" has advanced further to the right, so work is ongoing on rule language RIF, and query language SPARQL became an official W3C recommendation in 2008. Meanwhile OWL is being used more frequently by ontology builders.

The SW's history to date is largely one of standard-setting. However, it has also been argued that, analogous to other systems which have spread quickly and grown exponentially, what is needed is a "killer app" (i.e., an application that will meet a felt need and create a perception of the technology as "essential"). Less ambitiously, the SW's spread depends not only on having an impressive set of formalisms, but also software tools to use

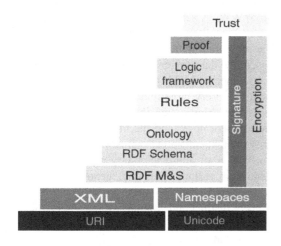

Fig. 2 The early layered view of the Semantic Web.

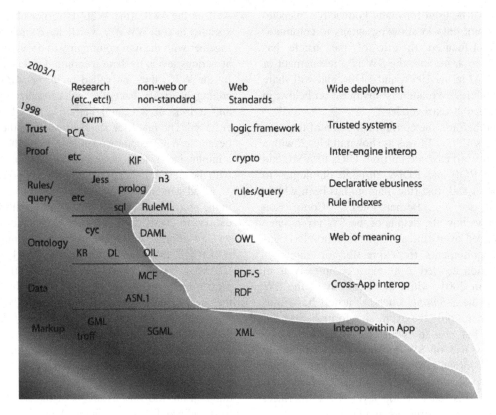

Fig. 3 A representation of the progress of semantic web development.

information represented in those formalisms.[49] The SW is clearly not, at the time of writing, an information resource in routine use. Nevertheless, there are some applications where SW technologies are serving valuable purposes, and we review some of these in the next section.

APPLICATIONS AND SYSTEMS

Properties of Systems

In general, SW projects tend to exhibit a few constant features. They generate new ontologies for the application domain (for example, art, or computer science), and use them to interrogate large stores of data, which could be legacy data or freshly harvested. Hence a body of evidence is building up that ontologies have an important role in mediating the integration of data from heterogeneous sources.

Furthermore, the results of SW projects are generally presented using custom-built interfaces. This hints at a very important research area, which is the development of scalable visualizers capable of navigating the graph of connected information expressed in RDF. As can be seen, the importance of applications and user interfaces was made clear in the latest version of the layered SW diagram (Fig. 1).

In this section we will look at active SW successes, focusing on application areas and types, then commercial/

real-world systems, before finally looking at some of the more successful academic efforts as judged by the SW development community itself.

Application Areas

There are areas where the SW is already an important tool, often in small focused communities with pressing information-processing requirements and various more or less common goals. Such communities can function as early adopters of the technology, exactly as the high energy physics discipline played a vital role in the development of the WWW. A series of case studies and use cases is maintained in w3.org's Web site.[54]

The most important application for SW technology is *e-science*, the data-driven, computationally intensive pursuit of science in highly distributed computational environments.[55] Very large quantities of data are created by analyses and experiments in disciplines such as particle physics, meteorology, and the life sciences. Furthermore, in many contexts, different communities of scientists will be working in an interdisciplinary manner, which means that data from various fields (e.g., genomics, clinical drug trials, and epidemiology) need to be integrated. Many accounts of distinct and complex systems (e.g., the human body, the environment) consist of data brought from disciplines varying not only in vocabulary, but also in the scale of description; understanding such systems, and the way in which events at the microscale affect the macroscale and *vice versa*, is clearly an important imperative. Many scientific disciplines have devoted resources to the creation of large-scale and robust ontologies for this and other purposes. The most well-known of these is the *gene ontology*, a controlled vocabulary to describe gene and gene product attributes in organisms, and related vocabularies developed by open biomedical ontologies.[56] Others include the protein ontology, the cell cycle ontology, Medical Subject Headings (MeSH, used to index life science publications), systematized nomenclature of medicine (SNOMED), and AGROVOC (agriculture, forestry, fisheries, and food).

E-government is another potentially important application area, where information is deployed widely, and yet is highly heterogeneous. Government information varies in provenance, confidentiality, and "shelf life" (some information will be good for decades or even centuries, while other information can be out-of-date within hours), while it can also have been created by various levels of government (national/federal, regional, state, city, and parish). Integrating that information in a timely way is clearly an important challenge (see for instance a pilot study for the United Kingdom's Office of Public Sector Information, exploring the use of SW technologies for disseminating, sharing, and reusing data held in the public sector.[57])

Commercial Activity

There is an increasing number of applications that allow a deeper querying of linked data. We have already discussed DBpedia,[36] DBLP,[37] and GeoNames.[38] Commercial applications are also beginning to appear. Garlik[58] is a company seeking to exploit SW-style technologies to provide individual consumers with more power over their digital data. It reviews what is held about people, harvesting data from the open Web, and represents this in a people-centric structure. Natural Language Processing is used to find occurrences of people's names, sensitive information, and relations to other individuals and organizations. Declaration of interest: Wendy Hall is chair of the Garlik Advisory Board. Twine[59] is intended to enable people to share knowledge and information, and to organize that information using various SW technologies (also, like Garlik, using Natural Language Processing). Twine's developer Nova Spivack has coined the term "knowledge networking" to describe the process, analogous to the Web 2.0 idea of 'social networking."

The increasing maturity of SW technology is being shown by the growing number of successful vendors of SW technology. We have already seen OWLIM,[31] which was developed by Ontotext, a semantic technology lab focused on technologies to support the SW and SW services based in Sofia, Bulgaria, and Montreal, Canada; Ontotext has been and is a partner in a number of major SW research projects.[60] Ontoprise, based in Karlsruhe,

Germany, is a software vendor for implementing SW infrastructure in large, distributed enterprises; its products include OntoBroker, which provides ontology support using the W3C recommended languages OWL, RDFS and SPARQL, and Semantic MediaWiki+, a collaborative knowledge management tool.[61] Asemantics, with offices in Italy, Holland, and the United Kingdom, uses a combination of Web 2.0 paradigms with SW technologies such as XML and RDF. The SW technologies are powerful representational tools but are often perceived as hard to use and search, so Asemantics attempts to exploit the perceived usability of Web 2.0 to present data in more widely accepted formats.[62]

Academic Work: The Semantic Web Challenge

Much of the major work in the SW has been carried out in the academic sphere, and in funded research projects between academic and commercial partners, and is reported in journals and conferences (see end of entry for a list of the more importance conferences). Any review of academic work in this field will inevitably be selective; for the purposes of this entry we will focus on a particular effort to nurture applications, the *Semantic Web Challenge*.

The SW Challenge was created in 2003, and associated with the International Semantic Web Conference (ISWC) of that year. Since then it has become an annual competition to create an application that shows SW technology in its best aspects, and which can act as a "benchmark" application. Hence the SW Challenge gives us a series of illustrative applications thought by researchers' peers to constitute best SW practice.[63]

To meet the criteria for the Challenge, a tool or system needs to meet a number of requirements,[64] which provide a useful characterization of the expectations governing an SW system, and are suggestive of the expected properties of SW applications. For instance, it should use information from sources that are distributed and heterogeneous, of real-world complexity and with diverse ownership. It should assume an open world, and that the information is never complete, and it should use some formal description of the meaning of the data. Optional criteria include a use of data in some way other than the creators intended, use of multimedia, and use of devices other than a PC. Applications need not be restricted to information retrieval, and ideally the system would be scalable in terms of the amount of data used and the number of distributed components cooperating. All these criteria indicate areas where SW systems would be expected to have an advantage.

The winners of the SW Challenge to date are as follows.

2003: CS AKTive Space (University of Southampton), an integrated application which provides a way to explore

Science–Semantic

the U.K. Computer Science Research domain across multiple dimensions for multiple stakeholders, from funding agencies to individual researchers, using information harvested from the Web, and mediated through an ontology.[65]

2004: Flink (Vrije Universiteit Amsterdam), a "Who's Who" of the SW which allows the interrogation of information gathered automatically from Web-accessible resources about researchers who have participated in ISWC conferences.[66]

2005: CONFOTO (appmosphere Web applications, Germany), a browsing and annotation service for conference photographs.[67]

2006: MultimediaN E-Culture Demonstrator (Vrije Universiteit Amsterdam, Centre for Mathematics and Computer Science, Universiteit van Amsterdam, Digital Heritage Netherlands and Technical University of Eindhoven), an application to search, navigate, and annotate annotated media collections interactively, using collections from several museums and art repositories.[68]

2007: Revyu.com (Open University), a reviewing and rating site specifically designed for the SW, allowing reviews to be integrated and interlinked with data from other sources (in particular, other reviews).[69]

CONTROVERSIES

The SW vision has always generated controversy, with a number of commentators being highly skeptical of its prospects. Let us briefly review some of the disputed issues.

The Semantic Web as "Good Old-Fashioned Artificial Intelligence"

One view holds that the SW is basically a throwback to the project to program machine intelligence which was jokingly christened by John Haugeland "GOFAI" (good old-fashioned AI). This proved impossible: so much of human intelligence is implicit and situated that it was too hard a problem to write down everything a computer needed to know to produce an output that exhibited human-like intelligence. For instance, if a human is told about a room, further explanations that a room generally has a floor, at least three walls, usually four, and a ceiling, and some method of ingress that is generally but not always a door, are not required. But a computer needs to be told these mundane facts explicitly—and similarly every time it is introduced to a new concept.[70]

One attempt to work around this problem is the Cyc project, set up in 1984, which aims to produce a gigantic ontology that will encode all commonsense knowledge of the type about the room given above, in order to support human-like reasoning by machines.[71] The project has always aroused controversy, but it is fair to say that over

two decades later, GOFAI is no nearer. The implicit nature of commonsense knowledge arguably makes it impossible to write it all down.

Many commentators have argued that the SW is basically a re-creation of the (misconceived) GOFAI idea, that the aim is to create machine intelligence over the Web, to allow machines to reason about Web content in such a way as to exhibit intelligence.[72,73] This, however, is a misconception, possibly abetted by the strong focus in the 2001 *Scientific American* article on an agent-based vision of the SW.[46] Like many GOFAI projects, the scenarios in that article have prominent planning components. There is also continuity between the AI tradition of work on formal knowledge representation and the SW project of developing ontologies (see below).

The SW has less to do with GOFAI as with context-based machine reasoning over content (and the provision of machine-readable data on the Web). The aim is not to bring a single ontology, such as Cyc, to bear on all problems (and therefore implicitly to define or anticipate all problems and points of view in the ontology definition), but rather to allow data to be interrogated in ways that were not anticipated by their creators. Different ontologies will be appropriate for different purposes; composite ontologies can be assembled from distributed parts (thanks to the design of OWL); and it is frequently very basic ontologies (defining simple terms such as "customer," "account number," or "account balance") that deliver large amounts of content. It is, after all, a matter of fact that people from different communities and disciplines can and do interact without making any kind of common *global* ontological commitment.[1,6,74]

Indeed, we can perhaps learn from the experience of hype and reaction that accompanied the development of AI. There has been a great deal of criticism of AI, but much has been learned from AI research and some AI methods and systems are now routinely exploited in a number of applications. The same may be expected of the SW. We should not expect to wake up one morning with the SW implemented and ready for use. Rather, a likelier model is that SW technologies will be incorporated into more systems "behind the scenes" wherever methods are needed to deal with signature SW problems (large quantities of distributed heterogeneous data).

Arguments for and against Ontologies

The importance of ontologies for the SW has been another point of friction with those who believe the program unrealistic. Ontologies are seen as expensive to develop and hard to maintain. Classification of objects is usually done relative to some task, and as the nature of the task changes, ontologies can become outdated. Classifications are also made relative to some background assumptions, and impose those assumptions onto the resulting ontology. To that extent, the expensive development of ontologies reflects the world view of the ontology builders, not necessarily the users. They are top-down and authoritarian, and therefore opposed to the Web ethos of decentralization and open conversation. They are fixed in advance, and so they don't work very well to represent knowledge in dynamic, situated contexts.[75–77]

Furthermore, say the critics, the whole point of the Web as a decentralized, linked information structure is that it reflects the needs of its large, heterogeneous user base which includes very many people who are naïve in their interactions. The infrastructure has to be usable by such people, which argues for simplicity. The rich linking structure of the current Web, combined with statistically based search engines such as Google, is much more responsive to the needs of unsophisticated users. The SW, in contrast, demands new information markup practices, and corporations and information owners need to invest in new technologies. Not only that, but current statistical methods will scale up as the number of users and interactions grows, whereas logic-based methods such as those advocated by the SW, on the other hand, scale less well (cf., e.g., Zambonini).[78]

Folksonomies

One development as part of the so-called Web 2.0 paradigm (of systems, communities, and services which facilitate collaboration and information-sharing among users) that has drawn attention in this context is that of the "folksonomy." Folksonomies have arisen out of the recent move to allow users to "tag" content on Web 2.0 sites such as the image-sharing site Flickr, and the video-sharing site YouTube. Having seen content, users are allowed to tag it with key words, which, when the number of users has become large enough, results in a structure of connections and classifications emerging without central control. Their promoters argue that folksonomies "really" express the needs of their users (since all the structure has arisen out of their user-based classifications), whereas ontologies "really" express the needs of authorities who can "impose" their views from the top-down.[76]

However, folksonomies are much less expressive than ontologies; they are basically variants on keyword searches. A tag "SF" may refer to a piece of science fiction, or to San Francisco, or something else from the user's private idiolect. Indeed, that ambiguity arises even if we make the unrealistic assumption of a monoglot English user community. Once we realize speakers of other languages will use a system, then there are further possible ambiguities—for instance, in German "SF" might refer to the Swiss television station Schweizer Fernsehen.

Resolving This Controversy

When a community is large enough and the benefits clear, then a large-scale ontology building and maintenance

program is justified. In a recent note, Berners-Lee argues that such conditions will be perhaps more frequently encountered than skeptics believe. On the very broad assumptions that the size of an ontology-building team increases as the order of the log of the size of the ontology's user community, and that the resources needed to build an ontology increase as the order of the square of community size, the cost per individual of ontology building will diminish rapidly as user community size increases. Of course these assumptions are not intended to be deeply realistic, so much as indicative of how the resource implications diminish as the community increases in size. Berners-Lee's moral: "Do your bit. Others will do theirs."[74]

Even so, not all ontologies need to be of great size and expressive depth. Certainly the claim that has been made that the SW requires a single ontology of all discourse on the model of Cyc, but this is not backed up by the SW community. Such an ontology, even if possible, would not scale, and in a decentralized structure like the Web its use could not be enforced. We should rather expect a lot of use of small-scale, *shallow* ontologies defining just a few terms that nevertheless are widely applicable.[74] Experience in building real-world SW systems often shows that expectations about the cost and complexity of the ontologies required are overblown, and the ontology-building process can be relatively straightforward and cheap.[79]

For example, the machine-readable friend-of-a-friend (FOAF) ontology is intended to describe people, their activities, and their relations to other people. It is not massively complex, and indeed publishing a FOAF account of oneself is a fairly simple matter of form-filling (using the FOAF-a-matic tool).[80] But the resulting network of people (showing their connections to other people) has become very large indeed. A survey performed in 2004 discovered over 1.5 million documents using the FOAF ontology.[81]

With respect to Folksonomies, it is important to note that ontologies and folksonomies serve different purposes. Folksonomies are based on word tags, whereas the basis for ontology reference is via a URI. One of the main aims of ontology definition is to *remove* ambiguity—not globally, for this may well be impossible, but rather within the particular context envisaged by the developer (see the section on "Symbol Grounding" below). Folksonomies will necessarily inherit the ambiguity of the natural language upon which they are based. And while folksonomies emerge from data-sharing practices, it is not necessarily the case the ontologies are authoritarian; rather, the latter should ideally be *rationalizations* of current sharing practice. This does entail departure from current practice, but not necessarily of great magnitude. Indeed, a strong possibility is to use cheaply gathered folksonomies as starting points for ontology development, gradually morphing the Web 2.0 structures into something with greater precision and less ambiguity.[82]

Symbol Grounding

An important aspect of the SW is that URIs must be interpreted consistently. However, terms and symbols are highly variable in their definitions and use through time and space. The SW project ideally needs processes whereby URIs are given to objects, such that the management of these processes is by communities and individuals, endorsed by the user community, who ensure consistency. This URI "ownership" is critical to the smooth functioning of the SW.[1]

But the process of *symbol grounding* (i.e., ensuring a fixed and known link between a symbol and its referent) is at best hard, and at worst (as argued by Wittgenstein, for instance) impossible.[83,84] Meanings do not stay fixed, but alter, often imperceptibly. They are delineated not only by traditional methods such as the provision of necessary and sufficient conditions, but also by procedures, technologies and instrumentation, and alter subtly as practice alters.

Any attempt to fix the reference of URIs is a special case of symbol grounding, and is consequently hard to do globally. It is certainly the case that attempting to resist the alteration in community practices and norms, and reformulation of meanings of terms, would be doomed.

Yorick Wilks has argued that since much knowledge is held in unstructured form, in plain text, automatic Natural Language Processing techniques, statistically based, can be used to "ground" meanings of terms for the SW.[73] Berners-Lee, on the other hand, maintains that the SW is necessarily based on logic and firm definitions (even if those definitions were imperfect, or highly situated and task-relative), not words, use patterns and statistics. Wilks' point is that the aim of defining terms in logic is too idealistic, and anyway depends on false assumptions about ordinary word meaning. Berners-Lee's counterargument is, in effect, that though meanings are not stable, they can be stable *enough* relative to individual applications and in particular contexts to allow the SW approach to work.

CONCLUSION

The SW has been somewhat misunderstood in some commentaries. Its aim is not to force users to accept large ontologies remote from data-sharing practice imposed by shadowy authorities. Neither is it intended to produce a theory of all discourse, or to reproduce GOFAI. Rather, it is intended to shift the emphasis of the Web from being a web of documents to a web of linked *data*. It is the development of formalisms and technologies facilitating the creation, sharing, and querying of linked data using sharable ontologies to establish common interpretations. For this reason, an alternative name for the SW is the *web of linked data*.

The SW is a work in progress. As it stands, the "buy in" to the SW has not yet produced the desirable network effects, although several disciplines are enthusiastic early adopters of the technology (e.g., the e-science community). And there are still several important research issues outstanding. It is not yet known how best to: 1) query large numbers of heterogeneous information stores at many different scales; 2) translate between, merge, prune, or evaluate ontologies; 3) visualize the SW; and 4) establish trust and provenance of the content.

As complex technologies and information infrastructures are developed, there is a dynamic feedback between requirements, analysis, engineering solutions, and hard-to-predict global behavior of human, machine, and hybrid systems. Understanding how basic engineering protocols governing how computers talk to each other can result in social movements at a very different level of abstraction is very hard, yet essential to realizing the SW vision. Indeed, such understanding, the defining purpose of the discipline of *Web Science*, is essential to ensuring that *any* Web-based information structure is beneficial.[5]

ACKNOWLEDGMENTS

The authors would like to thank Tim Berners-Lee, Nigel Shadbolt, James A. Hendler, Daniel J. Weitzner, Harith Alani, Marcia J. Bates, and an anonymous referee for helpful comments and discussions.

REFERENCES

1. Shadbolt, N.; Hall, W.; Berners-Lee, T. The Semantic Web revisited. IEEE Intell. Syst. **2006**, *21* (3), 96–101.
2. Fensel, D.; Bussler, C.; Ding, Y.; Kartseva, V.; Klein, M.; Korotkiy, M.; Omelayenko, B.; Siebes, R. Semantic Web application areas. In *7th International Workshop on Applications of Natural Language to Information Systems (NLDB 2002)*, Stockholm, Sweden, June 27–28, 2002, http://www.cs.vu.nl/~ronny/work/NLDB02.pdf, 2002 (accessed July 2008).
3. Fensel, D. *Ontologies: A Silver Bullet for Knowledge Management and Electronic Commerce*, 2nd Ed.; Springer: Berlin, Germany, 2004.
4. Berners-Lee, T. Relational databases on the Semantic Web, http://www.w3.org/DesignIssues/RDB-RDF.html, 1998 (accessed December 2007).
5. Berners-Lee, T.; Hall, W.; Hendler, J.; Shadbolt, N.; Weitzner, D. Creating a science of the Web. Science **2006**, *313* (5788), 769–771.
6. Berners-Lee, T.; Hall, W.; Hendler, J.A.; O'Hara, K.; Shadbolt, N.; Weitzner, D.J. A framework for Web Science. Found. Trends Web Sci. **2006**, *1* (1), 1–134.
7. Klyne, G.; Carroll, J.J.; McBride, B. Resource Description Framework (RDF): Concepts and abstract syntax, 2004 http://www.w3.org/TR/rdf-concepts/ (accessed December 2007).

8. Berners-Lee, T. Principles of design, 1998, http://www.w3.
    org/DesignIssues/Principles.html (accessed December 2007).

9. Berners-Lee, T.; Fielding, R.; Masinter, L. Uniform Resource Identifier (URI): Generic syntax, 2005, http://gbiv.com/protocols/uri/rfc/rfc3986.html (accessed December 2007).

10. Bray, T.; Paoli, J.; Sperberg-McQueen, C.M.; Maler, E.; Yergeau, F. *Extensible Markup Language (XML) 1.0*, 4ᵗʰ Ed.; 2006, http://www.w3.org/TR/xml/ (accessed December 2007).

11. Brickley, D.; Guha, R.V.; McBride, B. RDF vocabulary description language 1.0: RDF Schema, 2004, http://www.w3.org/TR/rdf-schema/ (accessed December 2007).

12. McGuinness, D.L.; van Harmelen, F. OWL Web Ontology Language overview, 2004, http://www.w3.org/TR/owl-features/ (accessed December 2007).

13. Antoniou, G.; van Harmelen, F. *A Semantic Web Primer*; MIT Press: Cambridge MA, 2004.

14. Dean, M.; Schreiber, G.; Bechhofer, S.; van Harmelen, F.; Hendler, J.; Horrocks, I.; McGuinness, D.L.; Patel-Schneider, P.F.; Stein, L.A. OWL Web Ontology Language Reference, 2004, http://www.w3.org/TR/owl-ref/ (accessed December 2007).

15. Smith, M.K.; Welty, C.; McGuiness, D.L. OWL Web Ontology Language guide, 2004, http://www.w3.org/TR/owl-guide/ (accessed December 2007).

16. Boley, H.; Kifer, M. RIF basic logic dialect, 2007, http://www.w3.org/TR/rif-bld/ (accessed December 2007).

17. Prud'hommeaux, E.; Seaborne, A. SPARQL query language for RDF, 2007, http://www.w3.org/TR/rdf-sparql-query/ (accessed December 2007).

18. Golbeck, J. Trust on the World Wide Web: A survey. Found. Trends Web Sci. **2006**, *1* (2), 1–72.

19. Bonatti, P.A.; Duma, C.; Fuchs, N.; Nejdl, W.; Olmedilla, D.; Peer, J.; Shahmehri, N. Semantic Web policies—a discussion of requirements and research issues. In *The Semantic Web: Research and Applications*, 3rd European Semantic Web Conference 2006 (ESWC-06), Budva, Montenegro, 2006; Sure, Y., Domingue, J., Eds.; Springer: Berlin, 2006.

20. O'Hara, K.; Alani, H.; Kalfoglou, Y.; Shadbolt, N. Trust strategies for the Semantic Web. In *Workshop on Trust, Security and Reputation on the Semantic Web*, 3rd International Semantic Web Conference (ISWC 04), Hiroshima, Japan, 2004, http://eprints.ecs.soton.ac.uk/10029/ (accessed December 2007).

21. Golbeck, J.; Hendler, J. Accuracy of metrics for inferring trust and reputation in Semantic Web-based social networks. In *Engineering Knowledge in the Age of the Semantic Web*, Proceedings of 14th International Conference, EKAW 2004, Whittlebury Hall, U.K., 2004; Motta, E., Shadbolt, N., Stutt, A., Gibbins, N., Eds.; Springer: Berlin, Germany, 2004; 116–131.

22. Groth, P.; Jiang, S.; Miles, S.; Munroe, S.; Tan, V.; Tsasakou, S.; Moreau, L. An architecture for provenance systems, http://eprints.ecs.soton.ac.uk/13216/1/provenanceArchitecture10.pdf, 2006 (accessed December 2007).

23. O'Hara, K.; Shadbolt, N. *The Spy in the Coffee Machine: The End of Privacy As We Know It*; Oneworld: Oxford, U.K., 2008.

24. http://creativecommons.org/about/ (accessed December 2007).

25. Weitzner, D.J.; Hendler, J.; Berners-Lee, T.; Connolly, D. Creating a policy-aware Web: Discretionary, rule-based access for the World Wide Web. In *Web and Information Security*, Ferrari, E., Thuraisingham, B., Eds.; Idea Group Inc: Hershey, PA, 2005.

26. http://jena.sourceforge.net/ (accessed December 2007).

27. http://sourceforge.net/projects/threestore (accessed December 2007).

28. Harris, S.; Gibbins, N. 3store: Efficient bulk RDF storage. In *Proceedings of the 1st International Workshop on Practical and Scalable Systems*, Sanibel Island, FL, 2003, http://km.aifb.uni-karlsruhe.de/ws/psss03/proceedings/harris-et-al.pdf (accessed December 2007).

29. http://www.oracle.com/technology/tech/semantic_technologies/index.html (accessed December 2007).

30. http://www.ontotext.com/owlim/ (accessed July 2008).

31. Kiryakov, A.; Ognyanov, D.; Manov, D. OWLIM: A pragmatic semantic repository for OWL. In *Web Information and Systems Engineering–WISE 2005 Workshops*, Proceedings of the Workshop on Scalable Semantic Web Knowledge Base Systems at WISE 2005, New York, November 2005; Dean, M., Guo, Y., Jun, W., Kaschek, R., Krishnaswamy, S., Pan, Z., Sheng, Q.Z., Eds.; Springer: Berlin, Germany, 2005; 182–192, http://www.ontotext.com/publications/ssws_owlim.pdf (accessed July 2008).

32. McBride, B. Jena: Implementing the RDF model and syntax specification. In *Proceedings of the 2nd International Workshop on the Semantic Web: SemWeb 2001*, World Wide Web Conference 2001, Hong Kong, May 2001; Decker, S., Fensel, D., Sheth, A., Staab, S., Eds.; CEUR-WS, Vol. 40, 2001, http://sunsite.informatik.rwth-aachen.de/Publications/CEUR-WS/Vol-40/mcbride.pdf (accessed July 2008).

33. Sirin, E.; Parsia, B.; Cuenca Grau, B.; Kalyanpur, A.; Katz, Y. Pellet: A practical OWL-DL reasoner. J. Web Semant. **2007**, *5* (2), 51–53.

34. http://kaon2.semanticweb.org/ (accessed July 2008).

35. Fensel, D.; Van Harmelen, F. Unifying reasoning and search to Web scale. IEEE Internet Comput. **2007**, *11* (2), 96, 94–95 (sic).

36. Auer, S.; Bizer, C.; Kobilarov, G.; Lehmann, J.; Cyganiak, R.; Ives, Z. DBpedia: A nucleus for a Web of open data. In *Proceedings of the 6th International Semantic Web Conference 2007*, Busan, South Korea, 2007, http://iswc2007.semanticweb.org/papers/715.pdf (accessed December 2007).

37. http://www4.wiwiss.fu-berlin.de/dblp/ (accessed December 2007).

38. http://www.geonames.org/ (accessed December 2007).

39. Connolly, D., Ed. Gleaning Resource Descriptions from Dialects of Languages (GRDDL), 2007, http://www.w3.org/TR/grddl/ (accessed December 2007).

40. Schröder, M.; Zovato, E.; Pirker, H.; Peter, C.; Burkhardt, F. W3C emotion incubator group report, 2007, http://www.w3.org/2005/Incubator/emotion/XGR-emotion/ (accessed December 2007).

41. Handschuh, S.; Staab, S., Eds. Annotation for the Semantic Web; IOS Press: Amsterdam, the Netherlands, 2003.

42. Troncy, R.; van Ossenbruggen, J.; Pan, J.Z.; Stamou, G.; Halaschek-Wiener, C.; Simou, N.; Tsouvaras, V. Image

annotation on the Semantic Web, 2007, http://www.w3.org/2005/Incubator/mmsem/XGR-image-annotation/ (accessed December 2007).

43. Handschuh, S.; Staab, S.; Ciravegna, F. S-CREAM—Semi-automatic CREAtion of Metadata. In *Knowledge Engineering and Knowledge Management: Ontologies and the Semantic Web*, Proceedings of 13th International Conference, EKAW 2002, Sigüenza, Spain, 2002; Gómez-Pérez, A., Benjamins, V.R., Eds.; Springer: Berlin, Germany, 2002; 358–372.

44. Vargas-Vera, M.; Motta, E.; Domingue, J.; Lanzoni, M.; Stutt, A.; Ciravegna, F. MnM: Ontology-driven semi-automatic and automatic support for semantic markup. In *Knowledge Engineering and Knowledge Management: Ontologies and the Semantic Web*, Proceedings of 13th International Conference, EKAW 2002, Sigüenza, Spain, 2002; Gómez-Pérez, A., Benjamins, V.R., Eds.; Springer: Berlin, Germany, 2002; 379–391.

45. Hendler, J.; Shadbolt, N.; Hall, W.; Berners-Lee, T.; Weitzner, D. Web Science: An interdisciplinary approach to understanding the World Wide Web. Commun. ACM **2008**, *51* (7), 60–69.

46. Berners-Lee, T.; Hendler, J.; Lassila, O. The Semantic Web. Sci. Am. May **2001**, http://www.sciam.com/article.cfm?articleID=00048144-10D2-1C70-84A9809EC588EF21 (accessed December 2007).

47. Berners-Lee, T. Foreword. In *Spinning the Semantic Web: Bringing the World Wide Web to its Full Potential*; Fensel, D., Hendler, J., Lieberman, H., Wahlster, W., Eds.; MIT Press: Cambridge, MA, 2003; xi–xxiii.

48. Golbeck, J.; Grove, M.; Parsia, B.; Kalyanpur, A.; Hendler, J. New tools for the Semantic Web. In *Knowledge Engineering and Knowledge Management: Ontologies and the Semantic Web*, Proceedings of 13th International Conference, EKAW 2002, Sigüenza, Spain, 2002; Gómez-Pérez, A., Benjamins, V.R., Eds.; Springer: Berlin, Germany, 2002; 392–400.

49. Alani, H.; Kalfoglou, Y.; O'Hara, K.; Shadbolt, N. Towards a killer app for the Semantic Web. In *The Semantic Web*, Proceedings of the International Semantic Web Conference 2005, Hiroshima, Japan, 2005; Gil, Y., Motta, E., Benjamins, V.R., Musen, M.A., Eds.; Springer: Berlin, 2005; 829–843.

50. Fensel, D.; Horrocks, I.; van Harmelen, F.; Decker, S.; Erdmann, M.; Klein, M. OIL in a nutshell. In *Knowledge Engineering and Knowledge Management: Methods, Models and Tools*; Proceedings of 12th European Knowledge Acquisition Workshop (EKAW 2000), Juan-les-Pins, France, October 2000; Dieng, R., Corby, O., Eds.; Springer: Berlin, Germany, 2000; 01–16, http://www.cs.vu.nl/~ontoknow/oil/downl/oilnutshell.pdf (accessed July 2008).

51. http://www.daml.org/about.html (accessed July 2008).

52. Patel-Schneider, P.; Horrocks, I.; van Harmelen, F. Reviewing the design of DAML + OIL: An ontology language for the Semantic Web. In *Proceedings of the 18th National Conference on Artificial Intelligence (AAAI02)*, Edmonton, Canada, 2002, http://www.cs.vu.nl/~frankh/postscript/AAAI02.pdf (accessed December 2007).

53. Connolly, D. Semantic Web update: OWL and beyond, 2003, http://www.w3.org/2003/Talks/1017-swup/all.htm (accessed December 2007).

54. http://www.w3.org/2001/sw/sweo/public/UseCases/ (accessed December 2007).

55. Hendler, J.; de Roure, D. E-science: The grid and the Semantic Web. IEEE Intell. Syst. **2004**, *19* (1), 65–71.

56. http://www.geneontology.org/ (accessed July 2008).

57. Alani, H.; Dupplaw, D.; Sheridan, J.; O'Hara, K.; Darlington, J.; Shadbolt, N.; Tullo, C. Unlocking the potential of public sector information with Semantic Web technology. In *Proceedings of the 6th International Semantic Web Conference 2007*, Busan, South Korea, 2007, http://iswc2007.semanticweb.org/papers/701.pdf (accessed December 2007).

58. https://www.garlik.com/index.php (accessed December 2007).

59. http://www.twine.com/ (accessed December 2007).

60. http://www.ontotext.com/index.html (accessed July 2008).

61. http://www.ontoprise.de/index.php?id=134 (accessed July 2008).

62. http://www.asemantics.com/index.html (accessed July 2008).

63. http://www.informatik.uni-bremen.de/agki/www/swc/index.html (accessed December 2007).

64. http://challenge.semanticweb.org/ (accessed December 2007).

65. Schraefel, m.m.c.; Shadbolt, N.R.; Gibbins, N.; Glaser, H.; Harris, S. CS AKTive Space: Representing computer science on the Semantic Web. In *Proceedings of WWW 2004*; New York, 2004, http://eprints.ecs.soton.ac.uk/9084/ (accessed December 2007).

66. Mika, P. Flink: Semantic Web technology for the extraction and analysis of social networks. J. Web Semant **2005**, *3*(2), http://www.websemanticsjournal.org/papers/20050719/document7.pdf (accessed December 2007).

67. Nowack, B. CONFOTO: A semantic browsing and annotation service for conference photos. In *The Semantic Web*, Proceedings of the International Semantic Web Conference 2005, Hiroshima, Japan, 2005; Gil, Y., Motta, E., Benjamins, V.R., Musen, M.A., Eds.; Springer: Berlin, Germany, 2005; 1067–1070.

68. Schreiber, G.; Amin, A.; van Assem, M.; de Boer, V.; Hardman, L.; Hildebrand, M.; Hollink, L.; Huang, Z.; van Kersen, J.; de Niet, M.; Omelayenko, B.; van Ossenbruggen, J.; Siebes, R.; Taekema, J.; Wielemaker, J.; Wielinga, B. MultimediaN e-culture demonstrator, 2006, http://www.cs.vu.nl/~guus/papers/Schreiber06a.pdf (accessed December 2007).

69. Heath, T.; Motta, E. Revyu.com: A reviewing and rating site for the Web of data. In *Proceedings of the 6th International Semantic Web Conference 2007*, Busan, South Korea, 2007, http://iswc2007.semanticweb.org/papers/889.pdf (accessed December 2007).

70. Haugeland, J. Understanding natural language. J. Philos. **1979**, *76*, 619–632.

71. Lenat, D.B. Cyc: A large-scale investment in knowledge infrastructure. Commun. ACM **1995**, *38* (11), 32–38.

72. Jones, K.S. What's new about the Semantic Web? Some questions. SIGIR Forum **2004**, *38*(2), http://www.sigir.org/forum/2004D/sparck_jones_sigirforum_2004d.pdf (accessed December 2007).

73. Wilks, Y. The Semantic Web: Apotheosis of annotation, but what are its semantics? IEEE Intell. Syst. **2008**, *23* (3), 41–49.

74. Berners-Lee, T. The fractal nature of the Web, 2007, http://www.w3.org/DesignIssues/Fractal.html (accessed December 2007).

75. Pike, W.; Gahegan, M. Beyond ontologies: Toward situated representations of scientific knowledge. Intl. J. Hum. Comput. Stud. **2007**, *65* (7), 674–688.

76. Shirky, C. Ontology is overrated: categories, links and tags, 2005, http://www.shirky.com/writings/ontology_overrated.html (accessed December 2007).

77. Stevens, R.; Egaña Aranguren, M.; Wolstencroft, K.; Sattler, U.; Drummond, N.; Horridge, M.; Rector, A. Using OWL to model biological knowledge. Intl. J. Hum. Comput. Stud. **2007**, *65* (7), 583–594.

78. Zambonini, D. The 7 (f)laws of the Semantic Web, 2006, http://www.oreillynet.com/xml/blog/2006/06/the_7_flaws_of_the_semantic_we.html (accessed December 2007).

79. Alani, H.; Chandler, P.; Hall, W.; O'Hara, K.; Shadbolt, N.; Szomsor, M. Building a pragmatic Semantic Web. IEEE Intell. Syst. **2008**, *23* (3), 61–68.

80. http://www.ldodds.com/foaf/foaf-a-matic (accessed December 2007).

81. Ding, L.; Zhou, L.; Finin, T.; Joshi, A. How the Semantic Web is being used: An analysis of FOAF documents. In *Proceedings of the 38th International Conference on System Sciences*, 2005, http://ebiquity.umbc.edu/_file_directory_/papers/120.pdf (accessed December 2007).

82. Mika, P. Ontologies are us: A unified model of social networks and semantics. J. Web Semant. **2007**, *5* (1), 5–15.

83. Harnad, S. The symbol grounding problem. Physica D **1990**, *42*, 335–346. http://users.ecs.soton.ac.uk/harnad/Papers/Harnad/harnad90.sgproblem.html (accessed December 2007).

84. Wittgenstein, L. *Philosophical Investigations*; Basil Blackwell: Oxford, U.K., 1953.

2. Berners-Lee, T. *Weaving the Web: The Past, Present and Future of the World Wide Web by Its Inventor*; Texere Publishing: London, U.K., 1999.

3. Berners-Lee, T.; Hall, W.; Hendler, J.A.; O'Hara, K.; Shadbolt, N.; Weitzner, D.J. A framework for web science. Found. Trends Web Sci. **2006**, *1* (1), 1–134.

4. Berners-Lee, T.; Hall, W.; Hendler, J.; Shadbolt, N.; Weitzner, D. Creating a science of the Web. Science **2006**, *313* (5788), 769–771.

5. Berners-Lee, T.; Hendler, J.; Lassila, O. The Semantic Web. Sci. Am. May **2001**. http://www.sciam.com/article.cfm?articleID=00048144-10D2-1C70-84A9809EC588EF21 (accessed December 2007).

6. Fensel, D. *Ontologies: A Silver Bullet for Knowledge Management and Electronic Commerce*, 2nd Ed.; Springer: Berlin, 2004.

7. Fensel, D.; Hendler, J.; Lieberman, H.; Wahlster, W. *Spinning the Semantic Web: Bringing the World Wide Web to its Full Potential*; MIT Press: Cambridge, MA, 2003.

8. Shadbolt, N.; Hall, W.; Berners-Lee, T. The Semantic Web revisited. IEEE Intell. Syst. **2006**, *21* (3), 96–101.

9. There are several important annual conferences for the SW community, including: the World Wide Web Conference (WWW); the International Semantic Web Conference (ISWC—pronounced Iss-wick); the European Semantic Web Conference. These conferences preserve their proceedings online.

10. The World Wide Web Consortium's Semantic Web activity page is at http://www.w3.org/2001/sw/, and contains references to interviews, manifestos and statements by key SW developers. It also maintains a useful site of case studies and use cases at http://www.w3.org/2001/sw/sweo/public/UseCases/. For Web Science, see http://webscience.org/.

BIBLIOGRAPHY

1. Antoniou, G.; van Harmelen, F. *A Semantic Web Primer*; MIT Press: Cambridge MA, 2004.

Science–Semantic

Semiotics

Marcel Danesi
Department of Anthropology, University of Toronto, Toronto, Ontario, Canada

Abstract

This entry deals with the main goals, theories, concepts, and practices of semiotics, as a science of meaning. Based on the fundamental notion of *sign*—anything that has the capacity to stand for something else (real or imagined)—semiotics has a long history behind it that overlaps with those of philosophy and language study. The main notions that undergird the practice of semiotics are examined closely here. These include denotation, connotation, opposition, text, code, and structure. Denotation is the intensional meaning assigned to a sign, while connotation refers to the extensional meanings it gains through usage. Opposition is the technique of sifting out minimal differences in meaning among signs so as to extrapolate an overall meaning structure from them. A text is a form constructed with signs in a structured fashion in order to convey some message; it includes verbal forms (such as books, conversations, etc.) and nonverbal forms (such as body language, paintings, etc.). Codes are the systems that organize the meanings that signs bear in social contexts (language, music, etc.), and structure is the notion that signs bear a patterned relation with each other and that it is through this very relation that they bear meaning.

INTRODUCTION

Semiotics is the discipline that aims to study signs and their functions. A *sign* is any physical form that stands for something other than itself to a specific individual or group in some specific context. A cross figure is such a form. It consists of two lines crossing at right angles. But most people who come across this form in our culture would hardly interpret it as a random (meaningless) shape consisting of two intersecting lines. Rather, they would tend to interpret it as standing for the arithmetical plus sign or for the religion of Christianity, among other things. It all depends on who uses it and in what context it is used. As a form occurring in a math book it would probably stand for the plus sign; as a figure made from two pieces of wood located on a church roof, it would stand instead for Christianity.

Today, semiotics is used mainly as methodological tool to study such sign-based phenomena as body language, art forms, discourses, visual communication, media, advertising, narratives, language, clothing, cuisine, rituals—in a phrase, anything that constitutes meaning-based social activity or behavior. For this reason, it is often referred to as the "science of meaning." One of its modern-day founders, the Swiss philologist Ferdinand de Saussure (1857–1913), defined it as the science concerned with "the role of signs as part of social life" and "the laws governing them."[1]

HISTORICAL SKETCH

The term *semiotics*—from Greek *sēmeiotikos* "observant of signs"—was coined by Hippocrates (ca. 460–370 B.C.E.), the founder of Western medicine, to designate the study of the symptoms produced by the human body. Hippocrates argued that the particular physical form that a symptom takes—a *semeion* ("mark")—constitutes a vital clue for finding its etiological source. The form stands not for itself, but for "something invisible"—a disease, malady, or ailment. The concept of *semeion* as a bodily or natural sign was expanded a little later to include human-made forms (such as words) that stood conventionally for ideas or cognitive states. Among the first to tackle the role of conventional signs in cognition was the Greek philosopher Plato (ca. 427–347 B.C.E.), who saw them as forms referring not to specific referents, but to all referents that resemble each other in some identifiable way. For example, the *circle* form does not refer to a singular thing (although it can if need be), but to anything that has the property "circularity." No matter what "size" the circle form has it is always interpreted as a "circle." For this reason, Plato argued that signs are not simple replacements for things—a particular drawing of a circle can be altered in size, but it will still be perceived as a circle because it possesses the property of circularity. Plato's pupil Aristotle (384–322 B.C.E.) argued instead that signs start out as practical devices that do indeed allow us to name singular (specific) things, rather than generic properties (circularity, roundness, etc.). We discover that things have such properties as we go along naming them. It is at such points of discovery that we create more abstract referential domains—words, symbols, etc.—indicating "categories" (plants, animals, objects, etc.).

Eventually, the question arose as to whether or not there was any connection between natural and conventional signs. The Stoics were among the first to deal with this question around 300 B.C.E., arguing that conventional

Encyclopedia of Library and Information Sciences, Fourth Edition DOI: 10.1081/E-ELIS4-120043687

signs are "evaluative structures," so to speak, that simply preserve for a specific group what people in that group assess to be useful or important; whereas symptoms (natural signs) are "response structures" produced by biology. The same question was taken up by St. Augustine (354–430 C.E.) in his *De Doctrina Christiana*, in which he describes natural signs *(signa naturalia)* as forms lacking intentionality and conventional ones *(signa data)* as products of human intentions. The former include not only bodily symptoms, but also the colors of plants, the signals that animals emit, and so on; the latter include not only words, but also gestures and the symbols that humans invent to serve their psychological, social, and communicative needs (pp. 24–56).[2]

For some reason, interest in signs waned shortly after St. Augustine's writings. It was rekindled in the eleventh century by the Scholastics. Using Augustine's philosophical ideas and Aristotelian logic as their frames of reference, they asserted that signs captured truths, not simply evaluated them (as the Stoics had claimed). So, a word such as *tree* captured the existence of something real and true—a specific and recognizable type of arboreal plant. But within Scholasticism there were some scholars—called *nominalists*—who argued that "truth" was a matter of subjective opinion and that signs captured, at best, only illusory and highly variable human versions of it. John Duns Scotus (ca. 1266–1308) and William of Ockham (ca. 1285–1349), for instance, stressed that signs, once invented, ended up referring to other signs producing a kind of existential circularity—a perspective that is strikingly akin to some modern theories of the sign. So, for the nominalists, the word *tree* is meaningful because users of the word believe that a particular plant requires identification. The same plant could easily have been subsumed under some other botanically named category (as a subspecies of that category). In effect, there is no truth, just our interpretation (or evaluation) of it. The renowned theologian St. Thomas Aquinas (ca. 1225–1274) countered, however, that one cannot deny that signs such as *tree* refer to real things. The names for these things may vary, but not the "truth" that they exist as such. At about the same time, the English philosopher and scientist Roger Bacon (ca. 1214–1292) developed one of the first comprehensive typologies of signs, claiming that, without a firm understanding of the role of signs in the construction of knowledge, discussing what truth is or is not would end up being a trivial matter of subjective opinion. The first step in understanding how information (raw facts) becomes knowledge is in understanding how signs are used to organize it. Plants constitute an information system, so to speak. They become part of organized knowledge (botany) the instant they are named. Naming the world of objects, events, things, plants, flowers, animals, beings, ideas, etc. allows people to organize the world conceptually, that is, to remember it through the words themselves. Without names the world would not have parts to it, at least in human cognition. Naming practices bring out what parts are useful or necessary to specific cultures and their knowledge schemes.

It was British philosopher John Locke (1632–1704) who first put forward the proposal of incorporating sign study, which he termed *semeiotics* (recalling Hippocrates's term), into philosophy in his *Essay Concerning Human Understanding* (1690).[3] For Locke, semeiotics was useful as an investigative instrument for philosophers, not as a distinct discipline. He thus defined it as the "doctrine" of signs, with *doctrine* meaning "system of principles." The idea of fashioning an autonomous discipline of sign study did not emerge until the late nineteenth century, when the Swiss philologist Ferdinand de Saussure (mentioned above) put such an idea forward in his *Cours de linguistique générale* (1916), a textbook compiled after his death. Saussure used the term *sémiologie* (English *semiology*) to designate the new discipline. He suggested that the main goal of semiology was to understand the social functions of signs—that is, to study how signs allow people to refer to things in their social environments in specific ways and how these permit people to interact meaningfully.

Today, Locke's term *(semeiotics)*, spelled *semiotics*, is the preferred one. It was reintroduced by another modern-day founder of the discipline, the American pragmatist philosopher Charles S. Peirce (1839–1914), becoming the term adopted by the International Association of Semiotic Studies in the year of its establishment, 1969. The term *significs*, coined by Victoria Lady Welby (1837–1912) in her correspondence with Peirce, is also used occasionally in the technical literature, but with a specific sense—the study of the relation of signs to the senses and the emotions. Although his writing style is rather dense, Peirce's ideas have come to constitute the theoretical platform upon which the study of signs is now elaborated.[4] Perhaps Peirce's greatest insight is that signs are "informed hunches" as to what something means in human terms. In other words, we sense a necessary psychological relation between the sign-forms we create and use and the things they stand for.

Following on the coattails of Saussure and Peirce, a number of key scholars developed semiotics into the sophisticated discipline that it has become today. Only a few can be mentioned here. The philosopher Ludwig Wittgenstein (1889–1951) suggested that signs were pictures of reality.[5] Each time we utter or hear a word such as *tree*, a generic image of the plant comes inevitably to mind. When we combine it with *apple*, that image is rendered more precise (in contrast to, say, a *fig tree*). Wittgenstein's view of the sign continues to inform a large part of semiotic theory and practice. The American semiotician Charles Morris (1901–1979) divided semiotic method into: 1) the study of sign assemblages, which he called *syntactics*; 2) the study of the relations between signs and their referents, which he called *semantics*; and 3) the study of the relation between signs and their social uses, which he called *pragmatics*.[6,7] The Russian-born

American semiotician Roman Jakobson (1896–1982) studied various facets of sign construction, but is probably best known for his semiotic model of communication, which suggests that sign exchanges in communication are hardly ever neutral but involve subjectivity and goal-attainment of some kind—that is, when we speak we intend to get something out of it, and the nature of the signs used bears this out.[8] The French semiotician Roland Barthes (1915–1980) illustrated the power of using semiotics for unmasking the hidden meanings in popular spectacles such as wrestling matches and Hollywood blockbuster movies (1957). French semiotician Algirdas J. Greimas (1917–1992) developed the branch of semiotics known as *narratology*, which studies the underlying structure of narratives.[9] The late American semiotician Thomas A. Sebeok (1920–2001) expanded the semiotic paradigm to include animal signaling systems, which he termed *zoosemiotics*, and sign use among all species (including plants), which has come to be called *biosemiotics*.[10] The interweaving and blending of ideas, findings, and scientific discourses from different disciplinary domains was, Sebeok claimed, the distinguishing feature of semiotics. Finally, Italian semiotician Umberto Eco (b. 1936) has contributed significantly to our understanding of how we interpret sign assemblages such as texts.[11] For example, a *closed* text, such as a traditional detective novel, revolves around clues that lead inescapably to the identity of the perpetrator of a crime. This is the goal of that type of text, unless it is constructed to accomplish something more (such as the mystery stories of Alfred Hitchcock). On the other hand, an *open* text, such as a novel by James Joyce or Virginia Woolf, leaves the interpretive domain open, since it does not lead to an inescapable conclusion (as does a detective novel).

MEANING

The underlying object of semiotic inquiry is, as mentioned, what *meaning* is and how it unfolds in human activities. What is meaning? A little reflection will reveal that *meaning* is a confusing term. As the psychologists Charles Ogden and I. A. Richards showed in their classic 1923 work, *The Meaning of Meaning*, there are at least 23 meanings of this word in English:[12]

He *means* to study jurisprudence. =	"intends"
A red light *means* stop. =	"indicates"
True love *means* everything. =	"has Importance"
The way she stared was full of *meaning*. =	"special import"
Does life have a *meaning*? =	"purpose"
What does that word *mean* to you? =	"convey"
And so on.	

To avoid ambiguity, the terms *semiosis* and *signification* are used instead by semioticians. The former refers to the psychological process itself of producing and recognizing specific forms as signs (p. 32, 41).[13] the latter is the

mental image that crops up in the brain the instant a sign is used. Signification involves two main meaning-making processes—reference and sense. Reference is the process itself of identifying something in the sign-form; sense is what that form elicits psychologically, historically, and socially. Signs (such as words) may refer to the same (or similar) things, known as *referents*, but they have different senses. For example, the "long-eared, short-tailed, burrowing mammal of the family Leporidae" can be called *rabbit* or *hare* in English. Both words refer essentially to the same kind of mammal. But there is a difference of sense between the two words—*hare* is the more appropriate term for describing the mammal if it is larger, has longer ears and legs, and does not burrow. Another difference is that a *rabbit* is often perceived to be a "pet," while a *hare* is unlikely to be perceived as such. The German philosopher Gottlob Frege (1848–1925) was among the first to point out the difference between sense and reference,[14] which he called *Sinn* and *Bedeutung* respectively. This same dichotomy was exemplified practically by philosopher Willard O. Quine (1908–2000). Think of a linguist who overhears the word *Gavagai* from the mouth of a native informant when a rabbit is sighted scurrying through the bushes, Quine (pp. 102–129)[15] suggests. The linguist cannot determine what the word refers to— "rabbit," "undetached rabbit parts," or "rabbit stage"— because all of these are senses associated with that word. The sense, therefore, will remain indeterminate unless it can be inferred from the context in which *Gavagai* occurs.

There is also another aspect of signification that merits mention here—definition. Definition is an analytical technique; it is a statement made about what something means consisting of words and other signs (for example, pictures). As useful as it is, definition leads inevitably to circularity. Take the dictionary definition of *cat* as "a small carnivorous mammal domesticated since early times as a catcher of rats and mice and as a pet and existing in several distinctive breeds and varieties." The problem with this statement is its use of *mammal* to define *cat*. In effect, it has replaced the latter with the former. So, what is the meaning of *mammal*? A *mammal*, it states elsewhere, is "any of various warm-blooded vertebrate animals of the class Mammalia." But this definition is hardly a viable solution. What is an *animal*? The dictionary defines *animal* as an *organism*, which it defines, in turn, as an individual form of *life*, which it then defines as the property that distinguishes living *organisms*. At that point the dictionary has gone into a referential loop, since it has employed an already-used concept, *organism*, to define *life*. This circular pattern surfaces in all domains of signification. It suggests that signs can never be understood in the absolute, only in relation to other signs.

In contemporary semiotics, the terms *denotation* and *connotation* are preferred to reference and sense. Consider, again, the word *cat*. The word elicits an image of a "creature with four legs, whiskers, retractile claws," etc. This is its *denotative* meaning. It allows users of the sign to determine if something real or imaginary under consideration is an exemplar of a "cat" or not. Denotative meaning thus divides the world or reference into yes-no domains—something is either a cat or it is not. The word *denotation*, incidentally, is derived from the compound Latin verb *de-noto* "to mark out, point out, specify, indicate." The noun *nota* ("mark, sign, note") itself derives from the verb *nosco* ("to come to know," "to become acquainted with" and "to recognize"). All other meanings of the word *cat* are *connotative*—as can be seen in "He's a real cool cat;" "She let the cat out of the bag;" and so on. These meanings are products of the historical associations forged between cats and socially significant concepts or processes. Connotation also encompasses emotional cues. Consider the word *yes*. In addition to being a sign of affirmation (denotative meaning), it can have various emotional senses (connotative meanings), depending on the tone of voice with which it is uttered. If one says it with a raised tone, as in a question, "Yes?" then it would convey doubt or incredulity. If articulated emphatically, "Yes!" then it would connote triumph, achievement, or victory.

Connotation is not an option, as some traditional philosophical and linguistic theories of meaning continue to sustain to this day; it is something we are inclined to extract at a *prima facie* level from a sign. The numbers 7 and 13 have specific denotative meanings—each digit stands for a specific quantity of things. But in our culture both invariably reverberate at the same time with connotative meanings such as "fortune," "destiny," "bad luck," and so on. Abstract concepts, such as *motherhood, masculinity, friendship*, and *justice*, are particularly high in connotative content. In 1957, the psychologists Charles Osgood, G. J. Suci, and P. H. Tannenbaum[16] showed this empirically by using a technique that they called the *semantic differential*, a technique consisting in asking a series of questions to subjects about a particular concept— *Is X good or bad? Should Y be weak or strong?* etc.— which they rate on seven-point scales. The ratings are collected and analyzed statistically in order to sift out any general pattern they might bear. Suppose that subjects are asked to rate the concept "ideal American president" in terms of the following scales: *Should the president be:* 1) *young or old?* 2) *practical or idealistic?* 3) *modern or traditional?* 4) *male or female?* and so on. A subject who feels that the president should be more "youngish" than "oldish" would place a mark toward the *young* end of the first scale; one who feels that a president should be "bland," would place a mark toward the *bland* end of the *attractive-bland* scale; and so on. If a statistically significant sample of subjects rated the president in this way, we would get a "connotative profile" of the American presidency in terms of the culture-based variations in sense that it evokes. Research using the semantic differential has shown, for example, that connotation is invariably culture-specific—a concept such as *noise* turns out to be a highly emotional one for the Japanese, who rate it consistently at the ends of the scales presented to them; whereas it is a fairly neutral concept for Americans, who tend to

rate it on average in the mid-ranges of the same scales. Connotation is not, therefore, open-ended; it is constrained by a series of culture-specific factors. Without such constraints, our signification systems would be virtually unusable.

Although it has a long history behind it in philosophy, the distinction between denotation and connotation, as we understand it today, was used for the first time by the American linguist Leonard Bloomfield in his seminal 1933 book called *Language*. This distinction was elaborated upon a little later by Danish linguist Louis Hjelmslev[17] and French semiotician in various works.

Semiotics also makes an important distinction between the terms *image* and *concept*. The former is the mental picture of a referent that is evoked when a sign is used; the latter is the culture-specific interpretation that is assigned to that picture. There are two types of concepts— concrete and abstract. The former is the concept that is formed when a sign refers to something that can be seen, heard, smelled, touched, tasted—that is, observed in some direct sensory way. The latter is the concept formed when the sign to something that cannot be perceived in such a direct sensory fashion. A "cat" constitutes a concrete concept because the existence of a real cat in the physical world can be perceived and thus easily pictured in the mind. On the other hand, "love" is an abstract concept because, although it can be experienced emotionally, it cannot be observed directly—that is, the emotion itself cannot be separated from the behaviors, states of mind it produces. The mental image that it evokes is, thus, abstract (imaginary).

The distinction between concrete and abstract concepts is only a general one. In actual fact, there are degrees and layers of concreteness and abstraction. At the highest level, called the *superordinate* level by psychologists, concepts are considered to have a highly general classificatory (abstract) function. So, for example, in the dictionary definition of *cat* (above), the related concept of *mammal* would be viewed as a superordinate concept, because it refers to the general category of animals to which a cat is perceived as belonging. Then, there is the *basic* or *prototypical* level, which is where the word *cat* itself would fit in. This is the level where basic types of mammals are classified—cats, dogs, goats, hogs, horses, etc. The third level, called the *subordinate* level, is where more detailed ways of referring to something occur. There are, in fact, many types (breeds) of cat—*Siamese, Persian, Abyssinian, Korat*, etc.—which allow us to refer to culturally meaningful differences in detail. However, such notions as levels and hierarchies in concept-formation are problematic, as Umberto Eco pointed out in his 1984 book *Semiotics and the Philosophy of Language*. The main difficulty, he suggested, is that decisions as to where a concept belongs in a hierarchy invariably end up being a matter of subjective choice.

Ultimately, the meanings that signs capture allow people to recognize certain patterns in the world over and over again. Signs are thus closely tied to social needs and aspirations, creating an ongoing dialogue between people that would otherwise never come into being—a fact emphasized by many semioticians, especially the Russian theorist Mikhail Bakhtin (1895–1975). Bakhtin went so far as to claim that signs gain meaning only as they are exchanged by people in actual social dialogue or discourse.[18] In effect, he maintained that all human meaning is constructed dialogically (socially).

SIGNS

Semiotic inquiry is guided by two fundamental models of the sign—known as Saussurean and Peircean. Saussure saw the sign as a binary form—a structure with two components, namely a physical part, such as the sounds that make up the word *cat*, called the *signifier*, and the concept that the sign elicits, called the *signified* (p. 101).[1] Saussure claimed, moreover, that there is no necessary psychological motivation or reason for creating the word *cat* other than the social need to do so. Any other signifier would have done the job just as effectively. This is why his model of the sign is also called "arbitrary." Peirce put forward a "triadic" model of the sign—a structure consisting of the actual physical sign-form, called the *representamen*, the thing to which it refers, termed the *object*, and the meanings that it elicits in real-world situations, called the *interpretant* (Peirce 1931–1958: Volume 2, 247–248, 307). The interpretant constitutes itself a "derived" sign, because it entails the further production of meanings (senses) arising from the context in which a sign is used. In our culture, a *cat* is considered to be a domestic companion, among other things; in others it is viewed primarily as a sacred animal; and in others still it is considered to be a source of food. Thus, while the sign refers to virtually the same mammal in different cultural contexts (no matter what name is used), its interpretant varies considerably.

Peirce also developed a comprehensive typology of signs, identifying 66 types in total. Newcomers to semiotics often react with perplexity to his typology, which consists of seemingly obscure and unfathomable notions such as *qualisigns*, *sinsigns*, and *legisigns*. But his terminological style is actually quite straightforward. As its name implies, a *qualisign* is a sign that draws attention to some *quality* of its referent (the object it represents). In language, an adjective is a qualisign since it draws attention to the qualities (color, shape, size, etc.) of things. In other sign systems, qualisigns include colors (painting), harmonies and tones (music), etc. A *sinsign* is a representamen that *singles* out a particular object—a pointing finger and the words *here* and *there* are examples of sinsigns. A *legisign* is a form that designates something by convention (literally "by law"). Legisigns include various kinds of symbols and emblems such as those used on flags and

logos. Unlike Saussure, Peirce viewed sign-creation as originating in the perception of some property in an object. For this reason, he called the initial act of sign-construction a "firstness" event. Firstness is, more technically, a tendency to forge signs as simulations of objects (or other sign-forms for that matter). The outcome is a sign that resembles what it stands for in some way. Peirce called such a sign an *icon*. Portraits are icons of human faces (and what they mean); onomatopoeic words are icons of sounds made by certain objects or actions (*drip*, *bang*, etc.); and so on. The referents of icons can be figured out even by those who are not a part of the culture, if they are told how icons simulate, resemble, or substitute them. A "secondness" tendency in sign-creation consists in relating objects in some way. He called signs that result from this tendency *indexes*. The pointing finger is a basic example of an index. When we point to something, we are in fact relating it to our location as pointers. If it is close by we refer to it as *near* or *here*. If not, we refer to it as *far* or *there*. Finally, a "thirdness" tendency consists in creating signs in historically based or conventional ways. Peirce called signs that result from this tendency *symbols*. The cross figure used to stand for Christianity is a perfect example of a symbol. Although it represents the figure of a cross on which Christ was crucified iconically, it is interpreted historically and conventionally as a sign standing for the religion that was founded after Christ's death.

Despite the obvious richness and breadth of Peircean sign theory, the Saussurean model continues to enjoy wide use among semioticians because it is a much more expedient one to apply, especially in the initial phases of analysis. Signifiers can easily be separated from contexts of occurrence and studied abstractly in relation to signifieds, albeit somewhat artificially. Peirce's model, however, has proven to be a more insightful and all-encompassing one in the development of a comprehensive theory of meaning.

STRUCTURE, TEXT, AND CODE

In order to extract meaning from a form, one must be able to recognize it as a sign in the first place. This means that it must have *structure*. Specifically, a form is a sign if: 1) it is physically distinctive; and 2) it is constructed in a predictable or recurring way. The former is called, more specifically, *paradigmatic* and the latter *syntagmatic* aspects of sign-structure. What keeps the words *cat* and *rat* recognizably distinct? It is, of course, the initial sound. The phonic difference between *c* (= /k/) and *r* (= /r/) is, in fact, what allows us to recognize the two words as different signs. Paradigmatic structure is a feature of all types of signs, not just words. In music, a major and minor chord of the same key are perceivable as distinct on account of a half tone difference in the middle note of the chord; the left and right shoes of a pair are identifiable as different in terms of the orientation of each shoe; raising the index and middle fingers in a vertical orientation can mean "victory," "peace" (among other meanings), but aiming the same two fingers in a horizontal way at someone would be interpreted instead as a threat; and so on.

The words *cat* and *rat* are legitimate signs, not only because they are recognizable as different in a specific way, but also because the combination of sounds with which they are constructed is consistent with English syllable structure. On the other hand, *pfat* would not be recognized as a legitimate word in English because it violates an aspect of such structure—English words cannot start with the cluster *pf*. Syllable structure is an example of *syntagmatic* structure. Syntagmatic structure too is found in the composition of all kinds of signs. In music, for instance, a melody is recognizable as such only if the notes follow each other in a certain way (e.g., according to the rules of harmony); two shoes are considered to form a pair if they are of the same size, style, and color; and so on.

The sign can take any form, or "size," we desire to give it—it can be something "small," such as a word or two fingers raised in a vertical way; or it can be something much "larger," such as a mathematical equation or a narrative. If we ask a mathematician what $c^2 = a^2 + b^2$ means, he or she would instantly recognize it as an equation (the signifier) standing for the Pythagorean theorem (the signified). If we ask someone who has just read a novel (the signifier), what he or she got out of it, we would receive an answer that reveals a perception of the novel as a form containing a hidden message or purpose (the signified).

In contemporary semiotic theory, such "larger signs" are called *texts*, rather than simply signs; and the meanings they encode are called *messages*. The term text embraces such things as conversations, letters, speeches, poems, myths, novels, television programs, paintings, scientific theories, musical compositions, and so on. Texts are composite structures (signs made up of smaller signs), but they are still signs, that is, they are not interpreted in terms of their constituent parts, but holistically as single meaning-bearing structures. This is why when we ask someone what a novel means, he or she couches the answer in terms of the message he or she extracts from it, not in terms of the words it contains.

Texts are used primarily to carry out *representation*—defined as the use of signs (words, pictures, sounds, etc.) to relate, depict, portray, or reproduce something perceived, sensed, imagined, or felt in some textual form. As an example, consider the concept of *sex*. This is something that exists in the world as a biological and emotional phenomenon. Perceiving it as something meaningful, humans across cultures have represented sex in various textual forms throughout their history. For example, in our culture, common textual representations of *sex* include: 1) a photograph of two people engaged in kissing

romantically; 2) a poem describing the various emotional aspects of sex; or 3) an erotic movie depicting the more physical aspects of sex. Each of these constitutes a specific kind of textual form. The meanings (messages) that each captures are built into it not only by its maker, but also by certain preexisting notions relative to the culture in which it was made. Representations of sex in, say, Paris are thus going to be different from representations of it Bombay or San Francisco. Moreover, the type of text or medium used to portray the object of sex also shapes its interpretation. Photographs can show fairly limited views of sexual activities, whereas movies can provide much more graphic detail. Finally, the ways in which people living in Paris, Bombay, or San Francisco will derive meaning from the representations of sex will vary widely. This is because they have become accustomed in their specific cultures to different perceptions of what sex is.

Text-making implies knowledge of how signs cohere into systems–words, figures, digits, sounds, etc. To enter into a conversation, for example, one would need to know the language system involved. This provides the signs (words, tones, etc.) and specifies the relations that these bear to each other for the purpose of making verbal messages. The term used in semiotics to refer to such a system is *code*. Language, dress, music, and gesture are examples of codes. These can be defined, more formally, as systems of signs that have specific paradigmatic and syntagmatic properties and, thus, can be used over and over to encode and decode texts. There are many kinds of codes. For example, *intellectual codes* contain signs in them (numbers, words, symbols, etc.) that allow for representational activities of a logical, mathematical, scientific, or philosophical nature; *social codes* (dress, gender, food, space, etc.) contain sign-structures for making messages in socially appropriate ways and for regulating interpersonal activities. Food codes, for example, underlie how people interpret certain foods as signifiers of various rituals, meanings, etc. This is the reason why many Christians say grace before starting a meal together or Jews say special prayers before partaking of wine and bread.

Codes may also have a *contextual* function. Consider a discarded and damaged beer can. If one were to come across this item on a sidewalk on a city street, one would no doubt view it as a piece of garbage or rubbish. But if one saw the very same object on a pedestal, displayed in an art gallery, and given a title such as "Waste," then one would be inclined to interpret it in a vastly different way. One would, in fact, interpret it as an artistic text, decrying a throw-away or materialistic society. Clearly, the can's physical context of occurrence and social frame of reference—its location on a sidewalk versus its display in an art gallery—will determine how we will interpret it. The art gallery is, in effect, a social code. This is why we interpret anything that is put on display within it as "art," rather than as something else (pp. 34–39).[19]

OPPOSITION

To identify forms as meaning-bearing structures, the so-called technique of *opposition* was used by Saussure in the *Cours*, where he called it *différence*. As we saw above, by opposing the word *cat* to the word *rat* we will be able to establish that the consonants /k/ and /r/ are meaning-signaling phonic cues in English. As a technique, opposition was further elaborated by a number of linguists who congregated in Prague in the early 1920s. The linguist Trubetzkoy,[20,21] for example, called word pairs such as *cat-versus-rat* that differed by only one sound in the same position *minimal pairs*. Opposition was also used by the same linguists to examine higher-level semantic *différences* such as synonymy (*big-large*), antonymy (*big-little*), taxonomy (*rose-flower*), part-whole relations (*handle-cup*), and so on. As C. K. Ogden (p. 18),[22] an early promoter of opposition theory claimed, "the theory of opposition offers a new method of approach not only in the case of all those words which can best be defined in terms of their opposites, or of the oppositional scale on which they appear, but also to *any* word." In the 1930s and 1940s, semioticians started noticing that oppositional structure was not confined to language. It cropped up in the analysis of nonverbal systems and codes as well. For example, in the integer system of numbers, oppositions include *positive-versus-negative*, *odd-versus-even*, and *prime-versus-composite*; in music, basic oppositions include *major-versus-minor* and *consonant-versus-dissonant*; and so on.

The Prague School linguists also argued that there were levels or orders of oppositions. In arithmetic, for example, the *addition-versus-subtraction* opposition is the basic one while the *multiplication-versus-division* opposition is a derived one—since multiplication is repeated addition and division repeated subtraction. The *addition-versus-subtraction* opposition is thus a first-order opposition and the derived *multiplication-versus-division* opposition a second-order opposition. In an analogous vein, French semiotician Algirdas J. Greimas later introduced the notion of the "semiotic square" to connect sets of oppositions.[9] Given a sign (for example, *rich*), Greimas claimed that we determine its overall meaning by opposing it to its contradictory (*not rich*), its contrary (*poor*), and its contradictory (*not poor*) in tandem. Also, as work with the semantic differential showed in the 1950s (mentioned above), there are also gradations within the binary oppositions themselves, which are due to culture-specific connotative processes. Anthropologist Claude Lévi-Strauss also entered the debate on opposition theory in the same decade by showing that pairs of oppositions often cohere into sets forming recognizable units. In analyzing kinship systems, Lévi-Strauss[23] found that the elementary unit of kinship was made up of a set of four oppositions: *brother* vs. *sister*, *husband* vs. *wife*, *father* vs. *son*, and *mother's brother* vs. *sister's son*. Lévi-Strauss suspected that

similar sets characterized units in other cultural systems and, thus, that their study would provide fundamental insights into the overall nature of human social organization.

Although the idea goes right back to Aristotle, the cognitive importance of opposition was noticed by the psychologists Wilhelm Wundt (1832–1920) and Edward B. Titchener (1867–1927), who were the ones to term it *opposition*. Its use in semiotics and linguistics is due, as mentioned, to Saussure and the Prague School linguists.[24–26] Since its introduction, the theory has often been criticized as being artificial and not really consistent with human psychology. However, already in the 1940s Jakobson[27] argued that the notion could, actually, be used to explain the psychology of language development. He noted that sound oppositions that occur frequently are among the first ones learned by children. Nasal consonants—/n/ and /m/—exist in all languages; and they are also among the earliest sounds acquired by children. On the other hand, consonants pronounced near the back of the throat are relatively rare and, seemingly, are among the last sounds to be acquired by children. In other words, the theory of opposition predicts the sequence of phonemic acquisition in children.

Research on metaphor since the latter part of the 1970s[28–31] has also serendipitously discovered that opposition theory has psychological validity. American linguist George Lakoff and philosopher Mark Johnson started the ball rolling by claiming that a simple linguistic metaphor such as "John is a gorilla" is really a token of something more general, namely, a conceptual metaphor that has the cognitive structure *people are animals*.[29] This is why we can also say that *John* or *Mary* or whoever we want is a *gorilla*, *snake*, *pig*, *puppy*, and so on. Each specific linguistic metaphor ("John is a gorilla," "Mary is a snake," etc.) is not an isolated example of poetic fancy. It is an instantiation of a more general conceptual metaphor—*people are animals*. The question becomes: How are such concepts formed? They are formed through *image schemata*.[32,33] The source for the *people are animals* conceptual metaphor seems to be an unconscious perception that human personalities and animal behaviors are linked in some way. In other words, it is the consequence of an ontological opposition: *humans-versus-animals*. This is yet another type of opposition—one in which the two poles are not contrasted (*night-versus-day*), but equated. This suggests that oppositional structure operates in a noncontrastive way at the level of figurative meaning.

POSTSTRUCTURALISM

The most severe critiques of opposition theory started in the 1950s, revolving around the relative notion of *markedness*.[34–37] In minimal pairs such as *night-versus-day*, the question becomes: Which of the two poles is the more basic one (culturally or psychologically)? The more basic (or default) one is called the *unmarked* pole and the other the *marked* pole. In pairs such as *night-versus-day* it is easy to identify *day* as the unmarked form and *night* as its marked counterpart. This fact comes out in many signifying forms and representations. For example, we ask "How many days are left before your birthday?" not "How many nights are left before your birthday?" Now, consider the *male-versus-female* opposition. In this case, the choice of one or the other as the unmarked pole is problematic and culture-specific. In patrilineal societies the unmarked form is *male*; but in matrilineal ones, as the Iroquois one,[38] it is *female*. This difference in markedness has social consequences. In English, gendered terms like *chairman*, *spokesman*, etc. were often cited in the not-too-distant past as examples of how the English language predisposed its users to view certain social roles in strict gender terms, with the masculine gender being considered the unmarked one. Feminist critics maintained (correctly) that English grammar and vocabulary were organized from the perspective of those at the center of the society—the men.

Some scholars, especially Michel Foucault (1926–1984) and Jacques Derrida (1930–2004), started to see opposition theory itself as flawed and the unwitting source of social inequalities.[39,40] Their refutations of this central structuralist technique led to the movement known as *poststructuralism*. To Derrida, the oppositions identified by linguists and semioticians were the result of an endemic logocentrism in western culture, not the result of some tendency present in the human brain. Saussure had emphasized that every sign is understandable in terms of its difference from other signs. In contrast to Saussure's idea of *différence*, Derrida invented the word *différance* (spelled with an "a," but pronounced in the same way), to intentionally radicalize Saussurean theory. With this term Derrida aimed to show that Saussure's so-called discoveries were unwitting biased ones, given the atmosphere of scientific logocentrism in which he operated, and which veiled from him the logic of *différance*—namely that a science of language cannot succeed because it must unfold through language and thus partake of the slippage (as he called it) it discovers.

Derrida argued that all sign systems are self-referential—signs refer to other signs, which refer to still other signs, and so on ad infinitum. Thus, what appears to be stable and logical to the language scientist turns out to be illogical and paradoxical. Many semioticians and linguists have severely criticized post structuralism. It has nevertheless had a profound impact on many fields of knowledge, not just semiotics and linguistics. So what do post structuralists analyze and how does post structuralism differ from traditional structuralist practice? From many points of view, post structuralism is really nothing more than structuralism expanded to include a few radical ideas. One of these is clearly logocentrism—the view that all human knowledge is constructed by linguistic categories.

Because written language is the fundamental condition of knowledge-producing enterprises, such as science and philosophy, these end up reflecting nothing more than the writing practices used to articulate them. In hindsight, there was nothing particularly radical in this poststructuralist position. Already in the 1920s, Jakobson and Trubetzkoy started probing the "relativity" of language oppositions in the light of their social and psychological functions. Basing their ideas in part on the work of German psychologist Karl Bühler (1879–1963), the Prague School linguists posited that language categories mirrored social ones. The goal of a true semiotic science, they claimed, was to investigate the isomorphism that manifested itself between sign and social systems.

In the end, the poststructuralist movement was, arguably, nothing more than a reaction to Saussureanism in its most radical forms. It was (and continues to be) of little or no interest to semioticians who work primarily within the framework of Peircean sign theory, which emphasizes the interpretive component in sign study.

SEMIOTICS AND INFORMATION

Above all else, semiotics is useful as an interdisciplinary tool. It has also been applied fruitfully to the information sciences see, for instance Brier[41] who gives an in-depth analysis of the "semiotics of information," as it may be called. Information can be defined simply as data that can be received by humans, animals, or machines. In various scientific theoretical frameworks, it is considered as something mathematically probabilistic—a ringing alarm signal, for instance, is said to carry more information than one that is silent, because the silent state is the "expected state" of the alarm system, while the former is its "alerting state" and thus carries maximum information about the referential domain the system is designed to encode. As is well known, the individual who developed the mathematical theory of information was the American telecommunications engineer Claude Shannon (1916–2001), who showed, essentially, that the information contained in a signal is inversely proportional to its probability—that is to say, the more probable a signal, the less information "load" it carries with it; the less likely, the more.

Shannon's model essentially depicts information transfer as a one-way process dependent on probability factors, that is, on the degree to which a message is to be expected or not in a given situation. It is appropriately called the "bull's-eye model" because a sender of information is defined as someone or something aiming a message at a receiver of the information as if in a bull's-eye target range. Shannon also introduced several key terms into the general study of information and communication: channel, noise, redundancy, and feedback. His model has, over the years, been useful in providing a terminology for describing aspects of communication and information systems, but it tells us nothing about how messages and meanings shape and ultimately determine the nature of human communication and knowledge-making events. The semiotician would ask: how does information become knowledge? The answer is that it is encoded in the form of signs and codes. Each code thus presents information according to its own particular kind of structure. This allows humans to interpret the world of objects and events in a specific way and, subsequently, to respond to it in specific ways. The innate semiotic modeling system of a species routinely converts the external world of information (sensory, affective, etc.) into internal states of knowing and remembering that are unique to the species. Access to those states without possessing the same mental modeling system is never going to be complete. To study modeling systems, a branch of semiotics, known as *biosemiotics*, has become dominant within the entire field.[42,43] Essentially, biosemiotics attempts to determine how each species converts information into self-serving knowledge through its innate system of semiosis—the ability to produce and use signs.

In the human world, however, information is assigned meaning, since it is meaningless in itself. This is accomplished by connecting it to some code or system of interpretation (language, science, mathematics, music, etc.), so that it can be utilized for some purpose. Information is useless without a semiotic key for interpreting and using it. It is, as its etymology suggests—from Latin *information* "a sketch, an outline"—nothing more than encoded *form*. Deriving *content* from this form requires knowledge of how it has been represented and how it has been used. Not only, but the relation between the representation of information and the information itself is so intrinsic that it is often impossible to differentiate between the two.

CONCLUDING REMARKS

Semiotics is, in a fundamental way, a study of how humans shape raw information into knowledge categories through sign-creation. We create signs in order to select from the raw flux of information that bombards our senses what we wish to remember from it. Although we create new signs to help us gain new knowledge and modify previous knowledge—that is what artists, scientists, writers, for instance, are always doing—by and large, we literally let our culture "do the understanding" for us. We are born into an already-fixed system of sign-use, called the *semiosphere* by the late Estonian semiotician Juri Lotman (1922–1993)—that will largely determine how we come to view the world around us.[44] Moreover, the semiosphere, like the biosphere, regulates human behavior and shapes evolution. But although they can do little about the biosphere, humans have the ability to reshape the semiosphere any time they want. This is why cultures are both restrictive and liberating. They are restrictive in that they impose upon individuals reared in them an already-fixed system

of signification. But cultures are also liberating because paradoxically they provide the textual resources by which individuals can seek new meanings on their own. The artistic, religious, scientific, and philosophical texts to which individuals are exposed in social contexts, moreover, open up the mind, stimulate creativity, and engender freedom of thought. As a result, human beings tend to become restless for new meanings, new messages.

REFERENCES

1. de Saussure, F. In *Cours de linguistique générale*; Bally, C.; Sechehaye, A., Eds.; Course in General Linguistics McGraw-Hill: New York, 1916/1958; Baskin, W., trans.
2. Deely, J. *Four Ages of Understanding: The First Postmodern Survey of Philosophy from Ancient Times to the Turn of the Twentieth Century*; University of Toronto Press: Toronto, ON, 2001.
3. Locke, J. *An Essay Concerning Human Understanding*; Collins: London, 1690.
4. Peirce, C.S. *Collected Papers of Charles Sanders Peirce*; Hartshorne, C., Weiss, P., Eds.; Harvard University Press: Cambridge, MA, 1931–1958; Vols. 1–8.
5. Wittgenstein, L. *Tractatus Logico-Philosophicus*; Routledge and Paul: London, 1922.
6. Morris, C. *Foundations of the Theory of Signs*; University of Chicago Press: Chicago, IL, 1938.
7. Morris, C. *Signs, Language and Behavior*; Prentice-Hall: Englewood Cliffs, NJ, 1946.
8. Jakobson, R. Linguistics and poetics. In *Style and Language*; Sebeok, T.A., Ed.; MIT Press: Cambridge, MA, 1960; 34–45.
9. Greimas, A.J. In *On Meaning: Selected Essays in Semiotic Theory*; Perron, P.; Collins, F., Eds.; University of Minnesota Press: Minneapolis, MN, 1987.
10. Sebeok, T.A. *Global Semiotics*; Indiana University Press: Bloomington, IL, 2001/2002.
11. Eco, U. *The Limits of Interpretation*; Indiana University Press: Bloomington, IL, 1990.
12. Ogden, C.K.; Richards, I.A. *The Meaning of Meaning*; Routledge and Kegan Paul: London, 1923.
13. Fisch, M.H. Peirce's general theory of signs. In *Sight, Sound, and Sense*; Sebeok, T.A., Ed.; Indiana University Press: Bloomington, IL, 1978; 31–70.
14. Frege, G. *Begiffsschrift eine der Aritmetischen nachgebildete Formelsprache des reinen Denkens*; Nebert: Halle, 1879.
15. Quine, W.O. *From a Logical Point of View; Nine Logico-Philosophical Essays*; Harvard University Press: Cambridge, MA, 1953.
16. Osgood, C.E.; Suci, G.J.; Tannenbaum, P.H. *The Measurement of Meaning*; University of Illinois Press: Urbana, IL, 1957.
17. Hjelmslev, L. *Essais linguistique*; Munksgaard: Copenhagen, 1959.
18. Bakhtin, M. In *The Dialogic Imagination*; Holquist, M., Ed.; University of Texas Press: Austin, TX, 1981.
19. Danesi, M. *The Quest for Meaning: A Guide to Semiotic Theory and Practice*; University of Toronto Press: Toronto, ON, 2007.

20. Trubetzkoy, N.S. Essaie d'une théorie des oppositions phonologiques. J. Psychol **1936**, *33*, 5–18.

21. Trubetzkoy, N.S. *Introduction to the Principles of Phonological Description*; Martinus Nijhoff: The Hague, 1968.

22. Ogden, C.K. *Opposition: A Linguistic and Psychological Analysis*; Paul, Trench, and Trubner: London, 1932.

23. Lévi-Strauss, C. *Structural Anthropology*; Basic Books: New York, 1958.

24. Hjelmslev, L. Note sur les oppositions supprimables. Travaux de Cercle Linguistique de Prague **1939**, *8*, 51–57.

25. Benveniste, E. Structure des relations de personne dans le verbe. Bulletin de la Société de Linguistique de Paris **1946**, *43*, 225–236.

26. Jakobson, R. Observations sur le classement phonologique des consonnes. *Proceedings of the Fourth International Congress of Phonetic Sciences*, Ghent, 1939; 34–41.

27. Jakobson, R. *Kindersprache, Aphasie und algemeine Lautgesetze*; Almqvist and Wiksell: Uppsala, 1942.

28. Pollio, H.; Barlow, J.; Fine, H.; Pollio, M. *The Poetics of Growth: Figurative Language in Psychology, Psychotherapy, and Education*; Lawrence Erlbaum Associates: Hillsdale, NJ, 1977.

29. Lakoff, G.; Johnson, M. *Metaphors We Live By*; Chicago University Press: Chicago, IL, 1980.

30. Lakoff, G.; Johnson, M. *Philosophy in the Flesh: The Embodied Mind and Its Challenge to Western Thought*; Basic: New York, 1999.

31. Fauconnier, G.; Turner, M. *The Way We Think: Conceptual Blending and the Mind's Hidden Complexities*; Basic: New York, 2002.

32. Lakoff, G. *Women, Fire, and Dangerous Things: What Categories Reveal About the Mind*; University of Chicago Press: Chicago, IL, 1987.

33. Johnson, M. *The Body in the Mind: The Bodily Basis of Meaning, Imagination and Reason*; University of Chicago Press: Chicago, IL, 1987.

34. Tiersma, P.M. Local and general markedness. Language **1982**, *58*, 832–849.

35. Eckman, F.R., Ed. *Markedness*; Plenum: New York, 1983.

36. Andrews, E. *Markedness Theory*; Duke University Press: Durham, 1990.

37. Battistella, E.L. *Markedness: The Evaluative Superstructure of Language*; State University of New York Press: Albany, GA, 1990.

38. Alpher, B. Feminine as the unmarked grammatical gender: Buffalo girls are no fools. Aust. J. Linguist **1987**, *7*, 169–187.

39. Foucault, M. In *The Archeology of Knowledge*; Sheridan Smith, A.M., Ed.; Pantheon: New York, 1972.

40. Derrida, J. In *Of Grammatology*; Spivak, G.C., Ed.; Johns Hopkins Press: Baltimore, MD, 1976.

41. Brier, S. *Cybersemiotics: Why Information Is Not Enough*; University of Toronto Press: Toronto, ON, 2008.

42. Sebeok, T.A.; Danesi, M. *The Forms of Meaning: Modeling Systems Theory and Semiotic Analysis*; Mouton de Gruyter: Berlin, 2000.

43. Barbieri, M., Ed. *Introduction to Biosemiotics: The New Biological Synthesis*; Springer: Dordrecht, 2007.

44. Lotman, Y. *Universe of the Mind: A Semiotic Theory of Culture*; Indiana University Press: Bloomington, IL, 1991.

Senegal: Libraries, Archives, and Museums

Bernard Dione
School of Librarianship, Archivists Information Science (EBAD), Cheikh Anta Diop University, Dakar, Senegal

Dieyi Diouf
Central Library, Cheikh Anta Diop University of Dakar, Dakar, Senegal

Abstract

The authors provide a historical overview of Senegalese libraries, archives, and museums, outlining patterns and trends from the French colonial period to the present. Topics covered include: national, public, academic, special, and school libraries as well as the National Archives of Senegal, regional archives, and major museums. The legal framework for these institutions is detailed. However, although comprehensive and well thought out library legislation was enacted in the 1970s, realization of the plans for a national library, and for a network of public libraries has been stalled due to the lack of funding. The authors also discuss the role of professional associations and the development and professional education in these three fields.

INTRODUCTION

Senegal is the westernmost country on the African continent and is located in the Sahel Region. It is bordered by the Atlantic Ocean to the West, Mauritania to the North, Mali to the East, and Guinea and Guinea Bissau to the South. Senegal almost completely surrounds the Gambia, which forms a virtual enclave within its borders. During the nineteenth century Senegal was a bridge-head for France's conquest of its African colonial empire and the coastal cities of Senegal were the first French colonial outposts in west Africa. In 1902, Dakar became the capital colonial French West Africa (Afrique Occidentale Française, or the AOF) which consisted of several additional colonies and territories. Citizens of Senegal were the first Africans to gain French citizenship rights. The French expansionism and the spread of Islam occurred simultaneously during the late eighteenth and nineteenth centuries have shaped modern Senegal (Fig. 1).[1]

The official language of government is French, but the country is characterized by cultural and linguistic diversity, with Wolof, Pulaar, Jola, Mandinka, and Serer also common languages. Senegal is a predominantly Muslim country with many Koranic schools, so Arabic is also an important language for reading and writing. The country's area is around 195,190 sq. km. and the Senegalese population was estimated at around 12,853,259 (in July 2008). The country's total literacy rate was about 39.3% (51.1% for males and 29.2% for females).[2]

LIBRARY AND INFORMATION PROFESSIONS

Systems and Services

A brief overview of legislation

In the early 1970s, the government of Senegal drew up a comprehensive legal framework for the promotion of reading and libraries and this legislation established the infrastructures for several important policy initiatives. By Act No. 71-58 and Act No. 71-53, the exemption of taxes on importation of books was adopted in 1971. By Decree No. 72-1316, a Conseil Superieur du Livre (High Book Council) was established. And 1 year later many institutions were created in order to promote literacy and a reading culture; these included:

- « Les Nouvelles Editions Africaines (NEA) » (New African Editions),
- The « Société de Presse, d'Edition et de Publicité (SONAPRESS) » (Society of Press, Publishing, and Publicity),
- « Les Nouvelles Imprimeries du Sénégal (NIS) » (New Printing Presses of Senegal),
- a the « Bureau Sénégalais du Droit d'auteur (BSDA) » (Senegalese Bureau of Author's Rights).

Act No. 73-52, dated December 4, 1973 was passed to protect literary and artistic rights. Then in 1980, two legal acts aiming to help the book sector were passed: Act No.

Encyclopedia of Library and Information Sciences, Fourth Edition DOI: 10.1081/E-ELIS4-120044835

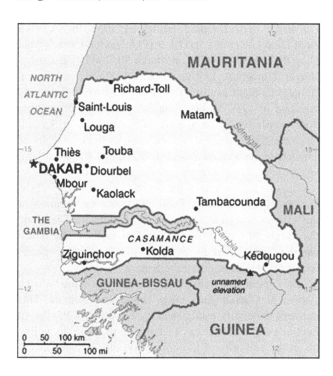

Fig. 1 Map of Senegal.
Source: *CIA world factbook*.https://www.cia.gov/library/publi
cations/the-world-factbook/geos/sg.html

80-37 and Act No. 80-79 dated August 25, 1980. These
acts instituted a value added tax exemption for periodicals
and newspapers, and for the importation and purchasing
of local raw materials used in the manufacturing of books
and newspapers in Senegal.

This legal framework for the promotion of literacy and
a reading culture was completed in 1976, by the legislation on libraries. During this period, important statements
of principle were formulated by the government for the
best applications of laws favoring open access to information for all.

The library profession in Senegal was given a legal
existence in 1969 by Decree No. 69-257, dated March 17,
1969 concerning the status of civil servants who work in
libraries and archives. Between 1975 and 1977 much of
the Senegalese legislation concerning library and documentation services were signed into law by the first
Senegalese president, the poet and French academician
Leopold Sédar Senghor (1906–2001).[3] The years 1976–
1977 represented an important turning point when seven
major legal documents were promulgated:

- Act No. 76-24, dated April 9, 1976 organizing the
  national library network,
- Act No. 76-30, dated April 9, 1976 establishing legal
  deposit,
- Decree No. 76-493 dated May 5, 1976 creating and
  organizing the National Library,
- Decree No. 76-494 dated May 5, 1976 creating a public lending library,

- Decree No. 76-1021 dated October 14, 1976
  establishing the Directorate of Public Libraries (Direction des Bibliothèques publiques) within the Ministry
  of Culture (Ministère de la Culture).
- April 6th, 1977, a National Center of Scientific and
  Technical Documentation [Centre National de Documentation Scientifique et Technique (CNDST)] was
  created by Decree No. 77-272, and
- Decree No. 69-257 was abrogated and replaced by the
  Decree No. 77-890, dated October 12, 1977 concerning
  in particular the status of civil servants in Archives and
  libraries.

All this legal texts were the results of the work of a
committee established in 1973.[4]

Around the same time, the Directorate of Public Libraries (Direction des Bibliothèques publiques) was merged
with the Directorate of Arts and Letters (Direction des
Arts et des Lettres) to become the Directorate of Arts,
Letters, and Libraries (Direction des Arts des Lettres et des
Bibliothèques). Raphael A. Ndiaye was appointed to implement these new policies. Unfortunately from the late 1970s
to the present, Senegalese libraries have suffered from a
lack of funding due to economic structural adjustment.
Most of the librarians employed in the public library network left for other positions, leaving theses small libraries
to be run by nonlibrarians. This situation still persists.

The legal framework remained stable until 2000 when,
by Decree 2000-947, a Directorate of Books and Reading
(Direction du livre et de la lecture) was created within the
Senegalese Ministry of Culture and, at the same time, a
professional librarian was appointed to manage the Directorate. Two years later, on April 3rd, 2002, Act No. 2002-
17, restoring the National Library was passed and another
act on the promotion of books and reading is under
preparation.

NATIONAL LIBRARY AND INFORMATION SERVICES

The National Library of Senegal exists only as a legal
entity. The Senegalese National Library was created by
Decree No. 76-493, dated May 5, 1976, but without facilities, budget, and staff. Three years later, the National
Library was made part of the National Archives of Senegal (by Letter No. 7820/PM/SGG/CI, dated October 5,
1979). The autonomy of this institution has been restored
legally by Act No. 2002-17, dated April 3, 2002.

Previously, in 1996, then President Abdou Diouf
decided to include a project to build a National Library
among the priorities of his government. A national task
force was named to work on the project, and a professional
librarian was appointed to manage it. The National
Library project was chaired by the head of the Directorate
of Books and Reading in the Ministry of Culture. Three

librarians, an assistant-librarian, a documentalist, and a computer scientist were also recruited for the project and funds were allocated for the constitution of the initial collection of the institution. The construction of the building of the National Library was begun in 1999, but the work was stopped by Abdoulaye Wade, the President of Senegal who was elected in 2000. The latter has decided to develop a new project and move it on another site.

To complete its information policy, the Senegalese Government, following the recommendations of the Conference of Ministers responsible for Application of Science and Technology to the Socioeconomic Establishment of Africa (CASTAFRICA meeting held in Dakar in 1974) decided to create a National Scientific and Documentation Center (CNDST). The decision was taken by the Council of Ministers on April 14th, 1975. The United Nations Development Programme and UNESCO were to help Senegal create this institution, and the CNDST was established by Decree No. 77-272, dated April 6, 1997. The objectives of this institution are to coordinate all the research activities of information and documentation services that constitute the links of the National Scientific and Technical Information Network [Réseau National de l'Information Scientifique et Technique—RNIST)], and to promote all actions of common interest that that could serve to strengthen the scientific and technical information services. In recent years, the CNDST has not really been visible in the information and documentation environment. The Scientific and Research Department even attempted to suppress the CNDST in 2005.

Academic and Research Libraries

Higher education in the former French West Africa was gradually put into place during the colonial period. The first stage of the process began in 1916 with the creation of the Jules Carde African School of Medicine and Pharmacy in Dakar (l'Ecole Africaine de Médecine et de Pharmacie Jules Carde de Dakar). Two decades later, in 1938 by the government of French West Africa created the French Institute for Black Africa [l'Institut Français d'Afrique Noire (IFAN)], which specialized in African research. The first director of IFAN was versatile young scientist named Théodore Monod (1902–2000). Monod laid the foundations for scientific research in French West Africa and saw to the establishment of the first research library in the region. During his 26 years as director of IFAN, Monod made it a priority to develop a good library collection, and by 1949 the size of the original collection had tripled.

Following World War II plans were made to extend higher education to Francophone countries, and Dakar was selected as the site for an inter-African program. In 1949, an undergraduate education program in chemistry/biology was opened. Finally, the Dakar Institute of Higher Education was created, which officially became the

University of Dakar on February 24, 1957, then Cheikh Anta Diop University in Dakar [l'Université Cheikh Anta Diop de Dakar (UCAD)] on March 30, 1987. The Gaston Berger University in Saint-Louis (L'Université Gaston Berger de Saint-Louis du Sénégal), whose cornerstone was laid in 1974 by President Senghor, did not open its doors until 1990. The number of universities in Senegal was recently enlarged by the creation of the University of Thiès (l'Université de Thiès) in 2005, and Regional University Centers in Bambey and Zuiguinchor in 2007.

The first collections of the current central library of the University Cheikh Anta Diop date from the creation of the African School of Medicine and Pharmacy. Therefore, the library of Cheikh Anta Diop University is the oldest and the most important university library in Francophone African countries south of the Sahara.

The central university library in Dakar is at the hub of a system of Cheikh Anta Diop University libraries. This network (officially established by Decree No. 95-197 of February 21, 1995) brings together all the libraries falling under the authority of the university; this includes a central library, 15 libraries of the Faculties (Schools), institutes or departments, and a photography collection. The central library of Cheikh Anta Diop University offers study spaces, modern technology and services (OPAC, Internet connection, WI-FI, etc.), and an encyclopedic collection of about 500,000 documents in all media. It also offers online access to digital collections.

The second largest university library system is found at the Gaston Berger University in Saint-Louis. This system offers a collection of about 70,000 items in the central library and 40,000 in the libraries of the training and research units (unités de formation et de recherche).

The recently created Universities of Ziguinchor and of Bambey have already set up university libraries and recruited librarians to manage them. Likewise, the Senegalese campus of Suffolk University offers information services. One can classify in this same category the library of the African Center for Post-Graduate Management Studies (Centre Africain d'Études Supérieures en Gestion — CESAG), a specialized management school.

All of these higher education libraries have joined together in the Consortium of Higher Education Libraries [Consortium des Bibliothèques de l'Enseignement Supérieur (COBES)]. University libraries constitute the most dynamic part of the library sector in Senegal. The university libraries in Dakar and in Saint-Louis, have at their disposal buildings and equipment that conform to international standards and they have integrated information technology into the service that they offer. Furthermore, they are managed by professionally qualified personnel.

Public Libraries

In 1976, the Senegalese government decided to create and organize a national public library network (by Decree No.

76-29, dated April 9, 1976). This legal framework was complemented by a second decree (Decree No. 76-1021, dated October 14, 1976) that created an administrative department, the Office for Public Libraries and by Act 76-30, dated April 9 establishing the Legal Deposit. The national public library network was a very ambitious project that included plans to create a public central library in the capital city Dakar, public regional libraries, public departmental libraries, district libraries, and rural libraries. But, this ambitious network remains to be built. In fact, the national library network, as it was initially conceived, was confined to 10 regional libraries integrated into Regional Cultural Centers and about 10 other municipal libraries integrated into the Departmental Centers of Physical Education and Sports (Centres Départementaux Education Physiques et Sportives). None of these libraries have equipment, separate facilities or professional staff and as a result they are unable to offer adequate library services. The collections are constituted by donations. The International Agency for Francophonie (Agence Internationale de la Francophonie) has established 16 Centers for Reading and Cultural Events [Centres de Lecture et d'Animation Culturelle (CLAC)] in two Senegalese regions. The first network installed in Thies region included seven of these centers; the second one in Kolda had nine centers. The Islamic Education, Scientific and Cultural Organization (ISESCO) has also established another network of 10 ISESCO CLAC for Arabic readers.

Beginning in 1990, eight libraries were created by the municipal authorities in Dakar and the city has plans to establish a network of 18 libraries. The total size of the collections of each of these small libraries is around 2000 books; 80% of the materials in these collections were donated by Canada. The remainder comes from a donation by the Franco-Senegal Alliance (Alliance Franco-Sénégalaise) and acquisitions made by the municipality.[5] Many other libraries have been set up by private associations. The Alliance Franco-Sénégalaise has established a network of five libraries in Dakar, Saint-Louis, Tambacounda, Ziguinchor, and Kaolack. In addition, libraries have been set up other agencies and organizations headquartered overseas (for example Service de Cooperation et d'Action Culturel de l'Ambassade de France, CAURIS, AFVP, Aide & Action, etc.). Local groups such as NGOs sports and cultural organizations, etc. have contributed to creating other libraries around the country.[5] In addition there are several libraries established by foreign cultural centers (Goethe Institute, British Institute, etc.).

As in the past, most of the public libraries services are located in the capital city Dakar, which is also the major commercial and cultural center of the country. Of the 83 public libraries listed by the Senegalese Library Association, Association Sénégalaise des Bibliothécaires, Archivistes et Documentalistes (ASBAD), about 43 (52%) are in Dakar. The list of all public library services is published on the Web site of the Minister of Culture (Ministère de la culture). http://www.culture.gouv.sn/article.php3?id_article=324/

School Libraries

Although they are an indispensable tool of education, school libraries still remain one of the weak links in the national network of reading resources. The absence of a legal framework clearly organizing school libraries seems to be recognized as a major obstacle to the development of school libraries in Senegal. Initiatives aimed at addressing this sector have been taken within the framework of two programs which are the Partnership Program for Effectiveness of Senegalese Schools (le Programme de Partenariat pour l'Efficacité de l'Ecole Sénégalaise) that concerns elementary schools and the Quality Education for All Program (le Programme Education de Qualité pour Tous) financed by the World Bank.[6]

Despite the efforts agreed to by aid associations for the development of education, such as Libraries, Reading, and Development (Bibliothèque, Lecture et Développement (BLD)), the situation on the ground still remains difficult. A 1991 study about libraries of public establishments in the Dakar Region found that facilities housing libraries were often reduced to one cramped room (7 × 5 m) serving both as the office of the librarian, the reading room, and the book stacks. As for the collections, these are often made up solely of textbooks or assigned novels that the students borrow at the beginning and return at the end of the school year.[6]

Special Libraries

Special libraries are more numerous but also more difficult to study. They are set up by specialized organizations and are not always accessible to the public. The specialized institutions and affiliated organizations of the United Nations (UNICEF, BIT, UNESCO-BREDA, World Bank, CINU) located in Dakar often have a library or a library and information service that one can research. Also, national, regional, or international research centers located in Senegal often set up a library. One can cite many examples of such research centers:

- The Senegalese Institute of Agricultural Research [l'Institut Sénégalais de Recherche Agricole (ISRA)],
- the Oceanographic Research and Documentation Center of Thiaroye [Centre de recherche et de Documentation Océanographique de Thiaroye (CRDOT)],
- the Institute of Food Technology [l'Institut de Technologie Alimentaire (ITA)],
- the Ecological Monitoring Center (le Centre de Suivi Ecologique), and

- the administrative, legal and historical library of the Directorate of the National Archives.
- The library of the Center for Research and Documentation in Saint-Louis (Centre de Recherche et de Documentation de Saint-Louis) comprises about 32,000 volumes;[7]
- The Council for Social Science Research in Africa (le Conseil pour la Recherche en Sciences Sociales en Afrique (CODESRIA)) offers a library and documentation center specializing in social sciences; and
- The Institute for Development Research [l'Institut de Recherche pour le Développement (IRD)] offers quality information services.

Finally, one could mention among special libraries and information services the libraries and information services of public administration. The Office of the President of the Republic, certain ministries, the Court of Cassation (highest civil court), and the la Cour des Comptes (a quasi-governmental organization that audits government accounts, assesses management of public agencies and advises the government), each have a library and an information service. Some of these services are managed by professional librarians.

Digital Library Collections and Services

A certain number of the projects offered by digital libraries have been developed in higher education and at the level of research centers. Academic and research librarians work more and more on projects such as Cyberdocs and SIST (Système d'Information Scientifique et Technique = Scientific and Technical Information System). Cyberdocs-UCAD is a platform developed by the central library of Cheikh Anta Diop University on the Cyberthèses (Digital Theses) platform. Cyberdocs-UCAD allows for the electronic processing and diffusion of theses and dissertations produced in the faculties (schools) and institutes attached to the university, whose authors have voluntarily deposited an electronic copy. It also permits placing online documents other than theses and dissertations. Its objective is to increase the value of the work of students and researchers, maximize the visibility of the contents, facilitate access to this information, and freely share the results of the research products of UCAD. A cooperative project of the French Foreign Ministry, SIST is aimed at making African research more easily available and thus promoting African expertise and putting the science in the service of development. It offers to researchers and to information professionals in 12 countries a platform for information, communication, and collaborative work. Since 2006 databases, Web sites, Senegalese bibliographic catalogs can be consulted through SIST Sénégal.

EDUCATION FOR LIBRARY AND INFORMATION SCIENCE

The Ecole des Bibliothecaires, Archivistes et Documentalistes (EBAD), http://www.ebad.ucad.sn/acces_dedies/etudiants/info_generales/historique.htm/ or the Senegalese School of Library, Archival and Information Studies is one of the oldest LIS education programs in Francophone Africa. It was created on March 28, 1962 as a French-speaking Regional Center for Library Training and inaugurated on December 4, 1963.[8,9] The first course began one month before its inauguration, on November 4, 1963 with 20 students: six from Senegal, two from Cameroon, one from Congo Brazzaville, two from Côte d'Ivoire (Ivory Coast), one from Dahomey (currently Benin), one from Guinea, one from Haute-Volta (Upper Volta, currently Burkina Faso), two from Madagascar, one from Mali, one from Chad, and two from Togo. The school still kept this regional orientation when it became the EBAD by Decree No. 67-1235 dated November 15, 1967 and became an Institute incorporated at Cheikh Anta Diop University. Initially, the training was focused on library science, but in 1971, a program on Archival studies was started and later a program on information science was established in 1975. Initially, EBAD awarded a diploma of proficiency in Librarianship, Archival studies, or Information science after a 2 year training period to holders of the Baccalaureate or an equivalent diploma. In 1982, another academic cycle (Final Honors) was created.

In 2007, Cheikh Anta Diop University decided to adopt the European curricular reform. To accomplish this, EBAD is transforming its degree programs into two cycles (Bachelor's and Masters). One of the objectives of this reform is to make its programs of study more compatible with programs in other countries; therefore with the help of The International Federation of Library Associations and Institutions (IFLA), Action for Development through Libraries Programme (ALP). EBAD, is working with newly established library schools of the Francophone countries to harmonize library curricula. Since 2000, EBAD has also been experimenting with distance learning and Internet courses through the project FORmation Continue en Information Informatisée en Réseau funded by the French agency for cooperation.

PROFESSIONAL ASSOCIATIONS

The existence of library associations in Senegal began when the International Association for the Development of Libraries in Africa was founded on September 13, 1957 in Saint-Louis, Senegal by E. K. Dadzie, and a small group of librarians working with other persons interested in promoting reading.[10] In Dakar, on March 18, 1975 another group of professional librarians founded, a second professional association named Association Nationale des

Bibliothécaires, Archivistes et Documentalistes Sénégalais. These two associations merged on July 9, 1988 to constitute the ASBAD. The aims of ASBAD are to advance the development of libraries, archives, and documentation centers in Senegal and to study concerns common to information professionals in the country.

ARCHIVES AND ARCHIVAL SCIENCE

A Brief Overview of Legislation

Just 2 years after independence, the government of Senegal established a legal framework that regulates the management and accessibility of archives. In 1962, the government ordered that all judicial archives more than 50 years old, be deposited in the National Archives (Decree No. 62-0215 of May 28, 1962). That same year, the President of the Council, Mamadou Dia, ordered the deposit of official archives and publications (in Circular No. 52 of August 16, 1962). A few years later, in 1968, a decree was issued regulating the deposit in the National Archives of notarized deeds (titles) more than 50 years old (Decree No. 68-342 of March 29, 1968). The elaboration of legal texts organizing deposits in the archives also continued. Thus, on March 16, 1976 a Circular of the Prime Minister was issued to regulate the deposit of official archives and publications, (Circular No. 00025) and 2 years later on April 28, 1978, another Circular established procedures for pre-archival records management in ministries and public services. Since 1977, the Archives of Senegal been transformed by statute, attaining the status of a Directorate attached to the Secretary General of the Government in the Bureau of the Prime Minister. Several other official texts organizing the archives were put into place after that date.

National Archives and Services

The Archives of Senegal were created as a subunit (Service) of the Archives of French West African (l'Afrique Occidentale Française/A.O.F.), which were established by Governor General William Ponty on July 1, 1913. Claude Faure, the first professional archivist to work in the French African colonies was hired that year. Over the next five decades this collection was maintained by a professional archivist who also provided training to the first African archivists.[9] Following the independence movement, these were the only archives in the French African colonies which were not taken back to France time of independence.

In 1958 when the government of Senegal, decided to transfer the capital from Saint-Louis to Dakar, the Archives of Senegal were transferred to the new capital where they were housed with the A.O.F. Archives.[11] Jean François Maurel, Conservator of the A.O.F. Archives,

remained in Senegal and assumed management of both archives. In 1970, the Archives of Senegal were attached to the Secretary General of the Government, which was a part of the Bureau of the Prime Minister.

By the 1970s, the need to provide the Archives of Senegal with an appropriate building became more and more evident and in 1973 a decree was issued that authorized the construction of a "House of Archives" (Maison des Archives) (by Decree No. 73-080 of January 27, 1973). This decree was never carried out but was extended by Decree No. 75-461 of April 26, 1975. Unfortunately, the construction of this "House of Archives," like that of the building destined to house the National Library, has remained until now an unfinished project due to the decision by President Abdoulaye Wade to halt construction. There are plans that both the National Library and the National Archives should eventually be integrated into a project for a larger cultural complex.

After the departure of Jean-François Maurel, Saliou Mbaye, archivist paleographer, educated at the l'Ecole des Chartes in Paris was named director of the archives. The Archival Service of Senegal (Le Service des Archives du Sénégal) became the Directorate of Archives of Senegal (la Direction des Archives du Sénégal) by Decree No. 77-615 of July 21, 1977. Raising the status of the Archival Service of Senegal to that of a Directorate marks an important step in the history of the Senegalies Archives (Law No. 81-02 relative to archives was passed on February 2, 1981). It was followed the same year by General Decree No. 81-430 of April 15, 1981, setting the conditions of organization and functioning of the Archives of Senegal and 2 years later by Decree No. 83-341 of April 1, 1983 devoted to access to documents in archives. This Law No. 81-02 of February 2, 1981 would not be repealed and replaced until 2006 by Law No. 2006-19 of June 30, 2006 relative to archives and administrative documents.

The Archives of Senegal occupy 12 km of shelf space separated into four principal sections according to the four principal collections (*fonds*):

- The Colonial Senegal collection (1816–1958);
- The A.O.F. collection (1895–1959);
- The collection of the Federation of Mali (1959–1960);
- The archives of independent Senegal (since 1958).

Article 7 of Law No. 81-02 of February 2, 1981 stipulates that "the Directorate of the Archives of Senegal is an organism of the State responsible for addressing all archival questions. It administers the national archives and the regional archives. It controls the archives of local collectivities." It is this disposition that established the Senegal collection to be subdivided into two parts: 1) central and regional archives, managed by the Directorate of the Archives and 2) archives of local collectivities placed under their control.

In principle, each Region should have at its disposal its own regional archival service. At the moment, five Regions are equipped with an archival service. These services are established within the services of the Regional Governors.

Since 1979, the Library of the Archives of Senegal houses the National Library Agency (l'Agence bibliothèque nationale) and receives the legal deposits instituted by Law No. 76-30 of April 9, 1976. The collection of the Library of the Archives is estimated at 27,300 works (books, reference works, microforms, and audiovisual documents and printed documents); this collection also includes 1515 titles of periodicals (both current and those which have ceased publication).

MUSEUMS AND MUSEOLOGY

Museums seem to have considerable difficulty in becoming integrated into Senegalese culture. According to an article published on June 8, 2006: "The Senegalese don't know the utility of museums or, in any case, only rarely visit them. In their place, it is rather tourists who flood into the museums after arriving by airplane."[12]

The museum sector in Senegal experiences a certain number of difficulties of which the most important seem to be: the absence of a legal framework, the timid politics of the government, the absence of a professional training school specialized in this domain, inadequate funding and the lack of public interest.

The most important museums of the country are concentrated in three cities: Dakar, Goree and Saint-Louis, Senegal.

The IFAN Museum is indisputably the most important museum because of its age, its building, and the size and diversity of its collection. It is located in Dakar at Soweto Place, opposite the National Assembly of Senegal. The building which it occupies was allotted to the offices of IFAN by Governor General Jules Brévié (by Decision No. 1958 of August 20, 1936). Currently, the IFAN Museum offers a permanent exhibition on the theme of the arts and cultural traditions of West Africa, temporary and thematic exhibits using the collections of the Museum, and collections conserved in the storerooms.

Dakar also contains two museums that focus on the military and on customs officials. The more important of these is the Armed Forces Museum (le Musée des Forces Armées), created in July 1996, whose mission is to collect, conserve, and spread the national historic and cultural patrimony in the military domain. It also possesses a library of 1200 volumes destined to serve as the basis for the creation of a future Center for the study and military history of West Africa (Centre d'études et d'histoire militaire de l'Afrique de l'Ouest).

With four establishments, the island of Goree occupies a choice place in the museum sector. The most celebrated is the House of Slaves of Goree (la Maison des esclaves de Gorée), which perpetuates the memory of one of the greatest human tragedies—slavery. The other museums of Goree are either the responsibility of IFAN or are private museums. The two museums administered by IFAN are the Historical Museum (le Musée Historique) that occupies the old Goree Fort and the Museum of the Sea (le Musée de la Mer). The Historical Museum of IFAN is devoted to the general history of Senegal from its origins to our days, illustrated by notable figures, whereas the Museum of the Sea concentrates on the sea, fishermen, and fishing tools.

Last but not least, there is the Henriette Bathily Museum (le Musée Henriette Bathily) devoted to women. The idea of creating a museum celebrating women dates from 1987, following a proposal by film maker Ousmane William Mbaye; however, the actual creation of the Henriette Bathily Museum did not occur until June 1994. Its establishment was justified, according to the words of its Director Annette Mbaye D'Erneville, by the fact that "(...) Women are the center of all communal life, for through their destiny is translated the destiny of an entire people, that her history (Herstory) sums up that of the whole society." This institution assigned itself the objective of making known the place and the role of Senegalese women in rituals and popular arts.[12] In addition to an Art Gallery, where permanent, temporary, and thematic exhibits are displayed, the Henriette Bathily Museum offers high quality artisanal products made by the women of the museum, and a workshop that introduces women to painting, batik, weaving, and traditional embroidery techniques. The museum employs 12 people and has a garden café as well as a shop. However, the proximity to the House of Slaves, which was perceived to be an advantage has proven to be a real challenge for the Museum of Women. In effect, the latter has a great deal of difficulty in becoming visible.

Finally, in Saint-Louis there is the Museum of the Center for Research and Documentation of Senegal (le Musée du Centre de Recherche et de Documentation du Sénégal). This Museum, the former IFAN Center inaugurated in 1956, is now a part of the Ministry of National Education. It covers three themes: ecology, history, and ethnology.

CONCLUSION

During the first decades following independence, Senegal established and developed EBAD, a well-respected professional school with a regional mission to train librarians, archivists, and documentalists who serve in institutions throughout Francophone Africa. In addition, the Senegalese government enacted a well thought out legal framework for establishing a national library and extending library services throughout the country. Unfortunately, neither the library network nor the national library have been realized due to difficult economic circumstances combined with the lack of strong political support.

Much work remains to be done in order for Senegal to be endowed with a library, archives, and museum network capable of collecting, processing, conserving, and making available the cultural and international patrimony of the country. Only university and research libraries have experienced a normal development, with collections and services that follow international standards and practices. And it is only the largest academic libraries and a few specialized research libraries (especially those in scientific fields) that have had enough financial support to employ modern information technology. Libraries of administrative services have often been treated as poor relatives while public libraries, school libraries, and all the other types of libraries have been sadly neglected and continue to suffer from a lack of adequate funding.

Given that political support is essential to the realization of these cultural institutions, it is of great concern that President Wade has halted work on the National Library and the House of Archives, declaring that neither of these were his projects. Faced with the situation of libraries, archives, and museums of Senegal, the words of the former President sound like a premonition when he noted in 1977 that:

> (...) the most difficult, you know, is not to decide, by decree and even by law, the creation of libraries and their complements, which are archives and museums; the most difficult, in any case the most important, is to create them effectively and, especially, to make them function effectively.[13]

Those professionals who are providing leadership for Senegalese libraries, archives, and museums have much advocacy work to do in order to persuade the government to support the development of a well-coordinated, effective system of information institutions. It must be noted that information technologies exercise a certain fascination and the discourse about the death of the book and libraries has reached Senegal where there continues to be debates about the need for printed materials at a time when access to the Internet is becoming somewhat more widespread. Even Senegalese political decision makers are becoming swayed by this technophile discourse, which is synonymous with modernity. The lure of technology has lead the political leaders to place greater emphasis on the acquisition of equipment rather than supporting efforts to set up viable information institutions. Digitization of documents is also becoming a growing trend in Senegal. Professionals in the libraries and information services must bring thoughtful reflection to the digitization projects and also consider other strategies for making information available to all.

ACKNOWLEDGMENT

Partial translation of this entry by Stephen C. Maack.

REFERENCES

1. Appiah, A.K., Gates, H.L., Eds., *Africana: The Encyclopedia of the African and African American Experience*; Basic Civitas Books: New York, 1999.
2. Senegal CIA World Factbook https://www.cia.gov/library/publications/the-world-factbook/geos/sg.html.
3. Lajeunesse, M.; Sene, H. "Legislation for library and information services in French-Speaking Africa Revisited". Int. Inform. Libr. Rev. **2004**, *36*, 367–380.
4. Ndiaye, R.A. "Politique culturelle et bibliothèques au Sénégal". BLIBAD: Bulletin de liaison à l'intention des bibliothécaires, archivistes et documentalistes africains **1979**, juin *No. 4*, 17–22.
5. Diongue Diop, M.; Diop, M.D. *Les Bibliothèques au Sénégal: état des Lieux*; Goethe Institute: Dakar, Senegal, 2003.
6. Samb, S. *Les Bibliothèques scolaires des établissements publics secondaires de la région de Dakar: étude de cas*; Université Cheikh Anta Diop de Dakar: Dakar, Senegal, 1991.
7. Fall, F.L. Les collections d'archéologie et d'histoire du Musée du CRDS de Saint-Louis. *ICMAH; Congrès = Congress, 14–19 Mars 1994*, Dakar, Sénégal 85–87 [Paris]: International Council of Museums, 1995.
8. Seguin, L. Regional center for the training of Archivists in Dakar. UNESCO Bull. Libr. **1964**, May–June *18*, 101–114.
9. Maack, M.N. *Libraries in Senegal: Continuity and Change in an Emerging Nation*; American Library Association: Chicago, IL, 1981.
10. Dadzie, K.E.W. Libraries, bibliography and archives in French-speaking Africa. UNESCO Bull. Libr. **1961**, October *15*, 242–253.
11. Mbaye, S.; Mbaye, S. "Les archives au service du développement: le cas des archives du Sénégal". Ethiopiques - Revue négro-africaine de littérature et de philosophie **1984**, *36*, 23–31.
12. Ndong, M. Les musées au Sénégal: La difficile communication entre le musée et le public: dossier publié dans le journal Le Quotidien du Jeudi 8 juin 2006. Available at http://www.lequotidien.sn/dossiers/article.CFM?article_id=590&var_doss=123/ (accessed December 24, 2007).
13. Senghor, L.S., 1977; Septembre La Bibliothèque comme instrument majeur du développement. Communication au Congrès jubiliaire de la Fédération internationale des Associations de Bibliothécaires. Bruxelles, 3–10.

BIBLIOGRAPHY

1. Aguolu, C.C. Librarianship in francophone West Africa. Int. Libr. Rev. **1982**, April *14*(2), 147–167.
2. Association Sénégalaise des Bibliothécaires, Archivistes et Documentalistes ASBAD. Rapport d'enquête sur les bibliothèques publiques au Sénégal, Dakar, Senegal.
3. Association Sénégalaise des Bibliothécaires, Archivistes et Documentalistes. ASBAD, 2001, Available at http://www.asbad.africa-web.org (accessed December 18, 2007).
4. Bousso, A. University of Dakar School for Librarians, Archivists and Documentalists. UNESCO Bull. Lib. **1973**, March–April *27*(2), 72–77 107.

5. Correa, A. Book hunger in schools. Focus. Int. Comp. Librariansh **1997**,*28*(2), 90–92.

6. Deschatelets, G.; Hamdouchi, A.; Sagna, O. A mini-international network for the production of computer-assisted learning material. J. Educ. Libr. Inform. Sci. **1991**, Summer/Fall *32*(1/2), 121–126.

7. Diop, M.D. Bibliotheques et politiques nationales d'information en Afrique de l'Ouest francophone. Libraries and national information policies in French speaking West Africa. Bulletin d'Informations de l'Association des Bibliothecaires Francais **1993**, (158), 72–77.

8. Gueye, N. *Répertoire analytique des textes et sites relatifs aux archives dans les pays francophones d'Afrique de l'Ouest*; EBAD: Dakar, 2005.

9. ICMAH. Congrès = Congress, 14–19 Mars 1994, Dakar, Sénégal.

10. Les archives en Afrique de l'Ouest : un patrimoine en mutation. Conférences de l'École des chartes, Mardi 24 février 2004 Available at (http://elec.enc.sorbonne.fr/document10.html/ visited 26/12/2007).

11. Maack, M.N. Books and libraries as instruments of cultural diplomacy in Francophone Africa during the Cold War. Libr. Culture. **2001**, Winter *36*(1), 58–86.

12. Maack, M.N. The colonial legacy in West African libraries: a comparative analysis. In *Advances in Librarianship*; Wesley, S., Ed.; Academic Press Inc.: New York, London, 1982; 173–245.

13. Maack, M.N. Libraries for the general public in French-speaking Africa: their cultural role, 1803–1975. J. Libr. Hist. **1981**, Winter *16*(1), 210–225.

14. Maack, M.N. Library research and publishing in Francophone Africa. IFLA J **1987**, *13*(1), 45–53.

15. Maack, M.N. The role of external aid in West African library development. Libr. Quart. **1986**, *56*(1), 1–16 s.

16. Mbaye, S. Oral records in Senegal. Am. Archivist. **1990**, Fall *53*(4), 566–574 s.

17. Mbaye, S. Problemes specifique aux archives en Afrique. Specific problems in African archives. Gazette des Archives **1982**, First Quarter (116), 20–29.

18. Ndiaye, R.A. Developpement de la bibliotheconomie dans le tiers monde (ALP). advancement of librarianship in the third world (ALP). IFLA. J. **1986**, *12*(4), 279–280.

19. Ndiaye, R.A. Oral culture and libraries. IFLA J. **1988**, *14*(1), 40–46.

20. Ndiaye, Theo La normalisation dans les bibliotheques universitaries d'Afrique. Standardisation in African university libraries. Afr. J. Acad. Librarianship **1984**, December 2(2), 41–43.

21. Ndong, M. "Les musées au Sénégal : La difficile communication entre le musée et le public : Dossier". Le Quotidien **2006**, Jeudi 8 juin Available at http://www.lequotidien.sn/dossiers/article.CFM?article_id=590&var_doss=123/ (accessed December 24, 2007).

22. Sagna, O. EBAD 1964–1994: premier bilan a l'heure de la sortie de la trentieme promotion. Training—EBAD 1964–1994: 30th graduating class, first evaluation. Documentaliste **94**, November/December *31*(6), 299–304.

23. Sene, H. Les bibliotheques en Afrique Occidentale Francaise: 1800–1958. Libraries in French West Africa: 1800–1958. Librarianship **1992**, October–December *42*(4), 306–329.

24. Sene, H. Le commerce du livre de langue arabe au Senegal jusqu'au debut du 20c siecle. Trade in books in the Arabic language in Senegal until the beginning of the twentieth century. Librarianship **1986**, June *36*(2), 146–159.

25. Takou–Ndogmo, M.L. *Les Sources de l'histoire des Archives et des Bibliothèques aux Archives nationales du Sénégal (1818–1983)*; Université Cheikh Anta Diop de Dakar: Dakar, Senegal, 1995.

26. Tavares, H.M.G.H. *La bibliothèque nationale du Sénégal: bilan et perspectives*; EBAD: Dakar, Senegal, 1995.

Sense-Making

Brenda Dervin
School of Communication, Ohio State University, Columbus, Ohio, U.S.A.

Charles M. Naumer
Information School, University of Washington, Seattle, Washington, U.S.A.

Abstract

This entry focuses on how research approaches labeled as sense-making or sensemaking are used to address user-oriented research relevant to the study of human information behaviors. This entry starts with a focus on the turn to sense-making in user studies and then reviews the historical and methodological roots and application contexts of the five most visible approaches that have addressed sense-making (or sensemaking) systematically in four fields: Human-Computer Interaction (HCI) (Russell's sensemaking); Cognitive Systems Engineering (Klein's sensemaking); Organizational Communication (Weick's sensemaking; Snowden's sense-making); and Library and Information Science (LIS) (Dervin's sense-making).

INTRODUCTION

This entry focuses on how research approaches labeled as sense-making or sensemaking are used to address user-oriented research relevant to the study of human information behaviors. This entry starts with a focus on the turn to sense-making in user studies and then reviews the historical and methodological roots and application contexts of the five most visible approaches that have addressed sense-making (or sensemaking) systematically in four fields: Human-Computer Interaction (HCI) (Russell's sensemaking); Cognitive Systems Engineering (Klein's sensemaking); Organizational Communication (Weick's sensemaking; Snowden's sense-making); and Library and Information Science (LIS) (Dervin's sense-making).

THE TURN TOWARD SENSE-MAKING IN USER STUDIES

Various terms referring to humans making something called "sense" are widely used in most human communities. We talk routinely of things that "make sense" and "do not make sense" and we ask others to "make sense."

Dictionary treatments of the term "sense" start with foundational emphases on basic human faculties of sensation and perception—sight, hearing, touch, taste, smell. These emphases focus on human faculties as transmitting tools that perceive in some way patterns of matter-energy, both inside the skins that enclose human bodies and outside in external environments.

Yet, dictionary definitions clearly branch out from here far beyond anchorings in human perceptual capacities to such definitions as: intelligibility, intuitive knowledge, capacity for mental feeling, natural understanding, practical soundness, wisdom, consciousness, impressions, emotional sensibility, meaning, signification, and reasonableness. Likewise, attention to the term "sense" as a verb shows wide range. To "sense" is defined foundationally as to perceive and more broadly to: feel, experience, be aware of, comprehend, grasp, ascribe meaning to, understand, interpret.

In the last two decades, theories and studies focusing on users and user interfaces with information, media, and technology systems have increasingly referred to the neoligisms "sense-making" or "sensemaking." In doing so, they all point in some way to their interests in how users make "sense" of the information resources systems actually or might provide. Different authors use one or the other of the two grammatical forms, most often deliberately. For sake of readability, sense-making will be used in this entry except in discussions of specific approaches when the forms preferred by specific authors will be used.

In understanding the differences in how the term sense-making is being used it is important to note how the full range of common parlance definitions have invaded scholarly treatments although very often in undefined ways. At one extreme, there is abundant attention to transmission theories of information processing asking whether humans are "sensing" what experts think they ought to. In transmission approaches to understanding users, focus starts with expert judgments of what is accurate, right, and proper in terms of information seeking, retrieving, and using. Experts draw these judgments out of normatively accepted knowledge-based domains. Usually, underlying these transmission assumptions is acceptance of a host of modernist assumptions about the nature of reality, information, and users that rest on often unstated agreements

Encyclopedia of Library and Information Sciences, Fourth Edition DOI: 10.1081/E-ELIS4-120043227

Semiotics–Slovakia

that the job of information-oriented systems is to encourage and facilitate human access to information assumed to map the orderliness that is "out there" in reality but may elude individual human senses because of lack of access, skill, tools, and expertise. This has meant that the patterned matter-energy that we humans call information, the packages into which we humans put that information (e.g., books, television, journals, blogs), and the systems we create to store, retrieve, and disseminate that information (e.g., libraries, databases, knowledge management systems, media institutions) have been assumed to be edifices against which humans can be measured in terms of standards such as accuracy, breath, depth, and skill of information processing. This tension between essentialist approaches to understanding human beings and interpretative approaches is in many ways at the center of the many versions of the so-called paradigm wars in the social sciences and humanities that marked the 1980s. While such discussions no longer take center stage, traces are very much still in evidence.[1–15]

At the other extreme, there is growing attention to what can be called communicative theories of information processing asking how humans are understanding, interpreting, finding insight, and making meaning. Here attention is redirected, again with myriad vocabularies to meaning-making—to the insights, interpretations, significations, and utilities humans construct from the contents and packages of the patterned matter-energy normatively called information.

In both kinds of theories of sense-making—transmission and communicative—emphasis is placed on both outcomes (the sense made) and processes (the hows of sense-making). The ways in which attentions to outcomes and processes have been defined, however, likewise reflect that same movement from sense as measured in terms of its deviation from expertise versus sense as understood as resulting from processes that must be studied as least in part communicatively rather than simply as resulting from transmission.

The purpose of this entry is to give an overview of how phenomena that are labeled with the term sense-making are being defined, studied, and applied in user studies focusing on information seeking and use. The difficulty in choosing what approaches to sense-making to focus on is that there has been over the past decade an explosion of interests in something authors call sense-making, now being applied to a whole host of information-related behaviors (e.g., processing, retrieving, searching, gathering, foraging, using, Web-browsing, rejecting, collaborating, risk-facing, and so on) and a host of potential applications (e.g., the design of libraries, media, software, Web sites, information packages, information-focused pedagogies, knowledge management tools, organizational environments, and collaboration interfaces). For brevity's sake, the abbreviation HIBs (Human Information Behaviors) will be used to stand in for the diverse sets of

behaviors both internal (e.g., cognitive, emotional, spiritual) and external (e.g., seeking, finding, foraging, retrieving) that are the focus of user studies.

The call for attending to sense-making in studying HIBs is most visibly present not only in the LIS field but also in the fields of Cognitive Systems Engineering, HCI, and Organizational Communication studies. At the same time, collaborations and mergings between institutions, scholars, and practitioners representing all these fields are making it increasingly difficult to fix a particular approach to sense-making as belonging only to a particular discourse. These convergences have been impacting LIS particularly as manifested in what has become known as the "information school movement" in which formerly homogenous LIS units have incorporated interdisciplinary expertise from a variety of social science, humanities, and engineering disciplines.

The difficulty in fixing a stable picture of what might be called a "sense-making" approach to studying HIBs is further muddied by the increasing frequency of comparisons executed without anchorings in historical and discourse community roots. Too often issues regarding differences between approaches are reduced simply to matters of the use of different methods or arriving at more encompassing and thus more valid overarching theories. Rarely is there acknowledgment that the various approaches are not defining or addressing sense-making as phenomenon in the same ways.

The intent of this entry is to differentiate between the most visible approaches that are attending to something called sense-making. This entry intentionally focuses deeply on historical roots and methodological differences and does not limit itself to the sense-making approach that 10 years ago all but dominated references to user studies in the LIS field—that is, Dervin's Sense-Making Methodology. Purpose is to attempt to make "sense" of the treatments of sense-making that focus in their different ways on studies relevant to LIS because they address user HIBs, albeit using a variety of labels in very different contexts to focus on very different kinds of HIBs.

DIFFERENT APPROACHES TO SENSE-MAKING

One recent avalanche in literatures relevant to study of users has begun to refer to sense-making as a key concept with no definitional explications at all. The term has simply been co-opted into popular applied social science mainstreams. There have been, however, relatively isolated discourse communities in different fields where the term has received systematic attentions. These efforts do not have the status of field-wide acceptance but rather occupy significant enclaves within four different fields. As named above, the most visible fields where sense-making attentions reside include: HCI, Cognitive Systems

Engineering, Organizational Communication Studies, and LIS.

In general, it must be said that authors in these different fields study what they call sense-making in very disciplinary-centric ways. Work has proceeded in relatively bounded discourse communities with specialized vocabularies, assumptions, and research contexts.[16–18] Authors may appear to address the same phenomena because they are using the same words (e.g., sense-making, information processing, users, retrieval, relevance) when in fact they mean very different and sometimes incommensurate things. This is additionally exasperated by recent practices of citing across these different approaches as if the differences do not make a difference.

Despite this background of interperspective confusion that is now a common feature of scholarly, research, and professional communities, in general, it is fair to say that all of those who have imported the term "sense-making" share common pulses. They have found accepted disciplinary vocabularies emphasizing cognition, attitude, opinion, information processing, and so on too confining. They have imbued into their projects at least in small measure a communicative sensibility—an interest in going beyond transmission assumptions regarding the interfaces between users and information systems. They share at least in small part a common attention to the idea that one reason research must move from transmission-based theories to communicative approaches is that our understandings of the ways in which information is useful to human life-facing have advanced beyond views drawn only from simplistic notions of modernity where already established and codified knowledge is seen as bridging all gaps. Instead, there is general acceptance of how complexity, uncertainty, and chaos theoretic approaches are needed—approaches that accept assumptions of the challenges human face as they move across time-space to changing environments and situations where knowledge as it is currently codified can rarely be complete enough to bridge all gaps.

Sense-Making in HCI

Human-Computer Interaction is a field, according to the Association for Computing Machinery (ACM)[19] "...concerned with the design, evaluation, and implementation of interactive computing systems for human use...." Those identified with HCI usually conduct research in academic, corporate, and governmental settings for application to practice, in particular to design of interactive computing systems including hardware and software interfaces.

The terms sense-making and sensemaking have no presence as of this writing in the Wikipedia entry on HCI.[20] However, there has been regular attention paid to sensemaking (using this grammatical form) by HCI researchers since at least 1993. The HCI sensemaking community traces its emphasis back to what seems to be the first use of the term presented in a paper at CHI1993 by Dan Russell, Mark Stefik, Peter Pirolli and Stuart Card.[21] Computer-Human Interaction (CHI) is an ACM special interest group.

In 1993, these authors were at PARC, the Palo Alto Research Center, Inc., a research and development company focusing in large part on human-computer interfaces. Much diffusion of a sensemaking emphasis has since ensued witnessed, for example, by PARC's listing of sensemaking as one of its 2008 research foci.[22]

Daniel Russell's (et al.) sensemaking

The Russell group's 1993 paper[21]—"The Cost Structure of Sensemaking"—defined sensemaking as:

> Making sense of a body of data is a common activity in any kind of analysis. Sensemaking is the process of searching for a representation and encoding data in that representation to answer task-specific questions. Different operations during sensemaking require different cognitive and external resources. Representations are chosen and change to reduce the cost of operations in an information processing task. The power of these representational shifts is generally underappreciated as is the relation between sensemaking and information retrieval.

With this paper and in their work since, the authors have most commonly examined the discrete cognitive steps, stages, and strategies with which users navigate databases seeking increasingly effective representations to support task-facings. The authors have been interested in understanding user sensemaking in specific information retrieval situations and then explaining and predicting user behavior so as to inform technology design choices. Typically, the research approach has involved qualitative and/or quantitative analysis of the online use histories of user engagements with particular database or software systems, sometimes coupled with in-depth interviewing and field observations.

All four authors have continued to pursue this research trajectory and have actively promoted understanding of sensemaking within the HCI community. Pirolli and Card, still working at PARC, have explored respectively sensemaking in relation to information foraging[23] and sensemaking as it relates to information visualization.[24] Other researchers from the HCI community such as George Furnas (University of Michigan) and Yan Qu (now at University of Maryland) have continued research programs focusing on much the same approach in varied contexts.[25–27]

In general, this approach to sensemaking focuses on what users do to make sense during specific task-related HCI that involve information retrieval in some form. Sometimes, user behavior is examined as it naturally occurs; sometimes it is examined in the context of specific design tools. The researchers have generally accepted that users do not navigate systems in orderly ways as prescribed by external experts. Russell and colleagues went to the essence of this community's focus in the call for papers for the CHI2008 Workshop on Sensemaking:[28]

> Making sense of the world is a ubiquitous activity, taking place around the margins of what we know....It arises when we change our place in the world or when the world changes around us. It arises when new problems, opportunities, or tasks present themselves, or when old ones resurface. It involves finding the important structure in a seemingly unstructured situation. It is an activity with cognitive and social dimensions, and has informational, communicational, and computational aspects.

Sense-Making in Cognitive Systems Engineering

The second field having a visible systematic literature invoking the term sensemaking (using this grammatical form) is Cognitive Systems Engineering. On the surface, the approach seems almost identical with the HCI approach because both have focused on improving technology design solutions to better serve human needs. The differences between the approaches are important, however, because they reflect differing disciplinary and historical origins.

The Cognitive Systems Engineering Consortium defines its focus as: "...a design discipline that uses analyses of work (practice, structure, purposes, and constraints) to inform the design of process and technology for Human-System Integration." It examines cognitive work, traditionally viewed as "the thinking associated with knowing, understanding, planning, deciding, and problem solving." It sees cognitive work as involving the interplay between perception, cognition, and action and "...the way the interplay establishes meaning."[29] Those focusing on sensemaking in this field generally work for industry, government (primarily military and defense), and academia and have backgrounds in psychology. They apply their expertise to designing more effective intersections between human cognitive competences, technologies, and work environments, particularly to computer and system designs.

Gary Klein's sensemaking

Gary Klein, a cognitive psychologist and leading figure in Cognitive Systems Engineering, has been the major proponent of this community's emerging focus on sensemaking. World-renowned for his pioneering work on decision making in natural settings, he was among those who concluded that laboratory models were not useful for understanding decision making in uncertainty

conditions.[30,31] He founded Klein Associates Inc., where he spearheaded a focus on naturalistic decision making.[32] In 2005, Klein Associates was acquired by engineering solutions development firm Applied Research Associates where Klein now serves as Chief Scientist.[33] In addition to much cited books, Klein's primary publication venue has been *IEEE Intelligent Systems*, top-cited journal in electronic and electrical engineering. IEEE considers itself the leading association for the advancement of technology. Originally IEEE referred to the Institute of Electrical and Electronics Engineers Inc., but now the organization is known simply by its acronym.[34]

The primary emphasis in Klein's work focuses on individual and team decision making. In a set of two 2006 coauthored papers, he described sensemaking as having "become an umbrella term for efforts at building intelligent systems."[35,36] Klein et al., were careful to explain that a broad definition of sensemaking as "how people make sense out of their experience in the world" could easily encompass or be confused with concepts often studied in psychology such as creativity, curiosity, comprehension, mental modeling, and situation awareness. Instead, the authors anchored themselves in this definition: "sensemaking is a motivated, continuous effort to understand connections (which can be among people, places, and events) in order to anticipate their trajectories and act effectively."

Klein's primary empirical method is what he calls Cognitive Task Analysis[37] (CTA) described in these terms: "In order to understand how people act upon the world around them, it is necessary to understand what goes on inside their heads....to find out how they think and what they know, how they organize and structure information, and what they seek to understand better." Cognitive Task Analysis focuses on eliciting understandings from decision-makers of the cognitive events, structures or models they use in situation assessment, sensemaking, decision making, and planning activities. With empirical evidence from a large corpus of studies, Klein and colleagues extracted a list of refutations of stereotypes about how domain practitioners make complex decisions in dynamic environments.[38] It is not so, they said, that: 1) data fusion and automated hypothesis generation aid sensemaking; 2) sensemaking is simply connecting the dots; 3) more information leads to better sensemaking; 4) it is important to keep an open mind; 5) biases are inescapable and prevent reliable sensemaking; and 6) sensemaking follows the waterfall model of how data leads to understanding.

Klein has emphasized that he studies sensemaking at macrocognitive not microcognitive levels. The macrocognitive positions people's problem solving behavior in terms of their views of complex sociotechnical systems while the microcognitive seeks to understand sequences of mental events. In a later paper, Klein and coauthors extrapolate their understanding of how sense making occurs in what they call a Data-Frame Model of

Sensemaking.[39] They emphasized, as Klein has continually done, that experts make decisions primarily through an "...understanding of the current situation, how it got there, and where it is going." However, the situational awareness here focuses not only on how the current situation invokes a working memory of the past but rather how experts make sense amid "...the growing suspicion" in the face of "...unexpected changes and surprises" that the "...current understanding is incorrect."

Using performance observations, interviews, and incident accounts, this research studies sensemaking as the process by which individuals and teams come to understand gaps between their initial accounts and new incoming data. The research focuses on how sensemakers get fixated on current explanations, investigate inadequacies, and then reframe accounts. The ultimate goal is what Klein and coauthors call Decision-Centered Design, in which sensemaking is one of a number of macrocognitive functions that are supported in design solutions.[40]

Sense-Making in Organizational Communication

There are two highly visible proponents of a focus on sense-making in organizational communication: Karl Weick and David Snowden. Weick deliberately uses the term sensemaking in order to convey the idea that the term is so all encompassing that it needs to be distinguished as a new concept.[16] Snowden uses both terms—sense-making and sensemaking—interchangeably to refer to a whole set of processes specifically addressed in his organizational interventions. While Weick and Snowden both focus on organizational communication and share many assumptions in common they come from different backgrounds and pursue their projects in distinctive ways.[41]

Karl Weick's sensemaking

Karl Weick is a social psychologist whose career has been mostly academic. He currently serves as professor of organizational behavior and psychology in the University of Michigan Ross School of Business. Drawing from his social psychologist's background, he emphasizes tensions inherent in organizational life such a threat versus rigidity, commitment versus decommitment, doubt versus self-fulfilling prophecy, and dissonance versus assurance. He brings this rich emphasis to bear on his central focus: "the conditions that precipitate the collapse of sensemaking in organizations."[42] In doing so, he attends with a broad and interdisciplinary reach to the intersections of literatures from social psychology, organizational studies, and communication. He generally works from theory to research practice but then turns his research results into recommendations for specific organizations and uses them as well to amplify his theoretic ideas.

He often cited 1996 book, *Sensemaking in Organizations*,[16] describes sensemaking as a process involving comprehending, constructing meaning, searching for patterns and frameworks, redressing surprise, and interacting with others in the pursuit of common understandings. Sensemaking, he emphasizes, should not be used as a synonym for interpretation which emphasizes a one-way relationship between interpreter and text. Sensemaking is also about authoring. It is not outcome but process—ongoing, social, retrospective, driven by plausibility rather than accuracy, and grounded in identity construction. It is about the enlargement of small cues. It is a search for contexts within which small details fit together and make sense. It is people interacting to flesh out hunches. It is a continuous cycling between particulars and explanations, with each turn giving added form and substance to the other. Sensemaking is concerned with how people "construct what they construct, why, and with what effects."[16]

Weick has generally applied his attention to sensemaking to those organizations that require acute mindfulness to avoid small errors, that is, High Reliability Organizations. He conceptualizes organizations as "...social structures that combine the generic subjectivity of interlocking routines, the intersubjectivity of mutually reinforcing interpretations, and the movement back and forth between these two forms by means of continuous communication."[16]

The emphasis on eliciting narratives which is a hallmark of Weick's approach is rooted in the central idea that storytelling is democratic: anyone can tell a story and anyone can criticize and analyze a story. "When people tell a story they are invoking a personal philosophy of reason, value, and action."[43] A narrative approach interrupts the privileged edifices of expert interpretation frozen in the past and requiring special technical skills for comprehension.

Weick's research approach is enacted through field studies involving both observation and interviews with primary emphasis on attending to narratives. Among the organizations he has researched have been jazz orchestras, firefighters, aircraft carriers, and power plants.[44] The research typically involves intensive and overtime observation and/or interviewing reconstructions of organizational events from different vantage points and different observers.[45,46] These are sometimes interspersed with workshop discussions with organizational representatives. Systematic analyses involve the use of triangulation of selected "interpretations" (usually those of multiple researchers) coupled with grounded theorizing approaches as espoused by Glaser and Straus.[47] Various paper and pencil data collection tools are sometimes used.

Research usually concludes with recommendations to specific organizations as well as mandates for organizational life. An example of the latter is the Weick. Sutcliffe, and Obstfeld emphasis on how organizations must focus not only on successes (which potentially lead to hubris) but on failures, doing so as a means of regular iterative review without fear of punishment.[48] Another example is

Semiotics–Slovakia

a call for fostering individually distinctive interpretations on what is going on and accepting diverse inputs in order to counteract oversimplification.

Weick's work in organizational sensemaking is highly diffused and cited. According to the ISI Web of Knowledge database (as of August 28, 2008), there are some 4600-plus journal articles that have cited his writings giving Weick a status within ISI as a "highly cited author."

David Snowden's sense-making

David Snowden's approach to sense-making shares much in common with that of Weick. Both have focused largely on organizational decision making, strategy development, and dealing with complexity. Both emphasize the value of narrative as a procedural response to complexity. Both pinpoint a need for organizations to move away from emphasizing top-down hierarchies to fluid structures responsive to changing and often elusive conditions.[41] Both use direct involvements via workshops and other interventions as an inherent core of their research-application processes.

In contrast with Weick, Snowden implements his approach not from within academia but from organizational settings. He has been identified as a major figure in the movement toward integration of humanistic approaches to knowledge management. He defines his project as naturalizing science-based approaches to decision theory and sense-making, bringing together both academic and practitioner perspectives. A native of Wales, he has a background in philosophy and business administration. He also makes frequent references to literacy and science fiction sources in his work.[41]

Formerly Director of the IBM Institute of Knowledge Management, Snowden is currently Founder and Chief Scientific Officer of United Kingdom-based Cognitive Edge, an international network of organizational consultants that focuses on rejuvenating management practices to better equip organizations to address intractable problems and uncertain and complex situations. Cognitive Edge's approach to research is based on action research principles.[49] The approach typically involves interacting with representatives in organizations using participatory and discovery methods so that issues and problems can be explored in a coevolutionary process.

In this context, sense-making is defined as "how we make sense of the world so we can act in it." Snowden and colleagues focus on developing and implementing tools and practices for analyzing narrative complexity in real organizational settings. One example is a branded software named "SenseMaker Suite" that provides tools for applying the themes of narrative, complexity, and networks directly into organizational analysis and practice. Snowden explicitly focuses on the development of specific alternative forms of organizational dialogue with labels

such as "Story Circles" and "Knowledge Discourse Points."[49]

The glue that holds much of this in place as described in Snowden's writings is an emphasis on "Cynefin"—a Welsh term referring as noun to habitat and as adjective to being familiar.[50,51] Cynefin is one of Snowden's organizing concepts, pointing to the idea that responding to complexity requires a sense of place that enables one to advance diverse views (i.e., different storytellings) and imagine narratives of what happened, what could have happened, and how to act differently in the future.[41,52–54]

From this anchoring in situated narratives, Snowden engages his organizational participants in differentiating between different kinds of sense-making gaps. One set of five distinctions involves differentiating between the simple, complicated, chaotic, complex, and disorderly. This framework might be used to gain insights into contentious issues, plan interventions to move situations from one domain to another, consider how to approach or manage different communities of practitioners, or develop strategies for knowledge retention.

In conjunction with the use of his various frameworks, Snowden employs action research methods such as contextualizations, narrative databases, convergences, and alternative histories. In his research, Snowden moves from a set of highly abstract philosophic premises to the dialogic practices and inventions he uses in his organizational interventions. From these he has developed tools for analyzing complexity in organizations that in turn gives feedback to his research emphases.

LIS

While LIS is the one field that most exhibits convergences between the various approaches to understanding sense-making, these convergences are of recent origin. Historically, the one approach to sense-making that has most marked LIS since 1986 is Dervin's. The germinal reference is the Dervin and Nilan review in the 1986 *Annual Review of Information Science and Technology* that called for a turn away from "traditional" approaches to studying users in which information is defined as objective, humans are seen as input-output processors, and the aim is to arrive at *trans*-situational propositions regarding information seeking and use.[4] The authors called instead for a turn to "alternative" approaches where information is defined as outcome of human constructing processes and humans are seen as making "sense" in response to changing and sometimes elusive conditions.

Since 1986, there has been an explosion of interests in user-oriented studies in LIS. This has led to the establishment of a special interest group in the American Society of Information Science and Technology focusing on information seeking and use (SIGUSE); and the founding of the European-based Information Seeking in Context

(ISIC) consortium that holds biannual conferences. Dervin has been frequently identified as instrumental in these developments and one of the key instigators of the shift from system-centered to user-centered research in information science.[55–59]

Brenda Dervin's sense-making

Dervin's disciplinary background is the field of communication.[60] Prior to her graduate studies she served as communication practitioner focusing on communicating with the urban poor. After graduate school she brought this specialty to the then Syracuse University School of Library Science, now incorporated in Information Studies. Since that time she has been located at the University of Washington (1972–1986) and Ohio State University Schools of Communication. Her emphasis has expanded from the poor to any communication efforts where experts attempt to communicate with nonexperts via their messages, procedures, or system designs. Dervin is often quoted as stating that in some context, we are all information poor.[61] For her, the biggest gap between users is not their differences as defined by outsiders but the yawning gap between nonexperts and expertise frozen in historical pasts and locked in specialized discourses.[62,63]

Dervin focuses broadly on phenomena she terms sensemaking and sense-unmaking. Her mandate is to understand how individuals engage internally (intrapersonally) and externally (interpersonally and via mediated communication) with the patterned matter energies that humans call by varied names—for example, observations, information, expertise, knowledge, wisdom. Since the 1970s, Dervin's writings have pivoted around a central theme—a call to focus on communication as communication rather than as transmission and to bridge gaps between research and practice with user-oriented research. Dervin's emphasis is applied to users and potential users by any other name, for example, patrons, audiences, patients, employees, citizens, leaders, constituents, customers, and so on. In addition to users of her work in LIS, Dervin's approach has been applied in numerous research communities, for example, pedagogy, media studies, public communication campaigns, citizen participation, development communication, and health communication.[63]

While her work has gone through developmental transitions since first being labeled as focusing on sensemaking,[4,64] in its current form it consists of a comprehensive theory of how dialogue must be conceptualized to work communicatively.[17,18,62] Dervin sees user research as an instance of dialogue. She aims to theorize human sense-making in the realm of what she calls "verbings" that rise above the specific noun-based idiosyncrasies of formalized information domains to the universals of how humans navigate the human condition where discontinuities are ever-present constants even in the most orderly of conditions.

She shares with all those who focus on sense-making a reach for attention to human beings in ways more holistic than traditional emphases have allowed. She also shares the common emphasis on humans making sense amid uncertainty, complexity, and chaos. She shares especially with Weick and Snowden their emphases on facilitating diverse voices to speak and be heard, their use of various philosophic inputs, and their emphases on narrative and storytelling. With Snowden, she shares an interest in inventing alternative systematic forms of communicative intervention.

What differs in Dervin's Sense-Making Methodology is that of all the approaches it is the only one that moves from a generalized set of philosophic premises to a fully explicated methodology and practice for studying and engaging sense-making. In addition, Dervin's approach is not anchored in specific research contexts but has been designed to be useful in any context that involves communicating intrapersonally, interpersonally, or via mediated means.

For Dervin, research is itself treated as sense-making and is not privileged as a special stance outside the phenomena it studies. What Dervin proposes is that understanding the sense-makings of others cannot be simply a matter of using open-ended queries and inviting alternative voices to the table. Rather, it requires a designed reframing of communicative processes, a reframing that explicitly attends to philosophic assumptions implemented in visibly aligned methods.

The most well-known example of the application of Dervin's Sense-Making is to the methodology's interviewing approaches.[62,65] These are all organized around a central Sense-Making Metaphor that draws together the approach's philosophic premises mandating that user studies attend systematically to: context, time, space, movement, gap, horizon, energy, power, history, experience, constraint, change (flexibility, caprice, chaos), and constancy (habit, inflexibility, rigidity). Briefly stated, these mandates require that users be studied as navigating situations while traversing two constant discontinuities of the human condition. The first is gappiness between times, spaces, and human as well as nonhuman entities that can never be bridged entirely with a priori information or instruction. The second is the struggle to sense-make one's own agency and to simultaneously sense-make one's engagements with external structures (e.g., communities, collectivities, organizations).

In its briefest form the metaphor is called the Sense-Making Triangle[62–64] linking situationally-based step-takings out of specific histories to the building of bridges (e.g., cognitive, emotional, spiritual, physical) across everpresent gaps and sensing outcomes (e.g., consequences, impacts, effects that help and/or hinder) that then in themselves become grounds for the next step-takings. This metaphor is not intended to suggest all human sense-making involves problem-solving or decision-making although these are conceptualized as among the possibilities.

Briefly, these philosophic assumptions mandate that sense-makers be seen as: changing as they move through time-space; navigating both certainty and uncertainty and the gaps between; sometimes confused, sometimes in doubt, and sometimes sure; struggling with how to be the same as others and yet be different; struggling, at least sometimes, with imposed structures and power constraints, albeit sometimes silently, sometimes unconsciously; sometimes acting as agents of structures, and sometimes acted on and resisting them.

In interviewing practice, these assumptions are applied in a series of different interviewing approaches conceptualized as implementing a fully developed theory of the interview.[62] Each of the approaches involves eliciting from informants situated narratives anchored in descriptions of internal and external movements through time-space. The various interviewing approaches, labeled with such names as the Micro-Moment Time-Line, Life-Line, Micro-Element Interview, and Help Chaining, all involve bracketing time-space in different ways. They serve different purposes depending on research, application, or dialogic context.

At the core of every interview is repeated uses of Sense-Making Triangulation where informants are anchored in specific time-space moments and asked a roster of questions—adapted with vocabularies suitable to informants and context—based on these core elements: What happened? How did it connect with your life/past/work? What questions, confusions did you struggle with? What ideas/conclusions/insights did you arrive at? What emotions or feelings did you have? How were you helped and/or hindered? How did you hope to be helped? How did this connect to constraints and power dynamics as you experienced them? The intent of the questioning is to insofar as possible keep researcher and expert nouns and understandings from being imposed during the interviewing process.

Over the years, rosters of central Sense-Making categories have emerged that are used for systematic analyses. The categories focus on "universals" of sense-making drawn from 30 years of projects across myriad contexts and applications. One example category set addresses how users see their micromoments of situated sense-making stopped at junctures requiring new or revised sense and/or abandoning old sense. The categories use such names as: decision, barrier, spin-out, wipe-out, tightrope, time passing, waiting, being chased by time, observing, moving. The category labels illustrate how the methodology attends to context-free universals even while mandating that user narratives be elicited in context and situationally anchored ways.

The various Sense-Making categories form a basis for Sense-Making's approach to Situational Contingency Analysis.[62,65] The primary gain from using this analytic approach to date has been to show repeatedly that users when seen through the lenses of their views of their situated movements in time-space are rarely well understood or predicted in traditional terms by measures that freeze individual users to attributes such as demography, personality, or cognitive style that transcend time-space. Likewise, users are rarely predicted well by attributes that freeze situations, tasks, domains, or contexts with expert driven framings that assume users see these as the same as they move through time-space.

The execution of Sense-Making informed studies have taken on many forms. All have interviewing as foundation, but administered in numerous ways—in person, by phone, online, text messaging, self-administered; executed in formalized surveys, laboratory settings, and in the field via participant observation and ethnographic approaches. The interviewing core has always involved the methodology's mandated structure of open-ended questions. Close-ended queries are sometimes added in ways consonant with the methodology's metatheoretic premises. Analyses involve both quantitative approaches including systematic content analyses and statistical displays, and qualitative approaches informed primarily by grounded theory[44] and use of Sense-Making's Situational Contingency Analysis. Some applications have involved field or laboratory experimentation focused on dialogic invention and intervention. In these cases, Sense-Making Methodology informs both the design of the communication inventions and the researching of their impacts.

While cited, according to the ISI Web of Knowledge, in more than 1000 journal articles, most references to Dervin's work uses it to document a generalized call for more user-oriented approaches. About 120 authors have gone beyond this general usage to systematically applying Dervin's approach in small or large part to research that has been applied to message, information, procedure, and system design; and to the design of communicative interventions for dialogue. Among the notable full-scale applications are a series of studies spearheaded by Dervin and funded by governmental agencies at the state and federal levels. Examples include Dervin's early studies of the everyday information needs of residents in Seattle in 1976[66] and California in 1984.[67] The most recent application is an Institute of Museum and Library Services (IMLS) funded study of college and university users in central Ohio.[68,69] Dervin has also supervised a large roster of doctoral dissertations that have applied the methodology to myriad kinds of users in varied contexts.

Some LIS anchored researchers who have given sustained attention to Dervin's approach include Savolainen[70,71] at the University of Tampere, Finland, particularly with his attentions to improving user studies of HIBs; Fisher and colleagues at the University of

Washington[72],[73] in their studies of the information grounds from which users move. In addition, the projects of a number of LIS researchers who have developed their own versions of a variety of user-oriented approaches to studying HIBs have drawn on Dervin particularly in the early stages of their projects. Examples include: Chatman;[74] Durrance;[75] Kuhlthau;[76] Nilan;[77] Ross;[78] and Solomon.[79–81] The most well-known application to design in LIS is Sense-Making Questioning originally presented as Neutral Questioning.[62,82] This approach to the procedures of the library reference interview is still being taught in many LIS schools and used actively in some library systems.[83]

SENSE-MAKING APPROACHES AS CLARION CALL

The approaches to sense-making described above have all been used in different contexts to focus on understanding HIBs, albeit using discourse-distinctive vocabularies, All have extracted recommendations for system designs and practices that will help humans better meet changing and often elusive situational conditions. All veer to the humanistic and veer away from the mechanistic. All move out of formerly accepted models of information exchange as transmission toward more interpretive, narrative, and phenomenological approaches.

At the same time, the approaches differ, sometimes subtly and sometimes distinctly. The fact that the approaches use common vocabularies belies how they proceed in quite different ways for quite different purposes. Some of the differences are easier to penetrate for they involve more readily identifiable differences in research intent and focus—who the research is conducted for; how it is used; what kind of HIBs it focuses on; in what kinds of contexts, situations or tasks; within the brackets of what time horizons; and, pointing to what kinds of outcome.

Other differences are far more subtle. Despite surface appearances of similarities, penetrating to the meanings deeply anchored within each of the different sense-making discourse communities takes time-consuming study. Deeply held assumptions are often unstated, understandably most often in approaches anchored in fields that privilege research applications to practice. Some approaches emphasize epistemology, focusing primarily on interpretive differences between sense-makers. Others emphasize ontology, focusing more on the different sense-making requirements of elusive and changing situations. Some focus at the micro level, some macro, and some both. All do a little bit of all these although sometimes only implicitly. The differences are a matter of emphasis in both articulation as well as procedure. More often than not, the tools that would allow the unraveling of these deeply rooted differences are themselves hidden beneath surfaces. Most efforts to compare and contrast assume essentialist meanings and, thus, execute approaches to dialogue based on transmission rather than communicative theories of communication.[17,18]

Clearly, while not all those who have turned to studying sense-making share an entirely common roster of assumptions, all have attempted to change traditional and accepted transmission oriented approaches in their research. They all reach as well to look at HIBs in ways that attend to complexity, chaos, and uncertainty. This a fundamental change and enlargement in the "paradigm" accepted for studying the human condition. Given the magnitude of this change and the challenges of the intellectual grounds that are being traversed, it is not surprising that there are inconsistencies, even contradictions, between the various approaches.

The move toward focusing on sense-making can be seen as having two major trajectories. One is a general trajectory in which the term sense-making serves as a clarion call, a marker of the growing energies directed at studying human beings and HIBs in more humanistic ways. The second trajectory is the way the term, in its various grammatical forms—sense-making and sensemaking—is being implemented to meet this clarion call in specific research and application contexts. The difficulty, for the reader attempting to grasp what sense-making is, is understanding that sense-making is not any one phenomena seen in any one way. The very difficulty of its defining and the inability to hold it still is itself a trace of the very sea-change in the understanding of HIBs toward which it may be said the sense-making movement directs research and design attention.

CONCLUSION

This entry has focused on how research approaches labeled as sense-making or sensemaking are used to address user-oriented research relevant to the study of human information behaviors Starting with a focus on the turn to sense-making in user studies, this entry reviews the historical and methodological roots and context applications of the five visible approaches that have addressed sense-making systematically in four fields: HCI (Russell's sensemaking); Cognitive Systems Engineering (Klein's sensemaking); Organizational Communication (Weick's sensemaking; Snowden's sense-making/ sensemaking); and LIS (Dervin's sense-making).

REFERENCES

1. Berlo, D.K. Communication as process: review and commentary. In *Communication Yearbook*; Transaction Books: New Brunswick, NJ, 1977; Vol. 1, 11–27.

Semiotics–Slovakia

2. Bruner, J.S. *Acts of Meaning*; Harvard University Press: Cambridge, MA, 1990.

3. Dervin, B., Foreman-Wernet, L., Eds. *Communication, a Different Kind of Horserace: Essays Honoring Richard F. Carter*; Hampton Press: Cresskill, NJ, 2003.

4. Dervin, B.; Nilan, M. Information needs and uses. Annu. Rev. Inform. Sci. Technol. **1986**, *21*, 3–33.

5. Dewey, J. *On Experience, Nature, and Freedom: Representative Selections;* Liberal Arts Press: New York, 1960.

6. Feyerabend, P. *Against Method: Outline of an Anarchistic Theory of Knowledge*; Humanities Press: London, U.K., 1975.

7. Feynman, R.P.; Robbins, J. *The Pleasure of Finding Things Out: The Best Short Works of Richard P. Feynman*; Perseus Books: Cambridge, MA, 1999.

8. Flyvbjerg, B. *Making Social Science Matter: Why Social Inquiry Fails and How It Can Succeed Again*; Cambridge University Press: Oxford, U.K., New York, 2001.

9. Foucault, M. *The Archaeology of Knowledge*; Pantheon Books: New York, NY, 1972.

10. Freire, P. *Pedagogy of the Oppressed*; Seabury Press: New York, 1970.

11. Gadamer, H.-G. *Truth and Method*; Seabury Press: New York, 1975.

12. Galtung, J. *Social Science—For What?*; Columbia University Press: New York, 1980.

13. Hayles, N.K. *Chaos Bound: Orderly Disorder in Contemporary Literature and Science*; Cornell University Press: Ithaca, NY, 1990.

14. McGuire, W.J. A perspectivist looks at contextualism and the future of behavioral science. In *Contextualism and Understanding in Behavioral Science: Implications for Research and Theory*; Rosnow, R.L., Georgoudi, M., Eds.; Praeger: New York, 1986; 271–301.

15. Toulmin, S. *Cosmopolis: The Hidden Agenda of Modernity*; The Free Press: New York, 1999.

16. Weick, K.E. *Sensemaking in Organizations*; Sage Publications: Thousand Oaks, CA, 1995.

17. Dervin, B. Human studies and user studies: a call for methodological inter-disciplinarity. Inform. Res. **2003**, *9*, (1, paper 166). Available at http://information.net/ir/9-1/paper166.html.

18. Dervin, B.; Reinhard, C. D.; Shen, F. S. Beyond communication—research as communicating: Making user and audience studies matter—paper 2. Inform. Res. **2006**, *12*(2, paper 287). Available at http://information.net/ir/12-1/paper287.html.

19. Association for Computing Machinery, 2008. Available at http://www.acm.org/about (accessed August 18, 2008) .

20. Wikipedia: Human-Computer Interaction, 2008. Available at http://en.wikipedia.org/wiki/Human-computer_interaction (accessed August 18, 2008).

21. Russell, D.M. The cost structure of sensemaking. Proceedings of the INTERACT '93 and CHI '93 Conference on Human Factors in Computing Systems; ACM: Amsterdam, the Netherlands, 1993.

22. PARC Human Information Interaction/HCI. Available at http://www.parc.com/research/projects/hii/default.html (accessed August 18, 2008).

23. Pirolli, P.; Card, S. Information foraging in information access environments. Proceedings of the SIGCHI Conference on Human Factors in Computing Systems; ACM Press/Addison-Wesley Publishing Co: Denver, CO, 1995; 51–58.

24. Card, S.K.; Pirolli, P.; Mackinlay, J.D. The cost-of-knowledge characteristic function: display evaluation for direct-walk dynamic information visualizations. Proceedings of the SIGCHI Conference on Human Factors in Computing Systems: Celebrating Interdependence; ACM: Boston, MA, 1994; 238–244.

25. Furnas, G.W.; Russell, D.M. Making sense of sense-making. CHI'05; ACM: Portland, OR, 2005.

26. Qu, Y. A sensemaking-supporting information gathering system. CHI '03 Extended Abstracts on Human Factors in Computing Systems; ACM: Ft. Lauderdale, FL, 2003.

27. Qu, Y.; Furnas, G.W. Sources of structure in sensemaking. CHI '05 Extended Abstracts on Human Factors in Computing Systems; ACM: Portland, OR, 2005.

28. Russell, D.M.; et al. Sensemaking workshop at CHI 2008, Available at http://dmrussell.googlepages.com/sensemakingworkshopchi2008.

29. Cognitive Systems Engineering Consortium. Available at http://kn. gd-ais.com/ASPs/CoP/EntryCoP.asp?Filter=GD-WB-CS (accessed August 18, 2008).

30. Klein, G.A. *Sources of Power: How People Make Decisions*; MIT Press: Cambridge, MA, 1998.

31. Klein, G.A. *The Power of Intuition: How to Use Your Gut Feelings to Make Better Decisions at Work*; Doubleday Business: New York, NY, 2004.

32. Klein Associates. Available at http://en.wikipedia.org/wiki/Klein_Associates (accessed August 18, 2008).

33. Applied Research Associates, Inc. Available at http://www.ara.com/ (accessed August 18, 2008).

34. IEEE: The world's leading professional association for the advancement of technology. Available at http://www.ieee.org (accessed August 18, 2008).

35. Klein, G.; Moon, B.; Hoffman, R.R. Making sense of sensemaking 1: alternative perspectives. IEEE Intell. Syst. **2006**, *21*(4), 70–73.

36. Klein, G.; Moon, B.; Hoffman, R.R. Making sense of sensemaking 2: a macrocognitive model. IEEE Intell. Syst. **2006**, *21*(5), 88–92.

37. Cognitive Task Analysis. Available at http://www.ara.com/capabilities/tech_cognitive.htm (accessed August 18, 2008).

38. Klein, G.; Ross, K.G.; Moon, B.M.; Klein, D.E.; Hoffman, R.R.; Hollnagel, E. Macrocognition. IEEE Intell. Syst. **2003**, *18*(3), 81–85.

39. Klein, G. et al. A data-frame theory of sensemaking. In *Expertise Out of Context,* Proceedings of the 6th International Conference on Naturalistic Decision Making; Hoffman, R.R., Ed.; Lawrence Erlbaum Associates: New York, 2007; 133–155.

40. Hutton, R.; Klein, G.; Wiggins, S. Designing for sensemaking: a macrocognitive approach. In *Computer Human Interactions 2008*; ACM: Florence, Italy, 2008.

41. Browning, L.; Boudes, T. The use of narrative to understand and respond to complexity: a comparative analysis of the Cynefin and Weickian models. Emerg. Complex. Organ. **2005**, *7*(3–4), 32–39.

42. Weick, K.E. Center for Positive Organizational Scholarship, University of Michigan Ross School of Business.

Available at http://www.bus.umich.edu/Positive/POS-Research/Contributors/KarlWeick.htm (accessed August 27, 2008).

43. Weick, K.E.; Browning, L.D. Argument and narration in organizational communication. J. Manage. **1986**, *12*, 249–59.

44. Weick, K.E.; Sutcliffe, K.M. *Managing the Unexpected: Assuring High Performance in an Age of Complexity*; Jossey-Bass: San Francisco, CA, 2001.

45. Weick, K.E.; Roberts, K.H. Collective mind in organizations: heedful interrelating on flight decks. Admin. Sci. Quart. **1993**, *38*, 357–381.

46. Eisenhardt, K.M. Building theories from case study research. Acad. Manage. Rev. **1989**, *14*(4), 532–550.

47. Glaser, B.G.; Strauss, A.L. *The Discovery of Grounded Theory: Strategies for Qualitative Research*; Aldine de Gruyter: New York, NY, 1967.

48. Weick, K.E.; Sutcliffe, K.M.; Obstfeld, D. Organizing and the process of sensemaking. Organ. Sci. **2005**, *16*(4), 409–421.

49. Cognitive Edge: Who We Are. Available at http://www.cognitive-edge.com/whoweare.php (accessed August 18, 2008).

50. Kurtz, C.F.; Snowden, D.J. The new dynamics of strategy: sense-making in a complex and complicated world. IBM Syst. J. **2003**, *42*(3), 462–483.

51. Snowden, D.J. Cynefin, a sense of time and place: an ecological approach to sense-making and learning in formal organizations. Proceeding of KMAC 2000. Available at http://www.knowledgeboard.com/library/cynefin.pdf (accessed August 28, 2008).

52. Snowden, D. Complex acts of knowing: paradox and descriptive self-awareness. J. Knowl. Manage. **2002**, *6*(2), 100–111.

53. Snowden, D.J.; Boone, M.E. A leaders framework for decision making—wise executive tailor their approach to fit the complexity of the circumstances they face. Harvard Bus. Rev. **2007**, *85*(11), 68.

54. Snowden, D.J. Managing for serendipity or why we should lay off 'best practices' in KM. Knowl. Manage. **2000**, *6*(8). Available at http://www.cognitiveedge.com/ceresources/articles/39_Managing_for_Serendipity_final.pdf (accessed August 28, 2008).

55. Vakkari, P. Information seeking in context: a challenging metatheory Information seeking in context. Proceedings of an International Conference on Research in Information Needs, Seeking, and Use in Different Contexts; Vakkari, P., Savolainen, R., Dervin, B., Eds.; Taylor Graham: London, U.K., 1997; 451–464.

56. Naumer, C.; Fisher, K.; Dervin, B. Sense-making: a methodological perspective. In *Computer Human Interactions 2008;* ACM: Florence, Italy, 2008.

57. Dalrymple, P.W. A quarter century of user-centered study: the impact of Zweizig and Dervin on Library Science research. Libr. Inform. Sci. Res. **2001**, *23*(2), 155–165.

58. Tidline, T.J. In *Dervin's Sense-Making in Theories of Information Behavior: A Researcher's Guide*; Fisher, K. E., Erdelez, S., McKenchie, L.E.F., Eds.; Information Today: Medford, NJ, 2005; Chapter 2.

59. Morris, R. Toward a user-centered information service. J. Am. Soc. Inform. Sci. **1994**, *45*(1), 11–30.

60. Barbato, C.; Dervin, B.L. In *Women in Communication: A Bio-bibliographic Sourcebook*; Signorelli, N., Ed.; Greenwood Press: Westport, CT, 1996 (1938).

61. Dervin, B. Communication gaps and inequities: moving toward a reconceptualization. In *Progress in Communication Sciences*; Dervin, B., Voigt, M., Eds.; Ablex: Norwood, NJ, 1980; 73–112.

62. Dervin, B. Interviewing as dialectical practice: sense-making methodology as exemplar, Paper Presented at International Association of Media and Communication Research Meeting, Stockholm Sweden, July 2008.

63. Dervin, B., Foreman-Wernet, L., Eds. *Sense-Making Methodology Reader: Selected Writings of Brenda Dervin*; Hampton Press: Cresskill, NJ, 2003.

64. Dervin, B. An overview of sense-making research: concepts, methods and results. Annual Meeting of the International Communication Association, Dallas, TX, 1983.

65. Song, M. Modeling situated health information seeking and use in context: the use of two approaches to grounded theorizing as applied to 81 sense-making methodology derived narrative interviews of health situation facing; Ohio State University, 2007.

66. Dervin, B.; Zweizig, D.; Banister, M.; Gabriel, M.; Hall, E. P.; Kwan, C. (with Bowes, J.; Stamm, K.). The development of strategies for dealing with the information needs of urban residents: Phase I: The citizen study. Final report of Project L0035J to the U.S. Office of Education; University of Washington, School of Communications: Seattle, WA, 1976; Vol. ERIC: ED 125640.

67. Dervin, B. *The Information Needs of Californians, 1984: Report #2: Context, Summary, Conclusions, Applications*; California State Library: Sacramento, CA, 1984–1905; (ERIC Document Reproduction Service No. ED 267 801).

68. Dervin, B., Reinhard, C.D., Adamson, S.K., Lu, T.T., Karnolt, N.M., Berberick, T., Eds. Sense-making the information confluence: the whys and hows of college and university user satisficing of information needs. Phase I: Project overview, the Three-Field Dialogue project, and state-of-the-art reviews. Report on National Leadership Grant LG-02-03-0062-03, to Institute of Museum and Library Services, Washington, DC, 2006; School of Communication, The Ohio State University: Columbus, OH. Available at http://imlsproject.comm.ohio-state.edu/imls_reports/imls_PH_I_report_list.html.

69. Dervin, B., Reinhard, C.D., Kerr, Z.Y., Song, M., Shen, F. C., Eds.; 2006; Sense-making the information confluence: the whys and hows of college and university user satisficing of information needs. Phase II: Sense-making online survey and phone interview study. Report on National Leadership Grant LG-02-03-0062-03 to Institute for Museums and Library Services, Washington, DC; School of Communication, Ohio State University: Columbus, OH. Available at http://imlsproject.comm.ohio-state.edu/imls_reports/imls_PH_II_report_list.html.

70. Savolainen, R. The sense-making theory: reviewing the interests of a user-centered approach to information seeking and use. Inform. Process. Manage. **1993**, *29*(1), 13–28.

71. Savolainen, R. Information use as gap-bridging: the viewpoint of sense-making methodology: research articles. J. Am. Soc. Inform. Sci. Technol. **2006**, *57*(8), 1116–1125.

72. Fisher, K.; Naumer, C. Information grounds: theoretical basis and empirical findings on information flow in social settings. In *New Directions in Human Information Behavior*; Spink, A., Cole, C., Eds.; Kluwer: Amsterdam, the Netherland, 2005.

73. Fisher, K.; Durrance, J.C.; Hinton, M.B. Information grounds and the use of need-based services for immigrants in Queens, NY: a context-based, outcome evaluation approach. J. Am. Soc. Inform. Sci. Technol. **2004**, *55*(8), 754–766.

74. Chatman, E. Framing social life in theory and research. New Rev. Inform. Behav. Res. **2000**, *1*, 3–17.

75. Durrance, J.C.; Souden, M.; Walker, D.; Fisher, K.E. Community problem-solving framed as a distributed information use environment: bridging research and practice. Inform. Res. **2006**, *11*(4), paper 262. Available at http://informationR.net/ir/11-4/paper262.html.

76. Kuhlthau, C.C. *Seeking Meaning: A Process Approach to Library and Information Services*, 2nd Ed.; Libraries Unlimited: Westport, CT, 2004.

77. Nilan, M.S. Cognitive space: using virtual reality for large information resource management problems. J. Commun. **1992**, *42*(4), 115–135, Autumn.

78. Ross, C.S. Finding without seeking: the information encounter in the context of reading for pleasure. Inform. Process. Manage. **1999**, *35*(6), 783–799.

79. Solomon, P. Discovering information behavior in sense making. 1. Time and timing. J. Am. Soc. Inform. Sci. Technol. **1997**, *48*(12), 1097–1108.

80. Solomon, P. Discovering information behavior in sense making. 2. The social. J. Am. Soc. Inform. Sci. Technol. **1997**, *48*(12), 1109–1126.

81. Solomon, P. Discovering information behavior in sense making. 3. The person. J. Am. Soc. Inform. Sci. Technol. **1997**, *48*(12), 1127–1138.

82. Dervin, B.; Dewdney, P. Neutral questioning—a new approach to the reference interview. Res. Quart. **1986**, *25*(4), 506–513.

83. Ross, C.S.; Nilsen, K.; Dewdney, P. *Conducting the Reference Interview*; Neal-Schuman Publishing, Inc.: New York, London, U.K., 2002.

Serbia: Libraries, Archives, and Museums

Staša Milojević
*Department of Information Studies, University of California, Los Angeles, Los Angeles,
California, U.S.A.*

Abstract

This entry provides a brief historical overview of the emergence of libraries, archives, and museums in
Serbia. It describes the current environment of these cultural and information institutions, including their
legislation, organization, staffing, collections, automation, and services. Representative institutional profiles are also given. The entry also discusses professional education in library science, library associations,
and interinstitutional cooperation.

INTRODUCTION

The Republic of Serbia is a country in Central- and Southeastern Europe. It is bordered by Hungary to the north,
Romania and Bulgaria to the east, Former Yugoslav
Republic of Macedonia and Albania to the south and Montenegro, Bosnia and Herzegovina, and Croatia to the west
(Fig. 1). Serbia is divided into 24 districts plus the City of
Belgrade. The districts and the City of Belgrade are further
divided into 161 municipalities.[1] Serbia has two prov-
inces: Kosovo (full official name Kosovo and Metohija)
and Vojvodina. The part of Serbia that is neither Kosovo
nor Vojvodina is called Central Serbia. Unlike the two
provinces, Central Serbia is not an administrative division.
Since the armed conflict and NATO intervention in 1999,
Kosovo has been governed by the United Nations Interim
Administration Mission. According to the 2002 census,
Serbia (without Kosovo) had a population of 7,498,001.[2]
Serbia is populated mostly by Serbs (82.9%). Significant
minorities include: Hungarians (3.9%), Bosniaks (1.8%),
Roma (1.5%), Croats (1%), and Slovaks (1%). The census
was not conducted in Kosovo. According to the *CIA World
Factbook*, Kosovo had an estimated population of
2,126,708 (Albanians 88%, Serbs 7%, and other 5%) in
2007. With 71,111 refugees from Croatia, 27,414 from
Bosnia and Herzegovina, and 206,000 Serbs and Roma
internally displaced from Kosovo, Serbia has the largest
refugee population in Europe. The official language is
Serbian, a Slavic language.

Serbia is on one of the major thoroughfares from Western Europe to Turkey and the Middle East. It is also
intersected by several major navigable rivers that connect
Serbia with Northern and Western Europe. Belgrade and
Novi Sad are major regional Danubian harbors. Serbian
terrain is extremely varied: to the north lies the rich fertile
Pannonian Plain. To the east, limestone ranges and basins,
and to the southeast mountains and hills. Over a quarter of
Serbia's landmass is covered by forests.

Although it had a favorable economic outlook at the
beginning of the process of economic transition in 1989,
years of mismanagement of economy, U.N. economic
sanctions (1992–1995), and the damage to the infrastructure and industry during the NATO airstrikes (1999) took
their toll. In 2000, Serbia's economy was only half the size
it was in 1990. And although its economy, with the GDP
for 2008 estimated at $80.717 billion and $10,985 per
capita PPP, is considered an upper-middle income economy by the World Bank, it still faces many problems, the
most prominent of which are high unemployment, high
export/import trade deficit, and considerable national debt.
Serbian economy is based mostly on various services,
industry, and agriculture.

Serbia is still developing its telecommunication infrastructure. In 2007 89% of households had fixed telephone
lines, and 74.5% of households had a cell phone.[3]

In 2008, 40.8% of households had a computer. One-
third of all households had the Internet connection, of
which 51.1% had a dial-up connection, 24.4% had Asym-
metric digital subscriber line (ADSL), and 23.2% had
cable Internet.[4]

HISTORICAL OVERVIEW

The Serbs, a Slavic people, settled the Balkans in the
seventh century. Timeline of major historical events is
provided in Appendix 1. They adopted Christianity in the
second half of the ninth century. From the eighth to the
twelfth century they inhabited the lands under the Bulgar-
ian and the Byzantine rule. In the twelfth century, under
the Nemanjić dynasty, Serbia became a kingdom with an
autonomous Orthodox Christian church. Saint Sava, son
of Stefan Nemanja, the founder of Nemanjić dynasty, is
accredited with writing the first Serbian prose, dealing
with the life of his father. He is also acknowledged for
laying the foundations of the national, religious, and

Encyclopedia of Library and Information Sciences, Fourth Edition DOI: 10.1081/E-ELIS4-120045446

Semiotics–Slovakia

Fig. 1 Map of Serbia.

cultural identity of Serbia. The most important libraries in the medieval Serbia were those in the monasteries of Studenica (twelfth century), Žiča (thirteenth century), Gračanica (fourteenth century), Dečani fourteenth century), and Manasija (fifteenth century). The most outstanding library was the collection of the monastery Hilandar (1199), which was founded by Serbian rulers on Mount Athos in Greece.

With the end of the Nemanjić dynasty in the fourteenth century the Serbian lands became fragmented among the competing nobility. The fragmentation made it harder to resist the advancement of the Ottomans who won two major battles against Serbs in 1371 and 1389. The country finally succumbed to the Ottoman Empire rule in the fifteenth century.

Under the Ottoman Empire rule the majority of Serbian population lived in the countryside, in small villages organized on traditional bases. The Orthodox church played a particularly important role by preserving the national identity and keeping the memory of the medieval Serbian kingdom. The center of the church was the Patriarchate of Peć (Province of Kosovo).

In the seventeenth century, Serbs helped Habsburg troops gain significant territory from the Ottomans. As the Habsburg forces were pushed back, Patriarch Arsenije III and over 30,000 families who feared massacre migrated with the retreating army to settle in the Habsburg lands. At the time of great migration in 1690 Serbs were promised freedom of religion and an autonomous church administration by the Habsburg ruler, Holy Roman Emperor Leopold I. Thus, Serbs had a relatively favorable status in the Habsburg

Empire. As in the Ottoman Empire, the church dignitaries were in practice the leaders of "shadow" Serbian secular government, with a Serbian metropolitan, established at Sremski Karlovci, at its head. Sremski Karlovci (Province of Vojvodina) became the foremost Serbian religious, cultural, and educational center. The first Serbian schools of higher education were established there.

The Orthodox church served as a major vehicle in the transmission and preservation of past traditions. It provided the only available education. Another method of the transmission of culture and history among illiterate peasants was by storytelling and oral epic and popular poetry. This oral literature had both historical and religious themes. The literary language at the time was the so-called Serbian-Slavonic, an artificial creation close to Church Slavic, but not to the speech of the common people. Vuk Stefanović Karadžić (1787–1864), the most important linguistic reformer and the great leader of the Serbian intellectual and literary renaissance, created both the modern Serbian literary language and the modern Serbian literature. He simplified Serbian orthography and introduced the "living" people's language into literature.

After the first (1804–1813) and the second (1815) uprising against the Ottomans, the social-political and economic development in Serbia was dynamic. First secular schools were being opened right after the first uprising, replacing monastery schools. By the end of the uprising, there were around 50 schools funded by local municipalities or by parents. The first higher education institution (Velika škola) was founded in Belgrade in 1808 to educate first civil servants.

After Serbia gained the autonomy within the Ottoman Empire in 1830 the conditions became favorable for the systematic development of education and the establishment of cultural and scientific institutions. During the first decades of the autonomy, the chief intellectual influence came from the Serbs living in the Habsburg Monarchy who became an important element in the new bureaucracy. One of the first institutions to be established by the newly formed Serbian government was the Printing press in 1831. It was followed by the foundation of the National Library in 1832; the first Serbian theater and its library in 1841; The Serbian Learned Society and its library in 1842; the Library of the Serbian Lyceum in 1844, and a number of reading rooms in Belgrade and larger towns in Serbia from 1846 onward. The appearance of reading rooms (čitališta) in Serbia during the 1840s was important for the history of books and libraries. The reading rooms were based on the models from Western Europe. They became the public cultural institutions established by the emerging middle class to serve their cultural, national, and political development.[5] There are records on 79 reading rooms that were active between 1846 and 1900. These reading rooms had the function of public libraries, although they were never funded by the state. The development of all types of libraries in Serbia was not the result of an organized state policy, but came out of the need for books by different types of users. The first official librarian, Filip Nikolić, was the first person to professionally organize the National Library in the period from 1853 to 1856. He set the foundations of cataloging for the library following the Austro-Hungarian regulations, and formulated the library's first set of procedures.

The country finally gained independence with the Treaty of Berlin in 1878. As a parliamentary monarchy Serbia went through a period of economic and cultural prosperity. The 1901 Law on National Library was very important for librarianship in Serbia. This law was based on best practices in librarianship from abroad (mainly Western Europe). It also defined the role of the National Library as well as public libraries. The libraries were considered educational institutions with the aim of supporting science and educating the population. The regulation regarding the state exam for National Library personnel from 1928 is the first regulation on the obligatory education for the librarians in Serbia. However, no formal or informal library training was provided until after the end of World War II.

Serbia joined union of states (soon to be named Yugoslavia) in 1918. Its capital, Belgrade, also served as the capital of the joint state. After World War II the monarchy in Yugoslavia was abolished and the Communist Party took power and established a socialist state. Serbia was one of six federal units ("the republics") of the state. Under the leadership of Josip Broz Tito (1892–1980) and his successors Yugoslavia pursued a policy of neutrality during the Cold War, managing to steer its path between the Warsaw Pact nations and the West. It became one of the founding members of the Non-Aligned Movement along with countries like India, Egypt, and Indonesia. Besides the close ties with developing countries, Yugoslavia maintained cordial relations with the United States and the Western European countries. It was the first communist country to open its borders to all foreign visitors, and to abolish visa requirements in 1967. After the breakaway from the Soviet sphere in 1948, Yugoslavia came up with its own form of communism that allowed for some degree of free market called "market socialism." People enjoyed far greater liberties than in the Soviet Union and Warsaw Pact states. The federal state dissolved in the early 1990s, with only Serbia and Montenegro remaining in the union. The following decade brought civil war in the region and economic destruction of the country which culminated in NATO bombing campaign in 1999. In 2000 democratic changes swept the country, and Serbia entered transitional phase with aspirations of joining the European Union. In 2006 both Serbia and Montenegro became independent states.

LIBRARIES

Libraries in Serbia today are organized in a system of central libraries performing coordinating functions. The system was set in place by 1960 Republic of Serbia Library Law. It is currently regulated by the 1994 Library Law. Central libraries manage library registers, create library catalogs, offer professional assistance, monitor professional activities, provide continuing education for library staff, analyze current conditions, and suggest improvements. The National Library of Serbia is the central library for all libraries in the country. Matica Srpska Library is the central library for all libraries in the province of Vojvodina, and University Library "Svetozar Marković" is the central library for all university, college, and research libraries in Central Serbia. This organization is regulated by the 1994 Resolution on Libraries performing coordinating functions. According to this Resolution, each county has a central library, a major public library, which oversees the functions of smaller public libraries. All coordinating activities are funded by the government. All central libraries contribute to and maintain "Serbian libraries network," a database containing statistics on all member libraries. At the end of year 2006 there were 2389 libraries in this network.

As a part of the coordinating activities, the National Library of Serbia and Matica Srpska Library conduct state professional examination of some 200 librarians twice a year. The central public libraries organize 10–20 seminars and 3–5 conferences for library staff under their jurisdiction. The National Library of Serbia, the Matica Srpska Library and the University Library "Svetozar Marković" are also the main leaders who implemented the project "Virtual Library of Serbia." The Virtual Library of Serbia[6] has: the union catalog with over 1.9 million bibliographic records; the online library catalogs of participating institutions; a database of libraries participating in the collaborative cataloging; bibliographies; and portals to electronic journals and online databases.

In 2005 central libraries formed the Association of Central Libraries of Serbia,[7] the role of which is enhancing coordinating functions. In 2007 the Association started the "Biblionet" project, an annual conference promoting both scholarly and professional contributions, proceedings of which are published by the Association.

The activity of libraries in Serbia is bounded by a set of laws regarding libraries, press, cultural property, and copyright. The major laws are: The Library Law from 1994; Cultural Property Law from 1994; Press Law and its amendments from 1991, 1993, and 1994; Civil Service Law from 1991; and Copyright Law from 2002. A number of new laws are in the process of being written: Culture Law, Library and Information Law, Cultural Property Law, and Legal Deposit Law.

The major library association in the country is Library Association of Serbia,[8] founded in 1947. The aim of the society is to promote the professional interests of librarians. The Association has been an International Federation of Library (IFLA) member since 1950. It has been publishing professional journal *Bibliotekar* since 1949. The

Association has also established several awards, the most important being "Stojan Novakovi·" for the best book on library and information science, and the "Best librarian" award. In the last 5 years, the Association has been organizing annual international conferences.

A new type of association, the Consortium of the libraries in Serbia for Cooperative Acquisition (KOBSON),[9] was formed in 2001. The idea for the creation of the consortium came from the directors of major academic and research libraries and the representatives from the Serbian Academic Library Association. The National Library's Center for scientific information took a leading role in founding and managing KOBSON. The primary aim of this consortium is cooperative acquisition of scientific journals in both print and electronic format. In 2003, through the funding from the Ministry of Science, Technology, and Development, the consortium purchased 800 printed works and obtained access to 9000 electronic titles. In 2002 the consortium became an active member of the Electronic Information for Libraries (eIFL) project, the aim of which is to enable access to full text databases to countries in transition. The first publisher to participate in the project was EBSCO, providing access to eight databases with approximately 5000 journals, primarily in social sciences and medicine. Today, the project is fully funded by the Ministry of Science, Technology, and Development and offers access to full text of 35,000 journals to 387 participating libraries of all types. It also provides access to electronic books through ebrary (offering access to 30,000 scientific books) and Oxford Scholarship Online (offering access to 1300 books).

National Library of Serbia

The National Library of Serbia[10] was founded in Belgrade in 1832 while parts of Serbia were still under the Ottoman rule. The library was first established as a town library, then served as the library of the State Printing Press (1833–1838), and as the library of Ministry of Education (1838–1870). However, from the very beginning it was receiving depository copies, thus acquiring the character of a national library. One of its missions from the outset has been to collect and preserve each Serbian book in order to document the national heritage. World War I brought losses to the library. Part of the collection was destroyed in Austrian bombing. In 1928 the library started producing the current national bibliography. In 1940 it started publishing *Glasnik Narodne biblioteke*, a refereed journal on library and information science, which is still being published.

However, World War II brought even harder blow to the library. The library was completely destroyed in German air raids on April 6, 1941. The reconstruction of the destroyed library began almost immediately, during the war at which time the library absorbed several collections (those of the Parliament, Senate, the Court, and the Saint Sava Society), as well as personal libraries of some of the literary figures and university professors.

In 1947 the library made its collection of 133,574 items again available to the public. The library was appointed the central library of the Republic of Serbia. In 1953 the Library Center, later to become the Department for the Promotion of Library Services was founded. In 1960 the library also added the Bibliographic Department, charged with compiling the Serbian retrospective bibliography; the Palaeographical Department, whose function was to describe and register South Slav Cyrillic manuscripts; and the Conservation Laboratory for the conservation and preservation of library materials. The library started the construction of the new building in the 1960s, which was inaugurated in 1972. In the following years the National Library started using various international standards, such as International Standard Bibliographic Description (ISBD) and Universal Decimal Classification (UDC). In 1987 the library started Cataloging-in-Publication service for monographs. In 1989 it established an online catalog for all new acquisitions, and the cataloging cards stopped being produced for new acquisitions in 1991. In 1996 the library got its local computer network and Internet access, as well as its first Web site.

The National Library is the central copyright depository of the country. It also serves as a research library. The library has the collection of 5 million volumes. Its collections relate to all fields of knowledge. In particular, it collects and catalogs materials published in and pertaining to Serbia. The main emphasis of the collection is preservation of the past and promotion of the cultural heritage. The library is also a central point for the deposit of international documents (of the World Health Organization, UNESCO, European Council, Organization for Security, and Cooperation in Europe). The library prepares both retrospective and current national bibliographies. It also maintains the union catalog.

After the democratic changes in 2000, the library tried to enhance its international activities, and the Center for International Cooperation gained a more prominent role. The National Library is cooperating with other national libraries. It is a member of International Federation of Library Associations, Conference of Directors of National Libraries, Conference of European National Libraries, European Bureau of Library, Information and Documentation Associations, Consortium of European Research Libraries, and Ligue des Bibliothèques Européennes de Recherche (LIBER).

Although, the library's main goal is to preserve accomplishments of the nation, its new and very important role is to help in building new democratic society by educating and informing the people of Serbia. Since this new mission includes building and promoting democracy and helping economic, social, and cultural revival of the country, a few new projects have been initiated to fulfill this goal. One of them has already been mentioned, the

KOBSON network for cooperative acquisition of print and electronic scientific journals. The library also took a leading role in reintroducing the cooperative cataloging efforts, which were halted in the 1990s. In 2003 it initiated project Virtual Library of Serbia,[11] the aim of which is to connect all online catalogs of libraries in Serbia. At the moment 91 libraries participate in this project.

In addition to the other functions, the library is a thriving cultural institution, offering film screenings, concerts, book readings, and exhibitions. It is also the center for professional library training. In its regulative role it gives accreditation to librarians and decides on rank and title given at promotion. It oversees public libraries in the country. It takes an active part in drafting and proposing laws pertaining not only to libraries, but to broader issues such as the book trade. By taking a visible role in the society, the library also promotes the profession of librarianship.

The library is active in the library community. It hosts information on the professional association on its Web site. It also provides information on accreditation, exams, continuing education classes, workshops, seminars, and talks. The library presents a number of awards annually to libraries, librarians, and authors. It publishes two journals and books on library and information science.

The Digital National Library of Serbia[12] has since 2003 grown to over half a million of digital documents organized into 70 collections. Ten collections are available through the European library portal,[13] while four collections are Open Archives Initiative compatible. One of the earliest projects was the Serbian Children's Digital Library,[14] which contains digital copies of 127 most notable Serbian children's books. The publishers granted copyright to post full-text in the form of scanned books.

Public Libraries

After World War II, public libraries were established in increased numbers as the result of government initiatives. Public libraries in Serbia serve four main functions: they provide for education-information needs of the people and they provide for their cultural and recreational needs. Another important activity performed by public libraries is the creation, development and, more recently, the digitization of local history collections. As of the end of 2005 there were 160 registered public libraries, 25 of which were central.[15] The legal status of public libraries is regulated by the Civil Service Act of 1991 and the Library Law of 1994. The public library is defined as an independent cultural institution established and funded by local municipalities. In 2007 public libraries had the professional staff of 1507. In 2006 they had 457,182 members, which is 6.10% of the entire population.[16] In order to help update library collections, in 2006 the Ministry of Culture purchased and distributed 62,082 books to all public libraries.

Public libraries have a lively programming activity. The most popular programs are exhibits, promotions of books, lectures, and round tables with wide range of topics.[17] A good example is a series of talks, lectures, and round tables of interest to a local community and a society in transition under the name "Tea on Thursdays at 6 P.M.," held in Jagodina Public Library in 2002 and 2003. This project was supported by the Fund for an Open Society as an example of a project that affirms libraries as centers of local communities. Public libraries also publish 14 titles of professional journals and magazines.[18]

Belgrade City Library[19] is the largest public library in Serbia. It was founded in 1929 and opened to public in 1931. In 1961 it became the central library for municipal libraries in Belgrade. It was the first public library in the country to implement an automated library system in 1987. Today, it has 14 different departments and divisions and coordinates a network of 13 municipal libraries and their branches covering 77 locations throughout the city. According to the 2007 Belgrade City Library network annual report, the staff of 300 served the population of close to 1,300,000 by managing the collection of close to 1,800,000 items. As the central public library in Belgrade, it serves in an advisory capacity, arranges exhibits of domestic and foreign books, arranges meetings with writers, and promotes lectures and discussions about new books.

Academic Libraries

The first institution of higher education in Serbia was the Serbian Lyceum founded in 1844. In 1863, the Lyceum transformed into a college, "Velika škola," and in 1905 into the University of Belgrade, absorbing the faculties of Philosophy, Law, and Technology. The Medical School, Faculty of Theology and Faculty of Agriculture were founded in 1919 and the Veterinary School in 1936. In 2008 the University of Belgrade had 2800 faculty and 90,000 students in its 31 faculties (separate legal entities within the university) and eight institutes and centers. Other major universities are University of Fine Arts, University of Novi Sad, University of Niš, and University of Kragujevac. Higher education in Serbia is undergoing major reforms in order to comply with the Bologna Declaration, the aim of which is to create the common European higher education system by making academic degree standards and quality assurance compatible throughout Europe.

Academic libraries differ from other libraries in that they belong to two systems: that of higher education (overseen by the Ministry of Education) and that of national library network (overseen by the Ministry of Culture). Academic libraries help universities fulfill their research and education functions. There are two models of academic libraries within the university, which is made up of separate legal entities, faculties, such as Faculty of

Law, Faculty of Philology, etc. Some faculties have central libraries, while the others have a large number of department libraries. Departmental libraries are created to better meet the specific needs of their users through the development of specialized collections and the types of services they provide. Department libraries are staffed with librarians with the appropriate subject background, usually holding the degrees from the departments they serve. In 2005, academic libraries had the professional staff of 509. Since most academic libraries are department or faculty libraries it is not surprising that 46% of academic libraries were one-person libraries, 29% of the libraries had staff of two, 18% had the staff of three or four, and only 8% had the staff of five or more.[20]

The legal status of academic libraries is governed by The Library Law, the University Law, and the Law on Scientific Research, as well as the statutes of their parent institutions. Libraries are also subject to the Cultural Property Law, Press Law, and Civil Service Law. According to the Library Law, minimum requirement for an academic library are a collection of at least 3000 volumes and one librarian. The newly founded academic libraries need to be funded by not less than 7% of their institution's budget for the first 5 years of their existence and 5% afterwards. All academic libraries receive depository copies of doctoral dissertations and master theses from their parent institutions.

The University Library "Svetozar Marković" in Belgrade[21] is the largest university library in the country and the central library of the University of Belgrade and Art University of Belgrade as well as the central library for all libraries in institutions of higher education and special libraries in research institutes in Central Serbia.[22] The network includes three central University libraries, 119 libraries at faculties and colleges and 98 libraries in

research institutes. As of 2007 the University Library had the staff of 96 and a collection of over 1.5 million volumes. The forerunner of The University Library "Svetozar Marković" in Belgrade was the library of the Serbian Lyceum. However, with the foundation of the University in 1905 the library was disassembled and the collection divided among a number of university institutes and the National Library. The library was reestablished in 1921, as the University Library. In 1926, through Carnegie funds, the new library building was constructed and the library regained its stature. It was the first purpose built library building in Serbia. The building is still being used (Fig. 2). After World War II the library introduced contemporary international methods and standards in the organization of the collection. Together with the National Library of Serbia it created Rules for cataloging which signified the beginning of collaborative cataloging efforts in Serbia. In 1977 the University Library became the central library for all libraries in institutions of higher education in Central Serbia. In 1987 the University Library became the center of the university information system. The library automation started in 1988, and its Web site came online in 1996.

Unlike specialized departmental and institute libraries which collect in their specialized areas, the University Library collects general works from all areas of science with an emphasis on social science and humanities. It is the depository library for all the doctoral dissertations granted in Serbia. The library also has a special museum-gallery with folk literature department, an archival collection of personal correspondence of prominent individuals from the seventeenth till the twentieth century, and a collection of old geographic maps and atlases.

There are two other central academic libraries: the Matica Srpska Library in Novi Sad for the libraries on the territory of the province of Vojvodina and the University

Fig. 2 The University Library Svetozar Marković in Belgrade.

of Priština library for the libraries on the territory of the province of Kosovo. The Matica Srpska Library is the first Serbian public and scientific library. With the establishment of the University of Novi Sad, the Matica Srpska Library[23] became the university library in 1960 and the central library for all academic libraries in province of Vojvodina. The Matica Srpska and its library were founded in 1826 in Budapest (Hungary), but the library was not opened to the public until 1838, when a wealthy citizen, Sava Tekelija, donated his collection of 4000 volumes; at that time it was known as Tekelianum. The library's holdings were further enriched through gifts, exchanges, and purchases. The first Serbian current bibliography was begun in the library in 1842. Throughout this period the library was located in Budapest except during the 1860s when it was transferred to Novi Sad where it remained till 1875. The library was finally moved to Novi Sad after World War II. The library automation started in 1989. In 2008 the library had the staff of 150 and a collection of over 3 million volumes. It has the largest collection of Serbian books from the fifteenth to the eighteenth century and the richest collection of the Serbian periodicals from the eighteenth and the first half of the nineteenth century. The University of Novi Sad had 1610 faculty and 43,259 students in 2007. In 2003 the University founded the Central Library of the University of Novi Sad.

The University of Niš was founded in 1965. Today, it is organized into 12 faculties with over 1400 faculty and 27,000 students.[24] The network of academic libraries in Niš consists of the University library "Nikola Tesla," founded in 1967, and 19 academic libraries. The University library Nikola Tesla has the collection of 80,000 books and 1200 titles of periodicals in print.

The University of Kragujevac Svetozar Marković was founded in 1976. Today, it is organized into 11 faculties and three centers with 600 faculty and 12,000 students. The network of academic libraries at the University of Kragujevac has the University library, founded in 1977, and 14 academic libraries. The University library has over 100,000 books and over 500 periodical titles in print.

In 1976 University of Belgrade Libraries Association was founded to help coordination among all the libraries of the university, however, it ceased to exist in the 1980s. In 1992, a new effort for better coordination resulted in the foundation of the Serbian Academic Library Association.[25] Its members are libraries from all six public universities, as well as the libraries of major research institutes. The association publishes two journals *Visokoškolske biblioteke* and *Infoteka: Časopis za informatiku i bibliotekarstvo*.

Special Libraries

According to the current Library Law special libraries are organizational units serving library functions within other organizations. In 2003 there were 228 registered special libraries. However, it can be claimed with certainty that the actual number is larger than that. In 2003 special libraries had close to 2.5 million volumes. The average special library collection is fairly small, around 10,000 volumes. The libraries had professional staff of 257.[26]

One of the largest special libraries is the Library of the Serbian Academy of Science and Arts.[27] The Serbian Academy of Science and Arts grew out of the Serbian Learned Society (1841) and the Serbian Royal Academy (1886). The library's collection started as a gift from Dimitrije Tirol, one of the first members of the society. Until 1952 the library was closed to the public, and only the members of the academy had access to it. Today the library is open to all researchers. With the collection of around 1.3 million volumes it is the fourth largest library in the country. It has a valuable collection of old and rare books with over 3000 titles. It also has a collection of 10,000 photographs of individuals active in the scientific and cultural life of the country in the nineteenth and twentieth centuries.[28]

In 2002 with cooperation with The Council of Europe, The Organization for Security, and Cooperation in Europe and Fund for an Open Society, the National Library of Serbia opened the Center for Law Information. The center is organized as a special collection within the National Library. It is an open stacks collection of official documents with the aim of making it available to wide audience. At the same time it serves the information needs of the legal professionals, members of the parliament, and law scholars by providing comprehensive legislative information pertaining to Serbia, Europe and the international law. A similar center was opened at the University library "Nikola Tesla" in Niš.

School Libraries

School librarianship emerged and developed professionally since 1945. In 1974 Law on the Elementary School stipulated that every school must have a library with the collection consisting of at least 2500 books. Under the current laws each elementary and high school is to have a library. School libraries today are subject to both laws on education and laws on libraries, where laws on education have primacy. There are 1342 school libraries in Serbia: 980 elementary school and 362 high school libraries.[29]

Larger school libraries developed into efficient media instructional centers. In 2006 the average elementary school library in Serbia had the collection of close to 9000 volumes. Library collections in elementary schools are divided into two separate collections: for students and for teachers. High school libraries have one collection for both students and teachers.

Among the major problems of school libraries are the lack of funds for the adequate development of the collections and the lack of permanent professionally trained staff. Prior to 2005 school library staff did not have to pass the state professional library exam if they passed the state professional teaching exam. Now school library staff needs to pass an exam for school librarians organized by the Ministry of Education.

LIBRARY EDUCATION

The first legal act to regulate library appointments was issued in 1928, requiring a civil service examination for the employment in the National Library. The requirements of this law were extended in 1929 to positions in the University Library in Belgrade.

Professional status for most library positions is attained primarily through a system of state professional examinations. These exams also serve as a form of continuing education. There are exams for librarians, senior library assistants, and library assistants. The exam is taken after at least 9 months at a position (for high school diploma holders) and a year at a position (for the associate and college degree holders). The exam must be taken during the first 3 years of employment. The exam consists of seven parts: 1) the constitution, library legislation, and legislation regarding preservation of old and rare books; 2) introductory knowledge of library science; 3) alphabetical catalog; 4) subject catalog; 5) introduction to information science; 6) introduction to bibliography; and 7) history of book, script, and libraries. Seminars for the preparation of the exam are organized by the National Library. Exams are held twice a year in the National Library in Belgrade and Matica Srpska Library in Novi Sad, the examiners are a committee appointed by the Ministry of Culture.

In 1948 the country's first library school, Secondary Library Science School, was founded in Belgrade marking the beginnings of regular library education. The school trained students for library assistant positions until it closed in 1979.

In 1962 at the Faculty of Philology (University of Belgrade), the department of library science was established offering an undergraduate degree. However, the department was closed after only two cohorts graduated.

The next attempt of bringing library education to universities was the establishment of interdisciplinary four-semester program for juniors and seniors from all the departments of the Faculty of Philology (University of Belgrade) in 1980. The courses included an introduction to library science; the organization of libraries; cataloging; bibliography; and the history of books and libraries. The program ceased to exist in 1990, when the Faculty of Philology University of Belgrade established the Department of Library and Information Science. The department offers undergraduate and graduate degrees. The department also offers the post-undergraduate certificate for school and special librarians. After the adoption of the Bologna Convention, the department introduced new classes on research methods, archives, and museology.[30]

The main institution of the continuing education for libraries is the National Library. The Educational center of the National Library offers Co-operative Online Bibliographic System and Services education, state exam preparation and different seminars and courses. University of Belgrade Library "Svetozar Marković" also organizes different lectures, seminars, courses, and workshops. Other institutions offering continuing education opportunities are the Department of Library and Information Science at the University of Belgrade, Matica Srpska Library, Serbian Library Association, and Serbian Academic Library Association.

ARCHIVES

Archival collections in Serbia began to develop throughout the country after 1918 and expanded after 1945. The Archives of Serbia was the only institution of this kind to exist in Serbia prior to 1918. Preservation of archival material in Serbia is regulated by the Cultural Property Law adopted in 1994. The Decree on the division of archival jurisdiction determines a geographical division of 34 archives within Serbia (20 in Central Serbia, five in Kosovo, and nine in Vojvodina). In addition to archives organized on the geographical jurisdiction, there are specialized archives (military, film, corporate, etc.) as well as in-house archival departments.

The contemporary Serbian archives network is comprised of the Archives of Serbia as a central archives, two provincial, 30 intermunicipal, and four city archives. The Archives of Serbia[31] was founded in 1900. It holds records from 512 institutions in Serbia, from Serbian government, from social and political organizations, and also from the University of Belgrade. It also holds records from companies, societies, associations as well as notable individuals. Today, it is responsible for archiving records produced by over 70 institutions. The archives signed an agreement with the Serbian Orthodox Church and The Ministry of Culture to preserve the clerical documents from 1830 onward.

The Archives collects records from the nineteenth century onward. There is only one older collection and some individual documents. The oldest record is *Dečanska povelja* from 1330. The archives has 937 major collections and 48 smaller collections.

The Archives is responsible for education of archivists by offering various courses. There is an exam at the end of each course, which has the character of the professional state exam. Since 1957 archive courses covering a variety of topics have been taken by 700 archivists. In 2008 the Archives started summer archives school. The Archives publishes the professional journal *Arhivski pregled*.

The Archives of the Serbian Academy of Science and Arts[32] began its work in 1841, but became an independent institution in 1952. The main mission of the archives is to collect records relevant to the history of the Academy and the history of Serbian people. The archives contains administrative documents of the Serbian Learned Society (1864–1892), Serbian Royal Academy (1887–1944), and two defunct institutes (Institute for the study of literature (1947–1954) and The institute for the study of villages (1948–1954). It also has minutes from the Serbian Academy of Science and Arts meetings as well as the meetings of its various bodies. The archives has four collections of documents: rare book and manuscript collection (collection of Serbian manuscript books and old print books from the thirteenth to the nineteenth century); historical collection (the largest collection with 15,071 signatures covering the medieval to modern period); ethnographic collection (collection of folk literature and ethnographic material from all parts of Serbia from the nineteenth and the twentieth centuries); and the oriental collection (collection of manuscript and print books in Turkish and Arabic from the fifteenth to twentieth centuries).

Besides the main archives in Belgrade, the Serbian Academy of Science and Arts also has archives in Sremski Karlovci. This archive has over 3 million records arranged in 44 fonds and 10 smaller collections covering the period from the mid-sixteenth century to the 1970s. This archive also contains documents important for the understanding of the political, cultural, and economic history of Serbs in the Habsburg Monarchy, with particular emphasis on churches and religious life, schools, education, literature, and arts. The first inventory for this archive was created in 1719.

Yugoslav Film Archives[33] is the national film archives founded in 1949. The archives today includes a museum and a library. In 1951 it became one of the founders and permanent members of The International Federation of Film Archives. The archive collects and preserves films and accompanying film material, photographs, posters, advertising material, documentation, props, and old equipment. The archives can be used by researchers of film and film theory. It takes an active part in educating general public and promoting film culture by organizing film screenings, lectures, round tables, and exhibits. The film collection has over 85,000 film copies, 80% of which are international. It also has a collection of documentary films pertaining to former Yugoslavia from the oldest film, *The 1904 Coronation of King Peter I*, up through the breakup of the country in 1992. It also has a valuable collection of Yugoslav movies, containing 90% of the entire production of former Yugoslavia since World War II. The library has over 21,000 books. Of special importance is the collection of scripts, scenarios, and dialog lists. The museum has a special theater that regularly shows films from its collection. In 2006 a small 18-seat theater was opened for digital media projections.

Historical Archives of Belgrade[34] was founded in 1945. Together with the Mathematical Institute of the Serbian Academy of Science and Arts, the archives is developing an archives description program based on application of the International Standard for Archival Description (General) [ISAD(g)] and the Document Type Description for the Encoded Archival Description. The Historical Archives also translated and made available archival metadata standards ISAD(g) and the International Standard Archival Authority Record for Corporate Bodies, Persons, and Families. The archives also translated and made available all resolutions of the International Council on Archives (1994–2007).

MUSEUMS

Churches and monasteries have large collections of valuable art objects. The oldest of these is the collection at the Serbian monastery Hilandar on Mount Athos in Greece from the beginning of the twelfth century. The first museums were founded as the result of initiatives taken by prominent Serbs. In the period between 1900 and 1945 numerous specialized museums (such as ethnographic, education, and military) as well as art galleries were opened. Altogether some 70 museums were founded. Unfortunately, many museum collections were partially or completely destroyed during World War II. The oldest gallery in Serbia is Matica Srpska Gallery in Novi Sad, founded in 1847 and opened to public in 1933.

Today, museums function within the legal framework of the Cultural Property Law.

The major professional association is Serbian Museum Association,[35] established in 2001. It continues the tradition of the previous association founded in 1962. The association has both individual and institutional members interested in the advancement of museology and museums. The association installs an annual award to the best museum and the best curator.

The National Museum

The National Museum Belgrade,[36] founded in 1844, is the oldest and most important museum in Serbia (Fig. 3). It initiated the first archeological excavations in Serbia in 1865 and started collecting world art in 1891. Today, the museum is the central institution in the museum network of Serbia. It is also a central museum for archeological, numismatic, and art collections dating before 1900. It is the central institution for the preservation of cultural property.

The museum has 34 archeological, numismatic, art, and historic collections. Its goal is to preserve, interpret and promote cultural heritage of Serbia and its neighbors. Apart from the archeological collection, the museum also has 1700 Serbian paintings from the eighteenth and

Fig. 3 The National Museum in Belgrade.

nineteenth centuries; 3000 Yugoslav paintings from 1889 to 1999; and international collection of 1100 mainly European paintings and sculptures from fourteenth to twentieth century. The museum holds Miroslav Gospel, the first preserved Serbian Cyrillic manuscript dating from around 1180 with miniatures of outstanding beauty. It has been registered in UNESCOs Memory of the World program in 2005.

In 1957 the museum opened new conservation lab. In 1997 it founded the school for conservation "Dijana." The school is now department for preservation and conservation.[37]

The museum has extensive educational activities. It organizes museum workshops for group visits by kindergarten and elementary school children. It also has guided tours and lectures for high school and college students.

In 1933 the museum started publishing the journal *Numizmatičar* and in 1937 the journal *Umetnički pregled.* Today, it publishes five journals: *Zbornik Narodnog muzeja u Beogradu: Arheologija, Zbornik Narodnog muzeja u Beogradu: Istorija umetnosti, Numizmatičar, Glasnik Društva prijatelja Narodnog muzeja u Beogradu,* and *Diana: Odeljenje za preventivnu zaštitu Narodnog muzeja u Beogradu.*

Art Museums and Galleries

The Museum of Applied Arts in Belgrade[38] was founded in 1950. The museum has over 35,000 artifacts. It is a central museum for the applied arts in Serbia. It has collections of jewelry, textile, costume, furniture, photography, glass, architecture, and modern applied arts.

The Museum of Modern Art was founded as a Modern Gallery in 1958. The museum collects and preserves Yugoslav artwork dating since 1900. The museum

researches new methods in the area of visual culture, history, and theory of art. It has the collection of paintings from 1900 to 1945; the collection of paintings after 1945; collection of sculptures; collection of prints; and the collection of new art media (photography, film, video, etc.).

The Museum of Naïve and Marginal Art in Jagodina[39] was founded in 1960. It contains about 2500 artworks from about 280 painters and sculptors. The museum organizes naïve art colonies and biennials.

The Gallery of the Serbian Academy of Science and Arts was opened in 1968. It is an organizational unit within the Academy. The gallery collects and preserves art objects owned by the Academy. It has paintings, prints, and sculptures of some 270 artists, 50 of them Academy members. The gallery organizes various art, science, and culture exhibits, public lectures, regular concert program and has a lively publishing activity. The gallery if funded by the academy, i.e., The Ministry of Science, Technology and Development. Some projects are funded by the Ministry of Culture, and the City of Belgrade Committee on Culture.

Science Museums and Galleries

The Natural History Museum,[40] founded in 1895, is one of the oldest museums and one of the oldest specialized scientific institutions in Serbia. It is the only natural history museum in the country, and with the collection of 1.5 million objects it is one of the largest natural history museums in southeastern Europe. Before the foundation of the museum, in the first half of the nineteenth century, a large number of natural history artifacts was held in the Lyceum. The first exhibit in the Museum was held in 1904 with the king present at the opening. The same year museum participated in the World Fair in Paris. During

World War I and World War II, parts of the collection were damaged or destroyed, including the museum archives and parts of the library. Today, the museum has 118 collections. It is one of the few museums in Serbia having a scientific research department. Its education department collaborates with numerous schools in Belgrade and Serbia. The museum also has a special library, one of the oldest scientific libraries in the country, founded in 1903. The museum has been publishing a scientific journal from 1948 to 1998. In 2008 it started publishing a new journal *Bulletin of the Natural History Museum in Belgrade*. The museum has also started the digitization project.

The Science and Technology Museum[41] was founded in 1989. The mission of the museum is the preservation of scientific and technological heritage in Serbia. Museum aims at popularizing science and enhancing scientific and technological culture by collecting, researching, preserving, and exhibiting objects related to science and technology.

The Science and Technology Gallery of the Serbian Academy of Science and Arts was founded in 1988, and started having exhibits in 1997. From 1997 till 2005 the program of the gallery, including exhibits and lectures was handled by the Science and Technology Museum. The gallery started organizing its own programs in 2006 with the emphasis on the history of science and technology in Serbia. The mission of the gallery is popularization of science and technology. The Gallery is also home to the Science and Technology Museum's special library.

The Nikola Tesla Museum[42] was founded in 1952. The museum holds personal documents and belongings of Nikola Tesla, making it the most significant institution for the study of life and work of this famous inventor. It has over 160,000 documents, over 2000 books and journals, 1200 historical technical artifacts, 1000 blueprints and drawings, and 1500 photographs and photographic plates of the original instruments. The museum has Nikola Tesla Archive, a unique collection of manuscripts, photographs, and scientific and patent documentation. The archive was registered in UNESCO's Memory of the World program in 2003. The museum also has Tesla's personal library with 786 book titles, 323 titles of periodicals, and about 70,000 newspaper clippings.

The Science and Technology Museum initiated the foundation of the Science and Technology Museum Association of Serbia in 1991. Through this association the museum coordinates 16 museums and collections in Serbia, including the Automobile Museum, the Aviation Museum, the Mining Metallurgy Museum, the Serbian Medical Museum, the Natural History Museum, the Agricultural Museum, and the Serbian Railway Museum. One of the accomplishments of the association is the creation of standards for processing technical cultural assets. As of 2003, the association started publishing a newsletter *NAVOJ*. Its primary goals are improving the cooperation among museums, contributing to the development of the profession, and informing expert and general public of the work that is being done for the protection of the technological heritage of Serbia.

Historical and Ethnographic Museums

The Historical Museum of Serbia was founded in 1963 to collect and preserve historical artifacts related to the economic, political, and cultural history of Serbia.

The Ethnographic Museum[43] was founded in 1901. It has been collecting artifacts from Serbia and the Balkans. In 1926 it started publishing the journal *Glasnik Etnografskog muzeja* which is still published today. The museum has one of the richest ethnographic libraries in the Balkans. It has an active educational unit and conducts ethnographic research. It also organizes workshops to teach the traditional crafts. Since 1992 the museum has been organizing the International Festival of Ethnographic Film.

CONCLUSION

Because of its location at the crossroads, Serbia was for centuries shaped by the cultural boundaries between the East and the West. Its cultural and information institutions shared its tumultuous history. Periods of greatness and prosperity were followed by periods of devastation. Throughout the history, wars would decimate the country's printed and cultural heritage and the institutions preserving that heritage. But, the institutions would soon rebuild and consolidate themselves and move forward. Such a history left the country constantly torn between striving for modernization and preserving its traditions and cultural heritage.

Present-day institutions started to be developed only in the midnineteenth century when the conditions became favorable for the systematic development of education and the establishment of cultural and scientific institutions. Chief intellectual influence for the development of these institutions came from the Western Europe, introduced to Serbia by the Serbs living in the Habsburg Monarchy. Thus, its first reading rooms were based on the models from Western Europe and the first library catalog in the National Library followed Austro-Hungarian regulation. The first libraries and museums were not result of an organized state policy, although the state supported them financial and developed appropriate legislation relatively early.

Much greater involvement of the state came during the communist rule after World War II. During that time Serbia organized a countrywide system of central libraries performing coordinating functions which is still in place. The system provides libraries greater visibility, streamlined funding, and more clout. It is also conducive to larger projects such as the reintroduction of cooperative cataloging through the Virtual Library of Serbia project or cooperative acquisition of scientific periodicals through the KOBSON project. In recent years Serbian libraries have increased cooperation with Western European countries.

APPENDIX

Table A.1 Timeline of Major historical events

Seventh century	Serbs, a Slavic people, settled the Balkans
Ninth century	Serbs adopted Christianity
Ninth century	Cyrillic alphabet introduced
Thirteenth century	Serbia became a kingdom with an autonomous Orthodox church
Fourteenth century	Serbia fell under the Ottoman Rule
1493	First Serbian printing office opened in Cetinje (Montenegro)
1494	First book printed in Serbian language
1690	Great migration of a part of Serbian population to Habsburg Empire
1768	First Serbian magazine published in Venice (Italy)
1791	First Serbian newspaper published in Vienna (Austria)
1808	Velika škola, the first higher education institution, was opened in Belgrade
1814	First grammar of the reformed language, *Pismenica*, by Vuk Karadžić was printed in Vienna (Austria).
1823	Srpska velika gimnazija (Serbian High Gymnasium) founded in Novi Sad
1825	First literary magazine, *Serbski letopis*, started in Buda (Hungary)
1826	Matica Srpska founded in Pest (Hungary)
1827	First bindery and bookstore opened in Belgrade
1830	Serbian principality granted a fully autonomous status by the Ottoman government
1831	State Printing Press established in Belgrade
1832	National Library founded; Legal deposit for the National Library introduced; First Serbian book printed by the state printing press in Belgrade
1834	First newspaper published in Serbia
1838	Licej Kneževine Srbije (Serbian Lyceum) founded
1842	Serbian Library Association founded; First Serbian current bibliography begun at Matica Srpska Library; Serbian Learned Society (Društvo Srpske Slovesnosti) founded; Library of the Serbian Learned Society founded
1844	Library of the Serbian Lyceum founded; National Museum Belgrade founded
1846	Reading room (čitalište) in Belgrade founded; First scientific journal published by the Serbian Learned Society
1847	Matica Srpska Gallery in Novi Sad founded

(Continued)

Table A.1 Timeline of Major historical events *(Continued)*

1853	First official librarian, Filip Nikolić, appointed in the National Library
1860	First private printing press opened
1867	Vuk Karadžić's new simplified orthography officially accepted
1869	First bibliography produced
1870	First Press Law
1871	Law dividing the National Library and the National Museum into separate institutions
1878	Serbia's independence from the Ottoman Empire recognized at The Congress of Berlin
1881	First law on The National Library
1891	Ministry of Education arranged interlibrary loan exchanges between the college library in Belgrade and the Court Library in Vienna
1895	Natural History Museum founded
1898	Law on the State Archives
1900	Archives of Serbia founded
1901	Law on the National Library and The Rules on Internal Organization and Work in the National Library; Ethnographic Museum founded
1918	Serbia joined the Kingdom of Serbs, Croats, and Slovenes
1928	Legal act to regulate library appointments requiring a professional examination for the employment in The National Library; National Library started producing the current national bibliography
1929	Kingdom of Serbs, Croats and Slovenes changed name to the Kingdom of Yugoslavia
1930	First union catalog of the University of Belgrade libraries created
1938	International standard format cataloging cards introduced
1940	Library journal, *Glasnik narodne biblioteke*, started being published
1941	National Library completely destroyed in German bombing
1945	Historical Archives of Belgrade founded
1946	Federal People's Republic of Yugoslavia proclaimed. Monarchy abolished
1947	Library Association of Serbia founded
1948	First library science degree program, Secondary Library Science School, founded in Belgrade
1949	Yugoslav Film Archives founded
1953	Library center (to become Department for the promotion of library services) founded in National Library
1958	Museum of Modern Art opened
1962	First undergraduate degree program in library science established at the University of Belgrade
1963	Name of the country changed to Socialist Federal Republic of Yugoslavia
1974	National Library started using UDC
1976	National Library accepted new international standards for bibliographic description, ISBD
1987	National Library started Cataloging-in-Publication service for monographs; Belgrade City Library implemented automated library system

(Continued)

Table A.1 Timeline of Major historical events *(Continued)*

1989	National Library started using the online catalog for all new acquisitions; Science and Technology Museum founded
1990	Department of Library and Information Science at the Faculty of Philology University of Belgrade founded
1991	Science and Technology Museum Association of Serbia founded
1992	Slovenia, Croatia, Bosnia and Herzegovina, and Macedonia gained independence from Yugoslavia
1992	Serbian Academic Library Association founded
1996	National Library established Internet access as well as its first Web site
1999	NATO bombing campaign; U.N. Administration of Kosovo
2001	Consortium of the libraries in Serbia for Cooperative Acquisition (KOBSON) formed
2003	National Library started Cataloging-in-Publication service for serials
2004	National Library became National ISSN center
2005	Association of Central Libraries of Serbia formed
2006	Serbia and Montenegro dissolved their union and became independent states

REFERENCES

1. CIA The World Factbook—Serbia. Available at https://www.cia.gov/library/publications/the-world-factbook/geos/ri.html.
2. Republika Srbija Republički zavod za statistiku. *Popis stanovništva, domaćinstava i stanova u 2002: Stanovništvo*; Beograd, 2003. Available at http://webrzs.statserb.sr.gov.yu/axd/Zip/VJN3.pdf (accessed September 2008).
3. Republika Srbija Republički zavod za statistiku. *Telekomunikacije*. Available at http://webrzs.statserb.sr.gov.yu/axd/drugastrana.php?Sifra=0005&izbor=odel&tab=47 (accessed September 2008).
4. Republika Srbija. Republicki zavod za statistiku. *Upotreba informaciono-komunikacionih tehnologija u Republici Srbiji 2008*, 2008. Available at http://webrzs.stat.gov.rs/axd/dokumenti/ict/2008/Naslovna/ICT_2008s.pdf (accessed September 2008).
5. Stamatović, D. *itališta u Srbiji u XIX veku*; Narodna Biblioteka Srbije: Belgrade, 1984.
6. The Virtual Library of Serbia. Available at http://vbsw.nbs.bg.ac.yu/cobiss/index-sc.html.
7. The Association of Central Libraries of Serbia. Available at http://www.nbs.bg.ac.yu/pages/arfticle.php?id=1318.
8. The Library Association of Serbia. Available at http://www.bds.rs/.
9. The Consortium of the Libraries in Serbia for Cooperative Acquisition (KOBSON). Available at http://nainfo.nbs.bg.ac.yu/Kobson/page/.
10. National Library of Serbia. Available at http://www.nbs.bg.ac.yu/.
11. Virtual Library of Serbia. Available at http://vbsw.nbs.bg.ac.yu/cobiss/.
12. The Digital National Library of Serbia. Available at http://www.digital.nbs.bg.ac.yu/scc/index.php.
13. The European Library. Available at http://www.theeuropeanlibrary.org.
14. Serbian Children's Digital Library. Available at http://digital.nbs.bg.ac.yu/knjige/decije/.
15. Milunović, D. Informacioni instrumenti u narodnim bibliotekama u Republici Srbiji. Available at http://www.nbs.bg.ac.yu/view_file.php?file_id=1894 (accessed September 2008).
16. Šekularac, V. Mreža javnih biblioteka u Srbiji u. 2006; godini. Available at http://www.nbs.bg.ac.yu/view_file.php?file_id=1918 (accessed September 2008).
17. Simović, D. Kulturna, obrazovna i prosvetna delatnost narodnih biblioteka u Srbiji u periodu 2001–2005 godine. Available at http://www.nbs.bg.ac.yu/view_file.php?file_id=2140 (accessed September 2008).
18. Simović, D. Analiza izdavačke delatnosti narodnih biblioteka u Srbiji 2001–2005 godine. Available at http://www.nbs.bg.ac.yu/view_ file.php?file_id=1896 (accessed September 2008).
19. Belgrade City Library. Available at http://www.bgb.org.yu.
20. Vukotić, B. Osoblje visokoškolskih i univerzitetksih biblioteka u Srbiji 2005 godine. Available at http://www.nbs.bg.ac.yu/view_file.php?file_id=1759 (accessed September 2008).
21. The University Library "Svetozar Marković". Available at http://www.unilib.bg.ac.yu/.
22. *Univerzitetska biblioteka "Svetozar Markovic" 2008 Izveštaj o radu za 2007*, Beograd 3.
23. Matica Srpska Library. Available at http://www.bms.ns.ac.yu/.
24. Mitrić, M. Univerzitetska biblioteka "Nikola Tesla" u Nišu. Glasnik Narodne biblioteke Srbije **2005**, *1/2005*, 211–226.
25. The Serbian Academic Library Association. Available at http://www.unilib.bg.ac.yu/zajednica01/index.php.
26. Milunović, D. Specijalne biblioteke u Republici Srbiji: Stanje i prioriteti razvoja sa predlogom mera za unapredjenje rada. Infoteka **2005**, *6* (3), 209–215.
27. The Library of the Serbian Academy of Science and Arts. Available at http://www.sanu.ac.yu/Biblioteka/Biblioteka.aspx.
28. Zečevic, M. Biblioteka srpske akademije nauka i umetnosti. Glasnik narodne biblioteke Srbije **2003**, *1/2003*, 257–264.
29. Marić, M. Uslovi rada—prostor, bibliotečka, tehnička i računarska oprema u školskim bibliotekama u Republici Srbiji. Available at http://www.nbs.bg.ac.yu/view_file.php?file_id=2114 (accessed September 2008).
30. Vraneš, A. From the history of the library and information science department of the Faculty of Philology of the University of Belgrade. INFOTHECA—J. Infor. Libr. **2008**, *9* (1–2), 5a–9a.
31. The Archives of Serbia. Available at http://www.archives.org.yu/.
32. The Archives of the Serbian Academy of Science and Arts. Available at http://www.sanu.ac.yu/Arhivi/Arhiv.aspx.

33. Yugoslav Film Archives. Available at http://www.kinoteka.org.yu/.
34. Historical Archives of Belgrade. Available at http://www.arhiv-beograda.org/.
35. Serbian Museum Association. Available at http://www.mds.org.yu/index.htm.
36. The National Museum. Available at http://www.narodnimuzej.org.yu/code/navigate.php?Id=1.
37. National Museum's Department for Conservation and Preservation Dijana. Available at http://www.ccdiana.org.yu/modules/home/content.php?group=2.
38. The Museum of Applied Arts. Available at http://www.mpu.org.yu/.
39. The Museum of Naïve and Marginal Art. Available at http://www.naiveart.org.yu/ (accessed September 2008).
40. The Natural History Museum. Available at http://www.nhmbeo.org.yu/ (accessed September 2008).
41. Science and Technology Museum. Available at http://www.muzejnt.org.yu/ (accessed September 2008).
42. Nikola Tesla Museum. Available at http://www.tesla-museum.org/meni_sl.htm (accessed September 2008).
43. Ethnographic Museum. Available at http://www.etnomuzej.co.yu/ (accessed September 2008).

Serials Collection and Management *[ELIS Classic]*

Sarah Sutton
Mary and Jeff Bell Library, Texas A&M University-Corpus Christi, Corpus Christi, Texas, U.S.A.

Abstract
This entry discusses the selection and management of serials in libraries. It provides an overview of the process of serials collection and management as well as current issues and controversies. Relevant definitions are provided as well as a brief history of serials management. Focus is on recent developments (standards, technologies) and their impact. Selection, acquisition, access, processing (including cataloging), maintenance, preservation, and weeding of serials in all formats are covered and important players in each process are identified.

INTRODUCTION

Serials are publications that are characteristically issued in discrete, separate parts without a predetermined date on which publication of successive issues will conclude. The parts are commonly differentiated from one another by numerical or chronological designations. Serials exist in the middle of the hierarchy of related terms; they are a type of continuing resource and encompass periodicals. These characteristics differentiate serials from other types of publications and are at the heart of the challenge that their collection and management presents to libraries.

The process of collecting and managing serials is cyclical rather than linear. Serials management is an open system subject to outside influences. Budgets set outside the library, technology, and in particular, changing users and user preferences directly impact what and how a library collects. Selection and management activities mirror the users' information seeking activities as is depicted in Fig. 1. The users' process is depicted in the inner cycle. An information need is identified and leads to information seeking and identification. Information identification can lead the users to the identification of new information needs or to obtain the identified information. Information obtained is used to create new information and/or for the identification of additional information or information needs. The outer cycle reflects (albeit simplistically) the cycle of serials information management. Serials are selected, acquired, and processed before they are made accessible to the user. Maintenance of serials requires both additional processing of issues that continued to be received over time as well as preservation of existing issues. Periodic weeding is often required as items to be preserved or discarded are identified. Selection is based on the users' information needs. Acquisition, processing, and the provision of access to serials support the users' information seeking and identification, and allows them to obtain information. Some but not all users will use the information they obtain to create new information which may then be selected for inclusion in the library collection.

This entry is organized on the basis of the cycle of serials management presented in Fig. 1. Issues and controversies among members of the serials information chain will be noted and explained as they arise in the text. For the most part, electronic serials are not dealt with separately but rather discussion of them is included in the discussion of the processes of serials selection and management, again with differentiations noted as needed. Although the introduction of electronic formats caused upheaval in the world of librarianship during recent decades, we have since, to some extent, become accustomed to rapidly changing formats; certainly they have become ubiquitous to users. Thus the focus should not be on formats alone but on the processes of selection and management with notation of the upheaval, etc. where it has recently been the greatest.

DEFINITIONS

A discussion of serials collection and management should begin with the precise definition of terms to be used in the discussion. Although often used interchangeably, definitions of the terms serial, periodical, and continuing resource are in fact different and hierarchically related to one another. The International Organization for Standardization (ISO), the body that assigns a unique International Standard Serial Number (ISSN) to serial publications, defines a serial as "a publication in any medium issued under the same title in a succession of discrete parts, usually numbered (or dated) and appearing at regular or irregular intervals with no predetermined conclusion."[1] The National Serials Data Program (NDSP) defines a serial as "print or nonprint publications issued in parts, usually bearing issue numbers and/or dates. A serial is

Semiotics–Slovakia

Encyclopedia of Library and Information Sciences, Fourth Edition DOI: 10.1081/E-ELIS4-120044625

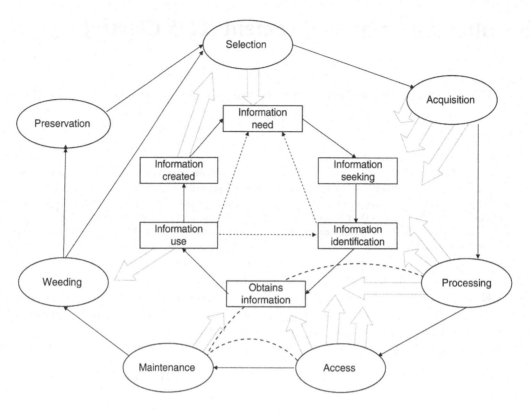

Fig. 1 The cycles of serials management and the user information process.

expected to continue indefinitely. Serials include magazines, newspapers, annuals (such as reports, yearbooks, and directories), journals, memoirs, proceedings, transactions of societies, and monographic series."[2] These definitions as well as definitions of serials from other authoritative sources like the second edition of the Anglo American Cataloging Rules (AACR2) have in common a number of characteristics that differentiate serial publications from other types of publications, namely:

- Successive parts
- Typically differentiated from one another by numerical or chronological designations
- No predetermined date of termination[2]

Serials exist in the middle of the hierarchy of related terms; they are a type of continuing resource and encompass periodicals. Continuing resources are defined in AACR2 as being "issued over time with no predetermined conclusion, including bibliographic resources issued successively in discrete parts and integrating resources into which updates are incorporated without remaining discrete. Examples include serials (periodicals, newspapers, etc.), monographic series, and updating loose-leaf services, databases, and Web sites."[2] The term periodical encompasses newspapers, popular magazines, scholarly journals, and trade magazines. They are, by definition, serials and thus share all of the characteristics of serials. They are usually intended to be published regularly (although in practice this may not always be the case).[3]

Typically, a newspaper is printed on newsprint, published daily or weekly,[2] and contains editorial comment, regular columns, advertising, and/or cartoons. Popular magazines can often be distinguished by being printed on glossy paper and contain a larger proportion of advertising than other categories of periodicals (since much of its costs is covered by advertising) and subscription rates are typically low.[2] Trade journals are usually intended for a specialized audience and often contain advertisements,[2] book reviews and listings of employment opportunities. Scholarly journals contain few, if any advertisements and are devoted to publishing the results of original research. Research articles are usually peer-reviewed, that is, they are critiqued by a panel of experts before they are accepted for publication.[3,4]

Although the physical form of periodicals has been used here as a distinguishing characteristic, almost all types of periodicals may also be published electronically. Serials published in electronic form are defined by the Library of Congress's Cooperative Online Serials (CONSER) program and AACR2 as being delivered online via a network.[1] It is important to note that other types of continuing resources are also often delivered online via a network and, in fact, this method of delivery is considered to be particularly effective for their timely delivery.

Almost every library's collection includes serials but the type and number varies widely from one library to the next. In general, public libraries collect fewer serials than do academic or special libraries. Public libraries spend far less of their budgets on serials (6% vs. 42% according to Black).[2] They may collect a larger proportion of popular periodicals (magazines, trade publications, and newspapers) to scholarly journals. Academic libraries collect more scholarly journals and, often, more trade publications than public libraries although, of course, all library serials collections are based on the needs and interests of their users. Scholarly journals are usually more expensive than trade publications (sometimes a great deal more expensive), thus a larger proportion of an academic library's budget is spent on serials subscriptions. The extent of serials collecting by special libraries (for example, law libraries and corporate libraries) is more difficult to generalize since it will depend on the population the library serves.

HISTORY

A comprehensive history of serial publications itself is beyond the scope of this entry. In addition to an excellent but relatively brief review of the history of the serial provided in the second chapter of Nisonger's *Managing Serials in Libraries*,[5] several useful and comprehensive books have been written on the subject including Davinson's *The Periodicals Collection*[6] and Houghton's *Scientific Periodicals: Their Historical Development*.[7] This section will focus on only the historical development of serials collection and management.

The first indexes developed at almost the same time as the first scholarly journal, around 1683 and the first abstracting service developed around 1830.[5] A number of currently well-known indexes developed during the later nineteenth century and early twentieth centuries: Poole's index to Periodical Literature which was published from 1848 to 1907, H. W. Wilson's Reader's Guide to Periodical Literature which began publication in 1900, and Ulrich's International Periodicals Directory which was initially published under the name "Periodicals Directory: A Classified Guide to a Selected List of Current Periodicals Foreign and Domestic in 1932."[5]

The late nineteenth century also saw initial forays into serials subscription management by agencies. Both the Faxon company (in the United States) and Blackwell's (in the United Kingdom) can trace their origins to this era. The earliest automated subscription services were introduced by Faxon and EBSCO in the 1980s.[9]

Bibliographic control of serials was hugely advanced in the 1960s and 1970s with the development of the ISSN and the ISSN Network. The ISSN Network consists of centers throughout the world which are responsible for the assignment of ISSNs and key titles both of which are unique identifiers and are immensely helpful in differentiating serials with similar titles. ISSNs can be assigned to a serial in any format.[5] In 2001, as the AACR2 chapter

dealing with serials was revised and renamed, ISSNs began to be assigned to continuing resources. In 2007 the standard for the creation and assignment of ISSNs was revised to include a linking ISSN or ISSN-L. The ISSN-L is a mechanism for bringing together the various formats in which a continuing resource may be published (each of which may have been assigned a unique ISSN). The ISSN-L is separate from the ISSN enabling it to be coded separately in metadata records. This provides for identification of a serial regardless of the number of different formats it is published in, by OpenURL services and in machine readable cataloging (MARC 21) records.[8]

Additional events in library automation that impacted serials management include the development of bibliographic utilities, integrated library systems, and the Online Public Access Catalog (OPAC). Bibliographic utilities like Online Computer Library Center (OCLC) and Research Libraries Information Network (RLIN) in the United States and Auto-Graphics, Inc. in Canada provide their members with access to a database of bibliographic records which they can download, create, and modify and which rely on machine readable cataloging as well as recording serials holdings information which facilitates interlibrary loan.[21] Noncomputer serials management systems were being developed in libraries as early as the 1940s but it would be the 1980s before computerized integrated library systems (ILS) would be developed. Initially this took place in libraries (mainly academic libraries). During the 1980s vendors like Readmore and Faxon began marketing their own ILS. Advances and widespread use of communication technologies like the Internet during the 1990s and 2000s provided libraries with greater and greater control over serials and all other library materials as well as for access to them through the OPAC.

SELECTION

Librarians, library staff members, and library users traditionally participate in serials selection either separately or through committees. The combination of selectors will vary by type of library (academic, public, special, etc.). In all cases, the users' needs are a primary selection criterion. Users may make their needs known directly, indirectly, or both. Direct communication of needs may occur through participation on selection committees or, as is often the case in academic libraries, through a program for faculty participation. Indirect communication of needs may occur through use which may or may not be formally measured.

Selection criteria related to user needs will reflect the mission of the institution and may include support for academic curricula and research, user interest, and relevance to the rest of the library collection. Additional selection criteria include access to the content through indexes, peer review of content (for scholarly journals), cost, anticipated level of use, publisher reputation, citation rates and impact factors, physical quality, level of topical coverage in relation to existing subscriptions, type and frequency of requests, longevity, availability elsewhere, reviews, availability of desired format, inclusion in core lists, and available space in the library. The exact combination of criteria a library uses will vary by type of library and, often, within a single library over time. Some selection criteria are more universal than others, particularly format and cost.

Format. The increasing ubiquity of electronic serials in the twenty-first century makes selection decisions regarding format more complex. Prior to the development of technologies that make the delivery of serials in electronic format attractive to both users and librarians, serials subscriptions were delivered in either print or microform. Print subscriptions were generally preferred and microforms were selected based on the library's need to either conserve shelf space or to preserve content or both. Electronic subscriptions provide similar space-saving advantages to microforms and can be made accessible to patrons inside and outside of the library building virtually 24 hours a day, 7 days a week. However licensing agreements for electronic subscriptions rarely allow libraries to preserve content locally. This loss of control over content preservation has created a fear among librarians that electronically subscribed content may disappear. Thus, despite the advantages of electronic serials, a library may elect to purchase serials in print or microform rather than or in addition to an electronic version.

Advantages and disadvantages of electronic subscriptions also vary depending on the type of serials being considered. The preceding discussion focused on periodicals including scholarly journals. Additional advantages exist for purchasing continuing resources in electronic format, and, in fact, there is a trend away from publication of continuing resources in print. Continuing resources in print require substantial library staff time to remove discarded pages and replace them with pages containing updated information. Examples of this include legal materials, medical materials, and business materials, particularly stock, bond, market, and industry information. The processing time required to make these materials available in print (printing, mailing, as well as in-library processing) delays users' access to time sensitive information. These disadvantages are eliminated by making them available electronically.

Cost. Serials subscription costs became a point of contention between publishers and libraries during the 1970s and 1980s when increases in annual subscription prices began to rise at a rate above (sometimes far above) the rate of inflation. Conditions that contribute to these increases are generally accepted to be increases in the volume of published research; increases in the number of serial publications; fluctuations in the rates of foreign currency exchange; and market dominance, particularly in the fields of science, technology, and medical, of a few, profit-oriented publishers. Also contributing is the cycle of subscription cancellations by libraries who can no longer afford a particular subscription, which results in publisher price increases made to make up for a smaller subscription base, which, in turn, results in another round of subscription cancellations by libraries, and so on. These conditions and the resultant rapidly increasing subscription costs are known as the serials crisis.

The serials crisis impacts academic and medical libraries to a greater extent than it does public libraries because more of their budgets are allocated to the purchase of serials. Academic libraries have responded by shifting funds previously earmarked for other types of library materials to their serials budgets. A 1992 study indicates that college library serials subscription expenditures increased from 31.13% of their budgets in 1973–1974 to 42.12% of their budgets in 1988–1989.[1] The annual Library Journal Periodicals Price Survey (published in the April 15 issue each year) reports changes in periodicals prices and predicts changes for the upcoming year. Other sources of serials subscription price increases are available from the Association of Research Libraries and the Association for Library Collections and Technical Services (ALCTS) division of the American Library Association (ALA).

Most academic libraries and many public libraries develop collection development policies to guide materials selection including serials subscriptions. A serials collection development policy typically includes a list and description of approved selection criteria. Serials collection development policies may also include guidelines for the acceptance of gift subscriptions and serial back issues. An academic library is likely to describe levels of colleting by subject discipline in its policy as well as strategies for conserving shelf space like setting specific lengths of retention for periodical back issues and for selecting titles for preservation. A serials collection development policy may also address the issue of access to versus ownership of serials titles (also known as just-in-case vs. just-in-time), that is, it may contain a plan for selecting which titles are relevant enough to require individual subscriptions (ownership) and which are only tangentially relevant and for which access may be provided via document delivery services like interlibrary loan or via a full text electronic aggregation (access but not necessarily ownership).

ACQUISITION

Once a serial has been selected, the next step in its management is to purchase a subscription, to acquire it. In simple terms, an order for a new subscription is placed by the library with the publisher; the publisher is paid for the subscription and subsequently begins delivery of issues to the library. At the end of the subscription period, the subscription is either renewed or cancelled. Seldom, however, is the process really this simple.

To begin with, a library is likely to have multiple subscriptions. Small public or special libraries may have as few as 10 or 20 subscriptions while large research libraries may have tens of thousands of subscriptions. In addition to a small number of serials subscriptions, small libraries generally have small staffs and while large research libraries have larger staffs, it is easy to see how ordering, renewing, tracking receipt of, and issuing payments for multiple serials subscriptions can begin to take up a great deal of library staff time in any library. For this reason, many libraries choose to purchase the services of a subscription agent to handle these functions for the library.

A subscription agent will typically place orders, make payments, and cancel or renew subscriptions on behalf of the library. The library pays one bill to the subscription agent for multiple subscriptions plus a service charge to the agent. The agent sends the library a list of subscriptions once a year for them to approve subscription renewals and make cancellations. The agent will also alert the library to changes in their subscriptions, for instance, changes to titles, publishers, subscription rates, and publication delays and will take some of the burden of communicating with the publishers about claiming missed issues of print serials and resolving access issues to electronic serials. A subscription agent handling a large proportion of a library's subscriptions can provide the library with valuable reports describing patterns in, for example, cost increases, delayed publications, and/or claims sent and fulfilled.

Recently, in response to increasing serials costs, libraries have begun to collaborate in the purchase of bundles of periodicals. Consortial purchases benefit libraries by providing them with buying power that they would not have individually and allow them to provide their users with access to periodicals that they would not otherwise have. Subscription agents often play a part in consortial purchases by providing centralized management of the titles included in the bundles and customized billing to consortia members who may pay different percentages of the total cost of the bundle based on their institution's estimated usage of titles in the bundle or number of users or both. Publishers benefit from the agent's management of title lists and by receiving a single payment for the bundled subscription. Consortia and member libraries benefit from the management of institutional title lists (which may vary among the consortia member libraries) and by the agent's ability to customize billing to each member library.

The services of a subscription agent generally apply to subscriptions to print, electronic, and sometimes microform serials and are considered to be worth the service fees charged. Care should be taken in selecting a subscription agent. Criteria for selecting a subscription agent include the quality of services provided and the agent's reputation and financial stability. The importance of an agent's financial stability became clear in 2002 when the divine/RoweCom/Faxon Library Subscription Service filed for bankruptcy leaving many libraries with paid but unfulfilled subscription orders.

PROCESSING

Check-In

Unlike monographic purchases, serials subscription purchases require constant tracking of receipt of multiple issues. This process is called check-in and occurs upon receipt by the library of each serial issue. In most libraries it is an automated process in which receipt of an issue is noted in the ILS where records of all of the materials owned by the library are stored and made available to users. Although check-in provides a record of receipt of materials purchased required by many institutions, there is some debate over whether check-in, particularly in the case of electronic serials, is worth the time spent on it by library staff. Some libraries have done away with check-in for serials issues in any format.

Check-in often alerts libraries to the existence of missing issues. Missing issues can then be requested directly from the publisher or from the publisher through the subscription agent. This process is called claiming. Claiming is often automated and conducted using the library's ILS. The ILS has the capability of creating a list or report of missing or late issues. The list can be printed and e-mailed or faxed to the subscription agent or publisher or it can be transmitted via electronic data interchange (EDI). EDI is a standard for structuring data so that it can be exchanged between computers quickly and efficiently. It is used by libraries and subscription agents for exchanging data required for claims as well as for prompt delivery of invoices.

Check-in also facilitates the provision of serials holdings information to users. Holdings information describes exactly which volumes and issues (or other parts) of a serial the library owns and/or provides access to. Also unlike monographic materials, libraries may provide multiple access points to serials. Holdings may be displayed in the OPAC but may also be displayed in separate lists. A current popular term for such a separate list is A-to-Z list, that is, a searchable alphabetical list of a library's or group of libraries' serial holdings. Another term for a list containing the serials holdings of two or more libraries is called a union list.

Cataloging

Although in libraries the term cataloging traditionally refers to the creation and maintenance of records containing bibliographic information in a library catalog (either paper or electronic) in order to provide access to the materials described in those records, maintaining bibliographic information describing serials (and other materials) in A-to-Z lists, union lists, and link resolvers as well as the OPAC can be (and is) described as cataloging. Cataloging of serials in the traditional sense is accomplished by most libraries through importing bibliographic records from a national bibliographic database like the OCLC. The Library of Congress's Program for Cooperative Cataloging Cooperative Online Serials (CONSER) program provides standards for traditional serials and continuing resources cataloging. These are used in conjunction with the standards for cataloging of other materials (including serials and continuing resources) described in AACR2 and MARC 21.

During the late twentieth century, as library catalogs began to be automated, some libraries chose not to include bibliographic records for serials in the OPAC but rather to provide lists of serials titles to display holdings and to shelve periodicals in alphabetical order by title in order to promote finding.[5] Advances in technology improved flexibility in OPACs and the emergence of electronic journals and the capability of OPACs to link to them have combined to make the inclusion of serials records in OPACs much more desirable and easily accomplished today. However, the question of whether or not to catalog serials lives on through the emergence of electronic journals and subsequent decisions required about ownership versus access.

Libraries in the early twenty-first century have the capability to make far more serials available to users electronically than they could in print and microform alone. The ability to purchase bundles of electronic serials either from publishers or from third party aggregators makes this possible. The time and staff required to catalog the much larger number of serials to which the library now provides access can be extensive. While catalog-ready MARC 21 records are often available for purchase with a bundle, some library resources are still required to download them and edit them to local standards. Libraries lacking the resources to purchase and process MARC 21 records for their electronic journal bundles often continue to elect to catalog in their OPACs only those journals to which they actually subscribe (as opposed to those to which they simply provide access).

Once the decision is made to include bibliographic records for serials in the OPAC, the library must determine the extent and level of cataloging. Libraries that shelve their print periodicals separately from the main collection and arrange them in alphabetical order by title may choose to catalog them to a lesser extent, with fewer subject headings and no classification numbers assigned, since neither are required in order to find the periodical on the shelf. Including classification numbers in periodicals' bibliographic records allows the library to arrange their print subscriptions in order by classification which has the advantage of collocating titles by subject (facilitating browsing) and either integrating them with the main

collection or not. This practice also allows the library to shelve more closely together periodicals that have undergone changes in title.

The fact that periodicals titles do change raises another issue with regard to cataloging. Until the first edition of the Anglo American Cataloging Rules (AACR) that was adopted in 1967, libraries used a method called latest entry cataloging to represent periodicals in their catalogs. In latest entry cataloging, all titles under which a single periodical has been published are integrated into a single bibliographic record which contains a complete history of the publication. The AACR and later, AACR2, calls for successive entry cataloging of periodicals. Successive entry cataloging requires the creation of a new bibliographic record for each new iteration of a periodical, for example, when the title or publisher changes. In successive entry cataloging, the new record is linked to the old record providing access to the title's publication history. Clearly, successive entry cataloging created the potential for large numbers of new bibliographic records. This was eventually seen to have resulted in too many new bibliographic records and the 2002 revision of AACR contained detailed instructions for catalogers regarding the differences between major title changes (when a new bibliographic record was required) and minor title changes (when an update to the existing bibliographic record would suffice and no new record was required).

The AACR2 and MARC 21 also call for separate bibliographic records to be created for each format in which a serial (and many other types of library materials) is available. MARC 21 Concise Format for Bibliographic Data in particular makes possible the differentiation of a wide variety of formats in which information may be contained. Each format has its own specific fields, thus the fields contained in a bibliographic record that describes material presented in electronic format will differ substantially from the fields in a record that describes material presented in print or in microform. In practice, it is argued, multiple bibliographic records describing the same material in different formats are confusing to library users. Thus some libraries choose to integrate the information from multiple records, that each describes material in a single format, into a single record that points to the library's holdings of that material in all formats. The debate has become particularly lively among serials librarians with the advent of electronic serials.

The future may hold still more changes for serials cataloging. During the 1990s, the International Federation of Library Associations' (IFLA) Study Group on Functional Requirements for Bibliographic Records (FRBR) developed a new conceptual model of the structure of the bibliographic record and its relationship with other records. In 2005, the Joint Steering Committee for Revision of AACR became the Joint Steering Committee for Development of Resource Description and Access (RDA) and began work on a new set of cataloging codes that encompass the FRBR conceptual model.

Advances in technology have provided libraries with tools for creating and maintaining list of serials subscribed to or for which access is available as well as for linking from those lists directly to the electronic version of a serial or a fuller description of the library's print and/or microform holdings. Two of these tools are link resolvers and federated search engines. These tools use the Z39.50 standard for metadata exchange to facilitate information retrieval at the article, issue, volume, and title levels for serials. Although not restricted to serials, a link resolver facilitates a users' search for full text of a journal article, for instance, based on data from a citation discovered in an electronic index among the library's electronic resources. Based on that data, the link resolver searches the library's resources for access to the full text of the cited article.

Both link resolvers and federated search engines contain databases (sometimes referred to as knowledge bases) of bibliographic records that describe the electronic journals and other electronic resources to which the library subscribes. Serially published information is described on the article, journal, and aggregation level. That is, a knowledge base may contain records that describe the bibliographic characteristics of articles, journals, and/or collections of journals. Rules for the creation of these records vary from system to system but every library that makes such finding tools available to their users must first populate the systems' knowledge base with records describing their holdings. In other words, they must catalog them.

ACCESS BEYOND THE CATALOG

As noted in the previous section, the trend in access to serials in libraries extends beyond the OPAC. Technology allows access to serials for library users via lists like union lists and A-to-Z lists, collections of serials titles from publishers and aggregators, federated search engines, and link resolvers. Libraries also provide access to serials through services like interlibrary loan, course reserves, and document delivery. But advances in technology also complicate the library's provision of such services.

Historically, more than half of all interlibrary loan transactions are for serials. In 1976, the U.S. House of Representatives commissioned an ad hoc committee to create guidelines for interlibrary loan. The committee, the National Commission on New Technological Uses of Copyrighted Work (known as CONTU), created guidelines that allow libraries to distribute not more than six articles per year from any one serial but limited the application of this rule to issues published within the past five years.[1]

While the availability of electronic serials improves the ability of academic libraries to work with faculty to make electronic versions of articles available to their students via the library's Web site, the Digital Millennium Copyright Act of 1998 requires that permission be obtained and fees be paid to the authors and/or publishers. The Copyright Clearance Center (CCC) (http://www.copyright.com) is a clearinghouse through which such permissions may be obtained and fees paid. Many libraries assist faculty in doing so by maintaining an account with the CCC and, sometimes, budgeting for the payment of fees through the CCC.

Protection of copyright is also at issue when libraries make electronic serials available to users. Publishers and aggregators require libraries to restrict access to electronic serials to authorized users. Although authorized users usually includes anyone within the walls of the physical library, remote users (e.g., those using the library's Web site from outside the library) are usually required to identify themselves somehow (authenticate) before being allowed access to an electronic serial via the library's Web site.

Restricting access to authorized users is currently accomplished by the library in several ways. The library may choose to register the Internet Protocol (IP) addresses of computer workstations within the library. Only those patrons who are using computer workstations whose IP addresses are recognized by the publisher or aggregator's servers are allowed access. This, however, requires that users be physically in the library in order to access electronic serials. Libraries may also choose to allow users who are outside the library building to access electronic serials by implementing a system of authorization. A list of authorized users is maintained in the library's ILS. Each time an off-site user wishes to access an electronic serial to which the library subscribes they are required to enter identifying information that matches information stored in their record in the ILS before being granted access.

Because of the restrictions placed on access to electronic serials, publishers and aggregators almost always require the library to sign a contract or license agreement in which the library agrees to restrict electronic serials access to authorized library users. The negotiation of license agreements is often seen as a cumbersome and time-consuming practice for librarians. Library participation in consortial purchases of electronic serials can alleviate this to some extent since license agreements for consortial purchases are usually negotiated once on behalf of all participating libraries. There is also currently a desire among librarians to develop a standard license agreement that would alleviate the need for every library to negotiate a new (and often different) license for every electronic serial subscription or bundle that is purchased. One such initiative is SERU: Shared E-Resources Understanding (http://www.niso.org/committees/seru).

Not all electronic serials publishers restrict access to their publications through the payment of subscription fees. Dubbed Open Access (OA) publications, these electronic serials are made freely available to anyone with

Internet access. OA publications may be (and many are) peer reviewed and contain reports of scholarly research. In lieu of garnering profit from subscription payments, many publishers require authors to pay a fee (upon acceptance of an article by reviewers or editors) for publishing in their journals. This practice remains controversial and has yet to gain the full acceptance of authors. In 2005, the U.S. National Institutes of Health (NIH) issued a policy that "requests and strongly encourages all investigators to make their NIH-funded peer-reviewed, author's final manuscript available to other researchers and the public" (NIH, 2005). A list of OA journals may be found in the Directory of Open Access Journals (DOAJ) (http://www.doaj.org/).

MAINTENANCE

Serials in all formats require maintenance in order to remain findable to users. Technological advances provide vastly improved means of serials maintenance. The adoption of ILS and OPACs in libraries in particular allows libraries to more accurately track and maintain serials.

Prior to migrating to the ILS, libraries tracked receipt of serials via KARDEX, a series of cards filed in alphabetical order by title on which the receipt of each new issue was recorded. Card catalogs provided information as to whether or not a library held a subscription to a serials title but a trip to the shelves (or microform cabinets) was required in order to discover whether the volume and issue sought was available. The ILS provides electronic check-in cards as well as linking between electronic check-in cards and bibliographic records. Electronic check-in cards are displayed in the OPAC (along with holdings statements) and provide information such as the expected date on which the next issue of a serial will be received and the status of each issue (e.g., on the shelf or at the bindery).

Use of an ILS in conjunction with EDI allows libraries not only to electronically transmit claims information to publishers and subscription agents but also to receive electronic invoices from them. Electronic receipt of invoices reduces the time required to obtain and process them. It also reduces human error in entering the volume and issue or other payment information into electronic payment or order records (which, like electronic check-in records are linked to bibliographic records) in the ILS since line items from electronic invoices can be downloaded automatically.

Tracking serials in an ILS dramatically improves the library's ability to identify not only late or missing issues but also to identify lapsed subscriptions. An ILS also has the capability of processing reports of library expenditures on serials, serials holdings by subject (which can be invaluable in selection), and circulation levels.

The adoption of the ILS is only one way in which automation assists libraries with serials maintenance. As noted above, links from bibliographic serials records have the capability to provide the user with links to electronic journals. But, as has also been noted, libraries often provide multiple access points to serials, all of which require some maintenance. For instance, when an electronic journal changes publisher, the new publisher information (and likely a new link) will need to be added to an A-to-Z list and the old information removed. When a publisher pulls a publication from an aggregation or bundle, this information must be edited in A-to-Z lists as well as in link resolvers and federated search engines. Luckily, most of these tools include some level of automated communication with aggregators and publishers so that many times the editing of records in knowledge bases happens as a matter of course.

ILS and other electronic tools that provide serials access also usually provide usage statistics which can be extraordinarily helpful in making selection and deselection decisions. Automated usage statistics for electronic serials have a reputation for being much more accurate than measures of print and microform serial usage. Usage of noncirculating print and microform serials collections in particular is notoriously difficult to measure accurately although use of radio frequency identification (RFID) technology in conjunction with the ILS offers more accuracy than do hand counts. Project Counting Online Usage of Networked Electronic Resources (COUNTER) is an international initiative that sets standards for the collection and reporting of usage statistics. It allows libraries to compare usage statistics reported by different vendors, publishers, and aggregators giving an assurance that all entities involved are using terms and statistics consistently. The provision of "COUNTER compliant" usage statistics is often a criterion used to evaluate a vendor of electronic serials.

Automation via ILS and other electronic tools allow libraries to more easily identify gaps in serials holdings. Gaps may occur in serial holdings in any format although they are most prevalent in print holdings. Filling gaps in print collections facilitates preservation by allowing libraries to bind full volumes of serials. Gaps in recent holdings may be filled via claiming but most publishers set a time limit beyond which they cannot guarantee their ability to fulfill a library's claim. Other means of filling gaps in print serials collections include back file purchases and participation in duplicate exchanges. Back file purchases, that is, the purchase of older issues of a serial, may be made from publishers or firms that specialize in providing fulfillment of older serials issues. Duplicate exchange services are groups of libraries which communicate the availability of duplicate issues (or issues that are to be pulled from a collection for other reasons) of print and microform serials. Communication is often accomplished electronically via e-mail or listserv. Needed issues are donated to the needy library for the cost of postage or shipping.

PRESERVATION

Print serials have long been preserved by binding loose issues in hard cover or by replacing print issues with microform (which has the advantage of saving shelf space). Preservation is particularly important for print serials, which are subject to loss or damage because of their size and shape, in order to provide continuing access to their contents.

Binding may be accomplished by a professional bindery or in-house. Professional binding being preferred since it generally ensures a more durable unit than does in-house binding, via binders, binder rings, and/or string and cardboard covers. In 1986, the Library Binding Institute published standards for library binding and they were included in American National Standards Institute/National Information Standards Organization (ANSI/NISO) standard Z39.78 for Library Binding. The standard describes the technical specifications for binding serial publications for libraries. For instance, a bound periodical should have a strong spine that is flexible enough to allow it to be opened face down on a copier or scanner so that a complete page image can obtained without breaking the spine.

As mentioned, an alternative to binding serials for purposes of preservation is replacing them in another, often more compact format from which individual pages or issues can be less easily removed. Traditionally this meant microform although during the late 1990s there was a surge of serials publication on CD-ROM. Both formats share the advantage of taking up less space in the library and the disadvantage of requiring the use of machinery in order to access the content (a reader printer in the case of microforms and a computer workstation with a CD-ROM drive and sometimes additional software in the case of a CD-ROM). One of the reasons for the short-lived popularity of serials preservation on CD-ROM was that it was followed so quickly by the widespread use of the Internet for delivery of serials.

The availability of serials on the Internet has sparked controversy in discussions of preservation. Electronic communications technology allows libraries to provide their users with access to more and more serial publications but, as noted above, the library does not necessarily own all of these publications. Librarians are understandably concerned about the loss of control over of their ability to provide their patrons with perpetual access to serials. License agreements prevent libraries from downloading the entire contents of one or more serial publications, even for purposes of preservation. Some license agreements for electronic journals provide for perpetual electronic access and some do not. Often, perpetual access rights can increase the cost of an electronic serial. And even if the publisher or aggregator promises perpetual access it is easy to imagine scenarios in which that access might be lost and the promise reneged upon (e.g., bankruptcy or even mergers between publishers).

In response to concerns over preservation of electronic content including serials, the Lots Of Copies Keep Stuff Safe (LOCKSS) program was initiated at Stanford University in 1999. It was released into production in 2004 and now is funded by contributions from the member libraries of the LOCKSS Alliance. LOCKSS allows libraries to create, preserve, and archive local collections thus promoting ownership of electronic information. "A library uses the LOCKSS software to turn a low-cost PC into a digital preservation appliance (a LOCKSS box) that performs four functions" (LOCKSS Web site): collect content, searches for changes in that content and makes replacements as necessary, provides access to stored content for library users, and provides Web-based administration that allows library staff to manage their LOCKSS box. LOCKSS allows libraries and publishers to retain their traditional roles in the serials information chain and provides for the safe keeping of otherwise ephemeral content.

The Controlled LOCKSS (CLOCKSS) initiative is a private LOCKSS network currently being pilot tested by seven host libraries. Whereas LOCKSS allows libraries to preserve their own collections, the function of CLOCKSS is to comprehensively preserve scholarly information and to make it available to the public if and when "no publisher has current responsibility for, nor is providing electronic access to selected content" http://www.clockss.org/clockss/Home. Current membership is made up of six U.S. and one U.K. libraries and eleven publishers. The pilot program is expected to conclude in 2008 at which time membership will be opened to additional libraries and publishers.

WEEDING

Although the technological advances of the late twentieth and early twenty-first centuries provide libraries with numerous alternatives to removing serials titles from their collections libraries can and do still weed. Shrinking shelf space and the publication of more and more new serials titles continue to make weeding or alternatives to weeding, like off-site storage, necessary. Users and user needs continue to change and serials titles that were relevant to users at the time they were selected often become less relevant and relatively more expensive to house and maintain. Weeding need not be a controversial or painful task in these days of electronic serials, especially if done on a consistent schedule, since alternatives like trading ownership for access or document delivery exist.

Criteria for weeding closely resemble criteria for selection and a well-written and maintained serials collection development policy can make weeding the serials collection less of a chore. Measured use of serials in all formats facilitates weeding. Unused titles may be replaced in a more compact format or made accessible via document delivery. In some disciplines, the information contained in serials will become obsolete more quickly than in others. On the other hand, some serials may be of greater historical value than others. Bound volumes are often lesser candidates for weeding because of the financial investment in their preservation. As in selection, support of user activity and/or interest should be considered as should availability of finding tools like indexes.

In addition to the alternatives to complete deselection from the library's collection mentioned above, a library may consider off-site storage for relatively low use print and microform serials. Larger libraries in particular may choose to store less used print or microform serials in a storage facility separate from or in a remote part of the main library. There are costs to be considered for this choice including the cost of the space in which the serials are housed; either in terms of rent or in terms of other uses to which the space might be put. Also to be considered is the cost in staff time in retrieving items from off-site or remote storage when they are requested by users. The cost of off-site storage of print and microform serials makes it less likely to be considered by smaller libraries.

CONCLUSION

The past two decades have been full of upheaval and change for serials management. New technologies allow libraries to make far more serials available to their users than ever before and to manage those serials more efficiently and effectively as well. Textbooks on the topic of serials management that were written in the 1990s often included a chapter or section containing predictions about the future of serials management. For example, Nisonger[5] correctly predicted the delivery of faculty research via university servers. Faculty research is being made available via institutional as well as disciplinary repositories like the California Digital Library, the Texas Digital Library, and the ArXiv.org Physics Archive.

Other predictions that have yet to come to pass include the full acceptance of the scholarly writing in electronic journals, required OA to articles describing the results of federally funded research, and the demise of the print and/or microform versions of serials. Some of these predictions may yet occur and may even already be occurring and some may never occur. The one constant that can currently be applied to serials selection and management is change.

REFERENCES

1. ISO, International Organization for Standardization. http://www.iso.org/iso/home.htm (accessed March 13, 2009).
2. Black, S. *Serials in Libraries Issues and Practices*; Libraries Unlimited: Westport, CT, 2006.
3. Joint Steering Committee for Revision of AACR and American Library Association. *Anglo-American Cataloguing Rules* Canadian Library Association; Ottawa, ON; American Library Association; Chicago: IL, 2002.
4. Hirons, J. Ed. CONSER Cataloging Manual. http://www.itsmarc.com/crs/manl1573.htm (accessed December 28, 2007).
5. Nisonger, T.E. *Management of Serials in Libraries*; Libraries Unlimited: Englewood, CO, 1998.
6. Davinson, D. *The Periodicals Collection*; Deutsch: London, 1978.
7. Houghton, B. *Scientific Periodicals their Historical Development, Characteristics, and Control*; Linnet Books: Hamden, CT, 1975.
8. Reitz, J.M. Online dictionary for library and information science ODLIS. *Libraries Unlimited*, http://lu.com/odlis/index.cfm (accessed December 28, 2007).

BIBLIOGRAPHY

1. ALCTS: Association for Library Collections & Technical Services, http://www.ala.org/ala/alcts/alcts.cfm (accessed December 28, 2007).
2. Black, S. *Serials in Libraries Issues and Practices*; Libraries Unlimited: Westport, CT, 2006.
3. Carter, R.C.; Hooks, J.D. *Implementing Online Union Lists of Serials: The Pennsylvania Union List of Serials Experience*; Haworth Press: New York, 1989.
4. CLOCKSS: Controlled LOCKSS, http://www.clockss.org/clockss/Home (accessed December 28, 2007).
5. Cole, J. *Serials Management in the Electronic Era: Papers in Honor of Peter Gellatly, Founding Editor of The Serials Librarian*; Haworth Press: New York, 1996.
6. Copyright Clearance Center, http://www.copyright.com/, (accessed December 28, 2007).
7. COUNTER: Counting Online Usage of Networked Electronic Resources, http://www.projectcounter.org/, (accessed December 28, 2007).
8. Davinson, D. *The Periodicals Collection*; Deutsch: London, 1978.
9. DOAJ: Directory of Open Access Journals. *Lund University Libraries*, http://www.doaj.org/ (accessed December 28, 2007).
10. Eaton, N.L. New challenges for technical services in the 21st century. In *Serials Management in the Electronic Era: Papers in Honor of Peter Gellatly, Founding Editor of The Serials Librarian*; Cole, J.; Williams, J.W., Eds.; Haworth Press: New York, 1996; 195–208.
11. Farrington, J.W. *Serials Management in Academic Libraries a Guide to Issues and Practices*; Greenwood Press: Westport, CT, 1997.
12. Ginsparg, P.; Los Alamos National, L.; Cornell, U. ArXiv.org e-Print archive. Cornell University, 1991, http://bibpurl.oclc.org/web/7130.
13. Healy, L.W.; Moen, W. Z39.50 a primer on the protocol. *NSIO Press*, 2007. http://www.niso.org/standards/resources/Z3950_primer.pdf (accessed December 28, 2007).
14. Hirons, J. CONSER cataloging manual. The Library Corporation, 2007, http://www.itsmarc.com/crs/manl1573.htm (accessed December 28, 2007).

15. Houghton, B. *Scientific Periodicals their Historical Development, Characteristics, and Control*; Linnet Books: Hamden, CT, 1975.

16. Johnson, V.A. *Organization of Serials Departments in University Libraries*; Graduate Library School: University of Chicago: Chicago, IL, 1973.

17. Joint Steering Committee for Revision of AACR, American Library Association. *Anglo-American cataloguing rules*; Canadian Library Association; American Library Association: Chicago, IL, 2002.

18. Joint Steering Committee for the Development of RDA, Joint Steering Committee for the Development of RDA, http://www.collectionscanada.gc.ca/jsc/index.html (accessed December 28, 2007).

19. LOCKSS: Lots of Copies Keep Stuff Safe, http://www.lockss.org/lockss/Home, (accessed December 28, 2007).

20. Lowell, F.K. From KARDEX to INNOVACQ: Serials control online. Ser. Libr. 1989, *16* (1/2), 17–27.

21. Moen, W. The ANSI/NISO Z39.50 protocol: Information retrieval in the information infrastructure, http://www.cni.org/pub/NISO/docs/Z39.50-brochure/ (accessed December 28, 2007).

22. National Institutes of Health. NIH public access. *National Institutes of Health Office of Extramural Research*, http://publicaccess.nih.gov/ (accessed December 28, 2007).

23. National Serials Data Program. *Library of Congress*, http://www.loc.gov/issn/ (accessed Decemebr 28, 2007).

24. Nisonger, T.E. *Management of Serials in Libraries*; Libraries Unlimited: Englewood, CO, 1998.

25. Organization NIS, Institute LB. Library binding. *National Information Standards Organization*, http://www.niso.org/standards/resources/Z39–78.pdf (accessed December 28, 2007).

26. Reitz, J.M.Online dictionary for library and information science ODLIS. *Libraries Unlimited,* http://bibpurl.oclc.org/web/4113 http://lu.com/odlis/ (accessed December 28, 2007).

27. *Serials Management and Library Education*; [computer program]. American Library Association: Version. Chicago, IL, 1978.

28. Task Force on a National Periodicals System. *Effective Access to the Periodical Literature: A National Program*; The Commission on Libraries and Information Science: Washington, DC, 1977.

29. Texas Digital Library. *Texas Digital Library* 2006. http://www.tdl.org/ (accessed December 28, 2007).

30. The Digital Millennium Copyright Act of 1998, *U.S. Copyright Office*, http://www.copyright.gov/legislation/dmca.pdf (accessed December 28, 2007).

31. Tillet, B. *What is FRBR?* Library of Congress: Washington, 2004.

32. Tuttle, M. Serials management. In *Guide to Technical Services Resources*; Johnson, P., Ed.; American Library Association: Chicago, IL, 1994; 120–135.

33. Tuttle, M.; Swindler, L.; Rosenberg, F.B. *Managing Serials*; JAI Press: Greenwich, CT, 1996.

34. University of California. California Digital Library: CDL, http://www.cdlib.org (accessed December 28, 2007).

Serials Vendors *[ELIS Classic]*

Karalyn Kavanaugh
Account Services Manager, EBSCO Information Services, Birmingham, Alabama, U.S.A.

Abstract

Libraries spend a substantial portion of their budgets on subscriptions to serial publications, such as journals, newspapers, yearbooks, and other periodical literature. Serials vendors do not house the publication issues; they act as the intermediary between the library and the publisher on behalf of the library. The consolidation of orders with one vendor makes serials management easier because of the combined, streamlined efforts made by the vendor on the customer's behalf with the publishers.

INTRODUCTION

Academic libraries spend 50%[1] or more of the materials budget on subscriptions, some of which are electronic journal subscriptions. Medical, public, school, corporate, and special libraries and organizations spend 20–40% of their materials budget on serials. The price of journals in all categories of library organizations has increased dramatically. In 2002, colleges and universities spent approximately 36% more for subscriptions than they did in 1998 (Table 1). With the growth of publications in print and online, higher periodicals prices, and the decline of materials budgets in the late twentieth century and early twenty-first century, the role of the serials vendor is an important one in the purchasing and management of serials.

OVERVIEW

What Is a Serials Vendor?

Serials vendors are also called subscription vendors, periodical vendors, subscription agents, jobbers or dealers, and in the early days field agents or trade agents. Serials vendors do not house the publication issues; they act as the intermediary between the library and the publisher on behalf of the library. There are many serials vendors in the world, but as larger agencies swallow the smaller ones, fewer choices remain. See the American Library Associations' publication, *International Subscription Agents*,[2] for a list of the world's serials vendors. This book provides information needed to help make vendor choices. It includes information such as phone numbers, fax numbers, cable addresses, and toll-free numbers. Services offered, handling charges, invoicing procedures, prepayment policies, the transition process when moving from one vendor to another, as well as the agent's technological capabilities are included. It is arranged alphabetically by agent and by country.

In a broad sense, a term used to refer to all types of suppliers of serial publications (i.e., both Continuation dealers and Subscription Agents), and to distinguish them from suppliers of monographs. The term sometimes is used in a narrow sense to refer to vendors who supply serials other than periodicals (i.e., continuation dealers) and to distinguish them from Subscription agents. Serials Acquisitions Glossary, prepared by the Serials Section Acquisitions Committee of the Association for Library Collections and Technical Services, Association for Library Collections and Technical Services, 1993. Copyright 1993 by the American Library Association.

How Vendors Work?

Almost any publication of a serial nature from any place in the world can be ordered through large serials vendors. Newsletters, reports, newspapers, periodicals, magazines, journals, annuals, and yearbooks are the standard fare. The consolidation of orders with one vendor makes serials management easier because of the combined, streamlined efforts made by the vendor on the customer's behalf with the publishers. With one invoice, one renewal list, and one monthly follow-up claiming system, subscriptions are managed more effectively (Fig. 1).

Because customers do not always have all the subscription orders ready at one time, vendors will accept orders throughout the year. Often, the vendor will work with the customer and publishers to arrange a common expiration date for as many publications ordered as possible, which makes the process a more efficient one. At the time of renewal, the serials vendor sends the customer a renewal list showing the expiration date(s). The list is sent about 6 months before the subscriptions expire. Once the customer reviews the list for changes and additions and sends it back, the serials vendor places the orders and pays publisher in time for the subscription

Encyclopedia of Library and Information Sciences, Fourth Edition DOI: 10.1081/E-ELIS4-120008917

Semiotics–Slovakia

Table 1 Five year price analysis from EBSCO information services, 2001. Five-year journal price increase history (1998–2002) data are based on proprietary sales data of select EBSCO subscription services customers of various library types. A sample of customers in good standing with a representative mix of U.S. and non-U.S. titles were selected for analysis

Library type	% of total titles	% of total expenditure	1998–1999 % increase	1999–2000 % increase	2000–2001 % increase	2001–2002 % increase	1998–2002 % increase
ARL							
U.S. titles	66.2	45.7	8.85	8.88	8.75	7.89	39.05
Non-U.S. titles	33.8	54.3	7.37	7.40	6.12	6.55	30.38
Total titles	100.0	100.0	8.02	8.06	7.30	7.16	34.20
College and university							
U.S. titles	77.7	58.6	8.92	8.83	8.44	8.21	39.10
Non-U.S. titles	22.3	41.4	7.94	7.62	6.31	6.74	31.82
Total titles	100.0	100.0	8.50	8.31	7.54	7.60	35.99
Academic medical							
U.S. titles	63.9	44.8	10.19	9.87	9.37	8.22	43.31
Non-U.S. titles	36.1	55.2	7.90	6.89	5.81	5.69	28.97
Total titles	100.0	100.0	8.87	8.16	7.36	6.81	35.02
Corporate							
U.S. titles	85.7	58.7	6.88	5.44	5.21	6.03	25.72
Non-U.S. titles	14.3	41.3	7.02	7.20	5.66	6.69	29.34
Total titles	100.0	100.0	6.95	6.15	5.39	6.30	27.19
Public library							
U.S. titles	95.3	85.3	3.92	3.34	3.25	4.76	16.15
Non-U.S. titles	4.7	14.7	5.65	6.12	5.04	6.08	24.93
Total titles	100.0	100.0	4.15	3.74	3.50	4.95	17.36

Ordering directly from publishers can be inefficient.

Ordering through a serials vendor reduces paperwork and saves staff time and money.

Fig. 1 Using a vendor versus ordering subscriptions directly with publishers, EBSCO Information Services, page 1.

to start the following year. This all seems fairly simple, but many exceptions arise when working with subscriptions. Publications aren't always published when the publisher says they will be. Titles can change names, change frequency, change format (i.e., from print to electronic), have delivery problems, be discontinued, suspend publication, resume publication, merge with other journals, split off into two or more journals, or cease entirely. Publishers go out of business, merge with other businesses, publish through an organization that sponsors them, or set up other publishing arrangements. All of these events play into managing subscriptions.

Serials vendors help keep track of these changes and communicate them to the customers.

Reasons to Use a Vendor

Approximately 95% of libraries use one or more serials vendors to manage subscriptions. Customers find the ease of ordering, paying, and renewing their entire list of subscriptions annually through an agency saves time and labor. A large international vendor allows access to information on foreign and domestic periodicals and will provide price quotations, catalogs, and offer their years of experience with foreign publishers and currencies. Vendors use the relationships they have established with publishers to communicate the needs of their customers.

Some serials vendors provide the customer with one salesperson, one account manager, and one customer service representative who provide continuity in managing subscriptions. Technology has allowed smaller vendors to have equal footing with larger vendors in many ways. E-mail or online ordering allows for "instant" orders. Orders, invoices, claims, renewal lists, and serials management reports can be produced from the information housed in most vendor databases. Not all aspects of the serials-ordering process can be handled electronically, however. Some publishers and vendors do not have electronic data interchange (EDI) capability.

Two advantages of using a large vendor are their strong relationships with publishers and the number of print and on-line publications found in their more comprehensive databases. International serials vendors are also more likely to be able to communicate with and provide payments to publishers in their own language and currency. The advantage to libraries is that when the vendor does this part of the process, it frees the librarian to perform other aspects of the job.

Research Library Needs

The decision by a research library to begin a subscription to a journal has long-term effects. It usually requires a commitment to that publication for many years because the library hopes to provide the information from that journal to its users to fulfill their research needs. Research libraries strive to provide historical materials for as many years as the information is valuable to the users, which often requires the purchase of a back file for the new journals to which they subscribe. Vendors can often acquire the necessary journal volumes for the customer.

Organizational/Corporate Subscriptions

Organizations and corporations subscribe to many publications through serials vendors. The subscription service works the same for organizations as it does for libraries, although often the publications are ordered for individual rather than organizational use. The organization gives the vendor the list of publications to order and the dates on which to start them. The vendor places the order with the publishers, pays for the subscriptions, and then invoices the organization for all the subscriptions ordered. The organization in turn pays the vendor's invoice. The vendor manages any problems that arise with orders or delivery of issues, which frees staff to do other jobs. This service also reduces the number of purchase orders and checks written that an organization might process if they were ordering each publication directly from the publisher. Libraries and other organizations may subscribe to thousands of subscriptions or as few as five. Although processing five checks to pay five publishers is not a huge task, writing thousands of checks to thousands of publishers is unmanageable and extremely costly and time-consuming. Accounting and business offices appreciate the services that serials vendors provide. Administrators can also track the flow of information coming into the organization based on reports provided by the serials vendor.

How Vendors Make Money

Serials vendors earn revenue from the discounts they receive from the various publishers whose titles are included in each customer's subscription order. By calculating the average publisher discount and comparing this to the estimated cost to service the customer's account, a vendor determines if a service charge or discount to the customer is warranted. The calculation is based on the mix of the list of titles ordered, those for which the publisher offers a discount versus those for which they do not. The current trend by publishers is to keep the discount formerly given to vendors, thereby making their titles "net" or "no discount" to customers. Some serials vendors have determined it is necessary to impose a "net title" charge, a flat fee, when the publisher does not give any discount to the vendor. This charge is intended to help the vendor recoup a portion of lost revenue. The vendor's concerns are to stay in business, stay solvent, serve their existing customers' needs, keep up with technology and expand their services while at the same time offering full service by handling all titles that publishers allow agents to order and service.

HISTORY

Subscription services have been around for many years. References in early library management books are few, but some references to vendor services have been noted since 1961. One of the first agencies to offer a consolidated subscription service to libraries was Frederick W. Faxon in 1886. The beginnings of EBSCO Information Services started in the late 1940s. Elton B. Stephens sold magazines door-to door to pay his way through college, and then continued by managing a periodical sales force through the Great Depression. The company he founded is now one of the largest serials vendors in the world.

New subscription agencies have started and others have expanded since the early 1960s. The U.S. federal government infused monies into research organizations to keep up with the rush to conquer space, which created programs that increased college enrollment. The number of serials titles published to support those programs led to larger library collections. Serials agents, such as Faxon, EBSCO, Moore-Cottrell, Hanson-Bennett, Franklin Square, Mayfair, Clark, Goldstein, Walter Johnson, Turner, and others, all small field agencies until that time, began to expand. As the publishing industry grew, so did libraries, library budgets, library buildings, etc., and likewise the need for a subscription agency to provide more journal titles and subscription management tools. Through the years, many agents bought smaller ones, both domestic and foreign, and the trend continues today. For example, EBSCO has purchased Franklin Square, Moore-Cottrell, Majors, McAinsh (Canada), Hill (New Zealand), Offilib (France), Lange and Springer (Germany), and others.

Publishers gave good commissions to field and trade agents in those days because the volume sold increased circulation. Higher circulation statistics allowed publishers to offer greater advertising opportunities and, in turn, reach greater sales and profit growth. As library orders grew, the commissions from publishers to agents did not. Often, the types of journals that were being ordered to support research were not those with advertising that would raise the publisher's revenue. Scientific, technical, and medical (STM) journals generally do not have advertising to boost revenue; therefore, publishers rely solely on paid subscriptions. Agents began adding a service charge to handle library accounts, their services to colleges, universities, research organizations and other types of libraries became more complex and even more essential. Commissions for handling such subscriptions are generally small. And most librarians believe that the service charge costs the library less than if it were to manage subscriptions in-house.

Early on, the management process was completely manual. Some agents kept records for orders to publishers in a card file called a wheeldex. Orders were hand-typed on $3'' \times 5''$ cards and filed in a box by publisher name. At the end of the week, they were counted by hand, photographed, and stored on microfilm. A summary of the orders and a check was typed and mailed to the publishers. All checks were hand-signed. Problem orders could be traced by reviewing the microfilm. Invoices to the customer were hand-typed and produced on a special ditto machine. They were hand-folded and mailed to customers biweekly. Renewal lists were produced at the same time as invoices and did not include prices. The renewal lists were filed by date and sent out approximately 6 months before time to renew. Follow-up reminder notices, when necessary, were sent approximately 3 months later. Automating to use of keypunch cards in the 1960s allowed agents to place orders and keep records rapidly. Some management reports were produced on the basis of keypunched data. Automatic renewal list generation was developed. By the early 1970s, three of the large U.S. subscription agencies, Faxon, EBSCO, and Franklin Square, were automated, making the placement of orders, invoicing, claiming, and report generation easier and more efficient.

Changes in Libraries

The past 20 years have seen a dramatic change in libraries. Card catalogs of library materials have been replaced with online catalogs. Serials and other information vendors now interface with all aspects of acquisition, databases access, and management of serials and reference materials. Few printed indexes are being published. Content in electronic format, such as databases with indexes and abstracts, full-text articles, and individual journals, are available. There is a movement toward providing more full-text information in electronic format through the World Wide Web, with less physical space being required for shelving (i.e., "the virtual library"). Books available in electronic format are accessible through library workstations, handheld devices, or personal computers. But readers continue to enjoy printed books and periodicals; libraries will likely continue to subscribe to a combination of print and (electronic) e-resources.

Naturally, serials vendors are expected to remain current with changing information access capabilities and are helping to lead the way. Some now handle e-databases, e-journals (full text), e-indexes and abstracts, e-tables of contents, pay-per-view articles, alerting services, e-books, e-payment and procurement services, and e-resource usage and analysis reports.

Libraries are looking to vendors to assist with archiving data and preserving materials, but publishers are reluctant to give data to vendors for storage and management. Librarians are creating their own electronic archives for serial and monographic materials. It is a challenge to librarians, publishers, and vendors to resolve the issue of archiving and preserving digital data.

Interfaces with Integrated Library Systems

To manage and maintain materials in their collections, most librarians use automated or integrated library systems (ILS). The ILS is used for the public access catalog, circulation system, interlibrary loan, collection management, and report writing. It is, therefore, important for librarians to choose a serials vendor with proven interfacing experience with their current or planned ILS. Electronic Data Interchange (EDI) invoices are provided by some vendors for payment through the customer's

Semiotics–Slovakia

serials acquisitions module. For an exact exchange of data, some serials vendors and system vendors apply EDI $\times$ 12 standards to their processes. Frequently used $\times$ 12 transaction sets are Invoice, 810; Publisher price list, 832; Purchase order, 850; Claim, 869; and Functional acknowledgement, 997.[3]

For the ILS to "talk" with the serials vendor database for claiming and invoicing, a link must be established between the two. Each record must have a vendor identification number and a Serial Item and Contribution Identifier (SICI) number, which is the ISSN from the bibliographic record. Several standards have been developed for library systems, as well as existing ones applied; these include the following: ANSI/NISO Z39; Electronic Data Interchange for Administration; Commerce and Transport (EDIFACT); and TRADACOMS (the UK standard for teleordering of books) with the help from the Serials Industry Systems Advisory Committee (SISAC). The International Committee for EDI in Serials (ICEDIS) was formed to standardize various parts of the routine exchange of business forms.

Serial orders in an ILS are different from book orders. Each book order is processed one time, and each order represents a unique item. The purchase order is entered into the ILS when the book is placed on order with a publisher; when the book arrives, it is processed and the bibliographic record is added to the catalog. Serial processing does not stop when the order is placed and the payment is made. A subscription is reordered each year and during the year issues arrive daily, weekly, biweekly, monthly, bimonthly, semimonthly, quarterly, annually, biannually, or even triannually. Each piece is received and recorded separately. Subscriptions might have billing adjustments or credits applied to them during the year. The ILS should be flexible enough to allow for all types of invoice activities and publication pattern changes.

Electronic Journals

At this time less than 10% of journals from the 60,000 active publishers in the world have developed electronic versions of their publications. Currently, electronic journals are primarily in the scientific, technical, and medical (STM) areas. As the titles change during the subscription term from print to print plus online or online only, some serials vendors provide the customer with updated information to adjust journal records in the ILS. As publishers become more comfortable with electronic publishing and provide access to the full text online, they usually change the offering to include a charge for online use. This charge is most often a percentage of the cost of the print publication. Initially some publishers required libraries to purchase print subscriptions to obtain the online full text.

Some large STM publishers offer their electronic journals only directly to libraries in a package, for a set fee. Because a serials vendor does not play its traditional role in the acquisition of these journals, this arrangement makes it difficult for a library's vendor to assist its staff with the management of those subscriptions. The librarian loses the benefit of vendor-supplied cost/invoice data on individual titles in the package as well as that of comprehensive serial management reports because those titles are acquired separately from the rest of their serial collection.

VENDOR SERVICES

Ordering

From the serial vendor's database of titles, the customer may choose from a few to thousands of titles. Orders usually can be placed through a Web-based ordering system, e-mail, fax, or produced in print form and mailed through the postal system. Large, international vendors handle most titles to which a customer might want to subscribe, currently approximately 260,000 titles from around the world. Most often, libraries order subscriptions for 1 year at a time, but subscriptions of 2- or 3-year terms are sometimes offered by publishers. Methods offered to aid in selection of publications typically include a print and/or online catalog of available titles, listing such information as title, price, publisher, ISSN, country of origin, currency, Library of Congress code, Universal/Dewey Code, term, where the publication is indexed, language, and publisher restrictions. Delivery options, such as surface, airmail, or electronic version, could also be included in the data.

Invoicing

Consolidated invoicing provided by a serials vendor reduces check writing and the numbers of invoices that accounting departments must handle. Consistent layout of the vendor's paper invoices and their inclusion of vital serial data usually make these documents valuable to librarians. Receipt of electronic invoices from the vendor through file transfer protocol (FTP) with EDI or EDIFACT standards also makes processing invoices easier.

Claiming

It is inevitable that some issues of a publication will not arrive at their destination as expected. For a research library with the purpose of collecting materials for research use, it is important to have every issue of every publication ordered. When an issue does not arrive as scheduled, the library staff must track it down to complete the volume for binding. Serials vendors take on the task of asking the publisher to send the issue that did not arrive. This is called "claiming." Claims are a major part of a vendor's service. Sometimes the customer judges the vendor solely on its claim resolutions. Serials vendors who have developed good claiming systems and a reputation for getting fast results for issues claimed on behalf of their customers often use this fact in marketing their services. Most serials vendors assign customer service representatives to handle individual accounts; they establish a relationship with the customer to better meet the customer's needs both in placing orders and resolving claims. Some integrated library systems and serials vendors have devised automated claiming procedures that pass from one system to another and onto the respective publisher, making claim resolution faster and more streamlined.

Renewals

Approximately 6 months before a subscription term ends, the serials vendor sends the customer a list of the titles ordered in the past year to use as a reminder to place renewal orders. After reviewing the list and making changes and additions, the customer sends it back to the serials vendor for renewal, allowing time for the orders to be entered. Once the vendor enters orders into its database, orders are sent with payment to the publishers in time to ensure uninterrupted service for the customer. Because it takes 6–10 weeks for a subscription to start, it is important for all parties to adhere to the renewal schedule to avoid gaps in service. By placing all orders at the same time, a customer pays one invoice for all of the subscriptions. The serials vendor pays each publisher with one transaction or money transfer for many customers' orders.

Reports

Serials vendors not only offer title choices, place orders, send invoices, communicate with publishers, and solve claiming issues, they also provide reports based on the customer's subscription list. Sorting subscription data in various ways allows the customer to evaluate the collection based on criteria such as cost, subject, or publisher. Reports can be designed to help librarians determine the titles published in a particular area of interest. Such reports can be programmed to show the titles on subscription or those to which the library does not subscribe. Collection managers can use these data to further develop the serial collection or to streamline it to better meet users needs. The vendor may allow the customer to use a fund/cost code to keep track of departmental expenditures. The vendor enters the designated fund/cost code and can then provide reports sorted accordingly to show the dollars spent in

that area of interest or for a specific customer department. Most serials vendors assign a subject or classification code to each entry in their title database so that reports can be produced by using various cataloging systems, such as the Library of Congress, the Dewey Decimal System, or the National Library of Medicine. Subscription price data collected by the vendor over time provides a way to review the collections based on cost history and pricing trends over a five year period. A customer may want to create lists by title, by cost per title, by country of origin, by publisher, by frequency of publication, and so forth, to meet their particular needs. The sorting and reporting capabilities are tremendous.

Services to Publishers

Serials vendors act as intermediaries between libraries and publishers and as partner with both. As many as 60,000 publishers work with serials vendors. Serials vendors develop relationships with publishers that are useful to their customers. Those relationships are based on a good understanding of each other's services and years of doing business together. The vendor can act on behalf of the library to solve claiming issues and to work out areas of mutual concern (e.g., a name change of a publication, a change in numbering sequence, or other significant changes affecting subscriptions).

Serials vendors not only provide services to libraries and other organizations but to publishers around the world. Vendors provide customers to publishers. Orders and claims information are sent from vendors to publishers in EDI format when the publisher has the capability to accept electronic data. This speeds up transactions and eliminates keying errors. From translating correspondence to delivering payment with the orders, publishers receive comprehensive subscription service from vendors. Some vendors are involved in the delivery of serial information in all formats from the content supplier to the user.

Relationships with Other Organizations

Serials vendors enjoy relationships with other organizations and associations such as the Serials Industry Systems Advisory Committee (SISAC), International Committee on EDI for Serials (ICEDIS), CONSER, and numerous library and information-related associations. These organizations work together to standardize procedures and operating practices in the publishing world and to foster relations and increase understanding among the many and varied parties playing key roles in the distribution of information. Groups such as the North American Serials Interest Group (NASIG), the Timberline Institute, The College of Charleston Conference, and the North Carolina Serials Interest Group bring together vendors, publishers, and librarians to discuss serial issues of mutual concern. Of interest to serials librarians might be the discussion list SERIALST, currently found at http://www.uvm.edu/~bmaclenn/serialst.html.

FUTURE ROLES

With the Internet and the Web-based services developed by serials vendors, customers can now generate renewal lists, management reports, and copies of invoices themselves. Serials vendors can interface with library systems such as SIRSI, Ex Libris, Innovative Interfaces, Inc., Endeavor/Voyager, and many more. EDI capabilities commonly assist technical service personnel in placing orders, paying invoices, and making claims. New automated business systems such as SAP, Ariba, Commerce One, and Oracle are being used in organizations. Each one can accept EDI to speed transactions, which helps manage information and library materials. Today more and more automated processes are being developed and used by key players in the serials industry. These greatly impact the efficiency of publisher, library, and serials vendor operations.

Future of Serials Vendors

Librarians want their vendor to be able to supply electronic journals and to negotiate the price and license agreement with the publishers. Some serials vendors include handling these requests as part of their basic services; others will do so in the future. Researchers want access to the top electronic journals in their fields. Customers expect serials vendors to provide a greatly expanded range of value-added services to assist with the myriad of tasks required to effectively manage electronic

journal subscriptions in addition to those for print publications. When ordering electronic journals for customers, the vendor needs to provide access services such as "turning on" (activating) the subscription. In the past, serials vendors worked primarily with serials and acquisitions departments in libraries and purchasing departments in organizations. Now they must also communicate with collection development staff, reference departments, campus legal departments, webmasters, and information systems staff. Other services that customers require for access to electronic journals include providing IP addresses to publishers, links to publisher websites, publisher contacts, contracts with consortia, and the archiving of license agreements.

A generic Standard License Agreement orchestrated by John Cox of John Cox Associates (UK), in association with five subscription vendors, is an example of the type of services serials vendors are providing to their customers. The license is in the form of a template that can be modified to accommodate the needs of libraries and corporations.

Libraries and other organizations have overwhelmingly embraced electronic content, and it continues to grow at breakneck speed (Fig. 2). Digitizing data (converting content into electronic format) enables a publisher to distribute content globally online and is provided through the operations of some serials vendors. The management of linking electronic journals to databases using OpenURL and SFX technology is taking place. The serials vendor continues to be the electronic serial manager for a library and can act as the aggregator of electronic information. Aggregators provide electronic gateways to many publishers' websites and full-text e-journals.

Publishers are looking for ways to control the financial stability of their companies and solutions to the concern

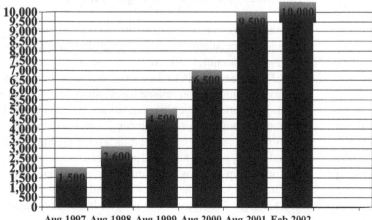

Fig. 2 Rise in number of electronic journals, EBSCO Information Services, page 9.

for preservation of materials. The issues of copyright and fair options to access are also critical to publishers. Serials vendors are working with the publishers and programmers, the courts and the librarians, and library organizations to keep these issues from colliding. All concerned parties are awaiting court decisions on various matters of copyright. Just as they have for decades with print publications, serials vendors play a vital role in the delivery of information in all formats, whereas librarians, vendors, and publishers continue to work together to reach their common goal of providing serial information to their users.

REFERENCES

1. Blixrud, J.C. *Bowker Annual, Library and Book Trade Almanac,* 46th Ed.; Bogart, D., Ed.; R.R. Bowker, 2001.
2. Wilkes, L.R. *International Subscription Agents,* 6th Ed.; American Library Association: Chicago, IL, 1994.
3. *Living with Electronic Data Interchange: Implementation and Practical Applications of EDI from the Perspective of the ILS Vendor, the Librarian, and the Book Vendor*; ALCTS, Automated Acquisitions/In-Process Control Systems Discussion Group Session at the ALA Midwinter Conference, January 26, 1996. Serials Review; Summer 1996; Vol. 22 (2), 107–109.

Shared Libraries

Ruth E. Kifer
Dr. Martin Luther King, Jr. Library, San Jose State University, San Jose, California, U.S.A.

Jane E. Light
Dr. Martin Luther King, Jr. Library, San Jose Public Library, San Jose, California, U.S.A.

Abstract

Shared libraries are partnerships between school libraries and public libraries, university libraries and public libraries, community college libraries and public libraries, and any number of other combinations of library organizations. This entry will discuss the shared library as a distinct library type, outlining the major political, fiscal, management, planning, information technology, public policy, and evaluation issues. Examples of shared libraries will be described as a means of illustrating differing management models and to identify areas of the world where joint libraries are most prevalent.

INTRODUCTION

Shared libraries or joint-use libraries as they are sometimes called have been in existence in the United States and other parts of the world for decades. Historically, these libraries have been school-housed libraries where the public library has located a community branch library in a school building. Increasingly, joint-use libraries include university, college, and community college libraries partnering with public libraries to create a shared-use facility that serves as the university or college's academic library and serves as either the main library or branch library of a public library system.

DEFINITIONS

Joint-use libraries can be defined in a number of different ways. Dr. Alan Bundy, past University Librarian at the University of South Australia and prolific writer on the topic defines a joint-use library as "a library in which two or more distinct library services providers, usually a school and a public library, serve their client groups in the same building, based on an agreement that specifies the relationship between the providers."[1] Ken Haycock, Director of the Graduate School of Library and Information Sciences at San José State University, defines dual-use libraries as "a common physical facility from which library services are provided to two ostensibly different communities of users."[2]

TYPES OF JOINT LIBRARIES

Virtually, any type of library can merge or partner with another type of library to form a shared-use or joint-use library. For example, there are and have been many joint school/public libraries in existence in rural areas of the United States and other parts of the world, specifically Australia and New Zealand since early in the twentieth century. The first Joint-Use Libraries International Conference held in 2007 included presentations representing many different kinds of joint-use libraries, including public, school, community college, university, health care, community center, municipal government, and vocational libraries—all partnering in some manner with another to form a shared-library space. These partnerships are similar in that two or more different library client groups are served from one shared-space facility while at the same time each is developed in a way unique to the local community needs, whether political, fiscal, or cultural.

POLITICAL AND FISCAL MOTIVATIONS

The impetus for the development of a shared-use library often comes from policy makers that perceive it as a way to address several goals and problems. Commonly, two different levels of government publicly fund such libraries. Sharing the costs of building, staffing, maintaining, and developing collections can be more cost effective than building and operating separate library facilities. In addition, the resources included in these buildings, including the collections, technology, staff, and facilities such as group study rooms and meeting rooms are readily available to more of the taxpayers who are the primary funders. Private, philanthropic funders may be more willing to contribute to a joint-use library. Policy makers are well aware that the access to information available today via the Internet makes it increasingly difficult to justify the barriers to access that exist when libraries serve more limited communities of users.

Encyclopedia of Library and Information Sciences, Fourth Edition DOI: 10.1081/E-ELIS4-120043278

Semiotics–Slovakia

Many school/public libraries are developed to serve rural population or communities that are growing and now have a need for both new schools and community amenities, such as parks and public libraries. Policy makers see an opportunity to place such amenities in one central convenient location.

BENEFITS AND OPPORTUNITIES

Every proposal for a joint-use library has the potential of synergy, of creating a whole that is greater than the sum of its parts. Fulfilling that potential begins with the intergovernmental agreement for construction, operation, and the building's physical design. The intergovernmental agreement will specify the mission of the library, the roles of the partners, their funding and staffing obligations, ownership of the building and its contents, its governance, and conflict resolution. It may have a finite length, or specify terms and conditions of termination of the agreement. The building design will reflect the terms of the agreement. For example, if the agreement stipulates that two libraries will operate as entirely separate entities, the building design will allow for separate entrances, collections that are in an area accessible only to a specific group of users, and different hours of service.

Dr. Alan Bundy has identified a number of specific ways in which joint-use libraries can provide more efficient use of public money. These include sharing of design, construction, and facility maintenance costs, sharing of staffing costs, and access to collections, including online resources. Less obvious, but also very important, is the opportunity to locate local history and archival information of interest to the entire community in one place and the possibility of providing more hours of service. Another advantage of having more staff members than the partners would each have in stand-alone facilities is that the skills, talents, and interests of the staff are broader and deeper. In a small joint-use library, staff may have more variety of tasks, as well as opportunities for professional growth and stimulation.[3]

OPERATIONAL ISSUES

Every joint-use library must address a number of the same issues about how the library will function. Many of these will be specifically included in the intergovernmental agreement; others will be developed as specific procedures or policies that are documented in supplementary agreements that can be modified by operational managers as needed. Operational policies, accompanied by specific procedures in larger or more complex shared libraries, must be developed for the entire range of services. These include in-house use and circulation of materials, use of computers and online resources, and collection development

policies. Licensing agreements for online resources need to provide for use by all library patrons. The partners will have to decide on ownership of collections (shared or separate). Most commonly, each partner retains ownership over materials purchased with its funds in order to ensure that the needs and requirements of its users are met. If shared, the partners must decide how the acquisitions budget will be apportioned to best meet the needs of all users.

The management and operation of technology in the shared library requires careful planning and ongoing attention. Often, one or both of the partners in a shared-use library operate other library facilities and therefore the joint-use library may be part of a larger network or networks. The holdings of the joint-use library and of other libraries in the network need to be included in an Online Public Access Catalog (OPAC). A shared-library Web site can present the library to all users as one library serving different user groups. Policies and procedures regarding use of computer resources must be set. As bandwidth requirements increase, the partners must develop and implement improvements to their network.

Library services and collections change more quickly now than in the past. The partners must have a way to alter these, as well as the way space is used in the library, as user needs change. In addition, provision for future expansion of the building should be addressed in the agreement and design. The library will eventually require renovation and replacement of building systems (i.e., lighting, electrical, heating, and air conditioning) and how the partners will share those costs should be included in their agreement. The partners must agree about building operations, including janitorial services, building maintenance and repair, security, and utilities. They must agree about who will provide these functions and how the costs will be shared.

Many joint-use libraries are located on a school, community college, or university campus. It is important that the building be sited in a way that makes its accessibility to both the campus community and the general public both clear and obvious. Often, this means that the library is located at the entrance to a campus or on an edge of the campus adjacent to the community. The College Hill Library in Colorado is a library shared by the City of Westminster and Front Range Community College. The library is located on the edge of the campus. A public parking lot is near the entrance to the first floor, designated as the Westminster Public Library. The second floor, allocated as the community college library, can be accessed via stair or elevator from the first floor, as well as from an entrance that faces the other community college buildings and student/staff parking.[4]

Key to the long-term success of a shared library is its ability to meet the needs of its different user groups and of the partner organizations to provide library services. Effective decision-making and administrative accountability are necessary. The administrative and staffing

Semiotics–Slovakia

model for the shared library will be identified in the intergovernmental agreement. There are several options, each of which brings with it operational challenges. A director can be employed by one of the partners that have agreed to be responsible for the management and operation of the shared library. All other staff are employed by that partner. In those cases, the second partner may have a consultative role in the selection and evaluation of the manager of the library and perhaps of the other staff too. In essence, the second partner is contracting for services from the first. The second partner may feel that the needs of its users or of the parent organization itself are difficult to assert and negotiate, especially as they change over the years. It is also possible that the contracting partner may lose commitment to and interest in the partnership over time.

In a second model, the intergovernmental agreement establishes a governing board consisting of representatives from the two partners. The governing board employs a director who reports to it. Generally, one partner acts as fiscal agent and employer of remaining staff, who report to the director. Staff previously employed by the partner that is not the fiscal agent may become employees of the fiscal agent, and in that case the specifics of a change of employment including salaries, benefits, seniority, and other terms and conditions must be worked out. The governing board sets the schedule of operation and other policies to meet the needs of both partners.

In a third staffing model, codirectors hired by each partner share the responsibility for managing the library. Each partner has employees working together under the direction of their respective codirector in the shared library. In these cases, issues of differing methods and standards for performance evaluation, varying job descriptions, career paths and pay scales, arise and must be dealt with. In addition, a staffing model that has employees of two jurisdictions working together requires that the codirectors and employees be flexible enough to create a shared organizational culture while participating effectively in the cultures of their parent institutions. It is essential that the codirectors be committed to the success of the shared library and can work as a team. Although administratively the most complex of the options, each of the codirectors is responsible for ensuring that the needs of their users and partner organization are met.[5]

ORGANIZATIONAL MODELS OF MANAGEMENT

University/Public Joint Libraries

Within the parameters of the various definitions given for shared libraries, a variety of university/public library models have been developed. NOVA Southeastern University, a private university, administers the Alvin Sherman Library, Research, and Information Technology Center, an integrated joint-use library with Broward County Public

Library system. In this scenario, the University manages the large shared facility including supervision of all staff and librarians who have become university employees. The County provided funding for the construction of the building, which opened in 2001 and provides funding to the University for operating expenses. All services and programs, as well as access to all collections, are available for all members of the community, both the university community and the Broward County community at large.

In St. Paul, Minneapolis, the Metropolitan State University Library and the Dayton's Bluff Branch of the Saint Paul Public Library System, cohabitate within a shared-use library facility. In this model, each of the library organizations controls, staffs, and manages their respective collections, services, programs, and other functions. Although library users aged 13 and up have reciprocal borrowing privileges from both collections, there are two circulation desks and two library cards. This model, where the public library leases space in the building from the University, is characterized as a partnership and not a merger.

A third model, unique to the previous two examples, is the Dr. Martin Luther King, Jr., Library (King Library), a partnership between the San José State University Library and the San José Public Library (Fig. 1). Like the Metropolitan State University Library and the City of St. Paul, the university library and the public library have retained their autonomy and identity as a university and a public library organization, respectively. However, like NOVA Southeastern University and Broward County Public Library, the libraries have merged services, programs, collections, and most significantly, staffing in four of the major functional areas of the library—circulation, information technology, reference, and technical services. All library users have access to all collections and reciprocal borrowing privileges, as well as use of the entire building. This hybrid model, where the shared library space is comanaged by two distinct and autonomous library organizations, is the largest such library in the world.

Joint School/Public Libraries

The most common type of joint-use library is the public school/public library combination. Research shows that there are common issues, advantages, and disadvantages to these partnerships, whether in the United States, Canada, or Australia. As with any type of library, the school library and the public library have missions and goals that are unique to their community, as it is defined. A public school librarian's goals are to support the school curriculum and to collaborate with classroom teachers to teach information literacy across the curriculum. The public library has a much broader mission—that of providing access to information, recreational resources, and lifelong learning for the entire community, not just the school-aged. Although these

Fig. 1 Photograph of Dr. Martin Luther King Jr., Library, joint university and public library, San José, California.

distinct missions can create tensions within a joint library, many such libraries have been highly successful. Dr. Ken Haycock identifies 10 criteria for potential success including the necessity for a legal written document, one librarian in charge of the library, a fully integrated facility, and a single independent decision-making board among others.[6]

JOINT LIBRARIES AROUND THE WORLD

South Australia has been a leader in the world in developing joint-use libraries and formulating strong public policy that supports school/community libraries. In addition to Australia, New Zealand, Sweden, and Canada, there is ongoing development and planning of such partnerships in England and Scotland. Although the United States has had school/public shared-use libraries since the early twentieth century, with the exception of the joint libraries in Florida and the San José model, the development of new joint-use libraries has been slow.

JOINT LIBRARIES AS REPLICABLE MODELS

The question regarding joint-use libraries that needs to be addressed is whether the models that now exist, as varied and unique as they are, can be replicated in other settings. The Dr. Martin Luther King, Jr., Library in San José, California, receives visitors from around the nation and the world. The impetus for many of these visits is a desire

on the part of a municipal official or university administrator who seeks to explore the idea of a joint library as a means to mitigate the costs of building a new library facility for their constituency. After 4 years, the King Library remains the largest joint library in the world and the number of joint university and public libraries has not grown significantly. Will the joint libraries now in existence serve as models for future development? Will other large metropolitan city libraries partner with large university libraries, thus building on the NOVA Southeastern University and San José State University partnerships with the public library systems in their regions? If this does not come to pass it may be because the joint library phenomenon is tied to the specifics of the region, the organizations, and the leadership at a given time in the history of the community. In each of the joint libraries that have been developed in the United States in recent years, there have been strong local leaders and unique regional factors that made the project both feasible and ultimately successful.

EVALUATION AND ASSESSMENT

Evaluation and assessment of libraries, their services, programming, access, collections, and relevance to library users is essential for creating truly library-user centered libraries. Academic libraries as integral players in the educational institutions within which they serve have been moving from identifying inputs and outputs to becoming more outcomes based. Joint libraries, regardless of the management model, are complex organizations requiring significant attention and intentionality with all decisions and new initiatives, whether they are specific to one or the other of the organizations, or to the joint operation. Evaluation and assessment in this context requires that not only the success of the joint library must be evaluated, but also the effectiveness of the services and support to the home constituency must also be examined critically. In order for the joint library to be successful, the service to the individual constituencies must be as good as or better than it was before the partnership. The Dr. Martin Luther King Jr., Library made provisions for the evaluation of the effectiveness of the merger well before the library opened. Surveys were conducted to measure the satisfaction level of library users prior to the merger and then twice after the merger. Overall, customer perceptions of the library programs had improved after the merger. As the library now begins to develop a more user-centric philosophy of service, a new approach to evaluation will be needed.

PUBLIC POLICY AND JOINT-USE LIBRARIES

Joint libraries have prospered in regions where public policy makers have advocated for such partnerships. This has occurred in South Australia, the United Kingdom, and in the United States. For example, in the United Kingdom, public policy actions have supported the development of many new joint libraries in the recent years. These joint initiatives are seen as politically attractive in light of New Labour policy initiatives.[7] Many of the joint-use libraries in the United States were initiated because of the expected cost savings and not because of explicitly stated public policy issues such as bridging the digital divide, building economic development in the community, the importance of a well-informed citizenry to participate in civic matters, the need to build social capital, or the public good inherent in providing lifelong learning opportunities for all of the community. As joint libraries evolve and demonstrate through research, evaluation, and assessment that the benefits to the communities are significant, these policy matters may become more explicit.

CONCLUSION

Shared libraries have developed around the world in response to local needs, strong and creative leadership, and actions of public policy makers. As these libraries evolve over time, and as new joint initiatives take shape, their efficacy will be determined. In each case, many of the same issues are of concern—those of staffing, budgeting, management, alignment of missions, development of policies and procedures, the use of emerging technologies to provide service, and access to collections. The benefits and opportunities, as well as the challenges that present themselves are considerable, thus making the joint library a significant institution in society.

REFERENCES

1. Bundy, A. Joint-use libraries—the ultimate form of cooperation. In *Planning the Modern Public Library Building*; McCabe, G., Kennedy, J., Eds.; Libraries Unlimited: Westport, CT, 2003; 129.
2. Haycock, K. Dual use libraries: guidelines for success. Libr. Trends **2006**, *54*(4), 488.
3. Bundy, A. Joint-use libraries—the ultimate form of cooperation. In *Planning the Modern Public Library Building*; McCabe, G., Kennedy, J., Eds.; Libraries Unlimited: Westport, CT, 2003; 137.
4. Sullivan, K. et al. Building the beginnings of a beautiful partnership. Libr. Trends **2006**, *54*(4), 573.
5. Call, I.S. Joint-use libraries: the issues—1997. Encycl. Libr. Inform. Sci. **1997**, *59*(suppl. 22), 268.
6. Haycock, K. Dual use libraries: guidelines for success. Libr. Trends **2006**, *54*(4), 492–493.
7. McNicol, S. What makes a joint-use library a community library?. Libr. Trends **2006**, *54*(4), 521.

BIBLIOGRAPHY

1. http://sjlibrary.org/ (accessed June 2007).
2. Breivik, P.S.; Budd, L.; Woods, R.F. We're married! The rewards and challenges of joint libraries. J. Acad. Librarianship **2005**, September *31*(5), 401–408.
3. Bundy, A. Joint-use libraries—The ultimate form of cooperation. In *Planning the Modern Public Library Building*; McCabe, G.B., Kennedy, J.R., Eds.; Libraries Unlimited: Westport, CT, 2003; http://www.library.unisa.edu.au/about/papers/jointuse.pdf (accessed June 28, 2007).
4. Bundy, A.; Amey, L. Libraries like no others: evaluating the performance and progress of joint use libraries. Libr. Trends **2006**, *54*(4), 501–518.
5. Call, I.S. Joint use libraries: the issues. Encycl. Libr. Info. Sci. **1997**, *59*(Suppl. 22), 265–276.
6. Childer, T. *San Jose King Library Metrics Project: Impacts of the Merger*, 2006; Unpublished internal report.
7. Conaway, P. Shared libraries. *Encyclopedia of Library and Information Science*, 2nd ed; Drake, M., Ed.; Marcel Dekker, Inc.: New York, 2003; Vol. 4, 2636–2642.
8. Dalton, P.; Elkin, J.; Hannaford, A. Joint use libraries as successful strategic alliances. Libr. Trends **2006**, *54*(4), 535–548.
9. Halverson, K.; Plotas, J. Creating and capitalizing on the town/gown relationship: an academic library and a public library form a community partnership. J. Acad. Librarianship **2006**, *32*(6), 624–629.
10. Haycock, K. Dual-use libraries: guidelines for success. Libr. Trends **2006**, *54*(4), 488–500.
11. Marie, K.L. One plus one equals three: joint-use libraries in urban areas—the ultimate form of library cooperation. Libr. Admin. Manage. **2007**, *21*(1), 23–28.

12. McNicol, S. What makes a joint use library a community library?. Libr. Trends **2006**, *54*(4), 519–534.

13. Peterson, C.A. Space Designed For Lifelong Learning: The Dr. Martin Luther King Jr. Joint-Use Library. Council on Library & Information Resources **2005**, February 56–65 http://www.clir.org/pubs/reports/pub129/peterson.html

(accessed January 3, 2006). Report no. 129 Retrieved January 3, 2006.

14. Smith, V. A further perspective on joint partnerships: a commentary on "Creating and Capitalizing on the Town/Gown Relationship.". J. Acad. Librarianship **2006**, *32*(6), 630–631.

Site Museums and Monuments

Destinee Kae Swanson
Adams Museum & House, Inc., Deadwood, South Dakota, U.S.A.

Abstract

This entry defines site museums and monuments and identifies the most commonly existing subtypes that fall within the definition of site museums and monuments. Examples of cultural patrimony from different regions of the world representing each type are included. The entry then provides a brief historical background, with specific reference to the role of site museums and monuments as agents of cultural unity and their subsequent vulnerability, particularly during times of war. This entry will also address legislation passed and organizations founded in the effort to protect the world's sites of cultural heritage. The entry then proceeds with an overview of some of the controversial issues concerning interpretation and preservation faced today by site museums and monuments and those charged with administering them. It ends by touching on the future prospects of site museums and monuments in an environment of globalization.

INTRODUCTION

Site museums and monuments are specific geographic locations with definite boundaries directly associated with notable events, people, or patterns of history and recognized by a particular group or entire culture for their significance relating to the history or prehistory of humankind. They are essentially institutions of public service and exist in the capacity of commemoration and/or education. As a result, these sites of cultural patrimony are often interpreted for the public through accompanying plaques, informational panels, related exhibits, or docent-led tours. Site museums and monuments exist in a variety of forms and types including commemorative monuments, structures, and landscapes; on-site museums (including house museums); and living history sites; some defy classification as a single type, embracing features or characteristics of two or more. Many are considered notable based on their status as the first, only, or oldest existing examples of their kind, but site museums and monuments hold especial value to societies and cultures for their authenticity of material and place—it is at such sites that visitors feel a mental and physical connection to the peoples and events of the past. Roy Rosenzweig and David Thelen explore the ways in which people, particularly Americans, use history in their daily lives and discuss the value of authenticity and immediacy that people associate with historic sites and museums as a central theme in their book, *The Presence of the Past: Popular Uses of History in American Life* (p. 12, 32, 105–106).[1]

This entry will discuss in broad terms the most widely represented types of site museums and monuments in the world today, with accompanying definitions and specific examples of each type. It will then provide a brief historical background, with specific reference to the role of site museums and monuments as agents of cultural unity and their vulnerability, particularly during times of war. This section will also address legislation passed and societies formed in the effort to protect the world's sites of cultural heritage. The entry will end with an overview of some of the controversial issues concerning interpretation and preservation faced today by site museums and monuments and those charged with administering them.

TYPES OF SITE MUSEUMS AND MONUMENTS

Commemorative Site Monuments and Landscapes

Commemorative monuments, structures, and landscapes are statuary (memorial statuary can take many different forms, e.g., cairns, cenotaphs, obelisks, and shrines) and architectural or geographic features situated on the original site of the commemorated event or a location directly associated with a notable person or a representative instance of a pattern of history. They are erected, preserved, or simply regarded by a collective body of people as a tribute or memorial to a historic event or personage, or as an extant example of a historic type or pattern. Interpretative text often accompanies these sites in an effort to formally communicate their intention, although many stand unaided by written explanation and are able to rely on the weight of their prominence, oral tradition, or other methods to convey their purpose. A closer examination of each subcategory listed above through specific examples will help illustrate the form and function of this class of cultural patrimony.

Commemorative site monument

Commemorative site monuments are man-made statuary, signage, or structures intended to indicate and memorialize

Encyclopedia of Library and Information Sciences, Fourth Edition DOI: 10.1081/E-ELIS4-120044098

Semiotics–Slovakia

either the actual geographic location of a historic event or a specific site associated with the activities of a notable person or pattern of history. The Monument to the Great Fire of London, commonly known as simply "The Monument," is a large-scale example of this type of cultural patrimony. The Monument was built in England near the site where the infamous fire of 1666 that razed London ignited, and was meant to forever symbolize the rebirth of the scorched cityscape. Construction of the 202-foot tall Doric column of Portland stone crowned by a gilded urn of fire was completed in 1677, and it has withstood the ravages of time, weather, and war with only routine maintenance and periodic repair. The sides of the monument feature relief carvings depicting the resulting destruction of the city, members of the Royal family at the time of the Great Fire, and other images and text chronicling this traumatic time in English history. This colossal column is a highly visible, permanent reminder of a city's resilience, and a wonderful example of a commemorative monument and structure. For further information on The Monument to the Great Fire of London, currently in the midst of routine repairs, refer to the Monument's Web site.[2]

Commemorative landscape

A commemorative landscape is a geographic area or feature with demarcated boundaries that is protected, preserved, or restored as a memorial to a directly associated event, person, or instance of a historical pattern; original and/or reconstructed architectural features and related monumental statuary are often present within their borders. The Homestead National Monument of America is a case in point of a commemorative landscape complex. This 163-acre site, administered by the National Park Service of the United States, is a tribute to westward migration and the settling of the frontier—a key period of American history. The Homestead National Monument preserves the original site in southeastern Nebraska of one of the first claims filed under the Homestead Act of 1862. The significance of the site has long been recognized; it was signed into legislative existence in 1936 by President Roosevelt. Several structures deemed to add depth to the site's story have since been added to the complex, including an 1867 log cabin from a neighboring homestead and an original one-room schoolhouse. Special events and school programs assist in educating the public about the historical meaning behind the Homestead National Monument. The National Park Service (NPS) of the United States, established in 1916 as a branch of the U.S. Department of the Interior, administers hundreds of historic sites across the country. For an excellent, albeit somewhat dated, narrative of the formation of NPS see Albright.[3] For site directions, hours of operation, and other pertinent information, refer to the National Park Service's Web site.[4]

Site Museums

A site museum is an edifice or locale situated on the actual geographic location of a directly associated event, person, or instance of a historical pattern; furthermore, it is a structure erected or a site protected in an effort to preserve the historical context for which the location is recognized as significant to the history or prehistory of humankind. Many site museums incorporate original architectural or artifactual archaeological components, while others utilize reproductions of originals that were not viable or new construction specifically tailored to preservational or educational purposes. Site museums can take several forms, from the traditional museum, to house museums, to active and inactive archaeological sites, to living history sites and complexes. A separate definition and accompanying example of each will better clarify this category of site museums and monuments.

Traditional site museum

A traditional site museum is an architectural feature preserved or designed for the purpose of commemorating, protecting, or promoting (either educationally or otherwise) a directly associated event, person, or instance of a historical pattern. They often house and/or interpret original artifacts or facsimiles of original artifacts from or relating to the associated event, person, or instance of a historical pattern. The National Civil Rights Museum is a prominent institution that aptly illustrates the form and function of a traditional site museum. The museum is housed in the former Lorraine Motel in Memphis, Tennessee (United States) where celebrated civil rights activist Martin Luther King, Jr., was assassinated in 1968. Officially opened to visitors in 1991, the National Civil Rights Museum incorporates authentic King artifacts, as well as other tokens and mementos related to both the national and global human rights movements. Here, the Martin Luther King narrative is used as a lens through which to tell the larger story of the global struggle for human rights. The creation of the museum served the dual purpose of ensuring that this historic property is preserved (the Lorraine Motel was a foreclosed property by 1982) and that its story is disseminated to the public. In this way, the National Civil Rights Museum is a wonderful example of a site museum that uses the authenticity and emotional weight of an actual historic site as the foundation for a larger commemorative or educational goal. For the most current information pertaining to this institution, refer to the National Civil Rights Museum's Web site.[5]

House museums

A house museum is a domestic structure that is directly associated with a historically significant person or family or exists as an outstanding example of architecture and is preserved for a commemorative or educational purpose; house museums generally hold and interpret original artifacts or facsimiles of original artifacts that formerly belonged or are related to the associated person or persons, or artifacts known to be contemporary to the structure's identified period of significance. The house museum movement is a flourishing aspect of historic preservation; the success of George Washington's Mt. Vernon under the leadership of Ann Pamela Cunningham is often recognized as the impetus for the popularity of the house museum in the United States. For an excellent summary of the house museum movement in the United States, with a particular focus on the contributions of women, see West.[6]

The Historic Adams House in Deadwood, South Dakota (United States), pictured in Fig. 1, is an 1892 Victorian mansion that has served as a house museum as defined in this paragraph since 2000. It is dedicated to the legacy of the families of Harris Franklin and W.E. Adams, both influential and philanthropic local businessmen and civic leaders who were among the first to arrive in the fledging gold camp of Deadwood—they are significant players in local history and, furthermore, their stories stand as excellent case studies of the industrious and successful Western entrepreneur. The artifact collection contained within and displayed at the Historic Adams House represents a nearly complete assemblage of domestic goods original to the structure that is used to tell the often-obscured story of Deadwood as a civilized oasis on the edge of the Western frontier. The contents of the Adams House are arranged much like they would have been when it was still a private residence, an interpretative technique employed often in house museums. House museums like the Historic Adams House reveal the more intimate details of history that are often excluded from other museum environments. Mary Kopco, *The Adams House Revealed* is a concise history of the Adams House

Fig. 1 The Historic Adams House in Deadwood, South Dakota (United States), former private residence and now house museum with an associated artifact collection interpreted for the visiting public through docent-led tours. (Photograph courtesy of the Historic Adams House, Deadwood, South Dakota.)

and its inhabitants, including a detailed description of the $1.5 million museum-quality restoration it underwent before opening its doors to the public.[7]

For those interested in further exploring the house museum genre, see Donnolley.[8] This compilation of essays explores various interpretative techniques employed by those who administer these institutions. For a European example, see the Brontë Parsonage Museum and Brontë Society's Web site[9] for information on the Brontë Parsonage Museum, a house museum located in Yorkshire (United Kingdom) that is preserved to both honor the memory of this famous family of nineteenth century literary giants and to educate the public about their private lives.

Outdoor Museums/Living History Sites

An outdoor museum or living history site (the two terms can be used interchangeably) is an original or reconstructed historic structure or complex of such associated structures that are used as an educational setting to present the visiting public with interpretative reenactments and displays of activities contemporary to the site's period of historic significance. Costumed interpreters are the most common medium used to convey information and conduct demonstrations for visitors. In order to be classified as a site museum, the outdoor museum must be located on the geographic location where the performed activities or reenactments actually took place at some point in the past, and must incorporate the original associated structures or facsimiles thereof. Many credit Sweden's Artur Hazelius as the pioneering force behind the outdoor museum; his Nordic Museum opened in the 1890s and utilized artifacts and representations of the past in an effort to instill native visitors with national pride. A short discussion of Hazelius' influence can be found in Murtagh.[10]

Colonial Williamsburg is perhaps the most well-known outdoor museum in the world. Situated on the location of the pre-Revolutionary capital of Virginia (United States), Colonial Williamsburg is a designated historic district within the larger city of Williamsburg. This expansive site museum encompasses 300 acres and 500 buildings (only 88 of which are contemporary to the interpreted time period, the rest are reconstructions). Visitors to the site can walk the streets and enter various structures to observe and interact with costumed interpreters who perform skilled trades, such as blacksmithing and millinery, as well as other activities that constituted daily life in the colonial era. From its beginnings, this ever-expanding cultural complex was intended to inculcate national pride and an appreciation for the merits of American democracy, seen by many to have roots in the colonial center of Williamsburg. While many experts would argue that Colonial Williamsburg does not present an accurate picture of the colonial landscape or colonial life, it remains a popular destination for thousands of visitors each year who seek to take a step into the past. Recent interpretative additions include a focus on the realities of life for Blacks under slavery, a sensitive issue that must be addressed accurately and fully, yet with sensitivity to those who must play the part of this exploited segment of society. Living history sites, when based on sound research and carried out with careful attention to detail, can serve as an invaluable purveyor of historical awareness for those who find traditional museums tedious and cerebral.

For the story of Williamsburg's colonial and early American prominence, its subsequent decay, and recent rise, see Kopper.[11] For a pictorial chronicle of Colonial Williamsburg's transformation from a decaying twentieth century city to a restored step-back-in-time, refer to Yetter.[12] Colonial Williamsburg has an in-depth Internet site that contains, among other features, a brief history of this outdoor museum, a virtual tour, and an online scholarly journal publication; refer to Colonial Williamsburg's Web site.[13]

Archaeological site museum

An archaeological site museum is an active or inactive archaeology site with an associated interpretative element (such as interpretative panels or placards or an on-site museum) protected, preserved, and at least periodically open to the public. (An archaeology site is a bounded geographic location that contains evidence of humankind's presence that is recorded and studied using scientific and historical methods. An active archaeology site is one that is the subject of ongoing research through continuing recordation and/or excavation; an inactive archaeology site is one that is not the subject of active research necessitating sustained onsite recordation and/or excavation.) Because they are accessible to the public, even if on a limited basis, archaeological site museums are especially vulnerable to the dangers of site looting and destruction—often by collectors who are aware of the value of archaeological artifacts in the underground economy. For this reason, those who administer archaeological site museums often employ such protective measures as observation decks or viewing windows that distance the visitor from the actual site. For an examination of the hazards faced by valuable cultural artifacts, refer to Brodie.[14]

The Pella Archaeological Site and Museum in Macedonia (Greece) is a captivating example of an inactive archaeological site museum. Visitors to Pella are presented with both an organic view of Grecian history through access to the original archaeological site, as well as an academically interpreted version of the evidence in the associated museum. The publicly accessible archaeological components at Pella allow visitors to view ancient Greek architectural features as originally uncovered by archaeologists,

some of which still contain intricate clay-tile mosaics. The associated museum, originally built in 1960 to house the artifacts excavated from Pella and the surrounding countryside and opened to the public in 1973, is located directly across the road from the archaeological site. Here visitors can view photographs and sketches resulting from archaeological digs that took place on-site and nearby, as well as original artifacts and facsimiles; they can also learn about the lives of the prosperous Macedonians who inhabited the site through interpretative text and panels. Several online sites are available that provide information about and photographs of the Pella Archaeological Site and Museum.[15,16]

Active archaeological sites that are also open to the public present a unique educational experience for visitors. The Town Creek Indian Mound Historic Site in North Carolina (United States) is a case in point. Comprehensive excavation at this American Indian ceremonial site commenced in 1937 and persisted for 50 continuous years, with intermittent archaeological research still carried out on a reduced scale—area students are yet able to take advantage of the opportunities presented by this culturally rich and artifactually dense site. In the 1950s and the 1960s, several key features identified by archaeologists at the Town Creek site were reconstructed using information gathered from the ongoing investigation; today, visitors can walk through the original landscape and view a ceremonial earthen mound, burial house, two temples, and the surrounding stockade. An on-site museum displaying actual excavated artifacts acquaints visitors with the history and culture represented by the Mound and serves as a gatehouse regulating entry into the site. Active archaeological site museums like North Carolina's Town Creek Indian Mound are able to educate the public on many different levels and in many different ways; they have something to offer everyone, from the casual history enthusiast to the graduate-level anthropologist and archaeologist. Archaeological, anthropological, and scientific information gathered at the Town Creek Indian Mound Historic Site has been the basis for much scholarship. For a comprehensive overview detailing the history of the site, from research methodologies employed to conclusions drawn, refer to Coe.[17,18]

Impact of archaeology on site museums and monuments: Although archaeological sites are often points of interest and a destination in and of themselves, many other sites have employed archaeological research methods for the purpose of gathering artifactual evidence; this evidence is then used to formulate a more complete understanding of the historic context at the site under investigation. To archaeologists, artifacts and monuments are an archive of past human activity, and are used in tandem with other historical and scientific sources to draw conclusions about the peoples, events, and recurring patterns of the past associated with the site. These conclusions are then used in various ways; sometimes they are simply conveyed to the public through narratives during tours and on interpretative panels, sometimes they are used as a basis for the reenactment of events and activities contemporary to the site (such as at living history sites), and sometimes they are used in efforts to reconstruct ruins and no longer existing architectural features and structures. In many ways, archaeology research methods remain central to the interpretation of the world's historic sites and structures. For an example of archaeology used in a practical manner, refer to Ford.[19] This article details how archaeologists and anthropologists in Britain used information obtained from archaeological excavations, along with environmental research, anthropology research, and comparisons with surviving contemporary structures to construct a blueprint to reconstruct the Silchester Church, which was to be used as a site museum upon completion.

HISTORICAL BACKGROUND

It would be impossible to create a comprehensive global timeline with specific dates and events chronicling the development of the site museum and monument as a cultural institution because they stand as universal features throughout place and time. The human phenomenon of commemoration crosses all boundaries of nationality, class, gender, sexual orientation, and religion; subsequently, site museums and monuments exist the world over, many are even thousands of years old. For these reasons, as well as in consideration of length constraints, we will limit our discussion of the historical background of the site museum and monument to a manageable time frame of roughly the last 200 years, written from the perspective of Western and, more specifically, European civilization and culture.

Site Museums and Monuments as Heritage

When discussing the reasons for societal interest in sites of cultural patrimony, including site museums and monuments, many scholars point to the emergence of the nation-state as a political and cultural entity as a major factor.[1,20] Now, people with different skin colors, who subscribed to different religions, and who were members of varying socioeconomic levels could identify with a larger group—one based strictly on the shared geographic boundary within which they lived. This new "nation" of otherwise divergent groups could develop yet deeper bonds on the basis of shared histories, made tangible in the form of site museums and monuments.[21] For example, the village of Oradour-sur-Glane, the French site of a 1944 invasion and massacre by Nazi invaders, was deemed a historic monument by the French parliament in 1946—just 2 years after the event took place. This village was preserved in its state of ruin to symbolize the collective instances of merciless destruction the French people suffered during World War II. Emotion-laden site museums

and monuments like Oradour-sur-Glane, be they mournful tributes or patriotic celebrations, serve as historical and cultural reference points around which groups of people can (literally and figuratively) gather. For an in-depth discussion of Oradour-sur-Glane as a commemorative landscape, refer to Farmer.[22]

Site Museums and Monuments as War Targets and Cultural Casualties

The cultural and emotional emphasis that individual nations and their peoples place on site museums and monuments have been, and continue to make them, prime targets during times of war, despite their often neutral meaning to those who seek to destroy them. Furthermore, the dangers faced by sites of cultural patrimony have grown exponentially with the historic emergence of "total war." Methods of combat that no longer avoid civilian areas or population-dense regions (where most historic sites and monuments are located) and advancements in weapons technology that make ultra long-range targeting effortless and exact place historic sites and monuments in escalating peril. As a case in point, the frequency of cultural casualties during the World Wars (particularly World War II and the Nazi-drive for world dominance), led to the coining of the phrase "martyred village," used to describe communities damaged by war. Oradour-sur-Glane, discussed earlier in this entry, is one such martyred village (see the section on "Site Museums and Monuments as Heritage").

Initially, nation-states and communities employed protective defense measures to safeguard specific cultural sites they perceived as most in danger; such tactics included removal and storage of stained glass and other fragile features and reinforcement of walls. But these methods soon proved ineffective. Cooperative treaties and other methods of international legislation were then put in place in an attempt to decrease cultural destruction. The most well-known examples are the successive global conferences known as the Hague Conventions, held in the Netherlands. Negotiations within the Hague Convention for the Protection of Cultural Property in the Event of Armed Conflict, held in 1954, led to treaties regulating the conduct of hostile enemies against and within the boundaries of those they oppose—specifically relating to those properties held as culturally significant by the nation on the defensive. Although conventions, agreements, treaties, and legislation have proved anything but failsafe in the ongoing effort to preserve the world's cultural heritage, they are a step in the right direction. For an examination and analysis of the destruction of sites of cultural patrimony during wartime, with a particular focus on Western Europe during and as a result of World War II, refer to Murtagh.[23] For a more modern example, see Sturges,[24] which includes a discussion of cultural destruction inflicted during the Balkan wars of the 1990s.

United States Federal Preservation Legislation

A society's values are reflected in the laws they formalize and regulate. So, by singling out legislation that directly pertains to the protection, preservation, and control of sites of cultural patrimony, we are able to see the recognition that site museums and monuments have gained nationally.

In the United States, a study of preservation-related laws shows that its leaders have identified America's cultural sites as vulnerable and in need of legislative safeguarding; U.S. law also illustrates the increased financial responsibility that the federal government has assumed to ensure the sustained existence of its cultural heritage. The Antiquities Act of 1906 was the forerunner to many later legislative acts in the United States. It gave the president the power to proclaim historically or scientifically significant public lands as national monuments, which simultaneously granted them federal protection and made them eligible for federal funding. The Antiquities Act of 1906 was a direct result of former United States' President Theodore Roosevelt's efforts to save prehistoric ruins and archaeological sites in the Southwest from destruction and looting.[23] Ten years later, the National Park Service Act of 1916 created the National Park Service to administer sites considered too large or too expensive for adequate private protection and preservation. The National Park Service is today an intricate agency that oversees over 80 million acres of public land in the United States—including many site museums and monuments.[25]

Probably the most significant piece of American legislation related to preservation is the 1966 National Historic Preservation Act. This act required that those planning any construction projects that rely in whole or in part on government funding must evaluate any possible impact the project may have on historical or archaeological sites (including those that could be defined as site museums and monuments) before any construction actually begins. (To download the complete text of the National Historic Preservation Act, last amended in 2000, go to "The National Historic Preservation Act of 1966, As Amended."[26] For a summary of Section 106 regulations, refer to "Section 106 Regulations Summary."[27]) The 1966 Act has served as a springboard for the formation of several other key preservation landmarks—such as the ever-expanding lists of the National Register of Historic Places and National Historic Landmarks and the post of State Historic Preservation Officer; all of which are dedicated to the identification, evaluation, and protection of America's cultural heritage. For a closer look at the history, key figures, and important legislation of the American preservation movement, refer to Stipe.[28]

Preservation Groups and Societies

In addition to federal legislation, several private and international groups and societies have been formed as part of the global effort to save sites of cultural heritage deemed significant to the history of humankind.

Cooperative efforts of private sector

One of the earliest private-sector preservation-minded groups that survives into the present day is the National Trust for Places of Historic Interest or Natural Beauty (more commonly known as simply "The National Trust"). Based in London (United Kingdom), The National Trust is a private charity started in 1895 dedicated to preserving and protecting cultural and environmental resources. As of today, it has over 3 million members and owns and oversees a collective area in excess of 623,000 acres (or 1.5% of the total land mass it serves in England, Wales, and Northern Ireland). National Trust properties include over 200 historic houses and gardens, many with associated collections. The inception and subsequent long-term success of the United Kingdom's National Trust has led to an American version, similarly titled the American National Trust for Historic Preservation. The American National Trust has a somewhat smaller preservational focus, forgoing an emphasis on natural landscapes to focus instead strictly on historic sites and communities. Since 1949, it has grown to include six regional offices and over 27,000 members. These two large and financially powerful organizations demonstrate the concern of the public sector over the need to preserve sites of cultural significance.[29,30]

International cooperative efforts

On an international level, the United Nations Educational, Scientific, and Cultural Organization (UNESCO), a United Nations' subsidiary organization, is a prominent example of cooperative steps taken between world powers to ensure the recognition and protection of human rights and freedoms. UNESCO was formed in 1945 on the heels of World War II and its accompanying worldwide destruction of human life and cultural property to encourage respect and collaboration between international powers. Since its inception, 198 nation-states have become voluntary members of UNESCO.[31]

A 1972 UNESCO convention established the list of World Heritage Sites in an effort to safeguard cultural and natural sites of "outstanding universal value" (as defined by internationally agreed-upon principles). The associated List of World Heritage in Danger identifies site of cultural patrimony that are threatened or impacted by natural, political, or other dangers, and provides funds to protect, preserve, and restore them. Many site museums and monuments in many parts of the world have benefited from UNESCO acknowledgment and financial backing. International efforts like UNESCO's embrace of World Heritage Sites are evidence of the growing global recognition of historic sites, monuments, and landscapes as vital cultural resources.[32]

Semiotics–Slovakia

ASSOCIATED CONTROVERSIAL ISSUES

Challenges of Interpretation

Site museums and monuments represent complex historical units, and there are countless different ways to view and interpret the historical meanings and human stories behind each site, and even more ways to convey these historical meanings and human stories to the public. Even sites that have been open for visitation for tens or even hundreds of years need to be periodically reevaluated in light of the latest research or restructured to accommodate current modes of thinking.

The freezing of time and landscapes

The overwhelming amount of historical information each site holds is often too complex for visitors to digest at one time; for this reason, those who administer most site museums and monuments focus on one key aspect, event, or time period associated with the site. The process of spotlighting one moment in time, an interpretative device often used at site museums and monuments, is sometimes referred to as "freezing time" or "landscape freezing"; and, although usually effective at simplifying a site's historical context, it is a technique that can also lead to the neglect (either intentionally or not) of other people or events that have also inhabited the same physical or historical space. To illustrate, landscape freezing is an interpretative technique often utilized at American Civil War battlefield sites. (For an examination of the contentious issue of landscape freezing in relation to a particular site, see Erika K. Martin.[33]) Here, a single day or event in history is spotlighted in a particular context, an interpretation sometimes erasing all acknowledgment of the people who lived, worked, and died natural deaths on the same physical space for generations prior to and after the Civil War. Historians agree that those site museum and monuments that employ the freezing of time or landscapes should reassess their interpretation to ensure that they are not overlooking people or events that audiences want or need in order to understand the significance of the site in an inclusive historical context.

Historical perspective

Site museums and monuments are cultural mediums that present the exciting opportunity of bringing to light histories and perspectives either purposely suppressed or pushed to the side in lieu of more popular or comforting depictions of associated events and peoples. Unfortunately, those who administer sites of cultural patrimony often choose to tell history from the perspective of the white male (sometimes obscuring or misrepresenting women and minorities in the process) or, worse yet, skim over or totally ignore parts of history that do not fit with either a political or personal agenda.

A famous example is Mount Vernon, the estate of American President George Washington located in Virginia (United States). This site monument only recently incorporated information on the realities of slavery, based in part on archaeological evidence, into their long-standing interpretation that had previously focused on the glorification of President Washington and his family.[34] Earlier presentations of history at Mount Vernon had avoided the topic of slavery, probably because it did not fit their profile of Washington as a dedicated and progressive statesman.

Those who visit site museums and monuments are reminded to consider that the presentations of history at these sites are constructed by fallible people, even if they are considered experts, and, as result, their interpretation of a site may be incomplete or biased. Visitors who are interested in the whole story should ask questions, view the evidence, and form their own conclusions.

Preservation Controversies

Identifying a cultural site, including those that fit the definition of site museum or monument, is the easy part of historic preservation; the difficult part is deciding how exactly to preserve that site, often a contentious and complicated process.

The restoration vs. original controversy

There are several schools of thought in the preservation field regarding the correct way to manage historic sites, structures, and monuments. Perhaps the most prevalent debate centers on the divergent methods of what could be termed "preventative preservation" and it's preservational opposite of "active conservation." Preventative preservation is the more organic approach to site management in which the genuine state of cultural patrimony is viewed as the most authentic and capable of conveying historic truth. Those who administer these sites focus their attention on retaining the original fabric and form. The only active measures taken at sites maintained under the tenets of preventative preservation are those intended to protect them from threats outside the scope of natural weathering, such as demolition or modern alteration.

In opposition to preventative preservation, the main objective of active conservation is returning a historic site, structure, or monument to its state during its recognized period of significance; it is a process that often involves restoration and/or reconstruction. The restored or reconstructed feature is often based on careful study of the historic and archaeological record; in many cases the untrained eye would never be able to point out the facsimile from the original.

Preservational purists argue that conservation is actually a type of destruction in which the authenticity of cultural heritage is compromised by the addition of artificial elements—even if they are exact copies of originals. Furthermore, many archaeologists look upon restoration as destroying the value of the sites as locales of viable artifactual documentation.[35] On the other hand, advocates of restoration contend that the viewer will gain a more complete understanding of history if they are able to see things "as they were," in addition to the more simple argument that restored sites are more aesthetically pleasing. Of course, preventative preservation and active conservation are extreme opposites, and a balance can be achieved by the resourceful preservationist who takes into account both sides of the debate.

Eastern vs. Western: The cultural factor

When examining the appearance, condition, and intended function of site museums and monuments worldwide, one must take into consideration the varying cultural beliefs and ideals that they represent. As an illustration of cultural disparities, let us look at a few global models through the eyes of a contemporary United States preservationist.

In the ancient Buddhist tradition of Sri Lanka, it was considered a commendable fulfillment of custom to carry out routine repair and maintenance of religious structures, which were built with the expectation that they would exist in perpetuity. This set of beliefs carries over into Buddhist tradition today, suggesting that, according to Western preservational notions, no Buddhist religious building is wholly original or authentic.[35] Next, let us consider current Brazilian culture in which the push for modernity consumes all aspects of society, and evidence of the antiquated past and native peoples is seen as negative. As a result, the demolition of structures Western preservationists would see as historically meaningful is freely carried out to make way for contemporary architecture.[36]

These two simplified cultural scenarios exemplify the notion that the preservation of cultural patrimony, including site museums and monuments, is not simply a matter of applying a standard set of universal rules. The ideals and traditions of all cultures must be respected, even if they do not align with our current belief system.

CONCLUSION

This entry has defined, with specific examples, the different types of site museums and monuments that are represented throughout the world, provided a brief historical background explaining the source of their significance, and, finally, presented a synopsis of some of the challenges of preservation and interpretation that they present. Readers will come away with an appreciation for the variety in form and function of these sites as a reflection of the diverse cultures that value them. Site museums and monuments exist as physical evidence of what a society perceives as worth saving, those monuments, landscapes, and sites that they feel are integral to their sense of self and their history.[37]

With the modern phenomenon of globalization (made possible by advances in science and technology), distances seem shorter and the world seems smaller; as a result, the human community has begun to realize that although their collective history has many different chapters in many different languages, it is all part of a story that must be saved.

REFERENCES

1. Rosenzweig, R.; Thelen, D. *The Presence of the Past: Popular Uses of History in American Life*; Columbia University Press: New York, 1998.
2. *The Monument: Great Fire of London 1666*. Available at http://www.themonument.info/index.html.
3. Albright, H.M. *The Birth of the National Park Service: The Founding Years, 1913–1933*; Howe Brothers: Salt Lake City, 1985.
4. *National Park Service, U.S. Department of the Interior: Homestead National Monument of America*. http://www.nps.gov/home/.
5. *National Civil Rights Museum*. http://www.civilrightsmuseum.org/.
6. West, P. *Domesticating History: The Political Origins of America's House Museums*; Smithsonian: Washington, DC, 1999.
7. Kopco, M.A. *The Adams House Revealed: The Restoration of a Historic Home*; Adams Museum & House, Inc.: Deadwood, SD, 2006.
8. Donnolley, J.F. *Interpreting Historic House Museums*; AltaMira Press: Walnut Creek, CA, 2003.
9. *The Brontë Parsonage Museum and Brontë Society*. Available at http://www.bronte.org.uk/.
10. Murtagh, W.J. Outdoor museums. In *Keeping Time: The History and Theory of Preservation in America*; Murtagh, W.J., Ed.; John Wiley & Sons, Inc.: Hoboken, NJ, 2006; 75–86.
11. Kopper, P. *Colonial Williamsburg, Revised*; Henry N. Abrams, Inc., Publishers: New York, 2001.
12. Yetter, G.H. *Williamsburg Before and After: The Rebirth of Virginia's Colonial Capital*; Colonial Williamsburg Foundation: Williamsburg, VA, 2004.
13. Colonial Williamsburg. Available at http://history.org/.
14. Brodie, N. *Illicit Antiquities: The Theft of Culture and Extinction of Archaeology*; One World Archaeology Series; Routledge: New York, 2002.
15. *Pella: Nature that Gave Birth to History*. http://www.pella.gr/pella_museumengl.htm .
16. *The Museums of Macedonia: Archaeological Museum, Pella*. http://www.macedonian-heritage.gr/Museums/Archaeological_and_Byzantine/Arx_Pellas.html.

17. Coe, J.L.; Burke, T.D.; Hogue, S.H.; Oliver, B.L.; South, S.; Trinkley, M.; Wilson, J.H. *Town Creek Indian Mound: A Native American Legacy*; University of North Carolina Press: Chapel Hill, NC, 1995.

18. *Historic Sites: Town Creek Indian Mound.* http://www.ah. dcr.state.nc.us/sections/hs/town/town.htm. *North Carolina.*

19. Ford, S.D. Silchester church: a dimensional analysis and a new reconstruction. Britannia **1994**, *25*, 119–126.

20. Lambourne, N. *War Damage in Western Europe: The Destruction of Historic Monuments During the Second World War*; Edinburgh University Press: Edinburgh, 2001.

21. Shackel, P., Ed. *Myth, Memory, and the Making of the American Landscape*; University Press of Florida: Gainesville, FL, 2001.

22. Farmer, S.B. Oradour-sur-Glane: memory in a preserved landscape. Fr. Hist. Stud. **1995**, *19*(1), 27–47.

23. Murtagh, W.J. *Keeping Time: The History and Theory of Preservation in America*; John Wiley & Sons, Inc.: Hoboken, NJ, 2006.

24. Sturges, P.; Rosenberg, D. *Disaster and After: The Practicalities of Information Service in Times of War and Other Catastrophes*; Taylor Graham: Los Angeles, CA, 1999.

25. *National Park Service, U.S. Department of the Interior.* http://www.nps.gov/.

26. *Advisory Council on Historic Preservation: The National Historic Preservation Act of 1966, As Amended.* http://www.achp.gov/nhpa.html.

27. Advisory Council on Historic Preservation: Section 106 Regulations Summary. http://www.achp.gov/106summary. html.

28. Stipe, R.E., Ed. *A Richer Heritage: Historic Preservation in the Twenty-First Century*; University of North Carolina Press: Chapel Hill, NC, 2003.

29. *The National Trust.* http://www.nationaltrust.org.uk/main/.

30. *National Trust for Historic Preservation.* http://www.nationaltrust.org/.

31. *United Nations Educational, Scientific and Cultural Organization.* http://www.unesco.org/.

32. World Heritage Site. Encyclopedia Britannica 2007 *Encyclopedia Britannica Online*. Available at http://search.eb.com/eb/article-9077491.

33. Sibert, E.K.M. The third battle of Manassas: Power, identity, and the forgotten African-American past. In *Myth, Memory, and the Making of the American Landscape*; Shackel, P., Ed.; University Press of Florida: Gainesville, FL, 2001; 67–84.

34. Beasley, J. The birthplace of a chief: Archaeology and meaning at George Washington birthplace national monument. In *Myth, Memory, and the Making of the American Landscape*; Shackel, P., Ed.; University Press of Florida: Gainesville, FL, 2001; 197–220.

35. Wijesuriya, G. Pious vandals: Restoration or destruction in Sri Lanka?. In *Destruction and Conservation of Cultural Property*; Layton, R.; Stone, P.G.; Thomas, J., Eds.; Routledge: London, 2001; 256–263.

36. Funari, P.P.A. Destruction and conservation of cultural property in Brazil: academic and practical challenges. In *Destruction and Conservation of Cultural Property*; Layton, R.; Stone, P.G.; Thomas, J., Eds.; Routledge: London, 2001; 93–101.

37. Sullivan, R. Evaluating the ethics and consciences of museum (1994). In *Reinventing the Museum: Historical and Contemporary Perspectives on the Paradigm Shift*; Anderson, G., Ed.; Rowman and Littlefield Publishers, Inc.: Lanham, MD, 2004; 257–263.

BIBLIOGRAPHY

1. Chambers, S.A. *National Landmarks, America's Treasures: The National Park Foundation's Complete Guide to National Historic Landmarks*; Preservation Press Series, John Wiley & Sons, Inc.: Hoboken, NJ, 1999.

2. Greeves, L. *History and Landscape: The Guide to National Trust Properties in England, Wales, and Northern Ireland*; The National Trust: London, 2006.

3. Kreps, C. *Liberating Culture: Cross-Cultural Perspectives on Museums, Curation, and Heritage Preservation*; Routledge: New York, 2003.

4. Messenger, P.M., Ed. *The Ethics of Collecting Cultural Property*; University of New Mexico Press: Albuquerque, NM, 1999.

5. Page, M. *Giving Preservation a History: Histories of Historic Preservation in the United States*; Routledge: New York, 2003.

6. Preziosi, D.; Farago, C. *Grasping the World: The Idea of the Museum*; Ashgate Publishing Co.: Burlington, VT, 2004.

Slovakia: Libraries, Archives, and Museums

Jela Steinerová
Department of Library and Information Science, Comenius University in, Bratislava, Slovak Republic

Juraj Roháč
Department of Archival Science and Auxiliary Historical Sciences, Comenius University in, Bratislava, Slovak Republic

Gabriela Podušelová
Slovak National Museum, Bratislava, Slovak Republic

Abstract

This entry presents a brief cultural history of Slovakia while concentrating on the development of libraries, archives, and museums and the related disciplines. An overview is provided of the multiple kinds of libraries, museums, and archives with particular attention given to major representative examples. The history of relevant legislation and policy is provided along with a discussion of the contemporary legislative environment. In conclusion, the tendency toward collaboration of libraries, archives, and museums is emphasized. Future plans for libraries, archives, and museums concentrate on national projects of cultural heritage digitization and building of digital cultural portals.

INTRODUCTION

The goal of this entry is to present the development of the cultural institutions of libraries, archives, and museums in Slovakia. A brief historical background is provided that highlights a few facts and events that have had an impact on literacy and culture in Slovakia. Library systems, networks of public archives, and networks of museums and galleries are presented as part of cultural life of the Slovak people. The main sections of the text discuss libraries, archives, and museums and their respective professions. Each section provides a brief historical overview, an outline of relevant legislation, and an introduction to some of the major cultural institutions. In conclusion, we emphasize the digitization activities in the cultural sector in Slovakia. The three types of institutions are converging through the development of national digital projects of cultural heritage, of specialized digital portals, and in an integrated portal of culture.

Brief Historical, Geographic, Economic, and Sociocultural Context

Slovakia (Slovenská republika, Slovak Republic) is a state in Central Europe situated in the Carpathian Basin, between the Danube River in the south and the Tatra Mountains in the north, which are part of the Carpathian mountain range. Slovakia shares borders with Poland to the north, the Czech Republic to the west, Hungary and Austria to the south, and with Ukraine to the east. The multicultural composition of the population is a result of Slovakia's geographic location: Slovaks (86%), Hungarians (9.7%), Roma, Czechs, etc. At present Slovakia has over 5.4 million inhabitants and its geographic area represents 48, 845 km^2. Slovakia is a parliamentary democratic republic. It is administratively divided into 8 regions and 79 districts. The regions are represented by larger cities such as Bratislava, Trnava, Nitra, Trenčín, Žilina, Banská Bystrica, Prešov, and Košice. The capital and the center of political, economic, cultural, and university life is Bratislava. After many transformations the present economic development has been marked by positive growth, especially since 2000 (Fig. 1).

The territory of Slovakia was inhabited since the Stone Age and among the first ethnic groups were Celts. Roman military stations, which formed part of Limes Romanus, were situated just south of the Danube. Starting in the fifth century the Slavs started to settle the territory. In the ninth century, the first Slavic states appeared beginning with the Great Moravian Empire. Later on, Slovakia became part of the Medieval Kingdom of Hungary and the Austro-Hungarian Empire. The foundations of old Slavic writings in the ninth century and the rise of libraries and book culture in the thirteenth and fourteenth centuries have played an important role in the cultural history of Slovakia.[1] The codification of literary Slovak language in 1843 and the national revival in 1848 represent milestones in cultural and historical development. In 1863, the Matica slovenská was established as an association and cultural institution aimed at defending the national and cultural interests of Slovaks in a multinational state. As part of the Matica slovenská, national library, archives, museum, and scientific institution foundations were

Encyclopedia of Library and Information Sciences, Fourth Edition DOI: 10.1081/E-ELIS4-120053471

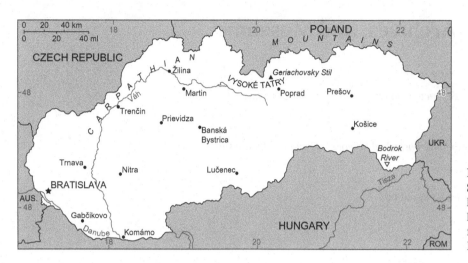

Fig. 1 Map of Slovakia.
Source: CIA World Fact Book. Retrieved from: https://www.cia.gov/library/publications/resources/the-world-factbook/geos/lo.html#wfbPhotoGallery Modal.

established. In the nineteenth century, a significant cultural contribution was made by the "Štúr generation": politicians, linguists, and literary intellectuals gathered around the leader L'udovít Štúr.

Slovakia became a part of Czechoslovak Republic at its establishment in 1918. In 1919–1945 the foundations of a systematic approach to building cultural institutions were laid. The first Czechoslovak Republic set the conditions for the operation of the state-supported cultural institutions including universities, theaters, libraries, and museums. After the end of World War II, the Czechoslovak Republic was reestablished falling under the influence of the Soviet Union. This had an impact on further economic, social, and cultural development of the country under communist ideology. Slovakia was a part of the Czechoslovak Socialist Republic. After 1989 and the fall of communism, Slovakia was released from Soviet influence in the common Czechoslovak Federative Republic. On January 1, 1993, the independent Slovak Republic was established on the principles of democracy and market economy. It became a member of the UNO and IMF, and in 2000, Slovakia joined OECD. In 2004 Slovakia entered NATO and became a part of the European Union. Politically and economically, Slovakia became a part of the European and Atlantic region.

LIBRARY AND INFORMATION PROFESSIONS, SYSTEMS, AND SERVICES

Brief Historical Outline

In 1919 the first library Act No. 430/19 Col. in Czechoslovakia was passed, which established public libraries in every municipality. Library activity was provided under systematic professional guidance.

In 1959 the Act No. 53/59 Col. was issued establishing the national system of libraries.[2] The unified system of libraries was composed of library networks including public, research, school, and academic libraries; libraries of

museums, archives, galleries, and ancient monuments; technical libraries; and libraries of the Slovak Academy of Sciences. The unified system of libraries was directed by the Matica slovenská. This centralized system of libraries, which was in existence from 1959 to 1989, has been marked by both the unification of professional library activities and ideological pressure. In addition, there existed a parallel system of technical and company libraries (referred to as a system of scientific, technical, and economic information), which provided information for enterprises and other institutions. Significant figures in Slovak librarianship include the bibliographers L'.V. Rizner, J. Čaplovič, and I. Kotvan in the field of incunabula.

A new stage of development of the Slovak library system began in 1993. Its main characteristics are decentralization, cooperation, and a new concept of digitization aimed at the coordination of information systems in both cultural and governmental institutions. International recommendations and standards, for example, UNIMARC, ISBD, AACR2, and ISO 2709, were adopted and applied to professional procedures, systems, and services. International professional cooperation has been strengthened especially within the framework of International Federation of Library Associations and Institutions (IFLA) and OCLC.

As early as the 1960s, Slovak libraries started to automate bibliographic procedures. In the 1970s Slovakia was one of the first former socialist countries that introduced an automated bibliographic system in the Matica slovenská. In the 1980s an advanced integrated library and information system IKIS was designed with the use of what were then new technologies. Efforts for coordinated automation since the 1990s have been embodied by the Czech and Slovak Library Information Network and other cooperative regional systems and networks (e.g., KOLIN).

Current Legislation and Present Library System

In 2000, a new Act No. 183/2000 on libraries was passed followed by subsequent acts amending legal deposits of publications (2001) and copyright act (2003). New integrated library systems of the third generation have been developed, such as library and information system of the 3rd generation (KIS3G). The library system of the Slovak Republic (SR) is part of the state information system and is included in building European electronic cultural systems. The library system comprises 9127 libraries, of which there are 2658 public libraries. In 2005 and 2006 new strategy for digitization and the integrated library and information system were introduced by the Slovak National Library (SNL).[3] The library system is composed of the national library, 12 research libraries, 37 academic libraries, public libraries, special libraries, school libraries, libraries of churches, and nonpublic military and prison libraries. Public libraries include 8 regional libraries, 29 district libraries, 106 city libraries, 271 municipal professional libraries, 2276 municipal nonprofessional libraries, and 2 private libraries for public use in Nové Zámky and Tornaľa. Special libraries are represented by 3 independent legal libraries, 118 medical libraries, 44 technical libraries, 23 agricultural libraries, and 89 libraries of museums and galleries. There are over 5000 school libraries.

The most important libraries established by the Ministry of Culture of the SR are Slovenská národná knižnica v Martine (the Slovak National Library in Martin, the SNL), Univerzitná knižnica v Bratislave (the University Library in Bratislava , the ULB), and three state research libraries in regional cities of Banská Bystrica, Košice, and Prešov. The same position is held by Slovenská knižnica pre nevidiacich Mateja Hrebendu v Levoči (the Matej Hrebenda Slovak Library for the Blind in Levoča). The independent special libraries are Knižnica pre mládež mesta Košice (the Library for Youth of the City of Košice) and Parlamentná knižnica NR SR v Bratislave (the Parliamentary Library of the National Council of SR in Bratislava). Important libraries in Slovakia also include Centrum VTI SR (the Centre of Scientific and Technical Information in Bratislava),

Ústredná knižnica Slovenskej akadémie vied (Central Library of the Slovak Academy of Sciences in Bratislava), Slovenská ekonomická knižnica Ekonomickej Univerzity v Bratislave (Slovak Economic Library of the University of Economics in Bratislava), Slovenská poľnohospodárska knižnica pri Slovenskej poľnohospodárskej univerzite v Nitre (Slovak Agricultural Library of the Slovak University of Agriculture in Nitra), and Mestská knižnica v Bratislave (the Municipal Library in Bratislava). Professional library activities are supported by two professional associations, namely, Spolok slovenských knihovníkov (the Slovak Librarians' Association, the SLA) and Slovenská asociácia knižníc (the Slovak Association of Libraries, the SAL). The SLA was established in 1946 and manages the professional activity at the level of individual membership and specialized professional sections. Annual conferences have been organized by the SLA since the 1970s. Since 1993 the SAL has been active as a professional coalition of institutions in which membership is based on the institution's function, for example, academic, public, and special libraries. Library policy emphasizes the coordination of services and systems and the objectives of supporting an information and knowledge society.

The Slovak National Library and the University Library

Slovak National Library

Slovenská národná knižnica (the Slovak National Library, the SNL) in Martin has evolved as part of the Matica slovenská[3] (Fig. 2). The complicated history of the Matica slovenská is tied to the social and political evolution of a number of changes in the form of government. In the nineteenth century its activities were interrupted, and in 1919 it was revived. The Matica has been developed both as a professional institution and as an association of

Fig. 2 The building of the Slovak National Library in Martin on the hill Hostihora (opened 1975).

people supporting Slovak culture. It has often resisted political influence and has undergone many organizational transformations. Following the Act No. 183/2000 the SNL has become independent from the Matica since 2000. It fulfills the tasks of the national library in the professional capacity of making national cultural and scientific heritage available through preservation of documents of Slovak origin (Slovak-subject documents—"slovaciká").

The library collections include 4.7 million documents. Historical library holdings contain incunabula, collections of prints, manuscripts, and other precious documents. Among the most precious documents are Confessionale by Antonin Florentin from 1477 (Fig. 3), Hungarian Chronicle by Johannes de Thurocz from 1488, and Pantheologia by Rainerius de Pisis printed in Basil in 1447 (Fig. 4). The most significant historical library holdings are the private libraries of M. Hamuljak and M. Rešetka and a historical library stock in Jasov. Apart from library materials, the collections of the SNL also include literary archives containing over 1.5 million items

and two literary museums. The oldest relic in the manuscript collections is the Glagolitic text on parchment from the twelfth century.

The SNL coordinates the library system in Slovakia. The SNL is also the national bibliographic agency, ISBN agency, and the leader of the KIS3G project.[4] The project is aimed at the development of an interoperable environment for the provision of library and information services in Slovakia. The SNL is engaged in many international professional activities including cooperation with European and other national libraries (e.g., The European Library [TEL]). The SNL has recently developed several other national and international projects such as the Slovak digital library, information for innovation, paper conservation research, and the Slovak digital edition of rare medieval codices, Memoria Slovaciae in the framework of UNESCO's Memory of the World Programme and the portal of the Slovak cultural heritage—Memoria slovaca.[3] The SNL is active in research in librarianship, bibliography, book culture, and literary archives and museums.

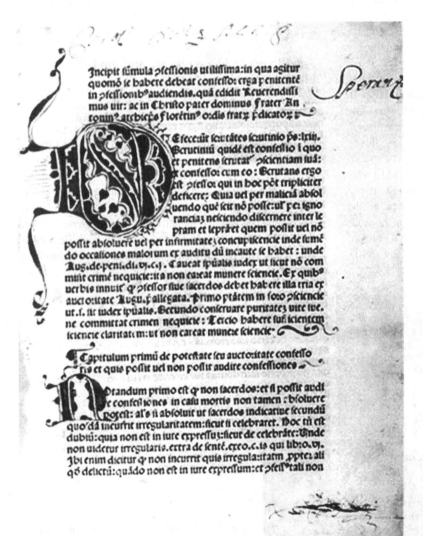

Fig. 3 Confessionale by Antonin Florentin from 1477.

Fig. 4 Pantheologia by Rainerius de Pisis. Basilae, Betholdus Ruppel, ca. 1477–1479.

University Library in Bratislava

Univerzitná knižnica v Bratislave is the next important institution in the library system of Slovakia.[5] It was established as part of the former Elisabethan University in 1912. In 1919 it was closely connected with the newly founded Comenius University. Until 1954 it also operated as the national library. In 1954 it became an independent research library fulfilling tasks of both national and international scope. The ULB holds collections of Slovak and foreign literature with an emphasis on both science and social sciences. Its collections contain over 2.4 million items. The historical collections include manuscripts and old prints, of which the most significant is the Bašagić collection of oriental manuscripts registered in the list of UNESCO's Memory of the World. The ULB is active in library, bibliographic, research, cultural, and educational tasks and coordinates the development of national union catalogs of periodicals. It houses the international UN, UNESCO, and NATO information centers.[6] The ULB is a member of international organizations such as IFLA,

and UNAL. The ULB is also at the center of coordination of information systems and registries in culture.[7] It is engaged in many international programs such as e-Culture and digitization on demand (DoD). The library is housed in historic buildings in the center of the Old Town of Bratislava, namely, the Palace of Hungarian Chamber (Fig. 5), the Leopold de Pauli Palace (Fig. 6), and the Clariseum (St. Clara's order convent). Since 2005, after the reconstruction of the historical premises, the ULB has become the Multifunctional Cultural and Library Centre and is also active in digitization of its historical collections.

Academic and Research Libraries

Academic libraries in SR developed along with university education after 1919. In 1990, a new act on higher education introduced democratic principles of education and democratic management of universities. Academic libraries started to implement automation more intensely, coordinated professional procedures, and improved services

Fig. 5 The building of the University Library in Bratislava—the Palace of the Hungarian Chamber.

academic information network SANET. Major university libraries include Univerzita Komenského v Bratislave (the Comenius University in Bratislava), Univerzita Pavla J. Šafárika v Košiciach (the P.J. Šafárik University in Košice), and Slovenská technická univerzita v Bratislave (the Slovak Technical University in Bratislava).

Research libraries are divided into general and specialized libraries. The universal (general) research libraries include state research libraries in the regional cities of Banská Bystrica, Prešov, and Košice. The independent specialized research libraries include Centrum VTI SR (the Centre of Scientific and Technical Information of the SR), Slovenská lekárska knižnica (the Slovak Medical Library), Ústredná knižnica SAV (the Central Library of the Slovak Academy of Sciences), Slovenská ekonomická knižnica pri EU (the Slovak Economic Library of the University of Economics), Slovenská pedagogická knižnica (the Slovak Pedagogical Library), Slovenská pol'nohospodárska knižnica pri SPU v Nitre (the Slovak Agricultural Library of the Slovak University of Agriculture in Nitra), and Slovenská lesnícka a drevárska knižnica vo Zvolene (the Slovak Library of Forestry and Wood Sciences in Zvolen).

The research and academic libraries are becoming part of the program on information innovation for the support of knowledge management and scientific and technical information.

Public Libraries

Public libraries in the SR have a complicated history. They emerged as municipal public libraries in 1919. After the act of 1959, they were professionalized and integrated into a unified system of libraries according to the act from 1959. Since 1990 changes in the organization of public libraries have been introduced as a result of the reorganization of local government authorities. There are four

providing access to quality foreign literature. At present, a majority of academic libraries in universities offer electronic catalogs, electronic resources, and value-added services for students, teachers, and researchers. Academic libraries are either centralized to provide service for the whole university or decentralized within single university units. Academic libraries are interconnected through the

Fig. 6 The building of the University Library in Bratislava—the Palace of Leopold de Pauli (1777).

basic types of public libraries: regional, county, city, and municipal. In accordance with the UNESCO Manifesto on public libraries, they take part in the democratization of culture and education in Slovakia. In 2005 the 2657 libraries of SR comprised 18.5 million library items. In 2013 more than 1.06 million of library users used libraries (19% of the whole population).[7]

Under new social and economic conditions, public libraries are being transformed into community centers that cooperate with regional cultural institutions. Examples of such public libraries include Mestská knižnica v Bratislave (the Municipal Library of Bratislava), Knižnica P.O. Hviezdoslava Prešov (the P.O. Hviezdoslav Library in Prešov), Knižnica Juraja Fándlyho v Trnave (the Juraj Fándly Library in Trnava), Krajská knižnica L'. Štúra vo Zvolene (the L'. Štúr County Library in Zvolen), Verejná knižnica Jána Bocatia v Košiciach (the Ján Bocatius Public Library in Košice), and municipal libraries in Piešt'any, Hlohovec, and Levice.

Education in Librarianship and Information Science

Since 1953 the education of librarians at the secondary level has been organized in the Škola knihovníckych a informačných štúdií (the School of Library and Information Studies) in Bratislava. In the course of its history, the school has provided part-time and further professional education as well as full-time program of study. The curricula have addressed librarianship, bibliography, archival studies, literary education, and scientific information. In1993, the contents of studies were changed. A program on information systems and services has since been established that provides focused study in library and business information systems. The school also currently offers graduate professional education to library and information workers. The school cooperates with similar foreign institutions and makes use of international programs for the modernization of the curriculum.

The Faculty of Arts of Comenius University in Bratislava provided the first university education of library and information professionals in 1951. Independent department of librarianship was established in 1961. The subject of Librarianship and Scientific Information was offered in combination with various disciplines and foreign languages. Since 1990, the contents and the form of studies have responded to national changes in higher education.

Katedra knižničnej a informačnej vedy Filozofickej fakulty Univerzity Komenského v Bratislave (the Department of Library and Information Science [DLIS] at the Faculty of Arts of Comenius University in Bratislava) provides education for library and information professionals within the library and information studies program at three levels—the bachelor's, master's, and doctoral levels. It is the most important professional institution in the area of university education and research. Following the

European curricular models, it provides the core for studies in the subjects of information seeking and retrieval, knowledge organization, and information systems. The new curricula represent information and media studies, literary communication, and book culture. The DLIS is involved with research projects. It is a member of the international association, the European Association of Library and Information Education and Research, and organizes international conferences (e.g., 1999, 2003, 2006). The staff is involved with international projects (e.g., DELOS-CEE), publishing, and lecturing at national and international conferences. In total approximately 1400 students graduated from the department since its inception. Information science in Slovakia since 1990 has grown largely through the research of DLIS at Comenius University in Bratislava. The research topics are focused on a new paradigm of information science, human information behavior, digital libraries, on updating the curricular content, and on information ecology.

Higher education for library and information workers at the levels of bachelor and master studies is also provided by new departments at Žilinská univerzita (the University of Žilina) in Žilina, Katedra mediamatiky a kultúrneho dedičstva (the Department of Mediamatics and Cultural Heritage), and until 2013 also Prešovská univerzita (the University of Prešov) in Prešov.

Library professional development is provided through training opportunities and workshops organized by the SNL, the Centre of Scientific and Technical Information (STI) SR, and DLIS. Professional development is also supported by the electronic information portal for library and information theory and practice InfoLib (since 2003)[8] and professional periodicals as Knižnica (library), as well as ITLib. Professional library associations and major research and public libraries take part in the continuing education of librarians as well.

Present State and Future Prospects

The present state of the library development in Slovakia can be characterized by continuing efforts at informatization and digitization. National programs of informatization are managed by the SNL and the Ministry of Culture of the SR. Recent topical strategies have focused on the provision of public Internet for libraries and schools, the development of common software, and support of small- and medium-sized libraries. Libraries are involved in European projects such as MINERVA, TEL-ME-MORE, e-Culture, DoD, DIGICULT, and TEL. International standards have been applied to the integration of memory institutions and to the preservation and presentation of cultural and scientific heritage. Digitization of Slovak cultural, scientific, and intellectual heritage is in progress based on UNESCO recommendations and those of the EU network of ministries of culture. Among the most important digitization projects are the illuminated codices from the Bratislava Chapter Library from the Slovak National Archives (SNA) and portions of the Arabic and Persian manuscript collections from the ULB—Bašagić Collection of Islamic Manuscripts. The goal of digitization is to develop value-added services in e-learning, content industry, and culture. The first results of this digitization project are available via the national library and information system KIS3G, registries of cultural institutions, and SNL portals such as the Slovak digital library[4] and Memoria slovaca, which provide digitized museum and archival objects.

ARCHIVES AND ARCHIVAL SCIENCE

Brief Historical Outline

The beginnings of archiving in Slovakia date back to the thirteenth century. The first historically documented public archives were founded at the so-called trustworthy locations—loca credibilia—and in medieval towns. Loca credibilia were public institutions that operated at chapter houses and convents in the Hungarian Kingdom and functioned as public notaries. Later on, loca credibilia were established in county/district archives, followed by the archives of mining and economic institutions. Private archives were the most common—feudal families' archives, archives of mansions, and church institutions. Guilds, and later on brotherhoods and organizations, also had their own archives. As Slovakia was part of the Hungarian Kingdom until 1918, no central archives were founded in the Slovak territory with the exception of the period between 1756 and 1785, when the royal/regional archives were moved to Bratislava due to the Turkish occupation of part of the territory of the Hungarian Kingdom. The idea of establishing the SNA originated in the Slovak national emancipation movement of the second half of the nineteenth century. Thereafter, the most important Slovak national cultural institutions such as the Matica slovenská, Muzeálna slovenská spoločnosť (the Slovak Museum Society), and Spolok svätého Vojtecha (St. Adalbert Association) began to develop archival documentation.

After establishing the Czechoslovak Republic, the Krajinský archív (the Regional Archives, 1928–1939) became the most important archives in Slovakia and was later replaced by Archív Ministerstva vnútra Slovenskej republiky (the Ministry of Interior of the Slovak Republic Archives, 1939–1945). Archív Slovenského národného múzea (the Slovak National Museum Archives) in Martin has operated continuously since 1929. The archives network in Slovakia was composed of county and municipal archives. However, at this time, it was impossible to establish either a private archiving organization or a central archiving institution or even to push through archival legislation.

The efforts to establish the central Slovak archives and archiving organization culminated in the second half

of the twentieth century. In 1948, Pôdohospodársky archív (the Agricultural Archives) was founded incorporating the collections of feudal families, mansions, and capitalist farms. In 1950, Ústredný banský archív (the Central Mining Archives) was established, and, eventually, Slovenský ústredný archív (the Slovak Central Archives) was founded in 1952 as a result of the activities of Slovenská archívna komisia (the Slovak Archiving Commission). Apart from processing archival documents and making them accessible, the Slovak Central Archives' main task was to supervise and coordinate the activities of regional, district, and municipal archives in Slovakia. In 1954 the Decree on archiving No. 29/1954 Col. was issued. It was the first legislation for archiving that created the unified archiving organization in the Czechoslovak Republic. Archiving in Slovakia was administered by Povereníctvo vnútra (the Home Affairs Authority) through Slovenská archívna správa (the Slovak Archives Administration). The archiving organization was composed of state central archives, state archives, district, municipal, special, and company archives. Church archives were also controlled by the state administration.

In 1975 the Act on archiving No. 149/1975 Col. was passed by the Slovak Parliament. As a result, archiving became part of the agenda of the Ministry of Interior of the Slovak Socialist Republic. The archives network consisted of the central archives (Štátny ústredný archív SSR, the Central State Archives of SSR, and Štátny ústredný banský archív, the State Central Mining Archives); the state regional archives in Bratislava, Nitra, Bytča, Banská Bystrica, Levoča, Prešov, Košice, and Archív hlavného mesta SSR Bratislavy (the Archives of the Capital City of Bratislava); 35 state district archives; Archív mesta Košice (the Archives of the City of Košice); archives of the organizations of special significance; and company archives. The armed forces' archives and the archives of armed security corps were administered by relevant ministries. Political parties, the national front, and trade unions established and administered their own archives. The Act on archiving considerably enhanced the professional character of the archives' activities. Štátny ústredný archív SSR became the main center for archival research. The new building of the Central State Archives of the SSR (today the Slovak National Archives) in Bratislava was established in 1983. In the 1960s and 1970s, modern technology became available and a new automated archiving system was created for recording, processing, and facilitating access to archival documents.

Current System and Legislation

Social and political changes that affected Slovak archiving after 1989 were reflected in amendments to the Act on archiving No. 332/1992 Col. More amendments were made in 1996 and 2001. Act No. 395/2002 Col. on archives and registries came into effect on January 1, 2003, as a result of the reform of the state administration in Slovakia, the changed territorial arrangement, the complex demands on the registry system, and the adaptation of the Slovak legal system to the legal system of the European Union. This amendment significantly modified the system of archives in Slovakia—since then the system has been made up of both public and private archives. The state archives now include 47 institutions: the two state central archives (i.e., the SNA and the State Central Mining Archives) and the 8 state archives of regional territorial jurisdiction and their 38 branches. The documentary legacy of the Slovak Republic held by the state archives amounts to over 25,000 archival collections of approximately 200,000 linear meters.

Other public archives include the archives of state administrative bodies, the archives of state budget and state subsidies organizations, municipal archives and the archives of self-governing regions, archives of legal entities established by law, and the archives of legal entities and corporate entities who serve as public administrative bodies. Private archives are constituted by the archives of legal entities and natural persons. Archiving lies within the purview of the Ministry of Interior of the Slovak Republic. Archives are under the jurisdiction of the Department of Archives and Registries, and the advisory body is the Scientific Archiving Council. The act on archives and registries was amended in 2007 by the Act No. 216/2007 Col.

Access to Archives

The terms of use and access to archived documents are defined by Act No. 395/2002 Col. and by the Decree of the Ministry of Interior of the Slovak Republic No. 628/2003 Col. Access to collections is limited and is determined by each archive based on a written application. Finding aids, available in both traditional and electronic forms, serve as guides through the collections, stock lists, and catalogs and provide analyses of collections.

The National Archives, State Archives, and Administration

As mentioned previously, the administrative body of archives in Slovakia is the Department of Archives and Registries of the Ministry of Interior of the Slovak Republic. The advisory bodies consist of the Professional Archives Council, the Heraldic Commission, the Acquisition Commission, and the Document Shredding Commission.

Slovenský národný archív (the Slovak National Archives) in Bratislava[9] is the largest and the most significant public archives in the Slovak Republic. It gathers, protects, processes, and makes accessible documents arising from the activities of the central bodies of the Slovak Republic and their predecessors and archival documents

of national importance. It is the central research and educational institution in archival science.

The Department of Early Resources and Collections administers the collections of state and administrative bodies before 1918; the archives of public figures, aristocratic families and mansions (the largest collection holds documents dating back to the thirteenth century), religious institutions, and loca credibilia; repositories of medieval documents; and a collection of maps and plans. The Department of New Resources and Collections administers the collections of the state and administrative bodies from the period of 1918 to 1968 as well as the collections of economic, legal, and financial organizations, political parties, associations, and unions. The Department of Prearchival Care methodologically supervises the central bodies of the state administration and of organizations of national importance in the area of registry, retention, and disposition activities. The Department of Reference Services provides public outreach and supports the use of archival documents for scientific, cultural, and administrative purposes. The department houses a study room, a library, and a film library. The Science and Research Section conducts research in archival science. The Department of Archival Preservation provides for the complex protection of archived documents and is an educational and research institution. The department also houses conservation and restoration laboratories, a photo laboratory, and a disinfecting chamber.

Outline of State and Specialized Public Archives in the Slovak Republic

State archives and their branches. The state archives collect, process, make accessible, and protect the resources of the state government and its administration, as well as the local governments and administrations including counties, agencies, committees, the justice system, army and security (including the gendarme and national security), finance, economy, agriculture, political parties, the educational system, health and social care, science, culture and history, religious organizations, significant families and mansions, prominent individuals, guilds, associations and interest organizations, and collections of other kinds of materials (registers, documents, maps and plans, sealing sticks, photographs, music materials, etc.).[10]

Branch archives hold the collections of the state and local government concerning the administration of towns, villages, local national committees, district offices, district national committees, and notary public offices. Additional materials relate to district courts, tax offices, economic associations and chambers, cooperatives, political parties and social organizations, schools (elementary, secondary, and professional), culture and national history, health care, prominent families and individuals, guilds, associations and interest organizations, and collections.

The State Central Mining Archives in Banská Štiavnica serves as the archive for mining, metallurgy, geological research, and related branches of the economy for the period between 1255 and 1991.

The Archives of the Capital City of Bratislava houses the records of the municipal administrative bodies, schools, health and social facilities, religious organizations, families and prominent individuals, guilds, associations and interest organizations of Bratislava. Of particular note are the records of the Council Office of the City of Bratislava from the thirteenth to the twentieth centuries.

The Archives of the City of Košice keeps the resources of state and local governing bodies from the thirteenth to the twentieth centuries. The Council Office of the City of Košice, with records dating from the years 1239 to 1922, is of prime importance. Additional resources include records of the district and municipal courts, the prosecutors' office, police headquarters, materials relating to factories and manufacturing from the sixteenth to the twentieth centuries, schools, health care and social facilities, religious organizations, cooperatives, political parties and social organizations, guilds and associations, and family and personal collections (e.g., King Ján Zápol'ský, 1537–1540). Other state archives are in Banská Bystrica, Bratislava, Bytča, Košice, Levoča, Nitra, Prešov, and other cities.

The specialized public archives keep a variety of materials concerning all aspects of social life. They include the archives of the central state administrative bodies, scientific, cultural, and educational institutions, as well as media archives. These archives include[10] Archív Slovenského národného múzea (the Slovak National Museum Archives), Ústredný archív Slovenskej akadémie vied (the Slovak Academy of Sciences Central Archives), Archív literatúry a umenia Slovenskej národnej knižnice (the Literature and Art Archives of the Slovak National Library), Vojenský historický archív (the Military History Archives), Archív pamiatkového úradu SR (the Archives of the Memorial Authority of the SR), Ústredný archív geodézie a kartografie (the Central Archives of Geodesy and Cartography), Archív Ústavu pamäti národa (the Archives of the Nation's Memory Institute of the SR), Národný filmový archív Slovenského filmového ústavu (the National Movies Archives of the Slovak Film Institute), Archív výtvarného umenia Slovenskej národnej galérie (the Visual Art Archives of the Slovak National Gallery), Archív Divadelného ústavu (the Theatre Institute Archives), Archív Univerzity Komenského (the Comenius University Archives), Archív Slovenskej technickej univerzity (the Slovak Technical University Archives), Archív Ekonomickej univerzity (the University of Economics Archives), Archív Národnej banky SR (the National Bank of the SR Archives), Archív Slovenského rozhlasu (the Slovak Radio Archives), Archív Slovenskej televízie (the Slovak Television Archives), Archív Kancelárie prezidenta SR (the Archives of the Office of President of the SR), Parlamentný archív (the Parliamentary Archives), Archív Ministerstva zahraničných vecí SR (the Ministry of Foreign Affairs of the SR Archives), Archív Zboru väzenskej a justičnej stráže SR (the Archives of the Corps of Prison and Justice Guards), and Archív Mincovne Kremnica (the Kremnica Mint Archives).

Archival Education

During the period of the Hungarian Kingdom, historians and lawyers used to work as archivists. Archival education was available only at universities abroad. The Czechoslovak Republic Štátna archívna škola (the State Archiving School) was founded in Prague in 1919. In 1950, archiving began to be studied at the Faculty of Arts of Comenius University in Bratislava. Starting in 1970, secondary extension lectures in archiving were given at the Secondary School of Librarianship in Bratislava. Later on pre-A-levels study of archiving were established at the same school. Since 2000, archiving can be studied at the independent Department of Archiving and Auxiliary Historic Sciences at the Faculty of Arts of Comenius University in Bratislava. The program of archiving and auxiliary historic sciences takes the form of bachelor's, master's, or doctoral studies. The study program provides courses in archiving, auxiliary historic sciences, administration history, national and world history, source languages (Latin, Old Slovak, Czech, Hungarian, German), information technologies, archived documents protection, and professional archival training. Since 1991 archiving can be studied at the Faculty of Philosophy of Prešov University. Graduates of university archiving programs can find jobs in public and private archives, registry centers, scientific institutions, central and local state administration, museums, libraries, galleries, publishing houses, newspapers, magazines, radio and television editor's offices, and educational and cultural institutions.

Organizations and Associations of Archivists

In 1990—Spoločnosť slovenských archivárov (the Association of Slovak Archivists) was founded in Bratislava. Its main aims are the development and improvement of Slovak archiving and the archive profession. It organizes professional conferences, functions as a permanent partner of the archiving bodies, and protects the interests and rights of its members. The association organizes annual national meetings of archivists, Archívne dni v SR (the Days of Archives in the Slovak Republic), which have international participation. It also publishes its own information bulletin—Fórum archivárov (the Archivists' Forum). Since 1980, Sekcia archívnictva a pomocných vied historických (the Archiving and Auxiliary Historic Sciences Section) has been active within the Slovenská historická spoločnosť pri Slovenskej akadémii vied (the

Slovak Historic Association at the Slovak Academy of Sciences), which organizes scientific conferences, symposiums, and exhibitions. It publishes proceedings of presentations from the events.

Archiving Magazine and Archiving Awards

Since 1966, the Department of Archives and Registries of the Ministry of Interior of the Slovak Republic has been publishing a professional magazine—Slovenská archivistika (Slovak Archiving). This periodical publishes research and professional articles on theory, the practice of archiving, and auxiliary historic sciences. Since 1979, the Ministry of Interior of the SR has awarded archivists P. Križko's Medal. Since 1998, the Ministry of Interior of the SR acknowledges achievements in the development of archiving by awarding the F.V. Sasinek's medal.

MUSEUMS AND MUSEOLOGY

Brief Historical Outline

The first collections of antiques and natural objects were established in Slovakia in the eighteenth century. At this time, Albert of Saxony-Cziesyn's collection was established in Bratislava (at that time the capital of the Hungarian Kingdom), and this collection now forms the basis of the Albertina museum in Vienna. Many historic artifacts were presented to the Magyar Nemzeti Múzeum in Budapest in the nineteenth century (1835). The first museum institutions in the Slovak territory, today's Múzeum mesta Bratislavy (the Bratislava City Museum) and Galéria mesta Bratislavy (the City Gallery of Bratislava), were founded in Bratislava in 1868. By 1918, museums in Košice (1872), Poprad (1886), Bardejov (1905), Ružomberok (1912), Trenčín (1876), Rožňava (1902), and Banská Štiavnica had been established. Between 1918 and 1945 museums were growing in number and in the size of their collections, and many were partly subsidized by the state. After 1948 all the museums were taken over by the state and fully subordinated to the policy and ideology of the communist party. New museums specializing in national history and special museums and galleries were established. The operation of museums was governed by the Act No.109/1961 Col. on museums and galleries, which confirmed the complete dependence of museums and galleries on the government's power.

As democracy was restored in the Slovak Republic after 1989, changes in museum administration and management were introduced. Act No. 115/1998 Col. on museums and galleries and objects of museum and gallery value altered the rights and duties of museums, galleries, and their founders and organizers. The decree of the Ministry of Culture of the Slovak Republic No. 342/1998 on professional administration of museum and gallery collections has largely determined how museum collections are professionally processed, including digitization of records.

The Slovak National Museum: History

Slovenské národné múzeum (the Slovak National Museum, the SNM) is one of the largest and oldest museum institutions in Slovakia.[11] The core collection was established through the Matica slovenská, which collected artifacts and objects from the past as evidence of the maturity of the Slovak nation. The institutional and professional foundations of the SNM were laid by the Muzeálna slovenská spoločnosť (the Slovak Museal Society, the SMS), which was founded in Martin in 1893. The SMS was established with the aim of collecting artifacts of the history and culture of the Slovak nation and of documenting natural history of Slovakia. The orientation of the SMS was determined by the founder of Slovak museum science, Andrej Kmeť, who gathered rich collections through his own activities and donated them to the museum. The museum collections grew primarily due to gifts of artifacts in many areas of study (history, ethnography, numismatics, art history, archaeology, botany, zoology, and mineralogy). The collections were displayed in the first museum building opened to the public in Martin in 1908. The museum in Martin operated as an association with no support from the government of the Hungarian Kingdom. The SMS has provided subsidies for museum-related research in Slovakia for several decades.

The status of the museum changed after the establishment of the Czechoslovak Republic in 1918. After 1919, the SNM began to receive subsidies from the state. The activities of the museum grew under Ján Geryk who became director in 1926; he expanded the collections and hired educated curators. The new museum building designed by the architect M.M. Harminc in Martin was opened in 1933. In the same year Národná galéria slovenská (the Slovak National Gallery) was opened followed by the first national historic and ethnographic expositions in 1938. In 1940 the memorial exposition of M.R. Štefánik, the cofounder of the Czechoslovak Republic, was opened.

After the establishment of the Czechoslovak Republic, the state authorities supported the development of education, science, and culture in Slovakia. Zemědělské muzeum (the Agricultural Museum) was founded in Bratislava in 1924, and Slovenské vlastivedné múzeum (the Slovak Museum of National History) opened in 1928. In 1940 the two museums had been merged into the Slovak Museum. The SNM in Martin and the Slovak Museum in Bratislava concentrated their collecting activities on enriching the collections with artifacts from all scientific fields, that is, archaeology, history, art history, arts and crafts, ethnography, zoology, botany, anthropology, mineralogy, and petrography.

Changes in managing museums in Slovakia occurred after 1948 when the SNM in Martin and the Slovak Museum in Bratislava were placed under the administration of the state by Act No. 12/1948 Col. This subsequently initiated the founding of new, regional museums specializing in national history. By Act No. 24/1948 Col., Slovenská národná galéria (the Slovak National Gallery) was established in Bratislava as the specialized museum institution for documenting the history of art in all possible times and forms of expression. The gallery's resources were based on the ancient art collections of the SNM in Martin and the Slovak Museum in Bratislava. Act No. 109/1961 Col. on museums and galleries merged the SNM in Martin and the Slovak Museum in Bratislava, thus creating the SNM based in Bratislava. The construction of the first national Slovak open-air museum of folk architecture in Martin began in 1967.

Specialized Museums

The SNM in Martin became the center of ethnographic research and the development of ethnography as a science. The institutions in Bratislava were transformed into the Archaeological Museum, the Historic Museum, the Music Museum, and the Museum of Natural History. In the 1990s, departments specializing in the documentation of ethnic and minority cultures began to be founded within the SNM, and these later became the independent specialized SNM museums. They include the Museum of Jewish Culture (1992), the Museum of Carpathian German Culture (1994), the Museum of Hungarian Culture in Slovakia (2001), and the Museum of Croatian Culture in Slovakia (2005). All are located in Bratislava.

In addition to the museums in Bratislava, SNM also oversees museums and sites elsewhere in the country.[12] The Museum of the Ukrainian–Ruthenian Culture (1956) is situated in Svidník and has been part of the SNM since 2002. The SNM in Martin includes the Museum of Czech Culture and the Museum of Roma Culture. The SNM also administers remarkable Slovak castles and palaces—for example, the Červený kameň Castle, the Krásna Hôrka Castle, the Spišský hrad (the Castle of Spiš) administered by the Spišské múzeum (the Museum of Spiš) in Levoča, the castle at Bojnice, the manor house in Betliar, and the Modrý Kameň Castle with the Múzeum bábkarských kultúr a hračiek (the Museum of Puppet Cultures and Toys). The SNM also administers two open-air museums—Múzeum slovenskej dediny (the Museum of the Slovak Village) in Martin and Múzeum ľudovej architektúry (the Museum of Folk Architecture) in Svidník. Other museums administered by the SNM include documenting historic turning points and important people in Slovak history—for example, the Museum of the SNR (Slovak Parliament) in Myjava and the Ľudovít Štúr Museum in Modra.

Slovak National Museum Collections

The collections of the SNM currently contain over 3.5 million objects documenting the development of nature and society across different eras and in all scientific disciplines. The collections of antiquities in the Archaeological Museum are particularly rich, containing materials from Egyptian, Greek, and Roman cultures (i.e., the lyceum collection), the Mohapl and Marcelová collections, and graves from the Roman period. These remarkable items of European and world significance are dated from the Bronze Age and include materials from the Halstattian and latent periods, the period of migration of nations, and up to the Middle Ages.

The specialized museums of the SNM hold collections documenting guild crafts, industry, transport and communications, education and science, and the life of urban families in the nineteenth and twentieth centuries including clothing and textiles. The collection of military objects is extensive as well. The numismatic collection of the Museum of History, containing over 100,000 items, is the largest in Slovakia. The collection contains some medals but predominantly consists of currency and coins dating from the Celtic period ("biatec") up to the twentieth century.

The collections of the SNM cover all historical periods in both fine art and arts and crafts—from rare Romanesque art to the nineteenth century art (burghers' portraits, realism). The Gothic and Baroque period collections are relatively rich containing the gallery of baroque portraits, the Danubian school, and ornamental sculptures from J.R. Donner's circle. The large group of arts and crafts objects consists of a variety of traditional materials—clay, glass, metal, wood, and textiles. It includes the collection of manufactured pottery from all of Slovakia, a collection of Holíč faience, a set of historical glass of Slovak provenance, and furniture dating from varied historical periods—from single pieces from the period of Renaissance to the furniture sets from the first half of the twentieth century. Artifacts of exceptional value include the original interiors preserved in their entirety at the castles of Krásna Hôrka and Červený Kameň, at the manor house of Betliar, and at the castle of Bojnice.

Documentation of the Political and Social Life of Slovakia

Apart from documenting the material culture and history of visual arts, the SNM concentrates on documenting the political and community life in Slovakia. The collections documenting the history of the national revival are very important, as are the collections documenting the Memorandum of the Slovak Nation (1861) and the iconography of Slovak industry. The SNM also administers the personal collections of important figures of science, culture, and art in Slovakia. The most important collections include the almost complete legacy of M. R. Štefánik, A. Dubček, A. Kmeť, the painter Martin Benka, the ethnographer and cinematographer K. Plicka, musicians J. L. Bella, E. Suchoň, A. Moyzes, and A. Albrecht. The archives of the SNM include many historic guild artifacts, historic maps, and documents on the history of museums and museum science in Slovakia. The SNM library is a specialized library containing literature on museology, museography, and museum book production in the Slovak Republic.

The ethnographic collections are predominantly concentrated in the Etnografické múzeum (the Ethnographic Museum) in Martin, in the Historické múzeum (the Museum of History) in Bratislava, and in the museums of national and ethnic minorities. Ethnographic collections comprise objects documenting traditional agriculture, sheep farming, apiculture, and woodcraft. The museums also hold extensive collections of folk pottery, crafts, jewelry, furniture, folk art (wooden sculptures and paintings on glass), and toys and collections documenting traditional customs. The largest of these are the collections of folk costumes and textiles. The culture of folk music is represented in the collections of Hudobné múzeum (the Music Museum). Natural history collections are predominantly located at the Prírodovedné múzeum (the Museum of Natural History) in Bratislava, which houses the largest collection of natural materials in Slovakia. It houses anthropological, botanical, mineralogical, paleontologic, and zoological collections. The museum administers a number of important collections, for example, Souček, Roubal, Hrubý, and Holuby. The most precious of the collections are the herbarium of the flying monk, Cyprián of Červený kláštor, from the eighteenth century and the herbarium of the father of Slovak museum science, A. Kmeť. The SNM also administers extensive libraries containing over 240,000 books, of which 31,059 are the historical library collections including several incunabula (a total of 1718 of them have been inventoried). The Museum at Betliar manor house administers the extensive library of the noble Andrássy family, containing over 14,000 items.

The SNM presents its collections in 63 permanent expositions and installs over a 100 exhibitions every year. The nature of Slovakia and the biodiversity of Earth are presented in the permanent displays of the Museum of Natural History in Bratislava. The most important archaeological collections are presented in the exhibit "Jewels of the Distant Past of Slovakia" at the Bratislava Castle. The wealth and diversity of the folk culture are presented through permanent expositions at the Ethnographic Museum in Martin and the open-air museums. The number of ethnic and national minorities in the history and culture of Slovakia is represented by permanent expositions at the same museums. At present there is no permanent display showing the historical, cultural, and social development in Slovakia, but there are some long-term exhibitions at the Bratislava Castle.

Publishing Activities of Slovak National Museum

The SNM publishes two specialized periodicals—the magazine Pamiatky a múzeá: Revue pre kultúrne dedičstvo (Monuments and Museums: Review for Cultural Heritage) determined for the general public and the magazine Múzeum (Museum) for museum workers and experts in cultural heritage protection. The monograph series *Ethnography, History, Archeology, and Natural Sciences* presents research findings and scientific activities. The series *Acta judaica slovaca* publishes documents on the history of Jews in Slovakia and on the holocaust. *Acta carpatho-germanica* documents the history and culture of Carpathian Germans. The journal of the *Little Library of Museum Science Literature* publishes literature for museum professionals and information for the public. The SNM also publishes guide books, brochures, and other printed materials for the use of expositions and exhibitions. Within Fonte´s, scientific surveys of the SNM collections are published. The SNM has been appointed to create the central registry of museum collections, using the special software ESEZ.

Museum and Gallery Network in the Slovak Republic

The museum and gallery network in the Slovak Republic consists of museum institutions differing in size, profile, specialization, collections, and topics of their expositions. They include specialized museums of national character, that is, mining, agriculture, forestry and woodcraft, military, literary, glassmaking, technological, post, coins and medals, education, physical education, transportation, police, and trading. National history museums concentrate on some of the regions of Slovakia but have a more narrow specialization, for example, tinkers' trade, papermaking, and fire-extinguishing technologies. Local museums and expositions map the history, folk culture, and people who came from a particular village. Most museums administer sites, which have been listed in the cultural heritage directory such as castles, palaces, manor houses, burghers' palaces, medieval town halls, technological monuments, archaeological sites, and open-air folk architecture museums.

There are almost 400 museums and galleries in Slovakia altogether. The museums in the SR administer over 15 million objects in their collections. Over 1000 exhibitions are prepared by the museums every year. In 2006 the museums in Slovakia were visited by 3.8 million visitors, and galleries were visited by 450,000 people.

Education in Museology and Professional Associations

Specialized studies in museology are provided by the Faculty of Philosophy at Constantine the Philosopher

University at Nitra (single-branch daily and external forms), by the Faculty of Arts at Comenius University in Bratislava (external study after completing the studies in bachelor's degree in related specializations, e.g., ethnology, history, archaeology), and by the Faculty of Humanities at Matej Bel University, Banská Bystrica (single-branch daily and external forms). Museum science is also offered at the Faculty of Natural Sciences, Comenius University as an elective course for students of biology. Postgraduate studies and continuing education of museums' employees is provided by the Cabinet of Museum Sciences of the SNM.

Since 1990 the museums in Slovakia have been associated through the Union of Museums in Slovakia, thus drawing from the traditions of the Czechoslovak Union of Museums (1919–1960). The Union of Museums is an association of museums with the shared purpose of supporting and developing the interests of museums, coordinating museum activities, and communicating with the administrators and founders of museums. Membership is voluntary and the seat of the union is in Banská Bystrica.

CONCLUSION

Libraries, archives, and museums and the corresponding professions evolved during the complex historical and cultural context of the development of the Slovak nation that has had numerous changes in the form of its government. At present Slovakia is becoming an active part of the European Union cultural and information arena.

Closer cooperation and the subsequent convergence of libraries, archives, and museums are inevitable. Information systems are successively integrated into a prospective national portal of culture as part of the European portal of culture, for example, the Central Registry of Museum Collections and Portal of Museums, the Central Registry of Visual Art Works, information systems of the Literary Information Centre, the Theatre Institute, the Music Centre, the Slovak Movies Database of the Slovak Film Institute, and the information system of the Slovak Design Centre.[7] Common strategic goals of these cultural systems are digitization of content, services, presentations, and broadcasting. The establishment of the center for digitization is planned as part of the SNL.

Strategies for the informatization of society emphasize more electronic resources for libraries, Internet for schools, development of public portals, services of e-government, and education in public administration. In 2006, the act on information systems of public administration was passed, and national strategies for information security and interoperability were formulated. The vision of digital cultural information services is focused on the development of a knowledge society with emphasis on innovation, human resources, education, and information literacy.

National Projects of Digitization in Cultural and Information Institutions in Slovakia

The complex digitization of documents and cultural objects has been developing in Slovakia since 2010 within the national project of informatization of society. The formal framework is represented by the operational program informatization of society.[13] The projects can be divided into digitization projects, including text documents and library collections, and restoration and conservation works. Other projects include infrastructural projects and supportive projects. The priority of digitization and digital archiving is part of the Strategy of Slovak Librarianship for the years 2015–2020 developed by the Ministry of Culture of the SR[20] and the new library law adopted in 2015.

Among the digitization projects, the most important is represented by the national project "Digital Library and Digital Archive"[14] led by the SNL in Martin (http://www.dikda.sk/). The goal of the project is to digitize more than 2.5 million objects, divided into documents and special documents (photographies, maps) of the SNL and the selected archival documents of the SNA. The project was supported by the European structural funding and other sponsors. Benefits of the project include mass digitization of documents and archival objects, building digitization workplace in Vrútky and conservation of precious documents and online services for public. Other connected digitization projects include digitizations of galleries (Slovak National Gallery, the project Digital Gallery) and museum collections (the project Digital Museum), film and audio materials (the Slovak Film Institute), and video materials, national monuments, and other memory collections. Other examples include such projects as the project of the Central Digital Archives (the University Library in Bratislava, long-term archival of digitized collections), the Memory of Slovakia, the National Centre of Excellence in Research and Protection of Cultural and Scientific Heritage (the Slovak National Library, Žilina University), or digitization of galleries (the Slovak National Gallery). All the digitization projects are in line with European tendencies of building digital libraries like Europeana and TEL and should establish closer cooperation in building digital collections, metadata harvesting, and provision of value-added services of digital libraries with respect to personalization, electronic publishing, and information sharing.

As for the electronic resources, the most important initiatives and projects are run by the Centre of the Scientific and Technical Information in Bratislava,[19] including the national project NISPEZ (the National Information System for Support of Research and Development in Slovakia—Access to Electronic Information Resources). All the projects are funded by the European Fund of Regional Development. In line with Horizon 2020, they support scholarly community in Slovakia, innovations, transfer of technologies, and open access to digital scholarly documents and data.

ACKNOWLEDGMENTS

The authors thank the directors of the national and university libraries, archives, and museums, as well as colleagues from libraries, archives, and museums and Comenius University in Bratislava for their help in compiling this entry. The text was compiled as part of the projects VEGA 1/2481/05 and KEGA 3/7275/09.

REFERENCES

1. Škvarna, Dušan, et al. Slovensko: dejiny, divadlo, hudba, jazyk, literatúra, ľudová kultúra výtvarné umenie, Slováci v zahraničí. Bratislava: Perfekt; Literárne informačné centrum, 2006. ISBN 80-8046-349-2. 383 p.

2. Katuščák, D.; Matthaeidesová, M.; Nováková, M. Informačná výchova: Terminologický a výkladový slovník. Odbor knižničná a informačná veda (Information education: Terminological dictionary. Library and Information Science) SPN: Bratislava, Slovakia, 1998.

3. Slovenská národná knižnica. Slovak National Library. 2016. (website). [online]. Rretrieved from: http://www. snk.sk/ (accessed December 9, 2016).

4. Slovenská knižnica. (Slovak Library). Portál ku katalógom a zbierkam slovenských knižníc. (Portal to catalogs and collections of Slovak libraries). (website). [online]. Slovak National Library 2011. Retrieved from: https:// www.kis3g.sk/o_projekte.html (accessed December 10, 2016).

5. Univerzitná knižnica v Bratislave. The University Library in Bratislave. 2016. (website). [online]. Retrieved from http://www.ulib.sk/sk (accessed December 9, 2016).

6. Trgiňa, T. The University Library in Bratislava. Bratislava, Slovakia: Univerzitná knižnica v Bratislave, 1919–2009, 131pp.; ISBN 978-80-89303-14-4.

7. Mojžiš, V.; Slančík, P.; Faklová, A.; Polakovič, B.; Kriššák, E. eCulture. Portál kultúry. Projekt budovania Registrov kultúrneho dedičstva a kultúrnych aktivít; (eCulture. Culture Portal. Project of Building Registries of Cultural Heritage and Cultural Activities); UKB: Bratislava, Slovakia, 2006.

8. Infolib. Portál pre knižničnú a informačnú teóriu a prax. [online]. Available at: http://www.infolib.sk/ (accessed 2014–11-13).

9. Slovenský národný archív. [online]. Slovak National Archives Available at: http://www.civil.gov.sk/snarchiv (accessed 2014–11-11).

10. Kollárová, Z.; Hanus, J. A Guide to the Slovak Archives; UNIVERSUM: Prešov, Slovakia, 1999.

11. Slovenské národné múzeum. Slovak National Museum. 2016. (website). [online]. Retrieved from: http://www. snm.sk (accessed 2016–12-09).

12. Okáli, I.; Okáli, I.; Podušelová, G.S. Sprievodca po múzeách a galériách (Slovakia. A Guide to Museums and Galleries), Bratislava, Slovakia, 1994.

13. Operačný program informatizácia spoločnosti. OPIS. 2016. (Operational program informatization of society). Retrieved from: http://www.opis.gov.sk (accessed 2016–12-09).

14. Digitálna knižnica a digitálny archív. DIKDA. 2016. Digital Library and Digital Archives. Projekt OPIS2 NP1. Retrieved from: http://www.dikda.sk/ (accessed December 9, 2016).

15. Birová, D. Slovenské knihovníctvo pod drobnohľadom. ITLIb 2012, 16 (4), 5–14.

16. Krištofová, K. Slovenská digitálna knižnica: Detašované pracovisko SBK, Vrútky. ITLib 2010, 2, 22–24.

17. Antalík, P.; Osuský, T. Štúdia uskutočniteľnosti. Operačný program Informatizácia spoločnosti. ITLib 2010, 2, 5–10.

18. Katuščák, D. Situačná správa o národnom projekte SNK: Digitálna knižnica a digitálny archív. ITLib 2012, 2, 5–9.

19. Turňa, J; Bilský, Ľ.; Vašková, E. Podpora vedy prostredníctvom národných projektov—súčasné a pripravované projekty CVTISR. In INFOS 2013: inovatívne knižnice a pamäťové inštitúcie. [online]. Spolok slovenských knihovníkov: Bratislava, Slovakia, 2013; 249–257. Available at http://www.infolib.sk/files/ Novy_portal_infolib_subory/janka_nemethyova/infos_2013/ infos_2013_zbornik.pdf (accessed December 7, 2016). ISBN 978-80-895886.

20. Gondová, D. 2015. Stratégia rozvoja slovenského knihovníctva na roky 2015–2020. [Development Strategy of the Slovak librarianship for the years 2015–2020]. In ITLib. 2015, Vol. 19, No. 1, 5–13.

Smithsonian Institution

Pamela M. Henson
Archives, Smithsonian Institution, Washington, District of Columbia, U.S.A.

Abstract

The Smithsonian Institution was established in 1846 for the "increase and diffusion of knowledge." It now consists of an array of 9 research institutes, educational resources, and 19 museums and a zoo; indeed, it is the largest museum complex in the world. The Smithsonian serves as the national museum of the United States, with collections in the arts, cultural studies, humanities, and science, welcoming 24.2 million visitors and 183.6 million Web visits in 2007. Since the 1970s, the Institution has been automating access to its collections and since 1995 has been disseminating information via its Web site at http://www.smithsonian.org.

INTRODUCTION

The Smithsonian Institution is a complex organization that is best known as a group of U.S. national museums. Established in 1846 with the bequest of an English scientist, James Smithson, the Institution is dedicated to the "increase and diffusion of knowledge" in the arts, humanities, and sciences throughout the world. The Institution consists of 19 museums, a zoological park, 9 research institutes, and a variety of special programs in support of its mission. The museums include the Anacostia Community Museum; Arts and Industries Building; Cooper-Hewitt, National Design Museum; Freer Gallery of Art; Hirshhorn Museum and Sculpture Garden; National Air and Space Museum (NASM) and the Steven F. Udvar-Hazy Center; National Museum of African-American History and Culture; National Museum of African Art; National Museum of American History; National Museum of the American Indian (NMAI) and the George Gustav Heye Center; National Museum of Natural History; National Portrait Gallery; National Postal Museum; Renwick Gallery; Arthur M. Sackler Gallery; Smithsonian American Art Museum; and the Smithsonian Institution Building or "Castle"; as well as the National Zoological Park. The research institutes are the Archives of American Art, Center for Earth and Planetary Studies of the NASM, Center for Folklife and Cultural Heritage, Conservation and Research Center of the National Zoological Park, Marine Station at Fort Pierce, Museum Conservation Institute, Smithsonian Astrophysical Observatory, Smithsonian Environmental Research Center, and Smithsonian Tropical Research Institute. In addition to its library, the Smithsonian houses 12 archival repositories including the Archives of American Art, Archives Center of the National Museum of American History, Archives of American Gardens, Eliot Elisofon Archives at the National Museum of African Art, Freer–Sackler Archives,

Hirshhorn Museum and Sculpture Garden Archives, NASM Archives, National Anthropological Archives (NAA) and Human Studies Film Archives (HSFA), NMAI Archives, Ralph Rinzler Archives of the Center for Folklife and Cultural Heritage Archives, and Smithsonian Institution Archives. This entry will introduce the reader to this complex organization and provide an overview of its information resources.

THE SMITHSONIAN INSTITUTION

On August 10, 1846, U.S. President James K. Polk signed the legislation founding the Smithsonian Institution as a public trust dedicated to the "increase and diffusion of knowledge." This legislation was the culmination of over a decade of debate among the general public and the U.S. Congress over a peculiar bequest. In 1829, an English chemist and mineralogist, James Smithson, died, leaving a will that stated if his heir died without heirs, his estate should go to the United States to found "in Washington, under the name of the Smithsonian Institution, an establishment for the increase and diffusion of knowledge among men." After his sole heir died in 1835, the United States was notified of this bequest, sparking a heated debate between states' rights advocates and federalists over whether such a national entity should be created, with the federalists prevailing. In 1836, the United States filed a claim for the Smithson estate in the British Court of Chancery which awarded the estate, valued at over $500,000 to the United States in 1838. Another decade passed, however, before the Smithsonian was actually created. Congressmen, educators, scientists, social reformers, and the general public all voiced opinions as to what they believed Smithson had meant by "the increase and diffusion of knowledge." Initially most Americans assumed that Smithson intended to found a university; thus debate

Encyclopedia of Library and Information Sciences, Fourth Edition DOI: 10.1081/E-ELIS4-120044506

Fig. 1 The Smithsonian Institution Building or "Castle," photograph by Ken Rahaim.
Source: From Smithsonian Institution.

centered on what type of school. Gradually other ideas were introduced—an observatory, a scientific research institute, a national library, a publishing house, or a museum. The final legislation represented a compromise among these ideas, leaving out only the university. The Smithsonian Institution was created as a trust instrumentality of the United States, not part of the three branches of government, managed by a self-perpetuating Board of Regents (see Fig. 1).

The Smithsonian Regents were given the responsibility to decide how to carry out Smithson's vague mandate and the broad legislation. Their first act was to build a home for the Institution, a Norman "Castle" designed by architect James Renwick Jr., located on the National Mall in Washington, District of Columbia. The Regents selected as the first chief operating officer or Secretary, Joseph Henry, a distinguished physicist from the College of New Jersey (now Princeton University) who was an expert on electromagnetic induction. During his years as Secretary (1846–1878), Henry focused on increasing knowledge through scientific research and diffusing knowledge through publication of *Smithsonian Contribution to Knowledge* and through international exchange of publications. He established a national network of weather observers that led to the founding of the National Weather Service. Although the enabling act called for it, Henry was reluctant to use the Smithson fund for a national library or museum. Thus in the 1860s, he transferred the library and art collection to the Library of Congress and Corcoran Gallery of Art, and had the provision for copyright deposit at the Smithsonian repealed from the legislation. Henry

accepted natural history collections, as necessary for research, but worried about the costs of maintaining a museum collection and exhibits. The U.S. government's collection of art works, historical memorabilia, and scientific specimens, then housed at the National Institute gallery in the Patent Office Building, was transferred to the Smithsonian in 1858. The Smithsonian agreed to care for the national collections if an annual appropriation was provided by the U.S. Congress, formally establishing the United States National Museum at the Smithsonian. The second Secretary, Spencer Fullerton Baird, turned his energies enthusiastically to creating a great national museum during his tenure from 1878 to 1887. As Smithsonian curator since 1850, Baird's goal was to compile for the U.S. National Museum a comprehensive collection of all natural resources of North America. Baird prepared all of the government exhibits for the Centennial Exposition in Philadelphia in 1876; this gave the Institution national visibility and persuaded the Congress to build the first U.S. National Museum Building, now known as the Arts and Industries Building. When the building opened to the public in 1881, it housed exhibits on art, history, and natural history. During Baird's tenure, the Bureau of American Ethnology was added to the Smithsonian's programs in 1879 to document Native American cultures rapidly vanishing from the West. During the tenure of the third Secretary, Samuel Pierpont Langley from 1887 to 1906, the Smithsonian Astrophysical Observatory was established in 1890, the National Zoological Park was established in 1891, and funding was secured for a new National Museum Building.

Charles Doolittle Walcott, paleontologist and director of the United States Geological Survey, succeeded Langley as the fourth Secretary from 1907 to 1927. Under Walcott, the new museum building, now known as the National Museum of Natural History, opened in 1910 to house natural history and art collections. A National Gallery of Art, now the Smithsonian American Art Museum, was formally created in 1920. In 1923 the Freer Gallery of Art also opened, housing industrialist Charles Lang Freer's collection of Asian art and the works of James McNeill Whistler.

The fifth Secretary, Charles Greeley Abbot, served from 1928 to 1944, through the Great Depression and World War II. The National Zoological Park used the Works Progress Administration and Public Works of Art program to construct new zoo buildings. During World War II, much of the National Museum collections were moved off-site for safekeeping. The Smithsonian housed the Ethnogeographic Board which provided the military with ethnographic and geographic information about little known areas of the world, especially the Pacific. After the war from 1945 to 1952, Alexander Wetmore, the sixth Secretary, oversaw a program of exhibits modernization at the National Museum. In 1946, the Canal Zone Biological Area was placed under Smithsonian aegis. Now known as the Smithsonian Tropical Research Institute, this research station in the Panama Canal was founded in 1923 to facilitate research on the tropics. The National Museum's growing aeronautical collection, which included Charles Lindbergh's *Spirit of St. Louis*, was formally designated the National Air Museum in 1946. The Smithsonian Traveling Exhibition Service was inaugurated in 1952 to facilitate exhibits at venues outside the Institution. During the 1950s, groundwork was laid for substantial growth in Smithsonian programs under the seventh Secretary Leonard Carmichael during 1953–1964. Carmichael secured the appropriation for a new museum building for the history collections, which opened in 1964 and is now the National Museum of American History. New wings were added to the Natural History Building in the 1960s to house additional collections. The Patent Office Building was transferred to the Smithsonian in 1958 to house the national art collections. A major capital improvement program was initiated at the National Zoological Park in the 1960s, and the Smithsonian Astrophysical Observatory was revitalized and transferred to Cambridge, Massachusetts, in 1955. After the launching of Sputnik in 1957, the observatory played a major role in the tracking of artificial satellites. S. Dillon Ripley, eighth Secretary from 1964 to 1984, oversaw a major expansion in Smithsonian programs. New museums included the Anacostia Community Museum (1967), the Cooper-Hewitt, National Design Museum, located in New York (1968), the National Portrait Gallery (1968), the Renwick Gallery (1972), the Hirshhorn Museum and Sculpture Garden (1974), the National

Museum of African Art (1979), the Sackler Gallery (1983), and the S. Dillon Ripley Center (1987). The Smithsonian American Art Museum moved to the newly renovated Patent Office Building in 1968. A new building for the NASM opened on July 4, 1976 in celebration of the Bicentennial of the American Revolution, and the Arts and Industries Building was renovated to recreate the Centennial Exposition in Philadelphia in 1876. In the 1970s, Smithsonian museums began the transfer of their collection records to automated database systems. In October of 1978, at the request of the U.S. Congress, the Smithsonian initiated a database inventory of all collections in its museums. In 1983, the survey was completed and had identified nearly 100 million objects and specimens.

New programs included the Office of Fellowships and Grants in 1964; The Smithsonian Associates and the Smithsonian Environmental Research Center in 1965; Office of Museum Programs in 1966; first Festival of American Folklife in 1967 and subsequently the Center for Folklife and Cultural Heritage; Conservation Analytical Laboratory in 1969 (now the Museum Conservation Institute), *Smithsonian* magazine, Smithsonian Institution Archives, and Archives of American Art in 1970; Smithsonian Marine Station at Link Port in 1971; Office of Elementary and Secondary Education in 1974 (now the Smithsonian Center for Education and Museum Studies); Office of Telecommunications in 1975; and Office of Horticulture in 1976. Expansions of existing programs included the Fred L. Whipple Observatory in Arizona in 1968; the Conservation and Research Center of the National Zoological Park in Front Royal, Virginia, in 1975; and the Museum Support Center in 1983 to house collections storage and handling. From 1984 to 1994, Robert McCormick Adams served as ninth Secretary, presiding over a period of consolidation and renewed emphasis on research. Museums founded during his tenure were the NMAI in 1989, located in both New York and Washington, District of Columbia, and the National Postal Museum in 1990. New research programs focused on the role of man in the environment, including the Biodiversity Program established in 1986 in conjunction with the United Nations Educational, Scientific, and Cultural Organization's Man and the Biosphere Program and the Mpala Research Station established in Kenya in 1992. The National Science Resource Center was established in 1985 in cooperation with the National Academy of Sciences to develop precollege curriculum resources in mathematics and science. Expansions of existing programs included the Arctic Studies Center established in the National Museum of Natural History in 1988 and a new observatory in Mount Harquehala, Hawaii, in 1991. In 1995, the Commission on the Future of the Smithsonian Institution issued its report, *E Pluribus Unum: This Divine Paradox*, setting forth its vision for the Smithsonian of the twenty-first century. When the tenth Secretary, I. Michael Heyman, took office in 1994, he turned his attention to disseminating information electronically and celebrating the 150th anniversary of the Institution in 1996. In 1995, the Smithsonian Institution's Home Page went live on the Internet, making the Institution's resources and exhibits available worldwide. Sesquicentennial programs included a traveling exhibit, "America's Smithsonian," and a celebration on the National Mall on August 10, 1996. Lawrence M. Small served as the eleventh Secretary from 2000 to 2007. In 2003, the Steven F. Udvar-Hazy Center of the NASM opened near Dulles Airport. Also in 2003, a National Museum of African-American History and Culture was established as part of the Smithsonian; the museum is projected to open on the Mall in 2015. In 2004, the NMAI opened on the Mall, complementing the small museum in New York City and the Cultural Resources Center in Suitland, Maryland. In 2007, biologist Cristián Samper was appointed Acting Secretary and served until the 12th Secretary, G. Wayne Clough assumed office on July 1, 2008.

Smithsonian Art Museums

There are eight Smithsonian art museums.

The Cooper-Hewitt, National Design Museum is located in the historic Carnegie Mansion in New York City and is the only museum in the nation devoted exclusively to historic and contemporary design. Through its over 200,000 objects, and educational and curatorial programs, the Museum studies the impact of design on daily life. The Museum's mission is to advance the public understanding of design across the twenty-four centuries of human creativity represented by the Museum's collection.

Located on the Mall, the Freer and Sackler Galleries house the strongest collection of Asian art in the world and are dedicated to fostering understanding of Asian art and culture. The Freer Gallery of Art contains art from China, Japan, Korea, South and Southeast Asia, and the Near East. Collections include Chinese paintings, Japanese folding screens, Korean ceramics, Indian and Persian manuscripts, and Buddhist sculpture. It also contains a collection of American art influenced by Asian art, including some 1300 works by James McNeill Whistler. A highlight of the Whistler holdings is the Peacock Room, a lavishly decorated dining room with a blue and gold peacock design that was once part of a London townhouse.

The Arthur M. Sackler Gallery houses the collection of some 1000 works of Asian art donated by Dr. Arthur M. Sackler, including early Chinese bronzes and jades, Chinese paintings and lacquerware, ancient Near Eastern ceramics and metalware, and sculpture from South and Southeast Asia. Acquisitions since 1987 have included the Vever Collection, an important assemblage of the Islamic arts of the book from the eleventh to the nineteenth century; nineteenth- and twentieth-century Japanese prints and contemporary porcelain; Indian, Chinese, Japanese, and Korean paintings; arts of village India; contemporary Chinese ceramics; and photography. The Sackler Gallery is connected by an underground exhibition space to the neighboring Freer Gallery of Art. Although their collections are stored and exhibited separately, the two museums share a director, administration, and staff. The Freer–Sackler Archives documents its areas of collecting.

The Hirshhorn Museum and Sculpture Garden, located on the Mall, is dedicated to contemporary art and culture, providing a national platform for the arts and artists. The museum collects, studies, and shares modern and contemporary art through acquisitions, archives, exhibitions, education and public programs, conservation, and research. Its collections, assembled originally by Joseph H. Hirshhorn (1899–1981), contain all media of modern art ranging from prints, drawings, paintings, sculpture, film, and video to multimedia and includes nearly 12,000 art works by such artists as Willem de Kooning, Helen Frankenthaler, Morris Louis, and Pablo Picasso. Its outdoor sculpture garden contains works such as Auguste Rodin's *Burghers of Calais* and Alexander Calder's *Six Dots over a Mountain*.

The National Museum of African Art, located on the Mall, fosters the discovery and appreciation of the visual arts of Africa. Its collections, originally assembled by Warren M. Robbins (1923–2008) embrace the diverse artistic expressions found throughout Africa, from ancient to contemporary times. Collection objects range from ceramics, textiles, furniture, and tools to masks, figures, and musical instruments. The arts of painting, printmaking, sculpture, and other media are well represented by living artists whose works highlight individual creativity, address global and local art trends, and innovatively transform artistic traditions into modern idioms. The Eliot Elisofon Photographic Archives is a research center with over 300,000 still photographic images documenting the arts, peoples, and history of Africa over the past 120 years.

The National Portrait Gallery tells the stories of America through depictions of the individuals who have shaped U.S. history and culture. Located in the Donald W. Reynolds Center for American Art and Portraiture in the historic Patent Office Building in northwest Washington, District of Columbia, the gallery uses the visual arts, performing arts, and new media to portray poets and presidents, visionaries and villains, actors, and activists who tell the story of American history. Notable among its collections is the Hall of Presidents, the only complete collection of portraits of U.S. presidents outside of the White House, with Gilbert Stuart's iconic "Lansdowne" portrait of George Washington. The collections include such figures as Sequoyah, Babe Ruth, George Gershwin, Marilyn Monroe, and Dr. Martin Luther King Jr.

The Smithsonian American Art Museum's Renwick Gallery collects, exhibits, studies, and preserves American crafts and decorative arts from the nineteenth to twenty-

Smithsonian–Society

first centuries. Housed in a historic architectural landmark designed by James Renwick for the original Corcoran Gallery of Art, across the street from the White House, the Renwick features unique work in clay, fiber, glass, metal, and wood. Selections from the Renwick's permanent collection of American crafts and decorative arts are displayed on a rotating basis in the second floor galleries. Popular works include Larry Fuente's *Game Fish*, Wendell Castle's *Ghost Clock*, and Albert Paley's *Portal Gates*. Temporary exhibitions of American crafts and decorative arts are shown on the Renwick's first floor. Special exhibitions highlight contemporary artists as well as traditions in American crafts.

The Smithsonian American Art Museum, located in the Donald W. Reynolds Center for American Art and Portraiture in the historic Patent Office Building in northwest Washington, District of Columbia, is dedicated to the art and artists of the United States. All regions, cultures, and traditions of the United States are represented in the museum's collections, research resources, exhibitions, and public programs. Colonial portraiture, nineteenth-century landscape, American impressionism, twentieth-century realism and abstraction, New Deal projects, sculpture, photography, prints and drawings, contemporary crafts, African-American art, Latino art, and folk art are featured in the collection. More than 7000 American artists are represented, including major artists such as John Singleton Copley, Winslow Homer, John Singer Sargent, Childe Hassam, Georgia O'Keeffe, Edward Hopper, Jacob Lawrence, Robert Rauschenberg, Nam June Paik, and Martin Puryear. Today the collection consists of more than 40,000 artworks in all media, spanning more than 300 years of artistic achievement. Digital images of over 20,000 of those objects are available online, and information about American art is available through the Joan of Art Web site and the museum's interactive blogs.

The Archives of American Art, colocated with the National Portrait Gallery and Smithsonian American Art Museum in the Reynolds Center, is dedicated to the collection, preservation, and study of papers and other primary records of the history of the visual arts in America. Its collections, comprising 15 million items, are the world's largest single source for such information. The collections include correspondence, journals, business papers, and other documentation of artists, dealers, critics, art historians, and art institutions from the eighteenth century to the present. They also include some 3000 oral history interviews, 500,000 graphic images, and 75,000 works of art on paper.

Smithsonian History Museums

There are eight Smithsonian history and culture museums.

The Anacostia Community Museum is a local center for African-American history and culture in southeast Washington, District of Columbia. The Museum explores American history, society, and creative expression from an African-American perspective. The museum encourages the collection, protection, and preservation of materials that reflect the history and traditions of families, organizations, individuals, and communities.

The Arts and Industries Building, which opened in 1881, was built as the first national museum of the United States. It was closed in 2006, pending renovations. Prior to closing, it housed the Smithsonian Institution Archives which collects the official records of the Smithsonian Institution, the papers of Smithsonian scholars and other staff members, and the records of related professional organizations. The Archives provides reference services to the general public and to staff of the Smithsonian Institution. The Archives maintains over 25,000 cubic feet of holdings, which include institutional records, personal papers, and special collections. Official records provide a comprehensive history of the development and activities of the Smithsonian; its role in nineteenth century American science, especially natural history; Smithsonian involvement with cultural and social issues; and the development of museums as institutions. Automated indexes and collection-level descriptions are available to more than 1100 collections in the Archives.

The National Museum of African-American History and Culture was legislated by the U.S. Congress in 2003 and is in the planning stages. The goals of the museum are to create an opportunity for those who care about or who are interested in African-American culture to explore this history; to help all Americans see how central African-American history is for everyone; to use African-American culture as a means to help all Americans see how their stories, their histories, and their cultures are shaped and informed by international considerations; and to serve as a place of collaboration, reaching beyond Washington to engage new audiences and to collaborate with the myriad of museums and educational institutions that have explored and preserved this important history. A site has been selected on the National Mall where the museum will open in 2015.

The National Museum of American History, Behring Center, uses its collections and scholarship to create a broader understanding of the United States and its many peoples. Its over 3 million objects cover such areas as the history of science, technology, and medicine, political history and history of domestic life. Iconic objects include the *Star-Spangled Banner*, the First Ladies Gowns, Dizzy Gillespie's angled trumpet, and Dorothy's ruby slippers from *The Wizard of Oz*. Its Archives Center preserves and provides access to documentary evidence of the American past, complementing the Museum's artifacts. More than 850 collections occupy some 12,000 feet of shelving; in addition to paper-based textual records, many Center collections contain photographs, motion picture films, videotapes, and sound recordings.

The NMAI has three components: a flagship museum on the National Mall in Washington, District of Columbia, which opened in 2003; the George Gustav Heye Center in New York City, located in the historic Customs Building, which features temporary exhibits; and a Cultural Resources Center in Suitland, Maryland, where Native Americans can view and use objects and consult the museum's archives. The NMAI is the first national museum dedicated to the preservation, study, and exhibition of the life, languages, literature, history, and arts of Native Americans. The museum works in collaboration with the Native peoples of the Western Hemisphere to protect and foster their cultures by reaffirming traditions and beliefs, encouraging contemporary artistic expression, and empowering the Indian voice. The museum's extensive collections, assembled originally by George Gustav Heye (1874–1957), encompass a vast range of cultural material—including more that 800,000 works of aesthetic, religious, and historical significance, as well as articles produced for everyday, utilitarian use. The collections span all major culture areas of the Americas, representing virtually all tribes of the United States, most of those of Canada, and a significant number of cultures from Central and South America as well as the Caribbean. Chronologically, the collections include artifacts from Paleo-Indian to contemporary arts and crafts. The museum's holdings also include film and audiovisual collections, paper archives, and a photography archive of approximately 90,000 images depicting both historic and contemporary Native American life.

The NASM located on the Mall in Washington, District of Columbia, maintains the largest collection of historic air and spacecraft in the world. It is also a center for research into the history, science, and technology of aviation and space flight, as well as planetary science and terrestrial geology and geophysics. The NASM Archives holds materials documenting the history of air and space flight, including a wide range of visual and textual materials, many emphasizing the technical aspects of air and spacecraft. The archival collection contains approximately 10,000 cubic feet of material including an estimated 1.75 million photographs, 700,000 feet of motion picture film, and 2 million technical drawings. The Mall museum houses such iconic objects as the Wright 1903 Flyer and Charles Lindberg's *Spirit of St. Louis*, Apollo 11 command module, and a moon rock. In 2004, its Steven F. Udvar-Hazy Center opened near Dulles Airport in Virginia to display collections that could not be viewed on the Mall, including the Boeing B-29 Superfortress *Enola Gay* and Space *Shuttle Enterprise*.

The National Postal Museum, a collaboration between the Smithsonian's National Philatelic Collection and the United States Postal Service, is located near Union Station in Washington, District of Columbia. Its exhibits feature stamps and philatelic items, vehicles that have carried the mail and a wide array of items from the history of America's postal system. The National Philatelic Collection was established at the Smithsonian in 1886 with the donation of a sheet of 10¢ Confederate postage stamps; today the collection totals more than 6 million items. In addition to one of the world's largest collections of stamps and philatelic materials, the National Postal Museum has postal history material that predates stamps, vehicles used to transport the mail, mailboxes and mailbags, postal uniforms and equipment.

Smithsonian Institution Building or Castle

The Smithsonian Institution Building or "Castle" was the first Smithsonian building, completed in 1855 on the National Mall. Designed by architect James Renwick in the Norman style, it is constructed of red Seneca sandstone and stands in sharp contrast to most of the classical marble buildings that dominate the nation's capital. In its early years, it housed all of the Institution's research and museum functions. Today it houses administrative offices and the Institution's Visitor Center where visitors can learn about the Institution's museums and research programs, and plan their museum visits.

Smithsonian Science Museums

There is one Smithsonian science museum, the National Museum of Natural History, as well as the National Zoological Park.

The National Museum of Natural History is the Institution's largest museum and is dedicated to inspiring curiosity, discovery, and learning about the natural world through its research, collections, exhibitions, and education outreach programs. The main building on the National Mall contains 1.5 million square feet of space overall with 325,000 square feet of exhibition and public space, and houses over 1000 employees. Among its 126.6 million artifacts and specimens are some of the oldest of the Institution's collections. The Museum includes a state-of-the-art collections storage facility in Suitland, Maryland; a marine science research facility in Ft. Pierce, Florida; and field stations as far away as Belize, Alaska, and Kenya. It also houses the NAA and the HSFA. The NAA is dedicated to preserving ethnographic, archaeological, and linguistic field notes, physical anthropological data, photographs, sound recordings, and other media created by American anthropologists. The Archives' holds 8250 linear feet of field notes, photographs, correspondence, journals, sound recordings, and works of art, and more than 53,000 digital images are now available. The HSFA is devoted to collecting, preserving, documenting, and disseminating a broad range of historical and contemporary ethnographic and anthropological moving image materials. The HSFA also collects related documentation including sound recordings, photographs, manuscripts and other associated texts, field notes, camera, and sound logs and production logs. Museum research activities are organized into seven departments, and a number of affiliated U.S. government agencies onsite contribute to the Museum's strength, including the Department of the Interior (U.S. Geological Survey Biological Resources Division), the Department of Agriculture (Systematic Entomology Laboratory), the Department of Commerce (National Marine Fisheries Service Systematics Laboratory), and the Department of Defense (Walter Reed Biosystematics Unit). The museum houses collections in anthropology, botany, geology and mineralogy, and zoology; among its iconic objects are the Hope Diamond and the Fenykovi elephant.

The National Zoological Park is located in Rock Creek Park in Washington, District of Columbia. Its mission is to demonstrate leadership in animal care, science, education, and sustainability through the highest quality animal care, research, and scientific knowledge in conserving wildlife, teaching people to protect wildlife, natural resources and habitats, and practicing conservation leadership. Its diverse collections includes animals from ants to elephants, representing habitats from tropical rainforest to local woodlands; it is perhaps best known for its Giant Pandas, Tian Tian, Mei Xiang, and Tai Shan. It has pioneered the conservation of such animals as the cheetah and the reintroduction of the golden lion tamarin. The zoo covers 163 acres and has 23 major buildings along with many smaller barns and support structures throughout the site. Its Conservation and Research Center, in Front Royal, Virginia, is dedicated to research on conservation, management, and reproduction of endangered species. Scientists at NZP's Conservation GIS Lab use satellite imagery and Geographic Information Systems (GIS) to identify, monitor, and fight habitat loss and species extinction globally. Collaborations with NASA, the U.S. Fish and Wildlife Service, and the U.S. Geological Survey allow Zoo scientists to utilize vast amounts of remotely-collected satellite images showing the condition of large and inaccessible areas—for example, the habitats and last strongholds for Asian elephants, giant panda, clouded leopard, and many other species. Zoo scientists integrate these data with their own extensive field research to monitor and assess the effects of habitat loss on these focal species.

In 2008, the Institution housed an estimated 137 million artifacts and specimens in its 19 museums, with over 126 million at the National Museum of Natural History (Table 1). The Institution shares its collections with some 152 affiliate museums in 39 states, the District of Columbia, Panama, and Puerto Rico. The Smithsonian endowment has grown to some $1 billion, part of a net operating budget in 2007 of $635 million, with about 70% in federal funds and the remainder in trust funds, including endowment, grants and contracts, and business income. In 2007 there were approximately 24.2 million visitors to the museums and National Zoo (see Table 2).

Table 1 Smithsonian Collections, 2007.

Museum	Collections
Anacostia Community Museum	8,781
Arthur M. Sackler Gallery	8,787
Cooper-Hewitt, National Design Museum	206,199
Freer Gallery of Art	28,450
Hirshhorn Museum and Sculpture Garden	11,536
National Air and Space Museum and S. F. Udvar-Hazy Center	47,579
National Museum of African Art	9,090
National Museum of American History	3,203,117
National Museum of American Indian and G. F. Heye Center	826,237
National Museum of Natural History	126,642,657
National Portrait Gallery	19,611
National Postal Museum	6,003,548
National Zoological Park	1,857
Smithsonian American Art Museum and Renwick Gallery	41,581
Other collections	48,283
Total collections	137,107,313

In 2007, a staff of nearly 6200 employees and nearly 6500 volunteers carried out its programs in 9 research institutes, 19 museums and zoological park in Washington, District of Columbia, across the continent, and around the world. The Institution employs specialists in the arts, culture, humanities and sciences, with employees in such categories as archivist, animal keeper, anthropologist, astrophysicist, biologist, curator, ecologist, education specialist, exhibits specialist, historian, horticulturalist,

Table 2 Smithsonian Visitors, 2007.

Building	Visitors
Anacostia Community Museum	37,000
Arthur M. Sackler Gallery	308,000
Arts and Industries Building	Closed
Cooper-Hewitt, National Design Museum	224,000
Freer Gallery of Art	590,000
Hirshhorn Museum and Sculpture Garden	740,000
National Air and Space Museum	6,000,000
National Air and Space Museum S. F. Udvar-Hazy Center	1,000,000
National Museum of African Art	310,000
National Museum of American History	Closed
National Museum of the American Indian	1,800,000
National Museum of the American Indian Heye Center	281,000
National Museum of the American Indian Cultural Resources Center	1,000
National Museum of Natural History	7,100,000
National Postal Museum	326,000
National Zoological Park	2,600,000
Renwick Gallery	132,000
S. Dillon Ripley Center	296,000
Smithsonian American Art Museum and National Portrait Gallery	786,000
Smithsonian Institution Building	1,600,000
Total visitors	24,200,000

librarian, network engineer, photographer, security guard, visual information specialist, woodcrafter, and writer/editor. Staff perform a wide range of duties in collections care, research, education, and public outreach. Volunteers perform a wide array of duties from museum docents, conservation technicians, and archives technicians to animal care assistants, and assist with research in the arts, culture, history, and science.

Since 1995, the Smithsonian has focused much of its energies on making its resources available to researchers, teachers, students, and the general public through the Internet, http://www.smithsonian.org. All research institutes, museums and the zoo have extensive Web sites, with 183.6 million visits in 2007. Museum exhibits are simultaneously presented in online format. Lectures and public programs are made available through podcasts. Information about the Institution's collections is being made available through online databases and digitization projects, such as Smithsonian Institution Research Information System (SIRIS, http://www.siris.si.edu). The National Portrait Gallery, for example, has an online database, the Catalog of American Portraits, a survey of American portraits in public and private collections across the United States and abroad, with information about the portrait and, often, a digital image of the art work, http://npgportraits.si.edu/eMuseumNPG/code/emuseum.asp.

Research collections of the National Museum of Natural History are available to the public via a standard Web interface with a total of 3,892,938 specimen records currently available. Of these records, 197,372 are extant type specimen records that represent more than 55% of the museum's extant biological type specimens, http://nhb-acsmith1.si.edu. Several of the museums have instituted monitored blogs on topics related to their collections, such as the Smithsonian American Art Museum's Eye Level, http://eyelevel.si.edu. The Smithsonian Libraries Galaxy of Knowledge, http://www.sil.si.edu/, contains digital copies of many of its resources. The Smithsonian Astrophysical Observatory makes a wide array of scientific resources available for researchers, but also operates the Chandra X-ray Observatory Center for teachers, students, and amateur astronomers at http://chandra.harvard.edu/. The Smithsonian Environmental Research Center has established a distance learning center with electronic field trips on ecology that can be used in the K-12 classroom, http://www.serc.si.edu/education/dl/index.jsp. The Smithsonian Tropical Research Institute has a long-term environmental monitoring program for marine and terrestrial environments and now makes its data available to researchers in real time, http://striweb.si.edu/esp/.

CONCLUSION

The Smithsonian Institution is the largest museum and research complex in the world. The bequest by English scientist James Smithson had a broad mandate, as did the Institution's enabling act, allowing the Institution to meet the needs of a young nation. Its complex of museums in the U.S. capital welcomes visitors from around the world without admission, displaying the arts, cultures, history, and the sciences. Its museums and research centers span the globe, and it disseminates its resources through its extensive Web sites.

ACKNOWLEDGMENTS

This information was compiled with assistance from the Smithsonian Institution Archives, National Collections Program, Web Services Division, Office of Public Affairs and Office of Programming, Management and Budget.

BIBLIOGRAPHY

1. Ewing, H.P. *The Lost World of James Smithson: Science, Revolution, and the Birth of the Smithsonian*; Bloomsbury Publishing: New York, 2007.
2. Field, C.R.; Stamm, R.E.; Ewing, H.P. *The Castle: An Illustrated History of the Smithsonian Building*; Smithsonian Institution Press: Washington, DC, 1993.
3. Hellman, G.T. *The Smithsonian: Octopus on the Mall*,; Greenwood Press: Westport, CT, 1978.
4. Henson, P.M. A national science and a national museum. In *Museums and Other Institutions of Natural History: Past, Present, and Future*; Leviton, A.E., Aldrich, M.E., Eds.; California Academy of Sciences: San Francisco, CA, 2004; 34–57.
5. Hinsley, C.M., Jr. *The Smithsonian and the American Indian: Making Moral Anthropology in Victorian America*; Smithsonian Institution Press: Washington, DC, 1994.
6. Jones, B.Z. *Lighthouse of the Skies: The Smithsonian Astrophysical Observatory: Background and History, 1846–1955*; Smithsonian Institution: Washington, DC, 1965.
7. Mergen, A. *From Bison to Biopark: 100 Years of the National Zoo*; Friends of the National Zoo: Washington, DC, 1989.
8. Meyer, A.E. *Charles Lang Freer and His Gallery*; Freer Gallery of Art: Washington, DC, 1970.
9. Oehser, P.H. *Sons of Science: The Story of the Smithsonian Institution and Its Leaders*; Henry Schuman: New York, 1949.
10. Oehser, P.H. *The Smithsonian Institution*; Praeger Publishers: New York, 1970.
11. Park, E., 1984; September 77–85 Secretary S. Dillon Ripley retires after twenty years of innovation. Smithsonian.
12. Reingold, N.,; Pierson, S.,; Molella, A.P., Eds.; *The Papers of Joseph Henry*; Smithsonian Institution Press: Washington, DC, 1972, 1975, 1979, 1981, 1985; Vols. 1–5.

13. Rivinus, E.F.; Youssef, E.M. *Spencer F. Baird of the Smithsonian*; Smithsonian Institution Press: Washington, DC, 1992.

14. Rothenberg, M.; Dorman, K.W.,; Millikan, F.R.; Jeffries, D.Y.; Shoenfeld, S.J., Eds.; *The Papers of Joseph Henry*; Smithsonian Institution Press: Washington, DC, 1992, 1996, 1998, 2002, 2004, 2007; Vols. 6–11.

15. Washburn, W.E. Joseph Henry's conception of the purpose of the Smithsonian Institution. In *A Cabinet of Curiosities: Five Episodes in the Evolution of American Museums*; Bell, W.J., Jr., Ed.; University Press of Virginia: Charlottesville, VA, 1967; 106–166.

Social Epistemology

Steve Fuller
Department of Sociology, University of Warwick, Coventry, U.K.

Abstract

"Social epistemology" is the social theory or social science of knowledge. After the field's bases in the Anglophone and Continental philosophical traditions are briefly explored, social epistemology's relevance to library and information science (LIS) is established. LIS presumes that knowledge is both an inherently collective product that ought to be made universally available. This is exemplified in the traditionally iconic status of the library. However, the library began to lose its salience in the Cold War, with the massification, technologization, and instrumentalization of knowledge, now renamed "information" to stress its relativity to decision-making contexts. The resulting stress on user-friendly information intensified after the Cold War, with the rise of neoliberalism. In this context, LIS has stood out in reasserting at a practical level the traditional universalist goals of social epistemology. In particular, Don Swanson's work on "undiscovered public knowledge" appears as a major achievement in applied social epistemology and a blow for "epistemic justice." It demonstrates the utility of breaking of default information search patterns that systematically neglect relevant literature in other fields. In the final section, *Wikipedia* is discussed as a self-organizing experiment in achieving the same effect by refusing to respect any claims to epistemic privilege.

PHILOSOPHICAL FOUNDATIONS AND RELEVANCE TO LIBRARY AND INFORMATION SCIENCE

"Social epistemology" literally means the social theory or social science of knowledge. That simple definition already says a lot. It implies that knowledge is *not* normally seen as intrinsically social; hence, "social" needs to be added to specify the field of inquiry. This point is worth noting because the image of knowledge as primarily acquired by individuals through their mental faculties (as perceptions, beliefs), who then combine with other such individuals, to construct more elaborate and durable knowledge products (such as theories, sciences), rests on a particular reading of the history of philosophy that is dominant only in the English-speaking world. For philosophers more influenced by French and German developments, knowledge is "always already" social in both its constitution and import. In the United States, this distinction is marked as "analytic" versus "continental" schools of philosophy.

For example, whereas English philosophers depict Descartes as someone whose skepticism was born of the potential unreliability of his senses and intellect, French and German philosophers stress the special relationship he claimed that we have with God, who in turn underwrites the general reliability of our senses and intellect. One consequence of this difference in emphasis is that in the English-speaking world "epistemology" is naturally aligned with the philosophy of mind, which focuses on what happens inside individual heads, while in the French- and German-speaking worlds it is more naturally aligned with the philosophy of science, which focuses of what happens between individuals in structured settings.

All of this matters to library and information science (LIS), which presupposes that knowledge is "always already" social. In other words, the relevant epistemological question is not whether we can possess knowledge but how can we come to possess it—specifically, what sorts of relationships do we need to forge with people, things, and processes to satisfy our epistemic needs. Accordingly, individual cognitive orientations can be understood as either normal or deviant expressions of preexistent culturally entrenched dispositions. While my personal experience may be unique, my public response to it is not. I know this because of the relative ease with which others can make sense of my response, even if they know little of my personal history. This does not mean that my response is completely predictable—but it can be contained within a relatively small range of possibilities. Without this strong sense of knowledge's social boundedness, LIS's capacity for systematically addressing society's various knowledge-based needs would be thrown into radical doubt. However, this still leaves open the question of whether the job of the LIS professional is to reinforce or to alter typical responses to recurrent knowledge-based needs. This may be the fundamental challenge that social epistemology poses to LIS.

It is clear that this challenge was grasped by those most closely associated with the emergence of social epistemology in LIS. Although social epistemology became a worldwide interdisciplinary concern only in the late 1980s

Encyclopedia of Library and Information Sciences, Fourth Edition DOI: 10.1081/E-ELIS4-120043254

Smithsonian–Society

with the establishment of a journal[1] and the publication of a book by that name,[2] it is now generally acknowledged that the prospects for a field called "social epistemology" were first broached in LIS as early as 1952 by Margaret Egan and Jesse Shera.[3] Indicative of the significance that social epistemology has acquired within LIS since its largely independent rediscovery by philosophers like Goldman,[4] Schmitt,[5] and Fuller[2] is the recent surge of interest in delineating the respective contributions of Egan and Shera to the development of the concept[6] and in demonstrating intellectual affinities between what LIS professionals and philosophers mean by social epistemology.[7]

Nevertheless, LIS professionals already had good reason to be concerned with the challenge posed by social epistemology in the third quarter of the twentieth century. The image of the library as the localized embodiment of the philosophical ideal of all knowledge available to all knowers was coming under severe strain, at both a material and an intellectual level. Materially, the book's status as the paradigmatic unit of knowledge was being eroded by the proliferation of specialist journals and other types of sources, many of which encoded knowledge in images rather than words. While some LIS visionaries like Paul Otlet and Suzanne Briet had seen the need for a more generic category of "document" to accommodate this inevitable expansion in knowledge-bearing materials, they did not anticipate the intellectual challenge to the very idea of universal knowledge, which continued to underwrite their cataloging schemes.

As the sources of knowledge became more diverse, the role of the LIS professional seemed to shift from a gatekeeper for generalists to a service provider for specialists. This shift was reflected in a shift in the academic training of LIS professionals from the humanities to the sciences. Both Egan and Shera had received their first degrees in English literature and considered LIS a career for generalists, yet they were faced with an increasingly computerized system of document storage and retrieval that was coded to favor specialist users. It seemed, then, that LIS professionals were fated to mediate user searches only in the context of instructing users in specialist categories, a service that might be provided in the future by a computerized "expert system" (Ch. 3).[8]

Social epistemology should be understood within LIS as a movement to mitigate, if not reverse, these trends, which are sometimes seen as having contributed to LIS's loss of professional status in various institutional settings. Indeed, in one of his last published pieces, Shera[9] warned of younger LIS professionals abandoning the librarian's traditional connoisseurship for a seemingly modern technology-driven expertise that only promised to render them obsolete in the long term. At a conceptual level, this problem was symbolized by the field's shift in focus from a philosophical conception of "knowledge" to a conception of "information" indebted, not always explicitly, to

Shannon and Weaver's communication theory.[10] According to this theory, information is defined relative to both the receiver and the medium of a message. Thus, a message is informative only if it makes a difference to the action taken by a given person in a given context. Such a stance implies a much more radical form of relativism than social epistemology licenses. Shannon and Weaver's theory seemed to deny that people need to know anything more than what will enable them to act decisively, which in turn presupposes that the best epistemic strategy for dealing with users in the long term is to provide them with information that offers the path of least resistance in the short term, and hence makes minimal demands on their default cognitive tendencies.

It is worth observing that the displacement of the library as the locus of universal knowledge that so concerned the early social epistemologists in LIS anticipated by a generation the more general displacement of academia as the seat of epistemic authority that is now associated with the "postmodern condition"[11] and the omnipresent "knowledge society."[12] Thus, today's knowledge users are frequently defined as "consumers" and, unsurprisingly, knowledge bases are increasingly demand-driven by particular classes of users, without any pretence to encompassing all knowledge users. This displacement of the library and the university can be explained in similar terms, namely, a decline in the salience of the nation-state as a frame of reference for defining the knower—that is, as a "citizen" who needs to be informed about things that go beyond his or her personal interests, simply by virtue of having a stake in a larger social order.

THE POSTMODERN CHALLENGE TO SOCIAL EPISTEMOLOGY: THE END OF UNIVERSAL KNOWLEDGE

The Cold War set the stage for the last strong state-based bid for universal knowledge, as the conflict between capitalism and socialism was sublimated through a "science race" between the United States and USSR. Egan and Shera[3] contributed to this discussion with the idea of a "macrocosmic bibliography," but its most important—albeit chequered—legacy has been the Science Citation Index (SCI), as first proposed by Eugene Garfield to the U.S. National Science Foundation (pp. 69–73).[13] From the standpoint of social epistemology, the most interesting feature of these proposals was their operationalization of "universality" as the multiple deployability of a common knowledge base so as to make maximum use of all that is already known. This would benefit not only the diverse interests of ordinary knowledge consumers but also frontline knowledge producers who when planning their research could avoid duplicating previous effort. At the same time, it marked a significant shift in the ideal exemplified by a universal knowledge base—from collective identity to individual efficiency—that, if anything, has acquired a greater salience in the post-Cold War neoliberal audit culture.[14]

Notwithstanding Shera's early concerns about the future of the library, and the LIS profession more generally, most pundits at the time took a more sanguine view about the emerging postmodern condition. Each regarded the image of the knowledge society as vindicating his own political perspective. For example, Fritz Machlup,[15] a classical liberal, believed that the increasing contribution of knowledge-based services to the economy pointed to the ultimate triumph of locally honed competences and individual initiatives over central state planning. On the contrary, Daniel Bell[16] argued, the prospect of computer-mediated production and distribution systems would perfect the welfare state's capacity to deal with the excesses of capitalism in order to bring about a just society. Finally, Alvin Gouldner,[17] a critical Marxist, held that the number of highly educated people required in the knowledge society, many in relatively marginal clerical positions, unwittingly created the conditions for what he called a "culture of critical discourse" that might eventually force a radical democratization of the social order.

To be sure, elements of Machlup's, Bell's, and Gouldner's punditry remain in play today, though not quite as any of them had hoped. The preoccupation with the assignment and protection of intellectual property speak to Machlup's vision; the increasing capacity of information technology to deliver services in an efficient and customized fashion address Bell's vision; and the use of the Internet to organize people worldwide to demonstrate against globalization and climate change bears out some of Gouldner's vision. However, what these "three wise men" missed in the realization of their respective visions is the idea that knowledge might lose some of its value as it is spread more widely.

As access is increased, the advantage one gains from having access diminishes. The upside is that it becomes more difficult, especially in the age of the Internet, for esoteric knowledge to be used as an instrument of power of others. The downside is that knowledge becomes so demystified that little value is placed on how we reach a conclusion as long as it is the one we wish to reach. Thus, today's knowledge societies marry a disrespect for expertise with a craving for credentials, resulting in a proliferation of what the historian David Noble[18] has called "digital diploma mills," such as the University of Phoenix, with its 300,000 student enrolment.

In short, the technological revolution in access embedded in a weakly regulated system of information transfer has turned the traditional normative conception of knowledge into what the political economist Fred Hirsch[19] originally called a "positional good", that is, a good whose value is determined more by its relative scarcity than its actual utility. Accordingly, the value of a Harvard education lies less in the content of its degree programs than in

the elite nature of its student selection process. An extension of the same point applies to the value of research published by a Harvard professor: The series of hoops through which one would have needed to jump to achieve that academic status does more to underwrite it as "knowledge" than its actual content, access to which for practical purposes might be acquired by less trying means.

Writing in what turned out to be the Golden Age of the welfare state, Hirsch believed that positional goods began to proliferate only after people had adequate access to goods that served the basic needs of living in a modern society. At that point, the struggle for survival yielded to the struggle for recognition—or, "Keeping up with the Joneses," to recall a resonant marketing slogan from the period. But Hirsch was wrong, at least with regard to knowledge, which exists as a positional good even though basic knowledge needs—even within academia—have yet to be serviced efficiently. Thus, the problem of knowledge utilization continues to loom large for social epistemology.[20] The problem has little to do with technical difficulties in the construction of search engines sufficiently responsive to a wide range of user needs. Rather, it relates to persistent, often discipline-based, biases that users—and specialist LIS professionals—bring to their searches that lead them down authorized paths that may do more to bolster an appearance of competence than directly address user needs. Thus, under the guise of what is sometimes called "information literacy," literatures may remain underutilized and user needs imperfectly addressed, as a presumption is created in favor of the "tried and tested."

This individual tendency is magnified at a collective level by the so-called principle of cumulative advantage, one of sociologist Robert Merton's[21] notorious euphemisms, whereby researchers tend to consult the work of those whose work has been worth consulting in the past to such an extent that new researchers come to be consulted only if they have been cited by those previously consulted. This results in a few researchers, typically with elite pedigrees, receiving a disproportionate amount of attention in any given field. Extreme instances of this tendency are in evidence when famous early adopters are given credit for a discovery or invention originally made by a more obscure figure. To be sure, this finding has been rationalized (especially by economists) in various ways, ranging from vague invocations of the "invisible hand" as an intellectual quality control mechanism to more *Realpolitik* suggestions that, in a competitive high-skill labor market, academic publication is indeed more about signaling competence than transmitting knowledge.[22]

Nicholas Rescher,[23] following in the footsteps of philosophy's most famous librarian, Gottfried Wilhelm von Leibniz, has coined the term "epistemetrics" to address these interpretive problems associated with the quantitative dimension of social epistemology. Perhaps because of his early mathematical training and Cold War links to systems theory and operations research, Rescher has been the analytic philosopher who over the past half-century has most consistently stressed themes of interest to LIS professionals. With that in mind, he has attributed to Herbert Spencer a "law of cognitive development," whereby an exponential rise in information corresponds to a linear growth of knowledge. Rescher here captures an idea that Marxists know as the "First Law of Dialectics," namely, that a sufficient number of elements in free combination will eventually produce structures with properties qualitatively different from those of the original elements. This "law" is meant to be applied very generally, so that the "elements" in question may include individual bits of information or containers of such bits (e.g., humans, computers, and other information processors).

A good historical example of Spencer's Law might be the step change in technological innovation that occurred in eighteenth century Britain that we now call the "Industrial Revolution," which is often attributed to a critical mass of skilled and literate individuals with the freedom to share their ideas and observations with each other. However, different mechanisms have been proposed to explain this transformation in social epistemology. Spencer's own *laissez faire* approach to political economy suggested trial and error, whereby the free elements collectively defined a market—or, more precisely, a clearinghouse—that selected better from worse ideas for further development, which then intensified the process of inquiry, resulting in a more rationalized and specialized division of labor. Of course, a similar selection can be applied to better and worse "bearers" of ideas, as implied by Merton's principle of cumulative advantage, in which case vital messages may be lost because the messenger is peremptorily shot, by virtue of possessing a poor or absent track record.

Economists, following Brian Arthur,[24] have distracted attention away from this possibility by focusing on the increasing returns on investment in a free market for ideas, which reinforces participants' commitment to the process, even if the ideas from which one benefits are not one's own. It is easy to get the impression that economists attracted by Merton's principle believe that the optimal solution for collective progress in the marketplace of ideas would be for original thinkers in obscure institutional positions to exchange their originality for mainstream acceptance by giving away their ideas to better placed thinkers to push them further while they themselves try to accommodate those ideas to mainstream thought so as to improve their own position. The reader is left to ponder the justice of a system that would reward both disrespect for individual achievement and respect for hierarchy in the guise of "peer review." To put a positive spin on Merton's principle, one might say that it encourages the merging of the roles of the composer and the performer than one regularly finds in the arts, whereby a noteworthy performer acquires much of the kudos that one might otherwise be reserved for the original composer.

APPLIED SOCIAL EPISTEMOLOGY: LIBRARY AND INFORMATION SCIENCE'S QUEST FOR EPISTEMIC JUSTICE

Unsurprisingly, LIS professionals, as guardians of knowledge as a material product and agents at the interface between producers and consumers of knowledge, have not been satisfied by such accounts. Perhaps most notably, Don Swanson[25] demonstrated the potency of a proactive social epistemology that refuses to take the unread as unworthy of being read. Though trained entirely in physics, Swanson, a library and information scientist at the University of Chicago, discovered that a plausible solution to an outstanding medical problem had been overlooked by the relevant specialists because it had been published in a journal that lay beyond their normal reading habits. Heartened by such findings, "knowledge managers" outside of academia have developed "data mining" procedures for accessing knowledge that, for the most part, academia has failed to exploit but could inspire industrial applications and patents.[8] However, there is no reason why such discovery procedures (or "retrieval strategies") should remain in the private sector and oriented solely toward commercial interests.

One cost-effective policy that LIS professionals could ensure in the name of social epistemology is that, in preparing grant proposals, researchers have identified the full range of precedents for the proposed work, in relation to which the research project would then be formulated. Such a policy would revive the original SCI concern to avoid the duplication of effort in an expanding knowledge system. Given the increasing specialization of today's researchers, research topics that potentially traverse several disciplinary boundaries may require LIS professionals as coprincipals to grant proposals to ensure not only the efficient utilization of the already available knowledge but also the comprehensive dissemination of the resulting research to relevant academic and nonacademic constituencies. This value-added character of LIS to the conduct of research is discussed below in terms of "epistemic justice" (pp. 24–29).[13]

Were the knowledge system organized from an LIS standpoint, no new research into a topic would be commissioned unless the already existing knowledge base had been exploited to its full extent. Thus, resource-intensive methods of original data generation and collection could be replaced, or at least deferred and attenuated, by the development of clever-automated search engines ("knowbots") with access to multiple disciplinary literatures. This policy would be very much in the spirit of Shera's vision of social epistemology, which would keep technological advances in LIS firmly under the control of its original humanist animus. Translated into practice, what Swanson[25] called "undiscovered public knowledge" supports the maintenance and use of institutional archives, in the face of increasing budgetary pressures to discard rarely consulted old books, serials, and other documents. The general failure of universities and other knowledge-based institutions to follow Swanson's precedent has resulted in an epidemic of "corporate amnesia," aka "mad archive disease."[26]

But it would be a mistake to conclude that corporate amnesia is merely the by-product of financially motivated negligence. It is also a design feature of science, akin to "planned obsolescence," whereby sciences with more clearly defined and rapidly advancing research frontiers have shorter citation half-lives. In other words, the relevance of each new text to the discipline's current state of play is evaluated quickly, clearly, and irreversibly. This implies a sharpening of the distinction between, so to speak, the discipline's "short-term" and "long-term" memory, corresponding to a division of labor between a practitioner and a historian of a discipline (pp. 6–9).[13] The influential historian and philosopher of science Thomas Kuhn went so far as to argue that the functional differentiation of practitioners and historians is constitutive of scientific progress, as it operationalizes the idea that science moves forward by leaving its past behind.[27] Indeed, Kuhn's contemporary and scientometrics' original theorist, Derek de Solla Price demonstrated that the harder the science, the sooner most of its literature is consigned to history. "Price's Index" implies that a sense of historicity is automatically generated by new literature falling, as David Hume said of his own first book, "still born from the presses" into oblivion (p. 27).[28]

Against this backdrop, LIS stands virtually alone among academic disciplines in its presumptive commitment to what might be called a "strong universalism" with regard to knowledge. LIS aims for knowledge that is "universal" not only in terms of validity but also availability, such that knowledge functions simultaneously as a source of authority and a mode of empowerment. This prospect animates what social epistemologists call "epistemic justice." Key to the administration of epistemic justice is a reduction in the gap between historian and practitioner knowledge, so as to minimize the power that expertise can exert over lay knowledge. After all, the faster the research frontier recedes from the view, the easier it is for one to be left behind; hence, the familiar phenomenon of a once active researcher who, after a few years in university administration, finds it impossible to return to her original field. This epistemic distance often appears as a layer of new jargon (expressed in both words and symbols) that functions as a barrier to latecomers, while allowing work to be redescribed as failed, primitive, or incomplete but, in any case, superseded by the new.

Philosophically speaking, a repository for all knowledge would entail access to, as courts demand of witnesses, "the whole truth and nothing but the truth." From the standpoint of social epistemology, LIS exists in the tension between the "whole" and the "nothing but" in the slogan. An expert-driven, discipline-based epistemic culture would have LIS focus on nothing but the truth, while a more consumer-driven, democratized epistemic culture would have the field cover truth as a whole. The former strategy is clearly more conservative than the latter, as a focus on nothing but the truth would allow, in statistical jargon, "false negatives," while a concern for the whole truth would allow "false positives." Hanging in the balance is whether LIS should reproduce the default search patterns of established disciplines. This would run the risk of peremptorily ignoring relevant work, or offer an independent and possibly more adventurous set of recommendations that itself would the risk of throwing up a lot of false leads but may end up, à la Swanson, reorienting more discipline-bound inquirers.

The two main philosophical approaches to social epistemology divide precisely on this point. On the one hand, some see the differentiation of knowledge into distinct expertises as a normal feature of the growth of knowledge. Often this process is depicted in terms of exfoliation or evolution, in both cases implying that expertise is an entitlement earned by those who have trained in and contributed to the discipline historically recognized as authorized to pronounce on a knowledge domain. From this standpoint, LIS professionals identify and police the boundaries separating these knowledge domains, directing users to the expert sources most relevant to their needs. Goldman[29] revealingly calls this position "epistemic paternalism," implying that an increasingly complex knowledge system requires that users be given increasing guidance on appropriate sources of knowledge. However, it takes for granted that the current division of cognitive labor is itself appropriate and necessary.

On the other hand, some philosophers, especially Fuller,[2,8] urge LIS professionals to adopt a more critical stance toward the historically contingent and institutionally entrenched character of existing disciplinary boundaries. From this standpoint, Swanson's "undiscovered public knowledge" draws attention to the increasing gaps between domains of knowledge that result from the tunnel vision induced by disciplinary specialization. But this must be distinguished from what the social science methodologist Donald Campbell[30] called the "fishscale model of omniscience," which implies that personal expertises overlap so that, taken together, there are no epistemic gaps in the community of inquirers.

While Campbell's point may describe the aggregate of people's actual knowledge bases, Swanson nevertheless captures people's tendency to interpret what they know of neighboring fields by the standards of their own fields, thereby limiting the prospects for those fields altering their own frame of reference. Here LIS professionals can facilitate the shifting between disciplinary frames, say, by the design of search engines that cross-classify cognate material so that users are forced to confront items they would not have otherwise deemed relevant to their inquiries. The result would be to shift users into a broader-gauged "browsing" mode, albeit within the general parameters of their original search. It would strike a small but reliable blow for epistemic justice.

WIKIPEDIA: A SELF-ORGANIZING EXPERIMENT IN EPISTEMIC JUSTICE

However, perhaps most extended experiment in epistemic justice underway is *Wikipedia*, the online encyclopedia, arguably most impressive collective intellectual project ever attempted—and perhaps achieved. It demands both the attention and the contribution of anyone concerned with the future of knowledge, not least LIS professionals. *Wikipedia*'s true significance has gone largely unremarked because of the speed with which it has become a fixture in cyberspace. Since its sixth anniversary in 2007, *Wikipedia* has consistently ranked in the top 10 most frequently viewed Web sites worldwide. As of mid-2007, everyday it is consulted by 7% of all 1.25 billion Internet users, and its rate of usage is growing faster than that of Internet usage as a whole.

Wikipedia is an encyclopedia to which anyone with a modicum of time, articulateness, and computer skills can contribute. Anyone can change any entry or add a new entry, and the results will immediately appear for all to see—and potentially contest. "Wiki" is a Hawaiian root that was officially added to English in 2007 to signify something done quickly—in this case, changes in the collective body of knowledge. Nearly 5 million "Wikipedians" have now contributed to 6 million entries, just over a third of which are in English and the other two-thirds in over 250 languages. Moreover, there is a relatively large hardcore of contributors: a good 75,000 Wikipedians have made at least five contributions in any given 30 day period. As to be expected of a self-organizing process, the quality of articles is uneven but not uniformly bad. Topics relating to sex and information technology have been elaborated in disturbingly exquisite detail, while less alluring matters have been left to lie fallow. Nevertheless, according to University of Chicago Law professor Cass Sunstein, *Wikipedia* is now cited four times more than the *Encyclopaedia Britannica* in U.S. judicial decisions. Moreover, *Nature*'s 2005 evaluation of the two encyclopedias in terms of comparably developed scientific articles found that *Wikipedia* averaged four errors to the *Britannica*'s three. That difference has been probably narrowed since then.

Unfortunately *Wikipedia* is not well served by boosters who trumpet *Wikipedia* as heralding the arrival of "Web 2.0." Whereas "Web 1.0" supposedly focused on the ease with which vast amounts of information of different kinds can be stored and transmitted in cyberspace, "Web 2.0" renders the whole process interactive, removing the final frontier separating the transmitter and receiver of information. Yet, we have been here before—in fact, for most of human history. The sharp divide between producers and consumers of knowledge began only about 300 years ago, when book printers secured royal protection for their trade in the face of piracy in a rapidly expanding market for literary products. The legacy of their success, copyright law, continues to impede attempts to render cyberspace a free marketplace of ideas. Before that time, there were fewer readers and writers but they were the same people with relatively direct access to each other's work (Ch. 2).[8]

A much smaller, slower, and more fragmented version of the Wikipedian community came into existence with the rise of the universities in twelfth and thirteenth century Europe. The large ornamental codices of the early Middle Ages gave way to portable "handbooks" designed for the lighter touch of a quill pen. However, the pages of these books continued to be made of animal hide, which could be easily written over. This often made it difficult to attribute authorship because a text might consist of a copied lecture in which the copyist's comments have been inserted and then perhaps altered as the book passed to other hands. *Wikipedia* has remedied many of these technical problems. Any change to an entry automatically generates a historical trace so entries can be read as what medieval scholars call a "palimpsest," a text that has been successively overwritten. Moreover, "talk pages" provide ample opportunity to discuss actual and possible changes. And of course, Wikipedians do not need to pass around copies of their text: Everyone owns a virtual copy of the same text. But *Wikipedia*'s spirit remains deeply medieval in its content policy.

Wikipedia content policy consists of three laws: 1) no original research; 2) neutral point of view; and 3) verifiability. They are designed for people with much reference material at their disposal but no authority to evaluate a knowledge claim beyond arguing from what is contained in that material. Such was the epistemic position of the Middle Ages, which presumed all humans to be mutually equal but subordinate to an inscrutable God. The most one could hope for, then, was a perfectly balanced dialectic. In the Middle Ages this attitude spawned scholastic disputation. In cyberspace the same practice, often dismissed as "trolling," remains the backbone of *Wikipedia*'s quality control. Thus, *Wikipedia* embodies a democratic medievalism. It does not respect claims to personal expertise in the absence of verifiable sources. To fully realize this ideal, participation in *Wikipedia* might be made compulsory for advanced undergraduates and master's degree candidates worldwide. The expected norms of conduct of these students correspond exactly to *Wikipedia*'s content policy: One is not expected to do original research but to know where it is and how to argue about it. Compulsory student participation would not only improve *Wikipedia*'s already impressive collective knowledge base but might help curb the elitist pretensions of researchers in the global knowledge system. If anything counts as "cutting-edge" social epistemology, then *Wikipedia* certainly must.

REFERENCES

1. Social Epistemology: A Journal of Knowledge, Culture and Policy. *Quarterly Journal*, Taylor & Francis: London, 1987.
2. Fuller, S. *Social Epistemology*; Indiana University Press: Bloomington, 1988.
3. Egan, M.; Shera, J. Foundations of a theory of bibliography. Libr. Quart. **1952**, *22* (2), 125–37.
4. Goldman, A. *Epistemology and Cognition*; Harvard University Press: Cambridge, MA, 1986.
5. Schmitt, F. Special issue on "Social Epistemology". Synthese **1987**, *73* (1), 1–204.
6. Furner, J. 'A Brilliant Mind': Margaret Egan and social epistemology. Libr. Trends **2004**, *52* (4), 792–809.
7. Zandonade, T. Social epistemology from Jesse Shera to Steve Fuller. Libr. Trends **2004**, *52* (4), 810–832.
8. Fuller, S. *Knowledge Management Foundations*; Butterworth-Heinemann: Woburn, MA, 2002.
9. Shera, J. Librarianship and information science. In *The Study of Information: Interdisciplinary Messages*; Machlup, F.; Mansfield, U., Eds.; Wiley: New York, 1983; 379–388.
10. Machlup, F.; Mansfield, U. *The Study of Information: Interdisciplinary Messages*; Wiley: New York, 1983.
11. Lyotard, J.-F. *The Postmodern Condition*; University of Minnesota Press: Minneapolis, MN, 1983 (Orig. 1979).
12. Stehr, N. *Knowledge Societies*; Sage: London, 1994.
13. Fuller, S. *The Knowledge Book: Key Concepts in Philosophy, Science, and Culture*; Acumen Press and McGill-Queens University Press: Chesham and Montreal, CA, 2007.
14. Fuller, S. A tale of two narratives: Prolegomena to an alternative history of library and information science. In *European Modernism and the Information Society*; Rayward, W.B., Ed.; Ashgate: Aldershot, 2007; 59–74.
15. Machlup, F. *The Production and Distribution of Knowledge in the United States*; Princeton University Press: Princeton, NJ, 1962.
16. Bell, D. *The Coming of Post-Industrial Society*; Basic Books: New York, 1973.
17. Gouldner, A. *The Future of Intellectuals and the Rise of the New Class*; Collier Macmillan: New York, 1979.
18. Noble, D.F. *Digital Diploma Mills*; New York University Press: New York, 2002.
19. Hirsch, F. *The Social Limits to Growth*; Routledge & Kegan Paul: London, 1976.
20. Jacobson, N. Social epistemology: Theory for the "Fourth wave" of knowledge transfer and exchange research. Sci. Commun. **2007**, *29*, 7–34.
21. Merton, R.K. *The Sociology of Science*; University of Chicago Press: Chicago, IL, 1977.
22. Fuller, S. Recent work in social epistemology. Am. Philos. Quart. **1996**, *33*, 149–166.
23. Rescher, N. *Epistemetrics*; Cambridge University Press: Cambridge, 2006.
24. Arthur, W.B. *Increasing Returns and Path Dependence in the Economy*; University of Michigan Press: Ann Arbor, MI, 1994.
25. Swanson, D. Undiscovered public knowledge. Libr. Quart. **1986**, *56* (2), 103–118.
26. King, R.G. *Mad archive disease: Archival spongiform encephalopathy, the loss of corporate memory, and the death of institutional archives*. Paper Delivered at the Combined SSA/CIMA Annual Meeting Flagstaff, AZ, 2002. Available at http://www.homestead.com/infomgmt/files/mad_archive_disease2.htm (accessed August 23, 2007).
27. Fuller, S. *Thomas Kuhn: A Philosophical History for Our Times*; University of Chicago Press: Chicago, IL, 2000.
28. De Mey, M. *The Cognitive Paradigm*; Kluwer: Dordrecht, 1982.
29. Goldman, A. *Knowledge in a Social World*; Oxford University Press: Oxford, 1999.
30. Campbell, D.T. *Methodology and Epistemology for Social Science*; University of Chicago Press: Chicago, IL, 1988.

Social Influences on Classification

Hope A. Olson
*School of Information Studies, University of Wisconsin-Milwaukee, Milwaukee,
Wisconsin, U.S.A.*

Abstract

The social and cultural influences on classification are evident in both the content and structure of classifications. In content, warrant, the basis on which content is determined, is most significant. Warrant is related to the purpose of the classification and has varied historically from the classical Greeks to the present. Warrant, whether it be what is written or published on a topic, what is taught, natural phenomena, or other factors is susceptible to all of the biases of the society that produces a classification. Biases of race, gender, orientation, geography, culture, language, and other factors are well-documented in relation to bibliographic classification. Bias occurs not only as a result of the warrant that determines content, but also as a result of classificatory structure. Classificatory structure may be culturally specific and the hierarchy typical of western classificatory structure can convey social influence through hierarchical force, ghettoization, and diasporization. Jesse Shera suggests the social importance of librarians and their role in classification. Combining Shera's theoretical stance with the historical/philosophical record and the empirical evidence of numerous studies in bibliographic classification, the link between society and classification is robust and of significance to the field of library and information science.

INTRODUCTION

Classification, whether knowledge classification or bibliographic classification, is now recognized as being governed by what can be described broadly as social influence. Within the term "social" can be included various aspects of a society, including, but not limited to, political, economic, ideological, and cultural factors. Increasingly, social influences have a global reach. The impact of social factors can be on the structure, the content of the classification, or, arguably, both. The mechanism that determines the content of a classification is warrant. The structure of a classification is found deeper in the metaphysical foundations that are dominant within the culture.

CLASSIFICATORY WARRANT

Warrant, in classification, is encompassed in the *Oxford English Dictionary*'s definition as a "justifying reason or ground for an action, belief, or feeling." Warrant in classification is generally found in the purpose for creating a classification scheme. That is, there is generally some agenda, overt or hidden, for the construction of the classification. That agenda will determine the source of the content and, possibly, its arrangement. Clare Beghtol wrote about bibliographic classification, but her description of warrant can apply as well to classification of knowledge or of phenomena:[1]

> In general, the warrant of a classification system can be thought of as the authority a classificationist invokes first

to justify and subsequently to verify decisions about what classes/concepts to include in the system, in what order classes/concepts should appear in the schedules, what units classes/concepts are divided into, how far subdivision should proceed, how much and where synthesis is available, whether citation orders are static or variable and similar questions. Warrant covers conscious and unconscious assumptions and decisions about what kinds and what units of analysis are appropriate to embody and to carry the meaning or use of a class to a classifier, ... The semantic warrant of a system thus provides the principal authorization for supposing that some class or concept or notational device will be helpful and meaningful to classifiers and ultimately to users of documents. (p. 110)

Historically, in western societies, classificatory warrant can be traced back to at least Aristotle. For example, in his *Generation of Animals* he based his zoological classification on animals' physical characteristics, specifically their form of reproduction, ranging from "generative slime" to human's viviparous live birth.[2] Once he established the categories of reproduction, Aristotle arranged them according to the young that they produced. Those species that produced progeny at the most fully developed level—mammals who give birth to largely functional young—were at the top. Animals that lay eggs were considered lower because the young needed the protection of the egg and parents to sit on it for warmth in order for it to survive. Whether or not this argument is convincing, it established a classification satisfying to humans. This approach to classification has been termed scientific, in that it is the result of scientific inquiry and reflects natural phenomena. However, it is not culturally

Encyclopedia of Library and Information Sciences, Fourth Edition DOI: 10.1081/E-ELIS4-120044536

neutral, in that it selects some particular characteristics as a basis and ignores others.

Late classical and medieval classifications of knowledge tended to have an educational purpose with main classes based on the seven liberal arts and Christian interpretations and expansions thereof; that is, on educational warrant. The classical education of free men from which our liberal (free) arts developed evolved into a codified set of topics employed by medieval scholars and, in much adapted form, into the framework for university education. Late Latin scholars ostensibly starting with Marcianus Capella in the fifth century began a tradition of encyclopedic works that presented knowledge in the mold of the liberal arts: the trivium consisting of grammar, rhetoric, and logic and the quadrivium consisting of geometry, arithmetic, music, and astronomy. Christian scholars, such as Boethius in the sixth century and Augustin, revised this tradition for their religious goals. Hugh of St Victor, a twelfth century educator and mystic, created a classification in his *Didascalicon* to guide students through readings in the liberal arts as a preparation for the ultimate study of theology. His educational goal was to aid students in their progress toward the ultimate goal of oneness with God. The framework offered by the seven liberal arts evolved from classical practices for teaching elite boys to fit the purposes of medieval Christian education. However, after over a millennium, an alternative framework for classification developed.

In the context of the renaissance rediscovery of classical texts and a concomitant revision of the structure of knowledge, Francis Bacon classified on the basis of existing recorded knowledge— epistemological warrant—to identify a new structure of knowledge and the gaps in it that merited investigation. His epistemological view saw sense-data being recorded in memory as history, transformed through imagination into poesy, and through reason into philosophy. This tripartite framework has structured much of western classification since. Denis Diderot and Jean le Rond d'Alembert took a Baconian approach in pursuing education as a road to reason in the classification of their Enlightenment *Encyclopedie*. Even Samuel Taylor Coleridge, who regarded Diderot as the anti-Christ, applauded the encyclopedists' use of Bacon's framework. Hegel rejected Bacon's classification of knowledge, but his classificatory warrant was similar to Bacon's in technique and his Being, Essence, and Idea end up being largely parallel to Bacon's History, Poesy, and Philosophy. Hegel and Bacon certainly come together in Melvil Dewey's universal library classification.[3] However, Hegel sought to reflect states of being rather than the process of knowing; his approach was ontological rather than epistemological.

These examples of warrant also illustrate a shift in the ordering of the classes. The seven liberal arts dominated the classical and medieval conceptions of knowledge and of the bibliographic schemes (such as Hugh's) of their time. With the Renaissance, the Baconian sequence became more prominent and influenced the major enumerative classifications of our time that are regarded as universal classifications, notably the Dewey Decimal Classification (DDC) and, arguably, the Library of Congress Classification (LCC).

In his *The Order of Things*, Michel Foucault[4] examines what is, in essence, warrant for arrangement of the content within this framework as it shifts from the medieval and renaissance to the classical period in Europe and from the classical period to the modern. What he finds in his studies across disciplines characterizes these changes as the transition from order based on resemblance in medieval and renaissance thought to order based on differences in identifiable characteristics in enlightenment thought and then from the latter to order based on the functions of systems in modern thought. In bibliographic classification, these stages make sense. As Alain Besson ([5], 24+) discusses, medieval bibliographic classification schemes were able to be simple because the collections were small. For broad categorization, similarity is a sufficient criterion. However, as collections grew, greater specificity came to be valued. Thus, beginning in the Enlightenment and carrying on to the enumerative schedules of DDC and LCC, differentiation is a key factor. Finally, function becomes crucial in the faceted classifications of modernity. It is apparent in Ranganathan's PMEST formula—personality, matter, energy, space, and time—in which each facet fulfills a function. Personality functions as the main topic; matter functions as the object acted upon; energy functions as a verb, an activity; space and time perform the function of defining context. Collectively they function as a system theoretically capable, in their flexibility, of representing the modern universal.

CLASSIFICATORY WARRANT AND SOCIAL INFLUENCES IN BIBLIOGRAPHIC CLASSIFICATION

Classic works on bibliographic classification set up a dichotomy between natural classification and artificial classification. Berwick Sayers ([6], §29+) called the source of warrant "the characteristic of classification." He divided the options into the artificial characteristic "in which some accidental property of the things classified is adopted as the characteristic of arrangement" (§35) and the natural characteristic "made upon the inherent properties in things; upon those properties without which a thing could not be the thing it is." (§36) In the former, a bat may be classified as a bird because it flies, while, in the latter, a bat does not have essential qualities of a bird and must, therefore, be classified elsewhere. Sayers' artificial classifications imply that characteristics may come from somewhere in the social, rather than the natural, order.

Henry Evelyn Bliss[7] also identified natural and artificial or purposive classifications. However, he acknowledged that natural classifications "may have a conceptual and often purposive warp in their fabric." (p. 149) Jesse Shera went further, proposing that classifications are invented rather than discovered, thus rejecting any universal pattern that can be reflected. Margaret Egan[8] put classification squarely in the social context: "[t]he study of bibliographic organization is, in effect, the study of the channels through which recorded knowledge flows, set against the background of evolving social and intellectual organization which determines where, how, and by whom that knowledge can be made effective in action." (p. 20)

In 1971, in an article provocatively titled "Misogynists All: A Study in Critical Classification," A.C. Foskett[9] stated bluntly that "... when one begins to examine almost any [classification] scheme it quickly becomes clear that, far from being objective, it is likely to reflect both the prejudices of its time and those of its author." What followed over the next three decades were critiques of mainstream classification schemes, most notably the DDC and the LCC, but also the Universal Decimal Classification (UDC) and others. Steve Wolf[10] began with a discussion of the gaps between the ideal of unbiased, objective, nonjudgmental classification schedules and the reality evidenced in LCC's and DDC's treatment of gays in the renegade collection *Revolting Librarians*. Thereafter, critiques began to appear in more mainstream professional journals, such as *Cataloging & Classification Quarterly* and *Library Resources & Technical Services*.

Critiques from the 1970s to the 1990s, suggesting bias based on culture, include documented bias regarding Africa,[11] Kenya,[12] African literature,[13,14] African history,[15] African languages,[16] African churches,[17] African studies,[18] and South Africa.[19] Other critiques relate to DDC and LCC treatment of Melanesian geography, ethnography, and languages;[20–22] Asia and the Pacific;[23] Arab-speaking countries;[24] and Turkey.[25] Indigenous cultures are poorly represented in mainstream classifications including DDC and LCC;[26,27] adaptations developed specifically to overcome existing biases for cultures such as Alaskan native cultures,[28] the Luiseno people of California;[29] and Canadian First Nations.[30]

Several of these critiques implied an imperialistic or colonial perspective, which was explicitly described as such by Martin.[23] Pacey gives the example of national literatures in historically colonized countries which may share the language of their colonizers, but the European literatures in that language are privileged in coming first and in having more space and more specific chronological subdivisions allotted to them, while colonial literatures are scattered across imperial and indigenous languages.[14] Muriuki puts this colonialism into the context of Kenyan libraries.[12] Amaeshi is explicit regarding this problem in relation to African literature in both DDC and LCC.[13] Lincoln[28] documents the issue of LCC patterns for "hyperborean languages of America and the kindred language of Asia" in asserting the need for a new distribution for Alaskan Native languages. Aderibigbe and Udoh note the narrow space and arbitrary alphabetical arrangement of African literature in LCC class PL that result in a miscellaneous sequence rather than one based on sound language groupings as is the case with European languages.[16]

Related to inappropriate distribution of topics is the lack of space sometimes allocated to cultures outside of a Eurocentric field of view. Henige discusses this broadly in relation to LCC,[15] Weinberg in both DDC and LCC,[31] and Bethel focuses specifically on African concepts, especially as used in the area of Black studies.[18] Soltani notes the poor appropriation of space to Iran, Arabic-speaking countries,[24] and Islam in both LCC and DDC. McConnell's studies[20–22] highlight the lack of specificity for Melanesian culture in DDC, such as the fact that there are only two numbers for Melanesian languages in Table 6 when Melanesia has over 1000 distinct languages. Yeh noted a similar problem the treatment of American Indian in LCC Class E–F.

Omission of topics is another way that social norms fail to express cultural differences. Dick and Burger[19] document this problem in regard to Africa in DDC as does Amankwe[11] in DDC, LCC, and Bliss's Bibliographic Classification. Afolabi examines it in detail in relation to African independent churches—a culturally-specific phenomenon.[17]

These problems of international cultural bias that result in omissions, in space allocated, and in inappropriate distributions of topics are especially troublesome where DDC has been used to organize national bibliographies.[32] Martin notes this problem specifically for the Asia-Pacific region.[23]

Other critiques address gender biases such as Ishbel Lochead's wide-ranging discussion[33] and Robert Mowery's look at women in literature in LCC.[34] Mowery noted that not only the classification, but also its application were at fault with over half of the books on literary history and criticism of women's writings being assigned to the literary numbers in classes PA-PT appropriate to women in literature. Sheila Intner and Elizabeth Futas explored how the shortcomings of LCC affect development of library collections for women's studies because it is a collection assessment tool as well as a browsing and collocation device.[35]

These various biases typically reflect social biases. Biases have tended to be in favor of the social mainstream. For example, the Christian bias in DDC which, even after some revision, allocates the 220s to the 280s to Christianity leaving only the 290s for all other religions. Or the DDC allocation of the 810s to American literature, a geographic distinction, when all other literatures are gathered according to language. LCC still places feminism with "Women. Feminism" (HQ1101+) hierarchically under

"The Family. Marriage. Women" between "Men" and "Life skills. Coping skills. Everyday living skills."

Going back as far as 1972, when Steve Wolf addressed the topic in the iconoclastic collection *Revolting Librarians*, bias in the placement of gays and homosexuality has been noted in both DDC and LCC. In 1981, Sanford Berman made the placement of homosexuality one of the major points in his critique of the nineteenth edition of DDC for its lack of specificity. Currently, in both DDC and LCC gay men and lesbians are still associated with sex rather than with demographically defined groups. In the previous edition, DDC21, gays were classified in 305.90664 under social groups (though relegated to the miscellaneous category "Persons by cultural level, marital status, sexual orientation, special social status"). At least gays were a social group as a primary defining characteristic. Now, however, gays are mixed in with 306.766 Homosexuality, which is in the hierarchy:

306	Culture and institutions
306.7	Sexual relations
306.76	Sexual orientation
306.766	Homosexuality

It comes between 306.74 "Prostitution" and 306.77 "Sexual and related practices" including "Masturbation," "Sodomy," "Oral sex," "Sadism," "Masochism," and "Transvestism." The focus of this part of the classification is clear. LCC also conflates gay people with homosexuality in HQ 75+ "Homosexuality, Lesbianism." Hierarchically it is under "Sexual minorities" (coming after "Sexual deviations") which is under "Sexual life." Under "Sexual minorities" is the list of topics: "Bisexuality," "Homosexuality. Lesbianism," "Transvestism," "Transsexualism," "Sadism, Masochism, Fetishism, Etc.," and "Prostitution."

Social influences can also have a progressive impact on classification. DDC originally, in 1876, had no number for the status of women (only for women's education and suffrage). By the eighth edition in 1913, "Woman's position and treatment" was given a place in "Customs, Costumes, Popular life" between "Etiquette" and "Gypsies, Nomads, Outcast races." Today's placement in 305.4 under social groups suggests that DDC has come a long way at least in some ways (Romany people are also now under social groups at 305.891497 while etiquette has appropriately remained inn the 390s under "Customs, etiquette, & folklore").

Foskett, in "Better Dead Than Read," a 1984 followup to his 1971 "Misogynists All" that kicked off much of this discussion, noted that there was some improvement in 13 years, but still much to do.[36] Perhaps for that reason, these studies of social and/or cultural bias continue, though at a diminished pace and often in a more specialized, closely-documented, and theoretical form. Jonathan

Furner and Anthony Dunbar used critical race theory to examine the classification of people of mixed race in DDC.[37] Eunice Kua, as recently as 2004, documented that DDC still has massive inequities in allocating space for non-Western languages and literatures that reflect the society in which DDC was contrived.[38] Lorraine Nero's study of the classification of popular Caribbean music[39] is another example of how mainstream classifications still neglect that which is outside of the social mainstream. In Nero's study, the fact that it is popular rather than classical music means that DDC and LCC are less able to accommodate. The ethnicity of the music further sets it apart.

The power of social influence is most easily seen in classification outside of one's own society. For example, the social and ideological values of the former Soviet Union are completely foreign to most of us. So it is easy to see that Soviet adaptations of UDC and the Soviet-born Bibliotechno-bibliograficheskaia Klassifikatsiia (BBK or Library-Bibliographical Classification) closely reflected their social context when they made Marxism-Leninism, The Party, and Dialectical Materialism into main classes. Their close response to social and ideological changes can be seen by the nearly instantaneous establishment of a class for "The Great Patriotic War" when the Soviet Union entered World War II with an initial subclass for "Comrade Stalin—Leader and Organizer" and then the complete disappearance of Stalin when Khruschev unseated the cult of the personality. Since the fall of the Soviet Union, those responsible for the BBK say that "[t]he radical changes of recent years which took place in political, ideological and socio-economic life in Russia, called for a critical revision of LBC [Library-Bibliographical Classification – BBK],"[40] acknowledging social influence on the classification.

From the early days of the Soviet Union, there was concern that a western classification such as UDC was too bourgeois, recognizing that not only does a classification reflect its society; the society is, in turn, influenced by classification. We cannot doubt that the current globalization of classification through sharing catalog records means that the mainstream western classifications used in most shared records are likely to influence the importing societies.

CLASSIFICATORY STRUCTURE

Not only do social and cultural influences affect the content of a classification scheme, they also affect its structure. For example, in dominant western culture, three characteristics build the pattern of classificatory structure and these characteristics reflect the logic that has developed as a hallmark of western culture beginning with the ancient Greek philosophers.[41] First, western classification presumes that categories within a classification should be mutually exclusive. That is, they should have impermeable boundaries. Second, western classification typically sequences topics within the classification (such as main classes or topics within a subclass) in a linear sequence such as abstract to concrete or vice versa. Third, western classification is hierarchical, with some topics being subordinate to others. Hierarchy is a logical result of arranging mutually exclusive categories in linear sequences that then, themselves, need to be arranged. Hierarchy is linear in a vertical sense. These three characteristics are not universal. For example, many indigenous cultures look at the world as a circle of being in which each entity plays an equally important role in the whole and the relationships between the entities may be more important than the entities themselves.[42] In another example of a culturally specific classification, Hur-Li Lee and Wen-Chin Lan describe how, in first century B.C.E. China, a scholar and royal family member, Liu Xin, and his father, Liu Xiang, constructed a classified catalog at the order of the Han emperor, Cheng.[43] The classification scheme developed for this catalog, known as the *Seven Epitomes*, was based on a canon of literature influenced by the political discourses of Han China and, in turn, influenced scholarship of the time and for the better part of the two following millennia.

The hierarchical classificatory structure dominant in mainstream western society is arguably culturally specific. It is a sort of intellectual infrastructure.

CONSEQUENCES OF HIERARCHICAL STRUCTURE

A hierarchical structure has ramifications that exhibit as much bias as the content derived from warrant. This bias may be simply a matter of hierarchical force, though it often comes in the form of the ghettoization and diasporization of topics that do not fit the original hierarchical structure constructed of main classes and subclasses.

A basic example of bias through hierarchical force is visible in the placement of gays in DDC noted above. Hierarchical force mandates that what is true of a class is also true of all of its subclasses. So if the class is "Sexual relations" then everything in that class is about sexual relations. By lumping gay people into the number for homosexuality, DDC is characterizing gays only according to one characteristic, their sexual relations, and not as multifaceted people.

Ghettoization is the problem of gathering and then isolating a topic rather than integrating it across the main classes. Because of the principle of hierarchical force, ghettoization can put a topic into a less than advantageous context. A classic instance is the treatment of Native Americans in classification. For example, in DDC, the general number for "American Native peoples" is 970.00497. Hierarchically, this number is under "Ethnic and national groups" under "History of North America."

The DDC relative index lists other numbers in the histories of more specific jurisdictions, but only four other numbers outside of history; these are for religion, civil rights, folk literature, and rodeo performers. In LCC, Indians of North America in general are classified in E75-E99, which is hierarchically under American history. The index lists other numbers only in collections of American prose literature, classes of persons in the arts in general, and bibliographies of literature on music by topic. In both *DDC* and *LCC*, Native Americans are separated from mainstream North American culture and are largely relegated to history as though there were no contemporary Aboriginal cultures.[26,27] The fact that the main classes are not easy umbrellas for cross-cultural topics can lead to ghettoization as the path of least resistance.

Diasporization occurs as different characteristics are used to make categories in a hierarchy more specific. For example, a group of people may be defined by different characteristics such as age, sex, class, ethnicity, etc. To create a hierarchical structure, groups are divided first by one characteristic, then a second, then a third. But only the groups with first characteristic will be gathered together. The others will be dispersed. DDC shows this in its classification of social groups. The basic arrangement is:

305	Social groups
305.2	Age groups
305.3	Men and women
305.4	Women
305.5	Social classes
305.6	Religious groups
305.7	Language groups
305.8	Ethnic and national groups
305.9	Occupational and miscellaneous groups

This works fine unless the groups are defined by more than one characteristic. Will African American male youths (to use DDC's example) be classed by race, sex, or age? To solve this problem, DDC includes a table of preference:

Unless other instructions are given, observe the following table of preference, e.g., African American male youths 305.235108996073 (not 305.3889607300835 or 305.896073008351):

Persons with disabilities and illnesses, gifted persons	305.908
Age groups	305.2
Groups by sex	305.3–305.4
Social classes	305.5
Religious groups	305.6
Ethnic and national groups	305.8
Language groups	305.7
Occupational and miscellaneous groups	305.9 (except 305.908)

So material about African American male youths will be classed with other youth, subdivided by sex and last by race. African American middle class women will be classified at 305.4855108996073 grouped with women, then middle class women, and finally African American middle class women. With ethnic and racial groups coming near the bottom of the table of preference, African Americans (and other ethnic and national groups) are scattered across social groups defined by age, sex, class, and/or religion. Language groups will be even more dispersed and miscellaneous groups, including immigrants and veterans, among others, will be the most dispersed. There is no valid way to bring all material about immigrants together as a social group as there is with people with disabilities, the first group in the table of preference.

Hierarchical force, ghettoization, and diasporization are examples of how classificatory structure, itself a product of social and cultural influence, is a vehicle for the views of a society.

CONCLUSION

Mai contends "that a classification is merely one particular explanation of the relationships in a given field that satisfied a group of people at a certain point in time." (p. 41)[44] He goes further to argue that only automatic classification generated from the documents themselves is objective (p. 42). There is certainly much evidence to confirm that classification as developed over millennia and manifested in mainstream bibliographic schemes is not objective, but reflects the society in which it is constructed and the biases in that society. The content of a classification scheme is influenced by its basis in the choice of what is used for warrant. Since literary warrant depends upon the biases manifested in whatever literature is being classified, even automatic indexing is subject to social influence, though it may be exempt from the influence of human classificationists. Classificatory structure as an intellectual infrastructure also reflects the epistemic presumptions of a culture or society.

Recently, so-called "folksonomies" created by social tagging seem to offer a more democratic, grassroots knowledge structure. Social or collaborative tagging is the assignment of typically uncontrolled keywords by users to photographs (http://flickr.com/), website bookmarks (http://delicious.com/), scholarly articles (http://citeulike.com/), products (http://www.amazon.com/), etc. The vocabulary used appears to be free from authority, but that does not mean that it is free from cultural bias. The structure turns out to fit a power law, Zipf-like distribution and the co-occurrence of terms shows a core, not only of terms, but also of relationships between terms Kipp[45] and Olson.[46] Research to explore whether or not this core reflects cultural bias still needs to be done, but it seems unlikely that such an unconsciously cultural product will escape cultural bias. However, only future study will tell.

That classification is an artifact crafted in a social context is evident. More difficult to assess is whether or not the reverse is the case. Does classification, in turn, influence a society? Or does it, at the very least, reinforce social norms? Those in power in the Soviet Union clearly believed that classification has that influence. In a different context, it does not take too great a leap of the imagination to envision a library user who, browsing the shelves, finds books about men in regard to any topic consistently classed before books about women on the same topic being influenced to accept it as a natural order. Of course, such a conclusion would involve proving causation. Proof may not be available, but Shera,[47] speaking on classification at the landmark Dorking conference, makes a convincing argument:

> Librarianship is a composite of many disciplines. In a limited sense, too, it is catalytic, for it can accelerate reaction wherever it serves. If it be true that recorded knowledge is autogenetic in that it begets more knowledge, then the librarian of the future may well be regarded as the geneticist of our intellectual life. (p. 26)

Shera's position suggests the social importance of librarians and their role in classification. Combining Shera's theoretical stance with the historical/philosophical record and the empirical evidence of numerous studies in bibliographic classification, the link between society and classification is robust and of significance to the field of library and information science.

ACKNOWLEDGMENTS

The author is pleased to acknowledge the invaluable assistance of Raina Bloom and reliance on earlier work in collaboration with Rose Schlegl and Shona Dippie.

REFERENCES

1. Beghtol, C. Semantic validity: Concepts of warrant in bibliographic classification systems. Libr Resource. Tech. Serv. **1986**, *30*(2), 109–125.
2. Aristotle, In *Generation of Animals*; Peck, A.L., Ed.; William H.: London, U.K., 1943; trans. William H.: London, UK.
3. Olson, H.A. Sameness and difference: A cultural foundation of classification. Libr. Resource Tech. Serv. **2001**, *45*(3), 115–122.
4. Foucault, M. *The Order of Things: An Archaeology of the Human Sciences*, Vintage Books: New York, 1970.
5. Besson, A. *Medieval Classification & Cataloguing*, Clover Publications: Biggleswade, U.K., 1980.
6. Sayers, W.C.B. *A Manual of Classification for Librarians & Bibliographers*, Grafton: London, U.K., 1926.
7. Bliss, H.E. *The Organization of Knowledge and the System of the Sciences*, Henry Holt: New York, 1929.

8. Egan, M.E. The library and social structure. Libr. Quart. **1956**, *25*(1), 15–22.

9. Foskett, A.C. Misogynists all: A study in critical classification. Libr. Resource. Tech. Serv. **1971**, *15*(2), 117–121.

10. Wolf, S. Sex and the single cataloger: New thoughts on some unthinkable subjects. In *Revolting Librarians*; West, C., Katz, E., Eds.; Booklegger Press: San Francisco, CA, 1972; 39–44.

11. Amankwe, N. Africa in the standard classification schemes. Libr Resource Tech. Serv. **1972**, *16*(2), 178–194.

12. Muriuki, M. Classification and subject cataloguing in Kenya: Including a short history of Kenyan libraries. Inter. Catalog. **1984**, October/December, 39–41.

13. Amaeshi, B. African literature as a new main class. Inter. Libr. Rev. **1985**, *17*, 39–50.

14. Pacey, P. The classification of literature in the Dewey Decimal Classification: The primacy of language and the taint of colonialism. Catalog. Classif. Quart. **1989**, *9*(4), 101–107.

15. Henige, D. Library of Congress subject headings: Is euthanasia the answer?. Catalog. Classif. Quart. **1987**, *8*(1), 7–20.

16. Aderibigbe, M.R.; Udoh, D.J.E. LC subclass PL8000-8844: A case for revision. Catalog. Classif. Quart. **1990**, *10*(3), 77–90.

17. Afolabi, M. Spiritual matters: Provision for independent African churches in general classification schemes. Inter. Classif. **1992**, *19*(4), 210–213.

18. Bethel, K.E. Culture keepers: Cataloging the Afrocentric way. In *Racial and Ethnic Diversity in Academic Libraries: Multicultural Issues*; Curry, D.A., Griswold Blandy, S., Martin, L.M., Eds.; Haworth Press: New York, 1994; 221–240.

19. Dick, A.L.; Burger, M. Transforming subject access: Some critical issues for South African information professionals. South African J. Libr. Inform. Sci. **1995**, *63*(2), 65–69.

20. McConnell, F. Classification of Melanesia: Proposals for revision of DDC, Table 2. Catalog. Classif. Quart. **1984**, *5*(1), 53–60.

21. McConnell, F. Languages of Melanesia: Problems and proposals classification. Catalog. Classif. Quart. **1985**, *5*(3), 57–66.

22. McConnell, F. Peoples of Melanesia: Proposals for revision of DDC 19, table 5. Catalog. Classif. Quart. **1985a**, *5*(4), 47–51.

23. Martin, G.S. The DDC in the Asia-Pacific region. *Dewey Decimal Classification: Edition 21 and International Perspectives*. Papers from a Workshop presented at the General Conference of the International Federation of Library Associations and Institutions (IFLA), Beijing, China, August, 19, 1996; Chan, L.M., Mitchell, J.S., Eds.; Forest Press: Albany, NY; 59–66.

24. Soltani, P. Translation and expansion of classification systems in the Arab Countries and Iran. Inter. Catalog. Bibliogr. Control **1996**, *25*(1), 13–15.

25. Baydur, G. Subject Indexing Practices in Turkey 61st IFLA General Conference, Conference Proceedings, Istanbul, Turkey August, 20–25, 1995. Available at http://www.ifla.org/IV/ifla61/61-bayg.htm.

26. Yeh, T.Y.-R. The treatment of the American Indian in the Library of Congress E-F Schedule. Libr. Resource Tech. Serv. **1971**, *15*(2), 122–131.

27. Young, M.L.; Doolittle, D.L. The halt of stereotyping: When does the American Indian enter the mainstream?. Ref. Librarian **1994**, *47*, 109–119.

28. Lincoln, T. Ethno-linguistic misrepresentations of the Alaskan Native languages as mirrored in the Library of Congress system of cataloging and classification. Catalog. Classif. Quart. **1987**, *7*(3), 69–90.

29. Herlihy, C.S.; Cocks, F. The Luiseno Culture Bank: Expanding the canon. Catalog. Classif. Quart **1995**, *20*(1), 61–81.

30. Hills, G. Multiculturalism and biculturalism: Native library progress in Canada and Greenland. *Native Libraries: Cross-Cultural Conditions in the Circumpolar Countries*; Scarecrow Press: Lanham, MD, 1997; 119–155.

31. Weinberg, B.H. A theory of relativity for catalogers. *Cataloging Heresy: Challenging the Standard Bibliographic Product*, St. John's University: Jamaica, New York, 1991; February 18. Proceedings of the Congress for Librarians, Weinberg, B.H., Ed.; Learned Information: Medford, NJ, 1992, 7–11.

32. Bell, B.L. The Dewey Decimal Classification system in national bibliographies *Dewey Decimal Classification: Edition 21 and International Perspectives*: Papers from a Workshop presented at the General Conference of the International Federation of Library Associations and Institutions (IFLA) Beijing, China August, 19, 1996; Chan, L.M., Mitchell, J.S., Eds.; Forest Press: Albany, New York, 59–66.

33. Lochhead, I. Bibliographic control of feminist literature. Catalog. Index **1985**, *76/77*, 10–15.

34. Mowery, R.L. The classification of African literature by the Library of Congress. Libr. Resource Tech. Serv. **1973**, *17*(3), 340–352.

35. Intner, S.S.; Futas, E. The role and impact of Library of Congress Classification on the assessment of Women's Studies collections. Libr. Acquis.: Pract. Theor. **1996**, *20*(3), 267–279.

36. Foskett, A.C. Better dead than read: Further studies in critical classification. Libr. Resource Tech. Serv. **1984**, *28*, 347–359.

37. Furner, J.; Dunbar, A.W. The treatment of topics relating to people of mixed race in bibliographic classification schemes: A critical race-theoretic approach. In *Knowledge Organization and the Global Information Society*, Proceedings of the Eighth International ISKO Conference, London, UK, July 13–16, 2004; McIlwaine, I.C., Ed.; Ergon Verlag: Würzburg, Germany, 2004; 115–120.

38. Kua, E. Non-Western Languages and Literatures in the Dewey Decimal Classification Scheme. Libri **2004**, *54*, 256–265.

39. Nero, L.M. Classifying the popular music of Trinidad and Tobago. Catalog. Classif. Quart. **2006**, *42*(3/4), 119–133.

40. Goltvisnkaya, T.S.; Sukiasyan, E.S. Library-Bibliographical Classification: On the path of renovation. Knowl. Org. **1993**, *20*(2), 77–79.

41. Olson, H.A. Exclusivity, teleology and hierarchy: Our Aristotelean legacy. Knowl. Org. **1999**, *26*(2), 65–73.

42. Olson, H.A. Cultural discourses of classification: Indigenous alternatives to the tradition of Aristotle, Durkheim and Foucault, Proceedings of the 10th ASIS SIG/CR Classification Research Workshop: Advances in Classification Research, v.10 October, 13, 1999; Albrechtsen, H., Mai,

J.-E., Eds.; Information Today, Inc. for the American Society for Information Science and Technology: Medford, NJ, 1999a; 91–106.

43. Lee, H.-L.; Lan, W.-C. Purposes and bibliographic objectives of a pioneer library catalog in China. Libr. Quart **2009**, *79*(2), 205–231.

44. Mai, J.-E. Classification in context: Relativity, reality, and representation. Knowl. Org. **2004**, *31*(1), 39–48.

45. Kipp, M.E.I.; Campbell, G.D. Patterns and inconsistencies in collaborative tagging systems: An examination of tagging practices, Proceedings of the ASIST Annual Meeting Austin, TX, 2006; Vol. 43, CD-ROM.

46. Olson, H.A.; Wolfram, D. Syntagmatic relationships and indexing consistency on a larger scale. J. Doc **2008**, *64*(4), 602–615.

47. Shera, J.H. Pattern, structure, and conceptualization in classification, Proceedings of the International Study Conference on Classification for Information Retrieval, Beatrice Webb House, Dorking, UK, May, 13–17, 1957; Aslib: London, UK; 15–27.

Social Informatics

Howard Rosenbaum
School of Library and Information Science, Indiana University, Bloomington, Indiana, U.S.A.

Abstract

This entry describes the concept of social informatics, delineates the research domain the concept is intended to cover, and explains its relevance for library and information science, updating Kling's 2003 description of social informatics in this Encyclopedia. After an initial definition of the term, a brief history of social informatics is presented from the origins of the term in the 1980s among Scandinavian scholars to the appropriation of the term by Kling and colleagues in the mid-1990s to its current status as a useful lens for researchers in a wide range of disciplines to use to study computerization in society. Three main approaches of social informatics are described after which some of the main insights that have emerged from social informatics research are discussed. The entry concludes with an assessment of the impact of and potential for social informatics in library and information science.

INTRODUCTION

Computers in various forms, cell phones, global positioning systems, and many other digital devices have become part of the routine fabric of many people's lives. Recent developments in ubiquitous computing, "which may be embedded in the environment, embedded in objects, worn, or carried by the user throughout everyday life," presage a future that moves beyond the computer as a desktop artifact[1] toward a scenario where people "have the same secure, personalized access to communications on devices everywhere, whether public or private, mobile or stationary."[2] These and other information and communication technologies (ICTs) have become key components of the large and complex infrastructures on which many different types of organizations depend. The pace of technological innovation continues to increase and as researchers and entrepreneurs work on Web 2.0 applications, for example, the effort led by Miller to develop the technologies that are forming the infrastructure of the "Semantic Web,"[3] there is already speculation about the next wave:

> The Semantic Web community's grandest visions, of data-surfing computer servants that automatically reason their way through problems, have yet to be fulfilled. But the basic technologies that Miller shepherded through research labs and standards committees are joining the everyday Web. They can be found everywhere–on entertainment and travel sites, in business and scientific databases–and are forming the core of what some promoters call a nascent 'Web 3.0.'[4]

This wave of innovation is sweeping over libraries and other information organizations and there is a small and growing literature about "library 2.0,"[5–7] a vision of a "next-generation library" based on "the application of interactive, collaborative, and multi-media Web-based technologies to Web-based library services and collections."[8] There is even some discussion among bloggers of "librarian 2.0."[9] As these activities intensify, one simple and profound question to ask is what this immersion in and dependence on ICTs is doing to us. This question is simple to ask and difficult to answer. In part, this is because it is difficult to study something that is both pervasive and routine; one of the implications of ubiquitous computing is that the object of study will eventually become invisible. In addition, a reliable approach is needed to study the ways in which people's work and play are affected by the ICTs they design and use that also allows researchers to understand the ways in which people are affecting the ICTs on which they rely. Research into computing and society requires an approach within which can be found the theories and concepts that will allow researchers to uncover these instances of mutual shaping. Social informatics is one useful approach that can do this because of its focus "on the social consequences of the design, implementation, and use of ICTs over a wide range of social and organizational settings" especially "the roles of ICTs in social and organizational change."[10]

This entry describes the concept of social informatics, delineates the research domain the concept is intended to cover, and explains its relevance for library and information science; it updates Kling's 2003 description of social informatics in this Encyclopedia.[11] After an initial definition of the term, a brief history of social informatics is presented from the origins of the term in the 1980s among Scandinavian scholars to the appropriation of the term by Kling and colleagues in the mid-1990s to its current status as a useful lens with which to study computerization in society. Three main approaches of social informatics are described after which some of the main insights that have

Encyclopedia of Library and Information Sciences, Fourth Edition DOI: 10.1081/E-ELIS4-120043526

emerged from social informatics research are discussed. The entry concludes with an assessment of the impact of and potential for social informatics in library and information science.

WHAT IS SOCIAL INFORMATICS?

To paraphrase a question asked by Kling in 1999,[12] what is social informatics and why does it matter in library and information science? Kling, Rosenbaum, and Sawyer recently defined social informatics as "the interdisciplinary study of the design, uses, and consequences of ICTs that takes into account their interaction with institutional and cultural contexts."[13] Lamb and Sawyer[14] describe social informatics as

A body of rigorous empirical research that focuses on the relationships among people, ICTs', and the social structures of their development and use. Social informatics studies engage a broad range of ICTs—from large, formal, organizational information systems such as medical records systems to everyday, informal, often highly-personalized devices such as mobile phones and personal digital assistants. In these studies, ICTs are seen as embedded within a larger social milieu that infuses meaning and purpose into their shaping and uses.

Social informatics focuses on the "the intended and unintended social and organizational consequences of ICT-enabled change and change efforts."[15] For these reasons, social informatics has a problem oriented focus[16]; although "multidisciplinary and methodologically diverse" it "can be considered to be distinctive through the common focus on a complex problem area; namely, computerization as sociotechnical complexity."[17]

Social informatics researchers are not typically interested in how to build or design ICTs. Instead, they want to understand the complex relationships that are involved when these ICTs are used in different types of social, cultural, organizational, and institutional contexts. Their objects of study include the ICTs, the people who design, set up, maintain, and use them, and the different settings in which they are used. Robbin and Day argue that social informatics researchers seek "to intervene in the social construction of the meaning, value, use and even design of technologies as shaped by discourse and education" and "to intervene in the practice of theory of ICTs by means of critical examination and discourse."[18] Horton, Davenport, and Wood-Harper add that "there is an implicit hope that the detailed analyses developed under the banner of social informatics will provide 'increased understanding' that will result in ICTs that are 'actually workable for people and can fulfill their intended functions'."[19] For these reasons, there is some overlap with cognate forms of intellectual inquiry such as knowledge management and

human–computer interaction, but the social informatics approach differs because its explicit focus on social, cultural, and organizational contexts within which people design, implement, and use ICTs, strongly orients researchers toward the use of social science theories, methods, and conceptual frameworks.

Social informatics matters because it addresses questions of fundamental importance in library and information science and other fields: given the types of situations described above, how can we best understand the complex relationships among people, the ICTs that they design and use, and the contexts in which design and use take place. In addition, Halavais asks:

How does the intended use of the technology relate to its use within ... existing social practices? In what ways, both intended and unintended, does the technology affect the structures of interaction and understanding within a community?[20]

HISTORY

The term "informatics" has been part of the academic lexicon for many years; Brookes argues that Lenin should be seen as the founder of informatics![21] Since the late 1970s[22] the term has been used to describe "the study of information content, representation, technology, and the methods and strategies associated with its use."[23] In early 1980s, however, the term acquired the modifier "social" when it was used by Norwegian social scientists whose work focused on the intersections among technology, organizations, and work. Roggen claims that "social informatics, the interdisciplinary field of informatics, ... [was] established as a science in 1982 by Stein Bråten" at the University of Oslo,[24] Ursul[25] and Robbin and Day[26] claim that it became a discipline soon after. The Faculty of Social Sciences at University of Ljubljana, Slovenia established a program in social informatics in 1985[27] stating that the term "relates to interaction between society and information-communication technologies" at macro and micro levels of analysis. Around this time, Kling, who had been studying computerization from a social science perspective in the United States since the 1970s, met with Bråten and Roggen in Norway where he learned about their new discipline and "its terms, concepts, theories, models, and research projects carried out by Bråten and his collaborators."[28]

In the mid-1990s, Kling and his colleagues were casting about for a label to describe more concisely the research in which he and like-minded researchers had been engaged. What had been called the "the social analysis of computing," "human-centered computing," the "social study of information technology," and the "sociology of computing" became "social informatics." According to Kling, Rosenbaum, and Sawyer,

In 1996, some participants in this research community agreed that the scattering of related research in a wide array of journals and the use of different nomenclatures was impeding both the research and the abilities of 'research consumers' to find important work. They decided that a common name for the field would be helpful. After significant deliberation, they selected 'social informatics.'[13]

Since then, there has been considerable activity, initially driven by Kling, that has included a 1997 NSF funded workshop that set a research agenda for social informatics, the introduction of a social informatics minitrack in the America's Conference for Information Systems (now called Social Theory in Information Research), panel discussions on social informatics at the Annual Meetings of the American Society for Information Science and Technology, special issues of the Information Society and the Journal of the American Society for Information Science, the formation of a Social Informatics Special Interest Group in the American Society for Information Science and Technology which held its fourth annual research symposium at the 2008 ASIST annual meeting, undergraduate and graduate courses about social informatics, and the establishment of several centers of social informatics at universities in the United States (the Rob Kling Center for Social Informatics at Indiana University) and Europe (the Center for Social Informatics at Napier University, Scotland). Social informatics research is alive and well and the movement Kling fostered "has grown to encompass a widening and interdisciplinary interest in research that carefully examines the ways in which ... ICTs ... are bound up in everyday social and organizational structures."[14]

ASSUMPTIONS

Social informatics research typically makes use of theories and methods of the social sciences. However, it is probably more accurate to say that social informatics is an approach to studying technology and society influenced by social science theory and method that cuts across many academic disciplines. Researchers working in information systems, library and information science, sociology, anthropology, communications, journalism, management, and other disciplines are using the concepts and tools of social informatics.[29] Despite this heterogeneity, there is a set of assumptions that is common to their work. These can be organized into assumptions about the embeddedness, duality, and configurability of ICTs.[30] The first, embeddedness, holds that the context matters; ICTs do not exist in social or technical isolation and are embedded in social, cultural, organizational, and institutional contexts.[31,32] A second and related assumption is that technology involves a fundamental duality wherein ICTs, the people who design and use them, and the contexts in which they are embedded are in relations of mutual shaping, an insight that has been important in the

work of Orlikowski.[33] Working from this assumption, social informatics research and theorizing "seeks to uncover and explain the coupling of technology and social order."[34] One implication of this assumption is that "the situated nature and uses of computing mean that context and use are bound up through practice: to report on use is to report on the situations of that use."[35] A related assumption about this duality emphasizes one dimension of mutual shaping. ICTs enable and constrain social actions and social relationships that are enacted within the contexts of design and use. Finally, ICTs are configurable. They are sociotechnical systems that can be interpreted and used in different ways in different settings.

APPROACHES TO SOCIAL INFORMATICS RESEARCH

There are three main approaches that characterize social informatics research. The first is normative and covers work that has as its main goal to influence practice. Researchers engaged in this type of work seek to provide empirically based findings that can be used to make recommendations intended to improve the work done by people designing, implementing, managing, and using ICTs. For example, some normative work is directed at designers and managers of ICTs, while other work seeks to influence people involved in setting ICT policy. The second is analytic and includes work that has is its main goal the development and refinement of theories of ICTs in their social, organizational, and cultural contexts. Analytic research "seeks to contribute to a deeper understanding of how the evolution of ICT use in a particular setting can be generalized to other ICTs and other settings."[36] This type of work is important because it results in the development of a body of theory and empirical work that forms the knowledge base of the discipline.

The third and perhaps most important approach is critical, covering work that examines "disjunctions between popular and professional claims about the social values and uses of [ITC] and the empirical reality of such."[37] Researchers adopting this approach call into question the conventional wisdom and assumptions about ICTs and, in doing so, employ "perspectives that do not automatically and uncritically adopt the goals and beliefs of the groups that commission, design, or implement specific ICTs."[36] Day argues that this critical impulse is at the heart of social informatics and, developed more deeply, can move the discipline in novel and rewarding directions because its "empirical objects ... can be as much conceptual constructs as empirical entities, and [its] central concern [can be] the examination of the notion of information as a culturally and historically specific conception of knowledge."[38] The critical approach easily incorporates genre and discourse analyses into the social informatics researcher's methodological tool kit as it becomes "ultimately, a discursive and cultural examination of the construction of meaning and concepts related to ICTs."[39]

KEY INSIGHTS FROM SOCIAL INFORMATICS RESEARCH

Some of what has been learned from almost 30 years of research into the interrelationships among technology, organizations, people and work now seems like common sense, but at the time these findings were being reported many were challenges to the conventional wisdom about computing and society. At the time of this writing, some of these findings have not yet had impacts on the design, implementation, and use of ICTs.

Based on the assumption of embeddedness, social informatics researchers have demonstrated empirically the mutual shaping that characterizes the relationships among people, ICTs, and the contexts of design and use. On the one hand, the context of ICT use directly affects the meanings and roles the technologies have for the people using them; for example, the same information system will be used differently in an elementary school and a government agency. In addition, the interpretations that people develop to help them grasp ICTs shapes their adoption and uses of these technologies. Such a set of conventions are necessary if the interactions enabled by the ICTs are to proceed smoothly.[40] The result is that the social and organizational contexts of ICTs play "a significant role in influencing the ways that people use information and technologies, and thus influence the consequences for work, organizations, and other social relationships."[32] A related insight also grounded in an assumption of embeddedness is that ICT use leads to multiple, and seemingly contradictory, effects. That the same ICT package can be implemented in two similar organizations and be used in different ways with different outcomes has been attributed to the differing contexts of use. This has been illustrated clearly by Orlikowski, who described two similar consulting firms that implemented the same software package and experienced two very different outcomes. The success of the software in one firm and the failure in the other was shown to be due to differences in non-technological organizational practices; in one form there were organizational incentives for employee participation and in the other there were not.[41]

There is also a set of insights about the nature of ICTs. The first is that ICTs are configurable—they are actually collections of distinct components. This means that different components and features are emphasized in different social and organizational settings. The second is that these configurations are not static. ICTs continue to evolve and change after they are implemented and sometimes in ways not anticipated by their designers. This is to be expected since there will be "ongoing adjustments of the technology and initiatives aimed at influencing the organizational context, for instance, training users, changing existing

procedures, and promoting the establishment of appropriate conventions for use."[42] This process has been called "technology-use mediation" and describes the efforts to align the structure and functioning of the ICTs with existing work and other organizational practices.[43] Walsham, for example, describes a police dispatch system that was modified by the people using it.[44] The process also has currency when considering the adoption and use of ICTs in social and domestic settings.

The third insight is that ICTs have trajectories that begin with their design and continue until they are no longer in use. It is therefore possible to study the evolution of an ICT configuration focusing on its history and future; a trajectory is composed of a social history and a trail of technological progress. These trajectories can be traced and studied, and although ICTs have the potential to be influential in social and organizational change, their trajectories often favor the status quo.[45] Finally, there is an insight that aligns well with fundamental assumption from the social construction of technology approach concerning the role of values and ideology in the design, development, and use of ICT; technology is not value neutral. ICT use has moral and ethical aspects and these have social and political consequences. In some cases, "IT applications can … shift the balance of influence and power in organizations by restructuring access to information, technical staff, and the kind of authority that informational resources can bring."[46] Consequently, the implementation and use of ICTs typically produce winners and losers. For example, in many organizations, the implementation of enterprise resource planning (ERP) systems has led to efficiencies, but also to changes in work routines that some employees do not like and, in more extreme cases, early retirement.

SOCIAL INFORMATICS AND LIBRARY AND INFORMATION SCIENCE

At the turn of the century, in a special issue celebrating the 50th anniversary of the *Journal of the American Society for Information Science* (now the *Journal of the American Society for Information Science and Technology*), Saracevic describes information science as "interdisciplinary in nature" and "inexorably connected to information technology" with a "technological imperative [that] is compelling and constraining" its development; in addition, information science "has a strong social and human dimension, above and beyond technology."[47] In the same issue, Bates identifies three "big questions" for library and information science (LIS), a "physical" question about the fundamental laws and features of recorded information, a "social" question about the ways in which people interact with and make use of information, and a "design" question about the ways in which access to information can be improved.[48]

It is clear that the assumptions and insights of social informatics as described above overlap with these descriptions of information science. As increasingly sophisticated ICT become integrated into information organizations, including libraries, the questions that social informatics researchers ask and the problems they investigate become increasingly relevant for LIS. For example:

- How is the introduction of new technologies changing work practices, organizational structure, and culture in libraries and other information organizations?
- How are libraries and other information organizations involved in relationships of mutual shaping with ICTs, particularly those outside these organizations?
- What can we learn by studying the discourses about technology and information organizations?
- What can a social informatics approach contribute to our understanding of problems of information seeking and use?
- Bishop and Van House have already argued for the value of a social informatics approach to digital libraries. What else can we learn about them?
- How can a social informatics approach lead to better understandings of fundamental concepts of LIS such as "information?"

CONCLUSION

Information and communication technologies have become essential components of many people's work and social lives. Within organizations, activities such as distance education, virtual teamwork, telecommuting, telemedicine, the outsourcing of organizational functions such as payroll management all depend on complex digital infrastructures supporting shifting configurations of ICTs. Outside of organizations, e-commerce, e-government services, electronic banking, and other networked electronic services are becoming increasingly commonplace parts of people's lives as they do their business in the world. Wikis, blogs, and social networking sites of all kinds are taking their places in people's social lives. As computers and other ICTs become ubiquitous and recede into the background, it becomes more important to analyze them from an approach that takes seriously their embeddedness in social and organizational contexts and social informatics is one useful way to do this.

Drawing on some 30 years of research into the relationships among computers conducted in the United States and a similar stream of work in Scandanavia, social informatics emerged as a research domain in the mid-1990s. Initially driven by Kling and colleagues social informatics, a label already with currency in Europe, defined a research domain that focused on the relationships of mutual shaping among ICTs, the people who design, implement, manage, and used them, and the social and organizational contexts with which the people and technologies are embedded. Social informatics has become a useful lens with which researchers in a variety of disciplines study ICTs, computerization, and society.

ACKNOWLEDGMENTS

Thanks to Ron Day and anonymous reviewer for their careful reading and useful suggestions.

REFERENCES

1. Consolvo, S.; Harrison, B.; Smith, I.; Chen, M.Y.; Everitt, K.; Froelich, J.; Landay, J.A. Conducting in situ evaluations for and with ubiquitous computing technologies. Int. J. Hum. Comput. Inter. **2007**, *22* (1 & 2), 103.
2. Shacham, R.; Schulzrinne, H.; Thakolsri, S.; Kellerer, W. Ubiquitous device personalization and use: The next generation of IP multimedia communications. ACM Trans. Multimedia Comput. Commun. Appl. **2007**, *3* (2), Article 12, 1.
3. Miller, E.; Swick, R. An overview of W3C semantic web activity. Bull. Am. Soc. Inform. Sci. Technol. **2003**, April/May, 8–12. http://www3.interscience.wiley.com/cgi-bin/fulltext/109859338/PDFSTART (accessed July 2007).
4. Borland, J. Smarter Web: New technologies will make online search more intelligent and may even lead to a "Web 3.0." Technol. Rev. **2007**, March/April. http://www.technologyreview.com/read_article.aspx?ch=specialsections&sc=web3&id=18306 (accessed July 2007).
5. Casey, M.E.; Savastinuk, L.C. Library 2.0: Service for the next-generation library. Libr. J. **2006**, September 1, *131*(14). http://www.libraryjournal.com/article/CA6365200.html (accessed July 2007).
6. Abrams, S. Web 2.0, Library 2.0, and Librarian 2.0: Preparing for the 2.0 World. OneSource: SirsiDynix. **2006**, January, *2*(1). http://www.imakenews.com/sirsi/e_article000505688.cfm (accessed July 2007).
7. Miller, P. Web 2.0: Building the new library. Ariadne **2006**, October, 45. http://www.ariadne.ac.uk/issue45/miller/ (accessed July 2007).
8. Maness, J. Library 2.0 theory: Web 2.0 and its implications for libraries. Webology **2006**, *3*(2). http://www.webology.ir/2006/v3n2/a25.html (accessed July 2007).
9. Stephens, M. Into a new world of librarianship. Tame The Web: Libraries and Technology (blog) 2007, January 26. http://tametheweb.com/2007/01/into_a_new_world_of_librarians.html (accessed July 2007).
10. Sawyer, S.; Rosenbaum, H. Social informatics in the information sciences: Current activities and emerging directions. Inform. Sci. **2000**, *3* (2), 89. http://inform.nu/Articles/Vol3/indexv3n2.htm (accessed July 2007).
11. Kling, R. Social informatics. In *Encyclopedia of Library and Information Science*; Marcel Dekker, Inc: New York, 2003; 2656–2661.
12. Kling, R. What is social informatics and why does it matter. D-Lib Mag. **1999**, *5*(1). http://www.dlib.org/dlib/january99/kling/01kling.html (accessed July 2007).

13. Kling, R.; Rosenbaum, H.; Sawyer, S. *Understanding and Communicating Social Informatics: A Framework for Studying and Teaching the Human Contexts of Information and Communication Technologies*; Information Today: Medford, NJ 2005; 6.

14. Lamb, R.; Sawyer, S. On extending social informatics from a rich legacy of networks and conceptual resources. Inform. Technol. People **2005**, *18* (1), 9.

15. Sawyer, S.; Eschenfelder, K.R. Social informatics: Perspectives, examples, and trends. Ann. Rev. Inform. Sci. Technol. **2002**, *36* (1), 428.

16. Kling, R.; Rosenbaum, H.; Sawyer, S. *Understanding and Communicating Social Informatics: A Framework for Studying and Teaching the Human Contexts of Information and Communication Technologies*; Information Today: Medford, NJ, 2005; 146.

17. Horton, K.; Davenport, E.; Wood-Harper, T. Exploring sociotechnical interaction with Rob Kling: Five 'BIG' Ideas. Inform. Technol. People **2005**, *18* (1), 51.

18. Robbin, A.; Day, R. On Rob Kling. In Berleur, J., Impagliazzo, J., Nurminen, M.I., Eds.; Social Informatics: An Information Society for All? In Remembrance of Rob Kling. 2006; 25–36, Maribar, Slovenia, 6.

19. Horton, K.; Davenport, E.; Wood-Harper, T. Exploring sociotechnical interaction with Rob Kling: Five 'BIG' Ideas. Inform. Technol. People **2005**, *18* (1), 55.

20. Halavais, A. Social informatics: Beyond emergence. Bull. Am. Soc. Inform. Sci. Technol. **2005**, *31* (5), 13. http://www.asis.org/Bulletin/Jun-05/helavais.html (accessed July 2007).

21. Brookes, B.C. Lenin: The founder of informatics. J. Inform. Sci. **1984**, *8*, 221.

22. Brookes, B.C. Informatics as the fundamental social science. In *New Trends in Documentation and Information*, Proceedings of the 39th FID Congress; Taylor, P.J., Ed.; University of Edinburgh, September 25–28, 1978. FID Publication 566. ASLIB: London, U.K., 1980; 20.

23. Sawyer, S.; Eschenfelder, K. Social informatics: Perspectives, examples, and trends. Ann. Rev. Inform. Sci. Technol. Inform. Today **2002**, 431.

24. Roggen, I. Home Page 2007. http://www.iss.uio.no/websociology/ (accessed July 2007).

25. Ursul, A.D. On the shaping of social informatics. Int. Forum Inform. Doc. **1989**, *14* (4), 10–18.

26. Robbin, A.; Day, R. On Rob Kling: The theoretical, the methodological, and the critical. In *Seventh International Conference "Human Choice and Computers" (HCC7)*, September, 21–23, 2006, Maribar, Slovenia.

27. The Faculty of Social Sciences, University of Ljubljana, Slovenia. Social Informatics. 2007. http://www.social-informatics.org/index.php?fl=0&p1=181&p2=5&p3=&id=197 (accessed July 2007).

28. Roggen, I. Personal communication, October 17, 2005.

29. Sawyer, S.; Rosenbaum, H. Social informatics in the information sciences: Current activities and emerging directions. Inform. Sci. **2000**, *3* (2), 89.

30. Kling, R.; Rosenbaum, H.; Sawyer, S. *Understanding and Communicating Social Informatics: A Framework for Studying and Teaching the Human Contexts of Information and Communication Technologies*; Information Today: Medford, NJ, 2005; 54.

31. Kling, R.; Rosenbaum, H.; Sawyer, S. *Understanding and Communicating Social Informatics: A Framework for Studying and Teaching the Human Contexts of Information and Communication Technologies*; Information Today: Medford, NJ, 2005; 16.

32. Kling, R. Social informatics. In *Encyclopedia of Library and Information Science*; Marcel Dekker, Inc: New York, 2003; 2656.

33. Orlikowski, W.J. The duality of technology: Rethinking the concept of technology in organizations. Organ. Sci. **1992**, *3* (3), 398–427.

34. Davenport, E. Social informatics in practice: A guide for the perplexed. Bull. Am. Soc. Inform. Sci. Technol. **2005**, *31* (5), 17. http://www.asis.org/Bulletin/Jun-05/davenport.html (accessed July 2007).

35. Sawyer, S. Social informatics: Overview, principles and opportunities. Bull. Am. Soc. Inform. Sci. Technol. **2005**, *31* (5), 10. http://www.asis.org/Bulletin/Jun-05/sawyer.html (accessed July 2007).

36. Sawyer, S.; Eschenfelder, K.R. Social informatics: Perspectives, examples, and trends. Ann. Rev. Inform. Sci. Technol. **2002**, *36* (1), 437.

37. Day, R.E. Kling and the "Critical": Social informatics and critical informatics. J. Am. Soc. Inform. Sci. Technol. **2007**, *58* (4), 575.

38. Day, R.E. Kling and the "Critical": Social informatics and critical informatics. J. Am. Soc. Inform. Sci. Technol. **2007**, *58* (4), 576.

39. Day, R.E. Kling and the "Critical": Social informatics and critical informatics. J. Am. Soc. Inform. Sci. Technol. **2007**, *58* (4), 578.

40. Bansler, J.P.; Havn, E. Technology-use mediation: Making sense of electronic communication in an organizational context. Scand. J. Inform. Syst. **2004**, *16*, 58.

41. Orlikowski, W.J. Learning from notes: Organizational issues in groupware implementation. In Proceedings of the Conference on Computer Supported Cooperative Work, ACM: New York, 1992; 362–369.

42. Bansler, J.P.; Havn, E. Technology-use mediation: Making sense of electronic communication in an organizational context. Scand. J. Inform. Syst. **2004**, *16*, 59.

43. Orlikowski, W.J.; Yates, J.; Okamura, K.; Fujimoto, M. Shaping electronic communication: The metastructuring of technology in the context of use. Organ. Sci. **1995**, *6* (4), 423.

44. Walsham, G. IT and changing professional identity: Micro studies and macro-theory. J. Am. Soc. Inform. Sci. **1998**, *49* (12), 1084.

45. Kling, R.; Rosenbaum, H.; Sawyer, S. *Understanding and Communicating Social Informatics: A Framework for Studying and Teaching the Human Contexts of Information and Communication Technologies*; Information Today: Medford, NJ, 2005; 95.

46. Kling, R. Social informatics. In *Encyclopedia of Library and Information Science*; Marcel Dekker, Inc.: New York, 2003; 2658.

47. Saracevic, T. Information science. J. Am. Soc. Inform. Sci. **1999**, *50* (12), 1052.

48. Bates, M. The invisible substrate of information science. J. Am. Soc. Inform. Sci. **1999**, *50* (12), 1048.

Social Justice in Library and Information Science

Bharat Mehra
School of Information Sciences, University of Tennessee, Knoxville, Tennessee, U.S.A.

Kevin S. Rioux
Division of Library and Information Science, St. John's University, Queens, New York, U.S.A.

Kendra S. Albright
School of Library and Information Science, University of South Carolina, Columbia, South Carolina, U.S.A.

Abstract

This entry presents an overview of social justice vocabularies, conceptualizations, and philosophies as they are represented in the history of library and information science (LIS) practice and research. Emphasis is placed on theoretical descriptions of both justice and social justice, and how these constructs are historically related to past and emerging trends in the LIS professions, with a main focus on social justice in regard to public library philosophy and practice in the United States. The entry also includes a discussion of information science research as it relates to the needs of disadvantaged populations.

INTRODUCTION

Traditions of fairness, open inquiry, service, and humanism have long characterized the library and information science (LIS) professions. Indeed, these and other altruistic stances are professional mandates in the varied representations of the discipline, providing important distinctions to the LIS domain. Although so far little has been written specifically about social justice in an LIS context,[1–3] the term is emerging as a useful conceptual tool to describe and analyze these qualitative aspects of LIS practice and research.

Presented here is an overview of social justice vocabularies, conceptualizations, and philosophies as they are represented in the history of LIS practice and research. Emphasis is placed on theoretical descriptions of both "justice" and "social justice", and how these constructs are historically related to past and emerging trends in the LIS professions, with a main focus on social justice in regard to public library philosophy and practice in the United States. The entry also includes a discussion of information science research as it relates to the needs of disadvantaged populations.

CONCEPTUALIZING SOCIAL JUSTICE

"Justice" is often used as a legal term that describes the administration and maintenance of fair laws.[4] The term "social justice" expands the notion of justice, referring to an ideal in which justice is achieved in every aspect of society, not simply the legal sphere.[5] Thus, in a socially-just society, individuals and groups are treated fairly and receive an equitable share of all of the benefits in society.

However, defining this "socially-just society" is problematic. Although social justice has been explored in philosophical, political, religious, and other contexts, no universally accepted, all-encompassing definition of "social justice" has emerged.

Historically, social justice has been concerned with the tensions between: 1) the individual's right to choose her/his own ends; 2) conflicts with other individuals' rights to make similar choices; and 3) the debate on individual rights vs. the good of the community. These tensions have existed in Western thought since the time of the classical Greeks.[6] For example, in his *Republic*, Plato reflected upon similar disputations in his model of justice intended to bring harmony to the city-state and establish rights for citizens.[7]

These notions of social justice were debated for hundreds of years (and continue to be), but the rights of individuals and the idea of the "common good" became particularly crucial issues during the vast social and political transformations of the nineteenth century. In the 1840s, the Thomistic Jesuit philosopher Luigi Taparelli coined the term "social justice" as a way to identify and conceptualize these tensions. He combined the words "social" and "justice" to refer to the intersecting tautology between the human rights of individuals and reconciling these rights to a society that is composed of groups.[8,9]

Taparelli's concept of social justice soon became part of ecclesiastic discourse on how societies should adjust to the Industrial Revolution. In 1891, Pope Leo XIII, a student of Taparelli, published the encyclical *Rerum*

Novarum (On the Condition of the Working Class), a key document in the early development of social justice philosophy. In this work, the Pope defended the efforts of labor unions to protect the rights of individual workers, urged nation-states to establish just societies through the protection of individuals' rights, and philosophically positioned the Catholic Church to address social issues and advocate for policies that promote class harmony, a position it retains today.[10,11]

As the twentieth century progressed, the concept of social justice was incorporated into secular discourses on human rights, policy, and public moral philosophy. This move from the religious sphere to the secular emphasized the "social" aspects of the affects, relationships, behavior, actions and interactions between people in society.[12] Social justice, thus, directs attention to the tangible reality of the social context in analyzing the implications of legal justice and its impact on the relations between people in every dimension of life.[13]

Furthermore, social justice inherits the etymological and conceptual origin of justice in terms of providing crucial reasons shaping one's beliefs and actions. It incorporates both the abstract issues of ethics and morality (related to beliefs), as well as the concrete actions that impact justice in a social context.[14] Consequently, social justice initiatives have recently emphasized progressive actions to bring positive changes in society that implement the abstract elements of justice (or typologies as further described in the entry).[15,16] Thus, specific social justice actions are viewed favorably as "progressive" when they provided impetus to a creation and development of those social conditions or environments that embodied the actualization of justice.[17,18] Philosophers, scholars, and activists draw close connections between this deconstructed meaning of social justice in terms of actions for change and a critical reflective process that questions traditional understandings and scrutinize existing values, practices, ideological frameworks, and processes to promote a progressive society.[19–21] Application of social justice as a critical framework and progressive mode of analysis has further been cemented in the twenty-first century.[22,23]

Presently, there are several movements throughout the world that are working toward various social justice goals.[24] These study and analyze social justice in terms of its legal, political, economic, criminal, civil, philosophical, linguistic, religious, historical, and sociocultural dimensions.[25] Also, they examine how social justice goals are shaping relationships and social exchanges in varied institutional, organizational, governmental, educational, community-based, group-related, familial, person-to-person, and other formal and informal settings.[26] Among these movements are LIS-specific examples, including the Campaign for the World's Libraries, Librarians Without Borders, and ProLiteracy Worldwide.[27] From these analyses, several interrelated typologies of

justice and social justice have been developed. The following are particularly useful typologies when considering social justice aspects of LIS practice and research.

Justice-as-Desert: Justice-as-desert theory propounds giving a person what s/he justly deserves.[28] It is considered integral to natural law that presents an understanding of justice as part of a systemic process of consequences which result from any option, decision, or action.[29] Justice-as-desert holds that justice provides individuals or groups with a consequence (e.g., goods, resources, etc.) that they deserve, merit, or are sanctioned to receive in society.[30]

Egalitarianism/Equity: Egalitarianism refers to the equal distribution of resources.[31] Equity enriches the concept of egalitarianism by considering political, economic, social, and cultural developments in society, and addresses limitations of treating all as equals without considering their historical or individual contexts that may lead to injustice and unfairness.[32]

Utilitarianism: The utilitarian perspective of justice favors the good of society over the good of the individual. Utilitarianism suggests that policies should maximize the welfare of the many, even if this results in the expense of an innocent few.[33]

Distributive Justice: Distributive justice refers to the appropriate distribution of resources, wealth, power, rewards, and respect among all or select stakeholders in a society.[34] This notion is based on theories of fairness, status, and right.[35]

Justice-as-Fairness: Justice-as-fairness presents the idea that societies must safeguard the rights of citizens based on rational and unbiased notions of fairness.[36] It was put forth by the American political philosopher John Rawls,[37] who asserts that fairness is based on principles of justice that: 1) ensure extensive and equal liberty; and 2) promote societal benefits to be arranged in such a way that the least disadvantaged persons obtain the greatest benefits possible.

Although justice and social justice theory are developed domains, LIS-specific social justice theory is in its infancy. Rarely is social justice explicitly articulated in LIS practice and research.[38] Yet ethical and moral imperatives have long been apparent in LIS.[39,40] The next section gives an overview of key social justice elements (i.e., fairness, humanism, individual rights, etc.) that have inhered within mainstream LIS constructs, practices, and research (e.g., intellectual freedom, service and diversity-related goals, community-based programs, etc.).[41,42] It is followed by a critique of mainstream LIS discourses within a social justice perspective that helps identify shortcomings and blind spots of the field. A critical point of view adds a deeper dimension of analysis that questions mainstream LIS ideologies and practices concerned with social justice values. Separating the two emphases in social justice and juxtaposing them provides for a stronger

Smithsonian–Society

and more balanced presentation of the issues. The former provides an understanding of the LIS professions in the United States in terms of their liberating role to seek social justice ideals in the services they developed for their various constituencies, while the latter presents an analysis in terms of a limited role of LIS professions to seek social justice outcomes in their work, constrained that they have been by curtailing sociopolitical, socioeconomic, and sociocultural circumstances during different times in their history.

The discussion presented in this entry on social justice elements in LIS and a critical analysis of the LIS professions from a social justice viewpoint includes only brief temporal snapshots in the history of LIS practice and research. An in-depth analysis of each historical moment and role of LIS is beyond the scope of this discussion since each time period and topic has been extensively addressed on its own terms; additionally, here the discussion is not meant to be all-encompassing in its extent and inclusion of all activities and roles of the LIS professions. The goal in this entry is to provide representational evidence to show the liberating and limited role of the LIS professions in addressing social justice criteria and impacts during various times.

The entry acknowledges that there have been multiple interpretations and meanings associated with the various times in the historical growth and development of the LIS professions in the United States. The intention here is to present one mode of analysis in discussing the liberating and limited role of the LIS professions to further a social justice agenda.

SOCIAL JUSTICE ELEMENTS IN LIS

In the United States, the library has evolved in direct response to the existing social, political, economic, and cultural conditions during different times.[43] These conditions influenced all dimensions of library development, particularly in regard to the library's role in furthering social justice.[44] They have also contributed in defining libraries functionally as institutionalized organizers of world knowledge and service providers of information to meet the needs of all members in society.[45] Tracing these central functionalities in the library institutions' activities show a connection between library practice and social justice elements, for example, in providing information access and outreach to underserved populations that runs deep in the history of American librarianship.[46]

The nineteenth century saw the dependency of democracy on capitalism sow the seeds for social justice to meet the needs of educated workers and informed citizenry.[47] Though not entirely based on a "capitalist agenda," American public schools and libraries responded to the social expectations in providing expanded collections and services to meet the demands of these intertwining needs.[48]

The concept of social justice was not yet developed, yet principles of equality, justice, and fairness of service were espoused by libraries, even though they had little control over their own fate since they were a voluntary institution (i.e., people did not have to use them) and highly dependent on public financing.[49] An increasing pressure to provide free access to information in the early nineteenth century[50,51] solidified middle class sympathy for the library, contributing to an expanded social justice agenda. Additionally, tax-funded library development in the mid-1800s represented the following liberating roles to further social justice elements in library work:[52]

- Library facilitation of social justice activities promoted equity in literacy services, supported fairness in information access to the middle-class, and incorporated elements of a welfare state in expanding their services to cater to all segments of their communities;
- Increased marketing efforts by the public library as "people's universities" allowed opportunities for all to learn[53] and where immigrants could Americanize so they could find jobs;[54]
- A growth in the community's stake in the public library as a result of its tax investment[55] provided a regular income for the public library and helped in its growth as a community's center, cultural hub, and agent of social justice.[56–60]

Important milestones and events for libraries in 1876 (e.g., founding of the American Library Association (ALA) and publishing of the *Library Journal*, first edition of the "Dewey Decimal Classification," and the U.S. Bureau of Education's "1876 Report" entitled *Public Libraries in the United States of America: Their History, Condition, and Management*)[61,62] provided liberating possibilities for social justice activities resulting from the library's increased power base in a consolidated professional body and development of organization and representation tools to meet the information needs of people on society's margins.[63]

During the period between 1890 and 1925, when semi-rural, small villages began growing into metropolises of more than one million inhabitants, libraries represented hope in the future and trust in progress.[64] Free public library service promoted literacy,[65] and the development of traveling libraries actualized the library's mission to provide service to far-flung immigrant communities.[66,67] For example, between 1896 and 1914, Lutie Stearns, a founder of the Wisconsin Free Library Commission, campaigned extensively engaging in lobbying amongst small-time elites (even though such political expediencies sometimes conflicted with her democratic ideals) for the establishment of public and traveling libraries.[68] It was such efforts and the vision motivating the actions that facilitated and consolidated the library's role as an information provider.[69]

Expansion of free library services and construction of library buildings with expanding collections, under the generous bequests of industry leaders and wealthy, civic minded men like Samuel J. Tilden, Andrew Carnegie, and others, provided yet another opportunity for the library to further its social ideals in reaching out to a greater number of people.[70] The generosity of industry leaders allowed libraries to extend their services in contribution towards the overall welfare of society (e.g., Carnegie libraries that were developed around the country) by creating jobs and furthering the economic wheels of a capitalist society, with its demanding appetite for a consuming middle class and literate working class.[71]

Martin[72] documents a rich and extensive history of the public library in the United States during the twentieth century as a reflection of prevailing sociocultural conditions during various times. For example, similar to the earlier periods, public library service in the twentieth century responded to a focused capitalist agenda to create a middle class with informed decision-making abilities, who could engage in productive work and contribute economically as a market segment owing to their significant buying potential.[73,74] Libraries played a significant role by portraying themselves as socially uplifting agents, developing library services to meet the needs of European immigrant populations during the foundation years (1900–1917), or during the era of depression and war (1930–1945), and afterwards, where the focus was on economic recovery and revitalization. During these times, the library provided liberating directions for social justice outcomes in nurturing just and fair ideals, expanding the base of impact to include outreach populations, creating a service-based ethics in the profession, and forging partnerships with community-based social justice agencies towards common goals.[75]

The twentieth century saw public libraries explore models and changing service philosophies to their patrons and user communities through lifelong learning, support for democracy and intellectual freedom.[76] In the early 1900s adult services in public libraries were part of an extension and outreach movement and later the national adult education program during 1920–1930[77] that extended the idea of library service to different under-served populations with "active transformations" of their collections, services, resources, and staff "into programmatic responses relevant to community served."[78] A series of essays in honor of Margaret E. Monroe identified the four basic adult services functions to include information, guidance, instruction, and stimulation,[79] the last considered "a library's response to community needs along the continuum from highly innovative to extensions of existing services."[80]

There were many library efforts to reach out to the poor and immigrant populations during the last century.[81,82] While the record is certainly mixed in terms of effectiveness of service, and not as extensive as one would hope,

several noteworthy efforts can be considered.[83] In *Libraries, Immigrants, and the American Experience*, Plummer Alston Jones Jr.[84] presents a thoughtful and well-documented volume on the historical interaction between American public libraries and immigrant communities from 1876 when the ALA was founded through 1948, when the ALA Committee on Work with the Foreign Born disbanded. Phyllis Dain[85] took issue with earlier critiques of libraries that essentially viewed them to be a creation of the social elite and recognized that a variety of people, including immigrants, believed in the value of reading and use of libraries. Gratia Countryman who led the Minneapolis Public Library from 1904–1936 and her contemporaries believed in social justice ideals making the library more user-friendly and open to all of the area's residents, regardless of age or economic position.[86] Similarly, many "revolting librarians" of the 1960–1970 era shared a similar faith in social justice ideals and reflective resistance towards expanding library service provision beyond its complacent boundaries and scope of activities.[87]

Historians of American librarianship (as well as in what later became identified as a related discipline of information science with the advent of computers during the closing half of the twentieth century) have traced its philosophical, theoretical, and sociohistorical roots to reveal directions for its future development.[88] These included social justice activities and initiatives, even though the rhetoric and vocabulary of "social justice" had not been significantly incorporated into the mainstream profession. For example, Shera's (1903–1982) work on the foundational principles of librarianship, the library's role in promoting literacy and its relationship to democracy, and identification of connections between librarianship, documentation, and information science have had a profound influence on the "conceptualization of public library service by the profession's leaders as it has been transmitted and reconfigured for each changing era."[89] Similarly, Ditzion[54] saw the library as an advocate for democracy and education to develop a reflective and engaged citizenry capable of sound decision-making and participation in a democratic life.[90]

The twentieth century saw a number of policy reports and guidelines published by the ALA and others that present ideals, professional tools, directions, bench marks, and codes of ethics to apply in current library practice on how to have a greater impact on the community in terms of a social justice discourse. For example, the *National Plan for Public Library Service*[91] developed and implemented by the ALA's Committee on Post-War Planning during 1947–1952, focused on the Public Library Inquiry, a professional legitimizing effort that served as an "exercise in identity creation that relied heavily on the role of the public library as a sustaining contributor to American democracy."[92] Post World War II library support programs (e.g., ALA's War on Poverty) during the next two decades helped strengthen professional interlibrary relationships and build national consensus on library service conceptualization and outreach mission definitions.[93] Several ALA publications during this time played a major role in shaping library ideals as rhetorical uplifters of the downtrodden, leading to extended dialogue, passionate discussion, and clarity in defining the library's perceived activism and its mission of serving poor people.[94,95]

Similarly, since 1968 when the ALA established a Coordinating Committee on Service to the Disadvantaged (that eventually became the Office for Literacy and Outreach Services), there have been several professional forums that were initiated to represent the needs of the underserved (e.g., the Subcommittee on Library Services to Poor and Homeless People, the Social Responsibilities Round Table (SRRT) and its Task Force on Hunger, Homelessness and Poverty, etc.).

Recently, there have also been non-mainstream efforts to return to the heritage of "traditional library service,"[96] serving the needs of diverse library users,[97] developing tangible measures of the impact of library and information services[98] on the lives of the disenfranchised, and "learning from the voices of the customers, the staff, the processes, and the organization."[99] These and other similar shifts have allowed for recent experimentation and implementation of progressive library activities targeted towards the needs of various disenfranchised populations based on race,[100,101] ethnicity,[102,103] class,[104,105] gender,[106,107] disability,[108,109] sexual orientation,[110,111] age,[112,113] and other variables associated with institutionalized social exclusion. It has provided for an appreciation of the convergence in ideals, motivations, and pragmatism in public library service delivery and its philosophy to meet the needs of specific communities based on local library planning and decision making.[114]

The lessons from the past are today providing libraries directions to develop a new approach that recognizes: 1) importance of outcome-based, socially relevant evaluation methods in assessing library services;[115] 2) value of local experiences and ontologies and their representation into formalized organizational tools of information; and 3) necessity in building equitable partnering efforts with disenfranchised constituencies.[116] This has been, in part, a result of external pressures from federal, regional, and local funding agencies (e.g., the National Institute for Museum and Library Services), that have incorporated the social relevancy of library projects as strict criteria in their missions and guidelines for grant proposals.[117] The funding of library projects with strong social relevance, in conjunction with leadership initiatives such as those spearheaded by the U.S. National Commission on Libraries and Information Science (NCLIS), are providing recognition and representation of the social value of libraries and librarians in circles of power. There is increasing external political expectations and pressure to provide the necessary support for libraries to expand their collections, services, programs, and other creative outreach partnering efforts for disadvantaged and underserved constituencies. This has called for the library's expanded role in social justice efforts to equalize power differentials in society and partner with underserved populations as equals who bring a change in their own lives with support from others (such as LIS professionals).[118,119]

Moreover, recent Library 2.0 efforts in the twenty-first century for information professionals to respond to constant contemporary changes by purposeful involvement of users in the design and evaluation of library and information services[120,121] has also provided some opportunities to expand the social justice missions in LIS work.[122] For example, Library 2.0 developments in the design of specific services, policies, procedures, programs, and technologies has required adopting participatory, collaborative and social applications via the Internet.[123] This has furthered social justice elements of building capacity, providing value to individual experiences, knowledge, and contributions, and thereby, shifted an earlier biased library service mission of helping people to "helping people help themselves."[38] It has resulted in efforts to equalize past power dynamics between the library and the library user and provided positive changes in public perception about the library, thereby increasing its role and function in society.[124]

CRITIQUE OF SOCIAL JUSTICE IN LIS

Libraries today are considered notable models of service to local and recently global communities, and are expected to be unequivocally immersed in pursuing this dictum.[125] But the implications of such a position for libraries, in terms of a social justice agenda, are not quite clear. LIS and its professional service orientation can be considered from a social justice perspective, specifically by examining the underlying power vested in libraries that has been historically perpetuated through a social contract in the American public sphere.[126]

The assumption is that as a public institution dedicated to represent diverse social constituencies, and because of its role to provide information based on the needs of those it characterizes as "marginalized," outside society's acceptable domains, the library acquires unstated power because of this mandate to serve.[127] For it is the library (as defined to include the institution and its library board, library director, and library staff) that decides its patrons or customer base and their information needs.[128] It is the library that plays the role of gatekeeper and determines what resources and information to include as a part of its collections, services, and programs.[129] This has developed a reputation of the traditional American library as an advocate of justice and a provider to the information needs of the underprivileged, based however, on sometimes biased conceptualizations and limited under-standing of people on society's margins solely in terms of their deficient characteristics.[130] Historically, as discussed in the following critique, such unfair library practices were not always effective in changing the sta-tus-quo, and instead, may have sometimes continued to perpetuate gaps between the haves and have-nots.[131]

Libraries as institutions that advance the "dominant cul-ture's ideology" and symbolize places for the privileged and select scholarly[132] can be traced back to the first "subscription library," established in 1731 by Benjamin Franklin and open to all who could afford the fees.[133] The nineteenth century provided an environment that offered a limited role for libraries to meet social justice criteria in their work, constrained that libraries were by curtailing sociopolitical, socioeconomic, and sociocultural circumstances of the times.[134] For example, the expanded collections and services in libraries of the times were ini-tially limited to only those who had the money to access them.[48] Owing to fee-structure, slavery, and a limited role of women in society, access to information was based on class and income, and subsequently on race and gender, amongst other variables.[135] The increasing pressure to provide free access to information in the early nineteenth century[50,51] and the solidified middle class sympathy for the library resulted in little connection with the needs of people on the ethnic margins (i.e., the indigenous Natives, Blacks and other people of color, and women from the lower middle classes).[136] Additionally, tax-funded library development in the mid-1800s to meet the whims and demands of the privileged classes[137] represented the fol-lowing limited role for libraries to further social justice:

- Library dependency on the public tax monies provided greater power to the growing middle class white popu-lation that had control over the library budget and became the guardians and dictators of the library's policies, programs, and collections,[138] leading to a minimal focus of library services to serve the informa-tion needs of others;[139]
- It led to increased library efforts in aggressive public relations and expansion in their services catering primar-ily to appease the largest and the loudest in the commu-nity since libraries perceived them to have the greatest influence over the allocation of tax revenues.[140]

Further, the important milestones and events for libraries in 1876 led to limiting inward-looking professional trends and practices of library leaders of the time to deliberately disengage with their local constituencies that has generated negative public criticism owing to their lack of perceived currency and relevance to everyday lives.[141] At the same time, the concept of "the public" in the public library of 1876 was understood as anything that was not in strictly private hands, open to any segment of the population.[142] A closer exploration of the culture and history during this

time suggests that the seemingly democratic notion of the "public" was more rhetorical rather than demonstrated action.[143] The "public" in public libraries was largely homogenized and "imagined"[144] to represent forces of economic, urban, and cultural development,[145] resonating with the religious beliefs and image of the majority.[146] Such a critique of the public library has been presented by Michael H. Harris and Gerard Spiegler,[147] who have asserted that Edward Everett and George Ticknor, advo-cates for the establishment of the Boston Public Library in 1852, were "elitists who supported libraries and education as one way of raising up an 'aristocracy of talent and intellect' which would provide benign and enlightened leadership to the masses." This image of some public libraries of the time reflected the profession's own market-ing agenda to retain favor with the growing middle class in order to hold-on to its tax support.[148]

Historical research indicates that women on the public library frontier were its strong backbone[149] actively involved in raising funds, lobbying for tax-support, and implementing outreach programs.[150] Yet, as in many levels of society at the time, women's role to improve society through libraries and their equal representation in the library was hampered by their lack of voting rights and status as second-class citizens.[151,152] It often led to an unfair position for women librarians, for example, even as late as 1903, when Gratia Countryman in Minneapolis became the first woman to head a major public library, her salary was set at $2000—$1000 less than her predecessor who was a white male.[153]

In addition, public library service to racial and ethnic minorities was far from equitable levels since these populations were quite "invisible" and faced many bar-riers to becoming recognized as part of the "public" domain that the library claimed to serve during this time.[154] For example, unequal and biased trends in public library services to non-white communities would continue till the 1960s shaped as they were by issues emerging from racial segregation and prejudice in their struggles for fair distribution, quality, quantity, and the development of ser-vices, collections, and availability of resources and opportunities.[155,156]

The funding and support of libraries by wealthy indus-trialists and capitalists had definite implications for improved service, accelerated progress, and library devel-opment;[157] it also resulted in the economic growth of the middle class that contributed in filling the pockets of the miniscule upper classes, who continued to grow richer and richer, strengthening their social control on the capital investments and industries, and thereby maintaining the status quo of widening socioeconomic gaps between those who had power and those who did not.[158] As Andrew Carnegie himself wrote, that he was motivated in part by the idea of public libraries making "men not violent revo-lutionists, but cautious evolutionists; not destroyers but cautious improvers."[159] A possibly well-intentioned and pacifist idea, though it makes one ponder if library support had alternatively come also from the government (via increased taxes from the upper classes) and federal, state, and local funding, instead of (or in addition to) donations from wealthy benefactors such as Carnegie and others, would libraries have been as dependent on the capitalists' agenda to maintain the status quo and social order and as likely to promote the goals of these elites?[160] Instead, we might have possibly witnessed more interaction between libraries and marginalized communities, shaping social change and social justice instead of taking a primarily reactive role.[161,162] But obviously, such a "what if" question may seem irrelevant today since library development did not historically go down that route, yet, it does call for challenging a purist interpretation of the noble motives and philanthropic activities of American capitalists in their support of public libraries during the times.

Similarly, parallel to earlier times, public library service in the twentieth century responded to (and was limited by) focused and encompassing capitalist motives that crippled democracy and developed an impotent middle class whose informed decision-making abilities, participation in productive work, and buying potential contributed in making the upper classes wealthy and widening the social, cultural, and economic gaps in society.[73,74] Embedded in a possibly unintentional hegemonic orchestration of profit-making for their wealthy benefactors, at this time, the development of libraries was limited in their inability to become truly culturally responsive agents.

Moreover, the vision of the library's role as an information provider was possibly facilitated without questioning the ingrained power imbalance between the library as provider and the disenfranchised population as the needy who required betterment and uplifting.[163] In this case, the community was viewed solely in terms of a unidirectional impact of library services on the community's knowledge-deficient and information-impoverished conditions.[164] This perspective assumed an active role for librarians and a passive role for the community as an inert receptor and consumer of library services. The activeness of libraries and the passiveness of a homogenized, deficient community perpetuated the profession's image of striving to improve the conditions of the needy members in society; helping those who were completely passive and helpless to better their own conditions. This perspective partially led to a failure of public libraries to significantly engage with a majority of disenfranchised Americans to actually use the libraries and adequately respond to new cultural and intellectual challenges of the day.[165] Contemporary trends recognize the limitations of past service-based ethics in the profession (e.g., biased language constructs reflecting imbalanced power dynamics) and are moving towards adopting more progressive concepts and practices (e.g., community engagement, community-based action research, collaborative learning, etc.).[166]

Historians of American librarianship have drawn flack in recent years for not taking a more aggressive stance to further social justice in their identification of future directions for the LIS professions in order to overcome the debilitating political and economic circumstances historically presented by a capitalist society. For example, critics of Shera's work identify important limitations in applying some of Shera's ideas into actual practice and creating library activities that could shape social conditions in the community and impact the everyday lives of disenfranchised people in meaningful ways.[167] Similarly, not only did Ditzion overlook the significance of key library developments including youth services librarianship,[168] he also ignored "long-standing gender stratification in the profession" (similar to other professions).[169] Also, Ditzion's view of librarianship as democratic agents limited the efforts by libraries to affect social change beyond the profession's self-conceptualization as a knowledge storehouse and information provider.[170]

Further, the post World War II library support programs and publications during the next two decades (e.g., ALA's War on Poverty) continued to remain essentially within the limited sphere of the national association, having little or no impact outside of library circles in local communities and at political and legislative levels of decision-making. For example, the National Plan for Public Library Service and other such subsequent efforts further perpetuated library efforts away from a social justice perspective in recommending public libraries to minimize their role among the lay public, and instead, focus more on gaining favor of only the most powerful opinion leaders in the community,[171,172] that invariably resulted in the possible exclusion of disenfranchised minorities and those outside the influence of library domains from receiving services.[173] An important note to make is that though the profession never completely endorsed this view nor was this strategy formally adopted by the ALA,[174] better services for opinion leaders is a de facto practice in many libraries (e.g., reflected in the contemporary practice of selective dissemination of information that focuses on providing the "right" information to important leaders and others in the community based on a study of their interests and topics of concern to gain their favor).[175]

Much professional energy and resources in the ALA were applied in dialogue and publications,[176] with little action that would affect any real change in the marginalized lives of the poor and the underserved.[177] Additionally, past ALA and other library initiatives have been criticized for their top-down focus on library leaders and administration, rather than facilitate any action for social change and extend involvement of others beyond "mainstream middle-class practices and values."[132] Similarly, ALA's efforts since the 1970s have encouraged professional discussion and conceptualization, identified national standards as "one fit" for all,[178] and built networks for librarians, strengthening ties within the "inner circle" of the privileged group, though it is debatable if in the past there have been any significant inroads beyond these bureaucratic and administrative policies and procedures.[179] For professional library avenues to represent dialogue about the underserved have included only very limited outside (beyond the profession) community members from the marginalized populations being discussed.[180] American Library Association's role at local community levels has thus been limited, and ALA representation and participation in external efforts at national, regional, and local levels in legal, policy, and political avenues has also been minimal.[181]

From a critical perspective, ALA's activities reflect its mission that focuses on efforts "to provide leadership for the development, promotion, and improvement of library and information services and the profession of librarianship in order to enhance learning and ensure access to information for all."[182] It has essentially been concerned with solely professional networking, internal mobilization, and creating limited political and public representation.[183] Contemporary democratic expectations to develop greater professional relevance of LIS warrant an expanded mission of ALA to include a proactive focus on outcome-based, community-level efforts that promote active participation of minorities and help develop stronger impacts on local communities.[81,82]

Over the years, there have been internal philosophical struggles in the ALA and the Public Library Association (PLA) towards realization for a process "that would reflect local community needs."[180] Lack of consolidated strategy, cultural inertia, and administrative lethargy have limited library professionals in only looking at the user in the life of the library, rather than the library in the life of the user.[184] Since the 1980s though the PLA decided to move toward a community-oriented, user-focused planning process for development of public library services,[185] and the first version of its planning manual recommended extensive needs assessment and community analysis; several iterations have emerged since but the goal is still (at least in principle) to establish guidelines to develop a best match between services and the localized needs of all members in different communities.[186]

As a result of a lack of consensus, however, libraries have been struggling to mobilize public opinion of library relevance and credibility for users, and to find ways to enable local communities to build and sustain capacity.[187] The recent non-mainstream efforts of "traditional library service" to serve the needs of diverse library users have also been partially successful, however, because they followed the traditional models of library service provision that did not go beyond knowledge organizers and information providers and struggled with classism and elitism "that pervade the library profession."[179]

Historical developments in information science research in the United States with its deep roots (philosophical, symbolic, and tangible) in librarianship[188] have incrementally allowed for an integration of social justice imperatives in the LIS professions though they also inherited a limited (and often slow) tendency to shape social justice outcomes.

Pioneers in the field of documentation, a precursor to information science, maintained a humanistic view in their work.[189] Paul Otlet, a central figure in the early documentation movement and his colleague Henri Lafontaine worked until the mid-1930s in developing universal organization schemes and storage and representational systems (e.g., library classification and library catalogs), promoting the notion that knowledge should be made available to anyone who needed it, and that organization and access to world knowledge could be integrated into efforts to promote a more peaceful and just world.[190,191]

Over the years, information organization and classification have been recognized and critiqued as tools for including and excluding, for validating and univeralization and reinforcing a dominant worldview, on the one hand, and for silencing and their transgressive potential to represent marginalized knowledge domains, on the other.[192,193] As a socially constructed tool, classification imbues power in its role as the "scaffolding of information infrastructures" to develop a systematic (though invariably biased) process of categorization and creating like and unlike groupings for understanding and retrieval purposes.[194,195] From the International Classification of Diseases, Library of Congress Subject Headings, Dewey Decimal Classification, to the Nursing Interventions Classification and race classification under apartheid in South Africa, amongst other examples, all categories and standards involve some form of bias and partiality. In order to further social justice ideals of fairness and equity in knowledge representation and information practice, the "knowing community" of LIS must continue to question the dominance of hierarchy and linearity, adopt fuzzy logic and web-like structures (instead of the pyramid), provide multi-lingual and metathesauri interfaces between standards, and augment traditional standards via cluster analysis to "enhance the situatedness of syntagmatic relationships," amongst other strategies, to rectify imbalances and better serve a diversity of users.[196]

A focus on access to information and information dissemination in the early twentieth century provided a conceptual opportunity and rhetorical space to question and philosophize the nature of LIS professions at a later date and to integrate social justice elements of fairness and equality for all.[197] At that time, however, such trends provided a broad, sweeping, and ambiguous goal of information access, leading to an unsatisfactory systems-centered approach for the design of information systems and services that was eventually found to be limited in meeting the information needs of users, especially in the scientific communities.[198] A particular focus was placed on the adaptation of users to information systems outputs rather than creating information systems that were user-driven.

Information was seen as objective, and users were seen as simple processors of information.

With the goal to improve information services,[199] the emergence of the user-centered paradigm in the 1980s as an alternative (or addition) to system-focused research and study of human information behavior in developing more effective and usable computer systems in information sciences[200] provided a shift in making people the focus of study, instead of systems and technologies. This had an indirect bearing upon social justice agendas. For example, understanding the user's perspective in information seeking and use[201,202] and in processes associated with information seeking, information gathering, and information giving,[203] the concept of usefulness in the assessment of information services[204] and the importance of psychological relevance and other relevance studies,[205] all represented fairness in social justice by acknowledging the existence of the human being involved in the interaction with systems and services, even if people were considered as abstract entities from a purely theoretical perspective.

Similarly, research on human interactions with information systems provided another area where a focus on user's problems in the process of information seeking situations,[206–208] and the user's evaluation of usefulness of information for resolution of the problem,[209–211] had limited relevance to social justice that does not narrowly view just one "problem" that LIS users face in their lives, as conceptualized and addressed in such work. A social justice construct regards the entire experience of users (including their economic, political, social, and cultural realities that limit their access and effective use of technology and information) as a "problem" (if one identifies the meaning of the word as a barrier or hindrance) to their well-being, advancement, and change in social status.[212,213] In such a context, evaluation of information provision must be taken into account in terms of meaningful integration and use of information within people's entire experience. Strategies to measure the effectiveness of information provision, and the usefulness of information resources and support mechanisms, must not identify them as isolated avenues, but their design, implementation and practice need to be expanded via studying their impacts in people's entirety of experiences in order to reflect what is really meaningful to people using them and how does it change their status and position in society.[214]

An important idea about focus on the personal meanings that users seek from the information[215–217] is relevant to social justice in terms of recognizing the personal experiences of users in their meaning-making process and decision-making. Here too, social justice translates the idea from a narrow application of meanings from "information" to making sense of meanings in relation to the entire experience of learning to further users' power and status in society.

The notion of construction of learning in information seeking as a process, and its dynamic nature, has been proposed in other prior work such as the analogous state of knowledge hypothesis,[218] where the researchers lay out the process of the user's information seeking from identification of the user's problem to finding a solution that satisfies the information need and solves the information problem. In situations where there is not a specific problem at hand, but the entire nature of experience has to be understood and negotiated (to improve one's "disenfranchised" sense of being), a broader framework is called for, to reflect the nuances and reality in the different and larger situation. Similarly, Taylor's significant work on information use environments[219] and levels of information need in terms of visceral (actual but unexpressed), conscious (internal description in the brain), formalized (formal statement of need), and compromised (presented question or query) also provide limited understanding of constructive process and learning experiences in its focused application of information seeking that bypasses social justice outcomes of larger economic/political/social changes in people's lives.

As noted by Case,[220] several researchers assert that understanding individual users' information needs is among the keys to improving information systems. Information needs are often described as being initiated by people's attempts to address everyday challenges or resolve uncertainties or knowledge insufficiencies. For example, Dervin[201,202] asserts that information behavior begins when a user acknowledges a gap in her/his knowledge of how to deal with a life situation. Marchionini[221] positions information seeking as a problem-solving activity "a process driven by life itself" (p. 128). Krikelas[203] describes information need as the general recognition of the existence of uncertainty. Understanding the cognitive processes in which users engage has also been recognized as an important way to improve information systems.[222–224] One of the most widely used frameworks for studying cognitive processes associated with information seeking and use is Dervin's Sense-Making approach. Sense-Making focuses on the notion that individuals who have information needs experience a cognitive gap that prevents them from making sense of a particular life situation, and they seek information to fill that gap. However, during this information search, an appropriate course of action is not indicated, and the individual is placed in a situation where "making sense fails." As the user collects information in the gap phase, s/he learns more about her/his situation, becomes better at interpreting it, and then is able to select a course of action or behavior that helps her/his make sense of the particular situation.[201,202] Dervin's sense-making triangle of situation-gap-use as a perspective to understand user's information seeking and use processes provides an opening view of social justice in focusing on the user and acknowledging peoples' information use to "make sense" of a "gap" in a specific "situation" that the user experiences.[225,226] Further, social justice must involve collecting information that addresses not one particular "gap" in a situation, but gaps in the entire reality of experience based on lack of knowledge and power to change one's state of being.

Pettigrew et al.[227] indicate that since the early 1990s, a key characteristic of information behavior research is a body of theory that emphasizes contextual interplays of cognitive, social, cultural, organizational, affective, and linguistic factors of information behavior. They assert that this research stream supports the notion that information behavior phenomena are part of the human communicative process. Study of context in information science research provided a recognition of the role of situational dynamics in the processes associated with people's interactions with various information systems and technologies.[228] Such work, important from a theoretical and descriptive point of view, has indirect bearing on social justice agendas in its identification of user's learning of information systems and services as a complex mechanism where individuals go through a dynamic process in learning about a particular subject or "becoming informed." It represents fairness by acknowledging the existence of the human being involved in the human–computer interaction.

Nahl[229] argues that cognitive processes are strongly connected to the emotions that users experience as they use information. Identifying an emerging affective paradigm in information behavior research, the researcher goes on to assert that given how deeply humans feel in response to information in newspapers, books, libraries, Internet, etc., it is critical that LIS professionals understand these emotions in order to maintain and improve information services for their constituencies. Affective aspects of information behavior are also often linked to Kuhlthau's information seeking process model (ISP), which describes the triad of thoughts, actions, and feelings associated with information seeking and use.[230] There is need to further this model via studying the role of the "classic triad" in the lives of "marginalized" and the information poor to examine how they negotiate and change their realities to represent social justice outcomes.

A wide variety of information behavior context studies have been published in recent years that are relevant to examinations of social justice in LIS. For example, Spink et al.[231] discussed word-of-mouth information seeking within multi-member, low-income African-American households. Hersberger[232] examined whether economically poor people are information poor. Chatman[104,105,233,234] explored the information needs, seeking, and use of under-served groups such as female prisoners and poor rural residents. Saumure and Given[235] investigated the information behavior of visually impaired students. Bilal[236] reported on how children used online search engines, and Mehra[237,238] examined the cross-cultural learning process of international students to propose "two-way" learning outcomes where both international students and American academicians/students learn from each other.

Broader contexts have also attracted the attention of LIS researchers. Van Dijk explored how information divides are emerging within and across demographic groups in all societies.[239] Others position librarianship as a tool of economic and social change in the developing world.[240–242] Seidelin and Jensen[243] presented frameworks for how libraries can be involved in efforts to minimize HIV/AIDS, poverty, and corruption.

These are but a few areas in current LIS research that reflect social justice philosophies, methods, and/or results. In the years to come, LIS professions will continue to engage in more of such work that use social justice parameters to frame, apply, and represent needs of underserved populations in society towards the design and development of fair, equitable, and just information systems and services that are meaningful to disempowered people and empower them to promote proactive changes in their lives.

CONCLUSION

Historically, a strong emphasis on humanism and fairness in both library practice and LIS research suggests that the first formative stages of a theory of social justice in LIS are clearly present. Future directions will include greater development of LIS-specific social justice theory in order to promote active and efficacious social justice agendas in the profession. We are seeing first steps in this direction as reflected in wide-ranging efforts to develop, test, and apply new concepts, terminologies, and methods (e.g., community informatics, community engagement, participatory action research, to name a few) that share intersecting elements with social justice to push the boundaries of traditional LIS conceptualizations towards more progressive outcomes.

The active involvement of LIS professionals working on society's margins in influencing positive social justice changes is imperative. Results of LIS involvement in select social justice activities can be evidenced in steady increases in library users and the increasing role of LIS professionals in shaping the form of library collections (e. g., fiction) and other services (e.g., local programming and events) to directly meet the needs of their local communities to empower their lives.[244]

In spite of these recent efforts, in sum, historically libraries and LIS research in the United States have been effective in bringing only moderate socially progressive changes in their communities, trapped that they have been within limited social justice parameters and constraints owing to their permitted roles within a socially structured fabric, community values, and academic streams of thought. Contemporary trends in twenty-first century LIS development, are however, showing a marked shift in attitudes, practices, management efforts, and planning to integrate social justice goals and outcomes in both practice and research. For example, positive changes and trends in LIS have included the use of computers in library and information environments to meet the information needs of various user/customer/patron/client constituencies (as variously defined) via their active and ongoing participation in assessment and evaluation of LIS services (e.g., library–community partnerships to host computer literacy training workshops, use of social tagging and Library 2.0 software, to name a few).[122] Such continued efforts to re-engage with local communities in terms of newly constructed modes of interaction will help to further integrate social justice ideals into LIS practices and build equitable relationships with people on society's margins to develop effective library services, programs, collections, and activities that are meaningful in the everyday lives of all members in society.

ACKNOWLEDGMENTS

The authors are grateful to Dr. Wayne A. Wiegand and Dr. Ramesh Srinivasan for their editorial comments to an earlier version of the library practice materials presented in this entry. We are also thankful to the editors and anonymous reviewers for their constructive suggestions and sharp insights.

REFERENCES

1. Mehra, B. Service learning in library and Information science (LIS) education: Connecting research and practice to community. Interact.: UCLA J. Inform. Educ. Stud. **2004**, *1*(1). Article 3, http://repositories.cdlib.org/gseis/interactions/vol1/iss1/art3/ (accessed January 2008).
2. Honma, T. Trippin' over the color line: The invisibility of race in library and information studies. Interact.: UCLA J. Inform. Educ. Stud. **2005**, *1*(2). Article 2, http://repositories.cdlib.org/gseis/interactions/vol1/iss2/art2/ (accessed January 2008).
3. Pyati, A.K. Critical theory and information studies: A Marcusean infusion. Pol. Futures Educ. **2006**, *4* (1), 83–89.
4. Lebacqz, K. *Six Theories of Justice: Perspectives from Philosophical and Theological Ethics*; Augsburg Publishing House: Minneapolis, MN, 1986.
5. Barry, B. *Why Social Justice Matters*; Polity Press: Cambridge, U.K., 2005.
6. Guillermina, J.; Wegener, B. Methods for empirical justice analysis: Part 1. Framework, models and quantities. Soc. Just. Res. **1997**, *10*(4), http://www.springerlink.com/content/73446x07w23p3686/ (accessed July 2007).
7. Plato *Republic*, Translated by Robin Waterfield, Oxford University Press: Oxford, U.K., 1984.
8. Behr, T.C. *Luigi Taparelli on the Dignity of Man*; Congresso Tomista Internatzionale: Rome, Italy, 2003. http://www.e-aquinas.net/pdf/behr.pdf (accessed January 2008).
9. Barry, B. *Theories of Justice*; University of California Press: Berkeley, CA, 1989.
10. Pontifical Council for Justice and Peace. *Compendium of the Social Doctrine of the Church*; USCCB Publishing: Washington, DC, 2005.
11. Massaro, Thomas S.J. *Living Justice: Catholic Social Teaching in Action (Come & See)*; Sheed & Ward: Lanham, MD, 2000.
12. Brighouse, H. *Justice (Key Concepts)*; Polity Press: Cambridge, U.K., 2005.
13. Fleishacker, S. *A Short History of Distributive Justice*; Harvard University Press: Cambridge, MA, 2005.
14. Vandenbroucke, F. *Social Justice and Individual Ethics in an Open Society: Equality, Responsibility, and Incentives (Studies in Economic Ethics and Philosophy)*; Springer: Berlin, Germany, 2001.
15. Glennon, F. Experiential learning and social justice action: An experiment in the scholarship of teaching and learning. Teach. Theol. Relig. **2003**, *7* (1), 30–37.
16. Merkel, W. Social justice and the three worlds of welfare capitalism. Eur. J. Sociol. **2002**, *43* (1), 59–91.
17. Opfer, V.D. Evaluating equity: A framework for understanding action and inaction on social justice issues. Educ. Pol. **2006**, *20* (1), 271–290.
18. Reid, C. Advancing women's agendas: A feminist research framework. Int. J. Qual. Met. **2004**, *3* (3), 1–15.
19. Kellner, D. *Boundaries and Borderlines: Reflections on Jean Baudrillard and Critical Theory*; 1989. http://www.gseis.ucla.edu/faculty/kellner/Illumina%20Folder/kell2.htm (accessed December 2004).
20. Habermas, J. *Justification and Application: Remarks on Discourse Ethics*, Translated by C. Cronin, The MIT Press: Cambridge, MA, 1993.
21. Froomkin, M.A. Habermas@discourse.net: Toward a critical theory of cyberspace. Harvard Law Rev. **2003**, *116*(3).
22. Arrigo, B.A. *Social Justice/Criminal Justice: The Maturation of Critical Theory in Law, Crime, and Deviance (Contemporary Issues in Crime and Justice Series)*, 1st Ed.; Wadsworth Publishing: Belmont, CA, 1998.
23. Toens, K. The dilemma of regress: Social justice and democracy in recent critical theory. Eur. J. Polit. Theor. **2007**, *6* (2), 160–179.
24. Clayton, M.; Williams, A., Eds.; *Social Justice*; Blackwell Publishing: Malden, MA, 2004.
25. Safety, A. *Value Leadership and Capacity Building*; Universal Publishers: Parkland, FL, 2004.
26. Murphy, S.M.; Wayne, S.J.; Liden, R.C.; Erdogan, B. Understanding social loafing: The role of justice perceptions and exchange relationships. Hum. Relat. **2003**, *56* (1), 61–84.
27. Samek, T. *Librarianship and Human Rights*; Chandos Publishing: Oxford, U.K., 2007.
28. Ross, M.; Miller, D.T., Eds. *The Justice Motive in Everyday Life*; Cambridge University Press: Cambridge, 2002.
29. Binmore, K. *Natural Justice*; Oxford University Press: New York, 2005.
30. Pojman, L.P.; Mcleod, O. *What Do We Deserve?: A Reader on Justice and Desert*; Oxford University Press: New York, 1999.
31. Rothbard, M.N. *Egalitarianism as a Revolt Against Nature and Other Essays*, 2nd Ed.; The Ludwig von Mises Institute: Auburn, AL, 2000.

32. O'Neill, S. Justice in ethnically diverse societies: A critique of political alienation. Ethnicities **2003**, *3* (3), 369–392.

33. Stein, M.S. *Distributive Justice and Disability: Utilitarianism against Egalitarianism*; Yale University Press: London, U.K., 2006.

34. Roemer, J.E. *Theories of Distributive Justice*; Harvard University Press: Cambridge, MA, 1996.

35. Tyler, T.R.; Boeckmann, R.J.; Smith, H.J.; Huo, Y.J. *Social Justice in a Diverse Society*; Westview Press: Boulder, CO, 1997.

36. Rawls, J. *Justice as Fairness: A Restatement*, 2nd Ed.; Kelly, E., Ed.; Belknap Press: Cambridge, MA, 2001.

37. Rawls, J. *A Theory of Justice*; Belknap Press: Cambridge, MA, 1971.

38. Mehra, B.; Albright, K.S.; Rioux, K. A practical framework for social justice research in the information professions; Proceedings of the 2006 Annual Meeting of the American Society of Information Science and Technology, Information Realities: Shaping the Digital Future for All, Austin, TX, November, 3–8, 2006.

39. Rioux, K.; Albright, K.S.; Mehra, B. Conceptualizing social justice in the information sciences. Proceedings of the 70th Annual Meeting of the American Society for Information Science and Technology 2007: Joining Research and Practice: Social Computing and Information Science 44, Milwaukee, WI, October, 18–25, 2007.

40. Gorman, M. *Our Enduring Values*; American Library Association: Chicago, IL, 2000.

41. Chaparro-Univazo, S. Where social justice meets librarianship: Truth commissions as information spaces for work and activism in international librarianship. Inform. Soc. Change **2007**, *25*, 33–38.

42. Mehra, B.; Robinson, W.C. The community engagement model in library and information science education: A case study of a collection development and management course. J. Educ. Libr. Inform. Sci. **2009**, *50* (1), 15–38.

43. Dain, P.; Stieg, M.F. Libraries and society: Research and thought. Libr. Trends **1979**, *27* (3), 221–224.

44. Mehra, B.; Srinivasan, R. The library-community convergence framework for community action: Libraries as catalysts of social change. Libri: Int. J. Libr. Inform. Sci. **2007**, *57* (3), 111–178.

45. Dain, P. The historical sensibility. Library history research in America. Libr. Cult. **2000**, *35* (1), 77–87.

46. Freeman, R.; Hovde, D.M., Eds. *Libraries to the People: Histories of Outreach*; McFarland: Jefferson, NC, 2003.

47. Tolzmann, D.H.; Hessel, A.; Peiss, R. *The Memory of Mankind: The Story of Libraries Since the Dawn of Time*; Oak Knoll Press: New Castle, DE, 2001.

48. Harris, N. Cultural institutions and American modernization. Libr. Cult. **1981**, *16* (1), 28–47.

49. Wiegand, W.A. Email communication dated July 4, 2006.

50. Utley, G.B. *The Librarians' Conference of 1853: A Chapter in American Library History*; American Library Association: Chicago, IL, 1951.

51. Black, A. The Victorian information society: Surveillance, bureaucracy, and public librarianship in 19th-Century Britain. Inform. Soc. **2001**, *17* (1), 63–80.

52. Maack, M.N. Gender, culture and the transformation of American librarianship, 1890–1920. Libr. Cult. Winter **1998**, *33*, 51–61.

53. Ditzion, S. *Arsenals of a Democratic Culture*; American Library Association: Chicago, IL, 1947.

54. Jones, P.A. *Libraries, Immigrants, and the American Experience*, Contributions in Librarianship and Information Science Series; Greenwood Press: Westport, CT, 1999.

55. Dewey, M. Relation of state to public library. In *American Library Philosophy: An Anthology*, Transactions and Proceedings of the Second International Library Conference, 1898; McCrimmon, B., Ed.; The Shoe String Press: Hamden, CT, 1975. http://juteux.net/rory/wbm7.html (accessed January 2008).

56. Change Institute, University of Maryland *Frontiers in Librarianship*; Contributions in Librarianship and Information Science Series; Greenwood Press: Westport, CT, 1969.

57. Anders, M.E. The development of public library services in the South-Eastern states, 1895–1960; Unpublished thesis; University of Michigan: Ann Arbor, MI, 1958.

58. Davies, D.W. *Public Libraries as Culture and Social Centers: The Origin of the Concept*; Scarecrow: Metuchen, NJ, 1974.

59. Phelps, W. *Autobiography, With Letters*; Oxford University Press: New York, 1939.

60. Weiss, M.J. *Reading in the Secondary Schools*; Odyssey: Gonic, NH, 1961.

61. Seavey, C. Images from the 1876 report; University of Missouri, 1998. http://www.coe.missouri.edu/~seaveyca/1876/ (accessed January 2008).

62. Breisch, K. *Henry Hobson Richardson and the Small Public Library in America: A Study in Typology*; MIT Press: Cambridge, MA, 1997.

63. Wiegand, W.A. *The Politics of an Emerging Profession: The American Library Association, 1876–1917*; Greenwood: Westport, CT, 1986.

64. Dain, P. *The New York Public Library: A History of Its Founding and Early Years*; New York Public Library: New York, 1972.

65. Whitehill, W.M. *Boston Public Library: A Centennial History*; Harvard: Boston, MA, 1956; 23.

66. Kane, M.E. *Yesterday in Riverdale Spuyten Duyvi*; Riverdale Neighborhood and Library Association: New York, 1947.

67. Constantino, R., Ed. *Literacy, Access, and Libraries among the Language Minority Population*; Scarecrow Press: Lanham, MD, 1998.

68. Pawley, C. Advocate for access: Lutie Stearns and the traveling libraries of the Wisconsin Free Library Commission, 1895–1914. Libr. Cult. **2000**, *35* (3), 434–458.

69. Drzewieniecki, W.; Drzewieniecki-Abugattas, J. Public library service to American ethics: The Polish community on the Niagara Frontier, New York. J. Libr. Hist. **1974**, *9*, 120–137.

70. Lagemann, E.C. *The Politics of Knowledge: The Carnegie Corporation, Philanthropy, and Public Policy*; Wesleyan University Press: Middletown, CT, 1989.

71. Van Slyck, A. *Free to All: Carnegie Libraries & American Culture, 1890–1920*; University of Chicago Press: Chicago, IL, 1995.

72. Martin, L. *Enrichment: A History of the Public Library in the United States in the Twentieth Century*; Scarecrow Press: Lanham, MD, 1998.

73. Cohen, E. *A Consumer's Republic: The Politics of Mass Consumption in Postwar America*; Alfred A. Knopf: New York, 2003.

74. D'Angelo, E. *Barbarians at the Gates of the Public Library: How Postmodern Consumer Capitalism Threatens Democracy, Civil Education and the Public Good*; Library Juice Press: Duluth, MN, 2006.

75. Barker, T.D. *Libraries of the South: A Report on Development*; American Library Association: Chicago, IL, 1936.

76. McCook, K de la P. Ch. 3 Public Library Growth and Values: 1918–2004. In *Introduction to Public Librarianship*; Neal-Schuman Publishers, Inc.: New York, 2004; 61–81.

77. Learned, W.S. *The American Public Library and the Diffusion of Knowledge*; Harcourt, Brace and Company: New York, 1924.

78. Heim, K.M. Adult services within the American Library Association: A historical examination of the move to synthesis. Renaissance Quart. **1991**, *30* (3), 386–394.

79. Schlachter, G.A. *The Service Imperative for Libraries: Essays in Honor of Margaret E. Monroe*; Libraries Unlimited: Littleton, CO, 1982.

80. McCook, K. de la P. *Introduction to Public Librarianship*; Neal-Schuman Publishers, Inc.: New York, 2004, 186.

81. Nauratil, M.J. *Public Libraries and Nontraditional Clienteles: The Politics of Special Services*; Greenwood Press: Santa Barbara, CA, 1985.

82. Jones, P.A. *Still Struggling for Equality: American Public Library Services with Minorities*; Libraries Unlimited: Santa Barbara, CA, 2004; 269.

83. Anonymous reviewer.

84. Jones, P.A. *Libraries, Immigrants, and the American Experience*; Greenwood Press: Westport, CT, 1999.

85. Dain, P. Ambivalence and paradox [the social bonds of the public library [reply to M. H. Harris]]. Lib. J. **1975**, *100*, 261–266.

86. Benidt, B.W. *The Library Book: Centennial History of the Minneapolis Public Library*; Minneapolis Public Library: Minneapolis, MN, 1984.

87. West, C.; Katz, E. *Revolting Librarians*; Booklegger Press: San Francisco, CA, 1972.

88. Battles, M. *Library: An Unquiet History*; W. W. Norton: New York, 2003.

89. Shera, J. *Foundations of the Public Library*; University of Chicago Press: Chicago, IL, 1949.

90. Gunselman, C.; Marvin, C.; Isom, M.F. Leaders of Oregon's library movement. Libr. Trends **2004**, *52* (4), 877–901.

91. Joeckel, C.; Winslow, A. *A National Plan for Public Library Service*; American Library Association: Chicago, IL, 1948.

92. Raber, D. *Librarianship and Legitimacy: The Ideology of the Public Library Inquiry*; Greenwood: Westport, CT, 1997.

93. Weibel, K. *The Evolution of Library Outreach, 1960–1975 and its Effects on Reader Services: Some Considerations*; University of Illinois, Occasional Paper 16; Graduate School of Library and Information Science: Urbana, IL, 1982.

94. Monroe, M. Reader services to the disadvantaged in inner cities. In *Advances in Librarianship*; Voight, M., Ed.; Seminar Press: New York, 1971; 253–274.

95. Lyman, H. *Literacy and the Nation's Libraries*; American Library Association: Chicago, IL, 1977.

96. Gaines, E. Let's return to traditional library service: Facing the failure of social experimentation. Wilson Libr. Bull. **1980**, *78*, 50–53.

97. Harrell, M. Serving diverse library users: The multicultural studies librarian at an urban research university. In *Diversity: Building a Strategic Future*, 3rd National Conference on Diversity in Academic Libraries, University of Iowa, April 4–6, 2002, http://www.lib.uiowa.edu/cicdiversity/papers.html (accessed January 2008).

98. Durrance, J.; Fisher-Pettigrew, K. Toward developing measures of the impact of library and information services. Ref. User Serv. Q. **2002**, *42* (1), 43–53.

99. Phipps, S. Beyond measuring service quality: Learning from the voices of the customers, the staff, the processes, and the organization. Lib. Trends **2001**, *49* (4), 635–662.

100. Guerena, S. *Library Services to Latinos: An Anthology*; McFarland: Jefferson, NC, 2000.

101. Baldwin, G. Public access to the internet: American Indian and Alaskan Native issues. In *Public Access to the Internet*; Kahin, B., Keller, J., Eds.; MIT Press: Cambridge, MA, 1995; 137–153.

102. Liu, M.; Redfern, B. Information-seeking behavior of multicultural students: A case study at San Jose State University. Coll. Res. Libr. **1997**, *58*, 348–354.

103. Stern, S. Ethnic libraries and librarianship in the United States: Models and prospects. In *Advances in Librarianship Volume 15*; Academic Press: New York, 1991; 77–102.

104. Berman, S. Foreword to *Poor People and Library Services*; Venturella, K.M., Ed.; McFarland: Jefferson, NC, 1998.

105. Chatman, E. The diffusion of information among the working poor; Unpublished dissertation; University of California: Berkeley, CA, 1983.

106. Harris, R. Searching for help and information: Abused women speak out. Libr. Inform. Sci. Res. **2001**, *23*, 123–141.

107. Olson, H.A. The feminist and the emperor's new clothes: Feminist deconstruction as a critical methodology for library and information studies. Libr. Inform. Sci. Res. **1997**, *19*, 181–198.

108. Klauber, J. Living well with a disability: How libraries can help. Am. Libr. **1998**, *29* (4), 52–55.

109. U.S. National Commission on Libraries and Information Sciences. *Library and Information Services for Individuals with Disabilities: An NCLIS Hearing in Washington DC July 8, 1999*; NCLIS Hearing: Washington, DC, 1999, http://www.nclis.gov/info/disabilities.hearing.final.pdf (accessed January 2008).

110. Norman, M. Out on loan. J. Libr. Inform. Sci. **1999**, *31* (4), 188–196.

111. Joyce, S.; Schrader, A. Hidden perceptions: Edmonton gay males and the Edmonton Public Library. Can. J. Inform. Libr. Sci. **1997**, *22* (1), 19–37.

112. Abif, K.; Obatala, O. At work in the children's room. In *Poor People and Library Service*; Venturella, Karen M., Ed.; McFarland: Jefferson, NC, 1998; 44–61.

113. Jones, P.; Shoemaker, J. *Do It Right: Best Practices for Serving Young Adults in School and Public Libraries*; Neal-Schuman: New York, 2001.

114. McClure, C. *Planning and Role Setting for Public Libraries: A Manual of Options and Procedures*; American Library Association: Chicago, IL, 1987.

115. Immroth, B.; McCook, K. de la P., Eds. *Library Services to Youth of Hispanic Heritage*; McFarland: Jefferson, NC, 2000.

116. Guerena, S.; Erazo, E. Latinos and librarianship. Libr. Trends **2000**, *49* (1), 138–181.

117. Burlingame, D. Fund-raising as a key to the library's future—Library finance: New needs, new models. Libr. Trends **1994**, *42* (3), 467–478.

118. Mehra, B. An Action Research (AR) manifesto for cyberculture power to "marginalized" cultures of difference. In *Critical Cyber-Culture Studies*; Silver, D., Massanari, A., Eds.; New York University Press: New York, 2006; 205–215.

119. Mehra, B. Library and information science (LIS) and community development: Use of information and communication technology (ICT) to support a social equity agenda. J. Commun. Dev. Soc. **2005**, *36* (1), 28–40.

120. Crawford, W. Library 2.0 and "Library 2.0." Cites Insights **2006**, *6*(2). http://cites.boisestate.edu/civ6i2.pdf (accessed November 2008).

121. Maness, J.M. Library 2.0 theory: Web 2.0 and its implications for libraries. Webology **2006**, *3*(2). http://www.webology.ir/2006/v3n2/a25.html (accessed November 2008).

122. Casey, M.; Savastinuk, L. *Library 2.0: A Guide to Participatory Library Service*; Information Today, Inc.: Medford, NJ, 2007.

123. Kalakota, R.; Robinson, M. *e-Business 2.0: Roadmap for Success, 2nd Ed.*; Addison-Wesley Professional: Indianapolis, IN, 2000.

124. Genoni, P.; Walton, G. *IFLA 116: Continuing Professional Development- Preparing for New Roles in Libraries: A Voyage of Discovery*; K. G. Saur: Munich, Germany, 2005.

125. Reed-Scott, J. *Scholarship, Research Libraries, and Global Publishing*; Hawthorn: Binghamton, New York, 1999.

126. American Library Association, *Keeping the Outreach Brand Viable*; American Library Association: Chicago, IL, 2004, http://www.ala.org/ala/olos/outreachresource/keepingoutreach.htm (accessed January 2008).

127. Frohmann, B. Discourse analysis as a research method in Library and Information Science. Libr. Inform. Sci. Res. **1994**, *16* (2), 119–138.

128. Vavrek, B. Is the American public library part of everyone's life? Am. Libr. **2000**, 60–64.

129. Stauffer, S. "She speaks as one having authority": Mary E. Downey's use of libraries as a means to public power. Libr. Cult. **2005**, *40* (1), 38–62.

130. Mehra, B.; Sandusky, R. Applications of community-based action research in elective courses: Partnering library and information science students with underserved populations to meet their information technology needs. In *The Service Connection: Library and Information Science Education and Service to Communities*; Roy, L., Ed.; ALA Editions: Chicago, IL, 2009.

131. Maack, M.N. Documenting one hundred twenty years of writings on women's entry, advancement, and struggle for equalization in librarianship (review essay covering *On Account of Sex: An Annotated Bibliography on the Status of Women in Librarianship (4 volumes) and The Role of Women in Librarianship, 1876–1976*). Libr. Q. **2002**, *72* (April), 241–246.

132. Malone, C. Toward a multicultural American public library history. Libr. Cult. **2000**, *35* (1), 77–87.

133. Korty, M.B. Benjamin Franklin and eighteenth-century American libraries. Trans. Am. Philos. Soc. New Ser. **1965**, *55*(9). The American Philosophical Society: Philadelphia, PA.

134. Martin, L.A. *Public Library: Middle Age Crises or Old Age?*; R. R. Bowker, LLC: New Providence, NJ, 1983.

135. Venezky, R.L. Steps toward a modern history of American reading instruction. Rev. Res. Educ. **1986**, *13*, 129–167.

136. McCullen, H. *American Libraries Before 1876*, Beta Phi Mu Monograph Series; Greenwood Press: Westport, CT, 2000.

137. Wiegand, W.A. Main street public library: The availability of controversial materials in the rural heartland, 1890–1956. Libr. Cult. **1998**, *31* (1), 131–132.

138. Goedeken, E. The rainbow survivors of some vanished grey moment of reality: A prospographical study of the Dictionary of American Library Biography and its supplement. Libr. Cult. **1995**, *30*, 155.

139. Wilson, P. *A Community Elite and the Public Library: The Uses of Information in Leadership*; Contributions in Librarianship and Information Science Series; Greenwood: Westport, CT, 1977.

140. Sturges, P. The public library and reading by the masses: Historical perspectives on the USA and Britain 1850–1900. In *Conference Proceedings of the 60th IFLA General Conference*, Buenos Aires, Argentina, August 21–27, 1994.

141. Rayward, W.B. The case of Paul Otlet, pioneer of information science, internationalist, visionary: reflections on biography. J. Libr. Inform. Sci. **1991**, *23*, 135–145.

142. U.S Bureau of Education. *Public Libraries in the United States of America: Their History, Condition, and Management*; Government Publications Office: Washington, DC, 1876.

143. Ryan, M. *Civic Wars: Democracy and Public Life in the American City During the Nineteenth Century*; University of California Press: Berkley, CA, 1997.

144. Anderson, B. *Imagined Communities: Reflection on the Origin and Spread of Nationalism*; Verso: London, 1983.

145. Ring, D. Men of energy and snap: The origins and early years of the Billings Public Library. Libr. Cult. **2001**, *36* (3), 397–412.

146. White, R. *It's All Your Misfortune and None of My Own: A History of the American West*; University of Oklahoma Press: Norman, OK, 1991.

147. Harris, M.H.; Spiegler, G. Everett, Ticknor and the common man: The fear of societal instability as the motivation for the founding of the Boston Public Library. Libri **1974**, *24*, 249–275.

148. Augst, T. The business of reading in nineteenth-century America: The New York Mercantile Library. Am. Quart. **1998**, *50*, 267–305.

149. Hildenbrand, S., Ed. *Reclaiming the American Library Past: Writing the Women In*; Greenwood Publishing Group: Westport, CT, 1996.

150. Malone, C. Quiet pioneers: Black women public librarians in the segregated south. Vitae Scholasticae **2000**, *19* (1), 59–76.

151. Brisley, M. Cornelia Marvin Pierce: Pioneer in library extension. Libr. Q. **1968**, *38*, 125–153.

152. Irine, B.J. *Sex Segregation in Librarianship: Demographic and Career Patterns of Academic Library Administrators* Contributions in Librarianship and Information Science Series; Greenwood Press: Westport, CT, 1985.

153. Pejsa, J. *Gratia Countryman: Her Life, Her Loves and Her Library*; Nodin Press: Minneapolis, MN, 1995.

154. Malone, C. Accommodating access: 'Colored' Carnegie libraries, 1905–1925, PhD thesis; University of Texas at Austin, 1996.

155. Malone, C.K. Books for black children: Public library collections in Louisville and Nashville, 1915–1925. Libr. Quart. **2000**, *70*, 179–200.

156. Malone, C.K.; Louise, S. Louisville free public library's racially segregated branches, 1905–35. Reg. Kentucky Hist. Soc. **1995**, *93* (2), 159–179.

157. Macleod, DavidI. *Carnegie Libraries in Wisconsin*; Arno Press, Inc.: New York, 1968.

158. Harris, M. Externalist or internalist frameworks for the interpretation of American library history—The continuing debate. J. Libr. Hist. **1975**, *10*, 106–110.

159. Wall, J.F. *Andrew Carnegie*; Oxford University Press, 1970; 821. Quoted in Harris. *op. cit.*

160. Jones, T. *Carnegie Libraries Across America: A Public Legacy*; John Wiley & Sons: New York, 1997.

161. Lorenzen, M. Deconstructing the Carnegie libraries: The sociological reasons behind Carnegie's millions to public libraries. Ill. Libr. **1999**, *81* (2), 75–78.

162. Bobinski, G.S. *Carnegie Libraries: Their History and Impact on American Public Library Development*; American Library Association: Chicago, IL, 1969.

163. Beck, N.R. The use of library and educational facilities by Russian-Jewish Immigrants in New York City, 1880–1914: The impact of culture. J. Libr. Hist. **1977**, *12*, 128–149.

164. Kaufman, M.; Alfonso, H.D. *Community Power and Grassroots Democracy: The Transformation of Social Life*; Zed Books: NJ, 1997.

165. Wiegand, W.A. *An Active Instrument for Propaganda: The American Public Library During World War I*, Beta Phi Mu Monograph Series; Greenwood Press: Westport, CT, 1989.

166. Mehra, B. Integrating socially-relevant projects and achieving meaningful community outcomes in required library and information science courses: From a service model to community engagement. In *The Service Connection: Library and Information Science Education and Service to Communities*; Roy, L., Ed.; ALA Editions: Chicago, IL, 2009.

167. Furner, J. Shera's social epistemology recast as psychological bibliology. Soc. Epistemol. **2002**, *16* (1), 5–22.

168. Jenkins, C. The history of youth services librarianship: A review of the research literature. Libr. Cult. **2000**, *35* (1), 103–140.

169. Hildenbrand, S. Library feminism and library women's history: Activism and scholarship, equity and culture. Libr. Cult. **2000**, *35* (1), 51–65.

170. Dodge, C. Taking libraries to the street: Infoshops & alternative reading rooms. Am. Libr. **1998**, *29* (5), 62–64.

171. Leigh, R. *The Public Library in the United States*; Columbia University Press: New York, 1950.

172. Berelson, B.; Janowitz, M. *Reader in Public Opinion and Communication*; Free Press: New York, 1950.

173. Wellisch, J. *The Public Library and Federal Policy*; Greenwood Press: Westport, CT, 1974.

174. Maack, M.N. Public libraries in transition: Ideals, strategies, and research. Libr. Cult. Winter **1994**, *29*, 75–94.

175. Weingand, D.E. *Administration of the Small Public Library*, 4th Ed.; American Library Association: Chicago, IL, 2001.

176. Berman, S. *Talking the Talk and Walking the Walk: What Libraries Say They Do But Frequently Don't*; School of Library and Information Science: University of Illinois at Urbana-Champaign, 1997, http://www.sanfordberman.org/biblinks/wtht.pdf (accessed January 2008).

177. Shorris, E. *Riches for the Poor: The Clemente Course in the Humanities*; W.W. Norton: New York, 2000.

178. Goodrich, J. Strategic planning at the Multnomah County Library: The past as prologue. Oreg. Libr. Assoc. Quart. **2000**, *6*(3), http://www.olaweb.org/quarterly/quar6–3/goodrich.shtml (accessed January 2008).

179. Berman, S. Foreword in *Intellectual Freedom and Social Responsibility in American Librarianship, 1967–1974*; Samek, T., Ed.; McFarland: Jefferson, NC, 2001.

180. McCook, K. de la P. Poverty, democracy and public libraries. In *Libraries & Democracy: The Cornerstones of Liberty*; Kranich, N., Ed.; American Library Association: Chicago, IL, 2001; 28–46.

181. Scrogham, R The American public library and its fragile future. New Libr. World **2006**, *107* (1220/1221), 7–15.

182. American Library Association: Our Association, http://www.ala.org/ala/ourassociation/ourassociation.htm (accessed January 2008).

183. Cronin, B. *Pulp Friction*; The Scarecrow Press, Inc.: Lanham, MD, 2003.

184. Zweizig, D. Predicting amount of library use: An empirical study of the role of the public library in the life of the adult public; PhD dissertation; Syracuse University: New York, 1973.

185. Pungitore, V.L.; Nowicke, C.E.; Tuten-Puckett, K.; Weinstein, F. *The Public Library Planning Process. Case Studies of its Implementation in Smaller Libraries: Final Report*; U.S. Department of Education: Washington, DC, 1991.

186. Stephens, A.K. *Assessing Public Library Planning Process*; Ablex Publishing: Norwood, NJ, 1996.

187. Nelson, S. *Strategic Planning for Results*, PLA Results Series; American Library Association: Chicago, IL, 2008.

188. Buckland, M. Documentation, information science, and library science in the USA. Inform. Process. Manage. **1996**, *32* (1), 63–76.

189. Rayward, W.B. The origins of information science and the International Institute of Bibliography/International Federation for Information and Documentation (FID). J. Am. Soc. Inform. Sci. **1997**, *48* (4), 289–300.

190. Rayward, W.B. UDC and FID: A historical perspective. Libr. Q. **1967**, *37* (3), 259–278.

191. Otlet, P. The organisation of the society of nations. In *International Organisation and Dissemination of Knowledge: Selected Essays of Paul Otlet*; Rayward, W. B., Ed.; Elsevier: Amsterdam, the Netherlands, 1990; 148–156.

192. Olson, H.A. *The Power to Name: Locating the Limits of Subject Representation in Libraries*; Kluwer Academic: Dordrecht, the Netherlands, 2002.

193. Bowker, G.C.; Star, S.L. Building information infrastructures for social worlds: The role of classifications and standards. In *Community Computing and Support Systems*; Springer: Berlin, Germany, 1998; 231–248.

194. Bowker, G.C.; Star, S.L. *Sorting Things Out: Classification and Its Consequences*; The MIT Press: Cambridge, MA, 2000.

195. Olson, H.A. Mapping beyond Dewey's boundaries: Constructing classificatory space for marginalized knowledge domains. In *How Classifications Work: Problems and Challenges in an Electronic Age [Special issue]*; Bowker, G.C., Star, S.L., Eds.; Libr. Trends **1998**, *47* (2), 233–254.

196. Olson, H.A. How we construct subjects: A feminist analysis. Libr. Trends **2007**, *56* (2), 509–541.

197. Shade, L.R. A gendered perspective on access to the information infrastructure. Inform. Soc. January/March **1998**, *14*, 33–44.

198. Waldrop, M.M. *The Dream Machine: J.C.R. Licklider and the Revolution that Made Computing Personal*; Penguin Non-Classics: New York, 2002.

199. Shera, J.H.; Cleveland, D.B. History and foundations of information science. Annu. Rev. Inform. Sci. **1977**, *12*, 249–275.

200. Dervin, B.; Nilan, M. Information needs and uses. Annu. Rev. Inform. Sci. **1986**, *21*, 3–33.

201. Dervin, B. From the mind's eye of the "user". In *Qualitative Research on Information Management*; Glazier, D., Powell, R., Eds.; Libraries Unlimited: Englewood, CO, 1992.

202. Dervin, B. *Sense-Making Methodology Reader: Selected Writings of Brenda Dervin*, Foreman-Wernet, L., Launterbach, E., Eds.; Hampton Press: Cresskill, NJ, 2003.

203. Krikelas, J. Information seeking behavior: Patterns and concepts. Drexel Libr. Q. **1983**, *19* (2), 361–371.

204. Saracevic, T.; Mokros, H.; Su, L. Nature of interaction between users and intermediaries in online searching: A qualitative analysis. Proc. 53rd ASIS Annu. Meet. **1990**, *27*, 47–54.

205. Harter, S. Psychological relevance and information science. J. Am. Soc. Inform. Sci. **1992**, *43*, 602–615.

206. Belkin, N.J.; Vickery, A. Interaction in information systems. In *Library and Information Systems Research Report 3*; British Library: London, U.K., 1985.

207. Borgman, C. Psychological research in human computer interaction. Annu. Rev. Inform. Sci. **1984**, *19*, 33–64.

208. Ingerwersen, P. *Information Retrieval Interaction*; Taylor Graham: London, U.K., 1992.

209. Belkin, N.J. The cognitive viewpoint in information science. J. Inform. Sci. **1990**, *16*, 11–15.

210. James, R. Libraries in the mind: How can we see users' perceptions of libraries? J. Libr. **1983**, *15*, 19–28.

211. Dervin, B. Useful theory for librarianship: Communication, not information. Drexel Libr. Q. **1982**, *13*, 16–32.

212. Adams, M. *Teaching for Diversity and Social Justice: A Sourcebook*; Routledge: New York, 1997.

213. Wronka, J.M. *Human Rights and Social Justice: Social Action and Service for the Helping and Health Professions*; Sage Publications, Inc.: Thousand Oaks, CA, 2007.

214. Bersellini, E.; Berry, D. The benefits of providing benefit information: Examining the effectiveness of provision of simple benefit statements on people's judgements about a medicine. Psychol. Health **2007**, *22* (1), 61–82.

215. Hollnagel, E.; Woods, D.D. Cognitive systems engineering: New wine in old bottles. Int. J. Man Mach. Stud. **1983**, *18*, 583–600.

216. Bates, M. The design of browsing and berry picking techniques for the on-line search interface. Online Rev. **1989**, *13*, 407–424.

217. Ingwersen, P. Cognitive perspectives of information retrieval interaction. J. Doc. **1996**, *52*, 3–50.

218. Belkin, N.; Oddy, R.; Brooks, H. ASK for information retrieval: Part I: Background and theory. J. Doc. **1982**, *38* (2), 61–71.

219. Taylor, R.S. Information use environments. In *Progress in Communication Sciences*; Ablex: Norwood, NJ, 1991; 217–255.

220. Case, D.O. *Looking for Information: A Survey of Research on Information Seeking, Needs, and Behavior*; Academic Press: New York, 2007.

221. Marchionini, G. *Information Seeking in Electronic Environments*; Cambridge University Press: New York, 1995.

222. DeMey, M. The cognitive viewpoint: Its development and its scope. In *CC 77: International Workshop on the Cognitive Viewpoint*; Ghent University: Ghent, Belgium, 1977.

223. DeMey, M. The relevance of the cognitive paradigm for information science. In *Theory and Application of Information Research*; Harbo, O., Ed.; Mansell: London, U.K., 1980.

224. Harmon, E.G.; Ballesteros, E.R. Unconscious cognition: The elicitation of deeply embedded information needs. In *Information Seeking in Context*, Proceedings of an International Conference on Information Needs, Seeking, and Use in Different Contexts, Tampere, Finland, Taylore Graham Publishing: London, U.K., 1997; 422–433.

225. Dervin, B. *An Overview of Sense-Making Research; Concepts, Methods, and Results to Date*; School of Communication, University of Washington: Seattle, WA, 1983.

226. Dervin, B. On studying information seeking methodologically: The implications of connecting metatheory to method. Inform. Process. Manage. **1999**, *35*, 727–750.

227. Pettigrew, K.; Fidel, R.; Bruce, H. Conceptual frameworks in information behavior. Annu. Rev. Inform. Sci. Technol. **2001**, *35*, 43–78.

228. Schamber, L.; Eisenberg, M.; Nilan, M. A re-examination of relevance toward a dynamic, situational definition. Inform. Process. Manage. **1990**, *26*, 755–776.

229. Nahl, D. The centrality of the affective in information behavior. In *Information and Emotion: The Emergent*

Affective Paradigm in Information Behavior Research and Theory; Nahl, D., Bilal, D., Eds.; Information Today, Inc.: Medford, NJ, 2007; 3–37.

230. Kuhlthau, C. *Seeking Meaning: A Process Approach to Library and Information Services*; Libraries Unlimited: Westport, CT, 2004.

231. Spink, A.; Bray, K.; Jaeckel, M.; Sidberry, G. Everyday life information seeking by low-income African American households: Wynnewood Healthy Neighborhood Project. In *Proceedings of the Second International Information Seeking in Context Conference*, Sheffield, United Kingdom, August 12–15, 1998; Department of Information Studies, University of Sheffield, U.K., 1998.

232. Hersberger, J Are the economically poor information poor? Does the digital divide affect the homeless and access to information. Can. J. Inform. Libr. Sci. **2002**, *27* (3), 44–63.

233. Chatman, E. *The Information World of Aging Women*; Greenwood Press: Westport, CT, 1992.

234. Chatman, E. The impoverished life-world of outsiders. J. Am. Soc. Inform. Sci. **1996**, *47*, 193–206.

235. Saumure, K.; Given, L. Digitally enhanced? An examination of the information behaviors of visually impaired post-secondary students. Can. J. Inform. Libr. Sci. **2004**, *28* (2), 25–42.

236. Bilal, D. Children's use of the Yahooligans! Web search engine. III. Cognitive and physical behaviors on fully self-generated search tasks. J. Am. Soc. Inform. Sci. Technol. **2002**, *52*, 1170–1183.

237. Mehra, B. *The Cross-Cultural Learning Process of International Doctoral Students: A Case Study in Library and Information Science Education*; Verlag Dr. Muller: Saarbruchen, Germany.

238. Mehra, B.; Bishop, A.P. Cross-cultural perspectives of international doctoral students: Two-way learning in library and information science education. Int. J. Prog. Educ. **2007**, *3*(1), http://inased.org/v3n1/mehrabishop.htm (accessed January 2008).

239. Van Dijk, J. *The Deepening Divide: Inequality in the Information Society*; Sage: Thousand Oaks, CA, 2005.

240. Mcharazo, A.; Koopman, S., Eds. *Librarianship as a Bridge to an Information and Knowledge Society in Africa*; K. G. Saur: Munich, Germany, 2007.

241. Miao, Q. To be or not to be: Public libraries and the global knowledge revolution. In *Libraries in the Information Society*; Ershova, T.V., Hohloy, Y.E., Eds.; K.G. Saur: Munich, Germany, 2002; 9–18.

242. Dasgupta, K. Libraries and librarians in India on the threshold of the third millennium: Challenges and risks. In *Libraries in the Information Society*; Ershova, T.V., Hohloy, Y.E., Eds.; K.G. Saur: Munich, Germany, 2002; 112–118.

243. Seidelin, S.; Jensen, T. *IFLA/FAIFE Theme Report: Libraries and the Fight Against HIV/AIDS, Poverty, and Corruption*, IFLA/FAIFE World Report Series No. 6; Copenhagen: Denmark, 2006.

244. Shulera, J.A. Public polices and academic libraries—The shape of the next digital divide. J. Acad. Libr. **2007**, *33* (1), 141–143.

Social Networks and Information Transfer

Caroline Haythornthwaite
Graduate School of Library and Information Science, University of Illinois at Urbana-Champaign, Champaign, Illinois, U.S.A.

Abstract
Information exchange, transfer and flow can often depend on the motivations of individuals who share that information. This in turn depends on the relationships they maintain with others, and the networks of information sharing resulting from their interconnections. This entry describes the attributes of social networks that facilitate or inhibit the exchange of information, how to discover these networks, and how different configurations of networks can constrain or facilitate information transfer.

INTRODUCTION

When people engage with others they transfer information. As they recount stories, discuss ideas, share opinions and experiences, they tell others about themselves, the activities they engage in, and the people with whom they engage in these activities. They transfer knowledge about processes, information about resources, and data about their experiences with others. This information can transfer in a one-to-one, one-to-many, or many-to-many distribution through conversation and instruction, by example or observation, and face-to-face or mediated through computer technologies. Each such transfer forms a connection with others based on a decision about what information to reveal, where, when and to whom. Such choices are tempered by expectations of who will hear or receive the information, how far the information might travel, how sensitive or timely the information is, and how well the speaker knows the audience. Patterns of connectivity, revealed by who transfers what kind of information to whom, are both formed and reinforced by existing knowledge of others. Together, the "ties" formed by information transfers between "actors" build "networks" with routes along which information travels, bridges that carry information from one social circle to another, and cul-de-sacs where information dead-ends or circulates repeatedly among the same set of friends.

This entry addresses the interplay between social networks and information networks, i.e., the way ties between individuals affect information transfer within social settings. The entry addresses who shares information with whom, what facilitates or inhibits information transfer, and how network configurations affect who receives what kinds of information.

INFORMATION NETWORKS

For the purposes of this entry, "information" is taken to refer to the intangibles of data, information, or knowledge, with no restriction on the type or purpose of the transfer, nor of the medium used for the transfer. Data on stock prices may be transferred by paper, phone, or e-mail, between brokers and clients or between friends, for investment and profit or for learning and fun. Information on health problems may transfer through online support groups, from doctor to patient, or among care-givers, for purposes of social support, medical intervention or symptom management. Knowledge on how to fix a car may be passed from parent to child through example and joint practice. In each case, while one can point to the conversation or the email text, it is not a tangible that has been transferred: the stock, the health problem, the car remain where they started. The information passes from one person to another while remaining with the originator. In this way, information networks have the potential to saturate as everyone in the network becomes aware of the same information.

As in most understandings of information, the potential for unlimited, undistorted transfer affects its value.[1] In some cases, value may be preserved in the timeliness and exclusivity of the information, e.g., in having inside information, and in restricting who has access. For other purposes, information is most beneficial when widely disseminated, e.g., as in the diffusion of health information or awareness of a product for sale. In that case, the goal is to facilitate information movement in a network. As will be discussed below, social network structures play a role in how easily information circulates, and thus our ability to transfer information easily to others or to retain control over its distribution.

Encyclopedia of Library and Information Sciences, Fourth Edition DOI: 10.1081/E-ELIS4-120044372

Mobilized or Accessible Information

Information transfer can happen in two ways: as direct transfers from one individual to another, or by common experience, e.g., co-attendance at events, lectures, etc. This distinction mirrors one made about social capital by Lin[2] between "mobilized" and "accessible" resources embedded in social structures. Mobilized resources are those that are brought into use for some outcome. For example, by asking others about job opportunities we bring out their knowledge for use in our job search. This is somewhat analogous to explicit knowledge, i.e., articulated information that we make a conscious effort to transfer. Accessible resources are those that are present in a network and potentially available for use. This is somewhat analogous to the idea of tacit knowledge, now considered at the network level. For example, the tacit knowledge of knowing how to behave in a social situation, or how to perform a particular routine task, is something that can be accessed by others, but is not normally explicitly discussed. According to Lin, social capital depends on the "resources embedded in a social structure; accessibility to such social resources by individuals; and use or mobilization of such social resources by individuals in purposive actions. Thus conceived, social capital contains three elements intersecting structure and action: the structural (embeddedness), opportunity (accessibility) and action-oriented (use) aspects" (p. 35).[2]

Building on this, we may think of information in terms of mobile and accessible forms. Mobile information includes transfers from one person to another of factual information, social support, skills, ideas, opinions, and collaborations, such as working together, socializing, or creating common understanding. By contrast, accessed information includes common knowledge created by living in the same culture, working in the same organization, or attending the same events. However, the information must be present in a network in order for it to be mobilized or accessible. Hence, the embeddedness of information in a network determines how much social capital (or we might say information capital) is possible for network members to access. Thus, too, the structures that connect the network to other larger circles of others also affect the social capital of a network. Lin's analyses[3,4] stress how network structures, for example cultural hierarchies, and the embeddedness of individuals within that structure, affect their access to resources, such as information on jobs. Since many of the resources that translate into social capital are accessed through information, there is much synergy in the work on social capital and on information transfer. We return to the ideas of mobilized and accessible information throughout this entry.

SOCIAL NETWORK FRAMEWORK

The basics of social networks are straightforward: "actors" maintain "relations" with others which form the "tie"

between them. The collective set of actors and ties forms the "network" of connections among all members of the particular social set. Analyses and visualizations of networks follow graph theory with the actors as the nodes and relations as lines between nodes. What follows is a brief description of these social network features. For more on social network analysis techniques, introductory texts, and edited collections, see the Bibliography section at the end of this entry.

Actors

Actors are connected by the individual relations they maintain—giving instructions, providing help, sharing resources. Collectively, this set of relations defines the tie between the actors. The challenge in examining networks is defining the set of actors to examine—i.e., the boundaries to the dataset or limit to the data collection—and the relation or set of relations to map. For studying information, many kinds of information transfer, exchange or sharing can be examined, from help on how to solve a problem to emotional support in a crisis. These different kinds of relations can describe different configurations within the network which in turn can affect the way information circulates the network as a whole.

In most cases the actors we are concerned with for information transfer are people: members of a team, employees in an organization, students in a school, or residents of a community. However, in network analyses, larger units can also function as nodes in the network. Thus, a school may be an actor in the network of educational institutions, a business may be an actor in an industry network. In these cases, information also flows and transfers, as schools receive new educational plans from boards, and businesses retain information for competitive intelligence. While the actors are different, the basic structures for analysis are the same, as are the considerations of what relations create ties between the actors, and how information transfers in networks.

Ties

A tie may consist of one relation only, and thus is entirely defined by the relation. However, most of our ties are predicated on more than one type of interaction, with the intensity and significance of each relation varying according to our particular relationship. This is the basis of the ideas of weak and strong ties. Weak ties are based on few relations of low intensity or significance. In voluntary (rather than kin-based) ties, weakly tied pairs interact infrequently, about few different things, and via few media, and their interactions involve little or no intimacy or self-disclosure.[5–9] By contrast, strong ties involve a variety of relations, from instrumental to personal, and tend to entail reciprocal interaction (e.g., favors are returned, whether in the same or a different form).

While the weak to strong continuum is relevant across all kinds of ties, relationships may be differentiated in terms of the combination of relations the actors maintain.[7,10] A strong work tie can exist that does not extend to social activity, a strong friendship tie can exist that has no work component; and we have kinship ties which remain even if socially or physically distant. The nature of the relationship is bound to affect the kind of information that is likely to transfer between actors, e.g., a work-only tie is unlikely to be a source of personal social support, a friend from outside work is unlikely to be a source of specialized information about that kind of work. Such information is not embedded in the structure of the tie, and thus not accessible to the actors. However, as will be discussed below, differences in what others have access to, is an important feature of information access. Thus, the friend may not know about your work, but they know about their own, and hence that information is accessible to you.

Three characteristics of relations help in assessing the nature of the tie: content, direction, and strength. "Content" refers to what is exchanged, shared or experienced together, for example, specific kinds of information, gossip, small services (e.g., babysitting), social support, cooperation and collaboration, or social services (e.g., helping neighbors). Information or resources may flow in one "direction" only, e.g., as one person gives instructions to another, or as experts show novices how to accomplish a task. Flow may also be two-way, as gossip flows back and forth, advice is both given and received, and group members keep each other aware of innovations relevant to their business. The "strength" of a relation refers to the frequency, intensity and importance of the exchange to the pairs involved; for example, communications may be daily, monthly or yearly, care may be given occasionally or full-time, and social support may be given for a minor or major crisis.

Networks

The ties formed between actors do not exist in isolation. Information transferred from one actor to another can be passed on again to others. Tracing the path the information takes describes the shape of the network. The resulting network may be dense with actors highly interconnected with others, a configuration associated with having high common knowledge because information can circulate through many channels. Or, the network may be sparse, indicating little mobilization of information among the actors. Density may appear in only some parts of the network, showing clusters and cliques of actors sharing information. Network configurations also show how particular actors may be positioned to affect information flow. Network structures and their impact on information flow are discussed further below. We turn now to considering what data to look at to assemble the network.

Data Collection

A major step in mapping networks is to determine the relation to ask about. This may be determined ahead of time, for example, if looking at the dissemination of a particular kind of health information, in using bibliometric data to examine scholarly communication,[11–13] or examining collaborations.[14] Or, the information transfer may be determined from the activities occurring among network members, e.g., in examining what kinds of interactions constitute a community,[15,16] a learning network[17,18] or a collaborative team.[10,14,19]

Data to describe the network can be gathered in a number of ways. One typical way of collecting social network data is to ask the actors about their information transfers: Who have you given support to during a major or minor crisis? Who learns from you and who do you learn from? Who do you discuss important matters with?[10,20,21] Other data sources include observations, legal and historical documents, and the wealth of traces left by our electronic activity, e.g., in e-mails (e.g., Diesner,[22] regarding who knew what and when in the Enron business scandal) or web linkages.[23]

Coauthoring and co-citation data reveal networks of collaboration, collegiality and common knowledge. Although beyond the scope of this entry to review, these data form the basis of studies of scientific collaboration and science knowledge for the fields of scientometrics and bibliometrics.[14,24,25] While the terms used to describe the coauthor or co-citation networks are slightly different from those used in social network analysis, the principles of connection through information use and co-orientation are the same (for discussion and comparison of social and citation networks, see White.[26] Applying this to online activity has given rise to the field of webometrics which parallels the field of bibliometrics.[27] Here again the distinction between mobilized and accessible information becomes apparent. Data may reflect mobilized information when individuals make a conscious effort to transfer information or knowledge, or connect to another's work, or the data may be drawn from accessible information, such as citation or web linking behaviors.

Network analysis also has another way to address accessible information. Asking who exchanges what information with whom produces a matrix of information exchange between people in the same social network, e.g., to and from every member of a class. This is known as a "one-mode network," and it shows mobilized information. Data may also be collected as a matrix of people by events, e.g., showing which scholars attended which conferences. These "two-mode networks" yield both the who-to-whom network of who attended conferences in common, and the event-by-event network that shows overlap in attendees. Thus, a two-mode network is a way to reveal accessible information networks.

With the data in hand, we can proceed to analyzing the social network data. In social network studies the unit of analysis is the relation—the interaction, exchange, transfer or sharing—that occurs between actors in the network. The kinds of questions that can be used to address information transfer are different from typical questions about aggregate behavior. With the kind of network data described above, we can ask questions such as:

- Who shares what kind of information with whom?
- Who uses what kind of technology to transfer that information, and with whom?
- What does it mean to get information directly from someone, or second or third hand?
- What facilitates, or inhibits information mobility within a network?
- How does information circulate in this social system?
- How does the nature of the tie between actors affect information transfer behavior?
- How do configurations of information sharing affect who gets what kinds of information?

We now turn to what social network studies have found about our understanding of information behaviors, and how asking questions such as those above helps inform our understanding of information transfer.

SOCIAL NETWORKS AND INFORMATION TRANSFER

Innovation

Social network studies have revealed a number of interesting and unexpected findings about information transfer. Perhaps the first such finding relates to diffusion of innovations. Where early impressions were of the isolated innovator, adopting new processes all on their own, research by Coleman, Katz, and Menzel[28] on the adoption of tetracycline, and the many studies on diffusion and adoption of innovations carried out by Rogers,[29] found that it is the individuals most connected to news sources who first becomes aware of an innovation, and those well-connected with others who have successfully used the innovation who are more likely to adopt it. Although early adopters may be alone in taking up the innovation, they have been embedded in an information network that leads them to be ready to adopt. Cohen and Levinthal[30] reinforced this point when they identified how some organizations are more ready to adopt innovations than others because of the preparedness of their employees. Attention to information circulating about their kind of work creates an "absorptive capacity" for innovation identification and adoption relevant to that work. Ahuja[31] also found that collaborative ties between organizations net an information payoff. She found that "collaborative linkages can provide access to knowledge spillovers, serving as

information conduits through which news of technical breakthroughs, new insights or failed approaches travels from one firm to another" (pp. 427–428).[31]

Social networks—who is connected to whom—matter in exposure to information, and in adoption decisions. While early adopters are well-embedded in information networks, later adopters have the example of those around them when adopting. They can see others' use, the visible results of that use, and hear about others' experiences with the innovation. Their adoption decision is heavily influenced by information from those around them. Rogers showed that influence is limited to those in close, trusted relationships with the potential adopter. Information on innovations received fourth or fifth hand is no more influential in adoption decisions than that received from mass media.

Rogers' work describes in detail the stages of innovation diffusion and adoption and also the attributes of early and late adopters. Earlier adopters are described as more cosmopolitan, and have higher socioeconomic status (higher education, income). In Cohen and Levinthal's terms, they have a higher absorptive capacity, based on their greater access to and readiness to recognize information useful for their purposes; in Lin's terms, they have access to greater social capital.

Strong and Weak Ties

Innovation studies show the role of strong and weak ties in information transfer. News sources (weak ties) are important for awareness of new trends; trusted sources (strong ties) are important for influencing adoption decisions. To investigate information transfer further, it is necessary to understand in more detail what composes a strong or weak tie. As noted above, the "strength of a tie" can be built on a number of different kinds of relations, but what differentiates a strong tie is the close association between the people who maintain that tie. When such pairs are asked about what they do together, they typically report more kinds of interaction, more intimacy and self-disclosure, and reciprocity in their behavior; recent studies also show they use more means of communication to maintain contact.[7,32] They exhibit a greater desire or need to communicate, get together, share experiences, and provide what they can for each other. These attributes are highly relevant for information transfer. Those in strong ties are more motivated to share with each other what information or other resources they have, and the exchange is more likely to be reciprocal. They create strong local bonds, with each actor within that network freely exchanging and sharing what they have so that all network members are aware of and informed by the same kind of information.

The limit to this strong local network is that the people who belong to it tend to be very similar (homogeneous). They share the same socioeconomic status, reinforced by where they live, where they travel, what kind of transport they use to get to work, the kind of news and television coverage they receive, what schools they attend, and the kinds of the media they use. Thus, exchanges among these people tend to pool information of a similar nature. Local groups may even further restrict information access by scheduling same-sex meetings (e.g., women's groups), or meetings held during daytime hours (thereby excluding working men and women).[33–35]

A key observation to be made about social networks in general is that time spent with one person or in one network reduces the amount of time you can spend with others. Thus, each conversational choice by necessity rules out another. Even though we often feel that the Internet has extended our ability to communicate with more, distant others, we need to ask how truly different these people are. A recent study by Hargittai of college students reveals systematic differences between users of different social networking sites in terms of ethnicity and parental education.[36] Hispanics and students were more likely than other ethnic groups to use MySpace, and Asians and Asian Americans more likely to use Xanga; students of parents with higher education levels were more likely to be Facebook users. These findings suggest that even online social enclaves are perpetuating interaction among similar others. Although we may now maintain more extended networks in absolute numbers, we need to continue to question whether these are really any more varied than before in who we meet and with whom we exchange information.

Weak ties are our alternate information route. Since we know these others less well, and hang out with them less frequently, both we and they can come in contact with information different from what we attain in our own networks. Weak ties thus act as a bridge between different social circles. In Granovetter's[5] words, this is the "strength of weak ties." As well as weak ties, individuals we know well may also function as such bridges, keeping one toe in different social worlds, particularly between work and home, and thereby bringing information from one world to the other. In the contemporary world, this also means bringing the means of access (i.e., computers) and skills about access from one world to another, and in particular from work or school to home. Studies by the U.S. National Telecommunications and Information Administration (NTIA), showed that in 2001, 77% of households where a computer or the Internet was used at work also used these at home, compared to 35% when these were not used at work.[37] Use of computers or the Internet at school provides similar ways to bring this information use knowledge into the household.[38,39] The relevant function here is the bridge between networks that hold different information, and the resulting shortening of the path length between those different resources and sources of information.

Small Worlds

In considering information received from remote others, we cannot ignore what has become known as the "small-world hypothesis." This idea that individuals are separated from others by only a short chain of others was first demonstrated by Milgram.[40] In his experiment, individuals in Nebraska were given letters and asked to pass them to people they knew by first name only on the way to getting them to Milgram's friend, a stockbroker in Boston. The average chain length, i.e., the number of people a letter passed through from source to destination, was six. Hence the phrase "six degrees of separation."

While Milgram's experiment has become legendary (not least in part due to the 1990 film by John Guare), there has been some question about whether this would hold in later studies because Milgram only included in his calculations data from completed chains (i.e., where letters reached the stockbroker). Newman[41] chose to examine the small world hypothesis based on data that was more readily available and more complete, He examined the network structure of coauthorship in scientific publications from 1995–1999 with data from four major databases (Medline for biomedical research, Los Alamos e-Print Archive for theoretical physics, Spires for high-energy physics, and NCSTRT for computer science). As found by Milgram, Newman also found that scientists were, on average, separated by six degrees. Newman's work builds on that of Watts and Strogatz[42,43] who created new models for networks that incorporate the clustering normally found in real-world networks. The Watts–Strogatz model has been used to show that a class of small-world networks exists defined by "some nontrivial local order, combined with just a fraction of long-range, random shortcuts" (p. 245).[43] The western U.S. electrical power grid, movie actor connections, and the neural network of the nematode *C. elegans* have been show to be small-world networks. As Watts[43] explains, this model has further been improved on by Jon Kleinberg to take into account that human social networks are "searchable." At the local level, this means we do not choose people randomly for association, but instead choose them purposefully for their information, resources, companionship, etc. At the global level, we also search purposively to achieve the resources necessary for our local networks.

The ideas of local clustering and widespread connection are common themes in social network analyses. The work by researchers such as Watts, Strogatz, Newman, and Kleinberg is providing models that can be used to compare real-world behaviors to models of predicted behaviors (for a review, see Börner.[44] This advance makes it more possible to compare and generalize across networks, and to test ideas such as Milgram's small world hypothesis. These models, when taken in conjunction with the explosion of data available online, are allowing greater progress to be made on analyzing human information behaviors. Although there is still a place for gathering data from individuals, automation makes it easier to collect and manage the data. As Newman[41] points out, while manual data collections provide detailed information on the structure of social networks, "data that are crucial to the understanding of information or disease propagation...the studies are labor intensive, and the size of the network that can be mapped is therefore limited—typically to a few tens or hundreds of people" (p. 404).[41] The new "network science" provides an important addition to the tools available to understand social networks and information behaviors, complementing smaller detailed studies by identifying characteristics that hold across multiple networks and very large datasets.

Roles and Positions

The work on network models also shows that it does not take many cross-cutting links to bring our information resources closer together. Work by Newman and colleagues (cited in Watts)[43] has shown that five random connections in a lattice model of a network can reduce path length by half, regardless of the size of the network. Although we know that human social networks do not conform to a lattice structure, cross-cutting connections are often found that bridge different social worlds. This is often deliberately implemented to achieve that effect, for example as negotiators are brought in to settle labor disputes, and as academic institutions favor hiring graduates from other universities. An entrepreneur may find a bridging position particularly profitable. Individuals who fill what Burt has called a "structural hole," benefit from brokering the relationship between others. Such individuals possess access to information in two worlds and can decide strategically what, how much, when, and to whom they will pass on information.

In social network terms, the entrepreneurs have a high "betweenness" score, because they sit strategically on the path that information needs to take to get from one end of the network to the other. Even if not profiting from such a position, they hold a key to information transfer in the network, often holding two parts of a network together. Again, in network terms, they are a "cutpoint"—a node that if removed leaves the network in two or more separate pieces. Network analyses that show whole network structure can reveal such positions and show where there is risk of information loss (and/or redundancy) in information routes.

Typical measures of actors examine how central an individual is in the network. The network "star" has contacts with many others, and can perform the role of passing on information or making introductions (e.g., Gladwell).[45] They exhibit a high "degree," i.e., a high number of connections to others. Some of these ties entail information that is primarily directed to them ("in-degree") and some entail information outbound from them ("out-degree"). A high in-degree indicates "prominence," i.e., others seek them out for advice, information, etc., and

a high out-degree indicates "influence," i.e., that their information is being sent out and received by others.

Across settings, many times we find people whose patterns of giving and receiving information look the same. Teachers perform the same kinds of information provision in relation to their students; libraries in different towns act in the same way in providing patrons with access to resources and the instruction necessary to use them. In these cases we see an "equivalence" in their information relations. When we discover this, we can identify particular "roles" and look for those again in other places. For example, technological gurus[46] are often identified as present in many organizations. These individuals act as information gateways, monitoring new technologies as they appear and bringing that information to others. Recent work also suggests the importance of information gatekeepers who know "who knows what". Studies of "transactive memory" show the importance to groups of knowing about themselves and where information resides within their own network.[47–50] Often the gatekeeper or guru role is informal, and does not appear on any organization chart. Thus, they can only be found by asking network questions about the information flow in the organization.

Empirical discovery of roles and network structures is an essential part of a social network analysis as it reveals what is happening among network members rather than what an outsider or an inside spokesperson says is happening. It can reveal aspects of network interaction that have been ignored or simplified by conventional descriptions of work processes or social interaction. For example, socializing, play, and off-task interaction are often considered to be distractions from work, taking time away from the job to be done. But the more we examine work groups, the more we find they maintain many relations, and seemingly off-task activities such as socializing actually allow people to get to know each other and their work styles, and create trust and understanding of how to work together as a group. More has yet to be done to understand the complicated interplay between multiple relations in sustaining interpersonal relationships, group functions, and network cohesion.

Network Structures

Actors within networks may demonstrate particular roles but they can only do that in relation to others in a network: the teacher acts in relation to students, the parent in relation to a child, a friend in relation to other friends. Even without a particular role, individuals' relations with others situate them in a position with respect to others in the network: the network star, the broker, the isolate are defined according to their ties (or lack of) with others in the network. In each case, the network demonstrates a shape that tells us how information travels, first between pairs, and then across the network as a whole.

Some of the first examinations of the effect of network structure on the circulation of information are those of Alex Bavelas and Harold Leavitt done in the 1940s and 1950s. In their laboratory setting, they compared information transfer between participants who were organized in a line, circle, Y or star shape. The communication structure was effected by isolating individuals and allowing them to pass messages to one or more others depending on the structure and their position in it (for further description, see Borgatti).[51] The most reported finding is that the star and Y structures were much faster at achieving common knowledge (knowing which symbol the team had been assigned), used fewer messages to achieve that result, and resulted in fewer errors. In short, these were found to be more efficient structures for circulating information toward common knowledge. Other findings are mentioned less often in discussions of these results. Borgatti reports that participants in the circle and line structures enjoyed themselves more. This suggests different structures may support different kinds of relationships—coworkers, collaborators, friends—and may be optimal for different kinds of tasks or outcomes. Getting work done can be frustrating if the system is inefficient and requires extra time, but a game may depend precisely on such obstacles to information transparency. Another result was that circle and line structure participants more readily said the group had a leader. Such a finding has implications for how an individual may secure a leadership position and what structures are most likely to support an emergent information leader.

Since these early experiments, studies have continued to reveal the impact of structural aspects of networks on information transfer. The simplest observation is that in networks with a high "density," i.e., a high number of connections among actors relative to the total possible number of connections, information transfers quickly and easily around the network because it can take nearly any route to get from one person to another. With low density, information is restricted to certain routes, and thus the likelihood of receiving that information depends on being strategically placed where the information is traveling. Highway and local road structures are an ideal analogy to explain this aspect of social networks. Superhighways carry lots of traffic, of all sizes, but do not connect all towns. Smaller roads connect more local regions, but carry limited traffic as slower speeds.

Continuing to view networks as roads, looking from above at the whole network we can see places where traffic (information) reaches a bottleneck because it all goes through only one central node (consider commuting across bridges, or traveling through airport hubs). Such a network has a high "centralization," i.e., a high coordination around one central point. "Cliques" of highly interconnected nodes may also be apparent, showing a group of actors who represent one of the local nonrandom orderings found in large networks. Larger aggregates may also be found as "clusters" or "components" in the network. Each of these

collective units appears because of their connectivity; actors within them are more likely to have and share access to the same resources and information.

The road analogy is also useful for understanding the effect that current structures have on future structures. Highways draw traffic and attract business and residences to locate close to these roads, creating and sustaining attention to these areas. Similarly, network structures reinforce themselves. Someone who is known for having particular kinds of information continues to be sought out for that information, increasing the number of people connected to that actor. New network structures are more likely to emerge and become sustained by people with a keen interest in communicating with each other, i.e., those with stronger ties. These individuals are more likely to spend the time negotiating new ways of communicating and coming to a joint understanding of how they will communicate in a process of "adaptive structuration."[17,32,52,53] Continued interaction also influences individuals' views of the network structure, and who knows what. Krackhardt and Kilduff[54] have shown that dyads within interacting triads (pairs within interacting sets of three people) have more similar views of social relationships among organization members than those in the same organization not in these triads. Taking this kind of common knowledge as information about the organizational culture, they concluded that, compared to a random selection, dyad relations within these interacting triads "predict higher levels of cultural agreement" (Krackhardt,[54] p. 288). Is this just because of stronger ties? Possibly, but their judgment is that "cliques lead to stronger ties and stronger ties lead to cliques in a reciprocating process that reinforces the relationship between Simmelian ties [three person ties] and agreement" (p. 288).[54]

Discussions of collaboration, community and groups, both offline and on, stress the development of common knowledge and shared understanding (e.g., in the development of communities of practice,[55] or in scientific collaborations),[14] with an emphasis on strong tie needs (e.g., in the development of computer tools to support work tasks). Once initiated, strong ties can perpetuate the structure they have created, but to get there requires initiating network connections. While strongly tied pairs can influence each other and pass on information and cultural knowledge to each other, how does information circulate to weak ties or to people with no tie between them? Research on media use by strong and weak ties suggests that a group-wide means of contact (regular meeting, conference, online listserv, etc.) can create such a connection.[17,32,56] Because those with no tie or only a weak tie are unlikely to be motivated to contact and influence each other, this means of contact needs to be established and initiated by an authority beyond the individuals themselves. Scheduling meetings, enrolling people in a listserv, or establishing a wiki creates "latent ties"—a "tie for which a connection is available technically but that has not yet been activated by social interaction." (p. 387).[32] A latent tie describes the accessible information that has potential to be mobilized. The common framework provides the ground on which latent ties can be activated into weak ties with attendant information transfer and mobilization, and potentially at least some will further be enabled into strong ties. Such frameworks may also serve to maintain dormant ties, making it easier to reactivate ties, or to tap into this network for information as needed.[57,58]

PERSONAL AND NETWORK OUTCOMES

What do actors gain (or lose) by belonging to networks, and what does the network as a whole gain by member engagement? It is generally accepted that individuals who engage with others in meaningful relationships benefit in terms of personal health and well-being reflected in social, emotional, economic, and health support. Networks gain in robustness and continuity in the face of change. Both aspects highlight the role of social capital.[2] Individuals in networks high in social capital gain access to both mobilized and accessible resources. These are "not possessed goods of the individual. Rather, they are resources accessible through one's direct and indirect ties" (p. 468).[3] The robustness of a network matters because social capital is found in a "durable network of more or less institutionalized relationships of mutual acquaintance and recognition."[59]

Robust networks are resilient to changes in parts, have structures that persist over time, and exhibit a stable social structure. They embody known rules of behavior and membership, increasing the likelihood that others in the network will act in an expected manner. This reduces the risk associated with making ties with others because it reduces uncertainty about how others will act and react. Known behaviors, and network conformity to them, also support self-policing, with members sharing the task of monitoring behavior, further reducing the likelihood of transgressions, as well as the burden on an individual to deal with such transgressions.[60,61] Social norms of behavior in society are one example, but such robustness is also enacted through laws and contracts and their enforcement.

While individuals gain from robust networks, there is also potential for constraint as the dense network allows more visibility of behaviors and thus the potential for more monitoring and reporting of transgressions. A nonsimple association exists on whether dense connectivity serves a positive or negative outcome, and this can vary with context.[62] Dense personal networks can contain anxiety-causing ties, or establish rigid roles that limit what individuals can do, thereby increasing stress and its negative effects on health. However, associations with others has benefits not only in access to information, but also in support structures. One benefit often mentioned is

that married people, particularly men, live longer than their unmarried counterparts. Although it is still debated whether health is the reason for marriage or the outcome, it appears that a good marriage contributes to a healthy lifestyle and thus longer life.[63]

That health and longevity appear to be associated with the size of personal networks explains recent concern over declines in the size of core discussion networks. Putnam[64] first warned of the loss of civic engagement, the basis of social capital in communities. More recently, McPherson, Smith-Lovin, and Brashears[65] used U.S. census data to compare the number of confidants people reported in 1985 and 2004. They found a significant drop, from 2.94 confidants on average in 1985 to 2.08 in 2004, and a much higher probability in 2004 that individuals would have no confidants at all. The percentage with only one or no confidant—a level described as having marginal or inadequate personal counseling—was found to have risen from 25% to 50% of the American population. Changes in work and home and consequent lack of connection to kin and local communities explain some of these changes, but, as the authors state, "[i]f we assume that interpersonal environments are important (and most sociologists do), there appears to have been a large social change in the past two decades" (p. 371),[65] and one that deserves our attention.

SUMMARY

Information, both accessible and mobilized, form an important basis of the social capital of our personal, social networks. Our access to information provides us with opportunities for work or play, and provides the basis for getting to know others to work with, be friends with, and gain support. Co-presence in a common environment— whether considered as a common geography, online space, or intellectual discipline—situates us in an accessible information space where social network relationships, i.e., connections created and maintained by people, can mobilize information so that it is shared among network members.

This entry has focused on how patterns of information sharing among people can be examined, and how interpersonal ties and networks structures affect the way information moves among members of a network. Individuals may occupy roles or positions that provide them with access to unique resources they can then pass on when and to whom they choose. Their choice of who to pass it to is likely to depend on how strongly they are engaged with others, favoring passing information to those with whom they are strongly tied and who are present in their close local circle. When they pass information to more distant others, it is likely the information will be new to that person or that social circle because of the differences in the experiences and information exposure across social circles.

The sum of all these contacts and information exchanges may be to increase the resources available to the network as a whole, adding to its stability and persistence, reinforcing its existing structure and culture, and generating social capital for all network members. While these outcomes are possible, some reservations exist about the benefits of highly dense, potentially socially controlling networks which may reinforce interaction only among similar others. At the same time that there is an equal concern that very sparse networks may contain insufficient support, with negative consequences for the health and well-being of individuals and their communities. In all, the social network data suggest striving for an optimal level of connectivity that promotes social capital without social control, and information access without information saturation and overload.

REFERENCES

1. Shapiro, C.; Varian, H.R. *Information Rules*; Harvard Business School Press: Boston, MA, 1999.
2. Lin, N. Building a network theory of social capital. Connections **1999a**, *22* (1), 28–51.
3. Lin, N. Social networks and status attainment. Ann. Rev. Soc. **1999b**, *25*, 467–487.
4. Lin, N.; Bian, Y. Getting ahead in urban China. Am. J. Soc. **1991**, *97* (3), 657–688.
5. Granovetter, M.S. The strength of weak ties. Am. J. Soc. **1973**, *78*, 1360–1380.
6. Granovetter, M.S. The strength of weak ties: A network theory revisited. In *Social Structure and Network Analysis*; Marsden, P.V., Lin, N., Eds.; Sage: Beverly Hills, CA, 1982; 105–130.
7. Haythornthwaite, C.; Wellman, B. Work, friendship and media use for information exchange in a networked organization. JASIST **1998**, *49* (12), 1101–1114.
8. Krackhardt, D. The strength of strong ties: The importance of *philos* in organizations. In Nohria, N., Eccles, R.G., Eds.; *Networks and Organizations: Structure, Form and Action*; Harvard Business School Press: Boston, MA, 1992; 216–239.
9. Marsden, P.V.; Campbell, K.E. Measuring tie strength. Soc. Forces **1984**, *63*, 482–501.
10. Haythornthwaite, C. Learning and knowledge exchanges in interdisciplinary collaborations. JASIST **2006**, *57* (8), 1079–1092.
11. Crane, D. *Invisible Colleges: Diffusion of Knowledge in Scientific Communities*; University of Chicago Press: Chicago, IL, 1972.
12. Lievrouw, L.A. Reconciling structure and process in the study of scholarly communication. In *Scholarly Communication and Bibliometrics*; Borgman, C.L., Ed.; Sage: Newbury Park, CA, 1990; 59–69.
13. Zuccala, A. Modeling the invisible college. JASIST **2006**, *57* (2), 152–168.
14. Sonnenwald, D.H. Scientific collaboration. Ann. Rev. Inform. Sci. Technol. **2007**, *41* (1), 643–681.
15. Wellman, B. The community question. Am. J. Soc. **1979**, *84*, 1201–1231.
16. Wellman, B. The network community: An introduction to networks in the global village. In *Networks in the Global Village*; Wellman, B., Ed.; Westview Press: Boulder, CO, 19991–48.
17. Haythornthwaite, C. Building social networks via computer networks: Creating and sustaining distributed learning communities. In *Building Virtual Communities: Learning and Change in Cyberspace*; Renninger, K.A., Shumar, W., Eds.; Cambridge University Press: Cambridge, U.K., 2002a; 159–190.
18. Haythornthwaite, C. Learning relations and networks in web-based communities. Int. J. Web Based Commun. **2008**, *4* (2), 140–158.
19. Haythornthwaite, C.; Lunsford, K.J.; Bowker, G.C.; Bruce, B. Challenges for research and practice in distributed, interdisciplinary, collaboration. In *New Infrastructures for Science Knowledge Production*; Hine, C., Ed.; Idea Group: Hershey, PA, 2006; 143–166.
20. Burt, R. Network items and the General Social Surveys. Soc. Netw. **1984**, *6*, 293–339.
21. Wellman, B.; Carrington, P.; Hall, A. Networks as personal communities. In *Social Structures: A Network Approach*, 2nd Ed.; Wellman, B., Berkowitz, S.D., Eds.; Cambridge University Press: Cambridge, U.K., 1997; 130–84.
22. Diesner, J.; Frantz, T.; Carley, K.M. Communication networks from the Enron email corpus. J. Comput. Math. Organ. Theor. **2006**, *11*, 201–228.
23. Park, H.W. What is hyperlink network analysis?: A new method for the study of social structure on the web. Connect. **2003**, *25* (1), 49–61.
24. Nicolaisen, J. Citation analysis. Ann. Rev. Inform. Sci. Technol. **2007**, *41* (1), 609–641.
25. Borgman, C.L.; Furner, J. Scholarly communication and bibliometrics. Ann. Rev. Inform. Sci. Technol. **2002**, *36* (1), 2–72.
26. White, H.D.; Wellman, B.; Nazer, N. Does citation reflect social structure?: Longitudinal evidence from the "Globenet" interdisciplinary research group. JASIST **2004**, *55* (2), 111–126.
27. Thelwall, M.; Vaughn, L. Webometrics. JASIST **2004**, *55*(14), whole issue.
28. Coleman, J.S.; Katz, E.; Menzel, H. *Medical Innovation: A Diffusion Study*; Bobbs-Merrill: Indianapolis, IN, 1966.
29. Rogers, E.M. *Diffusion of Innovations*, 4th Ed.; Free Press: New York, 1995.
30. Cohen, W.M.; Levinthal, D.A. Absorptive capacity: A new perspective on learning and innovation. Admin. Sci. Q. **1990**, *35*, 128–152.
31. Ahuja, G. Collaboration networks, structural holes, and innovation: A longitudinal study. Admin. Sci. Q. **2000**, *45* (3), 425–455.
32. Haythornthwaite, C. Strong, weak and latent ties and the impact of new media. Inform. Soc. **2002b**, *18* (5), 385–401.
33. McPherson, J.M.; Smith-Lovin, L. Sex segregation in voluntary associations. Am. Sociol. Rev. **1986**, *51* (1), 61–79.
34. McPherson, J.M.; Smith-Lovin, L. Homophily in voluntary organizations. Am. Soc. Rev. **1987**, *52*, 370–379.

35. Smith-Lovin, L.; McPherson, M.; Cook, J. Birds of a feather: Homophily in social networks. Ann. Rev. Soc. **2001**, *27*, 415–444.

36. Hargittai, E. Whose space? Differences among users and non-users of social network sites. JCMC **2007**, *13*(1), article 14. http://jcmc.indiana.edu/vol13/issue1/hargittai.html

37. National Telecommunications and Information Administration (NTIA.) *A Nation Online: How Americans are Expanding their Use of the Internet*; U.S. Department of Commerce: Washington, D.C., 2002. http://www.ntia.doc.gov/ntiahome/dn/anationonline2.pdf (accessed July 11, 2006).

38. Livingstone, S.; Bober, M. *UK Children Go Online: Final Report of Key Project Findings*; Economic and Social Research Council: London, U.K., 2005. http://news.bbc.co.uk/1/shared/bsp/hi/pdfs/28_04_05_childrenonline.pdf (accessed January 16, 2006).

39. Haythornthwaite, C. Digital divide and e-learning. In *Handbook of E-Learning Research*; Andrews, R.; Haythornthwaite, C., Eds.; Sage: London, U.K., 2007; 97–118.

40. Milgram, S. The small world problem. Psychol. Today **1967**, *1*, 62–67.

41. Newman, M.E.J. The structure of scientific collaboration networks. Proc. Nat. Acad. Sci. USA **2001**, *98* (2), 404–409.

42. Watts, D.J.; Strogatz, S.H. Collective dynamics of "small-world" networks. Nature **2004**, *393* (6684), 440–442.

43. Watts, D.J. The "new" science of networks. Ann. Rev. Sociol. **2004**, *30*, 243–270.

44. Börner, K.; Sanyal, S.; Vespignani, A. Network science. Ann. Rev. Inform. Sci. Technol. **2007**, *41* (1), 537–607.

45. Gladwell, M. Six degrees of Lois Weinberg. The New Yorker January 11, **1999**, http://www.gladwell.com/1999/1999_01_11_a_weisberg.htm (accessed December 8, 2007).

46. Allen, T.J. *Managing the Flow of Technology: Technology Transfer and the Dissemination of Technological Information within the R&D Organization*; MIT Press: Cambridge, MA, 1977.

47. Hollingshead, A.B.; Brandon, D.P. Potential benefits of communication in transactive memory systems. Hum. Commun. Res. **2003**, *29* (4), 607–615.

48. Moreland, R. Transactive memory: Learning who knows what in work groups and organizations. In *Shared Cognition in Organizations*; Thompson, L., Levine, J., Messick, D., Eds.; Lawrence Erlbaum Associates: Mahwah, NJ, 1999; 3–31.

49. Palazzolo, E.T. Organizing for information retrieval in transactive memory systems. Commun. Res. **2005**, *32* (6), 726–761.

50. Wegner, D. Transactive memory: A contemporary analysis of the group mind. In *Theories of Group Behavior*; Mullen, B., Goethals, G., Eds.; Springer-Verlag: New York, 1987; 185–208.

51. Borgatti, S. Communication structure and its effects on task performance, 1997. http://www.analytictech.com/mb021/commstruc.htm (accessed December 8, 2007).

52. DeSanctis, G.; Poole, M.S. Capturing the complexity in advanced technology use: Adaptive structuration theory. Organ. Sci. **1994**, *5* (2), 121–147.

53. Orlikowski, W.J. Knowing in practice: Enacting a collective capability in distributed organizing. Organ. Sci. **2002**, *13* (3), 249–273.

54. Krackhardt, D.; Kilduff, M. Structure, culture and Simmelian ties in entrepreneurial firms. Soc. Netw. **2002**, *24*, 279–290.

55. Wenger, E. *Communities of Practice: Learning, Meaning, and Identity*; Cambridge University Press: Cambridge, U.K., 1998.

56. Haythornthwaite, C. Social networks and Internet connectivity effects. Inform. Commun. Soc. **2005**, *8* (2), 125–147.

57. Cross, R.; Parker, A. *The Hidden Power of Social Networks*; Harvard Business School Press: Boston, MA, 2004.

58. Nardi, B.A.; Whittaker, S.; Schwarz, H. Networkers and their Activity in Intensional Networks. CSCW **2002**, *11* (1–2), 205–242.

59. Bordieu, P. The forms of capital. In *Handbook of Theory and Research for the Sociology of Education*; Richardson, J.G., Ed.; Greenwood: Westport, CT, 1986; 241–258.

60. Burt, R.S. The network structure of social capital. Res. Organ. Behav. **2000**, *22*, 345–423.

61. Smith, C.B.; McLaughlin, M.L.; Osborne, K.K. From terminal ineptitude to virtual sociopathy: Conduct control on Usenet. JCMC **1996**, *2* (4), http://www.ascusc.org/jcmc/vol2/issue4/smith.html.

62. Degenne, A.; Forsé, M. *Introducing Social Networks*; Sage: London, U.K., 1999.

63. University of Pittsburgh Medical Center. Can marriage help you live longer? 2006. http://www.upmc.com/HealthManagement/ManagingYourHealth/PersonalHealth/Men/?chunkiid = 43793 (accessed December 5, 2007).

64. Putnam, R.D. *Bowling Alone: The Collapse and Revival of American Community*; Simon & Schuster: New York, 2000.

65. McPherson, M.; Smith-Lovin, L.; Brashears, M.E. Social isolation in America: Changes in core discussion networks over two decades. Am. Soc. Rev. **2006**, *71*, 353–375.

BIBLIOGRAPHY

1. Barabasi, A. *Linked: The New Science of Networks: How Everything is Connected to Everything Else and What It Means For Business, Science, and Everyday Life*; Plume: New York, 2003.

2. Börner, K.; Sanyal, S.; Vespignani, A. Network science. Ann. Rev. Inform. Sci. Technol. **2007**, *41* (1), 537–607.

3. Degenne, A.; Forsé, M. *Introducing Social Networks*; Sage: London, U.K., 1999.

4. Garton, L.; Haythornthwaite, C.; Wellman, B. Studying online social networks. JCMC **1997**, *3*(1), http://www.ascusc.org/jcmc/vol3/issue1/garton.html.

5. Haythornthwaite, C. Social network analysis: An approach and set of techniques for the study of information exchange. Libr. Inform. Sci. Res. **1996**, *18* (4), 323–342.

6. Haythornthwaite, C. Social networks and online community. In *Oxford Handbook of Internet Psychology*; Joinson, A., McKenna, K., Reips, U., Postmes, T., Eds.; Oxford University Press: Oxford, U.K., 2007; 121–136.

7. Kilduff, M.; Tasi, W. *Social Networks and Organizations*; Sage: London, U.K., 2003.

8. Lin, N. *Social Capital: A Theory of Social Structure and Action*; Cambridge University Press: Cambridge, U.K., 2001.

9. Monge, P.R.; Contractor, N.S. *Theories of Communication Networks*; Oxford University Press: Oxford, U.K., 2003.

10. Scott, J. *Social Network Analysis: A Handbook*, 2nd Ed.; Sage: London, U.K., 2000.

11. Wasserman, S.; Faust, K. *Social Network Analysis*; Cambridge University Press: Cambridge, MA, 1994.

12. Watts, D.J. *Six Degrees: The Science of a Connected Age*; Norton: New York, 2003.

13. Watts, D.J. The "new" science of networks. Ann. Rev. Sociol. **2004**, *30*, 243–270.

14. *Networks in the Global Village*; Wellman, B., Ed.; Networks in the Global Village; Westview Press: Boulder, CO, 1999.

15. Wellman, B.; Berkowitz, S.D., Eds. *Social Structures: A Network Approach*; Updated Ed; JAI Press: Greenwich, CT, 1997.

Social Science Literatures and Their Users *[ELIS Classic]*

David Ellis
Department of Information Studies, Aberystwyth University, Wales, U.K.

Abstract

This entry reviews the impact that electronic communication and the availability of electronic information resources are having on social science literature and its users. The two key elements to this being the effect on literature and communication in the social sciences, and the effect on the use of social science literature. The perceptions of social scientists of electronic resources and their use are outlined, and the emergence of a hybrid communication system in the social sciences, through the phenomena of parallel publishing, is highlighted. The effects on social science information seeking behavior of the availability and use of electronic resources are explored with particular reference to the use of electronic journals and Internet resources. Although the main features of the information seeking patterns of social scientists appear generally unchanged, electronic resources are altering the nature of the social science literature base and affecting aspects of its use.

INTRODUCTION

Studies of social science literature and its users can be traced back to the series of projects undertaken in the United States in the 1960s by the American Psychological Association.[1] The results of these studies have been described by Garvey and Griffith[2–7] and by Garvey, Lin, and Nelson.[8–10] There was also a considerable amount of research carried out in the United Kingdom in the 1970s and early 1980s on information needs and information seeking behavior in the social sciences. In particular, in the Information Requirements of the Social Sciences (INFROSS) studies[11–15] and the Design of Information Systems in the Social Sciences (DISISS) projects.[16,17] These projects were followed up later by Hurych[18] and Slater.[19,20]

Because there are many different interpretations of what constitutes the social sciences and which disciplines or subjects should be included or excluded it can be difficult to provide a simple definition of social science literature and its users. Therefore it is probably better to work with reviews and frameworks that have been used to organize studies of social science literature and its use, and to accept that there will be some differences in the scope of these, which nonetheless does not detract from their utility in providing an overall understanding of the nature of social science literature and its use.

Hogeweg-De Haart[21–23] provides comprehensive reviews of social science information, social scientists use of literature, and information seeking behavior to the mid-1980s. These reviews include discussion of different interpretations and definitions of what constitutes the social sciences. More recently, Rosenbaum[24] and Janes[25] have provided frameworks and useful bibliographies of studies of social science literature and its users

from the 1970s through to the 1990s. Rosenbaum organizes studies of the literature of the social sciences according to the history of the social sciences and social science methodology; information needs and uses in the social sciences; scholarly communication and information exchange in the social sciences; literature and bibliography in the social sciences; and data resources in the social sciences. He also provides examples of studies of different subject literatures in the social sciences—library and information science; sociology; anthropology and psychology; politics and public administration; history and geography; economics, business and management; and education and communication. Janes' bibliography on social science information needs and use studies, has a separate category on INFROSS, DISISS, and associated articles, reflecting their key place in studies of social science information use, and then provides examples of general/academic social science information user studies; studies of applied social scientists; country studies; review/position articles on studies of social science information; general reviews of the user study approach; and bibliometric studies.

However, despite the utility of Hogeweg-De Haart's discussion and reviews, Rosenbaum's framework, and Janes' bibliography, they all focus on the conventional paper form of communication in the social sciences, and are concerned almost exclusively with paper resources and their use. They do not address the extent to which the use of electronic information resources and electronic communication have been, and are having, an impact on academic communication in the social sciences. The increasing availability of electronic information resources in the social sciences, and, in particular, the availability of material through the Internet, is altering the form of the social science information base and having an effect on its

Encyclopedia of Library and Information Sciences, Fourth Edition DOI: 10.1081/E-ELIS4-120043231

literature and use. The aim of this entry is to review how developments in electronic communication are affecting the pattern of communication in the social sciences, to assess the impact on the communication and information seeking behavior of social scientists, and to chart the extent to which the availability and use of electronic resources is altering both the nature and the use of social science literature, and, in particular, its effect on the production and use of the journal literature of the social sciences.

ACADEMIC COMMUNICATION AND THE SOCIAL SCIENCE LITERATURE

In the preface to his book Communication; the essence of science William Garvey recounts the following anecdote:

> James D Watson and Francis Crick discussed on the BBC how they made their discovery of the molecular structure of DNA, a discovery which led them along with Maurice Wilkins, to receive Nobel Prizes in 1962. In the course of their discussion they recalled the time when Maurice Wilkins had in his possession an x-ray photograph of DNA in the B form, which he was trying to keep Linus Pauling, Watson, and Crick from seeing until he had a chance to exhaust his own study of the photograph. "But," Crick said, "he had to eventually make public the photograph because communication is the essence of science."(p. ix).[26]

In this way Garvey and Griffith highlight the crucial role of communication in the development of science, in that, in the absence of communication of results and discussion of findings there would be no science as conventionally understood. Communication is, therefore, not an adjunct to science, but its essence. And at the heart of the scientific communication process they emphasize the place of peer review, in particular, its role in the development of the refereed journal article, which, for many, is the touchstone of scientific communication.

The origins of the contemporary refereed journal article can be traced to the late seventeenth century and beginning of the eighteenth century when the Philosophical Transactions of the Royal Society and the Journal de Scavans began to use the method. The role of peer review in both the creation and use of the social science literature by social scientists was examined by Ellis[27] and illustrates how both journal contributors and readers have quite a clear idea of the overall pattern of journal provision in their areas, as well as associated expectations about where their material might be published, and what kinds of material they would expect to find in which journals. These expectations relate both to the substantive topics, and to the type and quality of treatment of those topics.

"Rightly or wrongly I informally operate the belief that there is a small number of top quality journals in which the relevant stuff—the best relevant stuff appears—and therefore I don't need to go into those other journals in that detail.... There's a notion of quality, there are good journals" (p. 56).[27]

"You pick the journal depending upon first what is an appropriate journal for what you want to say and, given that, you tend to try and go for the most prestigious journal within that group" (p. 56).[27]

"Whatever the subject there are obvious journal to send it, typically I would send it to the one which I felt was the most prestigious in that area" (p. 56).[27]

The role of peer review for maintaining the quality of material published, particularly in relation to publication in the more prestigious journals in a field is widely recognized and understood. For many social scientists it is the principal defining role of peer review in the academic communication process.

"Usually you can tell on quality by the journal. On the whole you know what the reputation, reviewing procedures, and the rejection rates are. Journals have reputations, so if you know that if something appears in a reputable journal that it is going to have gone through screening procedures and it will probably be ok" (pp. 56–57).[27]

Those researching in an interdisciplinary area may find that their material may be appropriate to different types of journals dependent partly on their findings being of interest to the readers of the journals concerned. But this only serves to influence where the material might be directed, not the form in which it would be intended to publish, where again the refereed journal article predominated.

"The thrust of our work is in applied occupational psychology and appear in the occupational psychology journals. Occasionally we will make a discovery that we will put into more clinically and medically oriented journals" (p. 54).[27]

In some cases it can be difficult for a researcher working in an interdisciplinary area to choose which type of journal is most appropriate for the material. The choice may be critical both in terms of which journals to send the material to and for the way in which the material is written. It may be necessary to write in different ways for different audiences, and this can pose a dilemma for the researcher faced with this decision. But again this does not affect the preferred form of publication.

"Within industrial relations I was always in a terrible dilemma about whether to publish in the psychology journals or in the industrial relations journals, and, according to which I picked on, the study had to be written up in a completely different way" (p. 55).[27]

Even for those working in areas where this sort of dilemma does not arise, choosing an appropriate journal to send material to will usually involve more thought or consideration that that of simply reading through journals' notes for contributors. Journals often have tacit criteria, which are only apparent from reading several issues of the journal, and for those familiar with the journal and the field, these criteria may be easily identifiable, even if they are nowhere explicitly stated.

> Part of it is simply that, whatever the notes for contributors say, a particular journal tends to have a theme or themes. What happens is that papers that cite certain other papers tend to be located within that particular journal, rather than some other journal. Even though, in terms of the notes to the contributors, they might formally be just as appropriately placed there.... You get a tendency for a particular journal to repeatedly publish from people in this little sub-group of people who are citing each other and developing their own little sub-field (p. 55).[27]

For the traditional archival journal the refereeing process may be considered a device for maintaining the quality of the scientific archive, but it is important to recognize its other roles, such as directing papers from one journal to another, and ensuring that material is absorbed into the literature. It is not always the case that rigorous refereeing is appropriate for a journal. This depends on the function the journal has in the communication system. For the traditional archival journal the refereeing process may be the way to maintain the quality of the scientific archive. But other journals may have quite different roles to play and a too rigorous approach to reviewing material would be counterproductive, the different outlets complementing each other.

> Artificial Intelligence: this publishes long papers and is consequently not right up to the minute. There is a long publication lag. That meets one of the main requirements of any science of being a respectable archive source for major publications. That's all it does meet. It doesn't have any outlet worth speaking of for the shorter note. There is now something that is only semi-refereed and not archived, this serves the complementary purpose of publishing short notes of what is going on, what people are doing or hope to be doing, what the research application was, fairly informal accounts of conferences, who to write to for papers, it's right up-to-date. (p. 55).[27]

The refereeing process both in terms of the biases of journal editors and the judgments of referees does operate as a form of control on the type of material which is accepted for publication in a journal. As Paul Diesing[28] pithily observed:

> If one wonders about the remarkable uniformity of method displayed in certain journals and asks the authors of the articles why they write that way, they answer, "It's always done that way, that's science, isn't it? You do A, B, C, etc. Besides, we couldn't get it published any other way. Then there is the occasional anguished cry of the bewitched victim: One year of research down the drain to satisfy an editor's pet theory!" (p. 24).[28]

LITERATURE AND COMMUNICATION IN THE SOCIAL SCIENCES

Garvey and Griffith studied and documented almost every aspect of the academic communication process in psychology, including the role of prepublication, the steps involved in publication in a scientific journal article, and the nature of postpublication processing. They produced a comprehensive model of the scientific communication process in psychology from the inception of a project through its various stages of communication in literature. This model of the dissemination process was correctly seen as taking place over a long period of time, with, typically, journal publication taking place some three or more years after the inception of a project, and integration of the findings into the wider literature taking several more years. In their model, research is initiated, and preliminary results first communicated, in the form of preliminary reports. On completion of a project results were first communicated in seminars, colloquia, and other similar fora, with the first formal communication, postcompletion, being through conference presentations and the publication of papers in conference proceedings. The next stage in the formal communication of results took the form of the submission of a manuscript for review for publication as a journal paper. If the submission was successful, the next stage was the distribution of preprints, and appearance in the list of accepted manuscripts prior to the actual publication of the article in a journal. Journal publication was seen as key for disseminating the results of a project into the primary communication system and in the secondary communication system, through publication in current contents or through entries in indexing and abstracting services. Finally, the results of the research became part of the established body of knowledge in the subject area through reviews and citations in the literature.

Garvey and Griffith's studies were undertaken before the widespread application of computer technology in the scientific communication process. As Hurd[29] commented: "Computer based communication was not foreseen by the Garvey and Griffith's model, but any observer of contemporary research communities could not fail to see how scientists have assimilated information technologies into their daily routines" (p. 13).[29] Hurd offered a revised version of Garvey and Griffith's model, which envisaged the displacement of paper by electronic forms of communication, but without fundamental change to the features of the model. In Hurd's version, preliminary reports are substituted by listserv discussions. On completion of a research project, publication of results would take place through electronic conference reports, and their publication in electronic conference proceedings. In the place of conventional journal publication, Hurd envisaged an electronic version of the current paper publication model, with the submission of electronic manuscripts for review, the creation of electronic preprint databases, and, finally, electronic journal publication on the Internet. The transformation of the secondary literature was similarly seen to be that of replacing paper with electronic forms of communication. This would take place through the creation of electronic data sets, electronic articles in contents databases, and online indexing and abstracting databases. Hurd redraws the conventional paper model of communication, delineated by Garvey and Griffith, in a completely electronic form, and to some degree, developments in academic communication have mirrored this. But the evolution of the academic communication system has proceeded in a way which Hurd did not envisage, where publication in paper form and electronic form coexist, creating a hybrid communication system.

This has been documented by De Costa[30] in her study of the impact of computer usage on scholarly communication amongst academic social scientists. She identified a number of trends in scholarly communication in the social sciences, including the emergence of electronic journals, as well as the appearance of electronic books and the increasing use of the Internet and WWW pages to disseminate research results. De Costa highlighted the increasingly widespread phenomena of combining paper-based and electronic forms of communication in the form of parallel publishing. She found that parallel publishing was seen by some as offering the advantages of the efficiency of electronic delivery while retaining the economic advantages to the publisher of the existing paper product. As Meadows argued "Parallel publishing safeguards publishers' investments, since neither authors nor readers are likely to object to such an arrangement. It should also help toward a smoother transition from paper-based usage to electronic handling" (p. 154).[31] There are other economic and social arguments for the emergence of parallel publishing. McKnight and Price point out "Parallel publishing of an electronic version of a paper journal has enabled publishers to "test the water" for electronic journals. Since the paper journal already has a level of prestige, a readership and a back run, the electronic version can inherit these"(p. 126).[32] However, some advocate a wholesale move to electronic communication arguing that paper is no longer the most appropriate vehicle for academic communication. For example, Morton states

> Although printing has for three centuries been an agent of change in scholarly communication, we should remain mindful that central values of scholarly communication pre-dated the first learned journals; so, too, can they post-date the paper paradigm. The journal as we have known it was successful because it was the best technology available to do the job. This is no longer the case. Paper-based journals are no longer expedient because there is now a more effective and efficient technology than printing by

which to communicate among the extended scholarly community.[33]

Electronic journals provide a medium which is cheaper than the traditional printed journal, and which can be disseminated more efficiently and effectively than printed journals via the Internet. Electronic journals are relatively easy to compile, produce, and distribute, and, therefore, the period between submitting an article and having it published can be considerably reduced. In this respect, electronic journals can be seen as a way of overcoming one of the main drawbacks of the traditional printed journal, the long time lag between submitting an article and its actual publication—up to 2 years in some cases—which does not apply to anything like the same extent to publication in electronic form. Electronic journals, however, have not been universally recognized as legitimate publication outlets, or have not carried the prestige of the more established paper journals. This situation is changing, but the perception, was, and to a greater or lesser extent still is, that electronic journal publication is not of the same standard as publication in a paper journal. As Rowland commented in the 1990s: "At present some universities and grant giving institutions will not accept electronic publications for the author's credit. This situation is likely to change, but, for some time to come, researchers whose career is not fully established may wish to play safe by putting their best work in the best traditional journals" (pp. 247–248).[34] This perception was not restricted to universities and grant-giving institutions, the perception was shared by the academics themselves. Gomes and Meadows reported in their study of perceptions of electronic journals in British Universities

> The major sticking point for authors was the perceived lack of prestige of electronic journals. Most of those who commented on this saw the way forward as being parallel publication of journals, where the print version already possessed high prestige. Since this is currently the preferred policy of most publishers, parallel publishing can be expected to dominate in the immediate future (p. 180).[35]

In the mid-1990s Kling and Covi commented

> Scholarly publishing should be viewed as one part of the scholarly communications systems that connect authors and readers. In the extremes, world-class scholars (and national class scholars) are eager to have their works read (and appreciated) by their peers, and also by some larger disciplinary or cross-disciplinary audiences that usually number in the range of hundreds to thousands. In contrast, there are other scholars who are simply happy to publish periodically, or at least publish before receiving tenure or other professorial promotions. Scholars are very sensitive to the legitimacy and status of the journals (or publishing houses) that publish their work, but they vary in their

insistence in publishing in the journals that their peers regard most highly (p. 264).[36]

They correctly identified that the format of publication, electronic or paper, may not be the significant issue, but rather attitudes toward the two forms of publication in relation to perceptions of peer review and quality.

> As with paper publications, articles that are submitted to e-journals may be lightly edited or tightly reviewed by an editorial board with strong researcher standards. Today, many scholars are confused about the formats and intellectual quality of e-journals. In extreme cases, they feel that e-journals must be of lower intellectual quality than p-journals, because they sense something insubstantial and potentially transient—ghostly, superficial, unreal, and thus untrustworthy—in electronic media. In practice, some refereed e-journals publish high quality articles, but they are not well known by their existential critics (p. 265).[36]

This confusion seems to stem in part from the existence of a dichotomy between the form and the function of the journal in the academic communication system which has been examined by Smith.[37] Smith deconstructs the roles of the journal in academic communication, distinguishing between the journal's logical role in the communication process and its conventional paper format. Smith also differentiates between the explicit and implicit roles of the journal. The explicit roles he identifies as being editorial; exercising quality control of content and form; conferring recognition for work; and marketing and dissemination. The editorial role is mainly subject based, and is concerned with the selection of material. Although there may be some quality control of content undertaken by the editor, through triage, quality control of content is mainly carried out by the referees through peer review. The other explicit roles of the journal, which Smith identifies are quality control of the form of publication, including copy editing and general design, the things that taken together make a journal look professional. The role of conferring recognition of work is for many authors the preeminent role of the publication process, although, as Smith points out, for some the dissemination of information may rank higher. The more obviously commercial aspects of the process are marketing to readers and customers, and dissemination and delivery to purchaser or reader.

Smith identified the implicit roles of the journal as being subject defining; community defining; and archiving. In its subject defining role a journal, or the editorial board, helps to define the areas it serves directly through invited review papers and/or editorials; and indirectly through the decisions made on the papers chosen for inclusion. The second implicit role, community defining, is the role a journal plays in defining a subject community through its contributors and readership, in effect operating as a gatekeeper on communication through inclusion and exclusion. The third implicit role, archiving, is that of maintaining a record for posterity, mainly by libraries, and, as Smith points out, at no direct cost to the publishers, authors, or researchers.

The purpose of Smith's analysis was to present a model of the journal's function that could be used to underpin electronic alternatives to the traditional journal form. To retain the ends and purposes of the conventional peer review journal, but through different means and form. To this end Smith recommended the setting up of subject focal points and external advisory panels to take on the explicit and implicit roles of the journal, and, in particular to maintain the quality and reputation of the journal system in response to changes brought about by developments in electronic communication. Smith's analysis would suggest that the role and form of the academic communication system be separated to maintain quality control in a paperless environment. However, although technology has broken down the physical barriers between conventional paper publication and electronic publication, and provided opportunities for the rapid and widespread dissemination of the results of research, in ways which would have been impossible to contemplate even a decade or two ago, at the same time these barriers to publication have traditionally operated as a quality control or filtering mechanism on scientific communication. Academic publishers, by adopting the model of parallel publishing, have, in effect, created a duplicate system where the journal has maintained its place as the keystone of the academic communication system, but in a paper as well as electronic form.

USE OF SOCIAL SCIENCE LITERATURE

These developments in the production of the social science literature are reflected in changes in literature use by social scientists. In the 1980s Ellis[38] developed an empirically grounded model of information-seeking behavior and information use by social scientists which had six components: starting, chaining, browsing, differentiating, monitoring, and extracting. Ellis's model categorized existing practices in relation to social scientists literature use. This was later extended in studies of physicists and chemists to include the additional, related categories of verifying and ending.[39]

The premise of the model were that underlying the complex patterns of social scientists' information-seeking behavior were a relatively small number of different types of activity characterized as starting (activities characteristic of the initial search for information); chaining (following chains of citations or other forms of referential connection between material); browsing (semidirected searching in an area of potential interest); differentiating (using differences between sources as a filter on the nature and quality of material examined); monitoring (maintaining awareness of developments in a field through the monitoring of particular sources); and extracting (systematically working through a particular source to locate material of interest).

The original model was extended and developed in studies of the information-seeking behavior of other groups of researchers, in particular, those of physicists and chemists.[39] Despite the differing disciplinary backgrounds of the social scientists and the physicists and chemists, there was considerable similarity in general and detail between them in terms of their information-seeking behavior. The study of the chemists identified activities consistent with starting; chaining; browsing; differentiating; monitoring; and extracting as well as two other characteristics not highlighted in the study of the social scientists—verifying (checking that information is correct) and ending (characteristics of information seeking at the end of a project). The study of the physicists employed different terminology to that of the social scientists but it was clear that the activities themselves could be closely mapped to the characteristics of the original model—initial familiarization (activities undertaken at the earliest stages of information seeking); chasing (following up citation links between material); source prioritization (ranking sources based on perceptions of their relative importance); maintaining awareness (activities involved in keeping up-to-date); and locating (activities engaged in to actually find the information).

However, as with Garvey and Griffith's studies, Ellis's study of social scientists was based on the paper form of communication. Although some of the social scientists had made use of computer-based searches this was only to identify references from which more conventional forms of paper-based information-seeking behavior could begin. Even in the later studies of information seeking by physicists and chemists in the early 1990s, although electronic means of communication were available, the pattern of information seeking based on paper was still absolutely predominant: "In relation to the communication of research, the employment of electronic communication as a complement to or substitute for the traditional forms is, as far as can be discerned, virtually non-existent" (p. 366).[39] A decade later Meho and Tibbo[40] replicated Ellis's study in a Web environment. Collecting data through face-to-face and e-mail interviews they confirmed the activities of the Ellis model but also identified four additional categories: accessing information; networking; verifying; and information managing. In many respects, Meho and Tibbo confirm the relative robustness of the model of information-seeking behavior of social scientists over time, but differences are emerging as electronic communication takes a firmer hold on the academic communication process.

From the mid-1990s, with the advent of the Internet, the use of electronic information resources has increased exponentially. This development has been documented by Tenopir[41] who has provided an extensive overview and analysis of studies of the use and users of electronic library resources. Tenopir categorizes these studies into two broad types. The first type consists of large-scale studies, undertaken over a long period of time; the second comprises studies, which although not lesser in quality, were typically smaller in scale, or one-off projects. Only eight studies or groups of studies were placed into the first category. One of the most the most interesting of these, in terms of implications for social science literature use was that of SuperJournal.[42] The study, carried out in the United Kingdom, used logs, surveys, focus groups, and interviews to explore preference and reported behavior of students and faculty. The SuperJournal study identified seven categories of e-journal users: enthused; journal-focused; topic-focused; article-focused; bingers; explorers; and window shoppers. The study identified significant differences between scientists and social scientists. The enthused category, which consisted mostly of social scientists and graduate students, employed e-journals once or twice a month and searched a wide range of both journals and articles. Scientists tended to be more journal-focused, searching frequently but concentrating on only a few specific journal titles, half of which were full text, or article-focused, searching less often and only on one journal. Social scientists tended to be topic-focused rather than journal-focused, searched less often and searched by subject rather than specific journal. Social scientists tended to search through vertical chaining from table of contents, to abstract, to full text. Scientists would often search through vertical leaping table of contents to full text. "Social scientists seemed to be more task-driven than scientists; visited the library less often than scientists when new journals appeared; expressed less anxiety about keeping up to date".[41]

Interestingly, Tenopir notes that both scientists and social scientists valued the library as "the institution that provides them with journals."[41] With electronic journals being perceived as being useful for "keeping current with articles in the user's area of research; keeping up to date with what is being published more broadly in related areas; gathering background information on a new area on which the user might be embarking; preparing for a specific event such as writing an essay or grant proposal; or performing tasks associated with teaching such as writing or updating."[41] As Tenopir observes researchers "now use a variety of sources for articles, including electronic journals, print journals, Web sites of professional organizations and individuals"[41] but points out the findings of Lenares[43] and Rogers[44] that increase in e-journal usage is accompanied by a decrease in the frequency of use of print journals.[41] Significantly, Tenopir cites the finding of Speier[45] that

The perception that electronic journals are of lower quality than print is another problem that may be diminishing as a high percentage of peer-reviewed journals are digitized. In the late 1990s, business school faculty members surveyed reported they did not perceive e-journals to be as high quality as paper counterparts; their response changed, however, when they were asked to evaluate a well-respected print journal evolving to electronic format.[41]

But she contrasts this with the finding of Tomney and Burton[46] that "While more than 70% of the faculty members in a British university believe the quality of articles in e-journals is the same as in print journals, this same group cited the top disadvantage of e-journals as being the impression that electronic publication is not "real" publication."[41]

Tenopir records the findings of several studies that, in the social sciences, business school staff were early adopters of electronic journals, with finance and management information systems (MIS) faculty being most aware and economists the most enthusiastic users[45–47] while faculty in history, education and the arts were slower to adopt electronic journals.[41,46] Tenopir notes that the increasing availability of e-journals and full text databases is affecting information-seeking behavior: "As libraries make more e-journals and full text databases available to users, both browsing and searching remain important information seeking behaviors, but browsing by journal titles is decreasing while searching by topic is increasing."[41] Interestingly the information-seeking activities of categories of browsing, differentiating, and monitoring are evident in social scientists information-seeking patterns but this is being complemented by an increase in subject searching in electronic sources, as Tenopir points out "Most subject experts have a core group of journal titles that they browse, read from and recommend to students, but they read from a wider variety of journals through subject searching."[41] This is also affecting the balance between different activities, so that for example, "Although browsing and searching remain important information seeking strategies electronic journals (in particular, full-text databases) are causing a decrease in browsing titles while searching by topic has increased."[48,49] Browsing of core journals by tables of contents remains important, but searching by topic for additional journals and articles is increasingly popular, particularly in large, mixed-journal title databases and "experienced users also liked the ease of skimming and searching."[41] The increasing use of e-journals and journal title bases is increasing the demand for more with researchers expressing a "desire for more online materials, additional journal titles, a wider variety of special or out-of-the mainstream materials and complete volumes of back files of existing journals."[41,47–49]

The other key issue is the degree of confidence researchers place in the ability of electronic resources to fulfill the archival function. "Print is a proven archival format. Even those who prefer electronic access to journals (75% University of Michigan Faculty in economics, sociology, and anthropology), prefer books remain in print

format."[41,47] In the JSTOR study, which "received over 4000 responses from humanities researchers, social scientists and economists" more than 60% of the respondents "greatly value electronic journals...are comfortable using electronic resource, believe a variety of electronic resources are important to their research, and consider electronic databases invaluable."[41] But they were more qualified about their confidence of electronic sources to displace paper for archival purposes and, in particular, in relation to their perception of the effect on the archival function of the library. So that almost half agreed with the statement that "Regardless of what happens with electronic archives of journals, it will always be crucial for libraries to maintain hard-copy archives" while over half disagreed with the statement that "Assuming that electronic archives of journals are proven to work well and are readily accessible, I would be happy to see hard-copy archives discarded and replaced entirely by electronic archives."[41] Again, three-quarters of the respondents agreed with the statement that "With more and more journals becoming available electronically, it is crucial that libraries, publishers, or electronic databases archive, catalog, and protect these electronic resources."[41] Guthrie[50] concluded "faculty do not believe that a reliable solution for electronic preservation is in place"[41] and that the hard copy is needed for backup.

CONCLUSION

The picture which is emerging of the impact of electronic communication on social science literature and its use is a complex one. Technology and the Internet have altered the information landscape of the social sciences. The emergence of e-journals, full text databases, and e-books are altering the form of the social science literature base. Though conventional publication through paper journals and monographs continues to dominate much of academic communication in the social sciences, the availability of electronic means of communication is challenging that dominance. In some respects this is disguised by developments such as parallel publishing which offer an alternative model of communication to that of either the conventional paper model or that of full blown electronic communication. But the emergence of an electronic alternative to the paper model, even in the form of parallel publishing, offers different opportunities for information-seeking behavior. However, it is clear that traditional forms of information-seeking behavior are continuing to dominate. Features of the information seeking patterns of social scientists in the paper model are being replicated in the electronic information environment. But as electronic information resources offer alternative ways of interacting with social science literature, changes are beginning to emerge in effects on the information-seeking behavior of social scientists.

Some of these effects seem quite subtle such as the change in balance between browsing and searching in relation to electronic resources. Others appear more pronounced as researchers increasingly see opportunities for widening their information base through more extensive use of social science literature opened up by increasing the range and number of resources available electronically. Similarly, the initial reserve of many social scientists toward electronic journals appears to be diminishing, perhaps partly driven by the availability of respected journal sources electronically through parallel publishing. Ironically the growing use and acceptance of e-journal sources may be driven more by their inheritance of the prestige of their paper counterparts than by any recognition that electronic sources have superseded paper. Finally, the reservations expressed by social scientists about the reliability of electronic sources for the archival function seem to indicate a growing awareness that electronic sources may become an increasingly important constituent of the social science literature base.

ACKNOWLEDGMENT

The account of the role of peer review was based on interviews with social scientists in the University of Sheffield, from Ellis, D. The refereeing process. In: *Publish or Perish*. Hills, P. J. Ed.; Peter Francis: Soham, UK, 1987.

REFERENCES

1. American Psychological Association. *Reports of the Project on Scientific Information Exchange in Psychology*; American Psychological Association: Washington, DC, 1963–1969; 3 Vols.
2. Garvey, W.D.; Griffith, B.C. *An Overview of the Structure, Objectives and Findings of the American Psychological Association's Project on Scientific Information Exchange in Psychology*; American Psychological Association: Washington, DC, 1963.
3. Garvey, W.D.; Griffith, B.C. Scientific information exchange in psychology. Science **1964**, *146*, 1655–1659.
4. Garvey, W.D.; Griffith, B.C. Scientific communication: The dissemination system in psychology and a theoretical framework for planning innovations. Am. Psychol. **1965**, *20*, 157–164.
5. Garvey, W.D.; Griffith, B.C. Studies of social innovations in scientific communication in psychology. Am. Psychol. **1966**, *21*, 1019–1036.
6. Garvey, W.D.; Griffith, B.C. Scientific communication as a social system. Science **1967**, *157*, 1011–1015.
7. Garvey, W.D.; Griffith, B.C. Scientific communication: Its role in the conduct of and creation of knowledge. Am. Psychol. **1971**, *26*, 349–362.
8. Garvey, W.D.; Lin, N.; Nelson, C.E. Communication in the physical and social sciences. Science **1970**, *170*, 1166–1173.
9. Garvey, W.D.; Lin, N.; Nelson, C.E. Scientific communication behavior of social and physical scientists. Intl. Soc. Sci. J. **1971**, *23*, 256–261.
10. Garvey, W.D.; Lin, N.; Nelson, C.E. A comparison of scientific communication of social and physical scientists. Intl. Soc. Sci. J. **1971**, *23*, 256–272.
11. Bath University Library. *Investigation into Information Requirements of the Social Sciences. Research report*; Project head: Maurice B. Line. Senior research fellow: J. Michael Brittain. Research fellow: Frank A. Cranmer. Bath University Library: Bath, U.K., 1971; 2 Vols.
12. Bath University Library. *Towards the Improvement of Social Science Information Systems: Overview of Research Carried Out 1971–1975*; Bath University Library: Bath, U.K., 1980.
13. Line, M.B. The information needs and uses of social scientists: An overview of INFROSS. Aslib Proc. **1971**, *23*, 412–434.
14. Line, M.B. Information needs of the social sciences. INSPEL **1973**, *8*, 29–39.
15. Line, M.B.; Brittain, J.M.; Cranmer, F.A. *Information Requirements of Researchers in the Social Sciences*; Bath University of Technology Library: Bath, U.K., 1971; 2 Vols.
16. Line, M.B. Secondary services in the social sciences: The need for improvement and the role of libraries. Behav. Soc. Sci. Libr. **1980**, *1* (4), 263–273.
17. Line, M.B. *Towards the Improvement of Social Science Information Systems: Overview of Research Carried Out 1971–1975*; Design of information systems in the social sciences. Research reports series A. no. 1 Bath University: Bath, U.K., 1980.
18. Hurych, J. After Bath: Scientists, social scientists, and humanists in the context of online searching. J. Acad. Libr. **1986**, *12* (3), 158–165.
19. Slater, M. Social scientists' information needs in the 1980s. J. Docum. **1988**, *44* (3), 226–237.
20. Slater, M. *Information Needs of Social Scientists: A Study by Desk Research and Interview*; British Library Research and Development Department: London, 1989.
21. Hogeweg-De Haart, H.P. Characteristics of social science information: A selective review of the literature. Part I. Soc. Sci. Inform. Stud. **1983**, *3*, 147–164.
22. Hogeweg-De Haart, H.P. Social science and the characteristics of social science information and it users. Intl. Forum Inform. Docum. **1983**, *8* (1), 11–15.
23. Hogeweg-De Haart, H.P. Characteristics of social science information: A selective review of the literature. Part II. Soc. Sci. Inform. Stud. **1984**, *4*, 15–30.
24. Rosenbaum, H. Literature of the social sciences. http://www.slis.indiana.edu/faculty/hrosenb/www/L625/Intro1.html or http://memex.lib.indiana.edu/hrosenba/www/L625/Outline1.html (accessed May 2007).
25. Janes, M. IFLA bibliography on social science information needs and uses studies, http://www.ifla.org/VII/s5/project/Project_info-needs.htm (accessed May 2007).
26. Garvey, W.D. *Communication the Essence of Science*; Pergamon Press: Oxford, U.K., 1979.
27. Ellis, D. The refereeing process. In *Publish or Perish*; Hills, P.J., Ed.; Peter Francis: Soham, U.K., 1987; 47–63.
28. Diesing, P. *Patterns of Discovery in the Social Sciences*; Aldine: Chicago, IL, 1971.

Smithsonian–Society

29. Hurd, J.M. Models of scientific communication systems. In *From Print to Electronic: The Transformation of Scientific Communication*; Crawford, S.Y., Hurd, J.M., Willer, A.C., Eds.; Information Today: Medford, NJ, 1996; 9–33.

30. De Costa, S.S. *The Impact of Computer Usage on Scholarly Communication Amongst Academic Social Scientists*; PhD thesis, Loughborough University: Loughborough, Germany, 1999.

31. Meadows, A.J. Can we really see where electronic journals are going? Libr. Manag. **1997**, *18* (3), 151–154.

32. McKnight, C.; Price, S. *Authors and Electronic Journals*; British Library Research and Innovation Report, 126; The British Library Board: London, U.K., 1998.

33. Morton, B. Is the journal as we know it an article of faith?—An open letter to the faculty. Publ. Access Comput. Syst. Rev. **1997**, *8*(2), http://epress.lib.uh.edu/pr/v8/n2/mort8n2.html (accessed May 2007).

34. Rowland, F. The need for management of electronic journals. In *Scholarly Publishing: The Electronic Frontier*; Peek, R.P., Newby, G.B., Eds.; MIT Press: London, U.K., 1996; 243–250.

35. Gomes, S.; Meadows, A.J. Perceptions of electronic journals in British universities. J. Scholar. Publ. **1998**, *20* (3), 174–181.

36. Kling, R.; Covi, L. Electronic journals and legitimate media in the systems of scholarly communication. Inform. Soc. **1995**, *11*, 262–271.

37. Smith, J.W.T. The deconstructed journal—A new model for academic publishing. Learn. Publ. **1999**, *12*, 79–91.

38. Ellis, D. A behavioural approach to information retrieval system design. J. Docum. **1989**, *45*, 171–212.

39. Ellis, D.; Cox, D.; Hall, K. A comparison of the information seeking patterns of researchers in the physical and social sciences. J. Docum. **1993**, *49* (4), 356–369.

40. Meho, L.I.; Tibbo, H.R. Modelling the information seeking behavior of social scientists: Ellis's study revisited. J. Am. Soc. Inform. Sci. Technol. **2001**, *54*, 570–587.

41. Tenopir, C. *Use and Users of Electronic Library Resources: An Overview and Analysis of Recent Research Studies*. Report from the Council of Library and Information Resources, 2003, http://www.clir.org/pubs/reports/pub120/pub120.pdf (accessed July 2009).

42. SuperJournal. SuperJournal baseline studies report, http://www.superjournal.ac.uk/sj/baserept.htm (accessed May 2009).

43. Lenares, D. Faculty use of electronic journals at research institutions: Racing toward tomorrow. In Proceedings of the 9th National Conference of the Association of College and Research Libraries, Thompson, H.A., Eds.; Association of College and Research Libraries: Chicago, Il., 1999; 329–334.

44. Rogers, S.A. Electronic journal usage at Ohio State University. Coll. Res. Libr. **2001**, *62*, 25–34.

45. Speier, C.; Palmer, J.; Wren, D.; Hahn Faculty perceptions of electronic journals as scholarly communication: A question of prestige and legitimacy. J. Am. Soc. Inform. Sci. Technol. **1999**, *50*, 537–543.

46. Tomney, H.; Burton, P.F. Electronic journals: A study of usage and attitudes among academics. J. Inform. Sci. **1998**, *24*, 419–429.

47. Palmer, J.P.; Sandler, M. What do faculty want? Netconnect **2003**; Winter 26–28.

48. Sathe, N.A.; Grady, J.L.; Giuse, N.B. Print versus electronic journals: A preliminary investigation into the effect of journal format on research processes. J. Med. Libr. Assoc. **2002**, *90*, 235–243.

49. Tenopir, C.; King, D.W. Reading behavior and electronic journals. Learn. Publ. **2002**, *15*, 259–265.

50. Guthrie, K.M. Lessons from JSTOR: User behavior and faculty attitudes. J. Libr. Admin. **2002**, *36* (3), 109–120.

Social Science Professional Literatures and Their Users

Lynn Westbrook
School of Information, University of Texas at Austin, Austin, Texas, U.S.A.

Abstract

Focused on the individual's welfare, the five major social science professions include teachers and librarians (intellectual growth), social workers (daily life essentials), police officers (physical safety), and journalists (civic engagement). The information environments and experiences of these five critical professions involve information technology adaptation, information literacy concerns, and continuous professional development. The often stark divide between theoretically informed research and applied scholarship leaves practitioners with gaps in their connections between praxis and new research. As government and social policies, as well as economic influences, drive the need for evidence-based practice (EBP), those gaps in research application grow more important. For all five professions, information technology influences or even drives many professional activities.

INTRODUCTION

The social science professions are defined herein as those which focus on maintaining individuals' welfare in light of society's need for self-reliant, socially responsible members. The intellectual welfare of individuals is the responsibility of teachers and librarians who support lifelong learning. Social workers take on responsibility for welfare in the arena of daily life essentials. Police officers bear responsibility for individuals' safety. Journalists have responsibility for civic welfare by contributing to an informed citizenry. These fields tailor society's resources to the needs of individuals in an effort to, ultimately, build a healthy social fabric. Well-informed, self-reliant, secure, productive, and engaged individuals may need support from the social science professions at various points in their life span.

The intellectual, daily, physical, and civic lives of individuals are the *professional* responsibility of these groups as evidenced by the minimal characteristics of a profession. That is, each group maintains a code of ethics, requires specialized education, builds a corpus of knowledge constructed on theory, and supports professional associations involved in accreditation, standards, and professional development. All five of these professions have an established code of ethics. Although police and journalists may be hired in smaller organizations without the relevant baccalaureate degrees, those with the proper degrees are hired and promoted more quickly. The domain knowledge of each profession includes a substantial and interdisciplinary theoretical basis with doctoral programs in place to continue development of that knowledge base. Each of the five groups supports one primary and several secondary professional associations that address accreditation of educational programs. In the case of librarianship, that accreditation concerns graduate programs;

various police and criminal justice associations accredit not only the undergraduate programs but also the actual departments in individual municipalities.

Within the context of this definition of the "social science professions," this entry examines the information environment, common information behaviors, and primary information issues of each of these five social science professions. Teachers are examined in their primary and secondary school roles; university faculty's information issues are addressed elsewhere. Librarians in institutional settings of all types are included; entrepreneurial information industry individuals and other information specialists are not included. Social workers are included in their most traditional context although it must be recognized that lines may blur, in some jurisdictions, with public health and counseling professions. Municipal police officers involved in direct community protection and engagement are included; the larger governmental machinery, from the FBI to the judiciary, is excluded as its focus slides away from the individual within the community context. Journalists working in all formats are included.

TEACHERS

Teachers' actual information experiences and environments are studied relatively rarely. Piecing together a few in-depth studies, fragmentary case studies, examinations of professional development needs, and analyses of EBP creates a reasonable picture of their crowded information world. Their daily work entails an ever-increasing amount of statistical and narrative data on their students, including comparative data from a plethora of standardized tests, which can be analyzed along a number of variables such as socioeconomic status or geographic location. Gathering materials for incorporation into lesson plans and the

Smithsonian–Society

Encyclopedia of Library and Information Sciences, Fourth Edition DOI: 10.1081/E-ELIS4-120043467

overall curriculum has long been recognized as a critical aspect of their daily work, particularly when new material must be taught or standards change. Their professional growth includes locally mandated training, serials (both research and professional practice items), and optional training via conferences and similar organized functions. Their "community of practice" information network includes on-site colleagues, mentors, and extended networks in both local and digital channels. While some teachers have access to research databases and professional development collections in their own schools, nearby college campuses, or public libraries, most lack access to a substantive collection, much less a professional librarian prepared to assist in its use. Extremely limited time and low confidence in their ability to synthesize scholarly research are factors in their preference for research summaries that distill research into contextually relevant, brief, substantive overviews.[1]

Although biology teachers' experiences are probably not typical of the profession as a whole, their use of the Internet and a wide range of information resources in multiple formats is encouraging. Incorporating post-Internet resources into curriculum design is not, however, matched with an equally ready use of online databases, digital libraries, discussion lists, and other electronic resources designed to support teachers. Inadequate search skills and underutilized librarian connections underpin many of these concerns. Lack of search proficiency is confounded by a general lack of time in that many biology teachers believe any useful search will take an inordinate amount of time due to their undeveloped search skills. Resources which spark ideas and cover current information are particularly valued and a digital format is generally preferred.[2] A disciplinarily broader study of high school teachers indicates that they value the breadth, speed, and easy access of the Internet over the quality and depth of online databases although overwhelming responses to Internet searches severely discourages others.[3]

Using the scholarly research produced by university faculty and government agencies is part of many teachers' professional lives. That use, however, is circumscribed by their knowledge base, attitude, information need, and access to research. While research may move towards developing or refining theories, teachers are looking for concrete, practical strategies and tactics, which can be readily incorporated into their daily teaching. Primarily theoretical research study is unlikely to be viewed as worthwhile or contextually relevant. Research which provides strong and direct connections between findings and conclusions or echoes their own life experiences is more likely to be viewed as credible. The sustained opportunity to read, discuss, and engage with research increases both comprehension and understanding but is all too rare. Teachers generally lack physical access to research materials and the time with which to study them. In addition, access is curtailed by a limited sense of self-efficacy in

terms of both finding appropriate research and fully comprehending its implications.[1] The dense academic language, confusing references to theory, and narrow focus of scholarly studies also inhibit teachers' use of them.[4]

The "community of practice" aspect of information use is particularly powerful for teachers who address educational problems on many levels of their organizations. Through mentoring (both formal and informal), unit/department meetings, school-wide developments, and extensive interpersonal networking, teachers embed their daily practice in social communities of shared interest in educational practice.[5] Information which is generated by and integrated into this community of practice is more likely to be perceived as useful, credible, and accessible.[6] Harnessing this social network to support change however can backfire if opinion leaders are presented as administratively sponsored experts. Teachers are likely to become defensive, identifying characteristics of their own situations that invalidate the "expert" advice. Organically integrated change agents can disseminate both research and experiential information in a community of practice most effectively.[7] Contextualized, supported information seeking, use, and collaborative design develop in a social network of trusted colleagues, even in a primarily digital environment.[8]

Finally, teachers have long been inculcated with a tremendous sense of their responsibility for effective integration of information technology (IT) into the curriculum. The last two generations have received training, studied standards, designed techniques, developed curricula, taken workshops, and otherwise striven to master and keep ahead of the IT which permeates modern Western education.[9] The ability to search databases, manipulate statistical test data, browse the Web, and use the Internet for both communication and information dissemination are all viewed as part of their professional responsibility, much like mastery of their subject or grade area. An understandable reaction for some teachers, however, is a profound sense of futility. Since the schools rarely have high-quality hardware, intuitive software, customized professional development, or a full range of useful databases, even those who are willing to continually invest their rare fragments of unscheduled time in information skill improvement may find the return on their investment inadequate.

LIBRARIANS

Librarians' information environment and experiences are replete with paradoxes. They are the only social science profession which requires graduate work as the terminal degree but about two-fifths of the programs fail to require a course in research methods.[10] Although well aware of contextual influences on information experiences, research faculty sometimes fail to value the tacit knowledge of practitioners in their studies of user groups which leads, in turn, to research designs that librarians view as less than robust. The scholarly research literature is abundant, increasingly interdisciplinary, and theoretically grounded but practitioners and scholars agree that little of it is intended to be directly applicable to professional practice. Practitioners who conduct the applied research their colleagues desire produce, at times, substandard work due to a lack of research method preparation and experience. Despite a vibrant community of practice on local, regional, and national levels, librarians may tend to focus so narrowly on their own institutions that they fail to transfer knowledge from research studies to local settings.[11,12]

Related to these matters is the fact that information science (IS) is in its infancy as an academic discipline but it has readily subsumed librarianship and archives as "legacy" fields. As the term "legacy" implies, the associations are viewed by some as an unwelcome inheritance to be born only so long as is essential rather than as a germinal core contributing to the rich development of a new, integrated knowledge domain. Naturally, librarians find research streams generated by faculty who define their newly forming field by repudiating the quality, value, and relevance of librarianship as a profession unlikely to produce practical data or predictive theory. Other faculty and librarians embrace the potential for leveraging the breadth of IS as an evolutionary platform for major growth in librarianship through integrated, creative, responsive research and practice. As one extreme exemplar of the division, consider the impact ranking of the *Journal of the American Society for Information Science and Technology* (usually in the top 4–8) and the fact that most librarians never read it at all (p. 23);[12] (p. 237).[13] Faculty strive to publish in a journal that librarians rarely read. Other divisions, however, are not so sharp as evidenced by the high ranking (usually in the top 8–12) of *College & Research Libraries* which is read in full and regularly by academic librarians, many of whom receive it as part of their professional association membership.[12]

Within that rapidly developing context, librarians make moderate use of scholarly research for professional purposes. Through conferences, workshops, and journals they seek out distilled research findings that have been carefully transliterated from a theoretical to an applied focus. (Faculty in many IS programs are actively discouraged from contributing to any of these forums on the grounds that such efforts constitute service, rather than research dissemination, and service should be focused on the scholarly field rather than on practitioners.) Regularly reading the scholarly journals of their various professional associations, librarians are particularly interested in applied research on the integration and effective development of tools on the free Internet. Librarian/faculty research collaborations, generalizable studies, and evaluative case studies have long been touted as fruitful means of more deeply engaging librarians in research and, thereby, fostering their increased use of research in daily practice.[12]

Informal information networks among librarians are well developed in multiple channels including conferences, electronic discussion lists, e-mails, phone calls, wikis, blogs, RSS feeds, and virtual groups. Professional standards, in-house practice, digital resources, and even physical resources are deliberately sought, shared, and traded with in-house and external colleagues in the large community of practice. The experiences, insights, and opinions of these knowledgeable colleagues bear more authority than do empirical research findings.[13]

Professional development requirements for librarians demand sustained formal and informal information seeking, analysis, and application. Information technology design, development, deployment, and evaluation combine with established domain knowledge areas such as information literacy, organization, service, and management. As laws, technology, and user expectations develop, librarians struggle to anticipate the next learning curve. In addition to domain knowledge, professional capabilities in communication, strategic planning, customer care, and IT skills require continuous professional growth.[14] The wide range of knowledge domains and skill sets combined with the multi-role and even generalist-role of many librarians make simply keeping up with professional information a significant challenge. Seeking, filtering, evaluating, and incorporating a steady flood of information on current practice is insufficient when librarians also seek to anticipate user demand and IT developments. Trend analyses, experientially authoritative digests, and concept development works are valued for their contribution to professional development.[15]

SOCIAL WORKERS

Licensed, degreed social workers are almost universally mandated by states to continue their professional education through accumulation of continuing professional education (CPE) units. That fact alone provides an indication of the information demands made by their professional obligation to stay current with techniques and domain knowledge. Disseminating best practices, bolstering accountability, and strengthening society's opinion of the profession's quality, CPE activities are sanctioned by licensing boards who privilege certain formats, e.g., formal meetings such as workshops and conferences. Social workers actually believe they learn more from and change their practices based on informal formats, i.e., reading journals and peer consultation.[16]

As in the medical fields, IT is an increasing norm for the social worker. Striving to bring records into the field with sufficient accessibility, security, and accuracy to enhance client interactions, social work IT involves the use of customized databases, meta-analysis, visual files, and portable, wireless devices. Research suggests that acceptance of IT is more dependent on attitude than on IT efficacy. That is, social workers who believe in the potential value of the technology are far more likely to master, adopt, and fully incorporate it into their daily work. Developing that receptive attitude requires ceding elements of design control to those who must use the end-product, establishing peer-managed deployment teams (rather than using a top-down administrative approach), providing training that highlights client benefits rather than technology mechanics, rewarding effective or innovative adoption, and creating an ongoing support system for IT utilization. The journal reading and peer consultation mechanisms preferred by social workers will dovetail neatly with these IT development techniques.[17] As the subfield of social work informatics develops, many of these critical information issues may be addressed on a systemic, professional level rather than on an in-house, ad hoc level.[18]

Although social workers' information needs necessarily encompass a number of disciplines (e.g., medicine, law, education) for a number of populations (e.g., domestic violence survivors, veterans, cancer patients, seniors), there is little evidence that they have the information-seeking skills necessary to step easily into the research and practice literature of other fields to retrieve requisite information. Use of professional, rather than research, journals as well as official practice guidelines and directories is common. Their understanding of librarians' capabilities, resources, and services requires updating just as their online database and Internet search skills require development.[19] The two primary databases in field, *Social Work Abstracts* and *Social Service Abstracts*, complement each other so that both must be mastered for a thorough search.[20] The preference for interpersonal information seeking may undercut their utilization of research. Of course, simply getting access to the Internet, printers, e-mail, and baseline computers is still a major issue for many social workers—as is library access even in settings with specialized libraries, such as hospitals. Evidence of substantial interest in learning how to seek and identify useful information provides an additional area which might be incorporated into CPE planning.[19,21,22]

POLICE OFFICERS

The development of community policing[23] and data-driven police administration, including knowledge management initiatives,[24] has burgeoned in the post-9/11 world of law enforcement. The ability to mine the narrative files of individual police officers' incident reports as well as aggregated numeric data across an entire municipality requires a level of information management sophistication that is unprecedented in police work.[25–29] In larger municipalities, administrative police officers and civilian information systems analysts work on customized, integrated information networks for data analysis and

management. Cooperating with other first responders[30] as well as with national agencies, these high-level information exchanges require specialized training and IT. Administrative functions (e.g., budgeting, record keeping) and service delivery (e.g., dispatch, jail management) can be handled by civilian departmental employees in some settings.

On the street and in the detective units of police departments, however, individual officers face very different information needs. Individual officers work to keep up with legally mandated changes in guidelines, standard operating procedures, and criminal law. In those relatively few police departments which are accredited by the Commission for Accreditation of Law-Enforcement Agencies (CALEA), formal procedures and training requirements provide an infrastructure for that information distribution. In addition, CALEA approved departments tend to have a higher level of education required for new officers.[31] That education is increasingly an associate's degree and, in larger departments, a Baccalaureate in criminal justice or sociology. Generally a stronger educational base strengthens the potential for effective information seeking but, unfortunately, so little is known of the information experiences of patrol officers that no definite corollary can be established. Lynda Baker's study of information needs among female police officers involved in undercover prostitution work is unique in its examination of frontline officers' full range of information needs. Their heavy reliance on interpersonal information exchanges grows directly from the highly specific nature of the work and almost certainly does not reflect the information needs of all officers.[32]

The infrastructure required to implement an officer-level IT initiative in a police department is so complex that any change is likely to become institutionalized by the sheer weight of training requirements, regulations, procedures, and other legally required bureaucracy. The personnel training and adaptation issues become paramount when making a significant IT change.[33] As patrol officers incorporate IT into their daily work, often riding with a networked computer in the patrol car, their appreciation of information quality and timeliness is a significant factor in their acceptance of new IT. The ease of use and utility criteria originally identified as acceptance factors have been augmented in the last decade by these two new factors, an indication—perhaps—of an increasingly sophisticated incorporation of information into daily work.[34] Reports created by officers on digital forms can be automatically shared across departmental lines, trigger automated reminders for appropriate follow-up action, and feed into those larger aggregated systems mentioned earlier. Incorporating IT into a department causes inevitable personnel shifts, particularly a decline in the number of sworn officers and a rise in the number of civilian employees. Whether this is due to an IT-generated increase in officer efficiency or the budgetary drain of IT is yet to be determined.[35]

JOURNALISTS

The role of "citizen journalists" in documenting national catastrophes, such as hurricane Katrina, illustrate the information environment shifts experienced by professional journalists.[36,37] Using blogs, text messages, Google maps, e-government, and a combination of portable and desktop equipment, citizen journalists documented the disaster, disseminated information, and gathered the raw material of their analyses. The materials they send in to professional journalists connects these two groups directly, particularly in times of crisis.[38] Like the citizens who also strive to inform the wider public, many professional journalists have been making use of extensive IT (particularly portable devices), mining gray literature and government materials online, and vigorously maximizing the Internet's capabilities for both data gathering and communicating.

Unfortunately, a number of substantial difficulties continue to inhibit digital information seeking for some journalists. Recognizing the authority issues inherent in Internet-based information, journalists struggle to verify their findings despite a lack of sufficient contact information. Identifying high-quality information in a tsunami of options overwhelms some journalists and generates a reluctance to engage with the technology sufficiently to improve search skills. Accuracy, attribution, searchability, and easy access were sought but not always located by journalists in their Web work.[39] As recently as 2003, among some small, Oklahoma newspapers, particularly weekly papers, Internet access was still problematic due to cost or lack of a local provider. Others chose not to use it due to a lack of training although most had incorporated it to some extent.[40]

Librarians contribute to journalists' work in both the classroom and the newsroom. There are some indications that the entire research function is underdeveloped in nascent journalists due to a lack of search skills but academic librarians have been able to address these issues when curricular changes do not provide a more in-depth response.[41,42] Incorporating librarians into the newsroom information flow both increases effective use of digital information resources and enhances the connections between journalists and librarians.[43]

SUMMARY

In all five social science professions, the profound gap between scholarly research and applied research scars the information environment. Tenure requirements, the legitimate disciplinary need for sound theory development, and academia's tendency to place "soft" research fields toward the bottom of the prestige ladder combine to push some scholars in these fields to write for each other with minimal regard for the immediate utility of their work within the actual professions they study. Heavy workloads, minimal educational preparation, a sharp focus on their clients' immediate needs, and/or the constant struggle to keep abreast of externally imposed changes combine to push practitioners in these fields to seek out works which are "utilitarian, inspirational, provide immediate payoffs and meet local needs" (p. 453).[5]

EBP requires the systemic incorporation of empirically validated data (rather than personal experience) as a deciding factor in changing daily practice. Although potentially useful on the individual level, EBP in these social science professions generally requires such substantial effort to identify, gather, and analyze appropriate information that it is practiced on a more integrated level such as that of a department or entire organization. Analyses of the relatively sparse use of EBP suggest that information is more likely to be recognized as appropriate if practicing professionals have been involved in actually formulating the research questions and research design, rather than simply used as study participants (p. 454).[5] Legislatively mandated change, particularly when appropriately funded, is far more likely to effect change than is individual or even group-based efforts to identify and incorporate research in an EBP initiative. The IT complexities involved in manipulating, analyzing, storing, interpreting, and sharing data for EBP work calls on skills that are hardly universal and require use of software that still needs basic usability development.[44] The "workplace culture of action, not reflection, and the absence of information resources and skills" make EBP difficult at a time when social policy tends to require it with increasing insistence (p. 191).[27] Time constraints and a professional culture that values action to the exclusion of reflection make effective incorporation of research and praxis-based findings difficult to manage.

The social science professions impact critical aspects of our daily lives. On a larger scale, they are the living embodiment of social values and societal development. Regular, in-depth research on the information environment and experiences in which these professionals function should be recognized as a responsibility of IS scholars. By understanding and serving the information needs of these professions, we support society's responsibility for the minds, lives, and connections of all individuals.

REFERENCES

1. Williams, D.; Coles, L. Teachers' approaches to finding and using research evidence: an information literacy perspective. Educ. Res. 2007, 49(2), 185–206.
2. Perrault, A. An exploratory study of biology teachers' online information seeking practices. School Libr. Media Res. 2007, 10, 1–26. Available at http://www.ala.org/ala/aasl/aaslpubsandjournals/slmrb/slmrcontents/volume10/perrault_biologyteachers.cfm (accessed January 31, 2008).

3. Williams, T.; Grimble, B.; Irwin, M. Teachers' link to electronic resources in the library media center: a local study of awareness, knowledge, and influence. School Libr. Media Res. **2004**, *7*. Available at http://www.ala.org/ala/aasl/aaslpubsandjournals/slmrb/slmrcontents/volume72004/williams.cfm (accessed January 31, 2008).

4. Hemsely-Brown, J.; Sharp, C. The use of research to improve professional practice: a systematic review of the literature. Oxf. Rev. Educ. **2003**, *29*(4), 449–470.

5. Triggs, P.; John, P. From transaction to transformation: information and communication technology, professional development and the formation of communities of practice. J. Comput. Assist. Learn. **2004**, *20*, 426–439.

6. Cousins, J.; Leithwood, K. Enhancing knowledge utilization as a strategy for school improvement. Knowl. Creat. Diff. Util. **1993**, *14*(3), 305–333.

7. Wikely, F. Dissemination of research as a tool for school improvement. School Lead. Manag. **1998**, *18*(1), 59–73.

8. Recker, M. Perspectives on teachers as digital library users, consumers, contributors, and designers. D-Lib Mag. **2006**, *12*(9). Available at http://www.dlib.org/dlib/september06/recker/09recker.html (accessed January 31, 2008).

9. Barton, R.; Haydn, T. Trainee teachers' views on what helps them to use information and communication technology effectively in their subject teaching. J. Comput. Assist. Learn. **2006**, *22*, 257–272.

10. Park, S. Research methods as core competency. J. Educ. Libr. Inform. Sci. **2003**, *44*(1), 17–25.

11. Intner, S. Theory and practice or theory versus practice: fundamental issues and questions. In *Library Education and Leadership*; Intner, S., Vendergrift, K., Eds.; Scarecrow Press: Metuchen, NJ, 1990; 153–165.

12. Brown, C.; Spencer, B. The realities of relevance: a survey of librarians' use of library and information science research. Southeast Libr. **2004**, *52*(3), 17–30.

13. Brown, C.M.; Ortega, L. Information-seeking behavior of physical science librarians: does research inform practice. College Res. Libr. **2005**, *66*(3), 231–247.

14. Fisher, B.; Hallam, G.; Partridge, H. Different approaches – common conclusions: the skills debate of the 21st century. New Rev. Acad. Libr. **2005**, *11*(1), 41–52.

15. Hardesty, S.; Sugarman, T. Academic librarians, professional literature, and new technologies: a survey. J. Acad. Libr. **2007**, *33*(2), 196–205.

16. Smith, C.; Cohen-Callow, A.; Dia, D.; Bliss, D.; Gantt, A.; Cornelius, L.; Harrington, D. Staying current in a changing profession: evaluating perceived change resulting from continuing professional education. J. Soc. Work Educ. **2006**, *42*(3), 465–482.

17. Zhang, W.; Gutierrez, O. Information technology acceptance in the social services sector context: an exploration. Soc. Work **2007**, *52*(3), 221–231.

18. Parker-Oliver, D.; Demiris, G. Social work informatics: a new specialty. Soc. Work **2006**, *51*(2), 127–134.

19. Harrison, J.; Hepworth, M.; De Chazal, P. NHS and social care interface: a study of social workers' library and information needs. J. Libr. Inform. Sci. **2004**, *36*(1), 27–35.

20. Flatley, R.; Lilla, R.; Widner, J. Choosing a database for social work: a comparison of Social Work Abstracts and Social Service Abstracts. J. Acad. Libr. **2007**, *33*(1), 47–55.

21. Booth, S.; Booth, A.; Falzon, L. The need for information and research skills training support evidence-based social care: a literature review and survey. Learn. Health Soc. Care **2003**, *2*(4), 191–201.

22. Morgan, J.; Rankin, C. Early intervention and information use by mental health social workers. Ment. Health Learn. Disabil. Res. Pract. **2006**, *3*, 143–159.

23. Lumb, R.; Breazeale, R. Police officer attitudes and community policing implementation: developing strategies for durable organizational change. Polic. Soc. **2002**, *13*, 91–106.

24. Luen, T.; Al-Hawamdeh, S. Knowledge management in the public sector: principles and practices in police work. J. Inform. Sci. **2001**, *27*(5), 311–318.

25. Schroeder, J.; Xu, J.; Chen, H.; Chau, M. Automated criminal link analysis based on domain knowledge. J. Am. Soc. Inform. Sci. Technol. **2007**, *58*(6), 842–855.

26. Xu, J.; Wang, G.A.; Jiexun, L.; Chau, M. Complex problem solving: identity matching based on social contextual information. J. Assoc. Inform. Syst. **2007**, *8*(10), 525–545.

27. Chen, H.; Zeng, D.; Atabakhsh, H.; Wyzga, W.; Schroeder, J. COPLINK: managing law enforcement data and knowledge. Commun. ACM **2003**, *46*(1), 28–34.

28. Chen, H.; Chung, W.; Xu, J.; Wang, G.; Qin, Y.; Chau, M. Crime data mining: a general framework and some examples. Computer **2004**, *37*(4), 50–56.

29. Xiang, Y.; Chau, M.; Atabakhsh, H.; Chen, H. Visualizing criminal relationships: comparison of a hyperbolic tree and a hierarchical list. Decis. Supp. Syst. **2005**, *41*(1), 69–83.

30. Fedorowicz, J.; Gogan, J.; Williams, C. A collaborative network for first responders: lessons from the CapWIN case. Govern. Inform. Quart. **2007**, *24*, 785–807.

31. McCabe, K.; Fajardo, R. Law enforcement accreditation: a national comparison of accredited vs. nonaccredited agencies. J. Crim. Just. **2001**, *29*(2), 127–131.

32. Baker, L. The information needs of female police officers involved in undercover prostitution work. Inform. Res. **2004**, *10*(1). Available at http://InformationR.net/ir/10-1/paper209.html (accessed January 31, 2008), Paper 209.

33. Hauck, R.; Weisband, S. When a better interface and easy navigation aren't enough: examining the information architecture in a law enforcement agency. J. Am. Soc. Inform. Sci. Technol. **2002**, *53*(10), 846–854.

34. Colvin, C.; Goh, A. Validation of the technology acceptance model for police. J. Crim. Just. **2005**, *33*, 89–95.

35. Nunn, S. Police information technology: assessing the effects of computerization on urban police functions. Publ. Admini. Rev. **2001**, *61*(2), 221–234.

36. Piper, P.; Ramos, M. A failure to communicate: politics, scams, and information flow during hurricane Katrina. Searcher **2006**, *14*(6), 40–54.

37. Good, K. The rise of the citizen journalist. Feliciter **2006**, *52*(2), 69–71.

38. Masie, E. CNN newsroom in the midst of Katrina – "rapid development…content objects…learning implications". Publ. Libr. Quart. **2005**, *24*(2), 73–76.

39. Garrison, B. How newspaper reporters use the web to gather news. Newspap. Res. J. **2003**, *24*(3), 62–75.

40. Ketterer, S. Oklahoma small dailies, weeklies use Internet as reporting tool. Newspap. Res. J. **2003**, *24*(2), 107–113.

41. Drueke, J.; Steckfuss, R. Research skills for journalism students: from basics to computer-assisted reporting. Res. Strat. **1997**, *15*(2), 60–67.
42. Singh, A. A report on faculty perceptions of students' information literacy competencies in journalism and mass communication programs. Coll. Res. Libr. **2005**, *66*(4), 294–310.
43. Barreau, D. Integration of information professionals in the newsroom: Two organizational models for research services. Libr. Inform. Sci. Res. **2005**, *27*, 325–345.
44. Wayman, J. Involving teachers in data-driven decision making: Using computer data systems to support teacher inquiry and reflection. J. Educ. Stud. **2005**, *10*(3), 295–308.

BIBLIOGRAPHY

1. Barreau, D. Integration of information professionals in the newsroom: two organizational models for research services. Libr. Inform. Sci. Res. **2005**, *27*, 325–345.
2. Booth, S.; Booth, A.; Falzon, L. The need for information and research skills training support evidence-based social care: a literature review and survey. Learn. Health Social Care **2003**, *2*(4), 191–201.
3. Brown, C.; Spencer, B. The realities of relevance: a survey of librarians' use of library and information science research. Southeast Libr. **2004**, *52*(3), 17–30.
4. Colvin, C.; Goh, A. Validation of the technology acceptance model for police. J. Crim. Just. **2005**, *33*, 89–95.
5. Garrison, B. How newspaper reporters use the web to gather news. Newspap. Res. J. **2003**, *24*(3), 62–75.
6. Hardesty, S.; Sugarman, T. Academic librarians, professional literature, and new technologies: A survey. J. Acad. Librar. **2007**, *33*(2), 196–205.
7. Harrison, J.; Hepworth, M.; De Chazal, P. NHS and social care interface: a study of social workers' library and information needs. J. Librar. Inform. Sci. **2004**, *36*(1), 27–35.
8. Hauck, R.; Weisband, S. When a better interface and easy navigation aren't enough: examining the information architecture in a law enforcement agency. J. Am. Soc. Inform. Sci. Technol. **2002**, *53*(10), 846–854.
9. Hemsely-Brown, J.; Sharp, C. The use of research to improve professional practice: a systematic review of the literature. Oxf. Rev. Educ. **2003**, *29*(4), 449–470.
10. Perrault, A. An exploratory study of biology teachers' online information seeking practices. School Library Media Research **2007**, *10*, 1–26. http://www.ala.org/ala/aasl/aaslpubsandjournals/slmrb/slmrcontents/volume10/perrault_biologyteachers.cfm (accessed January 31, 2008).

Society for Scholarly Publishing (SSP)

Judy C. Holoviak
American Geophysical Union, Washington, District of Columbia, U.S.A.

October R. Ivins
Ivins eContent Solutions, Sharon, Massachusetts, U.S.A.

Lois Smith
Human Factors and Ergonomics Society, Santa Monica, California, U.S.A.

Abstract

The Society for Scholarly Publishing (SSP) is an international organization for both individuals and organizations that is dedicated to the facilitation of learning, communication, and the advancement of appropriate technologies for all who are involved with scholarly communication. The Society is unique in that it draws from all parts of the scholarly communication chain—authors, editors, librarians, information specialists, publishers (commercial, university, and society), printers, subscription agencies, and creators and vendors of various technology solutions. This article covers the Society's first thirty years, from its founding in 1978 and early history, its evolving organizational structure and programs, and its current and future plans for providing a forum to address challenges to scholarly publishers and producers.

INTRODUCTION

The Society for Scholarly Publishing (SSP) is an international membership organization for individuals and organizations that is dedicated to the facilitation of learning, communication, and the advancement of appropriate technologies for all who are involved with scholarly communication. The Society is unique in that it draws from all parts of the scholarly communication chain—authors, editors, librarians, information specialists, publishers (commercial, university, and society), printers, subscription agencies, and creators and vendors of various technology solutions. The SSP covers all aspects of scholarship, including the humanities, social science, science, technology, and medicine.

Any individual interested in the aims of the Society is welcome to join. The SSP originally targeted decision makers for membership. More recently, it created additional dues categories to encourage early and mid-career professionals, students, and librarians to join. A growing focus on networking and assistance in improving one's job performance is a hallmark of the Society. The tagline adopted in 2008 reflects the emphasis on individuals: "Innovative People Advancing Scholarly Communication."

The mission of SSP is to advance scholarly publishing and communication and the professional development of its members through education, collaboration, and networking among individuals in the field Fig. 1. The Society's logo, a globe with myriad points of connection, is a graphic representation of this central concept. The logo was designed by William Propert with what was then William Byrd Press. It was proposed for adoption and unanimously approved at the July 12, 1978 meeting of the Board of Directors. The minutes provide this description: "The points of the circumference of the circle represent the various communities the Society seeks to serve and the chords across the circle symbolize the interactions and lines of communication and interest among those communities."

The SSP was founded in 1978 for educational purposes. It is incorporated in the District of Columbia as a nonprofit corporation under section 501(c)(3) of the U.S. Internal Revenue Service (IRS) code. The SSP's Board added an organizational membership category in the mid-1990s. About 40% of the membership represents individuals who work for the 50 organizational member companies, which are evenly divided between scholarly societies, commercial and nonprofit publishers, vendors, and service providers. The membership in 2000 numbered 750; by 2008, it had grown to 1000. The majority of members reside in the United States and Canada, but more than a dozen other countries are also represented.

The 2008 annual budget was $750,000. All funding is generated from dues, Society programs (including exhibits and sponsorships), and some donations. The SSP has never been funded by outside sources, although a number of vendors have provided in-kind services over the years to help build the Society.

FOUNDING AND EARLY HISTORY

The SSP had a wealth of sources of inspiration leading to its formation. The earliest progenitor was the conference

Encyclopedia of Library and Information Sciences, Fourth Edition DOI: 10.1081/E-ELIS4-120044967

Fig. 1 The logos of the Society for Scholarly Publishing (used with permission of the SSP).

on the future of scientific and technical journals, sponsored by the Professional Communications Group of the Institute of Electrical and Electronics Engineers (IEEE) in May 1973.[1] The idea for the conference came from George Schindler, head of technical publications at Bell Laboratories. James M. Lufkin, manager of professional publications at Honeywell, Inc., served as general chair. At the close of the meeting, Lufkin declared the foundation of the Association of Learned Journal Editors, Publishers, and Users and automatically made each registrant at the conference a member.

Two IEEE-sponsored conferences followed in 1975 and 1977.[2,3] By 1977, the Lufkin-created association had shortened its name to Association of Scientific Journals (ASJ). At the insistence of its founder, the association had "no dues, no officers, and no formalities known to its members." Most of the participants at the first conference were engaged directly in publishing. By the 1975 conference, the list of participants had expanded greatly and included many librarians, information specialists, and vendors. The lively debates among this wider array of individuals influenced the founders of SSP and

were instrumental in determining the breadth of membership that SSP chose to serve.

A second source of inspiration came from a project devised and funded by the National Science Foundation (NSF) from 1974 through 1978, "Improving the Dissemination of Scientific and Technical Innovation," more commonly known as the Innovation Project.[4] The intent of this project was to document and share information about publishing and production procedures that would be of value to those concerned with scientific and technical journals. Two contractors were chosen by NSF to complete a survey of various organizations. The outgrowth of the survey was a planning guide to assist editors, publishers, and others involved with communicating scientific and technical results. This project had an interesting definition of innovation, as described in one of the letters seeking input for the survey: "Please understand that by 'innovation' we do not necessarily mean the leading edge of technology. Rather, we construe it to mean anything that has not yet become standard practice. Quite often, what is considered prosaic by one organization will be considered novel by another."

Preparation of the planning guide fell to the Capital Systems Group of Maryland. This independent management service organization was assisted by a technical advisory panel and, later, a user advisory panel. Several of those involved with the Innovation Project had also participated in the IEEE conferences. Among them was Jack Goellner, director of Johns Hopkins University Press, who suggested that the scholarly publishing community needed a lobbying organization independent of the various trade associations in existence. The voice of scholarly publishing was not being heard by Congress. This was the period of the omnibus revision to the U.S. Copyright Act.

Goellner's comment motivated Fred Spilhaus, executive director of the American Geophysical Union (AGU), who enlisted John Strawhorn as the Innovation Project manager at Capital Systems, as well as Judy Holoviak, director of publications at AGU. The three wrote a prospectus for SSP and recruited Mark Carroll, director of professional publications at the National Park Service, to serve as president pro tem. Other members of the pro tem board of directors were inducted, and the first board meeting was held in early spring 1978. The first annual meeting was held in Boston in June 1979, where Lufkin, as founder of ASJ, was formally designated godfather of SSP.[5]

The goals of the Society were summarized by its original mission statement:

> The mission of SSP is to draw together individuals involved in the process of scholarly communication. This process requires successful interaction of the many functions performed within the scholarly community. SSP provides the leadership for such interaction by creating opportunities for the exchange of information and opinions among scholars, editors, publishers, librarians,

printers, booksellers, and all others engaged in scholarly communication.

The original import is retained in the current mission statement.

CHALLENGES TO SCHOLARLY PUBLISHERS AND PRODUCERS

The founders of SSP recognized that the problems facing scholarly publishing could best be addressed by engaging all the key individuals in the information chain. Different branches of learning have special concerns. For example, publications dealing with chemistry and math must deal with specialized characters, which complicates typesetting and layout; geological publications must be able to reproduce complex maps; medical publications have stringent demands for reproduction of images. However, most of the problems of scholarly communication cut across disciplines. Handling the peer-review process in a timely and ethical way is a concern for all disciplines. Most scholarly publications rely heavily on volunteers to serve as editors and reviewers. Convincing volunteers to give of their valuable time is another common challenge for all areas of scholarship.

More recently, the producers and users of scholarly information are dealing with the costs and uncertainties of electronic publishing. This has set up an entirely new set of problems, not the least of which are lack of standards for production and delivery and the unknown costs of maintaining and upgrading archives when technology changes.

The SSP's founders believed that because many organizations involved in scholarly publishing are small and some are made up entirely of volunteers, sharing information and addressing common problems together should help make limited resources go further and should lead to better service overall for scholars. This foundation has served SSP well, creating a supportive atmosphere for addressing challenges posed by new technologies and business models such as open access, as well as anticipating future changes in order to ensure the long-term viability of all the professions represented by the SSP membership.

Although one of the inspirations for founding the Society was the sense that the scholarly publishing community should create its own lobbying organization, SSP has never attempted to influence legislation or public policy. Within 2–3 years of its formation, the Board of Directors took a formal action to abstain from any form of advocacy. The Board was concerned that no matter how carefully advocacy positions might be developed, they could easily become divisive because of the breadth of interests represented by the members. A small organization with a very diverse membership simply could not afford activities that might ultimately tear the Society apart. Lobbying has been left to more specialized associations. Successive boards have confirmed the wisdom of this decision.

ORGANIZATIONAL STRUCTURE

The officers and Board of Directors are elected by the membership. The individual chosen as president-elect automatically succeeds to presidency. Prior to 1996, the term of the president-elect and the president was 2 years each. In 1996, the term changed to 1 year for each position, and the individual then continued on the Board for an additional year as past president.

The other elected officer is the secretary-treasurer, who serves a 3-year term. There are nine elected directors, who serve 3-year terms, with three elected each year. The SSP officers for 2008–2009 are President October Ivins, Ivins eContent Solutions; President-Elect Raymond Fastiggi, Rockefeller University; Past President Susan Kesner, Copyright Clearance Center, Inc.; and Secretary-Treasurer Mady Tissenbaum, *Journal of Bone and Joint Surgery*.

The programs of the Society are managed by member volunteers under the guidance of the Board of Directors. SSP enjoys the active participation of many members who serve on committees, each of whom is responsible for critical programs and events serving all members' information and networking needs. Committee chairs and members are appointed by the president with the advice and consent of the Board. The president serves ex officio on all committees except the Nomination Committee. Each committee has a Board liaison, and committee chairs or cochairs are invited to Board meetings. Board meetings are held in conjunction with the annual meeting (May/June), the IN: Innovate, Interact, Inspire meeting (September) and in February.

At present, the SSP committees are as follows:

- SSP Annual Meeting Program Committee—plans and implements the SSP Annual Meeting
- SSP Development Committee—develops the exhibits and sponsorships program
- SSP Education Committee—plans and manages on-site and Web-based seminars and the Librarian Focus Group
- SSP Executive Committee—made up of Board members, acts for the Board of Directors between Board meetings
- SSP Finance Committee—makes recommendations regarding Society finances and investments
- SSP IN Committee—plans and implements the SSP IN: Innovate, Interact, Inspire Meeting
- SSP Marketing Committee—coordinates the promotional efforts of all committees

- SSP Membership Committee—solicits new members and monitors member satisfaction
- SSP Nominating and Awards Committee—prepares the slate of officer and Board candidates and identifies worthy individuals for awards
- SSP Organizational Collaboration Committee—guides the Board in decisions about collaborations with other organizations
- SSP Professional Development Committee—develops mentoring programs and administers the student and early career travel grant awards
- SSP Publications and Research Committee—oversees publications, the Web site, and development of research to provide key information to members
- SSP Web Site Development—coordinates planning for Web site technology and strategy
- SSP Web Site Editorial—maintains and updates Web site content

Since 1990, the administration of the Society has been managed by the Resource Center for Associations, an association management and consulting firm located in Wheat Ridge, Colorado. The position of executive director is held by Francine Butler, and David Stumph of Management Liaison. Ann Mehan Crosse, Associate Director, coordinates contributions from other key staff. Butler and Stumph are partners in the Resource Center for Associations.

STRATEGIC PLAN

Strategic plans over the years have served SSP well. A major initiative was implemented under the leadership of Susan Kesner in fall 2007, building on prior efforts led by publishing consultant Norman Frankel. A planning retreat of the Board and committee chairs produced a plan that addresses membership; marketing, communication, and visibility; programming; and governance, finance, and infrastructure. The plan is reviewed and updated at each Board meeting and has guided many of the changes already made and being planned. This initiative recognized and expanded the broader, more inclusive focus represented by, among other things, the establishment of Student and Early Career Travel Awards to the Annual Meeting, which was initiated in 2006 by Amy Brand, Harvard University Office of Scholarly Communication.

PROGRAMS OF THE SOCIETY

All programs of SSP are educational in nature. The Society organizes a variety of different-sized meetings. Over the years it has also had a varied publication program.

Meetings and Seminars

The SSP Annual Meeting is held in May or June each year. Until 1999, the venue was normally a major East Coast city with occasional excursions to the midcontinent and the West Coast. In 1999, a three-city rotation (Boston, San Francisco, District of Columbia area) was introduced, which simplifies site selection and arrangements. Attendance at recent annual meetings has been 650–770. The educational sessions normally last 2–2½ days with a combination of premeeting seminars, plenary sessions, and concurrent sessions on a wide range of topics. In past years, sessions were taped and participants as well as those unable to attend may purchase the tapes. The Board is revisiting this practice in light of new media options.

The educational sessions are designed to be of interest to both seasoned professionals and more junior colleagues. Topics are selected to cover the interests of authors, editors, librarians, publishers, and vendors. Sessions are often designed to look at a given problem from these different perspectives. Premeeting half-day and full-day seminars have a narrow topical focus and are more tutorial in nature than the plenary and concurrent sessions. Recently, many premeeting seminars have been concerned with issues related to new technologies.

About 30–40 exhibitors display their products and services at the annual meetings. Exhibitors are encouraged to participate fully in the educational sessions, and the schedule for the exhibit is set accordingly.

Each fall, SSP holds a 1–1½-day program for decision makers, formerly called the Top Management Roundtable (TMR). Leading-edge issues are the focus of the roundtable. The format allows for considerable discussion and debate. The originator of this very popular series was William Teare, a printing industry executive who served on the pro tem Board. To ensure uninhibited discussion, the TMR has only once been taped. The value of the TMR comes much more from the informal discussion than from the invited presentations.

In recent years, the TMR has become more like a small conference and has attracted a broader range of attendees. For several years, the meeting theme has focused on innovation, with speakers drawn from industries and communities outside scholarly communication. Beginning in 2009, the meeting was rebranded as the SSP IN: Innovate, Interact, Inspire Meeting.

Starting in 2007, the TMR was covered by a public Weblog (blog) written by Jill O'Neill, NFAIS. In 2008, blogging was continued and podcasting was added. This opening of the TMR discussions reflects the Society's mission to enhance the sharing of information to benefit all members.

SSP also sponsors 10–20 educational face-to-face or Web-based seminars each year. On-site seminars are held in the spring and fall as half-day or full-day events; often several seminars are scheduled back to back in the same facility to reduce travel costs for attendees. Attendance is limited to ensure ample time for questions and answers. Most seminars are designed to offer something of interest to managerial-level staff. Those designed for the novice are identified as such. The Society is experimenting with adding online communities to these events.

In 2005, SSP introduced the Librarian Focus Group. This member-only event enables publishers to interact with librarians who represent many types of libraries (medical, corporate, research, small college, etc.) to hear about effective ways to market content to libraries as well as explore budget forecasts, technology and interface preferences, changing user needs, and other current topics.

The SSP has also been a coorganizer of meetings. Partners have included the Association of American University Presses, Council of Biology Editors, the Association of Earth Science Editors, the International Federation of Scientific Editors' Associations, the Geoscience Information Society, and the North American Serials Interest Group.

Publications

The SSP published the proceedings of its first 11 annual meetings (1979–1989). Submission of an article was not mandatory for speakers, and there was no attempt to provide summaries of sessions for which the speakers did not submit articles. In 1990, the Board determined that it was too costly to continue this publication series. In its place, summary reports were published in the newsletter. Once tapes of the annual meeting sessions were available for sale, the publication of summary reports ceased.

The Society publishes a printed membership directory, which is available only to members. There is also an online membership directory. The information in this directory is intended for noncommercial use by SSP members only.

The Society has had three different newsletters during its history. The first, entitled *The Letter*, was published quarterly starting in 1980. However, quarterly publication meant that it was difficult to have timely news for Society members. In 1992, the Board decided to undertake a more ambitious publication, and a totally revamped newsletter was started under the title *Scholarly Publishing Today*. It was intended to be a bimonthly publication. *Scholarly Publishing Today* continued to be published nominally 6 times a year through 1996. This incarnation of the newsletter proved too great a time commitment for the volunteers who acted as editors, reporters, and production staff, and as a result, in 1997, only four issues were produced.

In 1997, the Board decided to put most of its publication efforts into a more extensive Web site (http://www.sspnet.org). A four-page printed newsletter, entitled *SSP Bulletin*, was also issued at that time. It provided information in a much abbreviated form and pointed members to the appropriate places on the SSP Web site for more

details. Publication of the *SSP Bulletin* ceased in 2000. To some extent, that publication served as "push technology" while the membership was getting accustomed to turning to the Web for news notes, articles, and technical information.

In 2006, SSP reached an agreement with the U.K.-based Association for Learned and Professional Publishers to cosponsor the publication of *Learned Publishing* (ISSN 0953-1513, Online ISSN: 1741-4857). The North American editor and several editorial board appointments are made by SSP. Priscilla Markwood, American Society for Investigative Pathology, the first editor appointed by SSP, was succeeded in 2008 by Janet Fisher, Publishers Consulting Group.

Led by volunteers Alix Vance, CQ Press, and John Shaw, Sage Publications, SSP invested in an extensive Web site redesign and moved to a new platform in 2007. The SSPNET.ORG Web site includes a Wiki workspace for committees and the Board. In addition to the online membership directory, a calendar of events, a job bank, and the means for conducting Society business, the SSP Web site contains a News page for information on topics of interest to those involved in the diverse areas of scholarly publication; Publications and Links, with access to a vast array of resources as well as members-only access to *Learned Publishing*; member news releases; Standards Watch, which provides information about the development and implementation of standards in the information industry; and the Services Directory, where members can list their services for hire.

With the launch of the redesigned Web site, *SSPN* founding Editor in Chief Barbara Meyers Ford, Meyers Consulting Services, and Managing Editor Lois Smith, Human Factors and Ergonomics Society, developed a new e-mail-format newsletter, *SSP News*. Published up to 8 times per year, it contains news and articles of interest to members. Currently, Meyers leads an editorial team that includes Associate Editor Patricia Baskin, *Neurology*, and Managing Editor Holly Manning, American Society for Clinical Pharmacology and Therapeutics.

In 2008, the Society launched a blog, The Scholarly Kitchen (http://scholarlykitchen.sspnet.org/), which is written by Kent Anderson, *New England Journal of Medicine*, as well as initial guest contributors Philip Davis, a doctoral student at Cornell University, and Howard Ratner, Nature Publishing Group.

FUTURE PLANS

The Society for Scholarly Publishing continues to grow and develop, helping its members continue to succeed as scholarly communication itself changes. Networking opportunities are perhaps best realized through service on committees, task forces, and publications. A member survey conducted in fall 2008, for which there was a 38% response rate, revealed that members gave the highest ratings to the annual meeting and other networking opportunities, in-person seminars, and the member directory. Analysis of survey responses indicates that what members need and expect from SSP is ongoing access to information that is relevant to how people do their jobs both strategically and practically. The consonance of that desire with SSP's mission statement suggests that the Society can look forward to at least another 30 years of success as it strives "to advance scholarly publishing and communication and the professional development of its members through education, collaboration, and networking among individuals in the field."

REFERENCES

1. Spilhaus, Jr., A.F. Conference summary. IEEE Trans. Prof. Commun. **1973**, *PC-16*(2), 50–53.
2. Special issue: Record of the 1975 IEEE conference on scientific journals. IEEE Trans. Prof. Commun. **1975**, *PC-18*(3), 85–308.
3. Special issue: Record of the 1977 IEEE conference on scientific journals. IEEE Trans. Prof. Commun. **1977**, *PC-20*(2), 49–136.
4. Meyers, B.E. The society for scholarly publishing. Sch. Publ. **1979**, *10*(3), 271–274.
5. Lufkin, J.M. Observations of a Godfather. *1979 SSP Proceedings*; Society for Scholarly Publishing: Washington, DC, 1980; 70–71.

Smithsonian–Society

Society for the History of Authorship, Reading and Publishing (SHARP)

Beth Luey
Fairhaven, Massachusetts, U.S.A.

Abstract

The history, organization, activities, and publications of the Society for the History of Authorship, Reading and Publishing (SHARP) are described.

INTRODUCTION

The Society for the History of Authorship, Reading and Publishing (SHARP) is an international association of scholars, librarians, and book trade professionals interested in the history of print culture in all its manifestations, from papyri to the World Wide Web. Founded in 1991, SHARP now has more than a thousand members in more than 20 countries, with every continent except Antarctica represented. Its activities include holding annual meetings and special conferences; maintaining a Web site and an electronic discussion list; offering prizes; and publishing a newsletter and an annual journal.[1]

HISTORY OF THE ORGANIZATION

The history of the book—also known as the history of print culture—has long been incorporated into a variety of academic disciplines, including bibliography, cultural and intellectual history, literary criticism, journalism, sociology, librarianship, business history, textual editing, legal history, and the history of education. The scholarly activities of book historians were thus scattered among a wide range of learned and professional societies, such as those of historians, educators, sociologists, librarians, and literary critics, and the professional organizations of publishers and booksellers. Despite this lack of formal unity, book historians around the world had undertaken large-scale research projects to study the national histories of the book. Such projects were under way in England, Scotland, Ireland, Wales, Germany, France, Canada, Australia, and the United States. Book historians thus felt the need for an organization to bring together those active in national projects as well as those interested in the history of print culture, regardless of academic discipline or professional activity. The purpose of such an organization would be to promote teaching and research in the field, and to enhance the visibility and status of the field itself. In 1991, two such scholars—Jonathan Rose, an American historian, and Simon Eliot, a British historian—organized the first conference dedicated exclusively to the history of the book. This conference, held at the Graduate Center of the City University of New York, marked the beginning of SHARP.

Perhaps because its origins lie in so many disciplines, SHARP maintains close ties with other scholarly and professional organizations, including the American Historical Association, the American Printing History Association, and the Modern Languages Association. In some cases (AHA and MLA, for example), these ties are formal, with joint sessions organized at meetings. In other cases, the links are more casual: SHARP maintains liaisons with more than a dozen other scholarly societies.

ORGANIZATION AND OFFICERS

The Society for the History of Authorship, Reading and Publishing is organized under a constitution that was revised in 2007. It provides for an executive council consisting of a president, vice president, treasurer, recording secretary, membership secretary, director of electronic resources, external affairs director, director for publications and awards, and one member at large. It is further governed by a board of directors with 15–20 members. All officers are elected. Standing committees are the nominating committee (elected), and two conference committees, one for local arrangements and the other for the program. The organization's daily business (membership and periodical fulfillment) is conducted by the Johns Hopkins University Press.

The founders of the organization, Jonathan Rose and Simon Eliot, served as its first two presidents. They were succeeded by James L. W. West III, Beth Luey, Robert Patten, and Leslie Howsam. Officers have generally been drawn from the Anglophone world, but the board of directors has been more inclusive. The international aspect of SHARP is most visible, however, in its conferences.

Encyclopedia of Library and Information Sciences, Fourth Edition DOI: 10.1081/E-ELIS4-120044830

ACTIVITIES

The Society for the History of Authorship, Reading and Publishing alternates its annual meetings roughly between North America and Europe, with focused meetings on other continents. North America meetings have been held in New York, Worcester (Massachusetts), Washington, Williamsburg, Vancouver, Claremont (California), Madison (Wisconsin), Minneapolis, and Halifax. European meetings have been held in London, Edinburgh, Cambridge, Oxford, Lyon, Mainz, and The Hague. In addition, meetings other than the annual conferences have been held in Calcutta, Cape Town, Sydney, Wellington, Venice, and Copenhagen.

Presentations at SHARP conferences are competitive, with proposals vetted by that year's program committee. The conferences are notable for the wide range of topics covered in presentations. Geographical coverage includes all continents; chronological coverage begins with the earliest scribal cultures and extends to the World Wide Web; genres discussed include children's books, literature, genre fiction, journalism, and propaganda; and topics covered include reading, authorship, illustration, bookselling, book design, marketing, book arts, printing technology, the economics of publishing, and book collecting. Roundtable sessions on teaching and curriculum are included in nearly every conference. Plenary speakers are distinguished scholars or creative writers chosen by the local arrangements committee. Another notable feature of SHARP conferences is the great variety of presenters. A panel might include the holder of an endowed professorship, a rare book dealer, and a graduate student. Although most papers are presented in English, some of the conferences have been bilingual, with simultaneous translation offered.

Between conferences, much of the conversation among SHARP members is conducted on the electronic discussion list, SHARP-L, through research questions, calls for papers, announcements of publications, and organizational business. Because members are located around the world, and because many of them are librarians at large research institutions, members are able to locate sources and have questions answered very efficiently. In addition, points of view from outside North America and northern Europe are represented, broadening and enlivening the discussions. The list is moderated and archived. It is open to nonmembers.

The Society for the History of Authorship, Reading and Publishing also maintains a Web site (http://www.sharpweb.org) that provides membership information, links to research projects, online resources (finding aids, research collections, and other materials), teaching syllabi and materials, and publications (periodicals, monographs, textbooks, and online collections).

The Society for the History of Authorship, Reading and Publishing offers three prizes, all presented at the annual meeting. The first prize established was the book history prize, renamed the George A. and Jean S. DeLong Book History Prize in 2004, when it was endowed by the DeLong family. The prize, administered by a changing panel of judges, is awarded annually to the author of the "best book on any aspect of the creation, dissemination or uses of script or print." The winners to date have been:

1997 Ellen Gruber Garvey, *The Adman in the Parlor* (Oxford University Press).
1998 Adrian Johns, *The Nature of the Book* (University of Chicago Press).
1999 Scott Casper, *Constructing American Lives* (University of North Carolina Press).
2000 Kevin Sharpe, *Reading Revolutions* (Yale University Press).
2001 Jonathan Rose, *The Intellectual Life of the British Working Class* (Yale University Press).
2002 Elizabeth McHenry, *Forgotten Readers* (Duke University Press).
2003 Janine Barchas, *Graphic Design, Print Culture, and the Eighteenth-Century Novel* (Cambridge University Press).
2004 Simone Murray, *Mixed Media* (University of Michigan Press).
2005 Heather Andrea Williams, *Self-Taught* (University of North Carolina Press).
2006 Rimi B. Chatterjee, *Empires of the Mind* (Oxford University Press, New Delhi).
2007 James Raven, *The Business of Books* (Yale University Press).

Because so much work in book history is the product of collaborative research, SHARP also gives an Award for Distinguished Achievement every other year. This award goes to an institution, a research team, or a project that has produced a printed volume or volumes or a digital product. The first award, given in 2004, was to *Bibles imprimés du XVe au XVIIIe siècle conservés à Paris*, a catalog of the early modern printed Bibles that survive in the main Parisian libraries, edited by Martime Delaveau and Denise Hillard. The 2006 award was shared equally by two projects: the Archive of Publishers' Records at the University of Reading Library, England, for its archival, research, and service contributions to book history; and the *Waterloo Directory of English Newspapers and Periodicals, 1800–1900*, a reference work essential to the study of print culture in the nineteenth century. The prize was not awarded in 2008.

Finally, SHARP gives an award each year to the best article on book history submitted by a graduate student to its annual journal, *Book History*. The winner receives a cash prize and publication in the journal.

PUBLICATIONS

The Society for the History of Authorship, Reading and Publishing publishes a quarterly newsletter and an annual journal. *SHARP News* (ISSN 1073–1725) includes essays, book and exhibit reviews, reports on the annual conference and other meetings of interest, calls for papers, conference announcements, a listing of new publications, notes and queries, and book history news. It is edited by Sydney Shep at Victoria University of Wellington, New Zealand.

In 1998, SHARP launched its annual peer-reviewed journal, *Book History* (ISSN 1098–7371 and ISBN varies year to year), whose first issue won the Council of Editors of Learned Journals prize for the best new journal. The journal's editors are Ezra Greenspan (Southern Methodist University) and Jonathan Rose (Drew University), who are advised by a 22-person editorial board. It is published by Penn State University Press, whose Web site provides the following description:

> *Book History* publishes articles on the history of the book, broadly defined as the history of the creation, dissemination, and reception of script and print. It will publish research on the social, economic, and cultural history of authorship, editing, printing, the book arts, publishing, the book trade, periodicals, newspapers, ephemera, copyright, censorship, literary agents, libraries, literary criticism, canon formation, literacy, literary education, reading habits, and reader response.[2]

Although articles are published in English and most frequently cover the Anglophone world, they have also included work on the history of print culture throughout the rest of the world, including the Netherlands, France, Russia, Finland, China, the Philippines, Japan, Latin America, India, Nigeria, and Germany. Subjects covered include popular literature, religious reading and publishing, bookselling, censorship, paratext, library history, publishing in wartime, translation, children's literature, reading practices, and quantitative research.

CONCLUSION

Although a relatively young organization, SHARP has achieved its founding goal of providing a forum for the advancement of book history as an international scholarly enterprise. Its membership continues to grow and expand geographically, and its conferences (annual and focused) are well attended. Its prize-winning journal, like SHARP itself, continues to expand the scope of its coverage.

REFERENCES

1. http://www.sharpweb.org.
2. http://www.psupress.org/journals/jnls_main.html.

Society of American Archivists (SAA)

Timothy L. Ericson
School of Information Science, University of Wisconsin-Milwaukee, Milwaukee, Wisconsin, U.S.A.

Steven L. Hensen
Rare Book, Manuscript and Special Collections Library, Duke University, Durham, North Carolina, U.S.A.

Abstract

The Society of American Archivists (SAA), founded in 1936, is North America's oldest and largest national professional archival organization that serves the education and information needs of more than 5000 individual and institutional members. The Society of American Archivists also provides national and international leadership for archivists on issues that relate to the identification, preservation, and accessibility of public and private records that have historical value. From ancient papyri to contemporary digital images, such records, created and preserved as evidence of communication, have been an integral aspect of human culture for thousands of years. Archivists traditionally have administered historical record formats such as photographs, moving image film, maps, and textual documents, but today they also deal with the emerging array of electronic communication media, such as audio and video recordings and "born digital" documents such as letters, memoranda, government reports, committee records, and blueprints. An important part of SAA's work also includes ensuring the preservation of a diverse and representative documentary heritage as well as promoting diversity within its membership and the archives profession as a whole. The Society of American Archivists advocates actively on behalf of archivists regarding issues such as access to public records that are important to the profession, and it cooperates with regional, national, and international archives organizations and such allied professional groups as those representing librarians, records managers, historians, and documentary editors.

INTRODUCTION

The Society of American Archivists (SAA), founded in 1936, is North America's oldest and largest national professional archival organization that serves the education and information needs of more than 5000 individual and institutional members. The Society of American Archivists also provides national and international leadership for archivists on issues that relate to the identification, preservation, and use of public and private records of historical value. Archival records encompass the entire range of documentation that human society and culture has created as evidence of communication—from ancient papyri to contemporary digital images. They include traditional and historical record formats such as photographs, moving image film, maps, and textual documents as well as the emerging array of electronic communication media, such as audio and video recordings and "born digital" documents such as letters, memoranda, government reports, committee records, and blueprints. An important part of SAA's work also includes ensuring the preservation of a diverse and representative documentary heritage as well as diversity within its membership and the archives profession as a whole. The Society of American Archivists also advocates on behalf of archivists regarding issues

such as access to public records that are important to the profession, and cooperates with regional, national, and international archives organizations and such allied professional groups as those representing librarians, records managers, historians, and documentary editors.

HISTORY OF THE SAA

The historical roots of SAA date back to the early nineteenth century. As early as 1810, Congress appointed a committee to "inquire into the state of the ancient public records of the United States," but no significant action resulted from the committee's findings beyond constructing three additional fireproof records vaults in which to store government records. At about the same time, the formation of local and state historical societies devoted to collecting the private papers and memorabilia of famous individuals as well as the official documents of government increased interest in finding more efficient ways of preserving their materials. By the early 1800s, one Ohio society developed a manner of protecting its documents in "air-tight metallic cases, regularly numbered and indexed, so that it may be known what is in each case without opening it." Following the Civil War, Congress

Encyclopedia of Library and Information Sciences, Fourth Edition DOI: 10.1081/E-ELIS4-120044954

despaired of finding an effective way of preserving the voluminous records of that conflict and instead allocated money to select the "important" documents and publish them in a massive 128-volume series titled *The War of the Rebellion*: *A Compilation of the Official Records of the Union and Confederate Armies*. There was no consistency in any of the early efforts to preserve historically valuable records and each archive developed its own system of organization and storage, with varying degrees of success. It was not until the end of the nineteenth century that archival theories and practices had evolved to the point at which practitioners at societies and associations began to share their knowledge with each other, taking the first steps toward formation of a distinct archives profession in the United States.

The American Historical Association (AHA), created in 1884, took on as one of its major priorities the development of standardized systems of archival organization by facilitating interaction among the various independent archives. The AHA created several subgroups, including the Historical Manuscripts Commission (1895), the Public Archives Commission (1899) and, in 1909, a Conference of Archivists that met annually in conjunction with the AHA. This Conference of Archivists worked to establish new archives, to promote and improve those already in existence, and to codify archival methodology. In 1912, the group began plans to publish a "Manual of Archival Economy" as a basic how-to text for archivists. Although the onset of World War I and other factors worked against the completion of this project, its beginning underscored the seriousness with which the Conference on Archivists viewed its responsibility to improve the care of historical records.

During this time there was also an increased awareness of the importance of archival records at the state level. Alabama established the country's first state archives in 1901, followed a year later by Mississippi. However, it was not until the 1930s that the federal government was moved to action. President Franklin D. Roosevelt's Work Projects Administration created the Historical Records Survey and funded the first-ever Survey of Federal Archives. In 1934, Congress followed this lead by founding the National Archives in an effort to centralize recordkeeping and preservation that previously had been the responsibility of individual government agencies.

Establishment of the National Archives was a watershed event in many ways. It signaled a stronger governmental recognition of and support for its responsibility to preserve its records. At the same time, members of the Conference of Archivists realized that a distinction should be made between historians and scholars (who used archival materials) and archivists (who organized, managed, and made records available for use by historians and others). Archivists came to recognize that they belonged to a distinct profession for which they needed their own professional association to advance their work and

promote their common interests. The Society of American Archivists was founded in December 1936, ". . .to promote sound principles of archival economy and to facilitate cooperation among archivists and archival agencies." A more democratic body than its predecessor, it opened its ranks not just to directors of large archival institutions, but to all "who are or have been engaged in the custody or administration of archives or historical manuscripts." Although the original membership of SAA was composed primarily of archivists who worked for government agencies in and around Washington, D.C., archives of all sizes and orientation—from small private and business archives to large historical collections—also were included.

Once born, SAA acted quickly. A president (A. R. Newsome) and a board of directors were elected by its initial 124 individual and 4 institutional members. In its first full year, membership increased to 243 archivists and institutions, and SAA began the practice of holding an annual convention at which professional papers were delivered, information was exchanged, and philosophies of archival organization were discussed. At the June 1937 convention, President Newsome outlined a course for SAA that has been followed to the present day: "To become the practical self-help agency of archivists for the solution of their complex problems" and "to strive to nationalize archival information and technique"; to seek "the solution of archival problems involving external relations with all archival agencies, with learned societies, and with the public"; and "to encourage the development of a genuine archival profession in the United States" in which SAA would "set training standards and advance archival administration through its meetings and publications." Primary among these publications was the society's journal of record, *The American Archivist*, whose premiere issue appeared in January 1938.

Volunteer members ran SAA under a tight economy during the final years of the Great Depression and throughout World War II. At war's end, SAA supported the formation of the International Council of Archives in order to encourage and facilitate exchanges among foreign and domestic archives. By the 1950s, SAA focused even greater attention on the necessity for codifying common archival techniques, such as selecting documents for preservation, and methods of organization and indexing. As the number of repositories and archives grew steadily, it became more and more important that systematic and consistent practices be widely adopted. These included criteria for identifying and prioritizing records (SAA formed a Committee on the Reduction of Archival Material in order to find ways to reduce the bulk of redundant or unnecessary material without jeopardizing the quality of information), sharing the most advanced techniques of document preservation, and standardizing the method of indexing and cataloging records.

As time passed, developments in technology offered some solutions to the problems of archival standardization, but also created even more complex issues. Improved or expanded technologies have been a vital concern of SAA throughout its history. In the pages of *The American Archivist* there are references to or articles on the photostatic copying of important and perishable documents (1939), the use of microfilm (1940), photocopying (1951), computers (1963), and automated information handling (1966). To solve problems of interinstitutional cooperation in automated formats, SAA in 1977 formed the National Information Systems Task Force, which explored common ground among archives of all sizes, subjects, and formats and that same year created the Archival and Manuscripts Control format of the United States Machine Readable Cataloging format, to enable archivists and manuscript curators to use a common language in creating online cataloging records for loading into bibliographic systems. In 1995, a group of archivists and description experts, working with the Bentley Historical Library, the Library of Congress, and several funding agencies, took the next step by developing an encoding standard for archival description and finding aids. This standard, called Encoded Archival Description, released in its full version in 1998, enables the sharing of detailed archival information via the World Wide Web.

Concurrently with the effort to develop a cataloging standard, SAA was involved in improving other standards within the profession. Previously records were in the hands of clerks, secretaries, public officials, and others who had little or no training in their care and preservation. Even after World War II few schools offered courses in archival theory and practice and there were no set professional guidelines outlining what should be included in an archival curriculum. Archivists agreed that they required specific knowledge and skills, but there was no clear path toward obtaining them. The Society of American Archivists became a strong advocate for improved archival education programs at the graduate level. In 1977, SAA formalized the first graduate education guidelines for university training of archivists, calling for a minimum three-course sequence within a library science or history graduate program. Since that time SAA's guidelines for graduate archival education programs have been revised and strengthened several times as the work of archivists became more complex and increasingly influenced by technology and the law.

Also in 1977, SAA began planning a more comprehensive continuing education curriculum by offering a series of workshops and seminars in conjunction with its annual meeting in Salt Lake City, Utah. The seminars focused on core archival responsibilities and were so popular that SAA laid plans to expand its continuing education program to reach those archivists who were already on the job. In 1980, a grant-funded "Basic Archival Conservation" program was started and proved to be very successful with on-the-job professionals who had never had formal education in this area. In 1982, SAA expanded this initiative by establishing a permanent education office at its Chicago headquarters in order to develop and coordinate a regular schedule of continuing education workshops, seminars, institutes and other offerings, both in conjunction with its annual meeting and throughout the year, frequently in conjunction with regional archival association meetings. The continuing education program has grown over the years and recently has begun to offer distance education learning opportunities as a cost-effective alternative for archivists who are not able to travel great distances for on-site workshops and seminars.

During the 1970s, SAA took the lead in developing a more extensive *corpus* of archival literature. Prior to that time, *The American Archivist* was the primary source of information on professional practice, along with literature from the National Archives (such as its staff information bulletins and circulars, a few monographs expanded from these publications, and translations of European classics such as the 1898 Dutch *Manual for the Arrangement and Description of Archives* that the National Archives coordinated). But in 1977 SAA undertook publication of a grant-funded "Basic Manual Series" that covered all aspects of core archival practice and served as guidebooks for a generation of archivists. This series was replaced in the mid-1980s with a series titled "Archival Fundamentals" and recently has been supplanted by a third set of core manuals for archivists (Archival Fundamentals II). In addition to these series of core manuals, SAA also has published books and monographs by contracting with individual authors and cooperating with other presses that publish in this area. Today SAA is the largest producer and distributor of archival literature in the world.

Its work in publishing *The American Archivist*, developing standards, planning and implementing conferences, initiating a basic manual series, and developing a continuing education program could not be sustained indefinitely with a part-time volunteer staff. In 1974, the SAA hired its first full-time executive director and established its national office on the Chicago campus of the University of Illinois. The subsequent hiring of editors, meeting planners, and other staff enabled SAA to achieve some of the goals that its members had long requested. A permanent staff also enabled SAA to become more effective in acquiring grant funding and completing strategic planning to guide future actions.

MEMBERSHIP INTEREST GROUPS

An increasing range of repository types and record formats has resulted in the creation of membership interest groups within SAA. Beginning in 1978, the Society established a series of Professional Affinity Groups that brought together archivists with common special interests. Twenty years later this initiative has developed into an extensive network of "Sections" and "Roundtables" that work within the Society. These groups undertake a variety of activities that typically include conducting business at the SAA annual meeting; submitting program proposals; producing directories, newsletters, and other publications; maintaining Web sites; and identifying and providing input to SAA regarding emerging issues and other areas of professional concern. The number and focus of Sections and Roundtables is member-driven and has evolved over the years. Currently these groups include the following:

Sections: Composed of SAA members who share a common interest resulting from the nature of their work or by the type of repository in which they are employed. Sections enable members to focus attention on and give voice to the concerns that fall within their particular area of interest. Sections focus expertise on the professional functions and responsibilities that archivists share to identify, administer, and promote the use of records of enduring value. Current sections include:

Acquisitions and appraisal—Serves as a forum for the discussion of issues and interests pertaining to the acquisition and appraisal of public records, private papers, and other archival or manuscript collections.

Archivists of religious collections—Composed of professional archivists who work for national, international, and local church organizations, religious societies and orders, and theological schools. The section's members are engaged in documenting the many facets of the private and public experience with faith as it is lived out through the institutional church, religious movements, and individual experience.

Business archives—Includes members who are employed in corporations or who administer records of corporations and businesses from an historical and archival standpoint. This section also maintains an online *Directory of Business Archivists*.

College and university archives—Composed of members who are employed or have an interest in the administration, organization, and care of records of institutions of higher education. The section has published an online publication entitled *Guidelines for College and University Archives*.

Description—Includes persons involved in the development of appropriate means to organize and describe manuscripts and archives so that they may be more easily used by researchers.

Electronic records—Functions as a locus of expertise, leadership, and information sharing for the profession regarding management and preservation of records in electronic form.

Government records—Composed of archivists whose primary concern is with the administration, organization, care, and use of government records at the local, state, or federal level.

Manuscript repositories—Serves as a forum for professionals employed by historical societies and similar repositories that collect records from a variety of private, family, or government organizations.

Museum archives—Includes persons responsible for the organization, preservation, and use of records located in museums.

Oral history—Members have a special interest in the administration and use of oral history interviews in the archival setting. This section also includes members who conduct oral history interviews and those who teach oral history methodology.

Preservation—Includes persons with a special interest in the problems presented by the deterioration, restoration, and preservation of archival materials in all formats.

Reference, access, and outreach—Brings together members who work with archival researchers, particularly those with reference responsibilities and those who have an interest in using archival and manuscript materials in exhibits and other public programs.

Visual materials—Composed of members who collect, arrange, describe, preserve, or interpret still photographs, moving images, art, and graphic material.

Roundtables, like SAA sections, enable professionals to focus their attention on concerns that fall within a particular area of interest. *Membership in roundtables is freely open to SAA members and non-members alike.* Roundtables function as communities of interest that generate ideas and meet the intellectual interests of their members. They focus expertise and interest on specific professional functions and responsibilities that archivists must perform to carry out their mission. Roundtables also provide channels of communication to the SAA membership and to the SAA Council on topical matters of concern. The creation of roundtables is also member-driven and they may exist as online communities that share information through electronic discussion groups. The current roster of SAA Roundtables includes:

Architectural records—Provides a forum for members to discuss issues related to preservation, access, and management of architectural records and related fields.

Archival educators—Facilitates the exchange of information about archival education programs throughout the United States and Canada and provides a forum for the discussion of issues relevant to those who teach courses and workshops in archival administration and related topics in academic institutions or other settings.

Archival history—Composed of those who have an interest in the history of the archives profession and who promote ways of studying this history.

Archives management—Brings together archivists from different institutional settings who share an interest in the identification and consideration of management and leadership issues and techniques that are important to archivists and archival institutions.

Archivists and archives of color—Provides a forum to identify and discuss concerns that racial minorities face and encourages an exchange of ideas by archivists with diverse racial backgrounds. The roundtable also promotes wider participation of minorities within the archives profession and promotes the preservation of archival materials pertaining to minorities. Members support the development of archival services and programs to minorities and seek funding for scholarships for minority students in library/information science master's degree programs.

Congressional papers—Provides a venue for discussing archival issues related to the acquisition, processing, and administration of the papers of members of the United States Congress.

Encoded archival description—Supports the implementation, use, and ongoing development of this international encoding standard for finding aids.

Issues and advocacy—Dedicated to monitoring current and emerging issues of concern to archivists and formulating for SAA Council's consideration responses to such issues.

International affairs—Identifies and addresses issues and concerns of archives and archivists throughout the world and provides a forum for discussion, dissemination, and promotion of issues related to international archival affairs.

Labor archives—Promotes communication among archivists and institutions concerned with records in the field of organized labor and develops cooperative strategies and guidelines to ensure comprehensive documentation of the labor movement.

LAGAR (*Lesbian and Gay Archives Roundtable*)—Includes archivists concerned with ensuring that the archival record includes documentation of lesbian, gay, bisexual, and transgender history and culture. Members work to ensure that LGBT archival issues are identified and visible within SAA and they serve as liaisons between independent LGBT archives and SAA.

Latin American and Caribbean Cultural Heritage Archives—Provides a forum to exchange ideas and provide support among US, Caribbean and Latin American archivists about the challenges and opportunities they face of acquiring, managing, and preserving their collections.

Local government records—Provides dialog among archivists concerned with the acquisition, administration, organization, preservation, and use of records from local government offices.

Lone arrangers—Provides education, stimulates communication, and encourages support among archivists working in "lone arranger" settings. The term "lone arranger" includes those working alone or with a very small staff.

Metadata and digital object roundtable—Promotes discussion, education, and collaboration among archivists who are interested in digital archival objects and the metadata that enables their access, management, and preservation.

Native American archives—Serves as a forum to educate archivists on the complexities and beauty of Native American archives throughout the western hemisphere and as a source of communication and support for archivists working with Native American collections.

Performing arts—Encourages the exchange of information on historical and contemporary documentation of music, dance, theater, and other performance media.

Privacy and confidentiality—Provides a forum for the discussion of privacy and confidentiality issues as well as their legal and ethical implications for archival practice.

Recorded sound—Serves as a forum for discussing the importance, preservation, and use of sound recordings in archival collections.

Records management—Encourages discussion of current issues in records and information management and promotes better understanding of the importance of collaborative efforts between archivists and records managers.

RLG (Research Libraries Group)—Promotes discussion and exchange of information about current RLG program initiatives and research projects affecting the archival community.

Science, technology, and health care—Provides a forum for archivists with similar interests or holdings in science, technology, and health care, including medicine, and provides an opportunity to exchange information, solve problems, and share successes.

Security—Focuses on issues relating to the prevention of theft in archival and manuscript repositories.

Visual materials cataloging and access—Provides a venue for archivists with visual collections to discuss cataloging and access issues.

Women archivists—Monitors the status of women in the archives profession and promotes the participation of women in all phases of SAA's activities and the profession as a whole.

Women's collections—Promotes the preservation and research use of records documenting women and networks archivists with holdings concerning or created by women.

DIVERSITY

In 2003, SAA established a Diversity Committee that works to ensure that the organization's services, activities, policies, communications, and products support the goal of a more diverse SAA and professional archival community. The Diversity Committee has been a catalyst for new initiatives that are developed in coordination with various

SAA groups. It also monitors, evaluates, advocates for, and reports on matters pertaining to diversity as it relates to the archives profession, including membership recruiting, program planning, documentation of minority groups, professional development, and cooperating with other organizations that have similar interests and aims.

The 2005 SAA Position Statement on Diversity affirms:

> The Society of American Archivists is committed to integrating diversity concerns and perspectives into all aspects of its activities and into the fabric of the profession as a whole. SAA is also committed to the goal of a Society membership that reflects the broad diversity of American society. SAA believes that these commitments are essential to the effective pursuit of the archival mission to ensure the identification, preservation, and use of the nation's historical record.

SAA further noted that, "The relevance of archives to society and the completeness of the national record hinge in part on the profession's ensuring that its members and the holdings of American repositories reflect more fully the diversity of society as a whole."

In support of its diversity activities, SAA also applied for and received a two-year grant, "Strengthening Tribal Archives Programs," that facilitated and supported the attendance and participation of Native American archivists in the Society's annual meeting.

GOVERNANCE AND MEMBER SERVICES

Today SAA maintains permanent headquarters in the Loop area of Chicago, staffed by an executive director and 11 other employees with responsibilities for production and sale of publications, meetings, membership development, financial operations, and continuing education. The Society is governed by a nine-member Council (serving three-year terms, with three new members elected each year) as well as a treasurer, vice-president/president-elect, and president, who presides over the meetings. Within the Council there is an executive committee consisting of the president, vice-president, treasurer, an at-large member elected from and by the Council, and the executive director. The Society of American Archivists also has a number of standing committees and boards that generally have more official, advisory, and administrative responsibilities than do the sections and roundtables and that help to oversee different aspects of the Society's operation. These include: *American Archivist* Editorial Board, Appointments Committee, Awards Committee, Committee on Education, Committee on Ethics and Professional Development, Committee on the Selection of SAA Fellows, Diversity Committee, Fellows Steering Committee, Membership Committee, Publications Board, Standards

Committee, and an annual meeting Program Committee and Host Committee.

An election is held in February of each year to elect an incoming vice-president/president-elect, a treasurer (once every 3 years), three incoming members of the Council, and members of the Nominating Committee.

The Society of American Archivists also supports a Mentoring Program that pairs new archivists with experienced professionals. The program is designed to assist those who are in the early years of their career or who are taking on new or additional responsibilities in their work. Every effort is made to pair those with similar professional positions and, when possible, geographical proximity. Although much of the mentoring activity occurs by telephone or e-mail, the Mentoring Program is also given a place in the annual meeting program so that mentors and protégés can meet in person and become better acquainted.

More than two dozen student chapters of the SAA have been established around the country since 1993. These chapters serve as a means of introducing new archivists into the profession, as well as enhancing education by providing an additional focus for students to discuss archival issues, identify with the profession, and engage in professional activities. The chapters also promote communication among student members and ultimately develop leaders of tomorrow's archives profession.

ADVOCACY OUTREACH AND COOPERATION

The Society of American Archivists continues to be actively involved in advocating on behalf of a wide range of professional issues related to the work of archivists. For example, SAA was one of a number of signatories to an *amicus curiae* brief arguing for allowing access to the papers of the "Unabomber." The SAA Council and officers were active in testifying and coordinating with 30 other archives and historical organizations opposing the process by which the Archivist of the United States was appointed in 2004, and SAA issued a public statement regarding the renewal of the USA PATRIOT Act. In cooperation with the National Coalition for History, SAA signed a letter supporting the permanent preservation of Guantanamo Bay detainee court case files and joined with other organizations in speaking out against *Executive Order 13233*, which gave former presidents and their heirs the right to keep White House papers secret indefinitely. Along with many other archives and historical organizations, SAA joined in supporting efforts to save records that had been damaged during Hurricanes Katrina and Rita, and co-signed with the Council of State Archivists and the National Association of Government Archives and Records Administrators a statement requesting cooperation in identifying and halting the sale of public records on eBay. In 2006, SAA issued a public statement, addressed to the Archivist of the United States, opposing the clandestine reclassification of public records that had previously been declassified and made available to researchers.

Hurricane Katrina also provided a catalyst for establishing an annual program, "MayDay: Saving Our Archives," designed to heighten awareness of the importance of preserving historical records. The Society of American Archivists also participates in "American Archives Month" each October and has developed a public relations kit that archivists can use to promote activities that support their programs.

The Society of American Archivists supports an active outreach program that makes information available to archivists and others who are not members of the Society. Many SAA publications, including the *Glossary of Archival and Records Terminology* and several sets of guidelines are available on its Web site to anyone interested in seeing them. Nonmembers are permitted to join SAA roundtables and view section and roundtable newsletters to facilitate networking with other archivists who share common interests. The Society of American Archivists's online employment bulletin, the most comprehensive source of information on jobs within the archives profession, is accessible by members and nonmembers alike.

CURRENT PUBLICATIONS

In addition to *The American Archivist*, the Society also publishes a bi-monthly newsletter, *Archival Outlook*, which carries news and articles of a more timely nature covering current business and actions of the Society; regular columns by the Society's president and executive director and the Archivist of the United States; national and international news relating to archives and archivists; a calendar of upcoming events of interest to archivists; and professional opportunities. Issues of *Archival Outlook* are available online from Vol. 53, 1, 1990 issue. Beginning in 2008, *The American Archivist* has been published both in print and online versions available to members and subscribers. Access to American Archivist Online is limited to SAA members and journal subscribers for a period of 3 years, after which issues become publicly available at no cost. The Society of American Archivists is in the process of making back issues available online as well.

In addition to these publications, the Society maintains an Internet site on the World Wide Web at http://www.archivists.org. This site carries detailed information about the Society, its various sections and roundtables, a membership directory (accessible only to SAA members), an employment bulletin, a full publications catalog, information on professional education and recognition, and news of the annual conference. The Web site includes a number of important publications, including a *Code of Ethics for Archivists*, *Guidelines for a Graduate Program in*

Archival Studies, *Guidelines for Archival Continuing Education Programs*, and *Glossary of Archival and Records Terminology*. Recently the SAA has added a number of case studies and classic monographs on archival management that are not available in print. The Web site also carries a list of "hot topics" covering news, reports, workshop information, a listing of SAA position statements and resolutions, and other topics of more immediate interest.

CONCLUSION

The Society of American Archivists, as the primary professional organization representing a large number of archivists, curators, special collections librarians, educators, and records managers in the United States today, often finds itself on the cutting edge of many important national policy issues as information—especially the digital transmission of that information—plays an increasingly central role in the economic, educational, and cultural life of the country and of the world. Thus the topics of electronic records, digitization, Internet access to the nation's documentary heritage, preservation (of both rapidly deteriorating original materials as well as digital copies of those materials) and copyright, intellectual property rights, and "fair use" are all issues with which today's archivists are much concerned and engaged, notwithstanding that basic issues of access, preservation, and use have been at the heart of the archival enterprise from its very beginnings. The Society of American Archivists is often asked to testify before Congress and participate in various national forums, organizations, and committees in which these issues are discussed and debated. As public awareness and wider use of primary sources via the Internet become more widespread and the issues of preservation and access concomitant to those uses become better understood, the SAA is optimistic about its growing visibility and importance in this arena and the additional opportunities this presents in meeting its mission.

BIBLIOGRAPHY

1. A*CENSUS: Archival Census and Educational Needs Survey in the United States. Available at http://www.archivists.org/a-census/. A comprehensive analysis of archivists and the archives profession conducted in 2004. The site includes the original questions and responses as well as several reports and analyses of the data.
2. Burckel, N.C. The society: From birth to maturity. Am. Archivist **1998 (Spring)**, *61* (1), 12–35 (A more analytical look at the history of the SAA membership demographics, annual meetings, and publications).
3. Cook, J.F. The blessing of providence on an association of archivists. Am. Archivist **1983 (Fall)**, *46* (4), 374–399 (An

excellent overview of the history of SAA from 1935 to 1974).

4. Publications relating to archival theory, standards, all aspects of the work of archivists, and the work of the Society in general. Available at http://www.archivists.org/catalog/ catalog/index.html. This catalog includes historical works as well as handbooks, monographs, and other publications on more contemporary issues.

5. Society of American Archivists official Web site. Available at http://www.archivists.org.

Sociology of Reading

Martine Poulain
*Department of Libraries and Documentation, National Institute for the History of Art (INHA),
Paris, France*

Abstract
This entry examines major themes and questions that have been the focus of sociology of reading from the early years of the twentieth century to the present. Theoretical works dealing with the history and sociology of reading are discussed as well as recent large scale surveys of readers in France, Britain, and the United States. The concluding sections deal the issue of functional illiteracy in developed countries and with the global impact of the Internet on reading.

INTRODUCTION

Reading has always been seen as somewhat suspect by religious and political authorities, even in the contemporary era. In the nineteenth century, the elites and the government were concerned with bringing literacy to the people, but at the same time they were troubled about the possible effect of uncontrolled reading. Until the 1920s efforts were made to prevent "bad reading" and to promote "good reading". Such attempts at control became futile in face of the rapid growth in the production of reading materials and the increased number of readers whose choices could not be controlled. However, by the twentieth century the perceived danger of reading had changed in character and what was considered "bad reading" was not the same. In addition, there was concern about the general decrease in reading due to competition from new leisure activities as well as new media. Nonetheless, educators sought to combat the commodification of reading by promoting "good authors." By the end of the century functional illiteracy was recognized as a problem, which, when combined with the diversification of writing (especially through web based media), led certain thinkers to decry the "death of reading."

Even though these ideological debates were rather sterile, the importance that societies accord to the practice of reading became apparent, and sociologists made an effort to describe and to analyze the meaning and value that ordinary readers accord to their reading. The resulting picture was much more nuanced than the utopian discourse of those who believed that the Internet would promote a growth of readership or the dystopian claims of those who deplored the demise of reading.

BAD READING, MARGINAL READERS

Scholars working in the field of book history and those in the sociology of reading both attempted to analyze the various discourses on reading ("discours sur la lecture")—i.e., those prescriptions and symbolic representations that surround individual reading practices and necessarily influence them. In 1902 a school teacher in Aisne complained:

> When all people know how to read…what will they read if one does not carefully, actively and severely monitor their reading. Too often what they are likely to read are those books and newspapers which…little by little sap authority in the name of liberty, exciting evil passions against authority of any kind: everyday they will read wild declarations against authority with renewed pleasure, as well as immoral novels which, by the means of cheap magazines (feuilletons) penetrate into the furthest village where they inflame the sensuality of youth and inspire in them…the unfettered desire for physical pleasure

(*Journal d'un instituteur de l'Aisne*, 1902, quoted in Poulain).[1] The ideas expressed by this teacher were not much different from those expressed during the same period by the clergy who especially feared the novel. For example, according to a 1903 Catholic manual: "The love of reading is one of the passions which, in our days especially, most torments the heart of the young girl, and this dangerous reading which offers another world to her is a stumbling block that is most difficult to avoid because of the strong attraction it has over her" (*Manuel des enfants de Marie Immaculée à l'usage des réunions dirigées par les filles de charité*, 1906, quoted in Chartier).[2] Likewise, a 1919 manual for virtuous young women warned that novel reading should be controlled because it distances the young girl from the real world: "After having read these stories which have penetrated her entire sensibility in an unhealthy fashion, where the imagination is over excited without the control of reason, where the heart is delivered up to a world of emotions and remains as if hypnotized…." After novel reading, the soul is empty and falls into a state of disenchantment and an indefinable

Encyclopedia of Library and Information Sciences, Fourth Edition DOI: 10.1081/E-ELIS4-120044947

Sociology–Special

malaise.[3] Certain kinds of reading were to be especially feared: newspapers whose political ideas were thought likely to lead people to revolt, and the novel, which takes women away from their duty and leads them to an uncontrollable universe of the imagination.

By the twentieth century other genres raised the fears of educators: the detective novel in France, in its "version noire" which originated in America; the comic book (bande dessinée), and science fiction—genres considered "minor" and dangerous, not part of what is considered "real" literature—at least not until they attain respectability and are admitted into the canon.

Certain readers have always been considered "weak readers" (lecteurs fragiles) incapable of putting adequate distance between themselves and the text, being completely absorbed in a simplistic identification with the characters in the novel. This term 'weak reader' was often applied to women readers of novels in the past, and to readers of Harlequin romances today. Certain categories of young people represent another group considered "weak readers" and among them especially young people from immigrant families living in the troubled suburbs of Europe.

THE BEGINNING OF THE SOCIOLOGY OF READING

Nicolas Roubakine (1862–1946), a Russian born scholar who emigrated to Switzerland in 1907, was influenced both by the illiteracy of the Russian masses and by World War I. As a result, Roubakine saw reading as a solution to all the evils that beset humanity. From this perspective, which he regarded as both scientific and activist, he produced numerous publications in an effort to understand various modes of book production as well as their content. However for Roubakine it was most important to understand the modes of "appropriation" of various kinds of works by readers—in other words, how readers interpreted what they read and applied it to their own lives. His grand ambition was to analyze world book production and guide the publishers so that they might produce works that exactly corresponded to the needs and expectations of readers. A utopian vision that was fortunately unrealizable!

It was also this double preoccupation, both scientific and political, that led sociologists in the United States to become interested in the effects of reading and other media on the population. The depression that began in 1929 strongly influenced researchers at the Graduate Library School (GLS) of the University of Chicago, as well as those working at the Gallup poll, which was founded in 1935 as the first institute for conducting large scale surveys. Researchers at GLS, like Douglas Waples and Bernard Berelson, had the ambitious goal of influencing political decisions so that the needs of the population

could be more adequately met. Using surveys they sought to find out who read, what they read, and why; in addition, this research attempted to identify the effect of reading on readers in relationship to socioeconomic circumstances of the time. These researchers observed that the economic crisis had motivated millions of Americans, whether or not they were unemployed, to use their public libraries and that all kinds of reading, but especially newspaper reading, had become a source of moral support for them. Overwhelmed by the effects of the economic depression, which they also saw as a crisis for democracy, the GSL researchers thought that by arriving at a better understanding of how books, newspapers, and radio were received by the public, their research could be used to improve "communication and understanding between the elite and the masses". In the study entitled *What Reading Does to People*, they stated "reading can furnish information and influence attitudes that can promote social tolerance, social cooperation and good government."[4] In Germany, these same preoccupations motivated librarian Walter Hoffmann in his attempt to analyze reading and readers.[5] Despite the utopian character of some of their ideas, researchers active during the 1930s and 1940s forged concepts are still useful today in the study of readers.

Beginning in the 1950s the sociology of books and reading and the history of the book both emerged as academic disciplines and, little by little, both fields have gained in sophistication and rigor. Large scale quantitative surveys on leisure and cultural activities were carried out and these studies allowed scholars to better understand the social landscape of reading. These large scale surveys greatly increased in number, especially after 1980, but such studies did not aid those researchers undertaking scientific analysis of reading practices. Nonetheless the abundance of such surveys is one of the signs of growing social concern surrounding questions dealing with the cultural level of people living in democratic societies. For more than half a century these democracies had been confronted with one preoccupying question in regard to reading: Why had the extension of years of schooling, the increase in the level of education, general economic growth, and the increase in leisure time "not" stimulated a more widespread practice of reading, if not a readership that was more cultivated and exigent?

DOMINANT READERS/DOMINATED READER

During the 1960s numerous sociological studies were produced in response to newly articulated social issues including:

- the necessity of recognizing "popular culture";
- the increased awareness of hegemony exercised by the "legitimate" or dominant culture; and

- the rejection of a "cultural order" in which the values and the hierarchies were those of the dominant class.

Many scholars drew on Richard Hoggart's pioneering book, *The Uses of Literacy: Aspects of Working Class Life* (Chatto and Windus, 1957). The British sociologist showed that the lower classes and the privileged elite related in very different ways to culture and cultural objects, such as writing. To understand this complex relationship to culture, Hoggart took a holistic approach that encompassed the entirety of life experience. For example, he found that among the poor, the modes of relating to texts, such as newspapers and "romans-photos," could be described as "oblique attention," casual, and at the same time an effective practice of reading. Thus the most frequent consumers of photo-romans were not taken in by them, but were able to distance themselves from what they read. The culture of the poor is not the same as the poverty of culture, as had been proposed—in part because access to high culture is of little concern to the poor whose values are elsewhere.

In his influential 1979 work entitled *La Distinction*, French sociologist Pierre Bourdieu (1930–2002) observed that the cultivated elite highly value the cultural distinction which legitimates their status whereas the lower classes prefer to adhere to the norms, interests, values and savoir-faire of their social group. Bourdieu wrote:

It must never be forgotten that the working-class 'aesthetic' is just one dominated 'aesthetic' which is constantly obliged to distinguish itself in terms of the dominant aesthetics. The members of the working class [and especially women] who can neither ignore the high-art aesthetic, which denounces their own "aesthetic," nor abandon their socially conditioned inclinations, but still less proclaim and legitimate them, often experience their relationship to aesthetic norms in a two fold and contradictory way.[5]

On the other hand, the cultural competence of

connaisseurs confers a self-confidence, which correlates with their certainty of having cultural legitimacy and the ease with which they can identify excellence. This produces a paradoxical relationship which is the result of the relative unawareness and the casual assurance in the familiarity that the upper bourgeoisie maintain with culture, that they regard as a kind of family inheritance to which they are the rightful heirs.[5]

The legitimacy of cultural products, including written works, is not an objective fact that arises from their inherent literary value, but rather a social construction that permits a small group to constitute the dominant elite.

As we have seen, on both sides of the Atlantic researchers were beginning to produce a body of scholarship that dealt with the social mechanisms at work in the creation, the diffusion and the sharing of cultural works. These studies also attempted to give space to other cultural practices, to other speech, and to other kinds of relationships with so called "dominant" texts.

READING, A CREATIVE ACT

Today the perspective of researchers is different from that of their predecessors. What has come to the foreground is an exploration of the mode of reception and appropriation of texts. French philosopher and theologian, Michel de Certeau (1925–1986), and cultural historian Roger Chartier (b. 1945) reaffirmed that reading is a creative activity for all categories readers. According to Michel de Certeau (*L'Invention du quotidien*, 1980) each reader, although equipped with unequal savoir-faire and unequal expectations, poaches on the land belonging to others "braconne sur les terres d'autrui."[6] An agent of creative activity, the reader is not simply a passive consumer, but rather someone who brings a text to life, and thus, in a certain fashion, creates a new text. According to noted philosopher Paul Ricoeur (1913–2005) each time a text is read it is a dynamic experience, an emigration through which the reader moves from configuration to reconfiguration of the world.[7] After reading the reader is transformed. According to Roger Chartier, reading affords a space for "distinction and disclosure" ("distinction" et "divulgation"), as well as "discipline and invention."[8,9]

In order to understand this, it is necessary to study the characteristics of the interactions between the printed book as an object (or now the computer screen), the text itself, and readers who engage in the act of reading within a particular context. Although the text itself might seem immutable, its mode of publication (form and format) and its reception by the reader is individualized and infinitely changeable—across time as well as contemporaneous with the period when the text was written. Even though reading (in terms of its objects, modalities, and benefits) can lead social cleavage, it can also be an instrument for social cohesion. There are no cultures that are so radically heterogeneous and antinomic that printed works cannot cross over boundaries among social groups and collectivities, which come together and differentiate themselves, set themselves apart, and at the same time share certain texts. The difference among these groups is constituted not in the objects of reading which can be radically heterogenous, but rather in the manner of reading and in the benefit drawn from the text, which can be varied and variable.

READING IN CRISIS IN DEVELOPED COUNTRIES

From the end of World War II through the late 1970s, the practice of reading expanded in most of the Western democracies on both sides of the Atlantic. But there were great changes during the 1980s and the situation today is paradoxical. Although the percentage of people holding advanced degrees has increased everywhere, and although the economic level of the population has improved (despite the growing gap between rich and poor) reading, and especially the reading of books, has diminished. In most countries the number of readers has hardly grown at all; furthermore there has been a marked decrease among avid readers who read several books a month. This decrease in reading is even more noticeable among regular readers: the proportion of avid readers has diminished, especially among students, youth, and those with advanced degrees. Even though young people remain the heaviest readers, they read less than the previous generation did when they were the same age. The only constant over time is the finding that women still read more than men, and girls more than boys. Paradoxically, in all the developed countries, the number of books published is still increasing, although the average number of copies printed is going down—a fact which underlines the rapid evanescence of the market for books. The overall earnings for publishers has increased, but so has the concentration in the book industry—causing independent publishers to experience more and more difficulties, sometimes even being forced to close or merge with another firm; meanwhile the number of scholarly works and "quality" books have declined precipitously.

Of course, reading is not limited to the reading of books. Newspapers, magazines, and electronic texts are also "reading objects." In a 2005 survey of 2000 adults in Great Britain (http://www.literacytrust.org.uk), 34% said they did not read books, a third had not bought a new book in the previous 12 months. However, 96% said they had read something in the past 7 days, whether books, magazines, newspapers or text messages. Furthermore, 47% of U.K. adults are registered with their local library. More amusing, some researchers actually questioned readers about books they found disappointing. A poll commissioned by Teletext in 2007 found the top fiction books that Britons were not able to finish;[10] these included:

1. *Vernon God Little*, D.B.C Pierre (35%)
2. *Harry Potter and the Goblet of Fire*, J.K Rowling (32%)
3. *Ulysses*, James Joyce (28%)
4. *Captain Corelli's Mandolin*, Louis De Bernieres (27%)
5. *Cloud Atlas*, David Mitchell (24%)
6. *The Satanic Verses*, Salman Rushdie (21%)
7. *The Alchemist*, Paulo Coelho (19%)
8. *War and Peace*, Leo Tolstoy (18%)
9. *The God of Small Things*, Arundhati Roy (16%)
10. *Crime and Punishment*, Dostoyevsky (15%)

To measure reading by only looking at the number of items read is certainly contestable (is it "better" to read 15 books than 12?). Attempting to discern the content of what is read is obviously more meaningful. From this standpoint, the reading of literary works is of special interest. The 2004 survey *Reading at Risk*[11] (http://www.nea. gov.news/news04/ReadingAtRisk.html) estimated that in the United States the number of readers of literary works decreased between 1992 and 2002, going from 54% to 45% among adults over 18 years old. This "dramatic decline" in the reading of literature, according to the hyperbolic statement in the survey, was accompanied by an overall decline in the reading of books: 61% of American adults read books in 1992 but only 56.5% in 2002—or a decline of a modest 4.5%. Among those who read books, 21% are considered "light" readers (1 to 5 books per year); 9% modest readers (6 to 10 books per year); 12% "frequent" readers (one book per month). As everywhere else, the decline is more marked among men, among individuals who are less educated, among young people from ethnic minorities, and among the economically disadvantaged. As in other countries, the most troubling finding is that the loss of interest in reading has increased over time.

The same phenomenon is seen in France where book reading has stagnated or decreased: 25% of the population over 15 does not read books. The proportion of "moderate" readers (10 books per year) increased from 24% in 1981 to 35% in 1997. This fact had first been interpreted by sociologists as progress (the transition from non-reader to reader), but is today considered as regressive because the proportion of avid readers declined: 22% of the adult population read more than 25 books per year in 1973, but by 1997 avid readers made up only 14% of the population. Even worse, across all demographic categories there is a marked decline in women readers. Nonetheless although the categories of French readers who read the most remain much the same (the highly educated, the privileged social classes, young people and students), these readers were found to read less than they did 20 years earlier.

Since 1980 all the developed countries have also confronted the problem of functional illiteracy. Here we must distinguish between the term illiteracy which designates those persons who have never learned to read or write and functional illiteracy which refers to the situation of those people who have a basic knowledge of reading, but have lost their reading skills due to the lack of practice or to poverty. The "discovery" of functional illiteracy was met with a great deal of shock and disbelief in developed countries. This resulted in many denunciations of the failure of democracy and its deficiencies. At the same time, the demographic profile of the functionally illiterate was often the archetype of the most disadvantaged—those people characterized by lack of knowledge and other social and economic deficiencies. Such analysis would not necessarily apply to much of the world's illiterate population, who may not perceive the acquisition of literary skills as essential to their daily lives. And in any context, the lack literacy skills does mean not being less of an active agent in their destiny or less capable of thinking.

Little by little tentative definitions of literacy levels became more rigorous in an effort to identify "functional illiteracy" or to describe the competencies expected of those who had finished primary school. Nonetheless attempts to quantify the number of illiterates remains problematic and statistics can vary from 5% to 15% of the population in Western countries. There has been a growing recognition that functional illiteracy is a serious problem, and its eradication should be considered imperative in developed countries that seek a broader dissemination of basic knowledge and competencies among the entire population.

THE END OF THE HUMANISTIC MODEL

Changes in reading patterns in contemporary societies should not be surprising. Even if some members of society still lack adequate literacy skills, reading has become an everyday activity, a widely shared practice that is no longer a mark of elite status. Young people in particular seem to take reading for granted and adopt a relativistic attitude toward what they read. In France a 1999 study of 1200 adolescents aged 14–17 revealed that these teens regularly engaged in reading, and with no compunction whatsoever, they reported reading all kinds of books as different as *Moliere* and Stephen King, *Camus* and *Never without my Daugher (Jamais sans ma fille)*. The researchers concluded that "rather than a crisis in reading, we are witnessing a mutation of the traditional model" and they advised that instead of complaining about this change one should take action to encourage all kinds of reading.[12] Young people do read, but they read differently, without reverence toward classic authors, and without embarrassment as to their choice of genres. In fact, they see reading as a cultural activity among others, and one that comes second to music. These researchers who conducted the 1999 study observed:

> The facts are clear: reading books now occupies a modest place among leisure activities of teens. It does not represent the preferred activity of any category of secondary school students, even among girls who are the heaviest readers—or among those girls who are good students and daughters of highly cultivated families. Of the adolescents surveyed, 26% placed reading among their three preferred leisure activities, but only 5% ranked reading in first place. The proportion of those who report reading little or not at all continues to increase over the course of time: by the fourth year of the survey these non-readers and light readers represented 72% of the boys and 40% of the girls. For the majority of teens surveyed, reading is not something vital, and it is not an act of reverence to the works that represent the literary heritage. Over the years young people have openly acknowledged reading fewer and

fewer titles from the literary canon and have increasingly cited titles popular among their peers. Without the least embarrassment they are willing to be seen by the researchers as non-readers or light readers. But this indifference that they show toward the central values of traditional humanism embodied in the literary canon does not signify that in their eyes reading is deprived of any value. They see reading as an activity like any other educational endeavor or recreational pastime, subject to changing needs and interests, to their individual life experience, and to pressure from their social network. Indifferent to those who consider reading "sacred" by identifying the practice of reading with reading of the literary canon, young people engage in a more realistic and practical approach. For them, reading is never invested with an a priori value: it is the individual situation that creates the need to read or the pleasure of reading, and determines how books are used. As much a product of the market economy as music or the cinema, reading does not benefit from any special status among the young.[12]

Furthermore, the researchers found that reading among young people decreases as they progress through the school curriculum, and worse still, it also decreases with the successful completion of schooling. This study showed that "students invest less time in reading as they spend more years in school…and reading continues to decline when they finish their studies. They read less in middle school and still less in secondary school."[12]

READING ELECTRONIC TEXT

At the same time that research on reading advances and policies to promote reading appear more and more complex, the Internet has been transforming the practice of reading and writing throughout the world. Electronic networks accessible through the Internet have exerted a profound influence on both the public sphere and private space.

The invasive presence of the Internet has produced all kinds of commentary, both positive and negative. There is unfortunately a lack of rigorous sociological research which would allow for a better comprehension of this technological and social revolution. Although there are a number of incisive and thoughtful commentaries, the debate on the social effects of the electronic revolution, whether their authors denounce or praise these changes, generally tend to be ideological discourses and not the result of solid empirical studies that analyze social behavior.

For some, the Internet is one of many indicators of social decadence; they assert that society cannot escape the pervasive influence of the market, which has been given free reign to invade the private space of individuals, as well as increasing the inequalities among social groups, and among rich and the poor countries. According to the naysayers, these phenomena will inevitably lead to the decline of book culture.

For others, the Internet is the best hope for global democracy—direct democracy that overturns long-standing political rules and national boundaries. The Internet has the potential to increase opportunities for creativity, invention, and social communication, and will therefore stimulate a redoubled use of writing, overcoming traditional divisions of labor. As a result each person will become at the same time a reader, author and editor, and will play dynamic role in each of these activities.

The sociological study of the impact of technological innovation on its users reveals that the use of these new technologies is rarely that which was envisioned by their inventors and producers. Users sometimes decide on quite different types of uses and their appropriation of new technologies goes through various phases as it evolves. In the end, the usage of technology is the result of a negotiation (sometime virtual) between what the technological tools allow, what the producers propose and what the users construct. This construction of usage is in and of itself, pluralistic and continually evolving.

Among the questions that need to be studied is a sociology of the practices used in reading text on a screen, the question of the relationship between reading and writing. In the reading of digital text, every reader becomes a reader-author. Writing now more than ever coexists with reading. In the world of print, the writing done by the reader is found on the margins of the page. Glosses, translations, commentary on a printed page are (almost illicit) examples of the use of writing for improving access to the text. Nonetheless the reader-as-writer is confined to the margins of the page. In the Internet world, rather than becoming an author, each reader, instead becomes a "librarian," who practices, thanks to hypertext, a kind of "meta-reading."

Another key question for the sociology of reading concerns the mutations between the relationship to knowledge and modalities of learning. The passage of the "Internaut" through various networks is a voyage in space, a journey into a territory far more vast than that allowed in the closed space of a book, and this new knowledge domain has of necessity modified the learning process. Passage through written text becomes boundless. For their own peace of mind, it will undoubtedly be necessary for the readers to reinstate some aspects of the experience of linear reading into the fluidity of reading electronic texts.

Finally, electronic text is silent and defies the oral. The Internet user ("l'Internaut") is alone, but connected to the entire world. In order to overcome the interdiction against the oral, s/he gives voice to the text by inventing chat, e-mail and listserves of all kinds—and by downloading music. But if each individual is a writer, each one is also deprived of the spoken word and this state could be aptly described as "interactive solitude." In the electronic environment, one is in a contradictory relationship with other: ever present, but always absent.

THE FUTURE OF READING

It is now a time of multiple reading practices and the traditional model of reading is not the dominant model. Even though sociology does not take a relativistic perspective, sociologists are attempting to find how each reader constructs meaning, and makes sense of the world. A constant within the contemporary sociology of reading concerns questions in regard to the dissatisfaction over the mastery of reading skills or the quality of reading in cultural situation of contemporary society. The study of the "discourse on reading," that a society defines or promotes has become an epistemological necessity, and is itself closely bound to society's hopes and fears.

The question posed by the Enlightenment as to why societies seek to promote reading is more than ever relevant today. When societies wish to enable everyone to master reading, is it the search for liberty, which comes through the emancipation of all? Or is society simply guided by pragmatic needs when it esteems that everyone should be information literate? Or is the motivation consumeristic—embodying the wish that the world of the imagination still be framed by the joy of novel reading?

In any case, one should not be surprised by the evolving forms, pleasures and benefits of reading. If the image of emancipatory literacy has lost its force, paradoxically it is because the diffusion of reading, despite some gaps or deficiencies, has been accomplished, and it has become clear that widespread literacy is not always synonymous with emancipation. No longer is reading inhibited or prohibited, except by the texts themselves, their unequal wealth or poverty. The more widespread reading becomes, the more it looses its symbolic image as a force for freedom. Nonetheless, this does not mean that reading is devalued, that is will disappear, or that the power of readers or reading will be diminished.

ACKNOWLEDGMENTS

This entry was translated by Mary Niles Maack.

REFERENCES

1. In *Pour une sociologie de la lecture: lectures et lecteurs dans la France contemporaine*; Poulain, M., Ed.; Editions du Cercle de la Librairie: Paris, France, 1992.
2. Chartier, A.-M. Hébrard, J. In *Discours sur la lecture, 1880–2000*; de Fraisse, E., Poulain, M., Pompougnac, J-C., Eds.; BPI-Centre Pompidou, Fayard: Paris, France, 2000; avec la collaboration.

3. Baeterman, J. BPI-Centre Pompidou, Fayard: Paris, France, 2000; *Les vertus de la jeune fille*; 1919, cité par Chartier, A-M.; Hébrard, J., *Discours sur la lecture, 1880–2000*, avec la collaboration de Fraisse, E., Poulain, M, Pompougnac, J-C.

4. Waples, D.; Berelson, B.; Bradshaw, F.R. *What Reading Does to People: A Summary of Evidence on the Social Effects of Reading and a Statement of Problems for Research*; University of Chicago Press: Chicago, IL, 1940.

5. Bourdieu, P. In *Distinction: A Social Critique of the Judgement of Taste*; Nice, R., Ed.; Harvard University Press: Cambridge, MA, 1984; 41 (originally published as: *La distinction: critique sociale du jugement* Ëditions de Minuit: Paris, France, 1979.).

6. de Certeau, M. In *The Practice of Everyday Life*; Rendall, S.F., Ed.; University of California Press: Berkeley, CA, 1984 (Translation of L'invention du quotidien [Paris]: Union générale d'éditions, [1980].).

7. Paul, R. In *Time and Narrative*; McLaughlin, K., Pellauer, D., Eds.; University of Chicago Press: Chicago, IL, 1984; (Translation of: *Temps et récit* (3 volumes) Seuil: Paris, France, 1983–1985.).

8. Roger, C., Ed. *The Cultural Uses of Print in Early Modern France*; Princeton University Press: Princeton, NJ, 1987; Lydia, G., Trans. (Translated from: Les Usages de l'imprimé (XVe–XIXe siècle.) Fayard: Paris, France, 1987.).

9. Roger, C. *Lectures et lecteurs dans la France*; Seuil: Paris, France, 1987.

10. National Literacy Trust. Survey Results on Reading Habits **2007**. Available at http://www.literacytrust.org.uk/Database/stats/readingstats.html (accessed November 15, 2008).

11. *National Endowment for the Arts. Reading at Risk: A Survey of Reading in America. Research Report 46*, June 2004; Available at http://www.nea.gov/news/news04/ReadingAt Risk.Html (accessed November 15, 2008).

12. Baudelot, C.; Cartier, M.; Detrez, C. *Et Pourtant, Ils Lisent*; Seuil: Paris, France, 1999.

BIBLIOGRAPHY

1. Bahloul, J. *Lectures Précaires: Etude Sociologique Sur Les Faibles Lecteurs*; Centre Georges Pompidou: Paris, France, 1988; Bibliothèque publique d'information.

2. Barbier-Bouvet, J.-F. *Publics à l'œuvre: pratiques culturelles à la Bibliothèque publique d'information du Centre Pompidou/Jean François Barbier-Bouvet, Martine Poulain*; BPI, Centre Pompidou/Documentation française: Paris, France, 1986.

3. Bloom, A. *Closing of the American Mind*; Simon and Schuster: New York, London, UK.; Sydney, Australia, 1987.

4. Chartier, A.-M. In *Discours sur la lecture, 1880–2000*; de Fraisse, E., Poulain, M., Pompougnac, J-C., Eds.; BPI-Centre Pompidou, Fayard: Paris, France, 2000; avec la collaboration.

5. Chartier, R.; Cavallo, G.; *Histoire de la lecture dans le monde occidental*; Seuil: Paris, France, 1997.

6. Mollier, J.-Y. *Où va le livre?*; La Dispute: Paris, France, 2007.

7. Poulain, M., Ed. *Pour une sociologie de la lecture: lectures et lecteurs dans la France contemporaine with Joëlle Bahloul*; Cercle de la librairie: Paris, France, 1988.

8. Poulain, M., Ed. *Lire en France aujourd'hui*; Editions du Cercle de la librairie: Paris, France, 1993.

WEB SITES

1. Hersent, J.F. *Direction du livre et de la lecture Sociologie de la lecture en France: état des lieux (essai de synthèse à partir des travaux de recherche menés en France)*, 2000; Juin http://74.125.95.104/search?q=cache:3sN7JgLT-fAJ: www.culture. gouv.fr/culture/dll/sociolog.rtf+%22Nicolas+Roubakine%22& hl=en&ct=clnk&cd=15&gl=us&client= firefox-a.

2. Signorini, A. *Permanent European Reading Watch—2002: The images of the keen reader in European research*, http://www.grinzane.net/Osservatorio2003/Osservatorio2003_ENG.html (accessed November 15, 2008).

Sociology of the Information Disciplines

Michael F. Winter
Shields Library, University of California, Davis, California, U.S.A.

Abstract

An overview of the sociology of the information disciplines is presented. The information disciplines are described and linked to the development of the social formation that sociologists refer to as "modernity." Development of several information disciplines is traced in relation to the phases of capitalism, the growth of the modern university, and the growth of information itself.

INTRODUCTION

This entry presents an overview of the sociology of the information disciplines (see the section "The Information Disciplines: Scope and Definition" for detailed enumeration). Its point of departure is a decisive break that occurred toward the end of the European Middle Ages, ushering in a new form of society. Economically, the break was triggered by the rise and rapid diffusion of modern capitalism; socially and historically, the advent of capitalist market economies brought about the new social formation that sociologists refer to as "modernity." (pp. 728–729),[1] (pp. 490–508),[2] (p. 9945).[3] Economically, modernity is closely associated with increasingly globalized commerce and trade. From a broadly social point of view, the coming of modernity introduces a new worldview and ethos of cosmopolitan scientific materialism. This worldview and ethos—in a word, this new culture—is accompanied by a strong ideological emphasis on the free circulation of both goods and ideas.

There is no clear consensus on the periodization of modernity: some writers begin with the rise of merchant capitalism in the fifteenth century, others emphasize the European Enlightenment of the mid-eighteenth century. Still others date the beginnings of modernity with the English industrial revolution of the 1780s. For present purposes, however, it is essential to point out that modernity is not only a historical phenomenon: it is also a distinct form of social organization (p. 727).[1]

Fortunately, the nature of the break, and the new form of society it inaugurated, is easier to identify than it is to specify its proper historical sequence. It is convenient to delimit a phenomenon by strategic contrast: human societies before modernity were dominated economically by agriculture, mining, and commerce. The division of labor was comparatively low, reflecting a simple, relatively undifferentiated occupational structure. Available technologies were also relatively simple, and did not change substantially over long periods. Politically, societies before modernity are marked by highly personalized power relations. Socially, they favor fixed hierarchical arrangements (e.g., in the family, the kin group, and the church). Culturally speaking, they rely heavily on oral communication leaving few fixed knowledge and information records, have low literacy levels (reading and writing are mostly confined to elites), education is family-based and informal, and they are governed largely by tradition (pp. 728–729).[1]

Modern societies, by contrast, are characterized by increasingly dynamic and rapid social change. They are dominated economically by the systematic and planned investment of surplus resources or capital. Initially invested and reinvested in processes of agriculture, mining, and commerce, the ceaseless flow of capital eventually dominates all economic production, distribution, and human services. The division of labor is complex and growing, reflecting the constant creation, abandonment, and subsequent recreation of enterprises and occupations. As rapidly as occupations become obsolete, new occupations take their place, destined to become obsolete themselves in relatively short order. There is in modernity a constant and mounting investment in the development of the sciences, and the use of scientific knowledge to invent new technologies that revolutionize production; modern societies are thus characterized by increasing reliance on rational forms of social action and organization (p. 727),[1] (p. 9945).[3] Politically speaking, modern societies depersonalize power relations, relying on complex, rationally structured, highly impersonal networks and organizations charged with oversight and regulation. Socially, many new opportunities for voluntary association arise, as individual ties to older hierarchical social relations loosen (pp. 728–729),[1] (pp. 490–508).[2] Culturally speaking, literacy levels rise slowly at first and then much more rapidly; formal educational institutions and mass education challenge the older tradition-based cultures of the family and the village. The increasing presence of literate populations places an emphasis on writing and printing; these means of formal communication are joined later by technologies of miniaturization like microprinting and digitization. All these challenge the

Encyclopedia of Library and Information Sciences, Fourth Edition DOI: 10.1081/E-ELIS4-120044668

supremacy of oral communication, and the traditions it perpetuated, instituting a much wider production of, and reliance upon, fixed knowledge and information records. The disciplines on which this entry focuses arise as occupational and organizational responses to vast increases in these knowledge and information records.

Because sociology itself originates as a reflective response to the rise and development of modern societies (p. 491),[3] it is well-positioned to frame and illuminate the rise and development of the modern information disciplines. Although the modern information disciplines themselves are a product of modernity as well, they focus on practical problems, and thus cannot provide on their own the reflective intellectual turn necessary to understand their historical and social significance. Because it is scarcely possible to survey all of a highly multiply paradigmatic field like sociology in such a brief compass, a suitable representative perspective needs to be identified; the sociological concept of modernity is ideally suited to this role. In addition to the above-mentioned enumeration of the scope of the information disciplines, the reader will find sections on the social character of disciplines in modern societies, the origins of the modern information disciplines in the disciplinary matrix of the university, the expansionist logic of modernity, the roots of the information disciplines in the continuing crises of modernity, and the dissolution of the nineteenth and twentieth centuries' disciplinary configuration. Drawing on recent work on discipline formation, dissolution, and reformation, it concludes by situating the contemporary information disciplines in an environment dominated by continuous innovation.

DISCIPLINES AND SOCIAL CONTROL IN MODERNITY: THE CASE OF KNOWLEDGE

"Discipline" (Lat. *disciplina*) refers to the instructional practices of defining, organizing, and transmitting knowledge. In modern times the discovery of new knowledge joins the list, and eventually takes pride of place. The knowledge transmitted, on the other hand, has been commonly referred to as "doctrine." Taken together, discipline and doctrine define the practical and theoretical aspects of formal or institutionalized education. Along with the new knowledge acquired, fundamental aspects of individual identity—cognitive, behavioral, and ethical—are restructured. Sociologists typically refer to this alteration of identity as "secondary-," "adult-," or "occupational-socialization," in contrast to an earlier phase in the formation of the self occurring during the "primary socialization" processes of childhood.

Disciplines, viewed as social formations, share two common goals: the first is to control a body of knowledge by subjecting it to systematic organization; and the second is to shape the consciousness and conduct of those who seek to apply this body of knowledge. This dual focus on the organization of the field and the socialization of the practitioner clearly identify disciplines as fulfilling key functions in the social control of knowledge.

Before the rise of the specialized information disciplines in more recent times much of this task of control was accomplished by two available means: specialization and classification.[4] Viewed singly, specializations act as primary filters, screening out much of the wider field of what is known (193ff.).[5] But when taken as an articulated system of categories, the overall arrangement of various branches of learning can be used to generate a template or grid providing a sense of cognitive integration, a kind of *de facto* classification scheme or outline of knowledge. In this grid, the names of the special fields double as organizing categories. Modernity provides a number of examples of these knowledge classification schemes that inspired the book and library classification schemes still in use today.[6] While originally based on the logic of deduction and arranged hierarchically, the reigning current schemes characteristically arrange categories by alphabetical (e.g., in the Library of Congress classification) or numerical sequence (e.g., in the decimal classifications), creating schemes immediately transparent to all literate persons.

Discipline(s), Knowledge, and Power

The brief outline sketched above highlights the role of specialized academic cultures in the creation, transmission, and control of formal knowledge. Some writers have taken a more expansive view of the concept of discipline, broadening it to the point where it is seen to work synergistically with all aspects of social control. In this view the social control of formal knowledge and its records rests on a deeper unconscious level of control conditioning both the knowledge and the entire range of social action simultaneously. The best-known of these writers is no doubt the French theorist and historian of the human sciences Michel Foucault (1926–1984), who saw the emerging disciplines of psychopathology, criminology, and pedagogy in early modern Europe working hand-in-glove with the rise of the social institutions of the asylum, the prison, and the school. Of particular significance to this entry is the frequent and increasing recourse found in this "knowledge/power" complex, to use a characteristically Foucauldian phrase, to gathering data, then recording and storing them for future use. The ensemble of these records constitutes a "field of documentation."[7] Notably, fields of documentation both provide disciplines with a rationally organized system of records, and at the same time furnish increasingly ubiquitous means for monitoring behavior. Thus, in the Foucauldian view, discipline refers not only to a field but also to a pervasive form of social control.

Although this significantly expanded use of discipline has not been used widely in the literature on the information fields, that use is increasing, and has been applied to

Sociology–Special

librarianship and museum studies with persuasive and striking results (p. 35),[8] (p. 10).[9] In this way, key organizations in information societies can be seen as agents of surveillance and bureaucratic control (p. 63).[9] By extension, librarianship assumes a role in collecting and providing access to records of many different kinds and at the same time studying, surveying, monitoring, and recording the behavior of library users (pp. 65–68).[9] Something of the same may be said of the realm of "material culture," the focus of museum collecting, and museum studies. Museums originated largely as the private collections of aristocrats and a small coterie of powerful bourgeois, but by the end of the eighteenth century, their collections began moving into monumental public settings. In these new venues, collections of art objects and artifacts attested to the rising power of the great nation-states of Europe and their expanding colonial empires. The museum, from serving as an arena of privileged wealth and taste, in modernity acquired the role of educating the population and at the same time helping to transform that population into a modern citizenry (p. 169).[10] Librarianship and museum studies, in this optic, appear as agents of control—of records, artifacts, and indeed of selves in their guises as library users or museum visitors. Much the same could be said of archivistics, the information sciences, informatics, and also of studies of readers, information users, and audiences.

THE INFORMATION DISCIPLINES: SCOPE AND DEFINITION

By the middle of the nineteenth century, the logic of expanding inquiry increasingly generated a need for new approaches and new occupational specializations to manage a constantly growing universe of knowledge records, including records containing data about users. Classification and specialization were no longer sufficient to supply the necessary organizational knowledge required for effective control. This entry draws attention to librarianship, archivistics, records management, bibliography and textual studies, document-type studies, social studies of information use, and museum studies, all sharing a broad, human-centered orientation, with quantitative methods making some inroads. The distinction between archivistics and records management is essential because, even though in North America the contrast between the two is not particularly sharp, it has for some time in Western Europe referred to two clearly distinguished fields.[11] To these we must add a newer, closely affiliated yet more quantitative and technical group: information science, information systems design, knowledge management, and informatics, where humanistic, historical, and interpretive approaches on the other hand are less prominent, though growing in importance. This rough classification follows Bates, who has also identified the more human-centered information

fields as "disciplines of the cultural record" and the more scientific group as "sciences of information"; we also adopt that typification here.[12]

The contrast between the disciplines of the cultural record and the information sciences recalls the familiar distinction, broadly speaking, between humanistic and scientific approaches to inquiry. In both cases, the contrast is at times a source of friction, but in the end fruitful. The friction comes from the contact between the older humanistic and the newer scientific styles of work. The tension is fruitful because the development of the information sciences, arriving on the scene relatively late, encouraged the older and more traditional disciplines of the record to treat records in more quantitative, calculative, and analytical ways. Where the more conservative, tradition-bound humanists viewed the text as largely fixed by authority, and thus alterable only with difficulty, reverence, and trepidation, information scientists approached texts and other knowledge records in a more practical, liberal, and open spirit. The tension is in any case counterbalanced by a common focus on acquiring, collecting, organizing, and preserving information in its recorded forms, in order to make records and their contents available to users.

For all the information disciplines, the increasing reliance on scientific approaches does much more than challenge older paradigms of humanism; it transforms many of the basic operations found in the institutional and organizational settings in which information work is so often carried out: libraries, archives, museums, public agencies, research institutes, think tanks, and businesses of different kinds. Although some of the characteristic tools and techniques used in these venues (for example, bibliographies, catalogs, schemes of document classification, and techniques for determining shelf location) preceded the coming of the information sciences, they were nonetheless thoroughly transformed thereby; and they were joined by many newer techniques and approaches (controlled vocabularies, numerous if often short-lived approaches to document retrieval, typed and later printed catalog and index entries, and eventually, by the 1950s, an increasing reliance on automation that continues unabated to the present). The newer techniques were by no means limited to those rooted in the applied versions of the natural sciences: so-called "rational" or "scientific" approaches to management and administration also left indelible marks.

The sociological significance of this distinction between the older humanism and modern science is large and pervasive, and reflective of epochal cultural changes. Initially crossing the divide between the field (and the laboratory) and the factory, science as method, technique, ethos, and worldview eventually moves into and colonizes the production, distribution, and use of records. This can also be seen in museum studies, which partly overlaps with librarianship, archivistics, and the information sciences. But the profile of museum studies ("museology," as it is also called) is complicated by the arrival of an altogether different incursion of modern scientific techniques for analyzing the artifacts of material culture, borrowed from physics, chemistry, and archaeology (124ff.).[13] The ancient status of the cultural record as exemplar of traditional authority is eclipsed, as the record itself, recast as a tool for practical exploitation, provides mundane opportunities for information-seeking. Not surprisingly, records in this context easily become commodities to be traded in knowledge- and information-intensive markets (p. 41).[8]

These informational commodities bear much more than traditional "use value," to borrow a standard concept from political economy: as commodities, they also become bearers of "exchange value" (pp. 358–359).[14] In the process, the work of the information professional reflects and increasingly incorporates the newer role of mediator between informational commodities and those wishing to use them and exchange them for profit. The shift to informational commodity mediator significantly challenges and partly displaces older text- and object-oriented curatorial and preservationist models of information work based on the traditions of intellectual craft labor and apprenticeship.

As records shift from tokens of intellectual authority to sources from which decontextualized facts, ideas, information, propositions, hypotheses, conjectures, knowledge-claims, and answers to queries may be extracted and used entirely outside the original context in which they appeared, the work situations of virtually all information professional are powerfully affected. Until well into the post-World War II era, the cultural gap between the older disciplines of the record and the new information sciences persisted. But since the 1960s, particularly in the English-speaking world, graduate and professional programs offering a kind of hybrid introduction to "library and information science" have attempted to fuse these two originally distinct approaches (3ff.).[15] The hybrid pattern fusing older approaches from humanism and the newer scientific methods is now not only characteristic of librarianship, but also of archivistics, museum studies, bibliographical and indexing services, publishing, and social studies of information use. (On archivistics, see Rumschöttel (p. 154);[16] on museum studies, see Hooper-Greenhill;[10] for an overview of the increasing significance of information science in all the information disciplines, see Buckland and Liu).[17]

THE INFORMATION DISCIPLINES: THEIR PLACE IN THE MODERN UNIVERSITY

Both the disciplines of the cultural record and the information sciences assumed characteristically modern forms by responding to the phenomenon widely known as the "information explosion," and more accurately described as a series of continuing explosions.[18] Triggered initially in the middle of the fifteenth century by the use of movable-type printing and a resulting shift from scribal to print culture, these surges were dramatically accelerated in the late eighteenth and early nineteenth centuries, and even more in the twentieth. In some cases, this led to the splitting off of new fields, as the problems of record control became too great for the established academic fields to handle on their own. Librarianship and the information sciences, especially in the hybrid form so often found in the library and information science graduate programs of the post-World War II period, bibliography and textual studies, and studies of readers or users of records come clearly to mind here. In other cases groups emerged within and remained partly dependent on older academic disciplines.

For example, archivistics and records management both not only bear the imprint of scientific history, corporate management, and public administration, but were also once subsumed under them (p. 46).[19] Museum studies, to take a different example, is significantly linked to cultural anthropology, history, art history, natural history, evolution and ecology, and archaeology (pp. 14–15).[20] On the whole, however, all achieved separate occupational identities and university affiliation only in relatively recent times. Museum studies is the youngest of the newcomers. Once rooted in the "master and apprentice" craft-dominated training models of the nineteenth-century museum, it did not even begin to establish degree programs in university settings until the 1920s, and it required several more decades for one of the first fully fledged university departments of museum studies to appear, in 1977 (pp. 424–426).[21]

The distinction between disciplines focused on the cultural record and the more quantitative information sciences can also be understood in terms of basic resource inequalities, a fixture of twentieth-century sociological writing (p. xii).[22] The disciplines of the cultural record stand to the information sciences much as the humanities and social sciences stand in relation to the better-funded and more politically powerful basic and applied natural sciences. This inequality may account for the keenness of the competitions and rivalries that establish carefully patrolled boundaries staking out professional jurisdictions.[14,23]

Despite key associations with older academic cultures, there is nonetheless a fundamental difference between these information fields and their older academic counterparts. The main difference is that the information disciplines are, in Bates' expression, "orthogonal": rather than occupying space in a continuum alongside them, they lie, so to speak, at a right angle to the older spectrum of disciplines, and focus in principle on the collective recorded output of all of them (p. 1044).[8,24] Neither primary producers nor distributors of content, they mediate between these poles, positioned to enable access, retrieval, content discovery, use, preservation, and control of the ever-increasing output (p. 1044),[24] (pp. 6–9).[25]

THE EXPANSIONIST LOGIC OF CAPITALIST MODERNITY

The origins of the modern disciplinary system, formed largely in the nineteenth and twentieth centuries, lie in a series of epochal transformations in which millennia of traditional agricultural economies and societies become overshadowed and eventually eclipsed by the development of capitalist modernity. Likewise with the informational fields arising in response to this development, the subject of modernity has occupied the attention of a great many scholars in many different fields. In this entry the focus is limited to a narrower range of key sociologists, social theorists, and some political economists of special importance to the development of sociological thought. Of particular note in this connection are Karl Marx (1818–1883), Max Weber (1864–1920), Emile Durkheim (1858–1917), and Georg Simmel (1858–1918). All were struck by the far-reaching effects exercised by the rise and spread of capitalism toward the end of the European Middle Ages, and how it displaced a much older, largely rural, much more static, and highly traditional society characterized by strong communal ties, the central presence of religious institutions, and relatively low levels of mobility. Marx and Engels memorably captured the fast-moving, highly mobile, and disorienting quality of capitalist societies in the *Communist Manifesto*, where they wrote: "all that is solid melts into air." These changes are all the more significant because although their origins lie in early modern Europe, a small and geographically relatively insignificant part of the world, their effect is revolutionary and their extent becomes distinctly global with the coming of the English industrial revolution.

The coming of capitalist modernity takes place in three phases: early modern mercantilism, eighteenth- and nineteenth-century industrialization, and a late nineteenth- and early twentieth-century second wave of industrialization sometimes called "reflexive modernization" (pp. 10ff.; p. 87),[26] and also "the second industrial revolution" (pp. 402–403).[27] While librarianship, bibliography, archivistics, and records management clearly have ancient lineages, their more characteristically modern forms do not emerge until the second and third of these three phases; and it is not until the third phase that much newer information disciplines like the information sciences, knowledge management, informatics, and museum studies make their appearance.

In early modernity, merchant capitalism, aided by the rise of modern banking and accounting, transformed and expanded commerce and the distribution of goods. In this phase, the older manuscript culture, with its characteristic "text and commentary" method (p. 101),[28] was transformed and substantially marginalized by the invention of movable-type printing in the mid-fifteenth century, permitting the production and distribution of large numbers of increasingly standardized texts. Nonetheless, movable-type printing remains for some time after its implementation firmly anchored in the culture of preindustrial craft production.

At this point in time, librarianship and archivistics were only barely emerging as occupations with distinct identities of their own, and not surprisingly they were frequently practiced by persons already involved with other lines of work: scholarship, religious vocations, administration, and letters, to cite the more common examples. The two pursuits were more often than not combined, if only because the collection and housing of both books and archival records so often occurred at the same location (p. 159).[29]

Materials selection still remained largely the province of the nonlibrarian. By the latter part of the fifteenth century, there were, however, early signs of the forms these nascent pursuits will later take: newly emerging bodies of knowledge like systematic and universal bibliography, bibliographic description, a much-increased reliance on alphabetical indexing, and the use of topical key words as organizational devices (pp. 126–128).[30] Closer to the end of this period, by the middle of the seventeenth century, as other early signs of the Enlightenment appear, formal treatises on librarianship, and the management of collections of records have begun to appear (p. 381).[31] Part of this specialized professional literature was necessarily devoted to the development of organizational tools for, as Le Gallois pointed out in a famous treatise of the day, "order is both the soul and the form of the library"; chief among these are the many classification schemes that, in the absence of any standard classifications, had to be custom-made to fit specific collections (pp. 381, 382–384).[31] And by the end of the seventeenth century, book and library classification schemes began to include special categories for this emerging professional literature (p. 181).[30]

Significantly, there is also the clear emergence of a frankly materialistic sensibility among practitioners. An important new idea of early modernity is that libraries must above all be dedicated to use, rather than the housing of sacred literary relics (p. 172),[30] (p. 385).[31] Librarians for their part openly avowed the need for material compensation for their work (p. 175).[30] Collection-building activity was focused heavily on exchanges, an expression of the idea of the book or text as a commodity to be traded (p. 176).[30] In a representative statement, the English librarian Thomas Durie wrote in a language clearly taken from the discourse of political economy: "for the increas' of the stock" librarians must mingle with persons "eminent in every science, to Trade with them…" And Durie went on to characterize the librarian in typical business terms as "a Treasurer and a Factor" who trades in "a useful commoditie" (p. 176).[30] Librarians, along with other types of workers, have become "employees" who are recruited from an increasingly fluid labor market. As such, they were free to enjoy social mobility, both geographic and occupational, and changed employers at will, seeking better pay and working conditions (p. 395).[31,32]

In the second phase, known as industrialization, capital expanded significantly by moving into production and exploiting artificial energy. The commercial capital accumulated in the period between 1400 and about 1750 provided necessary resources for a systematic exploitation of scientific and technical knowledge in production processes. Industrialization was no doubt also powered by a new religious and ethical zeal for applying scientific and technical advances in a wide variety of practical operations.[33] Noteworthy, advances in the technology of printing markedly increased the production and distribution of texts, providing even more commodities destined for an expanding, increasingly literate population. During this second phase of capitalist modernization, the early modern troika of theology, medicine, and law lost its dominant position in the university, where it was challenged and overshadowed by a wide variety of new fields imbued with the ethos of scientific exploration, discovery, and analysis.

Both socioeconomically and culturally, the profiles of the librarian and the archivist are strongly marked by the increasing dominance of the bourgeoisie. (This will later become true of museum curators as well.) The librarians of the period were clearly recruited almost exclusively from middle-class social strata, and only occasionally from the lesser nobility (p. 268),[30] (p. 386).[32] Not surprisingly, this socioeconomic profile is strongly imprinted by the bourgeois values of the time. The key value in this context is the belief that ideas and knowledge, along with the texts encoding them, must be allowed to freely circulate, just as goods in trade must be allowed to circulate. This deep ideological commitment, paired with an extensive grounding in the liberal arts and a thorough mastery of Latin, made them ideal members of scientific or learned societies where a materialist and secular spirit reigned, even further eclipsing the older influence of theology (p. 268).[30]

The period of industrialization also provides clear evidence of additional steps taken toward the formation of distinct occupational identities, at least for librarianship and archivistics. The first known instance of the term "library science," coined by a German writer, occurred in 1803; what is likely the first formal treatise on professional education appeared in 1820 (p. 313).[30] Indeed, the years following the French Revolution in 1789 are highly formative in other ways as well. There is a new reliance on examinations and formal certification procedures (p. 266).[30] The founding of the École des Chartes in 1821 provided government-certified professional education for librarians, archivists, and museum curators. Graduates enjoyed a virtual monopoly on appointments in libraries, archives, and major museums as early as 1839 (pp. 50–51),[19] (p. 392).[30] These developments in formal education in France, the United Kingdom, and Germany were accompanied by a parallel development in the professional literature (pp. 154, 156ff.).[29]

In the third phase of capitalist modernization, the processes that earlier transformed traditional agricultural societies began to push industrial society itself in new directions. When the forces of industrialization turn and begin to work on industrialization itself, capitalist modernity is said to enter a "reflexive" phase (p. 10).[26] Scientific advance, technological invention, and their combination penetrated the university and acquired a legitimacy previously denied. In this third phase, which gathers speed toward the end of the nineteenth and comes to fruition in the twentieth century, the forces that earlier transformed commerce and primary production begin to also transform the accumulation and management of information, especially in its recorded forms, as these become increasingly central to the management of advanced industrial societies (p. 403).[27]

It is largely in this third phase that the information disciplines become consolidated in forms more clearly recognizable today; during this period, they come together or "jell" as professionalizing occupations. The critical difference between the information disciplines in the nascent embryonic forms described above and the more recognizable shapes they assume in the last half of the nineteenth century is the forging of lasting links with formal, institutionalized, higher education. The information fields, among a number of other professionalizing occupations, moved into a growing middle ground between the shrinking bourgeoisie and the burgeoning industrial proletariat, claiming a special standing in the labor market based on expertise. For all these fields, the information disciplines included, university affiliation became essential. It not only provided a solid institutional disciplinary base for the generation and transmission of new knowledge but also and even more important from a sociological point of view, an acknowledged mark of competence, a recognized authenticity. And because the stamp of social legitimacy provided by affiliation with university programs facilitates social and economic success, professionalizing groups gained an important advantage in a competitive labor market. From a relatively small group of older traditional professions enjoying the benefits of professional privilege—chiefly theology, medicine, and law—the social and economic landscape of modernity became more heavily populated with new professional groups. In turn, all of these newer expertise-based occupations accumulated their own bodies of knowledge and staked claims to professional status and monopolies of control. Because these newer occupations grew rapidly thanks to the increasing circulation of capital, the bodies of knowledge, and the records they generated grew rapidly as well.

The increasing emphasis on certification, authenticity, and legitimacy by means of university affiliation subjects the information disciplines, in a way they had not been previously, to the powerful forces of bureaucratization ("rule by office," in the common formulation of the German sociologist Max Weber and a number of his colleagues). When librarians, archivists, and museum curators had been prepared and vetted by the much less formal mechanisms associated with the apprenticeship mode of craft labor, they had a more tenuous relation to centralized bureaucratic organization. The modern university, as it developed in the later stages of the industrial age, was by contrast a large and complex network of interdependent jurisdictions governed, like major corporations and state agencies, by rational techniques of administration. As such the university's operating philosophy was tailored to minimize the highly personal forms of authority and patronage characteristic of organizations before modernity. Thus, in this period, we find a common dual focus on organization and administration (pp. 728–729),[1] (pp. 490–508),[2] (p. 324).[30] The dual focus appears clearly in an influential treatise of the period, where it is argued that professional employees in the information fields should stress "the dependence of good service upon proper division of labor, smooth operation, and minimal paper work" (p. 325).[30] Because professional education for archivists not only acquired a formal affiliation with institutions of higher learning, but was also closely connected with major depositories, often government agencies, archivistics shows an even closer connection with the hierarchical complexities of bureaucracy (p. 65).[19]

Striking as it was, however, the constant increase in the size of the universe of records, an increase made possible by the constant expansion of capital, reflects and is partly overshadowed by an even larger expansionist social and cultural logic with an explosive dynamic of its own. The ongoing information explosions, in fact, were only one aspect of a larger cultural crisis. The writers of the nineteenth century—both literary and scholarly, particularly in the writings of those later identified as founders and forerunners of sociology—clearly struggled with an endemic sense of malaise in which individuals appear at the mercy of overwhelming social forces. That these individuals themselves unwittingly unleashed these forces only added to the drama. The march of industrial capitalism moved nineteenth-century writers and thinkers like Marx to liken the bourgeoisie—the flagship class of capitalist society—to a sorcerer whose creations behave like monsters; once created and let loose, they endlessly fashion and refashion society and us along with it. Max Weber likened bourgeois society itself, however rational and efficient it was in comparison to earlier social formations, to a cage of disenchantment. Durkheim identified and analyzed modernity's new social environment as lacking the reassuring compasses of community, religion, tradition, and clearly understandable social norms. And Simmel found in modernity a deep ambivalence toward the material and cultural abundance of modernity, which ironically dwarfed the individual's ability to understand and absorb it (for an overview of these trends, see Berman (pp. 27–29, 87–98).[34] The figures of speech vary, but the underlying concern is remarkably consistent: modern societies entrap and overwhelm the individual, burying it under an

avalanche of resources. Among these are the mounting populations of knowledge and information records, and the many techniques required to control them and navigate through them in order to retrieve relevant records. A century later the U.K.-based sociologist Anthony Giddens, sizing up the classical social theorists mentioned above and appraising advanced industrial society's obvious advantages along with its grave problems of control, refers to modernity as a "juggernaut" (p. 139).[35] We note here that the problems of dealing with exploding bodies of knowledge records are not autonomous developments, because they are grounded in larger social processes occasioning ceaseless change, disruption, and disorientation. Like the upstart academic fields of the nineteenth century which displace the earlier disciplinary matrix, the information disciplines emerge against the backdrop of this larger sense of crisis.

THE ORIGINS OF THE INFORMATION DISCIPLINES IN THE CULTURAL CRISES OF MODERNITY

Before modernity, ancestral forms of the disciplines of the cultural record appeared along with early systems of writing and are found, though in much smaller numbers, in ancient civilizations (p. 65).[9,36] Nonetheless, even the older fields of the cultural record did not begin to show a distinctively modern occupational identity until industrialization had substantially eroded the craft models of work operating in early modernity. The discipline originally called "documentation" or "documentalism," surfaces more or less *de novo* during the late nineteenth century; by about 1960, it became much more commonly called by its current name, "information science" (pp. 273ff.).[17] Developing separately, the disciplines of the record show varying patterns of growth. Librarianship's first training schools, university schools, professional associations, and certification procedures all date from the last quarter of the nineteenth century, the heyday of industrial modernity. Other common indicators of knowledge-intensive, discipline-based occupational development, like the development of formal codes of ethics, however, developed even later.

Even though archivistics has a long history, its professional associations did not appear until well into the twentieth century, about the same time that professional associations for information science appeared. Information science, of course, now has a number of university programs in force, but these developed only decades later than the library schools. The use of the archive as a public resource for scientific historical research, as opposed to a facility dedicated to the much older function preserving the records of ruling families, businesses, and governments (p. 162),[36] dates from the era of the French Revolution. Like the museum, the archive in modernity reflects the rising power of the bourgeois nation-state.[37,38] Archival training was once universally acquired in work settings, but in more recent times has become integrated into formal university curricula, and according to a recent report is no longer based exclusively in on-the-job training, but commonly requires an advanced professional degree for any real prospect of advancement. At the same time, the disciplinary context for the degree appears to have shifted from history departments, in the period from 1940–1960, to schools of library and information science, in the period between 1984 and 2000.[39,40] And while information science, born modern, may be dated from the early twentieth or the late nineteenth century at the earliest, a group of practitioners identifying themselves as such did not really emerge until the period between World Wars I and II (pp. 3ff.).[25]

Controlling the recorded output of the higher learning, by itself already a formidable task, turned out, however, to be only the beginning of the story. Intense social and political pressure for universities to become involved in solving a wide variety of practical problems inevitably spurred the pursuit and application of knowledge outside the academy. At the same time that capitalism transformed the university by revolutionizing its disciplinary matrix, it was also busy increasingly investing in a wide variety of business enterprises, and the public sector, in turn, developed vast networks of government agencies to regulate and facilitate enterprise. As offshoots of their many activities, these enterprises and agencies generate large quantities of additional records, some of them quite technical and specialized, and others aimed at wider audiences. Additionally, particularly in the period after World War II, an increasing number of enterprises specializing in mass communication, advertising, and entertainment generate an enormous amount of their own recorded content. All of these pushed the information disciplines into territory well beyond the academic sphere, and there were and continue to be appreciable growths in the need for information professionals in all these areas as well.

INNOVATION, HYBRIDIZATION, AND INTERDISCIPLINARITY

Marx and Engels were probably the first major social thinkers to characterize capitalist modernity as ceaseless transformation, but they were certainly not the last.[41] Their underlying idea, if not their precise language, was subsequently taken up by Friedrich Nietzsche (1844–1900), who along with Marx and Engels in turn exercised a strong influence on a number of subsequent writers, notably "political economists" and early sociologists like Max Weber, Werner Sombart (1863–1941), and somewhat later Joseph A. Schumpeter (1883–1950). Nietzsche and Weber recognized that Marx's and Engels' insight was clearly both sociological and historical, since it linked

the inherently transformative nature of capitalist societies with the risk-taking activities of the innovative entrepreneurs typically found in these societies (p. 224, n. 221).[33] Sombart and Schumpeter, on the other hand, used the Nietzschean concept of "creative–destruction" as a means for understanding the revolutionary role played by innovative entrepreneurialism in capitalist modernity.[41] This characteristic juxtaposition of innovation and destruction is at the root of capitalist societies' powerful nihilistic tendencies (pp. 98–105).[34]

Originally, this cycle of innovation, investment, and reinvestment to stimulate more innovation—this perpetual process of creative–destruction—was largely confined to economic goods production and distribution. The innovative approach to knowledge did not become socially dominant until industrialization began to revolutionize its own foundations (that is, in the third of these phases, referred to above as reflexive modernization or the second industrial revolution). (For the three stages, see the section "The Expansionist Logic of Capitalist Modernity"). In that third phase of development, the revolutionary transformation of economic production of earlier periods culminated in widespread rationalization processes. The end result is an expansion in the overall numbers of people producing, distributing, recording, and using knowledge and information. Note that the entrepreneur is the key player in initiating change, and that bureaucracy emerges as an organizational response to innovation.

Toward the end of the nineteenth century, and continuing well into the twentieth, the production and distribution of knowledge became increasingly modeled on the innovative entrepreneur; scholars, teachers, journalists, publicists, scientists, technocrats, and public intellectuals play increasingly important roles in knowledge-intensive, record-creating activities that are analogous to the activities of the innovator in goods production. These knowledge producers—to use a convenient shorthand to encompass all of them—innovate by a process aptly called "hybridization."[42,43] Hybridization proceeds by isolating congenial thematic strands or subfields from one larger field or discipline, and fusing one or more of them with strands or subfields from a different discipline. The result is not only a new subfield, but also a significantly more complex division of intellectual labor, and a further proliferation of records for the information disciplines to track and control (pp. 353–355).[14]

Moreover continuing innovation and specialization has the effect of blurring disciplinary boundaries that were once much more clearly delineated; the more rapidly the innovations appear and disappear, the shorter the half-life of the newer hybrids, and the more fluid the boundaries become (pp. xi–xii).[22] In some cases, hybrids coalesce into larger units, rivaling older disciplinary formations in size and complexity while they emerge as new disciplines or, perhaps more appropriately, "interdisciplines."[44] Numerous examples abound: the emergence of cultural studies, ethnic studies, women's studies, and disability studies, hybridized by crossing various strands from sociology, history, anthropology, literature, the arts, biology, and public health, spawning new bodies of literature in the form of books, journals, audiovisual resources, and Web sites, and eventually secondary and tertiary databases, search engines, and other discovery tools. But in many cases, no larger interdiscipline emerges, leaving an increasingly fragmented landscape of isolated hybrids, awaiting further combination.

In the information disciplines, one of the first of the hybrids to emerge as an interdiscipline was library and information science, fused with strands from traditional literary subfields like bibliography, textual analysis, and the study of readers and reading on the one side and on the other with "documentation studies," as it was known in the period from 1890 to about 1940, or information science, as it was known in the post-World War II period (pp. 168–169).[40] Library and information science during this period also emerged in contrast to a related but distinct interdiscipline, "computer and information science" (p. 9).[45] The difference between the two interdisciplines probably has less to do with issues of content or organization, and much to do with the underlying gender order of late modernity, since library and information science still attracts and holds a clear majority of females, while in computer and information science, on the other hand, precisely the opposite is true.[46]

Since the 1970s, a different pattern of convergence and hybridization has appeared along with the much more recent appearance of formal museum studies, sometimes called "the new museology" (p. 1).[20] In comparison to the patterns seen in earlier times, where librarianship, archivistics, and museum curation were often practiced in close connection with each other, in the late twentieth century, the three have often diverged. But the larger picture is far from clear, since there have been liberal borrowing relationships between museum studies, which have adopted concepts like "collection development" from librarianship (p. 135),[13] and archivistics and librarianship, which have in turn borrowed key concepts and techniques from museum studies (p. 106).[47] It is of course too early in this process to make confident predictions, but it is significant that in both North America and in Europe there is currently a movement to co-locate the information disciplines into one institutional setting for professional education, in effect stressing similarities and overlaps over differences (p. 73).[48] And in Europe there is evidence of an ambitious movement to combine advanced professional education in librarianship, information science, and archivistics into a single interdiscipline that will be able to function in virtually any setting requiring the systematic management of all kinds of information records (p. 323).[11] In the future, museum studies might well join them. At the same time, of course, it must be pointed out that the appearance of larger interdisciplinary

unities is by no means the whole story, since much more specialized, smaller, and relatively isolated hybrids continue to appear ("museum informatics," for example, and others of this kind).

CONCLUSION

The information disciplines today are, more than ever, shaped by the increasing ubiquity and spread of capitalist market societies. Perhaps for this reason, it has become commonplace, at least since about 1970, to call attention to the role of information and information records as exchangeable commodities, in contrast to earlier and possibly more traditional notions of information records as public goods offering various kinds of utility.[49,50] But we have seen that this view of information as commodity is actually very far from recent. When records and their contents acquire the status of exchangeable commodities, it means, among other things, that information disciplines and information professionals become part of a long economic chain connecting producer to end-user, and thus acquire some of the functions of the broker or trader, even though information professionals retain some of the older focus on the knowledge and information as public goods.

At the same time, however, knowledge and information records have more than utility (use value) and market value (exchange value). While their status as useful goods and economic commodities is beyond doubt, they have a distinctly sociological function not properly captured by this economic distinction, since they can also function, like any other object, as signs carrying a wide range of shared meanings. Thus, the record itself has a range of "sign values" (pp. 57–60),[51] (pp. 33–34),[52] and its presence and display figures in a larger social process of communication, quite independently of the much more specific communicative functions of its contents. This means that collections of records and how these are displayed can take on distinctly ideological functions. In consumerized market societies dominated by powerful and sophisticated technologies of information and communication, the information disciplines and the various venues in which information work is performed thus participate in a form of indirect advertising and display of the spectacular range of resources available in modern societies (p. 74).[9]

ACKNOWLEDGMENTS

The author would like to extend special thanks to Alexander Groth, David Michalski, Ellen R. Robert, Marcia Pankake, Aram A Yengoyan, and Luis Guarnizo for close readings and highly useful suggestions.

REFERENCES

1. Conley, D. *You May Ask Yourself: An Introduction to Thinking Like a Sociologist*; W.W. Norton: New York, London, 2008.

2. Macionis, J.J. *Society: The Basics*, 9th Ed.; Pearson Prentice Hall: Upper Saddle River, NJ, 2007.

3. Ong, A. Modernity: Anthropological aspects. In *International Encyclopedia of the Social and Behavioral Sciences*; Smelser, N., Baltes, P.B., Eds.; Elsevier: Amsterdam, the Netherlands, 2001; Vol. 15, 9944–9949.

4. Rothblatt, S. Universities in the history of the social sciences. In *International Encyclopedia of the Social and Behavioral Sciences*; Smelser, N., Baltes, P.B., Eds.; Elsevier: Amsterdam, the Netherlands, 2001; Vol. 23, 15983–15990.

5. Wilson, P. Interdisciplinary research and information overload. Libr. Trend. **1996**, *45*(2), 192–203.

6. Immroth, J.P. Library of congress classification. In *Encyclopedia of Library and Information Science*; Kent, A., Lancour, H., Daily, J.E., Eds.; Marcel Dekker, Inc.: New York, 1975; Vol. 15, 93–200.

7. Gutting, G. *Michel Foucault. Stanford Encyclopedia of Philosophy*, 2003. Available at http://plato.stanford.edu/entries/foucault (accessed January 2008).

8. Fyfe, G. Sociology and the social aspects of museums. In *A Companion to Museum Studies*; Macdonald, S., Ed.; Blackwell: Malden, MA, 2006; 33–49.

9. Black, A. The Victorian information society: Surveillance, bureaucracy, and public librarianship in 19th-century Britain. Inform. Soc. **2001**, *17*(1), 63–80.

10. Hooper-Greenhill, E. *Museums and the Shaping of Knowledge*; Routledge: London, U.K., 1992; New York.

11. Ketelaar, E. Archivistics research: Saving the profession. Am. Archivist **2000**, *63*, 322–340.

12. Bates, M.J. Defining the information disciplines in encyclopedia development. Inform. Res. **2007**, *12*(4). Available at http://InformationR.net/ir/12–4/colis/colis29.html (accessed November 2007).

13. Cossons, N. Professionals and museums 2. In *Museums 2000: Politics, People, Professionals, and Profits*; Boylan, P., Ed.; Routledge: London, U.K., 1992; 123–133, New York.

14. Winter, M.F. Specialization, territoriality, and jurisdiction: Librarianship and the political economy of knowledge. Libr. Trend. **1996**, *45*(2), 343–363.

15. Buckland, M.; Hahn, T.B. Introduction. In *Historical Studies in Information Science*; Buckland, M., Hahn, T.B., Eds.; Information Today, Inc.: Medford, NJ, 1998; 1–6.

16. Rumschöttel, H. The development of archival science as a scholarly discipline. Archival Sci. **2001**, *1*, 143–155.

17. Buckland, M.; Liu, Z. History of information science. In *Historical Studies in Information Science*; Hahn, T.B., Buckland, M., Eds.; Information Today, Inc: Medford, NJ, 1998; 272–295.

18. Johnson, E.; Harris, M. *History of Libraries in the Western World*, 3rd Ed.; Scarecrow Press, Inc.: Metuchen, NJ, 1976.

19. Posner, E. European experiences in training archivists. In *Archives and the Public Interest: Selected Essays*; Posner, E., Ed.; Public Affairs Press: Washington, DC, 1967.

20. Macdonald, S. Expanding museum studies: An introduction. In *A Companion to Museum Studies*; Macdonald, S., Ed.; Blackwell: Malden, MA, 2006; 1–15.

21. Boylan, P. The museum profession. In *A Companion to Museum Studies*; Macdonald, S., Ed.; Blackwell: Malden, MA, 2006; 415–441.

22. Weingart, P.; Stehr, N. Introduction. In *Practising Interdisciplinarity*; Weingart, P., Stehr, N., Eds.; University of Toronto Press: Toronto, ON, Canada, 2000; i–xvi.

23. Abbott, A. *The System of the Professions*; University of Chicago Press: Chicago, IL, 1988.

24. Bates, M. The invisible substrate of information science. J. Am. Soc. Inform. Sci. **1999**, *50*(12), 1043–1050.

25. Winter, M.F. *The Culture and Control of Expertise*; Greenwood Press: New York, 1988.

26. Beck, U. *The Risk Society: Towards a New Modernity*, Tr. Ritter, M.; SAGE: New York; London, U.K., 1986.

27. Muddiman, D. A new history of ASLIB, 1924–1950. J. Doc. **2005**, *61*(3), 402–428.

28. Znaniecki, F. *The Social Role of the Man of Knowledge*; Columbia University Press: New York, 1930.

29. Blasselle, B. La bibliothéconomie, théorie et pratique. In *Histoire des Bibliothèques Françaises: Les Bibliothèques de la Révolution et du XIXe Siècle*; Varry, D., Ed.; Promodis: Paris, France, 1991; 143–163.

30. Jackson, S.L. *Libraries and Librarianship in the West: A Brief History*; McGraw-Hill Book Co.: New York, 1974.

31. Jolly, C. Naissance de la "science" des bibliothèques. In *Histoire des Bibliothèques Françaises: Les Bibliothèques sous l'Ancien Régime, 1530–1789*; Vernet, A., Jolly, C., Eds.; Promodis: Paris, France, 1988; 381–385.

32. Caillet, M. Les bibliothécaires. In *Histoire des Bibliothèques Françaises: Les Bibliothèques sous l'Ancien Régime, 1530–1789*; Jolly, C., Ed.; Promodis: Paris, France, 1988; 373–389.

33. Weber, M. *The Protestant Ethic and the Spirit of Capitalism*, Tr. Kallberg, S.; Fitzroy Dearborn: Chicago, IL, 2001.

34. Berman, M. *All That Is Solid Melts into Air: The Experience of Modernity*; Penguin Books: Harmondsworth, U.K., 1988.

35. Giddens, A. *The Consequences of Modernity*; Stanford University Press: Stanford, CA, 1990.

36. Goody, J. *The Logic of Writing and the Organization of Society*; Cambridge University Press: Cambridge, U.K., 1986.

37. Dasher, O. Archives and historical databases. In *International Encyclopedia of the Social and Behavioral Sciences*; Smelser, N., Baltes, P.B., Eds.; Elsevier: Amsterdam, the Netherlands, 2001; Vol. 1, 643–646.

38. Markoff, J. Archival methods. In *International Encyclopedia of the Social and Behavioral Sciences*; Smelser, N., Baltes, P.B., Eds.; Elsevier: Amsterdam, the Netherlands, 2001; Vol. 1, 637–642.

39. Yakel, E.; Bastian, J. Graduate archival education and the A* census. Soc. Am. Archivists **2005**. Available at http://www.archivists.org/a-census/reports/YakelBastian-ACENSUS.pdf (accessed January 2008).

40. Buckland, M. Documentation, information science, and library science in the U.S.A. In *Historical Studies in Information Science*; Buckland, M., Hahn, T.B., Eds.; Information Today, Inc: Medford, NJ, 1998; 159–172.

41. Reinert, H.; Reinert, E.S. Creative destruction in economics: Nietzsche, Sombart, and Schumpeter. In *Friedrich Nietzsche (1844–1900): Economy and Society*; Backhaus, J.G., Drechsler, W., Eds.; Springer: New York, 2006; 55–85 S.l.

42. Dogan, M.; Pahre, R. *Creative Marginality: Innovation at the Intersections of the Social Sciences*; Westview Press: Boulder, CO, 1990.

43. Dogan, M. The hybridization of social science knowledge. Libr. Trend. **1996**, *45*(2), 296–314.

44. Klein, J.T. *Interdisciplinarity: History, Theory, and Practice*; Wayne State University Press: Detroit, MI, 1990.

45. Rayward, B. History and historiography of information science: Some reflections. In *Historical Studies in Information Science*; Buckland, M., Hahn, T.B., Eds.; Information Today, Inc: Medford, NJ, 1998; 7–21.

46. Gilley, J. Information science: Not just for boys anymore. Am. Libr. **2006**, *37*(6), 50–51.

47. Sola, T. Professionals and museums. In *Museums 2000: Politics, People, Professionals, and Profits*; Boylan, P., Ed.; Routledge: London, U.K., 1992; 101–113, New York.

48. Posner, E. Archival training in the United States. In *Archives and the Public Interest: Selected Essays*; Posner, E., Ed.; Public Affairs Press: Washington, DC, 1967; 58–77.

49. Debons, A.; Otten, K. Towards a metascience of information. J. Am. Soc. Inform. Sci. **1970**, *21*(1), 90–91.

50. Goulding, A. Information: Commodity or social good? J. Libr. Inform. Sci. **2002**, *33*(1), 1–4.

51. Baudrillard, J. The ideological genesis of needs. In *The Consumer Society Reader*; Schor, J., Holt, D., Eds.; The New Press: New York, 2000; 57–80.

52. Schor, J. *The Overspent American: Upscaling, Downshifting, and the New Consumer*; Basic Books: New York, 1998.

Software and Information Industry Association (SIIA)

Silje C. Lier
Software & Information Industry Association, Washington, District of Columbia, U.S.A.

Abstract

The Software and Information Industry Association (SIIA) is the principal trade association for the industries. In 1999, the Software Publishers Association, founded in 1984 by the current SIIA CEO, Ken Wasch, merged with the Information Industry Association, which had represented information industry publishers for a number of years, to create the SIIA as the primary trade association for the combined industries. SIIA has a three-pronged mission on behalf of the software and digital content industry: 1) promoting the common interests of the software and digital content industry as a whole, and its component parts; 2) protecting the intellectual property of its member companies, and advocating for a legal and regulatory environment that benefits the entire industry; and 3) informing the industry and the broader public by serving as a resource on trends, technologies, policies, and related issues that affect member firms and demonstrate the contribution of the industry to the broader economy. SIIA is organized into six major divisions: software, content, education, government affairs, antipiracy, and financial and information services. SIIA has more than 500 member companies that it brings together for useful discussions via large-scale and smaller conferences, as well as board, committee, and division-related planning sessions. It runs the CODiE Award Program, established in 1986 as a way for industry professionals to peer review each other's work and celebrate their achievements. SIIA is headquartered in Washington, D.C. and more information may be found on its Web site at http://www.siia.net.

INTRODUCTION

With today's ever-increasing technological advancements and the ubiquity of digital content and information, the software and information industry continues to flourish. As hi-tech firms grow and thrive as part of this ongoing industry success, a unifying thread is necessary for maintaining standards and providing support—the Software and Information Industry Association, or SIIA. Indeed, SIIA has proven itself as *the* principal trade association for the industry.

SIIA provides global services in government relations, business development, corporate education, and intellectual property protection to leading companies that are setting the pace for the digital age.

Further, SIIA has a three-pronged mission on behalf of the software and digital content industry. The first objective includes promoting the common interests of the software and digital content industry as a whole, as well as its component parts. As its second objective, SIIA protects the intellectual property of its member companies, and advocates a legal and regulatory environment that benefits the entire industry. Third, SIIA informs the industry and the broader public by serving as a resource on trends, technologies, policies, and related issues that affect member firms and demonstrate the contribution of the industry to the broader economy.

HISTORY OF SIIA

The SIIA was founded in April of 1984 by its current CEO, Ken Wasch, who was originally a lawyer at the U.S. Department of Energy. Wasch's interest in emerging software development contributed to his idea of creating a trade association for the then-nascent industry. In November of the previous year, he had sent letters of proposal to potential member companies, which outlined his overall plan for the association. The responses led to the establishment of the Software Publishers Association (precursor to SIIA) and the formation of the trade association's board of directors. In 1999, the Software Publishers Association merged with the Information Industry Association, which had represented information industry publishers for a number of years, and the SIIA was established as the primary trade association for the combined industries.

DEPARTMENTS WITHIN SIIA

The SIIA is organized into six major divisions: software, content, education, government affairs, antipiracy, and financial information services division, or FISD. These departments work collectively to uphold the trade association's mission and to provide benefits to member companies as a whole.

Software division: The software division of SIIA ensures the successful direction of member companies that are the driving vehicle behind contemporary software applications and services. The division provides a collaborative environment for company executives to adapt to changes within the industry and improve their companies. The division keeps up with industry trends and cutting edge research and provides members with the latest resources and opportunities.

Content division: The content division of SIIA provides leadership and support to member companies involved in the publishing and dissemination of digital content and related services. The content division also tracks emerging issues and trends in this arena.

Education division: SIIA's education division provides opportunities and marketing resources for member firms involved in education-related technology. The division also keeps up with education policy issues on a state and federal level. A main component of the education division is the K-20 Vision, an innovative initiative designed to increase learning efficiency through technological strategies and cutting-edge software.

Government affairs: The government affairs division protects member companies by tackling legal issues within the industry and actively working toward effective and successful policies on their behalf at the federal and state level. The division recognizes member concerns and represents their joint interests within a wide range of critical issues, including e-commerce regulation, privacy, and the protection of intellectual property.

Antipiracy: The antipiracy division of the SIIA works actively on minimizing software and content piracy by creating campaigns and educating the public about the legal consequences involved. The division also conducts a Corporate Antipiracy Program, which allows sources to anonymously report instances of piracy by a particular company. In addition, the Internet Antipiracy Program produces investigations of various auction Web sites for piracy occurrences.

FISD: The FISD allows exchanges, market data vendors, consumers and banks to communicate about issues involving the administration of financial information. FISD represents the industry by creating many networking events and opportunities for communication to ensure an understanding regarding the complexities of the marketing data industry.

SIIA MEMBERSHIP

Today, SIIA has more than 500 member companies and continues to enable members to come together for useful discussions via large-scale and smaller conferences, as well as productive board, committee, and division-related planning sessions. With a mix of large brand name companies as well as smaller start-up firms, members have the opportunity to network and share information. Membership also increases company visibility and promotes a positive corporate image. Further, members are represented when it comes to public policy and regulation issues.

THE CODIE AWARDS PROGRAM

The CODiE Award Program was established in 1986 as a way for industry professionals to peer review each other's work and celebrate their incredible achievements. The CODiE title originates from the common software word "code" in convergence with the symbol for information, "i." The CODiE's are held annually and have become *the* prestige of the industry, showcasing exceptional work, and setting high standards for products and services within the software and digital information industry. Products and companies nominated for an award undergo an impartial judging process, which then leads to finalists review process. Winners are announced at an awards gala each spring so that members of the industry can celebrate the success of the industry.

BIBLIOGRAPHY

1. *An Association CEO Who Founded His Association*; Bisnow on Business, Inc.: Washington, DC, November 15, 2007.
2. http://www.fisd.net/about/default.asp.
3. http://www.siia.net/default.asp.

ADDITIONAL RESOURCES

1. Additional information and resources may be found on the SIIA Web site. Available at http://www.siia.net.
2. SIIA is located at 1090 Vermont Ave NW, Sixth Floor, Washington DC, 20005.

Sound and Audio Archives

Mark Roosa
Pepperdine University, Malibu, California, U.S.A.

Abstract

This entry provides an overview of sound archives, including reasons why sound archives exist, their history and organization; types of sound recordings collected, methods of description, and access to and preservation of recorded sound materials. Recorded sound formats (e.g., cylinders, discs, long playing (LP) records, etc.) are covered in the context of how they have been (and are currently being) collected, described, preserved, and made available. Select projects and programs undertaken by regional, special, and national sound archives are covered. Professional associations that focus on sound archiving are described as are funding avenues for sound archives. Description is also included of work being carried out in the United States to modify copyright law to better enable sound archives to preserve their holdings for future generations of users.

INTRODUCTION

To a large extent, the rise of sound archiving directly parallels the development of recorded sound technology itself. Indeed, some of the earliest efforts to archive sounds came in the wake of the invention of the Edison phonograph in 1877, a device which recorded sound onto a wax cylinder. For an illustrated overview of sound record technology, http://history.sandiego.edu.[1] Archival safe keeping of sound recordings during this early period was tied to the commercial distribution of recordings of popular and classical music. As molded wax (and later plastic) cylinder production was limited, these artifacts from the early period of sound recording history have become increasingly rare and valuable. "In the 1890s it became possible to duplicate cylinders and discs on a large scale and, after the turn of the century, the commercial production of recordings really got under way."[1] Cylinders were collected chiefly by private individuals, museums, and historic societies. Federal institutions in the United States, such as the Smithsonian Institution and the Library of Congress, which housed centers for the study of folk culture, amassed large numbers of cylinder recordings. Many of these cylinders, made by anthropologists, musicologists, ethnomusicologists, and folklorists, recorded for the first time the words, sounds, music, and cultural expressions of Native Americans, Eskimos, and African Americans.

Recognizing a need to archive and preserve the growing number of cylinders in institutional hands, the Library of Congress launched the Federal Cylinder Project.

It began in June 1979, with three main goals:[1] to preserve wax cylinder recordings in federal collections by transferring them onto modern Mylar tape,[2] to document and catalog the recordings, and to disseminate the results of the project to the public, particularly to those culture groups from which the recordings were originally recorded [from a review by Richard Keeling which appeared in the Journal of American Folklore (101, 1988), 82].

In recent years, institutions and individual collectors have paid increasing attention to the preservation of cylinders as important artifacts. Several important projects aimed at providing increased public access to sounds recorded on these antique information carriers have been undertaken, including one notable initiative by the library at the University of California, Santa Barbara. The project, made possible through support from the Institute for Museum and Library Services, has produced a digital collection of nearly 8000 cylinder recordings held by the library's department of special collections. The digitized recordings can be freely downloaded or streamed from the library's Web site.[3]

RECORDING CULTURE

Elsewhere in the world, ethnographic and anthropological museums holding collections of cylinders have taken steps to identify and preserve collections of early recordings, including, for example, the Berlin Phonogramm-Archiv—one of the most significant collections of ethnographic recordings in Europe—which contains some of the earliest recordings of the indigenous peoples of Africa, North America, Asia, Australia, Oceania, and Europe. Today the Phonogramm-Archiv, which is part of the musicological section of the Ethnographical Museum, State Museum at Berlin, Prussian Cultural Heritage Foundation, holds, "more than 145,000 recordings of music representing the heritage of many cultures all over the world."[4]

Sound archives have also developed, "within research and educational institutions which took up sound

Encyclopedia of Library and Information Sciences, Fourth Edition DOI: 10.1081/E-ELIS4-120044485

Sociology–Special

recordings as yet another source of information in their specialized fields (e.g., music, ethnomusicology, and dialectology, political or social history)."[5] For example,

In 1890 the anthropologist Jesse Walker Fewkes pioneered the use of the phonograph when he recorded songs of the Passamaquoddy Indians. In Europe, the Hungarian Bela Vikar (1859–1945) is regarded as a pioneer for his work in recording traditional folk music and dialects. With the opening in 1899 of the Phonogrammarchive (Phonographic Archive) of the Academy of Science in Vienna, the first scientific sound archive in the world was established, having as its aim the systematic collection of this new type of source material by the production, acquisition and preservation of sound recordings for all areas of scholarship.[6]

The organization of sound archives in cultural institutions has developed along two chief lines. The *medium-centered* archive is one that collects recordings of like type, such as long playing (LP) phonograph records. The assumption here is that, "the needs of the medium take priority over any other consideration."[7] For certain formats such as early cylinders, the medium-centered approach can help in the long-term preservation of an endangered or artifactually important format. By contrast, the *content-centered* approach involves collecting recordings on the basis of how they relate to a particular topic or discipline. For example, an archive containing all known commercial recordings of works by Beethoven regardless of format would be an example of a content-centered approach.

Some examples of sound archives organized by content include:

- Linguistic
- Folklore
- Oral history
- Ethnographic
- Dialectic
- Music
- Ethnomusicology
- Bioacoustic (e.g., ornithology, etc.)
- Spoken word

Sound archives have also developed around national library and archives collection development mandates. For example, the British Library and the U.S. Library of Congress are both copyright depository libraries which are required by law to collect describe and preserve copies of all copyrighted materials in their respective countries. For these institutions, the business of sound archiving is integrated into the larger mandate of serving the public good by maintaining a collection of all items protected under copyright. Today, along with the Library of Congress in the United States, the British Library Sound Archive is one of the world's leading repositories of sound recordings in all genres and formats.

The sound archive holds over a million discs, 185,000 tapes, and many other sound and video recordings. The collections come from all over the world and cover the entire range of recorded sound from music, drama and literature, to oral history and wildlife sounds. They range from cylinders made in the late nineteenth century to the latest CD, DVD and mini disc recordings. We keep copies of commercial recordings issued in the United Kingdom, together with selected commercial recordings from overseas, radio broadcasts and many privately made recordings.[8]

Gronow notes, "The idea of a national collection of commercial recordings was first introduced in France, where the Phonotheque Nationale was founded in the 1930s."[9] In the United Kingdom, the British Institute of Recorded Sound collects not only commercial recordings but also wildlife sounds, documentary recordings, folk music, and broadcasts. In Sweden, the Arkivet for Ljud och Bild is the central archive for commercial recordings, radio and television broadcasts, and films. In Denmark, the Nationaldiskoteket is part of the National Museum. In the United States, the Motion Picture, Broadcasting and Recorded Sound Division of the Library of Congress, established in 1978,[9] serves as a national repository for sound recordings.

Large, broad-based national sound archives collections help assure that a representative cross-section of the total output of recorded culture produced in a particular country or region is collected, described, preserved, and made available. For those with particular research needs, however, large broadly focused collections may be of limited value. Instead, smaller topic-specific sound archives may be more useful to those perusing specific topics such as folk music, the spoken word, or jazz.

MUSIC FOR THE MASSES

With the introduction of the mass-produced Edison disc, manufactured by means of a stamping process, the availability of sound recordings skyrocketed. The Edison phonograph with its hand crank and ornate funnel-shaped horn rapidly became a fixture in households across America and around the world. Discs were aggressively marketed by the Edison Company. Competitors began to enter the scene and with this we see the rise of the so-called "format wars" which persist today. The competitive climate that defined the early years of commercial sound recording is described in great detail in Gelat's the Fabulous Phonograph: From Edison to Stereo (see the Bibliography entry by Besek, J.M.) Subsequent improvements in the disc manufacturing process enabled more grooves per inch to be added to a disc thus extending its playback time. Extended play enabled more varied repertory to be recorded. This significant improvement enabled extended popular and classical works to be recorded for the first time in their entirety usually on a series of discs. When packaged together these multidisc sets were referred to as record "albums." The push to increase disc program time led to the development of the LP record. Gronow notes [that] "In the 1950s, the introduction of the microgroove (long playing and single) record and the general improvement in the standard of living increased the demand for records, and for thirty years world sales increased."[2] The open reel tape format—the chief format for recording sound in a studio setting—was only moderately successful in the consumer market. More popular as a distribution medium was the Compact Cassette introduced by Philips in the 1960s for which many varied types of players were produced, including notably units fitted in automobiles.

A major change in the way in which sound was recorded came in 1979 with the introduction of pulse code modulation (PCM) recording technology. Pulse code modulation, the first digital music recording system for commercial use, was quickly adopted by recording studios because it was much better suited to studio recording, editing, and production than its analog counterpart. The digital compact disc (CD), and the CD player, was introduced in 1982. The CD remained the prevailing format collected by most popular and classical music sound archives throughout the 1980s and 1990s.

With the rise of the Internet as the primary means of distributing digital data (including text, moving images, and sound), the downloading of sound (currently in MP3 format) to computers and to portable devices (such at the Apple I Pod) is now a preferred means of accessing sound. This mode of delivery continues to gain in popularity each year as retail sales of CDs drop at a corresponding rate.

THE RISE OF MUSIC ARCHIVES

While initial efforts to archive sound began in step with the commercial development of the earliest sound recordings, the formal shaping of archives for the purposes of supporting research and to assure preservation of the cultural record is a more recent phenomenon. National libraries and archives, university libraries and archives, and private libraries and archives have each contributed uniquely to the development of a network of repositories for commercial and noncommercial sound recordings. Archives, such as the American Folklife Center at the Library of Congress (http://www.loc.gov/folklife/index.html), the Smithsonian Center for Folklife and Cultural Heritage (http://www.folklife.si.edu/index.html), and specialty archives such as the Rutgers Institute of Jazz Studies Archive (http://newarkwww.rutgers.edu/IJS/), state-based folk life centers, university-hosted centers, such as the Archives of Traditional Music at Indiana University (http://www.indiana.edu/~libarchm/) each play an important role in shaping a community responsible for collecting, preserving, and providing sustained access to recorded sound.

In Europe and in the United States, institutions holding substantial collections of sound recordings have aligned themselves with one another through participation in the work of professional associations such as the International Association of Sound Archives (IASA) and in the United States the Association for Recorded Sound Collections (ARSC). Within this latter organization resides the Association of Audio Archives a group composed of leading institutional sound archives, including those located at the New York Public Library, Yale University, Stanford University, and the Library of Congress.

SERVING USER NEEDS

The users of sound archives vary widely and extend beyond the realm of traditional scholarship. Writing on the role of sound archives in the field of Ethnomusicology, for example, Anthony Seeger notes, [that] "Scholars are not the only people who use archives. They are also used by musicians, students, members of the public interested in a certain part of the world or learning a language, members of the society recorded, and refugees." Seeger continues, "Field collections serve all these users better than commercial recordings because they usually provide more material and are closer to the original live performances than most commercial releases."[10]

Both private and corporate sound archives have contributed significantly to development of a network of sound repositories who serve a diverse range of needs. Symphony orchestras, for example, frequently possess archives which document live performances, rehearsals, and radio or television broadcasts. Jones and Trebble note that archives of sound recordings in broadcasting organizations (including the archives of the British Broadcasting Corporation, one of the world's leading broadcast archives) were not developed until the middle of the 1930s when recording techniques, such as instantaneous recording onto lacquer discs, began to be used in radio production.[11]

COLLECTING POLICIES

Collection development policies which set forth the type of material to be acquired by an archive are essential for effective collection management and for providing patrons with the materials they require. These written guidelines should be explicit and updated periodically. Jones and Trebble suggest the following questions be asked of items or collections being considered for acquisition:

- Is the recording likely to be of use in future broadcasts?
- Does the recording possess significance in sound, over and above the information and/or style of the script?

- Does the archive possess similar material and if so, does the new recording increase the value of the existing collection by providing additional examples, improved performances, or better technical quality?
- Is the recording technically suitable for preservation?
- Are there copyright, contractual, or other restrictions on the use of the recording?
- Should the recording be selected as a whole or in part?[12]

TECHNIQUES OF SOUND ARCHIVING

Effective technical processing of sound recordings is essential to providing sustained access to content. This involves making certain that procedures and policies are in place for the acquisition of materials. Written collection development guidelines which define the types of materials collected by an archive and preferred formats (e.g., 78s, LPs, CDs, etc.) are of fundamental importance. Such guidelines should also articulate retention and de-accession policies and procedures and provide archives staff with direction regarding how and when to copy recordings. Copying may be required when an item is deteriorated to the extent that information is at risk of being lost. Copying may also be carried out as a means of converting sound from an obsolete or noncompliant format to one that is supported by the archive. In addition, archives staff may copy for distribution provided they are in compliance with copyright law. In each case, procedures and guidelines are critical for the consistent and correct transfer of sound from one carrier to the next.

Correct documentation tailored to the level and type of access an archives wishes to provide is also of critical importance. This begins with compilation of a complete inventory of holdings. Once items are accounted for, cataloging and description can focus upon individual items or collections depending on the level of user access required. Cataloging or metadata records can be either minimal or full. This depends on a number of factors, including the relative importance or value of particular items to a collection. Indexing provides users a means for identifying specific performers, topics, and works within an archive's cataloged collections. A variety of cataloging standards have been used over the years to describe sound recordings. Two standards currently in common use are Machine-Readable Cataloging (MARC) and International Standard Bibliographic Description for Non-Book Material (ISBD NBM).

PRESERVATION AND ACCESS

Of equal importance in the responsible stewardship of sound is managing use of collections in ways that provide users with the resources they need while assuring good preservation. Effective preservation begins with development and use of written collection access policies which set forth the terms under which collections may be used, security guidelines, and care and handling policies. Such policies may also articulate the ways in which patrons may access recordings (onsite or remotely), how to use equipment, procedures for obtaining copies, etc. Depending on an archive's clientele and scope of activities, policies may also be needed to address such things as providing permissions for using sound recordings in publications, loan of materials for exhibitions, use of recordings for educational purposes, and broadcast.

SUPPORTING MATERIALS

A collection of sound recordings is of limited value without a catalog that enables a user to locate recordings of specific interest. Catalogs are usually organized by subject, author, genre, format, location, etc. Of special importance is supporting reference materials, such as bibliographies, discographies, and books or electronic resources pertinent to the types of recorded materials collected. Manufacturer catalogs, for example, can be invaluable reference sources for archives that collect commercially issued sound recordings.

PROFESSIONAL ASSOCIATIONS

The development and general availability of best practices for archiving sound recordings has been made possible in large part due to the growth of the profession of sound archivists. Today's sound archivist in search of information, best practices, and like-minded colleagues has a number of professional organizations to choose from. These associations and organizations serve as both convening bodies for professionals and clearing houses for information about sound archiving. In the United States, the ARSC, a nonprofit organization founded in 1966, is the largest professional association for sound archivists. As its Web site states, ARSC is, "dedicated to the preservation and study of sound recordings in all genres of music and speech, in all formats, and from all periods." Association for Recorded Sound Collections is unique in bringing together private individuals and institutional professionals. Archivists, librarians, and curators representing many of the world's leading audiovisual repositories participate in ARSC alongside record collectors, record dealers, researchers, historians, discographers, musicians, engineers, producers, reviewers, and broadcasters. The peer-reviewed ARSC *Journal*, first published in 1968, represents a wealth of landmark articles, papers, and reviews. The ARSC Newsletter delivers timely announcements, short articles, and a calendar of coming events. Topics explored in ARSC publications, at ARSC conferences, and on the ARSC List e-mail forum include, "preservation of sound recordings, access to recordings, audio conservation and restoration, biography, cataloging, discography, history and technology, archival practices, training and education, bibliography, copyright and intellectual property issues."[13] The work of ARSC and its members has made a tremendously positive impact on the management of sound archives in the United States. Several of its publications, such as the landmark study by Picket and Lemcoe, *Preservation and Storage of Sound Recordings* (1959, reprinted in 1991) are in wide use in both private and public sound archives throughout the world.

At the international level, IASA serves as the chief organization for sound archivists.

IASA was established in 1969 in Amsterdam to function as a medium for international cooperation between archives that preserve recorded sound and audiovisual documents. IASA has members from more than 60 countries representing a broad palette of audiovisual archives and personal interests which are distinguished by their focus on particular subjects and areas, e.g., archives for all sorts of musical recordings, historic, literary, folkloric and ethnological sound documents, theater productions and oral history interviews, bio-acoustics, environmental and medical sounds, linguistic and dialect recordings, as well as recordings for forensic purposes.[14]

International Association of Sound and Audiovisual Archives, which maintains operational relations with UNESCO, holds a conference each year in a different location. Committees responsible for various issues convene at these conferences. International Association of Sound and Audiovisual Archives publishes its *Information Bulletin* and *Journal* on a regular basis, as well as special publications on various topics. At the conference there are ample opportunities for sound archives professionals to gather, network, hear papers, present papers, visit exhibitions, and tour the libraries and archives of the host country.

ASSESSING THE STATE OF COLLECTIONS

During the twentieth century, collections of sound recordings especially those in academic settings have grown to support campus learning, teaching, and research. The relative state of these collections was not well understood until 2004 when the Council on Library and Information Resources (CLIR) undertook a survey of academic library repositories to better understand their preservation needs. Staff from more than 80 institutions responded to the CLIR survey which found that, "recorded sound collections on campuses are rich and diverse...and [that] campuses report increased demand for the use of audio in teaching and research. But with few exceptions, barriers to such use are high and institutional readiness for improving the condition and accessibility of audio holdings is

low, especially for rare and unique materials."[15] Respondents tended to identify lack of funding as the greatest barrier to access. Other commonly cited barriers included:

1) the absence of appropriate standards and tools for cost-effective inventory and bibliographic control; 2) the lack of effective and cost-efficient means of treating and reformatting analog materials; 3) the absence of clear mandates about how to provide access to valuable collections the rights to which are ambiguous or unknown; and 4) the lack of staff who are sufficiently trained and conversant in the genres, formats, and rights issues unique to recorded sound collections.[15]

PRESERVATION

Implicit in an archive's mission to provide sustained access to sound recordings is a deep-seated obligation to responsibly preserve its recordings so they are available for research, study, and enjoyment. To achieve this, an archive initially conducts a preservation needs assessment of its collections. Data derived from this work help an archive understand its preservation challenges and forge a strategy to address areas of concern.[16] Ideally this risk assessment and management process produces a series-coordinated measures to reduce risks to collections through preventive measures while providing remedial treatment for content in imminent danger of loss.

Preventive measures include making certain that the collection storage environment is conducive to long-term preservation of the media being stored. This begins with assuring the temperature and humidity levels are stable and within acceptable parameters for the materials being archived. It also requires that all materials (storage containers, record sleeves, tape storage boxes, etc.) which come in contact with the recordings are constructed of permanent and durable materials that will not interact adversely with the recordings they are designed to protect.

A frequent cause of damage to collections is through mishandling by staff and patrons. Investing in an educational program to address care and handling issues is money well spent, as it reduces unnecessary damage. Various manuals, bibliographies, and guides covering the care, handling, and storage of discs,[17] tapes,[18] and CDs[19] are available.

Due to the relatively unstable physical nature of many of the recorded sound formats that have been introduced over the years, and due to the increasing obsolesce of the hardware needed to play back some of these older formats, copying (or preservation reformatting) of endangered content is often the only viable remedial preservation option available. Several useful guides are available to assist archives personnel in this exacting work.[20] Preservation reformatting requires the skills of a trained individual (preferable a sound engineer), the correct equipment properly calibrated, and the investment of time and money.

Selected guidelines and best practices for the effective and accurate extraction of sound from older formats and its transfer (usually to digital systems) are described in *Capturing Analog Sound for Digital Preservation, Report of a Roundtable Discussion of Best Practices for Transferring Analog Discs and Tapes* (CLIR, March, 2006).[21] Another useful guide is *Sound Directions: Best Practices for Audio Preservation* by Mike Casey and Bruce Gordon (2007). Research and development into the art and science of extracting sound from antique or obsolete formats is ongoing. One recent effort, led by Dr. Carl Haber at the Lawrence Berkeley Labs in California, involves the use of techniques borrowed from high-energy particle physics to extract sound from grooved media using a noncontact method. This approach potentially eliminates the need for a traditional analog playback machine in the reformatting process.[22]

Following established guidelines and best practices for copying is a good starting point for extending the life expectancy of endangered recorded sounds. Following existing technical standards is also useful, including those developed by the Audio Engineering Society (AES).[23] Unfortunately, as the 2006 CLIR study mentioned above notes, due to the idiosyncrasies of individual application of these guidelines and standards and the variables associated with equipment used and personal preferences for attaining the "best sound" no firm technical standards for doing audio transfer have been universally adopted. Such as those which exist for more well – is tablished preservation techniques such as preservation-microfilming.

FUNDING AND SUPPORT

Because of the exacting and costly nature of much of the work associated with the preservation of sound recordings and the shortage—relative to the print world—of experts trained to do this work, institutions must often seek external sources of funding to accomplish their preservation objectives. Several federal agencies in the United States offer financial assistance for sound preservation.

The National Endowment for the Humanities (NEH), "an independent grant-making agency of the United States government dedicated to supporting research, education, preservation, and public programs in the humanities"[24] is one such agency. The National Endowment for the Humaniti offers, through its various program components, preservation support for humanities collections and resources and preservation education and training for individuals, organizations, and institutions.

The Institute for Museum and Library Services (IMLS) strives to, "provide leadership and funding for the nation's museums and libraries, resources these institutions need to fulfill their mission of becoming centers of learning for life crucial to achieving personal fulfillment, a productive workforce and an engaged citizenry."[25]

Both funding agencies offer, through their Web sites and program officers, a wealth of information and guidance to organizations seeking funding.

COPYRIGHT

Copying recordings for preservation and access purposes is a core activity in most sound archives. U.S. Copyright law provides a framework for legal copying. The Digital Millennium Copyright Act, enacted in 1998, amended portions of the copyright law to address the preservation practices of libraries and archives, but it was not a comprehensive revision. For example, direction concerning pre-1972 sound recordings not presently covered by federal copyright law was omitted from the revision. This prompted the Council on Library and Information Resources and the Library of Congress to publish a study in 2005 on this issue.[26] Concerned further with the exceptions and limitations applicable to libraries and archives under section 108 of the Copyright Act, the U.S. Copyright Office and the National Digital Information and Preservation Infrastructure and Preservation Program of the Library of Congress formed The Section 108 Study Group, "to conduct a reexamination of the exceptions and limitations applicable to libraries and archives under the Copyright Act, specifically in light of digital technologies."[27] Their report, published in March 2008, contains specific recommendations for amending copyright law to reflect the preservation and access needs of cultural repositories, including sound archives.

CHALLENGES OF THE DIGITAL ERA: MEETING USER NEEDS AND EXPECTATIONS

Since the late 1990s, the distribution of music has shifted from being format-based to being streamed or otherwise distributed digitally. Today's consumers increasingly expect their favorite music and sounds to be available through their choice of digital distribution channels. This shift in user expectations is impacting sound archives. As the format era draws to a close, sound archives interested in collecting contemporary music, for example, are being challenged to refocus efforts to address a media-less environment. Increasingly, the distribution of contemporary music will be on-demand, which is to say made available to users on a "pay-as-you-go" basis, downloaded from an Internet resource. Evidence of this trend can be seen to day in the degree to which commercial music distribution services (e.g., Apple I Junes, etc.) have proliferated. How long a commercial release remains available will depend directly on demand: if an item does not sell well, it will likely not remain available for long. Fundamental changes in the ways in which commercial recordings are distributed will challenge sound archives to develop new methods of harvesting content, including perhaps employing mechanisms for the automatic retrieval of digital content from creators, publishers, and aggregators.

Within the past decade, a growing number of libraries on academic campuses around the world have developed institutional digital repositories to preserve and provide sustained access to owned and leased scholarly material. Increasingly, these repositories are acquiring more and more sound content, much of it locally produced. This movement toward intuitions functioning as aggregators and stewards of distinctive, locally produced works represents perhaps a polar opposite to the prevailing practices of the twentieth century in which large regional or national sound archives served as the primary repositories of our recorded sound culture. The emergence of distributed models for archiving sound reflects the changing ways in which content is being created, aggregated, and used and also its value to the communities it serves.

Reflective of the proliferation of smaller institutions taking part in the archiving of sound, an increasing number of digital audio projects aimed at acquiring, describing, preserving, and distributing "born-digital" and digitally converted audio have appeared within the past 5–7 years. Several of these are noted at http://palimpsest. stanford.edu/bytopic/audio/ a Web site devoted to preservation and conservation. A particularly useful resource, developed by the University of Washington Libraries, "Digital Projects and Developing Technologies in Music and Media" (http://www.lib.washington.edu/music/projects.html) provides an overview of select digital audio projects, readings on digital audio technologies, information on music metadata (documentation), audio encoding and markup language, and other tools for the production and management of digital audio and video.

Along with the emergence of new models for archiving sound, several national efforts have also been mounted to create digital sound and moving image repositories and service centers. One such initiative is the National Audio Visual Conservation Center operated under the auspices of the Library of Congress. "Located at the foothills of the Blue Ridge Mountains in Culpepper, Virginia, the Library's newly completed Packard Campus of the National Audio-Visual Conservation Center provides underground storage for this entire collection on 90 miles of shelving, together with extensive modern facilities for the acquisition, cataloging and preservation of all audiovisual formats." In addition to being a national repository for sound and moving image formats where digital conversion takes place, the Culpepper facility is also designed to acquire, preserve, and make available "born-digital" sound and moving image content.

CONCLUSION

Moving forward, and facilitated to a large extent by tools which enable one to create a sizable archive of sound

recordings on one's laptop computer, one can easily imagine a time in the not-too-distant future when the infrastructure for sharing personal archives, globally mining institutional holdings, and rapidly accessing historical recordings from the collections of the great sound repositories of the twentieth century will be upon us. While there are significant cultural, institutional, and legal barriers to realizing this future, the technology needed to make possible this future is readily available today. With the strategic use of this technology directed toward providing seamless access to content, coupled with the continued good stewardship of those who are entrusted to care for recorded sounds wherever they reside, we may well reach that future sooner than expected.

REFERENCES

1. http://history.sandiego.edu/gen/recording/notes.html (accessed November 2008).
2. Gronov, P. Commercial recordings. In *Sound Archives, a Guide to Their Establishment and Development*; David, L., Ed.; IASA: Vienna, Austria, 1983; 77.
3. UCSB, http://cylinders.library.ucsb.edu/ (accessed November 2008).
4. UNESCO, http://www.unesco.org (accessed November 2008).
5. Schuursma, R. Approaches to the national organization of sound archives. In *Sound Archives, a Guide to Their Establishment and Development*; Lance, D., Ed.; IASA: Vienna, Austria, 1983; 1–9.
6. Schuller, D. Ethnomusicology. In *Sound Archives, a Guide to Their Establishment and Development*; Lance, D., Ed.; IASA: Vienna, Austria, 1983; 122.
7. Schuursma, R. Approaches to the national organization of sound archives. In *Sound Archives, a Guide to Their Establishment and Development*; Lance, D., Ed.; IASA: Vienna, Austria, 1983; 22.
8. British Library Sound Archive, http://www.bl.uk/collections/sound-archive/nsaabout.html (accessed November 2008).
9. Grenow, P. Commercial recordings. In *Sound Archives, a Guide to Their Establishment and Development*; Lance, D., Ed.; IASA: Vienna, Austria, 1983; 76.
10. Seeger, A. The role of sound archives. In *Sound Archives, a Guide to Their Establishment and Development*; Lance, D., Ed.; IASA: Vienna, Austria, 1983; 264.
11. Jones; Trebble Broadcasting. In *Sound Archives, a Guide to Their Establishment and Development*; IASA: Vienna, Austria, 1983; 76.
12. Jones; Trebble Broadcasting. In *Sound Archives, a Guide to Their Establishment and Development*; IASA: Vienna, Austria, 1983; 70–71.
13. ARSC, http://www.arsc-audio.org/ (accessed November 2008).
14. IASA, http://www.iasa-web.org/pages/00homepage.htm (accessed November 2008).
15. Smith, A.; David, R.A.; Karen, A. *Survey of the State of Audio Collections in Academic Libraries. Optimizing*

Collections and Services for Scholarly Use; Council on Library and Information Resources: Washington, DC, 2004; 10.

16. A particularly useful preservation needs assessment tool is FACET, http://www.dlib.indiana.edu/projects/sound directions/facet/index.shtml (accessed November 2008).

17. http://www.loc.gov/preserv/care/record.html (accessed November 2008).

18. http://www.clir.org/pubs/abstract/pub54.html (accessed November 2008).

19. http://www.clir.org/pubs/abstract/pub121abst.html (accessed November 2008).

20. Dale, R. *Audio Preservation: A Selective Annotated Bibliography and Brief Summary of Current Practices*; The Association: Chicago, IL, 1998.

21. Council on Library and Information Resources, National Recording Preservation Board (U.S.), and Library of Congress, *Capturing Analog Sound for Digital Preservation Report of a Roundtable Discussion of Best Practices for Transferring Analog Discs and Tapes. Optimizing Collections and Services for Scholarly Use*; Council on Library and Information Resources and Library of Congress: Washington, DC, 2006.

22. http://irene.lbl.gov/ (accessed November 2008).

23. http://www.aes.org/publications/standards/list.cfm for a list of AES standards (accessed November 2008).

24. NEH, http://www.neh.gov/whoweare/index.html (accessed November 2008).

25. IMLS, http://www.imls.gov/about/about.shtm (accessed November 2008).

26. Besek, J.M. *Copyright Issues Relevant to Digital Preservation and Dissemination of Pre-1972 Commercial Sound Recordings by Libraries and Archives*; Commissioned by the National Recording Preservation Board, Library of Congress; Council on Library and Information Resources and Library of Congress: Washington, DC, December 2005.

27. *The Section 108 Study Group Report. An Independent Report sponsored by the United States Copyright Office and the National Digital Information Infrastructure and Preservation Program of the Library of Congress*; United States Corporate Office: Washington, DC, March 2008, http://www.section108.gov/docs/Sec108ExecSum. pdf (accessed November 2008).

BIBLIOGRAPHY

1. Besek, J.M. *Copyright Issues Relevant to Digital Preservation and Dissemination of Pre-1972 Commercial Sound Recordings by Libraries and Archives. Optimizing Collections and Services for Scholarly Use*; Council on Library and Information Resources: Washington, DC, 2005.

2. Boston, G. *Archiving the Audio-Visual Heritage: Third Joint Technical Symposium: May 3–5, 1990, Canadian Museum of Civilization, Ottawa, Canada*; [S.l.]: Technical Coordinating Committee, 1992.

3. Council on Library and Information Resources, National Recording Preservation Board (U.S.), and Library of Congress. *Capturing Analog Sound for Digital Preservation Report of a Roundtable Discussion of Best Practices for Transferring Analog Discs and Tapes. Optimizing Collections and Services for Scholarly Use*. Council on Library and Information Resources and Library of Congress: Washington, DC, 2006.

4. Gelatt, R. *The Fabulous Phonograph; From Edison to Stereo*; Appleton Century: New York, 1966.

5. Lance, D. *Sound Archives: A Guide to Their Establishment and Development*; International Association of Sound Archives: Milton Keynes, England, 1983.

6. Pickett, A.G.; Lemcoe, M.M. *Preservation and Storage of Sound Recordings*; Library of Congress: Washington, DC, 1959.

7. Smith, A.; David, R.A.; Karen, A. *Survey of the State of Audio Collections in Academic Libraries. Optimizing Collections and Services for Scholarly Use*; Council on Library and Information Resources: Washington, DC, 2004.

8. Stielow, F.J. *The Management of Oral History Sound Archives*; Greenwood Press: Westport, CT, 1986.

9. Welch, W.L.; Leah, B.S.B.; Oliver, R. *From Tinfoil to Stereo: The Acoustic Years of the Recording Industry, 1877–1929*; University Press of Florida: Gainesville, FL, 1994.

South Korea: Archives and Libraries

Hyun-Yang Cho
Department of Library and Information Science, Kyonggi University, Suwon, South Korea

Eun Bong Park
Library Service Department, National Library of Korea, Seoul, South Korea

Soyeon Park
Department of Library and Information Science, Duksung Womens University, Seoul, South Korea

Jae-Hwang Choi
Department of Library and Information Science, Kyungpook National University, Daegu, South Korea

Seong Hee Kim
Department of Library and Information Science, Chung-Ang University, Seoul, South Korea

Jong-Yup Han
Research Information Team, KORDI, Seoul, South Korea

Abstract

This entry covers the development of libraries and archives in Korea, and with a focus on their current status and activities and their vision for the future. The authors present an overview of Korean institutional change, and describe recent government policies concerning libraries and archives. They also discuss various types of libraries as well as professional associations and educational programs for librarians and archivists.

FACTS ABOUT KOREA

The Korean Peninsula extends southward from the northeast of the Asian continent. The peninsula, with all of its some 3000 associated scattered islands, lies between 33° and 43° north latitude. The peninsula is surrounded by the Sea of the East (Sea of Japan) on the east, East China Sea to the south, and the Yellow Sea to the west, with the Korea Strait connecting the first two bodies of water. The country shares its northern borders with China and Russia along the Amnokgang (Yalu) and the Dumangang (Tumen) rivers. Its geographical location, bridging the continental Asia and the Pacific Ocean, has been considered by foreign powers to be strategically vital over the centuries (Fig. 1).

The peninsula and Korean islands have a total area of 222,154 square kilometers, similar in size to the United Kingdom (which covers 241,752 square kilometers). But as a result of the Korean War (1950–1953), the peninsula is divided into South Korea and North Korea by the Military Demarcation Line. South Korea, officially known as the Republic of Korea, occupies 45% of the total area of the peninsula, or 99,392 square kilometers, and is a little smaller than Iceland (which covers 103,000 square kilometers). About 70% of the peninsula is mountainous.

Despite its long recorded history, spanning over 5000 years, Korea remained a "Land of Morning Calm," as it was referred to by the great Indian poet and philosopher Rabindranath Tagore in the early twentieth century. But it broke the "calm" by successfully staging the Seoul Summer Olympic Games in 1988 and cohosting the World Cup finals in 2002. Korea joined the Organization for Economic Cooperation and Development (OECD) in 1996 to be its 29th member state, catching as a springboard for further progress into becoming an advanced economy.

Korea is a democratic republic. Its head of state is the President. The country currently maintains diplomatic relations with 186 nations. The size of the population was estimated at 48,294,000 as of July 2005. The average life expectancy reached 77.5 years (73.9 years for men and 80.8 years for women) as of the end of 2003. School attendance stands at 100% at the elementary level, 97.4% at the middle school level, 95.8% at the high school level, and 71.1% at the college and university level, respectively, as of the end of 2005. All elementary school graduates are eligible to attend middle school, 99.7% of the graduates actually enroll in middle school, and 82.1% of high school graduates enter colleges or universities. These percentages are the highest in the world, and Koreans have traditionally placed great importance on education. The nation's unusual enthusiasm for education has played a

Fig. 1   Map of South Korea.
Source: CIA World Factbook. https://www.cia.gov/library/publications/the-world-factbook/geos/ks.html.

vital role in its economic and social development despite a paucity of natural resources. The government is also making continued efforts to improve its educational system in order to cultivate high-quality human resources. Korea is also the most densely wired information technology (IT) powerhouse in the world, with the highest number of Internet subscribers and the second highest number of Internet users per 10,000 persons, respectively. According to the 2006 OECD Factbook, Korea's GDP was estimated at $1,005,300 million, ranking ninth among the OECD members at the end of 2004. With its GDP per capita income of $20,935, the nation is continuing to energetically advance toward becoming an economic power.

ARCHIVES AND ARCHIVAL SCIENCE

Introduction

This section focuses on the development of Korean National Archives & Records Service (NARS), and it also deals with legislation concerning NARS and with the government's efforts toward long-term planning for archives and public records management. The authors end this section with a brief discussion on archival educational programs, which are now offered in 16 Korean universities.

National Archives & Services

The National Archives & Records Service (NARS) is a national agency to collect and systematically manage the nation's important records. The NARS has the primary duty to preserve these records as a national critical cultural heritage and to ensure ready access to the essential evidence of the rights of the Korean people, the accountability of governmental activities, and national experiences.

Daejeon Headquarters of NARS is the primary institution designated to set up recordkeeping policies, to collect archives of the nation's history, to computerize the conventional records systems, to research and develop the technology of restoration and conservation, and to educate the records managers of governmental agencies at all levels. Daejeon Headquarters runs an Exhibition Hall, a Government Resources Library, and a Research Room for public services and outreach. The Daejeon repository is one of the National Archives repositories in Korea, which is located on the first and second basement floors at the government complex in Daejeon. This repository is especially dedicated to storing audio and visual materials. The repository also stores documents, museum artifacts for governmental administrations, government publications, Joseon Dynasty's historical archives, microfilms, and various kinds of audio and visual records.

Since 1984, the Busan repository has been the largest archival repository in Asia, with a special facility to protect archives and records from natural disasters and accidental negligence. The repository building is equipped with a heron gas fire-extinguishing system and double fireproof walls. This repository stores various types of records including ordinary documents, drawings/blueprints, microfilms, secret records, presidential records, as well as Joseon Dynasty's historical archives.

The research room at the Seoul office provides the public in metropolitan areas access to information that the archival collections hold. The services that Seoul Office provides are the same as those of Daejeon Headquarters. The Government Resources Library provides access service to government publications of all levels to the public as well as to government employees.

Archives Legislative History

A task force was organized to develop the Public Records Management Act in the NARS in 1997. A proposal for establishing the Public Records Management Act was sent to the President through the Administration Innovation Committee in 1997. Based on the advice from the parliamentary inspection of the governmental administration in 1997, NARS was also requested to establish a systematic master plan for management of public records such as legislation of Public Records Management Laws. The Legislation of the Public Records Management Laws was selected as one of the "New Government's 100 Major

Policies" by the Presidential Appointee Initiative in 1998. There were many efforts to exchange opinions with related institutions and to hold a conference about the details of the law in order to add more comprehensive contents in 1998. The Act was presented to and passed in the National Assembly in December 1998, promulgated in 1999, and went into force beginning in 2000. It was amended in 2007. Through this law, NARS encourages and supports government agencies to establish various archives and local records centers, and to maintain strong recordkeeping systems using the Records Classification/ Scheduling Scheme.

Archival Science as a Discipline

With the pressing need for both a consistent professional record management methodology and for training specialists to teach those methodologies, there is a rapid growth in the number of educational courses and institutions related to record management. There are now 16 universities in Korea that have graduate programs related to archival science. The majority of the programs consist of curricula that include courses on public administration, law, history, humanities, and social science, computer usage necessary in the age of information, introduction to record management, record management theories (organization, description, and evaluation thereof), research methodology for record management, the history of record management, Korean history of record management, and so on.

LIBRARY & INFORMATION PROFESSIONS, SYSTEMS, AND SERVICES

Introduction

This part includes the development of Korean libraries, their current status, and related activities. It covers specific facts about Korea; institutional changes, and policies concerning libraries; the present conditions of various types of libraries, library-related organizations; and librarianship education and libraries' activities in recent years.

Korean Library Administrative and Legal Systems

Korea has a presidential system. The nation has a three-tier administrative system consisting of the central government, provincial governments, and lower-level governments of counties, cities, and wards. The central government includes 22 ministries and 16 agencies as well as various committees under the supervision of the Prime Minister. In 1995, the nation introduced local autonomous rule and held the first popular election of local government leaders in more than 30 years. As of the end of 2005, local self-governing systems were divided into 16 provincial-

level governments and 234 lower-level governments. Under these regional and local governments a total of 3595 administrative units are being operated nationwide.

The governing system is reflected in the library management system. Libraries in Korea are largely divided into national libraries, academic libraries, school libraries, and public libraries. The National Library of Korea (NLK), Korea's leading library at the national level, runs under the supervision of the Ministry of Culture and Tourism; academic and school libraries operate under the Ministry of Education and Human Resources Development; and public libraries are legally under the administrative responsibility of the Ministry of Government Administration and Home Affairs and the Ministry of Education and Human Resources Development. However, the actual operations of public libraries are managed by provincial and lower-level governments and their offices of education. In short, Korean public libraries are managed by a dual system. At the central level, the Ministry of Government Administration & Home Affairs and the Ministry of Education & Human Resources Development are responsible for management of public libraries; at local levels, public libraries are divided into those administered by provincial and city governments and those administered by provincial and municipal education offices.

This complicated system dissuades libraries from being cooperative and supportive of each other in many areas, including policy coordination, staff training, personnel assignments, collection development, cooperative preservation of materials, and interlibrary loan. A need to streamline the system at the state level and transfer the managerial responsibility to a single government agency has certainly existed for some time, and calls for revising the law and creating a "powerful organization" to play a leading role in establishing, deliberating, and carrying out policies.

Korea follows a Constitutional law system. The Constitution takes precedence over laws, statutes, decrees, ordinances, and regulations. For libraries, the highest statute is the Library Act, accompanied by an enforcement decree and regulations. There are also various decrees and ordinances applicable to libraries of different kinds. But public libraries are managed according to the laws and regulations of respective local governments.

The Library Act, enacted in 1963, was Korea's first law governing libraries. The law was amended later three times. The Library Promotion Act, written in 1991 to supersede the Library Act, emphasized the "nurturing and promotion of libraries" and provided that "a library should be managed by a library professional." The Library and Reading Promotion Act, legislated in 1994, incorporated "promotion of reading," eventually obscuring its original meaning as an "exclusive statute for governing libraries."

The current "Library Act," which was revised in 2006, stipulates that the state and the local governments, as well as the national government, are responsible for management of libraries. It has the following four objectives: to strengthen the role of national libraries and the library-related policy of state and local governments; to broaden decentralization; to reduce gaps in knowledge and information; and to improve policy about library and information service to the handicapped. In particular, the "presidential committee for library and information policy" was organized to spearhead policy formulation, deliberation and implementation at a state level. Also, a "library research institute" was set up within the NLK.

Libraries in Korea

National Library of Korea

The National Library of Korea (NLK), founded in 1945, is Korea's foremost repository of books, documents, and other forms of recorded information. Its role is to establish a collection of materials representing the cultural and intellectual heritage of Korea, and to preserve the accumulated knowledge and wisdom of the nation for future generations. Compiling and distributing national bibliographies is an integral part of this activity. Along with its role as the nation's largest and most prominent library, the NLK also has the mission to seek to increase Korea's knowledge assets and information capabilities. In 2007, its number of collections reached 6.5 million items, some of which are national treasures.

This library has 228 employees, and is used by approximately 1,340,000 persons annually. With a nationwide library and archive database and a computerized catalog of its holdings, it has in place a full-featured e-library system covering its most essential processes and services. In October 2005, in the ceremony celebrating its 60th anniversary, the library proclaimed its vision, "Building a Powerful Knowledge-Based Nation," and unveiled its medium- and long-term development plans ("National Library of Korea 2010"). The plans laid out the roadmap toward the following three goals: fulfilling NLK's role as the nation's repository of the country's documentary heritage, serving as a center for distribution of knowledge resources, and becoming a platform for cooperation and exchange with libraries.

The NLK is currently at work on a project to build an information-age library, temporarily named "the National Digital Library," which is due for completion in 2009. The NLK will be open to the public, of course, open to the world via Internet in May of 2009. Meanwhile, it has been operating the new National Library for Children and Youth (NLCU) since May 2006, to help improve services for children and youth by linking school and public libraries. Even though the NLCU is under the control of NLK in terms of fiscal matters, it is almost operated independently from NLK and is located at a different area.

National Assembly Library

The National Assembly Library was established in 1952 during the Korean War. Serving the National Assembly as its primary source of information and supporting its legislative activities, the library has made major contributions to the promotion of democracy in Korea over the years. This library, with a collection of 2,761,481 volumes and 21,867 serial titles, is staffed by 275 employees as of the end of 2007, and 500,000 users visit there annually.

Its most important function is to gather, organize, and analyze information of both domestic and foreign origins, needed by the legislative body. As part of its role of national library, it also carries out activities such as compiling bibliographies of dissertations, theses, and periodicals to facilitate public access to information. A digital library project initiated in 1998 has equipped the library with a full-text database with close to 71,000,000 full-text images (equivalent to 600,000 volumes of books), quantities previously unprecedented in Korea. The database, accessed by as many as 706 universities, public institutions, and research institutes nationwide, has transformed it into a full-fledged national digital library.

The National Assembly Library's plans for the coming years include harnessing ubiquitous changing technologies for the improvement of its programs, processes, and system capabilities to better perform its role as an information gateway that connects citizens with the legislative body, on the one hand, and the legislative body with the executive body, on the other hand.

Supreme Court Library

The Supreme Court Library of Korea, as a library serving the judicial branch, is located within the Supreme Court, the highest judicial body in Korea. The library was formally established in 1989. With a dedicated staff of 75, the library has recently prepared the means to better meet information needs in legal fields through a project to build an integrated information system. Based on cross-linked databases of precedents from 1996 to the present, legal literatures and information, the system has brought about a major improvement in information accessibility and availability. More recently, the completion of an intercourt library network has enabled the Supreme Court Library to provide guidance to lower court libraries in a more efficient manner and to serve broader tiers of public with their information needs.

Academic libraries

The first academic library mentioned in recorded Korean history (Jongyeonggak) was set up in 1474 at Sungkyunkwan, a royal college of the Joseon Dynasty (1392–1910). In the late nineteenth century, the modern concept of education began in Korea. In May 1924, the first modern national college was created and named Kyongsong Imperial College, the predecessor of Seoul National University. In 1927, a library was added to the college, the first library affiliated with higher level schools in Korea. As of the end of 2007, Korea had a total of 516 college and university libraries. Among them, 14 have over one million volumes, and the Seoul National University Library keeps the largest collection with 3.4 million books and 16,000 serial titles. As the vital center of universities and colleges, academic libraries in Korea recently have undergone many changes and developments. First, academic libraries have increased the digitized portion of their collections, and they have focused on collecting, preserving, and managing digital contents. Second, they have decreased the portion of single volumes while enlarging academic journals and online databases. Third, academic libraries have strengthened cooperation with other libraries in their geographical vicinity to include libraries in other countries, such as Japan, China, and Russia. In particular, there is a growing trend among these libraries of sharing academic journals. Finally, academic libraries have adopted new technologies such as RFID (Radio Frequency IDentification), PDA (Personal Digital Assistant), and mobile phones in order to realize a "mobile campus (library)."

Public libraries

Korean public libraries are among the fastest growing in the world. The country's first modern concept of a public library dates back to the beginning of the 1900s. However, the development of Korean public libraries was suppressed during the Japanese colonial period (1910–1945) and the Korean War (1950–1953). In 1963, with the enactment of the first Library Act, Korean public libraries began to see a growth in numbers. During 1970–1990, Korea underwent dramatic social changes and achieved remarkable economic growth. These changes included an increase in the number of public libraries. Korea's public libraries grew exponentially over the last 40 years and also vastly improved the quality of their services. As of 2007, there are 564 public libraries in Korea. As stipulated by the Library Act, all Korean public libraries have built up a "Public Library Cooperation System" to promote interlibrary cooperation, share materials to provide better services, maximize the distribution and use of knowledge and information, and boost national competitiveness. In the future, Korean central and local governments have the following plans for improving the scale and scope of public library systems:

- Increase the number of public libraries to 750 by 2011 under the "Library Development Roadmap" announced by the Ministry of Culture and Tourism.

- Develop small-scale libraries to resolve library shortages.
- Pass the new Library Act to solve the problems in public library management and budget shortages.
- Continue to apply new technologies at public libraries.
- Use the NLCU adults to link all libraries specially fit for children.

School libraries

The modern concept of school libraries was introduced in Korea during the 1950s. At that time, a small number of progressive thinkers and school founders established libraries at several high schools in the southeastern part of Korea in order to upgrade overall education. The 1960s saw the systematic training and hiring of librarians at schools, leading to improvements in school libraries. In the 1990s, school libraries once again made remarkable progress, owing to legislative and governmental supports, and campaigns by civic groups. For example, in 1994, the enactment of the Library and Reading Promotion Act made it mandatory for schools to operate libraries. In March 2000, the Ministry of Education and Human Resources Development set up the "Comprehensive Library Informatization Plan." In order to carry out this plan, Digital Library System (DLS), a standardized school library information system, was developed in 2001. At the end of 2006, the portion of elementary schools with libraries nationwide was 86.2%, middle schools 91.8%, and high schools 99.9%, respectively, making an overall average of 95.0% (10,010 libraries). Korea's education system has adopted many recent alternatives, including new curricula and evaluation methods. To meet the changing needs, the Ministry of Education and Human Resources Development in 2002 formed the "Comprehensive Plan for Improving School Libraries." This plan allocated $6.4 million (60 billion won) annually over the 2003–2007 period to equip all elementary, middle, and high schools in Korea with their own libraries.

Special libraries

The first special library in Korea was the Railway Bureau Library, which was established in Seoul in 1920. In 1966, Korea's first engineering research house, Korea Institute of Science and Technology (KIST) was founded and led to the founding of many other research institutes in Korea. In the 1980s, R&D activities brought economic development and saw the expansion of special libraries covering different disciplines. Compared to other types of libraries, these special libraries are more advanced in providing up-to-date information. There were 663 special libraries in Korea at the end of 2006.

Librarianship Education in Korea

Librarians in Korea are divided into the following three categories, depending on their qualifications: first-grade professional librarians, second-grade professional librarians, and paraprofessional librarians. Usually, university graduates with the Bachelor's degrees in library and information science (LIS) are offered second-grade professional librarianships, and 2 year college graduates paraprofessional librarianships, respectively. A second-grade professional librarian can become a first-grade professional librarian by completing supplementary classes or a regular degree program after working in a library for a certain period of time. Also, a paraprofessional librarian can be promoted to a second-grade professional librarianship by taking a given education program after accumulating experience in library service. Korea's first undergraduate and graduate courses in library science were opened at Yonsei University in 1957, when Korea began formal education in LIS at the university level. As of 2006, LIS courses are taught in 6 junior colleges, 32 universities, and 24 graduate schools. Thirteen universities have doctoral programs and 17 graduate schools of education have majors in librarianship education. There are also three educational institutes for librarians that issue certificates.

Professional Associations

The representative professional association for librarians in Korea is the Korean Library Association, founded in 1945. The association has played a crucial role in strengthening the professional ability of librarians and thus helping Korean libraries to upgrade their services. The association currently is promoting the development of libraries and improving the interests of librarians, coordination of opinions about libraries, public relations, and creation and distribution of various rules and regulations, including the Korean Decimal Classification, the Korean Cataloging Rules. The association is also performing routine tasks such as producing and distributing the Korean Library Yearbook and the monthly magazine *Library Culture* as well as over 100 kinds of professional publications, hosting the annual national library conferences, and certifying librarians.

The association has two types of members, individual or institutional. Individual members are divided into ordinary members and lifetime members. Institutional members include the NLK, public libraries, academic libraries, school libraries, and special libraries. The membership totals 1375 individual members and 1001 institutional members as of November 2007.

The General Council of Members and the 14-member Board of Directors are responsible for governing the association. The council elects the president and the members of the Board of Directors. It is organized by delegates representing different regions and different categories of libraries. Affiliated with the association are 15 professional committees, three regional councils and seven councils of libraries of different kinds.

Library Activities in Recent Years

In recent years, many dynamic library act projects have flourished in Korea. These include the "Bookstart" movement, the "Miracle Library" project, "Children and Young Adult Services Programs," "Enhancing Library Services for the Disabled," the "Book Reading Seoul" project, the "One Book One City" movement, and the "Small Library" movement.

Bookstart was launched in Korea with a pilot program that ran from April to December 2003, under which books were given to 930 babies in the district of Jungnang-gu, Seoul. To operate the program, a civic organization called "Korean Committee for the Bookstart Movement" was formed. During the pilot period, in order to study the effects of the program, a research was carried out concerning 150 of the babies who had received books. From the latter half of 2004, the project set off as a number of local governments started their own Bookstart programs. Currently, Bookstart programs are conducted in many ways by local authorities in Seoul and countrywide.

The "Miracle Library" project is a movement to establish libraries so unique and dynamic that they are unlike any others in the world. The core of the project is to open libraries for children on the premise that all children have the right to grow up in a bright, sound, and safe environment. That is, the purpose of this project is to give all children anywhere in Korea same opportunity to use a library. The project grew out of the "Book Reading Program" initiated by a private broadcasting company in 2001. It reached a visible form with public donations; funds and resources donated by civic organizations and the private sector; and matching funds provided by local governments. The project is a unique model for private and public sector cooperation, whereby the private sector and the government build libraries together and have them operated by citizens and public servants.

"Service Program for Children and Young Adults" began in earnest in January 2004 according to a plan drawn by the KLA's Children and Young Adult Volunteer Committee. The major contents of the program include remodeling public libraries in rural areas to include children's libraries, training librarians in the art of storytelling, and workshops for children's librarians. The KLA (Korean Library Association) has taken charge of remodeling libraries in rural areas, and the storytelling program is a professional program organized by the Children and Young Adult Volunteer Committee for librarians at public and school libraries as well as small children's library managers and librarians to help them to strengthen services for children. Those who completed the program have organized a group called the Librarians' Blue Stories, which gathers once a month to work toward establishing storytelling hours for regular volunteer service.

"Enhancing Library Service for the Disabled" is the program that helps make it possible for blind people use library resources in a regular way. As of December 2005, the number of blind people in Korea stood at around 170,000, accounting for 0.35% of the population. Library services for the blind were limited until the Korean Braille Library opened, and public libraries began providing services for the disabled in 1984. However, services for the disabled remain weak. As for Braille libraries, there are only 34 public libraries, equipped with Braille reading facilities, as of February 2006. The new Library Act, legislated in 2006, includes a clause on the establishment of both a national library and a national support center for the blind under the control of the NLK. Impelled by inequality in disabled people's right to access information, this Movement is designed to provide better library services for the disabled, and thereby protect their human rights and help them to take more active part in society. In 2004, the Seoul Foundation for Arts and Culture (SAFC) inaugurated the "Book-Reading Seoul" project, proclaiming "Seoul Citizens Become One through Books" and "Unifying Seoul through Books." In this project, public libraries took the lead in organizing a variety of annual reading and cultural programs in Seoul. This is in response to the belief that libraries must become firmly established as the places to go to read books and at the same time satisfy people's demands for culture. This project influenced fixing Korean people's thoughts about libraries being centers for knowledge and information.

The "One Book, One City" movement in Korea started from a public library in a very small town, named Seosan Municipal Library in 2003. This movement has been spreading quickly and widely nationwide, proving to be a successful model for promoting reading in Korea. This program gained public support base and turned public libraries into ones like those found in advanced countries by developing them into local cultural movements that incorporate movements to promote reading. The "One Book, One City" movement could be a means to create a society where everybody reads many books and to make libraries in local communities more accessible, thereby establishing them as the reading centers of the country.

Currently there is a very important project to build more libraries in Korea, the so-called "Small Library" movement. This movement encourages civic organizations and private sectors to build small-scale libraries. The "Small Library" movement is a very dynamic library activity, naturally attracting more attention for social and cultural reasons. In the public sector, the central government has decided on a policy measure enabling the Ministry of Culture and Tourism and Korean Library Association to make use of public funds (lotto revenues) in order to establish 25 small libraries as a part of the official agenda in 2005. The private sector is also responding to building and operating libraries, with a particular focus on children's libraries. Small libraries in Korea are thus becoming an important means for expanding the number of libraries, either in the form of public and private sector cooperation or by each sector working separately.

CONCLUSION

Korea is a dynamic country that values information, knowledge, and reading in a digital age. Korea held successfully World Library and Information Conference (WLIC) in 2006, the world's largest and most prestigious gathering of library professionals. The 2006 WLIC was a good opportunity for participants from around the globe to take an interest in Korea. It not only helped to broaden the perspective of the Korean government and its citizens to the libraries of the outside world, but also served as an opportunity to radically shift thinking and conceptions of libraries and related areas.

BIBLIOGRAPHY

1. *Korea Library Yearbook*; Korean Library Association: Seoul, 2004–2008.
2. *Korean Library Association 60-Year History*; Korean Library Association: Seoul, 2005.
3. *National Archives of Korea.* Available at http://www.archives.go.kr (accessed February 1, 2009).
4. *National Library of Korea.* Available at http://www.nl.go.kr (accessed February 1, 2009).
5. Oh, K.-M.; Chang, Y. A study on the library & information science education and research development in Korea. J. Korean Soc. Inform. Manage **2006**, *23* (2), 185–206.
6. Yoon, H.-Y.; Jeong, D.-Y.; Yoon, H.-Y.; Chang, D.-H.; Kim, Y.-S. *Libraries in Korea: Past, Present and Future*; WLIC 2006 Seoul National Organising Committee: Seoul, 2006.

Spain: Libraries, Archives, and Museums

Lawrence J. Olszewski
OCLC Library, Dublin, Ohio, U.S.A.

Abstract

The purpose of this entry is to provide an overview of the current library, archives, and museum environment in Spain. Each library section—national, university, public, school, and special—as well the archives and museum sections, discusses administration, staffing, expenditures, collections, automation, and services, with trends when possible, and representative institutional profiles. It concludes with a discussion of professional education, associations, and cooperation.

INTRODUCTION

The Kingdom of Spain is a constitutional monarchy encompassing 85% of the Iberian Peninsula in south-western Europe, the Canary Islands, the Balearic Islands, and the cities of Ceuta and Melilla; with an area of almost 193,000 miles^2, it is the 3rd largest country in Europe (excluding Russia) and the 51st largest in the world (Fig. 1).

The official language is Castilian Spanish, though Catalan, Galician, and Basque are coofficial in their respective regions; compared to other European countries, English is less widely spoken or understood. Literacy hovers at 98%. The official 2006 census counts 44.7 million people. The country has almost 20 million Internet users. With the promulgation of the new constitution of 1978, Spain's 50 provinces are officially structured in 17 Autonomous Communities (plus the Northern African enclaves of Ceuta and Melilla), a reconfiguration of the 15 former historic provinces. Spain joined NATO in 1982 and the European Union in 1986.

Spain has made great social, political, and economic strides since Franco's demise in 1975; its GDP now ranks ninth in the world, ahead of such countries as South Korea, Australia, and the Netherlands.[1]

HISTORY

Despite the 600-year domination of the Roman Empire (200 B.C.E. to 400 A.D.) with a long-lasting cultural influence existing even today in architecture (Segovia aqueduct, several bridges) and the Latin-based Spanish language, Spain had no libraries to speak of until after the first Germanic tribes invaded the peninsula around 409 A.D. and the subsequent Visigoth kingdom that ruled the next 300 years. Like everywhere else in Europe, the first important libraries were established in monasteries as medieval bastions of culture. The culmination of Spanish medieval scholarship is the *Etymologies* of Saint Isidore of Seville (560–636), who compiled in that work a systematic comprehensive collection of knowledge available at the time. Because of his encyclopedic effort, he was proposed—unsuccessfully—as a patron saint of the Internet in 2003.

In 711 the Moors invaded Spain and by the tenth century had overrun the entire peninsula except for the far north. For almost 700 years the Moorish civilization, based in the Caliphate of Córdoba, was one of the most advanced cultural centers of Europe. The sumptuous library of Caliph al-Hakem II (ruled 961–976) allegedly had 400,000 volumes. The caliphate itself had a university, 70 libraries, several bookstores, and numerous collections of manuscripts unequalled anywhere in the world.[2]

The first attempt to create an academic library occurred in 1208, with the establishment of the University of Palencia, now disappeared; about 10 years later (1218), however, during the reign of Alphonse IX (1171–1230), the University of Salamanca was established, making it the oldest university in Spain still in existence and contemporary with the oldest in Europe (Bologna, Paris, Oxford). Later, in 1242 King Alphonse X the Wise (1221–1284) created the office of *estacionero* (stationer) to handle library collections in universities.

With the Renaissance and the accompanying growth of learning, some important universities were established in major urban areas: Seville (1505), Granada (1532), and Santiago de Compostela (1550). Around 1518, Ferdinand Columbus (1488–1539), the explorer's son, founded in Seville the Colombina Library, eventually with over 15,000 volumes, important as one of the first libraries to open its collection to the public. The legacy of this library exists today in the Seville diocese. On a grander scale was the library in the Escorial established by Philip II (1527–1598) in 1575. The Escorial, at once monastery, mausoleum, palace, and library, reflects the dour and austere character of its founder; the library eventually came to

Encyclopedia of Library and Information Sciences, Fourth Edition DOI: 10.1081/E-ELIS4-120043733

Fig. 1 Map of Spain.
Source: Central Intelligence Agency. World Factbook 2007. https://www.cia.gov/library/publications/the-world-factbook/geos/sp.html

house a major collection of priceless religious and historical manuscripts and materials.

The earliest bibliographic undertaking was that of Nicolás Antonio (1617–1684), whose *Bibliotheca Hispana Vetus* (*Library of Ancient Spain*, posthumously published in 1696) was an ambitious attempt to identify all books written in Spain from the Romans to 1500; its sequel *Bibliotheca Hispana Nova* (*New Library of Spain*, 1672) extended the compilation to 1670. Though somewhat limited by being written in Latin, these volumes are historically significant for the identification of many writers and works of the time, many now long forgotten.

The major event of the eighteenth century was the establishment of the Royal Library in 1711, which coincided with the founding of the Real Academia de la Lengua (Royal Academy of Language, 1714), the Real Academia de la Historia (Royal Academy of History, 1738), and several other cultural institutions as direct by-products of the Enlightenment. In 1771 it was decreed that the libraries of deceased ecclesiastics would be made available to seminarians, marking an important step into opening up theretofore private libraries.

During the nineteenth century the country continued to make progress toward the expansion of libraries and cultural institutions. In 1835 Prime Minister Juan Álvarez Mendizábal (1790–1853) enacted the *desamortización* (disentailment) of all church properties, including the extensive valuable library collections they contained. Those materials that survived the confiscation were eventually dispersed into various provincial and academic libraries. A major bibliographic effort was undertaken by Bartolomé José Gallardo y Blanco (1776–1852), whose *Ensayo de una biblioteca española de libros raros y curiosos* (*Essay of a Spanish Library of Rare and Unusual Books*, published posthumously from 1863–1889) represents the first major compilation of modern Spanish bibliography. He was also one of the first proponents of a national library system. In 1858 the supremacy of the National Library over other libraries was formalized, along with the creation of the first Spanish public library system. By 1885, there were 30 public libraries in Spain and by the end of the century, there were 14 university libraries.[3]

Despite advances in learning and greater availability of and access to the printed word, a devastating civil war, sandwiched between two dictatorships, slowed the pace of changes in libraries in the twentieth century. In 1902 the first set of formal cataloging rules was adopted. In 1931, though, in keeping with the progressive policies of the Second Republic (1931–1936), the first significant efforts to establish public libraries in Spanish cities were undertaken. Thus, by 1936, on the eve of the Civil War, the number of public libraries had increased to about 200.[4]

A hallmark of twentieth century intellectual thought was the provocative essay by philosopher José Ortega y Gasset (1883–1955) "La misión del bibliotecario" ("Mission of the Librarian," 1935, English translation 1961).

One of the landmarks of universal bibliography was the publication of the *Manual del librero hispano-americano* (*Manual of the Hispano-American Book Dealer*, 1948–1977), compiled by Antonio Palau y Dulcet (1867–1954) and edited posthumously, a 28-volume work that tracks publications of Spanish works from the invention of printing to the present.

LEGISLATION

Major legislation is as follows:

- 1978: The new constitution transferred the governance of public libraries from the national government to the newly created Autonomous Communities.
- 1983: Ley Orgánica de Reforma Universitaria (University Reform Law) 11/1983 modernized and reorganized universities, including granting them greater autonomy and allowing them to organize and develop and manage their own libraries and information policies.
- 1985: El Patrimonio Histórico Español (Law of Spanish Historical Heritage) 16/1985 established the current framework for libraries; also Royal Decree 565/1985 restructured the Ministry of Culture into three branches: the Centro de Coordinación Bibliotecaria (Center for Library Coordination), the Centro de las

Letras Españolas (Center for Spanish Letters) and Centro del Libro y la Lectura (Center for the Book and Reading).

- 1987: Royal Decree Reglamento de Museos de Titularidad Estatal y del Sistema Español de Museos (Regulation of Museums under State Ownership and of the Spanish System of Museums) 620/1987 established the current organization of Spanish museums.
- 1989: Royal Decree Reglamento de Bibliotecas Públicas del Estado y del Sistema Español de Bibliotecas (Regulation of Public Libraries of the State and of the Spanish System of Libraries) 582/1989 established the present Public Libraries of the State [the so-called Bibliotecas Públicas del Estados (BPEs)] and the Spanish Library System.
- 1991: Royal Decree 1581/1991 established the present statutes for the National Library.
- 2006: Ley Orgánica de Educación (Education Law) 2/2006 reorganized the structure of higher education in compliance with the Bologna Accord.

NATIONAL LIBRARY AND INFORMATION SERVICES

Libraries in general use IBERMARC format for cataloging, in use since 1976; those in Catalonia tend to use CATMARC. For classification, most use Universal Decimal Classification (UDC), by shelf position, or a combination of both. Several global ILS firms have a strong presence in Spain (Sirsi, Innovative Interfaces, VTLS, ExLibris). Two Spanish companies have the highest market share, however. The Absys product of Baratz Servicios de Teledocumentación S.A. is the Spanish library automation powerhouse; its more than 1000 installations include major government, royal academy, public, special, and university libraries, as well as library networks and museums. Eight university libraries participate in an Absys-user consortium called RUECA (Red Universitaria Española de Catálogs Absys, Spanish University Network of Absys Catalogs.) The other big player is 3000 Informática, with a strong customer base in regional public library systems, national archives, university libraries, and government.

Data consulted in the following discussion of the different library types came from four different sources: for the National Library, the National Library Web site; for public and special libraries, Library Statistics from Spanish Statistical Institute; for university libraries, REBIUN; and for school libraries, LibEcon.

The National Library's Web site is http://www.bne.es. The Spanish Statistical Institute's Instituto Nacional de Estadística, Estadísticas de Bibliotecas (http://www.ine.es), accessed June 2007, is released in December of odd years with data for the previous year; the current data are from 2004. In 2002 it changed its classification of libraries to

comply with ISO 2789 *Information and documentation— international library statistics*. REBIUN data (Red de Bibliotecas Universitarias. *Anuario de las bibliotecas universitarias y científicas españolas 2005* http://www. REBIUN.org/doc/estadisticas/ANUARIO%20REBIUN% 202005.pdf (accessed June 2007) was preferred for university libraries because of it currency (2005) and respect within the Spanish university library community. Data from the Spanish Statistical Institute's Estadísticas de Bibliotecas were used for the discussion of automation for university and research libraries since the REBIUN statistics do not measure that factor. Since neither the National Statistics Institute nor the Ministry of Culture tracks statistics for school libraries, data for that segment are difficult to obtain accurately. The most current and reliable data are from LibEcon (International Library Economics Research Study, http://www.libecon. org, accessed June 2007), based on 2002 grossed results. Data for archives are from the Ministerio de Cultura. Estadística de Archivos. http://www.mcu.es/ estadisticas/docs/capitulos_graficos/AEC2006/c_archivos 12.pdf (accessed June 2007). Data for museums come from the Ministerio de Cultura. Estadística de Museos y Colecciones Museográficas. http://www.mcu.es/estadis ticas/docs/capitulos_graficos/AEC2006/c_museos11.pdf (accessed June 2007).

National Library

Established in 1711 by King Philip V (1683–1746), the Royal Library was opened to the public on March 1, 1712 in the Royal Palace. In 1836 it changed its name to the National Library. It opened the doors to its present headquarters in Madrid on March 16, 1896, with a second, smaller location in Alcalá de Henares in 2000 (see Fig. 2). In 1716 the first charter for the National Library was issued and the beginning of the legal deposit system was created. Some famous literati have been directors, such as playwrights Leandro Fernández de Moratín (1811–1812), Manuel Bretón de los Herreros (1847–1854), Juan Eugenio Hartzenbusch (1862–1875), and Manuel Tamayo y Baus (1884–1898) and the noted scholars Agustín Durán (1854–1861), Marcelino Menéndez y Pelayo (1898–1912), whose personal library of 40,000 volumes in philology and literary history is among the finest ever assembled by one individual, Francisco Rodríguez Marín (1912–1930) and, during the Civil War, linguist Tomás Navarro Tomás (1936–1939).

Organization and structure

The National Library (http://www.bne.es) is the largest library in Spain and the center of the country's library system. It operates under statutes laid down by Decree 1581/1991, which were later slightly modified in 1997, 2000, 2001, and 2005. According to its Articles of Incorporation, it is mandated with three major functions:

Fig. 2 Facade of the National Library of Spain. © Alexandra Gnatush-Kostenko—Fotolia.com.

1. Compile, catalog, and preserve the bibliographic output produced in any language about Spain for the purposes of research, culture, and information.
2. Promote research through the study, lending, and reproduction of its bibliographic resources.
3. Disseminate information on Spain's bibliographic output received through the legal deposit system.

The mission of the National Library is the conservation, management, and diffusion of the Spanish bibliographic heritage, for the purposes of 1) transforming information into knowledge; 2) satisfying the needs of the research community; and 3) spreading the nation's historical memory to all Spanish citizens.

The recently developed 2006–2008 Strategic Plan enumerates the following six objectives:

1. Convert the National Library into a place of cultural discovery for all citizens.
2. Increase access to specialized information resources necessary for study and research and to improve services to users.
3. Analyze and plan for the management of collections in the library.

4. Promote the involvement of the Library in all professional arenas for the purpose of guaranteeing an active and enriching presence.
5. Assume a leadership role in innovation in the professional arena.
6. Develop the best organizational model for the fulfillment of library functions.

The library is headed by a Director General, responsible for strategic planning and overall direction for the library; a Technical Services Director who deals with the daily administration of the various working units; and a General Manager who supervises the financial and personnel operations. The library reports directly to the Minister of Culture.

Expenditures

Annual operating expenditures for the national library are broken down as follows:

• Staff	€12,103,130
• Materials	€7,932,327
• Other	€56,735
• Grand total	€20,092,192

Collections

Its collection is one of the largest in Europe and is especially strong in the humanities and social sciences; its breakdown by format is as follows:
Total holdings exceed 18 million items.

• Monographs	6,500,000
• Photographs	2,000,000
• Posters	800,000
• Prints	700,000
• Sound recordings	550,000
• Musical scores	500,000
• Postcards	500,000
• Ephemera	200,000
• Maps	134,000
• Journal titles	110,000
• Audiovisual	80,000
• Original drawings	45,000
• Manuscripts	30,000
• Newspapers	20,000
• Incunabula	3000
• Total Titles	12,172,000

The augmentation of the collections is enhanced considerably by the library's role as the curator of the national legal deposit system, whose current regulations were established in 1957. Every publisher is legally obligated to provide the library with one copy of every publication, but in reality the library often gets three copies: it keeps one for preservation and circulates the other two. This system is so effective that legal deposit items in all formats comprise 95% of the library's total collection. The relatively little remainder is obtained through direct purchase, exchange, and donations. In 2006 the library added almost 183,000 items to its collection, the largest category of which (55%) was in-print monographs.

Special collections

Among its priceless items is the only extant copy of the *Cantar de Mio Cid*, the early thirteenth century national epic; a manuscript of the Middle Ages masterpiece *El libro de buen amor* (Book of Good Love, 1368); the *Biblia Sacra Hispalense (Codex Toletanus)* (Holy Spanish Bible, Toledo Codex, 988 A.D.); and a tenth century copy of Saint Isidore's *Etymologies*.

- The Ephemera and Ex Libris (bookplate) Collections contain approximately 200,000 images of such collectables as matchboxes, wall calendars, labels from raisin and orange boxes, and cigar bands.
- The Cartography Collection consists of more than 134,000 maps (mostly of Spain); atlases; and specialized works in cartography, geography and astronomy, as well as descriptions of countries and travel writings.
- The heart of the Theater Collection's 55,000 volumes includes the personal libraries of several prominent scholars, in particular those of Juan Nicolás Böhl de Faber (1770–1863), Agustín Durán (1793–1862), and especially Pascual de Gayangos y Arce (1809–1897), who donated over 22,000 titles.
- The Africa Collection contains books, pamphlets, serials, manuscripts, photographs, postcards, maps, and graphics dealing primarily with the history and culture of North Africa.
- The library maintains two archival collections: one for the history of the library proper, and the other for the Junta Facultativa de Archivos, Bibliotecas y Museos (Archives, Libraries and Museums Supervisory Board).
- The library holds 1600 medieval codices.
- The Sala de Prensa y Revistas (Press and Journals Reading Room) contains paper, microfilmed, and digitized copies of more than 400 Spanish newspapers and serials.
- The Sala Cervantes (Cervantes Reading Room) is the library's rare book room, with over 13,000 ancient and modern manuscripts and incunabula, books printed from the sixteenth to eighteenth centuries, first editions from several epochs and especially materials relating to Cervantes and his works.

- The Sala Goya (Goya Reading Room) houses the art collection, with drawings, illustrated books, posters, photographs, art works, and maps.
- The Sala Barbieri (Barbieri Reading Room) contains the music collection, noted for its collection of scores, sound recordings, musical archives, and archived video games and computer programs.
- The Sala de Documentación Bibliotecaria (Library Documentation Reading Room) contains an extensive collection of 15,000 titles, both retrospective and current, in library science geared to the information professional.

Publications

1. The *Bibliografía española* (Spanish Bibliography) contains bibliographic records based on works which the National Library receives through the legal deposit program, including books, serial publications, maps, and music. Published since 1958, the monthly publication is available in print and online.
2. The Library also actively publishes works in its own right, usually of exhibitions that took place there. An outstanding example is the 2005 publication of *El Quijote: Biografía de un libro* (El Quijote: Biography of a Book), an elegant catalog of an exhibition that the Library sponsored in commemoration of the quadricentennial of Cervantes' masterpiece.

Databases and automation

- The Catálogo Bibliográfico (Bibliographic Catalog), called ADRIANA, is probably the library's most important database, containing over 3 million items and more than 10 million copies. It includes all works acquired since 1931, plus journals and nonprint materials from the collections. Users can export records using Z39.50 protocol.
- The Catálogo Autoridades (Authority File) contains over 400,000 records of personal names, corporate names, work titles, and subjects.
- The Directorio de Bibliotecas Españolas (Directory of Spanish Libraries), called DIBI, is an interactively searchable database containing information on over 10,000 of all types of libraries in the country with name, address, contact information, year founded, subject specialties, collections, services offered, and access policies.
- The Catálogo Colectivo de Publicaciones Periódicas (Union Catalog of Periodical Publications), or CCPP, is a union list of 88,000 serials held by 1100 Spanish libraries, with 370,000 records.
- Instrumenta Musicae: Catálogo Colectivo de Fondos Musicales del Siglo XIX (Union Catalog of Musical Resources from the 19th Century) contains 15,000

records representing 25,000 items of nineteenth century scores of all musical genres, plus monographs and facsimile editions. It represents a joint effort with seven Spanish American countries.

User services

In addition to the specialized reading rooms mentioned above, the library has a general reading room (Salón General), housing a reference collection and providing access to the bulk of the collection, newer works and copies of legal deposit items; the Sala de Información General (General Information Reading Room), where users can obtain permits and inquire about services; and the Sala de Información Bibliográfica (Bibliographic Information Reading Room), with access to general and specialized bibliographies, electronic databases, catalogs for other Spanish and foreign libraries, and a genealogy collection, as well as the card catalog which contains records for all monographs acquired through 1986.

The library has implemented a rather complex schema of five categories for library use, but in general, access is presently restricted to researchers, though at the time of this writing, management is considering having the government make the policy more open. In 2006 the library provided almost 19,000 researchers with passes to use the collection and hosted almost 130,000 readers, averaging 448 a day. The General Reading Room and the General Information Reading Room have the most visitors.

In the basement of the National Library is the recently renamed Museo de la Biblioteca Nacional (National Library Museum), formerly called Museo del Libro (Museum of the Book), which displays highlights of the collections and history of the library.

The National Library is also the ISSN national agent for Spain.

As for interlibrary loan, any publicly funded university, special or public library can borrow items from the library. Excluded from interlibrary loan are serials, reference works, manuscripts, and nonprint materials. The library will not make copies of works that are currently in print and will lend others that are still subject to intellectual property rights but only for research and not-for-resale purposes. The library attempts to supply a photocopy of a requested work if the original is not lendable.

Digitization

The library has undertaken several digitization projects:

- The most outstanding is undoubtedly the Hemeroteca Digital (Digital Newspaper Library), a copyright-free collection of over 500,000 pages from over 143 titles spanning the years 1772–1933.

- Other collections include digitized editions of *Don Quijote*, posters from the Republic and Civil War, Spanish cartography from the sixteenth to nineteenth centuries, Spanish iconography, and works of Francisco de Goya in the library.
- In late 2007 the library was scheduled to mount digitized versions of the top 100 works of Spanish literature, freely available on its Web site.

Cooperation

The library actively participates in national cooperative initiatives and sponsors conferences, workshops, and seminars; it also works closely with the major national library associations like the Federación de Asociaciones de Archiveros, Bibliotecarios, Museólogos y Documentalistas (Federation of Associations of Archivists, Librarians, Museologists, and Documentalists, ANABAD), the Federación Española de Sociedades de Archivística, Biblioteconomía, Documentación y Museística (Federation of Spanish Societies of Archives, Libraries, Documentation and Museology, FESABID), and the Asociación Española de Documentación e Información (Spanish Association for Documentation and Information, SEDIC). The National Library is also a major player in the international arena, of which the most important affiliations are the Consortium of European Research Libraries (CERL); the European Bureau of Library, Information and Documentation Associations (EBLIDA); the International Federation of Library Associations and Institutions (IFLA); the Ligue des Bibliothèques Européennes de Recherche (League of European Research Libraries, LIBER); and the European Library.

UNIVERSITY AND RESEARCH LIBRARIES

Administration and Staffing

Spanish university libraries are unique for three reasons. First, historically most campuses had decentralized libraries in the facultades (schools), some with sizeable collections; these libraries often held overlapping collections and duplicated operations with one another, and their existence was subject to the vagaries of departmental funding. Only recently have more universities established central libraries, but seven still do not have one. Second, most of the existing university libraries are of fairly recent origin. Though eight date from the seventeenth century or earlier (see Table 1), three-fourths (52) of all main university libraries today were founded since 1960 (see Table 2).

Finally, the Spanish higher education style of learning has always emphasized rote learning and memorizing professors' lectures with little emphasis placed upon inquiry into supplementary resources available from the library;

Table 1 Founding dates of the oldest University libraries.

Name of university	Year established
University of Salamanca	1254
University of Valladolid	1346
Complutense University	1499
University of Seville	1505
University of Granada	1532
University of Santiago de Campostela	1550
University of Saragossa	1583
University of Oviedo	1608

Source: Fatih, D., Ed. *Directory of University Libraries in Europe*, 2nd Ed.; Europa Publications: London, 2004; 293–331.

this mindset is slowly changing as university libraries are now modernizing their mission and establishing their importance as a premier component in the development of erudition on campuses.

Two-thirds of Spanish universities are public institutions; most of the private ones are run by the Roman Catholic Church.

The 68 university library administrative units of REBIUN have 688 service points (about ten per library).

The total staff of university libraries is 6681 persons, broken down into professionals (35%), support staff (51%), and student workers (14%).

Expenditures

Annual operating expenditures for university libraries are broken down as follows:

- Staff   €152,102,787
- Serials   €66,177,403
- Monographs   €33,195,024
- Databases   €13,522,152
- Other   €1,115,244
- Grand total   €266,112,610

Expenditures on staff comprise about 57% of total expenditures, a slight increase since 2000 (55%). Expenditures for electronic information comprise almost one-third (32%) across different materials accounts, a substantial increase since 2000 (8%). The average cost of a monograph in 2005 was €36 (a 33% increase over 10 years) and €275 for a journal subscription (a 46% increase).

Table 2 Number of central university libraries established by decade.

Decade	Number founded
1960s	7
1970s	12
1980s	4
1990s	27
2000s	2

Source: Fatih, D., Ed. *Directory of University Libraries in Europe*, 2nd Ed.; Europa Publications, 2004.

Collections

The total breakdown of university library collections by format is as follows:

- Books   35,676,734
- Electronic documents   3,374,450
- Graphics   2,125,639
- Microforms   1,238,708
- Serial titles   719,062
- Sound recordings   406,448
- Maps   334,112
- Videos and DVDs   277,544
- CD-ROMs   259,929
- Grand total   44,412,626

Books comprise 80% of university library collections, a decline of 10% from 2000, as university libraries are acquiring more nonprint materials. However, the annual net addition to the collection of about 1.4 million items has stayed fairly steady. Collections are relatively small by European and North American standards; although 8 universities have over 1 million volumes, 17 others have fewer than 100,000.

User Services

In general, use of library services, especially those for electronic materials, has increased exponentially since 2000. Visits to library Web pages, for example, increased 866% and library catalog searches were up 592% (likely due to a greater presence in 2005 than 5 years earlier). In contrast, however, total walk-in traffic was up at a more modest 26% increase and circulation even less, at 6%. University libraries are open 274 days a year and 71 hr a week on average, amounting to 5 hr more per year and 2 more per week than in 2000. The number of annual service transactions is as follows:

- Visits to Web pages   203,063,898
- Catalog searches   96,934,682
- Walk-ins   83,425,275
- Circulation   13,346,944

University libraries are net interlibrary borrowers, having borrowed 200,885 items in 2005 and lent 182,165. These figures represent a decrease from 2000, 29% in the case of borrowing and 34% in the case of lending, a decline due to the wider availability of resources in electronic formats.

Automation

University libraries have always been at the forefront of library automation, and all the REBIUN member libraries are automated to some degree. Indeed only 6 million volumes remain unconverted into the REBIUN database. Among all institutions of higher education, however, cataloging and circulation are the two functions with the heaviest penetration of automation in public libraries; almost 91% have automated their cataloging procedures and 76% have automated circulation. 63% have a Web page and 69% have Web-based OPACs. Presently 91% of academic libraries have Internet access.

Repesentative University Library Profiles

The selection of the representative libraries here and in the rest of the entry is based on the author's firsthand knowledge and on the consensus of evaluations from works cited in the bibliography.

Carlos III University

Established in 1989, the university took as its namesake the enlightened eighteenth century monarch Charles III (1759–88); the university's motto *Homo homini sacra res* ("Man is sacred for man") reflects that progressive humanistic heritage. The university's 19,000 students and 1000 full-time faculty are spread out over three campuses, but the María Moliner Library located in the southern Madrid suburb of Getafe serves the largest user base and has the largest collection; the library as a whole has over 422,000 monograph volumes and almost 4000 periodical subscriptions. The library employs 78 librarians. The library subscribes to a comprehensive collection of electronic resources and has seriously reduced its paper-based reference acquisitions. Interlibrary loan is very active; book lending is up and nonreturnables are down (due to campus-wide electronic access).

Complutense University

Third in historical prestige to the University de Salamanca but first in the size of its collections, the Complutense University dates from 1499 with its founding in Alcalá de Henares by Cardinal Francisco Jiménez de Cisneros (1436–1517), an instrumental figure in the publication of the first critical edition of the Bible, the *Biblia políglota complutense* [Polyglot Bible of Complutum (the Latin name for Alcalá de Henares), 1502–1517], for which was needed an extensive research collection. The university moved to Madrid in 1836. The library has 33 branches with a total of almost 3 million books, as well as a valuable manuscript collection. Yet for all its historical holdings, the library is very much in the vanguard of promoting electronic resources. It presently makes available over 31,000 electronic books, 21,000 e-journals, and a host of databases. Its most recent

claim to fame, however, is the 2006 agreement to join the Google Books Library Project, for which it has started contributing the texts of public domain works. This digitization effort follows on the heels of four earlier open access digitization projects: the Dioscórides Digital Collection of almost 3000 books and 40,000 images in the sciences and humanities; the Complutense E-prints Institutional Archive of 4000 theses; the Collection of Ancient Drawings from the Fine Arts Faculty Library, consisting of almost 300 drawings from 1752 to 1914; and the Portal of Complutense Scientific Journals, with full-text articles (currently around 23,000) from 67 scientific journals published by the University.

University of Salamanca

Founded in 1218 by King Alphonse IX (1171–1230) and reorganized in 1254 by his grandson King Alphonse X the Wise (1221–1284), the University of Salamanca is the oldest university in Spain still in existence. One of the most reputable Spanish universities, it is commendable for its collections; its library system has over a million volumes, including those of the 22 subject area libraries which have distinguished holdings for each of their specializations. Because of the university's early founding, its holdings of older and rare materials are outstanding; the library has over 2000 manuscripts, almost 500 incunabula, and 62,000 books printed before 1801.

Major Research Libraries

CSIC libraries

Created in 1939, the Consejo Superior de Investigaciones Científicas (Higher Council of Scientific Research), or CSIC (http://www.csic.es), is a network of 96 public research libraries reporting to the Ministerio de Educación y Ciencia (Ministry of Education and Science); spread out over 21 cities in ten Autonomous Communities, it is the largest research organization in the country. The combined total collection, especially strong in the pure and applied sciences, approaches 1.5 million volumes with over 56,000 periodical titles, all available through its union catalog, the Catálogos Informatizados de la Red de Bibliotecas del CSIC (Automated Catalog of the CSIC Library Network), called CIRBIC. All of its electronic resources are available remotely through its virtual library portal. Because of the heavy concentration on the sciences, 86% of the acquisitions budget goes to serial publications. Each library develops its own specialization and serves its own constituents, mainly the researchers in the specialized disciplines. It is the only nonuniversity institution member of REBIUN. Staff number around 200.

Ateneo Científico y Literario de Madrid (Scientific and Literary Athenaeum of Madrid)

The Ateneo was established as a political club and literary salon in 1835 and for years had been considered a hotbed of liberal ideas and progressive thought. Many of Spain's most famous writers, philosophers, and intellectuals were members at one time or another. The library is officially open only to the 3000 members, but with a very generous operating schedule, open daily from 9:00 A.M. to 1:00 A.M. and closed only 7 days a year. The library has four fairly identical reading rooms (one houses the extensive newspaper collection), with materials encased in wooden armoires. In addition to a collection of over 150,000 titles spread over 350,000 volumes, the library maintains several unique resources that one might not expect in a library of this sort, including a first edition of the *Encyclopédie* (1751–1777), 27,000 pamphlets, a 100,000-volume newspaper section, microfilmed pages from 3124 volumes, manuscripts dealing with the history of the Atheneum, over 1440 maps, and 249 letters. Many of its early pieces were duplicate castoffs from the National Library. Those Spanish writers and intellectuals who were members are especially well represented. The library also serves as the Atheneum archive, with rich holdings of the history of the institution, in-house publications, and catalogs of artist exhibitions, proceedings of conferences and texts of lectures that were given there. The library is beginning to digitize many of its rarer and more valuable historical materials and has almost completed retrospectively converting its holdings.

PUBLIC LIBRARIES

In 1931, in keeping with the progressive policies of the Second Republic (1931–1936), the Junta de Intercambio y Adquisición de Libros para Bibliotecas Públicas (Commission for Interchange and Acquisition of Books for Public Libraries) was created to supply books to libraries and to create public libraries in locations with a minimal number of inhabitants.

In 1947 the Servicio Nacional de Lectura (National Reading Service) was created to promote reading among the Spanish public. In 1953 the first bookmobiles began operation.

Three recent initiatives to advance the technological status of public libraries were

1. The PISTA Program (Promoción e Identificación de Servicios Emergentes de Telecomunicaciones Avanzadas (Promotion and Identification of Emerging Advanced Telecommunications Services) proposed to develop telecommunications in ten areas, including libraries and museums.

2. The Plan de Impulso de las Bibliotecas Públicas Españolas: las bibliotecas públicas, puertas de entrada a una Sociedad de la Información para todos (Plan for Boosting Spanish Public Libraries: Public Libraries as Doorways for Access to an Information Society for All*)* intended to provide all Spanish citizens with access to information, including improving Internet access.

3. Info XXI: la sociedad de la información para tod@s (The Inform@tion Society for All), established free access to information for all citizens.

Administration and Staffing

Libraries are governed by the Dirección General del Libro, Archivos y Bibliotecas (General Board of the Book, Archives and Libraries) under the Ministry of Culture. However, they are not administered centrally, but rather fall into three decentralized models.

1. Bibliotecas Públicas del Estado (State Public Libraries), called BPEs. These libraries are located in each one of the 52 provincial capitals. Though authorized federally, they are managed locally. They have the largest collections and provide the greatest variety of services to its users.

2. Bibliotecas Centrales de Comunidades Autónomas (Central Libraries of the Autonomous Communities). These libraries are like mini-national libraries for their regions, in that their mission is to collect everything published in and about their respective regions. These 13 libraries are entirely run by the Autonomous Communities, who authorize the creation of libraries and establish guidelines for managing them. The Balearic Islands, Canary Islands, Galicia, and the Basque Country are the only regions lacking one. Six—those in Aragon, Asturias, Cantabria, Castile-La Mancha, La Rioja, and Murcia—double as BPEs and perform functions more appropriate for that type of library as well.

3. Bibliotecas Públicas Municipales (Municipal Public Libraries). These libraries are the most numerous, numbering 4043 administrative units, representing 4812 service points. Every municipality with a population of at least 5000 people is mandated by law to set up a library, though some are libraries in name only. These libraries are created and administered with local funding. The municipal libraries in the largest cities have formed networks with branches scattered throughout the city. Some of these service points are located in very creative places, including Metro stations. In addition, 69 bookmobiles operate in several provinces.

Ranking of Municipal Public Library Administrative Units by Autonomous Community

Autonomous community	Number of administrative units	Rank by hnhabitants served
1. Andalusia	645	1
2. Valencia	458	4
3. Castile-La Mancha	438	9
4. Catalonia	412	2
5. Extremadura	394	13
6. Galicia	325	5
7. Castile and León	276	6
8. Basque Country	225	7
9. Aragon	213	11
10. Canary Islands	167	8
11. Balearic Islands	112	14
12. Asturias	103	12
13. Madrid	90	3
14. Navarre	80	15
15. Murcia	43	10
16. Cantabria	36	16
17. La Rioja	23	17
18. Ceuta	2	NA
19. Melilla	1	NA

All told, only 3% of the national population is without public library service.

Staffing

Total salaried staff is 10,406, of which 21% are professional librarians. Some of the workload is carried out by volunteers and student workers.

Expenditures

Annual operating expenditures for public libraries are broken down as follows:

• Staff	€29,218,269
• Materials	€60,201,778
• Other	€24,858,922
• Grand total	€114,278,453

The percentage allocated to staffing has remained fairly constant (68%) since 2000 (70%).

Collections

The item breakdown of collections in public libraries by format is as follows:

• Books and pamphlets	51,076,829
• Audiovisual materials	1,750,928
• Sound recordings	1,376,729
• Bound serials	1,185,920
• Microforms	557,983
• Electronic documents	435,623
• Other documents	390,016
• Graphics	185,868
• Sheet music	66,609
• Manuscripts	59,152
• Maps	30,438
• Grand total	57,116,095

Books comprise 89% of public library collections, down from 96% in 2000, because of the acquisition of more nonprint materials. Public libraries annually add about 3 million volumes to their collections.

User Services

As the name implies, these libraries, except in unusual cases, offer services free of charge, since national law requires that all basic public library services be available to users at no cost to users.

Public libraries had 9,811,766 registered users in 2004, a 37% increase since 2000 (7,172,882); an overwhelming majority (76%) are adults.

Total circulation transactions have increased 80% since 2000. Books and pamphlets continue to comprise the majority of circulation activity (61%). Circulation transactions are broken down by format as follows:

• Books and pamphlets	28,524,785
• Audiovisual materials	9,351,654
• Sound recordings	5,979,199
• Periodicals	1,721,117
• Electronic documents	1,220,726
• Other documents	201,477
• Grand total	46,998,958

Charging users overdue fines is not common.

Forty-one percent of libraries are open between 20 and 40 hr a week; another 32% are open between 10 and 20 hr. Only 12% are open longer than 40 hr a week.

Public libraries are net interlibrary lenders, having lent 167,713 items in 2004 and borrowed 151,747, almost exclusively to libraries within Spain. Lending has increased 8% since 2000. Libraries usually offer interlibrary loan to users free of charge.

Automation

Almost three-fourths of all public libraries perform at least one automated function. Cataloging and circulation are the two functions with the heaviest penetration of automation in public libraries; almost 60% have automated their cataloging procedures and 44% have automated circulation. Libraries that perform at least one automated function are broken down as follows:

- Cataloging   2427
- Circulation   1778
- Interlibrary loan   773
- Acquisitions   712
- Serials control   654
- Self checkout   211

Only 383 libraries (9%) have a Web page, but 1200 (30%) have Web-based OPACs. Presently three-fourths of public libraries have Internet access, most of whom make it freely available to users. The use of filtering software is not standard practice.

Representative Public Library Profiles

Library of Catalonia

Founded in 1907 in Barcelona, the Library of Catalonia serves as the legal deposit and bibliographic compiler of works published in and about the Catalonian region. With over an estimated 3 million documents, it is by far the largest and most research-oriented of the regional libraries and comes closest to defining the concept of a regional "national" library. Besides providing separate audiovisual, newspaper and art reading rooms, it houses the archives of the Catalan writer Joan Maragall (1860–1911) in his former residence. Among its many special collections are an extensive collection of the works of the medieval writer Ramon Llull (1235–1315) and the 4000-volume library of the noted Catalan poet Jacint Verdaguer i Santaló (1845–1902). In 2007 the library agreed, along with four other Catalan libraries, to digitize hundreds of public-domain works as part of the Google Books Project.

Pedro Salinas

The Pedro Salinas Public Library, one of the largest and most attractive of the 18 branches of the Madrid regional library system, is also one of the most typical. The circular structure encompasses two floors of stacks, reading rooms, a periodicals alcove, and a children's section. This particular branch claims to have 50,000 books, 94 serials, and 3000 AV materials and performs the services one would normally expect in a modern public library: reference, circulation, interlibrary loan, programming, and Internet access. Circulation policies, however, seem somewhat liberal: a passport is apparently all one needs to check items out. However, loan periods are somewhat more restrictive: three books for 30 days, and two DVDs videos, or CDs for

7 days. It even has what they call a "collective loan": educators can charge out up to a 100 books for up to 9 months, since the collections in school libraries are wanting.

SCHOOL LIBRARIES

Administration

School libraries have 2836 administrative units and 3429 service points.

Staffing

Total FTE library staff is 656, of which slightly more than half (342) are trained librarians. Based on these data, it appears that many school libraries are still drastically understaffed.

Expenditures

Annual operating expenditures for school libraries are broken down as follows:

- Staff   €95,122,072
- Materials   €36,802,178
- Other   €52,581,509
- Grand total   €284,505,759

The low attention paid to staffing is validated by the low budgetary allocations for staff (26%).

Collections

Books, by far the most numerous format, comprise 86% of school library collections, but audiovisual materials form an important collection component to complement the curriculum. The item breakdown of collections in school libraries by format is as follows:

- Books and bound periodicals   13,346,774
- Audiovisual materials   2,143,626
- Serial titles   43,858
- CD-ROMs   28,782
- Grand total   15,563,040

User Services

School libraries circulate 72,164,126 items a year to their users; with a served population of slightly over 10 million users, the circulation rate averages about seven items per user. Approximately 83,303,986 users visit the library annually, or about eight visits per user.

Automation

School libraries have automated only 31% of their records. About 62% are connected to the Internet.

SPECIAL LIBRARIES

Administration

The National Statistics Institute divides special libraries into two types. The first group consists of 414 libraries (with 486 service points) that serve special populations (for example, prisons and military). The other 1777, with 1957 service points, contain special collections and include the following specific types:

* Government   324
* Associations   292
* Archives and museums   261
* Health sciences   185
* Religious   155
* Research   147
* Corporate   73
* Other   340

For the purposes of this discussion, their features will be treated together.

Staffing

Total salaried staff is 5177, of which 31% are professional librarians, the remainder consisting of support staff and subject experts.

Expenditures

Annual operating expenditures for special libraries are broken down as follows:

* Staff   €67,399,901
* Materials   €41,802,597
* Other   €10,048,908
* Grand total   €119,251,406

The percentage allocated to staffing has increased considerably (56%) from what it was in 2000 (41%).

Collections

Books, though still the most numerous format, only comprise 42% of special library collections, considering the varied nature of the collections of these libraries. Special libraries annually add slightly over 1 million volumes to their collections. The item breakdown of collections in special libraries by format is as follows:

* Books and pamphlets   30,306,664
* Other documents   16,450,609
* Microforms   7,100,013
* Electronic documents   6,227,825
* Graphics   3,819,553
* Bound serials   3,584,088
* Audiovisual materials   1,770,559
* Sound recordings   1,162,511
* Manuscripts   911,101
* Maps   505,838
* Sheet music   159,371
* Grand total   71,998,132

User Services

Special libraries have 1,259,896 registered users; as expected, most (98%) are adults.

Even though these libraries circulate over 2 million items a year, circulation is not a major activity for them, since many of their materials are research based and for in-house use only. Books and pamphlets comprise the bulk of circulation transactions (55%). Circulation transactions are broken down by format as follows:

* Books and pamphlets   1,280,957
* Other documents   529,831
* Audiovisual materials   241,973
* Sound recordings   171,055
* Periodicals   95,478
* Electronic documents   30,739
* Grand total   2,350,033

Fifty-eight percent of libraries are open between 20 and 40 hr a week; only 1% is open longer than 40 hr a week.

Special libraries are net interlibrary lenders, having lent 402,453 items in 2004 and borrowed 136,954, almost entirely to libraries within Spain. Lending has increased 13% since 2000.

Automation

Cataloging is by far the function with the heaviest penetration of automation in special libraries; almost 64% have automated their cataloging procedures. Automated circulation, at 37%, is a distant second. The number of libraries that perform at least one automated function is broken down as follows:

- Cataloging   1411
- Circulation   818
- Serials   768
- Acquisitions   586
- Interlibrary loan   316
- Self checkout   182

567 libraries (26%) have a Web page, and slightly more (607, or 28%) have Web-based OPACs. Presently two-thirds of special libraries have Internet access.

GOVERNMENT LIBRARIES

At the national level, government libraries fall into two categories: those in the legislatures and those in the ministries. The congressional, or parliamentary, libraries, such as those of the Congress of Deputies and the Senate, serve the information needs of the legislators and generally are not open to the public. Likewise access to the collections in the libraries of the ministries is restricted to government staff. Several of these libraries have sizeable collections in their respective fields, especially those in the Ministries of Justice, Labor, and Agriculture. Government libraries also have the largest staff and expenditures of the special libraries.

Regional and provincial administrative units also have their own government libraries.

Reales Academias (Royal Academies)

The Spanish Royal Academies set standards and provide authority for each of their disciplines. Each one—fine arts, history, language, law, medicine, pharmacy, pure sciences, and social sciences—has its own library. The largest is that of History, with over 300,000 volumes; it is located in the former residence of the great nineteenth century scholar Marcelino Menéndez y Pelayo (1856–1912), who was the Academy's librarian (1893–1895) and director (1910–1912). Access to these libraries is restricted to qualified researchers only.

Palacio Real (Royal Palace)

The library in the Royal Palace was established during the reign of the enlightened monarch Charles III (1759–88), and achieved its present status when it split from the National Library in 1836. It is presently located in eight rooms on the first floor and basement of the palace. Along with the National Library and the library in The Escorial, it constitutes the third member of the triumvirate of prominent Spanish libraries and like them is open only to researchers. The main reading room consists of bibliographies and indexes to the collection, which specializes in primary source materials. Users can also access the collection through the Catálogo Colectivo del Patrimonio Bibliográfico Español (Union Catalog of the Spanish Bibliographic Heritage). The collections were augmented during the reign of Charles IV (1788–1808) through the acquisition of the private collection of Diego Sarmiento de Acuñas, the Count of Gondomar (1567–1626), of great historic value for its unique titles and his almost 20,000 very personal letters. The bulk of the 119,000 monographs are housed in an adjoining room encased in armoires, many dating from the initial occupancy. Its oldest printed book, *Rationale divinorum officiorum* (Account of the Divine Office, 1459), is one of over 260 incunabula. Almost 5000 manuscripts, some dating from the twelfth century, are stored in compact shelving in the basement. In addition the library has almost 5000 engravings, over 3000 maps, 4500 music scores, 1000 photos, and 4000 serials. The library is also known for the sumptuous binding of its materials, many of which are still bound in-house. The library publishes a quarterly bulletin, *Avisos: Noticias de la Real Biblioteca* (Notices: News of the Royal Library). Interlibrary loan is available for photocopies only. The professional staff consists of philologists and historians. Efforts are currently under way to digitize the manuscripts. The Royal Palace library also supplements the information resources of the nearby Monasterio de las Descalzas Reales (Convent of the Royal Barefoot Nuns) in central Madrid.

Museum Libraries

The Museo Nacional Centro de Arte Reina Sofía (Queen Sofia Center of Art National Museum)

Probably the most estimable museum library is that in the Queen Sofia Museum, called MNCARS (Museo Nacional Centro de Arte Reina Sofía, Queen Sofia Center of Art National Museum). The three-level building, in a new structure adjacent to the Madrid museum itself, opened in 2005. The library's collection strengths are in fine arts from 1900 and the related fields of history, museology, and architecture. The collection contains over 167,000 bibliographic records, including 111,000 monographs, 1500 serials, 1600 audiovisual materials, 6000 musical scores, and over 15,000 exhibition catalogs, plus numerous ephemera and artists' books. The library pursues a comprehensive collection policy for both current out-of-print materials, and strives to obtain and index Spanish journals relating to the history of Spanish art. The library has also begun a project to digitize its sheet music collection. With about 16,000 visitors a year, it is one of the few museum libraries in Spain that is freely open to the public.

Religious Libraries

Real Biblioteca del Monasterio de San Lorenzo de El Escorial (Royal Library of the Monastery of San Lorenzo of the Escorial)

Because it is housed in a working monastery, the Escorial library is probably the most famous ecclesiastical library in Spain, and one of the most important in Europe. The Escorial was built in 1562 as King Philip II's personal monastery, palace, and, later, mausoleum (most of the Spanish monarchs since Charles V are interred there) in San Lorenzo de El Escorial, about 25 miles from Madrid; the library was established 13 years later (1575). Access is restricted to researchers in philology, art, and history of various disciplines. Like the Royal Palace library, this other royal library has unique, specialized collections, whose treasures include tenth and eleventh century codices, autograph manuscripts of Saint Teresa of Ávila (1515–1582), and a copy of Alphonse X the Wise's (1221–1284) *Cantigas de Santa María* (Canticles of Holy Mary, 13th century). It compensates for its collection of only about 50,000 monographs with over 6000 manuscripts in Latin, Spanish, Arabic, Greek, Hebrew, French, Italian, and Portuguese; 700 incunabula; and another 25,000 rare books from the sixteenth and seventeenth centuries. Its two reading rooms include one for researchers, primarily consisting of reference books and indexes, and a much larger exhibition hall/library, which is part of the self-guided tour of the Escorial. This hall contains not only the collection in armoires, but also globes and other artifacts from Philip's personal collection. The ceiling is gorgeously painted with figures representing the medieval trivium and quadrivium, with philosophy and theology on either end, thus in sum illustrating all known realms of intellectual pursuit at the time of its creation. Collection growth is small, since its acquisitions policy is limited to reference materials and items relating to Philip II and the Escorial. Classification is by shelf location. Interlibrary loan is for photocopies only. The library has five staff.

DIGITAL AND VIRTUAL LIBRARY COLLECTIONS AND SERVICES

In addition to the various digital efforts that were discussed above under individual institutions, some of the other more important virtual and digital libraries are mentioned below.

- Biblioteca Digital de Catalunya (Digital Library of Catalonia). Founded in 1999 for the member institutions of CBUC, it provides access to 40 e-journals, e-books, and databases as well as to Catalan-specific content.
- Biblioteca Virtual Miguel de Cervantes (Miguel de Cervantes Virtual Library). A joint Project of the University of Alicante, the Santander Group and the Marcelino Botín Foundation, this ambitious project intends to digitize the most important works of Spanish and Spanish–American authors and make them freely available on the Internet. It incorporates four other virtual libraries: the Biblioteca Americana (American Library), with materials related to all aspects of Hispanic American literature and culture; Biblioteca de Signos (Sign Language Library), a unique resource of materials relating to sign language and the hearing impaired; the Biblioteca Joan Lluís Vives (Joan Lluís Vives Library), a digital library of Catalan language classics; and Literatura Infantil y Juvenil (Children's and Young Adult Literature), containing classics of Spanish-language children's literature.
- Universidad Oberta de Catalunya (Open University of Catalonia) Library. Users include those officially enrolled in the university as well as those who have established accounts. The library provides access to 252 databases and 7800 e-journals, mostly in the sciences. Physical resources number around 68,000 items. Founded in 1995 and a member of REBIUN, it is in the vanguard of electronic resources management.
- The Universidad Nacional de Educación a Distancia (National Distance Education University), called UNED, founded in 1972 with headquarters in Madrid, was one of the pioneers in the Open University concept. Its 68 service points provide virtual library services to over 188,000 students, faculty, and staff, the largest user base of any REBIUN member.

EDUCATION FOR LIBRARY AND INFORMATION SCIENCE

The first attempt at library education in Spain was the establishment of the Escuela de Diplomática (School for Diplomatics) in 1856, which granted a degree of archivist–librarian, until its demise in 1900. The Catalan writer Eugenio d'Ors (1881–1954) was instrumental in establishing the first library school in Barcelona, the Escola Especial de Bibliotecàries (Special School for Librarians), in 1915. In 1978 the Spanish government legislated universities the authority to grant the new degree of Diplomatura in Library and Information Science.[5] The first true graduate professional library degree, however, was not granted until 1992. So far library science education has consisted primarily of three levels: a 3-year Diplomatura (rather similar to a U.S. bachelor's degree), a 4- to 5-year Licenciatura (somewhat comparable to the U.S. master's degree), and occasionally the Doctorate. Twelve universities offer the Diplomatura, 11 offer the Licenciatura and 8 the Doctorate. This framework is undergoing major transition as Spain adopts the Bologna Agreement, a European Union accord passed in 1999 which standardizes higher education pedagogical practices and degrees granted throughout the Union and allows for degrees granted in one country to be recognized by the others. The deadline for Union-wide implementation is 2010, though the University of Salamanca and Carlos III have already implemented the degree in library and information science.

PROFESSIONAL ASSOCIATIONS

The first professional library organization was the Facultad de Archivistas, Bibliotecarios y Antecuarios (Faculty of Archivists, Librarians and Antiquarians), created in 1858.

Among the many professional library associations in Spain, the largest is the Federación Española de Sociedades de Archivística, Biblioteconomía, Documentación y Museística (Federation of Spanish Societies of Archives, Libraries, Documentation and Museology), known as FESABID (http://www.fesabid.org). Founded in 1988, it is a federation of 14 other library associations, thus with a total membership of over 7000 members. The biennial conference it sponsors is the largest gathering of information professionals in the country. The federation collaborates with these national professional organizations: the Federación de Gremios de Editores de España (Federation of Publishers Guilds in Spain), or FGEE; the Universitat Oberta de Catalunya (Open University of Catalonia), or UOC; the Centro Español de Derechos Reprográficos (Spanish Center for Reprographic Rights), or CEDRO; and the Asociación Española de Normalización y Certificación (Spanish Association of Standardization and Certification), or AENOR. Finally, FESABID is a member of the International Federation of Library Associations and Institutions (IFLA), the European Bureau of Library, Information and Documentation Associations (EBLIDA), and the International Council on Archives (ICA).

Another important association in this field is the Federación de Asociaciones de Archiveros, Bibliotecarios, Museólogos y Documentalistas (Federation of Associations of Archivists, Librarians, Museologists, and Documentalists), called ANABAD (http://www.anabad.com), itself a federation of four associations representing each of those disciplines. Founded in 1949, it publishes the quarterly *Boletín de ANABAD* (ANABAD Bulletin) as well as reports.

A final national association is the Asociación Española de Documentación e Información (Spanish Association for Documentation and Information), or SEDIC (http://www.sedic.es). Founded in 1975, it publishes two journals: the quarterly *Revista Española de Documentación Científica* (*Spanish Review of Scientific*

Documentation) and a more irregular *Boletín CLIP* (*CLIP Bulletin*) as well as directories of software and information service providers.

Regional Library Associations

In addition to these national associations, several Autonomous Communities also have library associations.

- Andalusia. Asociación Andaluza de Bibliotecarios (Andalusian Association of Librarians), AAB http://www.aab.es. Founded 1981. Publishes the quarterly *Boletín de la Asociación Andaluza de Bibliotecarios* (Bulletin of the Andalusian Association of Librarians).
- Asociación Andaluza de Documentalistas (Andalusian Association of Documentalists), AAD (http://www.aadocumentalistas.org). Founded 1990.
- Asturias. Asociación Asturiana de Bibliotecarios, Archiveros, Documentalistas y Museólogos (Asturias Association of Librarians, Archivists, Documentalists and Museologists), AABADOM (http://www.aabadom.org). Founded 1989. Publishes quarterly *Boletín* (Bulletin).
- Balearic Islands. Associació de Bibliotecaris, Arxivers i Documentalistes de les Illes Balears (Association of Librarians, Archivists and Documentalists of the Balearic Islands), ABADIB (http://www.abadib.es). Founded 1991.
- Basque Country. Artxibozain, Liburuzain eta Dokumentazainen Elkartea (Basque Association of Professionals in Archives, Libraries and Documentation Centers), ALDEE (http://www.aldee.org). Founded 1990.
- Catalonia. Col·legi Oficial de Bibliotecaris-Documentalistes de Catalunya (Official Association of Librarians-Documentalists of Catalonia, COBDC (http://www.cobdc.org). Founded 1985. Publishes the annual *Bibliodoc*, bimonthly *Document*, and the trimestrial *Item: revista de Bibliotecomia i Documentació* (Item: Review of Library Science and Documentation).
- Murcia. Asociación de Profesionales de la Información y Documentación de la Región de Murcia (Association of Professionals of Information and Documentation in the Murcia Region), curiously known as INDEX (http://www.indexmurcia.org). Founded 1998.
- Navarre. Asociación Navarra de Bibliotecarios (Navarre Association of Librarians), ASNABI (http://www.asnabi.com). Founded 1995. Publishes the annual *Revista TK* (TK Review).
- Valencia. Associació Valenciana d'Especialistes en Informació (Valencian Association of Information Specialists), AVEI (http://www.avei.org). Founded 1993. Publishes bimonthly *Métodos de Información* (Information Methods).

Subject Library Associations

- Asociación de Bibliotecas y Bibliotecarios de Arquitectura (Association of Architecture Libraries and Librarians), ABBA http://www.upv.es/pls/obib/est_arc. menu. With a membership of 38 libraries, it produces the ARCANO database of materials on architecture, engineering, and urban planning.
- Asociación Española de Documentación Musical (Spanish Association of Musical Documentation), AEDOM (http://www.aedom.org). Founded in 1993, it is the Spanish affiliate of the International Association of Music Libraries, Archives and Documentation Centers (IAML).

LIBRARY COOPERATION

The most important academic network is the Red de Bibliotecas Universitarias (Network of University Libraries), REBIUN (http://www.REBIUN.org). Its membership, currently at 69 institutions, includes virtually all public and private universities. Created in 1998 originally as a resource sharing network, in 2000 it launched REBIUN En Línea (REBIUN Online), ReBEL, its online union catalog. At the end of 2005, it contained over 7.7 million bibliographic records, 18.6 million titles, 35.7 million volumes, and 642,000 journal titles, serving over 1.8 million potential users. REBIUN is governed by the rectors of the member universities. Its annual publication of the statistics of its members (http://www.REBIUN.org/doc/estadisticas/ANUARIO%20REBIUN%202005.pdf) provides the most accurate and up-to-date data of university library collections, funding and use.

Five other major academic consortia are

- BUCLE. Bibliotecas Universitarias de Castile and León (University Libraries of Castille and León) http://www.ubu.es/biblioteca/bucle/. Five members. Founded 2002.
- BUGALICIA. Consorcio de Bibliotecas Universitarias de Galicia (Consortium of University Libraries of Galicia) http://www.bugalicia.org. Three members. Founded 2001.
- CBUA. Consorcio de Bibliotecas Universitarias de Andalucía (Consortium of University Libraries of Andalusia) http://www.upo.es/cbua/. Ten members. Founded 2001.
- CBUC. Consorci de Bibliòteques Universitàries de Catalunya (Consortium of University Libraries of Catalonia) http://www.cbuc.es/. Ten full and seven associated members. Founded in 1996, it is the oldest of the academic consortia.
- Madroño. Consorcio de las Universidades de la Comunidad de Madrid y de la UNED para la Cooperación Bibliotecaria (Consortium of the Universities of the Community of Madrid and the Nacional University of Distance Education for Library Cooperation). http://www.consorciomadrono.net. Seven members. Founded 1999. Madroño has implemented a courier-lending service available between member campuses with a promised maximum delivery time of 48 hr; it is also spearheading efforts at digitization, especially for open archives, theses, and journals unique to each member institution.

The major public library network REBECA, http://www.mcu.es/bibliotecas/MC/Rebeca/index.html is a cooperative cataloging database of more than 860,000 bibliographic records in which 19 BPEs and 8 Central Libraries participate.

In addition, some of the most important subject-based networks are

- Catálogo Colectivo del Patrimonio Bibliógrafico Español (Union Catalog of the Spanish Bibliographic Heritage) http://www.mcu.es/bibliotecas/MC/CCPB/index.html. Contains over 781,000 titles and over 2 million copies of printed works from the fifteenth to twentieth centuries from 722 libraries whose collections form part of the Spanish Bibliographic Heritage network.
- Coordinadora de Documentació Biomèdica (Consortium of Biomedical Documentation), CDB http://www.doc6.es/cdb/. Composed of most Catalonian health science libraries.
- DOCUMAT. http://wzar.unizar.es/documat/ccol.html. Composed of 17 libraries specializing in mathematics. The union catalog of approximately 90 libraries is maintained by the CSIC.
- MECANO. http://www.upv.es/pls/obib/est_mec.menu. Composed of 112 universities specializing in engineering, computer science and technology. Its union catalog of 18,000 journal titles and 4000 proceedings is maintained by the library at the Polytechnic University of Valencia.

ARCHIVES AND ARCHIVAL SCIENCE

Administration

Like libraries, archives are administered by the General Board of the Book, Archives and Libraries under the Ministry of Culture.

Archives can generally be categorized into five groups:

1. Historical archives, which includes the national and regional archives.
2. Government archives, mostly records kept at provincial and municipal governing bodies.

3. Ecclesiastical archives, found in cathedrals, monasteries, and bishoprics.
4. Peerage archives, containing the historical records of noble families.
5. Corporate archives, containing legal records and archives for corporations and nonprofit organizations.

However, there is no accurate current figure for the number of archives in Spain; available data are woefully out of date and suspiciously incomplete. The list compiled by the National Statistics Institute includes only the 11 archives administered by the Board; the data below reflect information available for those archives only.

These archives employ a total of about 450 staff, 22% of whom are archivists and 7% are librarians.

Expenditures

Total expenditures for these archives, both from national and regional sources, were 81 million euros, one-third of which went to staff.

Collections

The format breakdown of the collections of the state archives is as follows:

• Photographic images	8,363,267
• Parchments	296,996
• Maps	84,577
• Stamps	18,637
• Art works	16,244
• Audiovisuals	1103
• Other	367
• Total	8,781,191

Added to this total is a collection of 13 million digitized images.

User Services

About 10,000 visitors annually use these archives and 15,000 visit them over the Internet; over half of all research inquiries are requested by telephone. These institutions copy between 1 and 2 million documents annually.

Representative Archives Profiles

Archivo General de Simancas (General Archives of Simancas)

Founded in 1540, the Simancas Archives are the oldest of the three major national archives. Located near the former national capital of Valladolid, it was created by order of Emperor Charles V to store valuable documents in a castle

there; in 1572 Philip II had the famous architect Juan de Herrera (1530–1597) draw up sketches for an edifice to permanently house the collection. It thus ranks as one of the earliest officially sanctioned archives in the world. In 1844 it was permanently opened to the public for historical research, but a special pass is now required for admittance. The historically valuable collection of primary materials provides access to the written record of the Spanish monarchy from the time of Ferdinand and Isabella to the early nineteenth century (see Fig. 3).

Archivo General de Indias (General Archives of the Indies)

Established 200 years later (1785) by Charles III (1759–88) in Seville, the Indies Archives were created to pull together under one roof all the documents, previously dispersed in different locations, relating to the Spanish administration in its former American and Philippine colonies. Today the Archives contain more than 43,000 files, containing 80 million pages of primary documents, and 25,000 volumes of historically valuable material.

Archivo Histórico Nacional (National Historical Archives)

Founded in 1866 by Queen Isabel II (1830–1904) in Madrid, the National Historical Archives was housed in the National Library from the time the latter opened in 1896, but in 1952 it moved into its present seven-story location. Though the newest of the three, it has the largest collection, with over half a million items. Its collections basically continue where the Simancas Archives leave off, providing access to primary government records from the middle of the nineteenth century forward. The archives are also especially strong in church records, many dating from the eleventh century, as a result of the nineteenth century disentailment.

Associations

In addition to the national professional associations described above, mention should be made of one of the most active regional associations, the Asociación de Archiveros de Castilla y León (Association of Archivists of Castile and Leon), ACAL (http://www.acal.es). Founded in 1991, it publishes the quarterly *Archivamos* and the annual *Tabula*.

Education

Five universities offer advanced degrees in archival science.

Fig. 3 Simancas Castle that houses the General Archives of Simancas. © Nani—Fotolia.com.

MUSEUMS AND MUSEOLOGY

Administration

Museums are administered by the Dirección General de Bellas Artes y Bienes Culturales (General Board of Fine Arts and Cultural Assets) under the Ministry of Culture.

About one-third are private, primarily ecclesiastical. The bulk of the public ones are administered locally.

There are about 1367 museums of all types; although art and archeology comprise the largest percentage, numerous smaller, specialized ones exist throughout the country. For example, in addition to five bullfight museums, Spain is one of a handful of countries in the world with museums devoted to such unique topics as instruments of torture and playing cards.

The two Autonomous Communities of Valencia and Castile-León have the largest percentages of museums, about 12% each.

Total staffing is over 11,500, the bulk of which is dedicated to administrative and professional personnel (43%).

Expenditures

Total expenditures for museums, both from national and regional sources, are 337 million euros, almost one-quarter of which (21%) goes to staffing.

Collections

Museums house a total of about 34.6 million items, an average of about 37,000 per museum. The largest subject area is natural sciences and natural history, with almost 14 million items (about 40% of the total).

User Services

Almost all (98%) are accessible to the public. Total visitors number around 49 million a year, with attendance at fine arts museums by far the highest of all categories (almost one-third). Less than half (44%) have a library; about the same number (46%) give guided tours. Only half (49%) have a Web page, though 70% have some degree of automation. Forty-two percent engage in some variety of educational activities, both for children and adults; about 30% host conferences.

Representative Museum Profiles

Museo Nacional del Prado (National Museum of the Prado)

Construction of the Prado began in 1785 under the direction of the architect Juan de Villanueva (1739–1811). On November 10, 1819 it opened its doors as the Real Museo de Pintura y Escultura (Royal Museum of Painting and Sculpture); it became the Museo Nacional del Prado (National Museum of the Prado) in 1869 (see Fig. 4).

The Prado is one of the premier art museums in the world, especially outstanding for its collection of pre-twentieth century Spanish art. Permanently on exhibit are such masterpieces as Diego Velázquez' (1599–1660) *La familia de Felipe IV, o Las Meninas* (The Family of Philip IV, or the Ladies-in-Waiting, 1656), Francisco de Goya's (1746–1828) *El 3 de Mayo de 1808 en Madrid* (May 3, 1808, 1814), and Hieronymus Bosch's (1450–1516) *The Garden of Early Delights* (ca. 1504). In addition to exhibition catalogs, the library publishes an annual bulletin. To deal with overflow, since 1971 the Casón del Buen Retiro has displayed late nineteenth and

Fig. 4 Prado Museum. © jzoran—Fotolia.com.

early twentieth century paintings in an annex that was originally Philip IV's (1605–1665) seventeenth century hunting lodge.

Museo Nacional Centro de Arte Reina Sofia (Queen Sofia Center of Art National Museum) (MNCARS)

The collections of the Queen Sofia pick up where those in the Prado leave off, covering twentieth century Spanish art. Built in 1992 in a remodeled hospital, it was named after the present queen, a devoted patron of the arts. Now permanently exhibited here is probably the museum's most famous work, Pablo Picasso's (1881–1973) politically charged antiwar masterpiece *Guernica* (1937), under constant surveillance. The museum also has outstanding collections by the Spanish surrealists Salvador Dalí (1904–1989) and Joan Miró (1893–1983) and cubist Juan Gris (1887–1927). An addition built in 2005 houses a library and auditorium. Like the National Library and the Prado, the director reports directly to the Minister of Culture.

Thyssen-Bornemisza Museum

The third art museum in the same Madrid neighborhood (in fact visitors can see all three on the same combined discounted ticket) is the Thyssen-Bornemisza, which opened in 1992 in the former nineteenth century Villahermosa Palace. The main foci of the 1000 items on display are early European painting and twentieth century works, thus complementing the holdings of the other two nearby museums. The collection contains works that were donated, first the private collection of Baron Hans Heinrich Thyssen-Bornemisza (1921–2002), and then

that of his widow, Carmen (b. 1943). The museum publishes an irregular *Boletín de Noticias* (News Bulletin).

Museu Picasso (Picasso Museum)

Located in Barcelona, the Picasso Museum contains one of the largest single collections (over 3500 early works) dedicated to the Spanish master, who lived in Barcelona during 1895–1904. In 1970 Picasso personally donated over 900 of his works. It opened in 1963 in the gothic Aguilar Palace; four other former palaces were added later. The museum publishes guides to the collection and exhibit catalogs.

Guggenheim Bilbao Museum

Another noteworthy art museum is the Guggenheim, which opened in 1997 in Bilbao, capital of the Basque province of Vizcaya. As the name implies, it is part of the distinguished Guggenheim pedigree. The stunning architectural masterpiece that is a work of art in itself was designed by the noted architect Frank Gehry (b. 1929). The specialty of the collections is twentieth century art. The museum publishes exhibition catalogs and books dealing with the museum.

Museo de El Greco (El Greco Museum)

On a smaller scale in size but certainly not artistic import is the El Greco Museum in Toledo. Established in 1911 in a former home of the artist, the museum exhibits in one place many of the outstanding works of the Toledan native. The nearby Church of Santo Tomé displays what is perhaps El Greco's finest work, *El entierro del conde de Orgaz* (The Burial of Count Orgaz, 1586).

Museo Arqueológico Nacional (National Archeological Museum)

Founded by Queen Isabel II in 1867 in Madrid, this museum is probably the most notable archeological museum in the country. Its extensive time range runs from the Paleolithic era forward. Its most noteworthy single object is the Iberian stone sculpture, the Dama de Eche (c. 475 BCE), but the replica of the ceiling of the caves of Altamira with the prehistoric animal drawings is also a highlight. The museum publishes an annual bulletin.

Museo Nacional de Antropología. (National Anthropological Museum)

Located in Madrid, the Museum of Anthropology, Ethnology and Prehistory was founded in 1910 during the reign of King Alphonse XIII. Its present status came about as a merger in 1993 of the Museo Nacional de Etnología (National Ethnological Museum) and the Museo Nacional del Pueblo Español (National Museum of the Spanish People); in 2004 it split off again but kept its current name. The strength of this museum lies in the collections of objects from the former Spanish colonies, especially skulls, mummies, and skeletons. The museum publishes exhibition catalogs as well as *Anales* (Annuals).

Real Jardín Botánico (Royal Botanical Garden)

Founded in 1755 by Ferdinand VI, it moved into its present location near the Prado in 1781. Now part of the CSIC, it is noteworthy for both its extensive grounds and greenhouses as well as the botanical research conducted there. Its library of over 30,000 volumes, some of which are of great historical interest, is one of the finest in the field of botany. The garden publishes a biennial *Anales* (Annals).

Associations

In addition to the national and regional professional associations described above, mention should be made of two independent associations. The Asociación Española de Museólogos (Spanish Association of Museologists), AEM (http://www.museologia.net), was founded in 1993; it publishes a newsletter and the trimestral *Revista de Museología* (Museology Review). The Asociación de Casas-Museo y Fundaciones de Escritores (Association of House-Museums and Foundations of Writers), ACAMFE (http://www.acamfe.org), was founded in 1993; its membership consists of 52 houses and museums associated with Spanish literary and intellectual history.

Education

Three universities offer graduate degrees in museology.

CONCLUSION

In the 30 plus years since democracy has been restored in Spain, libraries, archives, and museums have made great strides in catching up with their continental neighbors. Expenditures, collections, and use of services are increasing in all libraries, with usage of electronic resources clearly leading the pack. The government has made a concerted effort to support institutions of higher education, public libraries, and museums; school libraries and some of the smaller special libraries are not so fortunate, though their situation is improving. Automation of collections and widespread access to the Internet are also a national priority. Digitization efforts are being seriously undertaken at the national and regional level to preserve the country's rich cultural heritage. Many libraries contain priceless manuscripts and other resources unequaled and unavailable elsewhere. Universities have implemented degreed programs in librarianship, archives, and museology. Libraries are beginning to appreciate the value of cooperation through the creation of networks that facilitate the sharing of resources and technology. Members have found an effective voice through their participation in professional associations, at both the federal and local level.

ACKNOWLEDGMENTS

The author would like to thank the following people who so generously and selflessly gave up their precious time to be interviewed: Adela d'Alòs-Moner, Director, Doc6; Ana María Ballester, Director, Ateneo de Madrid Library; P. José Luis del Valle Merino, Director, El Escorial Library; Pablo Andrés Escapa, Director, Royal Palace Library; Carmen López, Queen Sofía Museum Library; Teresa Malo de Molina y Martín-Montalvo, Technical Director, National Library of Spain; Eva María Méndez Rodríguez, Department of Library and Information Science, Carlos III University; Margarita Taladriz Más, Director, Carlos III University Library.

The author would also like to thank fellow librarians Barbara Clark and Paula Rumbaugh for their gracious willingness to read the manuscript and to provide suggestions for improvement.

REFERENCES

1. World Bank. http://siteresources.worldbank.org/DATASTA TISTICS/Resources/GDP.pdf.
2. Crow, J.A. *Spain: The Root and the Flower*, 3rd Ed.; University of California Press: Berkeley, CA, 1985; 57.
3. Carrión, M. Spain, libraries. In *Encyclopedia of Library and Information Science*, 1st Ed.; Kent, A., Lancour, H., Daily, J.

E., Eds.; Marcel Dekker, Inc.: New York, 1980; Vol. 28, 337.
4. Carrión, M. Spain, libraries. In *Encyclopedia of Library and Information Science*, 1st Ed.; Kent, A., Lancour, H., Daily, J. E., Eds.; Marcel Dekker, Inc.: New York, 1980; Vol. 28, 338.
5. Ruiz-Pérez, R.; López-Cózar, E.D. Education for cataloging in Spanish Universities: a descriptive and critical study. Catalog. Classif. Quart. **2006**, *41*(3), 294.

BIBLIOGRAPHY

1. Carrión Gútiez, M. *La Biblioteca Nacional*, Biblioteca Nacional: Madrid, Spain, 1996.
2. Colodrón, V. Country focus: Spain. Info. Eur. **2000**, *5*(2), 26–28.
3. *Directory of University Libraries in Europe*, 2nd Ed.; Faith, D., Ed.; Europe Publications: London, 2004; 293–331.
4. Escolar, H. *Historia de las bibliotecas*; Fundación Germán Sánchez Ruipérez: Madrid, Spain, 1985.
5. Escolar-Sobrino, H. Spain. In *World Encyclopedia of Library and Information Services*; 3rd Ed.; Wedgeworth, R., Ed.; American Library Association: Chicago, IL, 1993; 783–785.
6. Fundación Germán Sánchez Ruipérez, *Gua de Bibliotecas Pu´blicas Espan˜olas*, La Fundación: Madrid, Spain, 1996.
7. Gallo León, J.P. *Bibliotecas Espan˜olas: Gua del Usuario*; Alianza Editorial: Madrid, Spain, 2002.
8. Gómez Gómez, A.A. Pullman Country Report: Spain. Available at http://www.pulmanweb.org/countries/Spain. htm (accessed June 2007).
9. Mayol, C.; Massísimo, A. Libraries and librarianship in Spain. IFLA J. **1993**, *19*(2), 131–146.
10. Moscoso, P.; Extremeño, A. Country report: Spain. Manag. Info. **2000**, *7*(1), 42–52.
11. Sebastián, M.C.; Méndez Rodríguez, E.M.; Rodríguez Mateo, D. Information policies in Spain: towards the new "information society". Libri **2001**, *51*(1), 49–60.

Special Collections

Lynne M. Thomas
Northern Illinois University, DeKalb, Illinois, U.S.A.

Abstract
Special collections and manuscripts are discussed as an area of professional library practice, a subset of library materials encompassing rare books, archives, manuscripts, and any other materials handled outside of mainstream library work, and an institutional structure within libraries. Aspects of materials that make them eligible for special collections are outlined. The history of special collections, rare book rooms, and archives is briefly discussed, along with a brief history of professional special collections librarianship. Trends in modern special collections are described, emphasizing the uses of special collections in academic research libraries in the United States. Common professional practices and career paths for special collections' professionals, along with necessary skills, knowledge, and education for modern special collections work are also discussed.

INTRODUCTION

Special collections and manuscripts are discussed, both as an area of library practice and as a subset of library materials. The history of special collections and manuscripts in American libraries is discussed, along with the history of the profession of special collections and manuscripts librarianship. Major professional organizations and their influence on the field are noted. Trends in special collections librarianship are discussed, along with core competencies and skills necessary for special collections work. All references to "books" may be understood to include alternative materials formats that may also live in special collections. Special collections as a term is used in the modern sense, encompassing rare books, archives, manuscripts, and any other materials handled outside the mainstream activities of a research library.

DEFINITIONS

What Are Special Collections?

Special collections is a broad term for groupings of library materials that are handled separately from regular, circulating library collections, because of age, scarcity, market value, subject matter, condition, or physical format. We tend to think of special collections as rare books, manuscripts, and archives first, but special collections include many formats, including maps, games, original works of art, realia (nonbook objects, such as furniture, weaponry, or locks of hair), textiles, audiovisual materials, and digital materials, many of which are acquired in tandem with books, archives, and manuscripts as part of a dedicated collection. Area Studies collections (or portions of Area Studies collections) are also occasionally included under the broader umbrella of special collections, particularly when the materials collected require additional care and security.

The field of librarianship that includes the skills, knowledge, and education necessary to adequately service unusual materials is also referred to as special collections work. "Special collections" is often included in the name of departments that handle these materials. These departments (and at some institutions, stand-alone libraries) often have rules for accessing their materials that differ from the rest of the library. Special collections are generally noncirculating collections with requirements for reader registration. Unlike circulating collections, which often delete circulation records to protect user privacy, special collections typically track the use of materials and maintain those records as a long-term security measure. Ink pens, along with food and drink, are generally banned to prevent damage to materials. Coats, bags, and, in some cases, file folders and notebooks are also disallowed to discourage accidental or intentional theft. Users are encouraged to use pencils and notepaper, laptop computers, mobile devices, and occasionally cameras and/or scanners instead while using special collections materials. To protect the integrity of the bindings of books in use, patrons are often supplied with foam wedges or other book supports, along with light weights to help hold books open without leaning on them. White cotton gloves, however, unless readers are specifically working with photographs, are no longer typically in use, as they may snag and tear paper-based materials, and are difficult to keep clean. For materials that themselves have significant dust or damage, latex or nitrile gloves may be offered for use instead.

Special collections exist in all shapes and sizes, varying in budget, depth, and focus. Examples of more narrowly defined special collections include small collections of local history materials at a small-town public library, or

Encyclopedia of Library and Information Sciences, Fourth Edition DOI: 10.1081/E-ELIS4-120053478

Sociology–Special

the archives department of a community or 4-yr undergraduate college. Large stand-alone research and independent libraries devoted to special collections include the Beinecke Library at Yale University, the Rare Books Division of the Library of Congress, the Houghton Library at Harvard University, the Harry Ransom Center at the University of Texas-Austin, the Getty Research Center, the American Antiquarian Society, and the Newberry Library in Chicago. Between these two extremes, colleges and universities across the country, large urban public libraries, corporate archives, historical societies, and museums host special collections departments that serve their respective constituencies, while often providing research materials for the public at large.

What Is a Manuscript?

The term "manuscript" has meanings that have multiplied over time and across changing formats. The first meaning, taken directly from Latin, is simply "written by hand." "Manuscripts" can also refer to illuminated pages from the medieval era; longhand drafts of poems, stories, speeches, and novels; personal journals; and handwritten grocery lists. "Manuscript" also describes original materials, either handwritten or produced on a typewriter or computer, created by a writer, often with the intent of publication.[1] In the era of the personal computer, "manuscript" can refer to not only any and all versions of original digital files created by an author, but also the printed out, copyedited version of that file once it returns to the author from the editor. Codicology, the study of bound manuscripts ("codexes"), particularly from the medieval period, is often conducted in concert with paleography (studying the handwriting used on the manuscript), along with the study of decorations' illustrations added by hand. Christopher de Hamel has produced numerous books that discuss the history and production of illuminated manuscripts in greater detail. Manuscripts produced after the medieval period are also studied by historians and bibliographers, who use the tools of textual editing and analytical bibliography to reconstruct the life cycle of particular literary or historical works, from notes to published product, often working to create a complete or correct text (although the debate over what constitutes "complete" or "correct" is, in many scholarly circles, still under discussion). G. Thomas Tanselle and Jerome McGann, along with D. F. McKenzie, have produced a prodigious amount of scholarship on this topic, following in the footsteps of Fredson Bowers, R.B. McKerrow, and Philip Gaskell; much of the scholarship in this area is documented in the journals *Studies in Bibliography* and *TEXT*. As texts that would have traditionally been paper-based are increasingly born-digital, a new set of skills for their study, long-term care, and use, such as digital forensics and digital preservation, are increasingly necessary.

What Makes an Item or a Collection "Special"?

Special collections at individual institutions are formed using internally developed collection development policies. While these policies will differ from institution to institution—what's "rare" to one institution may be quite common to another—special collections materials in libraries do tend to share some common characteristics, with the preservation of artifactual integrity playing an overarching role. The Rare Books and Manuscripts Section (RBMS) of the American Library Association (ALA), along with the Antiquarian Booksellers' Association of America, has produced a brochure, "Your Old Books," that provides an overview of how materials are judged for inclusion in special collections. The Society of American Archivists (SAA) features brochures on donating both personal papers and organizational papers to repositories.[2]

Age

Old books often form the core of special collections, particularly when books are being initially selected from among circulating library collections. While age is not always the sole criterion for acquisition, library users and library staff recognize it as the most often easily recognizable (and logical) factor for why an item would be placed in special collections rather than allowed to circulate. There are some age guidelines that are quite common among special collections, particularly for published books: books published anywhere in the world before 1800, in the United States before 1865, and west of the Mississippi River before 1890 are usually candidates for special collections acquisition. Regionally or nationally based collections will often set additional guidelines, based upon the dates for the introduction of printing to the pertinent locale.

Market value

Materials that have significant market value nearly always end up in special collections to protect them from theft. The more security-conscious use policies of most special collections departments assure that expensive materials purchased with library or donor funds will remain in the library as intended. Placing expensive materials in special collections also may reduce the wear and tear of daily use, ensuring the longevity of the library's long-term investment.

The market for special collections materials can be volatile, with particular subject areas or authors moving in and out of fashion, and prices fluctuating accordingly. The two biggest factors for determining the market value of any given book are its physical condition and how many people or institutions are competing against each other to own it. Truly scarce materials are often more expensive than less scarce materials, but not always, if there is little market interest. Aspects of the physical book that may also affect its market value include its provenance (who owned it previously), markings in the book (is it signed by the author or illustrator?), and the presence or absence of dust jackets, particularly with modern first editions. Market value for books can also vary by where on the market the book is sold, whether at auction, through antiquarian booksellers, from private individual to private individual, through estate sales or used book stores, or through bookselling or broader sales and exchange websites. Any of these sales may take place in person, over the telephone, or through the web.

Provenance

Items are often placed in special collections because of their provenance, the history of the previous owners of the item. If a book was owned or used by someone famous, or infamous, the market value of that item may be greater than if its previous owner was not well-known. Markings made by previous owners, bookplates placed in the book, and binding choices made by previous owners may all provide reason to place an item in special collections. Some items become "special" because of their presence in famous collections, past and present. Other items become special because they were used by famous writers for specific purposes. For example, books owned by Sylvia Plath, including her dictionary, are part of the Sylvia Plath Collection at Smith College. That dictionary, a commercial edition from her time in college, has special value solely because it was owned and annotated by Plath.

Provenance is also particularly important for "high-spots" (expensive, culturally iconic items) such as Shakespeare First Folios, Gutenberg Bibles, The Ellesmere Chaucer manuscript (now held at the Huntington Library in California), Old Master drawings held at the Rosenbach Library and Museum in Philadelphia, or Burmese manuscripts held at Northern Illinois University. Items that cannot prove a clean provenance through an unbroken chain of ownership may have been stolen at some point in their existence. This can create headaches for auction houses, buyers, and sellers of expensive items as legitimate previous owners come forward to protest the sale of an item that was illegally taken from them and demand restitution. The 200-year-old discussion between the Greek and British governments over the Elgin Marbles, currently held at the British Museum, illustrates the thorny issues that occur when there is a dispute over an item's provenance.[3]

Format

Materials not in book format that require special handling and storage, such as archival materials, manuscripts, maps, and audio–visual materials, often end up in special collections. Having one department handle "unusual"

formats frees up library staff to process books for the main collections more efficiently than staff that must move from process to process based upon the format of the item in hand. Books more likely to be damaged through circulation, such as books with moving parts or significant numbers of maps or illustrations, are also likely candidates.

Some books are produced specifically for special collections, such as artists' books, livres d'artistes, and private press books. Artists' books use the book format to create a work of art, integrating all aspects of the book (type, paper, binding, illustration) into the artistic process, as a painter uses canvas, brush, paint, and framing to make a completed piece. Some artists create unique books, while others work in small runs of duplicates, creating anywhere from five to fifty copies of a particular piece, in keeping with the nature of the format. Livres d'artistes include original graphic art, often produced by famous artists such as Picasso, as illustrations to a text, but the illustrations are created separately from the whole book. Private presses may issue one or both kinds of these books; but many others focus instead on the act of letterpress printing, typographic design, and keeping particularly scarce texts, such as poetry, in print. Private presses often aim for a slightly wider distribution of their work, often printing anywhere from 100 to 1000 copies of a particular title for sale.

Subject matter

Many, if not most, individual special collections are formed around some kind of unifying subject theme, or different groups of themes, which vary from library to library. Most libraries hold groups of sometimes disparate collections that may or may not relate to one another in anything other than their need for special handling. The selected subject(s) may include particular author(s) (i.e., Gertrude Stein, James Weldon Johnson, Isaac Asimov, Audre Lorde, William Blake), organizations (individual corporations, churches, or departments at a university), types of materials (cookbooks, trade catalogs, sheet music, children's books, broadsides, dime novels) or specific topics, such as viticulture, women's history, poetry, dance, chemistry, law, or architecture. Politically volatile and sexually explicit materials are also more likely to be held in special collections for safekeeping because of the greater chance of their being mutilated or stolen by readers that disagree with their content.

Scarcity

When only a few extant copies of a book remain, or an item is unique, it makes sense to care for those materials differently than perhaps might be done with readily available materials, placing them in special collections to keep them from being destroyed by extensive handling. Artists' books, private press materials, limited editions, and the like often create scarcity because they are produced in limited numbers. Commercial publishers, particularly around the turn of the nineteenth century, often created "limited editions" of collected works of particular authors with ornate, matched bindings. This artificially created scarcity marks them among collectors as valuable and worth saving, ensuring the survival of individual copies. Everyday materials produced en masse, such as newspapers, broadsides, and paperback books, do not typically survive in such large numbers over time because individual owners deem them disposable. For historians interested in documenting quotidian life, this presents a dilemma, since primary materials for their research are, in some cases, more difficult to locate than materials already deemed "important" through contemporary marketing or criticism.

Condition

Placing fragile materials in special collections for safekeeping helps to extend their natural lifespan as original artifacts. Materials that do not circulate are less likely to be damaged through rough or continuous use. Patrons who use materials in a special collections setting handle them more carefully because of their "special" status. Additionally, removing fragile items from the circulating collection removes them from ready access; although they remain accessible, they are accessed less often in a special collections setting than sitting on a shelf in the circulating collection. Condition is also a preservation concern; to avoid contamination of other materials in the collection, materials that are moldy or mildewed should not be accepted into special collections if at all possible. Excessively fragile, brittle items require additional care in handling and storage and may require additional limitations on use, such as required use of surrogates, either photocopies or electronic.

While professional repair by a trained conservator can prolong the useful life of books that have been damaged, those books are no longer as close to their original state as books that have not had intervention. Condition, including the absence or presence of dust jackets for modern first editions, is paramount on the book-collecting market and drives the price for any given book. For the library market, depending upon collecting priorities, it may occasionally prove more advantageous, both for the collection and its resources, to acquire a gently used, less-expensive particular copy of a title, than none at all while holding out for a pristine but more expensive copy.

HISTORY AND PURPOSE

Foundations of Special Collections (through the 1980s)

While special collections, in the sense of materials handled separately from main collection materials, have

existed since the library at Alexandria, the term "special collections" dates back at least to the 1940s; libraries tended to maintain "rare book rooms" separate from manuscripts and institutional archives, with each earning its own issue of the journal *Library Trends*.[4]

Through the 1950s and 1960s, the special collections work focused on efficiently managing, organizing, and building collections, and how to distinguish one institution from another. From the 1970s through the 1990s, the profession emphasized library automation and physical preservation of rapidly deteriorating materials, as well as on theft prevention and security.[5] The broader term was in common parlance in the library literature of the 1980s, reflecting the growth, merger, and development of larger, more comprehensive departments that handle unusual materials over the previous three decades.[6]

The 2006 merger of the National Library of Canada and the National Archives of Canada, now combined to form the National Library and Archives of Canada, provides a recent example of this trend.[7] The terminology change, incorporating "rare books," "manuscripts," and "archives" under "special collections," was most recently codified through the RBMS of the Association for College and Research Libraries (ACRL), a division of the ALA. RBMS uses the term "special collections" and "special collections professionals" in their most recent guidelines submitted to ACRL, where they once used "rare books, manuscripts, and other special collections."[8]

The vast majority of special collections are tied to a parent institution: a university, a college, a city or town, a corporation. Special collections departments tied to institutions often began as "treasure rooms" or "rare books rooms" where particularly expensive or valuable volumes were kept under tighter supervision than items in the circulating collection, closely guarded by librarians, and handled only by distinguished, vetted visitors. This image of special collections persists, despite concerted efforts by the profession to dispel it. As special collections grew and evolved, the mission of the departments expanded, often in relation to resources provided by the "parent" institution, individual donors, or external funding agencies.

A few independent special collections libraries, such as the Morgan Library in New York, began as personal collections, later shared with the public through a philanthropic donation.[9] Other independent libraries became more special as their collections aged. When the Library Company of Philadelphia was established by Benjamin Franklin in 1733, it was a circulating subscription library. The books, imported from England, were not particularly rare in the modern sense, although they were too expensive to be acquired by most individuals. The library was originally designed to be a working collection of reference works for subscribers, who were often merchants and working men. As the collection aged, however, the materials became more scarce and valuable for historical research, and the modern version of the Library Company, although it retains its subscribers as donors, is an independent research library with a focus on American history and culture.[10] Many special collections now actively collect subsets of contemporary materials, developing deep collections that will become more special as they age.

Special Collections in the Contemporary Era (1990s–Present)

Modern special collections in the United States no longer serve only as "treasure rooms," collecting and holding particularly valuable materials securely for posterity and making them available to select scholars, or as storage areas for archives accessible to no one but the staff archivist. The possible audience for primary materials has been significantly expanded; both the SAA and the ALA recognized the importance of this expansion, issuing an initial joint statement of "Guidelines for Access to Original Research Materials" in 1994, revised in 2009.[11] Regardless of the parent institution's funding source (public, private, or some combination of the two), modern special collections now typically have a strong public service component at the core of their mission, educating the public about their materials through programs, exhibitions, publications, group and class visits, and digital projects. Just as libraries have limited resources and cannot be all things to all users, those responsible for special collections may find that they have to be selective about the types of public programming provided. For many departments, the continuing development of resources through fund-raising and grant-writing is also an integral part of special collections work. Digitization projects, a growing portion of the contemporary special collections landscape since the 1990s, have often been funded through grants. Future grant opportunities may also include projects to appropriately preserve digital special collections materials for long-term use.

Public programs and performances

Public programs, for many special collections, are an excellent way to reach out to communities beyond the small number of researchers interested in any given collection. Scholarly talks, live historical interpreters, literary readings, performances of music or plays held in the collections, and creative activities (such as crafts based upon items in the collection) emphasize the continuing relevance of the original artifacts to contemporary life. Public programs also raise the profile of the department and institution hosting the event.

Exhibitions and publications

Exhibitions of special collections materials allow for endless interpretation and reinterpretation of the artifacts involved. Rotating exhibits can showcase particular items, while safeguarding materials by limiting their exposure to light. Loaning to or borrowing from other special collections can extend local collections and draw new patrons to view larger, more robust exhibits. Akin to museum programs for exhibit loans, RBMS has endorsed guidelines for borrowing and lending exhibit materials.[12] Exhibitions need not be exclusively site-based; many special collections also provide online access to their exhibits, or leverage online exhibits to expand upon what can be shown in person.

Libraries may also provide enduring access to materials through publications such as exhibit catalogs, bibliographies, and collection guides. The Katharine Kyes Leab & Daniel J. Leab American Book Prices Current Exhibition Awards are presented annually by RBMS in recognition of excellence in exhibit catalog work, both paper-based and electronic.[13] While published bibliographies and collection guides may become outdated for special collections that continue to be developed, these publications can provide a snapshot of collections at given moments in time, particularly if they document major acquisitions. Exhibition catalogs based in single, comprehensive collections related to particular topics may also become standard reference works for the field.

Teaching and research

Contemporary special collections departments in the United States typically maintain a vigorous program of teaching and research. Digital facsimiles of special collections materials have become ubiquitous in teaching and research through numerous digital projects, allowing students and professors access to materials that would otherwise be inaccessible in person. Despite the usefulness of digital surrogates, particularly for laying academic groundwork for projects and making side-by-side comparisons in teaching, the surrogates cannot replace hands-on work with primary materials. Unique historical objects have physical characteristics that cannot be fully transferred to the digital realm. The conditions under which an item is produced influence its physical aspects and tell us its own history. Particular inks and paint color formulations used in medieval manuscript production, the feel of the "bite" of type when printing on vellum as opposed to paper, and the smell of "signature" glue that may identify a master bookbinder cannot be meaningfully replicated online. Physical characteristics of a particular artifact can only be fully integrated into its study when the artifact is physically present; without access to the original artifact, the story of that particular item is incomplete.

Classroom visits to special collections provide an important countermeasure to the digital world, grounding students in the physical realities and context of the original materials from which digital objects are drawn. This is particularly important as we continue to experience the aftereffects of mass digitization projects. Despite massive amounts of money, scanning, and bandwidth, it is unlikely that each and every book ever produced will be digitized, especially for materials placed in special collections because they didn't adhere as well to the specifications for a modern codex. It is unlikely that every set of archival records, three-dimensional artists' book, oversized atlas, or book with moving parts will be scanned. No cuneiform tablet, papyrus scroll, lap-desk, fountain pen, printing press, typewriter, or computer hard drive used for writing books in special collections will be sufficiently represented in digital form to replace the original.

There is a long tradition of scholarly research among special collections professionals, both based on the collections for which they are responsible, and in areas of their own intellectual interest. Whether they serve as faculty or as academic professionals at their own institutions, curators, catalogers, and archivists research collections for which they are responsible, add to them judiciously, document them for researchers through catalogs and bibliographies, and interpret them clearly for visitors. Scholarly research can also lead to better integration with teaching faculty at academic institutions, opening up the possibility for joint publications and collaboration on grant projects.

Public and scholarly access to special collections materials has grown through cooperative cataloging initiatives and web-based archival finding aids, but providing accurate, comprehensive information about special collections is still a challenge. In 2003, the Association of Research Libraries held a conference on the subject, which resulted in a white paper, an initiative to generate funding for "Exposing Hidden Collections," and an issue of *RBM* devoted to the topic.[14] From 2008 to 2014, the Council on Library and Information Resources sponsored a series of grants to enhance the discovery of hidden collections.[15]

Fund-raising and grant-writing

As library budgets have remained flat or dwindled, and the cost of library resources, particularly electronic journal databases, has increased in increments well exceeding inflation, fund-raising has become an integral part of special collections work for many professionals. Grant-writing has been a significant source of funding for special collections, particularly in providing access to materials already held. Many, if not most, early grant-funded digitization projects involved special collections materials. Many special collections departments also work closely with library friends groups, often providing tours and programming about their precious and unique materials to potential donors. In some cases, the library's friends group will be administered through the special collections department as well, particularly if there is no dedicated library fund-raising staff. Special collections is often a recipient of donations from friends groups, since a

common mission for friends is to purchase materials for the library that are too expensive for library budgets. Friends of the library may, in turn, become donors of in-kind special collections materials or financial support through endowments that support special collections acquisitions or preservation.

Security, preservation, and posterity

In addition to collection development work and public service, many special collections also provide additional security for high-risk items through vault storage and additional physical monitoring of materials use. Preservation and conservation of library materials is often part of the special collections mission. Larger special collections departments may have preservation and conservation professionals on-staff. Departments that do not have preservation staff on-site often still provide basic preservation advice to the library and the public, as well as referrals to local conservation professionals when necessary.

Special collections play a role in securing posterity for materials, both through preservation and security practices and through collection development choices. Careful collection development is paramount, as selection may indeed dictate the long-term survival of some contemporary, particularly ephemeral, materials. Materials selected for special collections placement are far more likely to survive longer, because they are more gently handled, accessed less frequently, and stored in more optimal conditions than in the main stacks.

SPECIAL COLLECTIONS IN PRACTICE

The Special Collections and Manuscripts Professional

Given the multitude of library tasks performed in a special collections setting, special collections professionals require a diverse skill set. Both the RBMS of the ALA and the SAA have produced guidelines that delineate core competencies for special collections professionals.[16] While each special collections professional may not need every single skill noted in these documents, they do provide an exhaustive listing of necessary skills for special collections professionals over the course of a career.

Core professional requirements

In addition to a bachelor's degree, positions in special collections at the entry level generally require an ALA-accredited master's degree in library and/or information science, SAA certification, or an advanced degree at the master's level in public history or a similar academic discipline. More advanced professional positions, particularly in libraries that maintain faculty rank for their librarians, may require an additional advanced degree in a subject specialization, either at the master's degree or doctoral level, depending upon the position and the institution in question.

Strong communication skills are essential in special collections. Only the largest special collections have internal staff dedicated to particular job functions such as technical services; many special collections professionals will find themselves working closely with technical services departments in their libraries, integrating workflow for special materials with those from the circulating collections. Modern special collections' outreach duties may include not only class visits, working with patrons and donors, and exhibitions, but also engaging with online patrons through the departmental presence on social media, highlighting individual items, collections, and events. Special collections professionals with acquisitions responsibilities must also work closely with a wide range of other professionals: book dealers, collectors, and, often, the creators of the works in question (authors, artists, etc.). Because these close working relationships always have the potential to produce conflicts of interest, both RBMS and SAA provide statements of professional ethics for special collections professionals.[17] Communication skills are especially important for those special collections professionals that also include fund-raising work in their job descriptions. Foreign languages are a significant asset in special collections work. Many special collections materials, particularly in rare book collections, are in languages other than English. (Significant numbers of books produced in Europe during the hand-press period were published in Latin, German, or French, for example). Some special collections are formed around area studies, collecting materials from particular geographic areas such as Southeast Asia or the Middle East. Linguistic ability in relation to collections served is crucial for both building the collection in question, and serving the readers that use it.

Every special collection is unique to its institution, and gaining knowledge of the collections is a central part of special collections work. Public service special collections professionals often serve as the interlocutor between researchers and the collections that they serve. Most special collections are closed-stack areas, with access restricted to authorized staff. While the scholarly discovery method of browsing the shelves in the hopes of serendipity is available in a special collections setting, it often requires an authorized staff member to be present with the patron. Public service and curatorial professionals often have the responsibility of interpreting aspects of the collections to users through classroom or group presentations and exhibit work. Cataloging professionals that work with special collections need collection knowledge to accurately integrate new materials; the

same holds true for those professionals with archival processing responsibilities.

Another particularly useful "foreign language skill" for special collections professionals, descriptive and analytical bibliography, uses formulae to describe the physical aspects of a book. This physical description of books requires some knowledge of the history of the book, including the history of the different technologies that make up the physical object: printing, typecasting and typesetting, bookbinding, and papermaking. A basic understanding of how to preserve paper-based materials, and materials in other formats as dictated by the collections served, is also required. In the modern special collections era, an understanding of the digital realm is also an essential skill set, not only for communicating effectively with colleagues, and making currently held materials more widely accessible, but also for participating in the long-term preservation of born-digital materials, particularly when charged with collecting contemporary materials produced after personal computing became widespread. Many of the special collections-specific skills described here can be acquired through classes in library and information science programs, through internships or practicum experiences in special collections departments, or through attendance at Rare Book School in Charlottesville, VA (which offers classes at satellite locations across the United States and in Europe).[18] Other professional development opportunities in particular topics are routinely offered through both RBMS and SAA, both nationally and regionally.

CONCLUSION: THE FUTURE OF SPECIAL COLLECTIONS

Special collections work has undergone significant changes since the formation of rare book rooms in the 1930s, with growth, consolidation, and a significant shift to accessing collection surrogates digitally. Daniel Traister suggested in his 2000 polemical essay on the future of special collections that to survive special collections professionals need to fundamentally change our approach, moving from guarding treasured materials from public abuse to making special materials as widely available as possible.[19] This shift continues with the advent of Web 2.0 tools, which advocate user-generated content as an integral part of the digital experience of any artifact.[20] The Association of Research Libraries sees special collections as a core ingredient in the research library of the future, codified in their Statement of Principles on Special Collections.[21] While the shift in attitudes has already begun in the profession, it remains to be seen whether the significant financial resources necessary to remain relevant in the digital age, both through continuing acquisitions and digitization, will be forthcoming.[22]

REFERENCES

1. Carter, J.; Barker, N. *ABC for Book Collectors*, 8th Ed.; Oak Knoll: New Castle, DE, 2004; 147.

2. http://rbms.info/yob.shtml (accessed Nov 2014); http://www2.archivists.org/publications/brochures/donating-family recs (accessed Nov 2014); http://www2.archivists.org/publications/brochures/donating-orgrecs (accessed Nov 2014).

3. http://www.britishmuseum.org/the_museum/news_and_press_releases/statements/parthenon_sculptures.aspx (accessed Nov 2014).

4. Downs, R.B. *Library Specialization..* Proceedings of an Informal Conference Called by the A.L.A. Board on Resources of American Libraries, May 13–14, 1941. Chicago, IL: American Library Association; Manuscripts and Archives, Ed. Vail, R.W.G., Library Trends 5:3 (Jan 1957); Rare Book Libraries and Collections, Ed. Peckham, H.H., Library Trends 5:4 (Apr 1957).

5. Berger, S.E. What is so rare...: Issues in rare book librarianship. Libr. Trends **Summer 1987**, *36* (1), 9–22.

6. Scham, A.M. *Managing Special Collections*; Neal Schuman: New York, 1987.

7. Doucet, M. Library and archives Canada: A case study of a national library, archives, and museum merger. RBM, **March 2007**, *8* (1), 61–66. http://rbm.acrl.org/content/8/1/61.full.pdf (accessed Nov 2014).

8. http://www.rbms.info/standards/index.shtml (accessed Nov 2014).

9. http://www.librarycompany.org/about/index.htm (accessed Nov 2014).

10. http://www.themorgan.org/about/history-of-the-morgan (accessed Nov 2014).

11. http://www2.archivists.org/statements/alasaa-joint-statement-on-access-to-research-materials-in-archives-and-special-collection (accessed Nov 2014).

12. http://www.ala.org/acrl/standards/specialcollections (accessed Nov 2014).

13. http://www.rbms.info/committees/exhibition_awards/index.shtml (accessed Nov 2014).

14. http://www.arl.org/storage/documents/publications/hidden-colls-white-paper-jun03.pdf (accessed Nov 2014).

15. http://www.clir.org/hiddencollections (accessed Nov 2014).

16. http://www.ala.org/acrl/standards/comp4specollect (accessed Nov 2014); http://www2.archivists.org/profession (accessed Nov 2014).

17. http://rbms.info/standards/code_of_ethics.shtml (accessed Nov 2014); http://www2.archivists.org/statements/saa-core-values-statement-and-code-of-ethics (accessed Nov 2014).

18. http://www.rarebookschool.org/ (accessed Nov 2014).

19. Traister, D. Is there a future for special collections? And should there be? A polemical essay. RBM, **Spring 2000**, *1* (1), 54–76. http://rbm.acrl.org/content/1/1/54.full.pdf+html (accessed Nov 2014).

20. Cohen, L.B. *Library 2.0 Initiatives in Academic Libraries*; Association of College and Research Libraries: Chicago, IL, 2007; Whittaker, B.M.; Thomas, L.M. *Special Collections 2.0: New Technologies for Rare Books, Manuscripts, and Archival Collections*; Libraries Unlimited: Santa Barbara, CA, 2009.

21. Association of Research Libraries Statement of principles: Special collections. 2003. Available at:http://www.arl.org/rtl/speccoll/speccollprinciples.shtml (accessed Nov 2014).

22. Hirtle, P. The impact of digitization on special collections in libraries. Libr. Cult. **2002**, *37* (1), 42–52. Available at: http://muse.jhu.edu/journals/libraries_and_culture/v037/37.1hirtle.html. (accessed Nov 2014); Proffitt, M.; Schaffner, J.K. *The Impact of Digitizing Special Collections on Teaching and Scholarship*; OCLC Research: Dublin, OH, 2008; http://www.oclc.org/content/dam/research/publications/library/2008/2008-04.pdf?urlm=162913 (accessed Nov 2014).

FURTHER READING

1. Antiquarian Booksellers Association of America, http://www.abaa.org/ (accessed Nov 2014).

2. Bowers, F. *Principles of Bibliographical Description*; Oak Knoll Press: New Castle, DE, 1995.

3. Carter, J. *ABC for Book Collectors*, 8th Ed.; Oak Knoll Press: New Castle, DE, 2004.

4. De Hamel, C. *A History of Illuminated Manuscripts*; Phaidon: London, U.K., 1997.

5. Gailbraith, S.K.; Smith, G.D. *Rare Books Librarianship: An Introduction and Guide*; Libraries Unlimited: Santa Barbara, CA, 2012.

6. Gaskell, P. *A New Introduction to Bibliography*; Oak Knoll Press: New Castle, DE, 2000.

7. McGann, J.J. *A Critique of Modern Textual Criticism*; University of Virginia Press: Charlottesville, VA, 1992.

8. McKenzie, D.F. *Bibliography and the Sociology of Texts*; Cambridge University Press: Cambridge, MA, 1999.

9. McKerrow, R.B. *An Introduction to Bibliography for Literary Students*; Oak Knoll Press: New Castle, DE, 1995.

10. Rare Books and Manuscripts Section, American Library Association, http://rbms.info (accessed Nov 2014).

11. Rare Book School Homepage. http://www.rarebookschool.org/ (accessed Nov 2014).

12. Society of American Archivists Homepage. http://www2.archivists.org/ (accessed Nov 2014).

13. Tanselle, G.T. *Textual Criticism and Scholarly Editing*; Bibliographical Society of the University of Virginia: Charlottesville, VA, 2003.

14. Theimer, K. ArchivesNext blog. http://www.archivesnext.com/ (accessed Nov 2014).

15. Theimer, K. *Description*. Innovative Practices for Archives and Special Collections Series; Rowan & Littlefield: Lanham, MD, 2014.

16. Theimer, K. *Reference and Access*. Innovative Practices for Archives and Special Collections Series; Rowan & Littlefield: Lanham, MD, 2014.

17. Theimer, K. *Outreach; Management*. Innovative Practices for Archives and Special Collections Series; Rowan & Littlefield: Lanham, MD, 2014.

18. Whittaker, B.M.; Thomas, L.M. *Special Collections 2.0: New Technologies for Rare Books, Manuscripts, and Archival Collections*; Libraries Unlimited: Santa Barbara, CA, 2009.

Special Collections and Manuscripts

Lynne M. Thomas
Rare Books and Special Collections, Northern Illinois University, DeKalb, Illinois, U.S.A.

Abstract

Special collections and manuscripts are discussed as an area of professional library practice, a subset of library materials encompassing rare books, archives, manuscripts, and any other materials handled outside of mainstream library work, and an institutional structure within libraries. Aspects of materials that make them eligible for special collections are outlined. The history of special collections, rare book rooms, and archives is briefly discussed, along with a brief history of professional special collections librarianship. Trends in modern special collections are described, emphasizing the uses of special collections in academic research libraries in the United States. Common professional practices and career paths for special collections professionals, along with necessary skills, knowledge, and education for modern special collections work are also discussed.

INTRODUCTION

Special collections and manuscripts are discussed, both as an area of library practice and as a subset of library materials. The history of special collections and manuscripts in American libraries is discussed, along with the history of the profession of special collections and manuscripts librarianship. Major professional organizations and their influence on the field are noted. Trends in special collections librarianship are discussed, along with core competencies and skills necessary for special collections work. All references to "books" may be understood to include alternative materials formats that may also live in special collections. Special collections as a term is used in the modern sense, encompassing rare books, archives, manuscripts, and any other materials handled outside of the mainstream activities of a research library.

DEFINITIONS

What Are Special Collections?

Special collections is a broad term for groupings of library materials that are handled separately from regular, circulating library collections, because of age, scarcity, market value, subject matter, condition, or physical format. We tend to think of special collections as rare books, manuscripts, and archives first, but special collections include many formats, including maps, games, original works of art, realia (nonbook objects, such as furniture, weaponry, or locks of hair), textiles, audiovisual materials, and digital materials, many of which are acquired in tandem with books, archives, and manuscripts as part of a dedicated collection. The field of librarianship that includes the skills, knowledge, and education necessary to adequately

service these unusual materials is also referred to as special collections work. "Special collections" is often included in the name of departments that handle these materials. These departments (and at some institutions, stand-alone libraries), often have rules for accessing their materials that differ from the rest of the library. Special collections are generally noncirculating collections with requirements for reader registration. Unlike circulating collections, which often delete circulation records to protect user privacy, special collections typically track the use of materials and maintain those records as a long-term security measure. Ink pens, along with food and drink, are generally banned to prevent contact with materials. Coats, bags, and, in some cases, file folders and notebooks are also disallowed to discourage accidental or intentional theft. Users are encouraged to only use pencils and notepaper or laptop computers while using special collections materials. To protect the integrity of the bindings of books in use, patrons are often supplied with foam wedges or other book supports, along with light weights to help hold books open without leaning on them. White cotton gloves, however, unless readers are working with photographs, are no longer typically in use, as they may snag and tear paper-based materials.

Special collections exist in all shapes and sizes, varying in budget, depth, and focus. Examples of more narrowly defined special collections include small collections of local history materials at a small town public library, or the archives department of a community or 4 year undergraduate college. Large stand-alone research and independent libraries devoted to special collections include the Beinecke Library at Yale University, the Rare Books Division of the Library of Congress, the Houghton Library at Harvard University, the Harry Ransom Center at the University of Texas-Austin, the Getty Research Center, the American Antiquarian Society, and the Newberry

Encyclopedia of Library and Information Sciences, Fourth Edition DOI: 10.1081/E-ELIS4-120044336

Sociology–Special

Library in Chicago. Between these two extremes, colleges and universities across the country, large urban public libraries, corporate archives, historical societies, and museums host special collections departments that serve their respective constituencies, while often providing research materials for the public at large.

What Is a Manuscript?

The term manuscript has meanings that have multiplied over time and across changing formats. The first meaning, taken directly from the Latin, is simply "written by hand." "Manuscripts" can also refer to illuminated pages from the medieval era; longhand drafts of poems, stories, speeches, and novels; personal journals, and handwritten grocery lists. "Manuscript" also describes the original materials, either handwritten, or produced on a typewriter or computer, created by a writer, often with the intent of publication.[1] In the era of the personal computer, "manuscript" can refer to not only any and all versions of original digital files created by an author, but also the printed out, copyedited version of that file once it returns to the author from the editor. Codicology, the study of bound manuscripts ("codexes"), particularly from the medieval period, is often conducted in concert with paleography (studying the handwriting used on the manuscript), along with the study of decorations illustrations added by hand. Christopher de Hamel has produced numerous books that discuss the history and production of illuminated manuscripts in greater detail. Manuscripts produced after the medieval period are also studied by historians and bibliographers, who use the tools of textual editing and analytical bibliography to reconstruct the life cycle of particular literary or historical works, from notes to published product, often working to create a complete or correct text (although the debate over what constitutes "complete" or "correct" is, in many scholarly circles, still under discussion). G. Thomas Tanselle and Jerome McGann, along with D.F. McKenzie, have produced a prodigious amount of scholarship on this topic, following in the footsteps of Fredson Bowers, R.B. McKerrow, and Philip Gaskell; much of the scholarship in this area is documented in the journals *Studies in Bibliography* and *TEXT*. As texts that would have traditionally been paper-based are increasingly born digital, a new set of skills for their study, care, and use will be necessary.

What Makes an Item Or a Collection "Special"?

Special collections at individual institutions are formed using internally developed collection development policies. While these policies will differ from institution to institution—what's "rare" to one institution may be quite common to another—special collections materials in libraries do tend to share some common characteristics, with the preservation of artifactual integrity playing an overarching role. The Rare Books and Manuscripts

Section (RBMS) of the American Library Association (ALA), along with the Antiquarian Bookseller's Association of America (ABAA), has produced a brochure, "Your Old Books," that provides an overview of how materials are judged for inclusion in special collections.[2]

Age

Old books often form the core of special collections, particularly when special collections are being initially separated from circulating collections. While age is not always the sole criteria for acquisition, it is the most often easily recognizable (and logical) factor for library users and library staff that explains why an item would be placed in special collections rather than be allowed to circulate. There are some age guidelines that are quite common among special collections, particularly for published books: books published anywhere in the world before 1800, in the United States before 1865, and west of the Mississippi River before 1890 are usually candidates for special collections acquisition. Regionally or nationally based collections will often set additional guidelines, based upon the dates for the introduction of printing to the pertinent locale.

Market value

Materials that have significant market value nearly always end up in special collections to protect them from theft. The more security-conscious use policies of most special collections departments assure that expensive materials purchased with library or donor funds will remain in the library as intended. Placing expensive materials in special collections reduces the wear and tear of daily use, ensuring the longevity of the library's long-term investment.

The market for special collections materials can be volatile, with particular subject areas or authors moving in and out of fashion, and prices fluctuating accordingly. The two biggest factors for determining the market value of any given book are its physical condition and how many people or institutions are competing against each other to own it. Truly scarce materials are often more expensive than less scarce materials, but not always, if there is little market interest. Aspects of the physical book that may also affect its market value include its provenance (who owned it previously), markings in the book (is it signed by the author?), and the presence or absence of dust jackets, particularly with modern first editions. Market value for books can also vary by where on the market the book is sold, whether at auction, through antiquarian booksellers, from private individual to private individual, through estate sales or used book stores, or through bookselling or broader sales and exchange Web sites. Any of these sales may take place in person, over the telephone, or through the Web.

Provenance

Items are often placed in special collections because of their provenance, the history of the previous owners of the item. If a book was owned or used by someone famous, or infamous, the market value of that item may be greater than if its previous owner was not well-known. Markings made by previous owners, bookplates placed in the book, and binding choices made by previous owners may all provide reason to place an item in special collections. Some items become "special" because of their presence in famous collections, past and present. Other items become special because they were used by famous writers for specific purposes. For example, books owned by Sylvia Plath, including her dictionary, are part of the Sylvia Plath Collection at Smith College. That dictionary, a commercial edition from her time in college, has special value solely because it was owned and annotated by Plath.

Provenance is also particularly important for high-spot items such as Shakespeare First Folios, Gutenberg Bibles, The Ellesmere Chaucer manuscript (now held at the Huntington Library in California), Old Master drawings held at the Rosenbach Library and Museum in Philadelphia, or Burmese manuscripts held at Northern Illinois University. Items that cannot prove a clean provenance through an unbroken chain of ownership may have been stolen at some point in their existence. This can create headaches for auction houses, buyers, and sellers of expensive items as legitimate previous owners come forward to protest the sale of an item that was illegally taken from them and demand restitution. The 200 year-old discussion between the Greek and British governments over the Elgin Marbles, currently held at the British Museum, illustrate the thorny issues that occur when there is a dispute over an item's provenance.[3]

Format

Materials not in book format that require special handling and storage, such as archives, manuscripts, maps, and audiovisual materials, often end up in special collections. Having one department handle "unusual" formats frees up library staff to process books for the main collections more efficiently than staff that must move from process to process based upon the format of the item in hand. Books more likely to be damaged through circulation, such as books with moving parts or significant numbers of maps or illustrations, are also likely candidates.

Some books are produced specifically for special collections, such as artists' books, livres' d'artistes, and private press books. Artists' books use the book format to create a work of art, integrating all aspects of the book (type, paper, binding, illustration) into the artistic process, as a painter uses canvas, brush, paint, and framing to make a completed piece. Some artists create unique books, while others work in small runs of duplicates, creating anywhere from 5 to 50 copies of a particular piece, in keeping with the nature of the format. Livres d'artistes include original graphic art, often produced by famous artists such as Picasso, as illustrations to a text, but the illustrations are created separately from the whole book. Private presses may issue one or both kinds of these books; but many others focus instead on the act of letterpress printing, typographic design, and keeping particularly scarce texts, such as poetry, in print. Private presses often aim for a slightly wider distribution of their work, often printing anywhere from 100 to 1000 copies of a particular title for sale.

Subject matter

Many, if not most, individual special collections are formed around some kind of unifying subject theme, or different groups of themes, which vary from library to library. Most libraries hold groups of sometimes disparate collections that may or may not relate to one another in anything other than their need for special handling. The selected subject(s) may be particular author(s) (i.e., Gertrude Stein, James Weldon Johnson, William Shakespeare, Isaac Asimov), organizations (individual corporations, churches, or departments at a university), types of material (cookbooks, trade catalogs, artists' books, sheet music, children's books, broadsides, dime novels) or specific topics, such as viticulture, women's history, poetry, dance, chemistry, law, or architecture. Politically volatile and sexually explicit materials are also more likely to be held in special collections for safekeeping because of the greater chance of their being mutilated or stolen by readers that disagree with their content.

Scarcity

When only a few extant copies of a book remain, or an item is unique, it makes sense to care for those materials differently than perhaps might be done with readily available materials, placing them in special collections to keep them from being destroyed by extensive handling. Artists' books, private press materials, limited editions, and the like often create scarcity because they are produced in limited numbers. Commercial publishers, particularly around the turn of the nineteenth century often created "limited editions" of collected works of particular authors with often ornate, matching bindings. This artificially created scarcity marks them among collectors as valuable and worth saving, ensuring the survival of individual copies. On the contrary, everyday materials produced en masse, such as newspapers, broadsides, and paperback books, do not typically survive in such large numbers over time because individual owners deem them disposable. For historians interested in documenting quotidian life, this presents a dilemma, since primary materials for their research are, in some cases, more difficult to locate than materials already deemed "important" through contemporary marketing or criticism.

Condition

Placing fragile materials in special collections for safekeeping helps to extend their natural lifespan as original artifacts. Materials that do not circulate are less likely to be damaged through rough or continuous use. Patrons who use materials in a special collections setting handle them more carefully because of their "special" status. Additionally, removing fragile items from the circulating collection removes them from ready access; although they remain accessible, they are less likely to be accessed as often in a special collections setting than sitting on a shelf in the circulating collection. Condition is also a preservation concern; to avoid contamination of other materials in the collection, materials that are moldy or mildewed should not be accepted into special collections if at all possible. Excessively fragile, brittle items require additional care in handling and storage, and may require additional limitations on use, such as required use of surrogates, either photocopies or electronic.

While professional repair by a conservator can prolong the useful life of books that have been damaged, those books are no longer as close to their original state as books that have not had intervention. Condition, including the absence or presence of dust jackets for modern first editions, is paramount on the book-collecting market, and drives the price for any given book. For the library market, depending upon collecting priorities, it may occasionally prove more advantageous, both for the collection and its resources, to acquire a gently used, less-expensive particular copy of a title, than none at all while holding out for a pristine but more expensive copy.

HISTORY AND PURPOSE

Foundations of Special Collections (through the 1980s)

While special collections, in the sense of materials handled separately from main collection materials, have existed since the library at Alexandria, the term "special collections" dates back at least to the 1940s; libraries tended to maintain "rare book rooms" separate from manuscripts and institutional archives, with each earning its own issue of the journal *Library Trends*.[4–6]

Through the 1950s and 1960s, special collections work focused on efficiently managing, organizing, and building collections, and how to distinguish one institution from another. From the 1970s through the 1990s, the profession emphasized library automation and physical preservation of rapidly deteriorating materials, as well as theft prevention and security.[7] The broader term was in common parlance in the library literature of the 1980s, reflecting the growth, merger, and development of larger, more comprehensive departments that handle unusual materials over the previous three decades.[8]

The 2006 merger of the National Library of Canada and the National Archives of Canada, now combined to form the National Library and Archives of Canada, provides a recent example of this trend.[9,10] The terminology change, incorporating "rare books," "manuscripts," and "archives" under "special collections" was most recently codified through the RBMS of the Association for College and Research Libraries (ACRL), a division of the ALA. RBMS uses the term "special collections" and "special collections professionals" in their most recent guidelines submitted to ACRL, where they once used "rare books, manuscripts, and other special collections."[11]

Most, but not all, special collections are tied to a parent institution: a university, a college, a city or town, a corporation. Special collections departments tied to institutions often began as "treasure rooms" or "rare books rooms" where particularly expensive or valuable volumes were kept under tighter supervision than items in the circulating collection, closely guarded by librarians, and handled only by distinguished, vetted visitors. This image of special collections persists, despite concerted efforts by the profession to dispel it. As special collections grew and evolved, the mission of the departments expanded, often in relation to resources provided by the "parent" institution, individual donors, or external funding agencies.

A few independent special collections libraries, such as the Morgan Library in New York, began as personal collections, later shared with the public through a philanthropic donation.[12] Other independent libraries became more special as their collections aged. When the Library Company of Philadelphia was established by Benjamin Franklin in 1733, it was a circulating subscription library. The books, imported from England, were not particularly rare in the modern sense, although they were too expensive to be acquired by most individuals. The library was originally designed to be a working collection of reference works for subscribers, who were often merchants and working men. As the collection aged, however, the materials held in it became more scarce and valuable for historical research, and the modern version of the Library Company, although it retains its subscribers as donors, is an independent research library with a focus on American history and culture.[13] Many special collections now actively collect subsets of contemporary materials, developing deep collections that will become more special as they age.

Special Collections in the Contemporary Era (1990s–Present)

Modern special collections in the United States no longer serve only as "treasure rooms," collecting and holding particularly valuable materials securely for posterity and making them available to select scholars, or as storage areas for archives accessible to no one but the staff archivist. The possible audience for primary materials has been significantly expanded; both the Society of American Archivists (SAA) and the ALA recognized the importance of this expansion, issuing a joint statement of "Guidelines for Access to Original Research Materials" in 1994.[14] Regardless of the parent institution's funding source (public, private, or some combination of the two), modern special collections now typically have a strong public service component as part of their mission, educating the public about their materials through programs, exhibitions, publications, group and class visits, and digital projects. Just as libraries have limited resources and cannot be all things to all users, those responsible for special collections may find that they have to be selective about the types of public programming provided. For many departments, the continuing development of resources through fundraising and grant-writing is also an integral part of special collections work. Digitization projects, a growing portion of the contemporary special collections landscape since the 1990s, have often been funded through grants. Future grant opportunities may also include projects to appropriately preserve digital special collections materials for long-term use.

Public programs and performances

Public programs, for many special collections, are an excellent way to reach out to communities beyond the small number of researchers interested in any given collection. Scholarly talks, live historical interpreters, literary readings, performance of music or plays held in the collections, and creative activities (such as crafts based upon items in the collection) emphasize the continuing relevance of the original artifacts to contemporary life. Public programs also raise the profile of the department and institution hosting the event.

Exhibitions and publications

Exhibitions of special collections materials allow for endless interpretation and reinterpretation of the artifacts involved. Rotating exhibits can showcase particular items, while safeguarding materials by limiting their exposure to light. Loaning to or borrowing from other special collections can extend local collections, and draw new patrons to view larger, more robust exhibits. Akin to museum programs for exhibit loans, RBMS has endorsed guidelines for borrowing and lending exhibit materials.[15] Exhibitions need not be exclusively site-based; many special collections provide access to their exhibits online.

Libraries may also provide enduring access to materials through publications such as exhibit catalogs, bibliographies, and collection guides. The Katharine Kyes Leab & Daniel J. Leab American Book Prices Current Exhibition Awards are presented annually by RBMS in recognition of excellence in exhibit catalog work, both paper-based and electronic.[16] While published bibliographies and collection guides may become outdated for special collections that continue to be developed, these publications can provide a snapshot of collections at given moments in time, particularly if they document major acquisitions. Often, bibliographies based in single, comprehensive collections related to particular topics become the standard for the field.

Teaching and research

Contemporary special collections departments in the United States typically maintain a vigorous program of teaching and research. Digital facsimiles of special collections materials have become ubiquitous in teaching and research through digital projects, and allow students and professors access to materials that would otherwise be impossible to study. Despite the usefulness of digital surrogates, particularly for laying academic groundwork for projects and making side-by-side comparisons in teaching, the surrogates cannot replace hands-on work with primary materials. Unique historical objects have physical characteristics that cannot be fully transferred to the digital realm. The conditions under which an item is produced influence its physical aspects, and tell us its own history. Particular inks and paint colors used in medieval manuscript production, the feel of the "bite" of type when printing on vellum as opposed to paper, and the smell of "signature" glue that may identify a master bookbinder cannot be meaningfully replicated online. Physical characteristics of a particular artifact can only be fully integrated into its study when the artifact is physically present; without access to the original artifact, the story of that particular item is incomplete.

Classroom visits to special collections provide an important countermeasure to the digital world, grounding students in the physical realities and context of the original materials from which digital objects are drawn. This is particularly important as we continue to experience the aftereffects of mass digitization projects. Despite massive amounts of money, scanning, and bandwidth, it is unlikely that each and every book ever produced will be digitized, especially those from special collections that were placed there because they did not adhere as well to the specifications for a modern codex. It is unlikely that every set of archival records, three-dimensional artists' book, oversized atlas, or book with moving parts will be scanned. No cuneiform tablet, papyrus scroll, lap-desk, fountain pen, printing press, typewriter, or computer hard drive used for writing books in special collections will be sufficiently represented in digital form to replace the original.

There is a long tradition of scholarly research among special collections professionals, both based on the collections for which they are responsible, and in areas of their own intellectual interest. Curators, catalogers, and archivists research the collections for which they are responsible, add to them judiciously, document them for researchers through catalogs and bibliographies, and interpret them clearly for visitors. Scholarly research can also lead to better integration with teaching faculty at academic institutions, opening up the possibility for joint publications and collaboration on grant projects.

Public and scholarly access to special collections materials has grown through cooperative cataloging initiatives and Web-based archival finding aids, but providing accurate, comprehensive information about special collections is still a challenge. In 2003, the Association of Research Libraries (ARL) held a conference on the subject, that resulted in a white paper, an initiative to generate funding for "Exposing Hidden Collections," and an issue of *RBM* devoted to the topic.[17] In 2008, the Council on Library and Information Resources (CLIR) launched a grant project to enhance the discovery of hidden collections.[18]

Fundraising and grant-writing

As library budgets have remained flat or dwindled, and library resources, particularly electronic serial databases, have gone up in cost increments well exceeding inflation, fundraising has become an integral part of special collections work for many professionals. Grant-writing has been a significant source of funding for special collections, particularly in providing access to materials already held. Many, if not most, early grant-funded digitization projects involved special collections materials. Many special collections departments also work closely with library friends groups, often providing tours and programming about their precious and unique materials to potential donors. In some cases, the library's friends group will be administered through the special collections department as well, particularly if there is not dedicated library fundraising staff. Special collections is often a recipient of donations from friends groups, since a common mission for friends is to purchase materials for the library that are too expensive for library budgets. Friends of the library may, in turn, become donors of in-kind special collections materials or financial support through endowments that support special collections acquisitions or preservation.

Security, preservation, and posterity

In addition to collection development work and public service, many special collections also provide additional security for high-risk items through vault storage and additional physical monitoring of materials use. Preservation and conservation of library materials is often part of the special collections mission. Larger special collections departments may have preservation and conservation

professional staff on-site. Departments that do not have preservation staff on-site often still provide basic preservation advice to the library and the public, as well as referrals to local conservation professionals when necessary.

Special collections play a role in securing posterity for materials, both through its preservation and security practices and through collection development choices. Careful collection development is paramount, as selection may indeed dictate the survival of some contemporary, particularly ephemeral, materials. Materials selected for special collections placement are far more likely to survive longer, because they are less handled, accessed less frequently, and stored in more optimal conditions than in the regular stacks.

SPECIAL COLLECTIONS IN PRACTICE

The Special Collections and Manuscripts Professional

Given the multitude of library tasks performed in a special collections setting, special collections professionals require a diverse skill set. Both the RBMS of the ALA and the SAA have produced guidelines that delineate core competencies for special collections professionals.[19] While each special collections professional may not need every single skill noted in these documents, they do provide an exhaustive listing of what may be generally necessary for special collections professionals.

Core professional requirements

In addition to a bachelor's degree, positions in special collections at the entry level generally require an ALA-accredited master's degree in library science, or an advanced degree at the master's level in history or a similar academic discipline. More advanced professional positions, particularly in libraries that maintain faculty rank for their librarians, may require an additional advanced degree in a subject specialization, either at the master's degree or doctoral level, depending upon the position and the institution in question.

Strong communication skills are essential in special collections. Only the largest special collections have internal staff dedicated to particular job functions such as technical services; many special collections professionals will find themselves working closely with technical services departments in their libraries, integrating workflow for special materials with those from the circulating collections. Special collections professionals with acquisitions responsibilities must also work closely with a wide range of other professionals: book dealers, collectors, and, often, the creators of the works in question (authors, artists, etc.). Because these close working relationships always have the potential to produce conflicts of interest, both RBMS and SAA provide statements of professional ethics for special collections professionals.[20] Communication skills are especially important for those special collections professionals that also include fundraising work in their job descriptions. Foreign languages are a significant asset in special collections work. Many special collections materials, particularly in rare book collections, are in languages other than English. Significant numbers of books produced in Europe during the handpress period were published in Latin, German, or French. Some special collections are formed around area studies, collecting materials from particular geographic areas such as Southeast Asia or the Middle East. Linguistic ability in relation to collections served is crucial for both building the collection in question, and serving the readers that use it.

Every special collection is unique to its institution, and gaining knowledge of the collections is a central part of special collections work. Public service special collections professionals often serve as the interlocutor between researchers and the collections that they serve. Most special collections are closed-stacks areas, with access restricted to authorized staff. While the scholarly discovery method of browsing the shelves in the hopes of serendipity is available in a special collections setting, it often requires an authorized staff member to be present with the patron. Public service professionals also often have the responsibility of interpreting aspects of the collections to users through classroom or group presentations and exhibit work. Cataloging professionals that work with special collections need collection knowledge to accurately integrate new materials; the same holds true for those professionals with archival processing responsibilities.

Another particularly useful "foreign language skill" for special collections professionals, descriptive and analytical bibliography, uses formulae to describe the physical aspects of a book. This physical description of books requires some knowledge of the history of the book, including the history of the different technologies that make up the physical object: printing, typecasting, bookbinding, and papermaking. A basic understanding of how to preserve paper-based materials, and materials in other formats as dictated by the collections served, is also required. In the modern special collections era, some understanding of the digital realm is also an essential skill set, not only for communicating effectively with colleagues, and making currently held materials more widely accessible but also for participating in the long-term preservation of born-digital materials. Many of the special collections-specific skills described here can be acquired through classes in library science programs, through internships or practicum experiences in special collections departments, or through attendance at Rare Book School in Charlottesville, VA (which offers classes at satellite locations across the United States and in Europe).[21] Other professional development opportunities in particular topics are routinely offered through both RBMS and SAA, both nationally and regionally.

CONCLUSION: THE FUTURE OF SPECIAL COLLECTIONS

Special collections work has undergone significant changes since the formation of rare book rooms in the 1930s, with growth, consolidation, and the shift to accessing collections digitally. Daniel Traister suggested in his 2000 polemical essay on the future of special collections that to survive special collections professionals need to fundamentally change our approach, moving from guarding treasured materials from public abuse to making special materials as widely available as possible.[22] This shift continues with the advent of Web 2.0 tools which advocate user-generated content as an integral part of the digital experience of any artifact.[23] The ARL sees special collections as a core ingredient in the research library of the future, codified in their Statement of Principles on Special Collections.[24] While the shift in attitudes has already begun in the profession, it remains to be seen whether the significant financial resources necessary to remain relevant in the digital age, both through continuing acquisitions and digitization, will be forthcoming.[25]

REFERENCES

1. Carter, J.; Barker, N. *ABC for Book Collectors*, 8th Ed.; Oak Knoll: New Castle, DL, 2004; 147.
2. http://www.rbms.info/yob.shtml.
3. http://www.britishmuseum.org/the_museum/news_and_press_releases/statements/parthenon_sculptures.aspx.
4. Downs, R.B., Ed. Library specialization Proceedings of an Informal Conference Called by the A.L.A. Board on Resources of American Libraries May, 13–14, 1941; American Library Association: Chicago, IL, 1941.
5. Vail, R.W.G. Manuscripts and archives. Libr. Trends **1957**, January 5(3).
6. Peckham, H.H. Rare book libraries and collections. Libr. Trends **1957**, April 5(4).
7. Berger, S.E. What Is So Rare...: Issues in Rare Book Librarianship. Libr. Trends **1987**, *36*(1), 9–22.
8. Scham, A.M. *Managing Special Collections*; Neal Schuman: New York, 1987.
9. Oder, N. Canada to merge national library and archives. Libr. J. **2002**, November 1 *127*(18), 15 http://www.libraryjournal.com/article/CA252316.html (accessed August 2008).
10. National library and archives merger finalized in Canada. Libr. J. **2004**, *129*(3), http://www.libraryjournal.com/article/CA426219.html (accessed August 2008).
11. http://www.rbms.info/standards/index.shtml.

12. http://www.librarycompany.org/about/index.htm.
13. http://www.themorgan.org/about/history.asp.
14. http://www.archivists.org/statements/alasaa.asp.
15. http://www.ala.org/ala/acrl/acrlstandards/borrowguide.cfm.
16. http://www.rbms.info/committees/exhibition_awards/index. shtml.
17. http://www.arl.org/bm~doc/hiddencollswhitepaperjun6.pdf.
18. http://www.clir.org/hiddencollections/index.html.
19. http://www.archivists.org/profession/overview.asp http:// www.ala.org/ala/acrl/acrlstandards/comp4specollect.cfm (accessed August 2008).
20. http://www.rbms.info/standards/code_of_ethics.shtml http:// www.archivists.org/governance/handbook/app_ethics.asp (accessed August 2008).
21. http://www.rarebookschool.org/.
22. Traister, D. Is there a future for special collections? And should there be? A polemical essay. RBM **2000**, *1*(1), 54–76 Spring, http://www.ala.org/ala/acrl/acrlpubs/rbm/ backissuesvol1no1/traister.PDF (accessed August 2008).
23. Laura, B. Cohen., Ed. *Library 2.0 Initiatives in Academic Libraries*; Association of College and Research Libraries: Chicago, IL, 2007.
24. Association of Research Libraries, Statement of principles: special collections **2003**, Available at http://www.arl.org/rtl/ speccoll/speccollprinciples.shtml (accessed August 2008).
25. Hirtle, P. The impact of digitization on special collections in libraries. Libr. Cult. **2002**, *37*(1), 42–52, Available at http://muse.jhu.edu/journals/libraries_and_culture/v037/ 37.1hirtle.html (accessed August 2008).

BIBLIOGRAPHY

1. Antiquarian Booksellers Association of America, Available at http://www.abaa.org/books/abaa/index.html (accessed August 2008).
2. Bowers, F. *Principles of Bibliographical Description*; Oak Knoll Press: New Castle, DL, 1995.
3. Carter, J. *ABC for Book Collectors*, 8th Ed.; Oak Knoll Press: New Castle, DL, 2004.
4. De Hamel, C. *A History of Illuminated Manuscripts*; Phaidon: London, 1997.
5. Gaskell, P. *A New Introduction to Bibliography*; Oak Knoll Press: New Castle, DL, 2000.
6. McGann, J.J. *A Critique of Modern Textual Criticism*; University of Virginia Press: Charlottesville, VA, 1992.
7. McKenzie, D.F. *Bibliography and the Sociology of Texts*; Cambridge University Press: Cambridge, 1999.
8. McKerrow, R.B. *An Introduction to Bibliography for Literary Students*; Oak Knoll Press: New Castle, DL, 1995.
9. Rare Books and Manuscripts Section, American Library Association, Available at http://www.rbms.info (accessed August 2008).
10. Rare Book School Homepage, Available at http://www. rarebookschool.org/ (accessed August 2008).
11. Society of American Archivists Homepage, Available at http://www.archivists.org/ (accessed August 2008).
12. Tanselle, G.T. *Textual Criticism and Scholarly Editing*; Bibliographical Society of the University of Virginia: Charlottesville, VA, 2003.

Special Librarianship

Susan S. DiMattia
DiMattia Associates, Stamford, Connecticut, U.S.A.

Abstract

Special librarianship is that portion of the broad profession of librarianship serving the people, subjects, and collections of information resources in limited subject areas. Unlike a public or academic library setting, where breadth of subject familiarity is expected, special librarianship operates in niche settings dealing with finance, law, publishing, health, and medicine, and other well-defined subject areas and organizations. Professional opportunities in special librarianship have both changed and grown over recent years. Technology has significantly multiplied the amount of available information. Users of information increasingly recognize their need for the assistance of expert information professionals to satisfy their requirement for locating complete, timely, and high quality information on which to base strategic decisions.

INTRODUCTION

This entry explores special librarianship; the qualities, philosophies, and competencies involved in that work; the associations and networks that help practitioners achieve excellence; and some of the major and evolving concepts of special librarianship. An attempt to suggest some of the changing roles and opportunities that may define the future of the profession concludes the entry.

HISTORICAL CONTEXT

Special collections and libraries began to appear in the early 1800s, in academic and government agency settings. The library at what is now the U.S. Military Academy at West Point, with its original emphasis in the late 1770s on engineering materials, is generally considered among the first of what can be considered a special academic library, followed by the science and engineering collections at such institutions as Rensselaer Polytechnic Institute. Through the years, the U.S. Department of State, the New York Chamber of Commerce, and several commercial firms established libraries to aid in meeting their missions and goals.[1] Although little is known about the people staffing many of these early special libraries, it is safe to assume that they were subject specialists rather than "librarians" in the sense that today we recognize those professionals with graduate level training in the collection, evaluation, and use of specialized information sources and the management of the libraries that house those resources (See the entry on "Special Libraries" p. 4966).

Evolution

Special librarianship has evolved over the past two or three decades arguably more than any other segment of the library profession. One of the drivers of this change has been the explosion of information technology and the opportunities and potential for gathering and sharing information that it has unleashed. In addition, as organizations, particularly those in the for-profit sector, have recognized the essential nature of and need for reliable, comprehensive actionable information, the support information professionals provide increasingly has become recognized as valuable and they have moved into strategic positions within their organizations. The terms special librarians and information professionals are used interchangeably in this entry, as they are in the literature of the profession.

Successful information professionals are those who are willing to embrace change, to continuously upgrade their competencies, and champion their value. At the time when the Internet was growing rapidly, people in management or purse-string-holder positions would question the need for information professionals if everyone in the organization had access to the Internet and everything on the Internet was free. Those professionals who had a ready answer to that annoying misperception have usually been able to survive. Those who were not prepared with a concise argument about the value of their expertise in an environment of exploding information were often at risk of losing their positions.

The Web Is Not All Free

The free Internet argument is one of the primary issues that continues to hover over special librarianship.

Mary Ellen Bates, one of the group of people in the profession classified as "super searchers," gave a Web seminar (webinar) in the Factiva series in 2004 on the topic "Convincing Your Boss That It's Not all Free on the Web." She quoted from several sources about the

Encyclopedia of Library and Information Sciences, Fourth Edition DOI: 10.1081/E-ELIS4-120044670

Sociology–Special

difficulty of finding accurate information on the Web. For example, with the billions of pages on the Web, search engines cannot retrieve everything. By one estimate, 50% of searches on the Web result in failure to retrieve the information sought. Among the many reasons for this low success rate may be that the search was not constructed well and/or the source selected was inappropriate, or that the source is not well indexed by search engines. These reasons, and more, point to the advisability of consulting an information professional. In a survey of information users by the information content consulting firm Outsell, reported in Bates' article, 85% of respondents considered themselves skilled searchers, but 52% said the desired information is too hard to find. Bates reminds readers that the "invisible Web," that portion of online sources that are not found by search engines, may actually contain up to 400 times more high-value information than the "visible Web."[2]

The Special Libraries Association (SLA) has defined, in the introduction to their "Competencies for Information Professionals of the 21st Century," the value of specialists in information management.

> In the information and knowledge age, specialists in information management are essential—they provide the competitive edge for the knowledge-based organization by responding with a sense of urgency to critical information needs. Information, both internally and externally produced, is the lifeblood of the knowledge-based organization and essential for innovation and continuing learning. Information sharing is also essential for any organization that is attempting to understand and manage its intellectual capital.... IPs [information professionals] play a unique role in gathering, organizing and coordinating access to the best available information sources for the organization as a whole. They are also leaders in devising and implementing standards for the ethical and appropriate use of information.[3]

By the mid-1990s, special librarianship began to move away from the physical space called the library. Services are provided as part of a project team or in a more virtual environment. Because funding is an ongoing concern of special librarianship, methods of recovering at least some costs of operations took the form of charge-backs to users and searches for fundraising opportunities. Through continuous training, practitioners added to the traditional jobs associated with special librarianship—materials selection; acquisition and organization of materials; reference, research, and retrieval services; and facilities planning. Responsibilities for preservation, digitization, and archiving; knowledge management; competitive intelligence; information architecture; metadata and data mining; informatics; strategic planning; technology issues represented by Web 2.0 and social networks; and other high-level information functions became part of the expected competencies. Excellent customer service is at the core of all of these activities. As

special librarians made themselves visible and demonstrated an understanding of the goals of the parent organization, as well as a willingness to join teams and committees in the organization, the more their value was recognized and their opportunities for advancement increased. Those special librarians who merged their knowledge of information with knowledge of the parent organization were most valuable. Moving from a reactive mode, where serving everyone was the goal, to an information and knowledge leadership role, special librarianship began to further specialize, in recognition of the fact that staff and resources would not grow along with the growth in need for services.

People point to the organizations that have disbanded their physical libraries, and there have been many of those. What is not as visible is the fact that many of the librarians have remained with the organization, reassigned to higher level analysis activities, working directly with project teams and specialized departments.

CAREER OPPORTUNITIES

Special librarianship is present in a broad range of organizations and institutions: nonprofits, such as museums, associations, and foundations; the financial and business environment, in banks, insurance companies, and manufacturing organizations; newspapers and other publishing ventures; law firms and health science settings attract information professionals possessing subject expertise, often requiring an advanced degree in the subject. Special subject units of large public libraries and universities are also employers of special librarians. Many professionals with special competencies work for vendors of products for the library community. Increasing numbers of professionals are working for themselves, as consultants and information brokers. The challenge for individual information professionals is to assess their personal skills and interests and then be open to opportunities that may present themselves from unexpected places.

In general, working conditions are quite good. The setting is often in a modern, well equipped office. The clientele is fairly predictable because it is common to admit people outside the organization by appointment only. The jobs within special librarianship can be stressful because of tight deadlines, understaffing, shifting organizational structures and objectives, and the need for long hours, among many other factors. Because so many organizations are now global in their activities, special librarians may find themselves working odd hours or shifts in order to provide services that "follow the sun."

One unique career option is that of "solo" librarian. In such a situation, the information professional works alone, possibly with occasional clerical assistance. Time management is a key concern to solo librarians since they are expected to do most of the jobs and provide most of the types of services of libraries with larger staffs.

According to the SLA 2008 salary survey, salaries for the information professionals who are association members outpaced inflation rates in the United States, Canada, and the United Kingdom. In Canada, the median percent change from the 2007 survey was 5.4%. In the United States it was 5.3%. In the United Kingdom, the change was 4.2%. In the United States, median salaries in the Middle Atlantic region, coming in at $79,125 (New York, New Jersey, Pennsylvania) and the Pacific region (California, Oregon, Washington) averaged 30% above those in the East South Central region, including Kentucky, Tennessee, Mississippi, and Alabama.[4]

Public Image

Librarians of all types find themselves fighting traditional stereotypes. Special librarianship is no exception. When a very visible source makes observations that combat those stereotypes, it is noteworthy.

In a December 2007 posting on the U.S. News and World Report Web site, librarianship, and special librarianship in particular, was listed in a positive light.

> Forget about that image of librarian as a mousy bookworm. Librarians these days must be high-tech information sleuths, helping researchers plumb the oceans of information available in books and digital records. It's an underrated career. Most librarians love helping patrons dig up information and, in the process, learning new things. Librarians may also go on shopping sprees, deciding which books and online resources to buy....

In the same article, "Special Librarian" is declared to be a "smart specialty." It explains,

> All sorts of organizations need librarians, not just universities and local governments. They work for law firms, prisons, corporations, and nonprofit agencies. In fact, special librarianship is the field's fastest-growing job market....[5]

Linking to a series of "Career Chemistry" articles provided on the U.S. News Web site during 2007, librarians are listed in the "Best Jobs for Investigative People" article, along with science researcher/professor, software engineer/developer, computer systems analyst/architect, and three jobs in the health sciences field.

Data organization, security, and archive management skills are in demand. The Topic of the Month in the December 2007 issue of Dialog's Quantum2 Highlights electronic newsletter for special librarianship, is "Managing Information." Expertise in three areas is recommended for those who want to increase their value in the workforce: taxonomies, records management, and information architecture. To achieve these skills, consider additional

education or collaborations with colleagues with skills complementary to yours, the Dialog consultants advise. This entry is part of a series on the concept of FUMSI (Find, Use, Manage and Share Information) (http://www.fumsi.com), a term that defines the purpose and philosophy of the work of special librarianship.[6]

ESSENTIAL ISSUES

Return on Investment

Always in the forefront of special librarianship is the term Return on Investment (ROI). The concept provides a framework for establishing a value for the work, services, and expertise of information professionals. It examines the resources (money, time, personnel, etc.) committed to providing information services compared with the value of the ultimate outcomes achieved by users of the information, using support from those information services.

Technology

All branches of librarianship wage a constant battle to keep abreast of changes in technology. New electronic information resources are introduced with great frequency. It is essential to be aware of what is being offered and to evaluate whether they are essential (have-to-have) products or whether they are optional (nice-to-have), decisions often based on the impact of high prices and constrained budgets. Special librarians also must make decisions about whether to acquire electronic products or paper products, when both are available.

The skill of negotiating the terms and prices for acquiring technology-based products can be difficult to master and add a complex dimension to the competencies of special librarianship.

Another technology-supported change in the delivery of information involves the elements of Web 2.0 and the social networks. Special librarianship is faced with decisions about whether RSS feeds, wikis, You Tube, and even more recent social networks are useful tools for communicating with potential customers.

As with all technology-related issues, user expectations, needs, and demands play a large role in decisions made and priorities determined. Providing excellent customer service is a hallmark of special librarianship.

End User Training

For many years, special librarians believed that if they taught their clients how to do database searches, for example, or even taught them to understand the nature of databases, it would be a threat to the existence of special librarianship. Herb White, the provocateur of the library profession, voiced that concern as late as 2006 when he said "Today, however, we seem determined to teach our clients everything we know, and I find that suicidal. Shouldn't we instead be teaching them what they shouldn't try to do on their own? Shouldn't we let them know where their brimming self-confidence...is misplaced?"[7]

Many people will agree with White's interpretation of the end user training dilemma. However, the paranoia of information professionals has waned after they discovered that by teaching their clients how to do the every-day, repetitive tasks, they were freed to do the more interesting, challenging, detailed research that showcases their unique talents and training. One information professional in the offices of a major technology company would tell her clients that when doing their own searches for information, if they had not found what they were looking for or if they were not comfortable with the validity of what they discovered, within 15 min., they were required to come to her. She said in all the times she used that rule, not a single person asked what was magical about 15 min. and no one asked who made the rule. She suspects they were relieved to comply without asking questions.

Teaching information literacy skills—the ability to find, evaluate, and effectively use information—to end users remains a key activity of special librarianship.

Knowledge Management

The concept of Knowledge Management (KM) began to be recognized late in the 1980s. It blossomed in response to the period when organizations were severely downsizing their middle management ranks, only to discover that much of the intellectual capital represented by those managers walked out the door with them. KM originated as an attempt to encourage everyone in an organization to share their knowledge/intellectual capital and the results of their projects. KM is the term for the conscious gathering, organizing, sharing, and analyzing of resources, documents, and people skills. Internal information is paired with external sources in an attempt to avoid duplication of effort on future projects, among other things, making knowledge a strategic asset. These segments of knowledge are referred to as "explicit" (recorded) and "tacit" (personal know-how and experience) and information sharing is key to the success of a KM program. The increasing sophistication of information technology made such programs possible. KM has become ubiquitous yet challenging to define uniformly from one organization to another. Many people maintain the concept has been at the core of special librarianship for a long time.

The Boeing Company defines KM as "a discipline that promotes finding, selecting, organizing, distilling and presenting information in a way that improves an employee's comprehension in a specific area of interest."[8] A Google search on the term KM results in a substantial list of definitions of the term culled from a wide variety of Web sites.

Competitive Intelligence

Competitive Intelligence (CI), as the term suggests, involves efforts to stay informed about the activities and innovations of competitor organizations. "Many corporate info pros find that Competitive Intelligence (CI) is a way to broaden their skills, raise their visibility, and more directly contribute to their firms' operations and direction."[9]

> Briefly defined, a complete CI program requires the ability to identify the needs of its key users (i.e., decision-makers) and define their key intelligence topics (KITs) and key intelligence questions (KIQs); plan and direct any CI projects or initiatives; conduct research using published sources (literature searches); conduct research using human sources (interviews and other primary material); analyze and package the results of the research using a range of models and tools; and share the findings of any research, analysis, and recommendations.[9]

According to a study conducted by the Competitive Intelligence Foundation, done in cooperation with its parent organization, the Society of Competitive Intelligence Professionals (SCIP), CI is increasing in visibility, as a standalone unit, although it still may be a small function with a limited budget. In many organizations, CI is the responsibility of nearly all personnel. The majority of respondents say they spend a significant portion of their time in analysis and secondary data collection. Company profiles, competitive benchmarking, and market or industry audits are the most frequent products of their work.[10]

Other Key Topics

Many additional terms and issues come into play in specific settings of special librarianship. Copyright in a digital age, globalization, outsourcing/offshoring, project management, and digitization are among them. Bioinformatics, an extension of the traditional roles of health information professionals, includes specializations required in hospitals and pharmaceutical and biotechnology industries, among other research and development environments.[11]

Anticipating and managing change presents a major challenge in special librarianship. Professionals strive to continue understanding the needs and goals of their organizations, revise their services and information resources to meet those needs and goals, and maintain their personal training and competencies to keep themselves up to the task of providing value and excellence.

CHARACTERISTICS

"Flexible" is among the most frequently used terms to describe special librarianship. In one job announcement for a researcher and information specialist, flexibility was called for because the job required working odd hours, including nights, overnights, and weekends. The job also required people who can handle multiple and varied research assignments and can work on tight deadlines in a fast-paced environment. Other terms used to describe top notch special librarians are proactive, tenacious, communicators, consultants, team players, accountable, trustworthy, entrepreneurial, and ethical. A special librarian is expected to be committed to continuous professional development, have excellent research skills, and then be able to evaluate and analyze the information retrieved and determine its relevance to a specific project or need. A customer focus goes without saying in an environment where satisfying the needs of the customer (or client, or patron—there is not universal satisfaction with a term that describes the users of an information service) is the primary reason for being.

By Any Name...

Groups of special librarians, particularly in North America, have grappled for years over the job title that will best suit the promotion of the information professionals and their value to an organization. One group is passionate about maintaining the term "librarian" because of its traditional identification with the reasons why some people joined the profession. The defenders of remaining with the tried and true term "librarian" believe that it is the actions, philosophies, qualities, and competencies possessed for information professionals that define practitioners and give special librarianship value, not the job titles by which they are called. Others believe that better salaries and greater opportunity for promotions and acceptance into the strategic work of the parent organization will result when librarians begin moving away from the traditional term that holds negative connotations and images in some environments. The debate seems not to be as strong and frequent outside North America, where "librarian" is a generally accepted term.

Several people have tried to document the specific job titles within specialized librarianship, but usually abandon the task when the numbers reach into the hundreds.

In a 1993 article in *Special Libraries* magazine, "What Will They Call Us in the Future?" Marydee Ojala, one of the original and most visible information consultants in the profession, reviews the opinions of several leaders in the field as they suggest possible job titles. Although the article is dated, the titles remain viable.[12] Among the more common titles found in Ojala's article, as well as some from more recent conversations, are:

Chief Information Officer
Director of Knowledge Management
InfoPro
Information Officer
Information Manager
Information Professional

Information Scientist
Knowledge Counselor
Knowledge Manager
Librarian

Some of the more unusual titles include:

Corporate Intelligence Professional
Cybrarian
Info Diva
Information Architect
Information Control Officer
Information Czar
Information Detective
Information Engineer
Information Oracle
Information Wizard
Informationist
Knowledge Coach
Knowledge Facilitator
Knowledge Services Specialist
Knowledge Thought Leader

The titles chosen by individual professionals are often a factor of the culture in which they work. In many settings, it is most appropriate to use the traditional term of "librarian" and then work diligently to create a new perception of what that job title means. In other settings, a more creative or descriptive title is appropriate.

ORGANIZATIONS

The successful practice of special librarianship relies heavily on networking, resource sharing, and lifelong learning. Professional organizations provide their members with opportunities for networking, resource sharing, leadership training, continuous professional development, impact on legislation and information policies, and other important issues. The organizations range from relatively small and specialized groups, such as the Theatre Library Association, Art Libraries Society of North America, and the Major Orchestra Librarians Association, to larger groups such as the SLA, with membership from around the globe. In all cases, these organizations provide information on their activities in a variety of ways, via Web sites (see a sampling of association Web sites at the end of this entry), blogs, newsletters, magazines, and special reports. In addition, most of them host annual conferences, conduct research, provide continuing education opportunities, and present awards and scholarships, among other activities.

Medical Library Association

The oldest of the specialized associations is the Medical Library Association (MLA), founded in 1898 by a group of four librarians and four doctors. It represents approximately 1200 institutions and 4000 health information professionals who operate in 23 subsections of the association. The sections focus on libraries in specialized fields such as cancer, chiropractic, consumer and patient health, dental, hospitals, pharmacy, and veterinary medicine. Regional Chapters increase the reach of the network. The Academy of Health Information Professionals (AHIP) is a unique credentialing program that provides the MLA members with professional development opportunities for which they achieve levels of recognition. Back issues of the *Journal of the Medical Library Association* (JMLA) are available on PubMed Central of the National Library of Medicine from 2002 to 2007. A new initiative, "Librarians without Borders," was formed in 2005

> to provide training in the field of information retrieval and library information assistance to people anywhere in the world, namely training on how to effectively conduct research using a library. The initiative also helps provide medical information for health care personnel responding to epidemics and natural and man-made disasters anywhere in the world.[13]

American Association of Law Libraries

The American Association of Law Libraries (AALL) was founded in 1906. Its purpose is to enhance the value of law libraries, foster the profession of law librarianship, and provide leadership in the field of legal information.[14] Members, numbering over 5000, are affiliated with law firms, law schools, corporate legal departments, courts, and government agencies. Thirteen Special Interest Sections provide opportunities for small groups to focus on areas of law librarianship such as academic law libraries, foreign and international law, legal history, private law libraries, and research instruction and patron services. Strong regional groups also are a membership benefit. Included in the AALL's long list of publications is *AALL Spectrum*, the monthly magazine of the association. Full issues are available on the association Web site, http://www.aallnet.org. The association conducts a biennial salary survey and publishes several reference works specific to the needs of law librarians. The "Competencies of Law Librarianship" are discussed elsewhere in this entry.[14]

SLA

The largest of the specialized associations is the SLA. Founded in 1909, during the annual meeting of the American Library Association at Bretton Woods, NH, the SLA now includes more than 10,000 members in 60 countries around the world. Among the 58 regional chapters, and attesting to the globalization of the association, are the Asian Chapter, Australia/New Zealand Chapter, the European Chapter, and the Sub-Saharan Africa Chapter. As is the case with its close counterparts, the SLA holds an annual conference, provides continuing education through an online initiative called Click University, gives several awards and scholarships, is active in monitoring Federal information policy developments, and issues publications in print and electronically. The SLA's official journal, *Information Outlook*, is available in print and online, through the association's Web site. Scanning back issues is an excellent way to determine the developments that define special librarianship of the twenty-first century. A salary survey and a document outlining the competencies expected of information professionals in the twenty-first century are among the special research reports published by the SLA. The latter product will be discussed later in this entry.[15]

Association of Independent Information Professionals

Alternative careers have become common for people in the special librarianship field. The Association of Independent Information Professionals (AIIP), founded in 1987, is an important association home for information brokers and independent researchers. Members may hold degrees in library science or may have advanced degrees in science, law, business, medicine, or other disciplines. AIIP arranges group discounts to information products, holds conferences and workshops and markets the concept of independent information professionals to potential clients. It also provides a strict code of ethical business practice. The ethics code includes statements on honesty, competence, and providing clients current and accurate information. Respecting client confidentiality and recognizing intellectual property rights are also major points in the code.[16]

Society of Competitive Intelligence Professionals

High ethical standards are a hallmark of the SCIP. The Society's Code of Ethics includes statements on avoiding conflicts of interest, accurately disclosing all relevant information when conducting a project, complying with all applicable laws, and providing honest and realistic recommendations and conclusions to clients.[17] The SCIP organization includes 20 regional chapters. Professional development needs of members is a primary focus and the annual conference is one venue for this activity. Established in 1986, the SCIP has approximately 3000 members representing practitioners, consultants, service providers, information specialists, and academic and government institutions. The Competitive Intelligence Foundation, a SCIP affiliate, conducts research on emerging issues and the *Journal of Competitive Intelligence and Management* represents the interests of the membership.[18]

Global Networks

Among the significant professional associations outside North America that include special librarians are the Australian Library and Information Association and the Chartered Institute of Library and Information Professionals, formed after a 2002 merger of two British associations, the Library Association and the Institute of Information Scientists. Both associations include specialized groups for various types of libraries and activities.

COMPETENCIES

Moving beyond informal lists of characteristics of special librarians and the job titles under which they work, several of the professional associations have created lists of competencies that identify superior information professionals. The documents may refer to "librarians," "information professionals," or "special librarians," among other titles, but they all apply to the trained information specialists that form the membership of each association. The competencies documents contain many common elements, in addition to specific competencies unique to the special group.

AALL

The AALL has a statement on the Web site, under Professional Education, a document approved in 2001. "Competencies are the knowledge, skills, abilities, and personal characteristics that help distinguish superior performance. These competencies may be acquired through higher education such as library and information science programs, through continuing education, and through experience."[14]

The AALL document is divided into two sections, the Core Competencies and the Specialized Competencies. According to the document, the Core Competencies "apply to all law librarians and will be acquired early in one's career." Among them are a commitment to excellent client service, recognition of the diversity of the client community, support for the culture and context of the parent institution, and knowledge of the legal system and legal profession. Twelve additional statements cover ethical behavior, leadership skills and creative thinking, risk taking, commitment to working with others to achieve common goals, excellent communication skills, and the pursuit of continuing education.

Under Specialized Competencies, there are five subsections, dealing with library management; reference, research, and client services; information technology; collection care and management; and teaching. The document sets forth some stringent expectations for the information professional who wants to be respected and valued by both clients and professional colleagues.

SLA

The SLA's "Competencies for Information Professionals of the 21st Century" was revised in 2003, building on the original version developed in 1997. It begins by defining an information professional:

> An information professional (IP) strategically uses information in his/her job to advance the mission of the organization. The IP accomplishes this through the development, deployment, and management of information resources and services. The IP harnesses technology as a critical tool to accomplish goals. IPs include, but are not limited to, librarians, knowledge managers, chief information officers, web developers, information brokers, and consultants.[15]

There is a strong emphasis on evidence-based practice in the competencies listed. Evidence-based practice is defined as "consciously and consistently making professional-level decisions that are based on the strongest evidence from research and best practice about what would work best for our clients."

The SLA competencies document is divided into sections on Professional Competencies, Personal Competencies, and Core Competencies.

The Core Competencies are essential for everyone. There are just two points in this section. "Information professionals contribute to the knowledge base of the profession by sharing best practices and experiences, and continue to learn about information products, services, and management practices throughout the life of his/her career." The second point states, "Information professionals commit to professional excellence and ethics, and to the values and principles of the profession." These two points anchor all other competencies included in the document.

Under the heading of "Professional Competencies" there are sections on managing information organizations, information resources, and information services, all while applying information tools and technologies.

Personal Competencies

> represent a set of attitudes, skills, and values that enable practitioners to work effectively and contribute positively to their organizations, clients and profession. These competencies range from being strong communicators, to demonstrating the value-add of their contributions, to remaining flexible and positive in an ever-changing environment.

The concepts of communication skills, proving value, being flexible, and managing change are among the characteristics most often mentioned as being essential to special librarianship.

MLA

In the "Platform for Change" developed by the MLA, there is a section on health information science knowledge and skills. "Health information professionals will posses varying levels of knowledge and skills in seven broad areas. No one individual can achieve mastery of all knowledge and every skill, but every organization will require collective expertise in all areas."[13] The seven areas are:

Health Sciences Environment and Information Policies
Management of Information Services in complex institutional environments
Health Science Information Services—understand information needs and analyze, evaluate, and synthesize information for those identified needs.
Health Science Resource Management—including identifying, collecting, evaluating, and organizing resources and using them effectively
Understand Information Systems and Technology
Instructional Support Systems—teaching ways to access, organize, and use information
Research, Analysis, and Interpretation

Even a quick review of the competencies set forth by three major associations at the core of special librarianship demonstrates the expectations for the people who chose to enter the profession. Society can be assured of the high level of professionalism and skill embodied in these professionals and should never consider asking, "Why do I need you?"

Employability

In her book, *Rethinking Information Work*, Kim Dority emphasizes the "lifetime employability" of information professionals by setting forth a list of actions professionals owe to themselves, to keep competitive and happily employed during their careers.

The concept of lifetime employability "involves continually developing new ways to contribute and grow professionally and seeking out opportunities to do so." Success "requires a sense of loyalty to your own professional goals. Although professional integrity mandates that we do our very best jobs for our employers and/or clients, we nevertheless must keep our own career goals moving forward at the same time."[19]

Among the career competencies on Dority's list are an understanding of who you are and who you want to be. This understanding must include an acceptance of the possibility of low pay, lack of respect, and lack of potential for growth; a focus on solutions; an understanding and acceptance of change without fear; adapting skills to the environment and understanding the environment; an ability to anticipate and willingness to look for opportunity; a willingness to take risks; and a commitment to continuous learning and reinventing of ourselves. All are essential qualities for satisfaction and success in professional careers.

EDUCATION

As information technology has become an increasing part of the job in special librarianship, it has raised confusing issues in library education. Should the master's level degree, which is the first rung on the professional ladder, concentrate on the core values and history of the profession, leaving the everyday needs of the job to be handled by on-the-job training, or should people graduate from Master of Library and Information Science (MLIS) programs fully able to function on their first day on the job? Employers would prefer the latter situation. However, given the limitations of the length of the curriculum and the expertise of the faculty in many graduate schools of library and information science, it is difficult to devise a curriculum that answers all needs and covers all bases. People graduate with the understanding that continuous professional education will be part of their future.

Because most graduate programs in the field require in the neighborhood of a year and a half to two years to complete the degree, it is obvious that not everything can be covered in that space of time. Should the curriculum include many of the traditional core courses of the profession, or should there be more availability of technology training and specialized topics? There is no universally accepted answer. In addition to such core courses as an introduction to the information professions, reference and cataloging (offered under several new titles to reflect the broader need to categorize information for quick and thorough retrieval), many schools offer focused courses on broad special librarianship as well as on the more specific areas of medical, law, art, and business librarianship. Multiple offerings teach information technology skills in tandem with more traditional content in some of the other courses in the curriculum.

The reality is, no matter how well prepared new employees may be, they will invariably face the need for additional training in order to move ahead in most environments. Constant updates on developments in technology and new products will be required. In law libraries, a law degree is often required or recommended for anyone who aspires to a management position. In the business and finance environment, an M.B.A. or similar advanced degree would be a plus. In many situations, competence in more than one language is a strong benefit, if not a requirement.

FUTURE PROSPECTS

Predicting the future of special librarianship is problematic. The only sure assumption is that change will continue at an accelerated pace and that professionals will be required to employ all of their skills of innovation and adaptability.

During the 2008 Leadership Summit sponsored by the SLA, delegates were divided into round table discussion groups with an assignment to envision the SLA as it should be in 2010. Leadership was highlighted as one key role for special librarianship moving into the immediate future. Participants thought that mentors and inspirational coaches should assist professionals in stepping out of the passive role in customer service, where the philosophy is to try and serve everyone. That service philosophy gives way to greater specialization in services aimed at specific user groups. Ongoing training in management, organizational politics, time management, relationship building, and communications, among other skills, will be essential. There will be a continuing need to educate users and potential users to the value special librarianship brings to an organization.The SLA will be instrumental in building partnerships and relationships based on trust and mutual respect, to the benefit of members.

Two management gurus to special librarianship have made strong statements about the unique contributions of information professionals. Herb White states emphatically that "We cannot have good libraries until we first have good librarians—properly educated, professionally recognized, and fairly rewarded."[20] Tom Davenport, in an article outlining the desirable characteristics represented by special librarianship, concludes,

> It is the professional librarian's expertise in managing information and working with users to identify, anticipate, and satisfy their information needs that transforms a passive collection into an information system used to support business decisions. A special library cannot exist without a librarian, and is only as good as the information professional managing it and the level of support and commitment from the parent organization.[21]

Because special librarians work in a broad range of institutions and organizations, they are subject to the same environmental and economic challenges as are their host organizations. For that reason, attempting to predict the future with any accuracy is problematic. What can be said with certainty is that current trends will accelerate, change will be continuous, and there will be new challenges around every corner.

Change Is a Given

"Is change an opportunity for librarians or is it a threat?" asks Pat McCauley in "From Librarian to Cybrarian: Coping with Accelerating Change in Libraries.... Will librarians assume a proactive role and act as change agents to bridge the gap between technology and the end user?" This is a common debate encountered by librarians. Will they step up and be proactive? McCauley, echoing many other writers, says librarians have to "strive to lead or we can decide to follow. None of us can choose to remain unchanged."[22]

It is encouraging to observe, working with new recruits to the profession, that they include a strong cadre of young leaders in special librarianship. The challenge will be for

them and those who have preceded them in the profession, to work together and build on the strengths of each other, in order to ensure that excellent customer service continues to be at the forefront of the philosophy of special librarianship and that, through that excellent service, there will be constant reinforcement of the concept that special librarians are essential members of the team that moves an organization forward to meet its goals and to anticipate the new challenges that lie ahead.

Dority, in the text cited earlier, looks at some terms that define the self-image of special librarians: energy, innovation, thought leadership, impact, engagement, passion, excitement, self-confidence, participation, entrepreneurial, collaboration, improvization, dynamic action, joy, contribution, laughter, politically astute, change agent, connected, adventurous, smart, resilient. The list provides a challenge to live up to, and an inspiring promise for the future of the profession.

> Each of these characteristics will be necessary for LIS practitioners in the coming years as the profession continues to be driven by new circumstances we can guess at now, as well as those we can't even imagine. We know the roles of...librarians will shift in response to demographic changes, technology advances, and funding issues, but what other disruptive changes are hiding in the wings? We know that fewer and fewer businesses are establishing and/or maintaining "traditional" corporate libraries, but what about the large number of information-based roles that are opening up in their stead?[19]

Eugenie Prime, for years the iconic head of libraries at Hewlett Packard, spoke at the 1998 Annual Conference of the SLA, a presentation frequently referenced because of the impact it had on the audience. Known for her direct approach, she outlined why she thought librarians don't reach their potential:

> The fault lies not in the inadequacy of our budgets, not in the myopia of upper management...not in sexism or gender symbolism, not in corporate restructuring/rightsizing/downsizing or any other sizing...but in ourselves....If we lack a fundamental certainty of who we are and what we are capable of doing...that uncertainty will leave us incapable of handling the complex changes of this Information Age.[23]

That analysis is just as valid, just as compelling in 2009 as it was a decade earlier. It gets at the core of expectations for special librarianship going into the future. It offers special librarians the platform and philosophy required to move into a successful future.

REFERENCES

1. Mount, E.; Massoud, R. *Special Libraries and Information Centers: An Introductory Text*, 4th Ed.; Special Libraries Association: Washington, DC, 1999; 10–11.

2. Bates, M.E. Convincing your boss that it's not all free on the web, Factiva webinar series, November 9, 2004, http://www.factiva.com/webinar/learning (includes audio and PowerPoint).

3. Special Libraries Association. Professional Development, Competencies, http://www.sla.org.

4. Latham, J.R. SLA's new salary survey includes CI compensation. Inform. Outlook **2008**, *12*(12).

5. Nemko, M. Librarian: Executive summary, U.S. News and World Report, http://www.usnews.com/articles/business/best-careers/2007/12/19/librarian (posted December 19, 2007).

6. Managing Information. Dialog's Quantum2 Highlights electronic newsletter, http://scientific.thomson.com/quantum/newsletter, December 2007.

7. White, H.S. Ruminations after retirement. Libr. J. **2006**, *131* (5), 53.

8. McCollum, D. Mark Twain and knowledge management. Inform. Outlook **2006**, *10* (9), 15–24.

9. Correig, C.C. Getting competitive: Competitive intelligence is a smart next step for information pros. Libr. J. **2006**, *131* (7), 52–53.

10. Fehringer, D.; Hohhof, B.; Johnson, T., Eds. *State of the Art: Competitive Intelligence*; Competitive Intelligence Foundation and Society of Competitive Intelligence Professionals: Alexandria, VA, 2007; Executive Summary athttp://www.scip.org/cifoundation.

11. Helms, A.J. Bioinformatics opportunities for health sciences librarians and professionals. J. Med Libr. Assoc. **2004**, *92* (4), 489–493.

12. Ojala, M. What will they call us in the future? Spec. Libr. **1993**, *84* (4), 226–229.

13. Medical Library Association, http://www.mlanet.org.

14. American Association of Law Libraries, http://www.aallnet.org.

15. Special Libraries Association, http://www.sla.org.

16. Association of Independent Information Professionals, http://www.aiip.org.

17. SCIP, http://www.scip.org.

18. Society of Competitive Intelligence Professionals, http://www.scip.org.

19. Dority, G.K. *Rethinking Information Work: A Career Guide for Librarians and Other Information Professionals*; Libraries Unlimited: Westport, CT, 2006.

20. White, H.S. Where is this profession heading? Libr. J. **1999**, *124* (19), 44–5.

21. Davenport, T. Functions worth following. Inform. Week **1995**, *527*, 158.

22. McCauley, P. From librarian to cybrarian: Coping with accelerating change in libraries. Ohio Media Spectrum **2000**, *51* (4), 31–6.

23. St. Lifer, E. Prime leadership. Libr. J. *123* (15), 36–38.

BIBLIOGRAPHY

Association Web Sites

1. American Association of Law Libraries, http://www.aallnet.org.

2. Association of Independent Information Professionals, http://www.aiip.org.

3. Australian Library and Information Association, http://www.alia.org.au.

4. Chartered Institute of Library and Information Professionals, http://www.cilip.org.uk.

5. The Major Orchestra Librarians Association, http://www.mola-inc.org.

6. Medical Library Association, http://www.mlanet.org.

7. Society of Competitive Intelligence Professionals, http://www.scip.org.

8. Special Libraries Association, http://www.sla.org.

9. Theatre Library Association, http://tla.library.unt.edu.

Book and Journal Sources

1. Bates, M.E. Convincing your boss that it's not all free on the web. Factiva webinar series2004November 9http://www.factiva.com/webinar/learning (includes audio and PowerPoint).

2. Correig, C.C. Getting competitive: Competitive intelligence is a smart next step for information pros. Libr. J. **2006**, *131* (7), 52–53.

3. Davenport, T. Functions worth following. Inform. Week **1995**, *527*, 158.

4. Dority, G.K. *Rethinking Information Work: A Career Guide for Librarians and Other Information Professionals*; Libraries Unlimited: Westport, CT, 2006.

5. Fehringer, D.; Hohhof, B.; Johnson, T., Eds. *State of the Art: Competitive Intelligence*; Competitive Intelligence Foundation and Society of Competitive Intelligence Professionals: Alexandria, VA, 2007; Executive summary at http://www.scip.org/cifoundation.

6. Helms, A.J. Bioinformatics opportunities for health sciences librarians and professionals. J. Med. Libr. Assoc. **2004**, *92* (4), 489–493.

7. Latham, J.R. An SLA salary survey first: European countries included. Inform. Outlook **2007**, *11*(11).

8. Managing Information. Dialog's Quantum2 Highlights electronic newsletter, December 2007, free subscription, http://scientific.thomson.com/quantum/newsletter.

9. McCauley, P. From librarian to cybrarian: Coping with accelerating change in libraries. Ohio Media Spectrum **2000**, *51* (4), 31–36.

10. McCollum, D. Mark Twain and knowledge management. Inform. Outlook **2006**, *10* (9), 15–24.

11. McGinnis, M. Bold, brazen, and bodacious. Inform. Outlook **2003**, (7), 6.

12. Mount, E.; Massoud, R. *Special Libraries and Information Centers: An Introductory Text*, 4th Ed.; Special Libraries Association: Washington, DC, 1999.

13. Nemko, M. Librarian: Executive summary, U.S. News and World Report, http://www.usnews.com/articles/business/best-careers/2007/12/19/librarian (posted December 19, 2007).

14. Ojala, M. What will they call us in the future? Spec. Libr. Fall **1993**; 226–229.

15. St. Lifer, E. Prime leadership. Libr. J. **1998**, *123* (15), 36–38.

16. White, H.S. Ruminations after retirement. Libr. J. **2006**, *131* (5), 53.

17. White, H.S. Where is this profession heading? Libr. J. **1999**, *124* (19), 44–45.

Index

A

AALL, *see* American Association of Law Libraries
AAM, *see* American Association of Museums
Aarhus Art museum, 1226
Aarhus State and University Library, 1216–1217, 1219
AASL, *see* American Association of School Librarians
AASL Hotlinks, 61
Abandoned Shipwreck Act of 1987, 1775
The Aboriginal and Torres Strait Islander Library and Information Resource Network (ATSILIRN) Protocols, 2041
Abridged WebDewey, 1259–1260
Absorption, distribution, metabolism, excretion, and toxicity (ADMET) testing, 837
Abstracts, 418–419
Academic art libraries, 251
Academic dishonesty
    definition, 3665
    faculty attitudes, 3668–3669
    individual differences, 3668–3669
    social factors, 3668
Academic e-mail messages, 2507
Academic law reviews, 2740
Academic Librarians Status Committee, 342
Academic libraries, 97, 2764, 3471–3472
    acquisitions units, organization of, 2918–2919
    administration, 9
    in Arab sector, 2548
    Armenia, 230–231
    in Australia, 384–385
    buildings, 10–11
    in China
        Peking University Library, 896
        Tsinghua University Library, 896–898
    in Croatia, 1125
    database integrators, 3472
    digital humanities (*see* Digital humanities)
    Ethiopia, 1498–1499
    external influence, 2–3
    in France, 1602–1603
    fund-raising and development
        access to donors, 2835
        annual fund, 2836–2837
        capital campaigns, 2838
        centralized *vs.* decentralized development, 2834–2835
        development activities, 2833–2834
        friends of libraries, 2836
        institutional barriers, 2834–2835
        institutionalization, 2839
        library director, role of, 2835
        literature, history of, 2832–2833
        major gifts, 2837
        planned giving, 2837–2838
        theoretical and philosophical foundations, 2839
        U.S. phenomenon, 2832
        Web communications, 2838–2839

games and gaming, 1639–1640
in Germany, 1695–1696
governance and hierarchy, 3–4
Greece, 1731–1732
history, 1–2
Hungary, 1922
in Israel, 2544–2545
Japan, 2562–2564
in Kazakhstan, 2582–2583
Kenya, 2596
Latinos, 2701–2702
library anxiety, 2785
Lithuania, 2951–2953
Mexican libraries, 3083–3086
mission, 1
in Moldova, 3125
music libraries, 3275
New Zealand libraries, 3375–3376
organizational structure, 4–5
personnel, 10
in Peru, 3608
professional associations, 3
resources and services
    expertise, 5–6
    public service, 7–8
    reference desk, 6–7
    technical services, 8–9
in Saudi Arabia, 3974
science and engineering librarians, 4009
Senegal, 4106
in Serbia, 4129–4131
Slovakia, 4177–4178
South Korea, 4310–4311
strategic planning (*see* Strategic planning, academic libraries)
Tunisia, 4628–4629
in Ukraine, 4642
in United Kingdom, 4703–4705
user privileges, 5
Venezuelan libraries, 4889–4890
Academic Library Advancement and Development Network (ALADN), 2834
Academic publications, 2826
Academic writing, 4548–4549
Academy of Beaux-Arts, 1594
Academy of Health Information Professionals (AHIP), 3035, 4356
Access control, *see* Authorization
Accessed information, 4236
Accessibility
    adaptive hardware and software, adults
        audiobooks and Playaways, 16
        audio description, 16
        Benetech, 16
        closed-circuit television, 15
        mouse challenges, 15
        outreach efforts, 16
        public meetings, signing for, 15–16
        screen reading software, 15
        talking books, 16
        TDDS and TTYS, 16

typing and voice recognition software, 15
virtual reference, 17
web conferencing platform, 17
Web sites, 16–17
audio/recorded books, 15
books by mail service, 14
Braille books, 15
building accommodations, 14
deposit collections, 14
homebound book delivery, 14
large print books, 14–15
services, 14
symbols, 4961, 4963
Access management, *see* Authorization
Access services, 173, 373, 895, 1910, 2912, 3472, 4735
Access to Knowledge (A2K) movement, 3386
Access-to-Own model, 1211
Accountability, 2055
Accounting in England and Scotland: 1543 to 1800, 645
Accreditation
    ALA, LIS programs
        Accreditation Process, Policies, and Procedures, 18, 20
        ALISE, 19–20
        ASPA Code of Good Practice, 18–19
        BEL, 19
        COA, 18–20
        Committee on Library Training, 19
        future prospects, 20–21
        Land Grant College Act, 19
        of postsecondary education, 19
        purpose of, 18
        standards, 18, 20
    of Canadian institutions, 19, 21
    fundamental assumptions of, 18
Accreditation Board for Engineering and Technology (ABET), 1434
Accredited Standards Committee (ASC), 413
Achenwall, Gottfried, 495
ACLU v. Reno, 2396
ACM, *see* Association for Computing Machinery
Acquisitions
    in academic libraries, 2918–2919
    approval plan vendors, 2919
    automated and integrated library systems, 2919
    bibliographic networks, development of, 2921
    definition, 2918
    EDI, 2919
    in public libraries, 2919
    purchasing decisions, 2918
    shared cataloging, 2921
    in small libraries, 2919
    in special libraries, 2918
Acquisitions Institute at Timberline Lodge
    collection development, 22
    facility, 2
    history and evolution, 22–23

Collaborative IR (CIR), 4880
Collaborative recommender systems
elicit preferences, 3861
predictions, 3862
recommendations, 3862
schematic representation, 3861
Collaborative Web browsing, 3443
Collabra, 1062
Collection development, 2333–2335
Collection Development and Evaluation Section
(CODES), 3909
*Collection Development Policies: for Libraries
& Visual Collections in the Arts*, 252
Collection maintenance, *see* Stack management
Collection Management Section (CMS), 329
*Collection of Letters for the Improvement of
Husbandry and Trade*, 1401
*Collection of Tracts, on the Subjects of Taxing
the British Colonies in America, and
Regulating their Trade*, 1402
Collections Australia Network (CAN), 3178
Collection-specific local vocabularies,
1078–1079
College archives, Hungary, 1925–1926
College Art Association (CAA), 255,
4933–4934
College Level Examination Program (CLEP),
1847
College library
in Australia, 384
bibliographic instruction/information literacy,
987–988
challenges, 983, 985
collection development, 985–986
history of, 983
information technology, development of,
983–985
interlibrary loan, 986–987
management, structure, and staff changes, 990
rare book collections, 3822
resources for, 354–355
standards, 988–990
in United Kingdom, 4705
College Library Directors Mentor Program, 990
College & Research Libraries (C&RL), 353
Collexis, 1768
Colon Classification (CC), 961, 967, 1534, 1536,
2669, 4466, 4475
Colonial Williamsburg, 3218, 4166–4167
Colon scheme, 574
Colorado Alliance of Research Libraries, 1209,
1212
Color formats, 1177
Color histogram, 4422–4423
Color illustration, 1945
Color management, 4943
Columbia River Basin Ethnic History Archive
(CRBEHA), 1783–1784
Comanaged libraries, 4160
COM cats, 2078–2079
COMEXAZ, 2699
Commemorative landscape, 4165
Commemorative site monuments, 4164–4165
Commercial and Financial Chronicle, 648, 1404
Commercial galleries, 243
Commercial journals, 2740
Commercial lending libraries, 4478

Commission for Accreditation of Law-Enforce-
ment Agencies (CALEA), 4258
Commission for Science and Technology
(COSTECH), 4508
Commission of Trade and Plantations, 646
Commission on Preservation and Access, 3725
Committee on Accreditation (COA), 18–20, 709
Committee on Archival Development (CAD),
2438
Committee on Best Practices and Standards
(ICA/CBPS), 2441
Committee on Copyright and Other Legal Mat-
ters (CLM), 2457–2458
Committee on Development and Intellectual
Property (CDIP), 5002
Committee on Freedom of Access to Informa-
tion and Freedom of Expression
(FAIFE), 2458
Committee on Institutional Cooperation (CIC),
1757, 1759
Committee on Museum Professional Training
(COMPT), 3219
Committee on Organization (COO), 76
Committee on Program Evaluation and Support
(COPES), 72–74
Committee on Reorganization, 339
Common Business-Oriented Language
(COBOL), 2272
Common Command Language (CML), 2345
Common communication format (CCF), 4627
Common Core State Standards (CCSS) Initia-
tive, 4002
Common Music Notation (CMN), 3267
Commonsense epistemology, 1456
Commonsense knowledge, 272
Commonwealth Archives Office, 119
Commonwealth Government archives, 185
Commonwealth Library Association (COMLA),
2597–2598
Commonwealth National Library, 381
Commonwealth Record Series (CRS), 3876
Commonwealth Scientific and Industrial
Research Organisation (CSIRO), 382
Communication channels, 2297
Communication engineering, 2051
Communication policy
administrative and judicial interpretation,
1008
competition, 1022–1023
competitive environment
cable, regulatory regime, 1016–1017
deregulate broadcasting, 1018–1019
hybrid technology, 1016
telecom regime, 1017–1018
cultural concerns
electronic media, 1013
radio, 1013
decision makers, 1008
goals
democracy, 1009
First Amendment, 1009–1010
intellectual property, 1010
policy mechanisms, 1008
postal roads, 1010
print technology, 1009
market, 1023–1024
market-oriented environment, 1007

national integration, mass media and
education
agricultural extension, 1011
land grant colleges and industrial education, 1011
mass media, 1010–1011
post-Civil War decision makers, 1010
public school movement, 1011
national security and defense
free speech and free market, 1015
limits on speech, 1015
networked information society, 1007
technological and socioeconomic developments, 1007
Telecommunications Act of 1996
Internet vision, 1019
legislative outcome, 1021–1022
103rd Congress, defeat in, 1020
104th Congress, retreat in, 1020
transportation, 1008
universal efficient interconnection via
regulation
defense technology, 1015
industrial economy, 1011
infrastructure, 1015
"must carry rules," 1014
public broadcasting, 1014
public service company, 1012
railroads and interstate commerce commission, 1012
spectrum licensing, 1014
telegraph, 1012
telephone, 1012–1013
voluntary censorship, 1013–1014
Communications, 144–145, 994–995,
2770–2771
and communication studies
contradictions, 1004–1005
IAMCR, profile of, 1001, 1004
ICA, profile of, 1001, 1003
institutionalization, phases of, 999–1001
mass and speech communication, 997–998
media, 998–999
NCA, profile of, 1001–1002
CSCW, 1055–1056
definitions of, 995–996
human communication, 2354
and mutual information, 2352–2354
organization, 4117–4118
PIALA, 3543
Communications Decency Act (CDA), 2396
Communicative memories, 1140
Communism, 4401
Communities of practice (COP), 1668, 2644,
2661–2662, 2754–2755, 3529, 4256
Community Access Program (CAP), 2039
Community archives, 4738
Community-based museums, 3237–3238
Community hospital library, 1872
Community informatics
community definitions, 1027–1028
emergence, 1031
Kling's definition, 1027
new directions, 1031
practitioners, 1027
researchers, 1027
roots of field

National Policy on Library and Information System (NAPLIS), 2001

National Program for Acquisitions and Cataloging (NPAC), 2965

National Programme for the Digitisation of Archival, Library and Museum Records, 1130

National Public Broadcasting Archives (NPBA), 1561, 1563

National-public libraries, 3321

National Register of Historic Places (NRHP), 1774

National Research and Education Network (NREN), 1551

National Research Council (NRC), 559, 660–661, 1673

National Sample Survey Organisation (NSSO), 1993

National Science Digital Library (NSDL), 2998, 3646, 4012, 4073

National Science Education Standards (NSES), 558

National Science Foundation (NSF), 555, 1029, 1392, 2217, 2517, 2772, 3646, 4263

National Science Foundation Act of 1950, 2217

National Scientific and Documentation Center (CNDST), 4106

National security, *see* Intelligence and Security Informatics

National Security Act of 1947, 2151

National Security Agency, 2151

National Security Archive (NSA), 2390

National Security Council (NSC), 2151–2152

National Security Laws, 785

National Serials Data Program (NDSP), 4139

National Society for the Study of Communication (NSSC), 2421

National Stolen Art File (NASF), 4577

National Stolen Property Act (NSPA) of 1934, 1153

National Storytelling Festival, Jonesborough, 4443

National Study of School Evaluation (NSSE), 64

National System of Public Libraries (NSPL), 4886

National System of Scientific, Technical and Organizational Information (SINTO), 3676

National Technical Information Center and Library, 1922

National Technical Information Service (NTIS), 1552, 1554

National Technical Institute for the Deaf (NTID), 1183

National Telecommunications and Information Administration (NTIA), 1279–1281, 2038

National Television and Video Preservation Foundation (NTVPF), 1579

National Terrorism Advisory Board, 4579

National Training Center and Clearinghouse (NTCC), 3035

National Training Information Service (NTIS), 687

National Trust, 4169, 4722–4723

National Union Catalog (NUC), 448, 769, 771

National War Museum of Scotland, 4719

National Zoological Park, 4194

Nation's Business, 650

Native American Graves Protection and Repatriation Act (NAGPRA) of 1990, 267, 1153, 1165–1166, 1169, 3167, 3245

Natural History, 644

Natural history museum, 1820, 3237, 4134
  Denmark, 1226
  Germany, 1704–1705
  Hungary, 1929
  India, 2021–2022
  London, 3224
  Madrid, 3152
  Tanzania, 4510
  United States, 5080

Natural language generation (NLG)
  applications, 430–431
  biography text, 432
  components, 431–432
  computational linguistics, 430
  current developments and outlook, 437–438
  dialogue situations, 431
  formal and computational properties, 430
  functional linguistics, 430
  linguistic variation
    aggregation, 435
    characterizations, 433
    discourse deixis, 435
    ideational representations, 434
    interpersonal control, 434–42
    lexicogrammar, 434–435
    linguistic abstraction, 434
    Penman text generation system, 434
    propositional content, 434
    semantic control, 434
    semantics, 434
    Sentence Plan Language, 434
    sentences, 435
    stratification, 433
    syntactic theory, 434
    textual control, 434–435
  macroplanning, 432
  message/text personalization, 433
  nonlinguistic material, 430
  non-NLG-based text production system, 433
  syntactic description, 430
  text planning, 436–437

Natural language processing (NLP), 274–275, 2201
  ANN
    advantages, 279–280
    cognitive models, 282
    connectionist/subsymbolic paradigm, 281
    disadvantages, 280
    formalisms, 281
    language-oriented disciplines, 281
    local and distributed representational schemes, 283
    meaning representation, 287
    physical symbol system, 281
    research paradigms, 283
    Rumelhart and McClelland model, 287–288
    sequential processing, 284–287
    symbolic paradigm, 281

applications, 3353

approaches
  connectionist approach, 3351
  hybrid approach, 3350
  similarities and differences, 3351–3353
  statistical approach, 3351
  symbolic approach, 3350–3351

definition, 3346

divisions, 3347

goal, 3346–3347

history, 3347–3348

human-like language processing, 3346

introspection, 3348

levels
  discourse, 3350
  lexical, 3349
  lower *vs.* higher levels, 3350
  morphology, 3349
  phonological analysis, 3349
  pragmatic, 3350
  semantic, 3350
  syntactic, 3349

origins, 3347

synchronic *vs.* sequential model, 3348

Natural Resource Monitoring Partnership (NRMP), 3312

Natural SEM, *see* Search engine marketing

Nauta, Doede, 2051–2052

Navigability affordance, 1118

Nazi memorabilia, 783

NBII, *see* National Biological Information Infrastructure

Nebraska Library Association, 920

Negative feedback, 1036

Neighboring rights, 1268

NELINET, 3922, 3924

NELLI, 2825

NEMO, *see* Network of European Museum Organisations

Neoclassicism, 1742

Neo-Schumpeterian approach, 2254

NESLI2, 2825

netLibrary e-books, 1209–1211

Netscape Collabra™, 1057

Networked European Deposit Library (NEDLIB), 1333

Networked Knowledge Organization Systems/Services (NKOS)
  aims and participants, 3366–3367
  special journal issues, 3368–3369
  workshops and special sessions, 3367–3368

"Networked Talent Model," 143–144

Network management
  activities, 3356
  ancillary support systems, 3357
  applications, 3356
  components, 3356
  dimensions, 3356
    accounting management, 3358
    configuration management, 3357–3358
    distributed computing systems, 3357
    fault management, 3357
    performance management, 3358
    security management, 3358–3359
  information and activity, 3362–3363
  LAN, 3356
  MAN, 3356

Office for Intellectual Freedom (OIF), 2387, 2391–2392

Office for Scientific and Technical Information (OSTI), 306

Office of Information and Regulatory Affairs (OIRA), 1550–1551

Office of Management and Budget (OMB), 1550–1551, 2154

Office of Research and Development (ORD), 3562

Office of Scholarly Communication (OSC), 365

Office of Scientific and Academic Publishing (OSAP), 365

Office of Scientific and Technical Information (OSTI), 1553

Office of Scientific Research and Development (OSRD), 2811

Official Gazette, 3561–3562, 3566

The Official Museum Directory, 4379

Official statistics, 495

Off-line storage, 4942

Ohio College Library Center (OCLC), 451, 1847, 2981; *see also* Online Computer Library Center

bibliographic network, 2981

cataloging system, 729–730

EMEA, 3400

WorldShare Record Manager, 1545

OhioLink, 987

Okapi BM-25 algorithm, 2205–2206

Okapi system, 3427–3428

Older adults' information needs and behavior

computers and Internet, 3410

everyday life information seeking, 3408, 3411

imperative for studying older age groups, 3407

information literacy (Fourth Age), 3409

information needs, 3408–3409

information sources, 3409

library-based research, 3407

old, definitions of, 3406–3407

residential communities, 3409–3410

Old Testament, 644

On2broker, 3458

OncologySTAT.com, 3472

On-demand books (ODB), 3735

One-clause-at-a time (OCAT) methodology, 1621

One Laptop Per Child (OLPC) program, 1283–1284

One-mode network, 4237

One-person librarian (OPL)

churches and synagogues, 3416

future, 3418–3420

history, 3413–3414

hospital librarians, 3415–3416

information brokers, 3416

law libraries, 3415

market researchers, 3416–3417

meaning, 3413

nontraditional sector, 3417

organization's goals, 3418

prison librarians, 3415

public librarians, 3416

school librarians, 3416

special libraries, 3414–3415

tasks, categories, 3417–3418

zoo librarians, 3416

One Thousand and One Nights, 853

One type, one printer theory, 1971

ONIX metadata upstream, 3395

Online Account Management Service, 683

Online bibliographic database, 4629

Online bibliographic retrieval, 2245

Online catalogs, 2079

Online Computer Library Center (OCLC), 2, 671, 733, 894, 984, 1390–1391, 1880, 2181, 2921, 3381, 3450–3452, 3454, 3916, 4472, 4578, 4774–4775, 4800

advocate for libraries, 3401–3402

Asia pacific, 3404

Canada, 3404

cataloging service, 3396–3397

DDC

Abridged WebDewey, 1259–1260

BISAC subject headings, 1261

Classify, 1262

development, 1260

Scorpion software, 1262

Subject Headings for Children and People, Places & Things, 1261

translations, 1260

WebDewey, 1259

WorldCat Collection Analysis service, 1258, 1262–1263

XML representations, 1260

digital collection services, 3400

eCONTENT, 3399

electronic books, 3399–3400

eSerials Holdings Service, 3398

Europe, Middle East and Africa, 3405

finances, 3394

Google, 3403–3404

governance

Board of Trustees, 3393–3394

contribution, 3392–3393

Global Council, 3394

Members Council, 3392–3393

membership, 3392

membership participation levels, 3393

WorldCat Principles of Cooperation, 3393

history, 3392

integrated library systems, 3400

Latin American and Caribbean, 3404–3405

outside United States, 3404

programs and research, 3400–3401

QuestionPoint, 3398–3399

reference and resource sharing, 3398

RLNs, 3921–3923

U.S. activity, 3404

WebJunction, 3402

WorldCat

bibliographic database, 3394

collection analysis, 3398

CONTENTdm collections, 3400

enrichment and quality control, 3395–3396

evolution, 3396

FirstSearch service, 3395

growth, 3396–3397

and information standards, 3396

Navigator, 3398

Online Union Catalog, 3394

Open WorldCat pilot program, 3402–3403

selection, 3398

statistics, 3395

web services, 3403

WorldCat Local, 3403

WorldCat.org, 3403

Online databases, 2240–2241

Online information exchange (ONIX), 4056

Online library instruction

assessment

economic viability, 3444

learner/instructor preferences, 3444

learning outcomes, 3444

usability, 3443

CAI, 3444

benefits, 3435

computer-assisted demonstration, 3434

independent learning tutorials, 3435

live assistance and hand-on, computer-based learning, 3434–3435

early days of distance education, 3434

history

emergence of distance education, 3432–3433

need for teaching librarian, 3432

online education as distance education, 3433

instructional opportunities

credit course, 3437–3438

discipline-specific online library instruction, 3437

intended audience, 3435

librarian professional development, 3438–3440

popular database and OPAC, 3436

in schools of library and information studies, 3438–3439

teaching information literacy skills, 3436–3437

virtual tour, 3436

internet, libraries and online learning

assessment of, 3443–3444

case for CAI, 3435

instructional opportunities for online library instruction, 3435–3439

predictors and predecessors, 3433

technology

chat, 3442–3443

collaborative Web browsing, 3443

conferencing software and courseware, 3442

reaching online learner through electronic mail, 3440, 3442

static Web pages, 3439

web site interaction, 3439–3441

Online Programming for All Libraries (OPAL), 17

Online public access catalogs (OPAC), 1–2, 250, 451–452, 487, 841, 1878, 2219–2220, 2240, 2847, 2854, 2947, 3399, 3435–3436, 4159, 4467–4468, 4789, 4978–4982

Boolean retrieval systems, 3422

vs. card catalog, 3450

database records, 3422

design, improvements, 3429

automated search heuristics, 3428

best-match retrieval approaches, 3427–3428

browse interface, 3426

catalog records, enhancement of, 3427

Participatory three-dimensional modeling
(P3DM), 1672–1673
Particle-induced X-ray emission (PIXE), 478
Partner institutions network, 535
Partnership libraries, 4160–4161
The Past as Prologue: *The Evolution of Art
Librarianship*, 249
Patchwriting, 3664
Patent Abstracts of Japan (PAJ), 3569
Patent Act of 1790, 3560
Patent Act of 1793, 3561
Patent Act of 1836, 3561
Patent and Trademark Depository Libraries
(PTDL), 3562
Patent and Trademark Depository Library Pro-
gram (PTDLP), 640
Patent Application Information Retrieval
(PAIR) system, 3566
Patent classification systems
IPC, 3566–3567
USPC, 3566–3567
Patent Cooperation Treaty (PCT), 815
Patent documents
AI patents, 3565
APC documents, 3566
certificates of correction, 3566
dedications, 3566
defensive publications, 3565
design/industrial designs, 3565
disclaimers, 3566
drawing, 3564
front page, 3563–3564
INID codes, 3564
kind codes, 3564
plant patents, 3565
reexamination certificates, 3566
reissue patents, 3565
SIRs, 3565–3566
specification, 3564
TVPP publications, 3566
utility models, 3565
utility patents, 3564–3565
Patent information
history
1790–1870, 3560–3561
1870–1970, 3561–3562
1970–2008, 3562–3563
monopoly right, 3560
patentability search, 3560
patent protection, 3560
WIPO, 3560
Patent Lens, 3570–3571
Patent Map Guidance, 3570
Patent Office Fire of 1836, 3561
Patents, 639–640, 815, 833–834; *see also* Patent
documents; Patent information
PatentScope, 3570
Patents Ordinance of 1924, 4513
PatFT patent database, 3566
Pathfinder Network (PFNET), 485, 931–932
PATRIOT Act, 2402–2403
Patron-driven acquisition (PDA), 415–416, 1209
Paul Banks and Carolyn Harris Preservation
Award, 331
Paul of Aegina, 3044
Paulo Montenegro Institute (IPM), 603
Peale, Charles Willson, 1818, 4767

Pedigree chart, 1656
PeerEvaluation, 47
Peer review, version control, 4898–4899
Peer-to-peer data grids, 3000
Peer-to-peer networks, 3652
Peircean sign theory, 4098, 4101
Peking University Library (PUL), 896, 903
Penman text generation system, 434
Pennsylvania Academy of Fine Arts, 4767
Pension Protection Act of 2006, 639
People–place–information trichotomy, 1512
People with disabilities and libraries
archives, 3575
barriers, 3573
cataloging and indexing, 3580–3581
collection development, 3580
disability
categories of, 3574
definition, 3573
disability rights movement, 3574
electronic resource accessibility
assistive technology, 3579
circulating equipment, 3579
library websites, 3578–3579
Tatomir Accessibility Checklist, 3578
vendor database, 3578
WCAG guidelines, 3578
for-profit sector, 3575
history, 3575–3576
language, 3575
legislation, 3575
museums, 3575
outreach, 3580
physical resource accessibility
physical books and media, 3577
services and programming, 3577–3578
space, 3576–3577
print disabilities, 3574
social model, 3573
staff training, 3579–3580
Perceived attributes, IT adoption
compatibility, 2296
complexity, 2293, 2296
observability, 2293, 2296
relative advantage
behavioral intention to use/actual usage,
2295
information quality, 2293–2294
IT quality, 2293
service quality, 2294–2295
user satisfaction, 2295
triability, 2296
Performance libraries, 3276–3277
Performing arts; *see also* Visual and performing
arts
archives
Center for Black Music Research, 4755
Folger Shakespeare Library, 4756
New York Public Library, 4756
definition, 4925
live and recorded elements, 4925
live events, 4925
Performing Arts Data Service (PADS), 297
Perseus Project, 1290
Persian illumination (1502–1736), 1955–1956
Persistent uniform resource locator (PURL),
2155

Personal anticipated information need (PAIN)
hypothesis, 2119
Personal construct theory, 2234
Personal health record (PHR), 86, 979, 3342
Personal information management, 2111
analysis
finding/refinding activities, 3588
information item and form, 3586
keeping activities map, 3588
meta-level activities, 3588
personal information collections, 3587
PSI, 3587
checkbox methodology, 3597
convergence and integration, 3599
e-mails, 3598–3599
factors, 3598
history, 3585–3586
information fragmentation, 3585
maintenance and organization, 3585
observant participation, 3598
PICs, 3584
practical methodologies, 3597
privacy, security and information, 3585,
3599
research
finding/refinding activity, 3588–3591
GIM and PIM social fabric, 3596
keeping activities, 3591–3593
meta-level activity, 3593–3596
search technology, 3599
user-subjective approach, 3598
Personality facet
levels of, 1536
rounds of, 1536–1537
PERsonalized and Successive Information
Search Tools (PERSIST), 1901
Personally identifiable information (PII), 1489
Personal space of information (PSI), 3587
Personnel Administration Section (PAS), 2844
Pertinence relevance judgments, 3943
Peru
libraries
academic libraries, 3608
education and professional associations,
3608
modern challenges, 3608–3609
National Library, 3606–3608
publications, 3607
public libraries, 3606–3608
school libraries, 3608
during Spanish domination, 3606
map of, 3606–3607
Pervasive information systems, 1488
Peschel, Oscar, 1687
Pests, 1150–1151
Peterborough library, 1839, 1843
Pew Global Attitudes project, 1061
Pew Research Center, 5028
Pew Research Institute's American Life Project,
841
PFNET algorithm, 485
Pharmacophore searching, 834–835
Phenomenography, 2754
Philadelphia Museum of Art, 1072, 3253
Philadelphia Peale Museum, 3243
Philosophical Transactions of the Royal Society,
646